THE TIMES

Guide to the House of Commons June 1987

Edited by Alan H Wood
The Times

Times Books

Published in 1987 by
Times Books Ltd
16 Golden Square
London W1R 4BN
© **Times Newspapers Ltd, 1987**

Typesetting by
London Post (Printers) Ltd

Compiled by: Andrew Burke, Derek Robinson,
Michael Vagg and Bernard West

Printed and bound in the UK by
Anchor Press
Tiptree
Essex

British Library Cataloguing in Publication Data

The Times guide to the House of Commons
    June 1987.
    1. Great Britain. *Parliament* —
Elections, 1987-
324.941'0858   JN956

ISBN 0-7230-0298-3

Contents

Her Majesty's Government

The Cabinet

**Prime Minister, First Lord of the
 Treasury and Minister for the
 Civil Service**
Mrs Margaret Thatcher

**Lord President of the Council and
 Leader of the House of Lords**
Lord Whitelaw

Lord Chancellor
Lord Havers

**Secretary of State for Foreign
 and Commonwealth Affairs**
Sir Geoffrey Howe

Chancellor of the Exchequer
Mr Nigel Lawson

Home Secretary
Mr Douglas Hurd

Secretary of State for Energy
Mr Cecil Parkinson

Secretary of State for Defence
Mr George Younger

Secretary of State for Wales
Mr Peter Walker

**Lord Privy Seal and Leader of the House
 of Commons**
Mr John Wakeham

Secretary of State for Social Services
Mr John Moore

**Chancellor of the Duchy of Lancaster
 and Minister for Trade and Industry**
Mr Kenneth Clarke

Secretary of State for Northern Ireland
Mr Tom King

**Minister of Agriculture, Fisheries and
 Food**
Mr John MacGregor

Secretary of State for the Environment
Mr Nicholas Ridley

Secretary of State for Employment
Mr Norman Fowler

**Secretary of State for Education
 and Science**
Mr Kenneth Baker

Chief Secretary to the Treasury
Mr John Major

Secretary of State for Scotland
Mr Malcolm Rifkind

**Secretary of State for Trade and
 Industry**
Lord Young of Graffham

Secretary of State for Transport
Mr Paul Channon

Departments of State and Ministers

AGRICULTURE, FISHERIES AND FOOD

Minister
Mr John MacGregor

Ministers of State
Mr John Gummer

Parliamentary Secretaries
Mr Donald Thompson
Lady Trumpington

DUCHY OF LANCASTER
Chancellor
Mr Kenneth Clarke

DEFENCE

Secretary of State
Mr George Younger

Minister of State for the Armed Forces
Mr Ian Stewart

**Minister of State for Defence
 Procurement**
Lord Trefgarne

**Under Secretary of State for the
 Armed Forces**
Mr Roger Freeman

**Under Secretary of State for
 Defence Procurement**
Mr Timothy Sainsbury

EDUCATION AND SCIENCE

Secretary of State
Mr Kenneth Baker

Minister of State
Mrs Angela Rumbold

Under Secretaries of State
Mr Robert Dunn
Lady Hooper
Mr Robert Jackson

EMPLOYMENT

Secretary of State
Mr Norman Fowler

Minister of State
Mr John Cope

Under Secretary of State
Mr John Lee
Mr Patrick Nicholls

ENERGY

Secretary of State
Mr Cecil Parkinson

Minister of State
Mr Peter Morrison

Under Secretary of State
Mr Michael Spicer

ENVIRONMENT

Secretary of State
Mr Nicholas Ridley

Ministers of State
**Minister for Water, Environmental
Protection, Countryside and Heritage**
Lord Belstead

Minister for Local Government
Mr Michael Howard

Minister for Housing and Planning
Mr William Waldegrave

Under Secretaries of State
Mr Christopher Chope
Mr David Trippier
Mrs Marion Roe
Mr Colin Moynihan
  (Minister for Sport)

FOREIGN AND COMMONWEALTH

Secretary of State
Sir Geoffrey Howe

Ministers of State
Mrs Lynda Chalker
Lord Glenarthur
Mr David Mellor

Minister for Overseas Development
Mr Christopher Patten

Under Secretary of State
Mr Timothy Eggar

HEALTH AND SOCIAL SECURITY

Secretary of State for Social Services
Mr John Moore

Ministers of State
Minister of Health
Mr Antony Newton

Minister for Social Security and Disabled
Mr Nicholas Scott

Under Secretaries of State
Mrs Edwina Currie
Lord Skelmersdale
Mr Michael Portillo

HOME OFFICE

Secretary of State
Mr Douglas Hurd

Ministers of State
Mr John Patten
Mr Timothy Renton
The Earl of Caithness

Under Secretary of State
Mr Douglas Hogg

LAW OFFICERS

Attorney General
Sir Patrick Mayhew

Lord Advocate
Lord Cameron of Lochbroom

Solicitor General
Sir Nicholas Lyell

Solicitor General for Scotland
Mr Peter Fraser

MANAGEMENT AND PERSONNEL OFFICE

**Prime Minister for the
  Civil Service**
Mrs Margaret Thatcher

**Minister of State, Privy Council
  Office and Minister for the Arts**
Mr Richard Luce

NORTHERN IRELAND OFFICE

Secretary of State
Mr Tom King

Minister of State
Mr John Stanley

Under Secretaries of State
Mr Peter Viggers
Lord Lyell
Mr Richard Needham
Dr Brian Mawhinney

PAYMASTER GENERAL'S DEPARTMENT

Paymaster General
Mr Peter Brooke

PRIVY COUNCIL OFFICE

**Lord President of the Council and
Leader of the House of Lords**
Viscount Whitelaw

**Lord Privy Seal and Leader
of the House of Commons**
Mr John Wakeham

SCOTTISH OFFICE

Secretary of State
Mr Malcolm Rifkind

Ministers of State
Mr Ian Lang
Lord Sanderson of Bowden

Under Secretaries of State
Mr Michael Forsyth
Lord James Douglas-Hamilton

TRADE AND INDUSTRY

Secretary of State
Lord Young of Graffham

**Chancellor of Duchy of Lancaster
and Minister of Trade and Industry**
Mr Kenneth Clarke

**Minister of State
Minister for Trade**
Mr Alan Clark

Under Secretaries of State
Mr John Butcher
Mr Francis Maude
Mr Robert Atkins

TRANSPORT

Secretary of State
Mr Paul Channon
Minister of State
Mr David Mitchell

Under Secretaries of State
Mr Peter Bottomley
Lord Brabazon of Tara

TREASURY

**Prime Minister, First Lord of the
Treasury and Minister for the
Civil Service**
Mrs Margaret Thatcher

Chancellor of the Exchequer
Mr Nigel Lawson

Chief Secretary
Mr John Major

**Parliamentary Secretary and
Government Chief Whip in the
House of Commons**
Mr David Waddington

Financial Secretary
Mr Norman Lamont

Economic Secretary (Minister of State)
Mr Peter Lilley

Paymaster General
Mr Peter Brooke

**Lord Commissioners (Government
Whips)**
Mr Michael Neubert
Mr Tony Durant
Mr Peter Lloyd
Mr Mark Lennox-Boyd
Mr David Lightbown

Assistant Government Whips
Mr Richard Ryder
Mr Kenneth Carlisle
Mr Alan Howarth
Mr David Maclean
Mr Stephen Dorrell

WELSH OFFICE

Secretary of State
Mr Peter Walker

Minister of State
Mr Wyn Roberts

Under Secretary of State
Mr Ian Grist

HM HOUSEHOLD

**Treasurer and Government Deputy
Chief Whip in Commons**
Mr David Hunt

Comptroller
Mr Robert Boscawen

Vice Chamberlain
Mr Tristan Garel-Jones

**Captain, Gentlemen-at-Arms
(Government Chief Whip in the
House of Lords)**
Lord Denham

Captain, Yeomen of the Guard
Viscount Davidson

Lords in Waiting
Viscount Long
Lord Hesketh
Lord Beaverbrook
Earl of Dundee
Earl of Arran

Second Church Estates Commissioner
Mr Michael Alison

The House of Commons

In this list of members returned to the House of Commons at the General Election on June 11, 1987 a † denotes a new member. The abbreviations used to designate political parties are:

C - Conservative; Lab - Labour; L/All - Liberal Alliance; SDP/All - Social Democratic Party Alliance; OUP - Official Unionist Party; SDLP - Social Democratic and Labour Party; UPUP - Ulster Popular Unionist Party; DUP - Democratic Unionist Party; SNP - Scottish National Party; Pl C - Plaid Cymru; PSF - Provisional Sinn Fein.

†Abbott, Ms Diana: *Hackney North and Stoke Newington*	Lab
Adams, Allen: *Paisley North*	Lab
Adams, Gerry: *Belfast West*	PSF
Adley, Robert: *Christchurch*	C
Aitken, Jonathan: *Thanet South*	C
Alexander, Richard: *Newark*	C
Alison, Michael: *Selby*	C
†Allason, Rupert: *Torbay*	C
†Allen, Graham: *Nottingham North*	Lab
Alton, David: *Liverpool, Mossley Hill*	L/All
Amery, Julian: *Brighton, Pavilion*	C
Amess, David: *Basildon*	C
†Amos, Alan: *Hexham*	C
Anderson, Donald: *Swansea East*	Lab
†Arbuthnot, James: *Wanstead and Woodford*	C
Archer, Peter: *Warley West*	Lab
†Armstrong, Ms Hilary: *Durham North West*	Lab
†Arnold, Jacques: *Gravesham*	C
Arnold, Tom: *Hazel Grove*	C
Ashby, David: *Leicestershire North West*	C
Ashdown, Paddy: *Yeovil*	L/All
Ashley, Jack: *Stoke-on-Trent South*	Lab
Ashton, Joseph: *Bassetlaw*	Lab
Aspinwall, Jack: *Wansdyke*	C
Atkins, Robert: *South Ribble*	C
Atkinson, David: *Bournemouth East*	C

B

Baker, Kenneth: *Mole Valley*	C
Baker, Nicholas: *Dorset North*	C
Baldry, Tony: *Banbury*	C

Banks, Robert: *Harrogate*	C
Banks, Tony: *Newham North West*	Lab
†Barnes, Harry: *Derbyshire North East*	Lab
Barnes, Mrs Rosie: *Greenwich*	SDP/All
Barron, Kevin: *Rother Valley*	Lab
Batiste, Spencer: *Elmet*	C
†Battle, John: *Leeds West*	Lab
Beaumont-Dark, Anthony: *Birmingham, Selly Oak*	C
Beckett, Mrs Margaret: *Derby South*	Lab
Beggs, Roy: *Antrim East*	OUP
Beith, Alan: *Berwick-upon-Tweed*	L/All
Bell, Stuart: *Middlesbrough*	Lab
Bellingham, Henry: *Norfolk North West*	C
Bendall, Vivian: *Ilford North*	C
Benn, Tony: *Chesterfield*	Lab
Bennett, Andrew: *Denton and Reddish*	Lab
†Bennett, Nicholas: *Pembroke*	C
Benyon, William: *Milton Keynes*	C
Bermingham, Gerald: *St Helens South*	Lab
Bevan, David Gilroy: *Birmingham, Yardley*	C
Bidwell, Sydney: *Ealing, Southall*	Lab
Biffen, John: *Shropshire North*	C
Biggs-Davison, Sir John: *Epping Forest*	C
Blackburn, John: *Dudley West*	C
Blair, Anthony: *Sedgefield*	Lab
Blaker, Sir Peter: *Blackpool South*	C
†Blunkett, David: *Sheffield, Brightside*	Lab
†Boateng, Paul: *Brent South*	Lab
Body, Sir Richard: *Holland with Boston*	C
Bonsor, Sir Nicholas: *Upminster*	C
Boothroyd, Miss Betty: *West Bromwich West*	Lab
Boscawen, Robert: *Somerton and Frome*	C
†Boswell, Timothy: *Daventry*	C
Bottomley, Mrs Virginia: *Surrey South West*	C
Bottomley, Peter: *Eltham*	C
Bowden, Andrew: *Brighton, Kemptown*	C
Bowden, Gerald: *Dulwich*	C
†Bowis, John: *Battersea*	C
Boyes, Roland: *Houghton and Washington*	Lab
Boyson, Sir Rhodes: *Brent North*	C
†Bradley, Keith: *Manchester, Withington*	Lab
Braine, Sir Bernard: *Castle Point*	C
Brandon-Bravo, Martin: *Nottingham South*	C
Bray, Dr Jeremy: *Motherwell South*	Lab
†Brazier, Julian: *Canterbury*	C
Bright, Graham: *Luton South*	C
Brittan, Leon: *Richmond, Yorks*	C
Brooke, Peter: *City of London and Westminster South*	C
Brown, Dr Gordon: *Dunfermline East*	Lab
Brown, Michael: *Brigg and Cleethorpes*	C
Brown, Nicholas: *Newcastle upon Tyne East*	Lab
Brown, Ronald: *Edinburgh, Leith*	Lab
Browne, John: *Winchester*	C

†Bruce, Ian: *Dorset South*	C
Bruce, Malcolm: *Gordon*	L/All
Buchan, Norman: *Paisley South*	Lab
Buchanan-Smith, Alick: *Kincardine and Deeside*	C
Buck, Sir Antony: *Colchester North*	C
†Buckley, George: *Hemsworth*	Lab
Budgen, Nicholas: *Wolverhampton South West*	C
†Burns, Simon: *Chelmsford*	C
Burt, Alistair: *Bury North*	C
Butcher, John: *Coventry South West*	C
†Butler, Christopher: *Warrington South*	C
Butterfill, John: *Bournemouth West*	C

C

Caborn, Richard: *Sheffield Central*	Lab
Callaghan, Jim: *Heywood and Middleton*	Lab
†Campbell, Menzies: *Fife North East*	L/All
†Campbell, Ronald: *Blyth Valley*	Lab
Campbell-Savours, Dale: *Workington*	Lab
Canavan, Dennis: *Falkirk West*	Lab
Carlile, Alexander: *Montgomery*	L/All
Carlisle, John: *Luton North*	C
Carlisle, Kenneth: *Lincoln*	C
†Carrington, Matthew: *Fulham*	C
Carttiss, Michael: *Great Yarmouth*	C
Cartwright, John: *Woolwich*	SDP/All
Cash, William: *Stafford*	C
Chalker, Mrs Lynda: *Wallasey*	C
Channon, Paul: *Southend West*	C
Chapman, Sydney: *Chipping Barnet*	C
Chope, Christopher: *Southampton, Itchen*	C
Churchill, Winston: *Davyhulme*	C
Clark, Alan: *Plymouth, Sutton*	C
Clark, Dr David: *South Shields*	Lab
Clark, Dr Michael: *Rochford*	C
Clark, Sir William: *Croydon South*	C
Clarke, Kenneth: *Rushcliffe*	C
Clarke, Thomas: *Monklands West*	Lab
Clay, Robert: *Sunderland North*	Lab
Clelland, David: *Tyne Bridge*	Lab
Clwyd, Mrs Ann: *Cynon Valley*	Lab
Cohen, Harry: *Leyton*	Lab
Coleman, Donald: *Neath*	Lab
Colvin, Michael: *Romsey and Waterside*	C
Conway, Derek: *Shrewsbury and Atcham*	C
Cook, Francis: *Stockton North*	Lab
Cook, Robin: *Livingston*	Lab
†Coombs, Anthony: *Wyre Forest*	C
Coombs, Simon: *Swindon*	C
Cope, John: *Northavon*	C
Corbett, Robin: *Birmingham, Erdington*	Lab

Corbyn, Jeremy: *Islington North* — Lab
Cormack, Patrick: *Staffordshire South* — C
Couchman, James: *Gillingham* — C
†Cousins, James: *Newcastle upon Tyne Central* — Lab
Cox, Thomas: *Tooting* — Lab
†Cran, James: *Beverley* — C
Critchley, Julian: *Aldershot* — C
Crowther, Stanley: *Rotherham* — Lab
†Cryer, Robert: *Bradford South* — Lab
Cummings, John: *Easington* — Lab
Cunliffe, Lawrence: *Leigh* — Lab
Cunningham, Dr John: *Copeland* — Lab
Currie, Mrs Edwina: *Derbyshire South* — C
†Curry, David: *Skipton and Ripon* — C

D

†Darling, Alistair: *Edinburgh Central* — Lab
Dalyell, Tam: *Linlithgow* — Lab
Davies, Denzil: *Llanelli* — Lab
†Davies, Quentin: *Stamford and Spalding* — C
Davies, Ronald: *Caerphilly* — Lab
†Davis, David: *Boothferry* — C
Davis, Terry: *Birmingham, Hodge Hill* — Lab
†Day, Stephen: *Cheadle* — C
Dean, Sir Paul: *Woodspring* — C
†Devlin, Timothy: *Stockton South* — C
Dewar, Donald: *Glasgow, Garscadden* — Lab
Dickens, Geoffrey: *Littleborough and Saddleworth* — C
Dicks, Terence: *Hayes and Harlington* — C
Dixon, Donald: *Jarrow* — Lab
Dobson, Frank: *Holborn and St Pancras* — Lab
†Doran, Frank: *Aberdeen South* — Lab
Dorrell, Stephen: *Loughborough* — C
Douglas, Richard: *Dunfermline West* — Lab
Douglas-Hamilton, Lord James: *Edinburgh West* — C
Dover, Den: *Chorley* — C
Duffy, Patrick: *Sheffield, Attercliffe* — Lab
Dunn, Robert: *Dartford* — C
†Dunnachie, Jimmy: *Glasgow, Pollok* — Lab
Dunwoody, Mrs Gwyneth: *Crewe and Nantwich* — Lab
Durant, Tony: *Reading West* — C
Dykes, Hugh: *Harrow East* — C

E

Eadie, Alexander: *Midlothian* — Lab
Eastham, Kenneth: *Manchester, Blackley* — Lab
Eggar, Timothy: *Enfield North* — C
Emery, Sir Peter: *Honiton* — C

†Evans, David: *Welwyn Hatfield*	C
Evans, John: *St Helens North*	Lab
Evennett, David: *Erith and Crayford*	C
Ewing, Harry: *Falkirk East*	Lab
†Ewing, Mrs Margaret: *Moray*	SNP

F

Fairbairn, Nicholas: *Perth and Kinross*	C
Fallon, Michael: *Darlington*	C
Farr, Sir John: *Harborough*	C
Fatchett, Derek: *Leeds Central*	Lab
Faulds, Andrew: *Warley East*	Lab
Favell, Anthony: *Stockport*	C
†Fearn, Ronald: *Southport*	L/All
Fenner, Dame Peggy: *Medway*	C
†Field, Barry: *Isle of Wight*	C
Field, Frank: *Birkenhead*	Lab
Fields, Terence: *Liverpool, Broadgreen*	Lab
Finsberg, Sir Geoffrey: *Hampstead and Highgate*	C
Fisher, Mark: *Stoke-on-Trent Central*	Lab
Flannery, Martin: *Sheffield, Hillsborough*	Lab
†Flynn, Paul: *Newport West*	Lab
Fookes, Miss Janet: *Plymouth, Drake*	C
Foot, Michael: *Blaenau Gwent*	Lab
Forman, Nigel: *Carshalton and Wallington*	C
Forsyth, Michael: *Stirling*	C
Forsythe, Clifford: *Antrim South*	OUP
Forth, Eric: *Worcestershire Mid*	C
Foster, Derek: *Bishop Auckland*	Lab
Foulkes, George: *Carrick, Cumnock and Doon Valley*	Lab
Fowler, Norman: *Sutton Coldfield*	C
Fox, Sir Marcus: *Shipley*	C
Franks, Cecil: *Barrow and Furness*	C
Fraser, John: *Norwood*	Lab
Freeman, Roger: *Kettering*	C
†French, Douglas: *Gloucester*	C
Fry, Peter: *Wellingborough*	C
†Fyfe, Mrs Maria: *Glasgow, Maryhill*	Lab

G

†Galbraith, Samuel: *Strathkelvin and Bearsden*	Lab
Gale, Roger: *Thanet North*	C
†Galloway, George: *Glasgow, Hillhead*	Lab
Gardiner, George: *Reigate*	C
Garel-Jones, Tristan: *Watford*	C
Garrett, Edward: *Wallsend*	Lab
†Garrett, John: *Norwich South*	Lab
George, Bruce: *Walsall South*	Lab

Gilbert, Dr John: *Dudley East*	Lab
†Gill, Christopher: *Ludlow*	C
Gilmour, Sir Ian: *Chesham and Amersham*	C
Glyn, Dr Alan: *Windsor and Maidenhead*	C
Godman, Dr Norman: *Greenock and Port Glasgow*	Lab
Golding, Mrs Llin: *Newcastle-under-Lyme*	Lab
Goodhart, Sir Philip: *Beckenham*	C
Goodlad, Alastair: *Eddisbury*	C
†Goodson-Wickes, Dr Charles: *Wimbledon*	C
†Gordon, Mrs Mildred: *Bow and Poplar*	Lab
†Gorman, Mrs Teresa: *Billericay*	C
Gorst, John: *Hendon North*	C
Gould, Bryan: *Dagenham*	Lab
Gow, Ian: *Eastbourne*	C
Gower, Sir Raymond: *Vale of Glamorgan*	C
†Graham, Thomas: *Renfrew West and Inverclyde*	Lab
†Grant, Bernie: *Tottenham*	Lab
Grant, Sir Anthony: *Cambridgeshire South West*	C
Greenway, Harry: *Ealing North*	C
†Greenway, John: *Ryedale*	C
Gregory, Conal: *York*	C
†Griffiths, Nigel: *Edinburgh South*	Lab
Griffiths, Peter: *Portsmouth North*	C
Griffiths, Sir Eldon: *Bury St Edmunds*	C
†Griffiths, Winston: *Bridgend*	Lab
Grist, Ian: *Cardiff Central*	C
†Grocott, Bruce: *Wrekin, The*	Lab
Ground, Patrick: *Feltham and Heston*	C
Grylls, Michael: *Surrey North West*	C
Gummer, John: *Suffolk Coastal*	C

H

Hamilton, Archibald: *Epsom and Ewell*	C
Hamilton, Neil: *Tatton*	C
Hampson, Dr Keith: *Leeds North West*	C
Hanley, Jeremy: *Richmond and Barnes*	C
Hannam, John: *Exeter*	C
Hardy, Peter: *Wentworth*	Lab
†Hargreaves, Andrew: *Birmingham, Hall Green*	C
Hargreaves, Kenneth: *Hyndburn*	C
Harman, Ms Harriet: *Peckham*	Lab
Harris, David: *St Ives*	C
Haselhurst, Alan: *Saffron Walden*	C
Hattersley, Roy: *Birmingham, Sparkbrook*	Lab
Hawkins, Christopher: *High Peak*	C
Hayes, Jeremy: *Harlow*	C
Hayhoe, Sir Barney: *Brentford and Isleworth*	C
Haynes, Frank: *Ashfield*	Lab
Hayward, Robert: *Kingswood*	C
Healey, Denis: *Leeds East*	Lab
Heath, Edward: *Old Bexley and Sidcup*	C

Heathcoat-Amory, David: *Wells*	C
Heddle, John: *Staffordshire Mid*	C
Heffer, Eric: *Liverpool, Walton*	Lab
†Henderson, Douglas: *Newcastle upon Tyne North*	Lab
Heseltine, Michael: *Henley*	C
†Hicks, Mrs Maureen: *Wolverhampton North East*	C
Hicks, Robert: *Cornwall South East*	C
Higgins, Terence: *Worthing*	C
Hill, James: *Southampton, Test*	C
†Hinchliffe, David: *Wakefield*	Lab
Hind, Kenneth: *Lancashire West*	C
Hogg, Douglas: *Grantham*	C
Hogg, Norman: *Cumbernauld and Kilsyth*	Lab
Holland, Stuart: *Vauxhall*	Lab
Holt, Richard: *Langbaurgh*	C
Home Robertson, John: *East Lothian*	Lab
†Hood, Jimmy: *Clydesdale*	Lab
Hordern, Sir Peter: *Horsham*	C
Howard, Michael: *Folkestone and Hythe*	C
Howarth, Alan: *Stratford-on-Avon*	C
Howarth, George: *Knowsley North*	Lab
Howarth, Gerald: *Cannock and Burntwood*	C
Howe, Sir Geoffrey: *Surrey East*	C
Howell, David: *Guildford*	C
Howell, Denis: *Birmingham, Small Heath*	Lab
Howell, Ralph: *Norfolk North*	C
Howells, Geraint: *Ceredigion and Pembroke North*	L/All
Hoyle, Douglas: *Warrington North*	Lab
†Hughes, John: *Coventry North East*	Lab
Hughes, Robert: *Aberdeen North*	Lab
†Hughes, Robert G.: *Harrow West*	C
Hughes, Roy: *Newport East*	Lab
Hughes, Sean: *Knowsley South*	Lab
Hughes, Simon: *Southwark and Bermondsey*	L/All
Hume, John: *Foyle*	SDLP
Hunt, David: *Wirral West*	C
Hunt, John: *Ravensbourne*	C
Hunter, Andrew: *Basingstoke*	C
Hurd, Douglas: *Witney*	C

I

†Illsley, Eric: *Barnsley Central*	Lab
†Ingram, Adam: *East Kilbride*	Lab
†Irvine, Michael: *Ipswich*	C
Irving, Charles: *Cheltenham*	C

J

†Jack, Michael: *Fylde*	C
Jackson, Robert: *Wantage*	C

†Janman, Timothy: *Thurrock* — C
Janner, Greville: *Leicester West* — Lab
Jessel, Toby: *Twickenham* — C
John, Brynmor: *Pontypridd* — Lab
Johnson Smith, Sir Geoffrey: *Wealden* — C
Johnston, Sir Russell: *Inverness, Nairn and Lochaber* — L/All
Jones, Barry: *Alyn and Deeside* — Lab
Jones, Gwilyn: *Cardiff North* — C
†Jones, Ieuan Wyn: *Ynys Mon* — Pl C
†Jones, Martyn: *Clwyd South West* — Lab
Jones, Robert: *Hertfordshire West* — C
Jopling, Michael: *Westmorland and Lonsdale* — C

K

Kaufman, Gerald: *Manchester, Gorton* — Lab
Kellett-Bowman, Mrs Elaine: *Lancaster* — C
Kennedy, Charles: *Ross, Cromarty and Skye* — SDP/All
Key, Robert: *Salisbury* — C
Kilfedder, James: *Down North* — UPUP
King, Roger: *Birmingham, Northfield* — C
King, Tom: *Bridgwater* — C
Kinnock, Neil: *Islwyn* — Lab
†Kirkhope, Timothy: *Leeds North East* — C
Kirkwood, Archy: *Roxburgh and Berwickshire* — L/All
†Knapman, Roger: *Stroud* — C
Knight, Dame Jill: *Birmingham, Edgbaston* — C
Knight, Gregory: *Derby North* — C
Knowles, Michael: *Nottingham East* — C
Knox, David: *Staffordshire Moorlands* — C

L

Lambie, David: *Cunninghame South* — Lab
Lamond, James: *Oldham Central and Royton* — Lab
Lamont, Norman: *Kingston upon Thames* — C
Lang, Ian: *Galloway and Upper Nithsdale* — C
Latham, Michael: *Rutland and Melton* — C
Lawrence, Ivan: *Burton* — C
Lawson, Nigel: *Blaby* — C
Leadbitter, Edward: *Hartlepool* — Lab
Lee, John: *Pendle* — C
Leigh, Edward: *Gainsborough and Horncastle* — C
Leighton, Ronald: *Newham North East* — Lab
Lennox-Boyd, Mark: *Morecambe and Lunesdale* — C
Lester, James: *Broxtowe* — C
†Lestor, Miss Joan: *Eccles* — Lab
Lewis, Terence: *Worsley* — Lab
Lightbown, David: *Staffordshire South East* — C
Lilley, Peter: *St Albans* — C

Litherland, Robert: *Manchester Central*	Lab
†Livingstone, Ken: *Brent East*	Lab
Livsey, Richard: *Brecon and Radnor*	L/All
Lloyd, Anthony: *Stretford*	Lab
Lloyd, Peter: *Fareham*	C
Lloyd, Sir Ian: *Havant*	C
Lofthouse, Geoffrey: *Pontefract and Castleford*	Lab
Lord, Michael: *Suffolk Central*	C
Loyden, Edward: *Liverpool, Garston*	Lab
Luce, Richard: *Shoreham*	C
Lyell, Sir Nicholas: *Bedfordshire Mid*	C

M

†Macdonald, Calum: *Western Isles*	Lab
MacGregor, John: *Norfolk South*	C
Macfarlane, Neil: *Sutton and Cheam*	C
MacKay, Andrew: *Berkshire East*	C
Maclean, David: *Penrith and the Border*	C
Maclennan, Robert: *Caithness and Sutherland*	SDP/All
Madden, Max: *Bradford West*	Lab
Madel, David: *Bedfordshire South West*	C
Maginnis, Kenneth: *Fermanagh and South Tyrone*	OUP
†Mahon, Ms Alice: *Halifax*	Lab
Major, John: *Huntingdon*	C
Malins, Humfrey: *Croydon North West*	C
Mallon, Seamus: *Newry and Armagh*	SDLP
†Mans, Keith: *Wyre*	C
Maples, John: *Lewisham West*	C
Marek, Dr John: *Wrexham*	Lab
Marland, Paul: *Gloucestershire West*	C
Marlow, Antony: *Northampton North*	C
Marshall, David: *Glasgow, Shettleston*	Lab
†Marshall, James: *Leicester South*	Lab
Marshall, John: *Hendon South*	C
Marshall, Michael: *Arundel*	C
†Martin, David: *Portsmouth South*	C
Martin, Michael: *Glasgow, Springburn*	Lab
†Martlew, Eric: *Carlisle*	Lab
Mates, Michael: *Hampshire East*	C
Maude, Francis: *Warwickshire North*	C
Mawhinney, Dr Brian: *Peterborough*	C
Maxton, John: *Glasgow, Cathcart*	Lab
Maxwell-Hyslop, Robin: *Tiverton*	C
Mayhew, Sir Patrick: *Tunbridge Wells*	C
†McAllion, John: *Dundee East*	Lab
†McAvoy, Thomas: *Glasgow, Rutherglen*	Lab
†McCartney, Ian: *Makerfield*	Lab
McCrea, Rev William: *Ulster Mid*	DUP
McCrindle, Robert: *Brentwood and Ongar*	C
McCusker, Harold: *Upper Bann*	OUP
†McFall, John: *Dumbarton*	Lab

†McGrady, Edward: *Down South*	SDLP
McKay, Allen: *Barnsley West and Penistone*	Lab
McKelvey, William: *Kilmarnock and Loudoun*	Lab
†McLeish, Henry: *Fife Central*	Lab
McLoughlin, Patrick: *Derbyshire West*	C
McNair-Wilson, Michael: *Newbury*	C
McNair-Wilson, Patrick: *New Forest*	C
McNamara, Kevin: *Hull North*	Lab
McTaggart, Robert: *Glasgow Central*	Lab
McWilliam, John: *Blaydon*	Lab
Meacher, Michael: *Oldham West*	Lab
†Meale, Alan: *Mansfield*	Lab
Mellor, David: *Putney*	C
Meyer, Sir Anthony: *Clwyd North West*	C
†Michael, Alun: *Cardiff South and Penarth*	Lab
†Michie, Mrs Ray: *Argyll and Bute*	L/All
Michie, William: *Sheffield, Heeley*	Lab
Millan, Bruce: *Glasgow, Govan*	Lab
Miller, Hilary (Hal): *Bromsgrove*	C
Mills, Iain: *Meriden*	C
Miscampbell, Norman: *Blackpool North*	C
†Mitchell, Andrew: *Gedling*	C
Mitchell, Austin: *Great Grimsby*	Lab
Mitchell, David: *Hampshire North West*	C
Moate, Roger: *Faversham*	C
Molyneaux, James: *Lagan Valley*	OUP
Monro, Sir Hector: *Dumfries*	C
Montgomery, Sir Fergus: *Altrincham and Sale*	C
†Moonie, Dr Lewis: *Kirkcaldy*	Lab
Moore, John: *Croydon Central*	C
†Morgan, Rhodri: *Cardiff West*	Lab
†Morley, Elliot: *Glanford and Scunthorpe*	Lab
Morris, Alfred: *Manchester, Wythenshawe*	Lab
Morris, John: *Aberavon*	Lab
Morris, Michael: *Northampton South*	C
Morrison, Charles: *Devizes*	C
Morrison, Peter: *Chester, City of*	C
†Moss, Malcolm: *Cambridgeshire North East*	C
†Mowlam, Dr Marjorie: *Redcar*	Lab
Moynihan, Colin: *Lewisham East*	C
Mudd, David: *Falmouth and Camborne*	C
†Mullin, Christopher: *Sunderland South*	Lab
†Murphy, Paul: *Torfaen*	Lab

N

Neale, Gerrard: *Cornwall North*	C
Needham, Richard: *Wiltshire North*	C
Nellist, David: *Coventry South East*	Lab
Nelson, Anthony: *Chichester*	C
Neubert, Michael: *Romford*	C
Newton, Tony: *Braintree*	C

Nicholls, Patrick: *Teignbridge*	C
†Nicholson, David: *Taunton*	C
†Nicholson, Miss Emma: *Devon West and Torridge*	C

O

O'Brien, William: *Normanton*	Lab
O'Neill, Martin: *Clackmannan*	Lab
Oakes, Gordon: *Halton*	Lab
Onslow, Cranley: *Woking*	C
Oppenheim, Philip: *Amber Valley*	C
Orme, Stanley: *Salford East*	Lab
Owen, Dr David: *Plymouth, Devonport*	SDP/All

P

Page, Richard: *Hertfordshire South West*	C
†Paice, James: *Cambridgeshire South East*	C
Paisley, Rev Ian: *Antrim North*	DUP
Parkinson, Cecil: *Hertsmere*	C
Parry, Robert: *Liverpool, Riverside*	Lab
Patchett, Terry: *Barnsley East*	Lab
†Patnick, Cyril: *Sheffield, Hallam*	C
Patten, Christopher: *Bath*	C
Patten, John: *Oxford West and Abingdon*	C
Pattie, Sir Geoffrey: *Chertsey and Walton*	C
Pawsey, James: *Rugby and Kenilworth*	C
Peacock, Mrs Elizabeth: *Batley and Spen*	C
Pendry, Tom: *Stalybridge and Hyde*	Lab
Pike, Peter: *Burnley*	Lab
Porter, Barry: *Wirral South*	C
†Porter, David: *Waveney*	C
Portillo, Michael: *Enfield, Southgate*	C
Powell, Raymond: *Ogmore*	Lab
Powell, William: *Corby*	C
Prescott, John: *Hull East*	Lab
Price, Sir David: *Eastleigh*	C
†Primarolo, Ms Dawn: *Bristol South*	Lab

Q

†Quin, Ms Joyce: *Gateshead East*	Lab

R

Radice, Giles: *Durham North*	Lab
Raffan, Keith: *Delyn*	C
Raison, Timothy: *Aylesbury*	C
Randall, Stuart: *Hull West*	Lab

Rathbone, John R (Tim): *Lewes*	C
Redmond, Martin: *Don Valley*	Lab
†Redwood, John: *Wokingham*	C
Rees, Merlyn: *Leeds South and Morley*	Lab
†Reid, Dr John: *Motherwell North*	Lab
Renton, Timothy: *Sussex Mid*	C
Rhodes James, Robert: *Cambridge*	C
Rhys Williams, Sir Brandon: *Kensington*	C
Richardson, Ms Jo: *Barking*	Lab
†Riddick, Graham: *Colne Valley*	C
Ridley, Nicholas: *Cirencester and Tewkesbury*	C
Ridsdale, Sir Julian: *Harwich*	C
Rifkind, Malcolm: *Edinburgh, Pentlands*	C
Roberts, Allan: *Bootle*	Lab
Roberts, Wyn: *Conwy*	C
Robertson, George: *Hamilton*	Lab
Robinson, Geoffrey: *Coventry North West*	Lab
Robinson, Peter: *Belfast East*	DUP
Roe, Mrs Marion: *Broxbourne*	C
Rogers, Allan: *Rhondda*	Lab
Rooker, Jeffrey: *Birmingham, Perry Barr*	Lab
Ross, Ernest: *Dundee West*	Lab
Ross, William: *Londonderry East*	OUP
Rossi, Sir Hugh: *Hornsey and Wood Green*	C
Rost, Peter: *Erewash*	C
Rowe, Andrew: *Kent Mid*	C
Rowlands, Edward: *Merthyr Tydfil and Rhymney*	Lab
†Ruddock, Mrs Joan: *Lewisham, Deptford*	Lab
Rumbold, Mrs Angela: *Mitcham and Morden*	C
Ryder, Richard: *Norfolk Mid*	C

S

Sackville, Thomas: *Bolton West*	C
Sainsbury, Timothy: *Hove*	C
†Salmond, Alexander: *Banff and Buchan*	SNP
Sayeed, Jonathan: *Bristol East*	C
Scott, Nicholas: *Chelsea*	C
Sedgemore, Brian: *Hackney South and Shoreditch*	Lab
†Shaw, David: *Dover*	C
Shaw, Sir Giles: *Pudsey*	C
Shaw, Sir Michael: *Scarborough*	C
Sheerman, Barry: *Huddersfield*	Lab
Sheldon, Robert: *Ashton-under-Lyne*	Lab
Shelton, William: *Streatham*	C
†Shephard, Mrs Gillian: *Norfolk South West*	C
Shepherd, Colin: *Hereford*	C
Shepherd, Richard: *Aldridge-Brownhills*	C
Shersby, Michael: *Uxbridge*	C
Shore, Peter: *Bethnal Green and Stepney*	Lab
Short, Ms Clare: *Birmingham, Ladywood*	Lab
Sims, Roger: *Chislehurst*	C

Skeet, Sir Trevor: *Bedfordshire North*	C
Skinner, Dennis: *Bolsover*	Lab
†Smith, Andrew: *Oxford East*	Lab
Smith, Christopher: *Islington South and Finsbury*	Lab
Smith, Cyril: *Rochdale*	L/All
Smith, John: *Monklands East*	Lab
Smith, Sir Dudley: *Warwick and Leamington*	C
Smith, Timothy: *Beaconsfield*	C
Smyth, Rev Martin: *Belfast South*	OUP
Snape, Peter: *West Bromwich East*	Lab
Soames, Nicholas: *Crawley*	C
Soley, Clive: *Hammersmith*	Lab
Spearing, Nigel: *Newham South*	Lab
Speed, Keith: *Ashford*	C
Speller, Tony: *Devon North*	C
Spicer, James: *Dorset West*	C
Spicer, Michael: *Worcestershire South*	C
Squire, Robin: *Hornchurch*	C
Stanbrook, Ivor: *Orpington*	C
Stanley, John: *Tonbridge and Malling*	C
Steel, David: *Tweeddale, Ettrick and Lauderdale*	L/All
Steen, Anthony: *South Hams*	C
†Steinberg, Gerald: *Durham, City of*	Lab
Stern, Michael: *Bristol North West*	C
Stevens, Lewis: *Nuneaton*	C
Stewart, Allan: *Eastwood*	C
Stewart, Andrew: *Sherwood*	C
Stewart, Ian: *Hertfordshire North*	C
Stokes, John: *Halesowen and Stourbridge*	C
Stott, Roger: *Wigan*	Lab
Stradling Thomas, Sir John: *Monmouth*	C
Strang, Gavin: *Edinburgh East*	Lab
Straw, Jack: *Blackburn*	Lab
Sumberg, David: *Bury South*	C
†Summerson, Hugo: *Walthamstow*	C

T

Tapsell, Sir Peter: *Lindsey East*	C
†Taylor, Mrs Ann: *Dewsbury*	Lab
Taylor, Edward (Teddy): *Southend East*	C
†Taylor, Ian: *Esher*	C
Taylor, John David: *Strangford*	OUP
Taylor, John Mark: *Solihull*	C
Taylor, Matthew: *Truro*	L/All
Tebbit, Norman: *Chingford*	C
Temple-Morris, Peter: *Leominster*	C
Thatcher, Mrs Margaret: *Finchley*	C
Thomas, Dafydd : *Meirionnydd Nant Conwy*	Pl C
Thompson, Donald: *Calder Valley*	C
Thompson, John: *Wansbeck*	Lab
Thompson, Patrick: *Norwich North*	C

Thorne, Neil: *Ilford South* — C
Thornton, Malcolm: *Crosby* — C
Thurnham, Peter: *Bolton North East* — C
Townend, John: *Bridlington* — C
Townsend, Cyril: *Bexleyheath* — C
Tracey, Richard: *Surbiton* — C
†Tredinnick, David: *Bosworth* — C
Trippier, David: *Rossendale and Darwen* — C
Trotter, Neville: *Tynemouth* — C
†Turner, Dennis: *Wolverhampton South East* — Lab
Twinn, Dr Ian: *Edmonton* — C

V

Vaughan, Sir Gerard: *Reading East* — C
†Vaz, Keith: *Leicester East* — Lab
Viggers, Peter: *Gosport* — C

W

Waddington, David: *Ribble Valley* — C
Wakeham, John: *Colchester South and Maldon* — C
Waldegrave, William: *Bristol West* — C
Walden, George: *Buckingham* — C
Walker, Cecil: *Belfast North* — OUP
Walker, Harold: *Doncaster Central* — Lab
Walker, Peter: *Worcester* — C
Walker, William: *Tayside North* — C
†Wall, Patrick: *Bradford North* — Lab
Wallace, James: *Orkney and Shetland* — L/All
Waller, Gary: *Keighley* — C
†Walley, Ms Joan: *Stoke-on-Trent North* — Lab
Walters, Dennis: *Westbury* — C
Ward, John: *Poole* — C
Wardell, Gareth: *Gower* — Lab
Wardle, Charles: *Bexhill and Battle* — C
Wareing, Robert: *Liverpool, West Derby* — Lab
Warren, Kenneth: *Hastings and Rye* — C
Watts, John: *Slough* — C
Weatherill, Bernard: *Croydon North East* — Speaker
Wells, Bowen: *Hertford and Stortford* — C
†Welsh, Andrew: *Angus East* — SNP
Welsh, Michael: *Doncaster North* — Lab
Wheeler, John: *Westminster North* — C
Whitney, Raymond: *Wycombe* — C
†Widdecombe, Miss Ann: *Maidstone* — C
Wiggin, Jerry: *Weston-Super-Mare* — C
Wigley, Dafydd: *Caernarfon* — Pl C
Wilkinson, John: *Ruislip, Northwood* — C
Williams, Alan J: *Swansea West* — Lab

†Williams, Alan W: *Carmarthen*	Lab
†Wilshire, David: *Spelthorne*	C
†Wilson, Brian: *Cunninghame North*	Lab
Winnick, David: *Walsall North*	Lab
Winterton, Mrs Ann: *Congleton*	C
Winterton, Nicholas: *Macclesfield*	C
†Wise, Mrs Audrey: *Preston*	Lab
Wolfson, Mark: *Sevenoaks*	C
Wood, Timothy: *Stevenage*	C
Woodcock, Michael: *Ellesmere Port and Neston*	C
†Worthington, Tony: *Clydebank and Milngavie*	Lab
†Wray, James: *Glasgow, Provan*	Lab

Y

Yeo, Timothy: *Suffolk South*	C
Young, David: *Bolton South East*	Lab
Young, Sir George: *Ealing, Acton*	C
Younger, George: *Ayr*	C

Big shadow Cabinet changes

Labour's general election campaign coordinator and shadow Chief Secretary to the Treasury, **Mr Bryan Gould** (Dagenham) topped the poll in the election for the new session's shadow Cabinet, results of which were announced on July 8 1987.

"Soft Left" supporters of Mr Neil Kinnock, the Labour leader, virtually swept the board. Four "Centre-Right" shadow Cabinet holders were defeated. Vacancies were also created by the retirement of Mr Denis Healey and the election of Mr Stanley Orme (Salford East) as new chairman of the Parliamentary Labour Party, an office which automatically gives him a shadow Cabinet seat.

Mr Gould obtained 163 votes out of the 220 Labour MPs who voted (229 ballot papers were issued). Others elected were (* denotes new member): Mr John Prescott (Hull East) 130 votes; Mr Michael Meacher (Oldham West) 127; Mr Gerald Kaufman (Manchester, Gorton) 115; Mr John Smith (Monklands East) 113; Mr Denzil Davies (Llanelli) 111; *Mr Robert Hughes (Aberdeen North) 106; *Mr Robin Cook (Livingston) 95; Mr Donald Dewar (Glasgow, Garscadden) 93; *Mr Frank Dobson (Holborn and St Pancras) 91; *Mr Gordon Brown (Dunfermline East) 88; Dr John Cunningham (Copeland) 88; *Ms Jo Richardson (Barking) 88; Dr David Clark (South Shields) 87; *Mr Jack Straw (Blackburn) 84.

Members of the shadow Cabinet defeated in the election were: Mr Barry Jones (Alyn and Deeside), who with 78 votes topped the list of those not elected; Mr Peter Shore (Bethnal Green and Stepney); Mr Peter Archer (Warley West); Mr Giles Radice (Durham North). Second and third of those not elected were Mr Tony Blair (Sedgefield) with 71 votes and Mr Tony Benn (Chesterfield) with 69 votes.

Other late news

Miss Betty Boothroyd (West Bromwich West, Lab) was on July 7 appointed the first woman Labour MP to be Deputy Speaker, being officially the Second Deputy Chairman of Ways and Means. She has announced she will not be seeking re-election to the National executive committee of the Labour Party.

Dame Jill Knight (Birmingham, Edgbaston, C) became the first woman vice-chairman of the 1922 Committee of Conservative backbenchers.

Mr David Heathcoat-Amory (Wells, C) has been appointed PPS to Mr Douglas Hurd, Home Secretary.

The General Election 1987

The general election of June 11, 1987 swept Mrs Margaret Thatcher, Prime Minister, back to Downing Street for an historic third successive victory. The Conservatives were returned to power with an overall majority in the Commons of 101, excluding the Speaker, and a majority over Labour of 146.

By June 12, Mrs Thatcher had her new cabinet in place, appointing Sir Michael Havers as Lord Chancellor - he was made a life peer - following the decision of Lord Hailsham to retire. Mr Norman Tebbit, chairman of the Conservative Party, left the Cabinet at his own request having expressed the desire to be able to spend more time with his wife who was paralysed in the Brighton bombing outrage in 1984. The Government chief whip in the last Parliament, Mr John Wakeham, also injured at Brighton, joined the Cabinet as Lord Privy Seal and Leader of the Commons, replacing Mr John Biffen.

Mr Cecil Parkinson, who resigned from the Cabinet in 1983, was recalled to it as Secretary of State for Energy and Mr Peter Walker was switched from that department to become Secretary of State for Wales. In the Principality and in Scotland the Conservatives fared badly. Mr Michael Jopling, Minister of Agriculture, Fisheries and Food, lost his job to Mr John MacGregor, Chief Secretary to the Treasury. Into the Cabinet in that post came Mr John Major.

The state of the parties in the Commons after the election compared with its composition at dissolution and after the 1983 general election is as follows:

	June 1987	Gains	Losses	Dissolution	June 1983
Conservative	375	12	29	392	397
Labour	229	27	6	206	209
Liberal	17	3	5	19	17
SDP	5	0	3	8	6
Scottish National	3	3	2	2	2
Plaid Cymru	3	1	0	2	2
Official Ulster Unionist	9	0	1	10	11
Democratic Unionist	3	0	0	3	3
Ulster Popular Unionist	1	0	0	1	1
Social Democratic and Labour	3	1	0	2	1
Provisional Sinn Fein	1	0	0	1	1
The Speaker	1	0	0	1	-
Independent	0	0	1	1	-
Seats vacant	-	-	-	2	-
Total	650	-	-	650	650

Details of seats that changed hands:

From Conservative to Labour — Aberdeen South; Bradford North; Bridgend; Cardiff West; Clwyd South West; Cunninghame North; Dewsbury; Edinburgh Central; Edinburgh South; Glanford and Scunthorpe; Halifax; Leicester East; Leicester South; Manchester, Withington; Newcastle upon Tyne Central; Newport West; Norwich South; Nottingham North; Oxford East; Renfrew West and Inverclyde; Strathkelvin and Bearsden; The Wrekin.

From Labour to Conservative — Battersea; Fulham (regained after Lab by-election win, 1986); Ipswich; Thurrock; Walthamstow; Wolverhampton North East.

From Alliance to Conservative — Cambridgeshire, North East (from L); Colne Valley (from L); Isle of Wight (from L); Portsmouth South (regained after SDP by-election win, 1984); Ryedale (regained after L by-election win, 1986); Stockton South (SDP).

From Alliance to Labour — Glasgow, Hillhead (from SDP); Leeds West (from L);

From SNP to Labour: Dundee East; Western Isles.

From Conservative to Alliance: Argyll and Bute (L); Brecon and Radnor (retained by L after 1985 by-election win); Fife North-East (L); Greenwich (retained by SDP after 1987 SDP by-election win); Southport (L).

From Conservative to SNP:
Angus East; Banff and Buchan; Moray.

From Conservative to Pl Cymru:
Ynys Mon.

From OUP to SDLP:
Newry and Armagh (held from 1985 by-election win); Down South.

Labour campaign looked better than it was

by Robin Oakley
Political Editor of *The Times*

Labour, by common accord, won the campaign in 1987. But it lost the election comprehensively. Mrs Thatcher not only became the first party leader in 150 years to win three consecutive General Elections, she also saw the Conservatives returned to office with another three figure majority.

Labour's increasingly self-confident campaign under a new leader succeeded in raising public interest in the party's chosen themes-- unemployment, education and health. Mr Neil Kinnock succeeded where Mr Michael Foot had failed in 1983 in re-establishing Labour as the main opponent of the Tory Government. Mr Bryan Gould, the party's campaign co-ordinator, Mr Peter Mandelson, Labour's communications director and Mr Larry Whitty, the general secretary, improved the party's presentation and deployed Labour's forces effectively.

In contrast with 1983, Shadow Ministers found themselves in the right place at the right time knowing exactly what was expected of them and there was little do-it-yourself policy making during the election. Discipline was tight, with union leaders little in evidence and the Left subdued . But for all that, the headline in *Labour Weekly* when it was all over told the story: "The dream shattered. Confidence which proved to be over confidence". The degree of appreciation for the achievements of the Thatcher Government in tackling inflation and union power , lifting living standards for those in work, building popular capitalism and restoring Britain's international reputation had been underestimated. Labour advanced, but only a little. Mr Kinnock's party still finished with 3 per cent less of the national vote than in 1979, the year of Mrs Thatcher's first triumph, and 40 fewer seats. And across a great swathe of Southern England it was the Alliance which remained in second place.

Labour increased its vote where it had least to gain, in Scotland, Wales and the North East, rather than eating into the Conservative marginals. It suffered from its unilateralist defence policy, from its readiness to reverse Tory trades union reforms and from the imprecision of its taxation policies. The campaign, in retrospect, proved to have looked better than it was.

Mr Kinnock did not emerge as a serious rival to Mrs Thatcher as a potential Prime Minister and despite that disciplined campaign with the bogeymen obligingly keeping quiet, Labour clearly failed to erase the extremist image acquired for it by some of its leading lights in local government. The so-called "Loony Left" effect was particularly evident in London where the Conservatives took two seats from Labour and regained another lost in a 1986 by-election.

It certainly was not all plain sailing for the Tories. Mr Norman Tebbit, the Conservative party chairman, who chose to bow out of the Cabinet as the election ended to spend more time with his wife Margaret, badly injured in the Brighton bomb blast, found himself under fire during the campaign, even from the Prime Minister, for a Tory effort which seemed to lack pace and panache. Ten days from polling, there were twitters in the high command amounting almost to panic and squabbles continued for some time afterwards about the quality of the advertising input from Saatchi and Saatchi and over which other advertising experts had been involved in the final week's slogans. But in the end Mr Tebbit's relaxed style was vindicated. As he was heard to remark: "If that's the sort of result you get with a 'lack-lustre' campaign then we must clearly fight more of them".

The Conservatives were worried, however, by an election triumph which left them without a single Tory M.P. in the inner cities of Manchester, Liverpool, Glasgow, Newcastle-upon-Tyne, Bradford, Leicester or Stoke, fuelling concern about the North/South divide. While the swing from Conservatives to Labour was 1. 5 per cent in England it was 5 per cent in Wales and 7. 5 per cent in Scotland, where the Tories lost 11 of the 21 seats they had held in 1983.

The Alliance was thrown immediately by the election result into an undignified and damaging squabble about whether the Liberals and SDP should merge into a single party. They had found themselves unable to mount an effective challenge after Labour had widened the gap between them from 5 per cent to 10 per cent in the opening week of the campaign. They failed to take advantage of their new parity of exposure on TV and their strategy was inconsistent. But despite the gloom and doom headlines about their efforts; they showed that they too have established a base vote among the British population.

23

It is a comment in itself that what was widely represented as an election catastrophe for them left the Alliance with only one seat less than in 1983 and with more than 7 million votes, less than 3 per cent below what they had achieved at the previous election with Labour in chaos.

The 1987 General Election was called soon after 2pm on Monday May 11. Media pressure and Westminster expectation had been allowed to build to such a pitch that the decision was inevitable. After leading the opinion polls for months the Tories had been waiting for local election results on May 7 as a final indicator. When those suggested that a Conservative victory was likely, though not absolutely certain, Mrs Thatcher had little option but to launch the contest. Her discussion at Chequers on Sunday May 10 with her "A team" of senior advisers spent little time on the election date, much more on how it was to be fought.

Justifying her decision to go to the country a year before she had to, risking a majority of more than 130, Mrs Thatcher said "I don't think I have been pushed into anything. It was best to end the uncertainty so that we can all plan for the future".

At 61, Mrs Thatcher signalled her intention of carrying on through the next Parliament and said that the Conservative manifesto would "set the course to go up to the end of this century".

Mr Denis Healey, Labour's Foreign Affairs spokesman, who was in Moscow at the time, made what was conceded to be the first gaffe of the campaign by announcing that the Soviet authorities were "praying" for a Labour victory.

By going for an early election the Conservative government had to abandon large chunks of its legislative programme to complete Commons business in time. Much of the Finance Bill was sacrificed, save for the 2p cut to a 27 per cent standard rate of income tax. From the Criminal Justice Bill, the centrepiece of the programme, only the measures to tackle serious fraud survived. Ministers had to drop key proposals on the private finance of public housing to get the Local Government Bill through.

Opinion remarkably static

The latest opinion poll put the Conservatives on 44 per cent, Labour on 33 per cent and the SDP/Liberal Alliance on 21. More than 80 per cent of voters claimed at the end of the campaign to have made up their minds before it started and, though there was considerable "churning" between the parties, opinion levels remained remarkably static during a contest enlivened by few major dramas.

The parties' campaign strategies were clear. The Conservatives were anxious to dispel complacency and to demonstrate that after two Parliaments they were not running out of steam. Their manifesto was to stress the radical nature of plans to revolutionise education, housing and the inner cities, with more power taken out of the hands of councils and local politicians and put into the hands of teachers, parents, tenants and developers.

Labour, heartened by an infinitely improved organisation and a slick new style of presentation centred on the red rose emblem, intended to concentrate on a moral crusade for job creation, health and education. This was to be based on a £3. 6 billion anti-poverty programme, financed by tax increases for the better off, and increased borrowing to provide for a £6 billion employment package.

The Alliance campaigned for a change in the electoral system to proportional representation, a package of constitutional reforms leading to more open government and for greater social spending, with a special tax to counter any inflationary take off.

As Parliament wound down to dissolution on May 18 the Alliance leaders appeared to have seized the initiative, catching headlines with selective leaks from their manifesto and a whirlwind tour of the regions, though opinion polls were to show that it was to little effect. The opposition lost its battle against the imposition of a guillotine on the bill to replace domestic rates in Scotland with a community charge on all adults, intended as a model to be extended to England and Wales after a Conservative victory. Labour was more successful in highlighting the issue of hospital waiting lists.

Challenged to a face to face TV debate by Mr Neil Kinnock, Mrs Thatcher told him that she would not give him the platform he was seeking.

Mr Kinnock confirmed his dominance of Labour's policy-making machinery on May 12 when the traditional Clause V meeting of the Shadow Cabinet and National Executive, often a traumatic affair, adopted with little wrangling a manifesto shorn of traditional left-wing commitments. Party conference calls for compensation to reimburse miners fined during the coal strike and surcharged councillors were dropped and past commitments to phase out nuclear power and to re-nationalise former State industries "privatised" by the Tories were modified. The hard Left were overwhelmingly defeated in votes on their attempts to commit Labour to withdraw Britain from the Common Market, to remove all US bases (not just nuclear ones) and the gradual dismantling of NATO and the Warsaw Pact. But Labour's unilateral disarmament policy, acknowledged as the most difficult part of its case to "sell" to the electorate, was not helped by General Bernard Rogers, NATO's Supreme Allied Commander Europe, when he said it would be the straw which broke the camel's back for the United States public and would lead to calls for their troops to be brought home.

The Conservatives, with Budget tax cuts about to feed through into pay packets, had a boost from the unemployment figures published on May 14 showing a further fall by 36,242 to stand at 3,107,128, with seasonally adjusted figures down for the tenth month in succession. Labour's spokesman Mr John Prescott hit back on what was to be a keystone issue for his Party throughout the campaign, criticising the government's alterations to the way in which jobless figures were collated and saying "Despite 19 fiddles and 750,000 people on temporary schemes, they still have not managed to cut unemployment".

Mrs Thatcher and Mr Kinnock both opened their campaigns outside Westminster on Friday, May 15. Mr Kinnock, whose powerful platform oratory was to be a major feature of the campaign, made the Prime Minister's professed desire for a fourth term a central issue, mocking what he called her yearning for immortality. She must not be allowed to go on and on and on, he said, reintroducing plans for schools, housing and health that had been abandoned 50 years before. At a Llandudno rally, he forecast the "last few weeks of that job-destroying, oil-wasting, truth-twisting, service-smashing, nation-splitting, bunch of twisters under a one-person government". Britain had taken a beating from a government with an "on your bike" employment policy, a "flag day" health service policy and a "jumble sale" education system and could not survive 13 years of that.

Mrs Thatcher, addressing Scottish Conservatives in Perth, pledged the Tories to an intensified drive for popular capitalism and warned that Labour would produce an "iceberg manifesto" with nine-tenths of its socialism invisible beneath the surface. Anticipating a Labour attack on the Tory health service record, she made the NHS a centrepiece of her speech, saying "I don't merely say the NHS is safe with us, [as she had done in 1983] I say the NHS is safe only with us". She claimed that Conservative policies of increasing choice and spreading ownership were "in tune with the deepest instincts of the British people".

Mrs Thatcher declared: "A vote for the Liberals or SDP? That's not a choice but a step into the unknown, into a no-man's land of confusion, uncertainty and parliamentary chaos. A Labour government? That's not a choice. It's a nightmare. "

In what was to prove, in Mr Kinnock's words, a "pretty mucky" election the first unpleasantness emerged that weekend with allegations about Liberal leader Mr David Steel and the wife of a close friend, rapidly followed by denials, apologies and the payment of hefty damages.

The Alliance manifesto, published on May 18, promised a "Great Reform Charter" including PR, a separate parliament for Scotland, fixed term parliaments, reform of the House of Lords, repeal of the Official Secrets Act and a new Ministry of Justice. Launching the document, Mr Steel and Dr David Owen, the SDP leader, in what was later widely agreed to have been a tactical mistake, concentrated their assault on the Conservatives, dismissing Labour as "unelectable and irrelevant".

Both the Alliance and Conservative strategies were built on the assumption, encouraged by opinion polls and the local government elections, that the Alliance would be challenging Labour for second place early in the campaign and might well surge past to become the major challenger to the Conservatives. But a strong Labour campaign in which Mr Kinnock's platform performances, American-style party election broadcasts and a well-orchestrated pursuit of the "caring" issues played a major role, instead restored Labour's position as the leading opposition party and the challengers, albeit at a distance, to the Conservatives. Both the Alliance and the Tories proved slow to adjust their tactics in response.

With early opinion polls showing a movement to Labour at the expense of the Alliance, the Tory and Labour manifestos were launched on Tuesday May 19.

Labour, in a much shorter programme than in 1983, promised a £12 billion package to tackle unemployment, poverty and crime. It included a national minimum wage, an £8 per week rise in pensions for couples and the borrowing of £3 billion more for spending on house building and the NHS. There was no mention, however, of Labour's plan to scrap the married man's tax allowance or to remove the £15,000 a year ceiling on national insurance contributions.

Defence row went on for days

The Tory manifesto included plans to allow parents and governors to opt to take their schools out of local education authority control and for council tenants to opt to have housing associations as their landlords instead. It also promised further privatisation — of the water authorities and electricity boards — and wider share ownership.

The Conservative manifesto infuriated the Alliance leaders, especially Dr Owen, by lumping them together with Labour as unilateralists and "fellow travellers". Demands that the "smear" be removed were ignored by the Prime Minister. She showed her sensitivity meanwhile by denying at a meeting of Tory candidates that the Conservatives were "uncaring". The defence row went on for days, much to Tory delight, with other parties objecting to much use of the Union Jack in a Conservative election broadcast. Said Dr Owen, "It really is sticking in our gullet this belief that only the Tories understand the national interest, only the Tories are patriotic".

For the Conservatives, the defence row served three purposes — drawing attention to Labour's unilateralism, reminding voters of the Alliance split on the issue the previous autumn, and drawing the Alliance into the thick of the party dogfight instead of allowing them to benefit as Mister Cleans on the sidelines while Labour and Tories conducted their habitual slanging match.

Labour secured a bonus meanwhile in a row over remarks about unemployment wrongly credited to Mr Norman Tebbit, the Conservative Party chairman, in a Labour advertisement. He had not used the words attributed to him, but as a triumphantly unearthed tape recording proved he had said it would be hard for the Tories to be re-elected with three million unemployed. Mr Tebbit had to defend himself against what Labour was forced to admit was a "paraphrase", but the result was that Labour succeeded in lifting unemployment, if only briefly, to the top of the election agenda.

When Mrs Thatcher launched her full election campaign at her adoption meeting on May 21 she made defence the centre of her attack on Labour. Polls showed the success of the Tory tactics. Those rating defence as a major issue increased by 13 per cent during the campaign. Labour meanwhile succeeded in lifting interest in the NHS and in education, two good issues for Mr Kinnock's party, by 6-7 per cent.

Remarks by Dr Owen suggesting that an Alliance government might maintain Trident after all if advised to do so by the Chiefs of Staff, helped to keep defence on the boil.

In the early days of the campaign the radical Tory manifesto proved a considerable embarrassment. Details of the education plans had clearly not been fully thought out and after remarks by the Prime Minister at her press conference appeared to suggest that "opted out" schools would be allowed to practice selection and to charge parents, the Tories were thrown on the defensive. Both Mr Baker, the Education Secretary, and Mrs Thatcher were forced to spell out that no fee paying or return to the 11+ was envisaged. Similar, though less damaging confusion followed a few days later over the ramifications of the new housing policy.

Meanwhile Mr Kinnock's tour of the provinces and the well-organised programme of speeches on jobs, health and education by shadow ministers showed the Labour machine back in fighting trim — even if it did owe more to Madison Avenue this time than to Keir Hardie. Mr Kinnock made his mark as a man of vigour, confidence and passionate concern about the plight of the less well-off in society.

The highlight of the presidential-style Labour approach was a hagiographical TV spectacular scripted by Colin Welland and directed by Hugh Hudson of *Chariots of Fire* fame. Concentrating entirely on the Labour leader and his wife and what his relatives and party figures had to say about him, it ended not with the slogan "Vote Labour" but simply with the word "Kinnock" — and was shown again, allegedly by popular demand, later in the campaign.

Meanwhile, Mr Kinnock was accused of dodging the national press by failing to appear for more than a handful of the traditional morning press conferences in London — a duty Mrs Thatcher continued to tackle with relish. But a fortnight after the election was called the Alliance was slipping as Mr Kinnock sold the voters a soft-focus only semi-Socialist Labour Party and the Tories were still searching for first gear.

Owen and Steel reacted by ceasing dual appearances on TV which they felt made them look silly. The Tories intensified their assault on Labour's defence policy after Mr Kinnock talked in a TV interview with Mr David Frost of Russian occupation. Though Labour's leader denied the interpretations, Tory ministers leapt in to deride him for embracing a policy of surrender followed by guerilla resistance in the Home Counties.

Labour blundered too over rates. When the Tories claimed that Labour was planning to move to capital value rating, instead of the existing system, party spokesmen denied it utterly. Only for *The Times* to reveal that it had been announced as official Labour policy in the briefing material issued to local government candidates a month before.

As the campaign wore on, with conflicting evidence from polls in the marginal seats, Labour seemed to close the gap slightly on the Tories while Alliance support stayed rooted at around 20-21 per cent. Their promised surge, 1983-style, resolutely refused to appear in the face of Labour's improved campaign. The Tories continued to play the defence card and to charge Mr Kinnock with running away. He suffered simultaneously from a bad cold and a bout of snappishness with journalists.

He knew defence was proving a weak point and subtly trimmed his position on Polaris on May 28, though announcing that he would be in Downing Street recalling the submarines within a fortnight. The Tories meanwhile found their performance criticised unusually for a lack of snap and professionalism.

Government supporters worried

Constant Labour claims that the Tories had a hidden economic agenda including plans to impose VAT on food, childrens' clothing and fuel prices eventually forced Mrs Thatcher into the commitment that there was no question of Britain under the Conservatives accepting the imposition of VAT on any of those items.

As the campaign moved into June, Mr Kinnock slipped again by underlining in a TV interview his desire for greater state control of industry, contrary to Labour's new image. But the Labour leader's growing confidence and style and the lacklustre Tory campaign began to worry government supporters. A Gallup poll in the *Daily Telegraph* suggested that the gap between Labour and the Tories had closed to 4 per cent and Thursday June 4 became what one senior Tory called "The day the Tory campaign wobbled". Harsh words were exchanged between Mrs Thatcher and Mr Tebbit. Lord Young was given a more intensive part to play in the campaign, co-ordinating Central Office and Downing Street and doubts were raised about the efficacy of the advertising campaign by Saatchi and Saatchi as the Prime Minister took advice from alternative ad-men. City prices dipped nervously as a BBC *Newsnight* poll raised the possibility of a hung Parliament.

Labour's confidence increased as public differences between Mr Steel and Dr Owen over the choice of potential coalition partners (one clearly preferred Labour, the other the Tories) scotched any hopes of an Alliance revival. Even Mr James Callaghan, an opponent of unilateralism who had wrecked Labour's 1983 campaign, stayed silent this time save for praising the vigour of Mr Kinnock's campaign.

But Labour had only flattered to deceive. Over the next few days the Party proved incapable of a convincing explanation of the full ramifications of its tax and benefit policies. There was confusion between Mr Kinnock and Mr Hattersley over the level at which Labour's tax and the national insurance proposals would start to bite — at £25,000, £15,000 or £10,000 a year. The Tory nerve recovered and Mrs Thatcher set off to Venice for a day to polish her world statesman image at the Economic Summit. Just before doing so she had given her Party jitters once more by mishandling press conference questions over her preference for private medicine and over hospital waiting lists, exploited by Labour over the case of Mark Burgess, a ten-year old whose heart operation had been postponed.

The final week of the campaign saw the most expensive advertising blitz ever launched in a British election with Tories and Labour taking page after page in the national press to sell their wares and condemn their opponents. The Tories who had begun high-mindedly with such a radical manifesto were forced back in the end to the old-fashioned cry of "Britain Is Great Again: Don't Let Labour Ruin It". Labour concentrated on the health service and on the Prime Minister's uncaring image.

Mrs Thatcher herself, a twitchier less confident leader than in 1983 for much of the campaign, came on strongly at the end with a series of TV and radio interviews. And though other Party leaders dismissed her Venice visit as "one cornetto photo opportunities" (David Owen) and the "grand banal" (Denis Healey), the other world leaders gave her what she wanted — a ringing endorsement of Thatcherite "sound money" policies and a condemnation of one-sided disarmament.

Employment Secretary Lord Young tried ably but unavailingly to entice the silent trades union leaders into the campaign and Labour, jabbed by Chancellor Lawson, continued to wriggle uncomfortably on taxation questions.

At their final rallies Mrs Thatcher called Labour a reckless party unfit to govern and played the Militant menace and the "Loony left" bogey, so beloved of Tory TV broadcasts, for all they were worth. Labour, she said, would destroy prosperity and return us to a "Strife-torn, strike-ridden, divided society".

Mr Kinnock, continuing to aim for the moral high ground, scorned Tory claims to be the party of the family and played up his youthfulness as the hope for the future. Where the Tories appealed to the pocket book he appealed to hearts and emotions, saying that Britain's children needed to live in a world that was not divided by privilege and poverty, not disabled by unemployment, not fractured by weak, partial and backward health and education systems.

The Alliance leaders, who had always drawn the least partisan, most impressive audiences, continued their increasingly despairing predictions of a last-minute surge in their favour and said that only the election of a substantial block of Alliance MPs could stop Mrs Thatcher enjoying "unfettered power" once again.

Two heads not better than one

In the end it turned out to have been a ritual election. The Tories opened with an 11 point lead, never dipped below the 40 per cent safety line, and held all but a fraction of their 1983 vote.

Labour, having once hit 37 per cent but only averaged 33 throughout, finished on 32 per cent. For all Mr Kinnock's fervour they had their second worst result since 1935 and still have a mountain to climb.

The Alliance edged up a couple of points to 23 per cent at the end but learned the hard way that rational appeals to the voter still require bite and passion to succeed. They learned too, that, in politics, two heads are definitely not better than one.

Mrs Thatcher sailed back into Downing Street, this time quoting Kipling instead of Francis of Assisi, with another three figure majority and the real prospect of going "on and on and on". The signs were that the decline of traditional class patterns, the spread of ownership and improved living standards for the 87 per cent in work had made the Conservatives the natural governing party, certainly so long as the anti-Conservative vote was split. But many Tories were left nonetheless with the distinctly queasy feeling that without Labour's self-inflicted wound of an unsaleable defence policy, Mr Kinnock and his Party might have made it a pretty close run thing.

The Conservatives immediately set about tackling the problems of the inner cities where they had done so badly, with the aims both of improving conditions for those who lived there and of pursuing Mrs Thatcher's mission to eradicate socialism in Britain by razing the last bastions of municipal Labour strength. The Alliance found itself with a constitutional crisis about its future shape and relationships. Labour meanwhile was left to sort out a conundrum. In a society of owner occupiers, an increasing number of share owners and 40 per cent white collar workers, how does a party which is financed and dominated by the trades unions and which appeals largely to council tenants and the less well off build the support it needs to achieve the enormous swing required for it to regain power-- especially if it remains wedded to a unilateralist defence policy which has twice been rejected conclusively by the British electorate?

U-turn took Tories out of doldrums

by Philip Webster
Chief Political Correspondent of *The Times*

If anyone believed that the 144 majority handed to Mrs Margaret Thatcher on June 9 1983 meant that her second term would be any less turbulent than the first, they could hardly have been more mistaken.

Far from getting the smooth ride some of her supporters expected, it was a Government which in it its early days stumbled from crisis to crisis, often giving the impression of uncertainty of purpose and lack of direction.

It was the Parliament that will be remembered most for its many episodes of high political, parliamentary and personal drama.

It was the Parliament when the Government was touched by scandal within weeks of its election; the Parliament when the IRA tried to wipe out the Cabinet as it slept at a conference hotel.

It was the Parliament when the affairs of a small helicopter company rocked the Government to its foundations and lost the Prime Minister two of her most able ministers; when the Government, armed with its labour legislation of this and the previous Parliament, took on the organized might of the National Union of Mineworkers, and won.

It was the Parliament when the Labour Party rose from the ashes of its worst election defeat since before the war to equip itself with a modern leader and image; when the Liberal-Social Democratic Party Alliance again threatened a breakthrough but finally flattered to deceive.

It was the Parliament of popular capitalism when millions more took shares in privatized companies like British Gas and British Telecom and bought their council homes; of steady economic growth, continued low inflation and, towards the end, of unemployment at last beginning to fall and nearing the three million mark.

It was the Parliament, at last, of the U-turn when the Government after years of preaching financial rectitude, suddenly broke its sacrosanct targets and found that it had £5 billion at its disposal to boost spending on health, education and housing.

But it was a Parliament which, despite all the setbacks along the way, ended for Mrs Thatcher like the one that preceded it - with a landslide victory for the Conservative Party.

When Mrs Thatcher gave her traditional pre-Christmas address to Conservative MPs in the 1922 Committee in 1984, she wished them a united new year. Her remarks were tinged with more than a little irony. Because there must have been times during the previous 18 months when she must have wondered what she had done to deserve such a rebellious band of backbenchers.

One of the Cabinet's first acts was to bring in an emergency £500m package of spending cuts. The Government suffered its first rebellion on the vexed question of MPs' pay, and it had a huge scare when its majority crashed to only 552 at the Penrith and the Border by-election caused by the elevation to the Lords of William Whitelaw.The voters were registering their dissatisfaction at having to return to the polls again so soon; but it was a warning shot to ministers.

On October 1, Neil Kinnock, at the age of 41, became the first Labour leader to be elected by the electoral college of trade unions, constituency parties and MPs. He secured an overwhelming 71.3 per cent of the vote, with Hattersley second on 19.3 per cent, Heffer on 6.3 per cent and Shore on 3.1 per cent. The so-called "dream ticket" was completed when Hattersley was elected deputy leader, securing 67.3 per cent of the vote against the left candidate, Michael Meacher, who received 27.9 per cent.

Kinnock was immediately given a comfortable majority on the ruling national executive and set about far-reaching plans to refashion Labour's policies and organization. He, too, was given a swift foretaste of the difficulties that lay ahead when James Callaghan, the former leader, and Denis Healey voiced doubts again about the defence policy on which Labour had fought the election. Although many of Labour's traditional left-wing commitments were dropped or changed in the years that followed, it was a non-nuclear policy to which Kinnock was personally attached but many others in his shadow cabinet were opposed that was to be put to the electorate in 1987.

With the Labour Party in good spirits after Kinnock's election, the Conservatives should have been meeting in triumph to celebrate the election victory at their Blackpool conference. But it did not turn out like that.

Shortly before the conference, Cecil Parkinson was to announce that he was the father of a baby expected the following January by his former secretary, Miss Sara Keays . The scandal dominated the week, although Parkinson, his ministerial colleagues and Mrs Thatcher hoped that he would be able to brave it. It was a long statement to *The Times* by Miss Keays which convinced the former party chairman that he would have to go to avoid further embarrassment to the Government. His departure from office distressed Mrs Thatcher and the possibility of his recall was to become a regular theme of Cabinet reshuffles throughout the Parliament. Norman Tebbit replaced Parkinson in his Cabinet post.

There followed the year of the revolts, as Conservative MPs seized upon issue after issue to flex their muscles.

Edward Heath, the former Prime Minister, led a revolt against the Government's legislation to cap the rates of high spending authorities. As a former chief whip, he was accused of disloyalty but Heath, whose icy opinion of Mrs Thatcher had never been a secret, retorted that he would not be a lackey.

Francis Pym, dismissed as Foreign Secretary just after the election, led a similar rebellion on the rate support grant settlement, and the Government was immediately embroiled in another controversry when it announced suddenly that the staff at the Government's communications headquarters at Cheltenham were being deprived of their right to union membership.

Neil Kinnock was in complete authority over his party. Its commitment to withdraw from the EEC was modified and a new policy structure giving a more decisive say to the party's MPs was being set up. By now, however, the miners' strike, which was to damage Labour's short and long-term fortunes, was under way. Unable and unwilling to give wholehearted backing to the strike, the Labour leadership was restricted to voicing concern over the way it was being policed. Kinnock called for a ballot "to bring cohesion to the actions of the National Union of Mineworkers." But with massive stockpiles of coal built up for just such an eventuality and miners continuing to work, the Government and the coal board had time on their side. They dug in for a long haul, refusing to intervene, believing that the time to strike a crippling blow against union militancy had arrived.

Back in the Commons, Heath and Pym and another former Cabinet minister, Sir Ian Gilmour, were at the forefront of opposition to the Government's legislation paving the way for the abolition in 1986 of the Greater London Council. To do that they needed a "paving" Bill cancelling the 1985 elections to the GLC and putting in nominated transitional bodies to run it in the final year of its life.

It just got through the Commons but was stopped dead in its tracks in the Lords. In a sensational revolt, peers voted to allow the elections to go ahead, ripping the heart out of the Bill. In the end, the Government was forced into the outcome they had sought to avoid, giving the GLC councillors an extra year of unelected office. It was, to date, the Government's worst legislative setback but more were to come.

While all this was going on, the Government was being hounded and harried over an event which it might reasonably have supposed would have passed into history, the sinking of the Argentine cruiser General Belgrano during the Falklands war.

Tam Dalyell, Labour MP for Linlithgow, was relentlessly pursuing Mrs Thatcher with his claim that the Belgrano was sunk for political not operational reasons, to scupper the Peruvian peace plan. A senior Ministry of Defence official named Clive Ponting was charged under the Official Secrets Act for allegedly passing official documents to Dalyell.

As the Labour leadership became involved in a campaign which Dalyell had for so long fought almost single-handedly, the Government admitted that the Ministry of Defence knew that the Belgrano had reversed course away from the task force on the day it was sunk, but that ministers were not informed of the change. The Government was further embarrassed in the new year when Ponting was acquitted.

Kinnock suffered the first big reverse of his leadership when his proposal to introduce a one-member one vote system for the reselection of MPs was defeated at the annual party conference. It meant that selections, for this Parliament at least, were to be left in the hands of often unrepresentative management committees of local parties. As events turned out, however, less blood was spilt than expected and only a handful of MPs were "deselected."

Then on October 12, 1984, at the end of the Conservatives' annual conference week came an event which transcended party politics. Early in the morning of Friday, October 12, an IRA bomb went off in the Grand Hotel, Brighton, where the Prime Minister and many of her Cabinet were staying.

It was an outrage that shocked the world. Five people, including Mrs Roberta Wakeham, wife of John Wakeham, the Government chief whip, and Sir Anthony Berry, the Conservative MP, were killed, and 31 injured. Mr Wakeham and Norman Tebbit were severely injured. Mrs Thatcher escaped unhurt and 12 hours after the attempt on her life she went into the conference hall to declare that terrorism would never defeat democracy.

Parliament resumed and the Government was quickly back in trouble with its MPs. There was a big rebellion over its plans for cuts in overseas aid, the threat of an even bigger one forced Sir Keith Joseph, then Secretary of State for Education and Science, to climb down on his plan to increase parental contributions to student grants, and Edward Heath led the backbench opposition to the Bill abolishing the GLC, when the Government's majority was slashed to 23, raising false hopes that the authority and the six metropolitan counties that disappeared with it might survive.

No surprise then that when a somewhat beleaguered prime minister went to offer her Christmas greetings to her MPs she should demand unity.

However, 1985 began with a sterling crisis. Interest rates rose and the pound fell to $1.10, and promised tax cuts were in jeopardy.

At the start of March, the pit strike ended in total defeat for Scargill and the striking miners. For the Government it was the turning-point of the Parliament. The picket line violence which scarred the dispute left a deep impression on the minds of the British public and ministers said privately that the

Government's victory would turn out to be as decisive in electoral terms as the victory in the Falklands war had been in the last Parliament.

It damaged Neil Kinnock and his party severely. Opinion polls suggested they got little credit for withholding their outright support from the strikers, but were damaged more by the antics of the far left who twice brought the Commons to a standstill with demonstrations over the strike. After the second, an exasperated Kinnock told his party: "My God. Maggie Thatcher could do with an attack like that every day." And he accused the left of self-indulgence.

The strike appeared to halt Labour's revival. By the turn of the year, after 10 months of the strike, almost all the progress made by Labour in the months following Kinnock's election had been reversed. And the Labour leader's standing among voters, particularly Labour supporters, fell. He could not win; he lost backing from those who felt he should have been stronger in his support for the NUM and those who wanted him to dissociate himself from the tactics of the union leadership. The lessons of the dispute were not lost on a weakened labour movement. Organized labour was not to take on the Government again in this Parliament.

But the Government's difficulties were far from over. Former ministers worried about its unemployment policies were joined by James Prior, a long-serving wet who had stood down from the Cabinet in the previous autumn's reshuffle. Francis Pym formed a new parliamentary grouping called Conservative Centre Forward which was expected to become the focus of anti-Thatcher discontent. But its launch was badly mishandled with divisions over tactics. Little was to be heard from it as the Parliament progressed.

The warning bells were ringing louder than ever when the Conservatives lost the Brecon and Radnor by-election to the Alliance, slipping to third place and having their general election share of the vote halved. It was the worst Tory by-election defeat since 1962; it was a contest dominated by the personality of the Prime Minister.

The Government's disarray was further underlined when about 100 backbenchers rebelled against its decision to grant top people's pay rises of up to 46 per cent. Never had a summer parliamentary recess been more welcome to a Government.

In the September of that year, Mrs Thatcher picked Norman Tebbit as her party chairman for the run-up to the next general election. She made Douglas Hurd Home Secretary and gave one of her favourites, Lord Young of Graffham, the crucial job of Secretary of State for Employment.

By now, Neil Kinnock had decided to take on the Militant leaders of Liverpool Council who had plunged the city towards bankruptcy in their budget confrontations with the Government. He electrified the Labour conference in Bournemouth with his most courageous leadership speech attacking Derek Hatton and the other Liverpool Militants.

"You end in the grotesque chaos, " he said, "of a Labour council hiring taxis to scuttle round the city handing out redundancy notices to its own workers." According to opinion polls, Kinnock's tough line won back for him from the voters much of the support that the miners' strike lost him. It was an onslaught that he was to press home. By the following year's conference, Hatton and other Militant leaders had been expelled from the Labour Party.

On November 15, 1985, Mrs Thatcher and Dr Garret Fitzgerald,the Irish Prime Minister, after 15 months of secret negotiations, signed the historic Anglo-Irish Agreement. The deal, denounced predictably by the Unionists as treachery, gave the Republic the right to contribute to policy in Northern Ireland for the first time since 1922. It set up a conference of British and Irish ministers to discuss political, security and legal matters affecting Northern Ireland. The Unionist MPs resigned their parliamentary seats in protest and fought by-elections on their opposition to the agreement.

Just before Christmas 1985, the biggest crisis of Mrs Thatcher's leadership hit the Government.

Westland Helicopters sought Government approval for a rescue deal with the American Sikorsky Corporation. Alone in the Cabinet, Michael Heseltine, the Secretary of State for Defence, preferred an agreement with European helicopter interests and embarked on an extraordinarily tenacious campaign to convince Parliament and the Cabinet that the American deal was against the national interest. Hampered by the scepticism of the Westland board and the refusal of the Government, most notably Mrs Thatcher, to take a collective view, Heseltine audaciously appealed to backbench MPs from both sides of the Commons to put pressure on the Cabinet.

The battle between the European consortium and the Americans raged into the new year with Heseltine publicly backing the Europeans. In an astonishing development, a highly confidential letter from the Solicitor General to Heseltine referring to inaccuracy in a letter written by Heseltine was officially leaked.

On January 9 Heseltine walked out of a cabinet meeting and resigned, accusing Mrs Thatcher of sabotaging attempts to launch the European rescue package. The Conservatives were dramatically split.

It was soon revealed that the leak of the Solicitor General's letter had been personally authorized by Leon Brittan, the Secretary of State for Trade and Industry. It was admitted that Mrs Thatcher's officials knew of the leak but not the Prime Minister herself. On January 24 Brittan resigned. The Westland affair had claimed its second Cabinet victim and it was the view of Conservative MPs that the Prime Minister's own image had taken a terrible pounding.

She was overruled in the Cabinet when her Cabinet colleagues insisted that the possible takeover of Austin Rover by Ford should be vetoed. Early in April the Labour Party gained a morale-boosting victory in a by-election at Fulham; and a few days later came the Government's most stunning legislative setback when 72 Tory MPs rebelled to kill a Bill to legalize Sunday trading.

That very same dramatic night, the Americans bombed targets in Libya in reprisal for terrorist attacks. Mrs Thatcher's decision to give the United States permission to use its bases in Britain to launch the strikes caused an outcry, and in an emergency Commons debate about 10 Conservative MPs rebelled.

So low had the Government's fortunes sunk that it was not really surprising when on May 8, 1986, the Conservatives lost the safe seat of Ryedale in Yorkshire, almost lost West Derbyshire, and suffered heavy defeats by the Alliance and Labour parties in the district council and London borough elections. John Biffen, the Commons leader, offered the view in a television interview that the Conservatives should enter the election with a "balanced ticket" to offset Mrs Thatcher's liabilities, a remark for which he was to suffer much later on. In a reshuffle, Mrs Thatcher swiftly promoted one of her best communicators, Kenneth Baker, to take over education from the retiring Sir Keith Joseph.

The other parties were not without their troubles. The Alliance had been trying for 18 months to hammer out a compromise on its defence policy. But when the report of a joint commission of both parties published a report recommending that a decision on whether Britain should replace Polaris should be left open, Dr Owen quickly made clear his disagreement with it. David Steel warned that the Alliance faced disaster unless its settled its differences but he was humiliated when his party assembly at Eastbourne passed a strongly anti-nuclear motion. Although Steel effectively disowned his assembly by pledging himself to the updating and maintenance of Polaris, the dispute appeared to do lasting damage to the Alliance.

With the talk now of an election, the spotlight again fell on Labour's defence policy. During a highly successful Labour conference, it was criticized by Caspar Weinberger, the United States Secretary of State, and the Conservatives made it the centrepiece of their attack on Labour at their annual conference in Bournemouth, a gathering which marked a dramatic transformation in the Government's fortunes.

Mrs Thatcher asked her ministers in their conference speeches to look beyond the next election and to set out their plans for another term. That combined with the defence attack appeared to pay quick dividends in the polls. A string of policy initiatives on housing, education, law and order and the inner cities left the Conservatives in much better heart than they would have dreamt possible a month before.

When MPs returned to the Commons after the summer recess there was already a strong whiff of electioneering in the air. The polls had the Conservatives just ahead, but they also suggested that people wanted more spent on the education and health services. The Government duly obliged. In a U-turn which some had thought would never come, the Government allowed its annual Star Chamber exercise of whittling down spending bids from ministers to fail, and agreed to an overshoot of spending of almost £5 billion. It was a somersault which shocked the monetarist purists on the Government side. It was wholly against the tenor of Lawson's Chancellorship, but it convinced MPs of all parties that an election was around the corner.

The Government, meanwhile, was reacting to the growing threat of the Aids epidemic. A special cabinet committee was set up under Lord Whitelaw to coordinate ministerial action. Labour was being dogged by the actions of a minority of left-wing "loony" councils. Kinnock was given a welcome target by the Government's attempts in Australia to stop the publication of a book by a former MI 5 employee, Peter Wright, but was not helped by having to make the admission that his office had been in contact with the defence lawyer in the case.

Kinnock made the first of two unhappy visits to the United States to explain his defence policy. The Government scrapped the GEC Nimrod aircraft early warning system on which £960m of public money had already been spent, but emerged practically unscathed, a stark contrast with similar controversies when the election was much further away.

The new year marked the beginning of the election campaign. Most Government decisions were seen in electoral terms. The polls were showing an increasing Conservative lead. The Government dropped controversial provisions to bring more competition into local authority services. The "loony left" issue took its toll on Labour when it lost Greenwich, a seat it had held for 50 years, to the Alliance. James Callaghan, in an intervention reminiscent of that which damaged Labour in the 1983 campaign, highlighted his objections to unilateralism in a Commons debate.

Everything seemed to be coming right for Mrs Thatcher. Some said she was lucky. Lawson produced an election budget, cutting 2p off income tax and paving the way for lower interest rates. Kinnock made an important concession on defence by making clear that cruise missiles could stay in Britain pending a superpower arms deal but when he saw President Reagan at the White House on March 27, he received a predictable rebuff for his policy.

His visit contrasted vividly with the Prime Minister's to Moscow the following week, a trip so successful that an exhilarated Prime Minister raised for the first time the prospect that she might want to go on to fight for a fourth term of office.

It was hard to believe that only a year before the Government, and particularly the Prime Minister, had been so deep in the doldrums. The Government dropped plans for the establishment of a low level nuclear waste dumping site. The independent nurses' pay award recommendation was met in full. The local election results on May 7 were better than the Conservatives dared hope. Just as they had in 1983, the Prime Minister and her most trusted advisers met at Chequers on the following Sunday to discuss the election date. On the Monday she went to the Palace.

House of Commons, June 1987

The parliamentary constituencies of the United Kingdom (England, Scotland, Wales and Northern Ireland) for election to the House of Commons are set out in alphabetical order. Constituencies in cities or towns (for example, Liverpool, Manchester, Glasgow, Cardiff, Belfast etc) are listed under that city or town.

Abbreviations used to designate the principal political parties contesting the election are: C — Conservative; Lab — Labour; L/All — Liberal/Alliance; SDP/All — Social Democratic Party/Alliance; SNP — Scottish National Party; Pl C — Plaid Cymru; Grn — Green Party; OUP — Official Unionist Party; DUP — Democratic Unionist Party; SDLP — Social Democratic and Labour Party; UPUP — Ulster Popular Unionist Party; PSF — Provisional Sinn Fein; All — Alliance Party (Northern Ireland); WP — Workers Party (Northern Ireland); WRP — Workers Revolutionary Party; RF (Red Front); Ind — Independent; Lny — Loony Official Monster Raving Party. Abbreviations of minor parties are given at the end of this constituency analysis along with abbrevations of political, trade union and other organizations mentioned in biographical details.

The percentage of the votes cast for each candidate and the majority in relation to the total poll in each constituency are calculated to the nearest decimal place, as is the percentage turnout.

The electoral register on which this General Election was fought came into effect on February 16 1987. The electorate figures for each constituency (along with those for 1983) consist of those eligible to vote when the register came into force plus the relevant proportion of those registered as becoming 18 years of age during the year. The relevant proportion used in 1987 was 115/364ths - the number of days the register had been in force on polling day. Ministers resign their directorships while holding office.

*Denotes members of the last Parliament.

Guide to election result tables

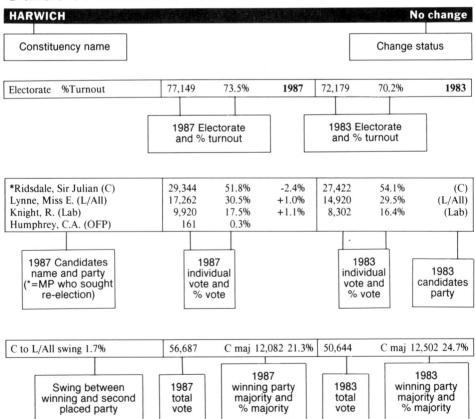

ABERAVON — No change

Electorate %Turnout	52,280	77.7%	1987	53,443	75.6%	1983
*Morris, J. (Lab)	27,126	66.8%	+8.0%	23,745	58.8%	(Lab)
Harris, Mrs M. (L/All)	6,517	16.0%	-4.3%	8,206	20.3%	(L/All)
Warrick, P. (C)	5,861	14.4%	-1.9%	6,605	16.3%	(C)
Howells, Miss A. (Pl C)	1,124	2.8%	-1.8%	1,859	4.6%	(Pl C)
L/All to Lab swing 6.1%	40,628	Lab maj 20,609 50.7%		40,415	Lab maj 15,539 38.4%	

Mr John Morris

Mr John Morris, QC, chief Opposition spokesman on legal affairs since 1983; Secretary of State for Wales, 1974-79. Returned to back-benches in 1981 after a spell as spokesman on Wales and then on legal affairs. Opposition spokesman on defence, 1970-74; Minister of Transport, 1966-68; Parliamentary Secretary, Ministry of Power, 1964-66. Member, Select Cmte of Privileges. Elected in 1959. Barrister; Recorder of Crown Court, 1982- . B Nov 1931; ed Acad of International Law, The Hague. Chmn, Welsh Lab group, 1970-71; Welsh parly party, 1972-73. Sponsored by Apex.
Mrs Marilyn Harris, analyst/programmer, BP Chemicals, Baglan Bay. Founder mbr, Aberavon Lib Assocn. B May 14 1945; ed Univ of Wales, Swansea. ASTMS.
Mr Paul Warrick, lawyer and company director. Member, Royal Borough of Kensington and Chelsea Cl, 1984- . B Sep 2 1944; ed Cheam Sch; Stowe Sch. Equity.
Ms Anne Howells, editor with Univ of Wales Press. Represents PlC women's section on party nec. Aged 31; ed St David's Univ Coll, Lampeter.

ABERDEEN NORTH — No change

Electorate %Turnout	63,214	69.9%	1987	63,049	65.0%	1983
*Hughes, R. (Lab)	24,145	54.7%	+7.6%	19,262	47.0%	(Lab)
Smith, R. (SDP/All)	7,867	17.8%	-6.9%	10,118	24.7%	(SDP/All)
Scanlan, Ms G.E.C. (C)	6,330	14.3%	-3.8%	7,426	18.1%	(C)
Greenhorn, P. (SNP)	5,827	13.2%	+3.9%	3,790	9.3%	(SNP)
				367	0.9%	(Other)
SDP/All to Lab swing 7.3%	44,169	Lab maj 16,278 36.9%		40,963	Lab maj 9,144 22.3%	

Mr Robert Hughes

Mr Robert Hughes, chief Opposition spokesman on transport since 1985 when elected to shadow cabinet; retained appointment even though defeated in 1986 shadow cabinet elections. Chief spokesman on agriculture, 1983-84; a transport spokesman, 1981-83. Vice-chmn, Tribune Gp, 1984- . Under Secretary of State for Scotland, 1974-75. Elected in 1970; contested North Angus and Mearns, 1959. B Jan 3 1932; ed Benoni HS, Transvaal, and Pietermaritzburg Technical Coll, Natal. Chmn, Anti-Apartheid Movement, 1976- ; founder member, CND. Member, Aberdeen Town Cl, 1962-71. Sponsored by AUEW.
Mr Robert Smith, estate manager. Member, Scottish CSD; Aberdeen city coordinator, Campaign for Fair Votes. B Apr 15 1958; ed Merchant Taylors Sch, London; Aberdeen Univ.
Ms Gae Scanlan, personnel consultant, fought this seat 1983. Chmn, Stocket Community Cl, Aberdeen. Senior vice-chmn, Inst of Marketing. CBI rep on industrial tribunals, Aberdeen Enterprise Trust, Publicity Club, City Centre Assocn. Mbr, Inst of Directors. B Oct 30 1951; ed Westbourne Sch for Girls, Glasgow; Strathclyde Univ.
Mr Philip Greenhorn, television engineer. B May 29 1947; ed Smithfield Primary Sch; Northfield Sec Sch; Aberdeen Radio Coll and Tech Coll. EETPU shop steward.

ABERDEEN SOUTH — Lab gain

Electorate %Turnout	62,943	67.1%	1987	57,540	68.7%	1983
Doran, F. (Lab)	15,917	37.7%	+7.8%	15,393	38.9%	(C)
*Malone, G.P. (C)	14,719	34.8%	-4.1%	11,812	29.9%	(Lab)
Philip, I.G. (SDP/All)	8,844	20.9%	-5.3%	10,372	26.2%	(SDP/All)
Weir, M.F. (SNP)	2,776	6.6%	+1.6%	1,974	5.0%	(SNP)
C to Lab swing 5.9%	42,256	Lab maj 1,198 2.8%		39,551	C maj 3,581 9.1%	

Mr Frank Doran

Mr Frank Doran, solicitor in Dundee, contested Scotland North East in 1984 Euro election. B Apr 13 1949; ed Aberdeen Univ. GMBATU.
Mr Gerald Malone, assistant Govt whip, 1986-87; PPS to Mr Leon Brittan, Secretary of State for Trade and Industry, 1985-86, and to Under Secs of State for Energy, 1985-86. Solicitor. MP for this seat 1983-87; contested Glasgow, Provan, Feb 1974; Glasgow, Pollok, Oct 1974; Roxburgh, Selkirk and Peebles, 1979; Glasgow, Hillhead, 1982 by-election. B Jul 21 1950; ed St Aloysius' Coll, Glasgow; Glasgow Univ. Former member, Select Cmtes on Energy and European legislation. Jt sec, Cons back-bench constitutional cmte, 1983-85.
Mr Ian Philip, chartered accountant and chmn, Aberdeen Shipbuilders Ltd, contested this seat for the Alliance in 1983 and Angus South for Labour in 1979; contested Scotland North East for SDP/All in 1984 Euro election. Treas, Scottish CSD, 1981-86. B Apr 8 1937; ed Sedbergh Sch; Oxford and Edinburgh Univs.
Mr Michael Weir, solicitor. Mbr, Angus DC, 1984- . B Mar 24 1957; ed Arbroath HS; Aberdeen Univ.

ALDERSHOT — No change

Electorate %Turnout	80,797	74.0%	**1987**	77,593	72.7%	**1983**
*Critchley, J.M.G. (C)	35,272	59.0%	+3.5%	31,288	55.4%	(C)
Hargreaves, R.A. (L/All)	17,488	29.2%	-4.6%	19,070	33.8%	(L/All)
Pearson, I.H. (Lab)	7,061	11.8%	+1.0%	6,070	10.8%	(Lab)
L/All to C swing 4.0%	59,821	C maj 17,784 29.7%		56,428	C maj 12,218 21.7%	

Mr Julian Critchley, writer, journalist and public affairs adviser, was elected in 1970; MP for Rochester and Chatham, 1959-64; contested seat, 1966. B Dec 8 1930; ed Shrewsbury, Sorbonne, and Pembroke Coll, Oxford. Chmn, Bow Group, 1966-67; jt vice-chmn, Cons back-bench defence cmte, since 1976; chmn, media cmte, 1976-80. Delegate to WEU (chmn, WEU defence cmte, 1974-77) and Cl of Europe; N Atlantic Assembly. Pres, Atlantic Assocn of Young Political Leaders, 1968-70.

Mr Roger Hargreaves is a town planner. B Apr 23 1948; ed Kingston Poly; Loughborough Univ of Tech. Nalgo.

Mr Ian Pearson, solicitor. Mbr, Rushmoor BC, 1986- . B May 30 1949; ed Farnham GS; Leicester Univ; Guildford Coll of Law. TGWU.

Mr Julian Critchley

ALDRIDGE-BROWNHILLS — No change

Electorate %Turnout	62,129	79.8%	**1987**	60,803	78.3%	**1983**
*Shepherd, R.C.S. (C)	26,434	53.3%	+2.6%	24,148	50.7%	(C)
Duncan, C. (Lab)	14,038	28.3%	+3.4%	11,864	24.9%	(Lab)
Betteridge, G. (SDP/All)	9,084	18.3%	-6.0%	11,599	24.4%	(SDP/All)
C to Lab swing 0.4%	49,556	C maj 12,396 25.0%		47,611	C maj 12,284 25.8%	

Mr Richard Shepherd, director of a retail food business in London, won the seat in 1979; fought Nottingham East, Feb 1974. Vice-pres, Inst of Environmental Health Officers, 1987- . B Dec 6 1942; ed LSE and The Johns Hopkins Univ - Sch of Advanced International Studies. Underwriting mbr of Lloyd's since 1974. Mbr, Select Cmte on Treasury and Civil Service, 1979-83; SE Economic Planning Cl, 1970-74; sec, Cons back-bench European affairs and industry cmtes, 1980-81. Director, Shepherd Foods (London) Ltd, Shepherd Foods (Marylebone) Ltd, and Partridges of Sloane Street Ltd.

Mr Clive Duncan, teacher, contested Chesham and Amersham 1983. B Aug 12 1950; ed Douai Abbey Sch; Oxford, Nottingham and Birmingham Univs. Has held Lab Pty branch and constituency posts. NUT.

Mr Glynn Betteridge, senior TV and video sales rep, Thorn EMI. B 1952; ed Willenhall Comprehensive Sch, Hednesford.

Mr Richard Shepherd

ALTRINCHAM AND SALE — No change

Electorate %Turnout	67,611	76.7%	**1987**	65,984	73.0%	**1983**
*Montgomery, Sir Fergus (C)	27,746	53.5%	+0.9%	25,321	52.5%	(C)
Mulholland, J. (L/All)	13,518	26.1%	-3.8%	14,410	29.9%	(L/All)
Hinder, D. (Lab)	10,617	20.5%	+4.5%	7,684	15.9%	(Lab)
				781	1.6%	(Other)
L/All to C swing 2.4%	51,881	C maj 14,228 27.4%		48,196	C maj 10,911 22.6%	

Sir Fergus Montgomery has been on the Select Cmtes on Home Affairs since 1983 and Commons Services since 1979; Select Cmte on Environment, 1979-83. Elected in Oct 1974; MP for Brierley Hill, 1967-Feb 1974, when he unsuccessfully contested Dudley West; MP for Newcastle upon Tyne East, 1959-64; contested Consett, 1955. Non-executive engineering company director; teacher, 1950-59. Member, exec cmte, UK branch of CPA, 1983- . B Nov 25 1927; ed Hebburn Methodist Sch; Jarrow GS; Bede Coll, Durham. Member, Hebburn UDC, 1950-58. Nat chmn, YCs, 1957-58. PPS to Mrs Thatcher as Secretary of State for Education and Science, 1973-74, and as Leader of the Opposition, 1975-76.

Mr John Mulholland, Asst Principal, St Helen's Coll, contested Stockton-on-Tees 1964 and 1962 by-election. Mbr, Runcorn RDC, 1959-62. Industrial relations arbitrator (Acas); Fellow, Inst of Personnel Management and BIM. B May 23 1933; ed St Mary's Coll, Middlesbrough; Manchester Univ, UMIST. NATFHE.

Mr David Hinder, corporate financial planner with an engineering and electronics company. B Nov 26 1954. Ed Leeds Univ and Manchester Business Sch. Worked in industry including production control, Leyland Cars. Main interests are the economy, regional and rural policy. APEX.

Sir Fergus Montgomery

ALYN AND DEESIDE — No change

Electorate %Turnout	58,674	80.4%	**1987**	56,618	78.1%	**1983**
*Jones, S.B. (Lab)	22,916	48.6%	+8.3%	17,806	40.3%	(Lab)
Twilley, N.J. (C)	16,500	35.0%	-2.2%	16,438	37.2%	(C)
Owen, E.C.H. (SDP/All)	7,273	15.4%	-6.2%	9,535	21.6%	(SDP/All)
Rogers, J.D. (Pl C)	478	1.0%	+0.1%	413	0.9%	(Pl C)
C to Lab swing 5.3%	47,167	Lab maj 6,416 13.6%		44,192	Lab maj 1,368 3.1%	

Mr Barry Jones, chief Opposition spokesman on Wales since 1983 when he was elected to the shadow Cabinet; employment spokesman, 1980-83. Under Secretary of State for Wales, 1974-79. Elected for this seat 1983; MP for East Flint, 1970-83; contested Northwich, 1966. Member, PAC, 1979-82. Teacher and former regional organizer, NUT. B Jun 1938; ed Hawarden GS and Bangor Coll of Education. Former UK delegate to Cl of Europe and WEU. Parly consultant to NUT. Former exec member, Wales Regional Lab Pty. PPS to Mr Denis Healey, 1972-74. Sponsored by TGWU.

Mr Nicholas Twilley, computer consultant, is editor and publisher of Conservative Micro News. Member, Mid-Sussex DC, 1984- . B Feb 8 1945; ed Westminster Sch.

Mr Eric Owen, barrister and author of legal textbooks, contested the seat 1983 and Cheshire West in 1984 Euro election. Community cllr, 1983-86. Member, SDP nat organisation cmte; former chmn, SDP Christian Forum; former vice-chmn, SDP Wales. B Dec 7 1946; ed Grove Park GS, Wrexham; Liverpool Univ.

Mr John Rogers, teacher, contested Flint East 1979 and Ebbw Vale Feb 1974. Founder, Cambrian Coast Line Action Gp. B Feb 1943; ed Glyndwr Sec Mod Sch, Rhyl; Rhyl GS; St Mary's Coll, Crosby; Leeds Univ.

Mr Barry Jones

AMBER VALLEY — No change

Electorate %Turnout	68,478	81.2%	**1987**	66,720	77.2%	**1983**
*Oppenheim, P.A.C.L. (C)	28,603	51.4%	+9.7%	21,502	41.7%	(C)
Bookbinder, D.M. (Lab)	19,103	34.4%	-0.9%	18,184	35.3%	(Lab)
Reynolds, S. (L/All)	7,904	14.2%	-7.1%	10,989	21.3%	(L/All)
				856	1.7%	(Other)
Lab to C swing 5.3%	55,610	C maj 9,500 17.1%		51,531	C maj 3,318 6.4%	

Mr Phillip Oppenheim, author and founder and director of What to Buy plc, was elected in 1983. Sec, Cons back-bench European Affairs cmte, 1986- ; Cons back-bench Party Organization cmte, 1985- ; all-pty Animal Welfare cmte. B Mar 20 1956; ed Harrow and Oriel Coll, Oxford. Member, cl, Parly IT Cmte. Vice-pres, Videotex Industry Assocn, since 1985. Son of Mrs Sally Oppenheim, retiring MP for Gloucester. Jt founder and co-editor, since 1980, of business consumer magazine covering high tech what to buy for business products.

Mr David Bookbinder has been leader of Derbyshire CC since 1981 and leader of the Lab gp since 1977 (elected to cl, 1973); member, Derby BC, 1969-74. Contested this seat 1983; High Peak Oct 1974 and 1979. B Mar 8 1941; ed sec mod sch; tech coll. Chmn, Derby Lab Pty, 1970-72; past chmn, Derby and Burton Co-operative Pty. Member, Allestree local Lab Pty since 1962, NCCL, British Humanist Assocn; League Against Cruel Sports, Nupe (member of its parly panel) and TGWU.

Mr Stewart Reynolds, a former teacher, is unemployed. Member, Cannock Chase DC, since 1982. B Jul 22 1947; ed Chesterfield Sch; Westminster Coll, Oxford; Open Univ.

Mr Phillip Oppenheim

ANGUS EAST — SNP gain

Electorate %Turnout	61,060	75.5%	**1987**	59,359	73.5%	**1983**
Welsh, A. (SNP)	19,536	42.4%	+6.4%	19,218	44.1%	(C)
*Fraser, P.L. (C)	17,992	39.0%	-5.0%	15,691	36.0%	(SNP)
Mennie, R. (Lab)	4,971	10.8%	+2.8%	4,978	11.4%	(SDP/All)
Mortimer, I. (SDP/All)	3,592	7.8%	-3.6%	3,497	8.0%	(Lab)
				239	0.5%	(Other)
C to SNP swing 5.7%	46,091	SNP maj 1,544 3.3%		43,623	C maj 3,527 8.1%	

Mr Andrew Welsh, Provost of Angus DC since 1984, was SNP MP for Angus South Oct 74-79., being SNP spokesman on housing, 1974-78, and SNP chief whip, 1978-79. Contested this seat 1983; Dunbartonshire Central, Feb 1974. Exec vice-chmn of SNP. responsible for local govt. Senior lecturer at Angus Tech Coll, Arbroath. B Apr 1944; ed Govan HS; Glasgow Univ.

Mr Peter Fraser, QC, became Solicitor General for Scotland in 1982. Elected for this seat 1983; MP for Angus South, 1979-83; fought Aberdeen North, Oct 1974. B May 29 1945; ed Loretto Sch; Gonville and Caius, Cambridge; Edinburgh Univ.

Mr Raymond Mennie is Labour group secretary and chief whip, Tayside Regional Council.; convenor, roads and transport cmte. Delegate, Scottish TUC. Shop steward and branch chmn. B Feb 21 1950; ed Lawside Academy.

Mr Ian Mortimer, engineer surveyor. Member, Monifieth TC, 1964-75; Angus CC, 1968-75; Dundee DC (as ind), 1977-84; chmn, Angus Burghs Assocn, 1974-75. B Apr 2 1932; ed Morgan Acad, Dundee; Dundee Coll of Tech.

Mr Andrew Welsh

ANTRIM EAST — No change

Electorate %Turnout	60,587	55.2%	**1987**	58,863	64.9%	**1983**
*Beggs, J.R. (OUP)	23,942	71.6%	+34.1%	14,293	37.4%	(OUP)
Neeson, S. (All)	8,582	25.6%	+5.7%	13,926	36.4%	(DUP)
Kelly, A. (WP)	936	2.8%	+1.3%	7,620	19.9%	(All)
				2,369	6.2%	(Other)
All to OUP swing 14.2%	33,460	OUP maj 15,360 45.9%		38,208	OUP maj 367 1.0%	

Mr Roy Beggs, a director of Larne Enterprise Development Company, was elected in 1983. Resigned seat in 1985 in protest at Anglo-Irish Agreement and retained it in 1986 by-election. Has served on PAC. Member for North Antrim, N Ireland Assembly, 1982-86; chmn, Economic Development Cmte, 1982-84. Member, Larne BC, 1973- ; Mayor of Larne, 1978-83. B Feb 20 1936; ed Ballyclare HS; Stranmillis Training Coll. Teacher, 1957-78; vice-principal, Larne HS, 1978-83. Pres, NI Assocn of Education and Library Boards, 1984-85. Chmn (1985-87) and vice-chmn (1981-85), NE Education and Library Bd; member of bd since 1973.

Mr Sean Neeson, former teacher, is Alliance Pty spokesman on economic affairs. B Feb 6 1946; ed St Malachys GS, Belfast; Queen's Univ. Member, Carrickfergus BC, 1977- *Details of 1986 by-election on Page 285*

Mr Roy Beggs

ANTRIM NORTH — No change

Electorate %Turnout	65,733	62.8%	**1987**	63,254	69.8%	**1983**
*Paisley, Rev I.R.K. (DUP)	28,383	68.7%	+14.6%	23,922	54.2%	(DUP)
Farren, S. (SDLP)	5,149	12.5%	-1.6%	10,749	24.3%	(OUP)
Williams, G. (All)	5,140	12.4%		6,193	14.0%	(SDLP)
Reagan, S. (PSF)	2,633	6.4%	-0.1%	2,860	6.5%	(PSF)
				451	1.0%	(Other)
SDLP to DUP swing 8.1%	41,305	DUP maj 23,234 56.2%		44,175	DUP maj 13,173 29.8%	

The Rev Ian Paisley, leader of the Democratic Unionist Party, has been MP for Antrim North since 1970. Resigned seat in 1985 in protest at Anglo-Irish Agreement and retained it in 1986 by-election. Mbr, European Parliament, 1979- ; N Ireland Assembly, 1982-86. Minister of Martyrs Memorial Free Presbyterian Church, Belfast, 1946- . Director, Voice Newspapers Ltd. Founded Protestant Unionist Party and sat as Protestant Unionist MP, 1970-74. B Apr 6 1926; ed Model School, Ballymena, and Reformed Presbyterian Theological Hall, Belfast. Ordained 1946. Won Bannside in 1970 and was a Stormont MP until 1972. Democratic Unionist member for North Antrim of NI Assembly, 1973-75, and UUUC member, NI Constitutional Convention, 1975-76.

Mr Sean Farren, lecturer, Univ of Ulster. Pty vice-chmn ,1975-1980; pty chmn, 1980-84. Mbr, Coleraine BC, 1977-81. SDLP Assembly man for N Antrim, 1982-86. Contested this parly seat 1979, 1983 and 1986 by-election.

Mr John Williams, community pharmacist. B Sep 24 1953; ed Ballymena Acad; Queen's Univ, Belfast. Sec, Ballymena Alliance Assocn.

Mr Sean Regan, former market trader. Aged 48. PSF cllr, Moyle DC, 1985- .

The Rev Ian Paisley *Details of 1986 by-election on Page 285*

ANTRIM SOUTH — No change

Electorate %Turnout	61,649	59.1%	**1987**	59,321	65.5%	**1983**
*Forsythe, C. (OUP)	25,395	69.8%	+24.1%	17,727	45.7%	(OUP)
Mawhinney, G. (All)	5,808	16.0%	+4.1%	10,935	28.2%	(DUP)
McClelland, D. (SDLP)	3,611	9.9%	+1.2%	4,612	11.9%	(All)
Cushinan, H. (PSF)	1,592	4.4%	+0.2%	3,377	8.7%	(SDLP)
				2,178	5.6%	(Other)
All to OUP swing 10.0%	36,406	OUP maj 19,587 53.8%		38,829	OUP maj 6,792 17.5%	

Mr Clifford Forsythe, former professional footballer with Linfield and Derry City, was elected in 1983. Resigned seat in 1985 in protest at Anglo-Irish Agreement and retained it at 1986 by-election. Party spokesman on transport and communications. B Aug 24 1929; ed Glengormley Public Elementary Sch. Plumbing and heating contractor. Exec member, UU Cl, 1980-83. Mbr, Newtownabbey BC, 1981-85 (mayor, 1983); NI Assembly, 1982-86; dep chmn, DHSS cmte of assembly, 1982-86. Chmn, Glengormley Chest, Heart and Stroke Assocn. Fellow, Industry and Parliament Trust.

Mr Gordon Mawhinney, chartered surveyor. B Jan 4 1943. Alliance Pty Assembly member South Antrim, 1982-86, being Alliance Chief Whip; chmn, pty environmental policy gp.

Mr Donovan McClelland, univ lecturer. Aged 39.

Mr Henry Cushinan, PSF mbr of Antrim BC, 1985- . Aged 30. Released from Maze prison in 1983 after serving six years for terrorist offences.

Details of 1986 by-election on Page 285

Mr Clifford Forsythe

ARGYLL AND BUTE — L/All gain

Electorate %Turnout	48,700	75.5%	**1987**	47,497	72.9%	**1983**
Michie, Mrs J.R. (L/All)	13,726	37.3%	+9.8%	13,380	38.6%	(C)
*MacKay, J.J. (C)	12,332	33.5%	-5.1%	9,536	27.5%	(L/All)
Shaw, R. (SNP)	6,297	17.1%	-7.5%	8,514	24.6%	(SNP)
Tierney, D. (Lab)	4,437	12.1%	+2.8%	3,204	9.3%	(Lab)
C to L/All swing 7.4%	36,792	L/All maj 1,394 3.8%		34,634	C maj 3,844 11.1%	

Mrs Ray Michie

Mrs Ray Michie, area speech therapist with Argyll and Clyde Health Board, contested the seat 1983 and Argyll 1979. Former vice-chmn, Scottish Lib Pty; former chmn, Argyll Lib Assocn. Mbr, Liberal/SDP commission on constitutional reform. B Feb 4 1934; ed Aberdeen HS for Girls; Lansdowne House Sch, Edinburgh; Edinburgh Sch of Speech Therapy.
Mr John MacKay was Under Secretary of State for Scotland in 1982-87, responsible for health and social work and (from 1985) home affairs; in Sep 1985 assumed responsibilities for education, agriculture and fisheries. MP for this seat 1983-87; MP for Argyll, 1979-83; contested Argyll, Oct 1974; Western Isles, Feb 1974. Principal teacher of mathematics, Oban HS, 1972-79. B Nov 15 1938; ed Dunoon and Campbeltown GSs; Glasgow Univ; Jordanhill Coll of Ed. Former chmn, Scottish Cons ed policy cmte; former sec, Scottish Cons MPs cmte; mbr, Oban TC and Burgh Treasurer, 1969-74; Argyll Water Bd, 1970-74. SSTA
Mr Robin Shaw, writer, craft cooperative director and guest house owner, fought Caithness and Sutherland 1979. B Apr 16 1937; ed Kilsyth Acad; Glasgow and Western Washington Univs. Chmn, Oban SNP. Former mbr, EIS.
Mr Desmond Tierney, research officer with Dumbarton DC; economics teacher. B Jan 1949; ed Heriot Watt Univ. Chmn, Scottish Medical Aid for Nicaragua.

ARUNDEL — No change

Electorate %Turnout	78,683	71.2%	**1987**	74,849	69.7%	**1983**
*Marshall, R.M. (C)	34,356	61.3%	+1.8%	31,096	59.6%	(C)
Walsh, Dr J.M.M. (L/All)	15,476	27.6%	-1.9%	15,391	29.5%	(L/All)
Slowe, P. (Lab)	6,177	11.0%	+2.8%	4,302	8.2%	(Lab)
				1,399	2.7%	(Other)
L/All to C swing 1.8%	56,009	C maj 18,880 33.7%		52,188	C maj 15,705 30.1%	

Mr Michael Marshall

Mr Michael Marshall was Under Secretary of State for Industry, 1979-81, and has been on Select Cmte on Defence since 1982. Chmn (1987-) and vice-chmn (1982-87), Parly Information Tech Cmte. Jt vice-chmn, British Gp, IPU, 1982- . Elected in Feb 1974; contested Hartlepool, 1970. Writer, broadcaster and chmn, Direct Business Satellite Systems Ltd. Managing partner, Marshall Consultants; non-exec director, Integrated Information Tech Ltd. Management consultant, Urwick Orr and Partners Ltd, 1969-74. B June 21 1930; ed Bradfield Coll, Harvard and Stanford Univs. Parliamentary adviser to BAe, Space and Communications Div, 1982- ; Cable and Wireless, 1982- ; Comsat General Corporation; Soc of West End Theatre, 1984- . Member, Select Cmte on Overseas Development, 1974-76; Nationalized Industries, 1976-79. Vice-chmn, Cons back-bench industry cmte, 1976-79. Mbr, Lloyd's.
Dr James Walsh, general practitioner, contested this seat 1983; Hove 1979 and Oct 1974, and Sussex West in 1979 Euro election. B Jan 11 1943; ed Wimbledon Coll; London Univ (London Hospital Medical Sch). Has served on Arun DC and Worthing DHA.
Dr Peter Slowe, lecturer in geography. Coordinator, exec, Lab finance and industry gp; ex-chmn, Camden local govt conference. B Mar 9 1953; ed Highgate Sch; Bristol and Oxford Univs. NATFHE.

ASHFIELD — No change

Electorate %Turnout	70,937	77.2%	**1987**	69,791	73.7%	**1983**
*Haynes, D.F. (Lab)	22,812	41.7%	-0.8%	21,859	42.5%	(Lab)
Coleman, B.G. (C)	18,412	33.6%	+3.0%	15,772	30.7%	(C)
Stein, Mrs F.B. (L/All)	13,542	24.7%	-2.1%	13,812	26.8%	(L/All)
Lab to C swing 1.9%	54,766	Lab maj 4,400 8.0%		51,443	Lab maj 6,087 11.8%	

Mr Frank Haynes, Opposition whip for the East Midlands since 1981, was elected in 1979. Mbr, Select Cmte on Parliamentary Commissioner for Administration (Ombudsman), since 1981. Coalminer, 1944-79; Southern Railway fireman, 1940-44. NUM branch official for 20 years; a mbr of the union for nearly 40 years. B Mar 8 1926; ed secondary schools in London. Mbr, Nottinghamshire CC, since 1965. Chmn, Central Notts Community Health Cl, 1974- . Sponsored by NUM.
Mr Barry Coleman, teacher. Mbr, Great Yarmouth BC, 1977- (Mayor, 1983-84; dep ldr of cl). B Jun 5 1943; ed Paston Sch, North Walsham.
Mrs Frances Stein, SRN, contested Ashfield 1983. Mbr, Ashfield DC 1976- ; regional health spokesman, East Midlands Pty Cl. B Jun 18 1941; ed Northampton Girls' Sch; Wingsthorpe.

Mr Frank Haynes

ASHFORD — No change

Electorate %Turnout			1987			1983
Electorate %Turnout	70,052	75.7%	**1987**	65,442	73.2%	**1983**
*Speed, H.K. (C)	29,978	56.5%	-0.3%	27,230	56.8%	(C)
Macmillan, N.N. (SDP/All)	14,490	27.3%	-0.5%	13,319	27.8%	(SDP/All)
Wiggins, M.J. (Lab)	7,775	14.7%	+1.8%	6,167	12.9%	(Lab)
Porter, Dr C.A. (Grn)	778	1.5%	+0.3%	569	1.2%	(Eco)
					651	1.4%	(Other)
SDP/All to C swing 0.1%	53,021	C maj 15,488 29.2%		47,936	C maj 13,911 29.0%	

Mr Keith Speed

Mr Keith Speed, company director and marketing consultant; Under Sec of State for Defence for Royal Navy, 1979-81; an Opposition spokesman on environment and local govt, 1975-79; Under Sec of State for Environment, 1972-74; Lord Commissioner of the Treasury (Govt whip), 1971-72; asst Govt whip, 1970-71. Mbr, Select Cmte on Defence, 1983- . Elected in Oct 1974; MP for Meriden, Mar 1968 to Feb 1974. Regular naval officer, 1947-56. B Mar 11 1934; ed Greenhill Sch, Evesham; Bedford Modern Sch; Dartmouth and Greenwich RNCs. Director, Westminster Communications Ltd (clients include Motor Cycle Assocn); Folkestone Water Co. Parly adviser, PAT, 1982- ; parly consultant, Assocn for Instrumentation Control and Automation Industry in UK; Machine Tool Assocn.
Mr Neil Macmillan, chief executive of a communications gp. B Mar 27 1946; ed Nairn Acad; Aberdeen Univ. Chmn, SDP policy cmte, 1981.
Mr Michael Wiggins, BR signal installer. B Aug 11 1939; ed in Ashford. Member, Ashford BC, 1974-87 (ldr, Lab gp, 1982-85; mayor, 1980-81); Kent Family Practitioner Cmte. NUR.
Dr Charles Porter, medical practitioner, contested Ashford 1983. B Apr 9 1936; ed Bryarston Sch, Dorset; Middlesex Hospital Medical Sch.

ASHTON-UNDER-LYNE — No change

Electorate %Turnout	58,440	74.0%	**1987**	58,963	71.6%	**1983**
*Sheldon, R.E. (Lab)	22,389	51.8%	+2.0%	20,987	49.7%	(Lab)
Cadman, H.L. (C)	13,103	30.3%	-1.2%	13,290	31.5%	(C)
Hunter, M.J. (L/All)	7,760	17.9%	+0.1%	7,521	17.8%	(SDP/All)
					407	1.0%	(Other)
C to Lab swing 1.6%	43,252	Lab maj 9,286 21.5%		42,205	Lab maj 7,697 18.2%	

Mr Robert Sheldon

Mr Robert Sheldon has chaired the Public Accounts Cmte of the Commons since 1983; also mbr, 1965-70 and 1975-79. An Opposition spokesman on Treasury and economic affairs, 1979-83; Financial Secretary to the Treasury, 1975-79; Minister of State, Treasury, 1974-75; Minister of State, Civil Service Dept, 1974. Former Opposition spokesman on Civil Service and machinery of govt. Mbr, Treasury and Civil Service Select Cmte, 1979-81; Public Expenditure Cmte, 1972-74; Fulton Cmte on Civil Service, 1966-68. Elected in 1964; contested Manchester, Withington, 1959. Director, Manchester Chamber of Commerce, 1964-74 and since 1979. B Sep 13 1923; ed elementary, GS, and tech colls; external graduate, London Univ. Chmn, NW group of Labour MPs, 1970-74. TGWU.
Mr Henry Cadman, senior lecturer in electrical engineering, Wigan Coll of Tech, contested Wigan 1983. B Apr 16 1935; ed Ashton-in-Makerfield GS; Liverpool Univ; Univ of Manchester Inst of Science and Tech. MIEE.
Mr Mark Hunter, leader of Liberal group on Tameside Metropolitan BC. Employed by *The Guardian* in Manchester.

AYLESBURY — No change

Electorate %Turnout	76,919	74.5%	**1987**	72,792	71.5%	**1983**
*Raison, T.H.F. (C)	32,970	57.5%	-0.5%	30,230	58.1%	(C)
Soole, M.A. (SDP/All)	16,412	28.6%	-0.8%	15,310	29.4%	(SDP/All)
Larner, Ms J. (Lab)	7,936	13.8%	+1.6%	6,364	12.2%	(Lab)
					166	0.3%	(Other)
SDP/All to C swing 0.1%	57,318	C maj 16,558 28.9%		52,070	C maj 14,920 28.7%	

Mr Timothy Raison

Mr Timothy Raison was Minister for Overseas Development, with the rank of Minister of State, Foreign and Commonwealth Office, 1983-86; Minister of State, Home Office, 1979-83; chief Opposition spokesman on the environment and member of shadow cabinet, 1974-77; spokesman on prices and consumer affairs, 1974-75; on social services and education, 1974; Under Secretary of State for Education and Science, 1973-74. Journalist and broadcaster. Director, Fleming Claverhouse Investment Trust; consultant to Robert Fleming Holdings. Elected in 1970. B Nov 3 1929; ed Dragon Sch, Oxford; Eton, and Christ Church, Oxford. Editor, Crossbow, 1958-60; New Society, 1962-68. Senior fellow, Centre for Studies in Social Policy, 1974-77. Former director, Private Patients Plan. Mbr, Richmond upon Thames BC, 1967-71.
Mr Michael Soole, barrister, fought this seat 1983. Mbr, CSD, 1984- . B Jul 18 1954; ed Berkhamsted Sch; Univ Coll, Oxford (Pres of Union).
Ms Julie Larner, mbr, Buckinghamshire CC. B Jul 31, 1951; ed Grange Sec Mod; Aylesbury CFE. TASS.

AYR — No change

Electorate	%Turnout		1987			1983
		66,450	79.9%	**1987**	65,010	76.7%	**1983**
*Younger, G.K.H. (C)		20,942	39.4%	-3.4%	21,325	42.8%	(C)
MacDonald, K. (Lab)		20,760	39.1%	+12.3%	13,338	26.8%	(Lab)
Moody, K.M. (L/All)		7,859	14.8%	-10.8%	12,740	25.6%	(L/All)
Weir, C. (SNP)		3,548	6.7%	+1.8%	2,431	4.9%	(SNP)
C to Lab swing 7.8%		53,109	C maj 182	0.3%	49,834	C maj 7,987	16.0%

Mr George Younger, Secretary of State for Defence, 1986- ; Secretary of State for Scotland, 1979-86, being a former Opposition spokesman on defence and mbr of shadow Cabinet, 1975-76; a spokesman on defence, 1974-75; Minister of State for Defence, 1974; Under Sec of State for Development, Scottish Office, 1970-73. Elected in 1964; contested North Lanarkshire, 1959. Scottish Cons whip, 1965-67. B Sep 22 1931; ed Cargilfield Sch, Edinburgh; Winchester Coll, and New Coll, Oxford. Former director, Tennant Caledonian Breweries Ltd, Glasgow.
Mr Keith MacDonald, teacher, contested the seat, 1983. B Feb 1953; ed Stirling Univ. Mbr, Kyle and Carrick DC, 1980- (ldr, Lab gp). EIS, NUT.
Mr Keith Moody, transport consultant; local govt official and member of Nalgo, 1951-84. Transport consultant. Mbr, Strathclyde Reg Cl, 1986- . B Nov 1 1934; ed Marsh Hill Primary Sch, Erdington; King Edward's GS, Birmingham. Fellow, Inst of Transport.
Mr Colin Weir, unit manager with Scottish Television. B 1947; ed Royal HS, Edinburgh. Mbr, SNP press and publicity cmte. ACTT.

Mr George Younger

BANBURY — No change

Electorate	%Turnout		1987			1983
		69,455	76.2%	**1987**	65,324	75.2%	**1983**
*Baldry, A.B. (C)		29,716	56.2%	+2.8%	26,225	53.4%	(C)
Rowland, D.C. (SDP/All)		12,386	23.4%	-3.4%	13,200	26.9%	(SDP/All)
Honeybone, J.A. (Lab)		10,789	20.4%	+1.4%	9,343	19.0%	(Lab)
					383	0.8%	(Other)
SDP/All to C swing 3.1%		52,891	C maj 17,330	32.8%	49,151	C maj 13,025	26.5%

Mr Tony Baldry, barrister, publisher and company director, was elected in 1983; contested Thurrock, 1979. PPS to Mrs Chalker, Minister of State for Transport and then for Foreign and Commonwealth Affairs, 1985- . B Jul 10 1950; ed Leighton Park and Sussex Univ. Director, Newpoint Publishing Gp Ltd, 1983- ; New Opportunity Press Ltd, 1975- . Dep chmn, Cons Group for Europe. Personal aide to Mrs Thatcher in Oct 1974 election; served in Leader of the Opposition's office, March-Oct 1975. Former mbr, Select Cmte on Employment; chmn, Bow Group standing cmte on employment. Mbr, Carlton Club political cmte. Awarded Robert Schumann Silver Medal, 1978, for contributions to European politics. Chmn, nat appeals cmte, National Childrens Home.
Mr David Rowland, airline pilot. Mbr, Oxford CC. Oxfordshire rep on ACC. Past chmn, Banbury SDP. B Dec 7 1946; ed Abbeydale GS, Sheffield. Balpa. Joined BOAC in 1969 and has been with British Airways Concorde fleet.
Mr Jim Honeybone, teacher, contested Cotswolds in 1979 Euro election. Mbr, Cherwell DC, 1979-83. B Mar 11 1938; ed King Edward's, Birmingham; Gonville and Caius, Cambridge. NUT.

Mr Tony Baldry

BANFF AND BUCHAN — SNP gain

Electorate	%Turnout		1987			1983
		62,149	70.8%	**1987**	60,403	67.0%	**1983**
Salmond, A.E.A. (SNP)		19,462	44.3%	+6.8%	16,072	39.7%	(C)
*McQuarrie, A. (C)		17,021	38.7%	-1.0%	15,135	37.4%	(SNP)
Burness, G.M. (SDP/All)		4,211	9.6%	-5.5%	6,084	15.0%	(SDP/All)
Livie, J.M. (Lab)		3,281	7.5%	-0.3%	3,150	7.8%	(Lab)
C to SNP swing 3.9%		43,975	SNP maj 2,441	5.6%	40,441	C maj 937	2.3%

Mr Alexander Salmond, energy economist with Royal Bank of Scotland plc, has been SNP vice-chmn since 1985. B Dec 31 1954; ed Linlithgow Acad; St Andrews Univ. BIFU.
Mr Albert McQuarrie, sec, Conservative back-bench fisheries sub-cmte, 1981-82, and vice-chmn, 1982-87. MP for this seat 1983-87; and for East Aberdeenshire, 1979-83; contested Caithness and Sutherland, Oct 1974, and Kilmarnock, 1966. Former mbr, Chairmen's Panel. Civil engineer; chmn, A McQuarrie and Son (GB) Ltd, since 1946, and director, Energy Exploration Ltd; consultant to Bredero Consultancy Ltd, Aberdeen and Epsom, 1976- . B Jan 1 1918; ed Greenock HS and Royal Coll of Science and Technology. Sec, Scottish Cons MPs, 1985- . Member, Select Cmte on Agriculture, 1983-85. Chmn, British-Gibraltar all-pty gp.
Mr George Burness, pharmaceutical chemist. Mbr, Highland Reg Cl, 1978-86 (chmn, finance cmte, 1982-86); Ross and Cromarty DC, 1980-84; Cromarty Firth Port Authority, 1980-83. B Apr 18 1943; ed Aberdeen GS; Robert Gordon's Inst of Tech.
Mr James Livie, lecturer in communications, Banff and Buchan CFE; teacher, 1980-85. B Dec 17 1948; ed Morgan Acad, Dundee; Dundee Univ; Dundee Coll of Ed. Mbr, Fraserburgh Community Cl.

Mr Alexander Salmond

BARKING — No change

Electorate	%Turnout		1987			1983
	51,639	66.9%	**1987**	52,362	65.4%	**1983**
*Richardson, Ms J. (Lab)	15,307	44.3%	+2.2%	14,415	42.1%	(Lab)
Sharp, W.K. (C)	11,898	34.4%	+4.1%	10,389	30.4%	(C)
Gibb, J.K. (L/All)	7,336	21.2%	-4.4%	8,770	25.6%	(L/All)
				646	1.9%	(Other)
Lab to C swing 0.9%	34,541	Lab maj 3,409 9.9%		34,220	Lab maj 4,026 11.8%	

Ms Jo Richardson

Ms Jo Richardson, Opposition front bencher on women's rights since 1983, has been a mbr of the Labour Party NEC since 1979; chairs its women's committee and formerly chaired its Black and Asian Advisory Group. Elected in Feb 1974; contested Harrow East, 1964; Hornchurch, 1959; Monmouth, 1955 and 1951. B Aug 28 1923; ed Southend HS for Girls. Former mbr, select cmtes on home affairs, nationalized industries, procedure and expenditure. Vicepres, CND; chmn, PLP Civil Liberties Group, 1975-79, and vice-chmn since 1979; mbr, exec cl, Nat Cl for Civil Liberties. Chaired Tribune Gp of Lab MPs, 1978-79 (sec, 1948-78, when it was known as Keep Left Gp and then Bevan Gp). Served on Hornsey BC and Hammersmith BC. ASTMS and Apex.
Mr Keith Sharp, company director. Ldr, Castle Point DC. B 1947; ed St Bonaventures GS, London. Mbr, British Rail Liaison Bd.
Mr John Gibb, company director, fruit importer, contested this setat 1983 and Ince, Oct 1974 and 1979; West Lancashire in 1979 Euro elections. B Sep 13 1926; ed St Egberts Coll, Chingford; Dolcoath Tech Coll, Camborne; King George V GS, Southport. Mbr, Lib International; Electoral Reform Soc.

BARNSLEY CENTRAL — No change

Electorate	%Turnout		1987			1983
	55,902	70.0%	**1987**	55,115	66.3%	**1983**
Illsley, E.E. (Lab)	26,139	66.8%	+7.0%	21,847	59.8%	(Lab)
Prais, Mrs V. (C)	7,088	18.1%	-2.9%	7,674	21.0%	(C)
Holland, Mrs S.A.M. (L/All)	5,928	15.1%	-4.1%	7,011	19.2%	(L/All)
C to Lab swing 4.9%	39,155	Lab maj 19,051 48.7%		36,532	Lab maj 14,173 38.8%	

Mr Eric Illsley

Mr Eric Illsley has worked for Yorkshire area NUM since 1978 and is now chief administrative officer. Has held local Lab Pty offices. B Apr 9 1955; ed Barnsley Holgate GS; Leeds Univ.
Mrs Vivien Prais, solicitor. B Dec 14 1941; ed LSE; Rome Univ.
Mrs Anne Holland, freelance translator. On an area education sub-cmte in Leeds; governor, Gledhow Primary Sch; cmte mbr of housing assocn. B Jul 22 1940; ed Queen Ethelburgh's Sch, Harrogate; Girton Coll, Cambridge.

BARNSLEY EAST — No change

Electorate	%Turnout		1987			1983
	53,505	72.6%	**1987**	53,611	67.3%	**1983**
*Patchett, T. (Lab)	28,948	74.5%	+8.2%	23,905	66.3%	(Lab)
Clappison, W.J. (C)	5,437	14.0%	-2.0%	6,413	17.8%	(L/All)
Griffiths, G.J. (L/All)	4,482	11.5%	-6.2%	5,749	15.9%	(C)
C to Lab swing 5.1%	38,867	Lab maj 23,511 60.5%		36,067	Lab maj 17,492 48.5%	

Mr Terry Patchett

Mr Terry Patchett, miner, has been on the Select Cmte on Social Services, since 1985. Elected in 1983. B Jul 11 1940; ed local schools. Jt vice-chmn, PLP energy cmte, 1985- . NUM Houghton Main branch delegate, 1966-83; mbr, Yorkshire Miners' Executive, 1976-83; Wombwell UDC, 1969-73. Former mbr, appeals tribunals, community health cl. NUM sponsored.
Mr James Clappison, barrister; mbr of Lloyd's. B Sep 14 1956; ed St Peter's Sch, York; Queen's Coll, Oxford.
Mr Geoffrey Griffiths, teacher. Mbr, Sheffield City Cl, 1978- . B Dec 11 1948; ed Bristol; Sheffield Coll.

BARNSLEY WEST AND PENISTONE — No change

Electorate %Turnout	61,091	75.6%	**1987**	60,648	73.2%	**1983**
*McKay, A. (Lab)	26,498	57.3%	+6.5%	22,560	50.8%	(Lab)
Duncan, A.J.C. (C)	12,307	26.6%	-0.9%	12,218	27.5%	(C)
Hall, R. (SDP/All)	7,409	16.0%	-5.6%	9,624	21.7%	(SDP/All)
C to Lab swing 3.7%	46,214	Lab maj 14,191 30.7%		44,402	Lab maj 10,342 23.3%	

Mr Allen McKay, the Opposition's Yorkshire whip since 1981, was elected for this seat in 1983; MP for Penistone, 1978-83. Mining electrical engineer, 1947-65; industrial relations trainee, NCB, 1965-66; asst manpower officer, Barnsley area NCB, 1966-78. Hon mbr, Yorkshire NUM. Unpaid parly consultant to British Assocn of Colliery Management. B Feb 5 1927; ed Hoyland Kirk Balk Sch; extra-mural dept, Sheffield Univ. Mbr, Hoyland Nether UDC, 1965-74 (chmn, 1973-74); Barnsley MBC, 1974-78.
Mr Alan Duncan, oil trader. B Mar 31 1957; ed Merchant Taylors' Sch, Northwood; St John's Coll, Oxford; Harvard Univ.
Mr Richard Hall, lecturer in art, design and general studies, York Coll of Arts and Tech. Borough cllr, 1986- . B 1942; ed Kitson Coll, Leeds; York Univ.

Mr Allen McKay

BARROW AND FURNESS — No change

Electorate %Turnout	69,288	79.0%	**1987**	67,896	75.2%	**1983**
*Franks, C.S. (C)	25,431	46.5%	+2.8%	22,284	43.6%	(C)
Phizacklea, P. (Lab)	21,504	39.3%	+4.6%	17,707	34.7%	(Lab)
Phelps, R.W. (SDP/All)	7,799	14.2%	-7.4%	11,079	21.7%	(SDP/All)
C to Lab swing 0.9%	54,734	C maj 3,927 7.2%		51,070	C maj 4,577 9.0%	

Mr Cecil Franks, solicitor, consultant and company director, was elected in 1983. Member, Manchester City Cl, 1975-84, being leader of Cons gp; Salford City Cl, 1960-74, leader of Cons gp. B Jul 1 1935; ed Manchester GS and Manchester Univ. Director, Pryde Investments Ltd. Mbr, North West RHA, 1973-75.
Mr Peter Phizacklea, unemployed foreman fabrication inspector in shipbuilding and engineering industry. Mbr, Cumbria CC, 1973- . Chmn, Lake District Planning Bd, 1981-85. B Apr 14 1937; ed Dowdales Sec Sch, Dalton-in-Furness. ASTMS.
Mr Richard Phelps was general manager, Central Lancashire New Town Development Corporation, 1971-86, when he retired. With Colonial Administrative Service, N Region and Fed Govt of Nigeria, 1948-57 and 1965-67; Principal, HM Treasury, 1957-59 and 1961-65; senior administrator, Hampshire CC, 1965-67; gen manager, Skelmersdale New Town Development Corporation, 1967-71. B Jul 26 1925; ed Kingswood Sch, Bath; Merton Coll, Oxford. Trustee, British Motor Industry Heritage Trust, 1985.

Mr Cecil Franks

BASILDON — No change

Electorate %Turnout	68,500	73.3%	**1987**	65,604	69.0%	**1983**
*Amess, D.A. (C)	21,858	43.5%	+4.9%	17,516	38.7%	(C)
Fulbrook, J.G.H. (Lab)	19,209	38.3%	+2.6%	16,137	35.6%	(Lab)
Auvray, R.M. (L/All)	9,139	18.2%	-7.5%	11,634	25.7%	(SDP/All)
Lab to C swing 1.1%	50,206	C maj 2,649 5.3%		45,287	C maj 1,379 3.0%	

Mr David Amess, a senior partner since 1981 in Employment Agency (Accountancy Aids), a specialist agency, and chmn of an executive search and selection company, was elected in 1983; contested Newham North West, 1979. B Mar 26 1952; ed St Bonadventure GS and Bournemouth Coll of Tech. Mbr, Redbridge BC, 1982- (vice-chmn, housing cmte). Trainee underwriter, 1974-76; head of temporary dept, Accountancy Personnel, 1979-81; senior consultant with Executemps Company Agency, 1979-81.
Mr Julian Fulbrook, barrister and lecturer in labour and social security law at LSE, contested this seat 1983 and Huntingdonshire 1979. Has acted for unions in industrial injuries cases. Mbr, Camden BC, 1978- ; chmn, Basildon Community Relations Cl, 1985- ; legal adviser, Soc for Prevention of Asbestosis and Industrial Diseases. B May 10 1948; ed Eltham Coll; Redruth Cty GS; Exeter and Cambridge Univs; Harvard Law Sch. TGWU.
Mr Ray Auvray, a principal careers officer, fought this seat 1979. Mbr, Essex CC, since 1985; Basildon DC, 1982-86. B Jun 23 1948; ed Bideford GS; Reading Univ; NE London Poly. Nalgo.

Mr David Amess

BASINGSTOKE — No change

Electorate	%Turnout		**1987**			**1983**
78,003	77.0%			71,975	76.8%	
*Hunter, A.R.F. (C)	33,657	56.0%	+4.7%	28,381	51.3%	(C)
Bennett, D. (SDP/All)	15,764	26.3%	-2.6%	15,931	28.8%	(SDP/All)
Daden, P. (Lab)	10,632	17.7%	-1.5%	10,646	19.3%	(Lab)
				344	0.6%	(Other)
SDP/All to C swing 3.6%	60,053	C maj 17,893 29.8%		55,302	C maj 12,450 22.5%	

Mr **Andrew Hunter** became a mbr of the Select Cmte on Environment in 1986; on Select Cmte on Agriculture, 1985. Elected in 1983; contested Southampton, Itchen, 1979. Asst master, Harrow, 1971-83. PPS to Lord Elton, Minister of State for Environment, 1985-86; sec, Cons backbench environment cmte, 1984-85. B Jan 8 1943; ed St George's Sch, Harpenden; Durham Univ and Jesus Coll, Cambridge. Member, CLA agriculture cmte, 1986- . Major in TAVR, 1973-84. Order of Merit (Govt of Poland in exile), 1980.

Mr **David Bennett**, director of a public affairs consultancy, contested Birmingham Yardley 1983 and Birmingham East in 1984 Euro election. Sec, Alliance Euro policy gp. B Oct 4 1948; ed Harold Malley GS, Solihull; Portsmouth Poly; John Hopkins Univ.

Mr **Peter Daden**, research and policy adviser with London Strategic Policy Unit. Former GLC industrial development officer. B Sept 9, 1946. Mbr, Basingstoke BC, 1982- (dep ldr, Lab gp); management cttee, Basingstoke Centre for Unemployed. School governor. TGWU.

Mr Andrew Hunter

BASSETLAW — No change

Electorate	%Turnout		**1987**			**1983**
68,043	77.6%			65,721	74.2%	
*Ashton, J.W. (Lab)	25,385	48.1%	+2.5%	22,231	45.6%	(Lab)
Selves, D.R.J. (C)	19,772	37.5%	-0.3%	18,400	37.7%	(C)
Smith, W.G. (SDP/All)	7,616	14.4%	-2.2%	8,124	16.7%	(SDP/All)
C to Lab swing 1.4%	52,773	Lab maj 5,613 10.6%		48,755	Lab maj 3,831 7.9%	

Mr **Joseph Ashton**, formerly a design engineer and now a journalist and broadcaster, was returned at a by-election in Oct 1968. Opposition spokesman on energy, 1979-81. Mbr, Select Cmte on Members' Interests, 1979-83, and Select Cmte on Members' Salaries, 1981-82. Asst Government whip, 1976-77; PPS to Mr Benn, 1974-76. Mbr, Sheffield City Cl, 1962-69. B Oct 9 1933; ed High Storrs GS, Sheffield; Rotherham Tech Coll. Mbr, Select Cmte on Nationalized Industries, 1974-76. Sponsored by AUEW (TASS). Columnist for *Sheffield Star*, 1970-75, 1979-80, *Labour Weekly*, 1971-82, *Daily Star*, 1979- . Holds two shares in Sheffield Wednesday FC on which no dividend has been paid since 1953.

Mr **David Selves**, financial consultant and author. B Aug 10 1949; ed Queen Elizabeth's GS, Barnet. Vice-pres, Mid-Sussex Cons Assocn. Member, Mid-Sussex DC, 1983-84.

Mr **William Smith**, a material control assistant, is chmn of Leicestershire and of Bassetlaw SDP. B Dec 22 1935; ed Wyggeston Sch, Leicester. Nalgo, serving on its West Midlands Gas Cmte; Nat Employees Gas Cmte, and W Midlands DC.

Mr Joseph Ashton

BATH — No change

Electorate	%Turnout		**1987**			**1983**
65,246	79.4%			64,325	74.4%	
*Patten, C.F. (C)	23,515	45.4%	-1.7%	22,544	47.1%	(C)
Dean, J.M. (SDP/All)	22,103	42.7%	+6.6%	17,240	36.0%	(SDP/All)
Smith, Ms J. (Lab)	5,507	10.6%	-4.5%	7,259	15.2%	(Lab)
Wall, D.N. (Grn)	687	1.3%	+0.4%	441	0.9%	(Eco)
				386	0.8%	(Other)
C to SDP/All swing 4.2%	51,812	C maj 1,412 2.7%		47,870	C maj 5,304 11.1%	

Mr **Christopher Patten**, Minister for Overseas Development, with the rank of Minister of State, Foreign and Commonwealth Office, 1986- ; Minister of State for Education and Science, 1985-86; Under Sec of State for N Ireland, 1983-85. Director of Cons Research Dept, 1974-79, and served in it, 1966-70; Cabinet Office, 1970-72; Voluntary Services Unit, Home Office, 1972; personal asst and political sec to Lord Carrington, chmn of Cons Pty, 1972-74. Elected in 1979; contested Lambeth Central, Feb 1974. B May 12 1944; ed St Benedict's Sch, Ealing; Balliol Coll, Oxford. PPS to Leader of the House, 1979-81; to Secretary of State for Social Services, 1981. Member, Select Cmtes on Defence and Procedure, 1982-83.

Mr **Malcolm Dean**, a journalist on *The Guardian* specialising in social policy. Special adviser to Sec of State for Social Services, 1978-79. Mbr, SDP anti-poverty cmte and Alliance social security cmte. B Jun 11 1939; ed Macclesfield GS; Ruskin Coll, Oxford; Chicago Univ. NUJ.

Ms **Jenny Smith**, housing aid worker for Shelter. Mbr, Avon CC, 1985- . B Aug 7 1938; ed Shaw House Sec Mod Sch, Newbury; Bristol Poly. ACTSS; NUPE.

Mr **Derek Wall**, lecturer and journalist. Mbr, Ecology Pty Cl, 1983-84. B May 26 1965; ed comprehensive sch; Inst of Archaeology; London Univ.

Mr Christopher Patten

BATLEY AND SPEN — No change

Electorate %Turnout	74,347	79.0%	**1987**	73,798	73.4%	**1983**
*Peacock, Mrs E.J. (C)	25,512	43.4%	+3.9%	21,433	39.6%	(C)
Woolmer, K.J. (Lab)	24,150	41.1%	+3.2%	20,563	38.0%	(Lab)
Burke, K. (SDP/All)	8,372	14.3%	-7.3%	11,678	21.6%	(SDP/All)
Harrison, A. (ML)	689	1.2%		493	0.9%	(Eco)
Lab to C swing 0.4%	58,723	C maj 1,362 2.3%		54,167	C maj 870 1.6%	

Mrs Elizabeth Peacock has been a mbr of the Select Cmte on Employment since 1983, the year she was elected for this seat. Parliamentary consultant to Nat Bedding Federation. Asst to exec director, York Community Cl, 1979-83; charitable trusts administrator, York, 1979-83. B Sep 4 1937; ed St Monica's Convent, Skipton. Magistrate. Mbr, N Yorkshire CC, 1981-84. Sec, Yorkshire Cons MPs, 1983- ; chmn, Cons back-bench party organisation cmte, 1986- ; vice-chmn, 1985-86. Vice-pres, Yorkshire area YCs, 1984-87; hon pres, Nat Assocn of Approved Driving Instructors, 1984- .
Mr Kenneth Woolmer was MP for Batley and Morley, 1979-83, contesting this seat 1983; Leeds North West, 1970. An Opposition spokesman on trade, 1981-83. Economist; lecturer, School of Economic Studies, Leeds Univ, 1983- ; previously lecturer at Leeds Univ and in Nigeria, 1963-79. Mbr, Select Cmte on Treasury and Civil Service, 1980-81; chmn, PLP finance and economic gp, 1981, and vice-chmn, 1982. B Apr 25 1940; ed Gladstone St County Primary Sch, Rothwell, Northants; Kettering GS; Leeds Univ. Mbr, Leeds City and Dist Cls, 1970-77; West Yorkshire Met CC, 1973-79. Chmn, Planning and Transportation Cmte, AMA, 1974-77. AUT, GMBATU.
Mrs Elizabeth Peacock   Mr Keith Burke, retail sales manager. B Jan 14 1938; ed Liversedge Sec Mod Sch.

BATTERSEA — C gain

Electorate %Turnout	66,979	70.7%	**1987**	65,938	66.6%	**1983**
Bowis, J.C. (C)	20,945	44.2%	+7.9%	19,248	43.8%	(Lab)
*Dubs, A. (Lab)	20,088	42.4%	-1.4%	15,972	36.4%	(C)
Harries, D.I. (SDP/All)	5,634	11.9%	-5.6%	7,675	17.5%	(SDP/All)
Willington, Mrs S.G. (Grn)	559	1.2%	+0.3%	539	1.2%	(NF)
Bell, A.B. (WRP)	116	0.2%		377	0.9%	(Eco)
				108	0.2%	(Other)
Lab to C swing 4.6%	47,342	C maj 857 1.8%		43,919	Lab maj 3,276 7.5%	

Mr John Bowis is public affairs director of the British Insurance Brokers' Assocn. Former education chmn, London borough of Kingston; on Greater London arts exec until 1985; mbr, Wandsworth CHC. B Aug 2 1945; ed Tonbridge Sch; Brasenose Coll, Oxford. ASTMS.
Mr Alfred Dubs was with the Opposition front brench team on home affairs, 1983-87, being spokesman on race relations and immigration. Former local govt officer. MP for this seat 1983-87, and for Battersea South 1979-83; contested Cities of London and Westminster, 1970; South Hertfordshire twice in 1974. Mbr, Select Cmte on Home Affairs and its sub-cmte on race relations and immigration, 1981-83. B Dec 1932; ed LSE. Mbr, Westminster City Cl, 1971-78; chmn, Westminster Community Relations Cl, 1972-77; jt vice-chmn, Greater London gp of Lab MPs, 1985-87. Sponsored by Cohse.
Mr David Harries, youth work trainer. Chmn, Battersea SDP; member, CSD and citizens rights working pty. B Dec 11 1949; ed Vyners GS, Ickenham, Middlesex.
Mrs Sally Willington, self-employed studio potter with retail shop, contested Battersea 1983. B May 25 1931; ed N London Collegiate Sch.
Mr John Bowis

BEACONSFIELD — No change

Electorate %Turnout	67,713	74.6%	**1987**	66,186	72.4%	**1983**
*Smith, T.J. (C)	33,324	66.0%	+2.2%	30,552	63.8%	(C)
Ive, D.H. (L/All)	11,985	23.7%	-1.8%	12,252	25.6%	(L/All)
Harper, K.J. (Lab)	5,203	10.3%	-0.4%	5,107	10.7%	(Lab)
L/All to C swing 2.0%	50,512	C maj 21,339 42.2%		47,911	C maj 18,300 38.2%	

Mr Timothy Smith, chartered accountant, was elected for this seat at the 1982 by-election; MP for Ashfield, 1977-79. PPS to Mr Leon Brittan, Home Secretary, 1983-85. Consultant to Price Waterhouse, *Accountancy Age* magazine, the Financial Intermediaries, Managers and Brokers Regulatory Assocn, and three other companies; former consultant to Inst of Chartered Accountants in England and Wales (being sec of its parly and law cmte, 1979-82). B Oct 5 1947; ed Harrow and St Peter's Coll, Oxford. Jt vice-chmn, Cons back-bench trade and industry cmte, 1986- , and its jt sec, 1985-86. Sec, Cons back-bench finance cmte, since 1985; Cons health and social services cmte, 1982-83; Cons small business cmte, 1982-83; mbr, Select Cmte on Social Services, 1982-83. Chmn, Coningsby Club, 1977-78.
Mr David Ive, solicitor, is vice-chmn, Lib Pty Home Office panel; former treas, British section, Amnesty International. Contested this seat 1983; Chipping Barnet, 1979. B Jan 2 1950; ed Highgate Sch; Birmingham Univ.
Mr Kenneth Harper, marketing manager. Former mbr, Welsh Cl for Labour; former chmn, Leyton CLP. B Dec 14 1956; ed Deeside HS; Portsmouth Poly. Sponsored by NUR.
Mr Timothy Smith

BECKENHAM — No change

Electorate %Turnout	60,110	73.6%	**1987**	58,719	70.0%	**1983**
*Goodhart, Sir Philip (C)	24,903	56.3%	-1.1%	23,606	57.4%	(C)
Darracott, C.G. (L/All)	11,439	25.9%	-0.7%	10,936	26.6%	(L/All)
Ritchie, K.G. (Lab)	7,888	17.8%	+2.3%	6,386	15.5%	(Lab)
				203	0.5%	(Other)
C to L/All swing 0.2%	44,230	C maj 13,464 30.4%		41,131	C maj 12,670 30.8%	

Sir Philip Goodhart has been chairman, Select Cmte on Sound Broadcasting, since 1983; mbr, Privileges Cmte and Select Cmte on Employment. Under Secretary of State for Defence, 1981; Under Secretary of State for N Ireland, 1979-81. Author and journalist, 1952-1956, *Daily Telegraph* and *Sunday Times*. Elected at 1957 by-election; contested Consett, 1950. B Nov 3 1925; ed Hotchkiss Sch, US, and Trinity Coll, Cambridge. Jt sec, 1922 Cmte, 1960-79. Sec, Cons defence cmte, 1967-72, chmn 1972-74, vice-chmn 1974-79. Chmn, all-pty parl gp on road safety, since 1983; Cons N Ireland cmte, 1976-79. Mbr, Advisory Cl on Public Records, 1970-79; exec cmte, British Cl, 1974-79; cl, Consumers' Assocn, 1959-68, and 1970-79, UK delegation to UN General Assembly, 1963, and N Atlantic Assembly, 1964-79.

Mr Colin Darracott is president and former chmn, London Lib Pty. Chmn (1986-87) and vice-chmn (1985-86), Lib Assembly cmte; member, Lib nat exec, serving on pty finance and administration bd. B 1949; ed City of Bath Boys Sch; Oxford Univ.

Mr Ken Ritchie, executive director, Appropriate Health Resources and Technologies Action Gp, a charity promoting health care in the Third World. B Dec 8 1946; ed Edinburgh and Aston Univs. Was systems analyst with ICI, War on Want researcher (now mbr of its cl) sec, UN Assn International Service overseas volunteer programme.

Sir Philip Goodhart

BEDFORDSHIRE MID — No change

Electorate %Turnout	80,673	78.6%	**1987**	75,558	76.9%	**1983**
*Lyell, N.W. (C)	37,411	59.0%	+2.1%	33,042	56.8%	(C)
Hills, N.C. (SDP/All)	14,560	23.0%	-4.0%	15,661	26.9%	(L/All)
Heywood, J. (Lab)	11,463	18.1%	+1.9%	9,420	16.2%	(Lab)
SDP/All to C swing 3.1%	63,434	C maj 22,851 36.0%		58,123	C maj 17,381 29.9%	

Sir Nicholas Lyell, QC, was appointed Solicitor General in Jun 1987; Under Secretary of State for Health and Social Security, 1986-87; PPS to Sir Michael Havers, Attorney General, 1979-86; a Recorder since 1985. Chmn and previously vice-chmn, executive, Society of Cons Lawyers, 1982-86. Elected for this seat 1983; MP for Hemel Hemstead, 1979-83; contested Lambeth Central, Oct 1974. Sec, Cons back-bench constitutional cmte, 1979. B Dec 6 1938; ed Stowe and Christ Church, Oxford. Mbr of Lloyd's; Select Cmte on Procedure (Finance), 1982-83. Vice-chmn, British Field Sports Soc, 1983-86.

Mr Nikolas Hills, account director in advertising and marketing consultancy. Chmn, North Bedfordshire SDP, 1983-84 and 1985-86; mbr, CSD, 1984-86; Tawney Society. B Apr 26 1950; ed Royal Liberty Sch, Gidea Park, Essex; NE London Poly.

Mr John Heywood, headmaster of comprehensive school. Convenor, Secondary Heads Assocn, Cambridgeshire; nat cl mbr, being salaries and conditions of service rep. B May 1 1937; ed Manchester GS; Lincoln Coll, Oxford.

Sir Nicholas Lyell

BEDFORDSHIRE NORTH — No change

Electorate %Turnout	73,536	77.2%	**1987**	71,491	75.2%	**1983**
*Skeet, Sir Trevor (C)	29,845	52.6%	+0.6%	27,969	52.0%	(C)
Lennon, Mrs J.V. (L/All)	13,340	23.5%	-2.8%	14,120	26.3%	(L/All)
Henderson, C.B. (Lab)	13,140	23.2%	+2.1%	11,323	21.1%	(Lab)
Slee, C.D. (OOBPC)	435	0.8%		344	0.6%	(Ind)
L/All to C swing 1.7%	56,760	C maj 16,505 29.1%		53,756	C maj 13,849 25.8%	

Sir Trevor Skeet, barrister and industrial consultant, won this seat in 1983; MP for Bedford, 1970-83; for Willesden, East, 1959-64; contested Llanelli, 1955, and Stoke Newington and Hackney North, 1951. Mbr, technical legislation cmte, CBI. B Jan 28 1918; ed King's Coll, Auckland, and Univ of NZ. Vice-chmn, Cons power and energy cmte, 1959-64; chmn, oil sub-cmte, 1959-64; chmn, Cons trade committee, 1971-74; mbr, Select Cmte on Wealth Tax, 1975-76; sec, all-pty group on airships, 1971-78; chmn, Cons Middle East cmte, 1973-78; mbr, all-pty group on minerals, since 1971; co-chmn from 1979. Vice-chmn, British-Brazilian Group and British-Japanese Group; sec, British-Nigerian Group; chmn (1985-), sec (1983-85) and mbr (1982-), steering cmte, Parly and Scientific Cmte. Consultant, Associated Portland Cement Manufacturers - Blue Circle Industries.

Mrs Janice Lennon, a teacher, 1970-77. Mbr, North Bedfordshire BC since 1974 and Bedfordshire CC since 1977. B Jan 25 1948; ed Putney HS; Cambridge and Nottingham Univs. In NUT when teaching.

Mr Bruce Henderson, contracts engineer. Mbr, Bedfordshire CC, 1981- . B Jul 30 1947; ed Kings Sch, Canterbury; Imperial Coll, London. Co-founder, Bedford Unemployed Workers Centre; vice-pres, Bedford RUFC. TASS.

Sir Trevor Skeet

BEDFORDSHIRE SOUTH WEST — No change

Electorate %Turnout	78,956	78.7%	**1987**	76,298	75.6%	**1983**
*Madel, W.D. (C)	36,140	58.2%	+3.1%	31,767	55.1%	(C)
Burrow, J.R. (SDP/All)	13,835	22.3%	-5.5%	16,036	27.8%	(SDP/All)
Dimoldenberg, P.H. (Lab)	11,352	18.3%	+1.1%	9,899	17.2%	(Lab)
Rollings, P.J. (Grn)	822	1.3%				
SDP/All to C swing 4.3%	62,149	C maj 22,305 35.9%		57,702	C maj 15,731 27.3%	

Mr **David Madel** has served on the Select Cmtes on European Legislation since 1986, Members' Interests since 1979, and Education, Science and the Arts, 1979-83. Parliamentary consultant to Banking Insurance and Finance Union; non-exec director of three companies; advertising exec, Thomson Organization, 1964-70. Elected for this seat 1983; MP for Bedford South, 1970-83; contested Erith and Crayford, 1965 by-election and 1966. B Aug 1938; ed Uppingham and Keble Coll, Oxford. Sec, Cons back-bench home affairs cmte, 1972-73. PPS to defence ministers, 1973-74. Chmn, Cons back-bench education cmte, 1983-85, jt vice-chmn, 1981-83; jt vice-chmn (previously jt sec), Cons back-bench employment cmte, 1974-81.
Mr **John Burrow,** barrister. B Jun 19 1950; ed Bishops Stortford Coll; Essex Univ.
Mr **Paul Dimoldenberg,** local govt officer with Southwark BC; mbr, Westminster City Cl, 1982- , chairing Lab gp. Vice-chair (1983), sec (1981-82), agent (1979), St Marylebone CLP. B Mar 3 1950; ed Bury GS; Central London Poly; Oxford Poly. RTPI, Nalgo.
Mr **Peter Rollings,** draughtsman. Mbr, Eaton Bray PC. B Oct 27 1955; ed Dunstable GS; Luton Coll of Tech.

Mr David Madel

BELFAST EAST — No change

Electorate %Turnout	54,628	60.2%	**1987**	55,581	70.0%	**1983**
*Robinson, P.D. (DUP)	20,372	61.9%	+16.6%	17,631	45.3%	(DUP)
Alderdice, Dr J. (All)	10,574	32.1%	+8.0%	9,642	24.8%	(OUP)
Cullen, F. (WP)	1,314	4.0%	+2.9%	9,373	24.1%	(All)
O'Donnell, J. (PSF)	649	2.0%	+0.2%	682	1.8%	(PSF)
				1,583	4.1%	(Other)
All to DUP swing 4.3%	32,909	DUP maj 9,798 29.8%		38,911	DUP maj 7,989 20.5%	

Mr **Peter Robinson,** who won the seat in 1979, has been deputy leader, Democratic Unionist Party, since 1980; was general secretary, 1975-80. Resigned seat in 1985 in protest at Anglo-Irish agreement and retained it in 1986 by-election. Mbr, N Ireland Assembly, 1982-86; chmn of its environment cmte. Mbr, Castlereagh BC, 1977- ; Deputy Mayor, 1978; Mayor, 1986. B Dec 29 1948; ed Annadale GS and Castlereagh CFE. Director, Crown Publications, Belfast, and hon director, Voice Newspapers Ltd.
Dr **John Alderdice,** consultant psychiatrist. B May 28 1955; ed Ballymena Acad; Queen's Univ Belfast. Chmn, Alliance policy cmte; East Belfast Alliance Assocn.
Mr **Joseph O'Donnell,** full-time PSF worker. Aged 35. Interned early 1970s and served prison sentence.
Details of 1986 by-election on Page 285

Mr Peter Robinson

BELFAST NORTH — No change

Electorate %Turnout	59,124	62.3%	**1987**	61,128	69.4%	**1983**
*Walker, A.C. (OUP)	14,355	39.0%	+2.8%	15,339	36.2%	(OUP)
Maginness, A. (SDLP)	5,795	15.7%	+1.7%	8,260	19.5%	(DUP)
Seawright, G. (Prot U)	5,671	15.4%		5,944	14.0%	(SDLP)
McManus, P. (PSF)	5,062	13.7%	+0.9%	5,451	12.9%	(PSF)
Lynch, S. (WP)	3,062	8.3%	+2.6%	3,879	9.1%	(All)
Campbell, T. (All)	2,871	7.8%	-1.3%	2,412	5.7%	(WP)
				1,134	2.7%	(Other)
SDLP to OUP swing 0.6%	36,816	OUP maj 8,560 23.3%		42,419	OUP maj 7,079 16.7%	

Mr **Cecil Walker,** a former sales manager, was elected in 1983; contested the seat, 1979. Resigned seat in 1985 in protest at Anglo-Irish Agreement and re-elected at 1986 by-election. Unsuccessfully contested N Ireland Assembly, 1973. B Dec 17 1924; ed Methodist Coll, Belfast. In timber business with James P. Corry & Co. Ltd, Belfast, from 1941; joinery sales manager, 1951-83; now retained in consultative role.
Mr **Alban Maginness,** barrister. Aged 37; ed St Malachy's Coll, Belfast; Queen's Univ, Belfast; Univ of Ulster. Mbr, Belfast City Cl, 1985- .
Mr **Paddy McManus,** former welder. Aged 44. Interned until Nov 1975. Unsuccessful PSF candidate for Belfast City Cl election, 1985.
Mr **Thomas Campbell,** partner in Belfast firm of solicitors. B Aug 31 1958; St McNissis GS, Garron Tower, Co Antrim; Queen's Univ, Belfast. Mbr for N Belfast, Belfast City Cl, 1985- ; Alliance Pty central exec.
Details of 1986 by-election on Page 285

Mr Cecil Walker

BELFAST SOUTH — No change

Electorate %Turnout	54,208	60.3%	**1987**	53,694	69.6%	**1983**
*Smyth, Rev W.M. (OUP)	18,917	57.8%	+7.9%	18,669	50.0%	(OUP)
Cook, D. (All)	6,963	21.3%	-2.7%	8,945	23.9%	(All)
McDonnell, Dr A. (SDLP)	4,268	13.0%	+4.4%	4,565	12.2%	(DUP)
Carr, G. (WP)	1,528	4.7%	+2.4%	3,216	8.6%	(SDLP)
McKnight, S. (PSF)	1,030	3.1%	+0.2%	1,107	3.0%	(PSF)
				856	2.3%	(Other)
All to OUP swing 5.3%	32,706	OUP maj 11,954 36.5%		37,358	OUP maj 9,724 26.0%	

The Rev Martin Smyth held seat for OUP at 1982 by-election caused by the murder of Rev Robert Bradford. Resigned seat 1985 in protest at Anglo-Irish Agreement and held it in 1986 by-election. Pty spokesman on health and social services; mbr, Select Cmte on Social Services, 1984-86. Mbr for Belfast South, NI Assembly, 1982-86; NI Constitutional Convention, 1975. B Jun 15 1931; ed Methodist Coll, Belfast; Magee Univ Coll, Londonderry; Trinity Coll, Dublin; Presbyterian Col, Belfast, and San Francisco Theological Seminary. Minister of religion without pastoral charge. Grand Master, Grand Orange Lodge of Ireland, 1972- ; Grand Master, Grand Orange Cl of World, 1974-82, and Pres, 1985- . Vice-pres, UU Cl, since 1974. Vice-chmn, all-pty cmte on Soviet Jewry, 1983- .
Mr David Cook, solicitor, contested this seat 1983; 1982 by-election; 1974. B 1944; ed Campbell Coll, Belfast; Pembroke Coll, Cambridge. Lord Mayor of Belfast, 1978-79. NI Assembly mbr for S Belfast, 1982-86.
Dr Alasdair McDonnell, GP in Belfast; mbr, Belfast City Cl, 1977-1981 and 1985- (ldr, SDLP gp, 1977-81). Fpught parly seat 1979, 1983 and 1982 and 1986 by-elections.
Mr Sean McKnight contested this seat 1983. PSF member, Belfast City Cl, 1984- (ldr, PSF gp).

The Rev Martin Smyth   *Details of 1986 by-election on Page 285*

BELFAST WEST — No change

Electorate %Turnout	59,324	69.1%	**1987**	59,750	74.3%	**1983**
*Adams, G. (PSF)	16,862	41.2%	+4.2%	16,379	36.9%	(PSF)
Hendron, Dr J.G. (SDLP)	14,641	35.7%	+11.1%	10,934	24.6%	(SDLP)
Miller, F. (OUP)	7,646	18.7%	+13.2%	10,326	23.3%	(Ind)
McMahon, Ms M. (WP)	1,819	4.4%	+0.2%	2,435	5.5%	(OUP)
				4,292	9.7%	(Other)
PSF to SDLP swing 3.4%	40,968	PSF maj 2,221 5.4%		44,366	PSF maj 5,445 12.3%	

Mr Gerry Adams was elected in 1983 but did not take his seat at Westminster. B Oct 6 1948; ed St Mary's GS, Belfast. President of Sinn Fein, since 1984; previously vice-pres. Elected, Northern Ireland Assembly, 1982, for West Belfast. Interned 1971, released in 1972 and flown to London for secret talks between republican movement and Secretary of State for Northern Ireland. Re-interned 1973. Attempted to escape from Long Kesh Prison and sentenced to 18 months imprisonment; released 1976. In Feb 1978 charged with membership of IRA; spent seven months imprisoned on remand but freed when charge was dropped. Served with exclusion order banning him from entering London for talks with the then GLC leader, Mr Kenneth Livingstone, Dec 1982. Exclusion order lifted when elected MP for Belfast West.
Dr Joseph Hendron, general practitioner, fought seat 1983. Aged 45. SDLP mbr, NI Convention, 1975, and of Assembly, 1982-86. Ldr SDLP gp, Belfast City Cl, 1985-.
Mr Frank Millar has been chief exec officer, OUP, since 1983. B Sep 27 1954. Press Officer OUP, 1981-1983; research asst, OUP at Westminster, 1977-81. Unsuccessful OUP candidate for NI Assembly in S Antrim, Oct 1982. Elected NI Assembly, Mar 1983 for S Belfast in by-election.

Mr Gerry Adams

BERKSHIRE EAST — No change

Electorate %Turnout	87,820	73.8%	**1987**	81,512	73.3%	**1983**
*MacKay, A.J. (C)	39,094	60.3%	+3.5%	33,967	56.8%	(C)
Murray, Mrs L.A. (SDP/All)	16,468	25.4%	-4.5%	17,868	29.9%	(SDP/All)
Evans, R.J.E. (Lab)	9,287	14.3%	+1.0%	7,953	13.3%	(Lab)
SDP/All to C swing 4.0%	64,849	C maj 22,626 34.9%		59,788	C maj 16,099 26.9%	

Mr Andrew MacKay, consultant to Morgan Grenfell and Co Ltd and to Willis Faber plc, a non-executive company director and former estate agent, was elected in 1983; MP for Birmingham, Stechford, from by-election 1977-79. PPS to Mr Tom King, Secretary of State for N Ireland, 1986- . Mbr, Select Cmte on Environment, 1985-86; nat exec, Cons Pty, 1979-82. Sec, Cons back-bench foreign affairs cmte, 1985-86; jt hon sec, Cons Friends of Israel parly gp, 1986. B Aug 27 1949; ed Solihull Sch. Mbr, Cons Pty nat exec, 1979-82. Consultant to Birmingham Housing Industries Ltd, 1973-83. Chmn, "Britain in Europe" campaign in Meriden constituency during 1975 referendum.
Dr Linda Murray, senior tutor/lecturer at Brunel Univ. Mbr, CSD; Sandhurst TC; Berkshire CC 1985- ; East Berkshire AHA. B 1949; ed local GS; City Univ, London.
Mr Robert Evans, middle sch dep head and Surrey CC advisory teacher in computers and microtechnology. Vice-chmn, Chertsey and Walton CLP; treas, Elmbridge Dist Lab Pty. B Oct 23 1956; ed Cty Sch, Ashford, Middlesex; London Univ Inst of Ed (Shoreditch Coll of Ed). NUT (pres, Leatherhead NUT, 1984-85).

Mr Andrew MacKay

BERWICK-UPON-TWEED — No change

Electorate %Turnout	54,378	77.3%	**1987**	53,585	77.8%	**1983**
*Beith, A.J. (L/All)	21,903	52.1%	-0.6%	21,958	52.7%	(L/All)
Middleton, T. (C)	12,400	29.5%	-3.5%	13,743	33.0%	(C)
Lambert, S. (Lab)	7,360	17.5%	+3.2%	5,975	14.3%	(Lab)
Pamphilion, N. (Grn)	379	0.9%				
C to L/All swing 1.4%	42,042	L/All maj 9,503 22.6%		41,676	L/All maj 8,215 19.7%	

Mr **Alan Beith**, Deputy Leader of Liberal Party and spokesman on foreign affairs 1985- ; chief Alliance spokesman on foreign affairs in 1987 election team. Won this seat, 1973 by-election; contested it 1970. Lib Chief Whip, 1976-85; education spokesman, 1977-83. Mbr, House of Commons Commission, 1979- ; Cmte on Privileges, 1986- ; Select Cmte on Procedure. B Apr 20 1943; ed King's Sch, Macclesfield; Balliol and Nuffield Colls, Oxford. Mbr, Cl of Europe and WEU, 1976-84; Gen Advisory Cl of BBC, 1974-84. Parly adviser to the AUT.
Mr **Terence Middleton**, sub-postmaster, contested Durham NW 1983 and Blaydon, 1979. Mbr, Gateshead MBC, 1975-82. B Sep 9 1944; ed St Cuthbert's GS, Newcastle upon Tyne; Ushaw Coll, Durham.
Mr **Stephen Lambert**, coll lecturer.Member, Newcastle Dist Lab Pty exec cmte and gmc, 1984-86. B Dec 15 1958; ed Gosforth East Sec Mod Sch; Gosforth HS; Warwick Univ; Bolton Coll of Ed. Nupe and NATFHE.

Mr Alan Beith

BETHNAL GREEN AND STEPNEY — No change

Electorate %Turnout	55,769	57.6%	**1987**	55,333	55.7%	**1983**
*Shore, P.D. (Lab)	15,490	48.2%	-2.8%	15,740	51.0%	(Lab)
Shaw, J.A. (L/All)	10,206	31.8%	+1.4%	9,382	30.4%	(L/All)
Maitland, Lady O.H. (C)	6,176	19.2%	+5.2%	4,323	14.0%	(C)
Gasquoine, Ms S. (Comm)	232	0.7%	-1.9%	800	2.6%	(NF)
				593	1.9%	(Other)
Lab to L/All swing 2.1%	32,104	Lab maj 5,284 16.5%		30,838	Lab maj 6,358 20.6%	

Mr **Peter Shore**, chief Opposition spokesman on Commons affairs, 1984- . Contested Lab leadership 1983. Mbr, shadow Cabinet, 1979- ; chief spokesman on trade and industry, 1983-84; Treasury and economic affairs, 1980-83; foreign and Commonwealth affairs, 1979-80. Mbr, Select Cmte on Commons Services, 1983- ; Select Cmte on Privileges. Sec of State for Environment, 1976-79; Sec of State for Trade, 1974-76. Chief spokesman on European affairs, 1971-74. Elected for this seat in 1983; MP for Stepney and Poplar, 1974-83, and Stepney, 1964-74; contested St Ives, 1950, and Halifax, 1959. B May 20 1924; ed Quarry Bank HS, Liverpool; King's Coll, Cambridge. Minister without Portfolio and Dep Leader of the House, 1969-70; Sec of State for Economic Affairs, 1967-69; Parly Sec, Min of Tech, 1966-67. TGWU.
Mr **Jeremy Shaw**, mbr, Tower Hamlets BC, 1982- . B Apr 18 1959; ed Latymer Sch, Edmonton; Queen's Coll, Oxford.
Lady **Olga Maitland**, journalist, chmn of Families for Defence 1983- ; vice-chmn, Why Campaign, 1987- . B May 23 1944; ed St Mary and St Anne's, Abbots, Bromley; Lycee Francais de Londres. NUJ.
Ms **Sarah Gasquoine**, nat women's organiser, Comm Pty. Printer; NGA. Aged 33.

Mr Peter Shore

BEVERLEY — No change

Electorate %Turnout	78,923	76.3%	**1987**	75,813	73.2%	**1983**
Cran, J.D. (C)	31,459	52.2%	-4.0%	31,233	56.3%	(C)
Bryant, J. (L/All)	18,864	31.3%	+0.0%	17,364	31.3%	(L/All)
Shaw, M. (Lab)	9,901	16.4%	+4.0%	6,921	12.5%	(Lab)
C to L/All swing 2.0%	60,224	C maj 12,595 20.9%		55,518	C maj 13,869 25.0%	

Mr **James Cran** is West Midlands director of the CBI and its former Northern director. Chief executive, Nat Assocn of Pension Funds, 1971-79. Contested Gordon, 1983; Glasgow, Shettleston, Oct 1974. Mbr, London borough of Sutton Cl, 1974-79. B Jan 28 1944; ed Ruthrieston Sch, Aberdeen; Aberdeen GS; Aberdeen Coll of Commerce; Kings Coll, Univ of Aberdeen. Sec, Scottish Cons back-bench cmtes, 1970-71.
Mr **John Bryant**, ldr of Alliance gp on Humberside CC; Hull City cllr. Contested Hull Central 1979. B Apr 1955; ed King Henry VIII GS, Coventry; Hull Univ. Formerly worked for *Hull Daily Mail*.
Mr **Martin Shaw**, sociology lecturer at Hull Univ and chair of Hull Univ Centre for Defence and Disarmament Studies. Chmn, Humberside CND; vice-chmn, Hull CND. B Jun 30 1947; ed LSE. AUT.

Mr James Cran

BEXHILL AND BATTLE — No change

Electorate %Turnout	65,288	77.4%	**1987**	61,785	72.9%	**1983**
*Wardle, C.F. (C)	33,570	66.4%	-0.9%	30,329	67.3%	(C)
Kiernan, R. (SDP/All)	13,051	25.8%	+2.3%	10,583	23.5%	(L/All)
Watts, D.K. (Lab)	3,903	7.7%	-0.2%	3,587	8.0%	(Lab)
				538	1.2%	(Other)
C to SDP/All swing 1.6%	50,524	C maj 20,519 40.6%		45,037	C maj 19,746 43.8%	

Mr Charles Wardle, elected in 1983, has been PPS to Mr Norman Fowler, Secretary of State for Social Services, since 1984. Mbr, Select Cmte on Trade and Industry, 1983-84. Director, Corporate Advisory Partnership Ltd; chmn, Benjamin Priest Group, 1977-84; managing director, 1974-77; director, 1972-74; in merchant banking, London, 1969-72; with American Express, New York, 1966-69. B Aug 23 1939; ed Tonbridge Sch; Lincoln Coll, Oxford; Harvard Business Sch. Chmn, governors, Charters-Ancaster Coll, Bexhill-on-Sea. Mbr, CBI Central Cl and CBI West Midlands Reg Cl, 1980-84; commercial and economic cmte, Engineering and Employers' Fed, 1980-83; Midlands cmte, Inst of Directors, 1980-83.
Mr Robert Kiernan, publisher. Founder mbr, SDP; mbr, exec cmte, Wealden SDP. B May 24 1940; ed Judd Sch, Tonbridge. Chmn, Horam PC.
Mr Derek Watts, schoolmaster. Mbr, Hastings BC, 1983-87; ex-chmn, Hastings and Rye CLP. B Nov 27 1943; ed Hastings GS; Southampton Univ. Chairs Hastings and Dist UNA. NAS/UWT.

Mr Charles Wardle

BEXLEYHEATH — No change

Electorate %Turnout	59,448	77.8%	**1987**	59,263	74.5%	**1983**
*Townsend, C.D. (C)	24,866	53.7%	+0.7%	23,411	53.1%	(C)
Standen, B.C. (L/All)	13,179	28.5%	-1.3%	13,153	29.8%	(L/All)
Little, J.F. (Lab)	8,218	17.8%	+0.6%	7,560	17.1%	(Lab)
L/All to C swing 1.0%	46,263	C maj 11,687 25.3%		44,124	C maj 10,258 23.2%	

Mr Cyril Townsend has been jt vice-chmn since 1985, and jt sec, 1982-85, of the Cons backbench defence committee. Chmn, all-party Freedom for Rudolf Hess campaign, Cl for Advancement of Arab-British Understanding, S Atlantic Cl, British-Cyprus parly group and, from 1977-83, the Bow Group standing cmte on foreign affairs; sec, Cons Middle East Cl. Elected in Feb 1974. Mbr, Select Cmte on Violence in the Family, 1976-77; Select Cmte on Foreign Affairs, 1982-83. Vice chmn, Friends of Cyprus, since 1980; political cmte, UNA, since 1980. B Dec 21 1937; ed Bradfield Coll, Berkshire; RMA Sandhurst. Employed in Cons Research Dept, 1970-74. Personal asst to Mr Edward Heath, 1968-70.
Mr Barry Standen, overseas mining dept manager, NCB, contested this seat 1983. Ldr, Alliance gp, Bexley BC. B Jan 22 1947; ed SE London Tech Sch; Kent Univ.
Mr Jim Little, retired transport manager, British Rail, contested Lewes Feb and Oct 1974, Thanet West 1979. B Oct 2 1927; ed St Mary's Christian Brothers Sec, Belfast. Ldr, Lab Gp, Kent CC. Chmn, Southern Regional Local Govt and Policy Cttee, Lab Pty; mbr, Nat Local Govt Advisory Cttee; Chartered Inst of Transport; Dartford and Gravesham HA; Gravesend Community Relations Cl.

Mr Cyril Townsend

BILLERICAY — No change

Electorate %Turnout	79,535	77.2%	**1987**	74,779	73.8%	**1983**
Gorman, Mrs T.E. (C)	33,741	54.9%	+1.2%	29,635	53.7%	(C)
Birch, M. (SDP/All)	15,755	25.6%	-1.6%	15,020	27.2%	(L/All)
Howitt, R. (Lab)	11,942	19.4%	+0.4%	10,528	19.1%	(Lab)
SDP/All to C swing 1.4%	61,438	C maj 17,986 29.3%		55,183	C maj 14,615 26.5%	

Mrs Teresa Gorman, founder and manager of a company making teaching equipment. Mbr, Conservative women's national cmte, 1983- ; Westminster City Cl, 1982-86 (cl rep on Age Concern). Chmn, ASP (Alliance of Small Firms and Self Employed People), a pressure gp for small businesses; also chmn of Amarant Trust, a registered charity for medical research. Has published research papers for Centre for Policy Studies. Stood in Streatham in Oct 1974 as Independent (Small Business) candidate. B Sep 1941; ed Fulham County Sch.
Mr Michael Birch, computer manager with publishing firm. Member, Basildon DC, 1986- . Cmte mbr and former sec, local SDP. Mbr, CSD. B Apr 3 1945; ed Sweyne Sch, Rayleigh, Essex.
Mr Richard Howitt, community worker in project with physically disabled people. Mbr, Harlow DC, 1984- . Chairs SE Economic Development Strategy Assocn, a gp of nine SE dist cls. B Apr 5 1961; ed comprehensive sch in Reading; Lady Margaret Hall, Oxford. Nalgo.

Mrs Teresa Gorman

BIRKENHEAD — No change

Electorate %Turnout	65,662	72.3%	**1987**	67,293	69.7%	**1983**
*Field, F. (Lab)	27,883	58.7%	+9.1%	23,249	49.6%	(Lab)
Costa, K.J. (C)	12,511	26.3%	-2.5%	13,535	28.9%	(C)
Kemp, R. (L/All)	7,095	14.9%	-5.9%	9,782	20.9%	(L/All)
				337	0.7%	(Other)
C to Lab swing 5.8%	47,489	Lab maj 15,372 32.4%		46,903	Lab maj 9,714 20.7%	

Mr Frank Field was an Opposition spokesman on health and social security,1983-84, and a spokesman on education, 1979-81. Elected in 1979; contested Buckinghamshire South, 1966. Director, Child Poverty Action Group, 1969-79, and of Low Pay Unit, 1974-80. Teacher at Southwark and Hammersmith CFEs, 1964-69. B Jul 16 1942; ed St Clement Danes GS; Hull Univ. Parly consultant to Civil and Public Services Assocn. Hounslow cllr, 1964-68. TGWU.
Mr Kenneth Costa, merchant banker. B Oct 31 1949; ed Christian Brothers' Coll; Cambridge Univ.
Mr Richard Kemp, an employment creation consultant, contested Runcorn in 1979. Mbr, Liverpool City Cl for nine years. Director of several small local businesses. B Jan 8 1953; ed Leeds Poly.

Mr Frank Field

BIRMINGHAM, EDGBASTON — No change

Electorate %Turnout	54,416	68.6%	**1987**	55,063	66.2%	**1983**
*Knight, Dame Jill (C)	18,595	49.8%	-3.9%	19,585	53.7%	(C)
Wilton, J. (Lab)	10,014	26.8%	+5.9%	8,167	22.4%	(SDP/All)
Binns, J.C. (SDP/All)	7,843	21.0%	-1.4%	7,647	21.0%	(Lab)
Simpson, P. (Grn)	559	1.5%	+0.1%	516	1.4%	(Eco)
Hardwick, S.T. (Ind C)	307	0.8%	+0.0%	293	0.8%	(Ind C)
				266	0.7%	(Other)
C to Lab swing 4.9%	37,318	C maj 8,581 23.0%		36,474	C maj 11,418 31.3%	

Dame Jill Knight has chaired the Conservative back-bench cmte on health and social services since 1982; sec, 1922 Cmte, 1983- , member of its exec cmte, 1979- . Elected in 1966; contested Northampton, 1959 and 1964. Housewife, lecturer and broadcaster. B Jul 9 1927; ed Fairfield Sch, Bristol; King Edward VI GS, Birmingham. Vice-Pres, Nat Union of Townswomen's Guilds, 1986- . Mbr, Northampton BC, 1956-66; Cl of Europe, 1977- ; WEU, 1977- . Member, Select Cmte on Race Relations and Immigration, 1969-72; Select Cmte on Home Affairs, 1980-83. Chmn, Lords and Commons all-pty family and child protection gp, 1978- .
Mr John Wilton, student and former structural engineer. B Jan 14 1947; ed Raines Foundation GS, Stepney; Bristol Poly; Birmingham and Keele Univs. Constituency and branch chmn and sec. ASTMS.
Mr Joseph Binns, insurance broker, contested this seat 1983, Birmingham West in 1984 Euro election and, for Labour, Gillingham 1966 and Bromley 1964. Chmn, W Midlands Inst of Export, 1980-83; W Midlands Inst of Credit Management, 1978-81. Nat treas, Inst of Credit Management, 1983- . Lab mbr, Greenwich BC, 1963-65. B May 29 1931.

Dame Jill Knight

BIRMINGHAM, ERDINGTON — No change

Electorate %Turnout	54,179	68.5%	**1987**	56,019	67.0%	**1983**
*Corbett, R. (Lab)	17,037	45.9%	+6.1%	14,930	39.8%	(Lab)
Johnston, P.J. (C)	14,570	39.2%	+0.1%	14,699	39.2%	(C)
Biddlestone, N. (SDP/All)	5,530	14.9%	-6.2%	7,915	21.1%	(SDP/All)
C to Lab swing 3.0%	37,137	Lab maj 2,467 6.6%		37,544	Lab maj 231 0.6%	

Mr Robin Corbett, an Opposition spokesman on home affairs, 1985- . Journalist; with IPC Magazines, 1969-74. Elected in 1983; MP for Hemel Hempstead, Oct 1974-79; contested the seat, 1966 and Feb 1974; West Derbyshire by-election, 1967. B Dec 22 1933; ed Holly Lodge GS, Smethwick. Mbr, Select Cmte on Home Affairs, 1983-85; chmn, PLP agriculture group, 1977-78; chmn, PLP home affairs group, 1984-86; vice-chmn, all-pty animal welfare gp, 1976-79; chmn, farm animal welfare coordinating cmte, 1977- . Jt sec, all-pty Anzac gp, 1985- ; PLP civil liberties group, 1974-79; mbr, NEC, NUJ, 1965-69. Fellow, Industry and Parliament Trust. NUJ. Sponsored by Usdaw.
Mr Paul Johnston, head of history and social studies at London Oratory School, SW6, contested Leigh 1983. B Feb 23 1945; ed Catholic Coll, Preston; Lancaster and Manchester Univs. Mbr, Wansdyke DC, Avon, 1976-79 (ldr, 1977-78).
Mr Neil Biddlestone, director of computer systems company and consultancy. Founder mbr, SDP; mbr, CSD, 1983-86; industrial, educational and constitutional reform policy gps. Chmn, Sutton Coldfield and Erdington SDP, 1982-85; school governor; B Sep 6 1939; ed King Edward VI GS, Aston; Aston and Birmingham Univs. Mbr, Inst of Metallurgists and a chartered engineer.

Mr Robin Corbett

BIRMINGHAM, HALL GREEN — No change

Electorate %Turnout	61,148	74.7%	**1987**	61,023	70.6%	**1983**
Hargreaves, A.R. (C)	20,478	44.9%	-4.2%	21,142	49.1%	(C)
Brook, Mrs E. (Lab)	12,857	28.2%	+0.8%	11,769	27.3%	(Lab)
Wilkes, M. (SDP/All)	12,323	27.0%	+3.4%	10,175	23.6%	(L/All)
C to Lab swing 2.5%	45,658	C maj 7,621 16.7%		43,086	C maj 9,373 21.8%	

Mr Andrew Hargreaves is assistant director of a bank. Contested Blyth Valley 1983. From 1977-81 was a fine art auctioneer and valuer with Christies. B May 15 1955; ed Eton; St Edmund Hall, Oxford.

Ms Eveline Brook, research fellow in mental health and poverty at Birmingham Univ. B May 7 1944; ed Bradford and Birmingham Univs. Mbr, Birmingham City Cl. Constituency and ward sec. Chairs, Birmingham Welfare Rights Gp; formerly chaired, Birmingham Standing Conference for the Single Homeless. Nupe.

Mr Michael Wilkes, univ lecturer. First SDP cllr on Birmingham City Cl, 1984- ; chmn, Birmingham area SDP, 1982-83; mbr, CSD, 1983-84. B Nov 9 1941; ed Birmingham Univ.

Mr Andrew
Hargreaves

BIRMINGHAM, HODGE HILL — No change

Electorate %Turnout	59,296	68.8%	**1987**	61,234	67.6%	**1983**
*Davis, T.A.G. (Lab)	19,872	48.7%	+1.1%	19,692	47.6%	(Lab)
Eyre, S. (C)	15,083	36.9%	+1.7%	14,600	35.3%	(C)
Hardeman, K.G. (L/All)	5,868	14.4%	-1.5%	6,557	15.8%	(L/All)
				529	1.3%	(Other)
Lab to C swing 0.3%	40,823	Lab maj 4,789 11.7%		41,378	Lab maj 5,092 12.3%	

Mr Terence (Terry) Davis has been an Opposition spokesman on industry since 1986; on Treasury and economic affairs, 1983-86; on health and social services, 1980-83. Parliamentary adviser to Inland Revenue Staff Federation. Elected for this seat 1983; MP for Birmingham, Stechford, 1979-83, and for Bromsgrove, 1971-74; contested that seat, 1970; Bromsgrove and Redditch, Feb and Oct 1974, and Birmingham, Stechford, 1977 by-election. Manager in motor industry, 1974-79. B Jan 5, 1938; ed King Edward VI GS, Stourbridge; London Univ; Michigan Univ. Mbr, Expenditure Cmte, 1973-74; Opposition whip, 1979-80. Mbr, Yeovil RDC, 1967-68. Sponsored by ASTMS.

Mr Stephen Eyre, barrister, has been a member of Solihull MBC since 1983. B Oct 17 1957; ed Solihull Sch; New Coll, Oxford.

Mr Kenneth Hardeman, director of catering company, contested Birmingham Ladywood 1983, 1979 and twice in 1974. Mbr, Birmingham City Cl and Birmingham DC, 1966-75. B Jan 21 1936; ed Slade Boys Sch, Handsworth; Erdington Tech.

Mr Terence Davis

BIRMINGHAM, LADYWOOD — No change

Electorate %Turnout	58,761	64.8%	**1987**	60,441	62.6%	**1983**
*Short, Ms C. (Lab)	21,971	57.7%	+6.7%	19,278	51.0%	(Lab)
Lee, S.T. (C)	11,943	31.3%	+4.3%	10,248	27.1%	(C)
Sangha, G. (SDP/All)	3,532	9.3%	-11.2%	7,758	20.5%	(L/All)
Millington, Mrs J. (Grn)	650	1.7%		335	0.9%	(Stop Dep)
				198	0.5%	(Other)
C to Lab swing 1.2%	38,096	Lab maj 10,028 26.3%		37,817	Lab maj 9,030 23.9%	

Ms Clare Short, elected in 1983, joined the Opposition front-bench employment team in 1985. Mbr, Select Cmte on Home Affairs, 1983-85. B Feb 5 1946; ed Keele and Leeds Univs. Director, Youthaid, 1979-83, and the Unemployment Unit, 1981-83. Mbr, Campaign Group of Lab MPs, and Tribune Group. Sponsored by NUPE.

Mr Timothy Lee, chartered surveyor and company chmn, is a mbr of W Midlands Cons Area Cl; finance officer, Birmingham District Cons Assocn. Specialist in charity law and compensation. B Aug 30 1948; ed Manley Hall, Staffordshire. Senior partner, Birmingham Practice Surveyors; chmn, A Edward Jones Ltd, silversmiths, Birmingham.

Mr Gurdial Sangha, managing director of a mortgage and insurance consultants. B Aug 10 1945.

Mrs Joyce Millington, retired teacher, is convenor of Green Pty education and population working gps; former branch sec. B Sep 17 1920; ed at GS in Newham; Birmingham Univ.

Ms Clare Short

BIRMINGHAM, NORTHFIELD — No change

Electorate %Turnout	73,319	72.6%	1987	74,326	71.2%	1983
*King, R.D. (C)	24,024	45.1%	+2.4%	22,596	42.7%	(C)
Spellar, J.F. (Lab)	20,889	39.2%	+1.7%	19,836	37.5%	(Lab)
Gordon, J. (SDP/All)	8,319	15.6%	-3.4%	10,045	19.0%	(L/All)
				420	0.8%	(Other)
Lab to C swing 0.3%	53,232	C maj 3,135 5.9%		52,897	C maj 2,760 5.2%	

Mr **Roger King** has been a member of the Select Committee on Transport since 1984; jt sec, Cons back-bench tourism cmte, 1985- ; vice chmn, all-party motor industry group, 1985- . Parly adviser to Retread Manufacturers Assocn. Elected in 1983; contested Cannock, Feb 1974. B Oct 26 1943; ed Solihull Sch. Auto engineering apprentice, British Motor Corporation, 1960-66; sales representative, 1966-74; had own motor products design, production and marketing business, 1974-81; self-employed distributor of motor products, 1982-83. Chmn, West Midlands YCs, 1972-74; West Midlands CPC, 1982 (vice-chmn, 1979-82).

Mr **John Spellar**, an EETPU official, was MP for Birmingham Northfield, 1982-83; contested Bromley 1970. Served on Select Cmte on Energy. B Aug 5 1947; ed Dulwich Coll and St Edmund Hall, Oxford. Mbr, Bromley BC, 1970-74.

Mr **John Gordon**, residential social worker, is a Birmingham representative on the CSD; chmn, Birmingham SDP policy cmte; Birmingham SDP spokesman on housing. B Oct 30 1958; ed Exhall Grange Sch, Coventry. Mbr, Social Care Assocn. Usdaw; former delegate to Birmingham Trades Cl.

Mr Roger King

BIRMINGHAM, PERRY BARR — No change

Electorate %Turnout	73,767	69.6%	1987	74,371	69.2%	1983
*Rooker, J.W. (Lab)	25,894	50.4%	-2.1%	27,061	52.6%	(Lab)
Taylor, J.D.B. (C)	18,961	36.9%	-1.3%	19,659	38.2%	(C)
Webb, D.D. (L/All)	6,514	12.7%	+3.4%	4,773	9.3%	(L/All)
Lab to C swing 0.4%	51,369	Lab maj 6,933 13.5%		51,493	Lab maj 7,402 14.4%	

Mr **Jeffrey Rooker**, a chartered engineer, became the main Opposition spokesman on housing and construction when he joined the front bench DOE team in 1984; previously spokesman on Treasury and economic affairs, 1983-84; on social security, 1979-83. Elected in Feb 1974. B Jun 5 1941; ed Handsworth Tech School and Coll; Aston and Warwick Univs. Former tool maker, production manager, and industrial relations and safety officer; lecturer, Lanchester Poly, Coventry, 1972-74. Mbr, cl, Inst of Production Engineers, 1975-81. Sponsored by ASTMS.

Mr **John Taylor**, barrister, was elected an officer of the Nat Cons Parly Candidates' Assocn in 1986; mbr, Solihull DC, 1985- . B Sep 21 1952; ed Moseley GS, Birmingham; Keele Univ; Inns of Court Sch of Law.

Mr **David Webb**, director of an import and export company, contested Birmingham Northfield 1983. B Apr 13 1935; ed Hitchin Boys' GS; London Univ; Cranfield Inst of Tech; Police Staff Coll, Bramshill. Police officer for 27 years, retiring as Superintendent in charge of Handsworth. Fellow, BIM and Inst of Sales and Marketing Managers.

Mr Jeffrey Rooker

BIRMINGHAM, SELLY OAK — No change

Electorate %Turnout	72,213	73.1%	1987	71,671	71.5%	1983
*Beaumont-Dark, A.M. (C)	23,305	44.2%	-0.7%	23,008	44.9%	(C)
Bore, A. (Lab)	20,721	39.3%	+4.9%	17,612	34.4%	(Lab)
Cane, Mrs C. (L/All)	8,128	15.4%	-5.3%	10,613	20.7%	(SDP/All)
Hackett, Ms M. (Grn)	611	1.2%				
C to Lab swing 2.8%	52,765	C maj 2,584 4.9%		51,233	C maj 5,396 10.5%	

Mr **Anthony Beaumont-Dark** is an investment analyst and senior partner of firm of stockbrokers. Elected in 1979; contested Birmingham, Aston, 1964 and 1959. B Oct 11 1932; ed Cedarhurst Sch, Solihull; Birmingham Coll of Arts; Birmingham Univ. Chmn, Birmingham Executive Airways Ltd; director, Cope Allman International Ltd, Wigham Poland (Midlands) Ltd and Birmid-Qualcast plc. Mbr, Select Cmte on Treasury and Civil Service, since 1979; Select Cmte on Procedure (Finance), 1982; Birmingham City Cl, 1957-67 (alderman from 1967); West Midland Met CC, 1973-80. Former sec, Cons backbench finance cmte.

Mr **Albert Bore**, physics lecturer, Aston Univ. Mbr, Birmingham City Cl (chmn, economic development cmte). B May 2 1946; ed Brighton Coll of Tech; Birmingham Univ.

Mrs **Charlotte Cane**, archaeologist; finds supervisor, Birmingham Univ field archaeology unit. B Jun 3 1958; ed St Helen's Sch, Northwood; Birmingham Univ.

Miss **Winifred Hackett**, retired univ lecturer, has contested local elections in Birmingham. Ed George Dixon Sch, Birmingham; Lady Margaret Hall, Oxford. Formerly AUT.

Mr Anthony
Beaumont-Dark

BIRMINGHAM, SMALL HEATH — No change

Electorate %Turnout	56,722	60.6%	1987	59,376	61.0%	1983
*Howell, D.H. (Lab)	22,787	66.3%	+3.2%	22,874	63.2%	(Lab)
Nischal, P. (C)	7,266	21.1%	+0.1%	7,622	21.0%	(C)
Hemming, J.A.M. (L/All)	3,600	10.5%	-5.3%	5,722	15.8%	(SDP/All)
Clawley, A. (Grn)	559	1.6%				
Sheppard, P.R. (Comm)	154	0.4%				
C to Lab swing 1.5%	34,366	Lab maj 15,521 45.2%		36,218	Lab maj 15,252 42.1%	

Mr Denis Howell, Opposition spokesman on sport, 1979- , serving with front-bench home affairs and environment teams. Director, Wembley Stadium Co Ltd; has own consultancy. Pres, Birmingham Olympic Games Cl, 1986. Minr of State for Environment and Minr for Sport and Recreation, 1974-79; Opposition spokesman on housing, local govt and sport, 1970-74; Minr of State for Housing and Local Govt, 1969-70, and Under Sec of State for Ed and Science, 1964-69, being Minr for Sport, 1964-70. Elected in 1961; MP for Birmingham, All Saints, 1955-59; contested Kings Norton, 1951. B Sep 4 1923; ed Gower St elementary sch; Handsworth GS. Mbr, Birmingham City Cl, 1946-56. Football League ref, 1956-70. Pres, Apex, 1971-83 (mbr since 1942). Sponsored by Apex.
Mr Paul Nischal, estate agent, contested the seat 1983. Founder chmn, Birmingham branch, Anglo Asian Cons Soc; mbr, W Midlands area exec cmte, 1983- .; B Oct 1944; ed in India. Gen Sec, Asian Peoples Welfare Soc.
Mr John Hemming, senior partnerin international software house, contested Birmingham, Hall Green 1983. B Mar 16 1960; ed King Edward's Sch, Edgbaston; Magdalen Coll, Oxford.
Mr Alan Clawley, technical support worker to voluntary organisations. B Dec 4 1943.

Mr Denis Howell

BIRMINGHAM, SPARKBROOK — No change

Electorate %Turnout	53,093	63.5%	1987	53,612	61.5%	1983
*Hattersley, R.S.G. (Lab)	20,513	60.8%	+0.9%	19,757	59.9%	(Lab)
Khan, N.A. (C)	8,654	25.7%	-2.3%	9,209	27.9%	(C)
Dimmick, R. (SDP/All)	3,803	11.3%	+0.9%	3,416	10.4%	(SDP/All)
Ambler, R. (Grn)	526	1.6%		305	0.9%	(Rev Com)
Khan, P. (RF)	229	0.7%		281	0.9%	(Ind)
C to Lab swing 1.6%	33,725	Lab maj 11,859 35.2%		32,968	Lab maj 10,548 32.0%	

Mr Roy Hattersley, elected Dep Ldr, Lab Pty in Oct 1983, becoming chief Opposition spokesman on Treasury and economic affairs; mbr, shadow Cabinet since 1979; chief spokesman on home affairs, 1980-83; on environment, 1979-80. Secretary of State for Prices and Consumer Protection and member of the Cabinet.1976-79; Minr of State for Foreign and Commonwealth Affairs, 1974-76. Spokesman on education, 1972-74; foreign and Commonwealth affairs, 1970-72, and defence, 1972. Minr of Defence for Administration, 1969-70; Under Sec of State for Employment and Productivity, 1968-69; Parly Sec, Min of Labour, 1967-68. Elected in 1964; contested Sutton Coldfield, 1959. Journalist and author. B Dec 28 1932; ed Sheffield City GS and Hull Univ. Visiting Fellow, Nuffield Coll, Oxford, 1984- .
Mr Nazir Khan, garage and supermarket proprietor; mbr, W Midlands CPC cmte. B 1956; ed Birmingham Poly. Acts as interpreter: Anglo/Urdu, Anglo/Swahili, and speaks Gujerati, Punjabi and Hindi.
Mr Robin Dimmick, radiographer. B Nov 24 1941.
Mr Rex Ambler, univ lecturer in theology. B Aug 20 1939; ed Beckenham and Penge GS for Boys; Oxford, Manchester and Amsterdam Univs.

Mr Roy Hattersley

BIRMINGHAM, YARDLEY — No change

Electorate %Turnout	56,957	73.9%	1987	57,707	72.1%	1983
*Bevan, A.D.G. (C)	17,931	42.6%	-0.6%	17,986	43.2%	(C)
Edge, G. (Lab)	15,409	36.6%	+0.3%	15,121	36.3%	(Lab)
Smith, L. (L/All)	8,734	20.8%	+1.3%	8,109	19.5%	(SDP/All)
				415	1.0%	(Other)
C to Lab swing 0.4%	42,074	C maj 2,522 6.0%		41,631	C maj 2,865 6.9%	

Mr David Gilroy Bevan, elected in 1979. Incorporated auctioneer, estate agent, valuer and surveyor, company director, parly adviser and leisure and recreation consultant. Mbr, Select Cmte on Transport, 1983- . B Apr 10 1928; ed Woodrough's Sch, Moseley; King Edward's Sch, Birmingham. Mbr, Birmingham City Cl, 1959-74; W Midlands CC, 1974-81. Chmn, Cons back-bench tourism cmte, 1984- ; previously vice-chmn; jt chmn, all-pty leisure and recreation cmte, 1979- ; jt sec, Cons urban affairs and new towns cmte, 1980- . Director, D'Avon Securities Ltd; Mortgage and Insurance Brokers (Midlands) Ltd and Four Oaks Estate Ltd (unremunerated). Parly adviser to Best Western Hotels. Fellow and past chmn (Midlands) and cl mbr, Incorporated Assocn of Architects and Surveyors; past chmn and fellow, W Midlands branch, Incorporated Soc of Valuers and Auctioneers.
Mr Geoffrey Edge, housing association manager and chmn of W Midlands Enterprise Board, was MP for Aldridge-Brownhills, Feb 1974-79. Mbr, Walsall BC, 1983- ; W Midlands CC, 1981-86; Milton Keynes BC, 1973-76; Bletchley UDC, 1972-74. B May 26 1943; ed Rowley Regis GS; LSE; Birmingham Univ. ASTMS and AUT.
Mr Leslie Smith, research student; volunteer counsellor, CAB. B 1963; ed Maypole Comprehensive, Birmingham; Hall Green Tech; Wolverhampton Poly.

Mr David Gilroy Bevan

BISHOP AUCKLAND — No change

Electorate %Turnout	72,147	74.1%	**1987**	71,142	72.1%	**1983**
*Foster, D. (Lab)	25,648	48.0%	+3.6%	22,750	44.4%	(Lab)
Wight, R. (C)	18,613	34.8%	-1.2%	18,444	36.0%	(C)
Irwin, G. (L/All)	9,195	17.2%	-2.4%	10,070	19.6%	(L/All)
C to Lab swing 2.4%	53,456	Lab maj 7,035 13.2%		51,264	Lab maj 4,306 8.4%	

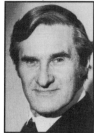

Mr Derek Foster was elected Labour Chief Whip in 1985; PPS to Mr Kinnock, Leader of the Opposition, 1983-85. An Opposition spokesman on social security, 1982-83; mbr, Select Cmte on Trade and Industry, 1980-82; assistant director of education in Sunderland, 1974-79. Elected in 1979. B Jun 25 1937; ed Bede GS, Sunderland; Oxford Univ. Former chmn, PLP finance and economic group. Chmn, North of England Development Cl, 1974-76. Mbr, Sunderland CBC, 1972-74; Tyne and Wear Met CC, 1973-77 and chmn of economic development cmte, 1973-76. Mbr of Salvation Army. Sponsored by Usdaw.
Mr Robin Wight is chmn of Wight Collins Rutherford Scott, advertising agency, formed in 1979. Copywriter, 1966-70; creative director, Richard Cope and Partners, 1970-79. Member, cl, Food from Britain. B Jul 6 1944; ed Cambridge Univ.
Mr George Irwin, chartered accountant, is in a management consultancy and accounting practice. District councillor, Richmondshire. B Aug 17 1938; ed St Cuthberts GS, Newcastle upon Tyne.

Mr Derek Foster

BLABY — No change

Electorate %Turnout	77,094	80.9%	**1987**	71,930	77.4%	**1983**
*Lawson, N. (C)	37,732	60.5%	+1.8%	32,689	58.7%	(C)
Lustig, R.E. (L/All)	15,556	25.0%	-3.0%	15,573	28.0%	(L/All)
Roberts, J.M. (Lab)	9,046	14.5%	+2.2%	6,838	12.3%	(Lab)
				568	1.0%	(Other)
L/All to C swing 2.4%	62,334	C maj 22,176 35.6%		55,668	C maj 17,116 30.7%	

Mr Nigel Lawson has been Chancellor of the Exchequer since 1983; Secretary of State for Energy, 1981-83; Financial Secretary to the Treasury, 1979-81; an Opposition spokesman on Treasury affairs, 1977-79. Journalist. Elected in Feb 1974; contested Eton and Slough, 1970. B Mar 11 1932; ed Westminster Sch; Christ Church, Oxford. Opposition whip, 1976-77. Special asst to Prime Minister (Sir Alec Douglas-Home), 1963-64; special political adviser, Cons Pty, 1973-74. Former mbr, Public Expenditure Cmte; Select Cmte on Wealth Tax. Editorial staff, *Financial Times*, 1956-60; City Editor, *The Sunday Telegraph*, 1961-63; Editor of *The Spectator*, 1966-70. Fellow, Nuffield Coll, Oxford, 1972-73.
Mr Richard Lustig is principal, Richard Lustig Associates, management consultants. Contested this seat 1983 and Derbyshire South East 1979. Has held office in Nalgo and IPCS. B Dec 17 1931; ed Salford GS; LSE.
Mr James Roberts, univ technician (museum studies), is a former chmn, Blaby CLP. Mbr, Leicestershire CC, 1981- (sec, Lab gp). Sec, Leicestershire Lab Pty. B Aug 28 1947; ed St Thomas Beckett GS, W Bridgford, Nottingham; Alderman Newton's GS, Leicester; Charles Keene Coll, Leicester. ASTMS.

Mr Nigel Lawson

BLACKBURN — No change

Electorate %Turnout	74,801	74.9%	**1987**	76,078	74.6%	**1983**
*Straw, J.W. (Lab)	27,965	49.9%	+5.2%	25,400	44.7%	(Lab)
Cheetham, Mrs A.C. (C)	22,468	40.1%	+0.7%	22,345	39.4%	(C)
Ali, M.A. (SDP/All)	5,602	10.0%	-4.4%	8,174	14.4%	(SDP/All)
				864	1.5%	(Other)
C to Lab swing 2.2%	56,035	Lab maj 5,497 9.8%		56,783	Lab maj 3,055 5.4%	

Mr Jack Straw has been in the Opposition front bench DoE team since 1983 as spokesman on local government; an Opposition spokesman on Treasury and economic affairs, 1980-83. Parliamentary adviser to AUT. Vice-pres, Assocn of DCs, 1984- ; mbr, Cl, Inst for Fiscal Studies, 1983- . Elected in 1979; contested Tonbridge and Malling, Feb 1974. Special adviser to Mrs Barbara Castle as Secretary of State for Social Services, 1974-76, and to Mr Peter Shore, Secretary of State for Environment, 1976-77. On staff of Granada TV (*World in Action*), 1977-79. Barrister. B Aug 3 1946; ed Brentwood Sch, Essex; Leeds Univ and Inns of Court Sch of Law. Pres, Nat Union of Students, 1969-71. Mbr, Islington BC, 1971-78; ILEA, 1971-74, its dep leader, 1973-74.
Mrs Anne Cheetham, company secretary of family business, contested Accington 1979. Treas, Area Cons Women's Cmte. B 1942; ed Convent of Ladies of Mary, Guildford; Weybridge Cty Tech Coll.
Mr Akbar Ali, chartered engineer employed by consulting engineer firm, Manchester. B Sep 15 1925; ed Osmania Univ, Hyderabad; Indian Inst of Science and Tech, Bangalore; Manchester Univ.

Mr Jack Straw

BLACKPOOL NORTH · No change

Electorate %Turnout	58,893	73.1%	**1987**	57,576	70.0%	**1983**
*Miscampbell, N.A. (C)	20,680	48.0%	-3.1%	20,592	51.1%	(C)
Curton, E. (Lab)	13,359	31.0%	+9.3%	10,440	25.9%	(L/All)
Heyworth, C.J. (L/All)	9,032	21.0%	-5.0%	8,730	21.7%	(Lab)
					514	1.3%	(Other)
C to Lab swing 6.2%	43,071	C maj 7,321 17.0%		40,276	C maj 10,152 25.2%	

Mr Norman
Miscampbell

Mr **Norman Miscampbell, QC,** has been a Crown Court recorder since 1977. Elected at by-election in 1962; contested Newton, 1959 and 1955. Former mbr, Select Cmte on the Environment. B Feb 20 1925; ed St Edward's Sch, Oxford, and Trinity Coll, Oxford. Mbr, Hoylake UDC, 1955-61.
Mr **Eric Curton,** a turner. B Nov 29 1929. Mbr, Lancashire CC; Blackpool Trades Cl; Blackpool Centre for Unemployed; Fylde CHC. AEU.
Mr **Christopher Heyworth** lectures at Blackpool and Fylde College of Further and Higher Education. Fought seat in 1983 and 1979. Chmn, Rebecca Heyworth Trust Fund to assist treatment and care of very sick children. B Jul 5 1946; ed Baines GS, Poulton-le-Fylde; Reading Univ; C F Mott Coll, Liverpool. Mbr, Blackpool BC, 1980-83; Blackpool DC, since 1986. NATFHE.

BLACKPOOL SOUTH · No change

Electorate %Turnout	57,567	73.5%	**1987**	56,201	69.8%	**1983**
*Blaker, Sir Peter (C)	20,312	48.0%	-2.5%	19,852	50.6%	(C)
Baugh, Mrs S. (Lab)	13,568	32.1%	+7.3%	9,714	24.8%	(Lab)
Allitt, J. (SDP/All)	8,405	19.9%	-4.1%	9,417	24.0%	(SDP/All)
					263	0.7%	(Other)
C to Lab swing 4.9%	42,285	C maj 6,744 15.9%		39,246	C maj 10,138 25.8%	

Sir Peter Blaker

Sir **Peter Blaker** was Minister of State for Armed Forces, 1981-83; Minister of State for Foreign and Commonwealth Affairs, 1979-81; Under Secretary of State for Foreign and Commonwealth Affairs, 1974; Under Secretary for Defence for the Army, 1972-74. An Opposition whip, 1966-67. Chmn, Cons back-bench foreign and Commonwealth affairs cmte, 1983- , vice-chmn, 1974-79; chmn, Hong Kong parly group, 1983- . Mbr, Select Cmte on Conduct of Members, 1976-77. Elected in 1964. Vice-pres, Cons Foreign and Commonwealth Cl, 1983- . B Oct 4 1922 in Hong Kong; ed Shrewsbury Sch, Toronto Univ; New Coll, Oxford (Pres of Union and Univ Law Soc). Barrister, company director, farmer, underwriting mbr of Lloyd's. Mbr, Cl for Arms Control, 1983- ; Freedom Assocn, 1984- . Vice-chmn, Peace through Nato, 1983- ; GB-USSR Assocn, since 1983. In foreign service, 1953-64.
Mrs **Sheilagh Baugh,** Dep Ldr, Lab gp, Blackpool Cl. B Dec 26 1948; ed Layton Hall Convent, Blackpool. Magistrate, 1983- . Mbr, Child Poverty Action Gp. Nupe.
Mr **Julian Allitt,** head of journalism at Lancashire Poly since 1984; director, Lancashire Cable TV Ltd and Merseyside Cablevision Ltd. Lobby correspondent for United Newspapers, 1975-82; head of news and current affairs at Red Rose Radio, 1982-84. B Jan 11 1946; ed Blackpool GS; Sheffield Univ.

BLAENAU GWENT · No change

Electorate %Turnout	56,011	77.2%	**1987**	55,948	76.8%	**1983**
*Foot, M.M. (Lab)	32,820	75.9%	+5.8%	30,113	70.1%	(Lab)
Taylor, A.R. (C)	4,959	11.5%	+0.3%	6,408	14.9%	(L/All)
McBride, D.I. (L/All)	3,847	8.9%	-6.0%	4,816	11.2%	(C)
Morgan, S. (Pl C)	1,621	3.7%	-0.1%	1,624	3.8%	(Pl C)
C to Lab swing 2.8%	43,247	Lab maj 27,861 64.4%		42,961	Lab maj 23,705 55.2%	

Mr **Michael Foot**

Mr **Michael Foot** was Leader of the Opposition, 1980-83; Deputy Leader, 1976-80; Lord President of the Council and Leader of the Commons, 1976-79; Secretary of State for Employment, 1974-76. Opposition spokesman on the power and steel industries, 1970-71; shadow Leader of the House principally concerned with Common Market legislation, 1971-72; from 1972-74 concerned with EEC affairs only. Elected for this seat 1983; MP for Ebbw Vale, 1960-83; MP for Plymouth Devonport, 1945-55; contested that seat, 1959, and Monmouth, 1935. Journalist and author; managing director, Tribune, 1945-74; editor, 1948-52 and 1955-60. B July 23 1913; ed Forres Sch, Swanage; Leighton Park Sch, Reading; Wadham Coll, Oxford (Pres of Union, 1933). Mbr, Lab Pty NEC, 1947-50 and 1972-83.
Mr **Andrew Taylor,** barrister. B Feb 14 1961; ed Tredegar Comprehensive Sch; Univ Coll, Cardiff.
Mr **David McBride,** chartered accountant. Mbr, Lib Pty Cl, 1979-82 and 1983- . B Jun 23 1960; ed Stockport Sch; Univ Coll, Swansea.
Mr **Stephen Morgan,** electrician at Panteg steel works, contested this seat 1983. Has served on Brynmawr TC. Aged 31.

BLAYDON — No change

Electorate %Turnout	66,301	75.7%	1987	65,481	73.2%	1983
*McWilliam, J.D. (Lab)	25,277	50.3%	+6.0%	21,285	44.4%	(Lab)
Nunn, V.P. (SDP/All)	12,789	25.5%	-0.8%	14,063	29.3%	(C)
Pescod, P.R. (C)	12,147	24.2%	-5.1%	12,607	26.3%	(SDP/All)
SDP/All to Lab swing 3.4%	50,213	Lab maj 12,488 24.9%		47,955	Lab maj 7,222 15.1%	

Mr John McWilliam has been an Opposition whip since 1984. Mbr, Commons Services Cmte, 1983- , and Select Cmte on Procedure, 1984- ; Select Cmte on Education, Science and the Arts, 1980-83. Chmn, PLP parliamentary affairs cmte, since 1983; deputy shadow Ldr of Commons, 1983-84. Elected in 1979; contested Edinburgh, Pentlands, Feb 1974. Chmn, Northern group, Lab MPs, 1985-86. Former Post Office engineer. B May 16 1941; ed Leith Acad, Heriott Watt Coll and Napier Coll of Science and Technology. Mbr, Edinburgh Corpn, 1970-75; treas, City of Edinburgh, 1974-75. Mbr, General Advisory Cl, BBC, 1984- ; Scottish Cl for Tech Ed, 1973-85; Commissioner for local authority accounts in Scotland, 1974-78. Sponsored by POEU, being mbr of union since 1957; branch sec, 1966-72.

Mr Paul Nunn, sports journalist with Newcastle Evening Chronicle, fought Gateshead East 1983. Former Gateshead SDP area sec; mbr, CSD. Chmn, Newcastle Hadrian Round Table. B Aug 28 1948; ed Woodhouse Grove Sch, Bradford; Bristol Univ. Mbr, Gateshead MBC; Blaydon Harriers; NUJ.

Mr Peter Pescod, solicitor and partner in Newcastle upon Tyne practice; mbr, Newcastle Law Soc standing cmte. B Jun 29 1951; ed Queen Elizabeth GS, Darlington; Newcastle Univ.

Mr John McWilliam

BLYTH VALLEY — No change

Electorate %Turnout	59,104	78.1%	1987	57,639	72.8%	1983
Campbell, R. (Lab)	19,604	42.5%	+3.0%	16,583	39.5%	(Lab)
Brownlow, Miss R.M. (SDP/All)	18,751	40.6%	+8.8%	13,340	31.8%	(SDP/All)
Kinghorn, Dr R. (C)	7,823	16.9%	-10.8%	11,657	27.8%	(C)
				406	1.0%	(Other)
Lab to SDP/All swing 2.9%	46,178	Lab maj 853 1.8%		41,986	Lab maj 3,243 7.7%	

Mr Ronald Campbell is an unemployed miner. Mbr, Blyth BC, 1969-74; Blyth Valley Cl, 1974- (chmn, environmental health, and vice-chmn, housing). Mbr, NUM, for 27 years and worked from age of 15 at Bates Pit, Blyth. B Aug 14 1943; ed Ridley HS, Blyth.

Miss Rosemary Brownlow, deputy head of comprehensive high school, fought this seat 1983. B Mar 4 1948; ed Sacred Heart GS, Newcastle; Leeds Univ. District councillor, 1983-87.

Dr Robert Kinghorn, university lecturer. Mbr, London Borough of Hounslow Cl, 1986- (Cons finance spokesman); London Borough of Islington Cl, 1968-70. B Aug 19 1942; ed Eastbourne Coll; Edinburgh and London Univs.

Mr Ronald Campbell

BOLSOVER — No change

Electorate %Turnout	65,452	77.3%	1987	64,769	72.7%	1983
*Skinner, D.E. (Lab)	28,453	56.2%	-0.1%	26,514	56.3%	(Lab)
Lingens, M.R. (C)	14,333	28.3%	+1.4%	12,666	26.9%	(C)
Fowler, M.H. (SDP/All)	7,836	15.5%	-1.3%	7,886	16.8%	(SDP/All)
Lab to C swing 0.8%	50,622	Lab maj 14,120 27.9%		47,066	Lab maj 13,848 29.4%	

Mr Dennis Skinner, a miner, 1949-70, is chairman of the East Midlands group of Labour MPs; chmn, Miners Group of Labour MPs, 1977-78. Elected in 1970. Mbr, Labour Party NEC, since 1978. B Feb 11 1932; ed Tupton Hall GS; Ruskin Coll, Oxford. Pres, Derbyshire Miners (NUM), 1966-70, and NE Derbyshire Constituency Labour Party, 1968-71. Mbr, exec cmte, Campaign Group Labour MPs, 1985-86; Clay Cross UDC, 1960-70; Derbyshire CC, 1964-70. Chmn, Bow Gp, 1984-85. Chmn, Tribune Group, 1973-74. Sponsored by NUM.

Mr Michael Lingens, business lawyer, is partner in a London law firm specialising in corporate and commercial transactions. Chmn, Bow Gp, 1984-85. B May 15 1957; ed St Edmunds Sch, Canterbury; Trinity Coll, Oxford. Mbr (for Colehill Ward), London Borough of Hammersmith and Fulham Cl, 1982-86

Mr Mark Fowler, commodity broker. Vice-chmn, Kensington SDP, 1884-86; nat sec, Young Social Democrats, 1983-84; London organiser, Tawney Soc, 1986- . B Nov 12 1958; ed Westminster City Sch; Central London Poly..

Mr Dennis Skinner

BOLTON NORTH EAST — No change

Electorate %Turnout	59,382	78.7%	**1987**	58,918	77.1%	**1983**
*Thurnham, P.G. (C)	20,742	44.4%	+1.2%	19,632	43.2%	(C)
White, F.R. (Lab)	19,929	42.6%	+4.8%	17,189	37.8%	(Lab)
Alcock, J.H. (SDP/All)	6,060	13.0%	-5.3%	8,311	18.3%	(SDP/All)
				290	0.6%	(Other)
C to Lab swing 1.8%	46,731	C maj 813 1.7%		45,422	C maj 2,443 5.4%	

Mr Peter Thurnham

Mr **Peter Thurnham**, chartered engineer and company director, was elected in 1983. Mbr, Select Cmte on Employment, 1983- ; jt sec, Cons back-bench employment cmte, 1986- . Mbr, cl, Policy Studies Inst, 1985- . B Aug 21 1938; ed Oundle; Peterhouse Coll, Cambridge; Cranfield Inst of Tech; Harvard Business Sch. Mbr, South Lakeland DC, 1982-84. Director, Wathes Holdings Ltd (chmn, 1972-) and subsidiaries; consultant to Electrical Contractors' Assocn and Institution of Civil Engineers. Jt vice-chmn, Cons back-bench smaller businesses cmte, 1986- ; vice-chmn, housing improvement sub-cmte, 1985- ; treas, all-pty chemical industry parly gp, 1985- . FIMechE.

Mr **Frank White**, executive director and industrial relations adviser, was MP for Bury and Radcliffe, Oct 1974-83; contested the seat Feb 1974; Bury North 1983. Asst Govt whip, 1976-78; Opposition whip, 1980-81; Opposition spokesman on church affairs, 1980-83; chmn, all-pty paper industry gp, 1979-83; chmn, NW Labour Gp, 1979-83; mbr, select cmte on employment, 1979-83; Bolton BC, 1963-74; Greater Manchester CC, 1973-75; NW regional executive Lab Pty, 1986- . B Nov 11 1939; ed Bolton Tech Coll. GMBATU.

Mr **John Alcock**, solicitor, contested this seat 1983. Mbr, Cheshire area SDP cmte, 1982- ; Stoke City Cl, 1983-84. B Dec 9 1947; ed Hanley HS; Worcester Coll, Oxford.

BOLTON SOUTH EAST — No change

Electorate %Turnout	65,932	74.9%	**1987**	67,527	73.6%	**1983**
*Young, D.W. (Lab)	26,791	54.3%	+6.0%	23,984	48.3%	(Lab)
Windle, S. (C)	15,410	31.2%	+0.6%	15,231	30.7%	(C)
Harasiwka, F. (L/All)	7,161	14.5%	-5.9%	10,157	20.4%	(L/All)
				296	0.6%	(Other)
C to Lab swing 2.7%	49,362	Lab maj 11,381 23.1%		49,668	Lab maj 8,753 17.6%	

Mr **David Young**, former teacher and insurance executive, was elected for this seat in 1983; MP for Bolton East, Feb 1974-83; contested Bath 1970, Banbury 1966, and South Worcs 1959. B Oct 12 1930; ed Greenock Acad; Glasgow Univ; St Paul's Coll, Cheltenham. PPS to Mr Mulley, Secretary of State for Defence, 1977-79. Former alderman, Nuneaton BC; mbr, Nuneaton DC; chmn, Coventry East Lab Pty, 1964-68. NUPE.

Mr **Stanley Windle**, electro plating engineer, fought Worsley 1983 and Farnworth 1979. B Feb 26 1925; ed Withington, Stockport and engineering training coll, London. Has served as chmn, N W Area Conservative Clubs.

Mr **Frank Harasiwka**, asst accountant. B 1959; ed Lords Coll, Bolton; Bolton Tech.

Mr David Young

BOLTON WEST — No change

Electorate %Turnout	69,843	80.0%	**1987**	67,354	78.1%	**1983**
*Sackville, T.G. (C)	24,779	44.3%	-0.8%	23,731	45.1%	(C)
Harkin, G.J. (Lab)	20,186	36.1%	+4.6%	16,579	31.5%	(Lab)
Eccles, D.T. (SDP/All)	10,936	19.6%	-3.8%	12,321	23.4%	(SDP/All)
C to Lab swing 2.7%	55,901	C maj 4,593 8.2%		52,631	C maj 7,152 13.6%	

Mr **Thomas Sackville** won this seat 1983; fought Pontypool 1979. With Deltec Banking Corporation, New York, 1971-74; Grindlays Bank, 1975-78; and International Bullion and Metal Brokers (London) Ltd, 1978- , being a divisional director, 1981- . Sec, all-pty cmte on drug abuse, 1984- ; former sec, Cons back-bench fisheries cmte. B Oct 26 1950; ed St Aubyn's, Rottingdean, Sussex; Eton Coll; Lincoln Coll, Oxford. Parly consultant to Metal Packaging Manufacturers Assocn. PPS to Minister of State, Northern Ireland Office.

Mr **Guy Harkin**, a senior industrial relations lecturer at Lancashire Poly; former WEA tutor and research fellow at Manchester Business Sch. B Feb 17 1947; ed Oxford Univ (Pres, Students Union, 1970); LSE. Dep ldr, Bolton Cl, 1983. Chmn, NW Local Govt Employers, 1984- .

Mr **David Eccles**, barrister, contested Leigh 1983. Mbr, CSD, 1981-86. B Mar 22 1953; ed GS; Clare Coll, Cambridge.

Mr Thomas Sackville

BOOTHFERRY — No change

Electorate %Turnout	75,176	75.8%	**1987**	72,370	73.1%	**1983**
Davis, D.M. (C)	31,716	55.7%	-2.0%	30,536	57.7%	(C)
Davies, Mrs J.D. (L/All)	12,746	22.4%	-2.4%	13,116	24.8%	(L/All)
Donson, R. (Lab)	12,498	21.9%	+4.4%	9,271	17.5%	(Lab)
L/All to C swing 0.2%	56,960	C maj 18,970 33.3%		52,923	C maj 17,420 32.9%	

Mr David Davis has been strategic planning director of Tate and Lyle plc since 1984. He was president, Zymaize, a large Canadian sweetener manufacturer, 1982-84; managing director, Tate and Lyle Transport, 1980-82; and financial director, Manbre and Garton, 1976-80. B Dec 23 1948; ed Warwick Univ (chmn, Univ Cons Assocn, 1971), London Business Sch (chmn of its assocn, 1972) and Harvard. Nat chmn, Fed of Cons Students, 1973-74; ex-officio member, Nat Union exec cmte and NUEC general purposes cmte. Mbr, CBI financial policy cmte, 1977-79; exec mbr, Industrial Soc, 1985. Originator, Tate and Lyle/Touche Ross student innovation awards.
Mrs Joan Davies, an exporting agent and consultant in educational materials; former lecturer in politics at Sandhurst. Lloyd's underwriter. Contested South Wales in Euro election, 1984. Ed Leeds Univ. Former mbr, IPCS.
Mr Roy Donson, town planner with Barnsley MBC. B Dec 7 1947; ed Leeds Sch of Town Planning; Leeds Coll of Art. School governor. Nupe.

Mr David Davis

BOOTLE — No change

Electorate %Turnout	71,765	72.9%	**1987**	75,354	68.3%	**1983**
*Roberts, A. (Lab)	34,975	66.9%	+13.9%	27,282	53.0%	(Lab)
Papworth, P.R. (C)	10,498	20.1%	-3.5%	12,143	23.6%	(C)
Denham, P. (SDP/All)	6,820	13.0%	-10.4%	12,068	23.4%	(SDP/All)
C to Lab swing 8.7%	52,293	Lab maj 24,477 46.8%		51,493	Lab maj 15,139 29.4%	

Mr Allan Roberts has been on the Select Cmte on Environment since 1983; chmn, PLP environment cmte, 1982- . Director, Stanley Road Advice Centre Co Ltd. Has served on City of Manchester Cl (former housing chmn). B Oct 28 1943; ed Droylesden, Little Moss Boys' County Sec Sch; Ashton-under-Lyne Coll of Education; Didsbury Coll of Education; Manchester Univ Extra-Mural Dept. Principal officer (child care), City of Salford Social Services Dept, 1976-79. Mbr, CND. Elected for Bootle 1979; contested Hazel Grove, Feb and Oct 1974. Former teacher, social worker and training officer.
Mr Peter Papworth, financial consultant and company director. B 1938; ed Wrekin Coll; RAF Command and Staff Sch. Local councillor since 1969 and former mayor.
Mr Paul Denham, lecturer, East Devon Coll of Further Ed. B Aug 10 1948.

Mr Allan Roberts

BOSWORTH — No change

Electorate %Turnout	77,186	81.3%	**1987**	73,097	78.2%	**1983**
Tredinnick, D.A.S. (C)	34,145	54.4%	-1.0%	31,663	55.4%	(C)
Bill, D.C. (L/All)	17,129	27.3%	+2.2%	14,369	25.1%	(SDP/All)
Hall, R.S. (Lab)	10,787	17.2%	-2.3%	11,120	19.5%	(Lab)
Freer, Mrs D. (Grn)	660	1.1%				
C to L/All swing 1.6%	62,721	C maj 17,016 27.1%		57,152	C maj 17,294 30.3%	

Mr David Tredennick, manager of family property company, contested Cardiff South and Penarth in 1983. Former research assistant to MPs. Marketing manager, Q 1 Europe Ltd (small business computers), 1979-81; consultant, Baird Communications, New York, 1978-79. B Jan 19 1950; ed Ludgrove Sch, Wokingham; Eton; Mons Officer Cadet Sch; Graduate Business Sch, Capetown Univ; St John's Coll, Oxford.
Mr David Bill is a mechanical engineer with GEC, Coventry. Mbr, Leicestershire CC, 1981- (dep ldr, Alliance gp); Hinckley and Bosworth BC, 1973- (ldr, Alliance gp). B Dec 8 1944; ed Paston GS, North Walsham; Coventry Tech Coll. TASS.
Mr Richard Hall, teacher. Mbr, Lincoln DC, 1982-86; chmn, Birchwood ward branch Lab Pty (Lincoln); county pty rep on East Midlands Reg Cl. B Apr 16 1951; ed St Giles Sec Mod Sch, Lincoln; Huddersfield and Sheffield Polys. NAS/UWT.
Mrs Diana Freer, social entrepreneur, freelance lecturer and writer, contested Leicestershire North West 1983. Mbr, Leics CC voluntary cmte to set up Springboard, a centre for unemployed in Coalville, Leics. B May 2 1935; ed Humphrey Perkins GS, Barrow-on-Soar; St Hugh's, Oxford Univ; Leicester Univ.

Mr David Tredennick

BOURNEMOUTH EAST — No change

Electorate %Turnout	75,232	70.5%	**1987**	70,771	66.6%	**1983**
*Atkinson, D.A. (C)	30,925	58.3%	+4.8%	25,176	53.4%	(C)
Millward, Dr J. (L/All)	16,242	30.6%	+1.4%	13,760	29.2%	(L/All)
Taylor, I.A. (Lab)	5,885	11.1%	+2.5%	4,026	8.5%	(Lab)
				4,142	8.8%	(Other)
L/All to C swing 1.7%	53,052	C maj 14,683 27.7%		47,104	C maj 11,416 24.2%	

Mr David Atkinson, partner, Exponential, public affairs advisers. PPS to Mr Paul Channon in his ministerial posts since 1979. Elected at 1977 by-election; contested Newham North West, Feb 1974, and Basildon, Oct 1974. B Mar 24 1940; ed St George's Coll, Weybridge; Southend Coll of Technology; the Coll of Automobile and Aeronautical Engineering, Chelsea. Nat YC chmn, 1970-71. Mbr, Essex CC, 1973-78; Southend CBC, 1969-72; Cl of Europe and WEU, 1979- . Pres, Christian Solidarity International, 1979-86; International Soc for Human Rights.
Dr John Millward, medical practitioner, contested this seat 1983. Ldr, Alliance group, Dorset CC; mbr, Bournemouth DC. B Jun 22 1933; ed Dudley GS; Keble Coll, Oxford; St Bartholomew's Hosp.
Mr Ian Taylor, lecturer in public administration and law. B Jan 2 1946; ed state schs in Bournemouth; Bournemouth Coll of Tech and Commerce; Reading and Brunel Univs. Sec, Bournemouth and District Fabian Soc; mbr, gen management cmte, Bournemouth East CLP. Sec, local cancer research charity. NATFHE.

Mr David Atkinson

BOURNEMOUTH WEST — No change

Electorate %Turnout	74,444	73.3%	**1987**	72,297	69.2%	**1983**
*Butterfill, J.V. (C)	30,117	55.2%	-1.7%	28,466	56.9%	(C)
Craven, P.G.M. (SDP/All)	17,466	32.0%	+1.7%	15,135	30.3%	(L/All)
Jones, R.W. (Lab)	7,018	12.9%	+0.4%	6,243	12.5%	(Lab)
				180	0.4%	(Other)
C to SDP/All swing 1.7%	54,601	C maj 12,651 23.2%		50,024	C maj 13,331 26.6%	

Mr John Butterfill, senior partner in a firm of chartered surveyors since 1977, is President, European Property Associates. Elected in 1983; contested Croydon North West, 1981 by-election; London South Inner in election to European Parliament, 1979. B Feb 14 1941; ed Caterham School; Coll of Estate Management, London. Jt vice-chmn, Cons backbench tourism cmte, 1984- , sec, 1983-84. Director, John Lelliott Development Ltd, Islef (Building and Construction) Ltd, and Conservation Investments Ltd and subsidiary companies; managing director, St Paul's Securities Group, 1971-79. Mbr, cmte, Cons Group for Europe; nat cl, European Movement, 1982- ; vice-chmn, Foreign Affairs Forum.
Mr Peter Craven, solicitor with practice in Bournemouth. County cllr. Mbr, CSD; SDP working pty on environment. B Apr 1943; ed local Bournemouth schools.
Mr Ron Jones, unemployed steelworker. B Aug 11 1935. Mbr, Gwent CC (chmn, leisure cmte); ISTC.

Mr John Butterfill

BOW AND POPLAR — No change

Electorate %Turnout	59,178	57.4%	**1987**	57,768	55.4%	**1983**
Gordon, Mrs M. (Lab)	15,746	46.4%	-3.2%	15,878	49.6%	(Lab)
Flounders, E. (L/All)	11,115	32.7%	+1.4%	10,017	31.3%	(L/All)
Hughes, D.C. (C)	6,810	20.1%	+4.0%	5,129	16.0%	(C)
Chappell, P.S. (WRP)	274	0.8%	+0.4%	596	1.9%	(NF)
				383	1.2%	(Other)
Lab to L/All swing 2.3%	33,945	Lab maj 4,631 13.6%		32,003	Lab maj 5,861 18.3%	

Mrs Mildred Gordon, retired teacher. Mbr, London Lab Pty executive, 1983-86 (women's cmte and anti-racism sub-cmte); joint chair, Greater London Lab Cmte's policy cmte, 1985-86; school govenor; former adviser on older women to GLC's women's cmte; has taught English, history, English as a second language in Brent and typing to prisoners in Holloway. B Oct 24 1923; ed GS in Stepney. NUT.
Mr Eric Flounders, company manager, contested this seat 1983, and Bethnal Green and Bow, 1979. Mbr, Tower Hamlets BC, 1978- , and leader of cl since 1986. B Aug 27 1947; ed Scarborough HS for Boys; Westminster Coll, Oxford.
Mr David Hughes, solicitor. B 1954; ed Millfield Sch; King's Coll, London.

Mrs Mildred Gordon

BRADFORD NORTH — Lab gain

Electorate %Turnout	67,430	72.7%	1987	66,349	70.8%	1983
Wall, C.P. (Lab)	21,009	42.8%	+12.0%	16,094	34.3%	(C)
*Lawler, G.J. (C)	19,376	39.5%	+5.2%	14,492	30.9%	(Lab)
Berkeley, A.M. (SDP/All)	8,656	17.7%	-7.8%	11,962	25.5%	(SDP/All)
				4,405	9.4%	(Other)
C to Lab swing 3.4%	49,041	Lab maj 1,633 3.3%		46,953	C maj 1,602 3.4%	

Mr Patrick Wall, hardware buyer for a mail order firm and previously stock controller and laboratory assistant, contested this seat 1983. President, Bradford Trades Cl, since 1973. Former mbr, Liverpool City Cl and Bingley UDC. B May 6 1933; ed Liverpool Inst GS. Author of report on access for disabled to public buildings.
Mr Geoffrey Lawler, a public relations executive, Was MP for this seat 1983-87. Jt vice-chmn, Cons back-bench employment cmte, 1986-87, and previously sec. Was consultant to Leedex Ltd, public relations practitioners. B Oct 30 1954; ed Colchester Royal GS; Richmond Sch, N Yorks; Hull Univ (pres, Students' Union, 1976-77). With Cons Central Office, 1978-82, being in Community Affairs Dept, 1978-80, and Research Dept, 1980-82. Hon pres, British Youth Cl, 1983- ; PR exec, Bulldog Publicity, 1982-83. Director (unpaid), DEM PR Ltd.
Mr Adrian Berkeley, sec and dep director, London region, Building Employers' Federation; asst director, East Midlands CBI, 1979-81. Contested Gedling 1983. Mbr, SDP nat cmte, 1982-84; CSD, 1982-84; Nottinghamshire CC, 1977-81. B May 14 1948; ed St Joseph's Acad, Blackheath; Trent Poly.

Mr Patrick Wall

BRADFORD SOUTH — No change

Electorate %Turnout	69,588	73.7%	1987	69,588	71.0%	1983
Cryer, G.R. (Lab)	21,230	41.4%	+3.9%	18,542	37.5%	(Lab)
Hall, G.T. (C)	20,921	40.8%	+3.5%	18,432	37.3%	(C)
Lindley, T. (SDP/All)	9,109	17.8%	-6.8%	12,143	24.6%	(SDP/All)
				308	0.6%	(Other)
C to Lab swing 0.2%	51,260	Lab maj 309 0.6%		49,425	Lab maj 110 0.2%	

Mr Robert Cryer was MP for Keighley, 1974-83; MEP for Sheffield, 1984- ; chmn, Jt Select Cmte on Statutory Instruments, 1979-83. Contested Darwen, 1964. Resigned in Nov 1978 as Under Secretary of State for Industry, to which he was appointed in 1976, in protest at decision to cut off public funds to a Merseyside workers' cooperative. Former tech coll lecturer. Mbr, Keighley BC, 1971-74. B Dec 3 1934; ed Salt HS, Shipley; Hull Univ. Vice-chmn, PLP defence cmte, 1980-83, and industry gp, 1982-83. Vice-pres (and founder), Keighley and Worth Valley Railway. TGWU since 1971; NATFHE, 1960-74.
Mr Graham Hall, fruit and vegetable merchant, contested this seat 1983. Mbr, Calderdale Cl, 1980-83. B Jun 30 1953; ed Crossley and Porter GS; Percival Whitley Coll.
Mr Trevor Lindley, personnel manager, was full-time N of England organiser, SDP, 1981-83; vice-chmn, Yorkshire and Humberside Reg Cl. With Lab Pty, 1969-81, being agent to Mr Roy Mason MP. Lab cllr in Barnsley, 1972-76. B Sep 20 1942; ed state schs; Ruskin Coll, Oxford; Sheffield Univ. ASTMS.

Mr Robert Cryer

BRADFORD WEST — No change

Electorate %Turnout	70,763	70.2%	1987	71,296	68.9%	1983
*Madden, M.F. (Lab)	25,775	51.9%	+12.2%	19,499	39.7%	(Lab)
Duncan-Smith, I. (C)	18,224	36.7%	+3.8%	16,162	32.9%	(C)
Moghal, M. (SDP/All)	5,657	11.4%	-15.7%	13,301	27.1%	(SDP/All)
				139	0.3%	(Other)
C to Lab swing 4.2%	49,656	Lab maj 7,551 15.2%		49,101	Lab maj 3,337 6.8%	

Mr Max Madden was an Opposition spokesman on health and social security, 1983-84. Labour Party director of publicity, 1979-82; previously press and information officer, British Gas Corpn, and journalist on the East Essex Gazette, Tribune, The Sun and Scotsman. Elected for this seat in 1983; MP for Sowerby, 1974-79; contested Sudbury and Woodbridge, 1966. B Oct 29 1941; ed Lascelles Sec Mod Sch, South Harrow; Pinner GS. Former mbr, Wandsworth BC. TGWU sponsored.
Mr Iain Duncan-Smith is a former captain in the Scots Guards.
Mr Manzoor Moghal, financial consultant. Chmn (1986-87), race relations cmte, Leicestershire CC. JP. Held various high civil offices in Uganda, 1960-72. Mbr, CSD, 1982-84. B Feb 2 1936; ed sch in Uganda; univ in Pakistan; Punjab Univ; FC Coll, Lahore. Managing director of family business in Uganda, 1957-72. Vice-chmn, Uganda Evacuees Assocn.

Mr Max Madden

BRAINTREE — No change

Electorate %Turnout	76,994	79.0%	**1987**	73,548	76.2%	**1983**
*Newton, A.H. (C)	32,978	54.2%	+1.6%	29,462	52.6%	(C)
Bing, I.G. (SDP/All)	16,121	26.5%	-2.1%	16,021	28.6%	(SDP/All)
Stapleton, B. (Lab)	11,764	19.3%	+0.5%	10,551	18.8%	(Lab)
SDP/All to C swing 1.9%	60,863	C maj 16,857 27.7%		56,034	C maj 13,441 24.0%	

Mr Antony Newton was appointed Minister for Health, with the rank of Minister of State, DHSS, in 1986; as Minister chairs NHS Management Bd; Minister for Social Security and the Disabled (also at DHSS), 1984-86; Under Secretary of State, DHSS, 1982-84; Lord Commissioner of the Treasury (Govt whip), 1981-82; Asst Govt whip, 1979-81. Elected in Feb 1974; contested Sheffield, Brightside, 1970. Economist. B Aug 29 1937; ed Friends' Sch, Saffron Walden; Trinity Coll, Oxford (Pres of Union, 1958). Governor, City Literary Inst; Felsted Sch. Vice-chmn, Fed of Univ Cons and Unionist Assocns. Jt sec, Cons back-bench health and social security cmte, 1976-79. Asst director, Cons Research Dept, 1970-74; head of economic section, 1965-70; research sec and then chmn, Bow Group, 1963-65.

Mr Inigo Bing, barrister, fought Braintree 1983 for SDP, and Beckenham 1970 for Lab. Former chmn, Lambeth area pty; mbr, CSD, citizens rights cmte, exec cmte of Tawney Soc; sec, SDP crime and policing working gp. Mbr (for Lab), Lambeth BC, 1971-78. B Apr 1 1944; ed St Olave's and St Saviour's GS, London; Birmingham Univ.

Mr Brian Stapleton, chartered accountant with own practice, contested Essex North East in 1984 Euro election. Mbr, Essex CC, 1985- ; Lab industrial planning gp, 1986; treas, Lab Pty computer advisory gp. Aug 5 1937; ed Wanstead HS; City Univ.

Mr Antony Newton

BRECON AND RADNOR — No change

Electorate %Turnout	49,394	84.4%	**1987**	47,277	80.1%	**1983**
*Livsey, R.A.L. (L/All)	14,509	34.8%	+10.5%	18,255	48.2%	(C)
Evans, J.P. (C)	14,453	34.7%	-13.5%	9,471	25.0%	(Lab)
Willey, F.R. (Lab)	12,180	29.2%	+4.2%	9,226	24.4%	(L/All)
Davies, J.H. (Pl C)	535	1.3%	-0.4%	640	1.7%	(Pl C)
				278	0.7%	(Other)
C to L/All swing 12.0%	41,677	L/All maj 56 0.1%		37,870	C maj 8,784 23.2%	

Mr Richard Livsey became the chief Alliance spokesman on the Countryside in the election team announced in Jan 1987. Liberal spokesman on agriculture since 1985; mbr, Select Cmte on Agriculture. Won this seat at 1985 by-election; contested the seat, 1983; Pembroke, 1979, and Perth and East Perthshire, 1970. Farmer; senior lecturer in farm management at Welsh Agricultural Coll, Aberystwyth, 1971-85. B May 2 1935; ed Talgarth County Primary Sch; Bedales Sch; Seale-Hayne Agricultural Coll; Reading Univ.

Mr Jonathan Evans, a solicitor and partner in Welsh law firm, contested Wolverhampton North East in 1979 and Ebbw Vale twice in 1974. B Jun 2 1950; ed Lewis Sch, Pengam; Howardian HS, Cardiff; Coll of Law, Guildford and Lancaster Gate.

Mr Richard Willey, mbr of Radnor DC, fought 1985 by-election. Chmn, constituency Labour Party. Researcher and writer specialising in education.

Dr John Davies, geologist and formerly in tourism, is unemployed. B May 3 1944; ed Allensbank Sec Sch, Cardiff; Llandaff Tech Coll; Chelsea Coll, London Univ.

Details of 1985 by-election at which L/All gained seat on Page 285

Mr Richard Livsey

BRENT EAST — No change

Electorate %Turnout	61,020	64.5%	**1987**	61,489	63.6%	**1983**
Livingstone, K.R. (Lab)	16,772	42.6%	-4.4%	18,363	47.0%	(Lab)
Crawley, Ms H.S. (C)	15,119	38.4%	+3.8%	13,529	34.6%	(C)
Finkelstein, D.W. (SDP/All)	5,710	14.5%	-2.4%	6,598	16.9%	(SDP/All)
Dooley, R.Q. (Ind Lab)	1,035	2.6%		289	0.7%	(Ind)
Litvinoff, M. (Grn)	716	1.8%		222	0.6%	(WRP)
				88	0.2%	(Other)
Lab to C swing 4.1%	39,352	Lab maj 1,653 4.2%		39,089	Lab maj 4,834 12.4%	

Mr Ken Livingstone was leader of the Greater London Council, 1981-86 when it was abolished; GLC mbr for Paddington, 1981-86, and for Hackney North, 1973-81. Joint editor, *Labour Herald*, 1981-85. Contested Hampstead, 1979. B Jun 17 1945; ed Tulse Hill Comprehensive Sch; Philippa Fawcett Coll of Ed. Former laboratory technician. Mbr, regional exec, London Lab Pty, 1974- ; Lambeth BC, 1971-78; Camden BC, 1978-82.

Ms Harriet Crawley, art dealer and writer, is director of a fine art company. B Sep 10 1948; ed King's Coll, London Univ. NUJ.

Mr Daniel Finkelstein chaired the Young Social Democrats, 1983-85. Mbr, SDP policy cmte; SDP communications cmte. Under-26 rep, SDP nat cmte; mbr, Tawney Soc nat cmte. Director, SDP youth campaign, 1985 and 1986. B 1962; ed LSE; City Univ Business Sch; Royal Coll of Arts.

Mr Miles Litvinoff, book editor. Co-chair, Brent Green Pty, since Feb 1987. B Dec 13 1950; ed City of London Sch; Liverpool Univ. Former NUJ Book branch FoC.

Mr Ken Livingstone

BRENT NORTH — No change

Electorate %Turnout	63,081	71.0%	1987	62,679	70.4%	1983
*Boyson, R. (C)	26,823	59.9%	+3.6%	24,842	56.3%	(C)
Patel, P. (Lab)	11,103	24.8%	+1.7%	10,191	23.1%	(Lab)
Mularczyk, C. (SDP/All)	6,868	15.3%	-5.3%	9,082	20.6%	(SDP/All)
Lab to C swing 0.9%	44,794	C maj 15,720 35.1%		44,115	C maj 14,651 33.2%	

Sir Rhodes Boyson

Sir Rhodes Boyson was Minister for Local Government, with the rank of Minister of State at the DoE, 1986-87; Minister of State, Northern Ireland, 1984-86; Minister for Social Security, with rank of Minister of State, DHSS, 1983-84; Under Secretary of State for Education and Science, 1979-83; an Opposition spokesman on education, 1976-79. Elected in Feb 1974; contested Eccles, 1970. Headmaster, 1955-74, including Highbury Grove Sch, 1967-74. B May 1925; ed Haslingden GS; University Coll, Cardiff; Manchester Univ; LSE and Corpus Christi Coll, Cambridge. Chmn, Nat Cl for Educational Standards, 1974-79; Churchill Press and Constitutional Book Club, 1969-79. Mbr, Waltham Forest BC, 1968-74; Haslingden Cl, 1957-61. Vice-chmn, Cons back-bench education cmte, 1975-76.
Mr Praful Patel, investment adviser and consultant. B Mar 7 1939; ed Uganda and India. Mbr, International Economic Advisory Panel, Indian Govt; Fabian Soc. ASTMS; ACTSS.
Mr Christopher Mularczyk, postgraduate researcher, is nat sec, SDP students; research asst to Mr John Cartwright MP. Mbr, Islington BC, 1986- . B Sep 8 1959; ed King Edward VII Sch, Sheffield; Leeds Univ.

BRENT SOUTH — No change

Electorate %Turnout	62,772	64.9%	1987	62,783	63.6%	1983
Boateng, P. (Lab)	21,140	51.9%	-1.4%	21,259	53.3%	(Lab)
Paterson, A.J. (C)	13,209	32.4%	+5.5%	10,740	26.9%	(C)
Harskin, M.T. (L/All)	6,375	15.7%	-3.3%	7,557	18.9%	(L/All)
				356	0.9%	(Other)
Lab to C swing 3.4%	40,724	Lab maj 7,931 19.5%		39,912	Lab maj 10,519 26.4%	

Mr Paul Boateng

Mr Paul Boateng, a solicitor, has been chairman, Afro-Caribbean Education Resource Project, since 1978; mbr, Lab Pty jt cmte on crime and policing, 1984- . Fought Hertfordshire West 1983. Mbr GLC, 1981-86 (chmn, Police Cmte, and vice-chmn, Ethnic Minorities Cmte, 1981-86). B Jun 14 1951; ed Ghana International Sch; Accra Acad; Apsley GS; Bristol Univ; Coll of Law. Chmn, Westminster Community Relations Cl, 1979-81; legal adviser, Scrap Sus Campaign, 1977-81; vice-pres, Waltham Forest Community Relations Cl, 1981- ; mbr, Lab Pty NEC sub-cmte on human rights, 1979-83; Home Office Advisory Cl on Race Relations, 1981-86; World Cl of Churches Commission on programme to combat racism, 1984- ; Police Training Cl, 1981-85; exec, NCCL, 1980-86; bd, English National Opera, 1984- . Governor, Police Staff Coll, Bramshill, 1981-84.
Mr Anthony Paterson, a solicitor, opposed Mrs Thatcher in 1979 election as Liberal. Research sec, Bow Gp. B May 16 1951; ed Winchester Coll; Worcester Coll, Oxford. Mbr, World Wildlife Fund Cl.
Mr Mike Harskin, journalist and director of labour unit at Liberal whips office, House of Commons. Co-founder of 'A New Direction', publishing co-operative. B Dec 19 1963; ed Wallington HS for Boys, Surrey; Harlow Tech Coll, Essex. NUJ.

BRENTFORD AND ISLEWORTH — No change

Electorate %Turnout	71,715	76.7%	1987	69,170	74.7%	1983
*Hayhoe, Sir Barney (C)	26,230	47.7%	+0.3%	24,515	47.4%	(C)
Keen, Ms A. (Lab)	18,277	33.2%	+4.0%	15,128	29.3%	(Lab)
Wilks, Dr D.M.W. (SDP/All)	9,626	17.5%	-4.6%	11,438	22.1%	(SDP/All)
Cooper, T. (Grn)	849	1.5%		427	0.8%	(NF)
				179	0.3%	(Other)
C to Lab swing 1.8%	54,982	C maj 7,953 14.5%		51,687	C maj 9,387 18.2%	

Sir Barney Hayhoe

Sir Barney Hayhoe was Minister for Health, with rank of Minister of State, DHSS, 1985-86; Minster of State, Treasury, with responsibilities for Civil Service, 1981-85; Minister of State, Civil Service Dept, 1981; Under Secretary of Defence for the Army, 1979-81; an Opposition spokesman on employment, 1974-79; PPS to Ld President and Ldr of Commons, 1972-74. Elected for Brentford and Isleworth, Feb 1974; MP for Heston and Isleworth, 1970-74; contested Lewisham South, 1964. Mbr of Lloyd's. B Aug 8 1925; ed elementary sch and Stanley Tech Sch, South Norwood; Croydon and Borough polytechnics. Jt hon sec (1970-73) and vice-chmn (1973-76), Cons Group for Europe. Vice-chmn, Cons Pty International Office, 1973-79; head of research section, Cons Research Dept, 1965-70. Mbr, Select Cmte on Race Relations and Immigration, 1971-73.
Mrs Ann Keen, an SRN. Former paper factory worker and health authority clerk. B Nov 26 1948; ed sec mod. Mbr, Socialist Health Organisation. Nupe.
Dr Michael Wilks, general practitioner, fought this seat 1983. Sec, Hounslow SDP, 1984-86; mbr, SDP health policy gp. B May 26 1949; ed St John's Sch, Leatherhead; St Mary's Hospital Medical Sch, London. BMA.

BRENTWOOD AND ONGAR · No change

Electorate %Turnout	67,521	79.0%	**1987**	65,976	76.6%	**1983**
*McCrindle, R.A. (C)	32,258	60.5%	+2.1%	29,484	58.4%	(C)
Amor, N.R. (L/All)	13,337	25.0%	-5.2%	15,282	30.3%	(L/All)
Orpe, J.W. (Lab)	7,042	13.2%	+1.8%	5,739	11.4%	(Lab)
Willis, Mrs M.E. (Grn)	686	1.3%				
L/All to C swing 3.7%	53,323	C maj 18,921 35.5%		50,505	C maj 14,202 28.1%	

Mr Robert McCrindle

Mr Robert McCrindle, an insurance broker, company director and consultant, has been on the Select Cmte on Trade and Industry since 1983; mbr, Select Cmte on Energy, 1979-83. Elected in Feb 1974; MP for Billericay, 1970-74; contested Thurrock, 1964, and Dundee East, 1959. B Sep 19 1929; ed Allen Glen's Coll, Glasgow. Parly adviser to British Insurance Brokers Assocn and British Transport Police Fed; consultant to Caledonian Aviation Group, since 1984. Chmn, Citybond Storage plc, and director, Stuart Hulse Associates Ltd, Travel Insight Ltd and Hogg Robinson Transport and Financial Services Ltd. Jt vice-chmn, Cons back-bench health and social services cmte, since 1979. Chmn, economic cmte, N Atlantic Assembly, 1980-84; mbr of UK delegation from 1977. Chmn, all-pty aviation group.
Mr Nicholas Amor, solicitor, contested the seat 1983. B Sep 26 1950; ed Great Baddon Sch; Magdelen Coll, Oxford; Guildford Law School. Member, Brentwood DC, 1982- .
Mr Jim Orpe, teacher, contested seat 1983. B Sep 27 1951; ed Colchester Royal GS; Colchester Inst; Essex Univ. Mbr, Colchester BC, 1978-82. NUT. Football referee.
Mrs Margaret Willis, horticulturalist. B Oct 12 1950; ed Bloomfield Collegiate GS; Cregagh Tech Coll; Writtle Agric Coll.

BRIDGEND · Lab gain

Electorate %Turnout	57,389	80.3%	**1987**	53,918	77.0%	**1983**
Griffiths, W.J. (Lab)	21,893	47.5%	+12.3%	15,950	38.4%	(C)
*Hubbard-Miles, P.C. (C)	17,513	38.0%	-0.4%	14,623	35.2%	(Lab)
Smart, R. (SDP/All)	5,590	12.1%	-11.1%	9,630	23.2%	(SDP/All)
McAllister, M s L. (Pl C)	1,065	2.3%	-0.8%	1,312	3.2%	(Pl C)
C to Lab swing 6.4%	46,061	Lab maj 4,380 9.5%		41,515	C maj 1,327 3.2%	

Mr Winston Griffiths

Mr Winston (Win) Griffiths, MEP for South Wales, 1979- ; a vice-pres, European Parliament, 1984-Jan 87, serving on regional policy; economic and monetary and industrial policy cmtes; sec, Intergp on Animal Welfare. B Feb 11 1943; ed Brecon Boys' GS; Univ Coll, Cardiff. Mbr, Vale of Glamorgan BC, 1973-76. Methodist Church lay preacher. NUT for 22 years, having taught in Tanzania; Geo Dixon GS for Boys, Birmingham, 1969-70; Barry Boys' Comprehensive Sch, 1970-76; and was head of history, Cowbridge Comprehensive Sch, 1976-79. Mbr, Cl for Preservation of Rural Wales.
Mr Peter Hubbard-Miles, PPS to Secretary of State for Wales, 1985-87, was MP for the seat,1983-87; contested Aberavon, Feb 1974. Mbr, Select Cmte on Welsh Affairs, 1983-85. B May 9 1927; ed Lewis' Sch, Pengam. Mbr, Mid-Glamorgan CC, 1974- ; Ogwr BC, 1974- ; Glamorgan CC, 1967-74; Porthcawl UDC, 1970-74.
Mr Russell Smart, economist and lecturer, was manual worker in engineering industry. SDP Welsh Cl employment spokesman. Fought seat 1983. B Aug 9 1931; ed Rhondda Tech Sch; Coleg Harlech; UCW, Cardiff. AUEW; NATFHE lay officer.
Ms Laura McAllister, student, chairs Pl Cymru youth movement. B Dec 10 1964; ed Bryntirion Comprehensive Sch; LSE. NUS.

BRIDGWATER · No change

Electorate %Turnout	67,480	78.2%	**1987**	64,225	74.8%	**1983**
*King, T.J. (C)	27,177	51.5%	-0.7%	25,107	52.3%	(C)
Clarke, C. (SDP/All)	15,982	30.3%	+0.3%	14,410	30.0%	(SDP/All)
Turner, J. (Lab)	9,594	18.2%	+0.4%	8,524	17.7%	(Lab)
C to SDP/All swing 0.5%	52,753	C maj 11,195 21.2%		48,041	C maj 10,697 22.3%	

Mr Tom King

Mr Tom King became Secretary of State for Northern Ireland in 1985; Secretary of State for Employment, 1983-85; Secretary of State for Transport, Jun-Oct 1983; Secretary of State for Environment, Jan-Jun 1983; Minister for Local Government and Environmental Services at DoE, 1979-83. Opposition spokesman on energy, 1976-79, and on industry, 1975-76. Vice-chmn, Cons industry cmte, 1974-75. Elected at 1970 by-election. B Jun 13 1933; ed Rugby and Emmanuel Coll, Cambridge. Chmn, Sale, Tilney and Co Ltd, 1971-79 (director, 1965-79); general manager, E. S. and A. Robinson, Bristol, 1964-69, joining company in 1956.
Mr Christopher Clarke, general manager. Mbr and dep ldr, Somerset CC; former mbr, Richmondshire DC. B Mar 24 1941; ed Westcliff-on-Sea HS; City of London Coll.
Mr John Turner, convenor for TGWU at British Cellophane Ltd, Bridgwater. Mbr, Sedgemoor DC, 1961-. Chmn, Sedgemoor Sports Cl.

BRIDLINGTON · No change

Electorate %Turnout	80,126	73.7%	**1987**	76,718	70.6%	**1983**
*Townend, J.E. (C)	32,351	54.8%	-3.0%	31,284	57.8%	(C)
Marshall, E.I. (SDP/All)	15,030	25.5%	-1.6%	14,675	27.1%	(SDP/All)
Bird, L.M. (Lab)	10,653	18.1%	+4.4%	7,370	13.6%	(Lab)
Myerscough, R.D. (Grn)	983	1.7%	+0.2%	803	1.5%	(Eco)
C to SDP/All swing 0.7%	59,017	C maj 17,321 29.3%		54,132	C maj 16,609 30.7%	

Mr John Townend

Mr John Townend, a wine merchant and chartered accountant. Mbr, Select Cmte on the Treasury and Civil Service, 1983- . Jt vice-chmn, Cons back-bench finance cmte, 1983- ; and of small businesses cmte, 1985- ; mbr, Select Cmte on Employment, 1980-81. Elected in 1979; contested Hull North, 1970. B Jun 12 1934; ed Hymers Coll, Hull. Mbr, Hull City Cl, 1966-74; Humberside CC, 1973-79 (ldr of opposition, 1973-77; ldr of cl, 1977-79); mbr, policy cmte, Assocn of County Cls, 1977-79; chmn, Humber Bridge Bd, 1969-71. Director, J Townend and Sons (Hull) Ltd and associated companies, and East Surrey Building Society; mbr of Lloyd's. Chmn, Yorks and Humberside Wine and Spirit Merchants Assocn, 1975-76. PPS to Minister of State for Social Security, 1981-83.

Dr Edmund Marshall, university lecturer, was Lab MP for Goole, 1971-83; fought Louth as Lib, 1966 and 1964. PPS to Home Secretary, 1976-79. Mbr, Wallasey CBC, 1963-65. B May 31 1940; ed Humberstone Foundation Sch, Cleethorpes; Magdalen Coll, Oxford; Liverpool Univ.

Mr Maxwell Bird, solicitor. Mbr, Humberside CC 1974- (chmn, education cmte 1981-). B May 29 1939; ed Malet Lambert HS, Hull; LSE. APEX.

Mr Richard Myerscough, teacher. B Apr 29 1946; ed Wynsford GS, Cheshire; St Paul's Teacher Training Coll; Open Univ. NUT; past pres, Bridlington Assocn.

BRIGG AND CLEETHORPES · No change

Electorate %Turnout	80,096	76.3%	**1987**	77,471	73.6%	**1983**
*Brown, M.R. (C)	29,723	48.7%	-2.0%	28,893	50.7%	(C)
Powney, I. (L/All)	17,475	28.6%	-0.7%	16,704	29.3%	(L/All)
Geraghty, T. (Lab)	13,876	22.7%	+2.7%	11,404	20.0%	(Lab)
C to L/All swing 0.7%	61,074	C maj 12,248 20.1%		57,001	C maj 12,189 21.4%	

Mr Michael Brown

Mr Michael Brown joined the Select Cmte on Energy in 1986. Elected for this seat 1983; MP for Brigg and Scunthorpe, 1979-83. Lecturer and tutor, Swinton Cons Coll, 1974-75; parliamentary assistant to MPs, 1976-79. B Jul 3 1951; ed Andrew Cairns County Sec Mod Sch, Littlehampton; York Univ. Vice-pres, York Univ Students' Union, 1971-72; vice-chmn, York Univ Cons Assoc, 1971-72. Jt sec, Cons back-bench N Ireland cmte, 1981- .

Mr Ian Powney, chartered accountant, contested Birmingham, Hall Green, Oct 1974, and The Wrekin, Feb 1974. B Nov 5 1950; ed Bishop Vesey's GS, Sutton Coldfield; Kent Univ. Mbr, Sutton Coldfield BC, 1972-74; West Midlands CC, 1973-77.

Mr Terence Geraghty has been leader of Humberside County Cl since 1984; mbr, 1973- ; Hull City Cl, 1970-76. Contested Boothferry, 1983. B Mar 14 1937; ed St Vincent's School. Former dock worker. Sponsored by TGWU.

BRIGHTON, KEMPTOWN · No change

Electorate %Turnout	60,271	74.5%	**1987**	60,877	71.5%	**1983**
*Bowden, A. (C)	24,031	53.5%	+2.4%	22,265	51.1%	(C)
Bassam, J.S. (Lab)	14,771	32.9%	+3.3%	12,887	29.6%	(Lab)
Berry, C. (L/All)	6,080	13.5%	-5.1%	8,098	18.6%	(SDP/All)
				290	0.7%	(Other)
C to Lab swing 0.5%	44,882	C maj 9,260 20.6%		43,540	C maj 9,378 21.5%	

Mr Andrew Bowden

Mr Andrew Bowden, a personnel consultant, has been chmn, all-party parly group for pensioners, since 1972; the all-party British Limbless Ex-servicemen's Assocn group, since 1975; and People to People International, since 1981. Won the seat in 1970; contested in 1966; Kensington North, 1964; Hammersmith, North 1955. Director, Council of International Cooperation; consultant to Buttram Energies Inc. Mbr, Select Cmte on Employment, 1979-83; Select Cmte on Abortion (Amendment) Bill, 1975-76; Select Cmte on Expenditure, 1973-74. B Apr 8 1930; ed Ardingly Coll, Sussex (member of its school cl since 1982). Pres, Captive Animals Protection Soc, since 1978. Nat chmn, YCs, 1960-61. Mbr, Wandsworth BC, 1956-62.

Mr Steven Bassam, local govt research officer and former social worker. B Jun 11 1953; ed Clacton Sec Mod; NE Essex Tech Coll; Sussex and Kent Univs. Ldr, Brighton BC, 1987- (Dep ldr, 1986-87; dep ldr, Lab gp, 1983-87). Nalgo.

Mr Christopher Berry, a chartered town planner, is Assistant Chief Planner, London Planning Advisory Cmte. B Mar 19 1948; ed Chatham House GS, Ramsgate; Stand GS, Manchester; N London Poly; Newcastle Univ. Univ of California, Los Angeles. Secretary, Liberal community relations panel; mbr, Liberal planning panel. Nalgo.

BRIGHTON, PAVILION   No change

Electorate %Turnout	58,910	73.7%	**1987**	59,769	69.3%	**1983**
*Amery, H.J. (C)	22,056	50.8%	-0.7%	21,323	51.5%	(C)
Hill, D.S. (Lab)	12,914	29.7%	+5.9%	10,191	24.6%	(SDP/All)
Carey, K.F. (SDP/All)	8,459	19.5%	-5.1%	9,879	23.9%	(Lab)
C to Lab swing 3.3%	43,429	C maj 9,142 21.1%		41,393	C maj 11,132 26.9%	

Mr Julian Amery

Mr Julian Amery is a member of the Select Cmte on Privileges. Minister of State, Foreign and Commonwealth Office, 1972-74; Minister for Housing and Construction, 1970-72; Minister of Public Building and Works, 1970; Minister of Aviation, 1962-64; Secretary of State for Air, from 1960; Under Secretary of State, Colonial Office, from 1958; Under Secretary of State, War Office, from 1957. Returned at 1969 by-election; MP for Preston North, 1950-66; contested the two-member Preston seat in 1945. Author, journalist and company director. B Mar 27 1919; ed Summerfields; Eton; Balliol Coll, Oxford. Director, Vaal Reefs Exploration & Mining Co Ltd and Western Deep Levels Ltd. Consultant to Sedgwick Forbes Overseas Group Ltd; adviser to Bank of Credit and Commerce International. Pres, Horn of Africa and Aden Cl, since 1984.
Mr David Hill, senior lecturer in education at West Sussex Inst of Higher Ed, contested this seat 1979. Journalist for *Labour Weekly* and *Tribune* covering West European elections. Mbr, East Sussex CC, 1981- (Lab gp ldr, 1982-); Brighton BC, 1975-76, 1979-83. B Oct 10 1945; ed Arlesey Cty Primary Sch, Beds; Westlain GS, Brighton; Manchester, London and Sussex Univs. NATFHE.
Mr Kevin Carey, overseas director, Royal Commonwealth Soc for Blind. B Nov 11 1951; ed Cardinal Allen GS, Liverpool; Downing Coll, Cambridge; Harvard Univ.

BRISTOL EAST   No change

Electorate %Turnout	63,840	78.7%	**1987**	66,296	73.8%	**1983**
*Sayeed, J. (C)	21,906	43.6%	+3.1%	19,844	40.5%	(C)
Thomas, R.R. (Lab)	17,783	35.4%	-1.5%	18,055	36.9%	(Lab)
Foster, D.M.E. (L/All)	10,247	20.4%	-0.8%	10,404	21.3%	(L/All)
Kingston, P.M. (NFFG)	286	0.6%		343	0.7%	(NF)
				311	0.6%	(Other)
Lab to C swing 2.3%	50,222	C maj 4,123 8.2%		48,957	C maj 1,789 3.7%	

Mr Jonathan Sayeed

Mr Jonathan Sayeed joined the Select Cmte on Environment in 1987. Elected for this seat 1983. Vice-chmn (since 1985) and former sec, Cons back-bench shipping and shipbuilding sub-cmte; sec, all-pty maritime gp. B Mar 20 1948; ed primary sch in Hampstead, London; Wolverstone Hall, Suffolk; RNC Dartmouth; Royal Naval Engineering Coll, Manadon. In Royal Navy, 1966-72; RNR, 1972-76. Trainee manager and manager, Marks and Spencers, 1972-73. Director, then chmn, insurance and shipping consultancy, 1973-82. Mbr of Lloyd's.
Mr Ronald Thomas, college lecturer, was MP for Bristol North-West, Oct 1974-79; contested the seat Feb 1974. B Mar 16 1929; ed Ruskin and Balliol Colls, Oxford. Mbr, Avon CC. ASTMS.
Mr Donald Foster, lecturer in science education and author of educational books, was elected to Avon CC in 1981 being leader, Alliance gp, 1981-86, and chairing its education cmte, 1986- . Associated with Bristol and Avon Community Enterprise. Mbr, ALC and NUT.

BRISTOL NORTH WEST   No change

Electorate %Turnout	72,876	79.4%	**1987**	72,996	76.9%	**1983**
*Stern, M.C. (C)	26,953	46.6%	+2.7%	24,617	43.9%	(C)
Walker, T.W. (Lab)	20,001	34.6%	+2.0%	18,290	32.6%	(Lab)
Kirkaldy, J.M.G. (SDP/All)	10,885	18.8%	-4.7%	13,228	23.6%	(SDP/All)
Lab to C swing 0.4%	57,839	C maj 6,952 12.0%		56,135	C maj 6,327 11.3%	

Mr Michael Stern

Mr Michael Stern, partner in firm of chartered accountants, was elected in 1983; fought Derby South, 1979. PPS to Mr Peter Brooke, Minister of State, Treasury, 1986- . Mbr, Select Cmte on Environment, 1986. Vice-chmn, West Country Cons MPs, 1983- ; chmn, unpaired Cons MPs; sec, Cons back-bench education cmte, 1984-85. B Aug 3 1942; ed Christ's Coll GS, Finchley. Co-opted mbr, London Borough of Ealing education cmte, 1981-83. Chmn, Bow Group, 1977-78; former political officer, treas and asst research sec, Bow Group, and managing director, Bow Publications. Treas, Finchley Cons Assocn, 1972-76, and Ealing, Acton Cons Assocn, 1982-83.
Mr Terry Walker, newsagent, was MP for Kingswood, Feb 1974-79; contested that seat 1983. Second Church Estates Commissioner, 1974-79. PPS at depts of health and trade. Mbr, Avon CC, 1981- (chmn, Avon Public Protection Cmte); wife also on Avon CC. B Oct 26 1935; ed Clarks GS, Bristol; Bristol Coll of Further Ed. TGWU.
Mr John Kirkaldy, lecturer at Salisbury Coll of Tech; part-time tutor/counsellor for Open Univ. Founder mbr, SDP; mbr, Kennet DC 1983- . B Jul 21 1947; ed Jamaica and Australia.

BRISTOL SOUTH — No change

Electorate	%Turnout		68,733	74.0%	**1987**	72,067	68.8%	**1983**
Primarolo, Ms D. (Lab)			20,798	40.9%	-3.1%	21,824	44.0%	(Lab)
Cutcher, P.S. (C)			19,394	38.1%	+3.0%	17,405	35.1%	(C)
Long, Mrs H.S. (SDP/All)			9,952	19.6%	+0.1%	9,674	19.5%	(SDP/All)
Vowles, G.R. (Grn)			600	1.2%	+0.5%	352	0.7%	(Eco)
Meghji, Ms C.M. (RF)			149	0.3%		224	0.5%	(Com)
						113	0.2%	(Other)
Lab to C swing 3.1%			50,893	Lab maj 1,404 2.8%		49,592	Lab maj 4,419 8.9%	

Ms Dawn Primarolo

Ms Dawn Primarolo, researcher. Mbr, Avon CC, since 1985. Sec, Bristol South East CLP; chair, Bristol District Lab Pty; SW rep, Nat Lab Women's Cmte. B May 2 1954; ed Thomas Bennett Comprehensive Sch, Crawley; Bristol Poly; Bristol Univ. ASTMS.
Mr Philip Cutcher is an engineer with Marcol Computer Systems, holding a share option in firm. Has contested two local government elections; personal asst to Bristol South candidate in 1983 election. B Oct 24 1951; ed Hornchurch GS; Leicester Univ; Cranfield Inst of Tech.
Mrs Hilary Long, former teacher, contested Bristol NW 1983. Founder mbr, SDP; former chmn, Bristol NW SDP; area chmn, Bristol SDP, 1984; mbr, SDP national cmte, 1984-87; arrangements cmte, CSD; area organiser, Nat Fed of Consumer Gps, 1972-74; member, BBC W of England Advisory Cmte, 1973-77; SW Gas Consumers Cl, 1977-83. B Nov 19 1936; ed Alice Ottley Sch, Worcester; Northampton HS; Wimbledon HS; Queen Mary Coll, London Univ; Froebel Inst, Roehampton.
Mr Glenn Vowles, science and maths teacher. B Jan 8 1962; ed Merrywood Boys' Sch; Trowbridge Tech Coll; Bristol Univ. NUT.

BRISTOL WEST — No change

Electorate	%Turnout		72,357	75.0%	**1987**	73,190	70.7%	**1983**
*Waldegrave, W.A. (C)			24,695	45.5%	-3.6%	25,400	49.1%	(C)
Ferguson, G.R.P. (L/All)			16,992	31.3%	+1.9%	15,222	29.4%	(L/All)
Georghiou, Mrs M.C. (Lab)			11,337	20.9%	+1.4%	10,094	19.5%	(Lab)
Dorey, Mrs G.A. (Grn)			1,096	2.0%	+0.3%	872	1.7%	(Eco)
Ralph, Ms V. (Comm)			134	0.2%		142	0.3%	(Ind)
C to L/All swing 2.7%			54,254	C maj 7,703 14.2%		51,730	C maj 10,178 19.7%	

Mr William
Waldegrave

Mr William Waldegrave became a Minister of State at the Department of Environment in 1985 holding responsibilities since Jun 1987 for housing and planning; Under Sec of State for Environment, 1983-85; Under Sec of State for Education and Science, 1981-83. Elected in 1979. Mbr, Central Policy Review Staff, Cabinet Office, 1971-73; on political staff at No 10 Downing Street, 1973-74; head of Mr Edward Heath's political office, 1974-75. With GEC Ltd, 1975-81. B Aug 15 1946; ed Eton; Corpus Christi, Oxford (Pres of Union and of Cons Assocn) and Harvard (Kennedy Fellow in Politics). Fellow of All Souls, Oxford, 1971-78, and since 1979.
Mr George Ferguson, architect, contested seat 1983. Mbr, Bristol City Cl, 1973-79. B Mar 22 1947; ed Rottingdean Sch, Sussex; Wellington Coll; Bristol Univ.
Ms Mary Georghiou, mbr, nat Lab women's cmte; 1987- ; chair, Bristol Lab women's cl; sec, Bristol W LP. B Jan 16 1946.
Dr Gundula Dorey, probation officer, contested Bristol NE 1979; Bristol E 1983. Co-chmn, Cl of Green Pty, 1987. B May 11 1942. NAPO.
Ms Veronica Ralph, unemployed. Mbr, W of England CP dist cmte. B Mar 25 1961.

BROMSGROVE — No change

Electorate	%Turnout		69,494	76.4%	**1987**	66,146	75.1%	**1983**
*Miller, H.D. (C)			29,051	54.7%	-1.5%	27,911	56.2%	(C)
Ward, J.D. (Lab)			12,366	23.3%	+2.6%	10,736	21.6%	(SDP/All)
Cropp, D.L. (SDP/All)			11,663	22.0%	+0.3%	10,280	20.7%	(Lab)
						716	1.4%	(Other)
C to Lab swing 2.0%			53,080	C maj 16,685 31.4%		49,643	C maj 17,175 34.6%	

Mr Hilary Miller

Mr Hilary (Hal) Miller, company director and consultant; a vice-chmn,Conservative Party, since 1984 with responsibilities for campaign organization and specialist services. Elected in 1983; MP for Bromsgrove and Redditch, Feb 1974-83; contested Bromsgrove in 1971 by-election and Barrow-in-Furness, 1970. B Mar 6, 1929; ed Eton, Merton Coll, Oxford, and London Univ. Jt chmn, all-pty motor industry group, since 1979. Director, Broadway Industrial Services Ltd and other companies; consultant to Glynwed Ltd. With Colonial Service in Hongkong, 1955-68. Fellow of the Economic Development Inst of World Bank. PPS to Secretary of State for Defence, 1979-81, to Chancellor of Duchy of Lancaster, 1981, to Mr John Gummer, Minr of State for Employment, and chmn of Cons Pty, 1984.
Mr Joe Ward, social worker. B Jun 2 1941; ed Holyrood Senior Sec, Glasgow; Co-op Coll, Loughborough; Selly Oak Coll, Birmingham. Was exec mbr and senior auditor, Lab Pty.
Mr David Cropp, head of special unit, Bartley Green Sch, Birmingham. Wyvern area SDP gen sec, 1984-86. B Aug 16 1946; ed Reading Sch; Birmingham and Warwick Univs.

BROXBOURNE — No change

Electorate %Turnout	70,631	75.2%	**1987**	67,387	74.0%	**1983**
*Roe, Mrs M.A. (C)	33,567	63.2%	+4.4%	29,328	58.8%	(C)
Yates, Ms E. (L/All)	10,572	19.9%	-3.9%	11,862	23.8%	(L/All)
Parry, P. (Lab)	8,984	16.9%	+0.5%	8,159	16.4%	(Lab)
				502	1.0%	(Other)
L/All to C swing 4.1%	53,123	C maj 22,995 43.3%		49,851	C maj 17,466 35.0%	

Mrs Marion Roe

Mrs Marion Roe was appointed an Under Secretary of State for Environment in Jun 1987. Elected in 1983; contested Barking, 1979. PPS to Mr John Moore, as Secretary of State for Transport, 1986-87, to Mr David Mitchell, Minister of State for Transport, 1986, and to Under Secretaries of State for Transport, 1985-86. Mbr, Select Cmte on Agriculture, 1983-85; sec, Cons back-bench horticulture cmte, 1983-85; jt sec, Cons back-bench organization cmte, 1985. B Jul 15 1936; ed Bromley HS; Croydon HS; English Sch of Languages, Vevey. Vice-pres, Women's Nat Cancer Control Campaign, since 1985; patron, UK nat cmte for UN Development Fund for Women, since 1985. Sponsored Prohibition of Female Circumcision Act 1985. Mbr, Bromley BC, 1975-78; GLC, 1977-86; BBC General Advisory Cl, 1986- ; IBA London advisory cmte, 1978-81; SE Thames Reg HA, 1980-84; Greater London area Cons local govt advisory cmte, 1978-82. Freeman, City of London.
Ms Eunice Yates, lecturer; business consultant. Director, Research Associates (Brentwood) Ltd. Fought Ilford S Oct 1974. B Apr 14 1944; ed N Manchester GS; Reading Univ.
Mr Philip Parry, lecturer in law. B Aug 10 1949; ed Coventry Poly; Warwick Univ. NATFHE.

BROXTOWE — No change

Electorate %Turnout	71,780	79.2%	**1987**	69,760	76.5%	**1983**
*Lester, J.T. (C)	30,462	53.6%	+0.1%	28,522	53.5%	(C)
Fleet, K. (Lab)	13,811	24.3%	+3.0%	13,444	25.2%	(L/All)
Melton, K.M. (L/All)	12,562	22.1%	-3.1%	11,368	21.3%	(Lab)
C to Lab swing 1.4%	56,835	C maj 16,651 29.3%		53,334	C maj 15,078 28.3%	

Mr James Lester

Mr James Lester was Under Secretary of State for Employment, 1979-81; mbr, Select Cmte on Foreign Affairs, since 1982. Founder mbr and current chmn, CARE (Conservative Action to Revive Employment). Parliamentary consultant to Direct Selling Assocn, Assocn of First Div Civil Servants and BAT Industries. Chmn, Cons back-bench employment cmte, 1983. Opposition whip, 1975-79. Elected for this seat 1983; MP for Beeston, 1974-83; contested Bassetlaw, 1968 by-election and 1970. B May 23 1932; ed Nottingham HS. Vice-chmn, all-pty gp on overseas development. Mbr, Notts CC, 1967-74. Delegate, Cl of Europe and WEU, 1974-75.
Mr Kenneth Fleet, chartered accountant, company director and secretary. B Nov 11 1932; ed Wycombe GS. Director, Bertrand Russell Peace Foundation and sec, Russell Press. Sec, Institute For Workers' Control. Former chm, Nottinghamshire Lab Pty; vice-chmn, Broxtowe CLP. ASTMS.
Mr Keith Melton, senior lecturer in international marketing, contested this seat 1983, Lincoln 1979 and Nottingham in 1984 Euro election. B Jun 10 1947; ed North Kesteven GS; UMIST.

BUCKINGHAM — No change

Electorate %Turnout	70,036	78.3%	**1987**	62,758	77.1%	**1983**
*Walden, G.G.H. (C)	32,162	58.6%	+1.7%	27,552	56.9%	(C)
Burke, C.M. (L/All)	13,636	24.9%	-3.2%	13,584	28.1%	(L/All)
Groucutt, M. (Lab)	9,053	16.5%	+1.5%	7,272	15.0%	(Lab)
L/All to C swing 2.5%	54,851	C maj 18,526 33.8%		48,408	C maj 13,968 28.9%	

Mr George Walden

Mr George Walden was Under Secretary of State for Education and Science 1985-87, as Minister for Higher Education. Former diplomat; principal private secretary to Lord Carrington and Dr David Owen, 1978-81; at British Mission, Peking, 1967-70; FCO, 1970-73; British Embassy in Paris, 1974-78; Fellow of Harvard Univ, 1981-82; head of policy planning, Foreign and Commonwealth Office, 1982-83. Elected in 1983. B Sep 15 1939; ed Latymer Upper Sch and Jesus Coll, Cambridge; postgraduate at Moscow Univ. PPS to Secretary of State for Education and Science, 1984-85; mbr, Select Cmte on Education and Science and the Arts, 1983-85. Former consultant to Samuel Montagu and Co Ltd.
Mr Martin Burke, teacher of business studies, was mbr, Hereford DC, 1979-84, being dep chmn, housing, 1982-83, and planning, 1983-84. B Jul 11 1953; ed Hereford HS; St Paul's Coll of Ed; Open Univ. NUT.
Mr Martyn Groucutt, teacher, contested the seat 1983. Mbr, Newcastle North CLP executive cmte; general management cmte, Northumbria Euro CLP and Monmouth CLP; vice chmn, Buckingham CLP. B Jul 24 1949; ed West Bromwich GS; Univ of Wales; Durham Univ. NUT.

BURNLEY — No change

Electorate %Turnout	65,956	78.8%	**1987**	66,542	76.3%	**1983**
*Pike, P.L. (Lab)	25,140	48.4%	+8.6%	20,178	39.7%	(Lab)
Elletson, H. (C)	17,583	33.8%	-4.4%	19,408	38.2%	(C)
Baker, R.H. (SDP/All)	9,241	17.8%	-4.3%	11,195	22.0%	(L/All)
C to Lab swing 6.5%	51,964	Lab maj 7,557 14.5%		50,781	Lab maj 770 1.5%	

Mr **Peter Pike** was elected in 1983, and joined the Select Cmte on the Environment in 1985; jt vice-chmn, PLP environment cmte, 1985- ; vice-chmn, PLP anti-apartheid gp. Production worker (Inspection), 1973-83. B Jun 26 1937; ed Hinchley Wood county sec sch; Kingston Tech Coll. Mbr, Merton and Morden UDC, 1962-63; Burnley BC, 1976-84, being Lab gp ldr, 1980-83. With Mullard (Simonstone) Ltd, 1973-83; Lab Pty organiser and agent, 1963-73; Twinings Tea, 1962-63; Midland Bank, 1954-62. GMBATU (shop steward, 1976-83). Mbr, Nat Trust, since 1974.
Mr **Harold Elletson,** journalist and publisher. Mbr, Lancashire CC, 1984- . B 1960; ed Eton; Exeter and Voronezh Univs. Co-founder of magazine *Lancaster Now.* Fluent in Russian.
Mr **Ronald Baker,** lecturer and marketing and training consultant, fought Bolton West 1983. Chmn, Bolton area SDP, 1981-83, and area cmte mbr, 1983-86. B Dec 24 1935; ed St Edward's GS, Liverpool; York Univ, Toronto; Lakeshore Teachers' Coll, Toronto; Keele Univ, Staffs. NATFHE.

Mr Peter Pike

BURTON — No change

Electorate %Turnout	73,252	78.5%	**1987**	71,849	75.9%	**1983**
*Lawrence, I.J. (C)	29,160	50.7%	-0.4%	27,874	51.1%	(C)
Heptonstall, D. (Lab)	19,330	33.6%	+3.8%	16,227	29.8%	(Lab)
Hemsley, K.A. (L/All)	9,046	15.7%	-3.4%	10,420	19.1%	(L/All)
C to Lab swing 2.1%	57,536	C maj 9,830 17.1%		54,521	C maj 11,647 21.4%	

Mr **Ivan Lawrence, QC,** has been on the Select Cmte on Foreign Affairs since 1983; mbr, Jt Select Cmte on Consolidation of Statutes, since 1974; Select Cmte on Social Services and Employment, 1974-79. Elected in Feb 1974; contested Peckham, 1966 and 1970. B Dec 24 1936; ed Brighton, Hove and Sussex GS; Christ Church, Oxford. Asst Recorder, 1983- . Chmn, Burton-on-Trent Artisan Dwelling Co Ltd. Vice-chmn, Cons back-bench home affairs cmte, 1982- , and legal cmte, 1979- . Chmn, all-pty anti-flouridation cmte, 1978- . Sec, all-pty cmte for release of Soviet Jewry, 1977- ; vice-chmn, Euro Interparliamentary Conference for Soviet Jewry, 1980- ; treas, Cons Friends of Israel parly group; mbr, Board of Deputies of British Jews; Cl of Justice, 1980- ; Cl, Statute Law Soc, 1985- ; W Midlands Cons Cl, 1985- . Vice-pres, Fed of Cons Students, 1981-83. Hon Pres, Nat Assocn of Approved Driving Instructors. Chmn, Burton Breweries Charitable Trust, 1982- .
Mr **Dennis Heptonstall,** lecturer. B May 3 1935. Mayor, Burton-on-Trent, 1980-81. Mbr, Burton DC 1973-83. Vice-chmn, Storham Housing Assn hostel for homeless young people. NATFHE.
Mr **Kenneth Hemsley,** a retired senior lecturer in teacher education, fought Eccles 1983. Occasional consultant-tutor to management and staff of youth training schemes. Mbr, Cheshire CC, Congleton BC, Congleton TC. B Feb 24 1926; ed Bridgnorth GS; Kirkby Coll of Ed; Manchester Univ.

Mr Ivan Lawrence

BURY NORTH — No change

Electorate %Turnout	67,961	82.5%	**1987**	66,065	79.6%	**1983**
*Burt, A.J.H. (C)	28,097	50.1%	+4.6%	23,923	45.5%	(C)
Crausby, D. (Lab)	21,186	37.8%	-2.4%	21,131	40.2%	(Lab)
Vasmer, D. (L/All)	6,804	12.1%	-2.2%	7,550	14.4%	(L/All)
Lab to C swing 3.5%	56,087	C maj 6,911 12.3%		52,604	C maj 2,792 5.3%	

Mr **Alistair Burt,** solicitor and consultant, has been PPS since 1985 to Mr Kenneth Baker at DoE and DES. Jt sec, Cons back-bench energy cmte, 1983-85; sec, North West Cons MPs, 1984- ; Parly Christian Fellowship, 1984- ; mbr, all-pty textile and paper cmtes. Elected in 1983. B May 25 1955; ed Bury GS; St John's Coll, Oxford. President, Oxford Univ Law Society, 1976. Mbr, Haringey BC, 1982-84, and Cons spokesman on community affairs.
Mr **David Crausby,** turner and full-time AEU convenor at Bolton engineering works of Beloit Walmsley. Mbr, Bury MDC 1979- ; former Bury rep on AMA. B Jun 17 1946.
Mr **David Vasmer** is political secretary for Assocn of Liberal Cllrs. Mbr, Liverpool City Cl, 1980-82. B Sep 2 1955; ed Kimbolton Sch, Cambridgeshire; Univ of Kent, Canterbury.

Mr Alistair Burt

BURY SOUTH — No change

Electorate %Turnout	65,039	79.7%	**1987**	64,827	76.1%	**1983**
*Sumberg, D.A.G. (C)	23,878	46.1%	+2.0%	21,718	44.0%	(C)
Boden, D. (Lab)	21,199	40.9%	+4.4%	17,998	36.5%	(Lab)
Eyre, D.A. (SDP/All)	6,772	13.1%	-6.5%	9,628	19.5%	(SDP/All)
C to Lab swing 1.2%	51,849	C maj 2,679 5.2%		49,344	C maj 3,720 7.5%	

Mr David Sumberg

Mr David Sumberg, solicitor and consultant partner, is parliamentary consultant to Northern Independent Bookmakers Assocn; adviser to Jackson and Lowe Ltd. Elected in 1983; fought Manchester, Wythenshawe, 1979. PPS to Solicitor-General, 1986- ; member, Jt Select Cmte with Hse of Lords on Statutory Instruments; sec, Cons back-bench food and drink industries sub-cmte. B Jun 2 1941; ed Tettenhall Coll, Wolverhampton; Coll of Law, London. Mbr, Manchester City Cl, 1982-84. Jt hon sec, Cons Friends of Israel parly gp, 1986. Former mbr, exec and cl, Manchester Youth and Community Service. Fellow, Industry and Parliament Trust.
Mr Derek Boden, electrical engineer for ICI and former merchant seaman radio officer. Mbr, Bury Cl 1972- ; B May 26 1937. ASTMS.
Mr Derek Eyre, probation officer. Chmn, Bury area SDP, 1986- ; Stoke-on-Trent area SDP, 1983-85; sec, Stoke Alliance cmte, 1983-85. B Jul 12 1952; ed sec mod sch. NAPO.

BURY ST EDMUNDS — No change

Electorate %Turnout	76,619	74.1%	**1987**	72,875	72.3%	**1983**
*Griffiths, Sir Eldon (C)	33,672	59.3%	+0.3%	31,081	59.0%	(C)
Harland, Sir Reginald (SDP/All)	12,214	21.5%	-6.9%	14,959	28.4%	(SDP/All)
Greene, C.L. (Lab)	9,841	17.3%	+4.7%	6,666	12.6%	(Lab)
Wakelam, Ms I.M.J. (Grn)	1,057	1.9%				
SDP/All to C swing 3.6%	56,784	C maj 21,458 37.8%		52,706	C maj 16,122 30.6%	

Sir Eldon Griffiths

Sir Eldon Griffiths has been parliamentary adviser to Police Fed of England and Wales since 1974 (also 1966-70) and of N Ireland since 1981. An Opposition spokesman on Europe, 1975-76; on trade and industry, 1974-75; Under Secretary of State for Environment and Minister for Sport, 1970-74; Parliamentary Sec, Ministry of Housing and Local Govt, 1970. Returned at 1964 by-election. Company director; adviser to Samuel Montagu Bank; consultant to Nat Caravan Cl and to Fed of Scale and Weighing Machine Manufacturers. B May 25 1925; ed Ashton GS; Emmanuel Coll, Cambridge. Chmn, Anglo-Iranian and Anglo-Polish parly groups; Indo-British Assocn. In Cons Research Dept, 1963-64. Chief European correspondent, *Washington Post,* 1961-63; editor, *Newsweek* magazine, 1956-63.
Sir Reginald Harland, Air Marshal; engineering and management consultant, fought this seat 1983. Mbr, CSD, 1982-85, and various cmtes. Consultant to Short Brothers plc, Belfast. B May 30 1920; ed Summerfields, Oxford; Stowe; Trinity Coll, Cambridge. Mbr, BIM cl, 1974-79 and 1981-86. Fellow, Royal Soc of Environmental Engineers (Pres, 1977-78).
Mr Christopher Greene, freelance political researcher, working for Mr George Foulkes, a Labour foreign affairs spokesman. B Jul 22 1954; ed Edinburgh Univ. TGWU.
Ms Julia Wakelam, solicitor. B May 23 1952; ed Sacred Heart Convent, Barnes; Ursuline Convent, Wimbledon; Ashby de la Zouch GS; Hull Univ.

CAERNARFON — No change

Electorate %Turnout	45,661	78.0%	**1987**	44,147	78.6%	**1983**
*Wigley, D.W. (Pl C)	20,338	57.1%	+4.4%	18,308	52.7%	(Pl C)
Aubel, F.F.E. (C)	7,536	21.2%	+0.1%	7,319	21.1%	(C)
Rhys Williams, D. (Lab)	5,632	15.8%	-3.6%	6,736	19.4%	(Lab)
Parsons, J.H. (L/All)	2,103	5.9%	-0.9%	2,356	6.8%	(L/All)
C to Pl C swing 2.2%	35,609	Pl C maj 12,802 36.0%		34,719	Pl C maj 10,989 31.7%	

Mr Dafydd Wigley

Mr Dafydd Wigley, president of Plaid Cymru, 1981-84. Won the seat, Feb 1974; contested Merioneth, 1970. Mbr, Select Cmte on Welsh Affairs, 1983- ; vice-chmn, all-pty social services support gp, 1985- ; mbr, all-party disablement group; sponsored Disabled Perons Act 1981; pres, Spastic Soc of Wales, 1985- ; vice-pres, Wales Cl for the Disabled. Awarded Grumshaw Memorial Award (1982) by Nat Fed of the Blind. An industrial economist; financial controller, Hoover Ltd, 1971-74; chief cost accountant and financial planning manager, Mars Ltd, 1967-71; on finance staff, Ford Motor Company, 1964-67. Mbr, Merthyr BC, 1972-74. B Apr 1 1943; ed Caernarfon GS; Rydal Sch, Colwyn Bay; Manchester Univ. Mbr, Nat Cmte for Electoral Reform; chmn, all-pty HoC reform gp, 1983- . ASTMS.
Mr Felix Aubel, Lampeter Univ researcher, was runner-up to Labour as the SDP/All candidate at Cynon Valley in the 1984 by-election and in 1983. B Sep 21 1960; ed Rhydfelen Welsh Medium Comprehensive Sch; St David's Univ Coll, Lampeter; Univ Coll, Cardiff.
Mr David Rhys Williams, teacher. Incoming Pres, Dyfedd NUT. Community cllr. Aged 39.
Mr John Parsons, solicitor and part-time town clerk, contested Ogmore 1983, Merioneth 1979. B Apr 19 1930; ed Machynlleth GS; Liverpool Univ.

CAERPHILLY — No change

Electorate %Turnout	64,154	76.5%	1987	63,479	74.5%	1983
*Davies, R. (Lab)	28,698	58.4%	+12.8%	21,570	45.6%	(Lab)
Powell, M.E. (C)	9,531	19.4%	-0.2%	10,017	21.2%	(L/All)
Butlin, M.G. (L/All)	6,923	14.1%	-7.1%	9,295	19.7%	(C)
Whittle, L.G. (Pl C)	3,955	8.1%	-5.5%	6,414	13.6%	(Pl C)
C to Lab swing 6.5%	49,107	Lab maj 19,167 39.0%		47,296	Lab maj 11,553 24.4%	

Mr Ronald Davies

Mr Ronald Davies, an Opposition whip, was further education adviser, Mid-Glamorgan CC, 1974-83; tutor-organiser, WEA, 1970-74, teacher, 1968-70. Elected in 1983. B Aug 6 1946; ed Bassaleg GS, Portsmouth Poly and Univ Coll of Wales, Cardiff. Mbr, Bedwas and Machen UDC and Rhymney Valley DC, 1969-84. NUPE sponsored.
Mr Michael Powell has his own driving school and music business. Mbr, Bridgend TC, 1979- (Mayor, 1984-85); Ogwr BC, 1979-83; Laleston Community Cl, 1979-85. B May 23 1948; Bridgend Boys' GS-Tech Sch; Exeter Univ. Equity and Driving Instructors' Assocn.
Mr Mike Butlin works for a computer manufacturer. Membership sec and constituency rep to reg pty exec and Euro constituency. Membership sec, Lloyd George Soc. B Jan 23 1942; ed Kingston Coll, Surrey. Mbr, British Computer Soc.
Mr Lindsay Whittle, housing officer, fought this seat 1983. Vice-chmn, S Wales Housing Assocn branch of Nalgo. Mbr, Rhymni Valley DC, 1976- ; Mid-Glamorgan CC, 1977-81; and Penyrheol Community Cl, 1985- . B Mar 24 1953; ed Caerffili Boys' GS.

CAITHNESS AND SUTHERLAND — No change

Electorate %Turnout	31,279	73.6%	1987	30,871	75.4%	1983
*Maclennan, R.A.R. (SDP/All)	12,338	53.6%	+1.6%	12,119	52.0%	(SDP/All)
Hamilton, R.L. (C)	3,844	16.7%	-5.9%	5,276	22.7%	(C)
Byron, A. (Lab)	3,437	14.9%	+0.7%	3,325	14.3%	(Lab)
MacGregor, K. (SNP)	2,371	10.3%	-0.7%	2,568	11.0%	(SNP)
Mowat, W.A. (Ind L)	686	3.0%				
Planterose, B. (Grn)	333	1.4%				
C to SDP/All swing 3.8%	23,009 SDP/All maj 8,494 36.9%			23,288 SDP/All maj 6,843 29.4%		

Mr Robert Maclennan

Mr Robert Maclennan, Alliance spokesman on agriculture and fisheries in the election team; SDP spokesman on home and legal affairs and N Ireland, 1983- , on Scotland, 1982-83, and on agriculture and fisheries, 1982-83. Mbr, nat steering cmte, SDP. Won seat for Lab in 1966; resigned in 1981 and joined SDP, retaining seat in 1983. Mbr, PAC, 1979- ; Estimates Cmte, 1967-69. Under Sec for Prices and Consumer Protection, 1974-79. An Opposition spokesman on foreign affairs, 1980-81; on Scotland, 1970-71, and on defence, 1971-72. Barrister. B Jun 26 1936; ed Glasgow Acad; Balliol Coll, Oxford; Trinity Coll, Cambridge; Columbia Univ, New York.
Mr Robert Hamilton, retired chartered accountant. B Aug 13 1921; ed Glasgow Acad.
Mr Allan Byron, fitter with the Atomic Energy Authority at Dounreay. B Apr 11 1950; ed Weymouth GS; Vale of Leven Acad; Thurso Tech Coll. AEU.
Mr Kerr MacGregor, lecturer in energy engineering; consultant on solar energy. B Jul 14 1940; ed Edinburgh and Strathclyde Univs. Chmn, Moorfoot Community Cl.
Mr Bernard Planterose, artist and ecologist. Warden for Royal Soc for Protection of Birds at two islands off Wester Ross since 1979. B Jun 10 1956; ed Eastbourne Coll, Sussex; Edinburgh Univ.

CALDER VALLEY — No change

Electorate %Turnout	73,398	81.1%	1987	71,309	78.5%	1983
*Thompson, D. (C)	25,892	43.5%	-0.1%	24,439	43.7%	(C)
Chaytor, D.M. (Lab)	19,847	33.4%	+6.4%	16,440	29.4%	(L/All)
Shutt, D.T. (L/All)	13,761	23.1%	-6.2%	15,108	27.0%	(Lab)
C to Lab swing 3.3%	59,500	C maj 6,045 10.2%		55,987	C maj 7,999 14.3%	

Mr Donald Thompson

Mr Donald Thompson was appointed Parliamentary Secretary, Ministry of Agriculture, Fisheries and Food in 1986; a Lord Commissioner of the Treasury (Govt whip), 1983-86; an asst Govt whip, 1981-83. Elected for this seat 1983; MP for Sowerby, 1979-83; contested it in both 1974 elections and Batley and Morley, 1970. Farmer and owner of contract butchering firm, 1952-74; director, 1979-86, and managing director, 1974-79, Armadillo Plastics, glass fibre manufacturers. B Nov 13 1931; ed Hipperholme GS. Mbr, West Riding CC, 1967-74; W Yorkshire CC, 1974-75; Calderdale MBC, 1975-79. Chmn, Cons Candidates' Assocn, 1972-74. Sec, Cons back-bench urban and new town affairs cmte, 1979-80.
Mr David Chaytor, senior lecturer. B Aug 1949. Calderdale cllr.
Mr David Shutt, chartered accountant, contested this seat 1983, Sowerby 1979, twice in 1974 and 1970. Mbr, Calderdale MBC, 1973- ; Mayor of Calderdale, 1982-83. B Mar 16 1942; ed Pudsey GS.

CAMBRIDGE — No change

Electorate %Turnout	69,336	78.0%	**1987**	67,018	75.2%	**1983**
*Rhodes James, R.V. (C)	21,624	40.0%	-1.5%	20,931	41.5%	(C)
Williams, Mrs S.V.T.B. (SDP/All)	16,564	30.6%	+0.9%	14,963	29.7%	(SDP/All)
Howard, C.J. (Lab)	15,319	28.3%	+0.1%	14,240	28.2%	(Lab)
Wright, Ms M.E. (Grn)	597	1.1%			286	0.6% (Loony Socy)
C to SDP/All swing 1.2%	54,104	C maj 5,060 9.4%		50,420	C maj 5,968 11.8%	

Mr Robert Rhodes
James

Mr Robert Rhodes James, historian, biographer, publisher and business consultant, was elected at 1976 by-election. Unpaid chmn, Buchan and Enright, publishers, 1982- ; chmn, History of Parliament Trust, 1983-. Mbr, Commons Services Cmte, 1983-. B Apr 10 1933; ed Sedbergh; Worcester Coll, Oxford. Asst clerk, House of Commons, 1955-61; senior clerk, 1961-64. Fellow, All Souls Coll, Oxford, 1964-68 and 1979- ; director, Inst for Study of International Organization, Sussex Univ, 1968-73; principal officer, exec office, UN Sec General, 1973-76. PPS, FCO ministers, 1979-82; Cons liaison officer for higher and further ed, 1979-85 (resigned) and since Sep 1986.

Mrs Shirley Williams, President of the SDP, 1982- ; one of the four joint leaders on its formation in 1981. Professorial Fellow, Policy Studies Inst, 1979-. SDP MP for Crosby, 1981-83; Lab MP for Hertford and Stevenage, Feb 1974-79, and for Hitchin, 1964-74. Sec of State for Education and Science, 1976-79; Sec of State for Prices and Consumer Protection, 1974-76, and also Paymaster General from Apr 1976; Minr of State, Home Office, 1969-70; Minr of State for Ed and Science, 1967-69; Parly Sec, Min of Labour, 1966-67. B Jul 27 1930; ed Summit Sch, Minnesota; St Paul's Sch, Hammersmith; Somerville Coll, Oxford; Columbia Univ, New York. Mbr, Lab Pty NEC, 1970-81.

Dr Christopher Howard, teacher. Mbr, Cambridge City Cl, 1979-87. B Mar 19 1952; ed Barry Boys' Comprehensive Sch; Bristol Univ; Peterhouse, Cambridge. NUT.

Ms Margaret Wright, poet and writer. B Feb 20 1940; ed Heaton HS, Newcastle; Bedford Coll, London Univ; Dept of Ed, Oxford Univ.

CAMBRIDGESHIRE NORTH EAST — C gain

Electorate %Turnout	74,231	77.4%	**1987**	69,894	76.3%	**1983**
Moss, M.D. (C)	26,983	47.0%	+6.2%	26,936	50.5%	(L/All)
*Freud, C.R. (L/All)	25,555	44.5%	-6.0%	21,741	40.8%	(C)
Harris, R.J. (Lab)	4,891	8.5%	-0.2%	4,625	8.7%	(Lab)
L/All to C swing 6.1%	57,429	C maj 1,428 2.5%		53,302	L/All maj 5,195 9.7%	

Mr Malcolm Moss

Mr Malcolm Moss, financial services company director, has served on Wisbech TC, 1979-87; Fenland DC, 1983-87; Cambridgeshire CC, 1985-87. Chmn, Mandrake Gp plc; chmn and managing director, Mandrake (Insurance and Finance Brokers) Ltd. B Mar 6 1943; ed Audenshaw GS; St John's Coll, Cambridge. Member, Fens Business Enterprise Trust; trustee, Wisbech Angles Theatre; vice-pres, Wisbech RFC Club and Wisbech Cricket and Hockey Club.

Mr Clement Freud was Liberal spokesman on education and on the arts and broadcasting, 1977-87; Alliance spokesman on arts, broadcasting and recreation in election team. MP for this seat, 1983-87; for Isle of Ely, 1973-83. Writer (former sports writer, cookery editor and columnist), broadcaster and lecturer. Rector of Dundee Univ, 1974-80. B Apr 24 1924; ed Dartington Hall and St Paul's Sch. NUJ, Equity. Sponsored Official Information Bill in 1978-79 session. Director, March Concrete Products Ltd; consultant to Grand Metropolitan Hotels. Was apprenticed to Dorchester Hotel and trained at Martinez Hotel, Cannes. Talk show broadcaster on food; appeared in award winning petfood TV commercial.

Mr Ron Harris, team leader with Cambridgeshire CC social services, contested this seat 1983. Mbr, Fenland DC, 1980-87. B Jul 12 1934; ed John Clare Sec Mod, Northampton.

CAMBRIDGESHIRE SOUTH EAST — No change

Electorate %Turnout	73,216	76.5%	**1987**	66,885	74.2%	**1983**
Paice, J.E.T. (C)	32,901	58.8%	+1.2%	28,555	57.6%	(C)
Lee, P.C. (SDP/All)	15,399	27.5%	-2.3%	14,791	29.8%	(SDP/All)
Ling, T.G. (Lab)	7,694	13.7%	+1.1%	6,261	12.6%	(Lab)
SDP/All to C swing 1.8%	55,994	C maj 17,502 31.3%		49,607	C maj 13,764 27.7%	

Mr James Paice

Mr James Paice is general manager and executive director of small company providing training, recruitment and management development services. Fought Caernarvon in 1979. B Apr 24 1949; ed Framlingham Coll, Suffolk; Writtle Agricultural Coll, Essex. Mbr, Suffolk Coastal DC, 1976-87 (cl chmn, 1982-83).

Mr Peter Lee, an area community education officer, was area SDP sec, Cambridgeshire, 1981-84. Mbr, CSD, 1981- ; SDP education policy gp; Cambridgeshire CC, 1985- (dep ldr and finance spokesman, Alliance gp). B May 16 1940; ed Latymer Upper Sch, Hammersmith; Keble Coll, Oxford. NATFHE.

Mr Tom Ling, lecturer. B July 16 1956; ed Cambridge and Essex univs. Mbr, Cambridge CC, 1986- (chmn, public health cttee). Has been chmn of Lab branch and dist parties and constituency sec. NATFHE.

CAMBRIDGESHIRE SOUTH WEST · No change

Electorate %Turnout	81,658	77.7%	**1987**	76,228	75.9%	**1983**
*Grant, Sir Anthony (C)	36,622	57.7%	+1.5%	32,521	56.2%	(C)
Nicholls, D.C. (L/All)	18,371	29.0%	-3.3%	18,654	32.2%	(L/All)
Billing, Ms J. (Lab)	8,434	13.3%	+1.7%	6,703	11.6%	(Lab)
L/All to C swing 2.4%	63,427	C maj 18,251 28.8%		57,878	C maj 13,867 24.0%	

Sir Anthony Grant was Under Secretary of State for Industrial Development, DTI, 1972-74; Under Secretary of State for Trade, DTI, 1970-72; Parliamentary Secretary, Board of Trade, 1970. Pres, Guild of Experienced Motorists. Elected for this seat 1983; MP for Harrow Central, 1964-83; contested Hayes and Harlington, 1959. Vice-chmn, Cons Party, with responsibilities for candidates, 1974-76. Company director and business consultant; adviser to Guild of Business Travel Agents, Barclays Bank plc and Bowring UK Ltd. B May 29 1925; ed St Paul's Sch and Brasenose Coll, Oxford. Freeman, City of London; Master of Guild of Freemen. Mbr, exec, 1922 Cmte, and chmn, Cons back-bench trade cmte, 1979-83. Opposition whip, 1966-70. Mbr, UK delegation to Cl of Europe (chmn of its economic cmte, 1980-84). Mbr, Select Cmte on Foreign Affairs, 1980-83.
Mr Derek Nicholls, lecturer in land economy, Cambridge Univ. Contested the seat 1983. B Apr 8 1939; ed Helston GS; Cambridge Univ.
Ms Judi Billing, teacher. Mbr, North Herts DC, 1980- (Dep ldr, :ab gp). B Feb 15 1951. School governor. NATFHE.

Sir Anthony Grant

CANNOCK AND BURNTWOOD · No change

Electorate %Turnout	68,137	79.8%	**1987**	66,188	77.4%	**1983**
*Howarth, J.G.D. (C)	24,186	44.5%	+3.5%	20,976	40.9%	(C)
Roberts, G.E. (Lab)	21,497	39.5%	+2.6%	18,931	36.9%	(Lab)
Stanley, N. (L/All)	8,698	16.0%	-6.1%	11,336	22.1%	(SDP/All)
Lab to C swing 0.5%	54,381	C maj 2,689 4.9%		51,243	C maj 2,045 4.0%	

Mr Gerald Howarth, international banker with Standard Chartered Bank from 1981, and a director, Richard Unwin International Ltd, since 1983, was elected in 1983. With Bank of America International, 1971-77; European Arab Bank, 1977-81. Mbr, Select Cmte on Parliamentary Commissioner for Administration, 1987- . B Sep 12 1947; ed Haileybury and ISC Junior Sch; Bloxham Sch, Banbury; Southampton Univ. Mbr, Hounslow BC, 1982-83. Jt sec, Cons back-bench aviation cmte, 1983- ; holds private pilot's licence. Parly consultant, Electric Cable Makers Confed.
Mr Gwilym Roberts was MP for Cannock, Feb 1974-83, and contested this seat in 1983; MP for Bedfordshire South, 1966-70; contested Conway 1964, Ormskirk 1959. B Aug 7 1928; ed Brynefail GS and Univ of Wales. Industrial consultant on computer methods, market and industrial research. Vice-pres, Inst of Statisticians, since 1978. PPS to DTI ministers, 1976-79. Former adviser to NATFHE.
Mr Neil Stanley is an NHS manpower planning officer. Mbr, Cannock Chase DC, 1978- (cl ldr, 1982-83); Staffordshire CC, 1985- . B Jun 11 1952; ed King Edward VI Sch, Stafford. Nalgo since 1972.

Mr Gerald Howarth

CANTERBURY · No change

Electorate %Turnout	76,062	74.0%	**1987**	73,464	70.0%	**1983**
Brazier, J.W.H. (C)	30,273	53.8%	-2.6%	29,029	56.5%	(C)
Purchese, J. (L/All)	15,382	27.3%	+1.5%	13,287	25.8%	(L/All)
Keen, Ms L.A. (Lab)	9,494	16.9%	+1.5%	7,906	15.4%	(Lab)
Dawe, S. (Grn)	947	1.7%	-0.2%	962	1.9%	(Eco)
White, Miss J.M. (ICN)	157	0.3%		226	0.4%	(Ind)
C to L/All swing 2.1%	56,253	C maj 14,891 26.5%		51,410	C maj 15,742 30.6%	

Mr Julian Brazier is a management consultant to industry; project manager with HB Maynard, management consultants. Fought Berwick-upon-Tweed in 1983. B Jul 24 1953; ed Wellington Coll, Berkshire; Brasenose Coll, Oxford. Chmn (1974) and former treas, Oxford Univ Cons Assocn. Former capt in TA. Mbr, Bow Gp. Has held party chmnship of Queen's Park Ward, Westminster North, and Christchurch branch, Streatham. Mbr, Friends of Westminster Cathedral. Marathon runner, as member of Frome Harriers.
Mr John Purchese runs a printing business, being a director of A and J Purchese Ltd; film sound recordist, 1953-70. Contested this seat 1983 and 1979. B Feb 21 1925; ed Steyning GS; Ardingly Coll, Sussex. In ACTT from 1947. Sec, East Bridge Deanery Synod. Chaired various road pressure groups, including A2 Group for 14 years, lobbying for Bridge bypass.
Ms Linda Keen, senior lecturer in local govt. B Oct 9 1947; ed Kent Univ. Former social worker, teacher, journalist. CAB worker. NATFHE.
Mr Steven Dawe, bookseller, contested Kent East in 1984 Euro election. Asst manager, Canterbury City Cl's community programme, 1984-85. B Jan 25 1956; ed Crypt Sch, Gloucester; Kent Univ.

Mr Julian Brazier

CARDIFF CENTRAL | No change

Electorate %Turnout	52,980	77.6%	**1987**	53,815	72.1%	**1983**
*Grist, I. (C)	15,241	37.1%	-4.4%	16,090	41.4%	(C)
Jones, J.O. (Lab)	13,255	32.3%	+8.1%	12,638	32.6%	(L/All)
German, M.J. (L/All)	12,062	29.4%	-3.2%	9,387	24.2%	(Lab)
Caiach, Ms S.M. (Pl C)	535	1.3%	-0.5%	704	1.8%	(Pl C)
C to Lab swing 6.2%	41,093	C maj 1,986 4.8%		38,819	C maj 3,452 8.9%	

Mr Ian Grist

Mr Ian Grist has served on the Select Cmte on MPs Interests since 1984 and the Select Cmte for Welsh Affairs, 1981-83, and since 1986; mbr, Select Cmte on Violence in the Family, 1977-79. Elected for this seat 1983; MP for Cardiff North, Feb 1974-83; contested Aberavon, 1970. PPS, Secretary of State for Wales, 1979-81. Information officer, Welsh Cons Party Office, 1963-74; Cons Research Dept, 1970-74. B Dec 5, 1938; ed Repton and Jesus Coll, Oxford. Mbr, Court of Governors, Univ of Wales, since 1983; Univ of Wales Inst of Science and Tech, since 1983. Chmn, Cons West African Affairs Cmte, since 1977; sec, Parly Friends of Welsh National Opera; vice-chmn, Assocn of Cons Clubs, 1978-82.
Mr Jonathan Jones, biology teacher. B Apr 19 1954; ed Ysgol Gyfun Rhydfelin; Norwich Univ; Univ Coll, Cardiff. Pres, Mid-Glamorgan NUT.
Mr Michael German, leader of Alliance gp on Cardiff City Cl to which he was elected in 1983, fought this seat in 1983 and Cardiff North, 1979 and Oct 1974. Teacher. Treas, Octavia Trust. B May 8 1945; ed St Illtyd's Coll, Cardiff; St Mary's Coll, London; Open Univ; Bristol Poly. NAS/UWT.
Dr Sian Caiach, orthopaedic surgeon. B Sep 8 1957; ed Gowerton primary schs; Hall Balk Sch, Barnsley; Charing Cross Hosp Medical Sch, London. MPU. ASTMS.

CARDIFF NORTH | No change

Electorate %Turnout	54,704	81.0%	**1987**	53,377	77.3%	**1983**
*Jones, G.H. (C)	20,061	45.3%	-1.8%	19,433	47.1%	(C)
Tarbet, S.H. (Lab)	11,827	26.7%	+6.7%	12,585	30.5%	(SDP/All)
Jeremy, A.W. (SDP/All)	11,725	26.5%	-4.0%	8,256	20.0%	(Lab)
Bush, Ms E.M. (Pl C)	692	1.6%	-0.8%	974	2.4%	(Pl C)
C to Lab swing 4.3%	44,305	C maj 8,234 18.6%		41,248	C maj 6,848 16.6%	

Mr Gwilym Jones

Mr Gwilym Jones, insurance broker, was elected in 1983. Director, Bowring Wales Ltd. Mbr, Select Cmte on Welsh Affairs, 1983- ; Cardiff City Cl, 1969-72 and 1973-83. B 1947; ed London and S Wales. Vice-pres, Kidney Research Unit for Wales Foundation, 1986- ; former chmn, S Wales Public Passenger Transport Operators; founder chmn, Friendship Force in Wales, 1978-81. Sec, Welsh Cons MPs, 1984- . Parliamentary election agent, Cardiff South East, Feb and Oct 1974.
Mr Stephen Tarbet, head of economics and business studies, Stanwell Comprehensive Sch, Penarth. B Oct 23 1954; ed Cantonian HS, Cardiff; Univ of Wales, Swansea; Cardiff colls. Sec, South Glamorgan and Cardiff West Lab Parties; chmn, Canton branch. GMBTU; NUT; pres, S Glamorgan NUT, 1986-87.
Mr Anthony Jeremy, solicitor, contested the seat 1983. Mbr, CSD; S Glamorgan CC, 1985- . B May 5 1936; ed Cardiff HS; Fitzwilliam Coll, Cambridge.
Mrs Eluned Bush, senior careers officer. Mbr, Pl Cymru nat cl; constituency sec; former nat exec mbr. B Mar 10 1944; ed Ferndale GS; Exeter and Reading Univs; Univ Coll, Cardiff.

CARDIFF SOUTH AND PENARTH | No change

Electorate %Turnout	58,714	76.4%	**1987**	59,520	71.0%	**1983**
Michael, A.E. (Lab)	20,956	46.7%	+5.5%	17,448	41.3%	(Lab)
Neale, G.J.J. (C)	16,382	36.5%	+0.6%	15,172	35.9%	(C)
Randerson, Mrs J.E. (L/All)	6,900	15.4%	-5.5%	8,816	20.9%	(L/All)
Edwards, Ms S.A. (Pl C)	599	1.3%	-0.3%	673	1.6%	(Pl C)
				165	0.4%	(Other)
C to Lab swing 2.4%	44,837	Lab maj 4,574 10.2%		42,274	Lab maj 2,276 5.4%	

Mr Alun Michael

Mr Alun Michael, community education officer. Mbr, Cardiff City Cl, 1973- (chief whip, Lab gp; chmn, finance cmte; vice-chmn, economic development cmte); Cardiff Trades Cl; bd of Cardiff and Vale Enterprise. Chmn, Butetown and Grangetown Citizens Advice Bureau. Journalist on *South Wales Echo*, 1966-71. B Aug 22 1943; Colwyn Bay GS; Keele Univ.
Mr Gareth Neale, college lecturer, contested Cardiff West 1974; Brecon and Radnor 1970, and Rhondda West by-election, 1967. Mbr, South Glamorgan CC, 1973- (ldr Cons gp). B Apr 12 1935; ed Barry GHS; UCW Wales, Aberystwyth; London Univ.
Mrs Jenny Randerson, further ed lecturer in business studies. Mbr Cardiff City Cl 1983- . Alliance energy spokesman for Wales. B May 26 1948; ed Wimbledon HS; Bedford Coll and Inst of Ed, London Univ. Chmn, Octavia Trust; magistrate; NATFHE.
Ms Sian Edwards, freelance translator and scriptwriter, fought this seat 1983. B Aug 30 1948; ed Ysgol Gymraeg St Fransis, Y Barri; Carmarthen Girls' GS; UCW, Aberystwyth.

CARDIFF WEST — Lab gain

Electorate %Turnout	57,363	77.8%	**1987**	58,538	69.6%	**1983**
Morgan, H.R. (Lab)	20,329	45.5%	+11.9%	15,472	38.0%	(C)
*Terlezki, S. (C)	16,284	36.5%	-1.5%	13,698	33.6%	(Lab)
Drake, R.G. (SDP/All)	7,300	16.3%	-9.1%	10,388	25.5%	(SDP/All)
Keelan, P.J. (Pl C)	736	1.6%	-0.4%	848	2.1%	(Pl C)
				352	0.9%	(Other)
C to Lab swing 6.7%	44,649	Lab maj 4,045 9.1%		40,758	C maj 1,774 4.4%	

Mr **Rhodri Morgan,** industrial analyst, is adviser to Labour Party economic planning commit- tees in Wales; former economic development officer for S Glamorgan CC; research and development officer in Welsh Office and DTI (1966-74); and EEC representative in Wales. B Sep 29 1939; ed state schs in Cardiff; Oxford and Harvard Univs. TGWU.
Mr **Stefan Terlezki,** former management consultant, was MP for this seat, 1983-87; contested Cardiff South East, Feb and Oct 1974, and South Wales in Euro elections, 1979. Mbr, Select Cmte on Welsh Affairs, 1983-87; jt sec, all-pty parly war crimes gp. B Oct 29 1927; ed Cardiff HS and Cardiff Coll of Food Technology and Commerce. Mbr, Cardiff City Cl, 1968-83; South Glamorgan CC, 1973-85; S Wales Police Authority, 1975-80; Welsh jt ed cmte, 1975-85; central cl, CPC. Chmn, Cardiff City FC, 1975-77.
Mr **Geoffrey Drake,** educational publisher with business interests also in audio-visual com- munications, fought Walsall South in 1966 for Lab. Chmn, Cardiff West SDP; mbr, CSD. B Apr 6 1937; ed Tonypandy GS; Swansea Univ.
Mr **Peter Keelan,** librarian at Univ Coll, Cardiff. Ed in Newport; London Univ; Welsh Coll of Librarianship. AUT local sec; represents PlC trade union section on pty nec.

Mr Rhodri Morgan

CARLISLE — No change

Electorate %Turnout	55,053	78.8%	**1987**	54,515	76.4%	**1983**
Martlew, E.A. (Lab)	18,311	42.2%	+4.7%	15,618	37.5%	(Lab)
Hodgson, W.G. (C)	17,395	40.1%	+2.8%	15,547	37.3%	(C)
Hunt, R.S. (SDP/All)	7,655	17.7%	-7.5%	10,471	25.1%	(SDP/All)
C to Lab swing 1.0%	43,361	Lab maj 916 2.1%		41,636	Lab maj 71 0.2%	

Mr **Eric Martlew,** personnel manager; unpaid director, Inward, promotion organization for NW England. Chmn, Carlisle CLP, 1980-85; mbr, Cumbria CC 1973- (chmn 1981-83); East Cumbria HA, 1981- ; Cumbria AHA, 1975-81 (chmn 1977-79); Carlisle City Cl, 1972-74. B Jan 3 1949; ed Harraby Sch, Carlisle. TGWU.
Mr **William Hodgson,** farmer and wine merchant, contested East Kilbride in 1979.B Aug 25 1937; ed Edinburgh Academy.
Mr **Richard Hunt,** area careers officer, Cumbria CC, contested the seat 1983. Founder mbr, SDP; mbr, CSD. B Mar 30 1942; ed in Australia.

Mr Eric Martlew

CARMARTHEN — No change

Electorate %Turnout	65,252	82.9%	**1987**	63,468	82.1%	**1983**
Williams, A.W. (Lab)	19,128	35.4%	+3.8%	16,459	31.6%	(Lab)
Richards, R. (C)	14,811	27.4%	-2.0%	15,305	29.4%	(C)
Edwards, H.T. (Pl C)	12,457	23.0%	-4.0%	14,099	27.0%	(Pl C)
Jones, G.G. (SDP/All)	7,203	13.3%	+2.3%	5,737	11.0%	(SDP/All)
Oubridge, G.E. (Grn)	481	0.9%	+0.2%	374	0.7%	(Eco)
				154	0.3%	(Other)
C to Lab swing 2.9%	54,080	Lab maj 4,317 8.0%		52,128	Lab maj 1,154 2.2%	

Mr **Alan W Williams** is a college lecturer in environmental science. B Dec 21 1945; ed Carmarthen GS; Jesus Coll, Oxford. Sec, Carmarthen Lab Pty, 1981-84; election agent, 1983. NATFHE.
Mr **Roderick Richards,** Welsh broadcaster and businessman. B Mar 12 1947; ed Llandovery Coll; UCW, Swansea. Director, Contemporary Systems Design. Member, Welsh Consumer Cl. Held Royal Marines short service commission, 1969-71.
Mr **Hywel Teifi Edwards,** lecturer, extra mural dept, Univ Coll, Swansea; lecturer and author on Welsh literature and the Eisteddfod. Mbr, Dyfed CC. Ed Univ Coll, Aberystwyth.
Mr **Gwynoro Jones,** asst education officer, W Glamorgan CC, was Lab MP for Carmarthen, 1970-74. Contested Gower by-election 1982. Lab Pty PRO in Wales, 1969-70; PPS to Roy Jenkins (Home Sec), 1974; first chmn, SDP Cl for Wales, 1982-85; mbr, SDP nat cmte 1981-84; jt chmn, Alliance cmte for Wales, 1983- ; chmn, SDP Cl for Wales policy cmte, 1985- ; mbr, Cl of Europe and WEU, 1974; CSD, 1982- . B Nov 21 1942; ed Gwenddraeth GS; Cardiff Univ.
Mr **G Oubridge,** Community cllr for Llanfynydd. Aged 35.

Mr Alan Williams

CARRICK, CUMNOCK AND DOON VALLEY — No change

Electorate %Turnout	56,360	75.8%	1987	55,925	74.3%	1983
*Foulkes, G. (Lab)	25,669	60.1%	+8.6%	21,394	51.5%	(Lab)
Stevenson, S. (C)	8,867	20.7%	-3.4%	10,024	24.1%	(C)
Ali, Mrs M. (SDP/All)	4,106	9.6%	-8.3%	7,421	17.9%	(SDP/All)
Calman, C.D. (SNP)	4,094	9.6%	+3.1%	2,694	6.5%	(SNP)
C to Lab swing 6.0%	42,736	Lab maj 16,802 39.3%		41,533	Lab maj 11,370 27.4%	

Mr George Foulkes, an Opposition spokesman on foreign and Commonwealth affairs 1985- ; spokesman on European and Community affairs, 1983-85. Won this seat 1983; MP for South Ayrshire, 1979-83; contested Edinburgh, Pentlands, Oct 1974, and Edinburgh West, 1970. B Jan 21 1942; ed Keith GS, Banffshire; Haberdashers' Aske's Sch; Edinburgh Univ. Member, Select Cmte on Foreign Affairs, 1981-83; delegate, Cl of Europe, 1979-81. Jt chmn, all-pty pensioners' group, 1983- ; sec-treas, 1979-83. Mbr, exec cmte, Scottish Lab Pty, 1981- ; Edinburgh Corpn, 1970-75; Lothian Reg Cl, 1974-79 (chmn, ed cmte). Apex.

Mr Struan Stevenson, farmer and company director, is ldr of Tory gp on Cosla. Mbr, Girvan DC, 1972-75; Kyle and Carrick DC, 1974- (Ldr of cl and chmn of policy and resource gp). B Apr 4 1948; ed Strathallan Sch; West of Scotland Agric Coll. Director, J & R Stevenson Ltd; Richard Demarco Gallery Ltd.

Mrs Maryum Ali, student taking a post-graduate diploma in social work at Glasgow Univ.

Mr Charles Calman, teacher, fought Kilmarnock and Loudoun 1983; Glasgow, Kelvingrove, Oct 1974; Ayr, Feb 1974. Mbr, SNP nat cl and nat assembly. B May 16 1928; ed Robert Douglas Memorial Sch, Scone; Langside CFE, Glasgow; Craigie Coll of Ed, Ayr. EIS.

Mr George Foulkes

CARSHALTON AND WALLINGTON — No change

Electorate %Turnout	69,120	75.0%	1987	68,682	72.0%	1983
*Forman, F.N. (C)	27,984	54.0%	+2.6%	25,396	51.3%	(C)
Grant, J.D. (SDP/All)	13,575	26.2%	-3.4%	14,641	29.6%	(SDP/All)
Baker, Mrs J.G. (Lab)	9,440	18.2%	+0.7%	8,655	17.5%	(Lab)
Steel, R.W. (Grn)	843	1.6%	0.0%	784	1.6%	(Eco)
SDP/All to C swing 3.0%	51,842	C maj 14,409 27.8%		49,476	C maj 10,755 21.7%	

Mr Nigel Forman was elected for this seat in 1983; MP for Carshalton, 1976-83; contested Coventry NE, Feb 1974. Jt vice-chmn, Cons finance cmte, 1983- ; vice-chmn, all-pty social science and policy cmte, 1984- ; member, Select Cmte on Science and Technology, 1976-79; sec, Cons back-bench cmtes on education, 1976-79, and energy, 1977-79. B Mar 25 1943; ed Dragon Sch, Oxford; Shrewsbury Sch; New Coll, Oxford; Coll of Europe, Bruges; Harvard and Sussex Univs. Asst director, Cons Research Dept, 1975-76; head of its external affairs section, 1974-75; and its European desk officer, 1971-74. Information officer, CBI, 1970-71. Member, Royal Inst of International Affairs; International Inst for Strategic Studies.

Mr John Grant, journalist, has been head of communications, EETPU, since 1984. Fought Islington North 1983 for SDP; Lab MP for Islington East 1970-74; and for Islington Central, Feb 74-83, resigning from Lab Pty in Oct 1981. SDP spokesman on industry, 1981-83. Labour Under Secretary of State for Employment, 1976-79; Under Secretary of State for Overseas Development, 1974-76; Parly Sec, Civil Service Dept, 1974. B Oct 16 1932; ed Stationers' Company's Sch, Hornsey. NUJ; EETPU.

Mr Nigel Forman

Mrs Joan Baker contested the seat 1983. B May 29 1932; ed GS. Former clerk. Mbr, Wandsworth Cl, 1962-64; Lambeth Cl, 1964-68.

CASTLE POINT — No change

Electorate %Turnout	65,992	75.1%	1987	64,023	71.3%	1983
*Braine, Sir Bernard (C)	29,681	59.9%	+1.4%	26,730	58.5%	(C)
Bastow, Ms A.P. (SDP/All)	10,433	21.1%	-3.7%	11,313	24.8%	(SDP/All)
Deal, W.A. (Lab)	9,422	19.0%	+2.3%	7,621	16.7%	(Lab)
SDP/All to C swing 2.5%	49,536	C maj 19,248 38.9%		45,664	C maj 15,417 33.8%	

Sir Bernard Braine, the Father of the House, is a member of the Cmte on Privileges; chmn, Select Cmtes on Overseas Aid and Development, 1970-74. Elected for this seat 1983; MP for Essex South East, 1955-83; for Billericay, 1950-55; contested Leyton East, 1945. Consultant, Police Superintendents Assocn of England and Wales and London. Visiting Professor, Baylor Univ, Texas, US. Opposition spokesman on foreign and Commonwealth affairs and overseas development, 1967-70; Parly Sec, Min of Health, 1962-64; Under Sec of State, Commonwealth Relations Office, 1961-62; Parly Sec, Min of Pensions and Nat Insurance, 1960-61. B Jun 24 1914; ed Hendon Cty Sch. Mbr, exec cmtr, UK branch, CPA. Governor, Commonwealth Inst, 1968-81, trustee since 1981. Chmn, Nat Cl on Alcoholism, 1973-82; British-German parly gp, 1970- ; British-Greek gp, 1979- ; all-pty Pro Life gp; all-pty Misuse of Drugs Cmte; and UK chapter, Soc of International Development, 1976-83. Vice-chmn, all-pty Human Rights parly gp. Pres, Soc for Defence of Unjustly Prosecuted; British Solidarity with Poland Campaign. FRSA, 1971.

Ms Anne Bastow, teacher, contested the seat 1983. Mbr, CSD, 1983-86; vice chair, South Sussex SDP, 1982-86. B Aug 20 1951; ed Carlton Univ, Ottawa.

Mr Bill Deal, unemployed. B Jul 30 1932; ed sec mod.

Sir Bernard Braine

CEREDIGION AND PEMBROKE NORTH | No change

Electorate %Turnout	63,141	76.5%	**1987**	60,523	77.8%	**1983**
*Howells, G.W. (L/All)	17,683	36.6%	-5.2%	19,677	41.8%	(L/All)
Williams, O.J. (C)	12,983	26.9%	-3.0%	14,038	29.8%	(C)
Davies, J.R. (Lab)	8,965	18.6%	+4.0%	6,840	14.5%	(Lab)
Davis, C.G. (Pl C)	7,848	16.2%	+3.3%	6,072	12.9%	(Pl C)
Wakefield, Ms M.A. (Grn)	821	1.7%		431	0.9%	(Eco)
L/All to C swing 1.1%	48,300	L/All maj 4,700 9.7%		47,058	L/All maj 5,639 12.0%	

Mr Geraint Howells, farmer, leader of Welsh Lib Pty since 1979- ; (Pres, 1974-78). Chmn, Lib by-election unit, 1987- . Alliance spokesman on Wales in election team; Lib spokesman on Wales and agriculture, 1976- . Elected for this seat 1983; MP for Cardigan, 1974-83; contested Brecon and Radnor, 1970. Mbr, Select Cmte on Welsh Affairs, 1979- . B Apr 15 1925; ed Ardwyn GS. Mbr, Cardiganshire CC, 1952-73. Welsh mbr, British Wool Marketing Bd; vice-chmn, 1971-83. Chmn, Wool Producers of Wales Ltd, 1977- .
Mr John Williams, chairman of family business and barrister. B May 17 1950; ed Harrow; Univ Coll, Oxford; Middle Temple. Mbr, Welsh Division, Inst of Directors; United Counties Agricultural Soc; Soc of Cymmrodorion.
Mr John Davies, teacher. Member, Walsall TC, 1970-74. B Jun 23 1937; ed Gwendraeth GS, Llanelli; St Luke's Coll, Exeter. NUT.
Mr Cynog Dafis, teacher, contested the seat 1983. Chmn, Dyffryn Teifi Housing Assocn. B Apr 1 1938; ed Aberavon Cty Sec Sch; Neath Boys' GS; UCW Aberystwyth.
Ms Marilyn Wakefield, describes herself as a domestic engineer, mother and politician. Contested Ceredigion and Pembroke North 1983; Mid and West Wales in 1984 Euro election. B Sep 13 1957; ed George Abbott County Comprehensive for Girls, Guildford.

Mr Geraint Howells

CHEADLE | No change

Electorate %Turnout	68,332	81.0%	**1987**	66,474	76.8%	**1983**
Day, S.R. (C)	30,484	55.1%	-0.7%	28,452	55.7%	(C)
Leah, A.B. (L/All)	19,853	35.9%	-1.5%	19,072	37.3%	(L/All)
Coffey, Ms A. (Lab)	5,037	9.1%	+2.1%	3,553	7.0%	(Lab)
L/All to C swing 0.4%	55,374	C maj 10,631 19.2%		51,077	C maj 9,380 18.4%	

Mr Stephen Day, sales executive with photographic processing laboratory, contested Bradford West 1983. Mbr, Otley Town Cl, 1975-76 and 1979-83; Leeds City Cl, 1975-80, being deputy whip and chairing education purchasing and careers advisory committees. B Oct 30 1948; ed Otley Sec Sch; Park Lane Coll, Leeds; Leeds Poly.
Mr Brian Leah, a food technologist, has been a mbr of Southport Met BC since 1973; Liberal gp ldr, 1980-84. In food industry over 30 years; employed by international cereal company. ASTMS.
Ms Ann Coffey, social worker. B Aug 31 1946. Mbr, Cheadle DC, 1984-. AHA representative. Nalgo.

Mr Stephen Day

CHELMSFORD | No change

Electorate %Turnout	82,564	82.2%	**1987**	78,849	79.4%	**1983**
Burns, S.H.M. (C)	35,231	51.9%	+4.3%	29,824	47.6%	(C)
Mole, S.G. (L/All)	27,470	40.5%	-6.5%	29,446	47.0%	(L/All)
Playford, C.E. (Lab)	4,642	6.8%	+1.7%	3,208	5.1%	(Lab)
Slade, A.C. (Grn)	486	0.7%		127	0.2%	(Ind)
L/All to C swing 5.4%	67,829	C maj 7,761 11.4%		62,605	C maj 378 0.6%	

Mr Simon Burns is policy research executive for the Institute of Directors; former director, What to Buy Ltd; personal and research assistant to Mrs Sally Oppenheim MP, 1975-80. Contested Alyn and Deeside, 1983. B Sep 6 1952; ed Christ the King Sch, Accra; Stamford Sch; Worcester Coll, Oxford. Sec, Oxford Univ Cons Assocn, 1972-75.
Mr Stuart Mole is assistant director of the Commonwealth Secretariat. Former personal assistant to Mr David Steel, the Liberal leader. Contested this seat 1983, 1979, Feb and Oct 1974. B Jan 15 1949; ed St Paul's Cathedral Choir Sch; St John's Sch, Leatherhead; Notting-ham, Oxford and London Univs. Mbr, Chelmsford BC, since 1972, being chmn, policy and resources cmte since 1983, the year he led Alliance to control cl. Former vice-chmn, Lib nat executive.
Mr Clive Playford, college lecturer, contested the seat 1983. Former social researcher with Docklands Forum and Low Pay Unit. Former BBC radio technician. B Jan 24 1953; ed Highbury Grove Sch; Essex Univ, LSE. NATFHE.

Mr Simon Burns

CHELSEA — No change

Electorate %Turnout	49,534	57.7%	**1987**	53,864	56.1%	**1983**
*Scott, N.P. (C)	18,443	64.6%	+1.3%	19,122	63.2%	(C)
Ware, Mrs J.M. (L/All)	5,124	17.9%	-5.5%	7,101	23.5%	(L/All)
Ward, D.J. (Lab)	4,406	15.4%	+2.6%	3,876	12.8%	(Lab)
Kortvelyessy, Ms N. (Grn)	587	2.1%		139	0.5%	(Ind)
L/All to C swing 3.4%	28,560	C maj 13,319 46.6%		30,238	C maj 12,021 39.8%	

Mr Nicholas Scott

Mr Nicholas Scott, Minister for Social Security and Minister for Disabled, 1987- ; Minister of State for Ireland, 1986-87; Under Secretary of State for N Ireland, 1981-86; Under Secretary of State for Employment, Jan-Feb 1974. Mbr of shadow Cabinet and chief spokesman on housing, 1974. Elected in Oct 1974; MP for Paddington South, 1966-74; contested Paddington, Feb 1974; Islington SW, 1964 and 1959. B Aug 5 1933; ed Clapham Coll. Chmn, Cons back-bench employment cmte, 1979-81. Mbr, 1922 exec cmte, 1978-81; Select Cmte on Environment, 1979-81.Pres, Greater London YCs, and Tory Reform Group. Mbr, Holborn BC, 1956-59 and 1962-65.
Mrs Jennifer Ware contested Battersea South Oct 1974. B Jan 1932; ed St Paul's Girls Sch, Hammersmith.
Mr David Ward, PLP campaigns officer. B May 12 1956; ed Bedford Coll; London Univ. Mbr, NEC sub-cmte on international affairs. NUJ.
Ms Niki Kortvelyessy, designer running a small business, represents Green Pty on CND parly and elections cmte. Mbr, coordinating team, London area pty gp; conciliation, arbitration and appeals cmte. B May 10 1947 in Budapest; ed in New Zealand.

CHELTENHAM — No change

Electorate %Turnout	79,234	78.9%	**1987**	76,068	75.9%	**1983**
*Irving, C.G. (C)	31,371	50.2%	-0.4%	29,187	50.6%	(C)
Holme, R.G. (L/All)	26,475	42.3%	+1.3%	23,669	41.0%	(L/All)
Luker, M. (Lab)	4,701	7.5%	-0.1%	4,390	7.6%	(Lab)
				479	0.8%	(Other)
C to L/All swing 0.9%	62,547	C maj 4,896 7.8%		57,725	C maj 5,518 9.6%	

Mr Charles Irving

Mr Charles Irving is consultant on public affairs for the Dowty Group; chmn, Western Travel; director, Norfolk Hotels Ltd, Irving Hotels Ltd, Chrisden Property Co Ltd and Sherborne Associates. Pres, Cheltenham and District Housing Assocn and chmn of two other housing assocns. Elected in Oct 1974; contested Bilston, 1970, and Kingswood, Feb 1974. Mbr, Cheltenham BC, 1947-74 (alderman, 1959-May 1967 and Sep 1967-74); Cheltenham DC, 1974 - ; (Freedom of borough, 1975, and Mayor of Cheltenham three times); Gloucestershire CC, 1948- ; (alderman, 1965-74); Gloucestershire AHA, 1974- . Ed Glengarth Sch, Cheltenham, and Lucton Sch, Herefordshire. Chmn, House of Commons catering sub-cmte, 1979- ; mbr, 1974- ; all-pty mental health gp. Mbr, Nat Cl for Care and Resettlement of Offenders.
Mr Richard Holme, chmn of the Constitutional Reform Centre, publisher and director of several companies. Contested this seat in 1983; Braintree. Oct 1974; and East Grinstead, 1964 and 1965 by-election. B May 27 1936; St John's Coll, Oxford. Political adviser to Mr David Steel; former president and vice-chmn of Lib Pty; member, Lib nat exec.
Mr Michael Luker, college lecturer. B Nov 28 1945; ed Cheltenham Sch of Architecture; Sir Thomas Rich's GS, Gloucester. NATFHE.

CHERTSEY AND WALTON — No change

Electorate %Turnout	71,448	75.5%	**1987**	70,210	72.5%	**1983**
*Pattie, G.E. (C)	32,119	59.5%	+1.2%	29,679	58.3%	(C)
Stapely, Ms S.K. (SDP/All)	14,650	27.2%	-0.3%	13,980	27.5%	(SDP/All)
Trace, H.G. (Lab)	7,185	13.3%	-0.2%	6,902	13.6%	(Lab)
				318	0.6%	(Other)
SDP/All to C swing 0.8%	53,954	C maj 17,469 32.4%		50,879	C maj 15,699 30.9%	

Sir Geoffrey Pattie

Sir Geoffrey Pattie was Minister for Information Technology, with the rank of Minister of State, DTI, 1984-87; Minister of State for Defence Procurement, 1983-84; Under Secretary of State for Defence Procurement, 1981-83; Under Secretary of State for Defence for the RAF, 1979-81. Elected in 1974; contested Barking, 1966 and 1970. B Jan 17 1936; ed Durham and St Catharine's Coll, Cambridge. Barrister. Member, General Synod of Church of England, 1970-75. GLC member for Lambeth, 1968-70. Mbr, PAC, 1976-79; vice-chmn (1976-78) and sec (1974-76), Cons back-bench aviation cmte; vice-chmn (1978-79) and jt sec (1975-78), Cons defence cmte. Vice-chmn, all-pty mental health gp, 1977-79.
Ms Sue Stapely, a solicitor specialising in family law, was the first woman to chair the 300 Group. Exec member, Women for Soc Dem and Soc Dem Lawyers. Hon legal advisor to CAB. Member, Law Soc; ACTT (when with BBC TV for eight years, being a former asst director on drama programmes). B Jul 11 1946; ed Haynes Sch, Haynes Park, Bedfordshire; Kingston Poly Sch of Law; Sch of Law Guildford.
Mr Harold Trace, retired college vice-principal. B Dec 13 1925; ed Birkenhead Park HS; Liverpool Univ. Former Lab Pty branch membership officer and press officer.

CHESHAM AND AMERSHAM · No change

Electorate %Turnout	71,751	77.3%	**1987**	69,980	75.9%	**1983**
*Gilmour, Sir Ian (C)	34,504	62.2%	+1.1%	32,425	61.0%	(C)
Ketteringham, A.T. (L/All)	15,064	27.1%	-4.0%	16,556	31.2%	(L/All)
Goulding, P.A. (Lab)	5,170	9.3%	+1.5%	4,150	7.8%	(Lab)
Darnbrough, Ms A.G. (Grn)	760	1.4%				
L/All to C swing 2.6%	55,498	C maj 19,440 35.0%		53,131	C maj 15,869 29.9%	

Sir Ian Gilmour

Sir Ian Gilmour was Lord Privy Seal and principal spokesman on foreign and Commonwealth affairs in the Commons, 1979-81; chief Opposition spokesman on defence, 1975-79; spokesman on N Ireland, 1974-75. Secretary of State for Defence, 74; Minister of State for Defence, 1972-74; Minister of State for Defence Procurement, 1971-72; Under Secretary of State for Defence for the Army, 1970-71. Chmn, Cons Research Dept, 1974-75. Elected in Feb 1974; MP for Norfolk Central, 1962-74. Journalist and barrister. Editor, Spectator, 1954-59. B Jul 8 1926; ed Eton; Balliol Coll, Oxford. Director, Gulf Development Co Ltd. Consultant to Robert Fraser and Partners Ltd.
Mr Andrew Ketteringham, marketing manager with TSB Gp, contested Brent North, 1979, and London NW in 1984 Euro election. Mbr, Chesham TC, 1982- ; chmn, Chesham Community Relations Cl. B Jul 15 1950; ed Lascelles Sec Mod Sch; Harrow County Boys' Sch; Hull Univ.
Mr Paul Goulding, barrister. B May 24 1960; ed Latymer Sch, Edmonton; Oxford Univ. Mbr, Soc of Lab Lawyers; Lab Campaign for Criminal Justice; Lab Housing Gp; Fabian Soc. GMBATU (MATSA).
Ms Ann Darnbrough, writer. B Apr 5 1931; ed Ellerslie, Gt Malvern.

CHESTER, CITY OF · No change

Electorate %Turnout	65,845	79.8%	**1987**	64,508	74.5%	**1983**
*Morrison, P.H. (C)	23,582	44.9%	-2.3%	22,645	47.1%	(C)
Robinson, D. (Lab)	18,727	35.6%	+7.4%	13,546	28.2%	(Lab)
Stunell, R.A. (L/All)	10,262	19.5%	-5.2%	11,874	24.7%	(L/All)
C to Lab swing 4.8%	52,571	C maj 4,855 9.2%		48,065	C maj 9,099 18.9%	

Mr Peter Morrison

Mr Peter Morrison was appointed Minister of State for Energy in Jun 1987; deputy chairman of Conservative Party since 1986; Minister of State for Industry at the DTI, 1985-86; Minister of State for State for Employment, 1983-85; Under Secretary of State for Employment, 1981-83; Lord Commissioner of the Treasury (Government whip) 1979-81; Opposition whip 1976-79. Elected in Feb 1974. Pres, Assocn of Cons Clubs; sec, North-West group of Cons MPs, 1975-76. Director, Witan Investment Company plc; former director of farming and hotel companies. B Jun 2 1944; ed Eton and Keble Coll, Oxford. Personal asst to Mr Peter Walker, 1966-67, and investment manager with Slater Walker Securities Ltd, 1968-70. Younger brother of Mr Charles Morrison, Conservative MP for Devizes.
Mr David Robinson, teacher. Dp ldr, Lab gp, Chester City Cl. B Sep 19 1946. NUT.
Mr Andrew Stunell is Councillors' Officer with Assocn of Lib Cllrs. Contested this seat, 1983 and 1979. Author of books on local govt finance and balance of power. Mbr, Chester City Cl, 1979- ; Cheshire CC, 1981- ; Alliance gp ldr, ACC. B Nov 24 1942; ed Surbiton GS; Manchester Univ; Kingston and Liverpool Polys. Nalgo, 1967-81; Staff Side, New Towns Whitley Cl, 1977-80. Baptist lay preacher.

CHESTERFIELD · No change

Electorate %Turnout	70,357	76.7%	**1987**	68,486	72.6%	**1983**
*Benn, A.N.W. (Lab)	24,532	45.5%	-2.6%	23,881	48.0%	(Lab)
Rogers, A.H. (L/All)	15,955	29.6%	+10.0%	16,118	32.4%	(C)
Grant, R.P. (C)	13,472	25.0%	-7.5%	9,705	19.5%	(L/All)
Lab to L/All swing 6.3%	53,959	Lab maj 8,577 15.9%		49,704	Lab maj 7,763 15.6%	

Mr Tony Benn

Mr Tony Benn, writer and broadcaster, was returned at the by-election in 1984. Opted for backbenches after 1979 election and then unsuccessfully contested deputy leadership of Labour Party in 1981 against Mr Healey. Mbr, Select Cmte on Privileges. Secretary of State for Energy, 1975-79; Secretary of State for Industry and Minister for Posts and Telecommunications, 1974-75; chief Opposition spokesman on trade and industry, 1970-74; Minister of Technology, 1966-70; Postmaster-General, 1964-66. MP for Bristol South East, 1950-60 and 1963-83, when he contested Bristol East. Debarred from Commons on death of his father, Viscount Stansgate, in Nov 1960, he won the by-election in May 1961, but an Election Court declared his Conservative opponent elected. He renounced his title for life under the Peerage Act and was re-elected in Aug 1963. Mbr, Lab Party NEC, 1959-60 and since 1962; chmn, 1971-72; executive cmte, Campaign Group of Labour MPs, since 1985. B Apr 3 1925; ed Westminster and New Coll, Oxford. NUJ.
Mr Tony Rogers, proprietor of self-catering apartments, contested South Hams 1983, Totnes 1979 and twice in 1974. B Apr 9 1938; ed Kingsbridge Sec Mod Sch. Mbr, Kingsbridge UDC, 1963-74; then served on Kingsbridge TC and South Hams DC (former mayor).
Mr Ronald Grant, chartered accountant and chmn of a publishing company and computer retailers. B Apr 8 1943; ed Coopers Foundation, Bow; Orange Hill GS, Edgware. Mbr, Harrow BC, 1982- (ldr of cl, 1987-).

CHICHESTER — No change

Electorate %Turnout	81,019	74.4%	**1987**	77,259	72.1%	**1983**
*Nelson, R.A. (C)	37,274	61.8%	-1.9%	35,482	63.7%	(C)
Weston, P.F. (L/All)	17,097	28.3%	+0.7%	15,365	27.6%	(L/All)
Morrison, D. (Lab)	4,751	7.9%	+0.7%	3,995	7.2%	(Lab)
Bagnall, I.F.N. (Grn)	1,196	2.0%	+0.5%	838	1.5%	(Eco)
C to L/All swing 1.3%	60,318	C maj 20,177 33.5%		55,680	C maj 20,117 36.1%	

Mr Anthony Nelson

Mr Anthony Nelson, merchant banker with N M Rothschild and Sons Ltd, 1969-73, was elected in Oct 1974; contested Leeds East, Feb 1974. B Jun 11 1948; ed Harrow; Christ's Coll, Cambridge. Consultant to European Investments and Development Ltd and to International Generics Ltd. Founder member, Nat Victims Assocn. PPS to Minister for Housing and Construction, 1979-83, and to Minister of State for Armed Forces, 1983-85. Member, Select Cmte on Science and Technology, 1975-79; sec, Cons back-bench industry cmte, 1974-75. Chmn, British-Canadian, British-Oman and British-UAE parly gps; vice-chmn, British-Saudi Arabia parly gp. Director (unpaid), Chichester Festival Theatre. Fellow, Royal Soc of Arts.
Mr Peter Weston, medical laboratory scientific officer, was agent at gen elections and a by-election, 1959-79. Mbr, Chichester City Cl, 1964-76 and 1979- ; Chichester DC, 1973- ; Mayor of Chichester, 1973-74. B Aug 15 1931; Chichester HS for Boys. Nalgo.
Mr David Morrison, fork lift driver. B Aug 2 1943; ed Midhurst Sec Mod. Has been constituency pty sec, vice chmn and agent; parish cllr.
Mr Nicholas Bagnall, self-employed remedial masseur, contested this seat 1979. Mbr, Plaistow PC, 1974- . B Dec 7 1943; ed Lancaster Royal GS; Downing Coll, Cambridge.

CHINGFORD — No change

Electorate %Turnout	56,797	76.7%	**1987**	56,228	72.7%	**1983**
*Tebbit, N.B. (C)	27,110	62.3%	+7.1%	22,541	55.1%	(C)
Williams, J.G. (L/All)	9,155	21.0%	-3.7%	10,127	24.8%	(L/All)
Cosin, Mrs M.I. (Lab)	6,650	15.3%	-2.4%	7,239	17.7%	(Lab)
Newton, Mrs E. (Grn)	634	1.5%	+0.3%	479	1.2%	(Eco)
				518	1.3%	(Other)
L/All to C swing 5.4%	43,549	C maj 17,955 41.2%		40,904	C maj 12,414 30.3%	

Mr Norman Tebbit

Mr Norman Tebbit became chairman of the Conservative Party in 1985; Chancellor of the Duchy of Lancaster, 1985-87; Secretary of State for Trade and Industry, 1983-85; Secretary of State for Employment, 1981-83; Minister of State for Industry, 1981; Under Secretary of State for Trade, 1979-81. PPS to Minister of State for Employment, 1972-73. Elected for this seat, Feb 1974; MP for Epping, 1970-74. B Mar 29 1931; ed Edmonton County GS. Served on former Select Cmte on Science and Technology; ex-chmn, Cons back-bench aviation cmte; former vice-chmn and sec, Cons back-bench housing and construction cmte; former sec, New Town MPs. Civil airline pilot, 1953-70; former elected official of Balpa. Asst director of information, NFBTE, 1975-79.
Mr John Williams, manpower planner. Mbr, Waltham Forest BC, 1982- . B Mar 22 1952; ed Highams Park Senior HS. TSSA.
Mrs Maggie Cosin, member, Camden Cl. B Jan 17 1941; ed Glasgow St Gillard's School; LSE. GMBATU. Former trade union organiser.
Mrs Elizabeth Newton, mature student. B Apr 20 1957; ed McEntee Senior HS, Walthamstow; Bush-Davies Theatre Sch, Romford; Queen Mary Coll, Univ of London. Former member of Equity and sec of CPSA sub-branch.

CHIPPING BARNET — No change

Electorate %Turnout	60,876	70.0%	**1987**	58,423	70.7%	**1983**
*Chapman, S.B. (C)	24,686	57.9%	+1.8%	23,164	56.1%	(C)
Skinner, J. (L/All)	9,815	23.0%	-3.1%	10,771	26.1%	(L/All)
Perkin, D. (Lab)	8,115	19.0%	+3.1%	6,599	16.0%	(Lab)
				747	1.8%	(Other)
L/All to C swing 2.4%	42,616	C maj 14,871 34.9%		41,281	C maj 12,393 30.0%	

Mr Sydney Chapman

Mr Sydney Chapman, a chartered architect and town and country planning consultant, has been a mbr of the Select Cmtes on Environment and House of Commons Services, since 1983. Elected for this seat in 1979; MP for Birmingham, Handsworth, 1970-Feb 1974; contested Stalybridge and Hyde, 1964. Vice-President, RIBA, 1974-75; member of council, 1972-77. Honorary mbr, Landscape Inst; Hon Fellow, Incorporated Assocn of Architects and Surveyors; Fellow, Faculty of Building. B Oct 17 1935; ed Rugby Sch; Manchester Univ. Mbr, exec cmte, Nat Union of Cons and Unionist Assocns, 1961-70; nat chmn, YCs, 1964-66. Originator of National Tree Planting Year, 1973; pres, Arboricultural Assocn, since 1983 (vice-pres, 1973-83); London Green Belt Cl, 1985- ; vice-chmn, Wildlife Link, 1985- . Non-exec director, Capital and Counties plc; parly consultant to Y J Lovell (Holdings) plc. PPS to Secretary of State for Transport, 1979-81, and to Secretary of State for Social Services, 1981-83. Chmn, Parliamentary Consultants Group, since 1980.
Mr James Skinner is an economist. Contested London North in 1984 Euro election. B Sep 8 1932; ed Eton; New Coll, Oxford; Florence Univ, Italy.
Mr Dave Perkin has spent four years post-graduate research studying nuclear physics. B Aug 7 1952; ed Oxford Univ. Mbr, CND; ASTMS.

CHISLEHURST — No change

Electorate %Turnout	55,535	75.5%	**1987**	54,567	72.7%	**1983**
*Sims, R.E. (C)	24,165	57.6%	+1.9%	22,108	55.7%	(C)
Younger-Ross, R.A. (L/All)	9,658	23.0%	-2.3%	10,047	25.3%	(L/All)
Ward, S.H. (Lab)	8,115	19.3%	+0.9%	7,320	18.4%	(Lab)
				201	0.5%	(Other)
L/All to C swing 2.1%	41,938	C maj 14,507 34.6%		39,676	C maj 12,061 30.4%	

Mr Roger Sims

Mr **Roger Sims** has been on the Select Committees on Education, Science and the Arts since 1984, and on Procedure, since 1980. A director, Inchcape International Ltd, 1981- ; consultant to Dodwell and Co Ltd for whom he worked as export manager; parly adviser to Scotch Whisky Assocn. Elected in Feb 1974; contested Shoreditch and Finsbury, 1966 and 1970. B Jan 27 1930; ed City Boys' GS, Leicester; St Olave's GS, London. PPS to Home Secretary, 1979-83. Jt sec, Cons back-bench home affairs cmte, 1976-1979; vice-chmn, Cons back-bench health and social services cmte, 1983- ; chmn, ASH parly gp, 1983- ; sec, British-Japanese parly gp, 1979- ; treas, British-Hongkong parly gp, 1983- . Member, Royal Choral Soc, 1950- ; Chislehurst and Sidcup UDC, 1956-62; central exec cmte, NSPCC, 1980- .

Mr **Richard Younger-Ross**, design consultant in architectural practice. Organising vice-chmn (1979-80) and sec gen (1980-81), NLYL; mbr, Lib Pty Cl, 1978-81; pty membership cmte, 1979-82; Home Counties candidates interviewing panel, 1979-82. B Jan 29 1953; ed Walton Boys' Sch, Walton-on-Thames; Ewell Tech Coll. Member, Howard League; Anti-Slavery Soc.

Mr **Selwyn Ward**, director of small publishing company, Optical World Ltd. Member, Bromley BC, 1982- . B May 20 1953; ed Westcliff HS for Boys; Manchester Univ.

CHORLEY — No change

Electorate %Turnout	78,541	76.9%	**1987**	72,841	79.2%	**1983**
*Dover, D.R. (C)	29,015	48.0%	-0.2%	27,861	48.3%	(C)
Watmough, A.J. (Lab)	20,958	34.7%	+4.2%	17,586	30.5%	(Lab)
Simpson, I.A. (L/All)	9,706	16.1%	-4.2%	11,691	20.3%	(SDP/All)
Holgate, A.S. (Grn)	714	1.2%	0.4%	451	0.8%	(Eco)
				114	0.2%	(Other)
C to Lab swing 2.2%	60,393	C maj 8,057 13.3%		57,703	C maj 10,275 17.8%	

Mr Den Dover

Mr **Den Dover**, a civil engineer and mbr of the Institution of Civil Engineers, has been on the Select Cmte on Transport since 1979. Elected in 1979; fought Caerphilly, Oct 1974. Director of Arcast Software Ltd; parly consultant to ASL Lane Ltd, B and R Taylor, CP Holdings. B Apr 4 1938; ed Manchester GS; Manchester Univ. Mbr, Barnet Cl, 1968-71. Pres, CTU nat engineering gp; former sec, Cons back-bench environment cmte; chmn, Cons urban affairs and new towns cmte, 1985- . Director of housing construction, GLC, 1977-79; contracts manager, Wimpey Laing, Iran, 1975-77; projects director, Capital and Counties Property Co Ltd, 1972-75; chief exec, 1971-72, dep chief exec, 1969-70, Nat Building Agency; with John Laing and Son Ltd, 1959-68.

Mr **Tony Watmough**, lecturer in general and communications studies. B Mar 27 1955; ed Wigan Tech Coll; Lancaster Univ; Bolton Tech Coll. NATFHE.

Mr **Ian Simpson**, insurance broker. Mbr, Wyre BC, 1983- ; Garstang TC, 1983- ; Mayor of Garstang, 1986-87. B Aug 9 1944; ed Clitheroe Royal GS for Boys. Rugby union coach.

Mr **Stephen Holgate**, self-employed, is a partner in offset and silk screen printing business. Contested Chorley 1983. B Jul 27 1954; ed Bridgewater Boys Sch, Worsley, Manchester. Former mbr, Sogat and Nalgo.

CHRISTCHURCH — No change

Electorate %Turnout	70,964	76.3%	**1987**	65,489	72.2%	**1983**
*Adley, R.J. (C)	35,656	65.9%	-1.2%	31,722	67.1%	(C)
McKenzie, Miss H.J. (SDP/All)	13,282	24.5%	-0.8%	11,984	25.3%	(SDP/All)
Longhurst, Ms C.E. (Lab)	5,174	9.6%	+2.0%	3,590	7.6%	(Lab)
C to SDP/All swing 0.2%	54,112	C maj 22,374 41.3%		47,296	C maj 19,738 41.7%	

Mr Robert Adley

Mr **Robert Adley**, director and marketing consultant, Commonwealth Holiday Inns of Canada Ltd, was elected for this seat in 1983; MP for Christchurch and Lymington, Feb 1974-83; MP for Bristol North East, 1970-74; contested Birkenhead, 1966, B Mar 2 1935; ed Falconbury and Uppingham. First chmn and founder mbr, Brunel Soc; mbr, cmte, National Railway Museum. Patron, SS Great Britain project. Trustee, Brunel Engineering Centre Trust. Chmn, all-pty tourism gp; all-pty publishing gp; British-Jordanian, British Hungarian and British-ASEAN parly gps. Vice-chmn, Cons back-bench transport cmte, 1975- . Mbr, nat cl, British Hotels, Restaurants and Caterers' Assocn. Director, General and Wholesale Representation Ltd, William Jacks plc and Alexander James and Dexter Ltd. Mbr, Select Cmte on Members' Interests, since 1979; Slough BC, 1966-69.

Miss **Hilary McKenzie**, public relations consultant, being account director with Malus PR, Taunton, Somerset. B Apr 2 1947; ed Notting Hill and Ealing HS (Girls' Public Day Sch Trust). Cmte mbr, Somerset area SDP. JP; NUJ.

Ms **Caralyn Longhurst**, communications lecturer. B Sep 24 1951; ed Lawnswood HS, Leeds; Bournemouth and Poole Coll CFE; Dorset Inst of HE; Southampton Univ. Mbr, Dorset Cty Service Training cmte. Exec mbr, Bournemouth and Christchurch Trades Cl.

CIRENCESTER AND TEWKESBURY — No change

Electorate %Turnout	84,071	77.9%	**1987**	80,067	74.9%	**1983**
*Ridley, N. (C)	36,272	55.4%	-1.8%	34,282	57.2%	(C)
Beckerlegge, P.T. (L/All)	23,610	36.0%	+1.9%	20,455	34.1%	(L/All)
Naysmith, J.D. (Lab)	5,342	8.2%	-0.6%	5,243	8.7%	(Lab)
Curtis, M.A. (Male OAP)	283	0.4%				
C to L/All swing 1.9%	65,507	C maj 12,662 19.3%		59,980	C maj 13,827 23.1%	

Mr Nicholas Ridley, Secretary of State for Environment, 1986- ; Secretary of State for Transport, 1983-86; Financial Secretary to the Treasury, 1981-83; Minister of State for Foreign and Commonwealth Affairs, 1979-81; Under Secretary of State for Trade, 1970-72; Under Secretary of State, Ministry of Technology, 1970. Chmn, Cons back-bench finance cmte, 1972-73, and jt vice-chmn, 1974-79. An Opposition spokesman on technology and trade, 1969-70, and on defence, 1965-66. Elected in 1959; contested Blyth, 1955. Civil engineer and former company director. B Feb 17, 1929; ed Eton and Balliol Coll, Oxford. Mbr, Royal Commission on Historical Manuscripts, 1967-79; exec cmte, Nat Trust, 1962-70; UK delegation, Cl of Europe and WEU, 1962-66.

Mr Philip Beckerlegge, solicitor, was re-elected to the Lib Pty nat exec in 1986. Contested this seat 1983 and 1979. Former constituency and regional pty chmn. Mbr, Cotswold DC, 1977-83. B Dec 20 1942; ed Tapton House GS, Chesterfield.

Mr Douglas Naysmith, medical scientist and lecturer, contested Bristol in 1979 Euro election. Mbr, Bristol City Cl, 1981- . B Apr 1 1941; ed Musselburgh Burgh Sch; George Heriot Sch, Edinburgh; Edinburgh and Yale Univs. Past international sec, British Soc for Immunology.

Mr Nicholas Ridley

CITY OF LONDON AND WESTMINSTER SOUTH — No change

Electorate %Turnout	57,428	58.2%	**1987**	67,773	51.8%	**1983**
*Brooke, P.L. (C)	19,333	57.8%	-1.3%	20,754	59.1%	(C)
Smithard, Ms J.C.G. (SDP/All)	7,291	21.8%	+0.8%	7,367	21.0%	(SDP/All)
Bush, Ms R.E. (Lab)	6,821	20.4%	+3.3%	6,013	17.1%	(Lab)
				985	2.8%	(Other)
C to SDP/All swing 1.1%	33,445	C maj 12,042 36.0%		35,119	C maj 13,387 38.1%	

Mr Peter Brooke became Paymaster General in Jun 1987; Minister of State, Treasury, 1985-87 but continues to have Treasury duties; Under Secretary of State for Education and Science, 1983-85; Lord Commissioner of the Treasury (Govt whip), 1981-83; asst Govt whip, 1979-81. Elected at 1977 by-election; contested Bedwellty, Oct 1974. B Mar 3 1934; ed Marlborough, Balliol Coll, Oxford (pres of union, 1957), and Harvard Business Sch. Vice-pres, NUS, 1955-56. Pres, Assocn of Prep Schs, 1980-83. Mbr, Camden BC, 1968-69. Former Swiss correspondent, *Financial Times*; former chmn, London firm of international management consultants. Mbr of Lloyd's.

Ms Jane Smithard, barrister; self-employed legal adviser to computer companies. Executive officer, Lord Chancellor's Dept, 1975-77; legal adviser with computer firms, 1977-84. Vice-chmn, Westminster South SDP. B May 2 1954; ed St Paul's Girls' Sch; St Mary's Hall, Brighton; Kingston Poly; Inns of Court School of Law.

Ms Ruth Bush, temporary office worker, former teacher and parly officer for Age Concern. B May 22 1946; ed Burgh Heath Meth Primary Sch, Surrey; Sutton HS; Oxford and York Univs. Former chair, Paddington Advice and Law Centre.

Mr Peter Brooke

CLACKMANNAN — No change

Electorate %Turnout	49,083	77.0%	**1987**	47,642	75.6%	**1983**
*O'Neill, M.J. (Lab)	20,317	53.7%	+8.0%	16,478	45.8%	(Lab)
Macartney, Dr A. (SNP)	7,916	20.9%	+1.9%	6,839	19.0%	(SNP)
Parker, J. (C)	5,620	14.9%	-3.2%	6,490	18.0%	(C)
Watters, Mrs A. (SDP/All)	3,961	10.5%	-6.8%	6,205	17.2%	(SDP/All)
SNP to Lab swing 3.0%	37,814	Lab maj 12,401 32.8%		36,012	Lab maj 9,639 26.8%	

Mr Martin O'Neil, former teacher and tutor. An Opposition spokesman on defence and disarmament 1984- ; a spokesman on Scotland, 1983-84. Mbr, Select Cmte on Scottish Affairs, 1979-83. Elected for this seat 1983; MP for Stirlingshire East and Clackmannan, 1979-83. B Jan 6 1945; ed Wardie Primary Sch, Trinity Acad, Heriot Watt Univ and Moray House Coll of Ed, Edinburgh. Sponsored by NGA.

Dr Allan Macartney, SNP vice-chmn (organization) 1985- ; international relations spokesman, 1983- . Social sciences staff tutor, Open Univ. Contested Tweeddale, Ettrick and Lauderdale 1983, Berwick and East Lothian 1979, and Renfrewshire West 1970. B Feb 1941; ed Elgin Acad; Tubingen, Marburg and Edinburgh Univs. AUT.

Mr James Parker, mining engineer, formerly with NCB, then consultant, now training to be a party agent. B Jul 2 1937; ed Bell-Baxter Senior Sec Sch; Heriot Watt Univ. Past member, NUM, Nacods, BACM.

Mrs Ann Watters, educational adviser. Founder mbr, SDP, with Fife area pty and Kirkcaldy branch. Mbr, Kirkcaldy DC, 1984- . B Sep 23 1926; ed St Leonard's Sch, St Andrews; Bedford Coll, London Univ. PAT.

Mr Martin O'Neil

CLWYD NORTH WEST — No change

Electorate %Turnout	66,118	75.2%	1987	62,503	73.1%	1983
*Meyer, Sir Anthony (C)	24,116	48.5%	-2.4%	23,283	51.0%	(C)
Thomas, K.L. (Lab)	12,335	24.8%	+8.5%	13,294	29.1%	(L/All)
Griffiths, O.G. (L/All)	11,279	22.7%	-6.4%	7,433	16.3%	(Lab)
Davies, R.K. (Pl C)	1,966	4.0%	+0.3%	1,669	3.7%	(Pl C)
C to Lab swing 5.5%	49,696	C maj 11,781 23.7%		45,679	C maj 9,989 21.9%	

Sir Anthony Meyer, former diplomat, won this seat in 1983; MP for Flint West, 1970-83, and for Eton and Slough, 1964-66. Mbr, Select Cmte on Welsh Affairs, 1979- .Underwriter at Lloyd's (non-active). Mbr, Chairmen's Panel, 1984- . Chmn, Franco-British parliamentary relations cmte, 1979- ; jt vice-chmn, Cons back-bench European affairs cmte, 1979-83 and since 1984; vice-chmn, Welsh Cons MPs, 1980-82 and since 1984. Trustee, Shakespeare Memorial National Theatre. B Oct 27 1920; ed Eton; New Coll, Oxford.In Foreign Services from 1946, including posts at Paris and Moscow embassies.

Mr Keith Thomas, part-time lecturer in trade union studies; retired microbiologist. Liaison officer, Clwyd CC Lab gp. B Aug 26 1929; ed Lincoln Sch and Liverpool Polytechnic. ASTMS.

Mr Gwyn Griffithss, solicitor, contested Caernarfon 1983. Vice-chmn, Welsh Lib Pty; member, Welsh Lib Pty policy cmte; Alliance cmte for Wales, 1981- . B Jul 30 1956; ed Tywyn Sch, Gwynedd; Univ of Wales, Aberystwyth. Mbr, Ct of Governors, Univ of Wales; Nat Trust.

Mr Karl Davies, Pl Cymru parly researcher since 1986. Chaired Welsh Language Soc, 1984-85. B Jul 26 1963; ed Univ Coll of Wales, Aberystwyth. TGWU.

Sir Anthony Meyer

CLWYD SOUTH WEST — Lab gain

Electorate %Turnout	58,158	81.1%	1987	55,792	77.3%	1983
Jones, M.D. (Lab)	16,701	35.4%	+8.0%	14,575	33.8%	(C)
*Harvey, R.L. (C)	15,673	33.2%	-0.6%	13,024	30.2%	(SDP/All)
Ellis, R.T. (SDP/All)	10,778	22.9%	-7.3%	11,829	27.4%	(Lab)
Jones, E.L. (Pl C)	3,987	8.5%	-0.1%	3,684	8.5%	(Pl C)
C to Lab swing 4.3%	47,139	Lab maj 1,028 2.2%		43,112	C maj 1,551 3.6%	

Mr Martyn Jones, microbiologist in the brewing industry and mbr of Institute of Biology. B Mar 1 1947; ed Grove Park GS, Wrexham; Liverpool and Trent Polys. Member, Clwyd CC, 1981- . Chmn, Clwyd Lab Pty. Area rep, TGWU.

Mr Robert Harvey, journalist. Mbr, Select Cmte on Foreign Affairs, 1984-87; Select Cmte on Welsh Affairs, 1983-84. Vice-chmn, Conservation Action to Revive Employment (CARE). MP for this seat, 1983-87; contested Caernarvon, Oct 1974, and Merioneth, 1979. B Aug 21 1953; ed Eton and Christ Church, Oxford. Consultant and writer for The Economist; asst editor, 1981-83 and staff correspondent, 1974-81. NUJ.

Mr Tom Ellis was MP for Wrexham, 1970-83, resigning from the Labour Party in 1981 to join the SDP. Pres, SDP Cl for Wales; mbr, CSD; SDP nat cmte. Contested this seat 1983, and West Flintshire, 1966. Mbr, European Parliament, 1975-79; contested Wales North in 1984 Euro election. Mining engineer. B Mar 15 1924; ed Ruabon GS; Univ Coll of N Wales; Nottingham Univ. Vice-chmn, Electoral Reform Soc. Mbr, Russell Cmte on Adult Ed.

Mr Eifion Lloyd Jones is a television producer and director. B Oct 13 1948; ed Ysgol Eifionydd, Porthmadog; Univ of Wales: Bangor and Aberystwyth.

Mr Martyn Jones

CLYDEBANK AND MILNGAVIE — No change

Electorate %Turnout	50,152	78.9%	1987	50,831	75.9%	1983
Worthington, A. (Lab)	22,528	56.9%	+12.1%	17,288	44.8%	(Lab)
Hirstwood, K. (C)	6,224	15.7%	-4.6%	9,573	24.8%	(SDP/All)
Ackland, R. (SDP/All)	5,891	14.9%	-9.9%	7,852	20.3%	(C)
Fisher, S. (SNP)	4,935	12.5%	+3.2%	3,566	9.2%	(SNP)
				308	0.8%	(Other)
C to Lab swing 8.4%	39,578	Lab maj 16,304 41.2%		38,587	Lab maj 7,715 20.0%	

Mr Tony Worthington, sociology lecturer at Jordanhill College of Education. Member, Strathclyde Reg Cl 1974- (chmn of finance); Scottish Community Ed Cl; chmn, Dumbarton and Argyll Deprivation Group; chmn, Strathclyde Community Business. Mbr, Scottish Community Education Cl, CND, Fabian Soc. B Oct 11 1941; ed City Sch, Lincoln; LSE; York and Glasgow Univs. GMBATU; Assocn of Colls of Ed in Scotland.

Mr Kenneth Hirstwood, manager, British Telecom. Mbr, Angus DC, 1983-86; Carnoustie Community Cl, 1979-83 (chmn, 1980-82); exec and finance cmtes, East Angus Cons Assoc; Carnoustie branch chmn, 1980-84. B Mar 3 1949; ed St Joseph's Coll, Dumfries. Soc of Telecom Executives.

Mr Rod Ackland, micro computer laboratory manager at Glasgow Univ, previously at Warwick Univ, contested Monklands West 1983; mbr, CSD; part-time tutor, Open Univ. B Apr 1945; ed Sussex and Oxford Univs. AUT.

Mr Stanley Fisher, teacher. B 1942; ed Aberdeen Univ.

Mr Tony Worthington

CLYDESDALE — No change

Electorate %Turnout	61,620	78.2%	**1987**	60,240	76.5%	**1983**
Hood, J. (Lab)	21,826	45.3%	+6.5%	17,873	38.8%	(Lab)
Robertson, R. (C)	11,324	23.5%	-4.7%	13,007	28.2%	(C)
Boyle, J. (SDP/All)	7,909	16.4%	-5.1%	9,908	21.5%	(SDP/All)
Russell, M. (SNP)	7,125	14.8%	+3.3%	5,271	11.4%	(SNP)
C to Lab swing 5.6%	48,184	Lab maj 10,502 21.8%		46,059	Lab maj 4,866 10.6%	

Mr Jimmy Hood

Mr Jimmy Hood, miner/coal face engineer in the Nottingham coalfield, previously at Douglas and Auchlochan collieries. Councillor for 14 years; was executive mbr, East Midlands Regional Lab Pty and in the Newark and Sherwood constituencies. A ward chmn, sec, political officer and election agent at various times. NUM branch president and secretary, 1973-84, and mbr of area political cmte. B May 16 1949; Lesmahagow higher grade sch; Coatbridge Tech Coll; Nottingham Univ WEA.
Mr Raymond Robertson, teacher, was chmn of Scottish YCs, 1982-84. Elder, Church of Scotland. B Dec 11 1959; ed Garrion Acad; Glasgow Univ; Jordanhill Coll of Ed. EIS.
Mr John Boyle, managing director of a tour operating company. B Feb 1 1952; ed Holy Cross HS; Blaus Coll, Aberdeen; Glasgow Coll of Tech.
Mr Michael Russell, executive director, Network Scotland Ltd; writer on rural and gaelic matters; founder of Celtic Film and TV Festival; chmn 'Save a Life in Scotland' campaign. Mbr, SNP publicity cmte and pty political broadcast sub-cmte; Western Isles SNP exec, 1979-82; Inverness CA exec, 1982-83. B Aug 9 1953; ed The Marr Coll, Troon; Edinburgh Univ. Sub Deacon, Episcopal Church in Scotland. TGWU.

COLCHESTER NORTH — No change

Electorate %Turnout	82,420	76.0%	**1987**	77,292	73.1%	**1983**
*Buck, Sir Antony (C)	32,747	52.3%	-0.7%	29,921	53.0%	(C)
Hayman, A. (SDP/All)	19,124	30.5%	+4.2%	14,873	26.3%	(L/All)
Green, R.A. (Lab)	10,768	17.2%	-1.2%	10,397	18.4%	(Lab)
				1,294	2.3%	(Other)
C to SDP/All swing 2.4%	62,639	C maj 13,623 21.7%		56,485	C maj 15,048 26.6%	

Sir Antony Buck

Sir Antony Buck, QC, has been chairman of the Select Committee on Parliamentary Commissioner for Administration (Ombudsman) since 1977; chmn, Cons back-bench defence cmte, since 1979; mbr, exec, 1922 Cmte, 1972 and since 1977. Non-exec director of firm of agricultural merchants. Under Secretary of State for Defence for the Royal Navy, 1972-74. Elected for this seat 1983; MP for Colchester, 1961-83. B Dec 19 1928; ed King's Sch, Ely, and Trinity Hall, Cambridge. Chmn, exec cmte of Cons Lawyers, 1979. Mbr, Assembly of Cl of European Union, 1975-77. Sec, Cons home affairs cmte, 1964-70; vice-chmn, 1970-72; chmn, 1972. PPS to Attorney General, 1963-64.
Mr Alan Hayman, television producer, is a founder mbr of SDP who has held various area party posts in NE Essex. Mbr, Essex CC, 1985- ; Essex Police Authority, 1985- . B Oct 12 1948; ed Brentwood Sch; Essex and London Univs. NUJ.
Mr Rod Green, teacher at comprehensive sch. B May 29 1943. Dist cllr 1978- ; planning spokesman, Lab gp. NUT.

COLCHESTER SOUTH AND MALDON — No change

Electorate %Turnout	84,392	75.3%	**1987**	79,582	73.3%	**1983**
*Wakeham, J. (C)	34,894	54.9%	+1.3%	31,296	53.6%	(C)
Stevens, J.W. (SDP/All)	19,411	30.6%	-2.2%	19,131	32.8%	(SDP/All)
Bigwood, Mrs S. (Lab)	9,229	14.5%	+0.9%	7,932	13.6%	(Lab)
SDP/All to C swing 1.8%	63,534	C maj 15,483 24.4%		58,359	C maj 12,165 20.8%	

Mr John Wakeham

Mr John Wakeham joined the Cabinet in Jun 1987 as Lord Privy Seal and Leader of the Commons; Parliamentary Secretary to the Treasury and Government Chief Whip, 1983-87; Minister of State, Treasury, 1982-83; Under Secretary of State for Industry, 1981-82; Lord Commissioner of Treasury (Govt whip), 1981; asst Govt whip, 1979-81. Chartered accountant and former company director. Elected for this seat 1983; MP for Maldon, Feb 1974-83; contested Wandsworth, Putney, 1970, and Coventry East, 1966. B Jun 22 1932; ed Charterhouse. Former sec, Cons small businesses cmte. Mbr of Lloyd's.
Mr John Stevens, retired philatelic auctioneer, contested this seat 1983 and Cleveland 1964. Founder mbr, SDP; has served on CSD; NE area SDP chmn, 1982-83. Mbr, Colchester BC, 1984- . B Aug 22 1932; ed Kingsbury GS, London; Magdalene Coll, Cambridge.
Mrs Sally Bigwood, local govt officer. B Jun 27 1947; ed Swindon Coll; Reading Univ; Chancery Lane Coll of Law.

COLNE VALLEY   C gain

Electorate %Turnout	70,199	80.1%	**1987**	69,634	76.2%	**1983**
Riddick, G.E.G. (C)	20,457	36.4%	+2.5%	21,139	39.8%	(L/All)
Priestley, N.J. (L/All)	18,780	33.4%	-6.4%	17,993	33.9%	(C)
Harman, J.A. (Lab)	16,353	29.1%	+3.3%	13,668	25.8%	(Lab)
Mullany, M.R. (Grn)	614	1.1%		260	0.5%	(Ind)
L/All to C swing 4.5%	56,204	C maj 1,677 3.0%		53,060	L/All maj 3,146 5.9%	

Mr Graham Riddick, sales manager, won this seat in 1987. B 1955; ed Stowe; Warwick Univ.
Mr Nigel Priestly, a solicitor, is a mbr of Meltham Town Council. Chairman, Colne Valley Liberal Assocn, 1984-85; has acted as local and general election agent for party. B Sep 22 1952; ed Lowerhouses Junior Sch; King James GS, Almondbury, Huddersfield; Warwick Univ; Law Soc Coll, Chester. Lay reader and parochial church cl member of St James Church, Meltham Hills.
Mr John Harman, teacher. Leader, Kirklees MDC 1986- ; mbr, West Yorkshire CC, 1981-86 (finance chmn); vice chmn, Huddersfield CLP, 1982-83; chmn, Huddersfield/Colne Valley coordinating, cmte 1983-84; mbr, W Yorks pty exec, 1981-86. B Jul 30 1950; ed St George's Coll, Weybridge; Manchester Univ; Holly Bank Coll, Huddersfield. NUT.
Mr Mark Mullany, countryside warden. Mbr, Greater Manchester Cl, 1985-86; Manchester City Cl, 1986- . B Jun 15 1960; ed Huddersfield New Coll; Gonville and Caius Coll, Cambridge. Nalgo.

Mr Graham Riddick

CONGLETON   No change

Electorate %Turnout	68,172	80.5%	**1987**	63,897	76.9%	**1983**
*Winterton, Mrs J.A. (C)	26,513	48.3%	-0.3%	23,895	48.7%	(C)
Brodie-Browne, I.M. (L/All)	18,544	33.8%	+2.4%	15,436	31.4%	(L/All)
Knowles, M. (Lab)	9,810	17.9%	-2.0%	9,783	19.9%	(Lab)
C to L/All swing 1.3%	54,867	C maj 7,969 14.5%		49,114	C maj 8,459 17.2%	

Mrs Ann Winterton was elected in 1983. Wife of Mr Nicholas Winterton, who became MP for the adjoining former Macclesfield constituency in 1971. B Mar 6 1941; ed Erdington GS for Girls. Mbr, West Midlands Cons Women's Advisory Committee, 1969-71. Joint Master, South Staffordshire Hunt, 1959-64.
Mr Iain Brodie-Browne, a charity director, contested Southport 1983 and Warrington 1979. B Jan 16 1953; ed Blackdown HS; City of London Poly.
Mr Mike Knowles, teacher. B Mar 18 1937. Sec, Cheshire Socialist Educnl Assoc. Former NUT shop steward and sec, Hackney Trades Cncl. Founder, Save the Walthamstow Marshes Campaign, 1979-82.

Mrs Ann Winterton

CONWY   No change

Electorate %Turnout	52,862	76.9%	**1987**	51,567	76.4%	**1983**
*Roberts, I.W.P. (C)	15,730	38.7%	-3.0%	16,413	41.7%	(C)
Roberts, J.R. (L/All)	12,706	31.2%	+0.4%	12,145	30.8%	(L/All)
Williams, Mrs E. (Lab)	9,049	22.3%	+5.2%	6,731	17.1%	(Lab)
Davies, R. (Pl C)	3,177	7.8%	-2.6%	4,105	10.4%	(Pl C)
C to L/All swing 1.7%	40,662	C maj 3,024 7.4%		39,394	C maj 4,268 10.8%	

Mr Wyn Roberts became Minister of State for Wales in Jun 1987; Under Secretary of State for Wales, 1979-87; Opposition spokesman on Welsh affairs, 1974-79; PPS to Secretary of State for Wales, 1970-74. Elected in 1983; MP for Conway, 1970-83. B Jul 10 1930; ed Beaumaris Cty Sch; Harrow; University Coll, Oxford. Journalist; formerly Welsh Controller, TWW (with company, 1957-68), and a former programme exec of Harlech Television. Jt sec, Cons backbench broadcasting cmte, 1974-79. Mbr, Court of Governors, Nat Library of Wales, Nat Musum of Wales, and Univ Coll of Wales, Aberystwyth, and of Gorsedd, Royal Nat Eisteddfod of Wales.
The Rev Roger Roberts, Methodist minister, was president, Welsh Liberal Party, 1981-84. Contested this seat 1983 and 1979. Mbr, Aberconwy BC, since 1976. B Oct 23 1935; ed John Bright GS, Llandudno; Univ Coll, Bangor; Handsworth Coll, Birmingham.
Mrs Betty Williams was elected to Gwynedd CC in 1976. Mbr, Lab Parliamentary Assoc. Sec, constituency pty. Age 42.
Mr Rhodri Davies has been planning solicitor with Anglesey BC since 1979; lecturer at Bristol Poly, 1971-79; articled with Anglesey County, 1969-71. B Nov 25 1947; ed Friars GS, Bangor; Univ of Wales, Aberystwyth. Mbr, Nat Union of Local Authority Secretaries.

Mr Wyn Roberts

COPELAND — No change

Electorate %Turnout	54,695	81.3%	**1987**	54,208	78.2%	**1983**
*Cunningham, J.A. (Lab)	20,999	47.2%	+3.0%	18,756	44.2%	(Lab)
Toft, A.R.M. (C)	19,105	43.0%	+3.1%	16,919	39.9%	(C)
Colgan, E.T. (SDP/All)	4,052	9.1%	-6.7%	6,722	15.9%	(SDP/All)
Gibson, R.A. (Grn)	319	0.7%				
Lab to C swing 0.0%	44,475	Lab maj 1,894 4.3%		42,397	Lab maj 1,837 4.3%	

Dr John Cunningham was elected to the shadow Cabinet in 1983 and made chief Opposition spokesman on the environment; an Opposition spokesman on industry, 1979-83. Under Secretary of State for Energy, 1976-79. Elected for this seat 1983; MP for Whitehaven, 1970-83. PPS to Mr James Callaghan, 1974-76. Former Research Fellow, Durham Univ. B Aug 4 1939; ed Jarrow GS and Bede Coll, Durham Univ. Full-time officer, GMWU, 1969-70; sponsored by the union. Mbr, Select Cmte on Science and Technology, 1970-76; Chester-le-Street DC, 1969-73. Industrial policy adviser to Albright and Wilson (UK) Ltd, to Leather Chemicals and to Dow Ltd. Fellow, Industry and Parliament Trust.
Mr Rex Toft is a Whitehaven solicitor and mbr, Cumbria CC.
Mr Edward Colgan, asst unit general manager, East Cumbria HA, managing a psychiatric hospital in Carlisle. Founder mbr, SDP; mbr, CSD. B May 3 1958; ed Leeds Univ.

Dr John Cunningham

CORBY — No change

Electorate %Turnout	66,119	79.6%	**1987**	63,067	77.5%	**1983**
*Powell, W.R. (C)	23,323	44.3%	+1.7%	20,827	42.6%	(C)
Feather, H.A. (Lab)	21,518	40.9%	+4.8%	17,659	36.1%	(Lab)
Whittington, T.G. (L/All)	7,805	14.8%	-5.4%	9,905	20.3%	(L/All)
				505	1.0%	(Other)
C to Lab swing 1.5%	52,646	C maj 1,805 3.4%		48,896	C maj 3,168 6.5%	

Mr William Powell, barrister, was elected in 1983. Mbr, Select Cmte on Procedure, 1987- . B Aug 3 1948; ed Lancing Coll; Emmanuel Coll, Cambridge. Mbr, Cl, British Atlantic Cmte, 1985- . Chmn, Cambridge Univ Cons Assocn, 1970; jt sec, Cons back-bench foreign affairs cmte, 1985. PPS to Minister for Overseas Development, 1985-86.
Mr Harry (Sandy) Feather, trade union officer with the Iron and Steel Trades Confederation and former steel worker. Mbr, TUC steel cmte and TUC pension cmte; Northamptonshire CC, 1968-71. B Aug 3 1938; ed Chiswick County Sch.
Mr Glynn Whittington, teacher; head of social and community studies dept, contested this seat 1983. B Feb 20 1943; ed Bells GS, Coleford, Glos; Battersea Tech; Hammersmith Coll of Art; Lanchester Tech; London Univ.

Mr William Powell

CORNWALL NORTH — No change

Electorate %Turnout	72,375	79.8%	**1987**	66,813	80.4%	**1983**
*Neale, G.A. (C)	29,862	51.7%	-0.7%	28,146	52.4%	(C)
Mitchell, M.N. (L/All)	24,180	41.9%	-1.1%	23,087	43.0%	(L/All)
Herries, Ms C. (Lab)	3,719	6.4%	+2.5%	2,096	3.9%	(Lab)
				364	0.7%	(Other)
L/All to C swing 0.2%	57,761	C maj 5,682 9.8%		53,693	C maj 5,059 9.4%	

Mr Gerrard Neale became chairman of the Campaign for Defence and Multilateral Disarmament in 1986. PPS to Mr Nicholas Ridley, Secretary of State for Environment, 1986- , and Secretary of State for Transport, 1985-86; to Minister for Consumer Affairs, 1981-82; to Minister of State for Trade, 1981-83. Elected in 1979; contested the seat, Oct 1974. Solicitor; director of Telephone Rentals Ltd, since 1979. B Jun 25 1941; ed Bedford Sch. Chmn, Buckingham Constituency Cons Assocn, 1974-76. Mbr, Milton Keynes Cl, 1973-79; mayor, 1976-77. Former mbr, Select Cmte on Environment.
Mr Michael Mitchell, teacher, who contested Torbay in 1979 and 1983, was chairman of Devon Liberal Party, 1982-84, and regional officer, Devon and Cornwall Liberal Party, 1976-84. B Apr 2 1949; ed Barnstaple Boys' Sec Sch; N Devon Tech Coll; Rolle Coll of Ed, Exmouth; Exeter Univ. Mbr, Exmouth UDC, 1971-74; East Devon DC, 1973-81. NUT.
Ms Christine Herries, unemployed teacher. B Jan 29 1947; ed Dereham HS, Norfolk; W Midlands Coll, Walsall. Chair, N Cornwall Lab Pty. NUT.

Mr Gerrard Neale

CORNWALL SOUTH EAST — No change

Electorate %Turnout	70,248	79.5%	1987	65,166	78.6%	1983
*Hicks, R.A. (C)	28,818	51.6%	-3.7%	28,326	55.3%	(C)
Tunbridge, I.P. (L/All)	22,211	39.8%	+0.8%	19,972	39.0%	(L/All)
Clark, P.A. (Lab)	4,847	8.7%	+3.8%	2,507	4.9%	(Lab)
				431	0.8%	(Other)
C to L/All swing 2.2%	55,876	C maj 6,607 11.8%		51,236	C maj 8,354 16.3%	

Mr Robert Hicks has been on the Select Cmte on European Legislation since 1976; also served on it, 1973. Parliamentary adviser, British Hotels, Restaurants and Caterers Assocn, since 1974; Milk Marketing Bd, since 1985. Elected for this seat 1983; MP for Bodmin, 1970-Feb 1974 and Oct 1974-83; contested Aberavon 1966. Asst Govt whip, 1973-74. B Jan 18 1938; ed Queen Elizabeth GS, Crediton; Univ Coll, London; Exeter Univ. Treas, Cons Middle East Cl, 1980- . Chmn, UK group, Parly Assocn for Euro-Arab Cooperation, 1983- ; West Country Cons MPs, 1976-77; vice-chmn, Cons back-bench agriculture cmte, 1972-73, and 1974-82; Cons back-bench cmte on Euro affairs, 1979-80. Lecturer in regional geography, Weston-super-Mare Tech Coll, 1964-70; teacher, St Austell GS, 1961-64.

Mr Ian Tunbridge, senior lecturer in geology and consultant geologist. B Nov 26 1953; ed Launceston Coll, Cornwall; Bristol and Reading Univs.

Mr Paul Clark, director of social services, East Cornwall. B Oct 3 1935; ed LSE. Chmn, Launceston Lab Pty, 1983; vice-chmn, N Cornwall CLP and Camelford branch; chmn, Launceston CND; cty rep, Ex-Services CND. Nupe.

Mr Robert Hicks

COVENTRY NORTH EAST — No change

Electorate %Turnout	67,479	70.6%	1987	67,037	69.2%	1983
Hughes, J. (Lab)	25,832	54.3%	+6.4%	22,190	47.8%	(Lab)
Prior, C. (C)	13,965	29.3%	+0.4%	13,415	28.9%	(C)
Wood, S. (L/All)	7,502	15.8%	-6.3%	10,251	22.1%	(SDP/All)
McNally, A. (Comm)	310	0.7%		342	0.7%	(WRP)
				193	0.4%	(Other)
C to Lab swing 3.0%	47,609	Lab maj 11,867 24.9%		46,391	Lab maj 8,775 18.9%	

Mr John Hughes, unemployed; former warehouse man and TGWU convenor at Unipart, Canley; chmn, Coventry NE CLP. Apprentice joiner before going into mining in which he became a mechanic at Keresley Colliery, Durham. Later at GEC factory, Humber at Leyland; Morris engines and then Unipart. Mbr, Coventry City Cl, 1974-82; chmn, dist Lab Pty, 1978-81. B May 29 1925.

Mr Charles Prior, man dir of training company. Qualified chartered accountant. B Oct 15 1947. Ed Marlborough. Mbr, Berkshire CC, 1985- ; National Fed of Small Businesses. Governor, Newbury Coll of FE.

Mr Stephen Wood, research fellow at Warwick Univ; employed at Macauley Inst for Soil Research, Aberdeen, 1983-86. Treas, Coventry SW Lib Assocn. B Jan 22 1958; ed Whitgift Comprehensive Sch, Grimsby; Liverpool Univ. Was vice-chmn, Macauley section, IPCS.

Mr Tony McNally, Midlands Dist Sec, Comm Pty. Former welder, shop stewards convenor and trades cl sec. Aged 42.

Mr John Hughes

COVENTRY NORTH WEST — No change

Electorate %Turnout	53,090	74.8%	1987	52,072	74.7%	1983
*Robinson, G. (Lab)	19,450	49.0%	+4.7%	17,239	44.3%	(Lab)
Powell, J. (C)	13,787	34.7%	-1.8%	14,201	36.5%	(C)
Jones, T. (SDP/All)	6,455	16.3%	-3.0%	7,479	19.2%	(L/All)
C to Lab swing 3.2%	39,692	Lab maj 5,663 14.3%		38,919	Lab maj 3,038 7.8%	

Mr Geoffrey Robinson was with the Opposition front bench team on trade and industry, 1983-86, with responsibilities for industry and previously regional affairs. On Select Cmte on Trade and Industry, 1983-84. Won by-election in 1976. Financial controller, British Leyland, 1971-72; managing director, Leyland Innocenti, Italy, 1972-73; chief executive, Jaguar Cars, Coventry, 1973-75; chief executive (unpaid), Triumph Motorcycles (Meriden) Ltd (a workers' cooperative), 1977-80, director 1980-82. Director (unpaid), W Midlands Enterprise Bd, 1980- , and Dudley Foundry Ltd. Research asst, Lab Pty, 1965-68. B May 25 1939; ed Emanuel Sch, Cambridge Univ, and Yale.

Mr James Powell, managing director of a ceramics company. B May 17 1949; ed Charterhouse; Trinity Hall, Cambridge.

Mr Tudor Jones, polytechnic lecturer, is a former chmn, North Oxford branch, Oxford area SDP. Contested Oxford City Cl and Oxfordshire CC elections 1984, 1985 and 1986. B Jan 25 1946; ed Univ Coll Sch, London; Jesus Coll, Oxford; Southampton Univ. NATFHE.

Mr Geoffrey Robinson

COVENTRY SOUTH EAST | No change

Electorate %Turnout	51,880	73.0%	**1987**	52,538	70.9%	**1983**
*Nellist, D.J. (Lab)	17,969	47.5%	+6.4%	15,307	41.1%	(Lab)
Grant, A. (C)	11,316	29.9%	-4.0%	12,625	33.9%	(C)
Devine, F. (SDP/All)	8,095	21.4%	-3.6%	9,323	25.0%	(L/All)
Hutchinson, N. (Grn)	479	1.3%				
C to Lab swing 5.2%	37,859	Lab maj 6,653 17.6%		37,255	Lab maj 2,682 7.2%	

Mr **David Nellist**, formerly a storeman, engineering and building supplies, was elected in 1983. Member, West Midlands County Council, 1982-86. B Jul 1952. AUEW-TASS.
Mr **Charles Prior**, managing director of a training company, is a member of Berkshire CC. B Oct 15 1947; ed Marlborough.
Mr **Frank Devine**, industrial relations manager with Alvis and formerly with Shell Oil and Unilever. Founder, SDP Friends of Ireland. B Dec 30 1954; ed Warwick Univ (Pres of Union, 1980-81). Personal interests include "annoying the Left by writing letters to the *New Statesman*."
Mr **Neil Hutchinson**, science teacher. B Sep 8 1937. NUT.

Mr **David Nellist**

COVENTRY SOUTH WEST | No change

Electorate %Turnout	65,567	78.7%	**1987**	65,077	75.9%	**1983**
*Butcher, J.P. (C)	22,318	43.3%	-1.7%	22,223	45.0%	(C)
Slater, R.E.G. (Lab)	19,108	37.0%	+5.1%	15,776	31.9%	(Lab)
Wheway, R. (L/All)	10,166	19.7%	-2.9%	11,174	22.6%	(SDP/All)
				214	0.4%	(Other)
C to Lab swing 3.4%	51,592	C maj 3,210 6.2%		49,387	C maj 6,447 13.1%	

Mr **John Butcher** became Under Secretary of State for Industry at the DTI in 1982. PPS to Mr Leon Brittan, Chief Secretary to the Treasury, 1981-82. Elected in 1979; contested Birmingham, Northfield, Feb 1974. Marketing executive and product manager, computer industry, 1968-79. B Feb 13 1946; ed Huntingdon GS and Birmingham Univ. Did research into guerrilla warfare and Nato at Inst of Strategic Studies. FRSA. Member, Birmingham City Cl, 1972-78; former parly adviser to Professional Assocn of Teachers.
Mr **Robert Slater**, further education lecturer, contested Burton 1983. Member, Leicester City Cl and ethnic minorities liaison officer, 1979- . B Dec 13 1948; ed George Gascoigne Sec Mod Sch, Walthamstow; Leicester Univ. NATFHE.
Mr **Robert Wheway** is an advisor on children's play provision. Member (Woodlands ward), Coventry City Cl, since 1985, being first Liberal elected to cl for 59 years. B Sep 15 1949; ed Bablake Sch, Coventry. ASTMS.

Mr **John Butcher**

CRAWLEY | No change

Electorate %Turnout	72,076	81.9%	**1987**	70,713	76.4%	**1983**
*Soames, A.N.W. (C)	29,259	49.5%	+1.5%	25,963	48.1%	(C)
Leo, P.J. (Lab)	17,121	29.0%	+2.8%	14,149	26.2%	(Lab)
Simmons, D.N. (SDP/All)	12,674	21.5%	-4.3%	13,900	25.7%	(SDP/All)
C to Lab swing 0.7%	59,054	C maj 12,138 20.6%		54,012	C maj 11,814 21.9%	

Mr **Nicholas Soames** was elected in 1983; contested Cental Dumbartonshire, 1979. Son of Lord Soames and grandson of Sir Winston Churchill. Non-executive director of Robert Fraser & Partners, bankers; two other Robert Fraser companies and of John Baily and Son (Poulterer) Ltd; adviser to Sedgwick Group (asst director to group, 1979-81). Jt sec, Cons back-bench foreign and Commonwealth affairs cmte, 1985- . B Feb 12 1948; ed St Aubyns, Sussex, and Eton. Legislative assistant to US senator, 1976-78; personal asst to Sir James Goldsmith, 1974-76; stockbroker, 1972-74; Equerry to Prince of Wales, 1970-72. Member, Select Cmte on European Legislation, 1983-84; PPS to Mr John Gummer, when Minister of State for Employment and chmn of Cons Pty.
Mr **Paul Leo**, business customer services manager. Mbr, West Sussex CC, 1985-; Thamesdown BC, 1980-82. B Jan 15 1959; ed Ealing GS; Ridgeway Comprehensive; The College, Swindon. Chmn, Swindon Youth Cl, 1979-82. ASTMS.
Mr **David Simmons**, general manager and vice-president of international operations for computer systems company, contested Coventry North East 1983, and Leicestershire in 1984 Euro elections. Former diplomat in India, North Vietnam and Brazil. Member, SDP third world gp and nat communications gp. B Jun 9 1945; ed Loughborough GS; Central London Poly. Formerly Apex and CPSA.

Mr **Nicholas Soames**

CREWE AND NANTWICH | No change

Electorate %Turnout	72,961	79.3%	**1987**	71,787	74.7%	**1983**
*Dunwoody, Mrs G.P. (Lab)	25,457	44.0%	+2.9%	22,031	41.1%	(Lab)
Browning, Mrs A.F. (C)	24,365	42.1%	+1.6%	21,741	40.6%	(C)
Roberts, Dr K.N. (SDP/All)	8,022	13.9%	-4.5%	9,820	18.3%	(SDP/All)
C to Lab swing 0.7%	57,844	Lab maj 1,092 1.9%		53,592	Lab maj 290 0.5%	

Mrs Gwyneth
Dunwoody

Mrs Gwyneth Dunwoody was chief Opposition spokesman on transport, 1983-85, and spokesman on the health service, 1981-83; previously in the front bench foreign affairs team. Mbr, Shadow Cabinet, 1983-85, and Labour Party NEC, since 1981, chairing its campaigns and communications cmte. In 1983 she declined a front-bench portfolio but was appointed by Mr Kinnock to co-ordinate party campaigns in Parliament and the country until 1985. Elected for this seat 1983; MP for Crewe, Feb 1974-83; Exeter, 1966-70; contested that seat, 1964. Mbr, European Parliament, 1975-79; Totnes BC, 1963-66. Parliamentary Secretary, Board of Trade, 1967-70. B Dec 12, 1930; ed Fulham County Sec Sch; Convent of Notre Dame. Director, Film Production Assocn of Gt Britain, 1970-74. Parly consultant, British Fur Trade Assocn; director, Dunwoody Computer Services. Sponsored by NUR.
Mrs Angela Browning, a training consultant, has served as the Western Area CPC chairman, and on the National Advisory Cmtes of the CPC and the Small Business Bureau. Fellow, Inst of Sales and Marketing Management. B Dec 4 1946; ed Reading and Bournemouth Colls of Technology.
Dr Kenneth Roberts, medical practitioner in pharmaceutical industry with Wellcome Foundation. Chmn, Crewe and Nantwich SDP. B Nov 19 1949; ed Sandbach Sch, Cheshire.

CROSBY | No change

Electorate %Turnout	83,914	79.6%	**1987**	83,274	77.9%	**1983**
*Thornton, G.M. (C)	30,836	46.1%	-1.1%	30,604	47.2%	(C)
Donovan, A.F.S. (SDP/All)	23,989	35.9%	-6.1%	27,203	42.0%	(SDP/All)
Cheetham, C.W. (Lab)	11,992	17.9%	+7.8%	6,611	10.2%	(Lab)
				415	0.6%	(Other)
SDP/All to C swing 2.5%	66,817	C maj 6,847 10.2%		64,833	C maj 3,401 5.2%	

Mr Malcolm Thornton

Mr Malcolm Thornton, a River Mersey pilot, 1955-79, won this seat in 1983; MP for Liverpool, Garston, 1979-83. B Apr 3 1939; ed Wallasey GS; Liverpool Nautical Coll. Member, Select Cmte on Environment, 1979-81; Select Cmte on Education and Science, 1985- . PPS to Mr Patrick Jenkin, as Secretary of State for Trade and Industry and for Environment, 1981-85. Parly consultant to Nalgo, BEC, NATFHE, System Drive Ltd and Keene Public Affairs Ltd. Mbr, Wallasey CBC, 1965-74; Wirral MBC, 1973-79. Chmn, Merseyside Met Districts liaison cmte, 1975-77; Education Cmte, AMA, 1978-79; CLEA, 1978-79. Member, Burnham Cmte, 1978-79. Former sec, Cons back-bench education cmte and of shipping and shipbuilding cmte. Former mbr, marine pilotage branch, TGWU.
Mr Scott Donovan, barrister. Founder mbr, SDP; chmn, Sefton area SDP; chaired 1981 Crosby by-election cmte. Mbr, Sefton MBC, 1982-86 (Alliance housing spokesman). B Jan 10 1948; ed St Mary's Coll, Crosby; New Coll, Oxford; univ in Washington DC, US.
Mr Chris Cheetham, personnel officer. B May 11 1949; ed St Mary's Coll, Crosby; Strathclyde Univ.

CROYDON CENTRAL | No change

Electorate %Turnout	55,410	70.5%	**1987**	56,531	68.6%	**1983**
*Moore, J.E.M. (C)	22,133	56.6%	+2.8%	20,866	53.8%	(C)
Prentice, Ms B.T. (Lab)	9,516	24.3%	+1.0%	9,045	23.3%	(Lab)
Burgess, T. (SDP/All)	7,435	19.0%	-3.8%	8,864	22.9%	(SDP/All)
Lab to C swing 0.9%	39,084	C maj 12,617 32.3%		38,775	C maj 11,821 30.5%	

Mr John Moore

Mr John Moore was appointed Secretary of State for Social Services in Jun 1987; Secretary of State for Transport, 1986-87; Economic Secretary to the Treasury, Jun-Oct 1983, and Financial Secretary, Oct 1983-86; Under Secretary of State for Energy, 1979-83. Elected in Feb 1974. Mbr, PAC, 1974-75. Former investment banker and stockbroker; former company director and chmn of Dean Witter International Ltd, 1975-79. Vice-chmn of Cons Party with responsibility for youth, 1975-79. B Nov 26 1937; ed Licensed Victuallers' Sch, Slough; LSE (Chmn, Cons Assocn; Pres of Union, 1959-60). Mbr, Merton BC, 1971-74. Lived in US 1961-65 where he was Precinct Captain (1962) and Ward Chmn (1964), Democratic Party. Non-underwriting member of Lloyd's.
Ms Bridget Prentice, teacher. B Dec 28 1952; ed Our Lady and St Francis Sch, Glasgow; Glasgow and London Univs. Chair, Lab gp, Hammersmith Cl. Chair, Fulham LP, 1982-85. NUT; GMBATU.
Mr Tyrrell Burgess, polytechnic reader and chmn, Tyrrell Burgess Associates Ltd, fought this seat 1983; and Croydon South for Labour in 1964. Chmn, Croydon SDP; additional member, ILEA. B Sep 7 1931; ed Royal Liberty Sch, Romford; Keble Coll, Oxford (Pres of Union, 1954).

CROYDON NORTH EAST — No change

Electorate %Turnout	63,129	69.7%	**1987**	62,923	67.5%	**1983**
*Weatherill, B.B. (Speaker)	24,188	55.0%		22,292	52.5%	(C)
Patrick, Ms C. (Lab)	11,669	26.5%	+4.1%	10,665	25.1%	(SDP/All)
Goldie, J.D. (SDP/All)	8,128	18.5%	-6.6%	9,503	22.4%	(Lab)
	43,985	Spk maj 12,519 28.5%		42,460	C maj 11,627 27.4%	

Mr Bernard Weatherill was chosen Speaker of the House of Commons in Jun 1983. Until then, he had been Conservative MP for this seat since 1964. Chmn, Commonwealth Speakers and Presiding Officers, 1986- ; pres, CPA, 1986. Deputy Speaker and Chairman of Ways and Means, 1979-83; Deputy Chief Opposition Whip, 1974-79; Government Deputy Chief Whip, 1973-74; Comptroller of the Household (whip), 1972-73; Vice-Chamberlain of Household (whip), 1971-72; Lord Commissioner of the Treasury (Govt whip), 1970-72; Opposition whip, 1967-70. Master tailor and former director of the family business. Freeman, City of London, and Borough of Croydon. B Nov 25 1920; ed Malvern Coll. Chmn, Guildford Cons Assocn, 1959-63; mbr, Nat Union of Cons Party, 1963-64. Mbr, Commons Services Cmte, 1970-79.
Ms Christine Patrick, market researcher. B Aug 3 1952; ed Newland HS, Hull; Oxford Univ. Croydon Sth constituency sec, 1985-86. ASTMS.
Mr Julian Goldie, insurance broker, contested the seat 1983. Founder mbr, SDP; chmn, Croydon SDP, 1986-87; treas, 1981-85. B Aug 3 1931; Clapham Coll, London. Branch officer, Clerical Workers Union, 1953-61.

Mr Bernard Weatherill

CROYDON NORTH WEST — No change

Electorate %Turnout	57,369	69.2%	**1987**	58,333	67.6%	**1983**
*Malins, H.J. (C)	18,665	47.0%	+4.7%	16,674	42.3%	(C)
Wicks, M.H. (Lab)	14,677	37.0%	+12.7%	12,582	31.9%	(L/All)
Rowe, L.A. (L/All)	6,363	16.0%	-15.9%	9,561	24.2%	(Lab)
				622	1.6%	(Other)
C to Lab swing 4.0%	39,705	C maj 3,988 10.0%		39,439	C maj 4,092 10.4%	

Mr Humfrey Malins, solicitor, was elected in 1983; contested Liverpool, Toxteth in both 1974 elections, and Lewisham East, 1979. B Jul 31 1945; ed St John's Sch, Leatherhead; Brasenose Coll, Oxford; Coll of Law, Guildford. Mbr, Mole Valley DC, 1973-82; chmn, housing cmte 1980-82. Jt vice-chmn, Cons back-bench legal cmte, 1986- ; jt sec, 1983-86. Member, Select Cmte on Consolidation Bills, since 1983.
Mr Malcolm Wicks, director Family Policy Studies Centre; worked in Home Office urban deprivation unit, 1974-77; research director and sec, study commission on the family, 1978-83. Served on social security working gps for Mr Michael Meacher. Mbr, Child Poverty Action Gp. TGWU.
Mr Leslie Rowe, deputy group accountant, Westminster Press Ltd. B 1952; ed Barton upon Humber GS.

Mr Humfrey Malins

CROYDON SOUTH — No change

Electorate %Turnout	65,085	73.7%	**1987**	64,482	71.0%	**1983**
*Clark, Sir William (C)	30,732	64.1%	-1.1%	29,842	65.1%	(C)
Morrison, I. (L/All)	11,669	24.3%	-2.8%	12,402	27.1%	(L/All)
Davies, G. (Lab)	4,679	9.8%	+2.0%	3,568	7.8%	(Lab)
Baldwin, P. (Grn)	900	1.9%				
L/All to C swing 0.8%	47,980	C maj 19,063 39.7%		45,812	C maj 17,440 38.1%	

Sir William Clark has been chairman of the Conservative back-bench finance cmte since 1979. Accountant, company director and consultant to Commercial Union Assurance Co Ltd, Life Insurance Assocn, Texaco Ltd and Tate and Lyle plc. Elected in Feb 1974; MP for Surrey East, 1970-74; for Nottingham South, 1959-66; fought Northampton, 1955. Member, Public Accounts Commission, 1983- . B Oct 18, 1917; ed London secondary sch. Jt dep chmn, Cons Pty, 1975-77; jt treas, 1974-75. Chmn, Select Cmte on Taxation, 1973, and member of former Select Cmte on Wealth Tax. An Opposition spokesman on Treasury affairs, 1964-66. Mbr, Wandsworth BC, 1949-53.
Mr Ian Morrison is an official of the Bank of England involved in banking supervision. Mbr, Epsom and Ewell BC, 1979-83; leader, Lib gp, 1980-83. B Dec 28 1951; ed Caterham Sch, Surrey (head boy and capt at rugby); Surrey Univ, Guildford (Pres of students' union).
Mr Geraint Davies, marketing executive. B May 3 1960; ed Llanishen Comprehensive Sch, Cardiff; Jesus Coll, Oxford Univ. Mbr (New Addington ward), Croydon BC. Exec mbr, Croydon Central CLP. Was Croydon North East Lab Pty asst sec. ASTMS.

Sir William Clark

CUMBERNAULD AND KILSYTH — No change

Electorate %Turnout	45,427	78.5%	**1987**	44,190	76.5%	**1983**
*Hogg, N. (Lab)	21,385	60.0%	+10.8%	16,629	49.2%	(Lab)
Johnston, T. (SNP)	6,982	19.6%	+2.2%	6,701	19.8%	(SDP/All)
Deans, C.S. (SDP/All)	4,059	11.4%	-8.4%	5,875	17.4%	(SNP)
Thomson, Mrs A.E. (C)	3,227	9.1%	-4.5%	4,590	13.6%	(C)
SNP to Lab swing 4.3%	35,653	Lab maj 14,403 40.4%		33,795	Lab maj 9,928 29.4%	

Mr **Norman Hogg**, Opposition Deputy Chief Whip 1983- ; Scottish Labour whip, 1982-83; chmn, Scottish group of Lab MPs, 1981-82. Mbr, Select Cmte on Commons Services, 1983- . Elected for this seat 1983; MP for East Dunbartonshire, 1979-83. Local govt official, Aberdeen TC, 1953-67. District officer, Nalgo, 1967-79; parly consultant to Nalgo. Mbr Select Cmte on Scottish Affairs, 1979-82. B Mar 12 1938; ed Causewayend Sch, Aberdeen; Ruthrieston Sec Sch, Aberdeen. TGWU.
Mr **Thomas Johnston**, teacher, contested Monklands East in 1983. Mbr, Cumbernauld and Kilsyth DC. B 1947; ed Glasgow Univ; Jordanhill Coll of Educ; London Univ. Pty spokesman on housing, 1985-87. Chmn, Cumbernauld North East SNP.
Mr **Colin Deans**, management consultant, contested Aberdeen North 1983. Founder member, SDP in Scotland; mbr, Scottish cmte and Grampian area; CSD. Director, Aberdeen Chamber of Commerce. B Oct 22 1941; ed in Nova Scotia, Canada and Scotland.
Mrs **Anne Thomson**, adult ed tutor; former primary sch teacher and teacher at sec special sch for mentally handicapped pupils. Has chaired Strathclyde East Euro constituency cl and been vice-chmn, W of Scotland area cl. Ed Glasgow Univ; Hamilton Coll of Ed.

Mr Norman Hogg

CUNNINGHAME NORTH — Lab gain

Electorate %Turnout	54,817	78.3%	**1987**	53,126	75.7%	**1983**
Wilson, B.D.H. (Lab)	19,061	44.4%	+9.8%	15,557	38.7%	(C)
*Corrie, J.A. (C)	14,594	34.0%	-4.7%	13,920	34.6%	(Lab)
Herbison, D.J. (SDP/All)	5,185	12.1%	-6.0%	7,268	18.1%	(SDP/All)
Brown, M. (SNP)	4,076	9.5%	+0.9%	3,460	8.6%	(SNP)
C to Lab swing 7.2%	42,916	Lab maj 4,467 10.4%		40,205	C maj 1,637 4.1%	

Mr **Brian Wilson**, journalist, investigative reporter, having written for *Glasgow Herald* and *The Observer*, and Scottish football correspondent of *The Guardian*. Contested Western Isles 1983, Inverness 1979 and Ross and Cromarty, Oct 1974. Founding editor and director, *West Highland Free Press* and first winner of Nicholas Tomalin Memorial Award for outstanding journalism. B Dec 13 1948; ed Dunoon Sch; Dundee Univ; Univ Coll, Cardiff. Mbr, exec cmte, Scottish Lab Pty. NUJ and TGWU.
Mr **John Corrie**, farmer. Mbr, Select Cmte on Scottish Affairs, 1979-87. MP for this seat 1983-87; MP for Ayrshire North and Bute, Feb 1974-83; contested Ayrshire Central, 1966, and Lanark North, 1964. Chmn, Scottish Cons MPs cmte, 1981-82. Mbr, Council of Europe and WEU, 1982-87; European Parliament, 1975-76 and 1977-79. An Opposition spokesman on Scotland, 1974-75; Opposition Scottish whip, 1975-76, resigning over devolution. B Jul 29 1935; ed George Watson's Coll, Edinburgh, and Lincoln Agricultural Coll, New Zealand.
Mr **Douglas Herbison**, head of European affairs at The Retail Consortium. Contested Cumbernauld and Kilsyth, 1983. B Jun 25 1951; ed London Univ.
Mr **Matthew Brown**, self-employed engineer and trainee lawyer. Former Provost of Cunninghame DC. B 1940.

Mr Brian Wilson

CUNNINGHAME SOUTH — No change

Electorate %Turnout	49,842	75.0%	**1987**	48,552	73.6%	**1983**
*Lambie, D. (Lab)	22,728	60.8%	+6.7%	19,344	54.1%	(Lab)
Gibson, E.R. (C)	6,095	16.3%	-4.9%	7,576	21.2%	(C)
Boss, J.A. (L/All)	4,426	11.8%	-6.0%	6,370	17.8%	(L/All)
Ullrich, Mrs K. (SNP)	4,115	11.0%	+4.2%	2,451	6.9%	(SNP)
C to Lab swing 5.8%	37,364	Lab maj 16,633 44.5%		35,741	Lab maj 11,768 32.9%	

Mr **David Lambie** has chaired the Select Cmte on Scottish Affairs since 1981; mbr from 1979. Sec, all-pty Cmte for Energy Studies, since 1980. Elected for this seat 1983; MP for Central Ayrshire, 1970-83; contested Ayrshire North and Bute, 1966, 1964 and 1959. Teacher, 1950-70. B Jul 13 1925; ed Kyleshill Sch; Ardrossan Acad; Glasgow and Geneva univs. Chmn, Scottish Lab Pty, 1964. Mbr, Select Cmte for Parliamentary Commssioner for Administration and Health Service, 1974-83. Chmn, Scottish parly Lab group, 1980. Chief negotiator on behalf of Scottish teachers in STSC, 1969-70; sec, Westminster branch, EIS, 1985- . Sponsored by USDAW.
Mr **Eric Gibson**, company director. B Feb 25 1943; ed Hawick HS; Scottish Coll of Textiles.
Mr **John Boss**, personnel officer with ICI since 1969 and with SW Gas Bd, 1965-69. Chmn, Cunninghame South Libs, 1985-86; community cllr, 1981- . B Dec 31 1940; ed Reading Sch; Trinity Coll, Dublin; LSE.
Mrs **Kay Ullrich**, paediatric social worker, fought this seat 1983. Nat sec, SNP/CND, 1984-86; Cunninghame South SNP press officer, 1978-87; chaired Ayr West branch, 1968-74. B May 5 1943; ed Ayr Acad; Queen's Coll, Glasgow. Qualified swimming coach.

Mr David Lambie

CYNON VALLEY — No change

Electorate %Turnout	49,621	76.7%	**1987**	50,284	73.4%	**1983**
*Clwyd, Mrs A. (Lab)	26,222	68.9%	+12.9%	20,668	56.0%	(Lab)
Butler, K.D. (SDP/All)	4,651	12.2%	-8.3%	7,594	20.6%	(SDP/All)
Bishop, M.A. (C)	4,638	12.2%	-2.0%	5,240	14.2%	(C)
Richards, Mrs D.L. (Pl C)	2,549	6.7%	-2.6%	3,421	9.3%	(Pl C)
SDP/All to Lab swing 10.6%	38,060	Lab maj 21,571 56.7%		36,923	Lab maj 13,074 35.4%	

Mrs Ann Clwyd, broadcaster and journalist, was elected chmn of the Tribune Group of Labour MPs in Nov 1986; chmn, PLP health and social security cmte, 1985- ; jt vice-chmn, PLP defence cmte, 1985- . Elected at by-election in 1984; contested Gloucester, Oct 1974, and Denbigh, 1970. Mbr, European Parliament, for Mid and West Wales, 1979-84; Lab Party NEC, 1983-84. Vice-chmn, Arts Cl of Wales, 1975-79, and Arts Cl of Gt Britain, 1975-80. B Mar 21 1937; ed Holywell GS, Queen's School, Chester, and Univ Coll, Bangor. Welsh correspondent, *The Guardian* and *The Observer*, 1964-79. Mbr, Royal Commission on NHS, 1976-79. Parly adviser to Soc of Telecom Executives. NUJ. Sponsored by TGWU.
Mr Keith Butler, commercial manager, Hereford United FC and previously with Worcestershire CCC. Mbr, CDS; Malvern Hill DC 1983- ; Broadheath PC; vice chmn, SDP area pty. B Dec 26 1953; ed King Edwards Sch, Witley, Surrey.
Mr Mark Bishop, barrister. B Jul 12 1958; ed The Leys Sch, Cambridge; Cambridge Univ; Inns of Court Sch of Law. Former chmn, Cambridge Univ Cons Assocn and past pres of Cambridge Union. C of E lay reader.
Mrs Dorothy Richards, senior social worker. Aged 38.

Mrs Ann Clwyd

DAGENHAM — No change

Electorate %Turnout	61,714	67.3%	**1987**	62,960	63.4%	**1983**
*Gould, B.C. (Lab)	18,454	44.4%	+5.2%	15,665	39.3%	(Lab)
Neill, R.J.M. (C)	15,985	38.5%	+6.7%	12,668	31.8%	(C)
Carter, J. (SDP/All)	7,088	17.1%	-9.9%	10,769	27.0%	(SDP/All)
				786	2.0%	(Other)
Lab to C swing 0.8%	41,527	Lab maj 2,469 5.9%		39,888	Lab maj 2,997 7.5%	

Mr Bryan Gould, an Opposition spokesman on trade and industry, 1983-86, was elected to the shadow Cabinet in 1986 becoming Lab's campaign coordinator and a spokesman on Treasury and economic affairs (shadow Chief Sec to the Treas); chmn, Lab economic policy group, from 1985. Presenter and reporter, *TV Eye*, Thames Television, 1979-83; fellow and tutor in law, Worcester Coll, Oxford, 1968-74; diplomatic service in Brussels, 1964-66, and in Foreign Office, 1964-66. Elected for this seat 1983; MP for Southampton, Test, Oct 1974-79; contested that seat, Feb 1974. B Feb 11 1939; ed Dannevirke HS, New Zealand; Victoria and Auckland Univs; Balliol Coll, Oxford. ASTMS.
Mr Robert Neill, barrister and company director, contested this seat in 1983. Leader, London fire and civil defence authority, 1985- ; mbr, Havering BC, 1974- ; former mbr GLC. B Jun 24 1952; ed Abbs Cross Sch, Hornchurch; LSE. Director of building firm and a local enterprise agency.
Mr John Carter, area manager of newsagency chain. B Jan 7 1942; ed Wirral GS; Chester CFE; Thurrock Tech Coll. BIM; Inst of Marketing.

Mr Bryan Gould

DARLINGTON — No change

Electorate %Turnout	65,940	80.8%	**1987**	65,233	77.1%	**1983**
*Fallon, M. (C)	24,831	46.6%	+2.0%	22,434	44.6%	(C)
O'Brien, O. (Lab)	22,170	41.6%	+3.8%	18,996	37.8%	(Lab)
Collinge, A. (L/All)	6,289	11.8%	-5.6%	8,737	17.4%	(SDP/All)
				108	0.2%	(Other)
C to Lab swing 0.9%	53,290	C maj 2,661 5.0%		50,275	C maj 3,438 6.8%	

Mr Michael Fallon was elected in 1983; contested Darlington by-election, 1983. Political researcher, writer and lecturer. B May 14 1952; ed Epsom Coll and St Andrews Univ. Political asst and adviser to Lord Carrington, 1974-77; EEC adviser, Cons Research Dept, 1977-79. Sec, Lord Home's cmte on future of House of Lords, 1977-78; assistant to Lady Elles, MEP, 1979-83. Jt managing director, European Consultants Ltd, 1979-81.
Mr Oswald (Ossie) O'Brian, director of workplace advisory service for the national charity, Alcohol Concern, was MP for this seat from the March by-election to the June election, 1983. Former director of studies at Loughborough Co-operative Coll and univ teacher. Mbr, Darlington BC, 1955-61; Darlington BC, 1973-76 (sec of Lab gp; chmn, personnel and development cmtes). B Apr 6 1928; ed St Mary's GS, Darlington; Durham Univ. Former pres, sec and treas, Darlington CLP; former mbr, regional exec. Past pres, Darlington Co-op Pty. ASTMS; formerly in GMBATU, AUT and NATFHE; active in trade union ed.
Mr Arthur Collinge, senior lecturer, contested Bishop Auckland 1983. Mbr, North Yorkshire CC; Alliance spokesman on economic development. B Jul 6 1939; ed Queen Elizabeth's GS, Blackburn; Univs of Wales and Durham. NATFHE.

Mr Michael Fallon

DARTFORD — No change

Electorate %Turnout	72,632	79.0%	**1987**	71,622	76.4%	**1983**
*Dunn, R.J. (C)	30,685	53.5%	+1.9%	28,199	51.6%	(C)
Clarke, B.J. (Lab)	15,756	27.5%	+0.7%	14,630	26.8%	(Lab)
Bruce, M.G. (SDP/All)	10,439	18.2%	-2.3%	11,204	20.5%	(L/All)
Davenport, K.J. (FDP)	491	0.9%	+0.2%	374	0.7%	(FDP)
				282	0.5%	(Other)
Lab to C swing 0.6%	57,371	C maj 14,929 26.0%		54,689	C maj 13,569 24.8%	

Mr Robert Dunn

Mr Robert Dunn was appointed an Under Secretary of State for Education and Science in 1983. Elected in 1979; contested Eccles, Feb and Oct 1974. Mbr, Southwark BC, 1974-78. Jt sec, Cons back-bench education cmte, 1980-83. B Jul 1946; ed Manchester Poly, Brighton Poly, and Salford Univ. Senior buyer, J Sainsbury, 1973-79, and adviser to company until he became a minister. PPS to Under Secretaries of State at DES, 1981-82, and to Mr Cecil Parkinson, 1982-83. Pres, Dartford YCs, 1976- ; Kent YCs, 1982-85; SE Area Cons Advisory Cmte for Education, 1982- ; Dartford Soc, 1982- . Vice-pres, Dartford branch, Kent Assocn for Disabled, 1979- . Former parly adviser to Professional Assocn of Teachers. Mbr, Select Cmte on Environment, 1981-82.
Mr Barrie Clarke, national political educ officer, Lab Pty; Chmn, Southern Region. B May 25 1944. Mbr, Kent CC; Medway DHA. School governor. Apex.
Mr Michael Bruce, educational consultant; head of sch of ed and teaching studies, Thames Poly, 1976-84. Mbr, CSD; SDP education policy gp; Tawney Soc; vice chmn, W Kent area pty, 1984- . B Jan 29 1937; ed Royal GS, Newcastle upon Tyne; New Coll, Oxford; Institut Britannique de Paris; Leicester Univ. NATFHE.

DAVENTRY — No change

Electorate %Turnout	69,241	78.2%	**1987**	64,314	76.8%	**1983**
Boswell, T.E. (C)	31,353	57.9%	+4.6%	26,357	53.3%	(C)
Miller, I.R. (L/All)	11,663	21.6%	-5.2%	13,221	26.8%	(SDP/All)
Koumi, Ms L.M.A.W. (Lab)	11,097	20.5%	+0.6%	9,840	19.9%	(Lab)
L/All to C swing 4.9%	54,113	C maj 19,690 36.4%		49,418	C maj 13,136 26.6%	

Mr Timothy Boswell

Mr Timothy Boswell, farmer, was special adviser to the Ministry of Agriculture, Fisheries and Food, 1984-86. Contested Rugby, Feb 1974. Agricultural specialist, Cons Research Dept, 1966-70, and head of economic section, 1970-73. B Dec 2 1942; ed Marlborough Coll and New Coll, Oxford. Chmn, Northants, Leics and Rutland NFU, 1983; former treas and chmn, Daventry Cons Assocn.
Mr Ian Miller, lobby group agent. Mbr (Towcester Div), Northamptonshire CC, 1981- ; Lib education panel. B Jan 17 1945; ed Denstone Coll, Uttoxeter; Reading Univ.
Ms Lesley Koumi, teacher. CLP sec, 1983-86; branch sec, 1981-86; chair, dist Lab Pty; sec, county and Euro parties. B Nov 6 1948; ed St Joseph's Convent GS, London and Essex Univ.

DAVYHULME — No change

Electorate %Turnout	65,558	77.3%	**1987**	64,363	74.6%	**1983**
*Churchill, W.S. (C)	23,633	46.6%	+0.6%	22,055	46.0%	(C)
Nicholson, J. (Lab)	15,434	30.4%	+3.6%	13,041	27.2%	(L/All)
Wrigley, D.I. (L/All)	11,637	23.0%	-4.2%	12,887	26.9%	(Lab)
C to Lab swing 1.5%	50,704	C maj 8,199 16.2%		47,983	C maj 9,014 18.8%	

Mr Winston Churchill

Mr Winston Churchill, author, journalist and mbr of Lloyd's, was Cons Party Coordinator for Defence and Multilateral Disarmament, 1982-84; mbr, Select Cmte on Defence, 1983- ; vice-chmn, Cons defence cmte, 1979-83; an Opposition spokesman on defence, 1976-78. Elected for this seat in 1983; MP for Stretford, 1970-83; contested Manchester, Gorton, by-election, 1967. B Oct 10 1940; ed Eton and Christ Church, Oxford. Sec, Cons back-bench foreign affairs cmte, 1973-76; mbr, exec, 1922 Cmte, 1979-85. Trustee, Winston Churchill Memorial Trust, 1968- , Nat Benevolent Fund for Aged, 1974- . Pres, Trafford Park Industrial Cl, 1971- . Governor, English Speaking Union, 1975-80. Cl member, Air League. IOJ.
Mr John Nicholson, Health Educ Cl researcher; formerly with Save the Children Fund and Equal Opportunities Commmission. Mbr, Manchester Cl, 1980- (Dep ldr, 1984-) B Dec 14 1954; ed Keele and Oxford Univs. ASTMS.
Mr Dennis Wrigley, principal of industrial management service. Former president, Assocn of Building Component Manufacturers. Contested this seat 1983; Stretford, 1979 and twice in 1974; High Peak, 1970, 1966, 1964 and 1961 by-election; Oldham East, 1959. B Jan 9 1930; ed Manchester GS; Manchester Reg Sch of Architecture. Lay preacher.

DELYN — No change

Electorate %Turnout	63,541	82.6%	1987	62,483	77.8%	1983
*Raffan, K.W. (C)	21,728	41.4%	-0.2%	20,242	41.6%	(C)
Hanson, D.G. (Lab)	20,504	39.1%	+9.7%	14,298	29.4%	(Lab)
Evans, D.J. (L/All)	8,913	17.0%	-8.8%	12,545	25.8%	(L/All)
Owen, D.J. (Pl C)	1,329	2.5%	-0.7%	1,558	3.2%	(Pl C)
C to Lab swing 4.9%	52,474	C maj 1,224 2.3%		48,643	C maj 5,944 12.2%	

Mr Keith Raffan

Mr Keith Raffan, freelance journalist and parliamentary correspondent, *Daily Express*, 1981-83, and leader writer, 1979-81, was elected in 1987; contested Dulwich, Feb 1974; East Aberdeenshire, Oct 1974. Mbr, Select Cmte on Welsh Affairs, 1983- ; vice-chmn, Cons back-bench party organization cmte, 1985- . B Jun 21, 1949; ed Robert Gordon's Coll, Aberdeen; Trinity Coll, Glenalmond, Perth; and Corpus Christi Coll, Cambridge. Pres, Welsh Cons Trade Unionists; vice-pres, Welsh YCs. Nat chmn, PEST, 1970-74. Introduced in 1985 private member's Bill that became Controlled Drugs (Penalties) Act. NUJ.
Mr David Hanson, regional manager with Spastics Society, contested Eddisbury 1983 and Cheshire West in 1984 Euro election. Mbr, Vale Royal DC, since 1983; wife also on cl. B Jul 5 1957; ed Verdin Comprehensive Sch, Winsford, Cheshire; Hull Univ. AEU/TASS.
Mr David Evans, lecturer in biology, contested Shropshire North 1983; Oswestry, 1979 and twice in 1974, and Wallasey, 1970. Mbr, Chester City Cl, since 1986. B Feb 28 1947; ed Teignmouth GS; Liverpool Univ.
Mr David Owen, quality assurance engineer with Rockware plc. B Dec 5 1949; ed Denbigh HS; Liverpool Univ.

DENTON AND REDDISH — No change

Electorate %Turnout	69,533	75.5%	1987	68,661	72.8%	1983
*Bennett, A.F. (Lab)	26,023	49.6%	+5.3%	22,123	44.3%	(Lab)
Slater, P. (C)	17,773	33.9%	-0.1%	16,998	34.0%	(C)
Huffer, T.I. (SDP/All)	8,697	16.6%	-5.2%	10,869	21.7%	(SDP/All)
C to Lab swing 2.7%	52,493	Lab maj 8,250 15.7%		49,990	Lab maj 5,125 10.3%	

Mr Andrew Bennett

Mr Andrew Bennett became an Opposition spokesman on education in 1983. Former teacher. Elected for this seat 1983; MP for Stockport North, Feb 1974-83; contested Knutsford, 1970. Mbr, Select Cmte on Members' Interests, 1979-83; Select Cmte on Social Services, 1979-83; chmn, Select Cmte on Statutory Instruments and Jt Select Cmte, 1983- . Mbr, Oldham BC, 1964-74. B Mar 9 1939; ed Birmingham Univ. NUT. Former chmn, PLP health and social services group; and sec, PLP civil liberties group.
Mr Peter Slater, marketing consultant. B Jul 9 1947; ed Broadway Sec Mod Sch, Cheadle; Mosley Hall GS, Cheadle; Bradford Univ. Mbr, Wandsworth BC, 1982- .
Mr Ian Huffer, barrister. B 1957; ed Oxford Univ. Mbr, Macclesfield BC, 1984- .

DERBY NORTH — No change

Electorate %Turnout	71,738	75.8%	1987	70,374	72.5%	1983
*Knight, G. (C)	26,561	48.9%	+5.2%	22,303	43.7%	(C)
Whitehead, P. (Lab)	20,236	37.2%	+0.4%	18,797	36.8%	(Lab)
Connolly, S.F. (L/All)	7,268	13.4%	-6.1%	9,924	19.4%	(L/All)
Wall, E. (Grn)	291	0.5%				
Lab to C swing 2.4%	54,356	C maj 6,325 11.6%		51,024	C maj 3,506 6.9%	

Mr Gregory Knight

Mr Gregory Knight, solicitor and proprietor of recording studio in Leicestershire, was elected in 1983. PPS to Mr David Mellor and the Earl of Caithness, Ministers of State, Home Office, from Jan 1987. Jt hon sec, Cons backbench employment cmte, 1985-86. B Apr 4 1949; ed Alderman Newton's GS, Leicester, and Coll of Law, Guildford. Mbr, Leicester City Cl, 1976-79; Leicestershire CC, 1977-83. Director, Leicester Theatre Trust.
Mr Philip Whitehead was an Opposition spokesman on education, 1981-83, and on arts, 1982-83. MP for this seat, 1970-83; contested West Derbyshire, 1966. Writer and television producr; chmn, Statesman and Nation Publishing; director, Consumers' Assocn. B May 30 1937; ed Rowsley elementary sch; Lady Manners Sch, Bakewell; Exeter Coll, Oxford. Mbr, Annan Cmte on future of broadcasting. Chmn, Fabian Soc, 1978-79; a founder of 76 Group for Broadcasting Reform, 1969; mbr, PLP liaison cmte, 1976-79; Select Cmte on Home Affairs, 1979-81; Select Cmte on Procedure, 1977-79; Cl of Europe, 1974-79. NUJ, NUR, ACTT.
Mr Stephen Connolly, unemployed, contested this seat 1983. Mbr, Derby CC. B Oct 4 1954; ed St Thomas More Sec Sch; Bemrose GS.
Mr Eric Wall, counsellor and therapist, stood at Derby South in 1983. Mbr, health working pty of Green Pty. B Oct 22 1938; ed Durham and Hull Univs.

DERBY SOUTH — No change

Electorate %Turnout	68,825	69.9%	1987	68,578	67.4%	1983
*Beckett, Mrs M.M. (Lab)	21,003	43.7%	+4.3%	18,169	39.3%	(Lab)
Leighton, P.F. (C)	19,487	40.5%	+2.1%	17,748	38.4%	(C)
Mellor, Mrs P.N. (SDP/All)	7,608	15.8%	-5.8%	9,976	21.6%	(SDP/All)
				297	0.6%	(Other)
C to Lab swing 1.1%	48,098	Lab maj 1,516 3.2%		46,190	Lab maj 421 0.9%	

Mrs Margaret Beckett

Mrs Margaret Beckett joined the Opposition front bench team on health and social security in 1984. Elected for this seat 1983; MP for Lincoln, Oct 1974-79; contested the seat, Feb 1974. Under Secretary of State for Education and Science, 1976-79; asst Govt whip, 1975-76; PPS to Minister of Overseas Development, 1974-75. Former metallurgist; principal researcher, Granada TV, 1979-83. B Jan 15 1943; ed Notre Dame HS, Norwich, and Manchester Coll of Science and Technology. Research asst, Lab Pty, 1970-74. Member, Lab Pty NEC, 1980-81 and 1985-86. Student apprentice, Dept of Metallurgy, AEI Manchester, 1961-66; experimental officer, Dept of Metallurgy, Manchester Univ, 1966-70. TGWU sponsored.
Mr Paul Leighton, broadcaster and journalist, has been a member of Matlock TC since 1983; chaired policy and finance cmte, 1984-87. First Town Mayor of Matlock, 1983-84. NUJ, 1974-79, being Radio Derby FOC, 1976-79; IOJ since 1979. Parochial church councillor. B Jun 28 1951; ed St Philip's GS, Edgbaston; Nottingham Univ.
Mrs Patricia Mellor, lecturer in further education. Member, 300 Group (national cmte 1985- ; chair of training cmte 1986-). Former Bolsover constituency sec; Scarsdale area party chair 1983-86. Member, national cmte of Women for Social Democracy 1985- ; CSD; former chmn, Derbyshire SDP. B Oct 31 1936; ed Dame Alice Harper Sch, Bedford; LSE; Nottingham Univ. NATFHE.

DERBYSHIRE NORTH EAST — No change

Electorate %Turnout	70,314	79.3%	1987	68,273	75.7%	1983
Barnes, H. (Lab)	24,747	44.4%	+3.6%	21,094	40.8%	(Lab)
Hayes, J.H. (C)	21,027	37.7%	+0.8%	19,088	36.9%	(C)
Hardy, S.P. (SDP/All)	9,985	17.9%	-4.3%	11,494	22.2%	(SDP/All)
C to Lab swing 1.4%	55,759	Lab maj 3,720 6.7%		51,676	Lab maj 2,006 3.9%	

Mr Harry Barnes

Mr Harry Barnes, lecturer in politics and industrial relations at Sheffield Univ; previously lectured at North Notts Further Ed Coll; former railway clerk. Member, CND; helped set up Dronfield Miners' Support Gp. B Jul 22 1936; ed Easington and Ryhope colliery schs; Oxford and Hull Univs (mature student). ASTMS.
Mr John Hayes is sales director of a Nottingham computer company. Member, Nottinghamshire CC, since 1985. B Jun 23 1958; ed Colfe's GS, SE London; Nottingham Univ.
Mr Stephen Hardy, company secretary and solicitor. Contested North East Derbyshire 1983. Member, Aslockton PC. B Jan 10 1948; ed Nottingham High Sch; Cambridge and Brussels Univs.

DERBYSHIRE SOUTH — No change

Electorate %Turnout	80,045	81.3%	1987	75,391	78.5%	1983
*Currie, Mrs E. (C)	31,927	49.1%	+5.3%	25,909	43.8%	(C)
Whitby, J.D. (Lab)	21,616	33.2%	+4.0%	17,296	29.2%	(Lab)
Edgar, J. (SDP/All)	11,509	17.7%	-9.3%	15,959	27.0%	(SDP/All)
Lab to C swing 0.6%	65,052	C maj 10,311 15.9%		59,164	C maj 8,613 14.6%	

Mrs Edwina Currie

Mrs Edwina Currie was appointed Under Secretary of State for Health and Social Security with responsibilities for the health of women in 1986; PPS to Sir Keith Joseph as Secretary of State for Education and Science, 1985-86. Teacher and lecturer in economics, economic history and business studies, 1972-81. Elected in 1983. Member, Select Cmte on Social Services, 1983-86. B Oct 13 1946; ed Liverpool Inst; St Anne's Coll, Oxford, and LSE. Vice-pres, Fed of Cons Students, 1983-84. Member, General Advisory Cl, BBC, 1985- ; Birmingham City Cl, 1975-84; Birmingham AHA, 1975-82; Birmingham Community Relations Cl, 1979-83.
Mr John Whitby, general manager, Derbyshire Co-operative Development Agency. Director, Co-operative Soc. B Dec 21 1945. TGWU; Nupe.
Mr John Edgar, industrial training consultant; chief executive of Drinks Industries' Training Assocn Ltd. Chmn, Lichfield SDP, 1985- ; sec, Derbyshire/Scarsdale SDP area party, 1986- . B Oct 16 1932; ed Annan and Dumfries Acads; Glasgow Univ; London Business Sch.

DER

DERBYSHIRE WEST — No change

Electorate %Turnout	70,782	83.1%	**1987**	68,668	77.4%	**1983**
*McLoughlin, P.A. (C)	31,224	53.1%	-2.8%	29,695	55.9%	(C)
Walmsley, C.R. (L/All)	20,697	35.2%	+8.2%	14,370	27.0%	(L/All)
Moore, W. (Lab)	6,875	11.7%	-5.4%	9,060	17.1%	(Lab)
C to L/All swing 5.5%	58,796	C maj 10,527 17.9%		53,125	C maj 15,325 28.8%	

Mr Patrick McLoughlin won the 1986 by-election; contested Wolverhampton South East 1983. Jt sec, Cons back-bench environment cmte, since 1986. Mineworker at Littleton Colliery, 1979-85; marketing official, NCB, 1985-86. B Nov 30 1957; ed Cardinal Griffin RC Sch, Cannock; Staffordshire Coll of Agriculture. Former nat vice-chmn, YCs. Mbr, Staffordshire CC, 1981-87; Cannock Chase DC, 1980-87. Nat vice-chmn, YCs, 1982-84. Consultant to CM Partnerships.

Mr Christopher Walmsley, producer and presenter with BBC Radio Manchester, contested the 1986 by-election and High Peak in Oct 1974. Mbr, Lib Pty Cl. B Jun 1943; ed St Joseph's Coll, Blackpool; Univ Coll, London (Pres of Union, 1969-70).

Mr William Moore, writer and former communications lecturer, contested the seat in by-election, May 1986, and in 1979; Erewash, 1983. Former mbr, Park planning bd. B Aug 1933; ed Birmingham Coll of Commerce; Sheffield Univ.

Mr Patrick McLoughlin

DEVIZES — No change

Electorate %Turnout	86,047	77.2%	**1987**	83,211	74.9%	**1983**
*Morrison, C.A. (C)	36,372	54.8%	+0.8%	33,644	53.9%	(C)
Siegle, Mrs L.E. (L/All)	18,542	27.9%	-1.0%	18,020	28.9%	(SDP/All)
Buxton, R.W. (Lab)	11,487	17.3%	+0.5%	10,468	16.8%	(Lab)
				234	0.4%	(Other)
L/All to C swing 0.9%	66,401	C maj 17,830 26.9%		62,366	C maj 15,624 25.1%	

Mr Charles Morrison is a mbr of the Select Cmte on Procedure. Farmer; director of Islay Estates and CA Morrison Farms Ltd; parliamentary adviser, British Scrap Federation; member of LLoyd's. Elected at 1964 by-election. B Jun 25 1932; ed Eton and Royal Agricultural Coll, Cirencester. Vice-chmn, Game Conservancy; mbr, cl, Salmon and Trout Assocn. Chmn, Nat Cmte for Electoral Reform, 1985- ; Young Volunteer Force Foundation, 1971-74. Elder brother of Mr Peter Morrison, Cons MP for City of Chester. Jt vice-chmn, Cons Middle East Cl; 1922 Cmte, 1974-83; mbr, exec cmte, 1972- ; chmn, Cons back-bench constitutional cmte, 1982-85; parly racing cmte; parly population cmte; former jt vice-chmn, Cons countryside conservation cmte; former chmn, Cons back-bench agriculture cmte. Pres, British Trust for Conservation Volunteers, 1973-78; chmn, 1972-78. Mbr, Wiltshire CC, 1957-64.

Mrs Linda Siegle, housewife, was elected to Dorset CC in 1985. B Jul 30 1945; ed Purley County GS for Girls; Guys Hosp, London. JP.

Mr Richard Buxton, account manager in computer industry. Mbr, Socialist Education Assn; Inst of Housing. Former Newham cllr. B Oct 11 1956. ASTMS.

Mr Charles Morrison

DEVON NORTH — No change

Electorate %Turnout	67,474	81.7%	**1987**	63,638	80.1%	**1983**
*Speller, A. (C)	28,071	50.9%	-4.2%	28,066	55.1%	(C)
Pinney, M.A. (L/All)	23,602	42.8%	+4.9%	19,339	37.9%	(L/All)
Marjoram, Ms A. (Lab)	3,467	6.3%	+0.6%	2,893	5.7%	(Lab)
				669	1.3%	(Other)
C to L/All swing 4.5%	55,140	C maj 4,469 8.1%		50,967	C maj 8,727 17.1%	

Mr Tony Speller has been chairman of the Westcountry gp of Cons MPs since 1983; mbr, Select Cmte on Energy, since 1982. Elected in 1979; contested the seat in Oct 1974. Chmn, The Copyshops of SW England, a family controlled drawing office, graphic art and printing chain. B Jun 12 1929; ed Exeter Sch; London and Exeter Univs. Member, Exeter City Cl, 1963-74. Chmn, all-pty alternative energy gp (Parligaes) since 19836; pres, catering industry liaison cmte, 1982- . Major, TA. Hon parly adviser to Caravan Club; the Nat Fed of Retail Newsagents; and Catering and Equipment Manufacturers Assocn.

Mr Aza Pinney, film maker and journalist; director, Euro-One Productions. Contested Dorset West 1964, 1966, West Derbyshire 1967, Devon West 1974 (Feb and Oct), and Devon in 1979 Euro-election. Referendum director, 1975. Mbr, Liberal EEC and agricultural policy panels. B Jul 3 1936; ed Port Regis Prep Sch; Eton; Christ Church, Oxford; Dorset Farm Inst. IoJ, NFU.

Ms Anni Marjoram, head teacher, special needs school for boys. B Dec 10 1949; ed Notre Dame Convent, Wigan; Bretton Coll, W Yorkshire.

Mr Tony Speller

DEVON WEST AND TORRIDGE — No change

Electorate %Turnout	74,550	78.7%	**1987**	70,648	76.0%	**1983**
Nicholson, Miss E.H. (C)	29,484	50.3%	-7.7%	31,156	58.0%	(C)
Burnett, J.P.A. (L/All)	23,016	39.2%	+4.2%	18,805	35.0%	(L/All)
Brenton, D.G. (Lab)	4,990	8.5%	+1.9%	3,531	6.6%	(Lab)
Williamson, F. (Grn)	1,168	2.0%		116	0.2%	(Ind)
				113	0.2%	(Other)
C to L/All swing 6.0%	58,658	C maj 6,468 11.0%		53,721	C maj 12,351 23.0%	

Miss **Emma Nicholson** has been a vice-chmn of the Conservative Pty since 1983, having special responsibility for women. Director of fund raising, Save the Children Fund, 1977-85; fund raising consultant to World Assocn of Girl Guides and Girl Scouts; member, boards, Netherlands Save the Children and French Save the Children, both of which she founded. Contested Blyth 1979. Computer programmer, being computer and general management consultant, McLintock Mann and Whinney Murray, 1969-73; previously programming instructor, systems analyst, ICL, 1963-66; computer consultant, John Tyzack, 1967-69. B Oct 16 1941; ed Portsdown Lodge Sch, Bexhill-on-Sea; St Mary's Sch, Wantage; Royal Acad of Music, London.

Mr **John Burnett**, solicitor, farmer, breeder of Devon cattle, and Royal Marines officer for seven years. B Sep 19 1945; ed Ampleforth; Coll of Law, London. Mbr, Law Soc; NFU.

Mr **David Brenton**, basket maker. B Aug 15 1945; ed St Luke's Coll, Exeter; Barnstaple GS. Has been chmn, Bideford branch, and chmn, Devon West and Torridge CLP. Mbr, Bideford TC. Former dep Mayor, Bideford. Founder mbr, conservation soc. NAS/UWT.

Miss Emma Nicholson

DEWSBURY — Lab gain

Electorate %Turnout	70,836	78.8%	**1987**	69,734	74.0%	**1983**
Taylor, Mrs W.A. (Lab)	23,668	42.4%	+7.1%	20,297	39.4%	(C)
*Whitfield, J. (C)	23,223	41.6%	+2.3%	18,211	35.3%	(Lab)
Mills, A. (SDP/All)	8,907	16.0%	-9.4%	13,065	25.3%	(SDP/All)
C to Lab swing 2.4%	55,798	Lab maj 445 0.8%		51,573	C maj 2,086 4.0%	

Mrs **Ann Taylor**, a housing corporation monitoring officer and part-time tutor with Open Univ, was MP for Bolton West Oct 1974-83 when she unsuccessfully contested Bolton North East; contested Bolton West Feb 1974. An Opposition front bencher on education as deputy to Mr Neil Kinnock, 1979-81; then in Opposition DoE team to speak on housing, 1981-83. PPS, Secretary of State for Education and Science, 1975-76, and Secretary of State for Defence, 1976-77; an asst Govt whip, 1977-79. Former teacher. B Jul 2 1947; ed Bolton Sch; Bradford and Sheffield Univs. Mbr, Select Cmte on Violence in the Family, 1975-76; on Wealth Tax, 1975-77; and on Sound Broadcasting, 1976-77.

Mr **John Whitfield**, solicitor and company director, was MP for this seat, 1983-87; contested Hemsworth, 1979. Expert on animal by-products industry. B Oct 31 1941; ed Sedbergh Sch and Leeds Univ. Specialist in taxation and company law. Sec and unpaid director, Caldaire Independent Hospital plc. Director, Cullingworth Textiles Ltd.

Mr **Alan Mills**, local govt officer, is a former elect cllr. Former senior officer, consumer protection services, former estates asst, former police officer. Mbr, CSD; past chmn, Wakefield Area SDP; chmn, Pontefract/Castleford constituency gp. B Oct 4 1937; ed Hemsworth GS. Chmn of his local parish cl and member, dist health authority.

Mrs Ann Taylor

DONCASTER CENTRAL — No change

Electorate %Turnout	69,699	73.7%	**1987**	71,039	70.8%	**1983**
*Walker, H. (Lab)	26,266	51.2%	+9.1%	21,154	42.0%	(Lab)
Rawlings, Miss P.E. (C)	18,070	35.2%	-1.9%	18,646	37.1%	(C)
Gore-Browne, J.A. (SDP/All)	7,004	13.6%	-7.3%	10,524	20.9%	(SDP/All)
C to Lab swing 5.5%	51,340	Lab maj 8,196 16.0%		50,324	Lab maj 2,508 5.0%	

Mr **Harold Walker** was elected Chairman of Ways and Means and Deputy Speaker in 1983. Elected for this seat in 1983; MP for Doncaster, 1964-83. An Opposition spokesman on employment, 1979-83; Minister of State, Department of Employment, 1976-79; Under Secretary of State for Employment, 1974-76; a spokesman on employment, 1970-74; Under Secretary of State, Department of Employment and Productivity, 1968-70; asst Government whip, 1967-68. Engineer. B Jul 12 1927; ed at council school and Manchester Coll of Technology. Sponsored by AUEW.

Miss **Patricia Rawlings**, who contested Sheffield Central in 1983, has been a member of the Conservative Women's National Cmte since 1984. Chmn, London branch, British Red Cross Soc; awarded Nat Badge of Honour in 1981 for services to nursing. Formerly with textile company specializing in exports and public relations. Mbr, Peace through Nato Cl; Video Classification Cl; Royal Inst of International Affairs; European Union of Women; International Inst of Strategic Studies. B 1939; ed Oak Hall, Haslemere; London Univ; LSE.

Mr **James Gore Browne**, solicitor. B Mar 26 1947; ed Dundee and Aston Univs.

Mr Harold Walker

DONCASTER NORTH | No change

Electorate %Turnout	72,986	73.1%	**1987**	72,184	69.9%	**1983**
*Welsh, M.C. (Lab)	32,950	61.8%	+9.0%	26,626	52.8%	(Lab)
Shepherd, R.J. (C)	13,015	24.4%	-3.2%	13,915	27.6%	(C)
Norwood, P. (SDP/All)	7,394	13.9%	-5.8%	9,916	19.7%	(SDP/All)
C to Lab swing 6.1%	53,359	Lab maj 19,935 37.4%		50,457	Lab maj 12,711 25.2%	

Mr Michael Welsh has served on the Select Cmte on Foreign Affairs since 1983. Former miner. Elected for this seat 1983; MP for Don Valley, 1979-83. Doncaster councillor since 1962. B Nov 23 1926; ed Woodlands elementary sch; Sheffield Univ (extramural studies) and Ruskin College, Oxford.
Mr Richard Shepherd, teacher examiner and tutor. Mbr, Charnwood BC, 1979- (vice-chmn, health and housing cmte, 1984-86; vice-chmn, policy and finance cmte, 1986-); Quorn PC, 1978- (chmn, 1981-83). B Oct 7 1948; ed St Dunstan's Coll, Catford; Trinity Hall, Cambridge; Nottingham Univ. Chmn, Loughborough CPC. Life mbr, Nat Trust. AMMA.
Mr Peter Norwood, self-employed marketing consultant and former teacher. B Oct 2 1928.

Mr Michael Welsh

DON VALLEY | No change

Electorate %Turnout	74,500	73.8%	**1987**	73,112	69.9%	**1983**
*Redmond, M. (Lab)	29,200	53.1%	+8.0%	23,036	45.1%	(Lab)
Gallagher, C.H. (C)	17,733	32.3%	-0.2%	16,570	32.4%	(C)
Whitaker, W.K. (L/All)	8,027	14.6%	-7.9%	11,482	22.5%	(L/All)
C to Lab swing 4.1%	54,960	Lab maj 11,467 20.9%		51,088	Lab maj 6,466 12.7%	

Mr Martin Redmond, a former heavy goods vehicle driver, was elected in 1983. B Aug 15 1937; ed Woodlands RC Sch and Sheffield Univ. Mbr, Doncaster BC, 1975- ; leader, 1982- ; chmn, Lab gp, 1982- . NUM delegate for many years; panel chmn, Doncaster pits, from 1975. Vice-chmn, Doncaster AHA. Mbr, exec cmte, Campaign Group of Lab MPs, 1985-86; CND. Sponsored by NUM.
Mr Charles Gallagher, company director. B Oct 15 1959; ed Harrow; Jesus Coll, Cambridge; London Business School.
Mr Wilfred Whitaker, lecturer in geography and urban studies/planning at Hull CFE and author, contested Selby 1983, Barnsley 1979, Normanton Oct 1974, and Keighley Feb 1974. Pres, Normanton Libs, 1974-77; sec, Howden/Boothferry Libs, 1982-83; parly spokesman, Selby, 1983-86. B Jan 1 1946; ed Morley GS; Hull Univ; Huddersfield Poly. Mbr, NATFHE, since 1968, being former branch chmn and holder of other offices. Life mbr and former adventure holiday leader for Youth Hostels Assocn; founder mbr, 813 Steam Loco Preservation Soc.

Mr Martin Redmond

DORSET NORTH | No change

Electorate %Turnout	72,844	79.1%	**1987**	67,524	76.6%	**1983**
*Baker, N.B. (C)	32,854	57.0%	-1.1%	30,058	58.1%	(C)
Tapper, Dr G.W. (L/All)	20,947	36.4%	+0.3%	18,678	36.1%	(L/All)
Hanley, J. (Lab)	3,819	6.6%	+1.4%	2,710	5.2%	(Lab)
				294	0.6%	(Other)
C to L/All swing 0.7%	57,620	C maj 11,907 20.7%		51,740	C maj 11,380 22.0%	

Mr Nicholas Baker, a solicitor specialising in company and commercial law and member of Lloyd's, was elected in 1979; contested Southwark, Peckham, Feb and Oct 1974. PPS since 1981 to ministers at MOD including Mr Michael Heseltine, Secretary of State, 1984-86. Partner in Frere Cholmeley, solicitors, 1973- . B Nov 23 1938; ed St Neot's Sch, Hampshire; Clifton Coll; Exeter Coll, Oxford. National service in Tanzania. Editor of Oxford Tory; pres, Oxford Carlton Club. Mbr, Select Cmte on Agriculture, 1986- ; Select Cmte on Consolidation Bills and Select Cmte on Statutory Instruments, 1979-83. Sec, Cons back-bench media cmte, 1980-81, and of legal cmte, 1979-81. Sec, 1970-71, and political officer, 1971-72, of Bow Gp.
Dr Geoffrey Tapper, general medical practitioner, contested the seat 1983. Mbr, North Dorset DC, 1975- ; parish cllr, 1968- . B Oct 4 1931; ed Kingswood Sch, Bath; Middlesex Hospital Medical Sch.
Mr Joseph Hanley, contracts manager. Chaired Dorset North Dist Lab Pty, 1986-87 and 1983-84; Blandford branch, 1985-87, also being branch sec, 1985-86. Has also been constituency sec and vice-chmn. B Apr 13 1949; ed St Francis Xavier's, Liverpool.

Mr Nicholas Baker

DORSET SOUTH — No change

Electorate %Turnout	72,855	75.5%	**1987**	68,998	72.7%	**1983**
Bruce, I. (C)	30,184	54.8%	-2.3%	28,631	57.1%	(C)
Ellis, B. (L/All)	15,117	27.5%	+0.5%	13,533	27.0%	(SDP/All)
Dench, Mrs B. (Lab)	9,494	17.2%	+1.6%	7,831	15.6%	(Lab)
Hayler, A. (Ind)	244	0.4%	+0.1%	151	0.3%	(Ind)
C to L/All swing 1.4%	55,039	C maj 15,067 27.4%		50,146	C maj 15,098 30.1%	

Mr Ian Bruce, recruitment and manufacturing consultant and company chairman, contested Burnley 1983, Yorkshire West in 1984 Euro elections. Nat chmn, Cons Prospective Candidates Assocn; founder of Trialogue, the Yorkshire candidates forum. B Mar 14 1947; ed Chelmsford Tech HS; Mid-Essex Tech Coll; Bradford Univ. Mbr, Colne Valley Cons Assocn and Kirklees Cons gp liaison cmte. Scout ldr.
Mr Brian Ellis, legal executive, is leader, Liberal gp, Weymouth and Portland BC; member since 1984. B Sep 15, 1950; ed Bridgwater Boys' Sch, Somerset.
Mrs Brenda Dench, nursing auxillary. Mbr, Weymouth and Portland BC, 1981- ; Dorset CC, 1982- . B Feb 27 1933; ed Moorend Lane Sec Sch, Birmingham. Nupe.

Mr Ian Bruce

DORSET WEST — No change

Electorate %Turnout	64,360	78.3%	**1987**	60,997	74.2%	**1983**
*Spicer, J.W. (C)	28,305	56.2%	-3.5%	27,030	59.7%	(C)
Jones, T. (L/All)	15,941	31.6%	+2.8%	13,078	28.9%	(L/All)
Watson, D. (Lab)	6,123	12.2%	+0.7%	5,168	11.4%	(Lab)
C to L/All swing 3.1%	50,369	C maj 12,364 24.5%		45,276	C maj 13,952 30.8%	

Mr James Spicer has been a vice-chmn of the Conservative Pty since 1985 and chmn, International Office; company director. Nat chmn, CPC, 1968-71. Mbr, Select Cmte on Agriculture, 1984-85; Select Cmte on European Secondary Legislation, 1974-75. Mbr, European Parliament, 1975-84, being elected MEP for Wessex, 1979-84; chief whip, European Democratic Gp, 1975-79; chmn, Cons Gp for Europe, 1975-78. B Oct 4 1925; ed Latymer. Elected in Feb 1974; contested Southampton Itchen by-election, 1971. Director, Fitness for Industry Ltd and Thames and Kennet Marina Ltd.
Mr Trevor Jones, retailer, was Mayor of Dorchester, 1982-83. Contested this seat 1983 and 1979, and Preston North, 1970. Mbr, West Dorset DC, 1973-83 and since 1986; Dorchester TC, since 1976. Former chmn, ALC. B Jun 21 1944; ed LSE.
Mr David Watson, an official of Nalgo, chairs the Dorset County and W Dorset Labour Parties; mbr, SW reg exec. Also chairs Dorchester Trades Cl; authority mbr, W Dorset HA. B May 24 1956; ed Nower Hill Comprehensive Sch; Stanmore Coll.

Mr James Spicer

DOVER — No change

Electorate %Turnout	68,997	79.8%	**1987**	67,922	77.6%	**1983**
Shaw, D.L. (C)	25,343	46.0%	-2.3%	25,454	48.3%	(C)
Love, S.S.E.W. (Lab)	18,802	34.1%	+3.3%	16,234	30.8%	(Lab)
Nice, G. (SDP/All)	10,942	19.9%	-0.3%	10,601	20.1%	(SDP/All)
				404	0.8%	(Other)
C to Lab swing 2.8%	55,087	C maj 6,541 11.9%		52,693	C maj 9,220 17.5%	

Mr David Shaw, chartered accountant, is founder and managing director of Sabrelance Ltd, a company which assists small businesses. Director of Invicta Sound, Kent's commercial radio station, and four other companies. Contested Leigh in 1979. Chmn, Bow Group, 1983-84. B Nov 14 1950; ed King's Coll Sch, Wimbledon, and City of London Poly. With Cooper and Lybrand, chartered accountants, 1971-79; County Bank, 1979-83. Vice-chmn, Kingston and Malden Cons Assocn, 1979-86. Mbr, Royal Borough of Kingston upon Thames Cl, 1974-78; Domesday national cmte.
Mr Stephen Love, headmaster of a community college, contested this seat 1983; Gillingham 1979. Chmn, Disabled Housing Trust; mbr, W Sussex ed cmte, 1977-87. B Aug 13 1934; ed Woodley Hill GS, Reading; Univ Coll, Oxford. Former adviser to IBA and to World Wildlife Fund. NUT.
Mr Geoffrey Nice, barrister, contested Dover 1983. Founder mbr, SDP. B Oct 21 1945; ed St Dunstan's Coll, Catford, Keble Coll, Oxford.

Mr David Shaw

DOWN NORTH — No change

Electorate %Turnout	65,018	62.8%	**1987**	61,574	66.2%	**1983**
*Kilfedder, J.A. (UPUP)	18,420	45.1%	-10.9%	22,861	56.1%	(UPUP)
McCartney, R. (Real U)	14,467	35.4%		9,015	22.1%	(All)
Cushnahan, J. (All)	7,932	19.4%	-2.7%	8,261	20.3%	(OUP)
				645	1.6%	(Other)
Uncalculated	40,819	UPUP maj 3,953 9.7%		40,782	UPUP maj 13,846 34.0%	

Mr James Kilfedder, leader of the Ulster Popular Unionist Party since 1980, was Speaker of the N Ireland Assembly, 1982-86. MP at Westminster for North Down since 1970, first as Official Unionist MP from 1970-Feb 1974, then Ind Unionist MP, Feb to Oct 1974 becoming Official Unionist MP from Oct 1974 until he resigned from the party towards the end of that Parliament. He retained the seat in 1979 becoming UPUP MP. Resigned seat 1985 in protest at Anglo-Irish agreement and re-elected in 1986 by-election. UU MP for Belfast West, 1964-66; former Chief Whip and Hon Sec, UU Parly. Party. Official Unionist member, NI Assembly, 1973-75; UUUC member, NI Constitutional Convention, 1975-76. Barrister. B Jul 16 1928, ed Portora Royal Sch, Enniskillen, and Trinity Coll. Dublin.

Mr John Cushnahan, leader of the Alliance Pty; former teacher, contested this seat 1983 and Belfast North 1979. B Jul 23 1948; ed St Mary's Christian Brothers Sch, Belfast; Queen's Univ; St Joseph's Coll of Ed. Assemblyman North Down, 1982-86.

Details of 1986 by-election on Page 285

Mr James Kilfedder

DOWN SOUTH — SDLP gain

Electorate %Turnout	71,235	79.4%	**1987**	66,968	76.6%	**1983**
McGrady, E.K. (SDLP)	26,579	47.0%	+7.8%	20,693	40.3%	(OUP)
*Powell, J.E. (OUP)	25,848	45.7%	+5.4%	20,145	39.2%	(SDLP)
Ritchie, Ms G. (PSF)	2,363	4.2%	-3.8%	4,074	7.9%	(PSF)
Laird, Miss S.E. (All)	1,069	1.9%	-1.7%	3,743	7.3%	(DUP)
O'Hagan, D. (WP)	675	1.2%	-0.5%	1,823	3.6%	(All)
				851	1.7%	(Other)
OUP to SDLP swing 1.2%	56,534	SDLP maj 731 1.3%		51,329	OUP maj 548 1.1%	

Mr Edward McGrady, chartered accountant, contested the seat 1983 and 1979. B 1943; ed St Patrick's GS, Downpatrick; Belfast Coll of Tech. Founder mbr and first chmn, SDLP, 1970-72. Mbr, N Ireland Assembly 1973, Convention 1975 and Assembly, 1982.

Mr Enoch Powell was returned for the seat in Oct 1974; resigned in 1985 in protest at the Anglo-Irish Agreement, and won the consequent 1986 by-election. Dismissed as defence spokesman for Opposition by Mr Heath in 1968 following speech on immigration. Contested Conservative leadership, 1965. Minister of Health, 1960-63; Financial Secretary to Treasury, 1957-58, resigning in protest at Govt spending. Parliamentary Secretary, Ministry of Housing and Local Government, 1955-57. MP for Wolverhampton South-West, 1950-1974. B Jun 16 1912; ed King Edward's HS, Birmingham, and Trinity Coll, Cambridge. Professor of Greek, Sydney University, 1937-39. Army, 1939-46, rising from private to brigadier.

Mrs Geraldine Ritchie, PSF mbr, Down DC, 1985- . Aged 28.

Mr Siobhan Laird, mbr, Alliance Pty central exec. B Sep 25 1962; ed Queen's Univ, Belfast; Ulster Univ, Jordanstown. Sec, Young Alliance.

Details of 1986 by-election on Page 285

Mr Edward McGrady

DUDLEY EAST — No change

Electorate %Turnout	75,206	72.3%	**1987**	74,765	71.3%	**1983**
*Gilbert, J.W. (Lab)	24,942	45.9%	+0.0%	24,441	45.8%	(Lab)
Jones, Mrs E. (C)	21,469	39.5%	+4.6%	18,625	34.9%	(C)
Monks, K. (SDP/All)	7,965	14.6%	-4.6%	10,272	19.3%	(SDP/All)
Lab to C swing 2.3%	54,376	Lab maj 3,473 6.4%		53,338	Lab maj 5,816 10.9%	

Dr John Gilbert, a mbr of Select Cmte on Defence since 1979, was Minister of State for Defence, 1976-79; Financial Secretary to Treasury, 1974-75; Minister for Transport, DoE, 1975-76. Non-exec company director, chartered accountant and economist. Elected for this seat, Feb 1974; MP for Dudley, 1970-74; contested Dudley by-election, 1968, and Ludlow, 1966. Opposition spokesman on Treasury matters, 1972-74. B Apr 5 1927; ed Merchant Taylors' Sch, Northwood; St John's Coll, Oxford, and New York Univ. Chmn, PLP defence group, 1981-83; vice-chmn, Lab Finance and Industry Group, 1983-85. Mbr, Cl for Arms Control; Amnesty International. GMBATU.

Mrs Elisabeth Jones, physiotherapist and beauty therapist, is training officer and former CPC chmn and officer, NW Hampshire Cons Assocn; vice-chmn, Hampshire Central Euro Cl. Mbr, Hampshire CC, 1985- ; Test Valley BC, 1976-83. Owner of clinic and training school. Chmn, British Assocn of Beauty Therapy and Cosmetology, 1982-84; international lecturer in health and beauty therapy. B Sep 22 1939; ed Glengara Park Sch, Dublin; Dublin Sch of Physiotherapy; Trinity Coll, Dublin; Bretlands Coll, Tunbridge Wells.

Mr Kevin Monks, researcher/student, has been in part-time employment at SDP HQ since 1985; research asst to Mr John Cartwright MP, 1986- ; previously a constituency organiser. B Feb 23 1962; ed Wallington HS, Surrey; Howardian HS, Cardiff; Reading Coll of Tech; Brunel Univ, W London.

Dr John Gilbert

DUDLEY WEST — No change

Electorate	%Turnout		81,789	79.1%	**1987**	77,795	75.9%	**1983**
*Blackburn, J.G. (C)			32,224	49.8%	+3.7%	27,250	46.2%	(C)
Titley, G. (Lab)			21,980	34.0%	+2.6%	18,527	31.4%	(Lab)
Lewis, G.P.T. (L/All)			10,477	16.2%	-6.3%	13,251	22.4%	(L/All)
Lab to C swing 0.5%			64,681	C maj 10,244 15.8%		59,028	C maj 8,723 14.8%	

Mr John Blackburn

Mr John Blackburn, sales director, Solway Engineering Co. Ltd, since 1965, and national sales manager with an international engineering company, 1965-79, is parliamentary adviser to Nat Assocn of Retired Police Officers. Elected in 1979. Chmn, Cons Friends of Israel parly group, 1986; mbr, Select Cmte on Home Affairs, 1980-83; jt vice-chmn, Cons back-bench cmte on arts and heritage, 1986- ; jt sec, 1980-86. Served in Royal Military Police, 1949-53; detective constable and then sergeant, Liverpool Police, 1953-65. B Sep 2 1933; ed Liverpool Collegiate Sch; Liverpool and Berlin Univs. Mbr, Wolverhampton Cl, 1970-80; Post Office Users' Nat Cl, 1972-80; Ecclesiastical Cl, 1979- . Freeman, City of London, 1980; City of Tel Aviv, 1981. FInstM, FISE, FInstMSM, and FRSA. Exec mbr, Traeth Coch Yacht Club. ASTMS since 1966; pres, Staffordshire branch, 1980-83.

Mr Gary Titley, campaign manager to Mr John Bird, MEP, contested Bromsgrove, 1983. Director, W Midlands Enterprise Bd. B Jan 19 1950; ed York Univ. Mbr, W Midlands CC, 1981-86. TGWU.

Mr Gerald Lewis, college counsellor at Dudley College of Technology, fought this seat in 1983 and Dudley East, 1979. B March 17 1926; ed at Aberdeen, Belfast and Aston, Birmingham, univs. Chmn, Dudley Lib Assocn; vice-chmn, West Midlands Lib Party. NATFHE.

DULWICH — No change

Electorate	%Turnout		56,355	69.3%	**1987**	56,596	67.2%	**1983**
*Bowden, G.F. (C)			16,563	42.4%	+1.9%	15,424	40.5%	(C)
Hoey, Miss C.L. (Lab)			16,383	42.0%	+6.3%	13,565	35.7%	(Lab)
Harris, Dr A.N.G. (SDP/All)			5,664	14.5%	-7.5%	8,376	22.0%	(SDP/All)
Goldie, A. (Grn)			432	1.1%		338	0.9%	(NF)
						336	0.9%	(Other)
C to Lab swing 2.2%			39,042	C maj 180 0.5%		38,039	C maj 1,859 4.9%	

Mr Gerald Bowden

Mr Gerald Bowden, who was elected in 1983, was principal lecturer in Dept of Estate Management, South Bank Polytechnic, 1972-83. Sec, Cons back-bench arts and heritage cmte, 1985- ; jt sec, Cons education cmte, 1985- . Barrister and chartered surveyor; mbr of Lloyd's. B Aug 26 1935; ed Battersea GS; Magdalen Coll, Oxford; Gray's Inn; Coll of Estate Management, London. GLC mbr for Dulwich, 1977-81. Mbr of TA until 1984 serving with rank of Lt-Colonel. Co-opted mbr, ILEA, 1981-85.

Ms Kate Hoey, physical education lecturer and adviser to Arsenal Football Club; former N Ireland Athlete; has run courses for London First Division assocn football clubs; taught politics in further ed colls. B Jun 21 1948; ed Belfast Royal Acad; London Univ.

Dr Andrew Harris, general medical practitioner. Mbr, CSD; SDP health policy cmte; chmn, Southwark area party 1984-85. B Mar 21 1951; ed King's Sch, Canterbury; Trinity Coll, Cambridge; St Thomas' Hospital Medical Sch. BMA.

Mr Alex Goldie, university researcher and lecturer in management. B 1929; ed London Univ; Thames Poly; Cranfield Inst of Tech. TA (awarded TD 1979).

DUMBARTON — No change

Electorate	%Turnout		58,968	77.9%	**1987**	57,373	75.1%	**1983**
McFall, J. (Lab)			19,778	43.0%	+6.3%	15,810	36.7%	(Lab)
Graham, R.F. (C)			14,556	31.7%	-0.1%	13,695	31.8%	(C)
Mowbray, R. (SDP/All)			6,060	13.2%	-9.6%	9,813	22.8%	(SDP/All)
Herriot, Ms J. (SNP)			5,564	12.1%	+3.4%	3,768	8.7%	(SNP)
C to Lab swing 3.2%			45,958	Lab maj 5,222 11.4%		43,086	Lab maj 2,115 4.9%	

Mr John McFall

Mr John McFall, assistant head teacher at a Glasgow comprehensive school. Founder and chair, West Dumbarton Community Involvement Project; founder of "Save the NHS" steering cmte; mbr, Gas Consumers' Cl, Scotland. B Oct 4 1944; ed local comprehensive school. Has chaired and been sec of CLP. Unpaid director, Dumbarton Equitable Co-operative Society. EIS; GMBATU; sponsored by Co-operative Party. Former sec, Trades Cl; now exec member.

Mr Robert Graham, Strathclyde Univ administrator since 1980 and lecturer in sociology, Glasgow Coll of Tech, 1971-78, fought Clydebank and Milngavie in 1983. B Aug 24 1936; ed High Wycombe Coll of Tech and Art; Essex Univ; Jordanhill Coll of Ed; Strathclyde Univ. Held Army short service commission, 1960-65; in diplomatic service, 1965-67. AUT.

Mr Richard Mowbray, economics lecturer, Paisley Coll of Tech, contested Glasgow Hillhead for Labour 1979. Mbr, CSD; Scottish SDP Cl, 1986-87; Scottish economic policy gp. B Sep 16 1946; ed Chesterfield GS; LSE; Glasgow Univ.

Mrs Jenny Herriot, the SNP spokesman on European affairs and mbr of its nat cl since 1982 and nat exec, 1982-84, fought Eastwood in 1983 and Strathclyde West in 1984 Euro election. B Jan 24 1944; ed Kirkcaldy HS; Glasgow Royal Infirmary.

DUMFRIES — No change

Electorate %Turnout	59,347	75.6%	**1987**	57,594	73.0%	**1983**
*Monro, Sir Hector (C)	18,785	41.9%	-2.7%	18,730	44.5%	(C)
Phillips, Ms C.W. (Lab)	11,292	25.2%	+4.3%	10,036	23.9%	(SDP/All)
McCall, J.R. (SDP/All)	8,064	18.0%	-5.9%	8,764	20.8%	(Lab)
McAlpine, T. (SNP)	6,391	14.2%	+3.5%	4,527	10.8%	(SNP)
Thomas, P.M. (Grn)	349	0.8%				
C to Lab swing 3.5%	44,881	C maj 7,493 16.7%		42,057	C maj 8,694 20.7%	

Sir Hector Monro

Sir Hector Monro, farmer and company director. Mbr, Select Cmte on Defence 1987- ; chmn, Scottish group of Cons MPs, 1983- .Mbr, Select Cmte on Procedure, 1983- . Under Secretary for Environment with responsibility for sport, 1979-81; Under Secretary of State, Scottish Office, 1971-74; Govt whip, 1970-71. Elected in 1964. B Oct 4 1922; ed Canford Sch; King's Coll, Cambridge.Pres, Scottish Rugby Union, 1976-77; Auto-cycle Union, 1983- . Hon Air Commodore, RAuxAF. Pres, Scottish Rugby Union, 1976-77; Auto-cycle Union, 1983- . RAF pilot, 1941-46; Hon Air Commodore, RAuxAF. Mbr, Nature Conservancy Cl, 1982- ; cl, Nat Trust for Scotland, 1983- .
Mrs Kate Phillips, tutor and organizer in adult education. B Sep 4 1946; ed Glasgow Univ (adult student). ASTMS.
Mr James McCall, publishing consultant. Contested this seat 1983. B Jan 3 1948; ed Ayr Acad; Glasgow Univ.
Mr Thomas McAlpine, director of electronics company, contested Clydesdale 1983; Lanark 1979 and again in 1974, Bothwell 1970. Nat exec vice-chmn, SNP. B Sep 23 1929; ed Dalziel HS; Glasgow Univ.

DUNDEE EAST — Lab gain

Electorate %Turnout	60,805	75.9%	**1987**	62,752	73.7%	**1983**
McAllion, J. (Lab)	19,539	42.3%	+9.4%	20,276	43.8%	(SNP)
*Wilson, R.G. (SNP)	18,524	40.1%	-3.7%	15,260	33.0%	(Lab)
Cook, P. (C)	5,938	12.9%	-2.6%	7,172	15.5%	(C)
von Romberg, Mrs M. (L/All)	2,143	4.6%	-3.0%	3,546	7.7%	(L/All)
SNP to Lab swing 6.5%	46,144	Lab maj 1,015 2.2%		46,254	SNP maj 5,016 10.8%	

Mr John McAllion

Mr John McAllion is convenor of Tayside Regional Council; former teacher in Dundee. B Feb 13 1948; ed St Andrews Univ; Dundee Coll of Ed. GMBATU.
Mr Gordon Wilson, SNP chairman since 1979 and the party's spokesman on economic affairs, was MP for this setat Feb 1974-87; contested it, 1973 by-election. Former partner in law practice. B Apr 16 1938; ed Douglas HS and Edinburgh Univ. Executive vice-chmn, SNP, 1972-73; senior vice-chmn, 1973-74; spokesman on energy, 1974; home affairs, 1975-76; and devolution, 1976-79; nat sec, SNP, 1963-71; dep leader, SNP parliamentary party, 1974-79. Rector, Dundee Univ, 1983-86.
Mr Paul Cook, managing director of travel company and personnel consultancy. Chmn, Banff and Buchan Cons Assocn; mbr, Scottish Cons Industry Cmte. B May 27 1949; ed Aberdeen GS; Robert Gordon's Inst of Tech. Mbr, Grampian Health Bd.
Dr Margo von Romberg, classics teacher, Webster's HS, Kirriemuir; part-time classics/English tutor in Edinburgh, 1977-85. Deputy convenor, Dundee Lib Assocn, 1987. B Jul 25 1942; ed Arbroath HS; St Andrews, Edinburgh and London Univs.

DUNDEE WEST — No change

Electorate %Turnout	61,926	75.4%	**1987**	62,703	74.4%	**1983**
*Ross, E. (Lab)	24,916	53.4%	+9.9%	20,288	43.5%	(Lab)
Donnelly, J.A. (C)	8,390	18.0%	-3.8%	10,138	21.7%	(C)
Morgan, A.N. (SNP)	7,164	15.3%	-1.7%	7,976	17.1%	(SDP/All)
Lonie, Mrs R. (SDP/All)	5,922	12.7%	-4.4%	7,973	17.1%	(SNP)
Mathewson, S.R. (Comm)	308	0.7%		302	0.6%	(Eco)
C to Lab swing 6.8%	46,700	Lab maj 16,526 35.4%		46,677	Lab maj 10,150 21.7%	

Mr Ernest Ross

Mr Ernest Ross has served on the Select Cmte on Standing Orders and the Unopposed Bills panel since 1981. Elected in 1979. Quality control engineer with Timex. B Jul 1942; ed St Joseph's and St Mary's Primary Sch, St John's Junior Sec Sch. Sponsored by AUEW (TASS).
Mr Alan Donnelly, gas operations technician at St Fergus gas plant. Chmn, Peterhead Community Cl; sec, Peterhead branch, Banff and Buchan Cons Assocn. B 1954; ed St Bede's Sec Sch, Jarrow; Hepburn Tech Coll; South Shields Marine. Became apprentice fitter on Tyneside; later joined Merchant Navy.
Mr Alasdair Morgan, computer project manager, fought Tayside North 1983. SNP nat treas since 1983. B Apr 21 1945; ed Breadalbane Acad, Aberfeldy, Perthshire; Glasgow Univ.
Mrs Rosemary Lonie, chemistry teacher. Mbr, CSD; chmn, Dundee and Angus area party 1984-86; former execi mbr, Campaign for a Scottish Assembly. B Jul 13 1939; ed Darlington High Sch; Durham and Dundee Univs. SSTA.
Mr Steve Mathewson, architectural technician. Mbr, Scottish cmte, Comm Pty; sec, Dundee area. Mbr, Scottish Div Cl, ASTMS; exec, Dundee Trades Cl. Aged 26.

DUNFERMLINE EAST | No change

Electorate %Turnout	51,175	76.6%	**1987**	49,881	72.0%	**1983**
*Brown, J.G. (Lab)	25,381	64.8%	+13.2%	18,515	51.5%	(Lab)
Shenton, C. (C)	5,792	14.8%	-4.0%	7,214	20.1%	(L/All)
Harris, Ms E. (L/All)	4,122	10.5%	-9.6%	6,764	18.8%	(C)
McGarry, Mrs A. (SNP)	3,901	10.0%	+2.8%	2,573	7.2%	(SNP)
				864	2.4%	(Other)
C to Lab swing 8.6%	39,196	Lab maj 19,589 50.0%		35,930	Lab maj 11,301 31.5%	

Dr Gordon Brown

Dr Gordon Brown has been an Opposition spokesman on regional affairs in the DTI front-bench team, since 1985. Elected in 1983. Chmn, Scot Lab Pty, 1983-84; mbr of its exec cmte, 1977-83. Mbr, Select Cmte on Employment, 1983-85. B Feb 20 1951; ed Kirkcaldy HS; Edinburgh Univ. Journalist with, then editor, current affairs dpt, Scottish Television, 1980-83; lecturer in politics, Glasgow Coll of Tech, 1976-80; temporary lecturer, Edinburgh Univ, 1975-76; rector, Edinburgh Univ, 1972-75. Hon Dir, 7:84 Theatre Co (Scotland). NUJ. Sponsored by TGWU.
Mr Clive Shenton, advocate, contested the seat 1983. B Oct 7 1946; ed Durban HS; RMA Sandhurst; Edinburgh Univ.
Ms Elizabeth Harris, teacher. Mbr, Dunfermline DC, 1984- ; nat exec, Scottish Lib Pty, 1986-; SLP housing and employment policy and Alliance education policy panels. Vice-chmn, Dunfermline Lib Assocn, 1982-84. B Apr 29 1957; ed Beath Senior HS; Dundee Coll of Ed; Open Univ.
Mrs Alice McGarry is vice-chair, Dunfermline East SNP. Mbr, Fife Reg Cl. B 1952; ed St Andrew's HS, Kirkcaldy. Mbr, Soc of Civil and Public Servants.

DUNFERMLINE WEST | No change

Electorate %Turnout	51,063	77.0%	**1987**	49,075	73.5%	**1983**
*Douglas, R.G. (Lab)	18,493	47.0%	+11.0%	12,998	36.0%	(Lab)
Gallie, P.R. (C)	9,091	23.1%	-6.0%	10,524	29.2%	(C)
Moyes, F.A. (SDP/All)	8,288	21.1%	-5.1%	9,434	26.2%	(SDP/All)
Hughes, G. (SNP)	3,435	8.7%	+1.0%	2,798	7.8%	(SNP)
				321	0.9%	(Other)
C to Lab swing 8.5%	39,307	Lab maj 9,402 23.9%		36,075	Lab maj 2,474 6.9%	

Mr Richard Douglas

Mr Richard Douglas, economic consultant on oil related matters and marine engineer. Mbr Select Cmte on Defence 1983- ; mbr, PAC, 1979-83; vice-chmn, Scottish gp of Lab MPs, 1986-. Elected for this seat 1983; MP for Dunfermline, 1979-83; MP for East Stirlingshire and Clackmannan, 1970 to Feb 1974; contested that seat, Oct 1974; Glasgow, Pollock, 1967 by-election; Edinburgh West, 1966; South Angus, 1964. B Jan 4 1932; ed Govan Sec Sch; Co-op Coll, Stanford Hall, Loughborough; Strathclyde Univ; LSE. Hpn lecturer, Strathclyde, 1980-. AEU. Sponsored by Co-op Pty.
Mr Philip Gallie, engineer in electricity supply industry. Contested Cunninghame South 1983. Mbr, Cunninghame DC, 1980-84. B Jun 3 1939; ed Dunfermline HS; Kirkcaldy Tech Coll. Elder, Church of Scotland. EPEA.
Mr Frank Moyes, consultant to RN on navigation systems, working on Polaris at Rosyth Dockyard. Contested Dunfermline W 1983. Dep ldr, Alliance Gp, Dunfermline DC, 1984- . B Jul 14 1942; ed St Johns Coll, Southsea; RGS, Guildford, Manchester Univ.
Mr Gordon Hughes, community worker. B 1943; ed Callendar Park and Moray House CFEs; Open Univ. Founder mbr, Heritage Soc.

DURHAM, CITY OF | No change

Electorate %Turnout	66,567	78.2%	**1987**	66,925	74.4%	**1983**
Steinberg, G.N. (Lab)	23,382	44.9%	+8.4%	18,163	36.5%	(Lab)
Stoker, D. (SDP/All)	17,257	33.2%	+0.6%	16,190	32.5%	(SDP/All)
Colquhoun, G.M. (C)	11,408	21.9%	-9.1%	15,438	31.0%	(C)
SDP/All to Lab swing 3.9%	52,047	Lab maj 6,125 11.8%		49,791	Lab maj 1,973 4.0%	

Mr Gerald Steinberg

Mr Gerald (Gerry) Steinberg, headmaster of a special school, has been on Durham City Cl for 11 years; sec, Lab gp for eight years; chmn, finance cmte. Agent to Durham MP 10 years and to Durham Euro MP five years. Sec, Durham CLP, 10 years. B Apr 20 1945; ed Whinney Hill Sec Mod Sch; Johnstone GS; Sheffield Coll of Ed; Newcastle Poly. NUT.
Dr David Stoker, historical researcher currently working at Sheffield Univ, contested this seat 1983. B 1952; ed King Edward VI Sch, Morpeth; Manchester Univ.
Mr Gordon Colquhoun, solicitor and partner in Winnard and Colquhoun of Dewsbury. B Jun 4 1954; ed Hutchesons' Boys GS, Glasgow; Barnfield HS and Sixth Form Coll, Luton and Leeds Univ. Mbr, Nat Trust, RSPB and Camra. Election agent, Barnsley West and Penistone, 1983.

DURHAM NORTH — No change

Electorate %Turnout	72,115	75.9%	**1987**	71,256	72.7%	**1983**
*Radice, G.H. (Lab)	30,798	56.2%	+5.3%	26,404	51.0%	(Lab)
Jeary, Dr D. (SDP/All)	12,365	22.6%	-2.5%	12,967	25.0%	(L/All)
Gibbon, N.C. (C)	11,602	21.2%	-2.8%	12,418	24.0%	(C)
SDP/All to Lab swing 3.9%	54,765	Lab maj 18,433 33.7%		51,789	Lab maj 13,437 25.9%	

Mr Giles Radice became chief Opposition spokesman on education in 1983 when he was elected to shadow Cabinet. Elected for this seat 1983; MP for Chester-le-Street, 1973-83; contested Chippenham, 1964 and 1966. An Opposition spokesman on employment, 1981-83; a spokesman on foreign affairs, 1981. Vice-chmn, Northern gp of Lab MPs, 1986- ; chmn, PLP employment gp, 1979-81. Mbr, Select Cmtes on Expenditure, 1974-79; Procedure, 1977-79; Employment, 1979-81. PPS to Mrs Shirley Williams, Secretary of State for Education and Science, 1978-79. Head of research dept, GMBATU, 1966-73. Chmn, Fabian Society, 1976-77, and mbr of its exec. B Oct 4 1936; ed Winchester and Magdalen Coll, Oxford. Mbr, cl, Policy Studies Inst, 1978-83. Sponsored by GMBATU.
Dr Derek Jeary, general medical practitioner. B 1948; ed Durham Johnston GS; Newcastle Univ.
Mr Nicolas Gibbon, parliamentary adviser to industry. B Aug 30 1954; ed St Alban's Sch, Herts; Surrey, Sussex and Munich Univs; Vienna Sch of Economics.

Mr Giles Radice

DURHAM NORTH WEST — No change

Electorate %Turnout	61,302	73.5%	**1987**	60,747	70.7%	**1983**
Armstrong, Ms H.J. (Lab)	22,947	50.9%	+6.3%	19,135	44.6%	(Lab)
Iceton, D. (C)	12,785	28.4%	-1.4%	12,779	29.8%	(C)
Foote Wood, C. (L/All)	9,349	20.7%	-4.9%	11,008	25.6%	(L/All)
C to Lab swing 3.9%	45,081	Lab maj 10,162 22.5%		42,922	Lab maj 6,356 14.8%	

Ms Hilary Armstrong, lecturer in community and youth work, has been on Durham CC since 1985; mbr, executive, North Regional Lab Pty; sec, Sunderland North, 1975-81; mbr of pty 26 years. Chair, ASTMS, Northern Division, 1981- . B Nov 13 1945; ed Monkwearmouth Comprehensive Sch; West Ham Coll of Tech; Birmingham Univ. Mbr, Anti-Apartheid Movement.
Mr Derek Iceton, chartered secretary, small business advisor and lecturer in finance and business administration. B May 27 1942; ed Hartlepool Tech Coll. Mbr, Derwentside DC. NATFHE.
Mr Chris Foote Wood, journalist, has run his own North Press News and Sports Agency since 1976. Contested this seat 1983; Durham 1979; Teeside, Middlesbrough, Oct 1974; Newcastle North, Feb 1974; County Durham in Euro elections, 1984 and 1979. B Dec 15 1940; ed Bury GS, Lancashire; King's Coll, Durham Univ; Open Univ. Mbr, Bishop Auckland UDC, 1967-74; Wear Valley DC, since 1973 (chmn, 1976-77, and ldr, 1976-79); Durham CC, 1973-77 and since 1985. Nalgo branch sec. NUJ branch sec; mbr, Freelance Industrial Cl; chief scrutineer, ADM (annual conference).

Ms Hilary Armstrong

EALING, ACTON — No change

Electorate %Turnout	67,176	71.0%	**1987**	62,078	72.2%	**1983**
*Young, Sir George (C)	25,499	53.4%	+4.2%	22,051	49.2%	(C)
Portwood, P.J. (Lab)	13,256	27.8%	+1.1%	11,959	26.7%	(Lab)
Brooks, S.R.D. (SDP/All)	8,973	18.8%	-4.8%	10,593	23.6%	(SDP/All)
				192	0.4%	(Other)
Lab to C swing 1.6%	47,728	C maj 12,243 25.7%		44,795	C maj 10,092 22.5%	

Sir George Young was an Under Secretary of State for Environment, 1981-86; Under Secretary of State for Health and Social Security, 1979-81; Opposition whip, 1976-79. Economist. Elected in Feb 1974. B Jul 16 1941; ed Eton and Christ Church, Oxford. Chmn, Acton Housing Assocn, 1972-79. Mbr, Select Cmte on Violence in Marriage, 1975. Mbr, GLC, 1970-73; Lambeth BC, 1968-71. Economic adviser, Post Office, 1969-74; Kobler Research Fellow, Surrey Univ, 1967-69; economist, NEDO, 1966-67.
Mr Philip Portwood, economic development officer with Camden Cl. Mbr, Ealing Cl, 1984- . B May 27 1958; ed Faraday Comprehensive S; Hull Univ. Mbr, cmte, East Acton community assocn; London Cycling Campaign. Nalgo.
Mr Stephen Brooks, personnel manager. B May 18 1954; ed Frimley and Camberley GS; Ruskin and Lincoln Colls, Oxford. Mbr, CSD; treas, Tawney Society; former chmn, Ealing SDP.

Sir George Young

EALING NORTH | No change

Electorate %Turnout	71,634	75.1%	1987	68,538	74.8%	1983
*Greenway, H. (C)	30,100	56.0%	+10.9%	23,128	45.1%	(C)
Benn, H.J. (Lab)	14,947	27.8%	-5.0%	16,837	32.8%	(Lab)
Miller, A.H.J. (L/All)	8,149	15.2%	-6.3%	11,021	21.5%	(L/All)
Fitzherbert, Mrs K. (Grn)	577	1.1%		306	0.6%	(BNP)
Lab to C swing 8.0%	53,773	C maj 15,153 28.2%		51,292	C maj 6,291 12.3%	

Mr Harry Greenway, former deputy headmaster. Mbr, Select Cmte on Education, Science and the Arts 1979- . Won the seat 1979; contested Stepney and Poplar, Feb and Oct 1974; Stepney, 1970. B Oct 4 1934; ed Warwick Sch; Coll of St Mark and St John, London; Caen Univ. Mbr, Cl of British Horse Soc, 1973- . Vice-chmn, Greater London Cons MPs, 1981- ; Cons back-bench education cmte, 1985-86 (sec, 1981-85 and 1986-); sec, Cons back-bench sports cmte, 1986- ; Cons back-bench arts and heritage cmte, 1986- ; Cons Nat Advisory Cmte on Education, 1981- . Chmn, all-pty adult ed cmte, 1979- ; member, cl, Open Univ, 1979- . AMMA.
Mr Hilary Benn, research officer with ASTMS, contested this seat 1983. Mbr, Ealing BC, 1979- . B Nov 26 1953; ed Holland Park Comprehensive Sch; Sussex Univ.
Mr Anthony Miller, personnel consultant, contested this seat 1983, Harrow Central 1970 and 1966, Streatham 1964. Mbr, Ealing BC, 1986- . B Dec 27 1934; ed Wells Cathedral Sch; Dulwich Coll; Sr John's Coll, Cambridge.
Mrs Kay Fitzherbert, social work consultant; journalist. Ed Oxford Univ; LSE.

Mr Harry Greenway

EALING, SOUTHALL | No change

Electorate %Turnout	74,843	69.7%	1987	71,441	71.4%	1983
*Bidwell, S.J. (Lab)	26,480	50.7%	-1.6%	26,664	52.3%	(Lab)
Truman, M.A. (C)	18,503	35.5%	+5.0%	15,548	30.5%	(C)
Howes, Mrs M. (L/All)	6,947	13.3%	-2.5%	8,059	15.8%	(L/All)
Lugg, R.F. (WRP)	256	0.5%		555	1.1%	(NF)
				150	0.3%	(Other)
Lab to C swing 3.3%	52,186	Lab maj 7,977 15.3%		50,976	Lab maj 11,116 21.8%	

Mr Sydney Bidwell has served on the Select Committee on Transport since 1979; Select Cmte on Race Relations and Immigration, 1968-79. Elected for this seat in 1974; MP for Southall, 1966-74; contested South West Hertfordshire, 1964; East Hertfordshire, 1959. B Jan 14 1917; ed elementary sch and evening classes and trade union movement. Lecturer; former tutor and organiser for National Cl of Labour Colls; previously railway worker. Former NUR and now TGWU. Chmn, Tribune Group, 1975. Vice-chmn, PLP transport group, 1977. Mbr, Southall BC, 1951-55. Sponsored by TGWU.
Mr Michael Truman, tax consultant. B Mar 27 1955; ed Loughborough GS; Quorn Rawlins Upper Sch; Manchester Univ; Chester Coll of Law. Director, Taxpartner Services.
Mrs Monica Howes fought Mid Bedfordshire in 1983. Served as Eastern Region representative on Lib Pty nat exec for four years and on Lib Pty Cl for six years. Mbr, 300 Group. B Sep 12 1938; ed Haberdashers' Aske's Sch; Johannesburg HS for Girls; Central London Poly.

Mr Sydney Bidwell

EASINGTON | No change

Electorate %Turnout	64,863	73.4%	1987	65,732	67.5%	1983
Cummings, J.S. (Lab)	32,396	68.1%	+9.7%	25,912	58.4%	(Lab)
Perry, W.J. (C)	7,757	16.3%	-0.2%	11,120	25.1%	(L/All)
Morpeth, G. (L/All)	7,447	15.6%	-9.4%	7,342	16.5%	(C)
C to Lab swing 5.0%	47,600	Lab maj 24,639 51.8%		44,374	Lab maj 14,792 33.3%	

Mr John Cummings, electrician at Murton Colliery, where he started work in 1958. Mbr, Easington DC, 1973- (leader, 1976-); mbr, Northumbrian Water Authority; vice-chmn, Coalfield Community Campaign. B Jul 6 1943; ed local schools. NUM; NUPE.
Mr William Perry, solicitor. Mbr, London borough of Merton Cl, 1980-86; Windsor and Maidenhead BC, 1974-79. Party service includes nat treas, Assocn of YC Cllrs; pres, Windsor and Maidenhead YCs; dep chmn, Windsor and Maidenhead political cmte. B Nov 19 1952; ed Malvern Coll; Univ Coll, Oxford; Coll of Law. Mbr, Carlton Club.
Lord Morpeth, former Regular Army officer. B Feb 15 1949; ed Eton; Balliol Coll, Oxford; Army Staff Coll.

Mr John Cummings

EASTBOURNE — No change

Electorate %Turnout	74,144	75.6%	**1987**	72,980	73.0%	**1983**
*Gow, I.R.E. (C)	33,587	59.9%	+0.8%	31,501	59.1%	(C)
Driver, P.G. (L/All)	16,664	29.7%	-4.1%	18,015	33.8%	(L/All)
Patel, A. (Lab)	4,928	8.8%	+1.7%	3,790	7.1%	(Lab)
Addison, Ms R. (Grn)	867	1.5%				
L/All to C swing 2.4%	56,046	C maj 16,923 30.2%		53,306	C maj 13,486 25.3%	

Mr Ian Gow

Mr Ian Gow was appointed Minister of State, Treasury, in Sep 1985, but resigned later in the year in protest at Anglo-Irish Agreeemnt; Minister for Housing and Construction, 1983-85; PPS to Mrs Thatcher, 1979-83. Solicitor; underwriting mbr of Lloyd's; director, Floyd Oil Participations plc; adviser to Cater Allen Holdings plc. Elected in Feb 1974; contested Coventry East, 1964, and Clapham, 1966. B Feb 11 1937; ed Winchester. Former mbr, Select Cmte on Wealth Tax and Select Cmte on Parliamentary Commissioner for Administration. Sec, Cons back-bench cmte on N Ireland, 1976-79; and constitutional cmte, 1977-79.
Mr Peter Driver, marketing director, Royal London Society for the Blind, contested Chelsea 1979. B Dec 1934; ed Epsom Coll.
Mr Ashok Patel, solicitor. B Jun 7 1955. Mbr, Amnesty International, Fabian Soc. TGWU; NCCL.

EAST KILBRIDE — No change

Electorate %Turnout	63,097	79.2%	**1987**	61,420	77.0%	**1983**
Ingram, A.P. (Lab)	24,491	49.0%	+11.9%	17,535	37.1%	(Lab)
Sullivan, D.R.E. (SDP/All)	11,867	23.7%	-4.2%	13,199	27.9%	(SDP/All)
Walker, P.M. (C)	7,344	14.7%	-9.6%	11,483	24.3%	(C)
Taggart, J.H. (SNP)	6,275	12.6%	+2.4%	4,795	10.1%	(SNP)
				256	0.5%	(Other)
SDP/All to Lab swing 8.0%	49,977	Lab maj 12,624 25.3%		47,268	Lab maj 4,336 9.2%	

Mr Adam Ingram

Mr Adam Ingram, full-time Nalgo district official and former systems analyst with South of Scotland Electricity Bd, contested Strathkelvin and Bearsden 1983. Mbr, East Kilbride DC, 1980- (ldr of cl, 1984-); Cosla Lab gp whip; Lab mbr of Cosla sub-cmtes on the Scottish Assembly and on equal opportunities. Former treas, East Kilbride Arts Cl; board mbr, East Kilbride Business Centre. B Feb 1 1947; ed Cranhill Sec Sch. Sponsored by TGWU.
Mr Denis Sullivan, assistant gen sec and editor, EIS, contested East Kilbride 1983. Mbr, Lab Pty, 1961-81; founder mbr, SDP; sec, SDP Cl for Scotland. B Mar 1 1945; ed St Augustine's Sch; Glasgow Sch of Art; Jordanhill Coll of Ed.
Mr Paul Walker, research assistant to Mr Allan Stewart, MP for Eastwood, and former civil servant, contested Motherwell South 1983. EETPU; nat officer, CTU. B Aug 26 1960; ed Glasgow HS; Glasgow Univ; Scottish Sch of Business, Strathclyde Univ.
Mr James Taggart, univ researcher, is SNP spokesman on social services and director of SNP's anti-Trident campaign. Former mbr, SNP nat exec. Contested Fife Central 1983. B 1943; ed St Mungo's Acad; Glasgow and Strathclyde Univs. Husband of Ms Jenny Herriot, SNP candidate in Dumbarton.

EASTLEIGH — No change

Electorate %Turnout	87,552	79.3%	**1987**	82,447	77.0%	**1983**
*Price, Sir David (C)	35,584	51.3%	+0.3%	32,393	51.0%	(C)
Kyrle, M.J. (L/All)	22,229	32.0%	+1.5%	19,385	30.5%	(L/All)
Bull, D.J.C. (Lab)	11,599	16.7%	-1.8%	11,736	18.5%	(Lab)
C to L/All swing 0.6%	69,412	C maj 13,355 19.2%		63,514	C maj 13,008 20.5%	

Sir David Price

Sir David Price, consultant to Union International Co Ltd and Institution of Industrial Managers (Vice-Pres, 1980-), has been on the Select Cmte on Social Services since 1983; Select Cmte on Transport, 1979-83. Jt vice-chmn, Cons back-bench arts and heritage cmte, 1979-81 and 1983- ; chmn, Parly and Scientific Cmte, 1973-75 and 1979-82, and its pres, 1975-79 and since 1982; Chmn and former vice-chmn, Cons shipping and shipbuilding sub-cmte, 1979- . Under Secretary of State for Aerospace, DTI, 1971-72; Parly Sec, Ministry of Aviation Supply, 1970-71; Parl Sec, Ministry of Technology, Jun to Oct 1970. Opposition spokesman on tech and science, 1964-70. Parly Sec, Bd of Trade, 1962-64. Elected in 1955. B Nov 20 1924; ed Eton; Trinity Coll, Cambridge (Pres of Union, 1948), and Yale Univ (Research Fellow). Dep Lieut, County of Hampshire. Served with Scots Guards during Second World War. With ICI Ltd, 1949-62; industrial consultant, 1964-70 and since 1972.
Mr Martin Kyrle, house master at comprehensive sch, contested this seat 1983, New Forest 1979, Christchurch and Lymington Feb 1974. B Mar 16 1933; ed Purbrook Park Cty HS; Southampton and Sussex Univs.
Mr David Bull, maths and computer teacher. B Nov 27 1952; ed Ipswich Civic Coll; Southampton Univ. Mbr, Southampton City Cl, 1979- .

EAST LOTHIAN — No change

Electorate %Turnout	65,046	78.7%	**1987**	62,581	76.2%	**1983**
*Home Robertson, J.D. (Lab)	24,583	48.0%	+4.1%	20,934	43.9%	(Lab)
Langdon, S.M. (C)	14,478	28.3%	-2.5%	14,693	30.8%	(C)
Robinson, A. (L/All)	7,929	15.5%	-5.4%	9,950	20.9%	(L/All)
Burgon-Lyon, A. (SNP)	3,727	7.3%	+2.9%	2,083	4.4%	(SNP)
Marland, A. (Grn)	451	0.9%				
C to Lab swing 3.3%	51,168	Lab maj 10,105 19.7%		47,660	Lab maj 6,241 13.1%	

Mr John Home
Robertson

Mr **John Home Robertson** has been an Opposition spokesman on Scottish agriculture since 1985; a spokesman on agriculture, 1984-85; Opposition Scottish whip, 1983-84. Elected for this seat 1983; MP for Berwick and East Lothian, 1978-83. Farmer. B Dec 5 1948; ed Ampleforth; West of Scotland Agricultural Coll. Mbr, Select Cmte on Scottish Affairs, 1979-83; chmn, Scottish group of Lab MP's, 1982-83, and of rural affairs group, Scottish PLP. Mbr, Berwickshire DC, 1974-78; Borders Health Board, 1975-78. Sponsored by TSSA.
Mr **Michael Langdon**, a chartered engineer and project engineer with Ferranti Ltd. B 1944; ed Royal HS, Edinburgh; Edinburgh and Oxford Univs. Elder of Church of Scotland. ASTMS.
Mr **Andrew Robinson**, chartered town planner with his own planning, environment and forestry consultancy; official in Kent Planning Dept, 1968-74. B Jul 23 1945; ed Manchester GS. Chmn, Scottish Lib environmental panel, 1985- .
Mr **Alexander Burgon-Lyon**, employed by Lothian Region as lecturer. Current chmn, East Lothian SNP. B 1936; ed Rugby Tech Coll; Napier Coll. SFHEA.
Mr **Angus Marland**, asst to director of Edinburgh Univ Centre for Human Ecology. Aged 38; ed Marlborough Coll, Wiltshire.

EASTWOOD — No change

Electorate %Turnout	61,872	79.4%	**1987**	59,378	76.2%	**1983**
*Stewart, J.A. (C)	19,388	39.5%	-7.1%	21,072	46.6%	(C)
Leishman, R. (SDP/All)	13,374	27.2%	-0.3%	12,477	27.6%	(SDP/All)
Grant-Hutchison, P.A. (Lab)	12,305	25.1%	+5.0%	9,083	20.1%	(Lab)
Findlay, J. (SNP)	4,033	8.2%	+2.4%	2,618	5.8%	(SNP)
C to SDP/All swing 3.4%	49,100	C maj 6,014 12.2%		45,250	C maj 8,595 19.0%	

Mr Allan Stewart

Mr **Allan Stewart** was an Under Secretary of State for Scotland, 1981-86, being Scottish minister for health and social work, 1981-82, for home affairs and environment, 1982-83, and for industry and education, 1983-86. Elected for this seat in 1983; MP for East Renfrewshire, 1979-83; contested Dundee East, 1970. Mbr, Select Cmte on Scottish Affairs, 1979-81. Economist. B Jun 1 1942; ed Bell Baxter HS, Cupar; St Andrews Univ and Harvard. Mbr, Bromley BC, 1974-76. Head of Regional Development Dept, CBI, 1971-73; Deputy Director (Economics), 1973-76; Scottish Sec, 1976-78; Scottish Director, 1978-79.
Mr **Ralph Leishman**, chartered accountant and management consultant, contested Cunninghame North 1983. Mbr, SDP Scottish economic policy gp. Vice-chmn, Glasgow North area SDP, 1981-82; chmn, Renfrewshire area SDP, 1983-86. B Jan 24 1957; ed Hillhead HS; Glasgow Acad; Glasgow Coll of Tech.
Mr **Peter Grant-Hutchison**, solicitor. B Jul 7 1956; ed Dundee Univ. Chmn, Muir Soc of Labour and Radical Lawyers; treas, Scottish Cl of Fabian Socs. ASTMS.
Mr **Alastair Findlay**, consultant surgeon with Argyll and Clyde Health Bd. SNP branch organiser. B 1935; ed Aberdeen Univ; Royal Coll of Surgeons.

ECCLES — No change

Electorate %Turnout	66,961	74.5%	**1987**	67,230	70.1%	**1983**
Lestor, Miss J. (Lab)	25,346	50.8%	+4.9%	21,644	45.9%	(Lab)
Packalow, Mrs M.E.J. (C)	15,647	31.3%	-1.8%	15,639	33.2%	(C)
Beatty, P.C.W. (SDP/All)	8,924	17.9%	-2.0%	9,392	19.9%	(L/All)
				485	1.0%	(Other)
C to Lab swing 3.3%	49,917	Lab maj 9,699 19.4%		47,160	Lab maj 6,005 12.7%	

Miss Joan Lestor

Miss **Joan Lestor**, director of Trade Unions Child Care Project since 1986; freelance lecturer; nursery school teacher, 1959-66, was Under Secretary of State for Education and Science, 1969-70 and 1975-76, resigning in protest at public spending cuts; Under Secretary of State for Foreign and Commonwealth Affairs, 1974-75; Opposition front bencher on women's rights and welfare, 1981-83. Chairs Defence for Children (UK), the children's rights gp; co-chmn, Jt Cmte against Racialism, 1978- ; mbr, CND nat cl, 1983- . Chmn, Lab Pty, 1977-78; vice-chmn, 1976-77; mbr, Labour NEC, 1967-82, chairing international cmte from 1978. MP for Slough, 1966-83; contested Lewisham West, 1964. B Nov 13 1931; ed Blaenavon Sec Sch, Monmouth; William Morris HS, Walthamstow; London Univ. Mbr, Wandsworth Cl, 1957-58; LCC, 1963-65. Sponsored by GMB.
Mrs **Joy Packalow**, teacher, TV writer and presenter of French language programmes. Interpreter, European Parliament, 1974. B 1947; ed St Joseph's Coll, Bradford; Hull Univ.
Mr **Paul Beatty**, medical physicist in the NHS and adviser to medical equipment manufacturers. Mbr, CSD; airports policy sub group; health and social services policy group. B Jan 25 1952; ed Handsworth GS; Univ Coll, London. Methodist local preacher. ASTMS.

EDDISBURY — No change

Electorate %Turnout	73,894	78.0%	**1987**	71,506	74.3%	**1983**
*Goodlad, A.R. (C)	29,474	51.1%	-2.3%	28,407	53.5%	(C)
Fletcher, R.I. (L/All)	13,639	23.7%	-1.9%	13,561	25.5%	(L/All)
Grigg, Mrs C. (Lab)	13,574	23.5%	+2.5%	11,169	21.0%	(Lab)
Basden, A. (Grn)	976	1.7%				
C to L/All swing 0.2%	57,663	C maj 15,835 27.5%		53,137	C maj 14,846 27.9%	

Mr Alastair Goodlad

Mr Alastair Goodlad, Under Secretary of State for Energy, 1984-87; a Lord Commissioner of the Treasury (Govt whip), 1982-84; an asst Govt whip, 1981-82. Elected for this seat 1983; MP for Northwich, Feb 1974-83; contested Crewe, 1970. Mbr of Lloyd's. B Jul 4 1943; ed St Faith's Sch, Cambridge; Marlborough Coll and King's Coll, Cambridge. Jt sec, Cons backbench trade cmte, 1978-79, jt vice-chmn, 1979-81; jt sec, N Ireland cmte, 1979-81; sec, all-pty heritage group, 1979-81; mbr, Select Cmte on Agriculture, 1979-81. Personal asst to Mr Peter Walker when Opposition spokesman on transport.
Mr Roderick Fletcher, freight liaison controller with British Rail, fought this seat 1983. B Jul 10 1943; ed King's Sch, Macclesfield. Mbr, Alsager TC, since 1979 (chmn, 1985-86); Congleton BC, since 1980 (ldr, Alliance gp, 1985- ; chmn, environmental health cmte, 1981-85). TSSA.
Mrs Catriona Grigg, chartered chemist and technical development manager. B Dec 8 1945. Sec, Helsby Village Soc; mbr, Helsby community centre management cmte.
Mr Andrew Basden, lecturer. B Jul 31 1948; ed George Heriot's Sch, Edinburgh; Dept of Electronics, Southampton Univ. Mbr, Frodsham PC, 1985-87. Expert in computer systems.

EDINBURGH CENTRAL — Lab gain

Electorate %Turnout	59,529	69.0%	**1987**	57,064	64.9%	**1983**
Darling, A. (Lab)	16,502	40.2%	+9.1%	14,095	38.0%	(C)
*Fletcher, Sir Alex (C)	14,240	34.7%	-3.4%	11,529	31.1%	(Lab)
Myles, A. (L/All)	7,333	17.9%	-7.8%	9,498	25.6%	(SDP/All)
Shaw, B. (SNP)	2,559	6.2%	+1.3%	1,810	4.9%	(SNP)
Hendry, Ms L.M. (Grn)	438	1.1%		119	0.3%	(Com)
C to Lab swing 6.2%	41,072	Lab maj 2,262 5.5%		37,051	C maj 2,566 6.9%	

Mr Alistair Darling

Mr Alistair Darling, advocate and member, Lothian Reg Cl (chmn, transport cmte, 1986-). B Nov 28 1953; Aberdeen Univ. Apex.
Sir Alexander Fletcher, Minister for Corporate and Consumer Affairs at DTI, with rank of Under Secretary of State, 1983-85; Under Secretary of State for Scotland, 1979-83; an Opposition spokesman on Scotland, 1977-79. Chmn, Select Cmte on Channel Tunnel Bill, 1986. Chartered accountant. Elected for this seat 1983; MP for Edinburgh North, 1973-83; contested West Renfrewshire, 1970. B Aug 26 1929; ed Greenock HS.
Mr Andrew Myles, health service administrator. Political organiser, Dundee Libs, 1983-86. B Oct 25 1957; ed Oxgangs Primary Sch, Edinburgh; Holt Sch, E Lothian; Merchiston Castle Sch; Dundee Univ (Pres, univ students' assocn, 1980-81). Nalgo, former steward.
Mr Brian Shaw, computer operator. Ex-nat sec, Young Scottish Nats. B Mar 8 1963; ed Firrwill HS and Napier Coll, Edinburgh. TASS shop steward; previously in CPSA.
Ms Linda Hendry, handloom weaver and spinning teacher and member of Guild of Weavers, Spinners and Dyers, contested Edinburgh South 1983; Lothians in 1984 Euro election. B Mar 7 1950; ed Dumfries Acad; Edinburgh Univ; Moray House Teachers' Training Cl.

EDINBURGH EAST — No change

Electorate %Turnout	48,895	74.1%	**1987**	51,156	70.4%	**1983**
*Strang, G.S. (Lab)	18,257	50.4%	+5.5%	16,169	44.9%	(Lab)
Renz, J.F. (C)	8,962	24.7%	-3.9%	10,303	28.6%	(C)
Aitken, Mrs J. (L/All)	5,592	15.4%	-5.6%	7,570	21.0%	(L/All)
Bovey, M. (SNP)	3,434	9.5%	+4.0%	1,976	5.5%	(SNP)
C to Lab swing 4.7%	36,245	Lab maj 9,295 25.6%		36,018	Lab maj 5,866 16.3%	

Mr Gavin Strang

Mr Gavin Strang has chaired the PLP defence cmte since 1985; chmn, Scottish Lab MPs, 1986- ; vice-chmn, 1985-86. Chmn, Labour Action for Peace, 1986- . An Opposition spokesman on agriculture, fisheries and food, 1979-82. Parliamentary Sec, Ministry of Agriculture, Fisheries and Food, 1974-79; Under Secretary of State for Energy, 1974. Elected in 1970. Member, Select Cmte on Science and Technology, 1970-74; Select Cmte on Agriculture, 1984- . An Opposition spokesman on trade and industry, 1973-74. Agricultural scientist. B Jul 10 1943; ed Morrison's Acad; Edinburgh Univ; Churchill Coll, Cambridge. Sponsored by TGWU.
Mr John Renz, an NHS manager, was hon sec, Edinburgh East Cons Assocn; also on nat exec, Scottish YCs. B Jul 11 1962; ed Portobello HS, Edinburgh; Heriot-Watt Univ. Deacon, Church of Scotland. Nalgo, being branch cmte member.
Mrs Judith Aitken owns a small business; former nurse. B Mar 1 1939; ed Avonbourne Sch for Girls. Chaired Central Fife Lib Assocn, 1986.
Mr Mungo Bovey, advocate and home affairs spokesman for SNP. Former elected member, SNP nat cl. B 1959; ed Jordanhill Coll Sch; Glasgow Univ.

EDINBURGH, LEITH — No change

Electorate	%Turnout	60,359	70.9%	**1987**	60,562	67.3%	**1983**
*Brown, R.D.M. (Lab)		21,104	49.3%	+9.6%	16,177	39.7%	(Lab)
Menzies, D.A.Y. (C)		9,777	22.9%	-3.4%	11,204	27.5%	(SDP/All)
Wells, Mrs S. (SDP/All)		7,843	18.3%	-9.2%	10,706	26.3%	(C)
Morrison, W. (SNP)		4,045	9.5%	+3.0%	2,646	6.5%	(SNP)
C to Lab swing 6.5%		42,769	Lab maj 11,327 26.5%		40,733	Lab maj 4,973 12.2%	

Mr Ronald Brown

Mr Ronald Brown was elected in 1979. Mbr, Select Cmte on Scottish Affairs, 1986- . Fitter. Chmn, Pilton branch, AUEW; former chmn, works cmte, Edinburgh District, South of Scotland Electricity Bd, and former shop stewards convenor, Parsons Peebles Ltd, Edinburgh. B Jun 1940; ed Ainslie Park HS and Bristo Tech Inst, Edinburgh. Mbr, Lothian Reg Cl, 1974-79; former mbr, Edinburgh TC. Mbr, Central Scotland Water Development Bd, 1974-79; Lothian and Borders Fire Bd, 1974-79. Sponsored by AUEW.
Mr Duncan Menzies, advocate, contested Midlothian 1983. B 1953; ed Edinburgh Acad; Cargilfield Sch; Trinity Coll, Glenalmond; Trinity Coll Sch, Ontario; Wadham Coll, Oxford; Edinburgh Univ.
Mrs Sheila Wells, hospital manager, is sec, Scottish Cl of SDP; vice-chmn, Edinburgh area pty. B Apr 9 1957; ed Gracemount HS, Edinburgh; Napier Coll, Edinburgh. Nalgo.
Mr William Morrison, stock controller, is an exec mbr, SNP trade union group; industrial organizer, Leith SNP. 1986. B May 30 1962; ed Uddingston GS, Glasgow; Napier Coll, Edinburgh. Usdaw.

EDINBURGH, PENTLANDS — No change

Electorate	%Turnout	58,125	77.7%	**1987**	59,295	73.4%	**1983**
*Rifkind, M.L. (C)		17,278	38.3%	-0.9%	17,051	39.2%	(C)
Lazarowicz, M. (Lab)		13,533	30.0%	+6.1%	12,742	29.3%	(SDP/All)
Smith, K.A. (SDP/All)		11,072	24.5%	-4.8%	10,390	23.9%	(Lab)
MacCormick, D.N. (SNP)		3,264	7.2%	+1.2%	2,642	6.1%	(SNP)
					687	1.6%	(Other)
C to Lab swing 3.5%		45,147	C maj 3,745 8.3%		43,512	C maj 4,309 9.9%	

Mr Malcolm Rifkind

Mr Malcolm Rifkind became Secretary of State for Scotland in 1986; Minister of State for Foreign and Commonwealth Affairs, 1983-86; Under Secretary of State, Foreign and Commonweath Office, 1982-83; Under Secretary of State for Scotland, 1979-82; Opposition spokesman on Scotland from 1975 until he resigned in 1977 over devolution. Elected in 1974; contested Edinburgh, Central, 1970. An advocate. B Jun 21 1946; ed George Watson's Coll, Edinburgh, and Edinburgh Univ. Mbr, Select Cmte on Overseas Development, 1978-79, and on European Secondary Legislation, 1975-76; Edinburgh Cl, 1970-74.
Mr Mark Lazarowicz, education officer for a voluntary organization. Mbr, Edinburgh DC, 1980- ; Lab Pty Scottish Exec, 1980- . Chairs Scottish War on Want. B Aug 8 1953.
Mr Keith Smith, soil scientist, contested this seat 1983. Co-chmn, Alliance Cmte for Scotland. B Feb 9 1940; ed King Alfred's Sch, Wantage; Durham and Reading Univs. Mbr, Berkshire CC, 1964-67; Wantage UDC, 1972-73.
Mr Neil MacCormick, Regius Professor of Public Law, Edinburgh Univ. Contested this seat 1983; Edinburgh N, 1979. Mbr, nat cl, 1978-84 and 1985-86. B May 27 1941; ed Glasgow HS; Glasgow Univ; Balliol Coll, Oxford.

EDINBURGH SOUTH — Lab gain

Electorate	%Turnout	63,842	75.7%	**1987**	62,517	71.7%	**1983**
Griffiths, N. (Lab)		18,211	37.7%	+9.1%	16,485	36.8%	(C)
*Ancram, M.A.F.J.K. (C)		16,352	33.8%	-2.9%	12,830	28.6%	(SDP/All)
Graham, D.A. (SDP/All)		10,900	22.5%	-6.1%	12,824	28.6%	(Lab)
Moore, Mrs R. (SNP)		2,455	5.1%	+0.1%	2,256	5.0%	(SNP)
Clark, Mrs R. (Grn)		440	0.9%	+0.1%	450	1.0%	(Eco)
C to Lab swing 6.0%		48,358	Lab maj 1,859 3.8%		44,845	C maj 3,655 8.2%	

Mr Nigel Griffiths

Mr Nigel Griffiths, information and welfare rights officer for mental handicap pressure gp. Chaired Edinburgh South CLP, 1977; sec, Lothian devolution campaign, 1977-78. Mbr, Edinburgh DC, 1980- (chmn, housing cmte, 1986-). B May 20 1955; ed Hawick Comprehensive Sch; Edinburgh Univ. Founder mbr (1981), Wester Hailes CAB; Lothian Anti-Eviction forum, 1982. TGWU shop steward, 1980-86. JP.
Mr Michael Ancram, advocate and former company director, was an Under Secretary of State for Scotland, 1983-87; MP for this seat, 1979-87; MP for Berwick and East Lothian, Feb to Oct 1974; fought West Lothian, 1970. B Jul 7 1945; ed Ampleforth; Oxford and Edinburgh Univs. Member, Select Cmte on Energy, 1979-83. Chmn, Scottish Cons Pty, 1980-83.
Mr David Graham, curriculum development officer, contested Edinburgh Leith for Alliance in 1983, and Roxburgh, Selkirk and Peebles twice in 1974 for Lab. Chmn, Alliance ed working pty, Scotland, 1985- . B Apr 4 1951; ed Royal Belfast Acad Inst; Edinburgh Univ.
Mrs Rina Moore, company secretary and former teacher, contested Edinburgh West twice in 1974; Edinburgh Central 1970. B 1937; ed Holy Cross Acad; Edinburgh Univ; Craiglockhart Training Coll.
Mrs Ruth Clark, freelance writer; former psychology teacher and researcher. Aged 50.

EDINBURGH WEST — No change

Electorate %Turnout	62,214	79.4%	**1987**	61,050	75.7%	**1983**
*Douglas-Hamilton, Lord J. (C)	18,450	37.4%	-0.8%	17,646	38.2%	(C)
King, D.G. (L/All)	17,216	34.9%	-2.2%	17,148	37.1%	(L/All)
McGregor, M. (Lab)	10,957	22.2%	+2.0%	9,313	20.1%	(Lab)
Irons, N. (SNP)	2,774	5.6%	+1.0%	2,126	4.6%	(SNP)
L/All to C swing 0.7%	49,397	C maj 1,234 2.5%		46,233	C maj 498 1.1%	

Lord James Douglas-Hamilton, advocate and author, second son of the 14th Duke of Hamilton, became Under Secretary of State for Scotland, Jun 1987. Lord Commissioner of the Treasury (Govt Whip), 1979-81; Scottish Conservative whip, 1976-79. Elected in Oct 1974; contested Hamilton, Feb 1974. B Jul 31 1942; ed Eton; Balliol Coll, Oxford (Pres of Union, 1964); Edinburgh Univ. Hon Pres, Scottish ABA, since 1975; Pres, Royal Commonwealth Soc in Scotland, since 1979; Pres, Scottish Cl, UNA, since 1981. Town cllr, Edinburgh, 1972-74.
Mr Derek King, manager with Housing Corporation, fought this seat 1983. Former treas, exec mbr and housing spokesman, Scottish Lib Pty. B Jul 27 1949; ed Harrow Cty GS, Middlesex; Lancaster Univ. Mbr, Edinburgh DC, 1980-84. ASTMS.
Mr Michael McGregor, telecoms planner for life assurance company, contested the seat 1979. B Jun 26 1940; ed Daniel Stewart's Coll, Edinburgh. Mbr Edinburgh Corpn, 1972-75. ASTMS.
Mr Norman Irons, partner in firm of consulting engineers. Chmn, Corstorphine branch, SNP. Mbr, Edinburgh City Cl, 1976- . B Jan 4 1941; ed George Heriot's Sch, Edinburgh.

Lord James
Douglas-Hamilton

EDMONTON — No change

Electorate %Turnout	66,080	72.5%	**1987**	64,809	68.9%	**1983**
*Twinn, I.D. (C)	24,556	51.2%	+8.7%	18,968	42.5%	(C)
Grayston, B.G. (Lab)	17,270	36.0%	-3.8%	17,775	39.8%	(Lab)
Lawson, M. (SDP/All)	6,115	12.8%	-4.1%	7,523	16.9%	(L/All)
				372	0.8%	(Other)
Lab to C swing 6.3%	47,941	C maj 7,286 15.2%		44,638	C maj 1,193 2.7%	

Dr Ian Twinn, who won this seat in 1983, was a senior lecturer in planning, South Bank Polytechnic, 1975-83. PPS to Minister of State for Industry, 1985- and to Dep Chmn, Cons Pty, 1986- . B Apr 26 1950; ed Netherhall Sec Mod Sch, Cambridge; Cambridge Boys GS; Univ Coll of Wales, Aberystwyth, and Reading Univ. Jt sec, all-pty Anglo-Greek parly gp; lighting industries gp. Sec, Cons back-bench food and drink industries sub-cmte. Former consultant to Social Survey (Gallup Poll); JSA Advertising Ltd. NATFHE.
Mr Bryan Grayston, compositor **and** sales executive in printing industry, contested Enfield North 1983. Mbr, Enfield BC, first serving on it 1962-68 and then 1971-78. B Jun 23 1938; ed Bush Hill Park Sec Mod Sch. Mbr, United Commercial Travellers Assocn/ASTMS. Governor of several Enfield schools.
Mr Michael Lawson, management consultant and company director. Vice-chmn, Enfield SDP. B Jun 15 1956; ed Oxford.

Dr Ian Twinn

ELLESMERE PORT AND NESTON — No change

Electorate %Turnout	71,344	81.0%	**1987**	69,992	75.8%	**1983**
*Woodcock, M. (C)	25,664	44.4%	-1.5%	24,371	45.9%	(C)
Jones, Miss H.M. (Lab)	23,811	41.2%	+8.6%	17,284	32.6%	(Lab)
Holbrook, S.A. (SDP/All)	8,143	14.1%	-7.4%	11,413	21.5%	(L/All)
Carson, D.J.E. (PRP)	185	0.3%				
C to Lab swing 5.1%	57,803	C maj 1,853 3.2%		53,068	C maj 7,087 13.4%	

Mr Michael Woodcock, company director, Lloyd's underwriter and author, was formerly senior consultant with an industrial training board. Accountant and former head of small business development unit. Mbr, Select Cmte on Trade and Industry, 1983- . Elected in 1983. B Apr 10 1943; ed Queen Elizabeth's GS, Mansfield. Director, University Associates International Ltd and Challenge Ltd; parly consultant to Chamber of Coal Traders. Mbr, manpower advisory cmte, NEDC. Fellow, Industry and Parliament Trust.
Miss Helen Jones, teacher, contested Shropshire North 1983, and Lancashire Central in 1984 Euro election. B Dec 24 1954; ed Chester Coll; University Coll, London; Liverpool Univ.
Mr Simon Holbrook, chemical engineer. Vice-chmn and sec, Wirral SDP; agent at 1983 gen election and 1984 Euro election. B Jul 21 1957; ed Mirfield HS; Loughborough Univ. ASTMS.

Mr Michael Woodcock

ELMET — No change

Electorate %Turnout	69,024	79.3%	**1987**	67,008	75.4%	**1983**
*Batiste, S.L. (C)	25,658	46.9%	-0.4%	23,909	47.3%	(C)
Burgon, C. (Lab)	20,302	37.1%	+5.3%	16,053	31.8%	(Lab)
Macarthur, J.D. (SDP/All)	8,755	16.0%	-4.9%	10,589	20.9%	(L/All)
C to Lab swing 2.9%	54,715	C maj 5,356 9.8%		50,551	C maj 7,856 15.5%	

Mr Spencer Batiste, solicitor and company director, is legal adviser to Cutlery and Silverware Assocn of UK; Law Clerk to Sheffield Assay Office. B Jun 5 1945; ed Carmel Coll, Sorbonne; Cambridge Univ. Elected in 1983; contested Euro constituency of Sheffield, 1979. Vice-chmn, Small Business Bureau, since 1983; mbr, cl of Sheffield Chamber of Commerce; cl of Sheffield Univ, 1982- . PPS to Sir Geoffrey Pattie, Minister of State for Information Technology, 1985-87. Sec, all-pty space cmte; Cons back-bench space cmte, 1983-85. Mbr, Select Cmte on Energy, 1985. Nat vice-pres, Cons Trade Unionists; pres (and former chmn), Yorkshire CTU. EETPU.

Mr Colin Burgon, teacher. B Apr 22 1948; ed St Michael's Coll, Leeds; City of Leeds and Carnegie Coll. School governor and former sec, Willington Common Residents' Assocn.

Mr John MacArthur, senior lecturer in agricultural economics; employed at Bradford Univ as Dep Director, Project Planning Centre for Developing Countries. Chmn, Elmet constituency SDP, 1981-85; area pty treas, 1985- . B May 22 1934; ed Reed's Sch and Caterham Sch, Surrey; Reading and Oxford Univs. AUT.

Mr Spencer Batiste

ELTHAM — No change

Electorate %Turnout	54,063	76.9%	**1987**	55,062	74.1%	**1983**
*Bottomley, P.J. (C)	19,752	47.5%	-0.4%	19,530	47.9%	(C)
Vaughan, D. (Lab)	13,292	32.0%	+2.7%	11,938	29.3%	(Lab)
Randall, E.J. (L/All)	8,542	20.5%	-1.6%	9,030	22.1%	(L/All)
				276	0.7%	(Other)
C to Lab swing 1.5%	41,586	C maj 6,460 15.5%		40,774	C maj 7,592 18.6%	

Mr Peter Bottomley was appointed Minister for Roads and Traffic, with rank of Under Secretary of State at Dept of Transport, in 1986; Under Secretary of State for Employment, 1984-86. PPS to Sec of State for Social Services, 1983-84; to Minister of State for Foreign and Commonwealth Affairs, 1982-83. Former industrial economist. Elected for this seat 1983; MP for Woolwich West, 1975-83; fought that seat, Feb and Oct 1974. B Jul 30 1944; ed mixed comprehensive, Washington, DC; Westminster Sch; Trinity Coll, Cambridge. Sec, Cons back-bench health and social services cmte, 1977-79; foreign and Commonwealth affairs cmte, 1979-81. Mbr, Select Cmte on Violence in the Family, 1976, and former mbr, Select Cmte on Overseas Development. Pres, CTU, 1978-80. Chmn, British Union of Family Organizations, 1973-80; Family Forum, 1980-82; trustee, Christian Aid, 1978-84. Member, cl, Mind, 1981-82. Wife is Cons MP for Surrey South West. TGWU (Transport House branch).

Mr David Vaughan, teacher. B Mar 1 1932; ed Firth Park GS, Sheffield; Goldsmith's Coll; London Univ. Mbr, Greenwich BC 1971-86. NAS/UWT. Former shop steward.

Mr Edward Randall, univ lecturer, contested this seat 1983. Mbr, Greenwich BC, 1982- . B Jul 13 1951; ed Durham Univ; LSE; St Thomas Hospital. NATFHE.

Mr Peter Bottomley

ENFIELD NORTH — No change

Electorate %Turnout	69,488	74.5%	**1987**	67,980	72.4%	**1983**
*Eggar, T.J.C. (C)	28,758	55.5%	+3.8%	25,456	51.7%	(C)
Upham, M. (Lab)	14,743	28.5%	+0.6%	13,740	27.9%	(Lab)
Leighter, Ms H. (SDP/All)	7,633	14.7%	-4.5%	9,452	19.2%	(L/All)
Chantler, M. (Grn)	644	1.2%	+0.6%	320	0.6%	(Eco)
				268	0.5%	(Other)
Lab to C swing 1.6%	51,778	C maj 14,015 27.1%		49,236	C maj 11,716 23.8%	

Mr Timothy Eggar was appointed an Under Secretary of State for Foreign and Commonwealth Affairs in 1985; PPS to Minister for Overseas Development, 1982-85; member, Select Cmte on the Treasury and Civil Service, 1979-82. Elected in 1979. Merchant banker (with European Banking Co, 1975-83); former director, Charterhouse Petroleum Ltd and former parliamentary adviser. B Dec 19, 1951; ed Winchester Coll; Magdalene Coll, Cambridge (chmn, Univ Cons Assocn, 1972); Coll of Law, London. Called to Bar, 1976. Vice-chmn, Fed of Cons Students, 1973-74. Personal asst to the then Mr William Whitelaw, 1974. Sec, Cons back-bench finance cmte, 1980-82; energy cmte, 1980-82.

Mr Martin Upham, research officer for ISTC, contested Harborough 1983. B Mar 11 1947; ed Manchester, Bristol, Hull Univs. Sec, Lab Parly Assocn.

Ms Hilary Leighter, management consultant. N London contact mbr, Women for Social Democracy; Putney membership sec, 1983-84. B Sep 21 1956; ed Claremont High Comprehensive Sch, Brent; New Hall, Cambridge. Governor, Bourne Primary Sch, Ruislip; mbr, Mount Vernon Hospital Defence Cmte.

Mr Timothy Eggar

ENFIELD, SOUTHGATE — No change

Electorate %Turnout	66,600	72.6%	**1987**	65,438	69.6%	**1983**
*Portillo, M.D.X. (C)	28,445	58.8%	+0.7%	26,451	58.1%	(C)
Harvey, N. (L/All)	10,100	20.9%	-2.5%	10,632	23.4%	(L/All)
Course, R. (Lab)	9,114	18.8%	+1.0%	8,132	17.9%	(Lab)
Rooney, S. (Grn)	696	1.4%		318	0.7%	(BNP)
L/All to C swing 1.6%	48,355	C maj 18,345 37.9%		45,533	C maj 15,819 34.7%	

Mr Michael Portillo

Mr Michael Portillo was appointed Under Secretary of State for Health and Social Security in Jun 1987; an asst Govt whip, 1986-87; PPS to Mr John Moore, Minister of Transport, 1986. Elected in 1984 by-election 1984; contested Birmingham, Perry Barr, 1983. Former oil industry consultant and TV political researcher. Mbr, Select Cmte on Energy, 1985-86; jt sec, Cons back-bench energy cmte and to Greater London Cons MPs, 1985-86. B May 26 1953; ed Harrow County Sch; Peterhouse, Cambridge. Special adviser to Mr David Howell, when Secretary of State for Energy; previously in Cons Research Dept; special adviser to Secretary of State for Trade and Industry, 1983, and to Chancellor of the Exchequer, 1983-84. Former consultant, Grieveson Grant (stockbrokers), British Airways, Building Employers Confed.
Mr Nicholas Harvey, parliamentary lobbyist with public relations consultancy. Member, Lib Party Cl; London Lib Pty exec, 1984-86; agent/organiser Finchley Lib Assocn, 1983-86; nat vice-chmn, ULS, 1981-82. B Aug 3 1961; ed Queen's Coll, Taunton; Middlesex Poly (Pres of Union, 1981-82). NUJ.
Mr Richard Course, campaigns director. Mbr, Enfield BC, 1986- . B Mar 23 1940. TGWU.

EPPING FOREST — No change

Electorate %Turnout	67,804	76.3%	**1987**	66,578	72.8%	**1983**
*Biggs-Davison, Sir John (C)	31,536	60.9%	+4.4%	27,373	56.5%	(C)
Humphris, A. (SDP/All)	10,023	19.4%	-5.4%	11,995	24.8%	(SDP/All)
Murray, S. (Lab)	9,499	18.4%	+1.2%	8,289	17.1%	(Lab)
Denhard, R. (Grn)	695	1.3%		452	0.9%	(Eco)
				330	0.7%	(Other)
SDP/All to C swing 4.9%	51,753	C maj 21,513 41.6%		48,439	C maj 15,378 31.7%	

Sir John
Biggs-Davison

Sir John Biggs-Davison, who has been chmn, Cons back-bench N Ireland cmte, since 1983, was an Opposition spokesman on N Ireland, 1976-78. Elected for this seat, Feb 1974; MP for Chigwell, 1955-74; contested Coventry South, 1951. Member, exec, 1922 Cmte. Author, journalist and broadcaster. B Jun 7 1918; ed Clifton Coll; Magdalen Coll, Oxford. Served Royal Marines and Pakistan administration. Former jt chmn, UK Falkland Islands parly group, 1977. Vice-chmn, Cons back-bench foreign and Commonwealth affairs cmte, since 1982; Cons constitutional cmte, since 1985. Jt vice-chmn, Cons Friends of Israel parly gp, 1986- ; chmn, British/Pakistan parly gp. Mbr, Cl of Europe and WEU, 1984-86. IOJ
Mr Anthony Humphris, economist and adviser to Mr Ian Wrigglesworth, SDP spokesman on Treasury and economic affairs; political aide to Mrs Shirley Williams, 1981-83; has also worked in industrial relations for CEGB. Lab candidate for West Kent in 1979 Euro election. Mbr, Oxford City Cl, 1972-76; Lab Pty, 1971-81; SDP, 1981- . B Nov 1 1950; ed Christ's Hospital Sch, Horsham; Brasenose Coll, Oxford. APEX, for whom he was head of research.
Mr Stephen Murray, teacher. B May 8 1959; ed Bristol Univ. Mbr, Epping Forest DC, 1982- (Ldr, Lab gp, 1984-); League Against Cruel Sports.

EPSOM AND EWELL — No change

Electorate %Turnout	70,683	75.4%	**1987**	70,630	72.0%	**1983**
*Hamilton, A.G. (C)	33,145	62.2%	+1.8%	30,737	60.4%	(C)
Joachim, Mrs M.J. (L/All)	12,384	23.2%	-3.4%	13,542	26.6%	(L/All)
Follett, Ms D.B. (Lab)	7,751	14.5%	+1.6%	6,587	12.9%	(Lab)
L/All to C swing 2.6%	53,280	C maj 20,761 39.0%		50,866	C maj 17,195 33.8%	

Mr Archibald
Hamilton

Mr Archibald Hamilton became Parliamentary Private Secretary to Mrs Thatcher, Prime Minister, in Jun 1987; Under Secretary of State for Defence Procurement in 1986-87; Lord Commissioner of the Treasury (Govt whip), 1984-86; assistant Govt whip, 1982-84. Elected at 1978 by-election; contested Dagenham, Feb and Oct 1974. Farmer; mbr of Lloyd's. B Dec 30 1941; ed Eton. Mbr, Cl of Royal Borough of Kensington and Chelsea, 1968-71. PPS to Secretary of State for Energy, 1979-81, and Secretary of State for Transport, 1981-82.
Dr Margaret Joachim, computer consultant, contested Finchley 1983; West Gloucestershire 1979. B Jun 25 1949; ed Brighton and Hove HS; St Hugh's Coll, Oxford; Birmingham Univ. Sex equality campaigner; chaired Fawcett Soc, 1984-87.
Ms Barbara Follett, a lecturer, contested Woking in 1983. B Dec 25 1942; ed at a high school in Cape Town. ASTMS.

EREWASH | | | | | | No change

Electorate %Turnout	76,545	77.4%	**1987**	73,355	75.7%	**1983**
*Rost, P.L. (C)	28,775	48.6%	+3.2%	25,167	45.3%	(C)
Jones, R.W. (Lab)	19,021	32.1%	+7.2%	13,848	24.9%	(Lab)
Moss, Ms C.P. (SDP/All)	11,442	19.3%	-2.9%	12,331	22.2%	(SDP/All)
				4,158	7.5%	(Other)
C to Lab swing 2.0%	59,238	C maj 9,754 16.5%		55,504	C maj 11,319 20.4%	

Mr Peter Rost

Mr Peter Rost has been on the Select Cmte on Energy since 1979. Director, Norcott Investments Ltd and Penrhos Electronics Ltd; investment adviser to General and Overseas Trust Ltd; parly consultant on energy matters for Associated Heat Services plc; consultant to 'Warmer' Campaign, Weleda (UK) Ltd, Natural Medicines Gp, and Thomas Moriarty Associates. Elected for this seat in 1983; MP for Derbyshire South-East, 1970-83; contested Sunderland North, 1966. B Sep 19 1930; ed Aylesbury GS; Birmingham Univ. Jt sec, Cons backbench cmte on trade, 1972-74, and of energy cmte, 1974-77. Treas, Anglo-German Parly Group, since 1974; Grand Cross, Order of Merit, Germany, 1979. FRGS (member of cl, 1980-83).
Mr Robert Jones, lecturer. B Apr 29 1940; ed Swanwick Sch; LSE; Birmingham Univ. Mbr, Derbyshire CC 1981- ; vice-chmn, social service cmte, 1985- . Sec, South-east Derbyshire Lab Pty, 1974-82. NATFHE
Ms Christine Moss, social worker. Mbr, CSD, since 1985; special interest gp on Third World. Responsible for introduction of joint membership as means of getting more women into politics. B Jan 12 1949; ed County HS for Girls, Romford; Hull and Nottingham Univs. Nalgo; previously Nupe.

ERITH AND CRAYFORD | | | | | | No change

Electorate %Turnout	59,292	75.4%	**1987**	56,066	73.5%	**1983**
*Evennett, D.A. (C)	20,203	45.2%	+8.1%	15,289	37.1%	(C)
Hargrave, C.F. (Lab)	13,209	29.5%	+2.2%	14,369	34.9%	(SDP/All)
Wellbeloved, A.J. (SDP/All)	11,300	25.3%	-9.6%	11,260	27.3%	(Lab)
				272	0.7%	(Other)
Lab to C swing 2.9%	44,712	C maj 6,994 15.6%		41,190	C maj 920 2.2%	

Mr David Evennett

Mr David Evennett, member of Lloyd's since 1976 and director of Lloyd's underwriting agency, won the seat in 1983; contested Hackney South and Shoreditch, 1979. Mbr, Select Cmte on Education, Science and the Arts, 1986- . Sec, House of Commons Motor Club, 1984-86. B Jun 3 1949; ed Buckhurst Hill County HS for Boys; LSE. Mbr, Redbridge BC, 1974-78.
Mr Colin Hargrave, teacher; barrister. Contested Bexley-Sidcup Feb 1974. B Oct 2 1943; ed Christ's Coll, Finchley; Mid Essex Tech Coll; LSE. Mbr, Bexley BC, 1974- (Ldr, Lab gp, 1982-). NUT.
Mr James Wellbeloved lost this seat as SDP MP in 1983. He was elected to it for Labour at the 1965 by-election but resigned from party and joined SDP in 1981. Under Secretary of State for Defence for the RAF, 1976-79; Opposition whip, 1972-1974. Commercial consultant; Director-General, National Kidney Research Fund. B Jul 29 1926; ed elementary sch and SE London Tech Coll. Mbr, Erith BC, 1956-65; London Borough of Bexley Cl; RACS Political Purposes Cmte, 1973-83. Nat vice-pres, Camping and Caravanning Club, since 1974. Director, Assocn of Former MPs, 1983- .

ESHER | | | | | | No change

Electorate %Turnout	62,117	76.9%	**1987**	61,745	73.1%	**1983**
Taylor, I.C. (C)	31,334	65.6%	+2.3%	28,577	63.3%	(C)
Barnett, A.J. (L/All)	12,266	25.7%	-2.4%	12,665	28.0%	(L/All)
Lucas, N.J.V. (Lab)	4,197	8.8%	+1.6%	3,250	7.2%	(Lab)
				664	1.5%	(Other)
L/All to C swing 2.3%	47,797	C maj 19,068 39.9%		45,156	C maj 15,912 35.2%	

Mr Ian Taylor

Mr Ian Taylor, chairman of the Conservative Group for Europe since 1985, is a director of Mathercourt Securities Ltd, an investment bank which also provides management services, and of World Trading and Shipping Ltd. Business consultant. Contested Coventry South East in Feb 1974. Chmn, Commonwealth Youth Exchange Cl, 1980-84, and vice pres since 1984; dep chmn, Vauxhall Cons Assocn, 1984-86. B Apr 18 1945; ed Whitley Abbey Sch, Coventry; Keele Univ; LSE - Ford Foundation Research Scholar. Hon sec, British Cons Assocn, Paris, 1976-78; mbr, Cons Nat Union exec and other nat cmtes, 1966-75; chmn, European Union of Christian Democratic and Cons Students, 1969-70; nat chmn, Fed of Cons Students, 1968-69.
Mr Anthony Barnett, director of marketing and advertising company. B 1943; ed Bishop Challenor Sch; LSE; Chicago Univ.
Mr Norman Lucas, lecturer. B May 29 1950.

EXETER | No change

Electorate %Turnout	75,208	80.6%	**1987**	73,441	78.0%	**1983**
*Hannam, J.G. (C)	26,922	44.4%	-2.1%	26,660	46.5%	(C)
Thomas, M.S. (SDP/All)	19,266	31.8%	+2.5%	16,780	29.3%	(SDP/All)
Vincent, J.A. (Lab)	13,643	22.5%	-0.3%	13,088	22.8%	(Lab)
Vail, R.J. (Grn)	597	1.0%	-0.4%	779	1.4%	(Eco)
Byles, N.D. (LAPP)	209	0.3%				
C to SDP/All swing 2.3%	60,637	C maj 7,656 12.6%		57,307	C maj 9,880 17.2%	

Mr John Hannam

Mr **John Hannam**, mbr, Govt advisory cmte on transport for disabled, 1983- , and sec, all-pty disablement group, 1974- . Won seat 1970. B Aug 2 1929; ed Yeovil GS; Open Univ. Chmn, Cons back-bench energy cmte, 1979- . Vice-chmn, British cmte of Rehabilitation International 1979- . Vice-pres, Disablement Income Gp; Royal Assocn for Disability and Rehabilitation. Mbr, cl, Action Research for the Crippled Child; Altzheimer's Disease Soc; Disabled Motorists Gp. Captain, Lords and Commons tennis club 1975- ; ski club, 1977-82. Mbr, Glyndebourne Festival Society; bd, National Theatre.
Mr **Michael Thomas**, communications consultant, was Lab MP for Newcastle upon Tyne East, Oct 1974-81 and SDP MP, 1981-83; contested E Hertfordshire 1970. Mbr SDP national cmte, 1981- ; chmn, SDP organisation cmte, 1981- , SDP by-election cmte, 1983- ; mbr, Alliance strategy cmte, 1983- . B May 24 1944; ed The Kings Sch, Macclesfield; Liverpool Univ. Collector of political and election memorabilia.
Mr **John Vincent**, univ lecturer. Mbr, Devon CC, 1981- . Jan 8 1947; ed Eltham Green Comprehensive; Sussex Univ. ASTMS.
Mr **Raymond Vail**, director of firm of recycled paper suppliers. B Jan 20 1958.

FALKIRK EAST | No change

Electorate %Turnout	52,564	75.0%	**1987**	52,045	72.3%	**1983**
*Ewing, H. (Lab)	21,379	54.2%	+6.5%	17,956	47.7%	(Lab)
Brookes, K.H. (C)	7,356	18.7%	-2.3%	7,895	21.0%	(C)
Halliday, R.N.F. (SNP)	6,056	15.4%	+3.4%	6,967	18.5%	(SDP/All)
Dick, Mrs E.G. (SDP/All)	4,624	11.7%	-6.8%	4,490	11.9%	(SNP)
				334	0.9%	(Other)
C to Lab swing 4.4%	39,415	Lab maj 14,023 35.6%		37,642	Lab maj 10,061 26.7%	

Mr Harry Ewing

Mr **Harry Ewing**, an Opposition spokesman on Scotland 1985- , was a spokesman on trade and industry, 1983-85, and on Scotland, 1979-83. Under Secretary of State for Scotland with responsibility for devolution and home affairs, 1974-79. Director, Cowdenbeath Football Club Ltd. Elected for this seat 1983; MP for Stirling, Falkirk and Grangemouth, Feb 1974-83; Stirling and Falkirk, 1971-74; fought East Fife, 1970. Post Office worker. B Jan 20 1931; ed and Beath HS, Cowdenbeath. Sponsored by UCW.
Mr **Kenneth Brookes**, UK manager of oil-related company. Mbr, Grampian Reg Cl, 1986- . B 1949; ed Frederick St Sch; Aberdeen Coll of Commerce; Aberdeen Univ; Northern Coll of Agriculture.
Mr **Ronald Halliday**, administrator at Stirling Univ, contested Edinburgh Central 1983. Convenor, SNP trade union gp. B Aug 16 1949; ed Boroughmis Senior Sec Sch, Edinburgh; Edinburgh Univ; Aberdeen Coll of Ed. Local exec mbr, AUT; Nalgo shop steward, 1980-84.
Mrs **Elizabeth Dick**, medical researcher, contested Dundee West 1983. Regional coordinator, Women for Social Democracy. Sec, local community cl. B Mar 17 1935; ed St Paul's Girls' Sch; St Anne's Coll, Oxford.

FALKIRK WEST | No change

Electorate %Turnout	50,222	76.7%	**1987**	49,402	74.0%	**1983**
*Canavan, D.A. (Lab)	20,256	52.6%	+7.0%	16,668	45.6%	(Lab)
Thomas, D.R.D. (C)	6,704	17.4%	-3.6%	7,690	21.0%	(C)
Goldie, I.R. (SNP)	6,696	17.4%	+4.4%	7,477	20.4%	(L/All)
Harris, M.J. (L/All)	4,841	12.6%	-7.9%	4,739	13.0%	(SNP)
C to Lab swing 5.3%	38,497	Lab maj 13,552 35.2%		36,574	Lab maj 8,978 24.5%	

Mr Dennis Canavan

Mr **Dennis Canavan**, mbr, Select Cmte on Foreign Affairs, 1982- . Jt vice-chmn, PLP foreign affairs cmte, 1985- ; PLP N Ireland cmte, since 1983; and PLP education and science cmte, 1983-85. Elected for this seat 1983; MP for West Stirlingshire, Oct 1974-83. Chmn, Scottish PLP gp, 1980-81; vice-chmn, 1979; treas, 1976-79; convenor of its education sub-cmte, 1976- . Head of maths dept, St Modan's HS, Stirling, 1970-74; asst headmaster, Holyrood HS, Edinburgh, 1974. Leader of Lab gp, Stirling DC, 1974, and mbr, 1973-74. B Aug 8 1942; ed St Columba's HS, Cowdenbeath, and Edinburgh Univ. EIS; sponsored by Cohse.
Mr **David Thomas**, medical student. B Jan 6 1964; ed Dundee HS; Edinburgh Univ. House mbr, Royal and Ancient Golf Club, St Andrews.
Mr **Ian Goldie**, senior language teacher employed by Strathclyde Region, contested Ayr 1983, and Scotland South in 1984 Euro election. Chmn, Lanark SNP; elected mbr, SNP nat cl. B Feb 8 1941; ed Hutchesons GS, Glasgow; Glasgow, Paris and Tubingen Univs. SSTA.
Mr **Marshall Harris**, director, Scottish Trust for UN and International Affairs, and Scottish officer, UN Assocn, 1955-86, contested this seat 1983 and Glasgow, Hillhead, 1979. B Mar 14 1928; ed Armadale Sec Sch and Lindsay HS, Bathgate; Glasgow Univ.

FALMOUTH AND CAMBORNE — No change

Electorate %Turnout	68,612	78.8%	**1987**	65,624	75.0%	**1983**
*Mudd, W.D. (C)	23,725	43.9%	-6.1%	24,614	50.0%	(C)
Marks, J.C. (SDP/All)	18,686	34.6%	+7.0%	13,589	27.6%	(SDP/All)
Cosgrove, J. (Lab)	11,271	20.9%	-0.4%	10,446	21.2%	(Lab)
Zapp, F. (Loony)	373	0.7%		582	1.2%	(MK)
C to SDP/All swing 6.5%	54,055	C maj 5,039 9.3%		49,231	C maj 11,025 22.4%	

Mr David Mudd, mbr, Select Cmte on Transport, 1981- ; sec, all-party minerals group, 1981- ; mbr, Unopposed Bills Panel, 1981-86; sec, Cons back-bench fisheries sub-cmte, 1974-75, and 1981-82. Won the seat in 1970. Journalist, author and consultant. PPS to Minister of State for Energy, 1979-81. Parly consultant to Nat Fed of Fruit and Potato Trades Ltd and to British Holiday and Home Parks Assocn Ltd; road safety consultant to Potters Ballotini Ltd. B Jun 2 1933; ed Truro Cathedral Sch. Mbr, Tavistock UDC, 1959-61. Sec, West Country Cons MPs, 1973-76. Editor *Cornish Echo*, 1950-52; on editorial staff of *Western Morning News*, 1953-54 and 1959-61.
Mr Jonathan Marks, barrister, contested Western-super-Mare in 1983 and Cornwall and Plymouth in 1984 Euro elections. Dep chmn, Kensington and Chelsea area party. Mbr, Social Dem Campaign for Racial Justice steering cmte; SDP working parties on citizens rights and on fisheries policy; Social Dem Lawyers Assocn. B Oct 19 1952; ed Harrow; University Coll, Oxford; Inns of Court Sch of Law.
Mr John Cosgrove, teacher, contested Cornwall and Plymouth in Euro election 1984. B May 22 1955; ed St Boniface's Coll, Plymouth; Trinity and All Saints' Coll, Leeds. NUT. Local cllr, 1985-87.

Mr David Mudd

FAREHAM — No change

Electorate %Turnout	76,974	78.2%	**1987**	71,901	73.7%	**1983**
*Lloyd, P.R.C. (C)	36,781	61.1%	-0.7%	32,762	61.8%	(C)
Slack, T. (L/All)	17,986	29.9%	-1.2%	16,446	31.0%	(L/All)
Merritt, M. (Lab)	5,451	9.1%	+1.9%	3,808	7.2%	(Lab)
L/All to C swing 0.2%	60,218	C maj 18,795 31.2%		53,016	C maj 16,316 30.8%	

Mr Peter Lloyd was appointed a Lord Commissioner of the Treasury (Govt whip) in 1986; an asst Govt whip, 1984-86. Former marketing manager of United Biscuits Ltd. Member of Lloyd's. Elected in 1979; contested Nottingham West, Feb and Oct 1974. B Nov 12 1937; ed Tonbridge Sch and Pembroke Coll, Cambridge. Chmn, Bow Group, 1972-73, research sec, 1970-72, and editor of *Crossbow*, 1974-76. Vice-chmn, Cons European affairs cmte, 1980-81; sec, Cons employment cmte, 1979-81; member, Select Cmte on Employment, 1983-84. PPS to Minister of State for N Ireland, 1982-83; to Secretary of State for Education and Science, 1983-84.
Mr Timothy Slack was director of the Foreign Office conference centre until it closed; former teacher abroad and as head of Bedales Sch, Petersfield. Contested 1984 Enfield Southgate by-election, Petersfield in Feb 1974. B Apr 1928; ed Winchester; New Coll, Oxford.
Mr Mike Merritt, tutor organiser in WEA. Former merchant seaman, miner and detective. B Apr 21 1942; ed Kent Univ (mature student); Bolton Coll of HE.

Mr Peter Lloyd

FAVERSHAM — No change

Electorate %Turnout	79,039	76.9%	**1987**	76,467	73.5%	**1983**
*Moate, R.D. (C)	31,074	51.1%	-2.0%	29,849	53.1%	(C)
Goyder, E.M. (SDP/All)	17,096	28.1%	+1.0%	15,252	27.1%	(SDP/All)
Dangerfield, P. (Lab)	12,616	20.8%	+1.0%	11,130	19.8%	(Lab)
C to SDP/All swing 1.5%	60,786	C maj 13,978 23.0%		56,231	C maj 14,597 26.0%	

Mr Roger Moate, insurance broker and director of Theatre Productions plc, Frank Bradford Holdings Ltd and subsidiaries, and Kent and City Holdings Ltd, won the seat in 1970; contested it, 1966. Former mbr, Statutory Instruments Cmte; former jt vice-chmn, Cons back-bench transport cmte. B May 12 1938; ed Latymer Upper Sch, Hammersmith. Vice-chmn, Greater London YCs, 1964-65; mbr, YC nat advisory cmte, 1963-66. Hon sec, British-Norwegian parly gp; British-American gp, 1974-81.
Mr Mark Goyder, distribution manager with Bowaters paper company. Mbr, Kent CC 1985- ; CSD; Tawney Society provisional cmte. B 1953; ed Rugby; Trinity Coll, Cambridge.
Mr Philip Dangerfield, polytechnic lecturer. Mbr, Swale BC and Faversham TC 1984- ; former vice chmn, Faversham CLP; mbr, Swale education advisory body; school governor. B Apr 7 1946; ed Boran GS, Sittingbourne; Southampton Univ. NATFHE.

Mr Roger Moate

FELTHAM AND HESTON · No change

Electorate %Turnout	81,062	73.7%	**1987**	78,366	69.8%	**1983**
*Ground, R.P. (C)	27,755	46.5%	+3.1%	23,724	43.4%	(C)
Hinds, C. (Lab)	22,325	37.4%	-2.0%	21,576	39.4%	(Lab)
Daly, J. (SDP/All)	9,623	16.1%	+0.2%	8,706	15.9%	(L/All)
				696	1.3%	(Other)
Lab to C swing 2.6%	59,703	C maj 5,430 9.1%		54,702	C maj 2,148 3.9%	

Mr Patrick Ground, QC, won the seat in 1983; contested Hounslow, Feltham and Heston in both 1974 elections and in 1979. Mbr, Select Cmte on MPs' Interests, 1983- . B Aug 9 1932; ed Beckenham and Penge County GS; Lycee Guy Lussac, Limoges; Selwyn Coll, Cambridge; Magdalen Coll, Oxford. Pres, Oxford Univ Cons Assocn, 1958. Mbr, Hammersmith BC, 1968-71. Chmn, Fulham Soc, 1975- .

Mr William Hinds, engineer, contested Gloucester in 1983. Apprenticeship with machine tool firm in Cheshire; then worked in Manchester. AEU convenor and shop steward for 20 years. B May 6 1945; ed Bauynulme Cty Jun Sch and Welacre Sec Mod Sch, Davyhulme.

Mr James Daly, senior lecturer in business studies, NE London Poly, contested Enfield North 1983. One of the original 12 members of nat steering cmte founding the SDP. Leader, Alliance group, Hounslow BC; former chmn, GLC transport cmte. B Oct 9 1936; ed Nottingham Univ.

Mr Patrick Ground

FERMANAGH AND SOUTH TYRONE · No change

Electorate %Turnout	68,979	80.3%	**1987**	67,880	88.6%	**1983**
*Maginnis, K. (OUP)	27,446	49.6%	+2.0%	28,630	47.6%	(OUP)
Corrigan, P. (PSF)	14,623	26.4%	-8.4%	20,954	34.8%	(PSF)
Flanagan, Mrs R. (SDLP)	10,581	19.1%	+2.6%	9,923	16.5%	(SDLP)
Kettyles, D. (WP)	1,784	3.2%	+2.1%	649	1.1%	(WP)
Haslett, J. (All)	941	1.7%				
PSF to OUP swing 5.2%	55,375	OUP maj 12,823 23.2%		60,156	OUP maj 7,676 12.8%	

Mr Kenneth Maginnis, former teacher, won the seat in 1983. Resigned in 1985 in protest at Anglo-Irish Agreement and retained it at 1986 by-election; also contested it 1981 by-election. Mbr, Select Cmte on Defence, 1983-85. B Jan 21 1938; ed Royal Sch, Dungannon, Co Tyrone; Stranmillis Teacher Training Coll, Belfast. Mbr, N Ireland Assembly, 1982-86; Dungannon DC, since 1981. Party spokesman on security. In UDR, 1970-81 (Commissioned 1972; gained rank of Major). Principal, Pomeroy Primary Sch, 1966-82.

Mr Paul Corrigan, aged 52, PSF mbr, Fermanagh DC 1985- (chmn of cl, 1985-86).

Mrs Rosemary Flanagan, teacher; head of careers dept in boys' sec sch. Fought this seat 1983.

Details of 1986 by-election on Page 285

Mr Kenneth Maginnis

FIFE CENTRAL · No change

Electorate %Turnout	56,090	76.2%	**1987**	54,389	72.5%	**1983**
McLeish, H.B. (Lab)	22,827	53.4%	+10.3%	17,008	43.1%	(Lab)
Aird, R.E. (C)	7,118	16.7%	-5.8%	9,214	23.4%	(L/All)
Little, Mrs T.M. (L/All)	6,487	15.2%	-8.2%	8,863	22.5%	(C)
Hood, D. (SNP)	6,296	14.7%	+4.5%	4,039	10.2%	(SNP)
				297	0.8%	(Other)
C to Lab swing 8.1%	42,728	Lab maj 15,709 36.8%		39,421	Lab maj 7,794 19.8%	

Mr Henry McLeish, local government officer and part-time university lecturer, contested North East Fife 1979. B Jun 15 1948; ed Buckhaven HS; Heriot Watt Univ, Edinburgh. Member and leader, Fife Regional Cl, 1978- ; regional cl director on Levenmouth Business Centre. Chmn, Kirkcaldy DC planning cmte, 1974-77. Sponsored by Nupe.

Mr Richard Aird, advocate, has held office in Putney and Edinburgh East Cons Assocns and Edinburgh branch, Soc of Cons Lawyers. B 1950; ed Loretto Sch; Edinburgh Coll of Commerce; London Poly; Exeter Univ; Inns of Court Sch.

Mrs Teresa Little, teacher, contested this seat 1983. Mbr, Fife Regional Cl, 1982-86. Sec and press officer, Dunfermline Lib Assocn, 1979-82. B Feb 15 1949; ed St Joseph's Convent, Girvan, Ayrshire; Edinburgh Univ. EIS.

Mr Daniel Hood, retired barrister, lecturer and economist, runs a small consultancy business with his wife. Contested Glasgow, Shettleston, 1983; and Scotland North East in 1984 Euro election. Mbr, Tayside Reg Cl; nec, SNP. B 1926; ed Whitehill Sch; Glasgow and London Univs. Former Dep Principal, Dundee Coll of Commerce; past pres, Scottish Further Ed Assocn.

Mr Henry McLeish

FIFE NORTH EAST — L/All gain

Electorate %Turnout	52,266	76.2%	1987	50,476	73.7%	1983
Campbell, W.M. (L/All)	17,868	44.8%	+4.6%	17,129	46.1%	(C)
*Henderson, J.S.B. (C)	16,421	41.2%	-4.9%	14,944	40.2%	(L/All)
Gannon, A.M.E. (Lab)	2,947	7.4%	+0.9%	2,442	6.6%	(SNP)
Roche, F.D. (SNP)	2,616	6.6%	-0.1%	2,429	6.5%	(Lab)
				242	0.7%	(Other)
C to L/All swing 4.8%	39,852	L/All maj 1,447 3.6%		37,186	C maj 2,185 5.9%	

Mr Menzies Campbell, QC, Liberal Party spokesman in Scotland on legal and home affairs, contested this seat 1983, East Fife 1979, and Greenock and Port Glasgow, twice in 1974. Chmn, Scottish Lib Pty, 1975-77. Advocate Depute, 1977-80; standing junior counsel to Army in Scotland, 1980-82. B May 22 1941; ed Hillhead HS, Glasgow; Glasgow Univ; Stanford Univ, California. International athlete: former captain, UK athletics team; former holder of UK 100 metres record; competed in Olympic and Commonwealth Games.

Mr Barry Henderson, management and systems consultant, was on the Select Cmte on Scottish Affairs, 1979-87. PPS to Economic Secretary to the Treasury, 1984-87. MP for this seat, 1983-87 ; for Fife East, 1979-83, and for East Dumbartonshire, Feb to Oct 1974; contested that seat, 1970, and Edinburgh East, 1966. B Apr 29 1936; ed Lathallan Sch; Stowe.

Mr Tony Gannon, unemployed. B Jun 13 1947; ed Kircaldy Coll of Tech; Stirling Univ.

Mr David Roche, architect; an asst director of tech services. Chmn, Eden local branch, SNP, Fife; NE Fife branch; the Campaign for a Scottish Assembly. B Mar 5 1941; ed St Michael's Coll, Irvine; Aberdeen Sch of Architecture. Nalgo.

Mr Menzies Campbell

FINCHLEY — No change

Electorate %Turnout	57,727	69.4%	1987	55,638	69.0%	1983
*Thatcher, Mrs M.H. (C)	21,603	53.9%	+2.9%	19,616	51.1%	(C)
Davies, J. (Lab)	12,690	31.7%	+4.9%	10,302	26.8%	(Lab)
Howarth, D. (L/All)	5,580	13.9%	-6.3%	7,763	20.2%	(L/All)
Buckethead, Lord (Gremloids)	131	0.3%		279	0.7%	(WFLOE)
St Vincent, Miss M. (GP)	59	0.1%		235	0.6%	(Loony Soc)
				222	0.6%	(Other)
C to Lab swing 1.0%	40,063	C maj 8,913 22.2%		38,417	C maj 9,314 24.2%	

Mrs Margaret Thatcher, the first woman Prime Minister and First Lord of the Treasury, took office on May 4 1979. Elected Leader of the Conservative Party and Leader of the Opposition in Feb 1975. Member of shadow Cabinet and chief Opposition spokesman on the environment, 1974-75; Secretary of State for Education and Science, 1970-74; chief Opposition spokesman on education, 1969-70; previously spokesman on transport, power, Treasury matters, housing and pensions; member, shadow Cabinet, 1967-70; Parliamentary Secretary, Ministry of Pensions and National Insurance, 1961-64. Elected for Finchley in 1959; contested Dartford, 1950 and 1951. Barrister (Lincoln's Inn, 1954; Hon Bencher, 1975) and research chemist, 1947-51. B Oct 13 1925; ed Grantham HS and Somerville Coll, Oxford, where she was treas and pres, Univ Cons Assocn. Freedom, Borough of Barnet, 1980; FRS, 1983.

Mr John Davies, director, educational publishers cl of The Publishers Assocn. B Apr 15 1941; ed Oxford and Sheffield Univs. Mbr, Barnet BC 1982- (ldr, Lab gp). Chmn, Phoenix Cinema Trust. Director, Copyright Licensing Agency. APEX; ASTMS.

Mr David Howarth, building society development representative, contested Durham North 1983. Mbr, Tyne and Wear CC, 1981-86. B Mar 23 1955; ed Queen Elizabeth's HS, Manchester; Rochdale Coll of Art and Design; Newcastle Poly.

Mrs Margaret
Thatcher

FOLKESTONE AND HYTHE — No change

Electorate %Turnout	64,406	78.3%	1987	67,802	70.6%	1983
*Howard, M. (C)	27,915	55.4%	-1.6%	27,261	56.9%	(C)
MacDonald, J.R. (L/All)	18,789	37.3%	+4.7%	15,591	32.6%	(L/All)
Anand, V.S. (Lab)	3,720	7.4%	-2.4%	4,700	9.8%	(Lab)
				318	0.7%	(Other)
C to L/All swing 3.1%	50,424	C maj 9,126 18.1%		47,870	C maj 11,670 24.4%	

Mr Michael Howard, QC, was appointed Minister of State for Environment, Jun 1987; Minister for Corporate and Consumer Affairs, with the rank of Under Secretary of State for Trade and Industry, 1985-87. Recorder from 1986. Elected in 1983; contested Liverpool, Edge Hill, 1966 and 1970. B Jul 7 1941; ed Llanelli GS and Peterhouse, Cambridge (Pres of Union, 1962). Mbr, Bow Group and chmn, 1970-71; chmn, Coningsby Club, 1972-73. PPS to Sir Patrick Mayhew, Solicitor General, 1984-85. Jt sec, Cons back-bench legal cmte, 1983-84; jt vice chmn, Cons employment cmte, 1983-84; vice-chmn, Soc of Cons Lawyers, 1985. Mbr of Lloyd's (ceased underwriting in Sep 1985).

Mr John MacDonald, QC, has been briefed to act in several notable human rights cases. Contested this seat 1983, and Wimbledon, 1970 and 1966. B Sep 26 1931; ed St Edward's Sch, Oxford; Queen's Coll, Cambridge.

Mr Vidya Anand, historian, author and community worker. B Sep 1 1939. ASTMS.

Mr Michael Howard

FOYLE | No change

Electorate %Turnout	70,519	69.0%	**1987**	67,432	77.5%	**1983**
*Hume, J. (SDLP)	23,743	48.8%	+2.8%	24,071	46.0%	(SDLP)
Campbell, G. (DUP)	13,883	28.5%	-1.9%	15,923	30.5%	(DUP)
McGuinness, M. (PSF)	8,707	17.9%	-2.4%	10,607	20.3%	(PSF)
Zammitt, Ms E. (All)	1,276	2.6%	+0.5%	1,108	2.1%	(All)
Mclaugh, E. (WP)	1,022	2.1%	+1.0%	582	1.1%	(WP)
DUP to SDLP swing 2.3%	48,631	SDLP maj	9,860 20.3%	52,291	SDLP maj	8,148 15.6%

Mr John Hume has been leader of the SDLP since 1979; deputy leader, 1970-79; founder mbr. Teacher. Won the seat in 1983; contested Londonderry, Oct 1974. B Jan 18 1937; ed St Columb's Coll, Londonderry; St Patrick's Coll, Maynooth. Mbr, European Parliament, 1979-, serving on bureau of Socialist Group. MP for Foyle, N Ireland Parliament, 1969-73. Elected for Londonderry to NI Assembly, 1973-75; NI Constitutional Convention, 1975-76; NI Assembly, 1982-86. Mbr, NI Forum, 1983-84. Minister for Commerce in NI power sharing executive, 1974.

Mr Gregory Campbell, former civil servant, contested this seat 1983. B Feb 15, 1953; ed Londonderry Tech Coll; Magee Coll. Member, NI Assembly for Londonderry, 1982-86. Ldr of DUP, Derry City Cl.

Mr Martin McGuinness is a member of the PSF nat exec. Contested this seat 1983. B May 23 1950; educated Christian Brothers Tech Coll. PSF assembly member Foyle, 1982-1986.

Ms Elizabeth Zammit, clerk and voluntary youth worker. B Sep 10 1958; ed Thornhill and Mount Carmel Girls GS, Strabane, Co Tyrone. Pty spokesman on consumer affairs.

Mr John Hume

FULHAM | C gain

Electorate %Turnout	54,498	77.1%	**1987**	51,833	76.1%	**1983**
Carrington, M.H.M. (C)	21,752	51.8%	+5.6%	18,204	46.2%	(C)
*Raynsford, W.R.N. (Lab)	15,430	36.7%	+2.7%	13,415	34.0%	(Lab)
Marshall, P.A.C. (SDP/All)	4,365	10.4%	-7.9%	7,194	18.2%	(L/All)
Grimes, Ms J. (Grn)	465	1.1%	+0.4%	277	0.7%	(Eco)
				331	0.8%	(Other)
Lab to C swing 1.4%	42,012	C maj	6,322 15.0%	39,421	C maj	4,789 12.1%

Mr Matthew Carrington, banker, regained seat for Conservatives in Jun 1987; contested the by-election in 1986 and Haringey, Tottenham in 1979. B 1947; ed French Lycee, London; Imperial Coll of Science and Tech, London Univ; London Graduate Sch of Business Studies.

Mr Nick Raynsford won this seat at the 1986 by-election. Became PPS to Mr Roy Hattersley, Dep Leader of the Opposition, 1986. Mbr, Select Cmte on Channel Tunnel Bill, 1986-87. Director of SHAC, the London Housing Aid Centre, 1976-86, being its research officer, 1974-76, and emergency officer, 1973-74. Gen sec, Soc for Co-op Dwellings, 1972-73; market research for A C Nielsen Co Ltd, 1966-68. B Jan 28 1945; ed Repton Sch; Sidney Sussex Coll, Cambridge; Chelsea Sch of Art. Member, London Borough of Hammersmith and Fulham Cl, 1971-75. ACTSS.

Mr Paul Marshall, investment fund manager. Research assistant to Mr Charles Kennedy, MP and editorial assistant to SDP newspaper. Sec, Putney SDP; member, SDP economics panel. B Aug 2 1959; ed St John's Coll, Oxford.

Details of 1986 by-election are on Page 285

Details of 1986 by-election are on Page 285

Mr Matthew
Carrington

FYLDE | No change

Electorate %Turnout	63,246	77.0%	**1987**	62,238	71.2%	**1983**
Jack, J.M. (C)	29,559	60.7%	-2.2%	27,879	62.9%	(C)
Smith, Mrs E.A. (L/All)	11,787	24.2%	-0.1%	10,777	24.3%	(L/All)
Smith, G. (Lab)	6,955	14.3%	+3.4%	4,821	10.9%	(Lab)
Fowler, H. (RCP)	405	0.8%		863	1.9%	(Ind)
C to L/All swing 1.0%	48,706	C maj	17,772 36.5%	44,340	C maj	17,102 38.6%

Mr Michael Jack, a sales director, is a mbr of the Mersey Regional Health Authority. Former nat chmn, YCs; former chmn, Nat Union of Students conference steering cmte. Contested Newcastle upon Tyne Central, Feb 1974. B Sep 17 1946; ed Bradford GS; Bradford Tech Coll; Leicester Univ. Sells horticultural produce to leading UK supermarket.

Mrs Anne Smith, director of Lancashire Enterprises, contested this seat 1983. Mbr, Lancashire CC, 1982- (ldr, Liberal gp); Fylde BC, 1979-; dist HA. B Mar 30 1929; ed private schs and GS.

Dr Geoffrey Smith, retired RAF Wing Commander and medical officer. Former asst opthalmic surgeon, Guy's Hospital. B Mar 27 1927; ed Cambridge Univ.

Mr Michael Jack

GAINSBOROUGH AND HORNCASTLE — No change

Electorate %Turnout	69,760	76.9%	1987	67,115	75.0%	1983
*Leigh, E.J.E. (C)	28,621	53.3%	+2.4%	25,625	50.9%	(C)
Grace, D.A. (L/All)	18,898	35.2%	-5.6%	20,558	40.8%	(L/All)
Naylor, R. (Lab)	6,156	11.5%	+3.8%	3,886	7.7%	(Lab)
				279	0.6%	(Other)
L/All to C swing 4.0%	53,675	C maj 9,723 18.1%		50,348	C maj 5,067 10.1%	

Mr Edward Leigh has been a member of the Select Cmte on Defence since 1983; chmn, Nat Cl for Civil Defence, 1980-82, and director, Coalition for Peace through Security, 1982-83; sec, Cons back-bench defence cmte, 1983-84; Cons back-bench agriculture cmte, 1983-85, and chmn, cereals sub-cmte, 1985- . Barrister; consultant to Nat Cold Storage Fed. Elected in 1983; contested Teesside Middlesbrough, Oct 1974. B Jul 20 1950; ed St Philip's Sch, Kensington; Oratory Sch; French Lycee, London; Durham Univ (pres of union and chmn, univ cons assocn). Mbr, Richmond BC, 1974-78; GLC, 1977-81; Cons Research Dept, 1973-75; and Mrs Thatcher's private office in charge of correspondence, 1975-76. Fellow, Industry and Parliament Trust.
Mr David Grace, public affairs consultant. B May 11 1951; ed Dover Coll; Magdalene and Wolfson Colls, Cambridge.
Mr Robin Naylor, economics lecturer. B Apr 10 1959; ed Caistor GS, Gainsborough; Oxford Univ. AUT.

Mr Edward Leigh

GALLOWAY AND UPPER NITHSDALE — No change

Electorate %Turnout	53,429	76.8%	1987	51,831	75.8%	1983
*Lang, I.B. (C)	16,592	40.4%	-4.3%	17,579	44.7%	(C)
Norris, S.F. (SNP)	12,919	31.5%	+0.6%	12,118	30.8%	(SNP)
McKercher, J. (L/All)	6,001	14.6%	+1.6%	5,129	13.1%	(L/All)
Gray, J. (Lab)	5,298	12.9%	+1.5%	4,464	11.4%	(Lab)
Kenny, D. (Retired)	230	0.6%				
C to SNP swing 2.5%	41,040	C maj 3,673 8.9%		39,290	C maj 5,461 13.9%	

Mr Ian Lang became Minister of State, Scottish Office, in Jun 1987; Minister for Industry and Home Affairs at Scottish Office, with rank of Under Secretary of State for Scotland, 1986-87; Under Secretary of State for Employment, 1986; a Lord Commissioner of the Treasury (Govt whip), 1983-86; asst Govt whip, 1981-83. Elected for this seat 1983; MP for Galloway, 1979-83; contested Ayrshire Central, 1970; Glasgow, Pollok, Feb 1974. B Jun 27 1940; ed Rugby and Sidney Sussex Coll, Cambridge. Former company director. Trustee, Savings Bank of Glasgow, 1969-74; West of Scotland TSB, 1974-83. Mbr, Select Cmte on Scottish Affairs, 1979-81. Vice-chmn, Scottish Cons Pty, 1983-87. Hon Pres, Scottish YCs, 1982-83. Mbr of Lloyd's. Mbr, Queen's Body Guard for Scotland (Royal Company of Archers), since 1974.
Mr Stephen Norris, master butcher and partner in family firm. Constituency organiser. B 1958; ed Douglas Ewart HS; Glasgow Univ.
Mr John McKerchar, managing director of own company producing health care products. Borders regional cllr. B May 11 1947; ed Burnage GS; Salford Univ.
Mr James Gray, welfare rights development officer. Sec, Pollokshields Lab Pty and Edinburgh Univ Labour Club. B Aug 4 1956; ed Stranraer Acad; Edinburgh Univ. Nalgo.

Mr Ian Lang

GATESHEAD EAST — No change

Electorate %Turnout	67,953	71.8%	1987	68,364	69.6%	1983
Quin, Ms J.G. (Lab)	28,895	59.2%	+10.9%	22,981	48.3%	(Lab)
Rogers, F.W. (C)	11,667	23.9%	-2.7%	12,659	26.6%	(C)
Rippeth, N.G. (SDP/All)	8,231	16.9%	-8.2%	11,920	25.1%	(SDP/All)
C to Lab swing 6.8%	48,793	Lab maj 17,228 35.3%		47,560	Lab maj 10,322 21.7%	

Ms Joyce Quin has been MEP for Tyne and Wear since 1979, being a mbr of the European Parliament's economic, agricultural and women's rights cmtes. Researcher, Lab Pty headquarters, 1969-72; then lecturer in French, Bath University, and in French and politics, Durham Univ. B Nov 26 1944; ed Whitley Bay GS (HS); Newcastle Univ; LSE. Sponsored by TGWU.
Mr Frank Rogers, retired school master, contested the seat 1983 and 1979. Mbr, Gateshead BC, 1952-65; North Tyneside MBC, 1975- . B Apr 4 1928; ed Gateshead GS; Oriel Coll, Oxford; external student, London Univ. Diocesan Reader, Church of England, since 1953. Mbr, Newcastle Soc of Antiquaries, Royal Inst of Philosophy, Freedom Assocn and Peace through Nato. AMMA.
Mr Noel Rippeth, teacher in Gateshead. Chmn, Gateshead SDP, 1983-86; mbr, CSD 1984- . B Dec 25 1939; ed Royal GS, Newcastle; Kings Coll, Newcastle; Durham and Open Univs. Chmn, local civic trust, local historian. Methodist local preacher. NAS/UWT.

Ms Joyce Quin

GEDLING | No change

Electorate %Turnout	68,398	79.1%	**1987**	66,656	75.4%	**1983**
Mitchell, A.J.B. (C)	29,492	54.5%	+0.4%	27,207	54.1%	(C)
Coaker, V.R. (Lab)	12,953	23.9%	+3.4%	12,543	25.0%	(SDP/All)
Morton, D. (SDP/All)	11,684	21.6%	-3.4%	10,330	20.6%	(Lab)
				186	0.4%	(Other)
C to Lab swing 1.5%	54,129	C maj 16,539 30.6%		50,266	C maj 14,664 29.2%	

Mr Andrew Mitchell, a banker, has been with Lazard Brothers and Co Ltd since 1979 using international and corporate finance experience in helping British firms to secure export orders against foreign competition; financial consultant since 1982 to El Vine Co Ltd, wine merchants and shippers. Contested Sunderland South in 1983. B Mar 23 1956; ed Rugby; Jesus Coll, Cambridge (Pres of Union, 1978). Chmn, Cambridge Univ Cons Assocn, 1977; the Coningsby Club, 1983-84; Islington North Cons Assocn, 1983-85..
Mr Vernon Coaker, teacher, contested Rushcliffe in 1983. Mbr, Rushcliffe BC, 1983- . B Jun 17 1953; ed Drayton Manor GS, London; Warwick Univ; Trent Poly.
Mr David Morton is full time in local politics. Mbr, Broxtowe BC; Nottinghamshire CC; chmn, Broxtowe SDP. B 1929; ed Rydal Sch; Leeds Univ. Was director, Cambridge school classics project, Cambridge Univ, from 1966; lecturer, Sch of Ed, Nottingham Univ, 1961-83.

Mr Andrew Mitchell

GILLINGHAM | No change

Electorate %Turnout	71,847	75.3%	**1987**	69,256	73.6%	**1983**
*Couchman, J.R. (C)	28,711	53.1%	+1.3%	26,381	51.7%	(C)
Andrews, L.R. (L/All)	16,162	29.9%	-0.6%	15,538	30.5%	(L/All)
Bishop, D.J. (Lab)	9,230	17.1%	-0.8%	9,084	17.8%	(Lab)
L/All to C swing 1.0%	54,103	C maj 12,549 23.2%		51,003	C maj 10,843 21.3%	

Mr James Couchman, director (since 1980) family licensed trade company, was elected in 1983; fought Chester-le-Street, 1979. Chmn, Bexley Health Authority, 1981-83. PPS to Mr Antony Newton, Minister for Social Security and then for Health, since 1984. B Feb 11 1942; ed Cranleigh Sch, Surrey; King's Coll, Newcastle upon Tyne; Durham Univ. Mbr, Bexley BC, 1974-82 (chmn, social services); Central Cl for Education and Training of Social Workers, 1976-80. Chmn, Bexley DHA, 1982-83. Governor, Nat Inst for Social Workers, 1976-80. Director, Chiswick Caterers Ltd. Freeman, City of London, and Vintner. NLVA. Former sec, Cons health and social services cmte; mbr, Select Cmte on Social Services, 1983-85.
Mr Leighton Andrews, lobbyist and charity director, is on the Liberal Party national executive (ex-vice-chmn of it) and the Liberal Party Cl; former vice-chmn, Lib Pty standing cmte. Former vice-pres, NUS. Director, 1987 International Year of Shelter for the Homeless. B Nov 8 1957; ed Poole GS; Univ Coll of N Wales, Bangor; Sussex Univ.
Mr David Bishop, a technical author, contested Tonbridge and Malling in 1983. B Jan 14 1941; ed technical coll. Mbr, Rochester on Medway City Cl, 1983- . (Ldr of the Opposition). TASS.

Mr James Couchman

GLANFORD AND SCUNTHORPE | Lab gain

Electorate %Turnout	72,816	78.0%	**1987**	71,962	73.5%	**1983**
Morley, E. (Lab)	24,733	43.5%	+6.2%	20,356	38.5%	(C)
*Hickmet, R.S. (C)	24,221	42.6%	+4.1%	19,719	37.3%	(Lab)
Nottingham, C. (SDP/All)	7,762	13.7%	-10.6%	12,821	24.2%	(SDP/All)
Trivedi, K.S. (Ind)	104	0.2%				
C to Lab swing 1.1%	56,820	Lab maj 512 0.9%		52,896	C maj 637 1.2%	

Mr Elliot Morley, remedial teacher at Hull comprehensive school, then head of the individual learning centre, won this seat in 1987. Mbr, Hull City Cl, 1979- . Ornithologist. B Jul 6 1952; ed St Margaret's CE HS, Liverpool. NUT, CND, Friends of the Earth, Greenpeace.
Mr Richard Hickmet, barrister and company secretary, was MP for this seat, 1983-87. Jt sec, Cons back-bench trade and industry cmte, 1984-85, 1986- ; Cons environment cmte, 1985-86. Mbr, Wandsworth BC, 1978-83; chmn, leisure and amenities cmte, 1980-83, when he privatised street cleansing, refuse collection and parks maintenance. B Dec 1 1947; ed Millfield, the Sorbonne and Hull Univ.
Mr Cyril Nottingham, master builder, contested the seat 1983. Labour member, Scunthorpe BC, 1966-83; former mayor of Scunthorpe; twice president, Master Builders' Assocn. B Sep 22 1927.

Mr Elliot Morley

GLASGOW, CATHCART — No change

Electorate %Turnout	49,307	76.4%	**1987**	51,055	75.8%	**1983**
*Maxton, J.A. (Lab)	19,623	52.1%	+10.7%	16,037	41.4%	(Lab)
Harvey, W.A. (C)	8,420	22.4%	-8.1%	11,807	30.5%	(C)
Craig, Miss M. (SDP/All)	5,722	15.2%	-7.3%	8,710	22.5%	(SDP/All)
Steven, W.A. (SNP)	3,883	10.3%	+4.8%	2,151	5.6%	(SNP)
C to Lab swing 9.4%	37,648	Lab maj 11,203 29.8%		38,705	Lab maj 4,230 10.9%	

Mr John Maxton

Mr John Maxton, an Opposition spokesman on Scotland 1985- ; chmn, PLP Treasury and Civil Service cmte, 1983, and of Scottish Labour MPs, 1983. Mbr, PAC, 1983-85. Gained the seat for Labour in 1979. Lecturer in social studies; chmn, Assocn of Lecturers in Colls of Ed, Scotland. Mbr, Socialist Educational Assocn; Select Cmte on Scottish Affairs, 1979-82. B May 5 1936; ed Lord Williams' GS, Thame, and Oxford Univ. Former parly representative, Civil Service Union and Scottish branch, Institute of Housing. EIS, ASTMS.

Mr William Harvey, mortgage and insurance broker, contested Glasgow Central 1983. Chmn, Glasgow Cons Assocn; chmn, Strathblane branch, Stirling. Church of Scotland Elder. B 1955; ed Woodside Sec Sch, Glasgow; Central Coll of Commerce, Glasgow; Glasgow Coll of Tech.

Miss Moira Craig, educational psychologist, contested Clydesdale 1983. Vice-chmn, area SDP and Scottish SDP cl; mbr, CSD. Founder mbr, Scottish Assocn of Local Govt and Educational Psychologists (pres, 1974-77). B 1929; ed Queen's Park Sch; Glasgow Univ; Jordanhill Coll of Ed.

Mr William Steven, senior science technician, contested this seat 1983. Mbr, SNP nat organisation cmte. B Jul 2 1955; ed Glenwood Sec Sch, Glasgow. Nalgo.

GLASGOW CENTRAL — No change

Electorate %Turnout	51,137	65.6%	**1987**	51,217	62.8%	**1983**
*McTaggart, R. (Lab)	21,619	64.5%	+11.4%	17,066	53.0%	(Lab)
Jenkin, B. (C)	4,366	13.0%	-5.9%	6,104	19.0%	(C)
Bryden, Dr J. (L/All)	3,528	10.5%	-6.2%	5,366	16.7%	(L/All)
Wilson, A. (SNP)	3,339	10.0%	-0.3%	3,300	10.3%	(SNP)
Brooks, A. (Grn)	290	0.9%		347	1.1%	(Com)
McGoldrick, J.P. (Comm)	265	0.8%	-0.3%			
Owen, D. (RF)	126	0.4%				
C to Lab swing 8.7%	33,533	Lab maj 17,253 51.5%		32,183	Lab maj 10,962 34.1%	

Mr Robert McTaggart

Mr Robert McTaggart won this seat at the 1980 by-election. Chmn, all-pty penal affairs cmte; PLP health and social security cmte. B Nov 2 1945; ed St Constantine's and St Bartholomew's Primary Schs; Holyrood secondary schs. Apprentice marine plumber, 1962-67; trigonometrical calculator, 1968-72, and pipework planner, 1972-80. EETPU shop steward, Govan Shipbuilders, 1971-77; mbr, Glasgow Corpn, 1974-75; DC, 1977-80.

Mr Bernard Jenkin, a venture capitalist, with Investors in Industry plc, 1986- , was a sales and marketing executive, Ford Motor Co Ltd, 1983-86. Research asst to Mr Leon Brittan MP, 1986- . B Apr 9 1959; ed Highgate Sch; William Ellis Sch; Corpus Christi Coll, Cambridge.

Dr John Bryden, community medical specialist. B Nov 20 1932; ed Kings Park, Glasgow; Rothesay Academy; Glasgow, Strathclyde and Edinburgh Univs.

Mr Alexander Wilson, health service servitor. B 1956; ed St Mirren Academy. Former mbr, Iverclyde DC. Chmn, Port Glasgow SNP. Nupe shop steward and branch chmn.

Mr Andrew Brooks, lecturer in computer science, Strathclyde Univ. Mbr, Scottish CND; Scientists Against Nuclear Arms. Aged 30; ed Edinburgh Univ.

Mr John McGoldrick, electrician, fought this seat 1983. Mbr, Scottish cmte, Glasgow exec cmte, Comm Pty. B Apr 9 1944; ed Holyrood Senr Sec Sch, Glasgow.

GLASGOW, GARSCADDEN — No change

Electorate %Turnout	47,958	71.4%	**1987**	50,589	69.1%	**1983**
*Dewar, D.C. (Lab)	23,178	67.7%	+11.5%	19,635	56.2%	(Lab)
Brophy, A. (SNP)	4,201	12.3%	+2.1%	6,161	17.6%	(SDP/All)
Begg, T.N.A. (C)	3,660	10.7%	-4.7%	5,368	15.4%	(C)
Callison, S. (SDP/All)	3,211	9.4%	-8.3%	3,566	10.2%	(SNP)
				218	0.6%	(Other)
SNP to Lab swing 4.7%	34,250	Lab maj 18,977 55.4%		34,948	Lab maj 13,474 38.6%	

Mr Donald Dewar

Mr Donald Dewar, chief Opposition spokesman on Scotland since 1983, was elected to the shadow Cabinet in 1984; a spokesman on Scotland, 1980-83. Chmn, Select Cmte on Scottish Affairs, 1979-81. Returned at the 1978 by-election; MP for Aberdeen South, 1966-70; contested the seat, 1964 and 1970. Solicitor; partner of Ross Harper and Murphy (solicitors). B Aug 21 1937; ed Glasgow Acad and Glasgow Univ (Pres of Union, 1961-62). PPS to President of Board of Trade, 1967. Mbr, Public Expenditure Cmte, 1978-79; PAC, 1966-68. Fellow, Industry and Parliament Trust. Sponsored by NUR.

Mr Andrew Brophy, solicitor, is chmn, Garscadden SNP, and a former local sec and organiser. B 1960; ed Glasgow Univ.

Mr Thomas Begg, in project/materials management; formerly employed in recently working in oil industry. Vice-chmn, Glasgow Pollok Cons Assocn. B Jun 7 1944; ed Uddingston GS; Strathclyde Univ. Church of Scotland elder; past mbr, Glasgow Junior Chamber of Commerce.

Mr Stuart Callinson, solicitor. Mbr, CSD; chmn, Scottish Young Social Democrats; former president, Glasgow Univ SDP. B Jun 19 1962.

GLASGOW, GOVAN — No change

Electorate %Turnout	50,616	73.4%	**1987**	51,754	71.6%	**1983**
*Millan, B. (Lab)	24,071	64.8%	+9.9%	20,370	55.0%	(Lab)
Ferguson, A. (SDP/All)	4,562	12.3%	-7.4%	7,313	19.7%	(SDP/All)
Girsman, Mrs J.R. (C)	4,411	11.9%	-7.5%	7,180	19.4%	(C)
McCabe, F. (SNP)	3,851	10.4%	+4.4%	2,207	6.0%	(SNP)
Chalmers, D. (Comm)	237	0.6%				
SDP/All to Lab swing 8.7%	37,132	Lab maj 19,509 52.5%		37,070	Lab maj 13,057 35.2%	

Mr Bruce Millan was chief Opposition spokesman on Scotland, 1979-83; mbr, shadow Cabinet, 1981-83. Secretary of State for Scotland, 1976-79; Minister of State for Scotland, responsible for Scottish Economic Planning Department, 1974-76. An Opposition spokesman on Scotland, 1973-74, and on industry, 1970-73. Under Secretary of State for Scotland, 1966-70; Under Secretary of State for Defence for the RAF, 1964-66. Elected for this seat 1983; MP for Glasgow, Craigton, 1959-83; contested the seat, 1955, and West Renfrewshire, 1951. Chartered accountant. Parly adviser, Inst of Chartered Accountants of Scotland. B Oct 5 1927; ed Harris Acad, Dundee. Mbr, Cl of Europe and WEU, 1984- . Sponsored by Apex.
Mr Alasdair Ferguson, insurance agent. B Dec 26 1955; ed Glasgow HS. Mbr, Nat Union of Insurance Workers.
Ms Janet Girsman, freelance journalist, director of electrical wholesale company and of her own public relations firm. Hon press officer, British Schools Exploring Soc. Ed Golphin and Latymer Schs; Harrow Sch of Art.
Mr Felix McCabe, teacher, has held various posts in the Craigton and Govan SNP branches. B Sep 25 1936; ed St Gerards Sec Sch, Govan, Glasgow; Strathclyde Univ. EIS.

Mr Bruce Millan

GLASGOW, HILLHEAD — Lab gain

Electorate %Turnout	57,836	72.4%	**1987**	57,016	71.9%	**1983**
Galloway, G. (Lab)	17,958	42.9%	+9.5%	14,856	36.2%	(SDP/All)
*Jenkins, R.H. (SDP/All)	14,707	35.1%	-1.1%	13,692	33.4%	(Lab)
Cooklin, B.D. (C)	6,048	14.4%	-9.1%	9,638	23.5%	(C)
Kidd, W. (SNP)	2,713	6.5%	+1.1%	2,203	5.4%	(SNP)
Whitelaw, A. (Grn)	443	1.1%		249	0.6%	(Ind C)
				378	0.9%	(Other)
SDP/All to Lab swing 5.3%	41,869	Lab maj 3,251 7.8%		41,016 SDP/All maj 1,164 2.8%		

Mr George Galloway, former chairman of the Scottish Labour Party, became gen sec of the charity War on Want in 1983. Sponsored by TGWU.
Mr Roy Jenkins, leader of the SDP, 1982-83; was Alliance election spokesman on Treasury affairs. Elected Chancellor of Oxford Univ, 1987. Won this seat in 1982; contested Warrington for SDP, 1981; Lab MP for Birmingham, Stechford, 1950-1976, and for Central Southwark, 1948-50. Pres, EEC Commission, 1977-81. Dep leader, Lab Pty, 1970-72; Home Secretary, 1974-76 and 1965-67; Chancellor of the Exchequer, 1967-70; Minister of Aviation, 1964-65. B Nov 11 1920; ed Abersychan GS; Univ Coll, Cardiff; Balliol Coll, Oxford.
Mr Brian Cooklin, English teacher, fought Edinburgh, Leith, 1983. *Mastermind* contestant. B Mar 26 1954; ed Hyndland Sec Sch, Glasgow; Glasgow Univ; Jordanhill Coll of Ed.
Mr William Kidd, housing official in Clydebank. Chmn, Hillhead SNP; vice-chmn, Hillhead West branch. B 1956; ed Central Coll of Commerce. Nalgo.
Mr Alastair Whitelaw, administrator at Glasgow Univ, contested this seat 1983. Aged 38.

Mr George Galloway

GLASGOW, MARYHILL — No change

Electorate %Turnout	52,371	67.5%	**1987**	51,847	65.5%	**1983**
Fyfe, Mrs M. (Lab)	23,482	66.4%	+11.3%	18,724	55.2%	(Lab)
Attwooll, Miss E.M.A. (L/All)	4,118	11.7%	-10.5%	7,521	22.2%	(L/All)
Roberts, G. (SNP)	3,895	11.0%	+3.9%	5,014	14.8%	(C)
Kirk, S.R.R. (C)	3,307	9.4%	-5.4%	2,408	7.1%	(SNP)
Spaven, D. (Grn)	539	1.5%		274	0.8%	(Com)
L/All to Lab swing 10.9%	35,341	Lab maj 19,364 54.8%		33,941	Lab maj 11,203 33.0%	

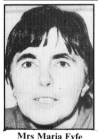

Mrs Maria Fyfe, lecturer in industrial relations. Mbr, Glasgow DC, 1980- (convenor, personnel cmte; former vice-convenor, finance cmte); Scottish Lab Pty exec, formerly chairing Scottish local govt cmte; Glasgow district and Maryhill parties. B Nov 25 1938; ed state primary and sec schools in Scotland; Strathclyde Univ. EIS and TGWU.
Miss Elspeth Attwooll, university lecturer in jurisprudence, contested the seat in 1979 and Oct 1974. B Feb 1 1943; ed Tiffin Girls GS, Kingston-upon-Thames; St Andrew's Univ. Former mbr, Scottish Lib Pty Exec; chmn, Greater Glasgow Lib Cl; Pres, Glasgow Univ Lib Club; vice-chmn Maryhill Lib Pty.
Mr Gavin Roberts, unemployed artist/teacher. Vice-chmn, Hillhead SNP and of Kelvingrove branch; mbr, SNP trade union gp. B 1956; ed Glasgow Sch of Art; Jordanhill Coll of Ed
Mr Simon Kirk, chartered engineer; plant engineer with ICI at Dumfries. B 1959; ed Felsted Sch; Christchurch Coll, Oxford. Son of late Sir Peter Kirk, who led the Cons Gp at the European Parliament when UK joined EEC.
Mr David Spaven, marketing manager in ScotRail freight dept. Scottish spokesman for Grn Pty. Aged 35. Glasgow cycling campaigner.

Mrs Maria Fyfe

GLASGOW, POLLOK — No change

Electorate %Turnout	51,396	71.7%	1987	53,217	68.2%	1983
Dunnachie, J. (Lab)	23,239	63.1%	+10.8%	18,973	52.3%	(Lab)
French, Mrs G. (C)	5,256	14.3%	-6.2%	7,441	20.5%	(C)
Shearer, J. (L/All)	4,445	12.1%	-5.3%	6,308	17.4%	(L/All)
Doig, A. (SNP)	3,528	9.6%	-0.3%	3,585	9.9%	(SNP)
Fogg, D. (Grn)	362	1.0%				
C to Lab swing 8.5%	36,830	Lab maj 17,983 48.8%		36,307	Lab maj 11,532 31.8%	

Mr Jimmy Dunnachie

Mr Jimmy Dunnachie, Rolls Royce engineer, mainly at its Hillington factory. Local councillor since 1972; mbr, Strathclyde Regional Cl, 1978- (vice-chmn, social work cmte, 1982-); Greater Glasgow Health Board. B Nov 17 1930. AEU (shop steward for 33 years).
Mrs Gillian French, buyer. Mbr, Bracknell DC. B Nov 16 1957; ed Eastwood HS, Renfrewshire; Aberdeen Univ (chmn, univ FCS). Also chaired NE Croydon YCs. ASTMS, previously member, exec, NUS (Scotland).
Mr James Shearer, jt managing director, Shearer Mormet Ltd. B Jan 11 1956; ed Shawlands Acad; Hutchesons' Boys GS; Glasgow Univ. Ex-chmn, Pollok YCs; former pres, Glasgow Univ Cons Club; convenor, Hillhead YLs.
Mr Andrew Doig, an assistant publican, has been on the SNP international relations cmte since 1981. Hon pres, Glas Univ Scottish Nationalist Assocn, 1983-84; elected mbr, SNP nat cl, 1985-86. B Dec 15 1961; ed Dennyloanhead Primary Sch; Denny HS; Falkirk Coll of Tech. Founder mbr, Scottish Socialist Soc, 1982. TGWU, WEA.
Mr Derek Fogg, senior lecturer in German and theatre studies, Glasgow Univ. Chmn, Glasgow gp, Amnesty International. Aged 60.

GLASGOW, PROVAN — No change

Electorate %Turnout	43,744	69.1%	1987	47,706	65.2%	1983
Wray, J. (Lab)	22,032	72.9%	+8.5%	20,040	64.4%	(Lab)
Ramsay, W. (SNP)	3,660	12.1%	+3.3%	4,655	15.0%	(SDP/All)
Strutt, Miss A. (C)	2,336	7.7%	-3.1%	3,374	10.8%	(C)
Morrison, J. (SDP/All)	2,189	7.2%	-7.7%	2,737	8.8%	(SNP)
				294	0.9%	(Other)
SNP to Lab swing 2.6%	30,217	Lab maj 18,372 60.8%		31,100	Lab maj 15,385 49.5%	

Mr James Wray, heavy goods vehicle driver. Mbr, Strathclyde Regional Cl, 1976- ; led the Gorbals rent strike and anti-dampness campaign; president, Gorbals United FC; St Enoch's Drug Centre; Scottish Ex-Boxers' Assocn. B Apr 28 1938. TGWU.
Mr William Ramsay, modern studies teacher. B 1955; ed Strathclyde Univ. EIS school rep.
Miss Anne Strutt, parliamentary lobbyist. B Dec 8 1955; ed Sherborne Sch for Girls, Dorset.
Mr John Morrison, solicitor. Mbr, Scottish Cl of SDP, 1986-87; chmn (1986-87) and sec (1986), Glasgow North SDP; convenor, Scottish SDP Students, 1983-84; pres (founder), Glasgow Univ SDP, 1981-82, 1983. B Jun 14 1962; ed North Kelvinside Sec Sch; Glasgow Univ.

Mr James Wray

GLASGOW, RUTHERGLEN — No change

Electorate %Turnout	57,313	77.2%	1987	59,209	75.2%	1983
McAvoy, T. (Lab)	24,790	56.0%	+7.7%	21,510	48.3%	(Lab)
Brown, R.E. (L/All)	10,795	24.4%	-3.4%	12,384	27.8%	(L/All)
Hamilton, G. (C)	5,088	11.5%	-6.5%	8,017	18.0%	(C)
Higgins, J. (SNP)	3,584	8.1%	+2.6%	2,438	5.5%	(SNP)
				148	0.3%	(Other)
L/All to Lab swing 5.6%	44,257	Lab maj 13,995 31.6%		44,497	Lab maj 9,126 20.5%	

Mr Thomas McAvoy

Mr Thomas (Tommy) McAvoy, engineering storeman, works for Hoover at Cambuslang. Mbr, Strathclyde Regional Cl, since 1982; chairs Strathclyde's Glasgow deprivation gp; vice-chmn, New Glasgow Division Community Development cmte. Former chmn, Rutherglen Community Cl and Fed of Tenants' Assocns; rep on Rutherglen Unemployed Workers Centre. B Dec 14 1943; ed St Columbkilles primary and junior sec schs. AEU.
Mr Robert Brown, solicitor, contested this seat 1983, 1979 and Oct 1974. Mbr, Glasgow DC, 1977-87 (leader, 1986 gp). B Dec 25 1947; ed Pinner Park primary sch, Harrow; Forgue primary, Huntly, Aberdeenshire; Gordon Schs, Huntly; Aberdeen Univ.
Mr Graeme Hamilton, local govt housing dept administrative supervisor. Member, exec, Rutherglen Cons Assocn. Reg cl candidate, 1986. Former chmn, British Youth Cl (Scotland). B Jun 20 1963; ed Hutchesons' GS, Glasgow. Nalgo.
Mr John Higgins is pres, Rutherglen SNP; mbr, SNP nat organization cmte. B 1944; ed Our Lady's HS, Motherwell. NUR.

121

GLASGOW, SHETTLESTON — No change

Electorate %Turnout	53,604	70.4%	**1987**	51,955	68.3%	**1983**
*Marshall, D. (Lab)	23,991	63.6%	+9.4%	19,203	54.2%	(Lab)
Fisher, J.M.S. (C)	5,010	13.3%	-5.9%	6,787	19.1%	(C)
MacVicar, J. (SNP)	4,807	12.7%	+4.8%	6,568	18.5%	(L/All)
Clarke, Miss P. (L/All)	3,942	10.4%	-8.1%	2,801	7.9%	(SNP)
				103	0.3%	(Other)
C to Lab swing 7.6%	37,750	Lab maj 18,981 50.3%		35,462	Lab maj 12,416 35.0%	

Mr David Marshall

Mr David Marshall joined the Select Cmte on Transport in 1985; mbr, Select Cmte on Scottish Affairs, 1981-83. Elected in 1979. Sec and treas, Scottish group of Lab MPs, 1981- ; jt vice-chmn, PLP transport cmte, 1983- ; jt chmn, parly road passenger transport gp, 1986- . B May, 1941; ed Larbert HS, Denny HS, Falkirk HS and Woodside Senior Sec Sch. Mbr, Glasgow Corp, 1972-75; Strathclyde Reg Cl, 1974-79 (Chmn, Manpower Cmte and COSLA Manpower Cmte). Former transport worker and shop steward. Sponsored by TGWU.
Mr Mark Fisher, solicitor in private partnership, is director of small family company, sec of various client companies, member of Dingwall Chamber of Commerce and of the Highland and Ross-shire and Sutherland Faculties of Solicitors. B Oct 1 1960; ed Allan Glen's Sch, Glasgow; Glasgow Univ. Mbr, Dingwall Choral Soc.,
Mr John MacVicar, a principal teacher of history with Strathclyde Region. Chmn, Cumbernauld branch, SNP; sec, Glasgow East End Community Transport Scheme. B 1947; ed Lancaster Univ; Moray House Coll.
Miss Pauline Clarke, lecturer, chairs Shettleston Lib Assocn. B Sep 19 1922; ed Glasgow and Strathclyde Univs; LSE; Jordanhill Coll.

GLASGOW, SPRINGBURN — No change

Electorate %Turnout	51,563	67.5%	**1987**	53,373	65.1%	**1983**
*Martin, M.J. (Lab)	25,617	73.6%	+8.9%	22,481	64.7%	(Lab)
O'Hara, B. (SNP)	3,554	10.2%	+2.1%	4,882	14.1%	(L/All)
Call, M. (C)	2,870	8.3%	-4.9%	4,565	13.1%	(C)
Rennie, D. (L/All)	2,746	7.9%	-6.2%	2,804	8.1%	(SNP)
SNP to Lab swing 3.4%	34,787	Lab maj 22,063 63.4%		34,732	Lab maj 17,599 50.7%	

Mr Michael Martin

Mr Michael Martin, a former trade union official and sheet metal worker, has served on the Select Cmte on Trade and Industry since 1983. Elected for Glasgow, Springburn, in 1979. Served on Glasgow Corporation, 1973-74, and Glasgow DC, 1974-79. B Jul 3 1945; ed St Patrick's Sch, Glasgow. PPS to Mr Denis Healey, when Deputy Leader of Lab Pty, 1981-83. Fellow, Industry and Parliament Trust. Sponsored by AUEW/TASS (craft sector).
Mr Brendan O'Hara, local govt officer. Mbr, SNP nat cl, 1986-87; chmn, Young Scottish Nationalists, 1984-86. B Apr 27 1963; ed St Andrews RC Comprehensive Sch, Glasgow. Nalgo; mbr, Glasgow District exec, Nalgo.
Mr Mark Call, business strategy consultant with London firm. Mbr, trade and shipping cmte, Bow Gp. Was chmn, Scottish Fed of Cons Students. B 1955; ed Frimley and Camberley GS; St Andrews Univ; European Business Sch, Fontainebleau.
Mr David Rennie, student; president, Glasgow Univ Students' Representative Cl. B Apr 28 1966; ed Bannerman HS, Glasgow; Glasgow Univ. President, Glasgow Univ Lib Club, 1985-86; pres, Glasgow Univ SRC, 1986-87; mbr, SLP exec, 1987- .

GLOUCESTER — No change

Electorate %Turnout	76,910	78.1%	**1987**	74,268	75.6%	**1983**
French, D. (C)	29,826	49.7%	+1.2%	27,235	48.5%	(C)
Hulme, D. (Lab)	17,791	29.6%	+3.5%	14,698	26.2%	(Lab)
Hilton, J. (L/All)	12,417	20.7%	-3.3%	13,499	24.0%	(SDP/All)
				739	1.3%	(Other)
C to Lab swing 1.1%	60,034	C maj 12,035 20.0%		56,171	C maj 12,537 22.3%	

Mr Douglas French

Mr Douglas French, barrister; director of an import-export company and managing director, Westminster and City Programmes Ltd, a financial seminar company, contested Sheffield, Attercliffe 1979. Special adviser to Sir Geoffrey Howe, Chancellor of the Exchequer, 1981-83, and personal assistant to him when shadow Chancellor, 1976-79; nat chmn, Bow Gp, 1978-79. B Mar 20 1944; ed Glyn GS, Epsom; St Catharine's Coll, Cambridge; Inns of Court Sch of Law.
Mr David Hulme, sixth form college teacher, contested Devizes 1983. Former vice-chair, Swindon CLP. B Jul 22 1952; ed public school; Oxford Univ; Inst of Ed. Mbr, Thamesdown DC, 1976-87; Swindon HA, 1982-87. NATFHE; TASS.
Mr Jeremy Hilton, scientific technician. B May 26 1955; ed Longlevens Sec Sch, Gloucester. Mbr, Gloucester City Cl, 1982-86 (chmn, planning cmte, 1985-86); Gloucestershire CC, 1985- (chmn, public protection and public transport cmtes).

GLOUCESTERSHIRE WEST — No change

Electorate	%Turnout			1987			1983
		77,994	81.1%	**1987**	74,266	79.6%	**1983**
*Marland, P. (C)		29,257	46.2%	+0.4%	27,092	45.8%	(C)
Nielson, P.E.S. (Lab)		17,578	27.8%	+3.1%	17,440	29.5%	(SDP/All)
Watkinson, J.T. (SDP/All)		16,440	26.0%	-3.5%	14,572	24.7%	(Lab)
C to Lab swing 1.4%		63,275	C maj 11,679 18.5%		59,104	C maj 9,652 16.3%	

Mr **Paul Marland**, a farmer, became a member of the Select Cmte on Agriculture in 1986. Elected in 1979; contested the seat, Feb and Oct, 1974, and Bedwellty, 1970. PPS to Minister of Agriculture, Fisheries and Food, 1983-86; PPS to Financial Secretary to the Treasury and to Economic Secretary, 1981-83. B Mar 19 1940; ed Gordonstoun Sch and Trinity Coll, Dublin. Former sec, Cons back-bench agriculture, fisheries and food cmte. Former mbr, North Cotswold RDC. Mbr of Lloyd's. NFU.

Mr **Peter Nielsen**, senior systems analyst, contested Oswestry 1979, South Worcestershire 1983, and Hereford and Worcester in 1984 Euro election. Chmn, Worcester CLP, 1973-76; mbr, West Midlands regional executive Lab Pty, 1975-77; Hereford-Worcester CC, 1977-82; Worcester City Cl, 1979-80. B Dec 7 1941; ed Handsworth Tech Sch, Birmingham; Bradford Univ. TGWU.

Mr **John Watkinson**, barrister and former TV reporter and teacher, was Lab MP for this seat, 1974-79, and contested it for SDP in 1983. Also fought Warwick and Leamington for Lab 1970. B Jan 25 1941; ed Bristol GS; Worcester Coll, Oxford. Former mbr, PAC and WEU; PPS in Home Office. Taught economics and politics at Repton and Rugby, 1964-71. TV reporter on BBC's *Money Programme*.

Mr Paul Marland

GORDON — No change

Electorate	%Turnout			1987			1983
		73,479	73.7%	**1987**	65,537	70.1%	**1983**
*Bruce, M.G. (L/All)		26,770	49.5%	+5.6%	20,134	43.8%	(L/All)
Leckie, P.R. (C)		17,251	31.9%	-10.1%	19,284	42.0%	(C)
Morrell, Mrs M.C. (Lab)		6,228	11.5%	+3.0%	3,899	8.5%	(Lab)
Wright, G.E. (SNP)		3,876	7.2%	+1.4%	2,636	5.7%	(SNP)
C to L/All swing 7.9%		54,125	L/All maj 9,519 17.6%		45,953	L/All maj 850 1.8%	

Mr **Malcolm Bruce** was Alliance election spokesman on employment; Liberal spokesman on energy, 1985- ; on Scotland, 1983-85. Mbr, Select Cmte on Scottish Affairs, 1983- . Jt editor, publisher and director, Aberdeen Petroleum Publishing, 1981-84; marketing director, Noroil Publishing House (UK) Ltd, 1975-81. Elected in 1983; contested W Aberdeenshire, 1979, and N Angus and Mearns, Oct 1974. B Nov 17 1944; ed Wrekin Coll, Shropshire; St Andrew's and Strathclyde Univs. Rector, Dundee Univ, 1986- . Dep chmn, Scottish Lib Pty, 1975-84.

Mr **Ross Leckie**, an associate of Stewart Wrightson Gp (UK) Ltd, contested Kilmarnock and Loudoun 1983 and Strathclyde E in 1984 Euro election. B 1957; ed Fettes Coll, Edinburgh; Corpus Christi Coll, Oxford; Royal Agricultural Coll, Cirencester.

Mrs **Morag Morrell**, freelance writer, contested Kincardine and Deeside in 1983. Mbr, Grampian Regional Cl. Chairs Aberdeen women's cl. B Apr 12 1932; ed primary schs; Arbroath HS.

Mr **George Wright**, an operation and maintenance technician, is sec, Grampian SNP liaison cmte. Mbr, Banff and Buchan DC, 1980-84. B May 28 1940; ed Lerwick Central Sch; Lauder Tech Coll. EETPU.

Mr Malcolm Bruce

GOSPORT — No change

Electorate	%Turnout			1987			1983
		68,113	74.8%	**1987**	64,877	71.6%	**1983**
*Viggers, P.J. (C)		29,804	58.5%	-2.1%	28,179	60.6%	(C)
Chegwyn, P.J. (L/All)		16,081	31.6%	+2.0%	13,728	29.5%	(L/All)
Lloyd, A. (Lab)		5,053	9.9%	+0.6%	4,319	9.3%	(Lab)
					241	0.5%	(Other)
C to L/All swing 2.1%		50,938	C maj 13,723 26.9%		46,467	C maj 14,451 31.1%	

Mr **Peter Viggers**, solicitor, member of Lloyd's and former company director, was appointed an Under Secretary of State for N Ireland in 1986; PPS to Solicitor General, 1979-83, and to Chief Secretary to the Treasury, 1983-86. Elected in Feb 1974. B Mar 13 1938; ed Portsmouth GS and Trinity Hall, Cambridge. Chmn, Campaign for Defence and Multilateral Disarmament, 1984-86; Cmte for Peace with Freedom, 1984-86. Delegate, N Atlantic Assembly, 1980-86. Jt sec, 1975-76, and vice-chmn, 1977-79, Cons energy cmte; has served as sec, Wessex group of Cons MPs. Former taxation adviser to NFBTE. Mbr, management cmte, RNLI, 1979- ; Bow Group.

Mr **Peter Chegwyn**, parliamentary consultant, fought this seat in 1983. Mbr, Gosport BC, Hampshire CC, League Against Cruel Sports, CPRE and Friends of the Earth. Former mbr, Medina BC, Isle of Wight. B Apr 9 1956; ed Worthing HS for Boys; Worthing Sixth Form Coll.

Mr **Alan Lloyd**, vehicle asembler. B Jul 13 1952; ed Taunton's Sch, Southampton. Exec mbr, Southampton Lab Pty. Mbr, Hampshire CC; Southampton City Cl. TGWU.

Mr Peter Viggers

GOWER — No change

Electorate %Turnout	58,871	80.7%	**1987**	56,693	78.7%	**1983**
*Wardell, G.L. (Lab)	22,138	46.6%	+8.6%	16,972	38.0%	(Lab)
Price, G.A.L. (C)	16,374	34.5%	-0.9%	15,767	35.3%	(C)
Elliott, D.H.O. (SDP/All)	7,645	16.1%	-7.3%	10,450	23.4%	(SDP/All)
Edwards, J.G.M. (Pl C)	1,341	2.8%	-0.4%	1,444	3.2%	(Pl C)
C to Lab swing 4.7%	47,498	Lab maj 5,764 12.1%		44,633	Lab maj 1,205 2.7%	

Mr Gareth Wardell

Mr **Gareth Wardell** has been chairman of the Select Cmte on Welsh Affairs since 1984. Former economics schoolmaster and college lecturer, he was elected for Gower at 1982 by-election. B Nov 29 1944; ed Gwendraeth GS and LSE. Tutor/counsellor in social science with the Open Univ, 1971-82; senior lecturer in geography, Trinity Coll, Carmarthen, 1973-82. Fellow, Industry and Parliament Trust. APEX.
Mr **Gerald Price**, barrister, contested Newport twice in 1974. B Sep 13 1948; ed Haileybury Coll, Hertford; Coll of Law, London.
Mr **Owen Elliott** probation service assistant and smallholder. Vice Pres, Glamorgan Fed of Young Farmers. B Aug 9 1949; ed Gowerton Boys GS, Swansea. Community cllr for eight years.
Mr **Jonathan Edwards**, barrister, is chmn of a company aiming to establish independent Welsh shipping company. B Feb 7 1952; ed Cheltenham Coll; Southampton Univ; Lincoln's Inn.

GRANTHAM — No change

Electorate %Turnout	79,434	75.0%	**1987**	75,047	73.5%	**1983**
*Hogg, D.M. (C)	33,988	57.1%	-0.4%	31,692	57.5%	(C)
Heppell, J.P. (L/All)	12,685	21.3%	-1.9%	12,781	23.2%	(L/All)
Gent, M.B. (Lab)	12,197	20.5%	+1.1%	10,677	19.4%	(Lab)
Hewis, Mrs P.A. (Grn)	700	1.2%				
L/All to C swing 0.7%	59,570	C maj 21,303 35.8%		55,150	C maj 18,911 34.3%	

Mr Douglas Hogg

Mr **Douglas Hogg**, elder son of Lord Hailsham of St Marylebone, the former Lord Chancellor, was appointed Under Secretary of State, Home Office, in 1986; an assistant Government whip, 1983-84. Elected in 1979. Barrister. Chmn, exec cmte, Soc of Cons Lawyers. B Feb 5 1945; ed Eton, Christ Church, Oxford (Pres of Union) and Lincoln's Inn. Mbr, Select Cmte on Agriculture, 1979-82; PPS to Chief Secretary of the Treasury, 1982-83.
Mr **James Heppell**, town planner and publisher, contested Stroud 1979, Gloucester 1970, Shipley 1966 and 1964. Former county and dist cllr in Gloucestershire and Kent. Methodist local preacher. B July 19 1938; ed Carres GS, Sleaford; Leeds Univ; Univ of Wales; City of London Poly. NATFHE.
Mr **Maurice Gent**, hosiery worker. B Apr 16 1935; ed Heage Sec Sch. Mbr, Amber Valley DC, 1980- (Dep ldr of cl, 1980-).

GRAVESHAM — No change

Electorate %Turnout	72,759	79.3%	**1987**	71,150	77.1%	**1983**
Arnold, J.A. (C)	28,891	50.1%	+2.7%	25,968	47.4%	(C)
Coleman, M.A. (Lab)	20,099	34.8%	+2.9%	17,505	31.9%	(Lab)
Crawford, R.I. (L/All)	8,724	15.1%	-4.6%	10,826	19.7%	(SDP/All)
				523	1.0%	(Other)
C to Lab swing 0.1%	57,714	C maj 8,792 15.2%		54,822	C maj 8,463 15.4%	

Mr Jacques Arnold

Mr **Jacques Arnold**, an international banker, has been a director of American Express Europe Ltd since 1985; assistant trade finance director, Midland Bank plc, 1984-85; regional director, Thomas Cook Gp, 1978-84. Contested Coventry South East in 1983. B Aug 27 1947; ed schools in Brazil and LSE. Mbr for Oundle division, Northamptonshire CC, 1981-85.
Mr **Martin Coleman**, solicitor and lecturer in law at Brunel University, contested Northampton South in 1983. Ldr of Brent Cl, 1982-84. Founder mbr, Assocn of London Authorities. Mbr, DoE Disablement Advisory Gp; mental health panel at Shenley Hospital. B Nov 19 1952; ed Worcester Coll, Oxford. AUT, CND and NCCL.
Mr **Iain Crawford**, parliamentary consultant. Mbr, exec, Lib Parly Assocn; ex-chmn, LSE Liberals; part-time researcher and administrator at Lib Pty HQ. Former hotelier and former chmn, Lochaber (Highland) Tourist Industry Marketing Assocn. B Jun 28 1947; ed Boroughmuir, Edinburgh; LSE.

GREAT GRIMSBY — No change

Electorate %Turnout	68,501	75.3%	**1987**	68,388	73.8%	**1983**
*Mitchell, A.V. (Lab)	23,463	45.5%	+9.2%	18,330	36.3%	(Lab)
Robinson, C.F. (C)	14,679	28.4%	-6.4%	17,599	34.9%	(C)
Genney, P.W. (SDP/All)	13,457	26.1%	-2.7%	14,552	28.8%	(SDP/All)
C to Lab swing 7.8%	51,599	Lab maj 8,784 17.0%		50,481	Lab maj 731 1.4%	

Mr Austin Mitchell

Mr Austin Mitchell has served on the Select Cmte on Treasury and Civil Service since 1979; chmn, PLP Treasury and Civil Service Cmte, 1985- ; previously vice-chmn. Opposition whip. Elected for this seat 1983; MP for Grimsby 1977 by-election to 1983. Journalist, Yorkshire Television, 1969-71 and 1973-77; presenter, BBC current affairs group, 1972-73. Sec, all-pty gp on TV in Commons, 1987- . B Sept 19, 1934; ed Woodbottom Cl School, Bingley GS, and Manchester and Oxford Univs. Vice-chmn, East Midlands Group of Lab MPs, 1986- . Fellow, Industry and Parliament Trust. PPS to Minister of State for Prices and Consumer Protection, 1977-79. Lecturer in history, University of Otago, Dunedin, New Zealand, 1959-63; senior lecturer in politics, Univ of Canterbury, Christchurch, New Zealand, 1963-67; Official Fellow, Nuffield College, Oxford, 1967-69. Director, Triangular Median Ltd. NUJ.
Mr Francis Robinson, former director, John Dickinson and Co, paper manufacturers, and former secretary of the British Paper and Board Industry Federation. Mbr, Buckinghamshire CC, 1979- (ldr, Cons gp, 1985-). B Apr 5 1931; ed Forres Prep Sch; Harrow; London Business Sch.
Mr Paul Genney, barrister, contested the seat 1983. Northern regional chmn; one of original 100 founder mbrs of pty. B Mar 14 1941; ed Wintringham GS, Grimsby; Bristol Univ.

GREAT YARMOUTH — No change

Electorate %Turnout	65,770	74.5%	**1987**	62,809	70.8%	**1983**
*Carttiss, M.R.H. (C)	25,336	51.7%	+1.3%	22,423	50.4%	(C)
Cannell, J. (Lab)	15,253	31.1%	+5.9%	11,223	25.2%	(Lab)
Maxwell, S.D. (SDP/All)	8,387	17.1%	-7.2%	10,803	24.3%	(L/All)
C to Lab swing 2.3%	48,976	C maj 10,083 20.6%		44,449	C maj 11,200 25.2%	

Mr Michael Carttiss

Mr Michael Carttiss, constituency agent for Yarmouth, 1969-82, won this seat in 1983. Mbr, Norfolk CC, 1966-85 (education cmte vice-chmn, 1972; chmn, 1980-85); Great Yarmouth BC, 1973-82 (Leader, 1980-82); East Anglian RHA, 1981-85. Chmn, Norfolk Museums Service, 1981-85. Commissioner, Great Yarmouth Port and Haven Commission, 1982-86. B Mar 11 1938; ed Filby County Primary Sch; Great Yarmouth Tech HS; Goldsmiths' Coll, London Univ; LSE. Teacher, 1961-69.
Mr John Cannell, bricklayer. Mbr, Gt Yarmouth Cl, 1979- . Vice chmn, East Anglia Region of TUC. Chmn, Gt Yarmouth Trades Cl. Former UCATT regional officer. B Feb 13 1946; ed Styles Comprehensive, Gt Yarmouth.
Mr Stuart Maxwell, public affairs consultant. B 1960; ed Whitgift Sch, Croydon and Univ Coll of Wales, Aberystwyth. Speech writer for Dr David Owen.

GREENOCK AND PORT GLASGOW — No change

Electorate %Turnout	57,756	75.4%	**1987**	59,437	74.2%	**1983**
*Godman, N.A. (Lab)	27,848	63.9%	+17.1%	20,650	46.8%	(Lab)
Moody, J.H. (L/All)	7,793	17.9%	-18.5%	16,025	36.3%	(L/All)
Pearson, T.J.D. (C)	4,199	9.6%	-0.1%	4,314	9.8%	(C)
Lenehan, T. (SNP)	3,721	8.5%	+1.8%	2,989	6.8%	(SNP)
				114	0.3%	(Other)
L/All to Lab swing 17.8%	43,561	Lab maj 20,055 46.0%		44,092	Lab maj 4,625 10.5%	

Dr Norman Godman

Dr Norman Godman, a teacher in Scottish further and higher education and former shipwright, won this seat in 1983; contest Aberdeen South, 1979. B Apr 19 1938; ed Westbourne Street Boys' Schl, Hull; Hull Univ; Herriot-Watt Univ. Mbr, Select Cmte on Scottish Affair, 1983- . Sponsored by TGWU. AUT.
Mr John Moody, art teacher; mbr, Inverclyde DC, 1984- . Chmn, Leith Libs, 1979-80; press officer (1982-84) and vice-chmn (1983-85), Inverclyde Lib Assocn. B Mar 23 1953; ed Redby Sec Mod Sch; Edinburgh Coll of Commerce; Sunderland Poly. EIS.
Mr Thomas Pearson, director of small retailing businesses. B Apr 1 1943; ed Hutchesons GS.
Mr Thomas Lenehan, self-employed in advertising; writer. B 1937; ed Strathclyde Univ. Joined SNP from Lab 1985; mbr (former Bailie), Glasgow DC, 1978-84. JP since 1979.

GREENWICH | No change

Electorate %Turnout	50,830	73.4%	**1987**	51,586	67.7%	**1983**
*Barnes, Mrs R.S. (SDP/All)	15,149	40.6%	+15.5%	13,361	38.2%	(Lab)
Wood, Mrs D.F.M. (Lab)	13,008	34.9%	-3.4%	12,150	34.8%	(C)
Antcliffe, J.G.C. (C)	8,695	23.3%	-11.5%	8,783	25.1%	(SDP/All)
Thomas, Ms J. (Grn)	346	0.9%		259	0.7%	(BNP)
Mallone, R. (Fellowship)	59	0.2%	-0.5%	242	0.7%	(Fellowship)
Clinton, Ms P. (Comm)	58	0.2%	-0.2%	149	0.4%	(Com)
Lab to SDP/All swing 9.4%	37,315 SDP/All maj 2,141 5.7%			34,944	Lab maj 1,211 3.5%	

Mrs Rosie Barnes, market researcher, won the by-election in Feb 1987, gaining the seat from Lab. Member, Cl for Social Democracy. B May 16 1946; ed Bilborough GS; Birmingham Univ.
Mrs Deirdre Wood contested the by-election in 1987. Mbr Ilea 1981- ; GLC, 1981-86. Chair, Ilea Staff Assocn.
Mr John Antcliffe, merchant banker. Contested this seat, Feb 1987 by-election. B 1961; ed Dulwich Coll; Corpus Christi, Cambridge. Mbr, Greenwich BC.
Ms Patricia Clinton, health visitor. Mbr, London dist cmte, Comm Pty; branch sec, Greenwich/Bexley Health Visitors Assocn. B Nov 9 1941; ed Western Infirmary, Glasgow; Canadian Red Cross Memorial Hospital; Croydon Coll.
Details of 1987 by-election won by SDP/All on Page 285

Mrs Rosie Barnes

GUILDFORD | No change

Electorate %Turnout	77,872	75.3%	**1987**	75,134	72.5%	**1983**
*Howell, D.A.R. (C)	32,504	55.5%	+0.4%	30,016	55.1%	(C)
Sharp, Mrs M.L. (SDP/All)	19,897	33.9%	+0.6%	18,192	33.4%	(SDP/All)
Wolverson, R.J. (Lab)	6,216	10.6%	-0.1%	5,853	10.7%	(Lab)
				425	0.8%	(Other)
C to SDP/All swing 0.1%	58,617	C maj 12,607 21.5%		54,486	C maj 11,824 21.7%	

Mr David Howell, economic consultant, journalist, author and non-executive company director, was Secretary of State for Transport, 1981-83; Secretary of State for Energy, 1979-81; Opposition spokesman on Home Office affairs and previously on Treasury and economic affairs and energy; Minister of State for Energy, 1974; Minister of State for N Ireland, 1972-74; Under Secretary of State for N Ireland, 1972; Under Secretary of State for Employment, 1971-72; Parliamentary Sec, Civil Service Dept, 1970-72; Lord Commissioner of the Treasury (Govt whip), 1970-71. Mbr, Select Cmte on Foreign Affairs. Elected in 1966; contested Dudley, 1964. B Jan 18 1936; ed Eton; King's Coll, Cambridge. Director of CPC, 1964-66. Ldr writer, *The Daily Telegraph*, 1960-64; Editor, *Crossbow*, 1962-64.
Mrs Margaret Sharp, economist and senior research fellow, science policy research unit, Sussex Univ, contested the seat 1983. Mbr, CSD; cmte, Tawney Soc; SDP economic and industrial policy cmtes; higher ed working gp. B Nov 21 1938; ed Tonbridge Girls' GS; Newnham Coll, Cambridge. AUT.
Mr Rob Wolverson, teacher. B Apr 26 1947; ed Wolverhampton GS; Cambridge, London and Leeds Univs. Chmn, Surrey Cty Lab Pty; sec, SW Surrey CLP, 1981-86. NUT.

Mr David Howell

HACKNEY NORTH AND STOKE NEWINGTON | No change

Electorate %Turnout	66,771	58.1%	**1987**	66,754	54.7%	**1983**
Abbott, Ms D.J. (Lab)	18,912	48.7%	-3.3%	18,989	52.0%	(Lab)
Letwin, O. (C)	11,234	28.9%	+0.3%	10,444	28.6%	(C)
Taylor, S.H. (SDP/All)	7,446	19.2%	+3.4%	5,746	15.7%	(L/All)
FitzPatrick, D.J. (Grn)	997	2.6%	+1.3%	492	1.3%	(Eco)
Anwar, Ms Y.T. (RF)	228	0.6%		426	1.2%	(Com)
				396	1.1%	(Other)
Lab to C swing 1.8%	38,817	Lab maj 7,678 19.8%		36,493	Lab maj 8,545 23.4%	

Ms Diane Abbott, a press officer with Lambeth BC, former civil servant and former employee of NCCL, Thames TV, Breakfast TV and ACTT. Mbr, Westminster Cl, 1982-86; Anti-Apartheid; CND; Campaign for Lab Pty Democracy. B Sep 27 1953; ed Harrow County Girls' GS; Newnham Coll, Cambridge. ACTT; NUJ.
Mr Oliver Letwin was special adviser to the Prime Minister's policy unit, 1983-86; special adviser to Secretary of State for Education and Science, 1982-83. Financial adviser and journalist. B May 19 1956; ed Eton; Trinity Coll, Cambridge. Adviser to overseas govts on privatisation of nationalised industries.
Mr Simon Taylor, public relations consultant. National organiser, SDP 1984 Euro election campaign; former sec, London region SDP. B Feb 7 1956; ed St Edwards Sch, Oxford; Durham Univ. Mbr, Euro Movement Cl; exec, Haemophilia Soc; founder of Euro Social Dem Youth.

Ms Diane Abbott

HACKNEY SOUTH AND SHOREDITCH · No change

Electorate %Turnout	70,873	55.4%	**1987**	71,304	53.8%	**1983**
*Sedgemore, B.C.J. (Lab)	18,799	47.8%	+4.5%	16,621	43.3%	(Lab)
Northcroft-Brown, M.C. (C)	11,277	28.7%	+5.4%	8,930	23.3%	(C)
Roberts, J.D. (L/All)	8,812	22.4%	+4.1%	7,025	18.3%	(SDP/All)
Green, D. (Comm)	403	1.0%		3,724	9.7%	(IL)
				2,058	5.4%	(Other)
Lab to C swing 0.5%	39,291	Lab maj 7,522 19.1%		38,358	Lab maj 7,691 20.1%	

Mr Brian Sedgemore, a barrister, researcher with Granada Television, 1979-83, and freelance journalist, was elected for this seat 1983; MP for Luton West, Feb 1974-79. Mbr, Treasury and Civil Service Select Cmte, since 1983. B Mar 17 1937; ed Newtown Primary Sch; Heles School, Exeter; Oxford Univ. PPS to Mr Tony Benn, 1977-78. Mbr, Wandsworth BC, 1971-74.
Mr Michael Northcroft-Brown, partner in furniture manufacturing company. B Aug 24 1955; ed Millfield Sch; London Coll of Furniture.
Dr Jeffery Roberts is head of European equities, Shroder Securities. Contested this seat 1983 and 1979. Mbr, London Borough of Hackney Cl, since 1980. B Jun 30 1943; ed Wasterloo GS, Liverpool; New Coll, Oxford; Univ of Wales.
Mr David Green, economics lecturer, contested this seat 1983. Mbr, exec cmte, Ldon Dist Comm Pty; co-opted mbr, Hackney Cl economic development cmte, 1981-84. B Aug 12 1952; ed St John's Coll, Cambridge. NATFHE; mbr, Inner London regional cl.

Mr Brian Sedgemore

HALESOWEN AND STOURBRIDGE · No change

Electorate %Turnout	78,017	79.4%	**1987**	76,403	76.4%	**1983**
*Stokes, J.H.R. (C)	31,037	50.1%	+1.7%	28,250	48.4%	(C)
Sunter, T.J. (Lab)	17,229	27.8%	+2.8%	14,934	25.6%	(SDP/All)
Simon, D.C.A. (SDP/All)	13,658	22.1%	-3.5%	14,611	25.0%	(Lab)
				582	1.0%	(Other)
C to Lab swing 0.5%	61,924	C maj 13,808 22.3%		58,377	C maj 13,316 22.8%	

Mr John Stokes was elected for the constituency in Feb 1974; MP for Oldbury and Halesowen, 1970-74; contested Hitchin, 1966; Gloucester, 1964. B Jul 23 1917; ed Haileybury; Queens Coll, Oxford. Served in Army, 1939-46 (major, Royal Fusiliers); personnel officer, ICI, 1946-51; personnel manager, British Celanese, 1951-59; dep personnel manager, Courtaulds, 1957-59; director, Clive and Stokes, personnel consultants, 1959-80. Mbr, Gen Synod of C of E, since 1985; Select Cmtee on Parliamentary Commissioner for Administration (Ombudsman), 1979-83; UK delegation, Cl of Europe and WEU, 1983- ; exec cmte, Oxford Soc. Chmn, general purposes cmte, Primrose League, 1971-85; vice-pres, Royal Stuart Soc; pres, W Midlands Cons Clubs, 1971-84.
Mr Tim Sunter, Dudley cllr. Mbr, Fabian Soc; Amnesty International. NUT.
Mr Crispin Simon, economics adviser and former teacher in India, contested Dudley East 1983. Founder mbr, SDP; mbr, City SDP. B Mar 25 1958; ed Westminster Sch; Lincoln Coll, Oxford.

Mr John Stokes

HALIFAX · Lab gain

Electorate %Turnout	73,392	77.7%	**1987**	72,747	75.1%	**1983**
Mahon, Ms A. (Lab)	24,741	43.4%	+6.0%	22,321	40.9%	(C)
*Galley, R. (C)	23,529	41.3%	+0.4%	20,452	37.4%	(Lab)
Cockcroft, F.L. (SDP/All)	8,758	15.4%	-6.4%	11,868	21.7%	(SDP/All)
C to Lab swing 2.8%	57,028	Lab maj 1,212 2.1%		54,641	C maj 1,869 3.4%	

Ms Alice Mahon, lecturer at Bradford and Ilkley Community College. Mbr, Calderdale MDC; local dist health authority; school governor. B Sep 28 1937.
Mr Roy Galley was on the Select Cmte on Social Services, 1983-87. MP for this seat, 1983-87; contested Dewsbury, 1979. Jt sec, Cons back-bench health and social services cmte, 1983-87. B Dec 8 1947; ed King Edward VII GS, Sheffield; Worcester Coll, Oxford. With North East Postal Bd, 1969-83, starting as management trainee and becoming Asst Controller (Projects). Mbr, Calderdale MBC, 1980-83. Chmn, Yorkshire YCs, 1974-76; Yorkshire CPC, 1982-83. Mbr, Soc of Public and Civil Servants.
Mr Laurence Cockcroft, an economist and self-employed consultant; former advisory economist to the World Bank and to govts of Zambia and Tanzania. Contested the seat 1983. Mbr, SDP working parties on wider share ownership, decentralisation and agriculture. B Jul 15 1943; ed Oundle; Cambridge.

Ms Alice Mahon

HALTON — No change

Electorate	%Turnout	73,848	78.3%	**1987**	72,743	73.3%	**1983**
*Oakes, G.J. (Lab)		32,065	55.5%	+9.0%	24,752	46.4%	(Lab)
Hardman, J. (C)		17,487	30.2%	-3.4%	17,923	33.6%	(C)
Clucas, Mrs H. (SDP/All)		8,272	14.3%	-5.7%	10,649	20.0%	(SDP/All)
C to Lab swing 6.2%		57,824	Lab maj 14,578 25.2%		53,324	Lab maj 6,829 12.8%	

Mr Gordon Oakes was an Opposition spokesman on the environment, 1979-83. Minister of State for Education and Science, 1976-79; Under Secretary of State for Environment, 1974-76; Under Secretary of State for Energy, 1976. Elected for this seat in 1983; MP for Widnes, 1971-83; and Bolton West, 1964-70; contested Bebington, 1959, and Manchester, Moss Side, 1961. Mbr, Select Cmte on Race Relations, 1968-70. B Jun 22 1931; ed Wade Deacon Sch, Widnes; Liverpool Univ. Public affairs consultant to 3M United Kingdom Ltd, the Pharmaceutical Society of Gt Britain, and the Caravan Club. Solicitor, not in practice. Mbr, Widnes BC, 1952-66; Mayor, 1964-65. Vice-pres, Assocn of County Cls, 1982- ; Environmental Officers' Assocn, 1973- ; Building Societies Assocn, 1984- . Chmn, all-pty energy efficiency gp, 1980- ; jt chmn, all-pty gp for licensing trade, 1986- ; vice-chmn, all-pty chemical industry group, 1981- ; mbr, exec cmte, UK branch of CPA, 1979- . Sponsored by TGWU.
Mr John Hardman, solicitor. B Mar 21 1954; ed Eccles GS; Exeter Coll, Oxford.
Mrs Flora Clucas, teacher. Mbr, CSD; Liverpool City Cl, 1986- ; Merseyside waste authority. B May 9 1947; ed Bellerive GS; St Mary's Coll of Ed, Bangor; Liverpool Inst of Higher Ed; Liverpool Univ. NAS/UWT.

Mr Gordon Oakes

HAMILTON — No change

Electorate	%Turnout	62,205	76.9%	**1987**	61,430	75.7%	**1983**
*Robertson, G.I.M. (Lab)		28,563	59.7%	+7.2%	24,384	52.4%	(Lab)
Mond, G.S. (C)		6,901	14.4%	-4.8%	9,365	20.1%	(L/All)
Mackay, T. (L/All)		6,302	13.2%	-7.0%	8,940	19.2%	(C)
Crossley, C. (SNP)		6,093	12.7%	+4.5%	3,816	8.2%	(SNP)
C to Lab swing 6.0%		47,859	Lab maj 21,662 45.3%		46,505	Lab maj 15,019 32.3%	

Mr George Robertson, main Opposition spokesman on European affairs, 1984- ; and a spokesman on foreign and Commonwealth affairs, 1981- ; on defence, 1980-81; and on Scotland, 1979-80. Vice-chmn, bd, British Cl, 1985- . Won by-election in 1978. Scottish organizer for the then GMWU, 1970-78. Member, cl, Royal Inst of International Affairs, 1984- ; British Atlantic Cmte, 1981- ; cl, Nat Trust for Scotland, 1976-82 and 1983-85; police advisory bd for Scotland, 1974-78. Governor, Scottish Police Coll, 1974-78. B Apr 12 1946; ed Dunoon GS and Dundee Univ. Sec, Manifesto group of PLP, 1979-84; chmn, Scottish Cl, Lab Party, 1977-78. Chmn, Seatbelt Survivors Club, since 1981. Mbr, board, Scottish Development Agency, 1975-78, and Scottish Tourist Bd, 1974-76. Sponsored by GMBATU.
Mr Gary Mond, corporate finance executive. Chmn, Greater London YCs, 1985-86; cl member, Bow Group; asst treas, Chelsea Cons Assocn. B May 11 1959; ed Univ Coll Sch, Hampstead; Trinity Coll, Cambridge. Former UK international butterfly swimmer.
Mr Tim McKay, chartered accountant. B Sep 17 1957; ed St Ronan's, Pollokshields, Glasgow.
Mr Christopher Crossley, a senior internal auditor, is vice-chmn, public relations cmte, Inst of Internal Auditors. B Mar 27 1950; ed Royal HS, Edinburgh.

Mr George Robertson

HAMMERSMITH — No change

Electorate	%Turnout	48,285	72.7%	**1987**	46,178	71.3%	**1983**
*Soley, C.S. (Lab)		15,811	45.0%	+3.5%	13,645	41.5%	(Lab)
Deva, N.J.A. (C)		13,396	38.1%	+2.6%	11,691	35.5%	(C)
Knott, S.H.J.A. (L/All)		5,241	14.9%	-0.1%	4,925	15.0%	(SDP/All)
Kirk, D.P. (Grn)		453	1.3%	+0.3%	1,912	5.8%	(Ind L)
Fitzpatrick, P.J.F. (RF)		125	0.4%		325	1.0%	(Eco)
Carrick, Miss M.M.A. (Humanist)		98	0.3%		250	0.8%	(NP)
					154	0.5%	(Other)
C to Lab swing 0.5%		35,124	Lab maj 2,415 6.9%		32,902	Lab maj 1,954 5.9%	

Mr Clive Soley, an Opposition spokesman on home affairs 1984- ; a spokesman on N Ireland, 1981-84. Elected for this seat 1983; MP for Hammersmith North, 1979-83. Probation officer, 1970-79; chmn, Alcohol Education Centre, 1977-83. B May 7 1939; ed Downshall Sec Med Sch, Ilford; Newbattle Abbey Adult Ed Coll; Strathclyde and Southampton Univs. Hammersmith cllr, 1974-78. Chmn, Alcohol Education Centre, 1977-84. Parliamentary consultant to Soc of Civil and Public Servants. Chmn, Lab Campaign for Criminal Justice, 1983- . Fellow, Industry and Parliament Trust. GMBATU .
Mr Joseph Deva, scientist, company director and co-founder of small businesses in London. Former mbr, Nat Consumer Cl; chaired Govt cmte on cheaper air travel; mbr, cmte seeking reform of European agriculture. B 1948; ed Loughborough Univ. Policy adviser to Cons leader on Ilea; governor of two Hammersmith schools.
Mr Simon Knott, senior partner of firm of stockbrokers, fought this seat as a Lib in 1983 against the Alliance candidate; also fought it in 1979; twice in 1974, and Barons Court in 1970, 1966, 1964 and 1959. B Jun 26 1931; ed Malvern Coll; Trinity Coll, Cambridge. Mbr, Hammersmith BC, 1967- . Former mbr, Lib Pty exec.

Mr Clive Soley

HAM

HAMPSHIRE EAST

No change

Electorate %Turnout	86,363	77.4%	**1987**	79,303	74.2%	**1983**
*Mates, M.J. (C)	43,093	64.5%	+1.7%	36,968	62.8%	(C)
Booker, R. (L/All)	19,307	28.9%	-2.8%	18,641	31.7%	(L/All)
Lloyd, C. (Lab)	4,443	6.6%	+1.1%	3,247	5.5%	(Lab)
L/All to C swing 2.2%	66,843	C maj 23,786 35.6%		58,856	C maj 18,327 31.1%	

Mr Michael Mates became chmn of the Select Cmte on Defence in Jan 1987; mbr since 1979. Partner in Chelsham Consultants whose clients include Estee Lauder Ltd, Performing Rights Society, London Oriental Carpets Ltd and other companies. Elected for this seat 1983; MP for Petersfield, 1974-83, prior to which he was in Army from 1954, resigning commission as Lt Col in 1974. Served on staff of Vice-Chief of Defence Staff. B Jun 9 1934; ed Blundell's; King's Coll, Cambridge. Master, Farriers' Co, 1986; liveryman from 1975, the year he piloted through Farriers Registration Act. Sec (1974-79) and vice-chmn (1979-81), Cons back-bench N Ireland cmte; vice-chmn, Cons back-bench home affairs cmte, 1979- ; chmn, all-pty Anglo-Irish gp, 1979- .

Mr Robert Booker, solicitor. Mbr, East Hampshire DC and Alton TC, 1983- . Chmn, Winchester Libs, 1984-85. Mbr, Lib Pty Cl, 1985. B May 9 1951; ed Royal Masonic Sch, Bushey; Leeds Univ; Sch of Law, Guildford.

Mr Colin Lloyd, teacher. B Apr 18 1958; ed Warwick and Bath Univs.

Mr Michael Mates

HAMPSHIRE NORTH WEST

No change

Electorate %Turnout	69,965	77.9%	**1987**	65,780	74.4%	**1983**
*Mitchell, D.B. (C)	31,470	57.8%	+0.4%	28,044	57.3%	(C)
Willis, I.H. (L/All)	18,033	33.1%	+0.6%	15,922	32.5%	(L/All)
Burnage, Ms A. (Lab)	4,980	9.1%	-1.0%	4,957	10.1%	(Lab)
C to L/All swing 0.1%	54,483	C maj 13,437 24.7%		48,923	C maj 12,122 24.8%	

Mr David Mitchell, Minister of State for Transport, 1986- ; Under Secretary of State for Transport, 1983-86; Under Secretary of State for N Ireland, 1981-83; Under Secretary of State for Industry, 1979-81. Elected for this seat 1983; MP for Basingstoke, 1964-83; contested St Pancras North, 1959. PPS to Secretary of State for Social Services, 1970-74; Opposition whip, 1965-67. Farming, 1945-50; businessman and wine merchant, 1951-79. B Jun 20 1928; ed Aldenham. Mbr St Pancras BC, 1956-59. Sec, Cons back-bench employment cmte, 1968-70; chmn, back-bench smaller business cmte, 1974-79; founder chmn, Small Business Bureau.

Mr Ian Willis, management consultant, contested this seat 1983. B Jul 9 1946; ed Harrow, RMA Sandhurst, and Christ Church, Oxford.

Dr Anne Burnage, social worker. B Jun 5 1948; ed St Joseph's Coll, Bradford; Univ Coll, Swansea; LSE. Nalgo; British Assoc of Social Workers.

Mr David Mitchell

HAMPSTEAD AND HIGHGATE

No change

Electorate %Turnout	63,301	71.5%	**1987**	66,554	66.9%	**1983**
*Finsberg, Sir Geoffrey (C)	19,236	42.5%	+1.3%	18,366	41.2%	(C)
Turner, P.J. (Lab)	17,015	37.6%	+3.9%	14,996	33.7%	(Lab)
Sofer, Mrs A. (SDP/All)	8,744	19.3%	-5.4%	11,030	24.8%	(SDP/All)
Weiss, G. (Rainbow)	137	0.3%		156	0.4%	(Poet)
Ellis, Ms S. (Humanist)	134	0.3%				
C to Lab swing 1.3%	45,266	C maj 2,221 4.9%		44,548	C maj 3,370 7.6%	

Sir Geoffrey Finsberg, vice-chmn, Cons Ptt, 1975-79, and 1983- . Vice-chmn, SE Regional Bd, Trustee Savings Bank, 1984- . Under Secretary of State for Health and Social Security, 1981-83; Under Secretary of State for Environment, 1979-81; Opposition spokesman on Greater London, 1974-79. Chmn, all-pty retail gp. Elected for this seat 1983; MP for Hampstead, 1970-83; contested Islington East, 1955. B Jun 13 1926; ed City of London Sch. Mbr Cl of Europe and WEU, 1983- ; Hampstead BC, 1949-65; Camden BC, 1964-74 (ldr 1968-70). Vice-chmn, Cons back-bench cmte on trade, 1972-73; mbr, Public Expenditure Cmte, 1974-79; exec, 1922 Cmte, 1974-79; cl of CBI, 1968-79 (chmn, Post Office panel); Post Office Users Nat Cl, 1970-77. Director, GUS Transport Ltd and Asda Property Holdings; consultant to OCS Gp of Companies Ltd.

Mr Phillip Turner, head of employment policy, British Coal, contested City of London and Westminster South twice in 1974. Leader, Camden Cl, 1982-86; mbr 1971- . B Jun 9 1939; ed Beckenham and Penge GS for Boys; Univ Coll, London. BACM.

Mrs Anne Sofer, journalist and former teacher, contested the seat 1983. SDP spokesman on education; mbr, SDP national policy cmte, 1982- . Member, GLC/Ilea, 1977-86; non-executive director, Channel Four, 1981-83; columnist of *The Times*. B Apr 19 1937; ed St Paul's Girls Sch; Swarthmore Coll, US; Somerville Coll, Oxford.

Sir Geoffrey Finsberg

129

HARBOROUGH — No change

Electorate %Turnout	74,700	79.3%	**1987**	72,177	75.9%	**1983**
*Farr, Sir John (C)	35,216	59.4%	-0.7%	32,957	60.1%	(C)
Swift, T.J. (L/All)	16,406	27.7%	+1.3%	14,472	26.4%	(L/All)
Harley, P. (Lab)	7,646	12.9%	+1.4%	6,285	11.5%	(Lab)
				1,082	2.0%	(Other)
C to L/All swing 1.0%	59,268	C maj 18,810 31.7%		54,796	C maj 18,485 33.7%	

Sir John Farr

Sir John Farr, a mbr of the Select Cmte on Standing Orders since 1981, was elected in 1959; contested Ilkeston, 1955. B Sep 25 1922; ed Harrow. Mbr of Lloyd's and landowner. Vice-chmn, Cons back-bench NI cmte, 1974-78; sec, Cons agriculture cmte, 1970-74; vice-chmn, 1979-84; sec, all-party conservation cmte, 1972- ; chmn, Anglo-Irish parl gp, 1977-80; British-Zimbabwe gp, 1980- ; British-Korea gp, 1984- ; all-party knitwear industries gp, 1979- . Member, UK delegation, WEU and Cl of Europe, 1973-78. Chmn, British Shooting Sports Cl, 1977-86; vice-pres, Shooting Sports Trust, 1972-86.
Mr Timothy Swift, research technologist, contested this seat 1983. B Jul 1 1957; ed Beauchamp Coll, Oadby; Leicester Univ. Mbr, Leicestershire CC and leader of Alliance gp, since 1981; Oadby and Wigston BC, 1983- . ASTMS.
Mr Philip Harley, teacher. Mbr, Leicester CC 1983- (chmn, transport cmte). B Jul 28 1953; ed Kent Univ. NUT.

HARLOW — No change

Electorate %Turnout	70,286	78.4%	**1987**	69,715	76.5%	**1983**
*Hayes, J.J.J. (C)	26,017	47.2%	+6.1%	21,924	41.1%	(C)
Newens, A.S. (Lab)	20,140	36.6%	+2.3%	18,250	34.2%	(Lab)
Eden-Green, Mrs M.C. (SDP/All)	8,915	16.2%	-8.0%	12,891	24.2%	(L/All)
				256	0.5%	(Other)
Lab to C swing 1.9%	55,072	C maj 5,877 10.7%		53,321	C maj 3,674 6.9%	

Mr Jeremy Hayes

Mr Jeremy Hayes, a barrister, won the seat in 1983. Jt vice-chmn, Cons back-bench constitutional cmte, 1986- ; jt sec, 1983-86. B April 20 1953; ed Oratory Sch and London Univ. Pres, Eastern Area YCs; vice-pres, Epping Forest YCs. Freeman, City of London; Liveryman, Worshipful Company of Fletchers; Freeman, Company of Watermen and Lightermen. Mbr, all-pty gps on human rights and human relations; Amnesty International. Sponsor of Video Recordings Act.
Mr Stanley Newens, MEP for London Central 1984- ; chmn, British Labour Gp at European Parliament, 1985- ; mbr political affairs and agriculture cmtes. MP for Epping, 1964-70, and for this seat, Feb 1974-83. Served on Select Cmte on Agriculture; chmn, Tribune Gp of Lab MPs, 1982-83. Teacher, 1956-65 and 1970-74; miner, 1952-55. B Feb 4 1930; ed Buckhurst Hill County HS; Univ Coll, London; Westminster Coll of Ed. Chmn, Eastern area gp of Lab MPs, 1974-83; PLP foreign and Commonwealth affairs gp, 1982-83. Director, London Co-op Soc, 1971-77, and pres, 1977-81. NUT.
Mrs Monica Eden-Green, part-time lecturer and tutor/councillor with Open Univ. Chmn, E Hertfordshire SDP, 1985-87; Bishops Stortford SDP, 1984-85. B Dec 9 1944; ed Tiffin Girls' Sch, Kingston-upon-Thames; Keele and London Univs. NATFHE.

HARROGATE — No change

Electorate %Turnout	75,761	74.1%	**1987**	72,815	69.0%	**1983**
*Banks, R.G. (C)	31,167	55.6%	-4.7%	30,269	60.2%	(C)
Leach, J.R. (SDP/All)	19,265	34.3%	+5.7%	14,381	28.6%	(SDP/All)
Wright, A.J. (Lab)	5,671	10.1%	-0.1%	5,128	10.2%	(Lab)
				479	1.0%	(Other)
C to SDP/All swing 5.2%	56,103	C maj 11,902 21.2%		50,257	C maj 15,888 31.6%	

Mr Robert Banks

Mr Robert Banks, a mbr of Lloyd's and company director, was elected in Feb 1974. Paddington cllr, 1959-65. B Jan 18 1937; ed Haileybury. Mbr, Select Cmte on Foreign Affairs and of sub-cmte on Overseas Development, 1982-83. Jt vice-chmn, Yorkshire Cons MPs, 1983- ; jt sec, Cons back-bench defence cmte, 1976-79. Chmn (1981-) and vice-chmn (1979-81), all-pty tourism group; chmn (1982-) and sec (1978-82), Anglo-Sudan all-pty group, 1982- . Mbr, Cl of Europe and WEU, 1977-81, and of N Atlantic Assembly, 1981- . PPS to Minister of State for Foreign and Commonwealth Affairs, 1979-82. Mbr, Alcohol Ed and Research Cl, 1982- . Principal, Princes Design Works; managing director Princes Design Works Ltd. Sponsored Licensing (Alcohol Education and Research,) Act 1981 and Licensing (Restaurant Meals) Act 1987.
Mr Jon Leach, solicitor. Mbr, Harrogate, Skipton and Ripon area SDP cmte, 1981- ; chmn, Craven district SDP, 1983-86; mbr, Craven DC, 1982-86. B Jul 19 1955; ed Ermysted's GS, Skipton; Univ of Wales, Cardiff; Coll of Law, Guildford.
Mr Andrew Wright, mature student of trade union and industrial studies, Northern Coll, Barnsley. Mbr, Knaresborough DC 1986- . B May 4 1953; ed King James's GS, Knaresborough. Nalgo.

HARROW EAST — No change

Electorate %Turnout	81,124	73.4%	1987	79,926	72.5%	1983
*Dykes, H.J.M. (C)	32,302	54.2%	+4.4%	28,834	49.8%	(C)
Brough, D.J. (Lab)	14,029	23.5%	+1.2%	16,166	27.9%	(L/All)
Gifford, Mrs Z. (L/All)	13,251	22.2%	-5.7%	12,941	22.3%	(Lab)
Lab to C swing 1.6%	59,582	C maj 18,273 30.7%		57,941	C maj 12,668 21.9%	

Mr Hugh Dykes

Mr **Hugh Dykes**, stockbroker, director and consultant. Mbr, Select Cmte on European Legislation, 1979-. Elected in 1970; contested Tottenham, 1966. Associate mbr, Quilter, Goodison, Stockbrokers, since 1978; chmn, ADA Video Systems Ltd, and director, Dixons Stores Far East Ltd; parly adviser to British Wine Producers Assocn, Dixon Group plc, Dewe Rogerson Ltd and BCCI SA. B May 17 1939; ed Weston-super-Mare GS and Pembroke Coll, Cambridge. Jt vice-chmn, Cons Friends of Israel parly gp, 1986-. Mbr, European Parliament, 1974-76. Mbr, Wider Share Ownership Cl. Chmn, Cons backbench European affairs cmte, 1979-81 (vice-chmn, 1974-79); sec, Anglo-French parly gp, since 1980; vice-pres (1981-) and chmn (1978-81), Cons Gp for Europe; jt hon sec, European Movement, 1982-87.
Mr **David Brough**, local govt officer, contested this seat 1983. Chmn and sec at various times of Harrow East CLP; mbr, Harrow BC, 1971-75. Chairs community rights project. B Oct 12 1947; ed Downer GS, Edgware; Univ Coll, London.
Mrs **Zerbanoo Gifford** chairs the Lib Pty community relations panel; mbr, Lib working group on status of women. Chairs Lib commission of inquiry into ethnic minority involvement in Lib Pty. Contested Hertsmere 1983. Housewife. B May 11 1950 in India of Zoroastrian parents; ed Roedean; Watford Coll of Tech; Open Univ. Mbr Harrow BC, 1982-86.

HARROW WEST — No change

Electorate %Turnout	74,041	74.5%	1987	73,151	72.3%	1983
Hughes, R.G. (C)	30,456	55.2%	+2.2%	28,056	53.0%	(C)
Bayliss, S.P. (SDP/All)	15,012	27.2%	-5.0%	17,035	32.2%	(SDP/All)
Bastin, C. (Lab)	9,665	17.5%	+2.8%	7,811	14.8%	(Lab)
SDP/All to C swing 3.6%	55,133	C maj 15,444 28.0%		52,902	C maj 11,021 20.8%	

Mr **Robert Hughes**, television news picture editor, contested Southwark and Bermondsey twice in 1983 and Stepney and Poplar, 1979. Mbr ,GLC, 1980-86, being deputy chief whip and Opposition spokesman on recreation and arts. Mbr, Hounslow BC, 1974-78. B Jul 14 1951; ed Spring Grove GS; Harrow Coll of Tech and Art. BETA and MUJ.
Mr **Stuart Bayliss**, international director of an insurance company, contested the seat 1983. Chmn, university sector, NUS executive, 1977-79; vice-chmn, British Youth Cl, 1978-80; national chmn, Cons Students, 1979-80. B Feb 22 1955; ed City of London Sch; Nottingham Univ.
Mr **Colin Bastin**, computer systems consultant, contested Wycombe 1983. B Mar 31 1948; ed Elliott Comprehensive Sch, Putney; SW London Coll, Tooting.

Mr Robert Hughes

HARTLEPOOL — No change

Electorate %Turnout	68,686	73.0%	1987	69,346	69.8%	1983
*Leadbitter, E. (Lab)	24,296	48.5%	+2.9%	22,048	45.5%	(Lab)
Catchpole, P.C. (C)	17,007	33.9%	-5.2%	18,958	39.1%	(C)
Preece, A. (L/All)	7,047	14.1%	-1.3%	7,428	15.3%	(SDP/All)
Cameron, I.J. (Ind)	1,786	3.6%				
C to Lab swing 4.1%	50,136	Lab maj 7,289 14.5%		48,434	Lab maj 3,090 6.4%	

Mr Edward Leadbitter

Mr **Edward Leadbitter**, mbr of the Commons Chairmen's Panel 1980-, and Select Cmte on Energy 1980-. Chmn, PLP transport group 1979-; held chmnship, from 1974, of PLP ports cmte and of Anglo-Tunisiam parly gp. Successfully sponsored Children's Home Registration Act, 1981. Elected in 1964. Teacher. B Jun 18 1919; ed state schools and Cheltenham Teacher Training Coll. Pres, Hartlepool Lab Party, 1958-62; mbr, West Hartlepool BC, 1954-67; Freeman of Hartlepool, 1981, and City of London, 1986. Mbr, Select Cmte on Science and Technology, 1969-78; Estimates Cmte, 1966-69. Spokesman for ASLEF.
Mr **Peter Catchpole**, a district general manager in NHS. B Sep 19 1947; ed Edgeware Sch; Orange Hill GS; London Univ. Nalgo.
Mr **Arthur Preece**, health service administrator and chartered secretary, is chmn of the Lib Pty health panel. Pres, Hartlepool Libs since 1984; chmn, Northern Lib Pty, 1982-84; former chmn, Berwick Lib Assocn. Lib agent for many local govt campaigns and by-election campaigner. B Feb 21 1929; ed High Storrs GS, Sheffield.

HARWICH — No change

Electorate %Turnout	77,149	73.5%	**1987**	72,179	70.2%	**1983**
*Ridsdale, Sir Julian (C)	29,344	51.8%	-2.4%	27,422	54.1%	(C)
Lynne, Miss E. (L/All)	17,262	30.5%	+1.0%	14,920	29.5%	(L/All)
Knight, R. (Lab)	9,920	17.5%	+1.1%	8,302	16.4%	(Lab)
Humphrey, C.A. (OFP)	161	0.3%				
C to L/All swing 1.7%	56,687	C maj 12,082 21.3%		50,644	C maj 12,502 24.7%	

Sir Julian Ridsdale, holder of the Order of the Sacred Treasure, Japan, has led parliamentary delegations to that country in most years from 1972-82; chmn, British-Japanese parly group, since 1964; London Japanese Soc, 1976-79. Elected at 1954 by-election; contested Paddington North, 1951. Adviser to Bank of Credit and Commerce, Shimizu Construction co and to Sir Robert McAlpine and Sons. Under Secretary of State, Air Ministry, 1962-64; Under Secretary of State for Defence for the RAF, 1964. B Jun 8 1915; ed Tonbridge, Sandhurst, and London Univ School of Oriental Languages. Chmn, Parly Gp for Engineering Development, 1985- ; vice-chmn, UN Parly Assocn, 1966-82. Mbr, PAC, 1970-74; N Atlantic Assembly, since 1979 being Vice-Pres, Political Cmte; Trilateral Commission, EEC, USA and Japan, since 1973. Deputy chmn, International Triangle, US-Europe-Japan, 1981-85.
Miss Elizabeth Lynne is an actress. B Jan 22 1948; ed Dorking County GS. Equity.
Mr Ralph Knight, electrical supervisor. Contested Harwich 1983. Mbr, Harwich TC and DC 1983- . B Sep 22 1934; ed in Manchester, Harwich and Colchester. TGWU.

Sir Julian Ridsdale

HASTINGS AND RYE — No change

Electorate %Turnout	72,758	71.8%	**1987**	69,747	68.9%	**1983**
*Warren, K.R. (C)	26,163	50.1%	-3.2%	25,626	53.3%	(C)
Amies, D.J. (L/All)	18,816	36.0%	+5.6%	14,646	30.5%	(L/All)
Hurcombe, Ms J. (Lab)	6,825	13.1%	-2.1%	7,304	15.2%	(Lab)
Howell, D. (Loony)	242	0.5%		503	1.0%	(Ind)
Davies, S.P. (NPR)	194	0.4%				
C to L/All swing 4.4%	52,240	C maj 7,347 14.1%		48,079	C maj 10,980 22.8%	

Mr Kenneth Warren, an aeronautical engineer, management consultant and company director, became chmn of the Select Cmte on Trade and Industry in 1983; mbr, Commons Services Cmte, since 1983. PPS to Secretary of State for Industry, 1979-81, and to Secretary of State for Education and Science, 1981-83. With Elliott Automation Ltd, 1960-69. Elected for this seat 1983; MP for Hastings, 1970-1973; contested St Pancras North, 1964. B Aug 15 1926; ed Midsomer Norton GS; Aldenham Sch; De Havilland Aeronautical Tech Sch; King's Coll, London, and LSE. Former branch officer, GMWU. Mbr, Cl of Europe, 1973-80; chmn, WEU science, technology and aerospace cmte, 1977-80. Mbr, Select Cmte on Science and Technology, 1970-79 (chmn, Offshore Engineering sub-cmte, 1975-76). Chmn, British/Soviet parly gp, 1986- ; Cons back-bench aviation cmte, 1977-77. Freeman, City of London; Liveryman, Coachmakers' and Harness Makers' Company and Guild of Air Pilots and Navigators.
Mr David Amies is manager of the Barbican estate and a company director. Contested this seat 1983; Havant and Waterloo 1979. B Feb 16 1942; ed Bexhill GS; Leeds Univ. Member, Rother DC, 1974-76; East Sussex CC, 1981- .
Ms Joy Hurcombe, teacher, contested Shoreham 1983. B Jan 8 1938; ed Hull and London Univs.

Mr Kenneth Warren

HAVANT — No change

Electorate %Turnout	76,344	74.6%	**1987**	73,096	72.1%	**1983**
*Lloyd, Sir Ian (C)	32,527	57.1%	+1.8%	29,148	55.3%	(C)
Cleaver, Mrs E.E. (SDP/All)	16,017	28.1%	-4.5%	17,192	32.6%	(SDP/All)
Phillips, J.A. (Lab)	8,030	14.1%	+2.1%	6,335	12.0%	(Lab)
Fuller, G.W. (Bread)	373	0.7%				
SDP/All to C swing 3.1%	56,947	C maj 16,510 29.0%		52,675	C maj 11,956 22.7%	

Sir Ian Lloyd has chaired the Select Cmte on Energy since 1979; mbr, Commons Services Cmte, 1983- . Elected for this seat 1983; MP for Havant and Waterloo, Feb 1974-83, and for Portsmouth, Langstone, 1964-74. Founder and first chmn, all-pty cmte on information tech, 1979-87; mbr, Select Cmte on Science and Technology, 1971-79; Vice-pres, Parly and Scientific Cmte, 1984-87 ; chmn, Cons back-bench shipping and shipbuilding sub-cmte, 1974-77. Economist. B May 30 1921; ed Michaelhouse, Natal; Witwatersrand Univ; King's Coll, Cambridge (Pres of Union, 1947) and Administrative Staff Coll, Henley. Director, Bricomin Investments Ltd; consultant to British & Commonwealth Holdings Ltd. Economic adviser to Central Mining and Investment Corpn, 1949-53; member, S African Bd of Trade and Industries, 1953-56. Mbr, UK delegation, Cl of Europe and WEU, 1968-72.
Mrs Elizabeth Cleaver, lecturer in accounting and finance, contested the seat 1983. Mbr, Hampshire CC, 1985- . B Jun 22 1935; ed Portsmouth HS; LSE. NATFHE.
Mr Jim Phillips, lecturer, contested Wight and Hampshire East in 1984 Euro election. Mbr, Havant BC, 1980- (Ldr, Lab gp). B Nov 13 1940; ed Portsmouth Coll of Tech; Open and London Univs. NATFHE.

Sir Ian Lloyd

HAYES AND HARLINGTON — No change

Electorate %Turnout	58,240	74.5%	**1987**	57,620	70.9%	**1983**
*Dicks, T.P. (C)	21,355	49.2%	+8.9%	16,451	40.3%	(C)
Fagan, P.F. (Lab)	15,390	35.5%	+5.6%	12,217	29.9%	(Lab)
Slipman, Ms S. (SDP/All)	6,641	15.3%	-13.7%	11,842	29.0%	(SDP/All)
				324	0.8%	(Other)
Lab to C swing 1.7%	43,386	C maj 5,965 13.7%		40,834	C maj 4,234 10.4%	

Mr Terence Dicks, a local government officer, was elected in 1983; contested Bristol South, 1979. Mbr, Select Committee on Transport, since 1986. B Mar 17 1937; ed Oxford Univ and LSE. Mbr, Hillingdon BC, since 1974 (deputy leader and housing chmn, 1982-84). Former head of Opposition secretariat and personal assistant to former leader of opposition on GLC, 1981-83. Employed by Ministry of Labour, 1959-66; Imperial Tobacco Co Ltd, 1952-59.
Mr Peter Fagan, toolmaker and shopkeeper. Mbr, Hillingdon BC, 1976- (ldr, Lab gp). B Jun 15 1932.
Ms Sue Slipman, director, Nat Cl for One Parent Families, since 1985. Mbr, SDP national, policy, health and social services cmtes; SDP urban policy and trades union reform gps; NCCL executive 1974-75; President, NUS 1975-78; vice chair, British Youth Cl 1977-78; negotiating officer, NUPE 1979-85; chair, Women for Social Democracy 1983-86; training chair, 300 Group 1985-86; mbr, London Voluntary Service Cl executive 1986- . B Aug 3 1949; ed Stockwell Manor Comp Sch; Univ of Wales; Leeds and London Univs.

Mr Terence Dicks

HAZEL GROVE — No change

Electorate %Turnout	65,717	81.6%	**1987**	63,630	77.2%	**1983**
*Arnold, T.R. (C)	24,396	45.5%	-0.6%	22,627	46.1%	(C)
Vos, A.M. (L/All)	22,556	42.0%	+0.1%	20,605	41.9%	(L/All)
Ford, J.G. (Lab)	6,354	11.8%	-0.2%	5,895	12.0%	(Lab)
Chapman, Ms F.K. (Grn)	346	0.6%				
C to L/All swing 0.3%	53,652	C maj 1,840 3.4%		49,127	C maj 2,022 4.1%	

Mr Tom Arnold, theatre producer, company director and publisher, has been a vice-chairman of the Conservative Party since 1983 with responsibility for the research and candidates' departments. Won this seat in Oct 1974; contested it, Feb 1974; Manchester, Cheetham, 1970. B Jan 25 1947; ed Bedales, Le Rosey (Geneva) and Pembroke Coll, Oxford. Jt vice-chmn and former sec, North West group of Cons MPs. PPS to Secretary of State for N Ireland, 1979-81, and to Lord Privy Seal, Foreign Office, 1981-82. Mbr, Society of West End Theatre. Director, Tom Arnold Ltd and other companies including Brintoak Investments Ltd, Aurum Press Ltd, Piccadilly Radio plc, Jackson Taylor International Gp Ltd, Scotts Restaurant plc, and Connaught Restaurants Ltd. Owner of musical and dramatic copyrights under Ivor Novello's will.
Mr Andrew Vos, barrister, contested this seat 1983. Mbr, Greater Manchester CC, 1984-86; Stockport MBC, 1983-87. B Jul 4 1956; ed Manchester GS; Jesus Coll, Cambridge; Coll of Law, London.
Mr Glyn Ford was elected MEP for Greater Manchester East in 1984; mbr, European Parliament Committee on External Economic Relations; senior research fellow, Manchester Univ. B Jan 28 1950; ed Reading and Manchester Univs. Mbr, Tameside MBC.

Mr Tom Arnold

HEMSWORTH — No change

Electorate %Turnout	54,951	75.7%	**1987**	54,323	68.6%	**1983**
Buckley, G.J. (Lab)	27,859	67.0%	+7.7%	22,081	59.3%	(Lab)
Garnier, E.H. (C)	7,159	17.2%	-2.4%	7,891	21.2%	(L/All)
Wooffindin, J.D. (L/All)	6,568	15.8%	-5.4%	7,291	19.6%	(C)
C to Lab swing 5.0%	41,586	Lab maj 20,700 49.8%		37,263	Lab maj 14,190 38.1%	

Mr George Buckley, miner at South Kirby Colliery. Member, Yorkshire regional TUC; Wakefield DC, 1973 - . B Apr 6 1935; ed in South Kirby and Leeds Univ. NUM.
Mr Edward Garnier, barrister. B Oct 26 1952; ed Wellington Coll; Jesus Coll, Oxford; Coll of Law, London. Parliamentary assistant to Sir Paul Hawkins, MP, 1984- . Mbr, Ilea sub-cmte of Greater London area Cons education advisory cmte; Wandsworth education cmte; Soc of Cons Lawyers.
Mr John Wooffindin, head of history dept, Ackworth Sch, contested this seat 1983. Member, Wakefield BC, 1982- . B Mar 4 1941; ed King James's GS, Huddersfield; Durham Univ. AMMA.

Mr George Buckley

HENDON NORTH | No change

Electorate %Turnout	55,095	65.8%	**1987**	54,505	68.0%	**1983**
*Gorst, J.M. (C)	20,155	55.6%	+5.7%	18,499	49.9%	(C)
Manson, Mrs J. (Lab)	9,223	25.5%	+1.8%	9,474	25.6%	(SDP/All)
Davies, Mrs E. (SDP/All)	6,859	18.9%	-6.6%	8,786	23.7%	(Lab)
				310	0.8%	(Other)
Lab to C swing 2.0%	36,237	C maj 10,932 30.2%		37,069	C maj 9,025 24.3%	

Mr John Gorst

Mr John Gorst has served on the Select Cmte on Employment since 1980; vice-chmn, Cons back-bench media cmte, since 1983; vice-chmn, all-pty war crimes cmte, 1987- ; sec, consumer protection cmte, 1973-74. Director, John Gorst & Associates Ltd, public affairs consultancy, since 1964, with clients including the British Amusements Caterers' Trade Assocn, Ladbroke Group Ltd, Radnor (Management Advisory Services) Ltd and Alfred Marks Group. Elected in 1970; contested Bodmin, 1966, and Chester-le-Street, 1964. B Jun 28 1928; ed Ardingly Coll; Corpus Christi Coll, Cambridge. Advertising and public relations manager, Pye Ltd, 1953-63. Founder (1964-80) and sec (1964-70), Telephone Users' Assocn; and also the Local Radio Assocn (sec, 1964-71).
Mrs Jenny Manson, tax inspector. B Nov 11 1948; ed St Georges Sch, Harpenden; Somerville Coll, Oxford. Mbr, Barnet BC. Has held various constituency and branch offices.
Mrs Elisabeth Davies, an advice bureau manager. Mbr, CSD, 1982-86; cmte mbr, Women for Social Democracy, 1984-86. B Sep 24 1937; ed Burlington Sch, Wood Lane, London; Newham Coll, Cambridge. ACTSS.

HENDON SOUTH | No change

Electorate %Turnout	54,560	63.8%	**1987**	53,929	65.3%	**1983**
Marshall, J.L. (C)	19,341	55.5%	+6.9%	17,115	48.6%	(C)
Palmer, M.O. (L/All)	8,217	23.6%	-6.7%	10,682	30.3%	(L/All)
Christian, Ms L. (Lab)	7,261	20.9%	-0.2%	7,415	21.1%	(Lab)
L/All to C swing 6.8%	34,819	C maj 11,124 31.9%		35,212	C maj 6,433 18.3%	

Mr John Marshall

Mr John Marshall, stockbroker and former university lecturer in economics, has been MEP for London North since 1979. Sec, Friendship with Israel Group, European Parliament. Contested Lewisham East, Feb 1974; Dundee East, 1964 and 1966. B Aug 19 1940; ed Glasgow Acad; St Andrews Univ. Mbr, Aberdeen Town Cl, 1968-70, and Ealing BC, 1971-86, chairing finance cmte, 1978-82, and local services cmte, 1982-84.
Mr Monroe Palmer, chartered accountant, contested the seat 1983 and 1979. Leader, Alliance gp, Barnet BC. B Nov 30 1938; ed Orange Hill GS, Edgware. Jt nat treas, Lib Pty, 1977-83; re-elected to Lib nat exec, 1986; former treas, Lib Parly Pty
Ms Louise Christian, solicitor. B May 22 1952; ed St Anne's Coll, Oxford. Mbr, regional exec, London Lab Pty. Was legal asst to former GLC police cmte. TGWU.

HENLEY | No change

Electorate %Turnout	65,443	74.9%	**1987**	62,120	72.9%	**1983**
*Heseltine, M.R.D. (C)	29,978	61.1%	+1.4%	27,039	59.7%	(C)
Madeley, J. (L/All)	12,896	26.3%	-3.0%	13,258	29.3%	(L/All)
Barber, M.B. (Lab)	6,173	12.6%	+3.1%	4,282	9.5%	(Lab)
				730	1.6%	(Other)
L/All to C swing 2.2%	49,047	C maj 17,082 34.8%		45,309	C maj 13,781 30.4%	

Mr Michael Heseltine

Mr Michael Heseltine was Secretary of State for Defence, 1983-Jan 1986, when he resigned over the future of the Westland helicopter company; Secretary of State for Environment, 1979-83. Shadow Cabinet chief spokesman on industry, 1974-76; chief spokesman on environment, 1976-79; spokesman on trade, 1974. Minister for Aerospace and Shipping, DTI, 1972-74; Under Secretary of State for Environment, 1970-72; Parliamentary Secretary, Ministry of Transport, 1970. Elected for this seat in Feb 1974; MP for Tavistock, 1966-74; contested Coventry North, 1964, and Gower, 1959. B Mar 21 1933; ed Shrewsbury and Pembroke Coll, Oxford (Pres of Union, 1954). Pres, YCs, 1982- . Chmn, Haymarket Press, 1966-70 and director, 1974-79; now consultant to Haymarket Publishing Gp.
Mr John Madeley, journalist and broadcaster, contested Petersfield 1979 and Christchurch and Lymington Oct 1974. Publisher and editor of *International Agricultural Development* magazine. Mbr, Gen Synod of C of E; Anglican reader. B Jul 14 1934; ed Bury GS; Manchester Univ.
Mr Michael Barber, charity director. Hackney cllr. B Nov 24 1955; ed Bootham Sch, York; Queen's Coll, Oxford. ASTMS.

HEREFORD — No change

Electorate %Turnout	67,075	78.0%	**1987**	64,051	75.8%	**1983**
*Shepherd, C.R. (C)	24,865	47.5%	-0.6%	23,334	48.1%	(C)
Green, C.F. (L/All)	23,452	44.8%	+1.4%	21,057	43.4%	(L/All)
Woodell, V.S. (Lab)	4,031	7.7%	+0.1%	3,690	7.6%	(Lab)
				463	1.0%	(Other)
C to L/All swing 1.0%	52,348	C maj 1,413 2.7%		48,544	C maj 2,277 4.7%	

Mr Colin Shepherd, marketing director of The Haigh Engineering Co Ltd, Ross-on-Wye, an engineering company, since 1963; also director of waste processing firm at Yeovil; parly adviser to Balfour, Beatty Power Construction Ltd. Elected in Oct 1974. B Jan 13 1938; ed Oundle; Caius Coll, Cambridge; McGill Univ, Montreal. Jt vice-chmn, Cons back-bench agriculture, fisheries and food cmte, since 1979; jt sec, 1976-82; vice-chmn, Cons horticulture sub-cmte, since 1985, previously sec. Mbr, Select Cmte on Commons Services, since 1979; chmn, library sub-cmte, since 1983. Mbr, cl, Royal Coll of Veterinary Surgeons, 1983- ; exec cmte, UK branch, CPA, 1987- ; sec, British-Yugoslavia and British-Canadian parly gps.

Mr Christopher Green, City of London Festival director and chairman, Ross Community Enterprise, contested this seat 1983 and 1979, Cheadle twice in 1974, and Surbiton, 1970. Former chmn, Liberal arts panel. B May 10 1943; ed Wrekin Coll, Shropshire; King's Coll, London Univ. NUJ

Mr Vivian Woodell, campaign organiser, coordinator of "Who Cares?" campaign against NHS cuts. Director, Oxford and Swindon Cooperative Society. B May 8 1962; educ Dragon Sch, Oxford; Westminster Sch; Bristol Univ. ASTMS.

Mr Colin Shepherd

HERTFORD AND STORTFORD — No change

Electorate %Turnout	75,508	77.7%	**1987**	68,615	75.6%	**1983**
*Wells, P.B. (C)	33,763	57.5%	+1.6%	29,039	56.0%	(C)
Wotherspoon, R.E. (SDP/All)	16,623	28.3%	-2.7%	16,110	31.0%	(SDP/All)
Sumner, Mrs P.R.E. (Lab)	7,494	12.8%	+0.8%	6,203	12.0%	(Lab)
Cole, G.C. (Grn)	814	1.4%		314	0.6%	(BNP)
				221	0.4%	(Other)
SDP/All to C swing 2.1%	58,694	C maj 17,140 29.2%		51,887	C maj 12,929 24.9%	

Mr Bowen Wells has served on the Select Committees on European Legislation and on Foreign Affairs since 1983. Elected for this seat 1983; MP for Hertford and Stevenage, 1979-83. Senior executive, Commonwealth Development Corpn, 1961-73. Owner and managing director, Substation Group Services Ltd, 1973-79. B Aug 4 1935; ed St. Paul's Sch, London; Exeter Univ; Regent St Poly Sch of Management. Jt sec, Cons back-bench trade and industry cmte, 1979-81 and since 1984, and vice-chmn, 1983-84. Sec, Cons back-bench employment cmte, 1981-82; PPS to Minister of State for Employment, 1982-83. Chmn, UN parly gp, 1983- ; British/Caribbean gp; sec, all-pty Overseas Development gp. Parly consultant to International Distillers and Vintners Ltd and to Geest Industries. Trustee, Ind and Parl Trust, 1985- .

Mr Ronald Wotherspoon, director of a small trade specialist computer systems company in Cambridge, contested this seat 1983. B Nov 18 1948; ed St Bonaventure Sch, London; Univ Coll, Swansea. A founder and former nat political director, Tory Reform Gp. Founder member, Crisis at Christmas.

Mrs Tricia Sumner, personal and research asst to Mr Norman Buchan, MP. B Apr 19 1947; ed Walthamstow HS; East Ham Tech Coll. Sec and cmte clerk, NEC/PLP policy cmte on arts, film and broadcasting gp. Sec, pol educ officer, chmn in various CLPs. TGWU.

Mr Graham Cole, gardener. B Feb 18 1955; ed Riversmead Comprehensive Sch, Cheshunt.

Mr Bowen Wells

HERTFORDSHIRE NORTH — No change

Electorate %Turnout	78,694	81.1%	**1987**	75,439	79.2%	**1983**
*Stewart, B.H.I.H. (C)	31,750	49.7%	+0.7%	29,302	49.0%	(C)
Binney, G.W. (L/All)	20,308	31.8%	-0.6%	19,359	32.4%	(L/All)
Gorst, A. (Lab)	11,782	18.5%	-0.1%	11,104	18.6%	(Lab)
L/All to C swing 0.6%	63,840	C maj 11,442 17.9%		59,765	C maj 9,943 16.6%	

Mr Ian Stewart was appointed Minister of State for the Armed Forces in Jun 1987; Economic Secretary to the Treasury, 1983-87; Under Secretary of State for Defence Procurement, Jan-Oct 1983; PPS to Chancellor of Exchequer, 1979-83. Elected for North Hertfordshire (known as Hitchin until 1983), Feb 1974; contested Hammersmith North, 1970. Former company director. B Aug 10 1935; ed Haileybury and Jesus Coll, Cambridge. Sec, Cons parly finance cmte, 1975-76 and 1977-79; member, Public Expenditure Cmte, 1977-79. County vice-pres, St John Ambulance Brigade for Herts, 1978- ; vice-pres, Hertfordshire Soc, 1974- . Trustee, Sir Halley Stewart Trust, 1978- . Mbr, cl, British Museum Soc, 1975-76; Life Governor, 1977, mbr of cl, Haileybury, 1980- . Director, British Numismatic Soc, 1965-75; mbr, British Academy Cmte for Sylloge of Coins of British Isles, 1967- . Fellow, Soc of Antiquaries.

Mr George Binney, head of management services, Courtaulds, 1984- ; consultant, McKinsey and Co, 1980-84. Barrister. B May 5 1953; ed Kings Coll Sch, Wimbledon; Peterhouse, Cambridge Univ; Coll of Law, London; European Business Sch, Fontainebleau.

Mr Alan Gorst, a director of social services. B Aug 30 1931; ed Epsom Coll; Boston and McGill Univs. Mbr, Herts CC. GMB.

Mr Ian Stewart

HERTFORDSHIRE SOUTH WEST — No change

Electorate %Turnout	75,643	77.7%	**1987**	74,371	75.8%	**1983**
*Page, R.L. (C)	32,791	55.8%	+2.2%	30,217	53.6%	(C)
Blair, I.M. (L/All)	17,007	28.9%	-3.0%	18,023	32.0%	(L/All)
Willmore, I. (Lab)	8,966	15.3%	+1.4%	7,818	13.9%	(Lab)
				307	0.5%	(Other)
L/All to C swing 2.6%	58,764	C maj 15,784 26.9%		56,365	C maj 12,194 21.6%	

Mr Richard Page was PPS to Mr John Biffen, when Leader of the Commons, 1982-87; to Secretary of State for Trade, 1981-82. Returned at 1979 by-election; contested Workington, Feb and Oct 1974; MP for Workington, 1976-79. Director of family company, Page Finance Ltd, since 1964, and associated companies. B Feb 22 1941; ed Hurstpierpoint Coll and Luton Tech Coll. Apprenticeship, Vauxhall Motors, 1959-64. Mbr, Banstead UDC, 1968-71.
Dr Ian Blair, physicist, contested Abingdon 1979 and Hertfordshire South West 1983. Mbr, Oxfordshire CC, 1981- . B May 9 1936; ed King George V Sch, Southport; Oriel Coll, Oxford; Liverpool Univ. C of E lay reader. IPCS.
Mr Ian Willmore, trade union researcher. B Nov 5 1958.

Mr Richard Page

HERTFORDSHIRE WEST — No change

Electorate %Turnout	78,966	80.9%	**1987**	76,597	79.5%	**1983**
*Jones, R.B. (C)	31,760	49.7%	+3.0%	28,436	· 46.7%	(C)
Hollinghurst, N.A. (SDP/All)	16,836	26.3%	-4.6%	18,860	31.0%	(SDP/All)
McBrearty, A. (Lab)	15,317	24.0%	+1.7%	13,583	22.3%	(Lab)
SDP/All to C swing 3.8%	63,913	C maj 14,924 23.4%		60,879	C maj 9,576 15.7%	

Mr Robert Jones, a civil engineering adviser, was elected in 1983; contested Teesside, Stockton, 1979; Kirkcaldy, Oct 1974. PPS to Mr Michael Spicer, Minister for Aviation, and Mr Peter Bottomley, Minister for Roads and Traffic, Dept of Transport, 1986- ; mbr, Select Cmte on Environment, 1983-86. B Sep 26 1950; ed Merchant Taylors' Sch; St Andrews Univ. Mbr, St Andrews BC, 1972-75; Fife CC, 1973-75; Chiltern DC, 1979-83. Vice-pres, Assocn of DCs, 1983- . Sec, Cons back-bench employment cmte, 1985-86; chmn, Cons organization cmte, 1985-86; mbr, Inland Waterways Amenity Advisory Cl;, 1985- ; vice-pres, Wildlife Hospital Trust, 1985- . Head of research, Nat House Building Cl, 1976-78; housing policy adviser, Cons Central Office, 1978-79; parliamentary adviser, Federation of Civil Engineering Contractors, 1979-83.
Mr Nicholas Hollinghurst, proprietor of ceramic tile distribution company, contested this seat 1983. Mbr, Dacorum BC, 1981- (ldr, All gp). B Sep 22 1945; ed St Anselm's Coll, Birkenhead; Univ of Manchester Instit of Science and Technology. Founder member, SDP.
Mr Tony McBrearty, local govt officer. Mbr, Haringey BC, 1975-86; GLC, 1981-86. Nalgo.

Mr Robert Jones

HERTSMERE — No change

Electorate %Turnout	73,367	75.4%	**1987**	72,997	73.7%	**1983**
*Parkinson, C.E. (C)	31,278	56.6%	+3.4%	28,628	53.2%	(C)
Brass, L.S. (L/All)	13,172	23.8%	-1.7%	13,758	25.6%	(L/All)
Ward, F. (Lab)	10,835	19.6%	+0.4%	10,315	19.2%	(Lab)
				1,116	2.1%	(Other)
L/All to C swing 2.6%	55,285	C maj 18,106 32.8%		53,817	C maj 14,870 27.6%	

Mr Cecil Parkinson was appointed Secretary of State for Energy in Jun 1987; Secretary of State for Trade and Industry after 1983 election resigning from Govt on Oct 14 1983. Paymaster General and chmn of Cons Party, 1981-83. Had additional post of Chancellor of the Duchy of Lancaster in 1982; Minister of State for Trade, 1979-81; an Opposition spokesman on trade, 1976-79; Opposition whip, 1974-76; asst Govt whip, 1974. Governor, Anglo-Indonesian Students Trust; pres, Anglo-Polish Cons Soc, 1986- . Pres, British Francophone Business Gp. Elected for this seat in 1983; MP for South Hertfordshire, Feb 1974-83, and for Enfield West, 1970-74; contested Northampton, 1970. B Sep 1 1931; ed Royal GS, Lancaster; and Emmanuel Coll, Cambridge. Chartered accountant; founder, former chmn and former director, Parkinson Hart Securities; former director, Sears Holdings plc; Babock International plc; Save and Prosper Group Ltd; Tarmac plc; and other commercial and charitable companies.
Mr Laurence Brass, solicitor, contested Edmonton in 1983, Finchley twice in 1974, Hornsey 1970, and London North in 1979 Euro elections. Mbr, Hertsmere BC, 1972-81. B Jul 26 1947; ed Clifton Coll, Bristol; Univ Coll, London. Mbr, Board of Deputies of British and Commonwealth Jews; Assocn of Lib Lawyers. Former exec member, London Lib Pty Cl.
Mr Frank Ward, works manager, Islington Building Works dept. Chartered builder; member, Inst of Management. B Feb 25 1938.

Mr Cecil Parkinson

HEXHAM

Electorate %Turnout	56,360	80.0%	**1987**	54,341	76.4%	**1983**
Amos, A.T. (C)	22,370	49.6%	-1.9%	21,374	51.5%	(C)
Robson, E.M. (L/All)	14,304	31.7%	+0.2%	13,066	31.5%	(L/All)
Wood, M.R. (Lab)	8,103	18.0%	+1.0%	7,056	17.0%	(Lab)
Wood, Mrs S.M. (Grn)	336	0.7%				
C to L/All swing 1.1%	45,113	C maj 8,066 17.9%		41,496	C maj 8,308 20.0%	

Mr Alan Amos, assistant principal of a college of further education and former head of agriculture at Conservative Central Office, contested Walthamstow 1983. Minutes sec, Cons back-bench agriculture cmte. Mbr, Enfield BC, since 1978 (dep ldr of cl and chmn of ed cmte, 1983-); chmn, London Boroughs Assocn ed cmte. B Nov 10 1952; ed St Albans Sch; St John's Coll, Oxford (Pres, Oxford Univ Cons Assocn). Sec, Nat Agricultural and Countryside Forum; chmn, political advisory cmte, Enfield-Southgate Cons Assocn. AMMA.

Mr Euan Robson, manager of the Scottish Gas Consumers' Cl since 1986, contested this seat 1983. Dep reg sec, Northern Gas Consumers' Cl, 1981-86. Mbr (for Humshaugh), Northumberland CC, 1981- ; Broomley and Stocksfield PC, 1976-79. Hon agent, Hexham constituency Lib Assocn, 1977-81. B Feb 17 1954; ed Trinity Coll, Glenalmond, Perthshire; Newcastle, Durham and Strathclyde Univs. Taught at King Edward VI Sch, Morpeth, 1976-79. Life mbr, Scot Nat Trust.

Mr Mike Wood, social worker. B Mar 3 1946; ed Leeds Univ.

Mr Alan Amos

HEYWOOD AND MIDDLETON

Electorate %Turnout	59,487	73.8%	**1987**	59,870	69.9%	**1983**
*Callaghan, J. (Lab)	21,900	49.9%	+6.6%	18,111	43.3%	(Lab)
Walker, R.E. (C)	15,052	34.3%	+0.5%	14,137	33.8%	(C)
Greenhalgh, I. (SDP/All)	6,953	15.8%	-6.3%	9,262	22.1%	(SDP/All)
				316	0.8%	(Other)
C to Lab swing 3.0%	43,905	Lab maj 6,848 15.6%		41,826	Lab maj 3,974 9.5%	

Mr Jim Callaghan was elected for this seat in 1983; MP for Middleton and Prestwich, 1974-83. Art lecturer at St John's Coll, Manchester, 1959-74. B Jan 28 1927; ed Manchester and London Univs. Mbr, Select Cmte on Education, Science and Arts, since 1983; Standing Orders Cmte, 1981-83; Middleton MBC, 1971-74. Football coach and referee.

Mr Roy Walker, lecturer at Bolton Inst of Higher Ed, contested Oldham East 1979 and Sheffield, Brightside, Oct 1974. Member, Bury MBC, 1982- ; Stockport MBC, 1973-80. B Feb 28 1943; ed Firth Park GS, Sheffield; Exeter, London and Manchester Univs. PAT.

Mr Ian Greenhalgh, master butcher, has held office as constituency and area SNP chmn. Founder mbr of party. Exec mbr, Chamber of Trade; Bolton Assocn, Nat Fed of Meat Traders. B Jul 9 1946; ed St Paul's C of E Primary Sch; Smithills Sec Mod Sch. Usdaw.

Mr Jim Callaghan

HIGH PEAK

Electorate %Turnout	69,926	80.5%	**1987**	67,358	78.5%	**1983**
*Hawkins, C.J. (C)	25,715	45.7%	-0.7%	24,534	46.4%	(C)
McCrindle, Ms J. (Lab)	16,199	28.8%	+2.8%	14,594	27.6%	(SDP/All)
Oldham, Dr J. (SDP/All)	14,389	25.6%	-2.0%	13,755	26.0%	(Lab)
C to Lab swing 1.7%	56,303	C maj 9,516 16.9%		52,883	C maj 9,940 18.8%	

Mr Christopher Hawkins, economist, was elected in 1983. Senior lecturer in economics, Southampton Univ, 1973-83. Research Division economist, Courtaulds, Coventry, 1961-66; with firm's head office economics dept from 1959. Consultant to Chelsea Building Soc. B Nov 26 1937; ed Bristol GS; Bristol Univ. Sec, Cons Action to Revive Employment. Mbr, Coventry City Cl, 1964-66.

Ms Jean McCrindle, tutor in history and politics, contested Sheffield, Hallam 1983. Chair, Broomhill ward Lab Pty; ASTMS and NATFHE branches. Nat Treas, "Women Against Pit Closures" 1984-85. B Apr 24 1937; ed St Andrews Univ, Scotland.

Dr John Oldham, medical practitioner. Chmn, SDP North West Regional Cl, 1985- ; founder and former vice-chmn, SDP health and social services assocn; chmn SDP primary care policy gp; mbr, CSD; SDP health and social services policy gp; A;liance jt commission on health. Adviser to SDP spokesman on health. B Aug 17 1953; ed Nelson GS; Manchester Univ. Mbr, BMA and Royal Coll of General Practitioners.

Mr Christopher
Hawkins

HOLBORN AND ST PANCRAS — No change

Electorate %Turnout	70,589	64.3%	**1987**	71,604	60.2%	**1983**
*Dobson, F.G. (Lab)	22,966	50.6%	+3.1%	20,486	47.5%	(Lab)
Luff, P.J. (C)	14,113	31.1%	+0.4%	13,227	30.7%	(C)
McGrath, S. (L/All)	7,994	17.6%	-3.8%	9,242	21.4%	(L/All)
Gavan, M.J. (RF)	300	0.7%		157	0.4%	(WRP)
C to Lab swing 1.3%	45,373	Lab maj 8,853 19.5%		43,112	Lab maj 7,259 16.8%	

Mr Frank Dobson

Mr Frank Dobson became in 1985, as a member of the Opposition's front bench DHSS team, chief spokesman on health; an Opposition spokesman on education, 1981-83. Elected for this seat 1983; MP for Holborn and St Pancras South, 1979-83. An assistant sec, local government ombudsman's office, 1975-79; mbr, Camden BC, 1971-76, leader, 1973-75. B Mar 15 1940; ed Archbishop Holgate GS, York, and LSE, of which he became a governor in 1986. Mbr, Chile Solidarity Campaign, 1979- ; and of nat cmte, Anti-Apartheid Movement, 1980- . NUR sponsored; chmn, NHS Unlimited, 1981- . Mbr, Select Cmte on Environment, 1979-81. Chmn, PLP Greater London group, 1983- . Sponsored by NUR.
Mr Peter Luff was head of Mr Edward Heath's private office, 1980-82; research assistant to Mr Peter Walker, 1977-79. Managing director of a public relations consultancy and company secretary of a family stationery firm. B Feb 18 1955; ed Windsor GS; Corpus Christi Coll, Cambridge.
Mr Simon McGrath, a mbr of the Lib Pty Cl and assembly cmte, is a manpower planning consultant. Ed City Univ, London. Has served as chmn, Assocn of Lib Trade Unionists, and been on the Lib nat exec.

HOLLAND WITH BOSTON — No change

Electorate %Turnout	65,539	72.3%	**1987**	63,562	71.0%	**1983**
*Body, Sir Richard (C)	27,412	57.9%	+2.6%	24,962	55.3%	(C)
Le Brun, Mrs C. (L/All)	9,817	20.7%	-8.6%	13,226	29.3%	(L/All)
Hough, J.D. (Lab)	9,734	20.5%	+5.1%	6,970	15.4%	(Lab)
James, D. (Local Voice)	405	0.9%				
L/All to C swing 5.6%	47,368	C maj 17,595 37.1%		45,158	C maj 11,736 26.0%	

Sir Richard Body

Sir Richard Body, elected for this seat in 1966, has been chairman of the Select Cmte on Agriculture since 1983, mbr since 1979; mbr, Jt Cmte on Consolidation Bills, 1975- . MP for Billericay, 1955-59; contested Leek, 1951, Rotherham, 1950, and Abertillery by-election, 1950. Barrister, farmer and underwriting mbr of Lloyd's. B May 18 1927; ed Reading Sch. Vice-pres, Small Farmers' Assocn, 1985- . Former officer of Cons back-bench sub-cmte on horticulture. Chmn, Open Seas Forum, since 1971. Jt chmn, cl, Get Britain Out (of EEC) Campaign, 1975. Pres, Cobden Club, 1981- ; vice-pres, Selsdon Group.
Mrs Carole Le Brun, teacher, contested the seat 1983. B Jan 31 1939; ed Doncaster HS; Kenton Lodge Training Coll, Newcastle; Open Univ. NAS/UWT.
Mr John Hough, contested Brigg and Cleethorpes 1983. Mbr of workers' cooperative. B Aug 22 1946. Was mbr, E Midland regional exec cmte, Lab Pty. Has worked in Africa on a government overseas aid programme.

HONITON — No change

Electorate %Turnout	77,259	76.4%	**1987**	72,232	74.5%	**1983**
*Emery, Sir Peter (C)	34,931	59.2%	-1.4%	32,602	60.6%	(C)
Tatton-Brown, G. (SDP/All)	18,369	31.1%	-2.0%	17,833	33.1%	(SDP/All)
Pollentine, S. (Lab)	4,988	8.4%	+2.2%	3,377	6.3%	(Lab)
Hughes, S. (Loony)	747	1.3%				
SDP/All to C swing 0.3%	59,035	C maj 16,562 28.1%		53,812	C maj 14,769 27.4%	

Sir Peter Emery

Sir Peter Emery has been chairman of the Select Cmte on Procedure since 1983 (member since 1972); mbr, Select Cmte on Trade and Industry, since 1979. Under Secretary of State for Energy, 1974; Under Secretary of State for Trade and Industry, 1972-74. Returned at 1967 by-election; MP for Reading, 1959-66; contested Poplar, 1951, and Lincoln, 1955. Mbr, N Atlantic Assembly, since 1983 (chmn, Science and Tech Cmte, since 1985). An Opposition spokesman on Treasury, economic affairs and trade, 1964-65. Jt founder, Bow Group, 1951. B Feb 27, 1926; ed Scotch Plains HS, New Jersey, US; Oriel Coll, Oxford. Mbr, Hornsey BC, 1951-58 (deputy mayor, 1957-58). Director, Shenley Trust Services Ltd, Purchasing Management Services Ltd, Direct Broadcast by Satellite Co Ltd and other companies. Chmn, Consultative Cl of Professional Management Organisations, 1964-72; director, Inst of Purchasing and Supply, 1961-72; sec general, Euro Fed of Purchasing, 1962-72.
Mr Gerald Tatton-Brown, farmer. Mbr, SDP national agricultural cmte. B 1951. NFU.
Mr Simon Pollentine, partner in retail greetings card firm. Town cllr. Honiton CLP press office, membership officer; mbr of its gmc and exec. Vice-chair and press officer, local pty branch. B Nov 1 1953; ed King's Sch, Ottery St Mary, Devon; Dorset Inst of Higher Ed.

HORNCHURCH · No change

Electorate %Turnout	62,397	75.3%	**1987**	61,741	73.7%	**1983**
*Squire, R.C. (C)	24,039	51.2%	+4.1%	21,393	47.0%	(C)
Williams, A.R. (Lab)	13,345	28.4%	+1.5%	12,209	26.8%	(Lab)
Long, M.L.C. (L/All)	9,609	20.4%	-4.3%	11,251	24.7%	(SDP/All)
				621	1.4%	(Other)
Lab to C swing 1.3%	46,993	C maj 10,694 22.8%		45,474	C maj 9,184 20.2%	

Mr **Robin Squire**, chartered accountant, has been on the Select Cmte on European Legislation since 1985. Gained Hornchurch for the Conservatives in 1979; contested the seat, Oct 1974. Mbr, board of Shelter, since 1982. Financial consultant to Lombard North Central plc, 1979- , being dep chief accountant with company, 1972-79; programme presenter, Capital Radio, 1982- ; parly adviser, Sea Containers, 1985- . B Jul 12 1944; ed Tiffin Sch, Kingston upon Thames. Chmn, Cons Gp for Electoral Reform, 1983-86 (vice-chmn, 1982-83); vice-chmn, Cons back-bench environment cmte, 1985- ; trade and consumer affairs cmte, 1980-83; sec, Cons back-bench European affairs cmte, 1979-80; mbr, Select Cmte on Environment, 1979-83; Sutton BC, 1968-82 (chmn, finance cmte, 1972-76; leader, 1976-79). Nat vice-chmn, YCs, 1974-75.

Mr **Alan Williams**, barrister and former teacher, contested the seat 1983. Mbr, Havering BC, 1986-. Former GLC mbr for Hornchurch; vice chmn, GLC planning cmte, 1981-86. B Nov 14 1945; ed Abingdon Sch; Bradford and Nottingham Univs. TGWU; formerly NUT.

Mr **Mark Long**, director of publicity and promotions consultancy, contested Dagenham 1979; cllr from 1985. B 1955; ed Robert Clack Tech Sch.

Mr Robin Squire

HORNSEY AND WOOD GREEN · No change

Electorate %Turnout	80,594	73.3%	**1987**	73,870	71.2%	**1983**
*Rossi, Sir Hugh (C)	25,397	43.0%	+0.5%	22,323	42.4%	(C)
Roche, Ms B.M.R. (Lab)	23,618	40.0%	+4.9%	18,424	35.0%	(Lab)
Eden, D. (SDP/All)	8,928	15.1%	-5.8%	10,995	20.9%	(SDP/All)
Crosbie, Ms E. (Grn)	1,154	2.0%	+0.4%	854	1.6%	(Eco)
C to Lab swing 2.2%	59,097	C maj 1,779 3.0%		52,596	C maj 3,899 7.4%	

Sir **Hugh Rossi** became chairman of the Select Cmte on Environment in 1983. Minister for Social Security and the Disabled, 1981-83; Minister of State for N Ireland, 1979-81; an Opposition spokesman and chmn of policy cmte on housing and land, 1974-79; Under Secretary of State for Environment, 1974; Lord Commissioner of the Treasury (Govt whip), 1972-74; asst Govt whip, 1970-72. Solicitor, legal consultant. Non-exec director, Bolton Building Soc and two companies. Elected for this seat in 1983; MP for Hornsey, 1966-83. B Jun 21 1927; ed Finchley Catholic GS and King's Coll, London Univ. Mbr, Haringey Cl, 1965-68; Hornsey Cl, 1956-65 (deputy mayor, 1964-65); Middlesex CC, 1961-65. Sec, Cons back-bench housing cmte, 1967-70; vice-chmn, legal cmte, 1970. Mbr, then dep leader, Govt delegation to Cl of Europe and WEU, 1970-73.

Ms **Barbara Roche**, barrister; head of Hackney Police Cmte support unit; previously with SE London law centre. Contested Surrey South West by-election 1984. Chaired Battersea CLP, 1981-85. B April 13 1954; ed comprehensive sch; Lady Margaret Hall, Oxford Univ.

Mr **Douglas Eden**, senior tutor in American studies, Middlesex Poly, contested Yorkshire South for Alliance in 1984 Euro election. Chmn, London SDP; vice-chmn, Social Democrats for Defence and Disarmament. Mbr, GLC, 1973-77. B Mar 5 1939; ed Columbia Univ, New York; LSE; London Univ. Chmn, Heathrow Airport consultative cmte, 1973- .

Sir Hugh Rossi

HORSHAM · No change

Electorate %Turnout	86,135	72.5%	**1987**	80,407	74.5%	**1983**
*Hordern, Sir Peter (C)	39,775	63.7%	+0.4%	37,897	63.2%	(C)
Pearce, Mrs J. (SDP/All)	15,868	25.4%	-1.5%	16,112	26.9%	(SDP/All)
Shrimpton, M. (Lab)	5,435	8.7%	+0.4%	4,999	8.3%	(Lab)
Metheringham, T. (Grn)	1,383	2.2%	+0.7%	925	1.5%	(Eco)
SDP/All to C swing 1.0%	62,461	C maj 23,907 38.3%		59,933	C maj 21,785 36.3%	

Sir **Peter Hordern** has served on the PAC since 1970; Public Accounts Commission, 1984- ; and the exec, 1922 Committee, 1968- . MP for Horsham, 1964-74 and since 1983; MP for Horsham and Crawley, 1974-83. Chmn, Cons finance cmte, 1970-72. Mbr of Lloyd's; London Stock Exchange, 1957-74. Director, Petrofina (UK) plc, since 1973 (chmn, 1987-); F. and C. Alliance Investment plc, since 1976 (chmn, 1986-); and T.R.Technology plc, since 1975. B Apr 18 1929; ed Geelong GS, Australia, and Christ Church, Oxford. Member, exec cmte, UK branch CPA, 1986- . Consultant to Fisons plc, House of Fraser plc and Pannell, Kerr, Forster.

Mrs **Jennifer Pearce**, psychiatric social worker with Surrey CC social services dept; former medical secretary. Founder mbr, SDP; vice chmn, Horsham SDP. B Aug 5 1941; ed Wimbledon Commercial Sch; W London Inst of Higher Ed.

Mr **Michael Shrimpton**, barrister. B Mar 9 1957; ed Queensland Univ, Australia; Univ of Wales. Has served with East Putney CLP as branch sec. TGWU; ACTSS.

Mr **Terence Metheringham**, systems analyst. B Jan 28 1955; ed Burnage HS, Manchester; City of London Poly; Kent Univ.

Sir Peter Hordern

HOUGHTON AND WASHINGTON — No change

Electorate %Turnout	77,906	71.2%	**1987**	75,686	66.9%	**1983**
*Boyes, R. (Lab)	32,805	59.1%	+7.4%	26,168	51.7%	(Lab)
Callanan, J.M. (C)	12,612	22.7%	-1.2%	12,347	24.4%	(SDP/All)
Kenyon, R.F. (SDP/All)	10,090	18.2%	-6.2%	12,104	23.9%	(C)
C to Lab swing 4.3%	55,507	Lab maj 20,193 36.4%		50,619	Lab maj 13,821 27.3%	

Mr Roland Boyes joined the Opposition's front bench environment team in 1985; jt vice-chmn, PLP defence cmte, 1985-86; mbr, Select Cmte on European Legislation, 1983- ; chmn, all-pty photography gp, 1987- . Elected for this seat 1983; MEP for Durham, 1979-84. B Feb 12 1937. Chmn, Tribune Gp, 1985-86. Teacher, 1961-74; assistant director, Durham County Social Services Dept 1975-79. Mbr, Peterlee TC, 1976-79; Easington DC, 1973-76. GMBATU.
Mr Martin Callanan, technical services manager. Mbr, Tyne and Wear CC, 1983-86. B Aug 8 1961; ed Heathfield Senior HS; Newcastle Poly.
Mr Rod Kenyon, personnel manager, contested this seat in 1983 and the 1985 Tyne Bridge by-election. B Jun 14 1945; ed Bootle GS; King George V Sch; Liverpool Poly. Nalgo.

Mr Roland Boyes

HOVE — No change

Electorate %Turnout	72,626	67.8%	**1987**	71,918	65.8%	**1983**
*Sainsbury, T.A.D. (C)	28,952	58.8%	-1.7%	28,628	60.5%	(C)
Collins, Mrs M.E. (SDP/All)	10,734	21.8%	-2.3%	11,409	24.1%	(L/All)
Turner, D.K. (Lab)	9,010	18.3%	+4.5%	6,550	13.8%	(Lab)
Layton, T.A. (SE)	522	1.1%		524	1.1%	(SEE)
				189	0.4%	(Other)
SDP/All to C swing 0.3%	49,218	C maj 18,218 37.0%		47,300	C maj 17,219 36.4%	

Mr Timothy Sainsbury was appointed Under Secretary of State for Defence Procurement in Jun 1987. A Government whip, 1983-87, being appointed a Lord Commissioner of the Treasury in 1985. Director, J Sainsbury plc, 1962-83; former director, Blackwell Press Ltd. Elected in 1973. B Jun 11 1932; ed Eton and Worcester Coll, Oxford. PPS to Secretary of State for the Environment, 1979-83, and to Secretary of State for Defence, 1983. Chmn, all-pty group for retail trade, 1979-83; all-pty cmte for release of Soviet Jewry, 1976-79, and vice-chmn, 1979-83; former jt hon treas, Cons Friends of Israel. Mbr, cl, RSA, 1981-83. Governor, Centre for Environmental Studies, 1976-79. Sponsored Indecent Displays (Control) Act 1981.
Mrs Margaret Collins, teacher. Mbr, West Sussex CC, 1985- . B Nov 10 1940; ed Brondesbury and Kilburn HS for Girls; Trent Park Training Coll; Sussex Univ. NUT.
Mr Don Turner, sales representative. Mbr, East Sussex CC; Brighton HA. B Jan 19 1935; ed Hove County GS; Open Univ.

Mr Timothy Sainsbury

HUDDERSFIELD — No change

Electorate %Turnout	66,413	75.5%	**1987**	68,174	71.1%	**1983**
*Sheerman, B.J. (Lab)	23,019	45.9%	+4.5%	20,051	41.4%	(Lab)
Hawkins, N.J. (C)	15,741	31.4%	-1.9%	16,096	33.2%	(C)
Smithson, J. (L/All)	10,773	21.5%	-3.4%	12,027	24.8%	(L/All)
Harvey, N.A.L. (Grn)	638	1.3%		271	0.6%	(Ind)
C to Lab swing 3.2%	50,171	Lab maj 7,278 14.5%		48,445	Lab maj 3,955 8.2%	

Mr Barry Sheerman, an Opposition spokesman on employment and education, 1983- . Chmn, PLP trade group, 1981-83. Elected for this seat 1983; MP for Huddersfield East 1979-83; contested Taunton, Oct 1974. B Aug 17 1940; ed Hampton GS; Kingston Tech Coll; LSE; London Univ. Lecturer. Mbr, PAC, 1981-83; chmn, Parly Advisory Cmte on Transport Safety, 1981- ; mbr, Loughor UDC, 1972-74; Lliw Valley BC, 1973-78. Fellow, Industry and Parliament Trust. Partner in Coptech (Cooperative technology). Sponsored by Co-op Pty.
Mr Nicholas Hawkins, barrister and legal consultant. B Mar 27 1957; ed Bedford Modern Sch; Lincoln Coll, Oxford.
Mr John Smithson is manager of Age Concern. Finance director, Liberal publications; editor of Radical Bulletin; treas, ALC; author of party's community campaign manual. Contested Brighouse and Spenborough, Oct 1974, and Richmond (Yorks), 1970. B Aug 15 1939; ed Penistone GS; King's Coll, Univ of London; Huddersfield Poly; Teesside Poly. Mbr, Kirklees MBC, since 1982; Pendle DC, 1973-76 (leader, 1974-75); Saltburn and Mauske UDC, 11966-69. ACTSS (shop steward, 1977-79).
Mr Nicholas Harvey, student nurse. B Aug 5 1964; ed Friary Grange Comprehensive Sch, Lichfield.

Mr Barry Sheerman

HULL EAST — No change

Electorate %Turnout	68,657	70.6%	**1987**	70,037	67.6%	**1983**
*Prescott, J.L. (Lab)	27,287	56.3%	+6.4%	23,615	49.9%	(Lab)
Jackson, P. (C)	12,598	26.0%	-2.6%	13,541	28.6%	(C)
Wright, T. (L/All)	8,572	17.7%	-3.8%	10,172	21.5%	(L/All)
C to Lab swing 4.5%	48,457	Lab maj 14,689 30.3%		47,328	Lab maj 10,074 21.3%	

Mr John Prescott, chief Opposition spokesman on employment 1985- ; elected to the shadow Cabinet in 1983, being chief spokesman on transport, 1983-85; Opposition spokesman on regional affairs, 1981-83; a spokesman on transport, 1979-81. Mbr, European Parliament, 1975-79 and leader of Labour delegation, 1976-79. Former official of the National Union of Seamen and sponsored by union; steward on passenger liners, Merchant Navy, 1955-63. Elected in 1970; contested Southport, 1966. B May 31 1938; ed Grange Sec Mod Sch, Ellesmere Port; Ruskin Coll, Oxford, and Hull Univ. Mbr, Select Cmte on Nationalised Industries, 1973-79. PPS to Mr Peter Shore, when Secretary of State for Trade, 1974-76.

Mr Philip Jackson, industrial chemist employed in safety dept of chemical manufacturer. Mbr, Great Grimsby BC, 1984- . Chmn, Great Grimsby CPC; vice-chmn, E Midlands area CPC; former chmn, Great Grimsby YCs. B Aug 28 1958; ed Grimsby Wintringham GS; Grimsby Coll of Tech. Mbr, Inst of Advanced Motorists.

Mr Timothy Wright, journalist and commercial vehicles sales rep. Humberside CC L/All gp sec and whip; gp spokesman on social services and planning and transportation. Mbr, Child Poverty Action Gp; Hull and Dist Cl for Racial Equality. B Mar 22 1952; ed Hessle HS; Darlington Coll of Tech. Past chmn and treas, Hessle Lib Assocn.

Mr John Prescott

HULL NORTH — No change

Electorate %Turnout	73,288	69.6%	**1987**	74,543	67.5%	**1983**
*McNamara, J.K. (Lab)	26,123	51.2%	+8.7%	21,365	42.5%	(Lab)
O'Brien, Miss A. (C)	13,954	27.3%	-3.1%	15,337	30.5%	(C)
Unwin, S.W. (SDP/All)	10,962	21.5%	-5.1%	13,381	26.6%	(SDP/All)
				222	0.4%	(Other)
C to Lab swing 5.9%	51,039	Lab maj 12,169 23.8%		50,305	Lab maj 6,028 12.0%	

Mr Kevin McNamara, an Opposition spokesman on defence and disarmament, 1982- . Lecturer in law. Elected for this seat 1983; MP for Hull Central, Feb 1974-83, and for Hull North, 1966-74; contested Bridlington, 1964. B Sep 5 1934; ed St Mary's Coll, Crosby, and Hull Univ. Mbr, UK delegation, N Atlantic Assembly, 1984- (vice-chmn of its economic cmte). Former chmn, PLP N Ireland gp; former mbr, Select Cmte on Foreign Affairs when he chaired its Overseas Development sub-cmte; UK delegation to Cl of Europe; Select Cmte on Procedure. Sec, TGWU parly gp. Sponsored by TGWU.

Miss Ann O'Brien, solicitor with a building society. Mbr, Leeds City Cl, 1984- ; mbr Blackburn BC for six years. B Jan 28 1950; ed Notre Dame GS, Blackburn; London Univ; Coll of Law, London.

Mr Stephen Unwin, univ lecturer, contested Hull West 1983; Humberside in Euro election 1984. Mbr, Hull Cl, 1981-82; Hammersmith and Fulham Cl, 1971-82. Contributor to SDP fishing policy. B Mar 5 1947; ed Bournemouth Sch; LSE. AUT.

Mr Kevin McNamara

HULL WEST — No change

Electorate %Turnout	55,636	67.6%	**1987**	57,702	63.5%	**1983**
*Randall, S.J. (Lab)	19,527	51.9%	+10.0%	15,361	41.9%	(Lab)
Humphrys, M.R.C. (C)	11,397	30.3%	-1.6%	11,707	31.9%	(C)
Bond, M. (SDP/All)	6,669	17.7%	-8.4%	9,575	26.1%	(SDP/All)
C to Lab swing 5.8%	37,593	Lab maj 8,130 21.6%		36,643	Lab maj 3,654 10.0%	

Mr Stuart Randall, who was elected in 1983, became an Opposition spokesman on agriculture, fisheries and food in 1985. PPS to Mr Roy Hattersley, shadow Chancellor, 1984-85. Consultant with Inter-Bank Research Organisation, 1968-71; manager with BSC (1971-76) and British Leyland (1976-80); then with Nexos Office Systems, 1980-81; Plessey Communications Systems, 1981-83. Contested South Worcestershire, Oct 1974, and Euro constituency of Midlands West, 1979. B Jun 22 1938; ed Univ of Wales. Sponsored by EETPU.

Mr Martin Humphrys contested the seat in 1983. Head of political studies, Bedford Sch. B Apr 13 1955; ed Chatham House; Downing Coll, Cambridge; Cambridge Dept of Ed. AMMA. Chmn, Bedford Rowing Club.

Mr Martyn Bond, European civil servant. Vice-chmn, Brussels SDP area party. B Oct 10 1942; ed Wincester; Cambridge Univ. Employed in press and private office of General Secretariat, EEC Cl of Ministers, 1974-81; with BBC in Berlin 1981-83; principal administrator in Cl of Ministers secretariat, 1983- .

Mr Stuart Randall

HUNTINGDON · No change

Electorate %Turnout	86,186	74.0%	**1987**	76,668	71.6%	**1983**
*Major, J. (C)	40,530	63.6%	+1.2%	34,254	62.4%	(C)
Nicholson, A.J. (SDP/All)	13,486	21.1%	-4.2%	13,906	25.3%	(L/All)
Brown, D.M. (Lab)	8,883	13.9%	+2.4%	6,317	11.5%	(Lab)
Lavin, B. (Grn)	874	1.4%	+0.6%	444	0.8%	(Eco)
SDP/All to C swing 2.7%	63,773	C maj 27,044 42.4%		54,921	C maj 20,348 37.0%	

Mr John Major was appointed Chief Secretary to the Treasury with a seat in the Cabinet, Jun 1987; Minister for Social Security and the Disabled, with rank of Minister of State at the DHSS, 1986-87; Under Secretary of State for Social Security, 1985-86; a Lord Commissioner of the Treasury (Govt whip), 1984-85; asst Govt whip, 1983-84. Elected for this seat 1983; MP for Huntingdonshire, 1979-83; contested St Pancras N, Feb and Oct 1974. Executive, Standard Chartered Bank, 1965-79; Associate of Inst of Bankers. B Mar 29 1943; ed Rutlish GS. Mbr, Lambeth BC, 1968-71; board of Warden Housing Assocn, 1975-83. Jt sec, Cons back-bench environment cmte, 1979-81. PPS to Ministers of State, Home Office, 1981-83. Parly consultant, Guild of Glass Engravers, 1979-83. Pres, Eastern Area YCs, 1983-85.
Mr Anthony Nicholson, history teacher. Chmn, North Beds SDP; Beds rep on CSD; Sec of Alliance Gp on North Beds BC. B Mar 31 1948; ed Chislehurst and Sidcup GS; Queen's Coll, Oxford; Jesus Coll, Cambridge. AMMA
Mr Dave Brown, Sogat '82 official. B Apr 8 1950; ed Staveley Sec Mod Sch, Chiswick.

Mr John Major

HYNDBURN · No change

Electorate %Turnout	60,529	80.5%	**1987**	59,341	77.4%	**1983**
*Hargreaves, J.K. (C)	21,606	44.4%	+2.1%	19,405	42.2%	(C)
Coombes, K. (Lab)	19,386	39.8%	-2.4%	19,384	42.2%	(Lab)
Strak, J. (SDP/All)	7,423	15.2%	+0.6%	6,716	14.6%	(SDP/All)
Smith, F. (Grn)	297	0.6%	0.0%	266	0.6%	(Eco)
				169	0.4%	(Other)
Lab to C swing 2.3%	48,712	C maj 2,220 4.6%		45,940	C maj 21 0.0%	

Mr Kenneth Hargreaves, office manager with Shopfitters (Lancashire) Ltd, Oswaldtwistle, 1963-83, was elected in 1983. Sec, Cons back-bench housing improvement sub-cmte, 1985- . B Mar 1 1939; ed St Mary's Coll, Blackburn; Burnley Municipal Coll; Manchester Coll of Commerce. Standard cost clerk, NCB, 1957-61; audit asst, Treasurer's Dept, Lancashire CC, 1961-63. Mbr, Oswaldtwistle UDC, 1965-74; Hyndburn BC, 1974-83; deputy leader, Cons gp, 1981-83. Associate, Inst of Chartered Secs and Administrators.
Mr Keva Coombes, solicitor, is convenor of the Labour gp on Liverpool City Cl; former leader of Merseyside DC.
Dr John Strak, lecturer and farmer. SDP agent in 1983 election. Mbr, Hyndburn BC, 1983 - ; ldr of Alliance gp. Chmn, Assocn Soc Dem Cllrs; sec, farm policy gp. B Aug 1 1951; ed Accrington GS; Aberdeen and Manchester Univs. NFU, AUT.
Mr Frank Smith is self-employed, selling organically grown food. Contested this seat 1983. Spent 10 years in chemical industry followed by two years doing practical conservation work. Sec, E Lancs Grn Pty, 1982- . B May 14 1952; ed Leeds Mod HS; Leeds Poly.

Mr Kenneth
Hargreaves

ILFORD NORTH · No change

Electorate %Turnout	60,433	72.6%	**1987**	60,248	71.3%	**1983**
*Bendall, V.W.H. (C)	24,110	54.9%	+3.6%	22,042	51.3%	(C)
Jeater, P. (Lab)	12,020	27.4%	+2.1%	10,841	25.2%	(Lab)
Tobbell, G. (SDP/All)	7,757	17.7%	-5.7%	10,052	23.4%	(SDP/All)
Lab to C swing 0.7%	43,887	C maj 12,090 27.5%		42,935	C maj 11,201 26.1%	

Mr Vivian Bendall has been a joint vice-chmn of the Cons back-bench employment cmte since 1984 (jt sec, 1981-84). Senior partner of Bendall's, surveyors and valuers; consultant to London Taxi Drivers' Assocn. Elected for this seat at 1978 by-election; contested Hertford and Stevenage, Feb and Oct 1974. B Dec 14 1938; ed Coombe Hill House, Croydon; Broadgreen Coll, Croydon. Mbr, Croydon BC, 1964-78; GLC, 1970-74. Chmn, Greater London YCs, 1967-68. Vice-chmn, Cons back-bench transport cmte, 1982-83; sec, foreign and Commonwealth affairs cmte, 1981-84.
Mr Paul Jeater, teacher. B Feb 5 1953; ed Thames Poly. Mbr, Redbridge BC, 1986- . Mbr, British/Granada friendship soc. NUT.
Mr Graham Tobbell, economist and senior lecturer in accounting; previously in NHS. Election agent 1983. Mbr, CSD; SDP health panel; past area pty chm. Chmn, NW Sussex SDP, 1983-86. B Mar 16 1950; ed Croydon schs; Essex Univ. APT and previously Nalgo.

Mr Vivian Bendall

ILFORD SOUTH — No change

Electorate %Turnout	58,572	71.8%	1987	58,208	70.6%	1983
*Thorne, N.G. (C)	20,351	48.4%	+2.9%	18,672	45.4%	(C)
Jones, K. (Lab)	15,779	37.5%	+3.2%	14,106	34.3%	(Lab)
Scott, R.J. (L/All)	5,928	14.1%	-5.4%	7,999	19.5%	(L/All)
				316	0.8%	(Other)
C to Lab swing 0.1%	42,058	C maj 4,572 10.9%		41,093	C maj 4,566 11.1%	

Mr **Neil Thorne**, chartered surveyor, consultant and Lloyd's underwriter. Mbr, Select Cmte on Defence, 1983- ; chmn, Nat Cl for Civil Defence, 1982- ; Commons motor club, 1985. Gained the seat in 1979; contested it, Oct 1974. B Aug 8 1932; ed City of London Sch and London Univ. Consultant to Hull and Co, chartered surveyors (senior partner of firm, 1962-76). Jt vice-chmn, Cons Greater London MPs. Mbr, TA, 1952-82. Mbr, Redbridge BC, 1965-68, and alderman, 1975-78; GLC, 1967-73. Chmn, Anglo-Nepalese all-pty parly gp, 1983- . Freeman and liveryman, City of London. Fellow, Industry and Parliament Trust.
Mr **Kenneth Jones**, local govt housing officer. Mbr, Redbridge BC, 1978- (dep ldr, Lab gp); chairs local health service campaign. Mbr, community relations cl. B Sep 2 1951. Nupe.
Mr **Ralph Scott**, contracts officer, contested the seat 1983 and 1979, and Leyton, Oct 1974. B Jan 10 1939; ed SE Essex County Tech Sch, Barking; NE London Poly. Nalgo.

Mr Neil Thorne

INVERNESS, NAIRN AND LOCHABER — No change

Electorate %Turnout	66,743	70.9%	1987	63,645	70.5%	1983
*Johnston, Sir Russell (L/All)	17,422	36.8%	-9.2%	20,671	46.1%	(L/All)
Stewart, D. (Lab)	11,991	25.3%	+11.0%	13,373	29.8%	(C)
Keswick, Mrs A.T. (C)	10,901	23.0%	-6.8%	6,448	14.4%	(Lab)
Johnson, N.P. (SNP)	7,001	14.8%	+5.0%	4,395	9.8%	(SNP)
L/All to Lab swing 10.1%	47,315	L/All maj 5,431 11.5%		44,887	L/All maj 7,298 16.3%	

Sir Russell Johnston, leader of the Scottish Liberal Party, 1974- , Liberal spokesman on Scotland, 1981- , Alliance spokesman on Scotland and Europe in the election team. Elected for this seat 1983; MP for Inverness 1964-83 MEP 1973-75 and 1976-79; contested Highlands and Islands in Euro-elections, 1979 and 1984. Delegate, Cl of Europe and WEU, 1985-86. Chmn, all-pty Scottish Gaelic parly gp; sec, UK-Falkland Islands gp; treas, British/Gibraltar gp. Former spokesman on foreign affairs and defence; former member, Select Cmte on EEC secondary legislation. B Jul 28 1932; ed Portree HS, Isle of Skye, and Edinburgh Univ, and Moray House Coll of Ed. Chmn, Scottish Lib Party, 1970-74; vice-chmn, 1965-70.
Mr **Dave Stewart**, social worker. Mbr, Lab Pty Scottish executive 1984- ; Nithsdale DC 1984-86. B May 5 1956; ed Paisley Coll; Stirling Univ. NUPE.
Mrs **Tessa Keswick**, director of Cluff Investments and Trading, a subsidiary of Cluff Oil. Mbr, Kensington and Chelsea BC, 1982-84. B Oct 15 1942; ed Woldingham and in Paris. Mbr, International Institute of Strategic Studies and contributor to Centre for Policy Studies.
Mr **Niall Johnson**, college lecturer, is SNP spokesman on Highland affairs. B Aug 14 1959; ed Paible Sec Sch, North Uist; Inverness Royal Acad; Inverness Coll. TGWU, IPCS, EIS.

Sir Russell Johnston

IPSWICH — C gain

Electorate %Turnout	68,165	77.1%	1987	67,292	75.4%	1983
Irvine, M.F. (C)	23,328	44.4%	+2.8%	22,191	43.7%	(Lab)
*Weetch, K.T. (Lab)	22,454	42.7%	-1.0%	21,114	41.6%	(C)
Nicholson, H.P. (SDP/All)	6,596	12.6%	-1.7%	7,220	14.2%	(L/All)
Lettice, D.T. (WRP)	174	0.3%		235	0.5%	(BNP)
Lab to C swing 1.9%	52,552	C maj 874 1.7%		50,760	Lab maj 1,077 2.1%	

Mr **Michael Irvine** contested Bishop Auckland in 1979. Barrister and son of the late Sir Arthur Irvine, Labour Solicitor General. B Oct 21 1939; ed Rugby; Oriel Coll, Oxford.
Mr **Kenneth Weetch** was mbr of Select Cmte on Parliamentary Commissioner for Administration, 1983-87. MP for this setat, Oct 1974-87; contested seat, Feb 1974, and Saffron Walden, 1970. Mbr, Select Cmte on Home Affairs, 1981-83; vice-chmn, PLP education, science and the arts cmte, 1986-87; and of PLP Agriculture Cmte, 1985-86. B Sep 17 1933; ed Newbridge GS and LSE. Principal lecturer in economic history; head of history department, Hockerill College of Education, Bishop's Stortford, 1964-74. Vice-pres, Building Societies Assocn; pres, Nat Houseowners Soc, 1975-78. PPS to Secretary of State for Transport, 1976-78. Sponsored by Cohse.
Mr **Hugh Nicholson**, chartered accountant with ICI at London HQ. Treas, NW Essex SDP, 1982-85. Mbr, working pty on tax and benefits, 1985-86. Mbr Northampton CB, 1968-71; Redbridge BC, 1974-75. B Jun 2 1941; ed Northampton Town and County GS.

Mr Michael Irvine

ISLE OF WIGHT | C gain

Electorate %Turnout	98,694	79.6%	**1987**	94,226	80.0%	**1983**
Field, B. (C)	40,175	51.2%	+4.8%	38,407	51.0%	(L/All)
Young, M. (L/All)	33,733	43.0%	-8.0%	34,904	46.3%	(C)
Pearson, K. (Lab)	4,626	5.9%	+3.5%	1,828	2.4%	(Lab)
				208	0.3%	(Other)
L/All to C swing 6.4%	78,534	C maj 6,442 8.2%		75,347	L/All maj 3,503 4.6%	

Mr Barry Field, company director. Mbr, Isle of Wight CC, 1986- ; Horsham DC, 1883-86. Founder mbr, Chichester branch of Cruse. Involved in Isle of Wight branch of Wessex Cancer Trust. Served in TA, including with 17 Port Regiment TCT Marchwood, Southampton. B Jul 7 1946; ed Bembridge Sch, Isle of Wight. Mbr, Island Sailing Club since 1964.
Mr Michael Young, company director and business executive, contested Penrith and the Border at the 1983 general election and by-election. B May 11 1945; ed Wellington GS, Shropshire; Univ of York. Mbr, companies committee of CBI. Director of a building materials products company.
Mr Kenn Pearson, financial planning consultant. Mbr, Southern Region executive cmte; Isle of Wight CLP general management cmte and executive cmte; political education officer, Isle of Wight CLP. B April 5 1940; ed St Marylebone GS; City of Westminster Coll, London; Corpus Christi Coll, Oxford. TGWU, previously with NGA.

Mr Barry Field

ISLINGTON NORTH | No change

Electorate %Turnout	58,917	66.5%	**1987**	59,984	61.6%	**1983**
*Corbyn, J.B. (Lab)	19,577	50.0%	+9.5%	14,951	40.4%	(Lab)
Noad, E.G. (C)	9,920	25.3%	+0.0%	9,344	25.3%	(C)
Whelan, A. (SDP/All)	8,560	21.8%	-0.5%	8,268	22.4%	(SDP/All)
Ashby, C. (Grn)	1,131	2.9%		4,091	11.1%	(Ind Lab)
				310	0.8%	(Other)
C to Lab swing 4.7%	39,188	Lab maj 9,657 24.6%		36,964	Lab maj 5,607 15.2%	

Mr Jeremy Corbyn, vice-chmn of the London Lab Pty, has been jt vice-chmn, London group of Labour MPs, and of the PLP health and social security cmte, since 1985. Nupe official, 1975-83; researcher for Tailor and Garment Workers Union, 1971-73, and for AUEW (Engineering Section). Elected in 1983. B May 26 1949; ed Adams GS, Newport, Shropshire. Mbr, Haringey BC, 1974-83 (chmn, Community Development Cmte 1975-78, Public Works 1978-79, Planning 1980-81, and 1982-83). Sec, PLP Central and Latin America gp; mbr, exec cmte, Campaign Group of Labour MPs. Trustee, N Islington Labour Party's Red Rose Labour Centre. Health spokesman for Nupe gp of Lab MPs; sponsored by Nupe.
Mr Ernest Noad, sales and marketing manager. Mbr, Croydon BC, 1978- (chmn, parks and recreational services cmte). B Nov 8 1951; ed St Joseph's Coll, SE London.
Mr Alan Whelan, deputy head of jt RC and C of E comprehensive sch in Richmond. Former press officer and vice-chmn, Ealing SDP. Chmn, Survive International Medical Aid and of Westminster Diocesan Adult Ed Cmte. B Mar 18 1947; ed St James's Christian Brothers Sch, Dublin; London Univ.
Mr Christopher Ashby, tutor. B Aug 15 1945; ed Claremont and Montgomery Sec Mod Schs; City of London Poly.

Mr Jeremy Corbyn

ISLINGTON SOUTH AND FINSBURY | No change

Electorate %Turnout	57,910	71.2%	**1987**	59,795	62.0%	**1983**
*Smith, C.R. (Lab)	16,511	40.1%	+3.8%	13,460	36.3%	(Lab)
Cunningham, G. (SDP/All)	15,706	38.1%	+2.8%	13,097	35.3%	(SDP/All)
Mitchell, A. (C)	8,482	20.6%	-6.1%	9,894	26.7%	(C)
Powell, P. (Grn)	382	0.9%		341	0.9%	(NF)
Dowsett, S. (SPGB)	81	0.2%	0.0%	102	0.3%	(IFP)
Early, Ms J. (HP)	56	0.1%		94	0.3%	(BNP)
				85	0.2%	(Other)
SDP/All to Lab swing 0.5%	41,218	Lab maj 805 2.0%		37,073	Lab maj 363 1.0%	

Mr Christopher Smith, an Opposition whip; chmn, PLP Home Affairs cmte, 1985- ; and jt vice-chmn, PLP environent cmte, 1985- ; sec, Tribune Gp of Lab MPs, 1985- . Mbr, Select Cmte on the Environment, 1983- . Former housing development worker. Elected 1983; contested Epsom and Ewell, 1979. B Jul 24 1951; ed George Watson's Coll, Edinburgh; Pembroke Coll, Cambridge (Pres of Union, 1972); Harvard Univ. Mbr, Islington BC, 1978-83; chief whip 1978-79, chmn of housing, 1981 and 1982-83. Chmn, Lab Campaign for Criminal Justice, 1985- ; mbr, exec cmte, NCCL, 1986- . Sponsored by ASTMS.
Mr George Cunningham, chief executive of the Library Assocn, was MP for this seat, Feb 1974-83, resigning from Labour in 1981 and joining the SDP, unsuccessfully contesting this seat 1983; Labour MP for Islington South West, 1970-74; contested Henley, 1966. Mbr, European Parliament, 1978-79. A Labour spokesman on home affairs, 1979-81. B Jun 10 1931; ed Dunfermline HS; Blackpool GS; Manchester and London Univs.
Mr Andrew R. Mitchell, barrister. Mbr, Haringey BC, 1984- . B Aug 6 1954; ed Haberdashers' Aske's Sch; Coll of Legal Ed.
Mr Peter Powell, actor. Mbr (Lab), Islington BC, 1982-86, resigning cl and pty, Mar 1986. B Apr 28 1934; ed Simon Langton Sch, Canterbury. Equity.

Mr Christopher Smith

ISLWYN — No change

Electorate	%Turnout		50,414	80.4%	**1987**	50,259	77.7%	**1983**
*Kinnock, N.G. (Lab)			28,901	71.3%	+12.0%	23,183	59.3%	(Lab)
Twitchen, J. (C)			5,954	14.7%	+0.6%	8,803	22.5%	(SDP/All)
Gasson, Ms J. (SDP/All)			3,746	9.2%	-13.3%	5,511	14.1%	(C)
Richards, A. (Pl C)			1,932	4.8%	+0.7%	1,574	4.0%	(Pl C)
C to Lab swing 5.7%			40,533	Lab maj 22,947 56.6%		39,071	Lab maj 14,380 36.8%	

Mr Neil Kinnock

Mr Neil Kinnock was elected leader of the Labour Party and leader of the Opposition in Oct 1983. Elected to shadow Cabinet in 1979 and was chief Opposition spokesman on education, 1979-83. Trade union tutor with the WEA, 1966-70. Elected for this seat 1983; MP for Bedwelty, 1970-83. Mbr, Labour Pty NEC, 1978- . B Mar 28 1942; ed Lewis Sch, Pengam, Glamorgan, and Univ Coll, Cardiff (Pres of union, 1965-66). PPS to Mr Michael Foot, Secretary of State for Employment, 1974-75; chmn, PLP Welsh group, 1977-78. Mbr, Public Expenditure Cmte, 1971-73; Select Cmte on Nationalized Industries, 1973-77. Director (unpaid), 7:84 (Socialist community theatre gp), 1979- ; Tribune Publications, 1974-82. Mbr, BBC General Advisory Cl, 1975-79. Sponsored by TGWU.
Mr John Twitchen, solicitor. Mbr, Southend on Sea BC, 1973-78. B Feb 19 1945; ed Westcliff HS for Boys.
Ms Jacqui Gasson, advice worker with CAB; mbr, Cardiff CHC and local consumer advisory cmte to Welsh Water Authority. Mbr, SDP health policy cmte. B Mar 15 1938; ed Tolworth GS, Kingston, Surrey; two Welsh Colls of FE; Univ Coll, Cardiff; Unist, Cardiff.
Mr Aneurin Richards, former chartered engineer with NCB. PLC housing spokesman. Mbr, Islwyn BC. Ed Univ Coll, Cardiff.

JARROW — No change

Electorate	%Turnout		62,845	74.4%	**1987**	63,770	71.4%	**1983**
*Dixon, D. (Lab)			29,651	63.4%	+8.2%	25,151	55.3%	(Lab)
Yeoman, P. (C)			10,856	23.2%	-1.5%	11,274	24.8%	(C)
Freitag, P. (L/All)			6,230	13.3%	-6.6%	9,094	20.0%	(L/All)
C to Lab swing 4.9%			46,737	Lab maj 18,795 40.2%		45,519	Lab maj 13,877 30.5%	

Mr Donald Dixon

Mr Donald Dixon is an Opposition whip; jt vice-chmn, PLP trade and industry group, and chmn of its shipbuilding and ship repair sub-cmte, 1985- ; former chmn, Northern group of Lab MPs; sec, trade union gp of Lab MPs. Shipyard worker, 1947-74; branch sec, GMBATU, 1974-79. Mbr, Select Cmte on Employment, 1979-83. Elected in 1979. B Mar 6 1929; ed Ellison Street Church of England Elementary Sch, Jarrow. Mbr, Jarrow BC, 1962-74 (leader, 1969-74); South Tyneside MDC, being chmn Lab gp and housing cmte, 1974-79. Freeman of Jarrow, 1972. Vice-pres, Jarrow and Hebburn Trades Cl. Mbr of and sponsored by GMB.
Mr Paul Yeoman, academic and farmer. B Dec 23 1954; ed Durham Johnstone GS; Durham Univ.
Mr Peter Freitag, business consultant and estate agent, fought Middlesbrough, 1979; Darlington twice in 1974; Tyne and Wear in 1979 Euro election. Chmn, Northern Lib Pty; former chmn, ALC; treas, Lib Euro Action Gp. B Apr 23 1929; ed Haberdashers' Aske's Sch. Mbr, Darlington DC, 1970-76; Durham CC, 1970-77 (ldr, Lib gp, 1973-77).

KEIGHLEY — No change

Electorate	%Turnout		65,831	79.4%	**1987**	63,678	78.9%	**1983**
*Waller, G.P.A. (C)			23,903	45.8%	+3.2%	21,370	42.6%	(C)
Rye, A. (Lab)			18,297	35.0%	-2.0%	18,596	37.0%	(Lab)
Wells, J.H. (L/All)			10,041	19.2%	-0.6%	9,951	19.8%	(L/All)
						302	0.6%	(Other)
Lab to C swing 2.6%			52,241	C maj 5,606 10.7%		50,219	C maj 2,774 5.5%	

Mr Gary Waller

Mr Gary Waller won this seat in 1983; MP for Brighouse and Spenborough, 1979-83; contested Rother Valley, Feb and Oct 1974. Journalist. B Jun 24 1945; ed Rugby and Lancaster Univ. Treas, Parly Information Technology Cmte, 1981- ; jt sec, Cons back-bench transport cmte, 1985- ; treas (1983-) and sec (1979-83), Yorkshire Cons MPs; sec, Cons back-bench sport and recreation cmte, 1979-81; mbr, Select Cmte on Transport, 1979-82; Jt Cmte on Consolidation Bills, 1982- . Sec, all-pty wool textiles group, 1979-84; chmn, 1984- ; dep chmn, Parly Food and Health Forum, 1985- . PPS to Secretary of State for Transport, 1982-83. Mbr, Nat Union exec cmte, 1976-77. Vice-chmn, Nat Assocn of Cons Graduates, 1970-73. Exec sec, Wider Share Ownership Cl, 1973-76.
Mr Alan Rye, advice and information worker at a parents' centre near Halifax; former teacher and social worker. Mbr, Bradford Cl, 1982- (chmn, Lab gp, 1985-86). B Mar 6 1943.
Mr John Wells, educational psychologist, contested this seat 1983. Mbr, West Yorkshire CC, 1981-86; Bradford MBC, 1985- ; parish cllr, 1979- . B Feb 26 1948; ed Colfe's GS; West Ham Coll of Tech; NE London Poly.

KENSINGTON — No change

Electorate %Turnout	48,212	64.7%	**1987**	49,854	62.3%	**1983**
*Rhys Williams, Sir Brandon (C)	14,818	47.5%	+1.5%	14,274	46.0%	(C)
Bousquet, B.T. (Lab)	10,371	33.2%	+3.7%	9,173	29.5%	(Lab)
Goodhart, W.H. (SDP/All)	5,379	17.2%	-4.9%	6,873	22.1%	(SDP/All)
Shorter, R.E. (Grn)	528	1.7%	-0.4%	649	2.1%	(Eco)
Carrick, Miss L. (Humanist)	65	0.2%		86	0.3%	(Ind)
Hughes, Mrs M. (PIP)	30	0.1%				
C to Lab swing 1.1%	31,191	C maj	4,447 14.3%	31,055	C maj	5,101 16.4%

Sir Brandon Rhys Williams was elected for this seat in Feb 1974; MP for Kensington South, 1968-74; contested Pontypridd, 1959, and Ebbw Vale, 1960 and 1964. Mbr, European Parliament, 1973-84. Mbr, Commons Select Cmte on Social Services, 1979-83. Industrial consultant. B Nov 14 1927; ed Eton. Vice-pres, British branch, European League for Economic Cooperation; asst director (appeals) Spastics Society, 1962-63. Consultant, Management Selection Ltd, 1963-71; formerly with ICI Ltd. Former vice-chmn, Cons back-bench health and social security and finance cmtes.
Mr Benjamin Bousquet, race relations officer, contested the seat 1983. B Nov 18 1938; ed Fircroft Coll, Birmingham. Vice-chmn, Black British Standing Cmte Against Apartheid in Sport. Mbr, Kensington and Chelsea BC, 1978- ; Black Londoners Action Cmte; Kensington Families Assn. Nalgo.
Mr William Goodhart, barrister, contested Kensington 1983. Helped produce the original SDP constitution. B Jan 18 1933; ed Eton, Cambridge; Harvard Law Sch. Husband of Mrs Celia Goodhart, SDP/All candidate at Kettering; brother of Sir Philip Goodhart, Cons MP for Beckenham.

Sir Brandon Rhys Williams

KENT MID — No change

Electorate %Turnout	72,456	71.9%	**1987**	66,510	71.4%	**1983**
*Rowe, A.J.B. (C)	28,719	55.1%	+1.7%	25,400	53.5%	(C)
Colley, G.D. (L/All)	13,951	26.8%	-0.3%	12,857	27.1%	(L/All)
Hazelgrove, J.A. (Lab)	9,420	18.1%	-0.7%	8,928	18.8%	(Lab)
				324	0.7%	(Other)
L/All to C swing 1.0%	52,090	C maj	14,768 28.4%	47,509	C maj	12,543 26.4%

Mr Andrew Rowe, founder and director of Cons Small Business Bureau, was elected in 1983. Mbr, Select Cmte on Employment 1983- ; jt sec, Cons back-bench employment cmte, 1983-86; vice-chmn, Cons back-bench environment cmte. Chmn, parly panel on personal social services; sec, all-pty franchising gp. B Sep 11 1935; ed Eton and Merton Coll, Oxford. Director of Community Affairs at Cons Central Office, 1975-79. Editor, *Small Business*, 1979- . Asst master, Eton Coll, 1959-62; Principal, Scottish Office, 1962-67; lectr, Edinburgh Univ, 1967-74; consultant to British Franchise Assocn; mbr, Swann Cmte, 1979-84; trustee, Community Service Volunteers; cl mbr, Save the Children Fund. Director, Milgate Publishing Ltd; adviser to Chevron Petroleum (UK) Ltd. Self-employed consultant and journalist, 1979-83. IoJ.
Mr Graham Colley is a solicitor with a family practice in Lambeth. Former Maidstone Lib fund raising officer. B Jun 19 1953; ed Nottingham HS; Univ Coll of Wales, Aberystwyth; Coll of Europe, Bruges; Coll of Law, Chester.
Mr Jack Hazelgrove, teacher. Mbr, Maidstone BC, 1984- (sec, Lab p). B Jul 4 1936; ed Brighton Hove and Sussex GS; Keble Coll, Oxford; City of London Poly. NUT.

Mr Andrew Rowe

KETTERING — No change

Electorate %Turnout	65,965	78.8%	**1987**	62,819	76.4%	**1983**
*Freeman, R.N. (C)	26,532	51.1%	+2.7%	23,223	48.4%	(C)
Goodhart, Mrs C.M. (SDP/All)	15,205	29.3%	-1.2%	14,637	30.5%	(SDP/All)
Minto, A.M. (Lab)	10,229	19.7%	-1.4%	10,119	21.1%	(Lab)
SDP/All to C swing 2.0%	51,966	C maj	11,327 21.8%	47,979	C maj	8,586 17.9%

Mr Roger Freeman was appointed Under Secretary of State for the Armed Forces in 1986. Elected in 1983; fought Don Valley, 1979. Chartered accountant. Executive director, Lehman Brothers International (UK) Ltd, 1972-86, and former director of other companies. B May 27 1942; ed Whitgift Sch; Balliol Coll, Oxford (Pres, Univ Cons Assocn, 1964). Former mbr, Select Cmte on Treasury and Civil Service. Former treas and cl member, Bow Group, and managing director, Bow Publications, 1968-69. Lecturer and conference chmn, Inst of Chartered Accountants. Mbr, Inst of Fiscal Studies.
Mrs Celia Goodhart, housewife, contested Kettering 1983; Northamptonshire in 1984 Euro election. Mbr, SDP Nat Cmte and Policy Cmte. B Jul 25 1939; ed St Michael's, Limpsfield, Surrey; St Hilda's Coll, Oxford. Former civil servant at MAFF and Treasury. Trustee, CPRE. Vice-pres, Women's Nat Cancer Control Campaign. Wife of Mr William Goodhart, SDP/All candidate at Kensington.
Mr Ashley Minto, social worker, contested Worthing 1983. Mbr, Southampton City Cl, 1979-82. B Jul 10 1954; ed Taunton's Sch, Southampton; Lancaster Poly; Southampton Univ. Nupe.

Mr Roger Freeman

KILMARNOCK AND LOUDOUN · No change

Electorate %Turnout	62,648	78.0%	**1987**	61,394	75.6%	**1983**
*McKelvey, W. (Lab)	23,713	48.5%	+4.9%	20,250	43.6%	(Lab)
Bates, Mrs A.K. (C)	9,586	19.6%	-5.1%	11,450	24.7%	(C)
Leslie, G. (SNP)	8,881	18.2%	+9.2%	10,545	22.7%	(SDP/All)
Kerr, P. (SDP/All)	6,698	13.7%	-9.0%	4,165	9.0%	(SNP)
C to Lab swing 5.0%	48,878	Lab maj 14,127 28.9%		46,410	Lab maj 8,800 19.0%	

Mr **William McKelvey** chaired the Scottish group of Labour MPs in the 1985-86 session; former executive mbr of gp. Served on Select Cmte on Scottish Affairs until 1986. Elected for this seat 1983; MP for Kilmarnock, 1979-83. Former full-time Lab Party and union official; chmn, Labour Action for Peace; mbr, Dundee DC. B Jul 1934; ed Morgan Acad; Dundee Coll of Technology. Sponsored by AUEW engineering section.

Mrs **Aileen Bates**, nurse teacher, is a steward of the Royal Coll of Nursing and mbr, CTU. B Apr 24 1947; ed Thurso HS; Glasgow Univ; Jordanhill Coll of Ed.

Mr **George Leslie**, veterinary surgeon. Exec vice-chmn (policy) of SNP, 1984- ; held the office, 1966-70. Fought Glasgow, Hillhead, 1983 and 1982 by-election; Glasgow, Pollok, 1970 and 1967 by-election; Glasgow, Craigton, 1966. Mbr, Strathclyde Reg Cl, 1976-78; Glasgow City Cl, 1968-71. B Nov 21 1936; ed Hillhead HS; Glasgow Univ.

Mr **Peter Kerr**, lecturer at Kilmarnock Coll, former labourer and engineering machinist. B Oct 10 1942; ed Kilmarnock GS and Acad; Glasgow Coll of Tech; Strathclyde Univ; Jordanhill Coll of Ed. Mbr, Lib Pty, 1978-85; joined SDP, 1985. EIS.

Mr William McKelvey

KINCARDINE AND DEESIDE · No change

Electorate %Turnout	63,587	75.2%	**1987**	59,552	71.5%	**1983**
*Buchanan-Smith, A.L. (C)	19,438	40.6%	-7.0%	20,293	47.7%	(C)
Stephen, N.R. (L/All)	17,375	36.3%	+7.0%	12,497	29.4%	(L/All)
Thomaneck, J.K. (Lab)	7,624	15.9%	+0.7%	6,472	15.2%	(Lab)
Duncan, Mrs F.E. (SNP)	3,082	6.4%	-1.3%	3,297	7.7%	(SNP)
Perica, Ms L.M. (Grn)	299	0.6%				
C to L/All swing 7.0%	47,818	C maj 2,063 4.3%		42,559	C maj 7,796 18.3%	

Mr **Alick Buchanan-Smith,** Minister of State for Energy, 1983-87; Minister of State for Agriculture, Fisheries and Food, 1979-83; Under Secretary of State, Scottish Office, 1970-74. Former Opposition spokesman on Scottish affairs, and mbr of shadow Cabinet from which he resigned in 1977, over devolution issue. Elected for this seat in 1983; MP for Angus North and Mearns, 1964-83; contested West Fife, 1959. Farmer. B Apr 8 1932; ed Edinburgh Acad, Glenalmond; Pembroke Coll, Cambridge; Edinburgh Univ.

Mr **Nicol Stephen**, solicitor, was election agent for this seat 1983. Mbr, Grampian Reg Cl, 1982- . B Mar 23 1960; ed Robert Gordon's Coll, Aberdeen; Aberdeen and Edinburgh Univs.

Mr **Jurgen Thomaneck**, lecturer and head of German dept, Aberdeen Univ. Mbr, Grampain Reg Cl; President, Aberdeen Trades Cl. B Jun 12 1941; ed Altes Gymnasium Flensburg Sch; Kiel, Tubingen and Aberdeen Univs. AUT.

Mrs **Frances Duncan** is a mbr of Tayside Reg Cl. B May 19 1942; ed Gordon's Sch, Huntly, Aberdeenshire.

Ms **Louise Perica** runs own company, Water Tiger Ltd, developing water purification techniques; former materials analyst for British N Sea Oil Corpn. Aged 32; ed Aberdeen Univ.

Mr Alick
Buchanan-Smith

KINGSTON UPON THAMES · No change

Electorate %Turnout	54,839	78.5%	**1987**	56,794	71.9%	**1983**
*Lamont, N.S.H. (C)	24,198	56.2%	+2.1%	22,094	54.1%	(C)
Hayes, R.M. (L/All)	13,012	30.2%	-2.2%	13,222	32.4%	(L/All)
Markless, R. (Lab)	5,676	13.2%	+1.0%	4,977	12.2%	(Lab)
Baker, J. (CPWSML)	175	0.4%		290	0.7%	(Eco)
				259	0.6%	(Other)
L/All to C swing 2.1%	43,061	C maj 11,186 26.0%		40,842	C maj 8,872 21.7%	

Mr **Norman Lamont** was appointed Financial Secretary to the Treasury in 1986; Minister of State for Defence Procurement, 1985-86; Minister of State for Industry, 1981-85; Under Secretary of State for Energy, 1979-81. An Opposition spokesman on industry, 1976-79, and on consumer affairs and prices, 1975-76. Merchant banker, N M Rothschild and Sons, 1968-79. Returned at 1972 by-election; contested Hull East, 1970. Sec, Cons back-bench health and social security cmte, 1972-74. B May 8 1942; ed Loretto Sch; Fitzwilliam Coll, Cambridge (Pres of Union), 1964). Chmn, Coningsby Club, 1970-71; Bow Group, 1971-72. Jt sec, Cons back-bench finance cmte, 1976.

Mr **Roger Hayes**, training consultant, fought this seat in 1983. Leader, Alliance gp, Kingston upon Thames BC, to which he was elected in 1982. Mbr, Medina BC, Isle of Wight, 1977-81. B Jun 23 1953; ed Faraday Comprehensive, East Acton; Isleworth Poly; Norwood Hall Inst of Horticulture; SW London Coll. Runs own training consultancy - R H Associates Training and Development Services. Chmn, Liberal Assembly cmte, 1985-86.

Mr **Robert Markless,** research administrator. B Feb 21 1950; ed Christ's Coll, Finchley; Leeds Univ. Apex.

Mr Norman Lamont

KINGSWOOD — No change

Electorate %Turnout	73,089	80.2%	**1987**	72,159	77.5%	**1983**
*Hayward, R.A. (C)	26,300	44.9%	+4.5%	22,573	40.4%	(C)
Berry, R.L. (Lab)	21,907	37.4%	+0.3%	20,776	37.1%	(Lab)
Whittle, Mrs P. (SDP/All)	10,382	17.7%	-4.8%	12,591	22.5%	(SDP/All)
Lab to C swing 2.1%	58,589	C maj 4,393 7.5%		55,940	C maj 1,797 3.2%	

Mr Robert Hayward

Mr Robert Hayward was elected in 1983; fought Carmarthen, Oct 1974. PPS to Minister for Corporate and Consumer Affairs, DTI, 1985- , and PPS to Minister of State for Industry, 1986- . Mbr Select Cmte on Energy, 1983-85. Personnel manager, Esso Petroleum, 1971-75; Coca Cola Bottlers, 1975-79; GEC Large Machines, 1979-82. B Mar 11 1949; ed Abingdon Sch; Maidenhead GS; Univ of Rhodesia. Nat vice-chmn, YCs, 1976-77; mbr, Coventry City Cl, 1976-78.

Mr Roger Berry, economics lecturer at Bristol Univ since 1978, contested Weston-super-Mare 1983 and Bristol in 1984 Euro election. Mbr, Avon CC, 1981- (dep ldr, Lab gp, 1985). B Jul 4 1948; ed Bristol and Sussex Univs. Mbr, IBA local advisory cmte, Bristol; Bristol Co-op Finance Co Ltd. AUT.

Mrs Pamela Whittle, education research assistant working on a survey of British dialect grammar. Sec, Reading East SDP, 1985-86. Mbr, West Berkshire area pty cmte, 1985-86. B Dec 30 1948; ed Monks Park Comprehensive, Bristol; Coll of Sarum St Michael, Salisbury; Open Univ.

KIRKCALDY — No change

Electorate %Turnout	53,439	76.5%	**1987**	53,078	71.9%	**1983**
Moonie, Dr L.G. (Lab)	20,281	49.6%	+9.3%	15,380	40.3%	(Lab)
Mitchell, I.G. (C)	8,711	21.3%	-5.0%	10,049	26.3%	(C)
Stewart, D. (SDP/All)	7,118	17.4%	-6.9%	9,274	24.3%	(SDP/All)
Mullin, W.A.R. (SNP)	4,794	11.7%	+2.7%	3,452	9.0%	(SNP)
C to Lab swing 7.2%	40,904	Lab maj 11,570 28.3%		38,155	Lab maj 5,331 14.0%	

Dr Lewis Moonie

Dr Lewis Moonie, community medicine specialist with Fife Health Bd. Mbr, Fife Regional Cl 1982-86 (vice-chmn, finance); bd member of local Co-operative Society. B Feb 25 1947; ed Grove Acad, Dundee; St Andrews and Edinburgh Univs. ASTMS and TGWU. Speaks French, Dutch and German.

Mr Iain Mitchell, advocate, contested Falkirk West 1983. Has served as vice-chmn, Edinburgh West Cons Assocn and mbr, Lothians Euro constituency cl. B 1951; ed Perth Acad; Edinburgh Univ.

Mr David Stewart, company director in telecommunications; formerly with British Telecom. Mbr, Kirkcaldy TC 1973-75; Fife Reg Cl, 1974-82. B Jan 23 1944; ed Viewforth HS; Kirkcaldy Tech Col. Election agent for this seat 1983; vice-chmn, SDP area pty, 1983- ; district gp chmn, 1982-86. POEU (now NCU), 1960-82.

Mr Roger Mullin, self-employed management consultant and Open University tutor. B 1948; ed Edinburgh Univ. Chmn, Scottish self-government college; former pty spokesman on sport.

KNOWSLEY NORTH — No change

Electorate %Turnout	52,960	74.2%	**1987**	55,606	69.5%	**1983**
*Howarth, G.E. (Lab)	27,454	69.9%	+5.4%	24,949	64.5%	(Lab)
Cooper, Ms R. (L/All)	6,356	16.2%	+1.4%	7,758	20.1%	(C)
Brown, R.C.A. (C)	4,922	12.5%	-7.5%	5,715	14.8%	(SDP/All)
Hallsworth, D. (RF)	538	1.4%		246	0.6%	(WRP)
L/All to Lab swing 2.0%	39,270	Lab maj 21,098 53.7%		38,668	Lab maj 17,191 44.5%	

Mr George Howarth

Mr George Howarth was elected at the 1986 by-election. Mbr, Select Cmte on Parliamentary Commissioner for Administration, 1987- . Director, Wales Cooperative Centre Voluntary Management Cmte. Former deputy leader, Knowsley Cl. B Jun 29 1949; ed in Huyton; Kirkby CFE; Liverpool Poly. Sponsored by AEU.

Miss Rosemary Cooper, who is employed in the Buying Division of Littlewoods chain stores, fought this seat in the 1986 by-election and Liverpool, Garston, 1983. Mbr, Liverpool City Cl, 1973- . B Sep 5 1950; ed Bellerive Convent; Liverpool Univ.

Mr Roger Brown, barrister. Mbr, Bury MDC 1982-86. B 1951; ed Sir William Borlases Sch, Marlow; Leeds Univ.

KNOWSLEY SOUTH — No change

Electorate %Turnout	65,643	74.1%	**1987**	68,114	70.3%	**1983**
*Hughes, S.F. (Lab)	31,378	64.5%	+10.7%	25,727	53.8%	(Lab)
Hall, A.J. (C)	10,532	21.6%	-7.5%	13,958	29.2%	(C)
Watmough, Mrs R. (SDP/All)	6,760	13.9%	-3.2%	8,173	17.1%	(L/All)
C to Lab swing 9.1%	48,670	Lab maj 20,846 42.8%		47,858	Lab maj 11,769 24.6%	

Mr **Sean Hughes**, an Opposition whip since 1984, won the seat in 1983; contested Crosby, Feb 1974. History teacher, 1970-83, being head of history dept, Ruffwood Comprehensive Sch, Kirkby, Merseyside, 1973-83. Former mbr, Select Cmte on Education, Science and Arts. B May 8 1946; ed West Park GS and Liverpool and Manchester Univs. Former mbr, Huyton DC and Merseyside CC.
Mr **Anthony Hall** is a housing manager. Mbr, Southampton City Cl, for seven years. B Dec 23 1956; ed Stockwood HS, Luton; Luton Sixth Form Coll; Southampton Univ.
Mrs **Ruth Watmough**, part-time solicitor's clerk in St Helens. B Feb 10 1949. Stood five times for local cl.

Mr Sean Hughes

LAGAN VALLEY — No change

Electorate %Turnout	64,873	64.1%	**1987**	60,099	67.5%	**1983**
*Molyneaux, J.H. (OUP)	29,101	70.0%	+10.8%	24,017	59.2%	(OUP)
Close, S.A. (All)	5,728	13.8%	+2.5%	6,801	16.8%	(DUP)
McDonnell, B. (SDLP)	2,888	6.9%	+0.5%	4,593	11.3%	(All)
Rice, P.J. (PSF)	2,656	6.4%	+2.1%	2,603	6.4%	(SDLP)
Lowry, J.T. (WP)	1,215	2.9%	+0.9%	1,751	4.3%	(PSF)
				809	2.0%	(Other)
All to OUP swing 4.2%	41,588	OUP maj 23,373 56.2%		40,574	OUP maj 17,216 42.4%	

Mr **James Molyneaux** became leader of the Ulster Unionist Parliamentary Party in 1974 and leader of the Ulster Unionist Party in 1979; leader, UUUC, 1974-77. Elected for this seat 1983; resigned it in 1985 in protest at Anglo-Irish Agreement and re-elected at 1986 by-election; MP for South Antrim, 1970-83. UU member for South Antrim, N Ireland Assembly, 1982-86. Former partner in family firm of letterpress printers. B Aug 27 1920; ed Aldergrove Sch, co Antrim. Dep Grand Master, Orange Order. Sovereign Grand Master, Commonwealth Royal Black Institution, 1971. Mbr, Antrim CC, 1964-73. Vice-pres, UU Cl, 1974. Vice-chmn, Eastern Special Care Hospital Cmte, 1966-73.
Mr **Seamus Close**, company secretary. Alliance Pty spokesman on local govt. B Aug 17 1947. Alliance Assembly mbr South Antrim, 1982-86. Mbr, Lisburn BC, 1973- .
Mr **Pat Rice**, head of Spanish Dept, West Belfast GS. Aged 46. PSF mbr, Lisburn Cl, 1985- .
Details of 1986 by-election on Page 285.

Mr James Molyneaux

LANCASHIRE WEST — No change

Electorate %Turnout	76,094	79.7%	**1987**	73,980	74.4%	**1983**
*Hind, K.H. (C)	26,500	43.7%	-2.5%	25,458	46.3%	(C)
Pickthall, C. (Lab)	25,147	41.5%	+7.7%	18,600	33.8%	(Lab)
Jermyn, R. (SDP/All)	8,972	14.8%	-5.2%	10,983	20.0%	(SDP/All)
C to Lab swing 5.1%	60,619	C maj 1,353 2.2%		55,041	C maj 6,858 12.5%	

Mr **Kenneth Hind**, barrister, was elected in 1983. PPS to Lord Trefgarne, Minister of State for Defence Procurement, 1986- . Sec, Cons back-bench legal cmte, 1986- . B Sep 15 1949; ed Woodhouse Grove School, Bradford; Leeds Univ (Pres of Union, 1971-72) and Inns of Court Sch of Law. Mbr, court, Leeds Univ, 1972-77; Assocn of Cons Lawyers; Liverpool Univ Senate. Hon vice-pres, Merseyside Chamber of Commerce; Central and West Lancashire Chamber of Industry and Commerce; Headingley Rugby Football Club.
Mr **Colin Pickthall**, lecturer. B Sep 13 1944; ed Univs of Wales and Lancaster. NATFHE.
Mr **Robert Jermyn**, clerk with Midland Bank. Founder mbr, SDP; mbr, West Lancashire DC 1986- ; branch organiser, Warrington Libs 1976-79. Mbr, SDP general mamagement cmte; election cmte, membership sec. B Sep 14 1941; ed Culford and Winersh GS. BIFU.

Mr Kenneth Hind

LANCASTER | No change

Electorate %Turnout	57,229	79.2%	**1987**	56,040	74.7%	**1983**
*Kellett-Bowman, Mrs M.E. (C)	21,142	46.7%	-3.6%	21,050	50.3%	(C)
Gallacher, J. (Lab)	14,689	32.4%	+7.5%	10,414	24.9%	(Lab)
Brooks, Mrs K.C. (L/All)	9,003	19.9%	-4.5%	10,214	24.4%	(L/All)
Jones, P.F.F. (Grn)	473	1.0%			179	0.4%	(Ind)
C to Lab swing 5.6%	45,307	C maj 6,453 14.2%		41,857	C maj 10,636 25.4%	

Mrs Elaine Kellett-Bowman, barrister, farmer and social worker, won this seat in 1970; contested Buckingham, 1966 and 1964; Norfolk South West, 1959 and 1959 by-election; Nelson and Colne, 1955. Mbr, European Parliament, 1975-84, being MEP for Cumbria from first European direct elections in 1979. B Jul 8 1924; ed Queen Mary's Sch, Lytham; The Mount, York, and St Anne's Coll, Oxford. Alderman, Borough of Camden, 1968-74. Mbr of Lloyd's; Press Council, 1964-68.
Mr Joe Gallacher, local authority economic development adviser. B Sep 1956. ASTMS.
Mrs Claire Brooks, solicitor, fought Skipton and Ripon in 1983, 1979, twice in 1974, and 1959; Cumbria and Lancashire North in 1984 Euro elections and Yorkshire North in 1979 Euro elections. Mbr, Liberal Pty nat exec and pty cl. Vice-pres, and former pres, WLF; former pres, NLYL and ULS. B Jun 20 1931; ed Settle Girls HS; Skipton Girls HSD; Univ Coll, London. Liberal group leader, Craven DC, 1976- (chmn, policy and finance cmte and of industrial development sub-cmte, 1986); mbr, Skipton TC, 1976- (Mayor of Skipton, 1985-86). Mbr, Law Society, British Legal Assocn.

Mrs Elaine Kellett-Bowman

LANGBAURGH | No change

Electorate %Turnout	79,193	78.8%	**1987**	77,387	75.0%	**1983**
*Holt, J.R. (C)	26,047	41.7%	0.0%	24,239	41.7%	(C)
Harford, P. (Lab)	23,959	38.4%	+7.0%	18,215	31.4%	(Lab)
Ashby, R.A.J. (L/All)	12,405	19.9%	-7.0%	15,615	26.9%	(L/All)
C to Lab swing 3.5%	62,411	C maj 2,088 3.3%		58,069	C maj 6,024 10.4%	

Mr Richard Holt was a personnel executive, 1965-81, with Rolls-Royce, William Hill Organisation, E Gomme Ltd, and Bowater Furniture; personnel consultant, since 1981. Mbr, Select Cmte on Environment, 1983- . Elected in 1983; contested Brent South, Feb 1974. B Aug 2 1931; ed Wembley County GS. Former Royal Navy seaman. Mbr, Brent BC, 1963-74; Wycombe BC, 1976- ; Bucks CC, since 1981; Thames Water Authority, 1981- ; Southern Provincial Sports Cl, 1981-84. Licensed bookmaker; consultant to Nat Assocn of Bookmakers and British Furniture Manufacturers Assocn. Fellow, Inst of Personnel Managment and mbr, British Inst of Management.
Mr Paul Harford, chemical process operator. Mbr, Cleveland CC, 1977- (chmn, highways cmte); Langbaurgh BC, 1973-85. Bus driver with Nat Bus Co, 1971-78. B Jun 1946. Sponsored by TGWU.
Mr Robin Ashby, self-employed public relations and marketing consultant, contested this seat 1983. B Jun 21 1947; ed Ipswich Sch; Birmingham and Aston Univs. Mbr, Middlesbrough BC, since 1981. Dep chmn, Northern Lib Pty, 1982-83. Former mbr, Steel Industry Management Assocn.

Mr Richard Holt

LEEDS CENTRAL | No change

Electorate %Turnout	59,019	64.8%	**1987**	63,299	61.7%	**1983**
*Fatchett, D.J. (Lab)	21,270	55.6%	+7.7%	18,706	47.9%	(Lab)
Schofield, D. (C)	9,765	25.5%	+2.0%	10,484	26.9%	(L/All)
Lee, Dr Karen (SDP/All)	6,853	17.9%	-8.9%	9,192	23.6%	(C)
Innis, W. (Comm)	355	0.9%			331	0.8%	(BNP)
				314	0.8%	(Other)
C to Lab swing 2.9%	38,243	Lab maj 11,505 30.1%		39,027	Lab maj 8,222 21.1%	

Mr Derek Fatchett, an Opposition whip until Jan 1987 when appointed to the front bench as deputy campaigns co-ordinator. Elected in 1983; contested Bosworth, 1979. Lecturer in industrial relations, Leeds Univ, 1971-83; chmn, PLP education, science and the arts cmte, 1985-86. B Aug 22 1945; ed Lincoln Sch; Birmingham Univ; LSE. Research officer, LSE, 1968-70; research fellow, Univ Coll, Cardiff, 1970-71. Mbr, Wakefield MDC, 1980-84. ASTMS; chmn, ASTMS parly cmte, 1985-86.
Mr David Schofield, further education college lecturer. Mbr, Leeds City Cl. B Oct 4 1944; ed Temple Moor GS, Leeds; Leeds and Newcastle Univs. NATFHE.
Dr Karen Lee, university teacher of chemical pathology. Sec, Leeds area SDP; mbr, CSD. B Nov 2 1956; ed Roundhay HS, Leeds; John Willmott GS, Sutton Coldfield; Leeds Univ. AUT.

Mr Derek Fatchett

LEEDS EAST — No change

Electorate %Turnout	61,178	70.2%	**1987**	63,611	66.3%	**1983**
*Healey, D.W. (Lab)	20,932	48.7%	+5.0%	18,450	43.8%	(Lab)
Sheard, J.S.W. (C)	11,406	26.5%	-2.8%	12,355	29.3%	(C)
Clay, Miss M.G. (L/All)	10,630	24.7%	-1.1%	10,884	25.8%	(L/All)
				475	1.1%	(Other)
C to Lab swing 3.9%	42,968	Lab maj 9,526 22.2%		42,164	Lab maj 6,095 14.5%	

Mr Denis Healey, chief Opposition spokesman on foreign and Commonwealth affairs, 1980- ; Deputy Leader of Labour Party, 1980-83; chief spokesman on Treasury and economics affairs, 1979-80. Unsuccesfully contested leadership of party in 1980 and 1976; won Deputy Leadership against Mr Benn in 1981. Chancellor of the Exchequer, 1974-79. Chief Opposition spokesman on Treasury matters, 1972-74; chief spokesman on foreign and Commonwealth affairs, 1970-72. Secretary of State for Defence, 1964-70. Elected for this seat in 1955; MP for Leeds South East, 1952-55; contested Pudsey and Otley, 1945. B Aug 30 1917; ed Bradford GS and Balliol Coll, Oxford. Mbr, European advisory board of NTT; Lab NEC, 1970-75 and 1980-83.
Mr Stuart Sheard, manager, contested Wakefield 1979. Fellow, BIM; graduate, Inst of Marketing. Office holder and divisional treas and divisional YC chmn, Batley and Morley. B Sep 13 1936; ed Batley GS; Huddersfield and Bradford Poly.
Miss Margaret Clay is general secretary of the Assocn of Liberal Cllrs. Contested this seat 1983; Leeds South East, 1979 and twice in 1974. B Apr 13 1947; ed County GS for Girls, Lewes, and Sheffield and Leeds Univs. Mbr, Leeds City Cl, 1978-80 and 1982- ; West Yorkshire Met CC, 1981-86.

Mr Denis Healey

LEEDS NORTH EAST — No change

Electorate %Turnout	64,631	75.3%	**1987**	65,226	70.7%	**1983**
Kirkhope, T.J.R. (C)	22,196	45.6%	-2.0%	21,940	47.6%	(C)
Crystal, P.M. (SDP/All)	13,777	28.3%	+0.2%	12,945	28.1%	(SDP/All)
Glover, O.B. (Lab)	12,292	25.3%	+1.5%	10,951	23.8%	(Lab)
Nash, Ms C.D. (Grn)	416	0.9%		128	0.3%	(A Corr)
				123	0.3%	(Other)
C to SDP/All swing 1.1%	48,681	C maj 8,419 17.3%		46,087	C maj 8,995 19.5%	

Mr Timothy Kirkhope, solicitor and company director, contested Darlington 1979 and Durham, Feb 1974. Former mbr, Northumberland CC. B Apr 29 1945; ed Royal GS, Newcastle-upon-Tyne; Coll of Law, Guildford. A northern organiser and speaker on defence for "Peace through Nato". Lawyer mbr of Mental Health Act Commission for its first three years. Holder of private pilot's licence.
Mr Peter Crystal, solicitor, contested this seat 1983; Mbr, SDP home affairs cmte; exec of SDLA. B Jan 7 1948; ed Leeds GS; Oxford Univ; McGill Univ, Montreal. Chair of Leeds SDP Friends of Israel.
Mr Bryn Glover, NHS physics technician. Mbr, nat exec, ASTMS and chair of race relations advisory cmte. B Sep 24 1942.
Mrs Claire Nash, librarian. B May 5 1953; ed Horsham HS; Southampton Univ.

Mr Timothy Kirkhope

LEEDS NORTH WEST — No change

Electorate %Turnout	68,227	75.7%	**1987**	68,004	71.3%	**1983**
*Hampson, K. (C)	22,480	43.5%	-3.0%	22,579	46.6%	(C)
Peters, B. (L/All)	17,279	33.5%	+4.5%	14,042	29.0%	(SDP/All)
Thomas, Ms J. (Lab)	11,210	21.7%	-0.5%	10,757	22.2%	(Lab)
Stevens, A. (Grn)	663	1.3%	-0.1%	673	1.4%	(Eco)
				437	0.9%	(Other)
C to L/All swing 3.8%	51,632	C maj 5,201 10.1%		48,488	C maj 8,537 17.6%	

Dr Keith Hampson has been vice-chairman of Youthaid since 1979; vice-president of WEA, since 1978, and of Assocn of Business Executives, since 1979. Jt sec, Cons back-bench defence cmte, 1985- . Elected for this seat 1983; MP for Ripon, 1974-83, which he contested at 1973 by-election. PPS to Mr Tom King as Minister for Local Government, 1979-83, and Secretary of State for Environment, 1983, and to Mr Michael Heseltine as Secretary of State for Defence, 1983-84. Consultant to AUT and to G.J.W. Ltd and educational adviser to Elydon Ltd, export projects consultants. Vice-chmn, Cons education cmte, 1976-79; mbr, Education Advisory Cmte for Unesco, 1980- . Personal asst to Mr Heath in 1966 election; assisted him at Bexley, 1970. B Aug 14 1943; ed King James I GS, Bishop Auckland, and at Bristol and Harvard Univs. Lecturer in American history, Edinburgh Univ, 1968-74.
Mr Barry Peters, lecturer. Cty cllr since 1981. B 1944; ed Birmingham, Bristol and Bath Univs.
Mrs Judith Thomas, secretary to Bradford community health cl. Mbr, Leeds City Cl 1980- ; former sec, Hitchin CLP; former vice-chair, NW Leeds CLP; former national sec, Gingerbread. B Mar 29 1942; ed Guildford High Sch; Southampton Univ. ASTMS.

Dr Keith Hampson
Mr Alan Stevens, office worker. B Feb 14 1955.

LEEDS SOUTH AND MORLEY — No change

Electorate %Turnout	60,726	71.6%	**1987**	60,864	67.9%	**1983**
*Rees, M. (Lab)	21,551	49.6%	+3.6%	18,995	45.9%	(Lab)
Holdroyd, Mrs T.C. (C)	14,840	34.1%	+2.3%	13,141	31.8%	(C)
Dawson, E.J.V. (SDP/All)	7,099	16.3%	-6.0%	9,216	22.3%	(SDP/All)
C to Lab swing 0.6%	43,490	Lab maj 6,711 15.4%		41,352	Lab maj 5,854 14.2%	

Mr Merlyn Rees

Mr Merlyn Rees, member of the Shadow Cabinet 1979-1983, was Opposition industry and employment policy co-ordinator, 1982-83. Chief Opposition spokesman on energy, 1981-82; on home affairs, 1979-81. Mbr, Cmte on Privileges, 1984- ; Select Cmte on Sound Broadcasting, 1983- ; all-pty gp on TV in Commons, 1987- ; vice-chmn, British American Parly Assocn. Home Secretary, 1976-79; Secretary of State for N Ireland, 1974-76. Chief Opposition spokesman on NI, 1972-74; an Opposition spokesman on Home Office, 1970-72. Under Secretary of State, Home Office, 1968-70; Under Secretary of State for Defence for the RAF, 1966-68, and for the Army, 1965-66. Elected for this seat in 1983; MP for Leeds South, 1963-83; contested Harrow East, 1955 and 1959. B Dec 18 1920; ed Harrow Weald GS, Goldsmith's Coll and LSE. Mbr, exec cmte, UK branch CPA, 1986-87; Franks Cmte on Falklands war, 1982-83, and Franks Cmte on Official Secrets Act, 1972. NUT; GMB.
Mrs Tessa Holdroyd, partner in firm of estate agents. Mbr, Cons Yorkshire area women's general purposes cmte; former vice-chmn, Colne Valley Cons Assocn. Mbr, Bow Group and of Gingerbread. B Jan 10 1939; ed St Andrews, Bedford; Brighton Poly.
Mr Edward Dawson, asst director, Conservation Society. B 1949; ed Open Univ.

LEEDS WEST — Lab gain

Electorate %Turnout	66,344	73.3%	**1987**	67,538	69.0%	**1983**
Battle, J.D. (Lab)	21,032	43.2%	+9.2%	17,908	38.4%	(L/All)
*Meadowcroft, M.J. (L/All)	16,340	33.6%	-4.8%	15,860	34.0%	(Lab)
Allott, P.D. (C)	11,276	23.2%	-3.7%	12,515	26.8%	(C)
				334	0.7%	(Other)
L/All to Lab swing 7.0%	48,648	Lab maj 4,692 9.6%		46,617	L/All maj 2,048 4.4%	

Mr John Battle

Mr John Battle, national coordinator for Church Action on Poverty, contested Leeds North West 1983. Mbr Leeds City Cl, 1980- (chmn, housing and urban development cmte). B Apr 26 1951; ed St Michael's Coll, Kirkby Lonsdale; Leeds Univ. ASTMS.
Mr Michael Meadowcroft was chief spokesman on housing and local government in the Alliance election team. Chmn, Lib Pty by-election unit, 1985-87; Lib spokesman on health, 1983-85; chmn, Lib Pty Assembly cmte, 1977-81. Mbr, Select Cmte on MPs Interests, 1986-87. MP for this seat, 1983-87; contested it, Feb and Oct 1974. Writer and journalist. B Mar 6 1942; ed King George V Sch, Southport; Bradford Univ. Mbr, Leeds City Cl, 1968-83; West Yorkshire Met CC, 1973-76 and 1981-83. Director, Leeds Grand Theatre and Opera House Ltd, 1971-83. Gen sec, Bradford Met Cl for Voluntary Service, 1978-83; asst sec, Joseph Rowntree Social Service Trust, 1970-78; sec, Yorkshire Lib Federation, 1967-70.
Mr Philip Allott, a regional sales manager for office equipment, was Mayor of Knaresborough in 1986. B Dec 22 1959; ed King James Sch, Knaresborough.

LEICESTER EAST — Lab gain

Electorate %Turnout	66,372	78.6%	**1987**	67,071	73.2%	**1983**
Vaz, N.K.A.S. (Lab)	24,074	46.2%	+9.1%	19,117	38.9%	(C)
*Bruinvels, P.N.E. (C)	22,150	42.5%	+3.5%	18,184	37.0%	(Lab)
Ayres, Mrs A.M. (SDP/All)	5,935	11.4%	-9.7%	10,362	21.1%	(SDP/All)
				1,429	2.9%	(Other)
C to Lab swing 2.8%	52,159	Lab maj 1,924 3.7%		49,092	C maj 933 1.9%	

Mr Keith Vaz

Mr Keith Vaz, solicitor with N Leicester Law Advice Centre, previously senr solicitor, Islington BC. Contested Richmond and Barnes 1983; Surrey West in 1984 Euro election. B Nov 26 1956; ed St Joseph's Convent, Aden; Latymer HS, Hammersmith; Gonville and Caius Coll, Cambridge; Coll of Law, Lancaster Gate. Chair, London Race Action Gp, 1984- ; Socialist Legal Services Campaign; London Trainee Solicitors Gp, 1982; Cambridge Fabian Soc, 1978. Mbr, Lab NEC working pty on Positive Action, 1984-85; nat cmte, Legal Action Gp, 1985- . Pres, Overseas Cricket Club of Leicestershire.
Mr Peter Bruinvels, management and parliamentary research consultant, was MP for this seat, 1983-87. Mbr, General Synod of C of E, 1985- ; Guildford Diocesan Synod, 1979- ; Bishop's Cl, 1985- . Jt vice-chmn (1986-87) and jt sec (1985-86), Cons back-bench education cmte; jt vice-chmn, Cons urban and new town affairs cmte, 1984-87. B Mar 30 1950; ed St John's Sch, Leatherhead; London Univ; Cl of Legal Ed. Freeman, City of London.
Mrs Aileen Ayres, revenue accounts clerk for British Midland Airways and former restaurant manager. Mbr, Leicester SDP cmte; Women for Social Democracy. B Oct 22 1936; ed Littleover Cty Sch; Derby CFE; Trent Poly.

LEICESTER SOUTH · Lab gain

Electorate %Turnout	73,236	77.0%	**1987**	73,573	72.3%	**1983**
Marshall, J. (Lab)	24,901	44.2%	+3.9%	21,424	40.3%	(C)
*Spencer, D.H. (C)	23,024	40.8%	+0.6%	21,417	40.3%	(Lab)
Pritchard, R. (L/All)	7,773	13.8%	-3.9%	9,410	17.7%	(L/All)
Fewster, B. (Grn)	390	0.7%	-0.2%	495	0.9%	(Eco)
Mayat, M.M. (Ind Lab)	192	0.3%	-39.9%	280	0.5%	(BNP)
Manners, Ms R.F. (WRP)	96	0.2%		161	0.3%	(WPWS)
C to Lab swing 1.7%	56,376	Lab maj 1,877 3.3%		53,187	C maj 7 0.0%	

Mr James Marshall was an Opposition spokesman on home affairs, 1982-83. MP for Leicester South, Oct 1974-83; contested seat, Feb 1974; Harborough, 1970. An assistant Govt whip, 1977-79. B Mar 13 1941; ed Sheffield City GS and Leeds Univ. Mbr, Leeds City Cl, 1965-68; Leicester City Cl, 1971-76 (leader, 1974). Lecturer.
Mr Derek Spencer, QC, was MP for this seat, 1983-87. Recorder of Crown Court since 1979; PPS to Sir Michael Havers, Attorney General, 1986-87, and to Mr David Mellor, Minister of State, Home Office, 1986. Jt sec, Cons back-bench legal cmte, 1985-86. B Mar 31 1936; ed Clitheroe Royal GS; Keble Coll, Oxford. Mbr, Camden BC, 1978-83; dep Cons leader, 1980-82. Vice-chmn, St Pancras North Cons Assocn, 1977-78.
Prof Robert Pritchard is a Professor of Genetics. B Jan 25 1930; ed King's Coll, London; Emmanuel Sch, London. AUT.

Mr James Marshall

LEICESTER WEST · No change

Electorate %Turnout	67,829	73.4%	**1987**	67,691	68.8%	**1983**
*Janner, G.E. (Lab)	22,156	44.5%	-0.3%	20,837	44.8%	(Lab)
Cooper, J.S.W. (C)	20,955	42.1%	+1.0%	19,125	41.1%	(C)
Edgar, W. (SDP/All)	6,708	13.5%	+0.7%	5,935	12.8%	(SDP/All)
				645	1.4%	(Other)
Lab to C swing 0.6%	49,819	Lab maj 1,201 2.4%		46,542	Lab maj 1,712 3.7%	

Mr Greville Janner, QC, a barrister and writer, has served on the Select Cmte on Employment, 1970-74, and 1983- ; mbr, Select Cmte on Procedure, 1984- . Non-exec director, Ladbroke plc. Elected in 1970; contested Wimbledon, 1955. B Jul 11 1928; ed Bishop's Coll Sch, Quebec; St Paul's Sch, London; Trinity Hall, Cambridge, and Harvard Law Sch. Pres, Board of Deputies of British Jews, 1979-85; Commonwealth Jewish Cl, 1983- ; Nat Cl for Soviet Jewry, 1979-85; Jewish Museum, 1985- ; vice-pres, Assocn of Jewish Ex-Servicemen and of Association for Jewish Youth, 1970- ; mbr, world exec, World Jewish Congress, 1986- , being Euro vice-pres, 1984-86; vice-chmn, all-pty parly cmte for release of Soviet Jewry, 1971- ; jt vice-chmn, British-Israel parly gp, 1983- ; sec, Uganda gp. Founder mbr, International Cmte for Human Rights in USSR. Pres, Retired Executives' Action Clearing House, 1982- ; chmn, all-pty parly industrial safety gp, 1975- ; jt hon sec, all-pty parly war crimes group. Mbr, Soc of Lab Lawyers, Magic Circle. NUJ.
Mr James Cooper, operational accounting.manager. Mbr, Solihull Cl (vice-chmn, ed cmte), 1982-86. B Aug 22 1951; ed Solihull Sch; Christ Church, Oxford.
Mr William Edgar, teacher. B 1958; ed Leicester Univ; North Staffs Poly.

Mr Greville Janner

LEICESTERSHIRE NORTH WEST · No change

Electorate %Turnout	70,633	82.9%	**1987**	68,510	81.1%	**1983**
*Ashby, D.G. (C)	27,872	47.6%	+3.0%	24,760	44.6%	(C)
Waddington, Mrs S.A. (Lab)	20,044	34.3%	+1.7%	18,098	32.6%	(Lab)
Emmerson, D.S. (L/All)	10,034	17.1%	-4.5%	12,043	21.7%	(L/All)
Michetschlager, Miss H.T. (Grn)	570	1.0%	-0.1%	637	1.1%	(Eco)
Lab to C swing 0.7%	58,520	C maj 7,828 13.4%		55,538	C maj 6,662 12.0%	

Mr David Ashby, barrister and non-executive company director, was elected in 1983. Mbr, Select Cmte on Parliamentary Commissioner for Administration, 1983- . B May 14 1940; ed Royal GS, High Wycombe; Bristol Univ. Sec, all-pty Anglo-Italy cmte; all-pty civil liberties gp; former sec, Cons back-bench legal and sports cmtes. Mbr, Hammersmith BC, 1968-71; GLC 1977-81 (chmn, legal and parliamentary cmte, 1978-79, and of housing cmte, 1979-81); ILEA, 1977-81.
Mrs Susan Waddington, adult education field officer. Mbr, Leicestershire CC 1973- (ldr and education chair, 1982-84; now dep ldr, Lab gp). B Aug 23 1944; ed Blyth GS, Norwich; Leicester Univ. Nupe.
Dr Stuart Emmerson, a lecturer in physics, is a Fellow of the College of Preceptors and associate mbr, BIM. B Apr 28 1949; ed Ashby-de-la-Zouch Boys' GS; Sidney Sussex Coll, Cambridge; Leeds Univ. Mbr, Anti-Apartheid Movement; Electoral Reform Society.
Miss Helen Michetschlager, self-employed violin maker. B Feb 10 1959; ed Hampstead Comp Sch; Newark Sch of Violin Making.

Mr David Ashby

LEIGH — No change

Electorate %Turnout	69,155	74.1%	**1987**	68,063	72.2%	**1983**
*Cunliffe, L.F. (Lab)	30,064	58.6%	+6.8%	25,477	51.9%	(Lab)
Browne, L.B.A. (C)	13,458	26.3%	-0.6%	13,163	26.8%	(C)
Jones, S.D. (SDP/All)	7,743	15.1%	-6.2%	10,468	21.3%	(SDP/All)
C to Lab swing 3.7%	51,265	Lab maj 16,606 32.4%		49,108	Lab maj 12,314 25.1%	

Mr **Lawrence Cunliffe**, an Opposition whip and a mbr of the nat exec NUM, was elected in 1979; contested Rochdale, Oct 1972 and Feb 1974; Former mbr, Commons Services Cmte. B Mar 25, 1929; ed St Edmund's RC Sch Worsley, Manchester. Engineer with NCB, 1949-79. Mbr, Farnworth BC, 1960-74; Bolton MDC, 1974-79. Sponsored by NUM; chmn, miners' parliamentary panel.
Mr **Louis Browne**, research student and part-time lecturer in law. B Aug 9 1963; ed St Anselm's Coll; Liverpool Poly; Balliol Coll, Oxford.
Mr **Steven Jones**, an accountant. Sec, Wigan area pty. Former nat officer, Young Social Democrats. B Sep 21 1958; ed Liverpool Blue Coat Sch.

Mr Lawrence Cunliffe

LEOMINSTER — No change

Electorate %Turnout	69,977	77.5%	**1987**	66,286	77.5%	**1983**
*Temple-Morris, P. (C)	31,396	57.9%	+0.9%	29,276	57.0%	(C)
Morris, S.C. (L/All)	17,321	31.9%	-6.0%	19,490	37.9%	(L/All)
Chappell, A.C.R. (Lab)	4,444	8.2%	+4.4%	1,932	3.8%	(Lab)
Norman, Ms F.M. (Grn)	1,102	2.0%	+0.7%	668	1.3%	(Eco)
L/All to C swing 3.4%	54,263	C maj 14,075 25.9%		51,366	C maj 9,786 19.1%	

Mr **Peter Temple-Morris**, barrister, company director and consultant, was elected in Feb 1974; contested Lambeth, Norwood, 1970, and Newport, 1964 and 1966. Nat treas, UN Assocn (UK), 1987-. Mbr, exec, British Gp, IPU, 1977- (chmn, 1982-85). Mbr, Select Cmte on Agriculture, 1982-83. B Feb 12 1938; ed Malvern; St Catherine's Coll, Cambridge. Sec, Anglo-Iranian parly gp, 1974- ; chmn, Anglo-Lebanese parly gp, 1983- ; treas, Anglo-Algerian parly gp, 1983- . Mbr, Royal Inst Internat Affairs. Chmn, Afghanistan Support Cmte, 1981-82. Freeman, City of London; Liveryman, Basketmakers' Co. Director J.K. Associates (Press Relations) Ltd, GEECO International Consultants Ltd; consultant to Perren Fire Protection Ltd; adviser to J E Hanger and Co Ltd.
Mr **Stephen Morris**, technical author; partner in software company. Mbr, Leominster DC, 1982- . B Nov 14 1955; ed Hereford Cathedral Sch; Exeter and Sussex Univs.
Mr **Christopher Chappell**, unemployed agricultural worker. Mbr, Herefordshire CHC; Hereford Cl for Voluntary Service. B Sep 19 1948; ed Down House Sch, Rye; Hampshire Coll of Agriculture. TGWU.
Ms **Felicity Norman**, teacher, contested this seat 1983; Hereford and Worcester in 1984 Euro election. B Jul 27 1946; ed St Margaret's and St Helen's, Hastings. NUT.

Mr Peter Temple-Morris

LEWES — No change

Electorate %Turnout	73,181	77.0%	**1987**	67,366	74.3%	**1983**
*Rathbone, J.R. (C)	32,016	56.8%	-1.6%	29,261	58.4%	(C)
Bellotti, D.F. (L/All)	18,396	32.6%	+2.0%	15,357	30.7%	(L/All)
Taylor, R.P. (Lab)	4,973	8.8%	+0.4%	4,244	8.5%	(Lab)
Sherwood, A.G.P. (Grn)	970	1.7%	-0.7%	1,221	2.4%	(Eco)
C to L/All swing 1.8%	56,355	C maj 13,620 24.2%		50,083	C maj 13,904 27.8%	

Mr **John R (Tim) Rathbone** was elected in Feb 1974. Mbr, Select Cmte on Sound Broadcasting, 1983- ; vice-chmn, all-pty gp on TV in Commons 1987- . B Mar 17 1933; ed Eton and Christ Church, Oxford, and Harvard Business Sch. Director, Charles Barker Gp Ltd, 1968-87. Chief publicity and public relations officer, Cons Central Office, 1966-68. Cl member, Nat Cmte for Electoral Reform. Former sec, Cons back-bench media cmte. PPS to Minister for Health, 1979-82; to Minister of Consumer Affairs, 1982-83; and to Minister for the Arts and Civil Service, 1985. Founding mbr, All-Party Cmte on Drug Misuse, 1984; Cons for Fundamental Change in S Africa, 1986. FRSA.
Mr **David Bellotti**, youth and community worker, contested this seat 1983 and Eastbourne 1979. Mbr, Lewes DC, 1979- ; E Sussex CC, 1981- (chmn, ed cmte, 1986-87). B Aug 13 1943; ed Exeter Sch; YMCA Nat Coll; Brighton Poly. Nat pres, Community and Youth Workers Union, 1976-78.
Mr **Ralph Taylor**, social services manager. B Apr 15 1945; ed Prescot GS, Merseyside; Birmingham, Liverpool, and Sheffield Univs. Mbr, South Yorkshire CC, 1981-83; Lab Disarmament Liaison Cmte. Nalgo; ASTMS.

Mr John R Rathbone

LEWISHAM DEPTFORD — No change

Electorate %Turnout	58,151	64.9%	**1987**	58,663	61.2%	**1983**
Ruddock, Mrs J.M. (Lab)	18,724	49.6%	+1.2%	17,360	48.3%	(Lab)
Punyer, M.C. (C)	11,953	31.7%	+0.1%	11,328	31.5%	(C)
Braun, Ms A.M.E. (SDP/All)	6,513	17.2%	-1.5%	6,734	18.8%	(SDP/All)
Makepeace, P.K. (Grn)	568	1.5%		317	0.9%	(BNP)
				173	0.5%	(Other)
C to Lab swing 0.6%	37,758	Lab maj 6,771 17.9%		35,912	Lab maj 6,032 16.8%	

Mrs **Joan Ruddock** chaired the Campaign for Nuclear Disarmament, 1981-85; vice-chair, 1985-86. Organiser, Reading Citizens Advice Bureau, 1979- ; Manpower Services Commission special programmes officer dealing with unemployed young people, 1977-79; director, Oxford Housing Aid Centre, 1973-77; with Shelter, 1968-73. B Dec 28 1943; ed Pontypool GS for Girls; Imperial Coll, London Univ. Sponsored by TGWU.
Mr **Martyn Punyer,** company secretary for national charity. Mbr, Lewisham BC, 1982-86 and 1986- . B 1955; ed St Dunstan's Coll, Deptford.
Mrs **Anne-Marie Braun,** formerly worked on a national newspaper's consumer advice and help service. Mbr, CSD; sec, SDP housing working party; exec member, Women for Social Democracy. Former mbr, Lambeth BC. B Jun 17 1947; ed St Mary's C of E Sch, Lewisham; Christs Hospital, Hertford; Somerville Coll, Oxford.

Mrs Joan Ruddock

LEWISHAM EAST — No change

Electorate %Turnout	59,627	73.9%	**1987**	61,216	69.5%	**1983**
*Moynihan, C.B. (C)	19,873	45.1%	+4.8%	17,168	40.4%	(C)
Profitt, M.R. (Lab)	15,059	34.2%	-1.7%	15,259	35.9%	(Lab)
Stone, Mrs V.W. (SDP/All)	9,118	20.7%	-1.3%	9,351	22.0%	(SDP/All)
				764	1.8%	(Other)
Lab to C swing 3.2%	44,050	C maj 4,814 10.9%		42,542	C maj 1,909 4.5%	

Mr **Colin Moynihan** was appointed Minister for Sport with rank of Under Secretary of State for Environment in Jun 1987. Elected for this seat in 1983. Mbr, Sports Cl, 1982-85. B Sep 13 1955; ed Monmouth Sch; Univ Coll, Oxford. Political asst to Mr Francis Pym, then Foreign Sec, 1982-83. Chmn, all-pty gp on Afghanistan, 1986-87. Sec Cons back-bench foreign and Commonwealth affairs cmte, 1983-85. Vice-chmn Cons back-bench sports cmte, 1985. Oxford double blue, rowing and boxing, 1976 and 1977. Won world gold medal for lightweight rowing, 1978; Olympic silver medal for rowing, 1980; world silver medal for rowing, 1981. Steward, British Boxing Bd of Control, 1979- ; governor, Sports Aid Foundation, 1980-82; trustee, Oxford Univ Boat Club, 1980-84; vice-chmn, Sports Aid Trust, 1983- .
Mr **Russell Profitt,** principal race relations adviser in Brent and former teacher, contested City of London and Westminster South 1979; former dep ldr, Lewisham BC. B Dec 22 1947 in Guyana and came to Britain in Aug 1961; ed Barnsbury Sec Sch and Goldsmith's Coll, London (pres of student union). Mbr, Labour Race Action Gp.
Mrs **Wendy Stone,** self-employed retailing/marketing consultant, currently with the marketing dept, National Maritime Museum, Greenwich; former senior buyer, Marks and Spencer. B Sep 7 1947; ed Christ's Hospital, Hertford; Newnham Coll, Cambridge.

Mr Colin Moynihan

LEWISHAM WEST — No change

Electorate %Turnout	62,923	72.3%	**1987**	63,043	70.3%	**1983**
*Maples, J.C. (C)	20,995	46.2%	+2.2%	19,521	44.0%	(C)
Dowd, J.P. (Lab)	17,223	37.9%	-0.5%	17,015	38.4%	(Lab)
Titley, Mrs S.C. (L/All)	7,247	15.9%	-0.9%	7,470	16.8%	(L/All)
				336	0.8%	(Other)
Lab to C swing 1.3%	45,465	C maj 3,772 8.3%		44,342	C maj 2,506 5.7%	

Mr **John Maples,** lawyer and businessman, was elected in 1983. B Apr 22 1943; ed Marlborough Coll, Wiltshire; Downing Coll, Cambridge Univ; Harvard Business Sch. Business consultant to Alexander Stenhouse Group. Contested GLC by-election at Vauxhall, 1980.
Mr **Jim Dowd,** communications systems engineer, contested Beckenham 1983. Mbr, Lewisham BC, 1971- ; Dep Mayor, 1987- ; former Lab chief whip. B Mar 5 1951. Formerly in ASTMS.
Mrs **Caroline Titley,** housing manager of a housing association. B Mar 17 1958; ed St Paul's Girls' Sch, London; Newnham Coll, Cambridge. Nalgo, housing associations branch.

Mr John Maples

LEYTON — No change

Electorate %Turnout	57,662	69.6%	**1987**	57,770	65.7%	**1983**
*Cohen, H.M. (Lab)	16,536	41.2%	-2.3%	16,504	43.5%	(Lab)
Banks, S. (L/All)	11,895	29.6%	+4.7%	11,988	31.6%	(C)
Gilmartin, D.N. (C)	11,692	29.1%	-2.5%	9,448	24.9%	(L/All)
Lab to L/All swing 3.5%	40,123	Lab maj 4,641 11.6%		37,940	Lab maj 4,516 11.9%	

Mr Harry Cohen became jt vice-chairman, PLP defence cmte in 1986. Accountant and local cl employee. Elected in 1983. B Dec 10 1949; ed secondary mod sch, part-time further education. Mbr, Waltham Forest BC, 1972- ; former chmn planning cmte; sec, Lab group. Mbr, Chartered Inst of Public Finance and Accountancy; Nalgo.
Mr Simon Banks, office worker, fought Plymouth, Sutton, twice in 1974. Mbr, Waltham Forest BC, 1982- ; leader, Alliance gp, 1982-87. B Nov 20 1946; ed Welwyn Garden City GS; King's Coll, Cambridge; Bristol Univ.
Mr David Gilmartin, dentist. Mbr, South Beds DC, 1982-87; Leighton Linslade TC, 1983-87; South Beds CHC, 1982-87. B Dec 29 1956; ed Trinity Coll, Dublin. BDA.

Mr Harry Cohen

LINCOLN — No change

Electorate %Turnout	77,049	75.6%	**1987**	72,887	74.6%	**1983**
*Carlisle, K.M. (C)	27,097	46.5%	+0.1%	25,244	46.4%	(C)
Butler, N.J. (Lab)	19,614	33.7%	+6.1%	14,958	27.5%	(Lab)
Zentner, P. (SDP/All)	11,319	19.4%	-5.6%	13,631	25.1%	(SDP/All)
Kyle, T.B. (RRPRC)	232	0.4%		523	1.0%	(Ind)
C to Lab swing 3.0%	58,262	C maj 7,483 12.8%		54,356	C maj 10,286 18.9%	

Mr Kenneth Carlisle was appointed an assistant Government whip in June 1987. Barrister, mbr of Lloyd's and farmer. PPS from 1983-87 to Mr Douglas Hurd as Minister of State, Home Office, Secretary of State for N Ireland, and Home Secretary; PPS to Minister of State for Energy, 1981-83. Elected in 1979. Mbr, Select Cmte on European Legislation, 1981-82; on Trade and Industry, 1980-82. B Mar 25 1941; ed Harrow; Magdalen Coll, Oxford. Sec, Cons back-bench trade cmte, 1980-81. Former vice-chmn, Bury St Edmunds Cons Assocn; chmn, CPC cmte, 1976-79. NFU.
Mr Nicholas Butler, an economist. Treas and vice chmn, Fabian Society. Former chmn, Streatham CLP; Labour Aid and Development Cmte. Chmn, ASTMS Westminster branch 1984-85. B Nov 22 1954; educ Blackpool GS; Trinity Coll, Cambridge.
Mr Peter Zentner, management consultant and author, contested Liverpool, Riverside, 1983. Mbr, SDP environment cmte, 1986- ; CSD, 1986- ; Haringey SDP area executive, 1983-86. B Aug 13 1932; ed Manchester GS; Gonville and Caius Coll, Cambridge.

Mr Kenneth Carlisle

LINDSEY EAST — No change

Electorate %Turnout	74,027	75.2%	**1987**	69,715	73.2%	**1983**
*Tapsell, Sir Peter (C)	29,048	52.2%	-1.1%	27,151	53.2%	(C)
Sellick, J.C.L. (L/All)	20,432	36.7%	-1.8%	19,634	38.5%	(L/All)
Stevenson, K. (Lab)	6,206	11.1%	+2.9%	4,229	8.3%	(Lab)
L/All to C swing 0.4%	55,686	C maj 8,616 15.5%		51,014	C maj 7,517 14.7%	

Sir Peter Tapsell, a member of the London Stock Exchange since 1960, has been a partner in James Capel and Co (London stockbrokers) since 1960. Mbr, cl, Inst for Fiscal Studies. Elected for this seat 1983; MP for Horncastle, 1966-83; for Nottingham West, 1959-64; contested Wednesbury, 1957. A front bench spokeman on Treasury and economic affairs, 1977-78, and on foreign and Commonwealth affairs, 1976-77. B Feb 1 1930; ed Tonbridge Sch; Merton Coll, Oxford. Librarian, Oxford Union, 1953; trustee, 1985-. Personal asst to Sir Anthony Eden, Prime Minister, during 1955 election. Chmn, Coningsby Club, 1957-58; hon mbr, Brunei Investment Advisory Bd, 1976-83. Vice-pres, Tennyson Soc.
Mr John Sellick, general manager, polythene printer/converter, contested this seat 1983; Louth in 1979, twice in 1974 and 1970. B Oct 1943; ed Knossington Grange; Oakham Sch, Rutland.
Mr Ken Stevenson, miner and former steel worker. Mbr, Bolsover DC. B Sep 11 1941.

Sir Peter Tapsell

LINLITHGOW
°No change

Electorate %Turnout	59,542	77.6%	**1987**	58,111	75.2%	**1983**
*Dalyell, T. (Lab)	21,869	47.3%	+2.3%	19,694	45.1%	(Lab)
Sillars, J. (SNP)	11,496	24.9%	+6.5%	8,333	19.1%	(C)
Armstrong-Wilson, T.R. (C)	6,828	14.8%	-4.3%	8,026	18.4%	(SNP)
McDade, Ms H. (SDP/All)	5,840	12.6%	-4.4%	7,432	17.0%	(SDP/All)
Glassford, J. (Comm)	154	0.3%	-0.2%	199	0.5%	(Com)
Lab to SNP swing 2.1%	46,187	Lab maj 10,373 22.5%		43,684	Lab maj 11,361 26.0%	

Mr Tam Dalyell

Mr **Tam Dalyell** was elected to the Labour Party NEC in 1986. Elected for this seat in 1983; MP for West Lothian, 1962-83; contested Roxburgh, Selkirk and Peebles, 1959. Opposition spokesman on science, 1980-82. Teacher and author; columnist *New Scientist.* B Aug 9 1932; ed Edinburgh Acad; Eton; King's Coll, Cambridge; Moray House Teachers' Training Coll, Edinburgh. MEP, 1975-79. Mbr Campaign Gp of Lab MPs, 1985-86. Vice-chmn, PLP, 1975-76; Scottish Labour MPs, 1973-75; chmn, PLP foreign affairs group, 1979-81. Mbr, cl, Nat Trust for Scotland. Sponsored by NUR.
Mr **James Sillars** is on the SNP nat exec; exec vice-chmn for policy, 1981-83. Lab MP for South Ayrshire 1970-79; resigned Lab Pty in 1976 helped found Scottish Lab Pty. Joined SNP in 1980. Former official, Fire Brigades Union. B Oct 1937; ed Newton Park Sch, Ayr; Ayr Acad; Open Univ. Vice-chmn "Yes for Scotland" in 1979 referendum.
Mr **Robert Armstrong-Wilson**, farmer and livestock haulier. President, Barrow YC 1960. B 1926; ed St Bees Sch; Ulverston Sch; Durham Univ.
Ms **Helen McDade**, veterinary surgeon. Mbr, Scottish Cl, SDP, 1985- ; CSD, 1986- ; nat exec, Campaign for Scottish Assembly, 1986- . B Dec 15 1958; ed Thurso HS; Edinburgh Univ. RCVS.

LITTLEBOROUGH AND SADDLEWORTH
No change

Electorate %Turnout	66,074	77.4%	**1987**	64,018	74.8%	**1983**
*Dickens, G.K. (C)	22,027	43.1%	+0.2%	20,510	42.8%	(C)
Davies, C. (L/All)	15,825	30.9%	-0.1%	14,860	31.0%	(L/All)
Stonier, P. (Lab)	13,299	26.0%	+0.7%	12,106	25.3%	(Lab)
				398	0.8%	(Other)
L/All to C swing 0.2%	51,151	C maj 6,202 12.1%		47,874	C maj 5,650 11.8%	

Mr **Geoffrey Dickens**, company director, was elected in for this seat in 1983; MP for Huddersfield West, 1979-83; contested Ealing North, Oct 1974, and Middlesbrough, Feb 1974. Mbr Select Cmte on Energy, 1985- . Vice-chmn, Assocn of Cons Clubs; vice-pres, NW Cons Clubs Cl. B Aug 26 1931; ed Harrow and Acton Tech Coll. Mbr, all-pty pensioners parly gp; all-pty childrens parly gp; campaigner for child protection. Holder of Royal Humane Soc Testimonial on Vellum for having saved the lives of children at sea. Mbr, Sandridge Parish Cl, 1961-73 (chmn, 1969-70); Hertfordshire CC, 1970-74; St Albans DC, 1967-73 (chmn, 1970-71).
Mr **Christopher Davies**, public relations consultant. Former chmn, Liverpool City Cl housing cmte. B 1954; ed Cheadle Hulme Sch; Cambridge and Kent Univs.
Mr **Paul Stonier**, asst director of housing, Tameside MBC. B Jul 27 1950; ed Manchester Poly; Liverpool Univ; LSE. Nupe.

Mr Geoffrey Dickens

LIVERPOOL, BROADGREEN
No change

Electorate %Turnout	63,091	75.9%	**1987**	63,826	72.1%	**1983**
*Fields, T. (Lab)	23,262	48.6%	+7.7%	18,802	40.9%	(Lab)
Pine, R. (L/All)	17,215	35.9%	+24.7%	15,002	32.6%	(C)
Seddon, M.R.G. (C)	7,413	15.5%	-17.1%	7,021	15.3%	(Ind L)
				5,169	11.2%	(SDP/All)
Lab to L/All swing 8.5%	47,890	Lab maj 6,047 12.6%		45,994	Lab maj 3,800 8.3%	

Mr **Terence Fields,** elected in 1983, was a fireman with the Merseyside County Fire Brigade, 1957-83. B Mar 8 1937; Major Street County Sec Sch; De La Salle GS, Liverpool. Vice-chmn, Bootle constituency Lab Pty; former mbr, Lab Pty NW reg exec cmte. FBU, Mbr FBU nat exec, 1977-83.
Mr **Richard Pine**, industrial relations adviser with Plessey, fought this seat as a Lib in 1983. Mbr, Liverpool City Cl, since 1976; dep leader, Alliance gp. B Dec 2 1953; ed Stowe; Keble Coll, Oxford. GMBATU-MATSA.
Mr **Mark Seddon**, stockbroker and mbr, Stock Exchange. Mbr, Knowsley BC, 1984- . B Mar 7 1959; ed St Edward's Coll, Liverpool; Liverpool Univ. ASTMS.

Mr Terence Fields

LIVERPOOL, GARSTON — No change

Electorate %Turnout	61,280	75.7%	**1987**	64,326	71.6%	**1983**
*Loyden, E. (Lab)	24,848	53.6%	+7.0%	21,450	46.6%	(Lab)
Feather, P.B. (C)	11,071	23.9%	-14.0%	17,448	37.9%	(C)
Isaacson, R. (SDP/All)	10,370	22.4%	+6.8%	7,153	15.5%	(L/All)
Timlin, K. (WRP)	98	0.2%				
C to Lab swing 10.5%	46,387	Lab maj 13,777 29.7%		46,051	Lab maj 4,002 8.7%	

Mr Edward Loyden

Mr Edward Loyden, re-elected in 1983; MP for the constituency, Feb 1974-79. Port worker, Mersey Docks and Harbour Co, 1946-74; Merchant Navy, 1938-46. B May 3 1923; ed Friary RC elementary sch, Liverpool. Mbr, Liverpool City Cl, 1960-74 and 1980- , (dep leader, 1983-;) Liverpool DC, 1973; Merseyside Met CC, 1973; Liverpool MDC, 1980-83. Pres, Liverpool Trades Cl, 1967; Merseyside Trades Cl, 1974. Member, nat exec, TGWU, from 1968 and mbr of union from 1946; sponsored by that union. Previously in NUS.
Mr Paul Feather, hotelier with Feathers Hotels and Catering Gp, including Feathers Catering and Event Management. Treas, Cons Candidates' Assocn. B Jun 26 1951; ed King David HS, Liverpool.
Mr Richard Isaacson, barrister. Sec, Liverpool area SDP; mbr, CSD; Liverpool City Cl 1986-. B Sep 7 1950; ed Liverpool Coll; Liverpool Univ.

LIVERPOOL, MOSSLEY HILL — No change

Electorate %Turnout	60,954	75.1%	**1987**	62,789	73.4%	**1983**
*Alton, D.P.P. (L/All)	20,012	43.7%	+2.8%	18,845	40.9%	(L/All)
Devaney, J.A. (Lab)	17,786	38.8%	+12.0%	14,650	31.8%	(C)
Lightfoot, W.M. (C)	8,005	17.5%	-14.3%	12,352	26.8%	(Lab)
				212	0.5%	(Other)
L/All to Lab swing 4.6%	45,803	L/All maj 2,226 4.9%		46,059	L/All maj 4,195 9.1%	

Mr David Alton

Mr David Alton was chief Alliance spokesman on N Ireland in election team. Appointed Liberal chief whip in 1985. Teacher of handicapped children, 1972-79. Elected for this seat 1983; won Liverpool, Edge Hill, at Mar 1979 by-election; served for six days until dissolution and re-elected in general election. Contested that seat, Feb and Oct 1974. Appointed political aide to Mr David Steel in Nov 1982 and Lib spokesman on inner cities; previously spokesman on environment and race relations. Served on Select Cmte on Environment. Treas, all-pty gp for HoC reform; jt chmn, Cl for Ed in the Commonwealth. Former pres, Nat League of YLs; pres, Liverpool Old People's Hostels Assocn; trustee of charity, Crisis at Christmas. B Mar 15 1951; ed Edmund Campion Sch, Hornchurch; Christ's Coll of Ed, Liverpool. Mbr, Liverpool City Cl, 1972-80 (dep ldr and housing chmn); Merseyside CC, 1973-77. Former member, NUT.
Mr Joe Devaney, building management officer. Mbr, Liverpool City Cl, 1984- . B Jul 5 1949.
Mr Warwick Lightfoot, economist and freelance journalist. B 1957; ed King Edward VI Sch, Totnes; Oxford Univ.

LIVERPOOL, RIVERSIDE — No change

Electorate %Turnout	53,328	65.3%	**1987**	61,638	62.4%	**1983**
*Parry, R. (Lab)	25,505	73.2%	+8.3%	24,978	65.0%	(Lab)
Fitzsimmons, S. (C)	4,816	13.8%	-5.9%	7,600	19.8%	(C)
Chahal, B.S. (SDP/All)	3,912	11.2%	-2.8%	5,381	14.0%	(SDP/All)
Gardner, Ms C.A. (Comm)	601	1.7%	+1.0%	261	0.7%	(Com)
				234	0.6%	(Other)
C to Lab swing 7.1%	34,834	Lab maj 20,689 59.4%		38,454	Lab maj 17,378 45.2%	

Mr Robert Parry

Mr Robert Parry was elected for this seat in 1983; MP for Liverpool, Scotland Exchange, Feb 1974-83 and Liverpool Exchange, 1970-74. Chmn, TGWU gp of Lab MPs, 1986-87; mbr, exec cmte, PLP trade union cmte. B Jan 8 1933; ed Bishop Goss RC School, Liverpool. Delegate to Cl of Europe, 1984- , and WEU, 1983- . Mbr, Standing Orders Cmte. Chmn, Merseyside group of Lab MPs, 1975-. Mber, Lverpool City Cl, 1963-74. President, Assocn for Democracy in Hong Kong, 1980- ; Kids in Need and Distress (KIND), 1981- . Vice-chmn, Liberation, 1981- ; Lab Action for Peace, 1983- . Mbr, exec cmte, International Cmte for Peaceful Re-unification of Korea, 1986- ; International Cmte for Human Rights in Syria, 1985- . Co-pres, International Cmte for Human Rights in South Korea, 1986- . TGWU and sponsored by union.
Mr Stephen Fitzsimmons, licensee; former security officer. B Aug 20 1956; ed Hillfoot Hey HS; Millbank Coll of Commerce. Chmn, Merseyside YCs, 1983-85.
Mr Baldev Chahal, unemployed telephonist, contested Ealing Southall Feb 1974 as an independent Sikh "Anti-Helmet" candidate. Former convenor, Turban Action Cmte UK. B Feb 6 1937; ed Punjab Univ; Univ of London.
Ms Katy Gardner, GP; on editorial bd, *Marxism Today*. B Feb 14 1950; ed Cambridge Univ; London Hosp. ASTMS.

LIVERPOOL, WALTON   No change

Electorate %Turnout	73,118	73.6%	**1987**	73,532	69.6%	**1983**
*Heffer, E.S. (Lab)	34,661	64.4%	+11.7%	26,980	52.7%	(Lab)
Clark, P.R. (L/All)	11,408	21.2%	-0.2%	12,865	25.1%	(C)
Mays, I.A. (C)	7,738	14.4%	-10.8%	10,970	21.4%	(L/All)
				343	0.7%	(Other)
L/All to Lab swing 6.0%	53,807	Lab maj 23,253 43.2%		51,158	Lab maj 14,115 27.6%	

Mr Eric Heffer

Mr Eric Heffer was chmn of the Labour Party, 1983-84; vice-chairman, 1982-83, and on its NEC from 1975-86. Senior Opposition spokesman on housing and construction, 1983-84, and on European and Community Affairs, 1981-83, while in shadow Cabinet 1981-84. Minister of State for Industry, 1974-75. In Opposition front bench team on Industrial Relations Bill, 1970-71; Opposition spokesman on employment, 1971-73. Elected in 1964. Carpenter-joiner; journalist. Was senior shop steward in shipyard and on large construction sites on Merseyside. B Jan 12 1922; elementary education. Mbr, and sponsored by, UCATT. Vice-chmn, League Against Cruel Sports. Mbr, Liverpool City Cl, 1960-66. Pres, Liverpool Trades Cl and Lab Pty, 1959-60 and 1964-65. Mbr, regional exec of Lab Pty before entering Parliament and of Lancs and Cheshire Fed of TUs.
Mr Paul Clark, partner in firm of solicitors, contested Cheadle in 1983, and Liverpool in Euro election, 1979. Mbr, Liverpool City Cl, 1976- . B May 7 1953; ed St Mary's Coll, Crosby; Liverpool Univ.
Mr Iain Mays, company director; founded computer software company in 1980. B 1954; ed John Fisher Sch, Purley; Queen Elizabeth and Imperial Colls, London.

LIVERPOOL, WEST DERBY   No change

Electorate %Turnout	60,522	73.4%	**1987**	63,088	69.5%	**1983**
*Wareing, R.N. (Lab)	29,021	65.3%	+10.8%	23,905	54.5%	(Lab)
Backhouse, J.E. (C)	8,525	19.2%	-8.3%	12,062	27.5%	(C)
Ferguson, M. (SDP/All)	6,897	15.5%	-2.4%	7,871	18.0%	(SDP/All)
C to Lab swing 9.6%	44,443	Lab maj 20,496 46.1%		43,838	Lab maj 11,843 27.0%	

Mr Robert Wareing

Mr Robert Wareing was a lecturer at various colleges, 1957-83, including the Central Liverpool College of Further Education, 1972-83. Elected for this seat 1983; contested Berwick-upon-Tweed, 1970, and Liverpool, Edge Hill, 1979 by-election and general election. Vice-chmn, British/Yugoslav parly gp, 1985- ; mbr, all-pty disablement gp. B Aug 20 1930; ed Ranworth Square Sch, Liverpool; Alsop HS, Liverpool; Bolton Coll of Ed; London Univ (external student). Mbr, Merseyside CC, 1981-86 (chief whip of Lab group, 1981-83, and chmn, economic development cmte, 1981-83). Vice-pres, AMA, 1984- . Chmn, Merseyside Economic Development Co Ltd, 1981-86. Pres, Liverpool District Lab Party, 1974-81. NATFHE and ASTMS. Mbr, parly cmte of ASTMS
Mr John Backhouse, founder and managing director, financial planning company. B 1955; ed Merchant Taylor's Sch; Kirkby Coll; Liverpool Poly.
Mr Malcolm Ferguson, mechanical engineer; planning engineer with CEGB. Mbr, Knaresborough East DC, 1986- ; Knaresborough TC 1986- . Chmn, Harrogate, Skipton and Ripon SDP area pty; mbr, CSD; SDP energy working pty. B Sep 14 1938; ed GS; Liverpool Univ. Mbr, Electrical Power Engineers' Assocn.

LIVINGSTON   No change

Electorate %Turnout	56,583	74.1%	**1987**	53,284	70.9%	**1983**
*Cook, R.F. (Lab)	19,110	45.6%	+7.8%	14,255	37.7%	(Lab)
McCreadle, R. (L/All)	8,005	19.1%	-5.5%	9,304	24.6%	(L/All)
Mayall, Dr M.N.A. (C)	7,860	18.7%	-5.4%	9,129	24.2%	(C)
MacAskill, K. (SNP)	6,969	16.6%	+3.1%	5,090	13.5%	(SNP)
L/All to Lab swing 6.7%	41,944	Lab maj 11,105 26.5%		37,778	Lab maj 4,951 13.1%	

Mr Robin Cook

Mr Robin Cook was member of the shadow Cabinet, 1983-86, being Opposition spokesman on European and Community affairs, 1983-85; campaigns coordinator, 1985-86. After defeat in shadow Cabinet elections in 1986, became a trade and industry spokesman; a spokesman on Treasury and economic affairs, 1980-83. Elected for this seat 1983; MP for Edinburgh Central, Feb 1974-83; contested Edinburgh North, 1970. Former tutor and organiser in adult education. B Feb 28 1946; ed Aberdeen GS; Royal HS, Edinburgh, and Edinburgh Univ. Mbr, Edinburgh Town Cl, 1971-74; sec, Edinburgh City Lab Pty, 1970-72. Former vice-chmn, PLP defence group. Sponsored by NUR.
Mr Robert McCreadie, law lecturer, contested Edinburgh South for Lab in 1983; joined Lib Pty from Lab Pty in 1985. B Aug 17 1948; ed Madras Coll, St Andrews; Edinburgh Univ; Christ's Coll, Cambridge. AUT.
Dr Mark Mayall, doctor of medicine and registrar in psychiatry, was research asst to Mr William Walker MP, 1984-87. B Dec 15 1958; ed St George's Coll, Weybridge; King's Coll, London; Westminster Hosp.
Mr Kenneth MacAskill, solicitor, contested this seat 1983. Mbr, SNP nat exec. B 1958; ed Linlithgow Acad; Edinburgh Univ. Apex.

159

LLANELLI — No change

Electorate %Turnout	63,845	78.1%	1987	63,826	75.4%	1983
*Davies, D.J.D. (Lab)	29,506	59.2%	+10.9%	23,207	48.2%	(Lab)
Circus, P.J. (C)	8,571	17.2%	-2.8%	9,601	19.9%	(C)
Shrewsbury, M.J. (L/All)	6,714	13.5%	-5.4%	9,076	18.9%	(L/All)
Price, A. (Pl C)	5,088	10.2%	-2.0%	5,880	12.2%	(Pl C)
				371	0.8%	(Other)
C to Lab swing 6.9%	49,879	Lab maj 20,935 42.0%		48,135	Lab maj 13,606 28.3%	

Mr Denzil Davies was elected to the shadow Cabinet in 1985; chief Opposition spokesman on defence and disarmament, 1983- ; chief spokesman on Wales, 1983; a spokesman on defence, 1982-83, on foreign and Commonwealth affairs, 1981-82, and on Treasury and economic affairs, 1979-81. Minister of State, Treasury, 1975-79. Barrister. Elected in 1970. B Oct 9 1938; ed Carmarthen GS and Pembroke Coll, Oxford. Lectured at Chicago and Leeds Univs. Mbr, Select Cmte on European Legislation, 1974-75; Select Cmte on Wealth Tax, 1974-75. Also served on PAC, Select Cmte on Corporation Tax and Jt Select Cmte on Delegated Legislation.
Mr Philip Circus, barrister and director for legal affairs, Institute of Practitioners in Advertising. Mbr, Richmond-upon-Thames BC, 1982-86. B May 8 1951; ed Westcliff HS; Ealing Coll of Higher Ed; Coll of Law; Southampton Univ.
Mr Martyn Shrewsbury, educational consultant, contested Swansea East in 1983. B Apr 7 1938; ed Burton GS; Dynevor Comprehensive; Manchester and Swansea Univs.
Mr Adrian Price teaches at his old school, the Amman Valley Comprehensive Sch. Aged 26. Attended Univ Coll, Aberystwyth.

Mr Denzil Davies

LONDONDERRY EAST — No change

Electorate %Turnout	71,031	68.7%	1987	67,365	76.3%	1983
*Ross, W. (OUP)	29,532	60.5%	+22.6%	19,469	37.9%	(OUP)
Doherty, A. (SDLP)	9,375	19.2%	+0.9%	12,207	23.8%	(DUP)
Davey, J. (PSF)	5,464	11.2%	-2.6%	9,397	18.3%	(SDLP)
McGowan, P. (All)	3,237	6.6%	+2.0%	7,073	13.8%	(PSF)
Donnelly, F. (WP)	935	1.9%	+0.3%	2,401	4.7%	(All)
Samuel, M.H. (Grn)	281	0.6%		819	1.6%	(WP)
SDLP to OUP swing 10.8%	48,824	OUP maj 20,157 41.3%		51,366	OUP maj 7,262 14.1%	

Mr William Ross, a farmer, was elected for this seat in 1983; MP for Londonderry, Feb 1974-83. Resigned seat in 1985 in protest at Anglo-Irish Agreement and was re-elected in 1986 by-election. Pty spokesman on agriculture and fisheries, and on local government. Mbr, Apprentice Boys of Derry, the Orange and Black Institutions; former sec, Mid-Londonderry Unionist Party. B Feb 4 1936; ed Dungiven Primary Sch.
Mr Arthur Doherty fought this seat 1983. Mbr, SDLP exec cmte, 1974-1980; chmn, Assocn of SDLP Cllrs.
Mr John Davey, unemployed. Aged 56. PSF mbr, Magherafelt DC, 1985- . Interned in the 1950s and early 70s.
Mr Patrick McGowan, art teacher and Alliance Pty spokesman on tourism. B Nov 2 1941; ed Dalriada Sec Sch, Ballymoney; Belfast Coll of Art; Hornsey Coll of Art, London. Member, Coleraine BC, 1981- .
Mr Malcolm Samuel, ecologist, contested this seat 1983. Pty spokesman on tropical rain forest and world federalism. Sec, Coleraine and North Antrim branch. B Sep 16 1953; ed Hendon and Wetherby; New Univ of Ulster.

Mr William Ross *Details of 1986 by-election on Page 285*

LOUGHBOROUGH — No change

Electorate %Turnout	73,660	79.2%	1987	70,668	77.7%	1983
*Dorrell, S.J. (C)	31,931	54.7%	+1.8%	29,056	52.9%	(C)
Wrigley, C.J. (Lab)	14,283	24.5%	+1.0%	12,876	23.4%	(Lab)
Fox, R.G. (SDP/All)	11,499	19.7%	-2.5%	12,189	22.2%	(SDP/All)
Gupta, R. (Grn)	656	1.1%	0.0%	591	1.1%	(Eco)
				228	0.4%	(Other)
Lab to C swing 0.4%	58,369	C maj 17,648 30.2%		54,940	C maj 16,180 29.5%	

Mr Stephen Dorrell was appointed an assistant Government whip in Jun 1987. Former company director. PPS to Mr Peter Walker, 1983-87; personal asst to Mr Walker in Feb 1974 election. Won this seat in 1979; contested Hull East, Oct 1974. B Mar 25 1952; ed Uppingham and Brasenose Coll, Oxford. Mbr, Select Cmte on Transport, 1983-85. Former jt sec, Cons back-bench finance cmte and N Ireland cmte; sec, Cons back-bench trade cmte, 1980-81. Mbr, bd, Christian Aid, 1985-.
Mr Christopher Wrigley, university teacher. Contested Blaby 1983. Leader, Lab Gp, Leicestershire CC; former Lab Gp deputy leader, Charnwood Borough Cl. Exec mbr, Loughborough Trades Council. B Aug 18 1947; educ Kingston GS; East Anglia and London Univs. AUT.
Mr Roger Fox, senior lecturer in economics, contested Cirencester and Tewkesbury for Lab, Feb 1974; and Staffordshire East for SDP in 1984 Euro election. Mbr (Lab)Kensington and Chelsea BC, 1971-78. B Feb 22 1939; ed King Edward VI GS, Birmingham; Ruskin Coll, Oxford; Warwick Univ. Mbr, National Heart and Chest Hospitals Special Health Authority, 1976- .
Mr Rama Gupta, yoga teacher. B Sep 1 1934; ed Punjab and Delhi Univs.

Mr Stephen Dorrell

LUDLOW — No change

Electorate %Turnout	66,187	77.1%	**1987**	63,256	74.6%	**1983**
Gill, C.J.F. (C)	27,499	53.9%	-1.8%	26,278	55.7%	(C)
Phillips, D. (L/All)	15,800	31.0%	-0.8%	14,975	31.7%	(SDP/All)
Harrison, K. (Lab)	7,724	15.1%	+2.5%	5,949	12.6%	(Lab)
C to L/All swing 0.5%	51,023	C maj 11,699 22.9%		47,202	C maj 11,303 23.9%	

Mr Christopher Gill is chmn of family business, F A Gill Ltd, engaged in meat processing and wholesaling; mbr, nat cl, Bacon and Meat Manufacturers' Assocn; cmte mbr, Fed of Fresh Meat Wholesalers. Former pres, Midlands West Euro Cons Cl; mbr, Wolverhampton BC, 1965-72; cl, Wolverhampton Chamber of Commerce, 1984-87. Runs livestock farm near Bridgnorth; cmte member, Bridgnorth NFU; mbr, CLA; life mbr, Rare Breeds Survival Trust, South Devon Herd Book Soc. B 1936; ed Shrewsbury Sch.
Mr David Phillips, director of Sales Management Ltd, contested Worcestershire South, 1983 and 1979, and Hereford and Worcester in 1984 Euro election. Chmn, W Midlands Lib Pty; convenor, W Midlands candidate approval panel; mbr, Lib Pty Cl. Lecturer for Electoral Reform Soc. B Feb 17 1933; ed Waverley GS.
Mr Keith Harrison is unemployed. B Feb 9 1943; ed Bedford Sch. Mbr, Shropshire CC (chmn, public transport subcmte and rights of way subcmte; vice-chmn, planning and transport cmte and planning subcmte).

Mr Christopher Gill

LUTON NORTH — No change

Electorate %Turnout	74,235	77.6%	**1987**	69,805	77.4%	**1983**
*Carlisle, J.R. (C)	30,997	53.8%	+5.5%	26,115	48.3%	(C)
Wright, M. (Lab)	15,424	26.8%	+0.6%	14,134	26.2%	(Lab)
Stephen, J.D. (SDP/All)	11,166	19.4%	-6.1%	13,769	25.5%	(SDP/All)
Lab to C swing 2.4%	57,587	C maj 15,573 27.0%		54,018	C maj 11,981 22.2%	

Mr John Carlisle was elected for this seat in 1983; MP for Luton West, 1979-83. Mbr, Select Cmte on Agriculture, 1985- . Consultant to Louis Dreyfus plc, since 1982; former director, Grafin Agriculture Ltd, Norfolk and York. Mbr, London Corn Exchange, 1970-79. B Aug 28 1942; ed Bedford Sch; St Lawrence Coll, Ramsgate; and London Univ. Vice-pres, Fed of Cons Students, 1986- . Chmn, Cons back-bench sport cmte, 1981-82, 1983-84, 1985- ; mbr, international exec cmte, Freedom in Sport. Sec, British-South Africa parly group, 1983- ; sec, Cons Africa Cmte, 1981-82; treas, British-Gibraltar group, 1981-82. Chmn, Mid-Bedfordshire Cons Assocn, 1974-76.
Mr Michael Wright, heavy goods vehicle driver/dustman. B May 14 1949; ed Luton Tech GS. Mbr, Bedfordshire CC 1981- (Dep ldr, Lab gp, and spokesman on transport, planning, environment). Senr shop steward., TGWU.
Mr David Stephen, executive, contested Luton North 1983. Was special adviser to Dr David Owen at Foreign and Commonwealth Office, 1977-79; director, Runnymede Trust, 1975-77; consultant to World Univ Service, Amnesty International, 1979-84; director, UK Immigrants Advisory Service; head of external relations, Commonwealth Development Corporation, 1984- ; mbr, bd of trustees, Action Aid. B Apr 3 1942; ed Luton GS; King's Coll, Cambridge; Essex Univ. Mbr, SDP defence and disarmament working pty.

Mr John Carlisle

LUTON SOUTH — No change

Electorate %Turnout	71,231	75.2%	**1987**	71,015	75.8%	**1983**
*Bright, G.F.J. (C)	24,762	46.2%	+4.4%	22,531	41.9%	(C)
McKenzie, W.D. (Lab)	19,647	36.7%	+3.4%	17,910	33.3%	(Lab)
Chapman, P. (L/All)	9,146	17.1%	-7.8%	13,395	24.9%	(L/All)
Lab to C swing 0.5%	53,555	C maj 5,115 9.6%		53,836	C maj 4,621 8.6%	

Mr Graham Bright, chairman and managing director of Dietary Foods Ltd since 1970, was elected in 1983; MP for Luton East, 1979-83; contested Dartford, Oct 1974; Thurrock, 1970 and Feb 1974. Chmn, Cumberland Packing Corp Ltd, Cumberland Foods Ltd and Mother Nature Ltd. Vice-chmn, bd, International Sweeteners Assocn. B Apr 2 1942; ed Hassenbrook County Sch and Thurrock Tech Coll. Mbr, Thurrock BC, 1966-79; Essex CC, 1967-70. Chmn, Eastern Area CPC, 1977-80; mbr, Nat CPC, 1980- ; patron, Eastern Area YCs, 1983. PPS to Home Office ministers, 1983- . Introduced Video Recordings Act, 1983. Mbr, Commons services cmte, 1982-84. Jt sec (1984-85) and former vice-chmn, Cons back-bench aviation cmte; jt sec, parly aviation gp, 1984- ; chmn, Cons back-bench cmte on smaller businesses, 1983-84; vice-chmn, Smaller Businesses Bureau, 1980- ; Cons food and drink sub-cmte, 1983-84.
Mr William McKenzie, chartered accountant. B Jul 24 1946; ed Reading Sch; Bristol Univ. Adviser to Mr Roy Hattersley, shadow Chancellor, on taxation; former partner in Price Waterhouse. Mbr, Luton BC, 1976- . (dep ldr, Lab gp). ASTMS.
Mr Peter Chapman, salesman. B 1959; ed Denbigh HS, Luton; Luton CFE. Mbr, Luton BC.

Mr Graham Bright

MACCLESFIELD — No change

Electorate %Turnout	76,093	77.4%	1987	73,082	75.0%	1983
*Winterton, N.R. (C)	33,208	56.4%	-3.0%	32,538	59.4%	(C)
Haldane, A.B. (L/All)	14,116	24.0%	+2.3%	11,859	21.6%	(L/All)
Pinder, Ms C. (Lab)	11,563	19.6%	+1.5%	9,923	18.1%	(Lab)
				488	0.9%	(Other)
C to L/All swing 2.7%	58,887	C maj 19,092 32.4%		54,808	C maj 20,679 37.7%	

Mr Nicholas Winterton

Mr **Nicholas Winterton** has been a mbr of the Select Cmte on Social Services since 1979, of the Select Cmte on Standing Orders since 1981, and of the Chairmen's Panel. Former company sales and general manager. Parliamentary adviser to Construction Plant-hire Assocn, Baird Textile Holdings Ltd, and BSM (Holdings) Ltd. Elected in 1971 by-election; contested Newcastle-under-Lyme, 1969 by-election and 1970. B Mar 31 1938; ed Bilton Grange Prep Sch and Rugby. Chmn, all-pty group for paper and board industry and all-pty gp for cotton and allied textiles. Vice-chmn, British-South Africa, British-Danish, and British-Swedish parly gps; all-pty Anglo-Austrian gp, Falkland Islands gp and British-Indonesia gp. Treas, all-pty British-Bahamas gp. Vice-chmn, Cons back-bench sports and recreation cmte, 1979-84. Freeman, City of London; member, Worshipful Company of Weavers; Warwickshire CC, 1967-72. His wife Ann is Conservative MP for Congleton.

Mr **Andrew Haldane**, senior lecturer in marketing at a polytechnic. B 1947; ed Worsley-Wardley GS, Swinton; Bradford and Salford Univs.

Ms **Caroline Pinder**, manager of information technology centre. B Dec 20 1949; ed Stockport Coll of Tech; Open Univ. Has worked as DHSS exec officer, welfare officer at Manchester Poly, gen sec, cl for voluntary service, Harlow, and freelance social researcher.

MAIDSTONE — No change

Electorate %Turnout	72,987	76.0%	1987	70,357	73.8%	1983
Widdecombe, Miss A.N. (C)	29,100	52.4%	+1.5%	26,420	50.9%	(C)
Sutton-Mattocks, C.J. (L/All)	18,736	33.8%	-3.2%	19,194	37.0%	(L/All)
Brooks, K.P. (Lab)	6,935	12.5%	+0.4%	6,280	12.1%	(Lab)
Kemp, Ms P.A. (Grn)	717	1.3%				
L/All to C swing 2.4%	55,488	C maj 10,364 18.7%		51,894	C maj 7,226 13.9%	

Miss Ann Widdecombe

Miss **Ann Widdecombe**, senior administrator at London University, contested Plymouth, Devonport, in 1983 and Burnley, 1979. Jt sec/research asst to Cons parly study gp on disablement benefits. B Oct 4 1947; ed Bath Convent; Birmingham Univ; Lady Margaret Hall, Oxford. Vice-chmn, Nat Assocn of Cons Graduates, 1976-78. Member, Runnymede DC, 1976-78; Cons nat advisory cmte on local govt, 1976-77.

Mr **Christopher Sutton-Mattocks,** barrister. B 1951; ed Winchester; Oxford Univ. Assisted party at Richmond 1974 and Fulham, 1979 and 1983.

Mr **Kevin Brooks,** unemployed. Mbr, Maidstone BC, 1984- (dep ldr, Lab gp, 1986-). B Sep 18 1963; ed Maidstone GS; LSE. Governor, Maidstone Girls GS.

Ms **Penny Kemp**, physical training teacher. Governor of Maidstone Girls GS. B May 10 1949; ed privately. Mbr, Headcorn PC.

MAKERFIELD — No change

Electorate %Turnout	70,819	75.8%	1987	69,176	73.7%	1983
McCartney, I. (Lab)	30,190	56.3%	+7.0%	25,114	49.3%	(Lab)
Robertson, L.A. (C)	14,632	27.3%	-0.7%	14,238	27.9%	(C)
Hewer, B. (L/All)	8,838	16.5%	-6.3%	11,633	22.8%	(L/All)
C to Lab swing 3.8%	53,660	Lab maj 15,558 29.0%		50,985	Lab maj 10,876 21.3%	

Mr Ian McCartney

Mr **Ian McCartney**, full-time Labour Party secretary/organiser in Wigan; former seaman and local government manual worker. Mbr, Wigan BC; chmn, Wigan Health Defence cmte; former member, Wigan Family Practitioner Cmte. B Apr 25 1951. Son of Mr Hugh McCartney, Labour MP Dumbartonshire East 1970-74; for Central Dumbartonshire Feb 1974-83; and for Clydebank and Milngavie 1983-87.

Mr **Laurence Robertson**, self-employed management consultant and director of Philip Gore (Bolton) Ltd. B Mar 29 1958; ed Farnworth GS.

Mr **Robert Hewer**, watchmaker. B 1947; ed Sec Mod Sch; Wigan Tech Coll; Open Univ.

MANCHESTER, BLACKLEY — No change

Electorate %Turnout	58,814	72.9%	**1987**	60,106	69.7%	**1983**
*Eastham, K. (Lab)	22,476	52.4%	+4.4%	20,132	48.1%	(Lab)
Nath, K. (C)	12,354	28.8%	-3.8%	13,676	32.6%	(C)
Showman, H. (SDP/All)	8,041	18.8%	-0.5%	8,081	19.3%	(L/All)
C to Lab swing 4.1%	42,871	Lab maj 10,122 23.6%		41,889	Lab maj 6,456 15.4%	

Mr Kenneth Eastham

Mr Kenneth Eastham, former planning engineer with GEC, Trafford Park, has served on the Select Cmte on Employment since 1983; jt vice-chmn, PLP employment cmte, 1985- . Elected in 1979. B Aug 11, 1927; ed Openshaw Tech Coll. Mbr, Manchester City Cl, 1962-80; deputy leader, 1975-79, and chmn, education cmte, 1978-79, and planning cmte, 1971-74. Mbr, NW Economic Planning Cl, 1975-79. Sponsored by AUEW.
Mr Krishan Kumar Nath is head teacher of Abingdon Junior School, Middlesborough. Was treas, sec and later chmn, Indian Assocn of Cleveland, from which he retired in 1979. Mbr, Cleveland Community Relation Cl holding various offices and becoming chmn, 1980. Mbr, exec cmte, Stockton South Cons Assocn; chmn of Kader Ward and of Anglo-Asian Cons Assocn of Cleveland. B Mar 23 1932 in India; ed Punjab, Durham and Hull Univs. NAHT.
Mr Harvey Showman, dentist. B Oct 5 1947; ed Manchester GS; Glasgow Univ.

MANCHESTER CENTRAL — No change

Electorate %Turnout	62,928	63.9%	**1987**	69,188	60.6%	**1983**
*Litherland, R.K. (Lab)	27,428	68.2%	+2.9%	27,353	65.3%	(Lab)
Banks, M.R.W. (C)	7,561	18.8%	-2.4%	8,868	21.2%	(C)
McColgan, B.W. (SDP/All)	5,250	13.0%	+1.2%	4,956	11.8%	(SDP/All)
				729	1.7%	(Other)
C to Lab swing 2.6%	40,239	Lab maj 19,867 49.4%		41,906	Lab maj 18,485 44.1%	

Mr Robert Litherland

Mr Robert Litherland, former sales representative for a printing firm, has represented the seat since Sep 1979. B Jun 23 1930; ed North Manchester HS for Boys. Mbr, Manchester City Cl, 1971- ; dep chmn, housing cmte; chmn, Manchester Direct Works Cmte, 1974-78. Dep chmn, Public Works Cmte, AMA, 1977-78. Sponsored by Sogat '82.
Mr Mathew Banks, mbr Wirral DC. Aged 26; ed RMA Sandhurst.
Mr Barry McColgan, chartered accountant, contested Knowsley North 1983 and, for Labour, Clitheroe Oct 1974 and Knutsford Feb 1974. Founder mbr, SDP. B 1946; ed St Thomas of Canterbury Sec Mod Sch, Salford; Salford Tech Coll; Hull and Manchester Univs; Manchester Business Sch. Chmn, Manchester Blackley Lab Pty, 1971-72; vice-chmn, Manchester North SDP, 1981-82.

MANCHESTER, GORTON — No change

Electorate %Turnout	64,243	70.4%	**1987**	64,645	67.9%	**1983**
*Kaufman, G.B. (Lab)	24,615	54.4%	+3.2%	22,460	51.2%	(Lab)
Kershaw, J. (C)	10,550	23.3%	-5.2%	12,495	28.5%	(C)
Whitmore, K.A. (L/All)	9,830	21.7%	+2.7%	8,348	19.0%	(L/All)
Lawrence, Ms P. (RF)	253	0.6%		333	0.8%	(Com)
				231	0.5%	(Other)
C to Lab swing 4.2%	45,248	Lab maj 14,065 31.1%		43,867	Lab maj 9,965 22.7%	

Mr Gerald Kaufman

Mr Gerald Kaufman became chief Opposition spokesman on home affairs in 1983; elected to the shadow Cabinet, 1980, being chief spokesman on the environment, 1980-83; previously spokesman on housing, 1979-80. Minister of State, Department of Industry, 1975-79; Under-Secretary of State for Industry, 1975; Under Secretary of State for Environment, 1974-75. Parliamentary press liaison officer for the Lab Party, 1965-70. Elected for this seat 1983; MP for Manchester, Ardwick, 1970-83; contested Gillingham, 1959, and Bromley, 1955. B Jun 21 1930; ed Leeds GS and Queen's Coll, Oxford. Asst sec, Fabian Society, 1954-55. Fellow, RSA. Political correspondent, *New Statesman,* 1964-65; political staff, *Daily Mirror,* 1955-64. Sponsored by GMBATU.
Mr John Kershaw, lecturer in law, Tamside Coll of Tech. Mbr, Manchester City Cl; chmn, Manchester, Gorton Cons Assocn and NW Area advisory cmte on education. Aged 37.
Mr Keith Whitmore fought this seat 1983. Mbr, Manchester City Cl, 1979- ; Greater Manchester Cl, 1981-86 (ldr, Lib gp). B Jun 15 1955; ed Chorlton HS; St John's CFE.

MANCHESTER, WITHINGTON · Lab gain

Electorate %Turnout	65,343	77.1%	**1987**	64,606	72.3%	**1983**
Bradley, K.J.C. (Lab)	21,650	42.9%	+8.8%	18,329	39.2%	(C)
*Silvester, F.J. (C)	18,259	36.2%	-3.0%	15,956	34.2%	(Lab)
Jones, Mrs A. (L/All)	9,978	19.8%	-6.4%	12,231	26.2%	(SDP/All)
Abberton, M.T. (Grn)	524	1.0%		184	0.4%	(Freedom)
C to Lab swing 5.9%	50,411	Lab maj 3,391 6.7%		46,700	C maj 2,373 5.1%	

Mr **Keith Bradley**, health service administrator with NW RHA. Mbr, Manchester City Cl, 1983- (chmn, environmental and consumer services cmte; vice-chmn, anti-poverty subcmte). City Cl director of Manchester Ship Canal and Manchester Airport plc. Sec, Manchester Withington Co-op Pty. B May 17 1950.
Mr **Fred Silvester**, mbr of the Public Accounts Cmte, 1983-87; Select Cmte on Procedure 1983-87. Elected for this seat Feb 1974; MP for Walthamstow West, 1967-70; contested that seat, 1966. Advertising exec and barrister. Political education officer, CPC, 1957-60. Opposition whip, 1974-76. Vice-chmn, Cons back-bench employment cmte, 1976-79. PPS to Secretary of State for Employment, 1979-81; and to Secretary of State for NI, 1981-83. B Sep 24 1933; ed Sir George Monoux GS, Walthamstow; Sidney Sussex Coll, Cambridge. Senior Associate Director, J Walter Thompson Co. Ltd; director, Advocacy Partnership. Elected to exec, 1922 Cmte, 1985. Mbr, Walthamstow BC, 1961-64.
Mrs **Audrey Jones**, company director and magistrate, is leader of Lib gp on Manchester City Cl to which she was elected in 1978. B Jan 3 1933; ed Levenshulme HS for Girls, Manchester. Director of local newspaper in South Manchester, started in 1978.

Mr Keith Bradley

MANCHESTER, WYTHENSHAWE · No change

Electorate %Turnout	58,287	72.1%	**1987**	60,995	69.6%	**1983**
*Morris, A. (Lab)	23,881	56.8%	+2.2%	23,172	54.6%	(Lab)
Sparrow, D.G. (C)	12,026	28.6%	-0.8%	12,488	29.4%	(C)
Butterworth, Ms J. (SDP/All)	5,921	14.1%	-1.9%	6,766	15.9%	(L/All)
Connelly, Ms S. (RF)	216	0.5%				
C to Lab swing 1.5%	42,044	Lab maj 11,855 28.2%		42,426	Lab maj 10,684 25.2%	

Mr **Alfred Morris**, Opposition spokesman on the disabled, 1979- ; Minister for the Disabled, 1974-79, with the rank of Under Secretary of State, DHSS. Chmn, World Planning Gp that drafted Charter for the 1980s for disabled people world wide, presented to all heads of govt in International Year of Disabled People, 1981. Elected in 1964; contested seat, 1959, and Liverpool, Garston, 1951. Chmn, parly Co-op gp, 1970-71 and 1983-85; member Nat Cl of Lab, representing Co-op movement, 1983- . Opposition spokesman on social services, 1973-74. Promoted Chronically Sick and Disabled Persons Act, 1970. B Mar 23 1928; ed Manchester elementary schs; Ruskin and St Catherine's Colls, Oxford; post-graduate studies at Manchester Univ. Pres, N of England Reg Associn for Deaf, 1980- ; trustee, Crisis at Christmas, 1982- ; patron, Disablement Income Gp, 1970- ; Motability, 1978- . Chmn, managing trustees, Parly Pensions Fund and H of C Members' Fund, 1983- . Member, Gen Advisory Cl, BBC, 1968-74 and 1984- . Adviser to Engineers' and Managers' Assoc.
Mr **David Sparrow**, barrister, practised at Hong Kong Bar, 1973-83. B Apr 12 1949; ed William Hulmes GS; Jesus Coll, Oxford.
Miss **Joan Butterworth**, polytechnic lecturer, Sec, Manchester area SDP. B Oct 2 ed Sale GS for Girls; Manchester Univ; l'Universite d'Aix-Marseille; Essex Univ. NATFHE.

Mr Alfred Morris

MANSFIELD · No change

Electorate %Turnout	66,764	78.4%	**1987**	65,277	70.7%	**1983**
Meale, J.A. (Lab)	19,610	37.5%	-3.0%	18,670	40.4%	(Lab)
Hendry, C. (C)	19,554	37.4%	+1.7%	16,454	35.6%	(C)
Answer, B. (SDP/All)	11,604	22.2%	-1.7%	11,036	23.9%	(SDP/All)
Marshall, B. (ML)	1,580	3.0%				
Lab to C swing 2.3%	52,348	Lab maj 56 0.1%		46,160	Lab maj 2,216 4.8%	

Mr **Alan Meale** has acted as parliamentary and political adviser to Mr Michael Meacher MP, chief Lab spokesman on social services; secretary of the Campaign Group of Labour MPs; author. Founder of Scotswood Link Programme for chronic unemployed in Newcastle-upon-Tyne and the Link specialist drugs rehabilitation projects. Sponsor of Campaign for Press and Broadcasting Freedom. Former member, AEU.
Mr **Charles Hendry**, public relations executive, contested Clackmannan 1983. B 1959; ed Rugby; Edinburgh Univ. Former vice-chmn, Fed of Cons Students for Scotland. Former research officer Bow Gp and former research asst to Cons MPs.
Mr **Barry Answer**, self-employed newsagent in Mansfield. Mbr, Notts CC, 1985- , being first SDP cllr. B Jul 8 1947; ed Whaley Thorns Cty Sec Mod Sch, Langwith, Derbyshire. Worked at Langwith Colliery for three years. Mbr, Newsagents' Fed; previously NUR and NUM.

Mr Alan Meale

MEDWAY No change

Electorate %Turnout	64,103	73.0%	**1987**	63,387	72.6%	**1983**
*Fenner, Dame Peggy (C)	23,889	51.0%	+2.1%	22,507	48.9%	(C)
Hull, V. (Lab)	13,960	29.8%	-0.3%	13,851	30.1%	(Lab)
Horne-Roberts, Mrs J. (SDP/All)	8,450	18.1%	-2.9%	9,658	21.0%	(SDP/All)
Rosser, Mrs J.V. (Grn)	504	1.1%				
Lab to C swing 1.2%	46,803	C maj	9,929 21.2%	46,016	C maj	8,656 18.8%

Dame Peggy Fenner

Dame Peggy Fenner was Parliamentary Secretary, Ministry of Agriculture, Fisheries and Food, 1981-86 and 1972-73. Elected for this seat 1983; MP for Rochester and Chatham, 1979-83 and 1970-Oct 1974; contested Newcastle-under-Lyme, 1966. Former mbr, Select Cmte for the Civil List and Public Expenditure Cmte. B Nov 12 1922; ed LCC elementary sch, Brockley and Ide Hill Sch, Kent. Co-chmn, Women's National Commission, 1983-86. Mbr, Sevenoaks UDC, 1957-71 (chmn, 1962-64); European Parliament, 1974-75; exec, Kent Borough and UDC Assocn, 1967-71; West Kent Divisional Exec Education Cmte, 1962-72.
Mr Vernon Hull contested Kent Mid 1983. Dist Sec, WEA. Former lecturer. B Oct 22 1947; ed Keele, Lancaster and London Univs. Mbr, Rochester City Cl. TGWU.
Mrs Jennifer Horne Roberts, barrister practising employment and commercial law; writer on employment and family law. Contested Fareham for Lab in Feb 1974; former mbr, Camden Cl. B Feb 1949; ed LSE. Member, 300 Gp.
Mrs Vivien Rosser, teacher (not practicing), mother and Open Univ student. B Nov 15 1951; ed W Midlands Coll of Ed. NAS/UWT and OUSA.

MEIRIONNYDD NANT CONWY No change

Electorate %Turnout	31,632	82.2%	**1987**	30,459	81.3%	**1983**
*Thomas, D.E. (Pl C)	10,392	40.0%	+0.8%	9,709	39.2%	(Pl C)
Jones, D.T. (C)	7,366	28.3%	-0.2%	7,066	28.5%	(C)
Roberts, H.G. (Lab)	4,397	16.9%	+1.8%	4,254	17.2%	(SDP/All)
Roberts, D.L. (SDP/All)	3,847	14.8%	-2.4%	3,735	15.1%	(Lab)
C to Pl C swing 0.5%	26,002	Pl C maj	3,026 11.6%	24,764	Pl C maj	2,643 10.7%

Mr Dafydd Thomas

Mr Dafydd Thomas, adult education tutor, broadcaster and writer. Pres of Plaid Cymru since 1984, was elected for this seat 1983; MP for Merioneth, Feb 1974-83; contested Conway, 1970. Former mbr, Select Cmte on Education, Science and the Arts. B Oct 18 1946; ed Ysgol Dyffryn Conwy and Univ Coll of N Wales. Became Plaid Cymru spokesman on social, educational and cultural policy in 1975; spokesman on agricultural and rural development, 1974.
Mr Dennis Jones, college lecturer, contested Caernarfon in 1983. Chmn, Wales cmte, Professional Assocn of Teacher. Mbr, CLA. B Aug 16 1949; ed Bala Boys GS; Essex Univ; Huddersfield Coll of Ed (Technical).
Mr Hugh Roberts, youth and schools officer with Snowdonia National Park Authority. B Apr 25 1948; ed Ysgol Ardudwy, Harlech; Ysgol Y Gader, Dolgellan; Bangor Coll. NALGO.
Mr David Roberts, farmer, contested this seat 1983. Mbr, SDP Cl for Wales; former chmn, Gwynedd area SDP. B Nov 15 1957; ed Tywyn Sch; King's Coll, London. Mbr, Campaign for Preservation of Rural Wales. NFU.

MERIDEN No change

Electorate %Turnout	78,444	73.9%	**1987**	74,161	71.6%	**1983**
*Mills, I.C. (C)	31,935	55.1%	+1.5%	28,474	53.7%	(C)
Burden, R.H. (Lab)	15,115	26.1%	+0.7%	13,456	25.4%	(Lab)
Parkinson, Ms C.E. (SDP/All)	10,896	18.8%	-1.3%	10,674	20.1%	(SDP/All)
				460	0.9%	(Other)
Lab to C swing 0.4%	57,946	C maj	16,820 29.0%	53,064	C maj	15,018 28.3%

Mr Iain Mills

Mr Iain Mills, elected in 1979, was marketing planning manager with Dunlop, responsible for marketing new tyre projects, 1964-79; responsible for all racing tyre development, 1966-70. Adviser to National Tyre Distributors Assocn and to Industrial Anti-Counterfeiting Gp. Parly adviser to Grant, Spencer, Caisley and Co; Novamark International Ltd; consultant to DIAL Ltd. Sec, Cons transport cmte, 1979- ; vice-chmn, all-pty transport safety gp, 1984- . B Apr 21 1940; ed Prince Edward Sch, Bulawayo, Rhodesia; Cape Town Univ. Mbr, Lichfield DC, 1973-74. Burgess, City of Glasgow. PPS to Minister of State for Industry, 1981, and to Mr Norman Tebbit, 1982- . Former mbr, Select Cmte on European Legislation. Treas, Commons Yacht Club.
Mr Richard Burden, Nalgo official in Midlands water industry. B 1954. Pres, York Univ Students Union, 1976-77. Mbr, War on Want.
Dr Christine Parkinson, inner city missioner; previously researcher in children's development. Chmn, Isleworth Alliance Gp, 1983-84; Birmingham area cmte, 1984-86; vice-chmn SDP Christian Forum, 1986- . B May 21 1943; ed Drayton Manor GS, London; Harrow Coll of Science and Tech; Barking Regional Coll of Tech; London Univ. Cellist, Birmingham Concert Orchestra.

MERTHYR TYDFIL AND RHYMNEY   No change

Electorate %Turnout	58,285	76.1%	**1987**	59,486	72.5%	**1983**
*Rowlands, E. (Lab)	33,400	75.3%	+8.0%	29,053	67.3%	(Lab)
Walters, N.M. (C)	5,270	11.9%	-0.7%	6,323	14.7%	(L/All)
Verma, P. (L/All)	3,573	8.1%	-6.6%	5,449	12.6%	(C)
Davies, Mrs J. (Pl C)	2,085	4.7%	-0.1%	2,058	4.8%	(Pl C)
				256	0.6%	(Other)
C to Lab swing 4.4%	44,328	Lab maj 28,130 63.5%		43,139	Lab maj 22,730 52.7%	

Mr Edward Rowlands

Mr Edward Rowlands, Opposition spokesman on energy 1980- ; an Opposition spokesman on foreign affairs, 1979-80. Minister of State, Foreign and Commonwealth Office, 1976-79; Under Secretary of State, FCO, 1975-76; Under Secretary of State, Welsh Office, 1974-75 and 1969-70. Elected for this seat in 1983; MP for Merthyr Tydfil, 1972-83, and for Cardiff North, 1966-70. Former lecturer in modern history and government. B Jan 23 1940; ed Rhondda GS, Wirral GS and King's Coll, London. Fellow, Industry and Parliament Trust. Mbr, governing body and exec, Commonwealth Inst, 1980- . Sponsored by Usdaw.
Mr Nicholas Walters, public relations consultant and director, Good Relations Gp plc. B May 16 1957; ed Downside; Exeter Univ. Mbr, nat exec, Nat Assocn of Cons Students, 1984 and 1985; chmn, Exeter Univ FCS, 1978. Mbr, Inst of International Affairs. Son of Mr Dennis Walters, MP for Westbury.
Mr Peter Verma, mining consultant and community worker. B 1941; ed in India.
Mrs Janet Davies, housewife, is senior vice-chmn, PlC. Contested Brecon and Radnor by-election 1985 and Pontypridd 1983. Mbr, Taff Ely BC. Aged 48; ed Trinity Coll, Carmarthen.

MIDDLESBROUGH   No change

Electorate %Turnout	60,789	71.0%	**1987**	62,950	66.5%	**1983**
*Bell, S. (Lab)	25,747	59.7%	+9.0%	21,220	50.7%	(Lab)
Orr-Ewing, R.J. (C)	10,789	25.0%	-2.6%	11,551	27.6%	(C)
Hawley, P.A. (L/All)	6,594	15.3%	-5.9%	8,871	21.2%	(L/All)
				207	0.5%	(Other)
C to Lab swing 5.8%	43,130	Lab maj 14,958 34.7%		41,849	Lab maj 9,669 23.1%	

Mr Stuart Bell

Mr Stuart Bell, a barrister, became an Opposition spokesman on Northern Ireland in 1984. Secretary, Solidarity group of Lab MPs, 1986. Elected in 1983; contested Hexham, 1979. B May 16 1938; ed Hookergate GS, Durham. Former journalist and novelist. Conseil Juridique and international lawyer, Paris, 1970-77. Mbr, Newcastle City Cl, 1980-83; Soc of Labour Lawyers; Fabian Soc, GMB. PPS to Mr Roy Hattersley, Dep Ldr of Opposition, 1983-84.
Mr Robert Orr-Ewing, barrister, but ceased practising in 1983 to start own legal and property business. Mbr, Kensington and Chelsea BC, 1982- ; deputy chmn, 1987- . B Dec 7 1953; ed Harrow; London Coll of Law. Served in TA, 1975-79. Governor, primary sch, 1986- .
Mr Philip Hawley is a local government officer. B Jan 27 1956; ed Hull Univ. Nalgo.

MIDLOTHIAN   No change

Electorate %Turnout	60,549	77.2%	**1987**	60,496	75.0%	**1983**
*Eadie, A. (Lab)	22,553	48.3%	+5.5%	19,401	42.7%	(Lab)
Dewar, A.R. (SDP/All)	10,300	22.0%	-7.1%	13,245	29.2%	(SDP/All)
Riddell, Dr F. (C)	8,527	18.2%	-3.6%	9,922	21.9%	(C)
Chisholm, I. (SNP)	4,947	10.6%	+4.4%	2,826	6.2%	(SNP)
Smith, I. (Grn)	412	0.9%				
SDP/All to Lab swing 6.3%	46,739	Lab maj 12,253 26.2%		45,394	Lab maj 6,156 13.6%	

Mr Alexander Eadie

Mr Alexander Eadie, an Opposition spokesman on energy and mainly on coal, 1979- ; Under Secretary of State for Energy, 1974-79; Opposition spokesman on energy, 1970-74. Sec, PLP miners' group and a former chmn of it; former chmn, parliamentary power and steel group. Former mbr, Select Cmte on Scottish Affairs. Elected in 1966; contested Ayr, 1959 and 1964. Former miners' agent. B Jun 23 1920; ed Buckhaven Senior Sec Sch, Fife, and technical coll. Has served on exec cmte, Scottish Reg Cl of Lab Pty; exec cmte, Scottish Area NUM; local govt for 20 years. Sponsored by NUM.
Mr Alan Dewar, solicitor, contested the seat in 1983. B Dec 9 1956; ed Lasswade HS, Midlothian; Dundee Univ. Writer to Her Majesty's Signet; partner in Thomson and Baxter, Edinburgh. Convenor, Scottish SDP constitutional and legal affairs policy gp.
Mr Frank Riddell, reader in chemistry, Stirling Univ. Mbr, Stirling DC, 1984- (ldr, Cons gp, 1985-). B 1940; ed Merchant Taylors Sch, Crosby; Liverpool Univ. Research fellow, Strasbourg Univ, 1965-67.
Mr Ian Chisholm, self-emploued marine electronics engineer. Chmn, City of Edinburgh SNP; Edinburgh SNP Club. B Apr 29 1945; ed Hawick HS; Leith Nautical Coll.
Mr Ian Smith, biomedical electronics engineer. B Jul 23 1955; ed Leith Acad. ASTMS.

MILTON KEYNES — No change

Electorate %Turnout	97,041	76.3%	**1987**	79,229	74.0%	**1983**
*Benyon, W.R. (C)	35,396	47.8%	-0.2%	28,181	48.0%	(C)
Rodgers, W.T. (SDP/All)	21,695	29.3%	+0.9%	16,659	28.4%	(SDP/All)
Brownfield-Pope, Ms Y.V.A. (Lab)	16,111	21.8%	-0.5%	13,045	22.2%	(Lab)
Francis, A.H. (Grn)	810	1.1%	+0.3%	494	0.8%	(Eco)
				290	0.5%	(Other)
C to SDP/All swing 0.6%	74,012	C maj 13,701 18.5%		58,669	C maj 11,522 19.6%	

Mr William Benyon

Mr William Benyon, an Opposition whip, 1974-76, was elected for this seat 1983; MP for Buckingham, 1970-83. Mbr, Commons Services Cmte, 1983- ; vice-chmn, Cons back-bench N Ireland cmte 1979- ; chmn, Cons forestry sub-cmte, 1986- . Farmer and landowner. B Jan 17 1930; ed RNC Dartmouth. Mbr, exec, 1922 Cmte, 1982-; Berkshire CC, 1964-74; Bradfield RDC, 1960-62; Cl of Reading Univ; Cl of Bradfield Coll; Royal Agricultural Soc of England.
Mr William Rodgers became vice-pres of the SDP in 1982. Spokesman on energy in Alliance election team. Labour Secretary of State for Transport, 1976-79; Labour MP 1962-81; resigned from pty in 1981 being one of the four joint leaders who formed the SDP. Fought Stockton North for SDP in 1983; MP for Stockton, Feb 1974-83, and for Stockton-on-Tees, 1962-74; contested Bristol West by-election, 1957. Minister of State, Treasury, 1969-70; Minister of State, Board of Trade, 1968-69; Under Secretary of State, Foreign Office, 1967-68; Under Secretary of State, Economic Affairs, 1964-67. B Oct 28 1928; ed Quarry Bank HS, Liverpool; Magdalen Coll, Oxford.
Ms Yvonne Brownfield-Pope, project worker, Milton Keynes welfare rights gp. B Feb 14 1951. ASTMS.
Mr Alan Francis, computer graphics system designer at Open Univ; director, Political Ecology Research Gp Ltd. Contested this seat 1983. B Jun 3 1948; ed Hitchen Boys' GS; Sussex Univ. AUT.

MITCHAM AND MORDEN — No change

Electorate %Turnout	63,089	75.7%	**1987**	63,535	73.1%	**1983**
*Rumbold, Mrs A.C.R. (C)	23,002	48.2%	+5.5%	19,827	42.7%	(C)
McDonagh, Ms S. (Lab)	16,819	35.2%	+6.4%	13,376	28.8%	(Lab)
Douglas-Mann, B.L.H. (SDP/All)	7,930	16.6%	-10.8%	12,720	27.4%	(SDP/All)
				539	1.2%	(Other)
C to Lab swing 0.5%	47,751	C maj 6,183 12.9%		46,462	C maj 6,451 13.9%	

Mrs Angela Rumbold

Mrs Angela Rumbold was appointed Minister of State for Education and Science in 1986; Under Secretary of State for Environment, 1985-86. Elected at 1982 by-election. PPS to Mr Nichollas Ridley, 1983-85. B Aug 11 1932; ed Notting Hill and Ealing HS; Perse School for Girls, Cambridge; and Kings Coll, London. Former company director and adviser. Mbr, Select Cmte for Social Services, 1982-83; Doctors and Dentists Review Body, 1979-82; Kingston upon Thames BC, 1974-83 (dep leader, 1976-82). Chmn, education cmte, Assocn of Met Authorities, 1979-80; Cl of Local Ed Authorities, 1979-80. Former mbr, Burnham Management Cmte and Assessment of Performance Unit, Dept of Education.
Ms Siobhain McDonagh, housing adviser with homeless person's unit, Wandsworth Cl. Local cllr. B Feb 20 1960; ed Essex Univ. Nalgo.
Mr Bruce Douglas-Mann, solicitor. Labour MP for North Kensington, 1970-74; Mitcham and Morden, Feb 1974-May 82 (joined SDP in 1981, resigned his seat and lost the resulting by-election). Contested St Albans, 1964 and Maldon, 1966 for Lab; Mitcham and Morden, 1983 for SDP. Mbr, CSD, 1984- ; Shelter bd, 1974- . B Jun 23 1927; ed Upper Canada Coll, Toronto; Jesus Coll, Oxford.

MOLE VALLEY — No change

Electorate %Turnout	67,715	77.0%	**1987**	65,067	75.0%	**1983**
*Baker, K.W. (C)	31,689	60.8%	-0.1%	29,691	60.8%	(C)
Thomas, Mrs S.P. (L/All)	15,613	29.9%	-0.7%	14,973	30.7%	(L/All)
King, C.M.B. (Lab)	4,846	9.3%	+0.8%	4,147	8.5%	(Lab)
L/All to C swing 0.3%	52,148	C maj 16,076 30.8%		48,811	C maj 14,718 30.2%	

Mr Kenneth Baker

Mr Kenneth Baker was appointed Secretary of State for Education and Science in 1986; Secretary of State for Environment, 1985-86; Minister for Local Government at DoE, with rank of Minister of State, 1984-85; Minister of State for Industry and for Information Technology, 1981-84; Parliamentary Secretary, Civil Service Dept, 1972-74. Elected for this seat 1983; MP for City of Westminster, St Marylebone, 1970-83; and for Acton, 1968-70; contested that seat, 1966, and Poplar, 1964. B Nov 3 1934; ed St Paul's Sch and Magdalen Coll, Oxford. Chmn, Hansard Soc, 1978-81. Former mbr, exec, 1922 Cmte. Mbr, Twickenham BC, 1961-63; PAC, 1969-70. PPS to Mr Edward Heath, 1974-75.
Mrs Susan Thomas, political campaigner, contested this seat 1983. B Dec 20 1935; ed Cranborne Chase Sch; Lady Margaret Hall, Oxford. Britisj Clothing Industries Cl for Europe chief exec, 1974-78.
Mr Christopher King, teacher. Mbr, Islington BC, 1975-82 and 1986- . B Nov 5 1948; ed Queen Mary's Sch, Basingstoke; Central Sch Speech and Drama; London Univ. NUT.

MONKLANDS EAST — No change

Electorate	%Turnout	49,644	74.8%	1987	49,030	73.1%	1983
*Smith, J. (Lab)		22,649	61.0%	+9.7%	18,358	51.2%	(Lab)
Love, J. (C)		6,260	16.9%	-7.0%	8,559	23.9%	(C)
Gibson, K. (SNP)		4,790	12.9%	+4.0%	5,721	16.0%	(L/All)
Grieve, Mrs S. (L/All)		3,442	9.3%	-6.7%	3,185	8.9%	(SNP)
C to Lab swing 8.4%		37,141	Lab maj 16,389 44.1%		35,823	Lab maj 9,799 27.4%	

Mr John Smith

Mr John Smith, QC, a member of the shadow Cabinet since 1979, has been chief Opposition spokesman on trade and industry since 1985; chief Opposition spokesman on employment, 1983-85; on energy, 1982-83; on trade 1979-82. Secretary of State for Trade, 1978-79; Minister of State, Privy Council Office, 1976-78; Minister of State for Energy, 1975-76; Under Secretary of State for Energy, 1974-75. Elected for this seat 1983; MP for North Lanarkshire, 1970-83; contested East Fife, 1961 and 1964. Advocate. B Sep 13, 1938; ed Dunoon GS and Glasgow Univ. Sponsored by GMB.
Mr John Love, regional administrator and accountant for Coatbridge firm of decorators, contested this seat 1983; Coatbridge and Airdrie Oct 1974 and 1979. Mbr, Monklands DC; former Ayr cllr. B Aug 1941; ed Airdrie Acad. Church of Scotland Elder; Boys' Brigade capt.
Mr Kenneth Gibson, fund raiser and advice worker. Treas, Glasgow Central SNP. B 1961; ed Stirling Univ.
Mrs Sandra Grieve, Scottish development officer of nat voluntary organisation; former organiser, Hamilton CAB. B May 17 1954; ed Uddingston GS; Bell Coll, Hamilton. Chmn, Strathclyde Regional Children's Panel; mbr, Scottish Women Liberal Cl.

MONKLANDS WEST — No change

Electorate	%Turnout	50,874	77.3%	1987	50,345	75.7%	1983
*Clarke, T. (Lab)		24,499	62.3%	+8.1%	20,642	54.2%	(Lab)
Lind, G. (C)		6,166	15.7%	-6.3%	8,378	22.0%	(C)
McQueen, Ms A. (SDP/All)		4,408	11.2%	-6.1%	6,605	17.3%	(SDP/All)
Bovey, K. (SNP)		4,260	10.8%	+4.3%	2,473	6.5%	(SNP)
C to Lab swing 7.2%		39,333	Lab maj 18,333 46.6%		38,098	Lab maj 12,264 32.2%	

Mr Thomas Clarke

Mr Thomas Clarke was elected for this seat in 1983; MP for Coatbridge and Airdrie, 1982-83. Mbr, Select Cmte on Scottish Affairs, 1983- . Chmn, PLP foreign affairs cmte, 1983-86. Former asst director, Scottish Film Cl and Scottish Cl for Educational Technology. Former pres, British Amateur Cinematographers' Central Cl. B Jan 10 1941; ed Columba HS, Coatbridge; Scottish Coll of Commerce. Mbr, Coatbridge Cl, 1964-74; Monklands DC, 1974; Provost of Monklands, 1974-82; pres, Convention of Scottish Local Authorities, 1978-80; vice-pres, 1976-78. GMBATU.
Mr Gordon Lind, principal guidance teacher. Mbr, Coatbridge BC, 1969-72. B 1945; ed Coatbridge HS; Strathclyde Univ; Jordanhill Coll of Ed.
Ms Anne McQueen, further education lecturer. Founder mbr, SDP. B Oct 1 1952; ed Coatbridge HS; Central Coll of Commerce, Glasgow.
Mr Keith Bovey is a vice-president of CND and president, Scottish CND. Solicitor. Fought Glasgow, Garscadden, 1978 by-election and Oct 1974; Glasgow, Hillhead, Feb 1974. B Jul 31 1927; ed Moorpark Sch, Renfrew; Paisley GS; Sch of Oriental and African Studies, London; Glasgow Univ.

MONMOUTH — No change

Electorate	%Turnout	58,468	80.6%	1987	56,112	78.8%	1983
*Stradling Thomas, Sir John (C)		22,387	47.5%	-1.6%	21,746	49.2%	(C)
Gass, Mrs K. (Lab)		13,037	27.7%	+6.0%	12,403	28.0%	(SDP/All)
Lindley, C.D. (SDP/All)		11,313	24.0%	-4.0%	9,593	21.7%	(Lab)
Meredudd, Mrs S. (Pl C)		363	0.8%	-0.3%	493	1.1%	(Pl C)
C to Lab swing 3.8%		47,100	C maj 9,350 19.9%		44,235	C maj 9,343 21.1%	

Sir John Stradling Thomas

Sir John Stradling Thomas was Minister of State, Welsh Office, 1983-85; Treasurer of HM Household and Govt Deputy Chief Whip, 1979-83; an Opposition whip, 1974-79; Lord Commissioner of the Treasury (Govt whip), 1973-74; asst Govt whip, 1971-72. Mbr, Select Cmte on Trade and Industry; Commons Services Cmte, 1979-83. Won the seat 1970; fought Cardiganshire, 1966; Aberavon, 1964. Farmer. B Jun 10 1925; ed Rugby and London Univ. Mbr, Carmarthen BC, 1961-64; NFU cl, 1963-70; chmn, Carmarthenshire NFU, 1964. Hon Associate, Royal Coll of Vet Surgeons and British Vet Assocn. Pres, Fed of Cons Clubs, 1984. Mbr, Select Cmte on Civil List, 1970-71.
Mrs Katrina Gass was elected to Gwent CC in 1985. Mbr, Brecon Beacons National Park cmte and North Gwent Community Health Cl. B Nov 9 1946. TGWU.
Mr Clive Lindley, company chairman and director Independent Radio News Ltd. Contested Leominster for Lab in Feb 1974; Monmouth (SDP) 1983; and South East Wales in 1984 Euro election. B Sep 22 1934; ed King Edward VII, Lytham. Chmn, *New Democrat* magazine.
Mrs Sian Meredudd, teacher. Mayor of Llandrindod. Ed Bristol Univ. Active in peace and anti-nuclear movements.

MONTGOMERY — No change

Electorate %Turnout	39,808	79.4%	**1987**	37,474	79.2%	**1983**
*Carlile, A.C. (L/All)	14,729	46.6%	+3.2%	12,863	43.3%	(L/All)
Evans, D.M. (C)	12,171	38.5%	-2.6%	12,195	41.1%	(C)
Llewellyn Jones, E.D.W. (Lab)	3,304	10.5%	+1.9%	2,550	8.6%	(Lab)
Clowes, C. (Pl C)	1,412	4.5%	-0.9%	1,585	5.3%	(Pl C)
				487	1.6%	(Other)
C to L/All swing 2.9%	31,616	L/All maj 2,558 8.1%		29,680	L/All maj 668 2.3%	

Mr Alex Carlile

Mr Alex Carlile, QC, was Alliance spokesman on legal affairs in its election team; Lib spokesman on home affairs and law, 1984- . Won the seat in 1983; contested Flint East, Feb 1974 and 1979. Mbr, Select Cmte on Parliamentary Commissioner for Administration, 1983- ; nat exec, Nat Cl for Civil Liberties. Recorder since 1986. B Feb 12 1948; ed Epsom Coll, Surrey, King's Coll, London, Inns of Court Sch of Law. Treas, all-pty UN parly gp; vice-pres, all-pty war crimes gp. Chmn, Welsh Lib Pty, 1980-82.
Mr David Evans, barrister on the Wales and Chester circuit. B Aug 13 1959; ed Kingsland Grange, Shrewsbury; Wrekin Coll, Telford; Mansfield Coll, Oxford; Inns of Court School of Law.
Mr Edward Llewellyn-Jones, teacher. Mbr, Ashfield DC; B Sep 9 1949; ed Durham and Cambridge Univs. NAS/UWT.
Dr Carl Clowes, director of planning, with Llanaelhaearn Community Cl, and specialist in community medicine, Powys HA, fought this seat in 1983 and 1979. Hon pres, Nat Language Centre. B Dec 11 1943; ed Bury GS; Manchester Univ medical sch; London Sch of Hygiene and Tropical Medicine.

MORAY — SNP gain

Electorate %Turnout	62,201	72.6%	**1987**	60,804	71.1%	**1983**
Ewing, Mrs W.M. (SNP)	19,510	43.2%	+7.9%	16,944	39.2%	(C)
*Pollock, A. (C)	15,825	35.0%	-4.2%	15,231	35.2%	(SNP)
Smith, C.R.C. (Lab)	5,118	11.3%	+4.1%	7,901	18.3%	(L/All)
Skene, D.G.M. (L/All)	4,724	10.5%	-7.8%	3,139	7.3%	(Lab)
C to SNP swing 6.1%	45,177	SNP maj 3,685 8.2%		43,215	C maj 1,713 4.0%	

Mrs Margaret Ewing

Mrs Margaret Ewing, an administrator, was SNP MP for Dunbartonshire East (then as Mrs Margaret Bain) from Oct 1974-79, contesting that seat Feb 1974 and Strathkelvin and Bearsden 1983. Dep leader of SNP 1984- . SNP spokesman on education and social services when an MP and served on Select Cmte on Violence in the Family. B Sep 1 1945; ed Biggar HS; Glasgow and Strathclyde Univs. NUJ.
Mr Alexander Pollock was PPS to Mr George Younger as Secretary of State for Scotland and Secretary of State for Defence, 1982-87. Mbr, Select Cmte on Scottish Affairs, 1979-82, and 1986-87. Advocate. MP for this seat 1983-87; MP for Moray and Nairn, 1979-83; contested it Oct 1974; West Lothian, Feb 1974. Former parly adviser to Inst of Professional Investigators. B Jul 21 1944; ed Glasgow Acad; Brasenose Coll, Oxford; Edinburgh Univ. Sec, British/Austrian parly gp, 1979-87. Mbr, Queen's Body Guard for Scotland, Royal Company of Archers, since 1984. Founder mbr, Thistle Group.
Mr Conal Smith, teacher. Aged 39; ed Aberdeen Univ. Founder, Moray YS. Mbr, exec, EIS.
Mr Danus Skene, teacher, contested Tayside North for Liberals, 1983; Kinross and West Perthshire for Labour in both 1974 elections. B Apr 2 1944; ed Sussex, Chicago and Aberdeen Univs. Mbr, Perth and Kinross DC, 1980-83.

MORECAMBE AND LUNESDALE — No change

Electorate %Turnout	55,718	76.1%	**1987**	53,238	72.9%	**1983**
*Lennox-Boyd, M.A. (C)	22,327	52.7%	-3.9%	21,968	56.6%	(C)
Greenwell, Mrs J. (SDP/All)	10,542	24.9%	-0.3%	9,774	25.2%	(SDP/All)
Smith, D. (Lab)	9,535	22.5%	+4.8%	6,882	17.7%	(Lab)
				208	0.5%	(Other)
C to SDP/All swing 1.8%	42,404	C maj 11,785 27.8%		38,832	C maj 12,194 31.4%	

Mr Mark Lennox-Boyd

Mr Mark Lennox-Boyd was appointed a Lord Commissioner of the Treasury (Govt whip) in 1986; an asst Govt whip, 1984-86. PPS to Mr Nigel Lawson, as Financial Sec to the Treasury, Secretary of State for Energy and Chancellor of the Exchequer, 1980-84. Barrister and former company director. Elected for this seat 1983; MP for Morecambe and Lonsdale, 1979-83; contested Brent South, Oct 1974. B May 4 1943; ed Eton and Christ Church, Oxford. Mbr, Select Committee on Energy, 1979-80.
Mrs June Greenwell, research nurse for S Cumbria HA. Mbr, Lancaster area SDP cmte; Cambridge City district cmte. B Jun 8 1939; ed Whitehaven GS, Cumbria; Newcastle Univ. RCN. Lecturer in health studies, Cambridgeshire CC.
Mr David Smith, a gardener. Mbr, Lancaster City Cl. Convenor, TGWU branch. B Apr 23 1945.

MOTHERWELL NORTH — No change

Electorate %Turnout	57,632	77.3%	**1987**	56,512	75.0%	**1983**
Reid, J. (Lab)	29,825	66.9%	+9.2%	24,483	57.8%	(Lab)
Currie, A. (SNP)	6,230	14.0%	+1.4%	6,589	15.5%	(C)
Hargrave, R. (C)	4,939	11.1%	-4.5%	5,970	14.1%	(L/All)
Swift, G. (L/All)	3,558	8.0%	-6.1%	5,333	12.6%	(SNP)
SNP to Lab swing 3.9%	44,552	Lab maj 23,595 53.0%		42,375	Lab maj 17,894 42.2%	

Dr John Reid, trade union official, was political research adviser to Mr Neil Kinnock, Leader of the Opposition, 1983-85; research officer, Scottish Labour Party, 1980-83. Organiser, Trade Unionists for Labour in Scotland. B May 8 1947; ed St Patrick's, Coatbridge; Stirling Univ. TGWU.

Mr Andrew Currie, a training adviser, has been on the SNP nat exec since 1978; SNP spokesman on environment; SNP vice-chmn (organisation), 1981-83. B Nov 30 1936; ed Paisley GS; Glasgow, Strathclyde and Open Univs. Mbr, Invergordon DC, 1973-75. ASTMS.

Mr Robert Hargrave, managing director of his own engineering company, contested this seat 1983. B 1939; ed Dalziel HS, Motherwell. Former works manager.

Mr George Swift, technical teacher employed by Strathclyde Reg Cl and previously by Lanark CC. Founder mbr (1980), Motherwell Dist Lib Assocn; former chmn, now sec. B Mar 9 1926; ed Dalziel HS; Coatbridge Tech Coll; Jordanhill Coll; Open Univ. SNP mbr, Burgh of Motherwell and Wishaw, 1949-52. Joined Libs 1980. Local preacher, Methodist Church. EIS.

Dr John Reid

MOTHERWELL SOUTH — No change

Electorate %Turnout	52,127	75.5%	**1987**	52,183	72.9%	**1983**
*Bray, J.W. (Lab)	22,957	58.3%	+5.9%	19,939	52.4%	(Lab)
Wright, J. (SNP)	6,027	15.3%	+5.5%	7,590	20.0%	(C)
Bercow, J.S. (C)	5,702	14.5%	-5.5%	6,754	17.8%	(L/All)
MacGregor, W.R. (SDP/All)	4,463	11.3%	-6.4%	3,743	9.8%	(SNP)
Somerville, R. (Comm)	223	0.6%				
SNP to Lab swing 0.2%	39,372	Lab maj 16,930 43.0%		38,026	Lab maj 12,349 32.5%	

Dr Jeremy Bray has been Opposition spokesman on science and technology since 1983; mbr, Select Cmte on Treasury and Civil Service, 1979-83. Consultant to Banking, Insurance and Finance Union and to Society of Telecom Executives. Elected in 1983; MP for Motherwell and Wishaw, Oct 1974-83; and for Middlesbrough West, 1962-70; contested Thirsk and Malton, 1959. Parliamentary Sec, Ministry of Technology, 1967-69, and to Ministry of Power, 1966-67. Mbr, Expenditure Cmte, 1978-79. Chmn, Fabian Soc, 1971-72. B Jun 29 1930; ed Aberystwyth GS; Kingswood Sch, Bath; Jesus Coll, Cambridge. Choate Fellow, Harvard. Director, Mullard Ltd, 1970-73. TGWU.

Mr James Wright, business management consultant, contested this seat 1983. Chmn, Clydesdale SNP. B 1942; ed Airdrie Acad.

Mr John Bercow, full-time vice-chmn, Cons Collegiate Forum. Mbr, Nat Union exec cmte, 1985- ; Lambeth BC, 1986- . B Jan 19 1963; ed Finchley Manorhill Sch; Essex Univ.

Mr Ross McGregor, technical officer with British Telecom. Founder mbr, SDP; member, SDP Scottish Cl. B Jan 2 1945.

Mr Robert Somerville, shop steward, Rolls Royce, E Kilbride. Vice-chair, Motherwell Trades Cl; Community cllr. Aged 51.

Dr Jeremy Bray

NEATH — No change

Electorate %Turnout	55,261	78.8%	**1987**	55,272	76.5%	**1983**
*Coleman, D.R. (Lab)	27,612	63.4%	+9.8%	22,670	53.6%	(Lab)
Howe, M.R.T. (C)	7,034	16.1%	-1.2%	9,066	21.4%	(SDP/All)
Warman, J. (SDP/All)	6,132	14.1%	-7.4%	7,350	17.4%	(C)
John, H. (Pl C)	2,792	6.4%	-0.8%	3,046	7.2%	(Pl C)
				150	0.4%	(Other)
C to Lab swing 5.5%	43,570	Lab maj 20,578 47.2%		42,282	Lab maj 13,604 32.2%	

Mr Donald Coleman, an Opposition spokesman on Wales, 1981-83, was elected in 1964. Mbr, Commons Chairmen's Panel, 1984- . Opposition whip, 1979-81, and 1970-74. Lord Commissioner of the Treasury (Govt whip), 1974-78; Vice-Chamberlain of Royal Household, 1978-79. PPS to Minister of State and then Secretary of State for Wales, 1967-70. Mbr, Select Cmte on Overseas Aid, 1969-74. Delegate, Cl of Europe and WEU, 1968-73. Metallurgist in Newport steel industry, 1954-64; sponsored by ISTC. B Sep 19 1925; ed Cadoxton Sch, Barry, and Cardiff Tech Coll. Tenor soloist and former mbr, Welsh Nat Opera Co. Parly adviser to Inst of Medical Laboratory Sciences.

Mr Martin Howe, barrister specialising in patents, copyrights and trade marks. Mbr, Hammersmith and Fulham BC, 1982-86 (chmn, planning cmte, 1985-86). B Jun 26 1955; ed Winchester; Trinity Hall, Cambridge.

Mr John Warman, boilermaker with BSC in Port Talbot. Vice-chmn, Neath area SDP. Mbr, Neath BC 1972- ; Press Cl; W Glamorgan Valuation Tribunal; Neath and Afan Health Cl. B Jun 20 1944; ed Cadoxton Sch, Neath; Swansea Tech Coll. GMB.

Mr Huw John, lecturer in motor vehicle technology at Neath Coll and broadcaster on motoring.

Mr Donald Coleman

NEWARK · No change

Electorate %Turnout	67,555	77.6%	**1987**	64,008	76.4%	**1983**
*Alexander, R.T. (C)	28,070	53.5%	-0.3%	26,334	53.8%	(C)
Barton, D. (Lab)	14,527	27.7%	+3.1%	12,051	24.6%	(Lab)
Emerson, G.A. (SDP/All)	9,833	18.8%	-1.8%	10,076	20.6%	(SDP/All)
				463	0.9%	(Other)
C to Lab swing 1.7%	52,430	C maj 13,543 25.8%		48,924	C maj 14,283 29.2%	

Mr Richard Alexander

Mr **Richard Alexander**, solicitor, gained this seat for the Conservatives in 1979; contested Lincoln, 1966 and 1970. B Jun 29 1934; ed Eastbourne GS; Dewsbury GS; Univ Coll, London; and Inst of Advanced Legal Studies, London Univ. Mbr, Bassetlaw DC, 1975-79; Retford BC, 1965-74; Notts CC, 1967-74; Select Cmte on Statutory Instruments, 1979- , and on Environ-ment, 1983- . Chmn, East Midlands Cons MPs, 1985- ; vice-chmn, all-pty Arts and Heritage parly gp. Former mbr, E Midlands Reg Economic Planning Cl and E Midlands Transport Users' Consultative Cmte. Director (unpaid), Ice Pick Ltd and Almawahe Ltd; consultant to Jones, Alexander and Co, solicitors, Retford (with whom he was senior partner, 1964-85), and to Rindalbourne Ltd.
Mr **David Barton**, college lecturer. B Nov 15 1946; ed Guildford GS; Kingston Poly. Ldr, Lab Gp, Newark and Sherwood DC. Former chmn, vice-chmn, sec, Newark CLP. NATFHE.
Mr **George Emerson**, farmer. Chmn, North Lincs area SDP 1984-87. Co-opted member GLC environmental planning cmte, 1970-71. B Aug 5 1943; ed Eton; Magdalen Coll, Oxford. NFU.

NEWBURY ° · No change

Electorate %Turnout	75,187	78.0%	**1987**	71,343	75.2%	**1983**
*McNair-Wilson, R.M.C. (C)	35,266	60.1%	+0.8%	31,836	59.3%	(C)
Rendel, D.D. (L/All)	18,608	31.7%	-3.3%	18,798	35.0%	(L/All)
Stapley, R.C. (Lab)	4,765	8.1%	+2.5%	3,027	5.6%	(Lab)
L/All to C swing 2.1%	58,639	C maj 16,658 28.4%		53,661	C maj 13,038 24.3%	

Mr Michael McNair-Wilson

Mr **Michael McNair-Wilson** was elected for Newbury in Feb 1974; MP for Walthamstow East, 1969-74; contested Lincoln, 1964. PPS to Minister of Agriculture, 1979-83. Mbr, Select Cmte on Nationalized Industries, 1974-79; Select Cmte on Education, Science and Arts, 1983-84 and 1986- ; Select Cmte on Mbrs' Interests, 1986- . First MP on kidney dialysis treatment. B Oct 12, 1930; ed Eton. Sec, Cons back-bench constitutional cmte, 1985- ; vice-chmn, Air Safety Gp, 1979- ; chmn, Cons Aviation Cmte, 1972-74; jt sec, UN Parly Group, 1970-72, and to Greater London Cons MPs, 1969-70. Public affairs consultant since 1979 to the McCann Consultancy, which incorporates Sidney-Barton with whom he has worked since 1955. Broth-er of MP for New Forest.
Mr **David Rendel**, financial analyst with Esso Petroleum, contested Fulham 1983 and 1979. Mbr, Newbury DC, 1987- . B Apr 15 1949; ed Eton and Oxford Univ.
Mr **Robert Stapley**, full-time trade union official. B Jul 29 1954; ed Owen's Sch, London; Exeter Univ.

NEWCASTLE-UNDER-LYME · No change

Electorate %Turnout	66,053	80.8%	**1987**	65,400	77.3%	**1983**
*Golding, Mrs L. (Lab)	21,618	40.5%	-1.5%	21,210	42.0%	(Lab)
Thomas, A.L. (L/All)	16,486	30.9%	+9.3%	18,406	36.4%	(C)
Ridgway, P.C.J. (C)	14,863	27.9%	-8.6%	10,916	21.6%	(L/All)
Nicklin, M.J. (Ex Lab Mod)	397	0.7%				
Lab to L/All swing 5.4%	53,364	Lab maj 5,132 9.6%		50,532	Lab maj 2,804 5.5%	

Mrs **Llin Golding**, who won the 1986 by-election, succeeded her husband, Mr John Golding, MP for the seat, 1969-86, who resigned when he became gen sec of the National Communica-tions Union. She had been his assistant, 1972-86, and formerly a radiographer. B Mar 21 1933; ed Caerphily Girls' GS; Cardiff Royal Infirmary Sch of Radiography. Mbr, North Stafford-shire District HA, 1983- ; sec, Newcastle District Trades Cl, 1976- . Former mbr, district Manpower Services Cmte. Nupe, former branch sec.
Mr **Alan Thomas**, lecturer in computer studies, fought this seat at the 1986 by-election and in 1983; Stoke-on-Trent Central, 1979 and Oct 1974. Mbr, Newcastle-under-Lyme BC, 1980- ; Staffordshire CC, 1981- . B Dec 1 1939; ed Wallasey GS; Hull and Keele Univs. NATFHE.
Mr **Peter Ridgway**, a bank financial services officer, contested Manchester, Blackley, 1983. Mbr, Newcastle-under-Lyme BC, 1986- . B Jun 24 1951; ed Langdale Junior Sch; Seabridge Sec Sch; Cauldon CFE. Mbr, Lloyds Bank Gp Staff Union.

Mrs Llin Golding

NEWCASTLE UPON TYNE CENTRAL — Lab gain

Electorate %Turnout	63,682	72.5%	**1987**	62,687	71.0%	**1983**
Cousins, J.M. (Lab)	20,416	44.2%	+8.4%	18,161	40.8%	(C)
*Merchant, P.R.G. (C)	17,933	38.8%	-2.0%	15,933	35.8%	(Lab)
Martin, Dr N. (SDP/All)	7,304	15.8%	-6.5%	9,923	22.3%	(SDP/All)
Bird, R.J. (Grn)	418	0.9%	-0.2%	478	1.1%	(Eco)
Williams, K. (RF)	111	0.2%				
C to Lab swing 5.2%	46,182	Lab maj 2,483 5.4%		44,495	C maj 2,228 5.0%	

Mr Jim Cousins has, since 1966, been a contract researcher and lecturer in steel, shipbuilding and inner city job markets for trade unions, the Commission on Industrial Relations and the Depts of Employment and Environment. Mbr, Tyne and Wear CC, 1973-86 (dep ldr, 1981-86); Wallsend Borough Cl, 1969-73. Founder, North Low Pay Unit. B Feb 21 1944; ed Oxford Univ; LSE. CND; ASTMS.

Mr Piers Merchant, journalist and editor of *Newsline*, the Cons Pty newspaper, 1982-84, was MP for this seat 1983-87; contested it, 1979. B Jan 2 1951; ed Nottingham HS and Durham Univ. On staff of *The Journal,* 1973-82, being news editor, 1980-82. Former Vice-chmn, all-pty parly AIDS gp; jt chmn, International Parly Gp on Human Rights; Free Flow of Information Cmte. Treas, northern group, Cons MPs; vice-chmn, Northern Area CPC. Treas, then chmn, Durham Univ Cons Assocn, 1970-73; chmn, Newcastle N Cons Assocn, 1981-83; pres, Newcastle Central Cons Assocn, 1982-83. NUJ, former FoC of Newcastle chapel.

Dr Nigel Martin, lecturer and vice-principal, Collingwood Coll, Durham Univ; research fellow, Downing Coll, Cambridge, 1971-75. Mbr, Durham CC, 1985- . B Apr 26 1945; ed Clee Humberstone Foundation Sch, Cleethorpes; Christ's Coll, Cambridge. AUT.

Mr Jim Cousins   **Mr Richard Bird**, polytechnic lecturer.

NEWCASTLE UPON TYNE EAST — No change

Electorate %Turnout	59,369	70.6%	**1987**	59,587	71.0%	**1983**
*Brown, N.H. (Lab)	23,677	56.4%	+10.9%	19,247	45.5%	(Lab)
Riley, Miss J.G.A. (C)	11,177	26.6%	-1.1%	11,755	27.8%	(C)
Arnold, P.J. (L/All)	6,728	16.0%	-10.7%	11,293	26.7%	(SDP/All)
Keith, J. (Comm)	362	0.9%				
C to Lab swing 6.0%	41,944	Lab maj 12,500 29.8%		42,295	Lab maj 7,492 17.7%	

Mr Nicholas Brown became an Opposition spokesman on legal affairs in 1985. Elected in 1983. Legal adviser, northern region of GMB, 1978-83. Mbr, Newcastle upon Tyne City Cl, 1980-84, serving on housing sub-cmte on slum clearance in east end of Newcastle. B Jun 13 1950; ed Swattenden Sec Mod Sch; Tunbridge Wells Tech HS; Manchester Univ.

Miss Jenny Riley, executive recruitment consultant, contested Wood Green, 1979. Mbr Croydon BC, 1986- ; mbr, GLC, 1977-81. Chmn, Cons Computer Forum, 1985- ; South London branch, Cons Friends of Israel. Mbr, Inst of Directors; British Computer Soc. B Apr 7 1946; ed St Mary's Hall, Brighton; Girton Coll, Cambridge. Former export planning manager with cigarette manufacturers, Carreras Rothmans and marketing executive at IBM; now managing consultant with Barry Latchford Associates, international recruitment consultants.

Mr Peter Arnold, an education officer, fought Rossendale, 1979, and Stockport North twice in 1974. B Aug 13 1944; ed Carlisle GS; Didsbury Coll of Ed, Manchester; London and Manchester Univs; Sunderland Poly. Gymnastics coach and judge. PAT.

Mr Joseph Keith, bus driver, is northern dist sec, Comm Pty, and mbr of its NEC. B Oct 22 1943; ed Bolam St Sec Mod Sch, Newcastle. TGWU shop steward.

Mr Nicholas Brown

NEWCASTLE UPON TYNE NORTH — No change

Electorate %Turnout	69,178	75.9%	**1987**	69,432	72.8%	**1983**
Henderson, D.J. (Lab)	22,424	42.7%	+5.1%	18,985	37.6%	(Lab)
Shipley, J.W. (L/All)	17,181	32.7%	+2.8%	16,429	32.5%	(C)
Tweddle, J.W. (C)	12,915	24.6%	-7.9%	15,136	29.9%	(L/All)
L/All to Lab swing 1.2%	52,520	Lab maj 5,243 10.0%		50,550	Lab maj 2,556 5.1%	

Mr Douglas Henderson, trade union official with GMB, was an executive mbr, Scottish Cl of Lab Pty, 1979-87; chaired cl, 1984-85. B Jun 9 1949; ed Waid Acad, Anstruther, Fife; Central Coll, Glasgow; Strathclyde Univ. Mbr, DATA, 1966-68 (branch sec); TSSA 1968-70 (recruitment officer) and GMB, 1973- .

Mr John Shipley, university administrator, contested this seat in 1983, Blyth twice in 1974, and Hexham, 1979. Mbr, Newcastle City Cl, since 1975; leader of Alliance gp. B Jul 5 1946; ed Whitby GS; Univ Coll, London (Pres of Union, 1968-69). AUT.

Mr John Tweddle, an electrical and grid control engineer with CEGB Operations Division, fought Huddersfield 1983. Mbr, West Yorkshire Met CC, 1977-86 (chmn, transportation, 1978-81; Cons chief whip, 1981-83). Treas, Elmet Cons Assocn; mbr, transport policy gp, 1983; Yorkshire area exec; Yorkshire and Northern area cls. B Jul 5 1948; ed St George's Coll, Weybridge; Birmingham and Huddersfield Polys. EPEA, technical rep.

Mr Douglas Henderson

NEW FOREST — No change

Electorate %Turnout	75,083	76.6%	**1987**	70,033	73.5%	**1983**
*McNair-Wilson, P.M.E.D. (C)	37,188	64.7%	-1.7%	34,157	66.4%	(C)
Karn, R. (L/All)	15,456	26.9%	+1.2%	13,232	25.7%	(L/All)
Hampton, J.I. (Lab)	4,856	8.4%	+0.5%	4,075	7.9%	(Lab)
C to L/All swing 1.4%	57,500	C maj 21,732 37.8%		51,464	C maj 20,925 40.7%	

Mr Patrick McNair-Wilson was elected for this seat in 1968; MP for Lewisham West, 1964-66. Chmn, Jt Lords and Commons Select Cmte on Private Bill Procedure, 1987- . Opposition spokesman on energy, 1974-76, and previously on the private steel sector; Opposition spokesman on fuel and power, 1965-66. Mbr, Select Cmte on Nationalized Industries, 1974, and on Science and Technology, 1968-70. Director, London Municipal Soc, 1960-63. Consultant to Union Carbide UK Ltd and to Fawley Plant of Re-Chem International Ltd. B May 28 1929; ed Hall Sch, Hampstead; Eton. Brother of MP for Newbury. PPS to Minister for Transport Industries, 1970-74.
Mr Roger Karn is a solicitor. B Sep 8 1953; ed King's Sch, Taunton; Trinity Coll, Cambridge.
Mr James Hampton, engineering lecturer. B Oct 6 1953; ed Surrey Univ. Mbr, Basingstoke Cl, 1980-84. Sec, New Forest CLP. NATFHE.

Mr Patrick McNair-Wilson

NEWHAM NORTH EAST — No change

Electorate %Turnout	60,787	64.1%	**1987**	62,463	62.1%	**1983**
*Leighton, R. (Lab)	20,220	51.9%	+2.2%	19,282	49.7%	(Lab)
Davis, P. (C)	11,984	30.7%	+3.0%	10,773	27.8%	(C)
Steele, Ms H. (L/All)	6,772	17.4%	-3.1%	7,943	20.5%	(L/All)
				794	2.0%	(Other)
Lab to C swing 0.4%	38,976	Lab maj 8,236 21.1%		38,792	Lab maj 8,509 21.9%	

Mr Ronald Leighton has been chmn of the Select Cmte on Employment since 1984 and of the PLP employment cmte since 1983; an Opposition whip, 1981-84. Printer. Regained seat for Labour in 1979; contested Horsham and Crawley, Feb 1974, and Middleton and Prestwich, 1964. Chmn, Labour's Common Market Safeguards Cmte, 1975- . B Jan 24 1930; ed Monteagle and Bifrons Sch, Barking; Ruskin Coll, Oxford. Sec, Labour Cmte for Safeguards on Common Market, 1967-70; director, Common Market Safeguards Campaign, 1970-73; national organiser of EEC referendum campaign for "No" vote, 1975. Sponsored by Sogat '82.
Mr Peter Davis is head of home affairs, Cons Research Dept; former product gp manager, Dylon International Ltd. Special adviser to Mr Kenneth Baker, when Sec of State for Environment, 1984-86. Mbr, Lambeth BC, 1978-84 (dep ldr, 1982; ldr of opposition, 1983-84). B Feb 25 1949; ed Archbishop Tenison's GS, Kennington; SW London Coll. Mbr, Inst of Marketing. Fluent in Danish.
Ms Harriet Steele, journalist. B 1964; ed Bolton Sch; Queen Mary Coll, London Univ. Chaired ULS, 1985.

Mr Ronald Leighton

NEWHAM NORTH WEST — No change

Electorate %Turnout	47,568	59.4%	**1987**	49,814	56.1%	**1983**
*Banks, T.L. (Lab)	15,677	55.4%	+8.8%	13,042	46.6%	(Lab)
Wylie, J.C. (C)	7,181	25.4%	+3.5%	6,124	21.9%	(C)
Redden, R.H. (SDP/All)	4,920	17.4%	-1.2%	5,204	18.6%	(SDP/All)
Harrison, Ms A. (Grn)	497	1.8%		3,074	11.0%	(Ind Lab)
				525	1.9%	(Other)
C to Lab swing 2.7%	28,275	Lab maj 8,496 30.0%		27,969	Lab maj 6,918 24.7%	

Mr Tony Banks joined the Select Cmte on Treasury and Civil Service in 1987; chmn, PLP arts cmte; UK/Nicaragua parly gp. Asst gen sec, Assocn of Broadcasting and Allied Staffs, 1976-83. Elected in 1983; contested East Grinstead, 1970; Newcastle North, Oct 1974; Watford, 1979. Chmn, GLC, 1985-86; and of its Arts and Recreation Cmte, 1981-83, and Gen Purposes Cmte, 1975-77; GLC member for Hammersmith, 1970-77, and for Tooting, 1981-86. Mbr, Nat Theatre Bd, 1981-85; English National Opera Bd; London Festival Ballet Bd. B Apr 8 1945; ed Archbishop Tenisons, Kennington; York Univ; LSE. Political adviser to Dame Judith Hart, Minister for Overseas Development, 1975; head of research, AUEW, 1969-75. Mbr, TGWU, by whom he is sponsored.
Mr John Wylie, chartered surveyor and chief executive, Dulwich estate. Mbr, Hammersmith and Fulham BC, 1974-82. B 1944; ed St Edward's Sch, Oxford; London Univ.
Mr Richard Redden, journalist, public affairs manager with British Telecom, contested Sevenoaks for Lab 1979. Former sec, Ravensbourne SDP; mbr, Micro SDP. B Dec 19 1942; ed Bromley GS; St Catherine's Coll, Oxford. NUJ.

Mr Tony Banks

NEWHAM SOUTH — No change

Electorate %Turnout	50,244	59.1%	**1987**	50,362	53.6%	**1983**
*Spearing, N.J. (Lab)	12,935	43.5%	-6.7%	13,561	50.2%	(Lab)
Fairrie, J. (C)	10,169	34.2%	+11.2%	6,250	23.1%	(SDP/All)
Kellaway, A.J. (SDP/All)	6,607	22.2%	-0.9%	6,212	23.0%	(C)
				993	3.7%	(Other)
Lab to C swing 8.9%	29,711	Lab maj 2,766 9.3%		27,016	Lab maj 7,311 27.1%	

Mr **Nigel Spearing** became chairman, Select Cmte on European Legislation in 1983; mbr from 1979. Mbr, Select Cmte on Foreign Affairs 1979- . Elected for this seat in May 1974 by-election; MP for Acton, 1970-Feb 1974; contested Warwick and Leamington, 1964. Teacher at Wandsworth Sch, 1956-68. B Oct 8 1930; ed Latymer Upper Sch, Hammersmith; St Catharine's Coll, Cambridge. Mbr, Select Cmte on Overseas Development, 1977-79 and 1973-74; on Procedure, 1975-78; on Members' Interests, 1974-75. Chmn, British Anti-Common Market Campaign, 1977-83; Pres, Socialist Environment and Resources Assocn (SERA), 1977-86. Co-opted on GLC planning and transport cmtes, 1966-73. NUT.
Mr **James Fairrie**, banker and former Army officer. Mbr, Wandsworth BC, 1981-86. B 1947; ed Downside Sch; RMC Sandhurst; Exeter Univ.
Mr **Alec Kellaway**, economist/business consultant on retailing and consumer spending, contested Newham North West 1983. Founder mbr, SDP; chmn, area SDP; sole SDP member, Newham Cl. B May 31 1953; ed East Ham GS; Christ Church, Oxford.

Mr Nigel Spearing

NEWPORT EAST — No change

Electorate %Turnout	52,199	80.1%	**1987**	52,503	76.6%	**1983**
*Hughes, R.J. (Lab)	20,518	49.1%	+9.5%	15,931	39.6%	(Lab)
Webster-Gardiner, G.R. (C)	13,454	32.2%	-0.9%	13,301	33.1%	(C)
David, Mrs F.A. (SDP/All)	7,383	17.7%	-7.9%	10,293	25.6%	(SDP/All)
Butler, G. (Pl C)	458	1.1%	-0.6%	697	1.7%	(Pl C)
C to Lab swing 5.2%	41,813	Lab maj 7,064 16.9%		40,222	Lab maj 2,630 6.5%	

Mr **Roy Hughes** became an Opposition spokesman on Wales in 1984. Elected for this seat 1983; MP for Newport, 1966-83. Former adminstrative officer in Coventry car firm, and officer in TGWU, 1959-66. B Jun 9 1925; ed Pontllanfraith Sec Sch; Ruskin Coll, Oxford. Mbr, Coventry City Cl, and sec, Coventry Lab Pty, 1962-66. Chmn, TGWU parliamentary group, 1968-69 and 1979-82; PLP steel group, since 1978; PLP sports group, 1974-83. PPS to Minister of Transport, 1974-75. Chmn, Welsh group of Lab MPs, 1986- ; vice-chmn, 1985-86. Mbr, Speaker's panel of chairmen, 1982-84, when he ws chmn, Welsh Grand Cmte.
Mr **Graham Webster-Gardiner** is chairman of the Conservative Family Campaign. Marketing director; hon sec, Marketing Society, 1981; chmn, postal cmte, British Direct Marketing Assocn, 1980. Fellow, BIM; mbr, Inst of Management Services. B Jul 4 1947; ed Selhurst GS, Croydon; Warwick Univ.
Mrs **Frances David**, teacher, contested this seat 1983. B Feb 4 1933; ed Sherborne Sch for Girls; St Hugh's Coll, Oxford. Mbr, CSD; vice-chmn, Welsh SDP and its ed spokesman. Mbr, Sec Heads Assocn.
Mr **Gareth Butler**, education adviser. Mbr, Ceredigion DC, 1987- . Ed Duffryn HS; Univ Coll, Aberystwyth. Former pres, students union.

Mr Roy Hughes

NEWPORT WEST — Lab gain

Electorate %Turnout	55,455	81.8%	**1987**	54,125	77.5%	**1983**
Flynn, P.P. (Lab)	20,887	46.1%	+9.4%	15,948	38.0%	(C)
*Robinson, M.N.F. (C)	18,179	40.1%	+2.1%	15,367	36.6%	(Lab)
Roddick, G.W. (L/All)	5,903	13.0%	-11.2%	10,163	24.2%	(L/All)
Bevan, D.J. (Pl C)	377	0.8%	-0.3%	477	1.1%	(Pl C)
C to Lab swing 3.7%	45,346	Lab maj 2,708 6.0%		41,955	C maj 581 1.4%	

Mr **Paul Flynn** is research officer for Mr Llewellyn Smith, Labour MEP for South East Wales. Has chaired broadcasting cl for Wales, and served on South Wales Docks Bd and cl, Univ Coll, Cardiff. Mbr, Newport Cl. B Feb 9 1935; ed St Illtyd's; Univ Coll, Cardiff. Nupe.
Mr **Mark Robinson** was Under Secretary of State for Wales in 1985-87; PPS to Secretary of State for Wales, 1984-85. Elected in 1983; contested South Yorkshire in Euro elections, 1979. Asst director, Commonwealth Secretariat, Marlborough House, 1977-83; personal and political asst to UN Secretary-General, Kurt Waldheim, 1974-77. Non-practising barrister. B Dec 26 1946; ed Harrow; Christ Church, Oxford (pres, univ Cons assocn, 1967), and Middle Temple. Mbr, Select Cmte on Foreign Affairs, 1983-84; hon sec, UN parly group, 1983-85; British-Canadian parly gp of CPA, 1983-85; treas, British-Caribbean parly gp of CPA, 1984-85; former sec, Welsh Cons MPs.
Mr **Winston Roddick**, QC, is chmn of the Alliance in Wales; president-elect, Welsh Lib Pty. Alliance spokesman on education in Wales. B Oct 2 1940; ed Caernarfon GS; Univ Coll, London.
Mr **Digby Bevan**, civil engineer employed by a Cardiff housing assocn. Aged 35. Worked overseas on irrigation projects.

Mr Paul Flynn

NEWRY AND ARMAGH | No change

Electorate %Turnout	66,027	79.2%	**1987**	62,387	76.0%	**1983**
*Mallon, S. (SDLP)	25,137	48.1%	+11.3%	18,988	40.0%	(OUP)
Nicholson, J.F. (OUP)	19,812	37.9%	-2.1%	17,434	36.8%	(SDLP)
McAllister, J. (PSF)	6,173	11.8%	-9.1%	9,928	20.9%	(PSF)
Jeffrey, W.H. (All)	664	1.3%		1,070	2.3%	(WP)
O'Hanlon, J. (WP)	482	0.9%				
OUP to SDLP swing 6.7%	52,268	SDLP maj 5,325 10.2%		47,420	OUP maj 1,554 3.3%	

Mr **Seamus Mallon** is vice chairman of the Social Democratic and Labour Party. Won this seat at by-election in 1986; contested it 1983. Teacher. B Aug 17 1936; ed Abbey GS, Newry; St Joseph's Coll of Ed, Belfast. Mbr, NI Assembly, 1973-74 and 1982; NI Convention, 1975-76; Irish Senate, 1981-82; Armagh DC, 1973- ; Irish Nat Teachers' Organisation..
Mr **James Nicholson** was MP for this seat, 1983-86, losing it in the by-election forced by theUnionist protest at the Anglo-Irish Agreement. B Jan 29 1945; ed Aghavilly Primary Sch. OUP Assembly mbr, 1982-86. OUP mbr, Armagh DC, 1976- .
Mr **James McAllister** contested the seat in the 1986 by-election and 1983. B 1944. PSF assembly mbr, Newry Armagh, 1982-1986; mbr, Newry and Mourne DC, 1985- .
Mr **William Jeffrey**, manager of advertising agency. B Feb 15 1934; ed Univ of Ulster, Jordanstown. Mbr, Belfast City Cl, 1977-81. Unsuccessful candidate in 1982 Assembly elections for Newry and Armagh.
Details of 1986 by-election at which SDLP gained seat on Page XXX.

Mr **Seamus Mallon**

NORFOLK MID | No change

Electorate %Turnout	73,893	78.2%	**1987**	68,953	75.3%	**1983**
*Ryder, R. (C)	32,758	56.7%	+0.8%	29,032	55.9%	(C)
Graham, G.J.E. (SDP/All)	14,750	25.5%	-0.5%	13,517	26.0%	(SDP/All)
Luckey, K. (Lab)	10,272	17.8%	+0.5%	8,950	17.2%	(Lab)
				405	0.8%	(Other)
SDP/All to C swing 0.6%	57,780	C maj 18,008 31.2%		51,904	C maj 15,515 29.9%	

Mr **Richard Ryder** was appointed an assistant Government whip in 1986. PPS to Secretary of State for Foreign and Commonwealth Affairs, 1984-86, and to Financial Secretary to the Treasury, 1984. Chmn, Cons Foreign and Commonwealth Cl, 1984- . Journalist and partner of family farming business. Political secretary to Mrs Thatcher, 1975-81. B Feb 4 1949; ed Radley; Magdalene Coll, Cambridge. Elected in 1983; contested Gateshead East in both 1974 elections. Former vice-chmn, Eastern Region Cl for Sport and Recreation.
Mr **Gavin Graham**, fish farmer. Mbr, Broadland DC, 1984- . Chmn, Mid-Norfolk SDP. B Jul 21 1947; ed All Saints, Bloxham; Liverpool Univ.
Mr **Keith Luckey**, railway guard. B Jul 8 1945; ed sec mod sch; Open Univ. Mbr, Peterborough City Cl, 1980- . NUR.

Mr **Richard Ryder**

NORFOLK NORTH | No change

Electorate %Turnout	69,790	77.5%	**1987**	65,101	74.6%	**1983**
*Howell, R.F. (C)	28,822	53.3%	-0.7%	26,230	54.0%	(C)
Anthony, N.R. (SDP/All)	13,512	25.0%	-1.8%	13,007	26.8%	(SDP/All)
Earle, A. (Lab)	10,765	19.9%	+0.7%	9,317	19.2%	(Lab)
Filgate, M.G. (Grn)	960	1.8%				
SDP/All to C swing 0.5%	54,059	C maj 15,310 28.3%		48,554	C maj 13,223 27.2%	

Mr **Ralph Howell**, a member of the Select Committee on the Treasury and Civil Service since 1982, was a nominated mbr, European Parliament, 1974-79. Farmer and underwriting mbr of Lloyd's. Chmn, Cons back-bench employment cmte, 1984- , and previously jt vice-chmn; jt sec, Cons agriculture, fisheries and food cmte, 1985- ; vice-chmn, Cons back-bench finance cmte, 1979-84; mbr, exec, 1922 Cmte, 1984- . Won seat for the Cons in 1970; contested it, 1966. B May 25 1923; ed Diss GS, Norfolk. Former local NFU chmn. Mbr, Mitford and Launditch RDC, 1961-74. Mbr, Cl of Europe Assembly, 1981.
Mr **Neil Antony**, personnel manager for a soft drinks manufacturer; previously in industrial relations dept of Ford Motor Co. B Nov 21 1956; ed King Edward VI Sch, Norwich; Durham Univ.
Mr **Tony Earle**, local government employee. B Aug 9 1941. Mbr, Nat Cmte of the Workplace Nurseries Campaign; Amnesty International. TWGU.
Mr **Michael Filgate**, social worker; E Norfolk Grn Pty coordinator; mbr, social welfare working pty. Parish cllr. B Apr 24 1950; HS and Coll in US; Reading Univ. Nalgo.

Mr **Ralph Howell**

NORFOLK NORTH WEST — No change

Electorate %Turnout	73,739	78.9%	**1987**	69,181	77.6%	**1983**
*Bellingham, H.C. (C)	29,393	50.6%	+7.1%	23,358	43.5%	(C)
Brocklebank-Fowler, C. (SDP/All)	18,568	31.9%	-5.7%	20,211	37.6%	(SDP/All)
Dignan, F. (Lab)	10,184	17.5%	-1.4%	10,139	18.9%	(Lab)
SDP/All to C swing 6.4%	58,145	C maj 10,825 18.6%		53,708	C maj 3,147 5.9%	

Mr Henry Bellingham, a barrister, was elected in 1983. B Mar 29 1955; ed Eton; Magdalene Coll, Cambridge; Inns of Court School of Law. Jt sec, Cons back-bench Northern Ireland Cmte, 1983- ; Cons smaller businesses cmte, 1983- . Mbr, nat board, Small Business Bureau, since 1982. Founder, West Norfolk Small Business Bureau, 1982. Mbr of Lloyd's; partner in family farming company.

Mr Christopher Brocklebank-Fowler, former managing director, Cambridge Corporate Consultants, was Conservative MP for King's Lynn 1970-74 and Norfolk North West from 1974, resigning from the party in 1981. Joined SDP, becoming spokesman on overseas aid and jt spokesman on foreign and Commonwealth affairs and agriculture, but was defeated in 1983. Contested West Ham North 1964. Chmn, SDP Third World policy cmte, 1981- ; mbr, SDP nat steering cmte, 1981-82. Vice-chmn, Centre for World Development of Education, 1980-83. Governor, Inst of Development Studies, 1979-81. B Jan 13 1934; ed Perse Sch, Cambridge.

Mr Frank Dignan, probation officer. B Oct 9 1957; ed St Michael's RC Coll, Leeds; Trinity and All Saints Coll, Leeds; Leeds Univ. Mbr, West Yorkshire CC, 1983-86. Director, Leeds Industrial Co-op Soc. GMBATU.

Mr Henry Bellingham

NORFOLK SOUTH — No change

Electorate %Turnout	78,372	81.0%	**1987**	73,523	77.2%	**1983**
*MacGregor, J.R.R. (C)	33,912	53.4%	-0.7%	30,747	54.2%	(C)
Carden, R.A.P. (L/All)	21,494	33.9%	+1.1%	18,612	32.8%	(L/All)
Addison, L. (Lab)	8,047	12.7%	-0.4%	7,408	13.0%	(Lab)
C to L/All swing 0.9%	63,453	C maj 12,418 19.6%		56,767	C maj 12,135 21.4%	

Mr John MacGregor was appointed Minister of Agriculture, Fisheries and Food in Jun 1987; joined Cabinet as Chief Secretary to the Treasury in 1985; Minister of State for Agriculture, Fisheries and Food, 1983-85; Under Secretary of State for Industry, 1981-83; a Lord Commissioner of the Treasury (Govt whip), 1979-81. Former director, Hill Samuel and Co Ltd, and Hill Samuel Registrars Ltd. Elected in Feb 1974. An Opposition whip, 1977-79. Mbr, PAC, 1974-75; Expenditure Cmte, 1975-77. Chmn, Bow Group, 1963-64. Sec, Cons back-bench finance cmte, 1976-77. B Feb 14 1937; ed Merchiston Castle Sch, Edinburgh; St Andrews Univ; King's Coll, London. Former journalist with New Society; special asst to Sir Alec Douglas-Home when Prime Minister, 1963-64, and head of Mr Heath's private office, 1965-68.

Mr Richard Carden, a systems engineer, contested the seat in 1983. B Jan 14 1942; ed King's Sch, Canterbury; Keble Coll, Oxford. Mbr, Norfolk CC, 1981- ; South Oxfordshire DC, 1973-76; Henley-on-Thames BC and TC, 1969-76.

Mr Lloyd Addison, restaurateur. County cllr, 1981-85. B Jul 3 1952; ed Downham Mkt Sec Mod Sch; King's Lynn CFE; East Anglia Univ. GMB.

Mr John MacGregor

NORFOLK SOUTH WEST — No change

Electorate %Turnout	74,240	76.0%	**1987**	70,398	73.1%	**1983**
Shephard, Mrs G.P. (C)	32,519	57.6%	+1.9%	28,632	55.7%	(C)
Scott, M. (L/All)	12,083	21.4%	-5.3%	13,722	26.7%	(L/All)
Page, Ms M. (Lab)	11,844	21.0%	+3.3%	9,072	17.6%	(Lab)
L/All to C swing 3.6%	56,446	C maj 20,436 36.2%		51,426	C maj 14,910 29.0%	

Mrs Gillian Shephard is chmn of the Norwich Health Authority and is involved in small family cattle and livestock business. Mbr, Norfolk CC, 1977- ; deputy leader of cl, 1981- . Norfolk representative on ACC. B Jan 22 1940; ed North Walsham Girls' HS, Norfolk; St Hilda's Coll, Oxford. Former Inspector of Schools and senior education officer. Mbr, exec cl and women's advisory cmte, Norwich South Cons Assocn; Cons Eastern Area women's and education advisory cmtes, 1978- ; nat cl, Centre for Family Policy Studies, 1980- ; special employment measures advisory group of MSC, 1980- ; Nacro juvenile crime advisory cmte, 1980- ; exec cmte, Norfolk Magistrates Assocn, 1973- ; Nat Cl of Mind, 1973- . Mental Health Act Commissioner, since 1983; chmn, Norfolk Museums Service, 1980- ; lecturer for Cambridge Univ extra mural bd in European subjects, 1973- . Fluent French speaker.

Mr Malcolm Scott, marketing executive, contested Norfolk South twice in 1974. B Nov 26 1946; ed St Joseph's Coll, Ipswich; Norwich City Coll.

Ms Mary Page, teacher and translator. Mbr, Breckland DC 1974-81; Thetford DC 1974-81 and 1985- ; Mayoress of Thetford 1980-81. B May 15 1944; ed Bournemouth Sch for Girls; Southampton and London Univs. Speaks French, German, Spanish, Italian and Polish.

Mrs Gillian Shephard   NAS/UWT.

NORMANTON — No change

Electorate %Turnout	62,899	74.8%	**1987**	61,249	70.4%	**1983**
*O'Brien, W. (Lab)	23,303	49.5%	+6.0%	18,782	43.6%	(Lab)
Smith, M.D.M. (C)	16,016	34.1%	+0.2%	14,599	33.9%	(C)
Macey, R.J. (SDP/All)	7,717	16.4%	-6.2%	9,741	22.6%	(SDP/All)
C to Lab swing 2.9%	47,036	Lab maj 7,287 15.5%		43,122	Lab maj 4,183 9.7%	

Mr **William O'Brien** has been a member of the Public Accounts Cmte since 1983 and the Select Cmte on Energy since 1986. Coalminer, 1945-83; NUM local branch official, 1956-83. Elected in 1983. Urban, county and metropolitan district councillor, 1951-83, serving on Wakefield DC, 1973-83. B Jan 25 1929; ed St Joseph's Sch, Castleford; Leeds Univ. Mbr, NUM, since 1946.
Mr **Michael Smith**, insurance executive. Chmn, Leeds Univ Cons Assocn. B 1948; ed Ifield GS, Crawley; Leeds Univ.
Mr **Richard Macey**, teacher. Chmn, Rother Valley SDP. B Oct 23 1944; ed Bristol GS; Sheffield Coll of Ed; Goldsmiths Coll, London Univ.

Mr William O'Brien

NORTHAMPTON NORTH — No change

Electorate %Turnout	69,294	74.6%	**1987**	68,370	72.0%	**1983**
*Marlow, A.R. (C)	24,816	48.0%	+1.0%	23,129	47.0%	(C)
Granfield, O.J. (Lab)	15,560	30.1%	+3.1%	13,269	27.0%	(Lab)
Rounthwaite, A.S. (L/All)	10,690	20.7%	-5.4%	12,829	26.1%	(L/All)
Green, M. (Grn)	471	0.9%				
Colling, S. (WRP)	156	0.3%				
C to Lab swing 1.1%	51,693	C maj 9,256 17.9%		49,227	C maj 9,860 20.0%	

Mr **Antony Marlow** has been a member of the Select Cmte on European Legislation since 1983. Former development manager with a grain shippers company. Gained seat for Cons in 1979; contested Normanton, Feb 1974, and Rugby, Oct 1974. Consultant for Gulf Centre for Strategic Studies. B Jun 17 1940; ed Wellington Coll; RMA Sandhurst; St Catharine's Coll, Cambridge. Jt sec, Cons back-bench defence cmte, 1985- ; former jt sec, Cons back-bench trade and consumer affairs cmte. Chmn, UK-Palestine all-pty parly group. Mbr, steering cmte, Cons European Reform Group. Former chmn, Daventry CPC cmte and East Midlands Area CPC working party.
Mr **Owen Granfield**, Apex Midland area organiser. Mbr, Northampton Cl, 1985- . Vice-Pres, Northampton Trades Cl. B Mar 23 1952; ed comprehensive sch and Manchester Poly.
Mr **Tony Rounthwaite**, general manager of Nere College Students Union, contested this seat, 1983 and 1979. Mbr, Northants CC, 1981- (ex-leader, Lib gp); Northampton BC, 1983- . Director, Hereward Radio; Northampton Royal Theatre. B Feb 6 1951; ed King's Sch, Tynemouth; Newcastle Poly. Former member Nupe.
Mr **Michael Green**, press officer. B Apr 27 1957; ed Northampton GS; Reading and Leicester Univs.

Mr Antony Marlow

NORTHAMPTON SOUTH — No change

Electorate %Turnout	76,071	75.2%	**1987**	68,910	72.6%	**1983**
*Morris, M.W.L. (C)	31,864	55.7%	+2.1%	26,824	53.6%	(C)
Dickie, J. (Lab)	14,061	24.6%	+1.5%	11,698	23.4%	(SDP/All)
Hopkins, G. (SDP/All)	10,639	18.6%	-4.8%	11,533	23.0%	(Lab)
Hamilton, Ms M. (Grn)	647	1.1%				
Lab to C swing 0.3%	57,211	C maj 17,803 31.1%		50,055	C maj 15,126 30.2%	

Mr **Michael Morris** has served on the Public Accounts Committee since 1979; mbr, Speaker's panel of chairmen, 1983- . Elected in Feb 1974; contested Islington North, 1966. Mbr, Select Cmte on Energy, 1982-85; vice-chmn, Cons back-bench energy cmte, 1981-. Director of Modern Personnel Ltd; consultant for AM International whose clients include Mars Corporation, Reckitt and Colman, Hill Samuel, Wood Mackenzie, the Glass and Glazing Federation, Underwoods (Cash Chemist) Ltd, Upjohn. B Nov 25 1936; ed Bedford Sch and St Catharine's Coll, Cambridge. Mbr, Cl of Europe and WEU, 1983- . PPS to Minister of State for N Ireland, 1979-81. Chmn, all-pty British-Sri Lanka, British-Singapore and British-Malaysia cmtes; vice-chmn, British-Indonesia cmte; treas, British-Thai and ASEAN cmte; sec, British-Burma cmte.
Mr **John Dickie**, teacher, contested Northamptonshire in 1984 Euro election. Mbr, Northampton BC, 1973- ; Labour whip. B Nov 28 1946; ed William Ellis Sch, London; Brighton Coll of Ed; Sussex Univ. NAS/UWT.
Mr **George Hopkins**, businessman. B Jul 1 1933; ed Keighley Boys' GS; RAF Coll Cranwell; RAF Staff Coll, Bracknell. Served in RAF 1955-71, leaving as Sq Ldr.
Ms **Margaret Hamilton**, community worker. B May 27 1945; ed Chiswick Poly; Open Univ. Mbr, Child Poverty Action Group. Nupe.

Mr Michael Morris

NORTHAVON — No change

Electorate %Turnout	78,483	80.2%	**1987**	73,553	78.0%	**1983**
*Cope, J.A. (C)	34,224	54.4%	+0.7%	30,790	53.7%	(C)
Willmore, Ms C. (L/All)	19,954	31.7%	+0.6%	17,807	31.1%	(L/All)
Norris, D. (Lab)	8,762	13.9%	-0.5%	8,243	14.4%	(Lab)
				499	0.9%	(Other)
L/All to C swing 0.0%	62,940	C maj 14,270 22.7%		57,339	C maj 12,983 22.6%	

Mr John Cope

Mr John Cope was appointed Minister of State for Employment, Jun 1987; Treasurer of HM Household and Government Deputy Chief Whip, 1983-87; Lord Commissioner of the Treasury (Govt whip), 1981-83; assistant Govt whip, 1979-81. Mbr, Select Cmte on Commons Services. Chartered accountant; former company director. Hon vice-pres, Nat Chamber of Trade. Elected for this seat 1983; MP for South Gloucestershire, Feb 1974-83; contested Woolwich East, 1970. B May 13 1937; ed Oakham School, Rutland. In Cons Research Dept and Central Office, 1965-1970, being personal asst to Cons Pty chmn, 1967-70. Special assistant to Secretary of State for Trade and Industry, 1972-1974. Former vice-chmn and sec, Cons back-bench smaller businesses cmte.
Ms Christine Willmore, barrister, is lecturer in law, Bristol Univ. Sec, ALC, 1984-86; vice-chair, 1986-87. Mbr, pty policy cmte, 1986-87; manifesto cmte, 1987; Northavon DC, 1983-87 (Ldr, Alliance gp, 1986-87). B Jan 24 1956; ed Godolphin and Latymer, London; Bristol Univ. AUT.
Mr Dan Norris, residential social worker and former teacher. B Jan 28 1966. Mbr, Socialist Ed Assocn; Fabian Soc; Nalgo; NAS/UWT.

NORWICH NORTH — No change

Electorate %Turnout	62,725	79.2%	**1987**	62,781	76.2%	**1983**
*Thompson, H.P. (C)	22,772	45.8%	+1.2%	21,355	44.7%	(C)
Honeyball, Ms M.H.R. (Lab)	14,996	30.2%	-2.2%	15,476	32.4%	(Lab)
Nicholls, T.P. (L/All)	11,922	24.0%	+1.4%	10,796	22.6%	(L/All)
				194	0.4%	(Other)
Lab to C swing 1.7%	49,690	C maj 7,776 15.6%		47,821	C maj 5,879 12.3%	

Mr Patrick Thompson

Mr Patrick Thompson, teacher and former engineer, was elected in 1983; contested Bradford North in both 1974 elections and Barrow-in-Furness, 1979. Jt sec, Cons back-bench energy cmte, 1985- ; mbr, Parly and Scientific Cmte, 1983- ; founder mbr, all-pty gp for engineering development, 1985- . B Oct 21 1935; ed Felsted Sch, Essex, and Emmanuel Coll, Cambridge. With English Electric Valve Co, 1959-60; sixth form physics master, Manchester GS, 1960-65, and at Gresham's Sch, Holt, 1965-83. Commissioned in King's Own Yorkshire Light Infantry on National Service, then five years in TA and 15 years in school's Combined Cadet Force; Major (retd); received Cadet Force Medal 1982. Mbr, Inst of Physics. AMMA.
Ms Mary Honeyball, director of a cl for voluntary service, contested Enfield, Southgate, 1983. Chaired Greater London Labour women's cmte, 1983-85; mbr, Co-op Retail Services SE Sector political cmte; Greater London Lab Pty reg exec cmte, 1980-82 and 1983-85; Barnet BC, 1978-86. B Nov 12 1952; ed Pate's GS, Cheltenham; Somerville Coll, Oxford. Nupe.
Mr Paul Nicholls, barrister, is legal officer to Commission for Racial Equality. Mbr, Lib Pty Cl and Community Relations Panel. Treas, Eastern Region Lib Pty. B Jul 2 1953; ed Cheltenham Coll; Brunel Univ (Pres of students' union, 1976-77); Cl of Legal Ed.

NORWICH SOUTH — Lab gain

Electorate %Turnout	64,421	80.6%	**1987**	64,100	76.4%	**1983**
Garrett, J.L. (Lab)	19,666	37.9%	+2.6%	18,998	38.8%	(C)
*Powley, J.A. (C)	19,330	37.3%	-1.6%	17,286	35.3%	(Lab)
Hardie, C.J.M. (SDP/All)	12,896	24.9%	+0.4%	11,968	24.4%	(SDP/All)
				704	1.4%	(Other)
C to Lab swing 2.1%	51,892	Lab maj 336 0.6%		48,956	C maj 1,712 3.5%	

Mr John Garrett

Mr John Garrett, management consultant, was MP for the seat, Feb 1974-83; an Opposition spokesman on industry and on Treasury affairs, 1979-83; PPS to Minister for the Civil Service and to Minister for Social Security, 11974-79. Mbr, Greenwich BC, 1970-74. B Sep 8 1931; ed Sir George Monoux Sch, London; Oxford and California (Los Angeles) Univs. Director, New Statesman Publishing Co; West Midlands Enterprise Board. TGWU.
Mr John Powley was MP for the seat, 1983-87; contested Harlow, 1979. Owner and director of a retail electrical, radio and television business, 1960-84. Mbr, Select Committee on Social Services, 1986-87; jt sec, Cons back-bench environment cmte, 1986-87. B Aug 3 1936; ed Cambridge GS; Cambridge Coll of Arts and Tech. Mbr, Cambridgeshire CC, 1977-77; Cambridge City Cl, 1967-79. Vice-pres, Assocn of Dist Cls, 1984- .
Mr Jeremy Hardie, chmn, National Provident Inst, since 1980 (director, since 1972; dep chmn, 1977), contested Norwich South 1983. Chmn of other companies, including Radio Broadland Ltd (Norwich commercial radio) since 1983. Mbr, cl, Oxford Centre for Management studies, 1978-85; Arts Council of GB, 1984- ; Peacock Cmte on financing BBC. B Jun 9 1938; ed Winchester Coll; New Coll, Oxford; Nuffield Coll, Oxford.

NORWOOD — No change

Electorate %Turnout	56,602	67.0%	**1987**	55,663	65.6%	**1983**
*Fraser, J.D. (Lab)	18,359	48.4%	+3.9%	16,280	44.6%	(Lab)
Grieve, D.C.R. (C)	13,636	36.0%	-0.7%	13,397	36.7%	(C)
Noble, M.M. (SDP/All)	5,579	14.7%	-2.7%	6,371	17.4%	(SDP/All)
Jackson, F.M. (RABIES)	171	0.5%		343	0.9%	(NF)
Hammond, R.J. (CD)	151	0.4%		123	0.3%	(Ind)
C to Lab swing 2.3%	37,896	Lab maj 4,723 12.5%		36,514	Lab maj 2,883 7.9%	

Mr **John Fraser** has been an Opposition spokesman on housing and construction since 1983; on trade, prices and consumer protection, 1979-83; Minister of State, Department of Prices and Consumer Protection, 1976-79; Under Secretary of State for Employment, 1974-76; an Opposition spokesman on home affairs, 1972-74. PPS to Mrs Barbara Castle, 1968-71. Won the seat in 1966; contested it, 1964. Solicitor. B Jun 30 1934; ed Sloane GS, Chelsea; Cooperative Coll, Loughborough; Law Soc School of Law. Mbr, Lambeth BC, 1962-68. Former chmn, PLP Greek Democratic Committee; former mbr, Select Cmtes on Education and Science and on Broadcasting of Proceedings. Former dep chmn, PLP environment group. GMB.
Mr **Dominic Grieve**, barrister. Mbr, Hammersmith and Fulham BC, 1982- . B 1956; ed Westminster Sch; Magdalen Coll, Oxford. Pres, Oxford Univ Cons Assocn, 1977.
Mr **Malcolm Noble**, deputy headmaster. Vice-chmn, Lambeth Central Lab Pty, 1972-8, before joining SDP. Contested Norwood (SDP) 1983; Cities of London and Westminster South (Lab) 1977. Sec, Clapham Lab Pty, 1969-70; former chmn, Norwood SDP. Mbr, Lambeth Cl, 1971-82. B Dec 30 1946; ed Peebles Burgh and Cty HS; London Univ.

Mr **John Fraser**

NOTTINGHAM EAST — No change

Electorate %Turnout	68,266	68.8%	**1987**	68,638	63.6%	**1983**
*Knowles, M. (C)	20,162	42.9%	+2.5%	17,641	40.4%	(C)
Aslam, M. (Lab)	19,706	42.0%	+4.9%	16,177	37.1%	(Lab)
Parkhouse, S. (L/All)	6,887	14.7%	-4.6%	8,385	19.2%	(SDP/All)
Malik, K. (RF)	212	0.5%		1,421	3.3%	(Ind C)
C to Lab swing 1.2%	46,967	C maj 456 1.0%		43,624	C maj 1,464 3.4%	

Mr **Michael Knowles** has been a member of the Select Cmte on European Legislation since 1983, the year he was elected to this seat; contested Merthyr Tydfil, Feb 1974, and Brent East, Oct 1974. PPS to Lord Elton, Minister of State for Environment and Minister for Planning, until his resignation in 1986. Former sales manager, export and home sales. B May 21 1942; ed Clapham Coll RC GS. Mbr, Kingston upon Thames BC, 1971-83; leader of cl, 1974-83. Mbr, Surbiton constituency exec, 1971-83, and Kingston constituency exec, 1974-83.
Mr **Mohammed Aslam**, chartered accountant, is a member of Nottinghamshire CC and was on the former Race Relations Board. An Asian, he became candidate when the Labour NEC chose him to replace black candidate Ms Sharon Atkins whom they suspended because of remarks she made about the party at a black sections rally.
Mr **Stephen Parkhouse**, physics and electronics teacher. Vice-chmn, Notts Alliance gp. B Jan 10 1951; ed Leeds, Leicester and Nottingham Univs. NAS/UWT.

Mr **Michael Knowles**

NOTTINGHAM NORTH — Lab gain

Electorate %Turnout	69,620	72.6%	**1987**	71,807	66.1%	**1983**
Allen, G.W. (Lab)	22,713	44.9%	+6.2%	18,730	39.4%	(C)
*Ottaway, R.G.J. (C)	21,048	41.6%	+2.2%	18,368	38.7%	(Lab)
Fernando, S.C. (SDP/All)	5,912	11.7%	-7.7%	9,200	19.4%	(SDP/All)
Peck, J.H. (Comm)	879	1.7%	-0.8%	1,184	2.5%	(Com)
C to Lab swing 2.0%	50,552	Lab maj 1,665 3.3%		47,482	C maj 362 0.8%	

Mr **Graham Allen**, trade union organiser, former GLC officer and Lab Pty research officer. National coordinator, political funds campaign for the trades union coordinating cmte, 1984-86. B Jan 11 1953; ed local schools in Nottingham. TGWU.
Mr **Richard Ottaway**, a solicitor and specialist in Admiralty law, has been a partner in a firm of solicitors since 1981; shipping consultant. MP for this seat, 1983-87. PPS to Ministers of State for Foreign and Commonwealth Affairs, 1985-87. B May 24 1945; ed Backwell Sec Mod Sch, Somerset; RNC Dartmouth; Bristol Univ. Chmn, research cmte, Cons Lawyers. Former cmte mbr, parly maritime gp and population and development gp. Mbr, International Commission of Jurists. Served in RN, 1961-70; RNR, 1970-80.
Mr **Sumal Fernando**, solicitor, contested Leicester West 1983. Mbr, CSD; former mbr, Leicester Cl for Community Relations; Leicester Business Centre ; first Asian candidateselected by SDP. Former adviser on immigration and nationality problems at SDP advice centre run by former SDP MP, Mr Tom Bradley. B Nov 16 1942; ed in Sri Lanka.

Mr **Graham Allen**

NOTTINGHAM SOUTH — No change

Electorate %Turnout	72,807	73.0%	**1987**	69,059	70.2%	**1983**
*Brandon-Bravo, N.M. (C)	23,921	45.0%	-0.9%	22,238	45.9%	(C)
Simpson, A. (Lab)	21,687	40.8%	+6.7%	16,523	34.1%	(Lab)
Williams, L.V. (SDP/All)	7,517	14.1%	-5.9%	9,697	20.0%	(L/All)
C to Lab swing 3.8%	53,125	C maj 2,234 4.2%		48,458	C maj 5,715 11.8%	

Mr Martin
Brandon-Bravo

Mr Martin Brandon-Bravo has been PPS to Mr John Patten since 1985. Elected in 1983; contested Nottingham East, 1979. Mbr, Nottingham City Cl, 1968-70 and 1976-87; bd of management, National Water Sports Centre, Nottingham, of which he is a founding mbr; former mbr, exec, Nat Rowing Cl. Pres, Notts international regatta; Nottingham and Union Rowing Club. Holds international umpire licence; mbr, International Umpires Commission. B Mar 25 1932; ed Latymer Sch. Director, Richard Stump Ltd (which he joined in 1952 rising to managing director, 1979-83), Nottingham and County Constitutional Club Co Ltd, and Nottingham and County Diary Co Ltd. Pres, Nottingham W Cons Pty, 1975-83.
Mr Alan Simpson, community relations officer; author of books and articles on racism and on housing policies. B Sep 20 1948. Former chmn, local CND branch. Sponsored by Nupe.
Mr Leighton Williams, economics lecturer at Trent Poly, contested Nottingham North 1983. Mbr, CSD; Assocn for a Social Democratic Europe; Tawney Soc; former chmn, Nottingham SDP; former chmn, area economic policy working pty on defence, foreign affairs and home affairs. B May 28 1955; ed King Edward VI Sch, Norwich; Univ Coll, Cardiff; Hertford Coll, Oxford.

NUNEATON — No change

Electorate %Turnout	68,287	80.4%	**1987**	66,072	77.2%	**1983**
*Stevens, L.D. (C)	24,630	44.9%	+4.4%	20,666	40.5%	(C)
Veness, Ms V.A. (Lab)	18,975	34.6%	+4.0%	15,605	30.6%	(Lab)
Trembath, A. (SDP/All)	10,550	19.2%	-8.7%	14,264	27.9%	(SDP/All)
Morrissey, Dr J. (Grn)	719	1.3%		504	1.0%	(Ind Lab)
Lab to C swing 0.2%	54,874	C maj 5,655 10.3%		51,039	C maj 5,061 9.9%	

Mr Lewis Stevens

Mr Lewis Stevens, self-employed management and industrial engineering consultant, was elected in 1983; fought seat 1979. Jt sec, Cons back-bench health and social services cmte, 1986- . Worked for engineering firms, 1958-79. Mbr, Select Cmte on Channel Tunnel Bill. Jt sec, Anglo-Finnish parly gp; mbr, exec cmte, engineering development parly gp. B Apr 13 1936; ed Oldbury GS, Worcestershire; Liverpool Univ; Lanchester Coll, Coventry. Mbr, Nuneaton BC, 1966-72; chmn, Nuneaton Cons Assocn, 1972-77 and 1981-83. Chmn, Midlands East, Cons Euro-constituency Assocn, 1978-82, pres 1982. Chmn of trustees, Albert Herbert Pension Fund.
Ms Valerie Veness, former nurse, contested Hornsey and Wood Green 1983. Formerly employed by *Tribune* newspaper. Mbr, Islington BC, 1985 (chaired women's cmte). B Aug 18 1945. Mbr, RSPCA; British Union for the Abolition of Vivisection.
Mr Andrew Trembath, teacher. Chmn, South Notts SDP, 1984-86; member, CSD. B Jun 2 1948; ed Carlton Le Willows GS, Gedling. AMMA.
Dr John Morrissey, medical practitioner, is gen sec, W Midlands Green and Ecology Parties, and convenor, Green Pty health working gp. B Jul 5 1950; ed St John's Coll, Cambridge; Birmingham Univ. Medical Practitioners' Union (ASTMS).

OGMORE — No change

Electorate %Turnout	51,255	80.0%	**1987**	51,378	76.9%	**1983**
*Powell, R. (Lab)	28,462	69.4%	+10.2%	23,390	59.2%	(Lab)
Barratt, M.F. (C)	6,170	15.0%	+0.3%	6,026	15.3%	(L/All)
James, Ms M. (SDP/All)	3,954	9.6%	-5.6%	5,806	14.7%	(C)
Jones, J.G. (Pl C)	1,791	4.4%	-3.5%	3,124	7.9%	(Pl C)
Spence, T.H. (Ind Lab)	652	1.6%	-57.6%	1,161	2.9%	(Eco)
C to Lab swing 4.9%	41,029	Lab maj 22,292 54.3%		39,507	Lab maj 17,364 44.0%	

Mr Raymond Powell

Mr Raymond Powell, an Opposition whip, became vice-chairman of the PLP agriculture cmte in 1986. Senior administrative officer, Welsh Water Authority, 1969-79. Elected in 1979. B Jun 19 1928; ed Pentre GS; Nat Cl of Labour Colls; LSE. With British Rail, 1945-50; shop manager, 1950-66. Chmn, Labour Party of Wales, 1977-78. Chmn, South Wales Euro constituency, 1980- . Former mbr, Select Cmtes on Employment and on Welsh Affairs. Sec, Welsh group of Lab MPs, 1984-87. Sec, all-pty Anglo-Bulgaria parly gp. Fellow, Industry and Parliament Trust. Sponsored by Usdaw.
Mr Michael Barratt, solicitor. B 1953; ed Havelock GS, Grimsby; Liverpool Poly. Chmn, Brighton CPC, 1985- .
Mrs Mair James, housewife, has chaired the Vale of Glamorgan area SDP since 1986; social and fund raising officer, 1983-86. B Feb 5 1934; ed Maestag GS. Sec, local charity.
Mr John Jones, miner, is chmn PlC constituency organization. Former mbr, Ogwr BC; former NUM lodge officer. Aged 27.

OLD BEXLEY AND SIDCUP — No change

Electorate %Turnout	50,831	77.1%	1987	50,255	74.1%	1983
*Heath, E.R.G. (C)	24,350	62.1%	+1.9%	22,422	60.2%	(C)
Pearce, T.H. (L/All)	8,076	20.6%	-5.4%	9,704	26.1%	(L/All)
Stoate, H.J.A. (Lab)	6,762	17.3%	+3.5%	5,116	13.7%	(Lab)
L/All to C swing 3.7%	39,188	C maj 16,274 41.5%		37,242	C maj 12,718 34.1%	

Mr Edward Heath

Mr **Edward Heath** was leader of the Conservative Party, 1965-75; Prime Minister 1970-74, and Leader of the Opposition, 1965-70, and from Feb 1974-75. Chief Opposition spokesman on Treasury and economic affairs, 1964-65, and chmn, party's policy cmte and research dept. Secretary of State for Industry, Trade and Regional Development, and President of the Board of Trade, 1963-64; Lord Privy Seal, 1960-63, being chief Foreign Office spokesman in Commons and leader of British team in negotiations to join EEC; Minister of Labour, 1959-60; Parliamentary Secretary to the Treasury and Govt Chief Whip, 1955-59; Deputy Govt Chief Whip, 1952-55; Govt whip, 1951-52. Elected for this seat 1983; MP for Bexley Sidcup, 1974-83, and for Bexley, 1950-74. B Jul 9 1916; ed Chatham House Sch, Ramsgate, and Balliol Coll, Oxford (pres of Union, 1939). Musician, international yachtsman and author. Member of Lloyd's. Mbr, Brandt Commission on the Third World, 1977-83.
Mr **Tom Pearce**, lecturer, sculptor and freelance cartoonist. Chmn, West Sussex Lib Pty. B Nov 21 1934; ed Porth County GS for Boys; Cardiff Coll of Art; Brentwood Coll of Ed.
Dr **Howard Stoate**, general practitioner. Vice-chmn, Dartford CLP, 1983-87; chmn, Dartford Fabian Soc. B Apr 14 1954; ed Kingston GS; Kings Coll, London Univ.

OLDHAM CENTRAL AND ROYTON — No change

Electorate %Turnout	65,277	69.2%	1987	67,177	66.9%	1983
*Lamond, J.A. (Lab)	21,759	48.1%	+6.7%	18,611	41.4%	(Lab)
Farquhar, J.A. (C)	15,480	34.3%	+0.2%	15,299	34.0%	(C)
Dunn, Mrs A. (SDP/All)	7,956	17.6%	-6.9%	11,022	24.5%	(SDP/All)
C to Lab swing 3.3%	45,195	Lab maj 6,279 13.9%		44,932	Lab maj 3,312 7.4%	

Mr James Lamond

Mr **James Lamond** was elected for this seat 1983; MP for Oldham East, 1970-83. Mbr, Speaker's panel of chmn, since 1979; served on Select Cmte on Members' Salaries. B Nov 29 1928; ed Burrelton Sch and Coupar Angus Sch. Engineering draughtsman, 1944-70. Mbr, Aberdeen Town Cl, 1958-70; leader, Lab gp 1967-70; Provost of Aberdeen, 1970-71; Lord Lieutenant of Aberdeen, 1970-71. Former mbr, PAC. Sponsored by AUEW (TASS) and a mbr since 1944. Vice-pres, World Peace Cl. Pres, British Peace Assembly.
Mr **Joseph Farquhar**, British Telecom engineer, fought this seat 1983. Mbr, Greater Manchester Cl, 1977-81; Oldham MBC, 1984- . B Feb 18 1945; ed Cowbridge GS, Glamorgan; Barnstaple GS, Devon; The Derby Sch, Bury, Lancs. Mbr, branch cmte, NCU(E), formerly POEU, 1968- .
Mrs **Ann Dunn**, peripatetic teacher of children with special educational needs. Mbr Oldham area pty cmte, 1982- ; CSD, 1984- . B May 6 1949; ed Hulme GS, Oldham; Cheshire CoE, Crewe; Keele Univ. Jt sec, Oldham Fed, PAT; Assocn of Soc Dem Trade Unionists.

OLDHAM WEST — No change

Electorate %Turnout	57,178	71.9%	1987	57,445	69.8%	1983
*Meacher, M.H. (Lab)	20,291	49.4%	+5.3%	17,690	44.1%	(Lab)
Jacobs, Mrs J.M. (C)	14,324	34.9%	-1.3%	14,510	36.2%	(C)
Mason, Miss M.R. (L/All)	6,478	15.8%	-3.5%	7,745	19.3%	(L/All)
				180	0.4%	(Other)
C to Lab swing 3.3%	41,093	Lab maj 5,967 14.5%		40,125	Lab maj 3,180 7.9%	

Mr Michael Meacher

Mr **Michael Meacher** contested the deputy leadership of Lab Pty in 1983. Elected to shadow Cabinet in 1983, becoming chief Opposition spokesman on health and social security. Under Secretary of State for Trade, 1976-79; Under Secretary of State for Health and Social Security, 1975-76; Under Secretary of State for Industry, 1974-75. Regained seat for Labour in 1970; contested Colchester, 1966. B Nov 4 1939; ed Berkhamsted Sch; New Coll, Oxford; and LSE. Mbr, Labour NEC, 1983- ; Select Cmte on the Treasury and Civil Service, 1979-83. Fellow, Industry and Parliament Trust. Sponsored by Cohse.
Mrs **Joan Jacobs**, a banker, contested Manchester, Wythenshawe, in 1983. Mbr, Manchester City Cl, 1980-84; South Manchester Community Health Cl. B Apr 12 1945; ed St Joseph's Convent HS, Manchester.
Miss **Mary Mason** was director of social services, Bolton MBC, 1973-82 when she retired. Contested Burnley 1964 and 1966. Bowden (Cheshire) UDC, 1961-74 (chmn, 1965-66); Bolton MBC, 1986- . Chmn, Greater Manchester Reg Lib Pty, 1983-86. B Apr 21 1924; ed Manchester HS for Girls; Girton Coll, Cambridge; Manchester Univ Training Dept.

ORKNEY AND SHETLAND | No change

Electorate %Turnout	31,047	68.7%	**1987**	30,087	67.8%	**1983**
*Wallace, J.R. (L/All)	8,881	41.7%	-4.3%	9,374	45.9%	(L/All)
Jenkins, R.W.A. (C)	4,959	23.3%	-2.3%	5,224	25.6%	(C)
Aberdein, J.H. (Lab)	3,995	18.7%	+5.7%	3,147	15.4%	(SNP)
Goodlad, J. (OSM)	3,095	14.5%		2,665	13.1%	(Lab)
Collister, G.K. (Grn)	389	1.8%				
L/All to C swing 1.0%	21,319	L/All maj 3,922 18.4%		20,410	L/All maj 4,150 20.3%	

Mr James Wallace was appointed Liberal spokesman on defence and deputy chief whip in 1985 and Alliance election team transport spokesman. Lib spokesman on energy, 1983-85, and on fisheries, 1983-87. Advocate. Elected in 1983; contested Dumfries, 1979; Euro candidate for South Scotland, 1979. Mbr, Commons Services Cmte, 1985- ; Liaison Cmte, 1985- . B Aug 25 1954; ed Annan Acad, Dumfriesshire; Downing Coll, Cambridge; Edinburgh Univ. Chmn, Edinburgh Univ Lib Club, 1976-77. Mbr, Scottish Lib nat exec, 1976-85; vice-chmn (policy), 1982-85. Hon pres, Scottish YLs, 1984-85.
Mr Richard Jenkins, sheep farmer, is pres, Dounby branch, Scottish NFU. B Apr 1 1951; ed Eton.
Mr John Aberdein, teacher; former herring fisherman and diver. Supervised sea-canoeing centre at Calshot, Hampshire, 1980-82. Was sec, Orkney Trades Cl; founder chmn, Orkney's first tenants assocn. B Mar 23 1946; ed Robert Gordon's Coll, Aberdeen; Aberdeen Univ. EIS.
Mr Grierson Collister, teacher. B Jul 31 1943; ed Battersea Col of Ed; London Univ.

Mr James Wallace

ORPINGTON | No change

Electorate %Turnout	59,608	78.5%	**1987**	58,759	76.0%	**1983**
*Stanbrook, I.R. (C)	27,261	58.2%	+1.0%	25,569	57.3%	(C)
Fryer, J.H. (L/All)	14,529	31.0%	-3.5%	15,418	34.5%	(L/All)
Cowan, S.J. (Lab)	5,020	10.7%	+3.0%	3,439	7.7%	(Lab)
				215	0.5%	(Other)
L/All to C swing 2.2%	46,810	C maj 12,732 27.2%		44,641	C maj 10,151 22.7%	

Mr Ivor Stanbrook, barrister, author and lecturer, has been a mbr of the Select Cmte on Home Affairs since 1983; sec, Cons back-bench home affairs cmte, 1974-77; jt vice-chmn, 1979-82. Chmn, Cons back-bench constitutional affairs cmte, 1985- ; jt vice-chmn, Cons back-bench N Ireland cmte, 1982- . Won Orpington in 1970; contested East Ham South, 1966. B Jan 13 1924; ed Willesden Central Sch; Birkbeck and Univ Colls, London Univ; Pembroke Coll, Oxford. Colonial district officer in Nigeria, 1950-60 (Asst Sec, Cl of Ministers, Lagos, 1954). Chmn, British-Nigerian all-pty group. Mbr, Court of Referees; exec cmte, UK branch, CPA, 1986- .
Mr Jonathan Fryer, writer, broadcaster and Third World development consultant, fought Chelsea 1983, and London South East in 1984 and 1979 Euro elections. B Jun 5 1950; ed Manchester GS; St Edmund Hall, Oxford. Mbr, Bromley BC, 1986- .
Mr Steven Cowan, teacher, contested Hampshire East 1983 and London South East in 1984 Euro election. Mbr, Ilea, 1982- . Sec, Tower Hamlet CLP, 1981-82. B Sep 6 1951; ed Balham Boys Sec Mod Sch, London; Charles Chute Sec Mod for Boys, Basingstoke. TGWU, NUT.

Mr Ivor Stanbrook

OXFORD EAST | Lab gain

Electorate %Turnout	62,145	79.0%	**1987**	63,613	73.9%	**1983**
Smith, A.D. (Lab)	21,103	43.0%	+5.7%	18,808	40.0%	(C)
*Norris, S.J. (C)	19,815	40.4%	+0.4%	17,541	37.3%	(Lab)
Godden, Mrs M. (L/All)	7,648	15.6%	-7.1%	10,690	22.7%	(L/All)
Dalton, D. (Grn)	441	0.9%				
Mylvaganam, P.S. (CC)	60	0.1%				
C to Lab swing 2.7%	49,067	Lab maj 1,288 2.6%		47,039	C maj 1,267 2.7%	

Mr Andrew Smith, an officer with the Oxford and Swindon Co-op Soc, contested this seat 1983. Mbr, Oxford City Cl, 1976- (chmn, planning cmte, 1984-87, and recreation cmte, 1980-83). Trustee, youth unemployment centre, Oxford. B Feb 1 1951; ed Reading GS; St John's Coll, Oxford. Usdaw, and on parly panel.
Mr Steven Norris, a director of four companies involved in transport, management services and computer engineering, was MP for this seat, 1983-87. PPS to Mr William Waldegrave at DOE, 1985-87; mbr, Select Cmte on Social Services, 1984-85. B May 24 1945; ed Liverpool Inst HS and Worcester Coll, Oxford. Mbr, Berkshire CC, 1977-85; Berkshire AHA, 1979-82; vice-chmn, W Berkshire Dist HA, 1982-85. Liveryman, Coachmakers and Coach Harness Makers Company.
Mrs Margaret Godden, computer programmer, contested this seat 1983. County cllr, 1985- . B Mar 29 1931; ed various local authority schs; Kings Coll, London. AUT.
Mr David Dalton works in the central fund raising divison of Oxfam. B Oct 26 1950; ed Manchester Univ. ACTSS.

Mr Andrew Smith,

OXFORD WEST AND ABINGDON — No change

Electorate %Turnout	69,193	78.4%	**1987**	67,413	74.0%	**1983**
*Patten, J.H.C. (C)	25,171	46.4%	-1.3%	23,778	47.7%	(C)
Huhne, C.M.P. (SDP/All)	20,293	37.4%	+4.0%	16,627	33.3%	(SDP/All)
Power, J.G. (Lab)	8,108	14.9%	-2.0%	8,440	16.9%	(Lab)
Smith, D. (Grn)	695	1.3%		544	1.1%	(Eco)
				474	1.0%	(Other)
C to SDP/All swing 2.7%	54,267	C maj 4,878 9.0%		49,863	C maj 7,151 14.3%	

Mr John Patten

Mr **John Patten** was appointed Minister of State, Home Office, in Jun 1987; Minister for Housing, Urban Affairs and Construction, with rank of Minister of State at DOE, 1985-87; Under Secretary of State for Health and Social Security, 1983-85; Under Secretary of State for N Ireland, 1981-83. Elected for this seat 1983; MP for Oxford, 1979-83. B Jul 17 1945; ed Wimbledon Coll and Sidney Sussex Coll, Cambridge. Lecturer, Oxford Univ, 1969-79; Fellow and tutor (1972-81) and Supernumary Fellow (1981-), Hertford Coll, Oxford. PPS to Ministers of State, Home Office, 1980. Mbr, Cl, Reading Univ; Oxford City Cl, 1973-76. Editor, Journal of Historical Geography, 1975-80.
Mr **Christopher Huhne**, economics editor, The Guardian, since 1980, and author, contested Reading East 1983. Brussels corr, The Economist, 1977-80. Mbr, SDP economic policy gp; tax and social security gp; B Jul 2 1954; ed Westminster; Sorbonne; Magdalen Coll, Oxford.
Mr **John Power**, library asst, contested Aylesbury 1979; Ox and Bucks in Euro elections 1984. Mbr, Oxford City Cl, 1979- ; Oxford CC, 1981-85. Mbr, AEU parly panel. B May 23 1938; ed E Oxford Sec Mod Sch; City of Oxford Tech Sch. AUEW.
Mr **Donald Smith**, computer software programmer; sec, Oxford Grn Pty. B Mar 17 1959; ed Torquay GS; UMIST.

PAISLEY NORTH — No change

Electorate %Turnout	49,487	73.5%	**1987**	50,464	68.6%	**1983**
*Adams, A. (Lab)	20,193	55.5%	+9.9%	15,782	45.6%	(Lab)
Laing, Mrs E.F. (C)	5,751	15.8%	-5.6%	8,195	23.7%	(SDP/All)
McCartin, Miss E.P. (SDP/All)	5,741	15.8%	-7.9%	7,425	21.4%	(C)
Taylor, I. (SNP)	4,696	12.9%	+4.9%	2,783	8.0%	(SNP)
				439	1.3%	(Other)
C to Lab swing 7.8%	36,381	Lab maj 14,442 39.7%		34,624	Lab maj 7,587 21.9%	

Mr Allen Adams

Mr **Allen Adams**, an Opposition whip, was elected for this seat in 1983; MP for Paisley, 1979-83. Computer analyst. B Feb 16 1946; ed Camphill HS, Paisley, and Reid-Kerr Tech Coll, Paisley. Mbr, Strathclyde Regional Cl, until 1980; vice-chmn, Strathclyde Social Services Cl, 1969-79. APEX.
Mrs **Eleanor Laing**, solicitor in legal dept of construction firm in London. Former mbr, exec, Edinburgh S Cons Assocn. Ed John Neilson Sch, Glasgow; St Columba's Sch, Kilmacolm; Edinburgh Univ.
Miss **Eileen McCartin**, a home economist employed by Strathclyde Reg Cl since 1975, contested this seat 1983. B May 6 1952; ed Notre Dame HS, Queens Coll, Jordanhill Coll and Coll of Tech, Glasgow. EIS, 1974-75; Nalgo, 1975- .
Mr **Ian Taylor**, welding engineer. Mbr, Renfrew DC; chmn, Inchinnan branch, SNP. B 1950; ed Glasgow and Paisley Tech Colls. TASS.

PAISLEY SOUTH — No change

Electorate %Turnout	51,127	75.3%	**1987**	52,031	72.5%	**1983**
*Buchan, N.F. (Lab)	21,611	56.2%	+14.7%	15,633	41.4%	(Lab)
Carmichael, A.M. (L/All)	5,826	15.1%	-9.0%	9,104	24.1%	(L/All)
Williamson, Miss D.A. (C)	5,644	14.7%	-6.0%	7,819	20.7%	(C)
Mitchell, J.R. (SNP)	5,398	14.0%	+1.0%	4,918	13.0%	(SNP)
				271	0.7%	(Other)
L/All to Lab swing 11.9%	38,479	Lab maj 15,785 41.0%		37,745	Lab maj 6,529 17.3%	

Mr Norman Buchan

Mr **Norman Buchan** was Opposition spokesman on the arts, 1983-87, when he was dismissed for continuing to advocate the retention of broadcasting as part of Labour's arts and media policy. Chief Opposition spokesman on agriculture, fisheries and food, 1981-83, and on social services, 1980-81. Minister of State for Agriculture, Fisheries and Food, Mar to Oct 1974, when he resigned. Opposition spokesman on agriculture, 1973-74, and on Scottish affairs, 1970-73. Under Secretary of State for Scotland, 1967-70. Elected for this seat 1983; MP for West Renfrewshire, 1964-83. Teacher. B Oct 27 1922; ed Kirkwall GS; Glasgow Univ. Chmn, board of Tribune, 1985- . Mbr, PAC, 1975. Former chmn, PLP Scottish group. Member, cl of Poetry Soc, since 1977. Sponsored by TGWU.
Mr **Alastair Carmichael**, hotel manager. B 1965; ed Islay HS; Glasgow Univ.
Miss **Dorothy Williamson**, personal/research asst to MP. B Feb 6 1960; ed Westbourne Sch for Girls, Glasgow; St Andrews Univ (editor, univ newspaper). Friend of the Tate Gallery.
Mr **James Mitchell**, joiner, Ucatt shop steward, contested this seat 1983. SNP gp ldr, Renfrew DC; former SNP exec vice-chmn for local govt. B 1942. Spokesman for 1820 Society.

PECKHAM — No change

Electorate %Turnout	59,261	55.6%	**1987**	59,128	54.5%	**1983**
*Harman, Ms H. (Lab)	17,965	54.5%	+2.9%	16,616	51.6%	(Lab)
Ingram, Mrs L.K.F. (C)	8,476	25.7%	+1.5%	7,792	24.2%	(C)
Shearman, R.H. (L/All)	5,878	17.8%	-3.9%	7,006	21.7%	(SDP/All)
Robinson, Miss D. (Grn)	628	1.9%			800	2.5%	(NF)
C to Lab swing 0.7%	32,947	Lab maj	9,489 28.8%	32,214	Lab maj	8,824 27.4%

Ms **Harriet Harman** joined the Opposition front bench team on social services in 1985. Elected for Peckham in 1982 by-election. Solicitor and civil rights campaigner. Member, PLP civil liberties group. B Jul 30 1950; ed St Paul's Girls Sch and York Univ. Legal officer, Nat Cl for Civil Liberties, 1978-82; Brent Community Law Centre, 1975-78. Sponsored by TGWU.
Mrs Kay Ingham is a financial consultant with the General Accident Group. B Dec 20 1957; ed Moorside HS; LSE.
Mr Richard Shearman, education officer, Design Cl. Mbr, Southwark BC, 1986- . B 1948; ed Skinners Sch, Tunbridge Wells; Cambridge and London Univs.

Ms Harriet Harman

PEMBROKE — No change

Electorate %Turnout	70,360	80.8%	**1987**	67,885	78.1%	**1983**
Bennett, N.J. (C)	23,314	41.0%	-5.9%	24,860	46.9%	(C)
Rayner, B.J. (Lab)	17,614	31.0%	+1.7%	15,504	29.2%	(Lab)
Jones, P.E.C. (L/All)	14,832	26.1%	+5.4%	10,983	20.7%	(SDP/All)
Osmond, O. (Pl C)	1,119	2.0%	-0.1%	1,073	2.0%	(Pl C)
				614	1.2%	(Other)
C to Lab swing 3.8%	56,879	C maj	5,700 10.0%	53,034	C maj	9,356 17.6%

Mr Nicholas Bennett is an education officer with the London Borough of Havering. Contested Hackney Central in 1979. B 1949; ed Sedgehill Sch, London; Southwark and Walbrook CFEs; North London Poly; London and Sussex Univs. Mbr, Lewisham BC, 1974-82 (leader of opposition, 1979-82); co-opted member, Ilea, 1978-81. Great grandfather was Tom Mann (1856-1941), leader of the 1889 dock strike and first gen sec, AEU; grandfather was features editor of *Daily Worker* until 1954.
Mr Bryan Rayner, research supervisor; Metropolitan Police officer, 1953-73; member, Dyfed-Powis Police Authority. Mbr, Dyfed CC, 1981- ; (dep ldr, Lab gp). B Jul 28 1936; ed Eastbourne Tech Sch; Univ Coll, Swansea. EETPU.
Mr Patrick Jones, medical laboratory scientific officer in NHS, contested the seat twice in 1974. Mbr, Pembrokeshire CC, 1970-75. B Jun 3 1939; ed Narberth GS; UCW, Aberystwyth. Nalgo.
Mr Ozi Osmond, artist and lecturer at Coll of Art, Carmarthen, contested this seat 1983. Aged 44.

Mr Nicholas Bennett

PENDLE — No change

Electorate %Turnout	63,588	81.8%	**1987**	64,483	79.7%	**1983**
*Lee, J.R.L. (C)	21,009	40.4%	-3.9%	22,739	44.2%	(C)
Renilson, Mrs S. (Lab)	18,370	35.3%	+3.0%	16,604	32.3%	(Lab)
Lishman, A.G. (L/All)	12,662	24.3%	+0.9%	12,056	23.5%	(L/All)
C to Lab swing 3.4%	52,041	C maj	2,639 5.1%	51,399	C maj	6,135 11.9%

Mr John Lee was appointed Under Secretary of State for Employment in 1986; Under Secretary of State for Defence Procurement, 1983-86. Chartered accountant and former company director. Elected for this seat in 1983; MP for Nelson and Colne, 1979-83; contested Manchester, Moss Side, Oct 1974. B Jun 21 1942; ed William Hulme's GS, Manchester. Vicechmn, NW Conciliation Cmte, Race Relations Bd, 1976-77. Chmn, cl, Nat Youth Bureau, 1980-83. Jt sec, Cons back-bench industry cmte, 1979-81; PPS to Mr Kenneth Baker, Minister of State for Industry, 1981-83, and to Mr Cecil Parkinson, Secretary of State for Trade and Industry, 1983. Former parly consultant to County Bank Ltd and National Bedding Fed.
Mrs Sylvia Renilson, youth and community worker. Mbr, Merseyside CC, 1981- . B Nov 27 1937. TGWU.
Mr Gordon Lishman is Head of Fieldwork, Age Concern England. Contested this seat 1983 and Bradford North twice in 1974, also Lancashire East in 1984 Euro elections. Director, Hebden Royd Publications Ltd; treas, Pendle Printing Society. B Nov 29 1947; ed Colne GS; Manchester Univ. Mbr, Northamptonshire CC, 1981-83. ACTSS.

Mr John Lee

PENRITH AND THE BORDER — No change

Electorate %Turnout	70,994	77.5%	1987	68,164	73.1%	1983
*Maclean, D.J. (C)	33,148	60.3%	+1.4%	29,304	58.8%	(C)
Ivison, D.J. (L/All)	15,782	28.7%	+0.8%	13,883	27.9%	(L/All)
Hutton, J.M.P. (Lab)	6,075	11.0%	-2.2%	6,612	13.3%	(Lab)
L/All to C swing 0.3%	55,005	C maj 17,366 31.6%		49,799	C maj 15,421 31.0%	

Mr **David Maclean** was appointed an assistant Government whip in Jun 1987. Security training consultant. Won the seat in Jul 1983 by-election caused by elevation to House of Lords of Mr William Whitelaw; contested Inverness, Nairn and Lochaber, 1983. PPS to Mr Michael Jopling, Minister of Agriculture, Fisheries and Food, 1986-87; mbr, Select Cmte on Agriculture, 1983-86. B May 16 1953; ed Fortrose Acad and Aberdeen Univ. Joined Securicor, 1975. Chmn, Addlestone branch of Chertsey and Walton Cons Assocn, 1979; chmn, Chertsey and Walton CPC, 1979.

Mr **David Ivison**, principal teacher of biology, Dumfries Academy. B Dec 24 1945; ed Carlisle GS; Newcastle Univ.

Mr **John Hutton**, lecturer and lawyer. B May 6 1955; ed Westcliff HS, Essex; Magdalen Coll, Oxford.

Mr David Maclean

PERTH AND KINROSS — No change

Electorate %Turnout	63,443	74.4%	1987	61,478	72.3%	1983
*Fairbairn, N.H. (C)	18,716	39.6%	-0.6%	17,888	40.2%	(C)
Fairlie, J.M. (SNP)	13,040	27.6%	+2.5%	11,155	25.1%	(SNP)
Donaldson, S. (L/All)	7,969	16.9%	-7.9%	10,997	24.7%	(L/All)
McConnell, J.W. (Lab)	7,490	15.9%	+5.9%	4,414	9.9%	(Lab)
C to SNP swing 1.6%	47,215	C maj 5,676 12.0%		44,454	C maj 6,733 15.1%	

Mr **Nicholas Fairbairn, QC,** was Solicitor General for Scotland, 1979-82. Mbr, Select Cmte on Scottish Affairs, 1983- . Elected for this seat 1983; MP for Kinross and West Perthshire, Oct 1974-83; contested Edinburgh, Central, 1964 and 1966. Vice-chmn, Scottish Cons MPs, 1983- . Journalist, painter, writer and broadcaster. Mbr, Cl of Edinburgh Festival, 1971- ; Cl of World Population Crisis, 1968-70; former mbr, Jt Select Cmte on Statutory Instruments. B Dec 24 1933; ed Loretto and Edinburgh Univ.

Mr **James Fairlie**, financial consultant. SNP spokesman on economic affairs; mbr, SNP nat exec, 1973- ; vice-chmn (policy), 1979-81; dep leader, 1981-84. Fought Dunfermline West 1983; Dundee West 1979 and twice in 1974. B May 16 1940; ed Perth Acad; Dundee Univ.

Mr **Stewart Donaldson**, investment analyst with Clydesdale Bank plc, fought Hamilton 1983 and Edinburgh Central, 1979. Vice-chmn (policy), Scottish Lib Pty, 1985-86, and Campaign for Scottish Assembly, 1983-85. B Dec 11 1953; ed Morrison's Acad, Crieff; Edinburgh Univ; Scottish Business Sch.

Mr **Jack McConnell**, teacher. Mbr, Stirling DC, 1984- . Chmn, Stirling Arts Council 1984-86. Mbr, central regional Lab Pty 1984-86. B Jun 30 1960; ed Arran High Sch; Stirling Univ.

Mr Nicholas Fairbairn

PETERBOROUGH — No change

Electorate %Turnout	84,284	73.5%	1987	78,957	73.3%	1983
*Mawhinney, Dr B.S. (C)	30,624	49.4%	+2.3%	27,270	47.1%	(C)
MacKinlay, A. (Lab)	20,840	33.6%	+4.6%	16,831	29.1%	(Lab)
Green, D.W. (L/All)	9,984	16.1%	-6.6%	13,142	22.7%	(SDP/All)
Callaghan, N.A. (Grn)	506	0.8%	-0.1%	511	0.9%	(Eco)
				155	0.3%	(Other)
C to Lab swing 1.1%	61,954	C maj 9,784 15.8%		57,909	C maj 10,439 18.0%	

Dr **Brian Mawhinney** was appointed Under Secretary of State for Northern Ireland in 1986. Radiation biologist. Gained seat for Cons in 1979; contested Teesside, Stockton, Oct 1974. B Jul 26 1940; ed Royal Belfast Academical Inst; Queens Univ, Belfast; Univ of Michigan, US; Univ of London. Mbr, Medical Research Cl, 1980-83; nat cl, Nat Soc for Cancer Relief, 1981-85; and exec of Cons Medical Soc. Mbr, Select Cmte on the Environment, 1979-82; former officer, Cons health and NI back-bench cmtes. PPS to Ministers of State, Treasury, 1982-84; and to Secretaries of State for Employment, 1984-85, and N Ireland, 1985-86. Former parly adviser, British Printing Industries Fed; vice-pres, Cons trade unionists nat cmte, 1984- ; mbr, General Synod of Church of England, 1985- . Former director, Servicemaster Hospital Services Ltd. AUT.

Mr **Andrew MacKinlay**, Nalgo trade union official, contested Croydon Central 1983, Surbiton twice in 1974, and London South and Surrey East in 1984 Euro election. Mbr, Chartered Inst of Secretaries and Administrators. B Apr 24 1949; ed Salesian Coll, Chertsey. Mbr, Kingston upon Thames Cl, 1971-78. Sponsored by TGWU.

Mr **David Green** contested the seat in 1979. Mbr Cambridge CC, 1985- ; Peterborough City Cl, 1982- . B 1949; ed Queen Edith's GS, Cambridge; in Belfast; Judd Sch, Tonbridge.

Dr Brian Mawhinney

PLYMOUTH, DEVONPORT · No change

Electorate %Turnout	64,741	76.9%	**1987**	61,813	76.0%	**1983**
*Owen, Dr D.A.L. (SDP/All)	21,039	42.3%	-2.1%	20,843	44.4%	(SDP/All)
Jones, T. (C)	14,569	29.3%	-4.6%	15,907	33.9%	(C)
Flintloff, I. (Lab)	14,166	28.5%	+7.5%	9,845	21.0%	(Lab)
				385	0.8%	(Other)
C to SDP/All swing 1.2%	49,774SDP/All maj 6,470 13.0%			46,980SDP/All maj 4,936 10.5%		

Dr David Owen

Dr David Owen has been Leader of the SDP since 1983. Secretary of State for Foreign and Commonwealth Affairs in Lab Government, 1977-79; resigned from Lab and was one of the joint leaders (the Gang of Four) of the SDP in 1981. SDP deputy leader, 1982-83; with overall responsibility for defence and foreign affairs. Mbr, Palme Commission on Disarmament and Security issues, 1980-82, and of Independent Commission on International Humanitarian issues, 1983- . Opposition spokesman on energy, 1979-80; Minister of State for Foreign and Commonwealth Affairs, 1976-77; Minister of State for Health, 1974-76; Under Secretary of State for Health, 1974. Elected for this seat in Feb 1974; MP for Plymouth, Sutton, 1966-74; contested Torrington, 1964. Opposition spokesman on defence, 1970-72, but resigned after disagreement on EEC policy. Under Secretary of State for Defence for the RN, 1968-70. B J 2 1938; ed Bradford Coll, Berkshire; Sidney Sussex Coll, Cambridge; St Thomas's Hosp, London. Patron, Disablement Income Gp, 1968- .
Mr Thomas Jones, founder and director of business systems company. Mbr, Plymouth Cl, 1973- . B 1938; ed Cardiff HS.
Mr Ian Flintoff, actor. B Jul 22 1937; ed Trinity Coll, Oxford. Ex-Kensingtona and Chelsea cllr.

PLYMOUTH, DRAKE · No change

Electorate %Turnout	51,186	76.6%	**1987**	52,383	74.3%	**1983**
*Fookes, Miss J.E. (C)	16,195	41.3%	-9.3%	19,718	50.6%	(C)
Astor, D. (SDP/All)	13,070	33.3%	+4.7%	11,133	28.6%	(SDP/All)
Jamieson, D. (Lab)	9,451	24.1%	+3.8%	7,921	20.3%	(Lab)
Barber, Ms P. (Grn)	493	1.3%		163	0.4%	(BNP)
C to SDP/All swing 7.0%	39,209	C maj 3,125 8.0%		38,935	C maj 8,585 22.0%	

Miss Janet Fookes

Miss Janet Fookes has been a member of the Select Cmte on Home Affairs since 1984 and of Speaker's panel of chairmen since 1976. Elected for this seat 1974; MP for Merton and Morden, 1970-74. Consultant to English Tourist Board. Chmn, RSPCA, 1979-81; vice-chmn, 1981-83; mbr of cl since 1975; chmn, parly gp for animal welfare, 1985- (sec, 1974-82). Teacher, 1958-70. B Feb 21 1936; ed Hastings and St Leonards Ladies' Coll, Hastings HS; Royal Holloway Coll, Univ of London. Served on former Expenditure Cmte. Vice-chmn, all-pty mental health group. Mbr, cls, Stonham Housing Association, 1980- ; SSAFA, 1980- ; and Nat Canine Defence League. Mbr, Hastings CBC, 1960-61 and 1963-70.
Mr David Astor, farmer and investment manager; director, Jupiter Tarbutt. Chmn, CPRE, 1983- . Mbr, SDP environment cmte, 1984- ; agriculture and rural affairs cmte, 1984- ; finance cmte, 1981-82. B Aug 9 1943; ed Eton; Harvard Univ. With United Newspapers, 1970-72; Housing Corporation, 1972-75; head of development, Nat Theatre, 1976-77. Grandson of Lady Astor, first woman MP.
Mr David Jamieson, deputy head teacher, contested Birmingham Hall Green Feb 1974. Mbr, Solihull Cl 1970-74. B May 18 1947; ed St Peter's Coll, Birmingham; Open Univ. NUT.

PLYMOUTH, SUTTON · No change

Electorate %Turnout	64,120	79.0%	**1987**	59,890	76.4%	**1983**
*Clark, A.K.M. (C)	23,187	45.8%	-9.4%	25,203	55.1%	(C)
Tidy, B. (L/All)	19,174	37.8%	+8.3%	13,516	29.6%	(L/All)
Maddern, R.D. (Lab)	8,310	16.4%	+2.1%	6,538	14.3%	(Lab)
				470	1.0%	(Other)
C to L/All swing 8.8%	50,671	C maj 4,013 7.9%		45,727	C maj 11,687 25.6%	

Mr Alan Clark

Mr Alan Clark was appointed Minister for Trade, with rank of Minister of State at the DTI, in 1986; Under Secretary of State for Employment, 1983-86. Barrister and historian. Elected in Feb 1974. B Apr 13 1928; ed Eton and Christ Church, Oxford. Jt sec, Cons back-bench home affairs cmte, 1982-83; vice-chmn, Cons back-bench defence cmte, 1980-83; mbr, Select Cmte on Sound Broadcasting, 1979-83.
Mr Bruce Tidy is sec to Cornwall Community Health Cl. Mbr, Restormer BC, 1983- (ldr, Alliance gp, 1985-). B Jul 9 1950; ed Cornwall Tech Coll; Exeter Univ. Nalgo; full-time officer, Nupe, 1974-77.
Mr Ralph Maddern, publisher (M/D Focus Publications) and former teacher and construction worker, contested Devon West in 1979. Mbr, Berkshire CC, 1981- , serving on ed and property cmtes. B May 3 1937; ed at schools and cols in Australia and Britain. Ucatt.

PONTEFRACT AND CASTLEFORD — No change

Electorate %Turnout	64,414	73.5%	**1987**	64,878	67.4%	**1983**
*Lofthouse, G. (Lab)	31,656	66.9%	+9.8%	24,990	57.1%	(Lab)
Malins, J.H. (C)	10,030	21.2%	-4.6%	11,299	25.8%	(C)
Taylor, M.F. (L/All)	5,334	11.3%	-5.8%	7,452	17.0%	(L/All)
Lees, D.M. (RF)	295	0.6%				
C to Lab swing 7.2%	47,315	Lab maj 21,626 45.7%		43,741	Lab maj 13,691 31.3%	

Mr Geoffrey Lofthouse, personnel manager with the NCB at Fryston, 1970-78, was elected at the by-election in Oct 1978. Mbr, Select Cmte on Energy, 1983- and jt vice-chmn, PLP energy cmte, 1985- . Sec, Yorkshire Labour MPs, 1985- . Started in mining industry as haulage hand. B Dec 18 1925; ed Featherstone Sec Mod Sch; Leeds Univ. Consultant to British Association of Colliery Management. Mbr, Pontefract BC, 1962-74, being Mayor, 1967-68; Wakefield MDC, 1974-79; NUM, 1939-64; Apex, 1970- ; BACM.
Mr Julian Malins, barrister. Mbr, City of London Court of Common Cl, 1981- ; Ilea, 1984-86. B May 1 1950; ed St Johns Sch, Leatherhead; Brasenose Coll, Oxford.
Mr Michael Taylor, teacher, contested Rossendale and Darwen 1983. Mbr, Calderdale MBC. B 1950; ed St Dunstan's Coll; New Univ of Ulster; Manchester Univ.

Mr Geoffrey Lofthouse

PONTYPRIDD — No change

Electorate %Turnout	61,255	76.6%	**1987**	60,883	72.7%	**1983**
*John, B.T. (Lab)	26,422	56.3%	+10.7%	20,188	45.6%	(Lab)
Swayne, D. (C)	9,145	19.5%	-3.4%	11,444	25.8%	(SDP/All)
Sain-Ley-Berry, P.G. (SDP/All)	8,865	18.9%	-7.0%	10,139	22.9%	(C)
Bowen, D.L. (Pl C)	2,498	5.3%	+0.7%	2,065	4.7%	(Pl C)
				449	1.0%	(Other)
C to Lab swing 7.1%	46,930	Lab maj 17,277 36.8%		44,285	Lab maj 8,744 19.7%	

Mr Brynmor John, who became chief Opposition spokesman on agriculture in 1984, was mbr of the shadow Cabinet, 1981-83, when he was chief Opposition spokesman on social security. Chief Opposition spokesman on Northern Ireland, 1979-80; on defence, 1980-81. Minister of State, Home Office, 1976-79; Under Secretary of State for Defence for the RAF, 1974-76. Elected in 1970. Solicitor. B Apr 18 1934; ed Pontypridd GS and Univ Coll, London. Specialized in industrial accident law.
Mr Desmond Swayne, schoolmaster and director of Brick Sculptures Co Ltd. B Aug 20 1956; ed Bedford Sch; St Andrews Univ. TA officer.
Mr Peter Sain-Ley-Berry, business consultant, contested Swansea West 1983. Sec, SDP Cl for Wales; mbr, CSD, 1985- . B May 9 1946; ed Magdalen Coll Sch, Oxford; Peterhouse, Cambridge; Birkbeck Coll, London. Director, Merlyn Foods Ltd. Principal in Welsh Office until 1982.
Prof Delme Bowen, university professor in biology, is vice-chmn, Pontyclun Community Cl. B Mar 20 1944; ed Univ Coll, Cardiff. AUT.

Mr Brynmor John

POOLE — No change

Electorate %Turnout	76,673	77.5%	**1987**	70,731	73.6%	**1983**
*Ward, J.D. (C)	34,159	57.5%	-0.8%	30,358	58.3%	(C)
Whitley, R.J. (SDP/All)	19,351	32.6%	+2.0%	15,929	30.6%	(L/All)
Shutler, M. (Lab)	5,901	9.9%	-0.8%	5,595	10.7%	(Lab)
				177	0.3%	(Other)
C to SDP/All swing 1.4%	59,411	C maj 14,808 24.9%		52,059	C maj 14,429 27.7%	

Mr John Ward, a chartered civil engineer and director of building companies Taylor Woodrow (Arcon) Ltd and Arcon Building Exports Ltd, was elected in 1979; contested Portsmouth North, Oct 1974. With Taylor Woodrow Ltd, 1958-79. B Mar 8 1925; ed Romford County Tech Sch and St Andrew's Univ. PPS to Financial Secretary to the Treasury, 1984-86. Delegate, Cl of Europe, 1983- . Vice-chmn, Cons back-bench trade and industry cmte, 1983-84; jt sec, industry cmte, 1982-83. Mbr, nat union exec, Cons Party, 1965-78, and central board of finance, Cons Party, 1969-78. Mbr, CPC Nat Advisory Cmte; European Movement; and Cons Group for Europe; founder mbr, Cons Commonwealth Cl; sec, Mediterranean group, 1955-60.
Dr Robert Whitley, pollution scientist with Wessex Water Authority since 1977; chemist with Anglian Water Authority, 1975-77. Mbr, CSD; SDP environment working group; chmn, local area party. B Feb 26 1951; ed Isleworth GS; Exeter Univ.
Mr Michael Shutler, social govt manual worker, contested Bournemouth East 1983. Sec, local Lab Pty and trades cl; treas, Hampshire Lab Pty; nat chmn, Socialist Countryside Group. Mbr, Ringwood Town Cl 1973- . B Aug 8 1937; ed Harbridge C of E Sch; Ringwood Secondary Modern. TGWU.

Mr John Ward

187

PORTSMOUTH NORTH — No change

Electorate %Turnout	80,501	74.8%	**1987**	77,923	72.9%	**1983**
*Griffiths, P.H.S. (C)	33,297	55.3%	+0.0%	31,413	55.3%	(C)
Mitchell, Mrs E. (SDP/All)	14,896	24.7%	+1.1%	13,414	23.6%	(SDP/All)
Miles, D. (Lab)	12,016	20.0%	-1.2%	12,013	21.1%	(Lab)
C to SDP/All swing 0.6%	60,209	C maj 18,401 30.6%		56,840	C maj 17,999 31.7%	

Mr Peter Griffiths has been on the Select Committee on MPs Interests since 1983. Elected for this seat in 1979; MP for Smethwick, 1964-66; fought Portsmouth North, Feb 1974, and Smethwick, 1959. Former headmaster and senior lecturer. B May 24, 1928; ed West Bromwich GS; City of Leeds Training Coll; London and Birmingham Univs. Mbr, Smethwick BC, 1955-64 (leader, Cons group, 1960-64) and alderman, 1964-66. Former president, YCs. Fullbright exchange professor of economics, Pierce Coll, Los Angeles, 1968-69.
Mrs Elizabeth Mitchell, town planner. Mbr, steering cmte, South East Hants SDP, 1981; sec, Portsmouth North SDP, 1986. Served on Dundee and Angus local authorities, 1973-76; became an officer of West Midlands CC, 1976-77, and Portsmouth DC, 1979-80. B Aug 14 1951; ed St Andrew's Univ; Edinburgh Coll of Art, Heriot Watt Univ.
Mr David Miles, personnel manager, Portsea Island Co-op Soc. B Jun 8 1954; ed Bedford Modern Sch; Oxford Univ. Mbr, Portsea Island Co-op Pty and Portsmouth Lab Pty (exec cmte member). NACO; formerly Apex.

Mr Peter Griffiths

PORTSMOUTH SOUTH — C gain

Electorate %Turnout	76,292	71.3%	**1987**	74,537	67.3%	**1983**
Martin, D. (C)	23,534	43.3%	-6.7%	25,101	50.0%	(C)
*Hancock, M.T. (SDP/All)	23,329	42.9%	+17.5%	12,766	25.4%	(SDP/All)
Gardiner, K. (Lab)	7,047	13.0%	-9.6%	11,324	22.6%	(Lab)
Hughes, R. (657 Party)	455	0.8%		554	1.1%	(Ind L)
				451	0.9%	(Other)
C to SDP/All swing 12.1%	54,365	C maj 205 0.4%		50,196	C maj 12,335 24.6%	

Mr David Martin is a director of family leisure/tourism business. Barrister, practising 1969-76. Contested Yeovil 1983. Mbr, Teignbridge DC, 1979-83. B Feb 5 1945; ed Kelly Coll, Tavistock; Fitzwilliam Coll, Cambridge.
Mr Michael Hancock was Alliance spokesman on planning in the election team. MP for this seat, 1984-87, winning it at by-election; also contested the seat in 1983. Engineer. B Apr 9 1946; ed Hampshire, Oxford and London. Mbr Portsmouth City Cl, 1971- ; Hampshire CC, 1973- , leading the Labour councillors, 1977-81, joining SDP in 1981. Mbr, SDP national executive, 1984- ; board of management, Salvation Army; governor, College of Art, Portsmouth.
Mr Keith Gardiner, teacher. B Oct 4 1949; ed Portsmouth Poly; Southampton Univ. NUT.
Details of 1984 by-election in which SDP/All won seat on Page 284

Mr David Martin

PRESTON — No change

Electorate %Turnout	64,459	69.0%	**1987**	64,969	71.9%	**1983**
Wise, Mrs A. (Lab)	23,341	52.5%	+5.7%	21,810	46.7%	(Lab)
Chandran, Dr R.T. (C)	12,696	28.5%	-3.2%	14,832	31.8%	(C)
Wright, J.P. (L/All)	8,452	19.0%	-2.5%	10,039	21.5%	(SDP/All)
C to Lab swing 4.5%	44,489	Lab maj 10,645 23.9%		46,681	Lab maj 6,978 14.9%	

Mrs Audrey Wise, former shorthand typist and lecturer, was MP for Coventry South West Feb 1974-79; contested Woolwich 1983. Mbr, Lab Pty NEC, 1982- (mbr of organisation, international, local govt, finance, communications and women's cmtes); vice-chair, Institute for Workers' Control; former chair, PLP social security gp; mbr, Select Cmte on Violence in the Family, 1976-78. B Jan 1935; ed Rutherford HS. Usdaw.
Dr Raj Chandran, general medical practitioner; managing director, Doctors Emergency Service, Derby, Chesterfield and Mansfield. B Sep 29 1938; ed Pasa Rd English Sch, Kuala Lumpur, Malaysia; Hindu Coll, Kokuril, Sri Lanka; Medical Sch, Colombo, Sri Lanka. Mbr, Ashfield DC, 1971-75; BMA. Major, RAMC (TA).
Mr John Wright, lecturer. Mbr, Preston BC, 1982- (dep ldr, Lib gp). Vice-chmn, Preston Lib Assocn; mbr, ALC. B Sep 18 1956; ed Preston Catholic Coll; East Anglia Univ. NATFHE.

Mrs Audrey Wise

PUDSEY — No change

Electorate %Turnout	71,681	78.0%	**1987**	70,583	75.8%	**1983**
*Shaw, J.G.D. (C)	25,457	45.5%	-0.2%	24,455	45.7%	(C)
Cummins, J.P.F. (L/All)	19,021	34.0%	-1.8%	19,141	35.8%	(L/All)
Taggart, N. (Lab)	11,461	20.5%	+2.7%	9,542	17.8%	(Lab)
				387	0.7%	(Other)
L/All to C swing 0.8%	55,939	C maj 6,436 11.5%		53,525	C maj 5,314 9.9%	

Sir **Giles Shaw** was Minister of State for Industry at the DTI, 1986-87; Minister of State, Home Office, 1984-86; Under Secretary of State for Energy, 1983-84, for Environment, 1981-83, and for N Ireland, 1979-81. Elected in 1974; contested Hull West, 1966. B Nov 16 1931; ed Sedbergh Sch and St John's Coll, Cambridge (Pres of Union, 1954). Formerly with Rowntree Mackintosh (marketing director, confectionery division, 1970-74) and former director, North Riding Motors. Vice-chmn, Cons prices and consumer affairs cmte, 1976-78; jt sec, all-pty wool textile group, 1978-79. Mbr, Select Cmte on Nationalised Industries, 1976-79; Flaxton RDC, 1957-64. Treas, Yorkshire Cons MPs, 1974-79.

Mr **Julian Cummins**, director of marketing company, contested this seat 1983. Mbr, Leeds City Cl, 1982- ; Lib Pty industry gp. B Jan 29 1955; ed Wellington Coll; King's Coll, Cambridge.

Mr **Neil Taggart**, mbr, Leeds City Cl, 1980- . B Dec 24 1951; ed Coleshill GS, Warwickshire; Leeds Univ. Chmn, Leeds Dist Lab Pty, 1980-81, and exec mbr 1978- . Chmn, Leeds NE CLP, 1981-84. Mbr, W Yorks PTA and W Yorks Police Authority. Apex.

Sir Giles Shaw

PUTNEY — No change

Electorate %Turnout	63,108	75.9%	**1987**	63,853	73.6%	**1983**
*Mellor, D.J. (C)	24,197	50.5%	+4.0%	21,863	46.5%	(C)
Hain, P.G. (Lab)	17,290	36.1%	+0.2%	16,844	35.9%	(Lab)
Harlow, Ms S. (L/All)	5,934	12.4%	-3.9%	7,668	16.3%	(L/All)
Desorgher, S. (Grn)	508	1.1%		290	0.6%	(NF)
				319	0.7%	(Other)
Lab to C swing 1.9%	47,929	C maj 6,907 14.4%		46,984	C maj 5,019 10.7%	

Mr **David Mellor** was appointed Minister of State, Foreign and Commonwealth Office, Jun 1987; Minister of State, Home Office, 1986-87; Under Secretary of State, Home Office, 1983-86; Under Secretary of State for Energy, 1981-83. Barrister. Won seat in 1979; contested West Bromwich East, Oct 1974. B Mar 12 1949; ed Swanage GS, Christ's Coll, Cambridge. Chmn, Cambridge Univ Cons Assocn, 1970. Sec, Cons back-bench legal cmte, 1979-81, and environment cmte, 1981; jt vice-chmn, Greater London Cons MPs, 1980-81.

Mr **Peter Hain**, research officer, Union of Communication Workers, since 1976, contested this seat 1983. Vice-chmn, Lab Co-ordinating Cmte. Civil rights and anti- apartheid campaigner. B Feb 16 1950; ed Pretoria Boys HS and Emanuel Sch, Wandsworth; Queen Mary's Coll, London Univ; Sussex Univ. Mbr, NCCL, CND, Apex.

Ms **Sally Harlow** is a computer software consultant. B Jun 18 1956; ed Christ's Hospital, Hereford; Luton Sixth Form Coll; Wadham Coll, Oxford. ASTMS.

Mr **Simon Desorgher**, musician, composer and teacher. Founder and organiser of Nettlefold Festival of Music, S London. B Dec 13 1951; ed Cheltenham GS; Royal Coll of Music.

Mr David Mellor

RAVENSBOURNE — No change

Electorate %Turnout	59,365	75.7%	**1987**	58,811	73.2%	**1983**
*Hunt, J.L. (C)	28,295	63.0%	-0.1%	27,143	63.0%	(C)
Campbell, G. (SDP/All)	11,376	25.3%	-1.7%	11,631	27.0%	(SDP/All)
D'Arcy, M. (Lab)	5,087	11.3%	+1.9%	4,037	9.4%	(Lab)
Waide, A. (BN)	184	0.4%		242	0.6%	(BNP)
SDP/All to C swing 0.8%	44,942	C maj 16,919 37.6%		43,053	C maj 15,512 36.0%	

Mr **John Hunt**, a former stockbroker, was elected for Ravensbourne in Feb 1974; MP for Bromley, 1964-74; contested Lewisham South, 1959. Member, Chairmen's Panel, 1980- ; Select Cmte on Home Affairs, 1980- , and its sub-cmte on race relations and immigration. Parly adviser to Nat Hairdressers' Fed. B Oct 27 1929; ed Dulwich Coll. Member, Bromley BC, 1953-65; mayor, 1963-64. Pres, Inst of Administrative Accountants. Former chmn, Greater London Cons MPs. Mbr, exec cmte, British gp, IPU; jt chmn, Indo-British parly group, 1979- ; British-Caribbean Assocn, 1968-77 and 1984- . Freeman, Haberdashers' Co and City of London. Mbr, BBC General Advisory Cl, 1975- ; London Stock Exchange, 1958-70; Cl of Europe and WEU, 1973-77.

Mr **Gareth Campbell**, solicitor; legal adviser, Nat Westminster Bank plc. Mbr, London borough of Sutton Cl, 1986- . B Jun 16 1952; ed Dulwich Coll; Bristol Univ. Member, Nat Cl for Electoral Reform.

Mr **Mike D'Arcy**, trade union officer. B May 26 1944; ed LSE. Fought Anerley local election, 1986. Has held various posts at branch, CLP and borough level. TGWU.

Mr John Hunt

READING EAST — No change

Electorate %Turnout	72,311	73.3%	1987	67,511	70.4%	1983
*Vaughan, Sir Gerard (C)	28,515	53.8%	+2.2%	24,516	51.6%	(C)
Baring, Mrs S.M. (SDP/All)	12,298	23.2%	-4.2%	13,008	27.4%	(SDP/All)
Salter, M.J. (Lab)	11,371	21.5%	+2.1%	9,218	19.4%	(Lab)
Unsworth, P.J. (Grn)	667	1.3%	+0.2%	519	1.1%	(Eco)
Shone, A.B. (CSOSMG)	125	0.2%		147	0.3%	(BNP)
				113	0.2%	(Other)
SDP/All to C swing 3.2%	52,976	C maj 16,217 30.6%		47,521	C maj 11,508 24.2%	

Sir Gerard Vaughan

Sir Gerard Vaughan was Minister of State for Trade (Minister for Consumer Affairs), 1982-83; Minister for Health, with rank of Minister of State, DHSS, 1979-82; an Opposition spokesman on the social services, 1975-79; Opposition whip, 1974-75. Mbr, Select Cmte on Education, Science and the Arts, 1983- . Consultant, lecturer, author and member of Lloyd's. Elected for this seat 1983; MP for Reading South, Feb 1974-83, and for Reading, 1970-74; contested Poplar, 1955. Chmn, Chingbury Ltd, a private family company, and Private Medical Centres plc; jt chmn, Spahealth Ltd, a medical film company; director, Healthfirst (Mutual of Omaha International). B Jun 11 1923; ed London Univ and Guy's Hosp. Pres, Cons Medical Soc. Liveryman, Worshipful Company of Barbers.
Mrs Susan Baring, former development officer, Richmond Fellowship for Mental Welfare and Rehabilitation. Mbr, Parole Bd; bd of visitors, Kingston Prison; vice-chmn, Central Cl of Probation Cmtes, 1979-82; Inner London Probation Cmte, 1983- ; cl, King's Coll, London; governing body, British Inst of Human Rights. B Jun 5 1930; ed Heathfield Sch, Ascot.
Mr Martin Salter, dep ldr, Reading BC. B Apr 19 1954; ed Sussex Univ.
Mr Philip Unsworth, electronics technician. B Jan 15 1946; ed Blackpool GS; Leeds and Leicester Univs; Reading Coll of Tech.

READING WEST — No change

Electorate %Turnout	70,391	72.2%	1987	66,080	72.5%	1983
*Durant, R.A.B. (C)	28,122	55.3%	+3.2%	24,948	52.1%	(C)
Lock, K.H. (L/All)	11,369	22.4%	-5.9%	13,549	28.3%	(L/All)
Orton, M.E. (Lab)	10,819	21.3%	+2.0%	9,220	19.3%	(Lab)
Wilson, E.P. (Grn)	542	1.1%		161	0.3%	(Ind)
L/All to C swing 4.6%	50,852	C maj 16,753 32.9%		47,878	C maj 11,399 23.8%	

Mr Tony Durant

Mr Tony Durant has been a Government whip since 1984, becoming a Lord Commissioner of the Treasury in 1986. Chmn, Cons nat advisory cmte on local govt, 1980-84; Cons back-bench environment cmte, 1982-84. Director and company secretary, audio visual aids business, 1970-84. Elected for this seat 1983; MP for Reading North, Feb 1974-83; contested Rother Valley, 1970. PPS to DoE and Secretary of State for Transport, 1983, to Secretary of State for Employment, 1983-84. B Jan 9 1928; ed Dane Court Prep Sch and Bryanston Sch, Dorset. Mbr, exec cmte, CPA, 1986- ; Select Cmte on Parliamentary Commissioner for Administration, 1974-83; chmn, all-pty gp on widows and single-parent families, 1977-85; mbr, Inland Waterways Advisory Cl, 1975-84; vice chmn, Parly Gp for World Govt, 1979-84. Mbr, Woking UDC, 1968-74; chmn, Woking and mbr, Surrey education cmte, 1969-74.
Mr Keith Lock is export manager with the Nabisco Group at Reading. Mbr, Newbury DC, 1973- ; Berkshire CC, 1985- . B Jun 29 1931; ed Colfe's Sch, London; Woolwich Poly.
Mr Michael Orton, coll lecturer in management studies and language in Buckinghamshire, contested Wokingham 1983. Mbr, Reading BC, 1975- (ldr, Lab gp, 1981-). B Sep 2 1948; ed King Edward VII Sch, Sheffield; Cambridge Univ; Manchester Business Sch. NATFHE.

REDCAR — No change

Electorate %Turnout	63,393	76.1%	1987	63,447	71.3%	1983
Mowlam, Miss M. (Lab)	22,824	47.3%	+6.8%	18,348	40.6%	(Lab)
Bassett, P.J. (C)	15,089	31.3%	-2.4%	15,244	33.7%	(C)
Nightingale, G. (SDP/All)	10,298	21.4%	-4.3%	11,614	25.7%	(SDP/All)
C to Lab swing 4.6%	48,211	Lab maj 7,735 16.0%		45,206	Lab maj 3,104 6.9%	

Dr Marjorie Mowlam

Dr Marjorie Mowlam, administrative officer at Northern College, Barnsley. Chmn, Tyne Bridge CLP, 1982-83; mbr, Socialist Education Assocn; Newcastle DLP. B Sep 18 1949; ed Coundon Court Comprehensive Sch, Coventry; Durham Univ; Iowa Univ, US. ASTMS.
Mr Peter Bassett, investment manager, contested the seat in 1983. Chmn and managing director, the London Exploration and Production Co Ltd. Mbr, Greenwich BC, 1978-82 (Cons chief whip, 1980-82); treas, London South Inner Euro constituency, 1982-83; nat treas, Tory Reform Gp, 1983-85. B Oct 31 1955; ed Malvern Coll; Queen's Coll, Cambridge.
Mr Glyn Nightingale, economics and business studies teacher, contested this seat 1983. Former chmn and vice-chmn, Middlesbrough Lab Pty; area convenor/sec, Cleveland SDP, 1981-84. Constituency chmn; mbr, CSD since formation, and of regional cl. B Mar 18 1943; ed Ashton-under-Lyne GS; Manchester Coll of Commerce; York Univ; Manchester Univ. NUT.

REIGATE — No change

Electorate	%Turnout	71,940	72.5%	**1987**	70,320	72.1%	**1983**
*Gardiner, G.A. (C)		30,925	59.3%	+0.2%	29,932	59.0%	(C)
Pamplin, Mrs E.A. (SDP/All)		12,752	24.4%	-2.4%	13,625	26.9%	(SDP/All)
Spencer, R.P. (Lab)		7,460	14.3%	+2.2%	6,114	12.1%	(Lab)
Brand, G. (Grn)		1,026	2.0%	0.0%	1,029	2.0%	(Eco)
SDP/All to C swing 1.3%		52,163	C maj 18,173 34.8%		50,700	C maj 16,307 32.2%	

Mr **George Gardiner** has chaired the Conservative back-bench cmte on European affairs since 1980; was sec, 1976-79, and vice-chmn, 1979-80. Journalist and public affairs consultant. Editor, *Conservative News*, 1972-79; author of a biography on Mrs Thatcher. MP for Reigate since Feb 1974; contested Coventry South, 1970. Non-exec director, public relations company. B Mar 3 1935; ed Harvey GS, Folkestone; Balliol Coll, Oxford. Mbr, Select Cmte on Home Affairs and Race Relations and Immigration sub-cmte, 1979-82. Former mbr, exec, 1922 Cmte. Chief political correspondent, Thomson Regional Newspapers, 1964-74.
Mrs **Elizabeth Pamplin**, employment development officer for Kensington and Chelsea Cl; visiting lecturer in corporate personnel policy, Central London Poly. Ed St Hugh's Coll, Oxford.
Mr **Robin Spencer**, road transport sales manager, contested Canterbury 1979. Former chmn and sec, Reigate CLP. Mbr, Canterbury City Cl, 1979-81; Reigate BC, 1983- . B Aug 7 1947; ed Woking GS; Bristol Univ. TSSA.
Mr **Graham Brand**, volunteer projects co-ordinator for community service volunteers. B Nov 1 1952; ed Horley Cty Sec Sch; Redhill Tech Coll.
Mr George Gardiner

RENFREW WEST AND INVERCLYDE — Lab gain

Electorate	%Turnout	56,189	80.5%	**1987**	53,510·	78.1%	**1983**
Graham, T. (Lab)		17,525	38.7%	+9.7%	13,669	32.7%	(C)
*McCurley, Mrs A.A. (C)		13,472	29.8%	-2.9%	12,347	29.5%	(SDP/All)
Mabon, Dr J.D. (SDP/All)		9,669	21.4%	-8.2%	12,139	29.0%	(Lab)
Campbell, C. (SNP)		4,578	10.1%	+1.4%	3,653	8.7%	(SNP)
C to Lab swing 6.3%		45,244	Lab maj 4,053 9.0%		41,808	C maj 1,322 3.2%	

Mr **Thomas Graham**, manager of firm of local solicitors; former engineer with Rolls-Royce. Mbr, Strathclyde Reg Cl. Aged 43.
Mrs **Anna McCurley** was mbr, Select Cmte on Scottish Affairs 1984-87. MP for the seat, 1983-87; contested West Stirlingshire 1979; Glasgow Central by-election, 1980. Teacher, 1966-72; college methods tutor, 1972-74. B Jan 18 1943; ed Glasgow HS for Girls; Glasgow and Strathclyde Univs; Jordanhill Coll of Education. Mbr, Strathclyde Reg Cl, 1978-82.
Dr **Dickson Mabon**, physician and company director, who was Labour's Minister of State for Energy, 1976-79, resigned from the party and joined the SDP in 1981, being its spokesman on energy, 1981-83. Mbr, SDP nat cmte. Fought this seat 1983; MP for Greenock and Port Glasgow, Feb 1974-83, and for Greenock, Dec 1955-74; contested Bute and North Ayrshire, 1951, and West Renfrewshire, 1955. Under Secretary of State for Scotland, 1964-67; Minister of State, Scottish Office, 1967-70. Chmn, Lab Cmte for Europe, 1974-76. B Nov 1 1925; ed state schs; Glasgow Univ.
Mr **Colin Campbell**, head teacher, is chmn, Renfrew West and Inverclyde SNP and of Kilbarchan branch, SNP. B Aug 31 1938; ed Paisley GS; Glasgow Univ; Jordanhill Coll of Ed.
Mr Thomas Graham

RHONDDA — No change

Electorate	%Turnout	60,931	78.3%	**1987**	62,587	76.2%	**1983**
*Rogers, A.R. (Lab)		35,015	73.4%	+11.7%	29,448	61.7%	(Lab)
Davies, G.R. (Pl C)		4,261	8.9%	-1.2%	8,078	16.9%	(SDP/All)
YorkWilliams, J.R. (SDP/All)		3,930	8.2%	-8.7%	4,845	10.2%	(Pl C)
Reid, S.H. (C)		3,611	7.6%	-0.8%	3,973	8.3%	(C)
True, A. (Comm)		869	1.8%		1,350	2.8%	(Com)
Pl C to Lab swing 6.5%		47,686	Lab maj 30,754 64.5%		47,694	Lab maj 21,370 44.8%	

Mr **Allan Rogers** has served on the Select Cmte on European Legislation since 1983; mbr, Channel Tunnel Bill Select Cmte, 1986; PAC, 1983- ; Select Cmte on Welsh Affairs, 1983- ; vice-chmn, Welsh gp of Lab MPs, 1986- . Elected for this seat 1983; former geologist; WEA tutor-organiser, 1965-70, and S Wales district sec, 1970-79. Fellow of Geological Soc. MEP for SE Wales, 1979-84; a vice-pres, European Parliament, 1979-81. B Oct 24 1932; ed Univ of Wales, Swansea. Mbr, Rhondda DC, 1965-71; Mid-Glamorgan CC, 1970-79. Chmn, Poly-technic of Wales. Vice-pres, Welsh anti-apartheid movement. CND. Sponsored by Cohse.
Mr **Geraint Davies**, pharmacist, contested the seat 1983. On local cl since 1983. B Dec 1 1948; ed Ysgol Gymraeg Ynyswen; Pentre GS; London Univ.
Mr **John YorkWilliams**, marketing manager; director, cable television, Hong Kong and Huaying Oil Telecoms Co. Active in Hong Kong SDP gp. B Feb 28 1948; ed Porth GTS; Bath and Wales Univs. Former chmn, Tower Hamlets SDP; member, CSD, 1981-84.
Mr **Stephen Reid**, data processing manager. Mbr, Basingstoke and Deane BC, 1978- (ldr, Cons gp). B 1951; ed Queen Mary's GS, Basingstoke; Fitzwilliam Coll, Cambridge
Mr **Arthur True**, retired electrician, fought seat in previous elections. Cty cllr. Aged 66.
Mr Allan Rogers

RIBBLE VALLEY   No change

Electorate %Turnout	62,644	79.1%	**1987**	59,982	76.8%	**1983**
*Waddington, D.C. (C)	30,136	60.9%	-2.6%	29,223	63.4%	(C)
Carr, M. (SDP/All)	10,608	21.4%	-1.7%	10,632	23.1%	(SDP/All)
Pope, G. (Lab)	8,781	17.7%	+4.2%	6,214	13.5%	(Lab)
C to SDP/All swing 0.5%	49,525	C maj 19,528 39.4%		46,069	C maj 18,591 40.4%	

Mr **David Waddington, QC**, was appointed Parliamentary Secretary to the Treasury and Government Chief Whip in Jun 1987; Minister of State, Home Office, 1983-87; Under Secretary of State for Employment, 1981-83; Lord Commissioner of Treasury (Govt whip), 1979-81. Elected for this seat 1983; MP for Clitheroe, 1979-83; for Nelson and Colne, 1968-Oct 1974; contested Heywood and Royton, 1966, Nelson and Colne, 1964, and Farnworth, 1955. Recorder of Crown Court, 1972- . B Aug 2 1929; ed Sedbergh Sch and Hertford Coll, Oxford. Former director, Padiham Room and Power Co Ltd; Progress Mill Ltd; J and J Roberts Ltd; and Wolstenholme Rink Ltd.
Mr **Michael Carr**, teacher, contested this seat 1983. Mbr, Ribble Valley BC, 1979-83. B Jan 31 1946; ed Catholic Coll, Preston; Margaret McMillan Memorial Coll of Ed, Bradford. Mbr, NAS/UWT, 1975- ; Lancs Fed NAS/UWT press sec, 1984-87; Rossendale Dist NAS/UWT sec, 1984- .
Mr **Greg Pope**, production worker. B Aug 29 1960; ed St Mary's Coll, Blackburn; Hull Univ.

Mr David Waddington

RICHMOND AND BARNES   No change

Electorate %Turnout	54,700	83.2%	**1987**	55,845	79.6%	**1983**
*Hanley, J.J. (C)	21,729	47.7%	+1.2%	20,695	46.5%	(C)
Watson, A.J. (L/All)	19,963	43.8%	-2.5%	20,621	46.4%	(L/All)
Gold, M.D. (Lab)	3,227	7.1%	0.0%	3,156	7.1%	(Lab)
Matthews, Ms C.M. (Grn)	610	1.3%				
L/All to C swing 1.9%	45,529	C maj 1,766 3.9%		44,472	C maj 74 0.2%	

Mr **Jeremy Hanley** has been a member of the Select Cmte on Home Affairs and its sub-cmte on race relations and immigration since 1983. Chartered accountant; lecturer and broadcaster. Chmn, Fraser Green Ltd; director of Financial Training Co Ltd and other companies. Parly adviser to Institute of Chartered Accountants in England and Wales. Elected in 1983; contested Lambeth Central, 1978 by-election and 1979. B Nov 17 1945; ed Rugby. Chmn, Cons Candidates' Assocn, 1982-83; jt vice-chmn (1985-) and jt sec (1983-85), Cons back-bench trade and industry cmte; sec, Greater London Cons MPs, 1986- ; mbr, Soc of Cons Lawyers company law reform cmte, 1976- ; Bow Group; European Movement; Mensa.
Mr **Alan Watson** was President, Liberal Party, 1984-85. Director of Wadlow Grosvenor International; chief executive, Alan Watson Communications Ltd. Broadcaster with London Weekend and then BBC TV, 1969-75; head of TV, radio and audio-visual division, Director-ate-General of Information, EEC, 1975-79. Contested this seat 1983; Richmond, Oct 1974 and 1979. B Feb 3 1941; ed Kingswood School, Bath; Jesus Coll, Cambridge.
Dr **Michael Gold**, journalist; editor of industrial relations journal. Treas, Richmond and Barnes CLP, 1986-87; vice-chmn, London West Euro CLP, 1987- . B Mar 23 1953; ed GSs in St Albans and Reading; St Peter's Coll, Oxford; Edinburgh Univ. NUJ.
Ms **Christina Matthews**, actress. B Apr 23 1952; ed Ursuline Convent HS, Wimbledon; St Anne's Coll, Oxford. Equity.

Mr Jeremy Hanley

RICHMOND (YORKS)   No change

Electorate %Turnout	79,277	72.1%	**1987**	75,196	68.7%	**1983**
*Brittan, L. (C)	34,995	61.2%	-1.4%	32,373	62.6%	(C)
Lloyd-Williams, D. (L/All)	15,419	27.0%	-0.7%	14,307	27.7%	(L/All)
Robson, F. (Lab)	6,737	11.8%	+2.1%	4,997	9.7%	(Lab)
C to L/All swing 0.4%	57,151	C maj 19,576 34.3%		51,677	C maj 18,066 35.0%	

Mr **Leon Brittan, QC**, who became Secretary of State for Trade and Industry in 1985, resigned in 1986 during the controversy over the future of the Westland helicopter company. Barrister; director, Sharp Technology Fund plc; adviser to Goldman Sachs International Group; consultant to International Generics Ltd. Chmn, Society of Cons lawyers, 1986- . Home Secretary, 1983-85; Chief Secretary to the Treasury with seat in Cabinet, 1981-83; Minister of State, Home Office, 1979-81. Elected for this seat 1983; MP for Cleveland and Whitby, Feb 1974-1983; contested Kensington North, 1966 and 1970. An Opposition spokesman on devolution and House of Commons affairs, 1976-79; appointed as an additional employment spokesman, Nov 1978. B Sep 25 1939; ed Haberdashers' Aske's Sch; Trinity Coll, Cambridge (Pres of Union, 1960); and Yale Univ. Editor, *Crossbow*, 1966-68. Chmn, Bow Group, 1964-65. Bencher, Inner Temple, since 1983.
Mr **David Lloyd-Williams**, antique dealer. Mbr, Richmond Cl, 1979- (Mayor, 1985-87); North Yorkshire CC, 1981- . B Mar 7 1944; ed Mount Grace Sch, Potters Bar. Chmn, GLC Staff Assocn Service Conditions Cmte, 1968-70.
Mr **Frank Robson**, farmer. Mbr, Darlington BC, 1979- . B Feb 28 1924; ed Queen Elizabeth GS, Darlington. Chmn, Darlington District Lab Pty, 1985- . TGWU.

Mr Leon Brittan

ROCHDALE · No change

Electorate	%Turnout	68,703	74.6%	**1987**	66,976	70.8%	**1983**
*Smith, C. (L/All)		22,245	43.4%	-2.7%	21,858	46.1%	(L/All)
Williams, D. (Lab)		19,466	38.0%	+7.9%	14,271	30.1%	(Lab)
Condie, C. (C)		9,561	18.6%	-3.7%	10,616	22.4%	(C)
					667	1.4%	(Other)
L/All to Lab swing 5.3%		51,272	L/All maj	2,779 5.4%	47,412	L/All maj	7,587 16.0%

Mr Cyril Smith was Liberal spokesman on employment and on social services, 1979-85 and 1976-77, previously chief whip. Gained the seat for Liberals in 1972 by-election; contested seat, 1970. B Jun 28 1928; ed Rochdale GS. Managing director, Smith Springs (Rochdale) Ltd, 1963-87, now non-exec director of company to whom he sold it. A production manager, 1958-63; newsagent, 1954-58; Lab Pty agent at Ashton-under-Lyne and Heywood and Royton, 1950-55; Lib Pty agent, Stockport, 1948-50; rejoined Lib Pty 1967. Mbr, Rochdale BC, 1952-75; Mayor of Rochdale, 1966-67. Former mbr, Select Cmte on Commons Services and catering sub-cmte. Deputy Chancellor, Lancaster Univ, 1978-86.

Mr David Williams, lecturer in trade union law, former scrapyard labourer and British Rail waiter. Contested Colne Valley 1983. Mbr, Rochdale Cl, 1979- . B May 1 1949; ed Newcastle and Manchester Univs; Colton Coll of Ed. NATFHE.

Mr Clive Condie, project manager, Manchester Airport plc; worked as planning asst and asst projects officer for former Manchester International Airport Authority. B Jul 19 1960; ed Hulme Hall Sch, Cheadle Hulme; Cheadle Hulme Sch; Stirling Univ.

Mr Cyril Smith

ROCHFORD · No change

Electorate	%Turnout	76,048	78.1%	**1987**	69,392	73.5%	**1983**
*Clark, M. (C)		35,872	60.4%	+2.6%	29,495	57.8%	(C)
Young, P. (L/All)		16,178	27.3%	-4.9%	16,393	32.1%	(L/All)
Weir, D. (Lab)		7,308	12.3%	+2.3%	5,105	10.0%	(Lab)
L/All to C swing 3.7%		59,358	C maj	19,694 33.2%	50,993	C maj	13,102 25.7%

Dr Michael Clark, a management consultant with PA Management Consultants Ltd since 1981, has been on the Select Cmte on Energy since 1983; jt sec, Cons back-bench energy cmte, 1986- . Industrial chemist with ICI and Smiths Industries, 1960-69; with PA International Management Consultants, 1969-73; marketing manager, St Regis Paper Co, 1973-78; director, Courtenay Stewart International, 1978-81. Elected for this seat 1983; contested Ilkeston, 1979. B Aug 1935; ed King Edward VI GS, Retford; King's Coll, London; Univ of Minnesota; St John's Coll, Cambridge, and Univ of Minnesota. Mbr, cl, parliamentary information technology, 1984- ; hon sec, Parly and Scientific Cmte, since 1985; all-pty gp for chemical industry, 1985- ; and Anglo-Nepalese Soc, 1985- . Mbr, Cambridge Cons Assocn, 1969-83, being treas, 1975-78; vice-chmn, 1978-80; chmn, 1980-83. Mbr, Cons Eastern Area exec cl, 1980-84. Elected Fellow, King's Coll, London, 1987.

Mr Philip Young, journalist; former editor, *Liberal News*. B 1948; ed South Kent Coll of Tech, Ashford.

Mr David Weir, engineer. Mbr, Essex CC; Rochford DC. B Feb 6 1932; ed Logie Central Sch, Dundee.

Dr Michael Clark

ROMFORD · No change

Electorate	%Turnout	55,668	72.9%	**1987**	55,758	69.8%	**1983**
*Neubert, M.J. (C)		22,745	56.0%	+2.6%	20,771	53.4%	(C)
Smith, N.J.M. (Lab)		9,274	22.8%	+3.6%	10,197	26.2%	(L/All)
Bates, J.H. (L/All)		8,195	20.2%	-6.0%	7,494	19.3%	(Lab)
Gibson, F.J. (Grn)		385	0.9%		432	1.1%	(NF)
C to Lab swing 0.5%		40,599	C maj	13,471 33.2%	38,894	C maj	10,574 27.2%

Mr Michael Neubert became a Lord Commissioner of the Treasury (Govt whip) in 1986; asst Govt whip, 1983-86. PPS to Lord Cockfield, Secretary of State for Trade, 1982-83; PPS to other ministers, 1980-82. Sec, Cons back-bench trade cmte, 1975-79; Cons prices and consumer affairs cmte, 1974-79. Elected in Feb 1974; contested Romford 1970, Hammersmith North 1966. Former travel and industrial consultant. B Sep 3, 1933; ed Queen Elizabeth's Sch, Barnet; Bromley GS; Downing Coll, Cambridge. Mbr, Bromley BC, 1960-63; 1964-68; alderman, 1968-74; leader, 1967-70; mayor, 1972-73.

Mr Nigel Smith, teacher, contested Chichester Feb and Oct 1974 and Essex South East 1979. Mbr, Basildon Cl, 1975-79; Southend Cl, 1985- . B Oct 9 1947; ed Manchester Poly; Kent State Univ, US.

Mr John Bates, barrister, is chairman of the Liberal Party environment panel. Contested this seat 1983 and 1979. In TA. B May 29 1951; ed Harrow; Inns of Court Sch of Law.

Mr Michael Neubert

ROMSEY AND WATERSIDE — No change

Electorate %Turnout	79,136	79.0%	**1987**	70,782	75.8%	**1983**
*Colvin, M.K.B. (C)	35,303	56.4%	-0.2%	30,361	56.6%	(C)
Bloss, A.T. (SDP/All)	20,031	32.0%	+0.9%	16,671	31.1%	(SDP/All)
Roberts, S.J. (Lab)	7,213	11.5%	-0.8%	6,604	12.3%	(Lab)
C to SDP/All swing 0.6%	62,547	C maj 15,272 24.4%		53,636	C maj 13,690 25.5%	

Mr Michael Colvin, PPS to Ministers of State, Foreign and Commonwealth Office, 1983-85, and to Mr Richard Luce, Minister for the Arts, since 1985. Won this seat in 1983; MP for Bristol North West, 1979-83. Farmer, landowner, company director and public house licensee. Mbr, Select Cmte on Employment, 1981-83. Part-time mbr, Cons Research Dept, specializing in aviation, 1975-79. Sec, West Country Cons MPs, 1982-83; chmn, 1983. Qualified pilot and parachutist. B Sep 27 1932; ed Eton, RMA Sandhurst, and Royal Agricultural Coll, Cirencester. Mbr, Andover Cl, 1965-73; Test Valley Cl, 1973-75. Vice-chmn, Southern Sports Cl, 1968-73. Director, Accrep Ltd. Chmn, Cons aviation cmte, 1982-83; vice-chmn, Cons back-bench cmte on small businesses, 1980-83; sec, Cons shipping and shipbuilding cmte, 1981-83.
Mr Alan Bloss, freelance interpreter, being mostly at UN organizations in Geneva and Vienna since 1979. Contested this seat 1983. B Mar 19 1938; ed Palmer's Sch, Grays; London Univ.
Mr Stephen Roberts, mortgage broker. Constituency membership sec and trade union liason officer; mbr, Lab coordinating cmte. B Oct 25 1960; ed Park Burn Comp Sch, Guildford; Belair Scho of Drama. TGWU.

Mr Michael Colvin

ROSS, CROMARTY AND SKYE — No change

Electorate %Turnout	52,369	72.7%	**1987**	48,401	72.6%	**1983**
*Kennedy, C.P. (SDP/All)	18,809	49.4%	+10.9%	13,528	38.5%	(SDP/All)
Spencer Nairn, F. (C)	7,490	19.7%	-14.0%	11,824	33.7%	(C)
MacMillan, M.M. (Lab)	7,287	19.1%	+5.2%	4,901	14.0%	(Lab)
Gibson, R.M. (SNP)	4,492	11.8%	-2.1%	4,863	13.8%	(SNP)
C to SDP/All swing 12.4%	38,078	SDP/All maj 11,319	29.7%	35,116	SDP/All maj 1,704	4.9%

Mr Charles Kennedy became chief Alliance spokesman on health and social security in its election team; SDP spokesman on health and social security and on Scotland, since 1983; mbr, Select Cmte on Social Services, since 1986. Won the seat in 1983 when on a Fulbright scholarship teaching speech communication and British politics in Indiana Univ. Chmn, SDP Cl for Scotland. B Nov 25 1959; ed Lochaber HS, Fort William; Glasgow Univ (Pres of union, 1980-81). Chmn, Glasgow Univ Social Democratic Club, 1979-80. Won British Observer mace debating tournament, 1982. Occasional adviser to Engineering Employers' Fed. Formerly worked as radio news reporter and broadcaster in Inverness.
Mr Frank Spencer Nairn, farmer and chartered accountant, has business interests in holiday cottages and a sheep and deer farm. Member of Lloyd's. Community cllr since 1982. B May 10 1949; ed Eton; Magdalene Coll, Cambridge; Graduate Sch of Business, Capetown Univ. Member, Scottish NFU, serving on Inverness area exec cmte. Fly fisherman.
Mr Michael MacMillan, solicitor. Constituency and branch chmn and sec. B Mar 14 1941; ed Conon Bridge Primary Sch; Dingwall Academy. GMB.
Mr Robert Gibson, secondary school teacher, is on the SNP nat exec; party spokesman on land policy. Fought Inverness in Feb 1974. B Oct 16 1945; ed Dundee Univ. EIS.

Mr Charles Kennedy

ROSSENDALE AND DARWEN — No change

Electorate %Turnout	75,038	80.3%	**1987**	74,401	77.8%	**1983**
*Trippier, D.A. (C)	28,056	46.6%	-0.5%	27,214	47.0%	(C)
Anderson, Mrs J. (Lab)	23,074	38.3%	+6.5%	18,393	31.8%	(Lab)
Hulse, P.J. (L/All)	9,097	15.1%	-6.1%	12,246	21.2%	(L/All)
C to Lab swing 3.5%	60,227	C maj 4,982 8.3%		57,853	C maj 8,821 15.2%	

Mr David Trippier was appointed an Under Secretary of State for Environment in Jun 1987; Under Secretary of State for Trade and Industry, 1983-85, moving to Dept of Employment as Under Secretary of State in 1985 but remaining Minister for Small Businesses. Former stockbroker and member of Stock Exchange from 1968. Elected for this seat 1983; MP for Rossendale, 1979-83; fought Rochdale in 1972 by-election and Oldham West, Feb and Oct 1974. B May 15 1945; ed Bury GS. Mbr, Rochdale Cl, 1969-78. Jt sec, Cons back-bench defence cmte, 1980-82; sec, all-pty footwear cmte, 1979-83. PPS to Minister for Health, 1982-83. Nat vice-chmn, Assocn of Cons Clubs, 1980-84. Chmn, Rochdale YCs, 1965, and chmn, SE Lancs YC, 1966. Former director, financial planning company.
Mrs Janet Anderson, assistant to Mr Jack Straw MP; former personal asst to Mrs Barbara Castle, MEP. B Dec 6 1949; ed Kingsfield Comp, Bristol; Central London Poly. TGWU, CND.
Mr Peter Hulse, project engineer with aircraft manufacturer. Mbr, Preston BC. B 1951; ed Smallwood Manor and Denstone Coll, both in Uttoxeter; Oxford Univ.

Mr David Trippier

ROTHERHAM — No change

Electorate	%Turnout	61,521	69.2%	**1987**	61,165	67.0%	**1983**
*Crowther, J.S. (Lab)		25,422	59.7%	+5.4%	22,236	54.3%	(Lab)
Stevens, J.C.C. (C)		9,410	22.1%	-3.6%	10,527	25.7%	(C)
Bowler, P.J. (L/All)		7,766	18.2%	-1.8%	8,192	20.0%	(L/All)
C to Lab swing 4.5%		42,598	Lab maj 16,012 37.6%		40,955	Lab maj 11,709 28.6%	

Mr Stanley Crowther

Mr Stanley Crowther, elected at a by-election in 1976, has been a member of the Select Cmtes on Trade and Industry and on Procedure since 1983, and on the Chairmen's Panel since 1984. Jt vice-chmn, PLP trade and industry cmte, 1985- ; chmn, Yorkshire group of Labour MPs, 1985- . B May 30 1925; ed Rotherham GS and Rotherham Coll of Technology. Freelance journalist from 1951; previously with *Rotherham Advertiser* and *Yorkshire Evening Post*. Mbr, Rotherham BC, 1958-59 and 1961-76; Mayor of Rotherham, 1971-72, and 1975-76; chmn, planning cmte, 1964-76; chmn, Yorkshire and Humberside Development Assocn, 1973-76. Mbr, exec, Town and Country Planning Assocn, 1973- . Former parly adviser to British Reclamation Industries Confed. Sponsored by TGWU.
Mr John Stevens, merchant banker. B 1955; ed Winchester; Magdelen Coll, Oxford.
Mr Peter Bowler, a sales representative for Colgate-Palmolive Ltd, fought this seat 1983. Director, Yorkshire Wildlife Trust Ltd. Mbr, Amber Valley DC, 1976-81; Ripley TC, 1976-81, being leader of Lib gp. B Oct 19 1952; ed Ripley Tech Sch, Derbyshire. Mbr, British Assocn of Nature Conservationists, Greenpeace, Friends of the Earth.

ROTHER VALLEY — No change

Electorate	%Turnout	66,416	75.6%	**1987**	65,127	71.9%	**1983**
*Barron, K.J. (Lab)		28,292	56.4%	+9.9%	21,781	46.5%	(Lab)
Rayner, P.R. (C)		12,502	24.9%	-3.2%	13,156	28.1%	(C)
Boddy, J.R. (SDP/All)		9,240	18.4%	-7.0%	11,903	25.4%	(SDP/All)
Driver, M.R. (WRP)		145	0.3%				
C to Lab swing 6.5%		50,179	Lab maj 15,790 31.5%		46,840	Lab maj 8,625 18.4%	

Mr Kevin Barron

Mr Kevin Barron has been PPS to Mr Kinnock, Leader of the Opposition, since 1985. Coal miner, 1962-83. Elected in 1983. Mbr, Select Cmte on Energy, 1983-86. B Oct 26 1946; ed Maltby Hall Sec Mod Sch; Ruskin Coll, Oxford. Pres, Rotherham and District TUC. Was NUM delegate for Maltby colliery. Sponsored by NUM.
Mr Paul Rayner is a management consultant and managing director of his own company advising on the use of computers; past chmn, Computer Retailers' Assocn. B Oct 25 1946; ed Leeds GS; Bristol Univ. Past chairman, Yorkshire Area CPC; former vice-chmn, Bristol Univ Cons Assocn.
Mr John Boddy, management consultant, contested Rother Valley 1983 and Greater Manchester West in 1984 Euro election. B Apr 7 1930; ed Burnley GS; LSE.

ROXBURGH AND BERWICKSHIRE — No change

Electorate	%Turnout	43,140	77.2%	**1987**	41,702	75.8%	**1983**
*Kirkwood, A.J. (L/All)		16,388	49.2%	-1.1%	15,920	50.3%	(L/All)
Fox, Dr L. (C)		12,380	37.2%	-2.4%	12,524	39.6%	(C)
Luckhurst, T. (Lab)		2,944	8.8%	+1.5%	2,326	7.4%	(Lab)
Douglas, M. (SNP)		1,586	4.8%	+2.1%	852	2.7%	(SNP)
C to L/All swing 0.6%		33,298	L/All maj 4,008 12.0%		31,622	L/All maj 3,396 10.7%	

Mr Archy Kirkwood

Mr Archy Kirkwood was Alliance election team spokesman on overseas development; Liberal spokesman on health and social security since 1985; former Scottish Lib Pty spokesman on fisheries. Elected in 1983. Sec/treas, all-ptyt pensioners gp; treas, all-pty gp on AIDS; ,br, Royal College of Nursing parly panel. Lawyer. B Apr 22 1946; ed Cranhill Sec Sch, Glasgow; Heriot-Watt Univ, Edinburgh. Trustee, Joseph Rowntree Social Service Trust, since 1985. Aide to Mr David Steel, 1971-75 and 1977-78.
Dr Liam Fox, medical practitioner; former registrar, Hairmyres Hospital, East Kilbride, senior houseman at Billshill Maternity Hospital, and junior house doctor, Glasgow Royal Infirmary. Chmn, West of Scotland YCs, 1983-84. B 1961; ed St Bride's HS, East Kilbride; Glasgow Univ (Pres, Univ Cons Club, 1982-83).
Mr Tim Luckhurst, parly adviser to Shadow Secretary of State for Scotland, Mr Donald Dewar. B Jan 8 1963; ed Peebles HS; Robinson Coll, Cambridge Univ. Mbr, parly branch NUJ. Adviser to PLP Cmte on Abolition of Domestic Rates.
Mr Marshall Douglas, accountant and audit manager. Treas, Tweeddale, Ettrick and Lauderdale SNP; sec, Tweeddale East branch. B 1957; ed Scottish Coll of Textiles.

RUGBY AND KENILWORTH — No change

Electorate %Turnout	76,654	79.6%	**1987**	74,501	78.1%	**1983**
*Pawsey, J.F. (C)	31,485	51.6%	+0.7%	29,622	50.9%	(C)
Airey, J. (Lab)	15,221	24.9%	+2.3%	15,381	26.4%	(L/All)
Owen-Jones, D.R. (L/All)	14,343	23.5%	-2.9%	13,180	22.7%	(Lab)
C to Lab swing 0.8%	61,049	C maj 16,264 26.6%		58,183	C maj 14,241 24.5%	

Mr James Pawsey

Mr James Pawsey, non-executive director of vending machine group, was elected for this seat 1983; MP for Rugby, 1979-83. Chmn, Cons back-bench education cmte, 1985- ; mbr, Select Cmtes on Energy, 1983-87; on Parliamentary Commissioner for Administration, since 1983; on Environment, 1981-82; Parly Scientific Cmte, 1882- ; exec, IPU, 1984- . Mbr of Lloyd's; Inst of Directors. B Aug 21 1933; ed Coventry Tech Sch; Coventry Tech Coll. Ex-pres, Warwickshire Assocn of Parish Cls. Mbr, Rugby RDC and Rugby BC, 1964-74; Warwickshire CC, 1974-79. Sec, Cons back-bench health and social services cmte, 1982-83. PPS to DES, 1982-83; DHSS, 1983-84; Minister of State for N Ireland, 1984-86. Mbr, HoC Cons Euro Reform Group and Cons Middle East Cl. Sec, British Solidarity with Poland Campaign, 1982- ; British/Greek parly gp, 1984- ; British/Portuguese parly gp, 1984-. Treas, Parly Assocn for Euro-Arab Cooperation; British/Bangladesh parly gp, 1984- .
Mr John Airey, senior lecturer in trade union studies, Warley Coll of Technology. B Jun 29 1949; ed Walton-le-Dale County Secondary Schl; Ruskin Coll; Pembroke Coll, Oxford Univ. TGWU.
Mr David Owen-Jones, barrister, contested this seat 1983 and Carmarthen twice in 1974. B Mar 16 1949; ed Llandovery Coll; Univ Coll, London.

RUISLIP, NORTHWOOD — No change

Electorate %Turnout	56,365	77.7%	**1987**	56,378	72.9%	**1983**
*Wilkinson, J.A.D. (C)	27,418	62.6%	+3.1%	24,498	59.6%	(C)
Darby, Mrs D. (L/All)	10,447	23.9%	-4.1%	11,516	28.0%	(L/All)
Smith, Ms H.A. (Lab)	5,913	13.5%	+1.1%	5,105	12.4%	(Lab)
L/All to C swing 3.6%	43,778	C maj 16,971 38.8%		41,119	C maj 12,982 31.6%	

Mr John Wilkinson

Mr John Wilkinson was chmn, Cons back-bench aviation cmte, 1983-85, and vice-chmn, Cons defence cmte, 1983-85; chmn, Cons space sub-cmte, 1986- , and vice-chmn, 1983-85. Previously held other offices on these cmtes. PPS to Minister of State for Industry, 1979-80; to Secretary of State for Defence, 1981-82. Business consultant, being chmn, EMC Communications Ltd; lecturer and author. Elected for Ruislip-Northwood 1979; MP for Bradford West, 1970-Feb, 1974; contested that seat, Oct 1974. B Sep 23 1940; ed Eton; RAF Coll, Cranwell; Churchill Coll, Cambridge. Flying instructor at Cranwell, 1966-67, and Stansted, 1974-75. Held executive posts with aircraft companies, 1975-79. ADC to Commander 2nd Allied Tactical Air Force, Germany, 1967. Chmn, European Freedom Cl, 1982- ; Anglo-Asian Cons Soc, 1979-82; Horn of Africa Cl, 1984- . Delegate to Cl of Europe (chmn, space sub-cmte, since 1984) and WEU (chmn, cmte on scientific, tech and aerospace, since 1986), 1979- . Mbr, Select Cmtes on Race Relations and Immigration and on Science and Tech, 1972-74.
Mrs Doreen Darby is on the Lib Pty Environment Panel. Mbr, Chiltern DC, 1979-83; Chalfont St Peter PC, 1979- . B Nov 6 1926; ed Queen Elizabeth's Girls' GS, Barnet; Trafalgar Sch for Girls, Montreal.
Ms Hazel Smith, mature student. B May 26 1954. Former Colchester and Lambeth cllr.

RUSHCLIFFE — No change

Electorate %Turnout	72,797	80.0%	**1987**	70,333	76.9%	**1983**
*Clarke, K.H. (C)	34,214	58.8%	-2.7%	33,253	61.5%	(C)
George, L. (SDP/All)	13,375	23.0%	-1.1%	13,033	24.1%	(L/All)
Tipping, S.P. (Lab)	9,631	16.5%	+3.1%	7,290	13.5%	(Lab)
Wright, Ms H. (Grn)	991	1.7%	+0.7%	518	1.0%	(Eco)
C to SDP/All swing 0.8%	58,211	C maj 20,839 35.8%		54,094	C maj 20,220 37.4%	

Mr Kenneth Clarke

Mr Kenneth Clarke, QC, was appointed Chancellor of the Duchy of Lancaster and chief Commons spokesman for the DTI in Jun 1987; joined Cabinet in 1985 as Paymaster General and Minister for Employment, being dept's chief spokesman in Commons; Minister for Health, with rank of Minister of State, DHSS, 1982-85; Parliamentary Secretary (1979-81) and Under Secretary of State (1981-82) for Transport. Elected in 1970; contested Mansfield, 1966 and 1964. An Opposition spokesman on industry, 1976-79, and social services, 1974-76; Lord Commissioner of the Treasury (Govt whip), 1974; asst Govt whip, 1972-74. Barrister. B Jul 2 1940; ed Nottingham HS, Gonville and Caius Coll, Cambridge (Pres of Union, 1963). Pres, YCs, 1986-87. Chmn, Fed of Cons Students, 1963-65. Research sec, Birmingham Bow Group, 1966-67. PPS to Solicitor General, 1971-72
Mr Laurence George, commercial lawyer. B Mar 3 1954; ed Bootham Sch, York; Nottingham Univ; Coll of Law; City of London Poly.
Mr Simon Tipping, social worker. Mbr, Nottinghamshire CC 1981- . B Oct 24 1949; ed Hipperholme GS; Nottingham Univ. NUPE.
Ms Heather Wright, social worker. B Feb 19 1947; ed West Cornwall Sch, Penzance; Westonbirt Sch, Tetbury; Edinburgh Univ; Chiswick Poly.

RUTLAND AND MELTON · No change

Electorate %Turnout	77,846	76.8%	**1987**	75,180	73.3%	**1983**
*Latham, M.A. (C)	37,073	62.0%	+1.6%	33,262	60.3%	(C)
Renold, R.C. (L/All)	14,051	23.5%	-3.6%	14,909	27.0%	(L/All)
Burke, L.C. (Lab)	8,680	14.5%	+2.9%	6,414	11.6%	(Lab)
				532	1.0%	(Other)
L/All to C swing 2.6%	59,804	C maj 23,022 38.5%		55,117	C maj 18,353 33.3%	

Mr Michael Latham

Mr Michael Latham, on Public Accounts Cmte since 1983 when he was elected for this seat; MP for Melton, Feb 1974-83; contested Liverpool, West Derby, 1970. Housing adviser to Y J Lovell Group since 1985 (director, Lovell Homes Ltd, 1975-85); advisor on parly affairs to Builder Group Ltd and regular contributor to *Building* magazine. B Nov 20 1942; ed Marlborough Coll; King's Coll, Cambridge. Mbr, Advisory Cl on Public Records, 1985- ; Select Cmte on Energy, 1979-82; Public Expenditure Cmte, 1974-79; Jt Cmte on Statutory Instruments, 1974-75; Jt Ecclesiastical Cmte of both Houses, 1974- . Vice-chmn, Cons back-bench environment cmte, 1979-83; sec, countryside conservation cmte, 1977-83. Vice-pres, Building Socs Assocn, 1981- . Mbr, Westminster City Cl, 1968-71. Vice-pres (1985-) and chmn (1982-85), Cons Friends of Israel. Chmn, British/Israel parly gp, 1981- , and of exec cmte, Anglo/Israel Assocn, 1986- . Trustee, Oakham Sch, 1987- .
Mr Robert Renold, chartered design and quality engineer, fought Leicester South 1983. Mbr, Leicestershire CC, since 1985. First Lib elected in Leicester since 1962 representing ward with 70 per cent Asian electorate. B Apr 20 1952; ed Gordonstoun; Birmingham Univ; Cranfield Inst of Tech.
Mr Chris Burke, engineering supervisor. B Sep 9 1952; ed Garston, Liverpool. Gen elec agent, 1983. Chmn, Stamford CLP, 1985-87. RAF, 1970-82. AEU.

RYEDALE · C gain

Electorate %Turnout	83,205	79.2%	**1987**	78,388	71.8%	**1983**
Greenway, J.R. (C)	35,149	53.3%	-5.8%	33,312	59.2%	(C)
*Shields, Mrs E.L. (L/All)	25,409	38.6%	+8.1%	17,170	30.5%	(L/All)
Beighton, J. (Lab)	5,340	8.1%	-2.2%	5,816	10.3%	(Lab)
C to L/All swing 6.9%	65,898	C maj 9,740 14.8%		56,298	C maj 16,142 28.7%	

Mr John Greenway is senior partner in own firm of insurance brokers; lecturer and writer on financial matters. Mbr, North Yorkshire CC, since 1985; North Yorkshire police cmte. Governor of several schools. B Feb 15 1946; ed Sir John Deane's GS, Northwich, Cheshire. Metropolitan police officer, 1965-69. A vice-pres, York City Football Club; a governor of York Theatre Royal.
Mrs Elizabeth Shields was the Alliance election team spokesman on the disabled. MP for this seat 1986-87 after winning by-election; contested seat 1983, and Howden, 1979. Teacher, 1954-86; head of department at Malton Sch, N Yorkshire, 1976-86. B Feb 27 1928; ed Whyteleafe Girls' GS; Univ Coll, London; Avery Hill Coll of Ed. Mbr, Ryedale DC, since 1980; Malton and Norton Civic Soc. Patron, Norton Boys' Club.
Mr John Beighton, medical representative. B Jan 31 1959; ed sec sch. Contested N Yorks CC election 1985.
Details of 1986 by-election won by L/All on Page 285

Mr John Greenway

SAFFRON WALDEN · No change

Electorate %Turnout	73,185	79.0%	**1987**	69,385	76.9%	**1983**
*Haselhurst, A.G.B. (C)	33,354	57.7%	-0.2%	30,869	57.8%	(C)
Hayes, M.P. (L/All)	16,752	29.0%	-0.3%	15,620	29.3%	(SDP/All)
Gifford, R. (Lab)	6,674	11.5%	+0.2%	6,078	11.4%	(Lab)
Hannah, G.B. (Grn)	816	1.4%		797	1.5%	(ACM)
Smedley, W.O. (CMNHY)	217	0.4%				
L/All to C swing 0.1%	57,813	C maj 16,602 28.7%		53,364	C maj 15,249 28.6%	

Mr Alan Haselhurst

Mr Alan Haselhurst, member of Select Cmte on European Legislation; chmn, Cons backbench aviation cmte, 1986- ; vice-chmn, 1983-86. Vice-chmn, Cons education cmte, 1983- . PPS to Secretary of State for Education and Science, 1979-82. Chmn, trustees, Community Projects Foundation, 1986- (trustee from 1982); chmn, Rights of Way Review Cmte, 1983- . Elected at 1977 by-election; MP for Middleton and Prestwich, 1970-Feb 74. Consultant to Electronic Engineering Assocn, Albright & Wilson Ltd, Evan Steadman Communications Group, Barrington Jay and Co, Shandwick Consultants Ltd and Johnson Matthey plc. B Jun 23 1937; ed King Edward VI Sch, Birmingham; Cheltenham Coll; Oriel Coll, Oxford (Pres, Univ Cons Assocn, 1958, and sec, treas and librarian of Union, 1959-60). Nat chmn, YCs, 1966-68.
Mr Mark Hayes, architect, is chmn, Liberal housing panel. Mbr, Lib Pty Cl; former mbr, Cambridge City Cl; former vice-chmn, British Youth Cl. B 1956; ed Watford GS; Jesus Coll, Cambridge.
Mr Robert Gifford, teacher. Mbr, Milton Keynes BC, 1987- . Has served as CLP chmn and press officer. B Oct 25 1952; ed Swansea and Exeter Univs; London Inst of Ed. NUT.
Mr George Hannah, furniture restorer, contested Bermondsey, 1983 by-election, and Norwich North, 1979. B Aug 18 1941; ed Kelvinside Acad, Glasgow; East Anglia Univ, Norwich.

197

ST ALBANS — No change

Electorate %Turnout	75,281	80.2%	**1987**	72,849	78.2%	**1983**
*Lilley, P.B. (C)	31,726	52.5%	+0.5%	29,676	52.1%	(C)
Walkington, A.S.B. (L/All)	20,845	34.5%	-2.5%	21,115	37.0%	(L/All)
McWalter, A. (Lab)	6,922	11.5%	+0.6%	6,213	10.9%	(Lab)
Field, Ms E.V. (Grn)	788	1.3%				
Pass, W.H. (CPRP)	110	0.2%				
L/All to C swing 1.5%	60,391	C maj 10,881 18.0%		57,004	C maj 8,561 15.0%	

Mr Peter Lilley

Mr Peter Lilley was appointed Economic Secretary to the Treasury in Jun 1987; PPS to Mr Nigel Lawson, Chancellor of the Exchequer, 1984-87; PPS to Lord Bellwin and Mr William Waldegrave, Ministers for Local Govt, Jan-Oct 1984. Investment adviser on North Sea oil and other energy industries, 1972-84. Elected in 1983; contested Haringey, Tottenham, Oct 1974. Consultant director, Cons Research Dept, 1979-83. B Aug 23 1943; ed Dulwich Coll and Clare Coll, Cambridge. Former director, Greenwell Montague Stockbrokers Ltd and Great Western Resources Ltd. Mbr, Select Cmte on Treasury and Civil Service, 1983-84; sec, Cons back-bench energy cmte. Fellow, Inst of Petroleum, since 1978.
Mr Sandy Walkington, corporate planner; co-ordinator of media relations for Texaco oil company, contested this seat 1983. Formerly worked in Commons as head of research, Parly Lib Pty. B Dec 5 1953; ed Cheltenham Coll; Trinity Hall, Cambridge; Coll of Law, London (Grays Inn); Tulane Univ, New Orleans. Mbr, St Albans DC.
Mr Tony McWalter, lecturer in philosophy and logic. Dist cllr, 1979-83. B Mar 20 1946. NATFHE. Sponsored by Co-op Pty.
Ms Elaine Field. B Aug 14 1956; ed Finchley Cty GS; Finchley Manorhill Comprehensive Sch.

ST HELENS NORTH — No change

Electorate %Turnout	70,836	76.3%	**1987**	71,059	74.5%	**1983**
*Evans, J. (Lab)	28,989	53.7%	+5.8%	25,334	47.9%	(Lab)
Libby, Miss M.J. (C)	14,729	27.3%	-3.1%	16,075	30.4%	(C)
Derbyshire, N.P. (L/All)	10,300	19.1%	-2.7%	11,525	21.8%	(L/All)
C to Lab swing 4.5%	54,018	Lab maj 14,260 26.4%		52,934	Lab maj 9,259 17.5%	

Mr John Evans

Mr John Evans has been an Opposition spokesman on employment since 1983, and a mbr of the Labour Party NEC since 1982. PPS to Mr Michael Foot, then Leader of the Opposition, 1980-83; an Opposition whip, 1979-80; asst Govt whip, 1978-79. Elected for this seat 1983; MP for Newton, Feb 1974-83. MEP, 1975-79; chmn, European Parliament regional policy and transport cmte, 1976-78. Former mbr, PAC. Fitter in shipbuilding and other industries, 1955-65 and 1968-74. B Oct 19 1930; ed Jarrow Central Sch. Mbr, Hebburn UDC, 1962-74, chmn 1972-73, leader, 1969-74, and of South Tyneside MDC, 1973-74. Sponsored by AEU.
Miss Melinda Libby, advertising executive. B 1958; ed St Paul's Girls Sch; Girton Coll, Cambridge.
Mr Neil Derbyshire, lecturer, fought this seat 1983 and Dewsbury, 1979. Mbr, Merseyside CC, 1982-86. B Oct 18 1951; ed Huddersfield and Liverpool Polys.

ST HELENS SOUTH — No change

Electorate %Turnout	69,449	71.3%	**1987**	69,172	70.6%	**1983**
*Bermingham, G.E. (Lab)	27,027	54.6%	+7.7%	22,906	46.9%	(Lab)
Brown, A.J. (C)	13,226	26.7%	-0.4%	13,244	27.1%	(C)
Briers, P.J. (SDP/All)	9,252	18.7%	-3.7%	10,939	22.4%	(SDP/All)
				1,780	3.6%	(Other)
C to Lab swing 4.1%	49,505	Lab maj 13,801 27.9%		48,869	Lab maj 9,662 19.8%	

Mr Gerald
Bermingham

Mr Gerald Bermingham, a barrister, was elected in 1983; contested South East Derbyshire, 1979. Mbr, Select Cmte on Home Affairs, 1983- ; jt vice-chmn, PLP home affairs cmte, 1985- . B Aug 20 1940; ed Cotton Coll, North Staffordshire; Wellingborough GS; Sheffield Univ. Mbr, Sheffield City Cl, 1975-79; 1980-82. Mbr, SERA, NCCL, and Campaign for Criminal Justice. APEX. TGWU.
Mr Tony Brown, self-employed builder, contested St Helens 1979; mbr, St Helens DC, 1974- . B Jul 5 1933; ed Rainford Sec Mod Sch; St Helens Tech Coll.
Mr Philip Briers, senior training advisor, Engineering Industry Training Bd, contested the seat 1983. Mbr, Bold PC, 1987- ; former chmn, St Helen's area SDP; former asst sec, St Helen's Lab Pty; former Lab mbr, St Helen's MBC (chmn, education cmte). B May 28 1948.

ST IVES — No change

Electorate	%Turnout	67,448	77.2%	**1987**	64,012	73.8%	**1983**
*Harris, D.A. (C)		25,174	48.3%	-3.0%	24,297	51.4%	(C)
Carter, H.H.J. (SDP/All)		17,619	33.8%	-0.9%	16,438	34.8%	(SDP/All)
Hope, I. (Lab)		9,275	17.8%	+6.6%	5,310	11.2%	(Lab)
					1,227	2.6%	(Other)
C to SDP/All swing 1.1%		52,068	C maj	7,555 14.5%	47,272	C maj	7,859 16.6%

Mr David Harris, mbr of Select Cmte on Agriculture, 1983- ; sec, Cons back-bench fisheries sub-cmte, 1985- ; jt vice-chmn, Westcountry Cons MPs, 1983- . Journalist. Elected in 1983; contested Mitcham and Morden, Feb 1974. MEP for Cornwall and Plymouth, 1979-84, being Cons spokesman in European Parliament on regional policy. B Nov 1 1937; ed Mount Radford Sch, Exeter. Mbr, GLC, for Bromley and for Bromley, Ravensbourne, 1968-77, and chmn of council's Thamesmead cmte, 1971-73. Worked for *The Daily Telegraph* Westminster, 1961-69, being chief political correspondent, 1976-79; chmn, parliamentary lobby journalists, 1977-78; previously on *Western Morning News* and *Express and Echo*, Exeter. NUJ.
Mr Harold Carter contested the seat 1983. Marketing consultant and in venture capital; marketing and policy adviser to Dr David Owen. Mbr, CSD, 1984-86. B Feb 6 1952; ed Rugby; Caius Coll, Cambridge (Pres of Union, 1974); Nuffield Coll, Oxford; Insead, Fontainebleau. Chmn, Wakeham Trust. Consultant with Boston consulting gp, 1982-83; trade finance officer, Chase Manhattan Bank, 1977-80.
Mr Ian Hope, fire brigade sub-officer. Mbr, Penwith DC 1984- ; Cornwall CHC; vice chmn, local CLP 1980- . B Jan 17 1941; ed Falmouth C of E Sch; Falmouth GS. FBU.

Mr David Harris

SALFORD EAST — No change

Electorate	%Turnout	58,087	66.0%	**1987**	63,946	62.3%	**1983**
*Orme, S. (Lab)		22,555	58.8%	+5.1%	21,373	53.7%	(Lab)
McFall, C.W.H. (C)		10,499	27.4%	-2.4%	11,832	29.7%	(C)
Keaveney, P. (SDP/All)		5,105	13.3%	-2.2%	6,190	15.5%	(SDP/All)
Murray, S.G. (WRP)		201	0.5%	-0.5%	417	1.0%	(WRP)
C to Lab swing 3.7%		38,360	Lab maj	12,056 31.4%	39,812	Lab maj	9,541 24.0%

Mr Stanley Orme, member of shadow Cabinet since 1979, has been chief Opposition spokesman on energy since 1983; on industry, 1980-83, and on health and social security, 1979-80. Elected for this seat 1983; MP for Salford West, 1964-83; contested Stockport South, 1959. Minister for Social Security, with a seat in the Cabinet, 1976-79; Minister of State, DHSS, 1976; Minister of State for N Ireland, 1974-76. Engineer. B Apr 5 1923; ed elementary and tech schs, Nat Cl of Lab Colls and WEA classes. Mbr, Sale BC, 1958-64. Sponsored by AEU; former shop steward; chmn, AEU parly gp of MPs.
Mr Hamish McFall, financial public relations consultant. B Jul 4 1959; ed Eton; York Univ; RMA Sandhurst. Was chmn, York Univ Cons Assocn; founder, univ industrial soc. Officer in Royal Armoured Corps Reserve. Sch governor.
Mr Patrick Keaveney, gas board service engineer. Former mbr, Young Social Democrats nat cmte; has worked for Jesse Jackson in US. B Jul 7 1961.

Mr Stanley Orme

SALISBURY — No change

Electorate	%Turnout	76,221	75.6%	**1987**	74,189	72.8%	**1983**
*Key, S.R. (C)		31,612	54.9%	+1.4%	28,876	53.5%	(C)
Mitchell, P.A. (SDP/All)		20,169	35.0%	-5.2%	21,702	40.2%	(L/All)
Seabourne, Ms T.E. (Lab)		5,455	9.5%	+3.7%	3,139	5.8%	(Lab)
Fletcher, S.W. (Ind)		372	0.6%	+0.5%	182	0.3%	(W Reg)
					86	0.2%	(Other)
SDP/All to C swing 3.3%		57,608	C maj	11,443 19.9%	53,985	C maj	7,174 13.3%

Mr Robert Key was an asst master at Harrow, 1969-83; political sec to Mr Edward Heath, the former Prime Minister, 1984-85. PPS to Mr Alick Buchanan-Smith, Minister of State for Energy, 1985- . Mbr, Select Cmte on Education, Science and Arts, 1983-86. Sec, Cons backbench cmte on arts and heritage, 1983-84. Chmn, Cl for Education in Commonwealth, 1985- . Patron, 'Turning Point', 1985- . Elected in 1983; contested Camden, Holborn and St Pancras South, 1979. B Apr 22 1945; ed Sherborne Sch; Clare Coll, Cambridge. Chmn, Harrow Central Cons Assocn, and vice-chmn, London Central Euro constituency, 1980-82. Mbr, Cons Pty nat union exec, 1981-83. Founder chmn, Alice Trust for Autistic Children, 1977-82. Member, UK Nat Commn for UNESCO, 1984- . Consultant, Scott, Wilson, Kirkpatrick, consulting engineers. A director, Acad of St Martin-in-the-Fields.
Mr Parry Mitchell, chmn of United Leasing plc, contested Ealing, Acton 1983. Member, CSD; SDP industry and finance working gp; communications cmte; chmn, high tech working gp. B May 6 1943; ed Christ's Coll GS, Finchley; London and Columbia Univs.
Ms Teresa Seabourne, policy adviser to ILEA; former full-time asst to Mr Christopher Smith MP. Mbr, Lab Pty computer advisory gp; economic strategy editorial bd. B Apr 17 1959; ed Westwood St Thomas Sch, Salisbury; Southampton Univ.

Mr Robert Key

SCARBOROUGH — No change

Electorate %Turnout	74,612	73.2%	1987	72,362	71.3%	1983
*Shaw, Sir Michael (C)	27,672	50.7%	-3.6%	27,977	54.3%	(C)
Callan, Mrs H. (SDP/All)	14,046	25.7%	-1.5%	14,048	27.2%	(SDP/All)
Wolstenholme, M. (Lab)	12,913	23.6%	+5.1%	9,545	18.5%	(Lab)
C to SDP/All swing 1.0%	54,631	C maj 13,626 24.9%		51,570	C maj 13,929 27.0%	

Sir Michael Shaw, chartered accountant, has been on the Public Accounts Cmte since 1979 and Speaker's panel of chairmen since 1979. President, Society of Conservative Accountants. Elected in Feb 1974; MP for Scarborough and Whitby, 1966-74, for Brighouse and Spenborough, 1960-64; fought that seat in 1959, Dewsbury 1955. Mbr, European Parliament, 1974-79. Consultant to Costain Group plc. B Oct 9 1920; ed Sedbergh. Served on Select Cmtes on Members' Salaries and on Members' Interests. Chmn, Yorks area Cons, 1965-66. Vice-chmn, Cons trade and industry cmte, 1967-74; chmn, Yorks Cons MPs, 1983-87.
Mrs Hilary Callan, researcher and lecturer. B Oct 27 1942; ed Bradford Girls' GS; St Paul's Girls' Sch, London; Somerville Coll, Oxford; and in Brazil, Australia and New Zealand.
Mr Mark Wolstenholme, teacher at Scarborough VI Form Coll. Sec, Scarborough CLP, 1986-87. B Sec Mod Sch, Blackpool; Blackpool and Fylde CFE; Sussex Univ; Bolton Inst of HE. TGWU.

Sir Michael Shaw

SEDGEFIELD — No change

Electorate %Turnout	60,866	76.1%	1987	61,702	72.9%	1983
*Blair, A.C.L. (Lab)	25,965	56.0%	+8.5%	21,401	47.6%	(Lab)
Hawkins, N.B.S. (C)	12,907	27.8%	-1.3%	13,120	29.2%	(C)
Andrew, R.I. (SDP/All)	7,477	16.1%	-6.5%	10,183	22.6%	(SDP/All)
				298	0.7%	(Other)
C to Lab swing 4.9%	46,349	Lab maj 13,058 28.2%		45,002	Lab maj 8,281 18.4%	

Mr Anthony Blair, a barrister, has been an Opposition spokesman on Treasury and economic affairs, since 1984. Won the seat in 1983; contested Beaconsfield by-election, 1982. B May 6 1953; ed Durham Choristers Sch; Fettes Coll, Edinburgh, and St John's Coll, Oxford. Sponsored by TGWU.
Mr Nigel Hawkins became political correspondence secretary to the Prime Minister at 10 Downing St in 1984. Export sales manager, Marlow Ropes Ltd, 1978-82; desk officer, Cons Research Dept, 1982-84. B Oct 10 1954; ed Tonbridge Sch; Buckingham Univ. Associate, Inst of Chartered Shipbrokers.
Mr Ralph Andrew, runs an agricultural seed company. Mbr, CSD; chmn, Richmond and Hambleton area SDP; mbr, Hambleton DC, 1983- ; North Yorkshire CC, 1985- . B Jan 1935; ed local GS.

Mr Anthony Blair

SELBY — No change

Electorate %Turnout	71,378	77.7%	1987	65,365	72.1%	1983
*Alison, M.J.H. (C)	28,611	51.6%	-5.1%	26,712	56.7%	(C)
Grogan, J.T. (Lab)	14,832	26.7%	+6.2%	10,747	22.8%	(L/All)
Longman, J.E.F. (L/All)	12,010	21.7%	-1.1%	9,687	20.5%	(Lab)
C to Lab swing 5.6%	55,453	C maj 13,779 24.8%		47,146	C maj 15,965 33.9%	

Mr Michael Alison became PPS to the Prime Minister in 1983; Minister of State for Employment, 1981-83; Minister of State for N Ireland, 1979-81. An Opposition spokesman on environment, 1978-79, and on home affairs, 1975-78. Elected for this seat 1983; MP for Barkston Ash, 1964-83. Under Secretary of State for Health and Social Security, 1970-74. B Jun 27 1926; ed Eton; Wadham Coll, Oxford; Ridley Hall, Cambridge. Mbr, Expenditure Cmte, 1974-75; Kensington BC, 1956-59. Research officer, foreign section, Cons Research Dept, 1958-64.
Mr John Grogan, research asst of Lab gp, Leeds City Cl; was asst to Dr Barry Seal MEP and to ldr, Wolverhampton Cl. B Feb 24 1961; ed St Michael's Coll, Leeds; St John's Coll, Oxford. Mbr, Lab economic strategies gp.
Mr Ford Longman, retired HM Inspector of Community Ed; life mbr and past branch sec, Ministry of Health, Assocn of First Diivision Civil Servants. Mbr (for Tadcaster West), North Yorks CC. B Dec 8 1928; ed Watford GS; RAF and Cambridge Tech Coll; London, Open and Leeds Univs; York Art Coll.

Mr Michael Alison

SEVENOAKS — No change

Electorate %Turnout	73,179	76.4%	**1987**	71,327	73.7%	**1983**
*Wolfson, G.M. (C)	32,945	58.9%	+0.5%	30,722	58.4%	(C)
Jakobi, S.R. (L/All)	15,600	27.9%	-0.7%	15,016	28.6%	(L/All)
Green, G.A. (Lab)	7,379	13.2%	+1.0%	6,439	12.2%	(Lab)
				416	0.8%	(Other)
L/All to C swing 0.6%	55,924	C maj 17,345 31.0%		52,593	C maj 15,706 29.9%	

Mr Mark Wolfson, a director of Hambros Bank Ltd since 1973, and its head of personnel, 1970-85, was elected in 1979; contested Islington North, Feb 1974; City of Westminster, Paddington, Oct 1974. B Apr 7 1934; ed Eton and Pembroke Coll, Cambridge. Mbr, Select Cmte on MPs' Salaries, 1981-82; jt sec, Cons back-bench cmte on employment, 1981-83. PPS to Minister of State for N Ireland, 1983-84, and to Minister of State for Defence Procurement, 1984-85. Mbr, parly delegation to Nicaragua, 1982. Worked (1957-60) for Canadian Pacific Railway for two years and as a teacher in an Indian reservation in British Columbia. Head of Brathay Hall Centre, Lake District, 1962-66; head of youth services, Industrial Soc, 1966-69.
Mr Stephen Jacobi, solicitor, contested this seat 1983, Cambridgeshire 1979 and twice in 1974, Windsor and Maidenhead 1966, Cities of London and Westminster by-election 1965, Battersea North 1964. B Mar 1935; ed Malvern Coll; Clare Coll, Cambridge; Swansea Coll of Tech. Served as chmn, Lib Pty race relations panel.
Mr Graham Green, solicitor, was elected to Kent CC in 1981. Sec, Kent Cty Lab Pty; vice-chmn, Gravesham CLP; mbr, Gravesend and Dist Community Relations Cl. B Feb 16 1954; ed Springhead Sch, Northfleet; Bristol Univ. ASTMS.

Mr Mark Wolfson

SHEFFIELD, ATTERCLIFFE — No change

Electorate %Turnout	67,051	72.9%	**1987**	64,203	69.7%	**1983**
*Duffy, A.E.P. (Lab)	28,266	57.8%	+6.3%	23,067	51.5%	(Lab)
Perry, G.J. (C)	11,075	22.7%	-2.9%	11,455	25.6%	(C)
Woolley, Mrs H.E. (SDP/All)	9,549	19.5%	-3.3%	10,241	22.9%	(SDP/All)
C to Lab swing 4.6%	48,890	Lab maj 17,191 35.2%		44,763	Lab maj 11,612 25.9%	

Mr Patrick Duffy was an Opposition spokesman on defence, 1979-81 and 1983-84; Under Secretary of State for Defence for the Royal Navy, 1976-79. Elected in 1970; MP for Colne Valley, 1963-66; contested Tiverton, 1950, 1951 and 1955. Economist and consultant. B Jun 17 1920; ed LSE and Columbia Univ. Served in Fleet Air Arm, 1940-46. Lecturer at Leeds Univ, 1950-63 and 1967-70. Chmn (previously vice-chmn), PLP defence cmte, 1983-85 and of PLP economic affairs and finance group, 1965-66 and 1974-76. Member, Public Expenditure Cmte, 1970-76, and chmn of its trade and industry sub-cmte; vice-chmn, PLP NI Group, 1974 and 1982. PPS to Sec of State Defence, 1974-76. Member, North Atlantic Assembly, 1979- , being chmn of its defence cooperation sub-cmte, 1983- . Sponsored by GMBATU.
Mr John Perry, product manager in computer and printing industry. Member, Wolverhampton BC, 1983-87. Chmn, Wolverhampton NE Cons Assocn, 1983-86; vice-chmn, Scottish Fed of Cons Students, 1980. B Nov 23 1958; ed Wolverhampton GS; Dundee Univ (Sec to union, 1979-80).
Mrs Helen Woolley, landscape architect employed by Sheffield local authority. Member, CSD; Third World Assocn; SDP sports policy cmte. B Nov 15 1956; ed King Edward VI Camphill GS, Birmingham; Newcastle Univ. Nalgo; Associate of Landscape Inst.

Mr Patrick Duffy

SHEFFIELD, BRIGHTSIDE — No change

Electorate %Turnout	64,982	68.7%	**1987**	67,260	65.5%	**1983**
Blunkett, D. (Lab)	31,208	69.9%	+11.9%	25,531	58.0%	(Lab)
Glyn, Miss M.C. (C)	7,017	15.7%	-2.2%	10,322	23.4%	(L/All)
Leeman, J.A. (L/All)	6,434	14.4%	-9.0%	7,888	17.9%	(C)
				286	0.6%	(Other)
C to Lab swing 7.0%	44,659	Lab maj 24,191 54.2%		44,027	Lab maj 15,209 34.5%	

Mr David Blunkett, who contested Sheffield, Hallam, in Feb 1974, became the Labour leader of Sheffield City Cl in 1980, serving on the authority, 1970-87; also on South Yorkshire CC, 1973-77. Mbr, Labour Pty NEC, 1985- , chairing its local govt cmte. He has also been dep chmn, AMA. B Jun 6 1947; ed Royal Nat Coll for the Blind, Shrewsbury; Richmond CFE, Sheffield; Sheffield Univ; Huddersfield Coll of Ed (Tech). Shop steward, 1967-69; presently member of NATFHE and Nupe. Worked for E Midlands Gas Bd, and later as industrial tutor at Barnsley Coll of Tech.
Miss Mary Glyn, insurance auditor. Member, Chelsea YCs. B 1963; ed St George's Sch, Ascot; York Univ.
Mr John Leeman, teacher. Vice-chmn, East Yorkshire and Humberside area Lib Pty; mbr, Lib Pty Cl; Holderness BC. B Apr 3 1952; ed Riley Tech HS, Hull; Endsleigh Coll of Ed, Hull.

Mr David Blunkett

201

SHEFFIELD CENTRAL — No change

Electorate %Turnout	61,156	62.5%	1987	66,769	61.6%	1983
*Caborn, R.G. (Lab)	25,872	67.7%	+7.6%	24,759	60.2%	(Lab)
Oxley, B. (C)	6,530	17.1%	-2.1%	7,969	19.4%	(SDP/All)
Hornby, Ms F.C. (SDP/All)	5,314	13.9%	-5.4%	7,908	19.2%	(C)
Dingle, C.T. (RF)	278	0.7%		296	0.7%	(Com)
Petts, K.E. (Comm)	203	0.5%		226	0.5%	(Rev Com)
C to Lab swing 4.8%	38,197	Lab maj 19,342 50.6%		41,158	Lab maj 16,790 40.8%	

Mr Richard Caborn

Mr **Richard Caborn** was elected in 1983; MEP for Sheffield, 1979-84; chmn, British Labour Pty group. Mbr, Select Cmte on European Legislation, 1983- ; Select Cmte on Trade and Industry. B Oct 6 1943; ed Hurlfield Comprehensive Sch, Sheffield; Granville Coll of Further Ed, and Sheffield Poly. Vice-chmn, Tribune Group, 1986-87. Convenor of shop stewards, Firth Brown Ltd, 1967-79. Vice-pres, Sheffield Trades Cl, 1968-79. Sponsored by AEU. Chmn, Sheffield District Lab Pty. Mbr, BBC Advisory Cl, 1975-78.
Mr **Brian Oxley**, local govt officer. Former treas, Derby North Cons Assocn, and former sec of its political cmte; co-founder, Derby City YCs. B Sep 2 1959; ed Lees Brook Sch, Derby; Queen Mary Coll, London Univ. Stood in Derby City elections, 1982, and Derbyshire CC elections, 1985. Nalgo.
Ms **Fiona Hornby**, teacher at Frome Coll, Somerset. Founder mbr, SDP; former SE Sussex area pty chmn; former mbr, CSD. B Sep 26 1953; ed Bexhill GS; Lewes Tech Coll; Warwick and Sussex Univs.
Mr **Keith Petts**, welfare rights worker. Aged 35. Nupe.

SHEFFIELD, HALLAM — No change

Electorate %Turnout	74,158	74.7%	1987	72,878	72.8%	1983
Patnick, C.I. (C)	25,649	46.3%	-4.3%	26,851	50.6%	(C)
Gold, P.J. (L/All)	18,012	32.5%	+4.1%	15,077	28.4%	(L/All)
Savani, M.C. (Lab)	11,290	20.4%	+0.7%	10,463	19.7%	(Lab)
Spencer, Ms L.M. (Grn)	459	0.8%		656	1.2%	(Ind C)
C to L/All swing 4.2%	55,410	C maj 7,637 13.8%		53,047	C maj 11,774 22.2%	

Mr Cyril Patnick

Mr **Cyril Patnick** is director of a textile company responsible for special projects and developments. Mbr, Cons nat local govt advisory cmte; nat exec, Cons Party; Sheffield City Cl (former deputy leader). Leader, Cons group, S Yorkshire CC, until its abolition in 1986. Contested Sheffield Hillsborough, 1979 and 1970. B Oct 1929; ed Central Tech Sch and Sheffield Poly. Mbr, Hallam and Attercliffe Cons Assocn; vice-pres, Attercliffe Division Cons Pty. Governor, Sports Aid Foundation, Yorkshire and Humberside.
Dr **Peter Gold**, lecturer in Spanish studies at Sheffield City Poly, is a mbr of the Lib Pty foreign affairs policy panel and of the S Atlantic Cl. B Jun 20 1944; ed Harrow County GS; Christ Church, Oxford. APT.
Mr **Mukesh Savani**, personnel officer with Rotherham MBC. B Mar 8 1955; ed in Uganda; King Edward VII Sch, Sheffield; Sheffield Univ. Mbr, Sheffield City Cl, 1982-. ASTMS. NUPE.
Mrs **Leela Spencer**, ballet teacher, housewife, mother. B Apr 18 1954; ed Grandison Coll.

SHEFFIELD, HEELEY — No change

Electorate %Turnout	73,931	72.0%	1987	74,659	70.5%	1983
*Michie, W. (Lab)	28,425	53.4%	+7.6%	24,111	45.8%	(Lab)
Mearing-Smith, N.P. (C)	13,985	26.3%	-3.6%	15,743	29.9%	(C)
Moore, P. (SDP/All)	10,811	20.3%	-4.0%	12,813	24.3%	(SDP/All)
C to Lab swing 5.6%	53,221	Lab maj 14,440 27.1%		52,667	Lab maj 8,368 15.9%	

Mr William Michie

Mr **William Michie**, former maintenance electrician and laboratory technician, became redundant in 1981; was unemployed, 1981-83, and was elected for this seat in 1983. Vice-chmn, Yorkshire gp of Lab MPs, 1985- . B Nov 24 1935; ed Abbeydale Secondary Sch, Sheffield. Mbr, Sheffield City Cl, 1970-84 (chmn, planning, 1974-81; employment, 1981-83, group sec and chief whip, 1974-83); South Yorkshire CC, 1974-1986 (chmn, area planning, 1974-81). Sponsored by AEU, former shop steward of union, which he joined in 1952.
Mr **Nicholas Mearing-Smith**, investment banker and director, Counties Securities Ltd. Mbr, Bristol City Cl, 1976-79. Former nat vice-chmn, YCs. B Mar 8 1950; ed Watford Boys GS; Bristol Univ.
Mr **Peter Moore**, power transmission engineer with CEGB. Mbr, Aston PC, 1984- ; former chmn, Rotherham area SDP. B Apr 5 1947.

SHEFFIELD, HILLSBOROUGH — No change

Electorate %Turnout	76,312	78.0%	**1987**	74,422	75.4%	**1983**
*Flannery, M.H. (Lab)	26,208	44.0%	+6.8%	20,901	37.2%	(Lab)
Chadwick, D. (L/All)	22,922	38.5%	+4.0%	19,355	34.5%	(L/All)
Sykes, J.D. (C)	10,396	17.5%	-10.8%	15,881	28.3%	(C)
L/All to Lab swing 1.4%	59,526	Lab maj 3,286 5.5%		56,137	Lab maj 1,546 2.8%	

Mr **Martin Flannery** has been on the Select Cmte on Education, Science and Arts since 1981. Consultant to NUT; mbr, nat exec, NUT, 1970-74. Teacher from 1946-74, being head teacher from 1969. Chmn, PLP NI cmte, since 1983. Elected in Feb 1974. B Mar 2 1918; ed De La Salle GS; Sheffield Coll of Ed. Chmn, Tribune Group of Lab MPs, 1980-81; former chmn, PLP education, science and arts cmte; former sec, PLP Chile group. ASTMS and NUT.
Mr **David Chadwick**, college lecturer, fought this seat 1983; Penistone, 1979, 1978 by-election, and twice in 1974; Blackpool South, 1970; Nelson and Colne By-election, 1968. Mbr, Sheffield City Cl, 1975- (Lib gp ldr); S Yorkshire CC, 1980-85 (Lib gp ldr); Blackpool CBC, 1968-72. B Sep 2 1939; ed Blackpool CFE; Bolton Coll of Ed. NATFHE, being sec NATFHE liaison cmte, Rotherham BC,and vice-chmn BC jt consultative cmte.
Mr **John Sykes**, company director with interests in petroleum retailing, agriculture and property. Cons Pty service as chmn, YC assocn, and mbr, area cl. B Aug 24 1956; ed St David's Sch, Huddersfield; Giggleswick Sch, N Yorkshire.

Mr **Martin Flannery**

SHERWOOD — No change

Electorate %Turnout	71,378	81.9%	**1987**	69,091	76.3%	**1983**
*Stewart, A.S. (C)	26,816	45.9%	+4.9%	21,595	41.0%	(C)
Bach, W.S.G. (Lab)	22,321	38.2%	-1.6%	20,937	39.7%	(Lab)
Thompstone, S.R. (SDP/All)	9,343	16.0%	-3.3%	10,172	19.3%	(SDP/All)
Lab to C swing 3.2%	58,480	C maj 4,495 7.7%		52,704	C maj 658 1.2%	

Mr **Andrew Stewart**, a farmer, was elected in 1983 and became a mbr of the Select Cmte on Agriculture. B May 27 1937; ed Strathaven Acad, Lanark, and W of Scotland Agricultural Coll. Mbr, Nottinghamshire CC, 1974-83; Caunton Parish Cl, 1973-83. Former chmn of governors, Rufford Comprehensive and Notts Coll of Agriculture. Mbr, Newark branch, NFU, since 1961, and of county exec cmte, since 1966; Newark and Notts Agricultural Soc.
Mr **William Bach**, a barrister, contested this seat 1983, and Gainsborough, 1979. B Dec 25 1946; ed Oxford Univ. Mbr, Leicester City Cl, 1976-87 (chmn, finance cmte; Lab chief whip). Treas, Leicester West CLP, 1974-86; chmn, Leicester Dist Lab Pty, 1975-76.
Mr **Stuart Thompstone**, univ lecturer, contested Newark 1983. Organiser of SDP launch in Notts; sec, Notts SDP, until 1983; mbr, CSD. B Oct 18 1941; ed The HS, Newcastle-under-Lyme; Forfar Acad; RAF Coll, Cranwell; Sch of Slavonic and East European Studies, London Univ; LSE. AUT.

Mr **Andrew Stewart**

SHIPLEY — No change

Electorate %Turnout	68,705	79.2%	**1987**	67,584	77.0%	**1983**
*Fox, Sir Marcus (C)	26,941	49.5%	-0.2%	25,866	49.7%	(C)
Wallace, W.J.L. (L/All)	14,311	26.3%	-1.4%	14,421	27.7%	(L/All)
Butler, C.R.B. (Lab)	12,669	23.3%	+1.7%	11,218	21.6%	(Lab)
Harris, C.M. (Grn)	507	0.9%	+0.1%	521	1.0%	(Eco)
L/All to C swing 0.6%	54,428	C maj 12,630 23.2%		52,026	C maj 11,445 22.0%	

Sir **Marcus Fox** is a director of a number of companies and consultant to various others. Vice-chmn, 1922 Cmte, 1984- ; jt vice-chmn, Yorkshire Cons MPs. Chmn, Commons Cmte of Selection, 1984- . Under Secretary of State for Environment, 1979-81; Opposition spokesman on transport, 1975-76, on environment, 1974, and housing, 1974-75; Lord Commissioner of the Treasury (Govt whip), 1973-74; asst Govt whip, 1972-73. Elected in 1970; contested Dewsbury, 1959, and Huddersfield West, 1966. B Jun 11 1927; ed Eastborough Cl Sch, Dewsbury; Wheelwright GS, Dewsbury. Mbr, Select Cmte on Members' Salaries, 1981-82; Select Cmte on Race Relations and Immigration, 1970-72. A Cons Pty vice-chmn with responsibility for candidates, 1976-79. Mbr, Dewsbury CBC, 1956-63.
Mr **William Wallace**, deputy director, Royal Institute of International Affairs, is vice-chmn of the Liberal policy cmte, adviser to Mr David Steel, the Liberal leader, and member of the Alliance working gp which in 1986 drafted *Partnership for Progress*. Contested this seat 1983; Manchester, Moss Side, twice in 1974; Huddersfield West, 1970. B Mar 12 1941; ed St Edward's Sch, Oxford; King's Coll, Cambridge; Cornell Univ, US; Nuffield Coll, Oxford.
Dr **Christopher Butler**, general practitioner. B Nov 7 1942; ed Hallcroft Sch, Ilkeston; Univ Coll, London; Univ Coll Hospital, London. Nat coordinator, MPU/ASTMS.

Sir **Marcus Fox**

SHOREHAM — No change

Electorate %Turnout	71,318	77.5%	**1987**	69,720	73.7%	**1983**
*Luce, R.N. (C)	33,660	60.9%	-0.8%	31,679	61.6%	(C)
Ingram, J.A. (L/All)	16,590	30.0%	-1.0%	15,913	31.0%	(L/All)
Godwin, P. (Lab)	5,053	9.1%	+1.8%	3,794	7.4%	(Lab)
L/All to C swing 0.1%	55,303	C maj 17,070 30.9%		51,386	C maj 15,766 30.7%	

Mr Richard Luce

Mr Richard Luce was appointed Minister for the Arts in 1985, also being Minister of State, Privy Council Office, with responsibilities for the Civil Service. Resigned in Apr 1982 as Minister of State for Foreign and Commonwealth Affairs, a post he had held since 1981, over Argentina's invasion of the Falkland Islands. Re-appointed Minister of State, Foreign and Commonwealth Office, 1983-85. Under Secretary of State for Foreign and Commonwealth Affairs, 1979-81; an Opposition spokesman on foreign and commonwealth affairs, 1977-79; an Opposition whip, 1974-75. PPS to Sir Geoffrey Howe, then Minister for Trade and Consumer Affairs, 1972-74. Elected for Arundel and Shoreham in 1971 and for this seat in Feb 1974; contested Hitchin, 1970. B Oct 14 1936; ed Wellington Coll; Christ's Coll, Cambridge; Wadham Coll, Oxford. Former company chmn.
Mr Julian Ingram, advertising executive, Abbot Mead Vickers, contested this seat 1983. B Apr 17 1956; ed Worthing GS; Worthing Sixth Form Coll; LSE. Former director of travel company.
Mr Paul Godwin, trade union officer. Mbr, Hove BC, 1979- . B May 2 1952; ed Brighton, Hove and Sussex GS. TGWU.

SHREWSBURY AND ATCHAM — No change

Electorate %Turnout	70,689	77.0%	**1987**	66,554	74.0%	**1983**
*Conway, D.L. (C)	26,027	47.8%	-1.7%	24,397	49.5%	(C)
Hutchison, R. (L/All)	16,963	31.2%	-0.9%	15,773	32.0%	(L/All)
Owen, Mrs E. (Lab)	10,797	19.8%	+1.4%	9,080	18.4%	(Lab)
Hardy, G. (Grn)	660	1.2%				
C to L/All swing 0.4%	54,447	C maj 9,064 16.6%		49,250	C maj 8,624 17.5%	

Mr Derek Conway

Mr Derek Conway became a mbr of Select Cmte on Agriculture in 1986. Serves in the TA being Major, 5th Bn (TA) Light Infantry. Principal organiser, national fund for research into crippling diseases, 1974-83. Elected in 1983; contested Newcastle upon Tyne East, 1979; Durham, Oct 1974. B Feb 15 1953; ed Beacon Hill Boys' School; Gateshead Tech Coll and Newcastle Poly. Nat vice-chmn, YCs, 1973-75. Mbr, nat executive, Cons Party, 1971-81; Cons nat local govt cmte, 1979-83; Tyne and Wear Met CC, 1977-83 (leader, 1979-82); Gateshead BC, 1974-78; executive, British Youth Cl; board, Northern Arts, 1980-83; board, Washington Development Corporation, 1979-83; North of England Development Cl, 1979-83; board, Newcastle Airport, 1980-83.
Mr Robert Hutchison is a writer and social researcher; research fellow, Policy Studies Inst, 1982-86. B Mar 28 1941; ed St Paul's Sch; Trinity Coll, Dublin; Univ of East Anglia; Birkbeck Coll, London.
Mrs Elizabeth Owen, biologist. Mbr, Shropshire CC, 1981- (Chairs primary and special ed cmtes; vice-chair, social services cmte). B Jan 13 1948.

SHROPSHIRE NORTH — No change

Electorate %Turnout	77,122	75.5%	**1987**	73,333	72.7%	**1983**
*Biffen, W.J. (C)	30,385	52.2%	-1.3%	28,496	53.4%	(C)
Smith, G. (L/All)	15,970	27.4%	-4.1%	16,829	31.6%	(L/All)
Hawkins, R. (Lab)	11,866	20.4%	+5.6%	7,860	14.7%	(Lab)
				135	0.3%	(Other)
L/All to C swing 1.4%	58,221	C maj 14,415 24.8%		53,320	C maj 11,667 21.9%	

Mr John Biffen

Mr John Biffen was Lord Privy Seal and Leader of the Commons, 1983-87; Lord President of the Council and Leader of the Commons, 1982-83; Secretary of State for Trade, 1981-82; Chief Secretary to the Treasury, with a seat in the Cabinet, 1979-81; chief Opposition spokesman on energy and industry, 1976-77. In Nov 1978, appointed spokesman on small businesses and self-employed. Elected for this seat 1983; MP for Oswestry, 1961-83; contested Coventry East, 1959. Economist. B Nov 3 1930; ed Dr Morgan's GS, Bridgwater; Jesus Coll, Cambridge. Chaired, Commons Privileges Cmte; mbr, Public Accounts Commission, 1983-87. Former mbr, Select Cmte on Procedure; PAC; Select Cmte on Nationalised Industries. With Economist Intelligence Unit, 1960-61; Tube Investments Ltd, 1953-60.
Mr Gordon Smith, civil engineer; Sheriff of Chester, 1986-87; mbr, Chester City Cl, 1978- (Lib housing spokesman). B Dec 14 1941; ed Bury GS; Leeds Univ. Nalgo.
Mr Rob Hawkins, teacher. B Mar 25 1949; ed in Worthing; Kesteven Coll of Ed.

SKIPTON AND RIPON — No change

Electorate %Turnout	72,199	77.8%	**1987**	69,421	74.9%	**1983**
Curry, D.M. (C)	33,128	59.0%	-1.6%	31,509	60.6%	(C)
Cooksey, S.J. (L/All)	15,954	28.4%	-3.2%	16,463	31.6%	(L/All)
Whitfield, T.L. (Lab)	6,264	11.2%	+3.4%	4,044	7.8%	(Lab)
Williams, Ms L.S. (Grn)	825	1.5%				
L/All to C swing 0.8%	56,171	C maj 17,174 30.6%		52,016	C maj 15,046 28.9%	

Mr David Curry

Mr **David Curry**, freelance journalist, has been MEP for Essex North East since 1979. A vice-chmn and European Democratic Group and Conservative spokesman, European Parliament Budgets Cmte, since 1984, and rapporteur-general on the 1986-87 EEC budget. Chmn, EP Agriculture Cmte, 1982-84; previously EDG spokesman on it. Contested Morpeth in both 1974 elections. B Jun 13 1944; ed Ripon GS and Corpus Christi Coll, Oxford. In 1975 appointed Brussels correspondent, *Financial Times*, covering EEC and Benelux affairs and European Parliament. Became Paris correspondent in 1976; in 1978 appointed Foreign News Editor, London. Mbr, cl, Centre for European Agriculture Studies, Wye College, since 1983.
Mr **Stephen Cooksey** became president of Yorkshire Lib Fed in 1986, being a fed officer since 1975. Mbr, Lib Pty Cl and nat exec. Lib gp ldr since 1981 and Alliance gp ldr since 1985 on Leeds City Cl. Lib cllr since 1971 having served on Horsforth DC and West Yorkshire CC. Contested Pudsey 1979 and twice in 1974; Leeds South 1970. B Jan 1944; ed Middlesbrough HS; Leeds Univ.
Mr **Timothy Whitfield**, community relations officer. Chmn, Bradford CHC. B May 10 1952; ed Hitchin GS, Reading and Bristol Univs. ASTMS.

SLOUGH — No change

Electorate %Turnout	73,424	75.9%	**1987**	71,907	71.5%	**1983**
*Watts, J.A. (C)	26,166	46.9%	+4.0%	22,064	42.9%	(C)
Lopez, E. (Lab)	22,076	39.6%	+2.7%	18,958	36.9%	(Lab)
Goldstone, M. (SDP/All)	7,490	13.4%	-5.1%	9,519	18.5%	(SDP/All)
				853	1.7%	(Other)
Lab to C swing 0.6%	55,732	C maj 4,090 7.3%		51,394	C maj 3,106 6.0%	

Mr John Watts

Mr **John Watts**, chartered accountant, joined the Select Cmte on Treasury and Civil Service in 1986. Mbr, Hillingdon BC, 1973-86, being leader of the cl, 1978-84, and opposition leader, 1976-78. Won this seat in 1983. Parly adviser to Institute of Actuaries; consultant to Rank Hovis McDougall plc and to Reddy Siddiqui Khokhar and Co, chartered accountants. B Apr 19 1947; ed Bishopshalt Sch, Hillingdon; Gonville and Caius Coll, Cambridge. Chmn, Cambridge Univ Cons Assocn, 1968; Uxbridge Cons Assocn, 1973-76. Mbr, Cl of Brunel Univ, 1982- . PPS to Mr Ian Gow, when Minister for Housing and Construction, 1984-85, and Minister of State, Treasury, 1985.
Mr **Edward (Eddie) Lopez**, full-time political organiser with the Labour Party; trained as chartered accountant before being full-time organiser in Norwood. B Feb 7 1942; ed Affra Primary Sch, Brixton; Alleyns Sch, Dulwich. NULO and GMB.
Mr **Michael Goldstone** runs an exercise equipment supply company. Mbr, CSD, 1981-86; Merton area SDP cmte; SW London magistrate probation cmte. B Apr 28 1937; ed Whitgift Sch, Croydon.

SOLIHULL — No change

Electorate %Turnout	78,123	75.1%	**1987**	73,677	71.4%	**1983**
*Taylor, J.M. (C)	35,844	61.1%	+0.3%	31,947	60.8%	(C)
Gadie, G.E. (L/All)	14,058	24.0%	-3.7%	14,553	27.7%	(L/All)
Knowles, Mrs S.E. (Lab)	8,791	15.0%	+3.4%	6,075	11.6%	(Lab)
L/All to C swing 2.0%	58,693	C maj 21,786 37.1%		52,575	C maj 17,394 33.1%	

Mr John Mark Taylor

Mr **John Mark Taylor**, solicitor, consultant and company director, became jt vice-chmn, Cons back-bench European affairs cmte, in 1986 (jt sec, 1983-86); mbr, Select Cmte on Environment, since 1983; vice-chmn, Cons back-bench sports cmte, 1985- . Adviser to Fed of Master Builders. Elected for this seat in 1983; contested Dudley East, Feb and Oct 1974; MEP for Midlands East, 1979-84, being Cons EEC budget spokesman in European Parliament, 1979-81, and group deputy chmn, 1981-82. B Aug 19 1974; ed Bromsgrove Sch. Mbr, Solihull CBC, 1971-74, and W Midlands CC, 1973-86 (leader of opposition, 1975-77; leader of cl, 1977-79). Vice-pres, AMA, since 1979; mbr, W Midlands Economic Planning Cl, 1978-79.
Mr **Geoffrey Gadie** is a regional manager with Leyland Parts Division. Former vice-chmn, Worksop Lib Assocn; founding chmn, Lowdam and Doverbeck Lib Assocn. B Mar 2 1944; ed Barton GS, S Humberside; Sheffield Poly. Mbr, BIM, since 1973.
Mrs **Susan Knowles**, marketing manager for automotive company company - Partco Ltd, is vice-chair of Solihuill Lab Pty, having previously held other offices. Former sec and treas, Midlands Central Euro-constituency Lab Pty. B Feb 27 1953; ed Nortre Dame Convent GS, Blackburn; Manchester Univ. Apex.

SOMERTON AND FROME | | | | | | No change

Electorate %Turnout	68,773	79.4%	**1987**	64,695	76.7%	**1983**
*Boscawen, R.T. (C)	29,351	53.7%	-0.7%	26,988	54.4%	(C)
Morgan, R.G. (L/All)	19,813	36.3%	+0.5%	17,761	35.8%	(SDP/All)
Kelly, I.S. (Lab)	5,461	10.0%	+0.2%	4,867	9.8%	(Lab)
C to L/All swing 0.6%	54,625	C maj	9,538 17.5%	49,616	C maj	9,227 18.6%

Mr Robert Boscawen

Mr Robert Boscawen was appointed Comptroller of the Royal Household in 1986; Vice-Chamberlain of Royal Household (Govt whip), 1983-86; Lord Commissioner of the Treasury (Govt whip), 1981-83; assistant Govt whip, 1979-81. Elected for this seat 1983; MP for Wells, 1970-83; contested Falmouth and Camborne, 1966 and 1964. Underwriting mbr of Lloyd's. B Mar 17 1923; ed Eton and Trinity Coll, Cambridge. Mbr, Select Cmte on Expenditure and its employment and social services sub-cmte, 1974; vice-chmn, Cons health and social security cmte, 1974-79. Mbr, London executive cl, NHS, 1956-65. Served in Coldstream Guards, 1941-50.
Mr Rowland Morgan, chartered civil engineer and lecturer, contested Woodspring 1983, Weston-super-Mare 1979, Bedwellty twice in 1974. Mbr, Lib nat exec; chmn, Western Counties Regional Lib Pty, 1983-86. B Dec 2 1934; ed Tredegar GS; Manchester Univ. Cty cllr from 1977; dist cllr from 1979.
Mr Ian Kelly, local government officer. Treas, Avon County Lab Pty; mbr, Bristol NW constituency executive and general cmtes. B Dec 13 1964; ed Wintringham Comprehensive; Bristol Poly. ACTSS (TGWU).

SOUTHAMPTON, ITCHEN | | | | | | No change

Electorate %Turnout	72,687	75.8%	**1987**	72,233	73.2%	**1983**
*Chope, C.R. (C)	24,419	44.3%	+2.8%	21,937	41.5%	(C)
Denham, J.Y. (Lab)	17,703	32.1%	+5.0%	16,647	31.5%	(SDP/All)
Mitchell, R.C. (SDP/All)	13,006	23.6%	-7.9%	14,324	27.1%	(Lab)
C to Lab swing 1.1%	55,128	C maj	6,716 12.2%	52,908	C maj	5,290 10.0%

Mr Christopher Chope

Mr Christopher Chope was appointed an Under Secretary of State for the Environment in 1986. Elected in 1983. PPS to Mr Peter Brooke, Minister of State, Treasury, 1985-86. Ldr, Wandsworth BC, 1979-83; mbr, 1974-83; chmn, housing cmte, 1978-79. Barrister. B May 19 1947; ed St Andrew's Sch, Eastbourne; Marlborough Coll; St Andrew's Univs. Jt sec, Cons environment cmte, 1983-86; former sec, Cons back-bench shipping and shipbuilding sub-cmte; mbr, Select Cmte on Procedure, 1984-86; exec cmte, Soc of Cons Lawyers, 1983-86.
Mr John Denham, nat campaign officer for War on Want, contested this seat 1983. Mbr, Hampshire CC, 1981- . Former head of youth affairs, British Youth Cl; also worked for Friends of the Earth. B Jul 15 1953; ed comprehensive sch; Southampton Univ. TGWU.
Mr Richard Mitchell, lecturer in business studies, was MP for this seat from 1971 by-election to 1983, when he fought it for SDP. Lab MP for Southampton, Test, 1966-70; contested that seat 1964, and New Forest, 1959. Former chmn, S Hampshire SDP. Mbr, European Parliament, 1975-79; Select Cmte on Education and Science, 1968-70; Chairmen's Panel, 1979-83; Southampton City Cl, 1955-67. Former dep headmaster. B Aug 22 1927; ed Godalming GS; Southampton Univ. Postal chess player; has played for Gt Britain.

SOUTHAMPTON, TEST | | | | | | No change

Electorate %Turnout	73,918	76.4%	**1987**	74,668	73.1%	**1983**
*Hill, S.J.A. (C)	25,722	45.6%	+0.4%	24,657	45.2%	(C)
Whitehead, A.P.V. (Lab)	18,768	33.3%	+5.2%	15,311	28.1%	(Lab)
Rayner, Miss V. (L/All)	11,950	21.2%	-5.6%	14,592	26.7%	(SDP/All)
C to Lab swing 2.4%	56,440	C maj	6,954 12.3%	54,560	C maj	9,346 17.1%

Mr James Hill

Mr James Hill, a director of two family private companies, regained the seat for the Conservatives in 1979; held seat, 1970-Oct 1974; contested it, 1968. Mbr, Select Cmtes on European Legislation, 1979-83; Trade and Industry, 1979-83; Expenditure, 1972-73. Delegate and Govt whip to Cl of Europe and WEU, 1980-85. Pres, Motor Schools Assocn, 1980-85; member, cl, Inst of Advanced Motorists, 1982-85. Chmn, HoC Flying Club. B Dec 21 1926; ed Regents Park Sch, Southampton; North Wales Naval Training Coll; Southampton Univ. Chmn, Cons backbench housing improvement sub-cmte, since 1985; sec, Cons back-bench cmte on housing and construction, 1971-73; Cons industry cmte, 1979-81. Mbr, European Parliament, 1973-75, being chmn of its cmte for regional policy and transport; Southampton City Cl, 1966-70 and 1976-79.
Mr Alan Whitehead, director of charity, the British Inst of Industrial Therapy. Mbr, Southampton City Cl (ldr since 1984). B Sep 15 1950; ed in Isleworth; Southampton Univ. Mbr, Labour Co-ordinating Cmte. Nupe.
Miss Vivienne Rayner, public relations, marketing and employment consultant. Cty cllr from 1985. B 1950; Godolphin and Latymer; Nottingham Univ.

SOUTHEND EAST — No change

Electorate %Turnout	59,073	69.3%	1987	57,690	67.6%	1983
*Taylor, E.M. (C)	23,753	58.0%	+2.2%	21,743	55.8%	(C)
Berkeley, H.J. (SDP/All)	9,906	24.2%	-4.2%	11,052	28.4%	(SDP/All)
Scully, D.R. (Lab)	7,296	17.8%	+1.9%	6,188	15.9%	(Lab)
SDP/All to C swing 3.2%	40,955	C maj 13,847 33.8%		38,983	C maj 10,691 27.4%	

Mr Edward Taylor

Mr Edward (Teddy) Taylor has been jt sec, Cons back-bench home affairs cmte, since 1983. Elected at the 1980 by-election; MP for Glasgow, Cathcart, 1964-79; contested. Glasgow, Springburn, 1959. Journalist, adviser and company director. Chief Opposition spokesman on Scotland, 1977-79; Under Secretary of State (Development) for Scotland, 1974, and in 1970-71 when he resigned in disagreement with Govt policy on EEC. Sec, Cons European Reform Gp, 1980- . B Apr 18 1937; ed Glasgow HS and Glasgow Univ. Industrial relations officer, Clyde Shipbuilders' Assocn, 1959-64. Mbr, Glasgow City Cl, 1960-64; mbr, Select Cmte on Trade and Industry, 1983-85; Select Cmte on Environment, 1982-83. Adviser to Port of London Police Fed and to Lawrence Building Co; director, Shepherd Foods Ltd and Ansvar (Temperance) Insurance Co. Vice-chmn, Cons back-bench trade and consumer affairs cmte, 1981-83. NUJ.
Mr Humphry Berkeley, director of a medical charity, was Conservative MP for Lancaster 1959-66, having contested Southall for the Conservatives 1951. Joined Lab Pty 1970; contested North Fylde for Lab Oct 1974; joined SDP 1981. Patron, International Centre for Child Studies, 1984- . B Feb 21 1926; ed Dragon Sch, Oxford; Malvern Coll; Pembroke Coll, Cambridge.
Mr David Scully, teacher. Director, Thurrock Business Services (secretarial). Sec, Thurrock Dist Lab Pty. Cllr since 1984. B Aug 22 1938; ed City GS, Lincoln; London Univ. NAS/UWT.

SOUTHEND WEST — No change

Electorate %Turnout	68,415	75.3%	1987	67,486	71.7%	1983
*Channon, H.P.G. (C)	28,003	54.4%	-0.1%	26,360	54.5%	(C)
Grant, G. (L/All)	19,603	38.1%	+0.2%	18,327	37.9%	(L/All)
Smith, Ms A. (Lab)	3,899	7.6%	0.0%	3,675	7.6%	(Lab)
C to L/All swing 0.2%	51,505	C maj 8,400 16.3%		48,362	C maj 8,033 16.6%	

Mr Paul Channon

Mr Paul Channon was appointed Secretary of State for Transport in Jun 1987; Secretary of State for Trade and Industry, 1986-87; Minister for Trade, with rank of Minister of State at the DTI, 1983-86; Minister for the Arts, 1981-83; Minister of State, Civil Service Dept, 1979-81; chief Opposition spokesman on the environment, 1974-75; spokesman on consumer affairs, 1974; Minister for Housing and Construction, 1972-74; Minister of State for N Ireland, Mar-Nov 1972; Under Secretary of State for Environment, 1970-72; Parly Sec, Ministry of Housing and Local Govt, Jun-Oct 1970; Opposition spokesman on arts and amenities, 1967-70. Elected at 1959 by-election, succeeding his father. B Oct 9 1935; ed Lockers Park, Hemel Hempstead; Eton, and Christ Church, Oxford. Former director, CSE Aviation, Arthur Guinness and Son.
Mr Gavin Grant, membership and promotions campaigner for Cl for Protection of Rural England, fought this seat 1983. Chmn, Lib Parly Assocn, 1987- . Director of political publishing company. B Jun 20 1955; ed Roan Sch for Boys, Greenwich; Reading Univ.
Ms Angela Smith, political officer with League Against Cruel Sports. B Jan 7 1959; ed Leicester Poly.

SOUTH HAMS — No change

Electorate %Turnout	78,583	78.6%	1987	74,276	74.9%	1983
*Steen, A.D. (C)	34,218	55.4%	-1.9%	31,855	57.2%	(C)
Chave, R.F. (L/All)	21,072	34.1%	-0.9%	19,454	35.0%	(L/All)
*Hamilton, W.W. (Lab)	5,060	8.2%	+1.3%	3,824	6.9%	(Lab)
Titmuss, C.G. (Grn)	1,178	1.9%	+1.0%	518	0.9%	(Eco)
Langsford, T.C. (Loony)	277	0.4%				
C to L/All swing 0.5%	61,805	C maj 13,146 21.3%		55,651	C maj 12,401 22.3%	

Mr Anthony Steen

Mr Anthony Steen, community worker and youth leader, barrister and Lloyd's underwriter, has been coordinator, Chmn's Unit for Marginal and Critical Seats, Cons Central Office, since 1982; former director, European Centre for Urban Regeneration. Won the seat 1983; MP for Liverpool, Wavertree, 1974-83. Adviser to British Midland Airways, Manx Airlines, Logan Air, British Islands Airways plc, the English Vineyards Assocn and to a firm of management consultants. B Jul 22 1940; ed Westminster Sch. Sec, Westcountry Cons MPs, 1986- . Jt nat chmn, Impact 80s Campaign; chmn, all-pty cycling gp, 1979- ; Commons and Lords cycle club; sec, parly Caribbean group, 1979- . Member, cl, Nat Playing Fields Assocn; vice-chmn, Task Force Trust; chmn, Outlandos Trust, 1981- . Vice-pres, International Centre of Child Studies; Ecology Building Society.
Mr Robert Chave, accountant. B 1952; ed Exeter Sch; S Devon Tech; Portsmouth Poly.
Mr William Hamilton was MP for Central Fife, 1974-87; for West Fife, 1950-74; contested that seat in 1945. Former teacher. B Jun 26 1917; ed Washington GS, co Durham, and Sheffield Univ. Mbr, European Parliament, 1975-79. Author of My Queen and I, 1975.
Mr Christopher Titmuss, teacher. B Apr 22 1944; ed John Fisher Sch, Purley, Surrey; Wat Thao Kol Monastery, Thailand.

SOUTHPORT — L/All gain

Electorate %Turnout	71,443	76.3%	**1987**	70,089	72.5%	**1983**
Fearn, R.C. (L/All)	26,110	47.9%	+7.4%	25,612	50.4%	(C)
Thomas, N.M. (C)	24,261	44.5%	-5.9%	20,573	40.5%	(L/All)
Moore, Ms A. (Lab)	3,483	6.4%	-1.9%	4,233	8.3%	(Lab)
Walker, J.R.G. (Grn)	653	1.2%		374	0.7%	(SBILP)
C to L/All swing 6.7%	54,507	L/All maj 1,849 3.4%		50,792	C maj 5,039 9.9%	

Mr **Ronald Fearn**, senior asst bank manager, contested this seat in 1979, twice in 1974, and 1970. Has served on Southport TC, Sefton and Merseyside MDCs and Merseyside CC. B Feb 2 1931; ed Norwood Road County Sch and King George V GS, Southport. Past Chmn, Inst of Bankers, Southport area. BIFU.
Mr **Nigel Thomas**, barrister, contested Carmarthen in 1983 and 1979. B Mar 18 1952; ed Whitland GS, Carmarthen; Univ Coll of Wales, Aberystwyth; Emmanuel Coll, Cambridge. Has served as asst sec, Soc of Cons Lawyers; founded its student branch. Tutored in land law at Univ Coll, London.
Ms **Audrey Moore**, local govt officer. B Apr 27 1946; ed Open Univ.
Mr **Justin Walker**, asst sales manager, Liverpool Tanning Co Ltd. Green Party national agent, 1982-85. TA officer, 1975-84. B Dec 13 1955; ed Charterhouse. Active supporter of CND and Greenpeace.

Mr Ronald Fearn

SOUTH RIBBLE — No change

Electorate %Turnout	72,177	82.5%	**1987**	72,401	77.7%	**1983**
*Atkins, R.J. (C)	28,133	47.2%	-1.9%	27,625	49.1%	(C)
Roebuck, D.F. (Lab)	19,703	33.1%	+6.5%	14,966	26.6%	(Lab)
Holleran, J.A. (L/All)	11,746	19.7%	-4.6%	13,690	24.3%	(L/All)
C to Lab swing 4.2%	59,582	C maj 8,430 14.1%		56,281	C maj 12,659 22.5%	

Mr **Robert Atkins** was appointed an Under Secretary of State for Trade and Industry in Jun 1987. Former sales executive with Rank Xerox (UK) Ltd. Won this seat in 1983; MP for Preston North, 1979-83; contested Luton West, Feb and Oct 1974. PPS to Lord Young of Graffham as Minister without Portfolio and Secretary of State for Employment, 1984-87; PPS to Minister of State for Industry, 1982-84. Jt chmn, all-pty cmte for reform of licensing hours, 1986-87; jt sec, Cons back-bench defence cmte, 1979-82; vice-chmn, Cons aviation cmte, 1979-82. B Feb 5 1946; ed Highgate Sch. Former parly consultant to Parliamentary Monitoring Services Ltd (expenses only). Mbr, Haringey BC, 1968-77. Nat pres, Cons Trade Unionists, 1984-87. Pres, Lancashire YCs, 1984-86; chmn, Hornsey YCs, 1967-69; vice-chmn, Greater London YCs, 1969-70 and 1971-72.
Mr **David Roebuck**, union official, former postman, former officer in RN. Mbr, Preston BC; chmn, Preston HA and Police Liaison Cmte. B Jan 16 1946; ed state schs in Dulwich; Open Univ. Sponsored by UCW.
Mr **Alan Holleran**, a representative, has been on South Ribble BC since 1986. Chmn, Pemwortham Lib Assocn, 1983-86. B Sep 16 1936; ed St Mary's, Blackburn.

Mr Robert Atkins

SOUTH SHIELDS — No change

Electorate %Turnout	60,754	70.7%	**1987**	61,924	66.2%	**1983**
*Clark, D.G. (Lab)	24,882	57.9%	+11.4%	19,055	46.5%	(Lab)
Fabricant, M.L.D. (C)	11,031	25.7%	-5.2%	12,653	30.9%	(C)
Meling, Mrs M. (SDP/All)	6,654	15.5%	-7.2%	9,288	22.7%	(SDP/All)
Dunn, E.G. (Dem)	408	0.9%				
C to Lab swing 8.3%	42,975	Lab maj 13,851 32.2%		40,996	Lab maj 6,402 15.6%	

Dr **David Clark**, elected to shadow cabinet in 1986 and appointed to new and separate portfolio of Opposition spokesman on environmental protection and development. Elected for this seat in 1979; MP for Colne Valley, 1970-Feb, 1974; contested Manchester, Withington, 1966, and Colne Valley, Feb and Oct 1974. An Opposition spokesman on agriculture, 1972-74, defence, 1980-81, and on environment, 1981-86. B Oct 19 1939; ed Windermere GS and Manchester and Sheffield Univs. Forester and univ lecturer. Chmn, Northern Gp of Lab MPs, 1986- ; chmn, Open Spaces Soc, 1979- ; pres, Northern Ramblers; exec mbr, Nat Trust; pres, Northern region of YHA; cl mbr, Friends of Lake District and World Wildlife Fund UK. Adviser to Homeowners Friendly Soc. Sponsored by Nupe.
Mr **Michael Fabricant**, economist and director of broadcasting electronics gp. Chmn, Brighton Pavilion Cons Pty. B Jun 12 1950; ed Loughborough, Sussex and London Univs, and postgraduate research economics at Univ of Southern California.
Mrs **Margaret Melling**, a deputy head teacher. B Nov 16 1945; ed St Anthony's GS, Sunderland; Bede Coll, Durham Univ; Open Univ; Newcastle and Sunderland Polys. Community health cllr, 1972-80; mbr, CSD; BBC Radio Newcastle advisory panel; Sunderland Cl, NAS/UWT. Founder, in 1976, South Tyneside Women's Aid. Ind mbr, S Tyneside Met CC, 1972-80.

Dr David Clark

SOUTHWARK AND BERMONDSEY — No change

Electorate %Turnout	55,438	64.9%	**1987**	55,839	61.7%	**1983**
*Hughes, S.H.W. (L/All)	17,072	47.4%	-2.4%	17,185	49.9%	(L/All)
Bryan, J. (Lab)	14,293	39.7%	+4.8%	12,021	34.9%	(Lab)
Heald, O. (C)	4,522	12.6%	-0.4%	4,481	13.0%	(C)
Power, P.N. (Comm)	108	0.3%		474	1.4%	(NF)
				308	0.9%	(Other)
L/All to Lab swing 3.6%	35,995	L/All maj 2,779 7.7%		34,469	L/All maj 5,164 15.0%	

Mr Simon Hughes was chief Alliance spokesman on health in its election team and on Church of England affairs; Liberal spokesman on environment from 1983. Won this seat at the 1983 by-election. Director, Cambridge University Mission Trust Ltd; barrister. B May 17 1951; ed Woodford C of E Primary Sch, Cheshire; Westgate Sch, Cowbridge, Glamorgan; Llandaff Cathedral Sch, Cardiff; Christ Coll, Brecon; Selwyn Coll, Cambridge; Inns of Court Sch of Law; Coll of Europe, Bruges. Pres, NLYL, 1986- (vice-pres, 1983-86); vice-pres, ULS, 1983- ; jt pres, British Youth Cl, 1983-84; vice-chmn, Parly Youth Affairs Lobby, 1984- . Mbr, Assocn of Lib Lawyers, 1977-85; steering cmte, Campaign for Fair Votes, 1983- ; Gen Synod of Church of England, 1984-85; NCCL. Chmn, Lib Pty home affairs panel, 1981-83.
Mr John Bryan, bricklayer. Mbr, Southwark BC, 1982- (dep ldr of cl, 1985-86). B Jun 26 1951; ed St Joseph's Primary Sch; St Michael's Sec Sch. Ucatt.
Mr Oliver Heald, barrister. B Dec 15 1954; ed Reading Sch; Pembroke Coll, Cambridge.
Mr Nigel Power, video worker. Aged 26.

Mr Simon Hughes

SPELTHORNE — No change

Electorate %Turnout	72,967	74.1%	**1987**	72,236	71.0%	**1983**
Wilshire, D. (C)	32,440	60.0%	+7.6%	26,863	52.4%	(C)
Cunningham, Mrs M. (SDP/All)	12,390	22.9%	-3.1%	13,357	26.0%	(SDP/All)
Welfare, D.F.J. (Lab)	9,227	17.1%	+1.6%	7,926	15.5%	(Lab)
				3,141	6.1%	(Other)
SDP/All to C swing 5.4%	54,057	C maj 20,050 37.1%		51,287	C maj 13,506 26.3%	

Mr David Wilshire is a political consultant; formerly personnel officer, teacher and owner of group of small businesses. Visiting lecturer, Institute of Local Govt Studies, Birmingham Univ, and co-director, political management programme, Brunel Univ. B Sep 16 1943; ed Kingswood Sch, Bath; Fitzwilliam Coll, Cambridge. Mbr, Wansdyke DC, Avon, 1976-87 (leader, 1981-87); Avon CC, 1977-81.
Mrs Mavis Cunningham, lecturer, contested Twickenham in Oct 1974. Mbr, SDP housing policy cmte. B Nov 11 1934; ed Cockburn HS, Leeds; Leeds Univ. Wife of Mr George Cunningham, SDP candidate at Islington S and Finsbury.
Mr Damien Welfare was political research officer with GLC, 1981-86; mbr GLCSA. B Dec 19 1957; ed Cambridge Univ.

Mr David Wilshire

STAFFORD — No change

Electorate %Turnout	72,431	79.5%	**1987**	70,570	76.5%	**1983**
*Cash, W.N.P. (C)	29,541	51.3%	+0.1%	27,639	51.2%	(C)
Phipps, C.B. (SDP/All)	15,834	27.5%	+2.8%	13,362	24.7%	(SDP/All)
Hafeez, Ms N. (Lab)	12,177	21.2%	-2.5%	12,789	23.7%	(Lab)
				212	0.4%	(Other)
C to SDP/All swing 1.3%	57,552	C maj 13,707 23.8%		54,002	C maj 14,277 26.4%	

Mr William Cash, a solicitor, was elected at May 1984 by-election. Member, Select Cmte on European Legislation, 1985- ; Select Cmte on Statutory Instruments, 1986- . B May 10 1940; ed Stonyhurst Coll; Lincoln Coll, Oxford. Adviser to British Foundry Assocn, Inst of Legal Executives, Society of Company and Commercial Accountants, Cl for Complementary and Alternative Medicine, and Legal Studies and Services Ltd. Jt vice-chmn (1985-87) and sec (1984-85), Cons cmte on constitutional affairs; sec, all-pty cmte on East Africa, 1984- . Chmn, all-pty mte on widows, 1984- ; general purposes cmte, Primrose League, 1985- ; vice-chmn, Cons Small Business Bureau, 1984- ; jt sec, Cons back-bench smaller businesses cmte, 1985- ; sec, Cons back-bench employment cmte, 1986- . Mbr, exec cl, Royal Commonwealth Soc, 1984- ; director, Ironbridge Gorge Museum, 1980- .
Dr Colin Phipps, petroleum geologist, oil and gas consultant, company director and farmer in Herefordshire, contested Worcester for SDP in 1983; Lab MP for Dudley West, Feb 1974-79; also fought Walthamstow East, 1969 by-election. Chmn, West Midland Reg Cl of SDP; member, nat cmte, SDP, 1985- ; policy cmte, 1987- . B Jul 23 1934; ed Townfield elementary sch, Hayes Middlesex; Acton Cty Sch; Swansea GS; Univ Coll, London; Birmingham Univ.
Ms Najma Hafeez, lecturer in English. Mbr, Birmingham City Cl (chairs ed cmte and social services sub-cmte). B Aug 10 1956; ed Birmingham Poly.
Details of 1984 by-election on Page 284

Mr William Cash

STAFFORDSHIRE MID — No change

Electorate %Turnout	71,252	79.4%	**1987**	67,425	77.5%	**1983**
*Heddle, B.J. (C)	28,644	50.6%	-1.4%	27,210	52.1%	(C)
St Hill, C.R. (Lab)	13,990	24.7%	+2.3%	13,330	25.5%	(L/All)
Jones, T.A. (L/All)	13,114	23.2%	-2.3%	11,720	22.4%	(Lab)
Bazeley, J.G. (Ind C)	836	1.5%				
C to Lab swing 1.9%	56,584	C maj 14,654 25.9%		52,260	C maj 13,880 26.6%	

Mr John Heddle, company director, consultant surveyor and mbr of Lloyd's, has chaired the Conservative national local govt advisory cmte since 1984; mbr, Cons Pty Nat Union Exec, 1984- . Vice-pres, Building Societies Assocn. Elected for this seat 1983; MP for Lichfield and Tamworth, 1979-83; contested Bolton East, Oct 1974; Gateshead West, Feb 1974. B Sep 15 1943; ed Bishop's Stortford Coll; Coll of Estate Management; London Univ. Chmn, Cons back-bench environment cmte, since 1983 and its jt sec, 1979-83; Bow Gp Environment Cmte, 1980. Mbr, Select Cmte on Environment, 1982-83; Kent CC, 1973-80; International Real Estate Fed, 1972- . Freeman, City of London. Fellow, Rating and Valuation Assocn; Inst of Directors; Royal Soc of Arts. Hon Fellow, Incorporated Assocn of Architects and Suerveyors. Consultant partner, Elliott Son and Boyton, chartered surveyors.
Mr Crispin St Hill, race and community relations adviser; teacher by profession. Mbr, Islington BC, 1971-81; Islington Lab Pty gmc, 1971-76. B Oct 25 1933; ed St Mary's Coll, St Lucia, West Indies; Inns of Court Sch of Law; Bedford Coll, London. TGWU.
Mr Tim Jones, barrister, contested this seat 1983; Warwick and Leamington, Feb and Oct 1974. B Apr 20 1951; ed Jesus Coll, Cambridge; LSE; Coll of Law.

Mr John Heddle

STAFFORDSHIRE MOORLANDS — No change

Electorate %Turnout	74,302	80.4%	**1987**	72,466	77.2%	**1983**
*Knox, D.L. (C)	31,613	52.9%	-0.8%	30,079	53.7%	(C)
Ivers, Mrs V. (Lab)	17,186	28.8%	+4.6%	13,513	24.1%	(Lab)
Corbett, J.P. (SDP/All)	10,950	18.3%	-3.8%	12,370	22.1%	(SDP/All)
C to Lab swing 2.7%	59,749	C maj 14,427 24.1%		55,962	C maj 16,566 29.6%	

Mr David Knox, economist and management consultant, won this seat in 1983; MP for Leek, 1970-83; contested Birmingham, Stechford, 1964 and 1966, and Nuneaton by-election, 1967. Mbr, Speaker's Panel of Chairmen, 1983- ; Select Cmte on European Legislation, 1976- . B May 30 1933; ed Lockerbie Acad; Dumfries Acad; London Univ. Vice-chmn, Cons Pty, 1974-75. Jt sec, Cons back-bench finance cmte, 1972-73; sec, Cons trade cmte, 1974; vice-chmn, Cons employment cmte, 1979-80 (sec, 1976-79). Vice-chmn, Cons Group for Europe, 1984-87.
Mrs Vera Ivers has worked as nurse, mental welfare officer, social worker, CAB organiser and community worker for elderly. Mbr, Staffordshire Moorlands DC, 1981- ; Staffordshire CC 1985- . B Dec 16 1931; ed NE London Poly. ASTMS.
Mr James Corbett, a barrister, contested Erewash in 1983 and Cheshire East in 1984 Euro elections. Founder mbr, SDP; mbr, CSD; sec, Nottingham East SDP. B May 10 1952; ed Sloane Sch, Chelsea; Exeter Univ; Inns of Court Sch of Law. Nupe.

Mr David Knox

STAFFORDSHIRE SOUTH — No change

Electorate %Turnout	79,261	78.2%	**1987**	73,038	75.8%	**1983**
*Cormack, P.T. (C)	37,708	60.9%	+1.7%	32,764	59.2%	(C)
Oborski, Mrs F. (L/All)	12,440	20.1%	-3.4%	13,004	23.5%	(L/All)
Bateman, P. (Lab)	11,805	19.1%	+1.8%	9,568	17.3%	(Lab)
L/All to C swing 2.5%	61,953	C maj 25,268 40.8%		55,336	C maj 19,760 35.7%	

Mr Patrick Cormack has been on the Commons chairmen's panel since 1983; mbr, Commons Services Select Cmte. Writer, company director, consultant and former teacher. Elected for this seat Feb 1974; MP for Cannock, 1970-74; contested Grimsby, 1966; Bolsover, 1964. B May 18 1939; ed St James's Choir and Havelock Schs, Grimsby, and Hull Univ. Jt chmn, all-party heritage group, since 1979; chmn, parly gp of Anti-Slavery Society, since 1987; Cons Arts and Heritage Cmte, 1979-83; Cl for Independent Education, since 1980; mbr, Historic Buildings Cl, 1979-84; cl Georgian Gp, 1985- ; cl, Winston Churchill Memorial Trust, 1983- . Non-exec chmn, Aitken Dott Ltd (The Scottish Gallery) of Edinburgh; director, Historic House Hotels Ltd, and Aitken Dott Ltd (Art in Business). Mbr, Select Cmte on Education, Science and Arts, 1979-83; Royal Commission on Historical Manuscripts and Lord Chancellor's Cmte on Public Records, 1979-84; Worshipful Company of Glaziers. Fellow, Soc of Antiquaries, since 1978. Rector's Warden, St Margaret's Church, Westminster, 1978- . Freeman, City of London; Hon. Citizen of Texas. IOJ.
Mrs Frances Oborski, teacher, contested Walsall North by-election 1976. Mbr, Wyre Forest DC, 1973- . B Nov 25 1945; ed Bassaley GS, Newport, Gwent; Worcester Coll of Ed; Birmingham Univ; Open Univ. NAS/UWT (former national officer, UWT).
Mr Philip Bateman, railman. B Mar 14 1950; ed in Wolverhampton.

Mr Patrick Cormack

STAFFORDSHIRE SOUTH EAST — No change

Electorate %Turnout	66,176	79.4%	**1987**	63,324	76.5%	**1983**
*Lightbown, D.L. (C)	25,115	47.8%	-2.9%	24,556	50.7%	(C)
Gluck, Miss E. (SDP/All)	14,230	27.1%	+6.0%	13,658	28.2%	(Lab)
Spilsbury, D. (Lab)	13,230	25.2%	-3.0%	10,220	21.1%	(SDP/All)
C to SDP/All swing 4.4%	52,575	C maj 10,885 20.7%		48,434	C maj 10,898 22.5%	

Mr David Lightbown was appointed a Lord Commissioner of the Treasury (Government whip) in Jun 1987; an assistant Government whip, 1986-87. Former chief engineer and director of Hampson Industries plc. Elected in 1983. B Nov 30 1932; ed Derby Sch of Art; Derby Tech Coll. Mbr, Lichfield DC, 1975-87, ldr, 1977-83; Staffordshire CC, 1977-85, dep ldr, 1979-83. Dep chmn, Lichfield and Tamworth Cons Assocn; former chmn, Staffordshire Dist Cls Assocn; served on policy cmte of ACC; former exec mbr, W Midlands Chamber of Commerce; former govenor, N Staffordshire Poly and Keele Univ. Manager of his village football team until he became an MP.
Miss Elisabeth Gluck, chairman, Programmes Ltd. Mbr, CBI, Inst of Directors and 300 Gp. B Mar 5 1956; ed Queen's Coll; St Martin's Sch of Art; Brighton Poly. Was art therapist at Holloway Prison.
Mr David Spilsbury, teacher. Exec mbr, Birmingham Trades Cl. B Dec 8 1939; ed Moseley GS, Birmingham; Bulmershe Coll of Ed, Reading. NUT, previously AUEW-TASS.

Mr David Lightbown

STALYBRIDGE AND HYDE — No change

Electorate %Turnout	67,983	74.2%	**1987**	67,916	70.5%	**1983**
*Pendry, T. (Lab)	24,401	48.4%	+2.8%	21,798	45.5%	(Lab)
Greenwood, R.N. (C)	18,738	37.1%	+0.7%	17,436	36.4%	(C)
Ashenden, P.J. (SDP/All)	7,311	14.5%	-2.9%	8,339	17.4%	(L/All)
				294	0.6%	(Other)
C to Lab swing 1.1%	50,450	Lab maj 5,663 11.2%		47,867	Lab maj 4,362 9.1%	

Mr Tom Pendry has chaired the all-party football cmte since 1980 and PLP sports cmte since 1984; an Opposition spokesman on overseas development, 1981-83, and on NI, 1979-81; on devolution and regional affairs, 1982-84. Under Secretary of State for N Ireland, 1978-79; Lord Commissioner of the Treasury (Govt whip), 1974-77. Opposition whip, 1971-74. Mbr, Select Cmte on MPs' Interests, 1983- ; former mbr, Public Expenditure Cmte. Mbr, nat advisory cmte, Duke of Edinburgh's Award Scheme; Speaker's Conference on Electoral Reform, 1973-74. Full-time official, NUPE, 1960-70. Elected in 1970. B Jun 10 1934; ed St Augustine's Ramsgate; Oxford Univ. Mbr, Paddington BC, 1962-65; UK delegation, WEU and Cl of Europe, 1973-75. Sponsored by NUPE.
Mr Richard Greenwood, local businessman. Mbr, Tameside MBC, 1983- . B Jun 26 1957; ed Sedbergh Sch; Manchester Univ.
Mr Peter Ashenden, certified accountant with own consultancy; chief accountant with plastics manufacturing firm, 1969-83. Mbr, High Peak BC, May 1987- . Treas, North and West Derbyshire SDP, 1981- . B Oct 31 1944; ed Gravesend GS; Open Univ.

Mr Tom Pendry

STAMFORD AND SPALDING — No change

Electorate %Turnout	70,560	77.8%	**1987**	65,955	74.4%	**1983**
Davies, J.Q. (C)	31,000	56.5%	0.0%	27,728	56.5%	(C)
Bryan, Ms R. (L/All)	17,009	31.0%	-1.6%	15,972	32.6%	(SDP/All)
Lowe, P.E. (Lab)	6,882	12.5%	+1.6%	5,354	10.9%	(Lab)
L/All to C swing 0.8%	54,891	C maj 13,991 25.5%		49,054	C maj 11,756 24.0%	

Mr Quentin Davies is a director of Morgan Grenfell and Co Ltd, merchant bankers, and of certain group subsidiaries. Contested Birmingham, Ladywood by-election, 1977. B May 29 1944; ed Dragon Sch, Oxford; Gonville and Caius Coll, Cambridge; Harvard Univ, US.
Ms Rebecca Bryan, investment analyst with merchant bank, fought Hampshire East 1983. Nat chmn, ULS, 1980; mbr, Lib Pty defence panel; former mbr, Lib nat exec; former governor of LSE Court. B Jan 18 1960; ed St Martin's Sch, Solihull; Solihull Sixth Form Coll; LSE.
Mr Peter Lowe, senior lecturer in public finance, Leicester Poly. B Dec 12 1945; ed Univ Coll, Swansea; Leicester Univ.

Mr Quentin Davies

STEVENAGE No change

Electorate %Turnout	69,525	80.5%	**1987**	67,706	77.9%	**1983**
*Wood, T.J.R. (C)	23,541	42.1%	+2.6%	20,787	39.4%	(C)
Stoneham, B.R.M. (SDP/All)	18,201	32.5%	-3.6%	19,032	36.1%	(SDP/All)
Withers, M.R.C. (Lab)	14,229	25.4%	+1.4%	12,673	24.0%	(Lab)
				236	0.4%	(Other)
SDP/All to C swing 3.1%	55,971	C maj 5,340 9.5%		52,728	C maj 1,755 3.3%	

Mr Timothy Wood

Mr **Timothy Wood** resigned as a senior project manager with the international computer firm ICL, whom he joined in 1963, when he won this seat in 1983. PPS to Mr John Stanley, then Minister of State for Armed Forces, 1986- ; jt sec, Cons back-bench environment cmte, 1985-86. B Aug 13 1940; ed King James's GS, Knaresborough; Manchester Univ. Mbr, Bracknell DC, 1975-83; leader, 1976-78. Chmn, Wokingham Cons Assocn, 1980-83; vice-chmn, Thames Valley Euro constituency cl, 1979-83. Mbr, exec cmte, Nat Assocn of Cons Graduates, 1973-78; Bow Group cl, 1968-71 and 1972-73; board, Bracknell Development Corp, 1977-82.

Mr **Benjamin Stoneham**, director of personnel/industrial relations, Portsmouth and Sunderland Newspapers plc, fought this seat for the Alliance in 1983; Lab candidate Saffron Walden, 1979 and 1977 by-election. Mbr, SDP nat cmte, 1986- ; CSD; study gps on environment and employer participation; Herts CC, 1985- . B Aug 24 1948; ed Christi Coll, Cambridge; Warwick Univ. With NCB, 1975-79, includg two years as personal aide to Sir Derek Ezra, then chmn; education officer, NUR, 1979-82.

Mr **Malcolm Withers** contested Lincoln 1983 and Rutland and Stamford, 1979 and 1974. Financial journalist. Member, Rutland DC, 1974-82; Lincoln CC, 1984-86. B Mar 12 1936; ed St Clement Danes GS, London; Leicester Univ. NUJ.

STIRLING No change

Electorate %Turnout	57,836	79.4%	**1987**	56,302	75.7%	**1983**
*Forsyth, M.B. (C)	17,591	38.3%	-1.7%	17,039	40.0%	(C)
Connarty, M. (Lab)	16,643	36.2%	+8.3%	11,906	27.9%	(Lab)
McFarlane, I. (L/All)	6,804	14.8%	-9.1%	10,174	23.9%	(L/All)
Lawson, I.M. (SNP)	4,897	10.7%	+2.5%	3,488	8.2%	(SNP)
C to Lab swing 5.0%	45,935	C maj 948 2.1%		42,607	C maj 5,133 12.0%	

Mr Michael Forsyth

Mr **Michael Forsyth** was appointed an Under Secretary of State for Scotland in Jun 1987. Former company director. Won this seat 1983. Mbr, Select Cmte on Scottish Affairs, 1983-87; PPS to Sir Geoffrey Howe, Foreign Secretary, 1986-87; vice-chmn, Cons back-bench environment cmte, 1985-86. Mbr, Westminster City Cl, 1978-83; exec cmte, Nat Union of Cons and Unionist Assocn, 1975-77. B Oct 16 1954; ed Arbroath HS; St Andrews Univ. Chmn, Fed of Cons Students, 1976-77.

Mr **Michael Connarty**, teacher of handicapped children, contested Stirling 1983. Mbr, Stirling DC 1977- (ldr, 1980-); exec cmte, Scottish Lab Pty; chmn, Scottish local govt cmte; chmn, district sports cl. B Sep 3 1947; ed Stirling and Glasgow Univs; Jordanhill Coll of Ed. EIS.

Mr **Iain MacFarlane**, university lecturer in psychology, contested West Stirlingshire in 1979. Cllr, Central Region, 1982- . B Mar 16 1942; ed King's Park Primary and Sec Sch, Glasgow; Glasgow Univ. AUT (mbr, nat exec, 1985-86; Scottish exec, 1982- , and sec, local branch, 1982-85).

Mr **Iain Lawson**, proprietor of pest control company in Paisley, contested Dumbarton for Cons in 1983, Glasgow Garscadden in 1979 and 1978 by-election. Joined SNP on day Gartcosh steel mill closed. Elected mbr, SNP nat cl. B 1952; ed Clydebank HS.

STOCKPORT No change

Electorate %Turnout	60,059	78.1%	**1987**	58,908	74.6%	**1983**
*Favell, A.R. (C)	19,410	41.4%	-0.8%	18,517	42.1%	(C)
Haines, Mrs S. (Lab)	16,557	35.3%	+6.3%	12,731	29.0%	(Lab)
Begg, J.L. (SDP/All)	10,365	22.1%	-5.5%	12,129	27.6%	(SDP/All)
Shipley, M. (Grn)	573	1.2%	+0.4%	369	0.8%	(Eco)
				194	0.4%	(Other)
C to Lab swing 3.5%	46,905	C maj 2,853 6.1%		43,940	C maj 5,786 13.2%	

Mr **Anthony Favell**, a solicitor, company director and Halifax Building Society agent, was elected in 1983; contested Bolsover, 1979. PPS to Mr John Major, when Minister for Social Security and the Disabled, 1986-87. B May 29 1939; ed St Bees, Cumbria, and Sheffield Univ. Mbr, Select Cmte on Social Services, 1985-86; jt sec, Cons back-bench health and social services cmte, 1985-86. Mbr, exec, Nat Union of Cons and Unionist Pty, 1982-83. Treas (1985-) and vice-chmn (1984-85), Assocn of Cons Clubs, 1984- .

Mrs **Shirley Haines**, health visitor (SRN), contested 1986 Ryedale by-election, Selby 1983, and York in 1984 Euro election. Mbr, North Yorkshire CC; elected to York City Cl, 1983. B May 7 1939; ed Newland HS, Hull; Hammersmith Hosp; Surrey Univ. Nupe.

Mr **John Begg**, teacher in Manchester, contested Denton and Reddish 1983. Mbr, CSD. B Mar 21 1946; ed Oakham Sch; Aston Tech Coll; Leeds Univ. NAS/UWT.

Mr **Michael Shipley**, sec sch teacher, contested this seat 1983. Mbr, Grn Pty ed policy gp; founding chmn, Stockport Grn Pty, 1980-83. B Jul 8 1945; ed NE London poly; Salford Univ; Worcester Coll, Oxford. Sch rep AMMA.

Mr Anthony Favell

STOCKTON NORTH — No change

Electorate %Turnout	70,329	75.4%	**1987**	70,277	70.3%	**1983**
*Cook, F. (Lab)	26,043	49.1%	+12.0%	18,339	37.1%	(Lab)
Faber, D.J.C. (C)	17,242	32.5%	-0.8%	16,469	33.3%	(C)
Bosanquet, N.F.G. (SDP/All)	9,712	18.3%	-11.3%	14,630	29.6%	(SDP/All)
C to Lab swing 6.4%	52,997	Lab maj 8,801 16.6%		49,438	Lab maj 1,870 3.8%	

Mr Francis Cook

Mr Francis Cook was a construction project manager with Capper-Neill International; former teacher, transport manager, gravedigger and Butlins redcoat. Elected in 1983. Mbr, Select Cmte on Employment, since 1983. B Nov 3 1935; ed Corby Sch, Sunderland; De La Salle Coll, Manchester; Inst of Ed, Leeds. Chmn, Stockton Lab Pty, 1981-83. Fellow, Industry and Parliament Trust. Sponsored by AUEW (TASS).
Mr David Faber was, until the start of the election, working in the campaigning dept, Conservative Central Office. Worked within pty for three years, including as personal asst to deputy chmn. Mbr of Lloyd's. B Jul 7 1961; ed Eton; Balliol Coll, Oxford. Grandson of the late Lord Stockton of Chelwood (Mr Harold Macmillan).
Mr Nicholas Bosanquet, senior research fellow at York Univ, contested Slough 1983. Former mbr, SDP urban policy and housing working parties; joined SDP in 1981; mbr, Camden Cl, 1974-82; former economic advisor to Nat Bd for Prices and Incomes and Royal Commission on Distribution of Income and Wealth. B Jan 17 1942; ed Cambridge Univ; LSE.

STOCKTON SOUTH — C gain

Electorate %Turnout	75,279	79.0%	**1987**	73,790	72.1%	**1983**
Devlin, T.R. (C)	20,833	35.0%	-1.5%	19,550	36.7%	(SDP/All)
*Wrigglesworth, I.W. (SDP/All)	20,059	33.7%	-3.0%	19,448	36.6%	(C)
Scott, J.M. (Lab)	18,600	31.3%	+5.0%	13,998	26.3%	(Lab)
				205	0.4%	(Other)
SDP/All to C swing 0.7%	59,492	C maj 774 1.3%		53,201	SDP/All maj 102 0.2%	

Mr Timothy Devlin

Mr Timothy Devlin, barrister, serves on the committee of the Cons Foreign Affairs Forum. B Jun 13 1959; ed Dulwich Coll; LSE; City Univ, London; Inns of Court Sch of Law, and Financial Training Ltd. Also educated in France. Hardwicke and Thomas More Scholar at Lincolns Inn.
Mr Ian Wrigglesworth, SPD spokesman, 1983-87, on industry and economic affairs, was Alliance election spokesman on trade and industry. SDP spokesman on home affairs, 1982-83, and on industry, 1981-82. Lab Opposition spokesman on Civil Service, 1979-80; PPS to Mr Roy Jenkins, then Home Secretary, 1974-76. Labour MP for Teeside, Thornaby, from Feb 1974-81, then joined SDP; won this seat for SDP in 1983. Divisional director, Smiths Industries Ltd; with Cleveland Management and Marketing; consultant to Assocn of First Division Civil Servants; adviser to Barclays Bank plc. B Dec 1939; ed Stockton GS; Stockton-Billingham Tech Coll; Coll of St Mark and St John, London.
Mr John Scott, head of dept of management and professional studies, Stockton-Billingham Tech Coll. Mber, Thornaby-on-Tees, BC 1960-68 (mayor 1966-67); Stockton-on-Tees BC, 1974- (mayor 1981-82). Vice chmn, Northern Region Cls Assocn. B Oct 18 1925; ed Blackpool GS; Lincoln Coll, Oxford. Bd mbr, Northern Development Cmte and Cleveland Youth Business Centres. TGWU.

STOKE-ON-TRENT CENTRAL — No change

Electorate %Turnout	65,987	68.8%	**1987**	66,934	65.9%	**1983**
*Fisher, M. (Lab)	23,842	52.5%	+4.5%	21,194	48.1%	(Lab)
Stone, D. (C)	14,072	31.0%	+1.7%	12,944	29.4%	(C)
Cundy, I. (SDP/All)	7,462	16.4%	-5.0%	9,458	21.4%	(SDP/All)
				504	1.1%	(Other)
C to Lab swing 1.4%	45,376	Lab maj 9,770 21.5%		44,100	Lab maj 8,250 18.7%	

Mr Mark Fisher

Mr Mark Fisher became Opposition spokesman on the arts in Jan 1987; chmn, PLP education, science and arts beck-bench cmte, 1984-86, and of PLP arts sub-cmte, since 1984; vice-chmn, PLP Treasury cmte, 1983-84; previously an Opposition whip. Elected for this seat 1983; contested Leek, 1979. Mbr, Select Cmte on Treasury and Civil Service, 1983-86. Documentary film producer and script writer, 1966-75; principal, Tattenhall Centre of Education, 1975-83. B Oct 29 1944; ed Eton and Trinity Coll, Cambridge. Mbr, Staffordshire CC, 1981- ; NUT and Socialist Educational Assocn.
Mr David Stone, chartered accountant in private practice, is vice-chmn, CPC nat cmte, and a member of the Nat Union exec cmte. Personal assistant to Mr Norman Tebbit during Oct 1974 and 1979 general elections. Chmn, Greater London CPC, 1980-82; mbr, Primrose League; former area YC officer. Mbr, Camden BC, 1982-86. B May 1953; ed Hasmonean GS.
Mr Iain Cundy, systems engineer, employed by GEC Electrical Projects Ltd, Rugby. Mbr, West Midlands and nat SDP cls; former treas, membership sec and press officer, Coventry area SDP; sec, Limehouse Gp. B Feb 20 1964; ed Bristol Cathedral Sch; Warwick Univ. ASTMS.

STOKE-ON-TRENT NORTH — No change

Electorate %Turnout	74,184	72.9%	**1987**	75,251	71.0%	**1983**
Walley, Ms J.L. (Lab)	25,459	47.1%	+0.8%	24,721	46.3%	(Lab)
Davies, R. (C)	16,946	31.3%	+0.4%	16,518	30.9%	(C)
Simmonds, S.J. (SDP/All)	11,665	21.6%	-1.2%	12,186	22.8%	(SDP/All)
C to Lab swing 0.2%	54,070	Lab maj 8,513 15.7%		53,425	Lab maj 8,203 15.4%	

Ms **Joan Walley** is a vice-president of the Inst of Environmental Health Officers. Holds diploma in community work and degree in social admin. Formerly chaired Norwood Labour Party; mbr, London borough of Lambeth Cl, 1982-86. ACTSS (TGWU). Member of pty for 14 years. B Jan 23 1949; ed Biddulph GS; Hull Univ; Univ Coll, Swansea.
Mr **Reginald Davies,** adminsitration manager, food industry. Former Labour cllr, Leek UDC. Joined Conservatives in 1979. Mbr, Leek TC, 1979- ; mayor, 1980. B 1942; ed Abbey Hulton and Carmountside Schs, Stoke-on-Trent.
Mr **Stephen Simmonds**, convenor of Staffordshire Nat Union of Students. Mbr, Newcastle BC, May 1987- ; N Staffs area SDP exec, 1985-87; vice-chmn, Newcastle-under-Lyme SDP gp, 1986-87; chmn, Keele Univ SDP Students, 1984-87. B May 18 1955; ed Beal GS, Redbridge, Essex; Middlesex Poly; Essex and Keele Univs.

Ms Joan Walley

STOKE-ON-TRENT SOUTH — No change

Electorate %Turnout	70,806	73.7%	**1987**	70,600	69.6%	**1983**
*Ashley, J. (Lab)	24,794	47.5%	-0.5%	23,611	48.0%	(Lab)
Hartshorne, D. (C)	19,741	37.8%	+4.2%	16,506	33.6%	(C)
Wild, P. (L/All)	7,669	14.7%	-3.7%	9,050	18.4%	(L/All)
Lab to C swing 2.4%	52,204	Lab maj 5,053 9.7%		49,167	Lab maj 7,105 14.5%	

Mr **Jack Ashley,** journalist and broadcaster, is chmn of the all-party Lords and Commons disablement group. Founder and pres, Hearing and Speech Trust, 1985- . Parly consultant to Soc of Telecom Executives. Mbr, Lab Pty NEC, 1976-78. Elected in 1966; contested Finchley, 1951. PPS to Secretary of State for Economic Affairs, 1967-70; and to Secretary of State for Social Services, 1974-79. Labourer and crane driver, 1936-46; shop steward; BBC radio producer, 1951-57, and senior TV producer, 1957-66. B Dec 6 1922; ed St Patrick's Elementary Sch, Widnes; Ruskin Coll, Oxford; Gonville and Caius Coll, Cambridge (Pres of Union, 1951). Mbr, PLP liaison committee, 1977-78; nat exec, Chemical Workers' Union, 1946-47; General Advisory Cl, BBC, 1967-69; Widnes BC, 1946-47. Sponsored by GMB.
Mr **Dennis Hartshorne**, lecturer. Mbr, Birmingham City Cl, 1982- . B Jan 2 1946; ed Heanor GS; Lancaster and Leicester Univs.
Mr **Peter Wild**, manager of high street dry cleaner shop. B 1963; ed Yew Tree HS, Northenden, Manchester; S Trafford CFE; Keele Univ.

Mr Jack Ashley

STRANGFORD — No change

Electorate %Turnout	64,429	57.6%	**1987**	60,232	64.9%	**1983**
*Taylor, J.D. (OUP)	28,199	75.9%	+27.1%	19,086	48.8%	(OUP)
Morrow, A.J. (All)	7,553	20.3%	+4.6%	11,716	30.0%	(DUP)
Hynds, Miss I.E. (WP)	1,385	3.7%		6,171	15.8%	(All)
				2,143	5.5%	(Other)
All to OUP swing 11.3%	37,137	OUP maj 20,646 55.6%		39,116	OUP maj 7,370 18.8%	

Mr **John D Taylor**, a chartered engineer, was elected in 1983; resigned seat in 1985 in protest at Anglo-Irish Agreement and retained it at 1986 by-election. Mbr, European Parliament, since 1979, serving on political affairs and agriculture cmtes; resigned from European Democratic (Conservative) Group in Jan 87 in protest at Anglo-Irish Agreement and joined European Right Group. UU EEC spokesman in Hse of Commons. Unpaid chmn of six companies and a housing association including Tyrone Printing Co Ltd and Ulster Gazette (Armagh) Ltd; publisher of Tyrone Courier, Ulster Gazette, Armagh Standard, Armagh Advertiser, Dungannon News. Partner, G D Taylor and Associates, architects and civil engineers, 1966-74. B Dec 24 1937; ed Royal Sch Armagh; Queen's Univ, Belfast. Mbr, Stormont, 1965-72; NI Assembly, 1973-75; NI Constitutional Convention, 1975-76; NI Assembly, 1982-86; Select Cmte on European Legislation, 1983-86. Cabinet minister for Home Affairs in NI Govt, 1970-72.
Mr **Patrick Morrow**, farmer, is dep ldr, Alliance Pty and its spokesman on agriculture. B Jul 17 1928. Mbr, Castlereagh BC, 1973- ; Alliance pty Assembly member East Belfast, 1982-86.
Details of 1986 by-election on Page 285

Mr John D Taylor

STRATFORD-ON-AVON | No change

Electorate %Turnout	81,263	76.5%	**1987**	76,649	72.9%	**1983**
*Howarth, A.T. (C)	38,483	61.9%	+1.0%	34,041	60.9%	(C)
Cowcher, D.G. (L/All)	17,318	27.9%	-1.0%	16,124	28.8%	(L/All)
Rhodes, R.H. (Lab)	6,335	10.2%	-0.1%	5,731	10.3%	(Lab)
L/All to C swing 1.0%	62,136	C maj 21,165 34.1%		55,896	C maj 17,917 32.1%	

Mr Alan Howarth

Mr Alan Howarth was appointed an assistant Government whip in Jun 1987. Elected for this seat 1983. PPS to Sir Rhodes Boyson, Minister of State for N Ireland and then Minister for Local Govt, 1985-87; sec, Cons back-bench arts and heritage cmte, 1984-85. Public affairs adviser to Baring Brothers and Co Ltd, 1982-87; former parly consultant to GRC Europe Ltd and to Time Manager International. Governor, Royal Shakespeare Theatre, since 1984. B Jun 11, 1944; ed Rugby and King's Coll, Cambridge. Vice-chmn, Cons Pty, 1980-81; director, Cons Research Dept, 1979-81; personal asst, chairmen, Cons Pty, 1975-79. Senior research asst to Field Marshal Montgomery on I *History of Warfare*, 1965-67. Asst master, Westminster Sch, 1968-74.
Mr George Cowcher, senior planner with design and build company. B 1954; ed Kingswood Sch; Newcastle Univ.
Mr Robert Rhodes, team manager in Birmingham mental handicap social services, contested Chichester 1983. B May 4 1949; ed Cheltenham GS; Gloucestershire Royal Sch of Nursing; Birmingham Poly. Mbr, Warwickshire CC, 1981-85; N Warwickshire DHA, 1981-84. Nupe (branch sec, 1977-80).

STRATHKELVIN AND BEARSDEN | Lab gain

Electorate %Turnout	62,676	82.2%	**1987**	60,500	79.4%	**1983**
Galbraith, S. (Lab)	19,639	38.1%	+12.5%	17,501	36.4%	(C)
*Hirst, M.W. (C)	17,187	33.4%	-3.1%	13,801	28.7%	(L/All)
Bannerman, J. (L/All)	11,034	21.4%	-7.3%	12,308	25.6%	(Lab)
Paterson, G. (SNP)	3,654	7.1%	-2.1%	4,408	9.2%	(SNP)
C to Lab swing 7.8%	51,514	Lab maj 2,452 4.8%		48,018	C maj 3,700 7.7%	

Mr Samuel Galbraith

Mr Samuel Galbraith, neuro-surgeon, Institute of Neurological Sciences, Glasgow. Mbr, Medical Campaign against Nuclear Weapons; Scottish Medical Campaign for Nicaragua. President, Medical Practitioners Union and of NEC of ASTMS; Health Centre Appeal Fund. B Oct 18 1945; ed Glasgow Univ.
Mr Michael Hirst, chartered accountant, was MP for this seat, 1983-87. Mbr, Select Cmte on Scottish Affairs, 1983-87. Vice-chmn, Scottish Cons Pty, 1987- . Contested Dunbartonshire East, 1979; Dunbartonshire Central, Feb and Oct 1974. Consultant to Peat, Marwick, Mitchell and Co in which he was a partner until he became MP. B Jan 2 1946; ed Glasgow Acad; Glasgow Univ; Iceland Univ as exchange scholar. Chmn, Scottish Cons Candidates' Assocn, 1978-81. PPS to Under Secretaries of State for Energy, 1985-87.
Mr James Bannerman, pharmacist, is director of family pharmacy; pres, Pharmaceutical Soc, 1974-76. Mbr, Strathclyde Reg Cl, 1982- . B May 24 1935; ed Glasgow Acad; Strathclyde Univ.
Mr Gil Paterson manages his motor company in Bishopbriggs. Contested Glasgow Central 1980 by-election. Mbr, Strathclyde Reg Cl, 1975-78. SNP spokesman on sport; member, SNP nat exec; ldr, SNP rates action gp. B 1942; ed Possilpark Sec Sch.

STREATHAM | No change

Electorate %Turnout	60,519	69.5%	**1987**	60,032	65.4%	**1983**
*Shelton, W.J.M. (C)	18,916	44.9%	-1.6%	18,264	46.5%	(C)
Tapsall, Mrs A. (Lab)	16,509	39.2%	+7.7%	12,362	31.5%	(Lab)
Tuffrey, M. (L/All)	6,663	15.8%	-5.4%	8,321	21.2%	(L/All)
				321	0.8%	(Other)
C to Lab swing 4.7%	42,088	C maj 2,407 5.7%		39,268	C maj 5,902 15.0%	

Mr William Shelton

Mr William Shelton was an Under Secretary for State for Education and Science, 1981-83. Mbr of Lloyd's and director, Saracen Consultants Ltd; former chmn of advertising agency. Mbr, Select Cmte on MPs' Interests. Elected for Streatham in Feb 1974; MP for Clapham, 1970-74. B Oct 30 1929; ed Radley Coll; Worcester Coll, Oxford; Tabor Univ, Mass; and Texas Univ. GLC councillor for Wandsworth, 1967-70; chief whip, ILEA, 1968-70. PPS to Mrs Thatcher when Leader of the Opposition, 1975-79. Vice-chmn, Cons education and foreign affairs cmtes, 1979-81.
Mrs Anna Tapsall, home care organiser in Clapham area of Lambeth borough; former actress, nurse, welafare worker. Previously active with Bedford Cl for Community Relations. Aged 51. Chaired Lambeth Nalgo for four years; shop steward.
Mr Michael Tuffrey, chartered accountant, is research officer to Alliance peers, House of Lords. Vice-chmn, London Lib Pty; mbr, ALC, Lib ecology gp, Assocn of Lib trade unionists. B Sep 30 1959; ed Douai Sch, Reading; Durham Univ. Mbr, GLC/ILEA, 1985-86. Apex.

STRETFORD | | | | | No change

Electorate %Turnout	57,568	71.9%	**1987**	57,448	70.0%	**1983**
*Lloyd, A.J. (Lab)	22,831	55.2%	+10.3%	18,028	44.9%	(Lab)
Dougherty, D. (C)	13,429	32.4%	-1.6%	13,686	34.1%	(C)
Lee, D. (SDP/All)	5,125	12.4%	-7.9%	8,141	20.3%	(SDP/All)
				336	0.8%	(Other)
C to Lab swing 6.0%	41,385	Lab maj 9,402 22.7%		40,191	Lab maj 4,342 10.8%	

Mr **Anthony Lloyd** became chairman of the PLP foreign affairs cmte in 1986; mbr, Select Cmte on Home Affairs and its sub-cmte on race relations and immigration, since 1985; Social Services Select Cmte, 1983-85; jt vice-chmn, PLP home affairs cmte, 1985- ; sec, NW Gp of Lab MPs. Lecturer, Dept of Business and Admin, Salford Univ, 1979-83. B Feb 25 1950; ed Stretford GS, Nottingham Univ and Manchester Business Sch. Mbr, Trafford DC, 1979-84. Sponsored by NGA.
Mr **Daniel Dougherty**, bank official, fought Liverpool, Broadgreen, in 1983. Chmn, NW Area Cons Trade Unionists; nat vice-chmn, CTU banking and finance gp. B Jan 16 1948; ed St Oswald's RC Sch, Liverpool and Bankfield. Mbr, Merseyside CC, 1977-81. Mbr and former office rep, BIFU.
Mr **Dennis Lee**, computer engineer. Founder mbr, Bolton area SDP; treas, Bolton NE SDP. B Aug 28 1936; ed St Andrew's Sch, Rugby; Rugby Tech Coll; Bolton Inst of Tech; Salford Univ. Represented Lancashire in athletics; treas, Bolton Harriers. ASTMS.

Mr Anthony Lloyd

STROUD | | | | | No change

Electorate %Turnout	81,275	80.6%	**1987**	77,528	77.7%	**1983**
Knapman, R. (C)	32,883	50.2%	-1.1%	30,896	51.3%	(C)
Walker-Smith, A.A. (L/All)	20,508	31.3%	-0.6%	19,182	31.9%	(L/All)
Levitt, T. (Lab)	12,145	18.5%	+1.7%	10,141	16.8%	(Lab)
C to L/All swing 0.3%	65,536	C maj 12,375 18.9%		60,219	C maj 11,714 19.5%	

Mr **Roger Knapman** is a chartered surveyor. B Feb 20 1944; ed Allhallows Sch, Lyme Regis; Royal Agricultural Coll, Cirencester.
Mr **Adrian Walker-Smith**, manager in firm of mail order publishers, contested City of London and Westminster South in 1983. B Oct 22 1947; ed London Univ.
Mr **Tom Levitt**, teacher. Mbr, Cirencester TC 1983- . B Apr 10 1954; educ comprehensive sch in Leek; Lancaster and Oxford Univs. NUT.

Mr Roger Knapman   *199L*   *16,031 .*

SUFFOLK CENTRAL | | | | No change

Electorate %Turnout	79,199	76.2%	**1987**	75,641	74.4%	**1983**
*Lord, M.N. (C)	32,422	53.7%	+0.2%	30,096	53.5%	(C)
Dale, T. (L/All)	16,132	26.7%	-0.6%	15,365	27.3%	(L/All)
Walker, M. (Lab)	11,817	19.6%	+0.3%	10,828	19.2%	(Lab)
L/All to C swing 0.4%	60,371	C maj 16,290 27.0%		56,289	C maj 14,731 26.2%	

Mr **Michael Lord** has been PPS to Mr John MacGregor, as Minister of State for Agriculture and then Chief Secretary to the Treasury, since 1984. Arboricultural consultant; parly consultant to British Printing Industries Fed. Sec, Cons back-bench forestry sub-cmte, since 1983; mbr, Select Cmte on Agriculture, 1983-84. Elected in 1983; contested Manchester, Gorton, 1979. B Oct 17 1938; ed William Hulme's GS, Manchester; Christ's Coll, Cambridge. Mbr, Bedfordshire CC, 1981-83; North Bedfordshire BC, 1974-77. Vice-pres, Arboricultural Assocn; mbr, BIM.
Mr **Thomas Dale**, director of public relations company and former international officer of Lib pty, contested Harwich 1959, 1964, 1966 and 1970. Mbr, Essex CC; Tendring DC; exec cmte, ACC, and former chmn of its consumer affairs cmte. B Mar 14 1931; ed Gosfield Sch; LSE; Univ of London Inst of Ed. Former mbr, Apex.
Mr **Mark Walker**, administrator for NUR; former railman. B Mar 6 1959; ed Stratton Upper Sch, Biggleswade, Bedfordshire.

Mr Michael Lord

SUFFOLK COASTAL | No change

Electorate %Turnout	75,684	77.9%	**1987**	71,521	75.0%	**1983**
*Gummer, J.S. (C)	32,834	55.7%	-2.6%	31,240	58.2%	(C)
Miller, Mrs J.M. (SDP/All)	17,554	29.8%	+0.6%	15,618	29.1%	(SDP/All)
Reeves, Mrs S.A. (Lab)	7,534	12.8%	+0.1%	6,780	12.6%	(Lab)
Holloway, J.W. (Grn)	1,049	1.8%				
C to SDP/All swing 1.6%	58,971	C maj 15,280 25.9%		53,638	C maj 15,622 29.1%	

Mr John Gummer

Mr John Gummer became Minister of State for Agriculture, Fisheries and Food in 1985; Paymaster General, 1984-85; Minister of State for Employment, 1983-84, being chairman of Conservative Party, 1983-85; Under Secretary of State for Employment, Jan-Oct 1983. Elected for this seat 1983; MP for Eye, 1979-83, and for Lewisham West, 1970-Feb 1974; contested Greenwich, 1964 and 1966. Lord Commissioner of the Treasury (Govt whip), 1981-83; asst Govt whip, 1981. Mbr, General Synod, C of E, since 1979. B Nov 26 1939; ed King's Sch, Rochester; Selwyn Coll, Cambridge (Pres of Union, 1962). Chmn, Fed of Cons Students, 1961. Mbr, ILEA, 1967-70. A vice-chmn, Cons Pty, 1972-74. PPS to Mr James Prior, Minister of Agriculture, 1971, and to Secretary of State for Social Services, 1979-81. Publisher, writer and broadcaster; chmn, Selwyn Shandwick International, 1976-81; Siemssen Hunter, 1979-80, and a director, 1973-80.
Mrs Joan Miller, housewife. Vice-chmn, South Suffolk SDP, 1986- ; S Suffolk area sec, 1983-85; Euro election organiser, Suffolk and SE Cambs, 1984. Mbr, East Bergholt PC, 1983-. B Feb 13 1950; ed Rosebery GS, Epsom; Warwick Univ. Vice-chmn, East Bergholt Community Cl, 1981-85.
Mrs Sue Reeves, shop steward and sch governor. B Mar 31 1943. Mbr, CND and Nalgo.

SUFFOLK SOUTH | No change

Electorate %Turnout	81,954	77.6%	**1987**	76,209	76.3%	**1983**
*Yeo, T.S.K. (C)	33,972	53.4%	+2.8%	29,469	50.6%	(C)
Bradford, C.M.N. (L/All)	17,729	27.9%	-3.4%	18,200	31.3%	(L/All)
Bavington, A.C. (Lab)	11,876	18.7%	+0.6%	10,516	18.1%	(Lab)
L/All to C swing 3.1%	63,577	C maj 16,243 25.5%		58,185	C maj 11,269 19.4%	

Mr Timothy Yeo

Mr Timothy Yeo was director of the Spastics Society, 1980-83, and on its exec cl, 1984-86; director, Worcester Engineering Co Ltd, 1975-86 (now consultant to Worcester Group plc). Elected in 1983; fought Bedwellty, Feb 1974. Mbr, Select Cmte on Social Services, since 1985. B March 20 1945; ed Charterhouse; Emmanuel Coll, Cambridge. Jt sec, Cons back-bench finance cmte, 1984- . Formerly taught agriculture in Tanzania. Treas, International Voluntary Service, 1975-78, now a vice-pres; trustee, Tanzania Development Trust, since 1980. Led campaign to save Tadworth Court Children's Hospital, Surrey; chmn, Tadworth Court Trust, since 1984. Mbr, Independent Development Cl on Mental Handicap. Chmn, Charities VAT Reform Gp, 1982- .
Mr Christopher Bradford is a mbr of the Lib Pty education panel. Mbr, Cambridgeshire CC for 16 years and until recently leader of its Alliance group.
Mr Tony Bavington, secondary teacher of English, presently writing Ph.D in literature at Essex Univ. Mbr, Babergh DC, 1985- (ldr, Lab gp, 1986-); Gt Cornard PC, 1983- . B Jun 20 1948; ed Goldington Sec Mod, Bedford; Stratton GS, Biggleswade; Luton Coll of Tech; Leeds Univ; Doncaster Coll of Ed; Essex Univ. NAS/UWT.

SUNDERLAND NORTH | No change

Electorate %Turnout	75,674	70.5%	**1987**	78,520	66.5%	**1983**
*Clay, R.A. (Lab)	29,767	55.8%	+9.5%	24,179	46.3%	(Lab)
Picton, I.S. (C)	15,095	28.3%	-4.2%	16,983	32.5%	(C)
Jenkinson, T. (L/All)	8,518	16.0%	-5.3%	11,090	21.2%	(L/All)
C to Lab swing 6.9%	53,380	Lab maj 14,672 27.5%		52,252	Lab maj 7,196 13.8%	

Mr Robert Clay

Mr Robert Clay, a bus driver with Tyne and Wear Passenger Transport Executive, 1975-83, was elected in 1983. Secretary, Campaign Gp of Lab MPs. B Oct 2 1946; ed Bradford Sch; Gonville and Caius Coll, Cambridge. Was sec, Sunderland and District Lab Pty. Branch chmn, GMB, 1977-83.
Mr Iain Picton, parliamentary officer with Building Employers' Confederation, contested Rochdale 1979. Chmn, Tory Reform Gp, 1983-87; personal asst to Mr Michael Heseltine in 1983 election; mbr, nat union exec, 1979-82; nat chmn, YCs, 1981-82. B Aug 31 1951; ed Alleyne's Sch, Stevenage; Liverpool Univ. Mbr, Lambeth BC, 1982-86 (Cons spokesman on race relations and police).
Mr Terence Jenkinson, joint proprietor of sub-Post Office. B 1930; ed Pendower Commercial Sch; Newcastle Municipal Coll of Commerce.

SUNDERLAND SOUTH — No change

Electorate %Turnout	74,947	71.1%	**1987**	75,124	66.6%	**1983**
Mullin, C.J. (Lab)	28,823	54.1%	+8.4%	22,869	45.7%	(Lab)
Howe, G.E. (C)	16,210	30.4%	-4.2%	17,321	34.6%	(C)
Hudson, K. (SDP/All)	7,768	14.6%	-5.1%	9,865	19.7%	(SDP/All)
Jacques, D.N. (Grn)	516	1.0%				
C to Lab swing 6.3%	53,317	Lab maj 12,613 23.7%		50,055	Lab maj 5,548 11.1%	

Mr Christopher Mullin, journalist and political novelist, was editor of *Tribune*, 1982-84. Contested Kingston upon Thames in Feb 1974, and Devon North in 1970. B Dec 12 1947; ed St Joseph's Coll, Birkfield, Ipswich; Hull Univ. Sub-editor, BBC World Service, 1974-78. Executive mbr, Campaign for Labour Party Democracy, 1975- ; mbr, Labour Co-ordinating Committee, 1978-82; Lab NEC working pty on media, 1978-82. ASTMS and NUJ.
Mr George Howe, lecturer and engineer. B Jul 1 1936; ed Sunderland Poly; Toronto Univ. NATFHE.
Mr Keith Hudson, insurance agent with London and Manchester Insurance Co. Sec, North Tyneside SDP. B Feb 19 1947; ed Dudley Cty Sec Sch.
Mr Neil Jacques, education officer in museums, contested Newcastle Central 1983. Nat sec, Grn Pty; NE rep on Grn Pty Cl. B Feb 28 1955; ed Wycliffe Coll, Glos; Trinity and All Saints Coll, Leeds. Nalgo; mbr Newcastle City branch exec; convenor, museum stewards.

Mr Christopher
Mullin

SURBITON — No change

Electorate %Turnout	45,428	78.3%	**1987**	46,949	71.3%	**1983**
*Tracey, R.P. (C)	19,861	55.9%	+1.3%	18,245	54.5%	(C)
Burke, D.T. (SDP/All)	10,120	28.5%	+0.1%	9,496	28.4%	(SDP/All)
McGowan, A. (Lab)	5,111	14.4%	-1.1%	5,173	15.5%	(Lab)
Vidler, Ms J. (Grn)	465	1.3%	+0.3%	551	1.6%	(Eco)
SDP/All to C swing 0.6%	35,557	C maj 9,741 27.4%		33,465	C maj 8,749 26.1%	

Mr Richard Tracey was Minister for Sport, with the rank of Under Secretary of State for Environment at the DoE, 1985-87. PPS to Mr Geoffrey Pattie, 1984-85. Public affairs adviser, 1978-83; BBC radio and television news and current affairs presenter, 1966-78. Sec, Cons media cmte, 1983-84; Cons gp of London MPs, 1983-84. Won the seat 1983; contested Northampton North, Oct 1974. B Feb 8 1943; ed King Edward VI Sch, Stratford-upon-Avon; Birmingham Univ. Chmn, London SW Euro Constituency, 1979-81; dep chmn, Greater London area Cons Party, 1981-83; member, nat union exec cmte and policy group for London, 1981-83; Economic Research Cl, since 1981. Freeman, City of London.
Mr Tom Burke, visiting lecturer, contested Brighton Kemptown 1983. Director, Green Alliance, 1982- ; head of policy and research, Earthlife Foundation, 1986- ; director, Earth Resources Rsearch, 1975- . B Jan 5 1947; ed Liverpool Univ; St Boniface's Coll, Plymouth.
Mr Allister McGowan, local govt officer - careers service, chairs Surbiton Lab Pty and Kingston and Surbiton Lab Pty local govt cmte. Co-opted member, Kingston ed cmte. B Mar 22 1950; ed Leicester and Birmingham Univs. Nalgo: Pres (and ex-chair), Surrey Cty branch.
Ms Jean Vidler, company director London area treas, Grn Pty. B Oct 9 1951; ed Arnold County HS, Notts; S Wilts GS for Girls; St John's Sch, Singapore.

Mr Richard Tracey

SURREY EAST — No change

Electorate %Turnout	59,528	77.2%	**1987**	58,485	74.1%	**1983**
*Howe, Sir Geoffrey (C)	29,126	63.4%	+0.5%	27,272	62.9%	(C)
Anderson, M.A.J. (L/All)	11,000	23.9%	-3.4%	11,836	27.3%	(L/All)
Davis, M. (Lab)	4,779	10.4%	+0.6%	4,249	9.8%	(Lab)
Newell, D. (Grn)	1,044	2.3%				
L/All to C swing 1.9%	45,949	C maj 18,126 39.4%		43,357	C maj 15,436 35.6%	

Sir Geoffrey Howe, QC, was appointed Secretary of State for Foreign and Commonwealth Affairs in 1983; Chancellor of the Exchequer, 1979-83; chief Opposition spokesman on Treasury and economic affairs, 1975-79, and a spokesman on social services, 1974-75; Minister for Trade and Consumer Affairs, 1972-74; Solicitor General, 1970-72. Elected for this seat, Feb 1974; MP for Reigate, 1970-74, and Bebington, 1964-66; contested Aberavon, 1955 and 1959. B Dec 20 1926; ed Winchester and Trinity Hall, Cambridge. Pres, Nat Union of Cons and Unionist Assocns, 1983-84. Director, EMI Ltd, 1976-79; Sun Alliance and London Insurance Group, 1974-79; AGB Research Group, 1974-79. Mbr, General Cl of Bar, 1957-61.
Mr Michael Anderson, personnel adviser with Shell UK Ltd, fought Epsom and Ewell in 1983, 1979 and 1978 by-election. Mbr, Lib Pty Cl, LPA cmte. B Sep 4 1930; ed Perse Sch, Cambridge; Emmanuel Coll, Cambridge.
Mr Michael Davis, graphic designer, contested Hampshire NW 1983. GMC sec, NW Hants; vice-chair, Surrey East. Mbr, Test Valley DC, 1979-83. B Oct 14 1951; ed South Borough Sec Sch, Maidstone; Maidstone Coll of Art. NUJ.
Dr David (Herb) Newell, scientist, contested Reigate 1983. Surrey cty coordinator, Grn Pty. B Jul 18 1955; ed Oxted Cty Sch, Surrey; NE Surrey Coll of Tech; London Univ.

Sir Geoffrey Howe

SURREY NORTH WEST — No change

Electorate %Turnout	83,083	72.5%	**1987**	78,377	70.2%	**1983**
*Grylls, W.M.J. (C)	38,535	64.0%	-0.2%	35,297	64.1%	(C)
Brodie, C. (L/All)	14,960	24.8%	-1.1%	14,279	25.9%	(L/All)
Cooper, J. (Lab)	6,751	11.2%	+1.3%	5,452	9.9%	(Lab)
L/All to C swing 0.5%	60,246	C maj 23,575 39.1%		55,028	C maj 21,018 38.2%	

Mr Michael Grylls

Mr Michael Grylls, chairman of the Small Business Bureau since 1979, has been chmn of the Cons back-bench trade and industry cmte since 1981; vice-chmn, 1975-81. Elected in Feb 1974; MP for Chertsey, 1970-74; contested Fulham, 1964 and 1966. Chmn, Le Carbone (UK) Ltd; director, Stirling Winthrop Co Ltd; consultant to Assocn of Authorised Public Accountants, Biwater Shellabear, Digital Equipment Co Ltd and other companies; adviser to Unitary Tax Campaign and to Omec International; hon leader, parly panel, and parly spokesman, Inst of Directors, 1979- . B Feb 21 1934; ed RNC Dartmouth and univs in Paris and Madrid. Mbr, Select Cmte on Overseas Development, 1972-77; GLC, 1967-70 (deputy leader of ILEA, 1969-70); St Pancras BC, 1959-62.
Mr Charles Brodie is finance manager with Wang (UK); former director, MAC (Scotland), consultants. Fought Ayr 1983, Dundee East 1979 and Oct 1974. B May 8 1944; ed Morgan Acad, Dundee; St Andrew's Univ. Vice-chmn, Scottish Lib Pty, 1980-81 and 1982-83; mbr, Scottish Lib Pty exec, 1974-81.
Mr John Cooper, playwright and lawyer. B Sep 15 1958; ed Newcastle Univ. Most recent play, *Burning Point*, about life in the inner city. Mbr, Writers Guild; Soc of Lab Lawyers.

SURREY SOUTH WEST — No change

Electorate %Turnout	73,018	78.4%	**1987**	69,875	74.5%	**1983**
*Bottomley, Mrs V.H.B.M. (C)	34,024	59.5%	-0.3%	31,067	59.7%	(C)
Scott, G.D. (L/All)	19,681	34.4%	+2.3%	16,716	32.1%	(L/All)
Evers, J.K.P. (Lab)	3,224	5.6%	-2.5%	4,239	8.1%	(Lab)
Green, M.J. (Ind C)	299	0.5%				
C to L/All swing 1.3%	57,228	C maj 14,343 25.1%		52,022	C maj 14,351 27.6%	

Mrs Virginia Bottomley

Mrs Virginia Bottomley was elected at the 1984 by-election; contested Isle of Wight, 1983. PPS to Mr Christopher Patten as Minister of State for Education and Science and Minister for Overseas Development, 1985- . Vice-chmn, Nat Cl of Carers and their Elderly Dependants, since 1982; exec mbr, Church of England Children's Soc, 1978-83. Magistrate in inner London juvenile courts since 1975; chmn, Lambeth Juvenile Court, since 1980. Psychiatric social worker, Maudsley Hospital, and Brixton and Camberwell Child Guidance Units, 1973-84. B Mar 12 1948; ed Putney HS; Essex Univ; LSE. Sec, Cons back-bench employment cmte, 1985. Member, Cons women's nat cmte, 1982-83; governor, Foundation for Age Research, 1985- ; psychiatric social worker in child guidance unit, 1973-84. Wife of Mr Peter Bottomley, MP for Eltham.
Mr Gavin Scott, writer and TV journalist, fought this seat at the 1984 by-election. Director, Tigerlily Film and Video Productions. B Apr 25 1950; ed collegiate sch and Victoria Univ, Wellington, New Zealand.
Mr John Evers, postman; mbr, general cmte and exec cmte, Sutton and Cheam Lab Pty; Sutton BC, 1982-86. B Nov 13 1954; ed Wandsworth Comprehensive Sch. Chairs Sutton branch, UCW; former mbr, Natsopa clerical chapel, *The Times*.
Details of 1984 by-election on Page 284

SUSSEX MID — No change

Electorate %Turnout	80,147	77.2%	**1987**	77,005	74.7%	**1983**
*Renton, R.T. (C)	37,781	61.1%	-0.3%	35,310	61.4%	(C)
Westbrook, N.S.E. (L/All)	19,489	31.5%	-0.8%	18,566	32.3%	(L/All)
Hughes, R. (Lab)	4,573	7.4%	+1.4%	3,470	6.0%	(Lab)
				196	0.3%	(Other)
L/All to C swing 0.2%	61,843	C maj 18,292 29.6%		57,542	C maj 16,744 29.1%	

Mr Timothy Renton

Mr Timothy Renton was appointed Minister of State, Home Office, in Jun 1987; Minister of State for Foreign and Commonwealth Affairs, 1985-87; Under Secretary of State for Foreign and Commonwealth Affairs, 1984-85. Former director of building, investment and insurance companies. PPS to Sir Geoffrey Howe, Chancellor of Exchequer and then Foreign Sec, 1983-84; to Mr John Biffen, Chief Sec to Treasury and Secretary of State for Trade, 1979-82. Mbr of Lloyd's. Elected in Feb 1974; contested Sheffield Park, 1970. B May 28 1932; ed Eton and Magdalen Coll, Oxford. Nat Pres, Cons Trade Unionists, 1980-84. Chmn, Cons Foreign and Commonwealth Cl, 1982-84; Cons back-bench employment cmte, 1981-82; vice-chmn, Cons back-bench trade cmte, 1974-79. Mbr, Select Cmte on Nationalized Industries, 1974-79; BBC General Advisory Cl, 1982-84; Cl, Roedean Sch, 1982- . With wife, has tree nursery in Sussex. Apex.
Mr Nicholas Westbrook, chief executive, Youth Training Resources Ltd, contested Aldershot 1983 and 1979, Plymouth Devonport Oct 1974. B May 26 1948; ed Peter Symonds Sch, Winchester; Framlingham Coll, Suffolk; Heriot-Watt Univ.
Mr Robert Hughes, social services grants officer. B Aug 30 1960; ed Nottingham Univ.

SUTTON AND CHEAM — No change

Electorate %Turnout	63,850	76.6%	**1987**	63,099	74.3%	**1983**
*Macfarlane, D.N. (C)	29,710	60.8%	+3.6%	26,782	57.1%	(C)
Greig, R.D. (L/All)	13,992	28.6%	-6.6%	16,518	35.2%	(L/All)
Monk, Ms L. (Lab)	5,202	10.6%	+3.0%	3,568	7.6%	(Lab)
L/All to C swing 5.1%	48,904	C maj 15,718 32.1%		46,868	C maj 10,264 21.9%	

Mr Neil Macfarlane was Under Secretary of State for the Environment and Minister for Sport, 1981-85; Under Secretary of State for Education and Science and Deputy Minister for the Arts, 1979-81. Chmn, Sports Aid Foundation. Now with public affairs dept of British Gas Corpn. Director, Bradford and Bingley Building Soc. Parliamentary and public affairs adviser, Professional Golfers' Assocn; vice-pres, European Tournament Players Division, PGA. Member, R and A, MCC, Essex CCC. Non-exec chmn, Chelsea Restaurant plc. Regained seat for Cons, Feb 1974; contested East Ham North, 1970; Sutton and Cheam by-election, 1972. B May 7 1936; ed St Aubyns, Woodford Green, and Bancrofts Sch, Woodford Wells. Mbr, Select Cmte on Science and Technology, 1974-79; former sec, Cons back-bench cmtes on energy, Greater London and on sport and recreation.
Mr Robert Greig, NHS administrator. B May 3 1957; ed Alcester GS; Bath Univ.
Ms Loraine Monk, welfare rights advice worker; vice-chair, local pty; sec, women's section and local govt cmte. Mbr, Greater London Women's Cl; coopted mbr, Kingston cl's women's cmte. B Nov 9 1955; ed sec mod sch; tech coll; Newcastle and Oxford Univs.

Mr Neil Macfarlane

SUTTON COLDFIELD — No change

Electorate %Turnout	72,329	74.5%	**1987**	67,695	71.8%	**1983**
*Fowler, P.N. (C)	34,475	64.0%	-1.4%	31,753	65.4%	(C)
Bick, T. (L/All)	13,292	24.7%	-1.6%	12,769	26.3%	(L/All)
McLoughlin, P. (Lab)	6,104	11.3%	+3.0%	4,066	8.4%	(Lab)
L/All to C swing 0.1%	53,871	C maj 21,183 39.3%		48,588	C maj 18,984 39.1%	

Mr Norman Fowler was appointed Secretary of State for Employment in Jun 1987; Secretary of State for Social Services, 1981-87; Secretary of State (1981) and Minister (1979-81) of Transport; chief Opposition spokesman on transport, 1976-79; chief spokesman on social services, 1975-76; joined shadow cabinet, 1975; a spokesman on home affairs, 1974-75. PPS to Secretary of State for N Ireland, 1972-74. Journalist on The Times, 1961-70, being its Home Affairs Correspondent, 1966-70. On editorial board of Crossbow, 1962-70. Elected for this seat, Feb 1974; MP for Nottingham South, 1970-74. B Feb 2 1938; ed King Edward VI Sch, Chelmsford; Trinity Hall, Cambridge. Chmn, E Midlands Area CPC, 1970-73. Mbr, Select Cmte on Race Relations and Immigration, 1970-74. NUJ.
Mr Timothy Bick, human resources adviser. Mbr, Warwickshire CC, 1981- (ldr, Alliance gp, 1983-); exec cl, ACC, 1985- . Press officer, Warwick and Leamington Lib Assocn, 1978-81. B Sep 5 1955; ed Leamington Coll for Boys; Lincoln Coll, Oxford (Chmn, Univ Lib Club, 1975).
Mr Peter McLoughlin, operations manager with an automotive components company. B Jun 17 1942; ed Hatfield Poly; Bradford Univ Management Centre.

Mr Norman Fowler

SWANSEA EAST — No change

Electorate %Turnout	57,200	75.4%	**1987**	57,285	71.5%	**1983**
*Anderson, D. (Lab)	27,478	63.7%	+9.3%	22,297	54.4%	(Lab)
Lewis, R.D. (C)	8,140	18.9%	-0.9%	8,762	21.4%	(L/All)
Thomas, Rev D.W. (L/All)	6,380	14.8%	-6.6%	8,080	19.7%	(C)
Reid, C. (Pl C)	1,145	2.7%	-1.1%	1,531	3.7%	(Pl C)
				294	0.7%	(Other)
C to Lab swing 5.1%	43,143	Lab maj 19,338 44.8%		40,964	Lab maj 13,535 33.0%	

Mr Donald Anderson, a barrister, has been an Opposition spokesman on foreign affairs since 1983. Vice-chmn, exec, IPU and CPA, since 1985; Assocn of West European Parliamentarians for Action against Apartheid, 1984- . In diplomatic service, 1960-64; lecturer at University College, Swansea, 1964-66. Elected for this seat, Oct 1974; MP for Monmouth, 1966-70. PPS to Attorney General, 1974-79. Chmn, Welsh Lab Gp, 1977-78; Select Cmte on Welsh Affairs, 1981-83 (mbr, 1979-83); PLP environment cmte, 1974-76 and 1977-79. B Jun 17 1939; ed Swansea GS and University Coll, Swansea. Consultant (unpaid) to Royal Soc of Chemistry. Mbr, Kensington and Chelsea BC, 1971-75. Methodist local preacher. Pres, Gower Society, 1976-78. Sponsored by NUR.
Mr Richard Lewis, newsagent. Mbr, Swansea City Cl, 1973- . B Jan 25 1939; ed Queen's Coll, Taunton.
Mr Wynford Thomas, priest in charge, Waunwen, Swansea - Church in Wales. Contested Colchester Feb 1974, Pembroke 1970. Mbr, Cwmbwrla DC; chmn, Swansea East Lib Pty. B Mar 10 1948; ed Gowerton GS, Swansea; Univ Coll of Wales, Aberystwyth.
Mr Clive Reid, pharmacist in Morriston, contested this seat 1983. Aged 46; ed Welsh Sch of Pharmacy, Cardiff.

Mr Donald Anderson

SWANSEA WEST — No change

Electorate %Turnout	59,836	76.1%	**1987**	58,237	73.5%	**1983**
*Williams, A.J. (Lab)	22,089	48.5%	+6.4%	18,042	42.1%	(Lab)
Evans, N.M. (C)	15,027	33.0%	-3.6%	15,692	36.6%	(C)
Ford, M. (L/All)	7,019	15.4%	-3.3%	8,036	18.8%	(SDP/All)
Williams, N. (Pl C)	902	2.0%	+0.1%	795	1.9%	(Pl C)
Harman, Mrs J.V. (Grn)	469	1.0%	+0.4%	265	0.6%	(Eco)
C to Lab swing 5.0%	45,506	Lab maj 7,062 15.5%		42,830	Lab maj 2,350 5.5%	

Mr Alan Williams

Mr Alan J Williams, deputy Opposition spokesman on Commons affairs, 1984- ; an Opposition spokesman on trade and industry, 1983-84; Civil Service, 1980-83; Wales, 1979-80. Minister of State for Industry, 1976-79; Minister of State, Prices and Consumer Protection, 1974-76. Opposition spokesman on education and science, 1970-73; consumer affairs, 1973-74. Parly Sec, Ministry of Technology and Power, 1969-70; Under Secretary of State, Dept of Economic Affairs, 1967-69. Elected in 1964; contested Poole, 1959. B Oct 14 1930; ed Cardiff HS; Cardiff Coll of Tech; London and Oxford Univs. Economics lecturer. Director, Job Creation Ltd; adviser to Institution of Plant Engineers; adviser (unpaid) to Assocn of First Division Civil Servants, 1982- , and to TSSA.
Mr Nigel Evans, newsagent and grocer. Mbr, West Glamorgan CC, 1985- . B Nov 10 1957; ed Dynevor Sch; Univ Coll, Swansea.
Mr Martyn Ford, barrister. Mbr, West Glamorgan CC, 1985- ; chmn, West Glamorgan local authority, 1982-83. Chmn, Swansea West Lib Assocn, 1984. B May 27 1954.
Mr Nigel Williams, business consultant, contested Gower 1983. Aged 32.
Ms Julie Harman, development officer. Aged 32. Co-chair, W Glamorgan Grn Pty.

SWINDON — No change

Electorate %Turnout	86,150	77.8%	**1987**	76,833	74.1%	**1983**
*Coombs, S.C. (C)	29,385	43.8%	+4.7%	22,310	39.2%	(C)
Johnston, Ms G. (Lab)	24,528	36.6%	-0.1%	20,915	36.7%	(Lab)
Scott, D.J. (SDP/All)	13,114	19.6%	-4.6%	13,743	24.1%	(SDP/All)
Lab to C swing 2.4%	67,027	C maj 4,857 7.2%		56,968	C maj 1,395 2.4%	

Mr Simon Coombs

Mr Simon Coombs, a marketing executive with British Telecom, 1970-83, won this seat in 1983. Parly consultant to Blick International. PPS to DoE ministers, 1984-85, and to Mr Kenneth Baker at the DTI, 1984. Sec, parly cable TV gp, 1986- . Mbr, all-pty road study group and motor industry group; British-American parly group, 1983- ; Commonwealth Parly Assocn, 1983- ; courts of Reading and Bath Univs. Sec, British/Malawi parly gp, 1985- ; parly Food and Health Forum, 1985- . B Feb 21 1947; ed Wycliffe Coll and Reading Univ. Mbr, Reading BC, 1969-72 and 1973-84; Southern Electricity Consultative Cl, 1981-84. Pres, Wiltshire YCs, 1984- ; chmn, Wessex Area Cons Pty, 1980-83, and Wessex Area YCs, 1973-76.
Ms Gaye Johnston, social services policy planner, contested Langbaurgh 1983, Cleveland and Whitby Feb 1974, and Scarborough and Whitby 1970. Former nat sec, Labour Campaign for Mental Health. Mbr, Darlington BC, 1979-83; Nupe since 1970. B Dec 13 1943; ed Ackworth Friends Sch, Pontefract; Bristol, Liverpool, Leeds and Durham Univs.
Mr Derek Scott, economist in oil industry, contested the seat 1983. Economic adviser to Mr James Callaghan when Ldr of Opposition, and to Mr Denis Healey at Treasury. Member, SDP economic policy cmte and of CSD. Formerly at NEDO. B Jan 17 1947; ed Liverpool Univ; LSE; Birbeck Coll, London. London borough cllr, 1974-78. ASTMS.

TATTON — No change

Electorate %Turnout	71,904	76.7%	**1987**	68,747	74.3%	**1983**
*Hamilton, M.N. (C)	30,128	54.6%	+0.0%	27,877	54.6%	(C)
Gaskin, Ms B. (SDP/All)	13,034	23.6%	-3.6%	13,917	27.2%	(SDP/All)
Blears, Ms H.A. (Lab)	11,760	21.3%	+3.1%	9,295	18.2%	(Lab)
Gibson, M.G. (FP)	263	0.5%				
SDP/All to C swing 1.8%	55,185	C maj 17,094 31.0%		51,089	C maj 13,960 27.3%	

Mr Neil Hamilton

Mr Neil Hamilton, barrister (non-practising), was elected in 1983; contested Abertillery, Feb 1974, and Bradford North, 1979. PPS to Mr David Mitchell, Minister of State for Transport, since 1986. Former European and parly affairs director, Inst of Directors. Parly consultant to Brewers' Soc and to Nat Assocn of Licensed Opencast Operators. Vice-pres, League for Introduction of Canine Controls, since 1984; Fed of Cons Students, 1986- . B Mar 9 1949; ed Amman Valley GS; Univ Coll of Wales, Aberystwyth; Corpus Christi, Cambridge. Vice-chmn, Small Business Bureau, 1985- ; jt vice-chmn (1984-86) and sec (1983-84), Cons back-bench trade and industry cmte; sec, all-pty UK/Anzac group, 1984- .
Mrs Brigid Gaskin, principal educational psychologist with Tameside MBC since 1974; with Luton Corporation, 1970-74, contested Greater Manchester East in 1984 Euro election. Chmn, Manchester SDP. B Aug 22 1935; ed Nat Univ of Ireland; Queen's Univ, Belfast; Gottingen Univ, W Germany; Birkbeck Coll, London.
Ms Hazel Blears, solicitor with Manchester City Cl. Mbr, Sayard City Cl, 1984- ; sec, Sayard jobs and industry campaign. B May 14 1956. Nalgo and TGWU(ACTSS).

TAUNTON | No change

Electorate %Turnout	74,145	79.4%	**1987**	70,359	75.5%	**1983**
Nicholson, D.J. (C)	30,248	51.4%	-1.5%	28,112	52.9%	(C)
Cocks, M.A.K. (SDP/All)	19,868	33.7%	+4.5%	15,545	29.2%	(SDP/All)
Reynolds, Dr G. (Lab)	8,754	14.9%	-3.0%	9,498	17.9%	(Lab)
C to SDP/All swing 3.0%	58,870	C maj 10,380 17.6%		53,155	C maj 12,567 23.6%	

Mr David Nicholson is deputy director, Association of British Chambers of Commerce; in Conservative Research Dept, 1972-82, and a former Asst Principal, Dept of Employment. Contested Walsall South, 1983; Islington borough elections, 1978, 1982, 1986. B Aug 17 1944; ed Queen Elizabeth's GS, Blackburn; Christ Church, Oxford. Co-editor, *The LS Amery Diaries, Vol I*, published in 1980.
Mr Michael Cocks, financial consultant, contested the seat 1983. Mbr, exec cmte, Kensington and Chelsea SDP area pty. Cons mbr, Kensington and Chelsea BC, 1964-71 and 1974-80. Former mbr, London Stock Exchange. B Oct 16 1936; ed Eastwood and Beaufort Lodge Prep Schs, Barnet; Westcliff HS; Peterhouse, Cambridge.
Dr Gary Reynolds, medical doctor, Commonwealth Secretariat Health Programme. Former branch sec, North Sydney (Australia); Wimbledon. Mbr, medical campaign against nuclear weapons. B Aug 28 1949; ed North Sydney Boys' High Sch; faculty of medicine, Univ of New South Wales. MPU/ASTMS.

Mr David Nicholson

TAYSIDE NORTH | No change

Electorate %Turnout	53,985	74.7%	**1987**	51,972	72.6%	**1983**
*Walker, W.C. (C)	18,307	45.4%	-5.7%	19,269	51.0%	(C)
Guild, K.J.N. (SNP)	13,291	32.9%	+8.6%	9,170	24.3%	(SNP)
Regent, P.F. (L/All)	5,201	12.9%	-6.3%	7,255	19.2%	(L/All)
Whytock, J. (Lab)	3,550	8.8%	+3.3%	2,057	5.4%	(Lab)
C to SNP swing 7.2%	40,349	C maj 5,016 12.4%		37,751	C maj 10,099 26.8%	

Mr William Walker has served on the Select Cmtes on Scottish Affairs and on Parliamentary Commissioner for Administration since 1979, and on the Private Bill Cmte. Scottish Cons Pty defence spokesman since 1981. Chmn, all-pty scout gp; vice-chmn, Cons back-bench aviation cmte, 1985- ; former jt vice-chmn, European Affairs cmte. Chmn of Walker Associates, his own management, marketing and design consultancy company, and of Ulster Airways Ltd and Ulster Airways Inc. Elected for this seat 1983; MP for Perth and East Perthshire, 1979-83; contested Dundee East, Oct 1974. B Feb 20 1929; ed Logie and Blackness Schs, Dundee; Trades Coll, Dundee; Coll of Arts, Dundee; and Coll for Distibutive Trades, London. Former senior gliding instructor, Air Cadet Gliding Sch; holds RAFVR commission; parly adviser (unpaid) to British Gliding Assocn and to Soc of Procurator Fiscals; also adviser to Nat Fed of Site Operators. Fellow, BIM, Inst of Personnel Management, RSA.
Mr Kenneth Guild, coll lecturer, contested Gordon in 1983. Member, Dundee DC. B Feb 13 1946; ed Harris Acad, Dundee; RNC Dartmouth; Dundee Univ. EIS.
Mr Peter Regent, sculptor and writer, is a district councillor, NE Fife. B Dec 8 1929; ed Thetford GHS; Keble Coll, Oxford.
Mr William Walker   **Mr Jim Whytock**, local authority gardner. B Jul 25 1954.

TEIGNBRIDGE | No change

Electorate %Turnout	71,872	80.3%	**1987**	67,515	77.5%	**1983**
*Nicholls, P.C.M. (C)	30,693	53.2%	-0.8%	28,265	54.0%	(C)
Ryder, R.D. (L/All)	20,268	35.1%	-3.2%	20,047	38.3%	(L/All)
Greenwood, J. (Lab)	6,413	11.1%	+3.9%	3,749	7.2%	(Lab)
Hope, A. (Loony)	312	0.5%		241	0.5%	(Loony Soc)
L/All to C swing 1.2%	57,686	C maj 10,425 18.1%		52,302	C maj 8,218 15.7%	

Mr Patrick Nicholls was appointed an Under Secretary of State for Employment in Jun 1987. Solicitor. Elected in 1983. PPS to Mr John Gummer, Minister of State for Agriculture, 1986-87; to Home Office ministers, 1984-86. B Nov 14 1948; ed Redrice Coll, Andover, and Coll of Law, Guildford. Steward, British Boxing Bd of Control, since 1985. Mbr, East Devon DC, 1980-84. Jt sec, Cons backbench legal cmte, 1983-84; sec, Westcountry Cons MPs, 1984-85.
Mr Richard Ryder, psychologist and animal rights campaigner, fought Buckingham 1983. Chmn, RSPCA, 1977-79. B Jul 3 1940; ed Sherborne Sch; Cambridge, Columbia and Edinburgh Univs.
Mr Justin Greenwood, research assistant. Vice-chmn and sec, Nottingham South CLP. B May 17 1960; ed Newton Abbot GS; Nottingham Univ (chmn, Univ Lab Club). GMB.

Mr Patrick Nicholls

THANET NORTH — No change

Electorate %Turnout	69,723	72.2%	**1987**	66,678	68.8%	**1983**
*Gale, R.J. (C)	29,225	58.0%	-0.4%	26,801	58.4%	(C)
Cranston, N.R.M. (SDP/All)	11,745	23.3%	-3.4%	12,256	26.7%	(SDP/All)
Bretman, A.M. (Lab)	8,395	16.7%	+2.5%	6,482	14.1%	(Lab)
Condor, D.R. (Grn)	996	2.0%		324	0.7%	(BNP)
SDP/All to C swing 1.5%	50,361	C maj 17,480 34.7%		45,863	C maj 14,545 31.7%	

Mr **Roger Gale**, producer with Thames Television, 1979-83, and director of BBC children's television, 1976-79; producer, BBC radio current affairs, 1973-76. Parliamentary consultant for Scottish and Newcastle Breweries plc; voluntary consultant, Operation Raleigh. Elected in 1983; fought Birmingham, Northfield, in 1982 by-election. Founder mbr, East Kent Development Assocn, 1984- . B Aug 20 1943; ed Southbourne Prep Sch; Hardye's Sch, Dorchester, and Guildhall Sch of Music and Drama. Mbr, nat cmte, CTU, 1979- . Former chmn, all-pty parly gp, Fund for Replacement of Animals in Medical Experiments. Jt sec, back-bench tourism sub-cmte, 1985- ; back-bench media cmte, 1985- . Equity, NUJ, ACTT.
Mr **Nicholas Cranston**, international banker. Chmn, Oxford Univ SDP, 1982; sec, Westminster S SDP, 1983; mbr, exec, City SDP. B Aug 19 1960; ed Eton; Trinity Coll,Oxford.
Mr **Alan Bretman**, newsagent and bookseller; teacher. B Sep 13 1949; ed Sir Geo Monoux GS, London; Cambridge and Nottingham Univs. Mbr, Queenborough TC, 1983-87 (chmn, 1984-87). Chair, Faversham CLP, 1986-87.86.
Mr **David Conder**, asst sec at CI for the Protection of Rural England. Contested Canterbury 1983. B Jan 5 1953; ed Gresham's Sch, Holt; Univ Col North Wales, Bangor.

Mr Roger Gale

THANET SOUTH — No change

Electorate %Turnout	62,761	73.7%	**1987**	61,989	70.0%	**1983**
*Aitken, J.W.P. (C)	25,135	54.3%	-2.1%	24,512	56.5%	(C)
Pitt, W.H. (L/All)	11,452	24.8%	+0.7%	10,461	24.1%	(L/All)
Wright, C. (Lab)	9,673	20.9%	+1.5%	8,429	19.4%	(Lab)
C to L/All swing 1.4%	46,260	C maj 13,683 29.6%		43,402	C maj 14,051 32.4%	

Mr **Jonathan Aitken**, author and journalist, was elected for this seat in 1983; MP for Thanet East, Feb 1974-83; contested Meriden, 1966. Chmn, Aitken Hume plc, since 1981, and a director of the group's principal subsidiary and associated companies; director, TV-am plc, since 1981, and Al Bilad (UK) Ltd. Foreign correspondent, *Evening Standard*, 1966-71. Managing director, Slater Walker (Middle East), 1973-75. B Aug 30 1942; ed Eton and Christ Church, Oxford. Mbr, Select Cmte on Employment, 1979-82. Pres, London Road Runners Club, 1984- ; chmn, British-Saudi Arabian parly group. Former sec, Cons broadcasting and communications cmte.
Mr **Bill Pitt**, MP for Croydon NW, 1982-83, having won that seat at by-election; contested that seat 1979 and twice in 1974. Lib spokesman on home affairs, 1982-83. B Jul 1937; ed London Nautical Sch; South Bank Poly. Mature student/writer. Former chmn, London Lib Pty. Former jt vice-chmn, all- pty cmte against racialism.
Mr **Chris Wright**, lithographic scanner and planner. B Jun 14 1947. Mbr, Croydon HA; Westminster Disablement Bd; NCCL; League Against Cruel Sports; Co-op Pty; CND; NGA.

Mr Jonathan Aitken

THURROCK — C gain

Electorate %Turnout	67,594	71.5%	**1987**	66,300	67.7%	**1983**
Janman, T.S. (C)	20,527	42.5%	+7.1%	17,600	39.2%	(Lab)
*McDonald, Miss O.A. (Lab)	19,837	41.0%	+1.9%	15,878	35.4%	(C)
Benson, D.S. (SDP/All)	7,970	16.5%	-5.2%	9,761	21.7%	(SDP/All)
				1,671	3.7%	(Other)
Lab to C swing 2.6%	48,334	C maj 690 1.4%		44,910	Lab maj 1,722 3.8%	

Mr **Timothy Janman**, IBM salesman; previously in industrial relations with Ford Motor Co. B Sep 9 1957; ed Sir William Borlase GS; Nottingham Univ. In YCs, Ilford South; Fed of Cons Students, Nottingham. Mbr, Selsdon Gp.
Dr **Oonagh McDonald** was an Opposition spokesman on Treasury and economic affairs, 1983-87; a spokesman on defence and disarmament, 1981-83. MP for this seat, 1976-87; contested South Gloucestershire, Feb and Oct 1974. B Feb 1938; ed Roan School for Girls, Greenwich; East Barnet GS, and King's Coll London. Lecturer in philosophy, Bristol Univ, 1965-76. Mbr, PAC, 1977-78; PPS to Chief Secretary of the Treasury, 1977-79; mbr, Select Cmte on Employment, 1981. Mbr, industial policy sub-cmte (1976-83) and finance and economic affairs sub-cmte (1978-83) of Lab Pty NEC. ASTMS. Sponsored by Usdaw.
Mr **Donald Benson**, transport lecturer and author, contested the seat 1983. B Feb 10 1926; ed Palmers Endowed Sch for Boys, Grays. With Port of London Authority, 1951-70, becoming exec officer in charge of training; senior lecturer with Essex ed cmte, 1970-82. Fellow, Inst of Transport Administration, MCIT.

Mr Timothy Janman

TIVERTON — No change

Electorate %Turnout	68,210	79.7%	**1987**	63,828	77.5%	**1983**
*Maxwell-Hyslop, R.J. (C)	29,875	54.9%	+0.2%	27,101	54.8%	(C)
Morrish, D.J. (L/All)	20,663	38.0%	-0.8%	19,215	38.8%	(L/All)
Northam, Ms J.A. (Lab)	3,400	6.3%	-0.1%	3,154	6.4%	(Lab)
Jones, W.J. (LO)	434	0.8%				
L/All to C swing 0.5%	54,372	C maj 9,212 16.9%		49,470	C maj 7,886 15.9%	

Mr Robin
Maxwell-Hyslop

Mr Robin Maxwell-Hyslop has served on the Select Cmte on Trade and Industry since 1979; also mbr, Select Cmte on Procedure, 1978- ; Select Cmte on Standing Orders, 1977- . Elected at 1960 by-election; contested Derby North, 1959. With Rolls-Royce Aero Engines 1954-60, being personal asst to director of Sales and Service following graduate apprenticeship and two years in Export Sales Dept. B Jun 6 1931; ed Stowe and Christ Church, Oxford. Chmn, Anglo-Brazilian parly group. Jt sec, Cons aviation cmte, 1972-79.
Mr David Morrish, lecturer at Exeter Univ, fought this seat 1983 and 1979; Exeter twice in 1974 and in 1970. Mbr, Devon CC, 1973- (cl ldr, 1985-); Exeter City Cl, 1961-74; exec cmte, ACC; Devon Sea Fisheries Cmte; Lib Ecology Gp; Electoral Reform Soc. Former chmn, Devon Lib Pty. Governor, Bicton Coll of Agriculture. B May 17 1931; ed Sutton HS, Plymouth; Exeter Univ; Wisconsin Univ, US. AUT.
Ms Jean Northam, lecturer in further ed. B Mar 7 1941. Chairs Devon SEA; former borough cllr; sch governor. NATFHE.

TONBRIDGE AND MALLING — No change

Electorate %Turnout	76,797	77.8%	**1987**	72,549	74.7%	**1983**
*Stanley, J.P. (C)	33,990	56.9%	+0.8%	30,417	56.1%	(C)
Ward, M.J. (SDP/All)	17,561	29.4%	-1.8%	16,897	31.2%	(SDP/All)
Still, D.G. (Lab)	7,803	13.1%	+0.3%	6,896	12.7%	(Lab)
Easter, M.D.S. (BN)	369	0.6%				
SDP/All to C swing 1.3%	59,723	C maj 16,429 27.5%		54,210	C maj 13,520 24.9%	

Mr John Stanley

Mr John Stanley was appointed Minister of State for Norther Ireland in Jun 1987; Minister of State for the Armed Forces at the Ministry of Defence, 1983-87; Minister for Housing and Construction, with rank of Minister of State at the DoE, 1979-83; PPS to Mrs Thatcher, 1976-79. Former consultant to RTZ Industries Ltd. Elected in Feb 1974; contested Newton, 1970. B Jan 19 1942; ed Repton and Lincoln Coll, Oxford. Mbr, Select Cmte on Nationalized Industries, 1974-76; sec, Cons backbench industry cmte, 1974-75; vice-chmn, 1975-76. Research associate, International Inst for Strategic Studies, 1968-69; in Cons Research Dept, 1967-68.
Mr Michael Ward, public affairs officer wwith Gas Consumers Cl, was Lab MP for Peterborough, Oct 1974-1979; contested that seat in 1966 (when he lost by three votes after seven recounts), 1970 and Feb 1974, when he lost by 22 after four recounts. Former press officer with ILEA. Mbr, Commons expenditure cmte, 1976-79, and of its Education, Arts and Home Office sub-cmte. Lab mbr, Romford BC and successor Havering BC, 1958-78; alderman, 1971-78; ldr of cl, 1971-74. Vice-chmn, West Kent Area SDP. B Apr 7 1931; ed Royal Liberty GS, Romford, and Manchester Univ. NUJ.
Mr Derek Still, diesel engineer. Local cllr. B Aug 1 1938; ed Tunbridge Wells Tech Coll.

TOOTING — No change

Electorate %Turnout	68,116	71.2%	**1987**	68,083	67.5%	**1983**
*Cox, T.M. (Lab)	21,457	44.2%	+1.5%	19,640	42.7%	(Lab)
Winter, M.A. (C)	20,016	41.3%	+4.3%	16,981	37.0%	(C)
Ambache, J.N. (SDP/All)	6,423	13.2%	-4.9%	8,317	18.1%	(SDP/All)
Vickery, Mrs M. (Grn)	621	1.3%		355	0.8%	(NF)
				654	1.4%	(Other)
Lab to C swing 1.4%	48,517	Lab maj 1,441 3.0%		45,947	Lab maj 2,659 5.8%	

Mr Thomas Cox

Mr Thomas Cox was an assistant Government whip 1974-77; Lord Commissioner of the Treasury (whip) 1977-79. Delegate to Cl of Europe and WEU, 1985- . Elected in 1983; MP for Wandsworth, Tooting, Feb 1974-83, and for Wandsworth Central, 1970-74; contested Stroud, 1966. B 1930; ed state schools and LSE. Electrician. Former alderman, Fulham BC. Sponsored by EETPU.
Mr Martin Winter, partner in firm of solicitors. B Apr 13 1954; ed St Edmund Hall, Oxford. Mbr, Wandsworth CHC; bd of management, Tooting youth project; law centre in Lambeth. Governor of Ernest Bevin Sch; coordinator of local neighbourhood watch.
Mr Jeremy Ambache, social services manager, Croydon, previously in social services with Birmingham City Cl, at Hammersmith and Fulham, Brent. Chmn, Putney SDP. B Dec 16 1946; ed Beadles Sch; Sussex and York Univs. Nalgo.
Mrs Monica Vickery, housewife and local pty fundraiser. B Mar 3 1940; ed Surbiton HS; Tolworth County Sec Sch; Wimbledon Tech. Has contested Ilea election.

TORBAY | No change

Electorate %Turnout	70,435	76.3%	**1987**	67,337	72.6%	**1983**
Allason, R.W.S. (C)	29,029	54.0%	+1.4%	25,721	52.6%	(C)
Bye, N.D. (L/All)	20,209	37.6%	-1.6%	19,166	39.2%	(L/All)
Taylor, G.R. (Lab)	4,538	8.4%	+1.2%	3,521	7.2%	(Lab)
				500	1.0%	(Other)
L/All to C swing 1.5%	53,776	C maj 8,820 16.4%		48,908	C maj 6,555 13.4%	

Mr Rupert Allason, author and historian, contested Battersea, 1983, and Kettering, 1979. Editor, Intelligence Quarterly, and book publisher. B Nov 8 1951; ed Downside Sch, Bath; Grenoble and London Univs. NUJ.
Mr Nicholas Bye manages hotel and business dept of estate agency. B 1960; ed Montpelier Sch, Paignton; Kings Coll, Taunton; Oxford Univ. Former press officer, Torbay Debating Soc.
Mr Gerald Taylor, student at Essex Univ. B Feb 9 1958; ed Shaldon Primary Sch; Teignmouth GS; Ruskin Coll, Oxford. Chmn, Teignbridge CLP, 1984-85; served as chmn and press officer, Teignmouth Lab Pty. Nalgo.

Mr Rupert Allason

TORFAEN | No change

Electorate %Turnout	59,896	75.6%	**1987**	58,739	74.4%	**1983**
Murphy, P.P. (Lab)	26,577	58.7%	+11.4%	20,678	47.3%	(Lab)
Blackburn, G.R. (L/All)	9,027	19.9%	-8.4%	12,393	28.3%	(L/All)
Gordon, R. (C)	8,632	19.1%	-3.2%	9,751	22.3%	(C)
Evans, Ms J. (Pl C)	577	1.3%	-0.8%	896	2.0%	(Pl C)
Witherden, M. (Grn)	450	1.0%				
L/All to Lab swing 9.9%	45,263	Lab maj 17,550 38.8%		43,718	Lab maj 8,285 19.0%	

Mr Paul Murphy, lecturer in government at Ebbw Vale CFE, contested Wells in 1979. Mbr, Torfaen BC, 1973-87 (chmn, finance cmte, 1976-86). B Nov 25 1948; ed St Francis Sch, Abersychan; West Monmouth Sch, Pontypool; Oriel Coll, Oxford. Constituency party secretary, 1972-87. Mbr, Co-op Pty, WEA, Socialist Ed Assocn. Sponsored by TGWU.
Mr Graham Blackburn, engineer and general manager, BSC (Industry) Cardiff workshops, contested this seat 1983. Exec chmn, Welsh Lib Pty cmte, 1979-81. B Mar 25 1939; ed Newport HS; St Catharine's Coll, Cambridge. Mbr, Steel Industry Management Assocn.
Mr Robert Gordon, solicitor in private practice. Mbr, Watford BC, 1982- ; gp ldr, 1984-86; dep ldr, 1983-84. B Mar 29 1952; ed Watford GS; Sussex Univ; Coll of Law, Guildford and Lancaster Gate. Dep chmn, Watford Cons Assocn, 1984-86; primary sch governor.
Ms Jillian Evans speaks for PlC on Peace and international affairs. Aged 28; ed Univ Coll, Aberystwyth; Poly of Wales.
Mr Melvin Witherden, community development worker, is sec, Torfaen Green Pty. Sec, Cwmbran Community Press Ltd, a community cooperative. B Jan 11 1948; ed Maidenhead GS; St Catharines Coll, Cambridge. Formerly NUJ.

Mr Paul Murphy

TOTTENHAM | No change

Electorate %Turnout	76,092	66.1%	**1987**	67,944	63.4%	**1983**
Grant, B. (Lab)	21,921	43.6%	-8.4%	22,423	52.0%	(Lab)
Murphy, P.L. (C)	17,780	35.4%	+5.1%	13,027	30.2%	(C)
Etherington, S. (L/All)	8,983	17.9%	+1.6%	6,990	16.2%	(L/All)
Nicholls, D. (Grn)	744	1.5%		652	1.5%	(Ind C)
Nealon, P. (Gaitskell Lab)	638	1.3%				
Dixon, Ms C.L. (WRP)	205	0.4%				
Lab to C swing 6.8%	50,271	Lab maj 4,141 8.2%		43,092	Lab maj 9,396 21.8%	

Mr Bernie Grant was leader of Haringey Cl, 1983-87; dep leader, 1982-83; elected to cl, 1978. Won nomination for seat from Mr Norman Atkinson, MP for Tottenham for more than 20 years. Strong supporter of black sections in Labour Party. B Feb 17 1944 in Georgetown, Guyana; emigrated to UK 1963; ed Tottenham Tech Coll; Heriot Watt Univ, Edinburgh. Former British Rail clerk, telephonist and Nupe area officer before being Newham senior district housing officer (community relations) from 1985. Chairs Broadwater Farm panel; governor, three local schools. Nupe.
Mr Peter Murphy, chartered surveyor, contested this seat 1983. Mbr, Haringey BC, 1986- . B 1946; ed St Mary's RC GS, Crosby. Son of Liverpool docker.
Mr Stuart Etherington is director of a voluntary organisation. B Feb 26 1955; ed Sondes Place Sch, Dorking, Surrey.
Mr Donald Nicholls, teacher. B Jul 8 1950; ed Stamford Sch; Bedford Coll of Ed; Middlesex Poly. NATHFE.

Mr Bernie Grant

TRURO — No change

Electorate %Turnout	72,432	79.9%	**1987**	68,514	79.6%	**1983**
*Taylor, M.O.J. (L/All)	28,368	49.0%	-8.3%	31,279	57.3%	(L/All)
St Aubyn, N.F. (C)	23,615	40.8%	+2.7%	20,799	38.1%	(C)
King, J.R. (Lab)	5,882	10.2%	+5.6%	2,479	4.5%	(Lab)
L/All to C swing 5.5%	57,865	L/All maj 4,753 8.2%		54,557	L/All maj 10,480 19.2%	

Mr **Matthew Taylor**, who won this seat at the 1987 by-election, was economic policy research-er for the Parliamentary Liberal Party and research assistant to the late Mr David Penhaligan, MP for the seat 1974-86. Mbr and sec, Alliance tax and benefits reform working party; Alliance public expenditure working gp. B Jan 3 1963; ed St Paul's Sch, Truro; Treliske Sch, Truro; Univ Coll Sch, London; Lady Margaret Hall, Oxford (Pres of student union).
Mr **Nicholas St Aubyn**, merchant banker, contested the by-election in March 1987. Mbr, Westminster City Cl, 1982- . B 1955; ed Eton and Trinity Coll, Oxford.
Mr **John King**, teacher and writer. Contested Truro by-election Mar 1987. Chmn, Camborne branch Lab Pty; Kerrier district Lab Pty; former chmn, Camborne TC. Mbr, Cornish Gorsedd. B Feb 14 1948; ed in Bishopshalt, Hillingdon and Middlesex; Bristol and Manches-ter Univs. NUT.
Details of 1987 by-election on Page 285

Mr Matthew Taylor

TUNBRIDGE WELLS — No change

Electorate %Turnout	76,291	74.3%	**1987**	73,709	72.7%	**1983**
*Mayhew, Sir Patrick (C)	33,111	58.4%	+0.2%	31,199	58.3%	(C)
Buckrell, Mrs D.A. (L/All)	16,989	30.0%	0.0%	16,073	30.0%	(L/All)
Sloman, P.L. (Lab)	6,555	11.6%	+0.3%	6,042	11.3%	(Lab)
				236	0.4%	(Other)
L/All to C swing 0.1%	56,655	C maj 16,122 28.5%		53,550	C maj 15,126 28.2%	

Sir **Patrick Mayhew**, QC, was appointed Attorney General in Jun 1987; Solicitor General, 1983-87; Minister of State, Home Office, 1981-83; Under Secretary of State for Employment, 1979-81. Elected in Feb 1974; fought Dulwich, Camberwell, 1970. Commissioner of Church of England. B Sep 11 1929; ed Tonbridge Sch and Balliol Coll, Oxford (Pres of Union, 1952). Mbr, exec, 1922 Cmte, 1976-79, and jt vice-chmn, Cons back-bench home affairs cmte, 1976-79.
Mrs **Dorothy Buckrell**, grants officer, London boroughs grants unit. Mbr, Surrey CC. B 1941; ed Willows Sch, Morden; Exeter Univ.
Mr **Peter Sloman**, housing officer. Mbr, Gravesham BC, 1983- (ldr, Lab gp). B Mar 2 1960; ed Gravesend Sch for Boys; Thames Poly. Nalgo.

Sir Patrick Mayhew

TWEEDDALE, ETTRICK AND LAUDERDALE — No change

Electorate %Turnout	37,875	77.2%	**1987**	37,075	77.8%	**1983**
*Steel, D.M.S. (L/All)	14,599	49.9%	-8.5%	16,868	58.5%	(L/All)
Finlay-Maxwell, Mrs S. (C)	8,657	29.6%	+0.7%	8,329	28.9%	(C)
Glen, N. (Lab)	3,320	11.4%	+3.7%	2,200	7.6%	(Lab)
Lumsden, A. (SNP)	2,660	9.1%	+4.1%	1,455	5.0%	(SNP)
L/All to C swing 4.6%	29,236	L/All maj 5,942 20.3%		28,852	L/All maj 8,539 29.6%	

Mr **David Steel** was elected Leader of the Liberal Party in July 1976. Liberal chief whip, 1970-74. Former mbr, Select Cmte on Privileges. Elected for this seat 1983; MP for Roxburgh, Selkirk and Peebles, 1965-83; contested that seat, 1964. Former Lib spokesman on foreign affairs. Sponsored the Abortion Act, 1967, and mbr, Select Cmte on Abortion (Amendment) Bill, 1975-76. Pres, Anti-Apartheid Movement in Great Britain, 1966-69; chmn, Scottish Advisory Cl of Shelter, 1968-72. Journalist and broadcaster. B Mar 31 1938 in Scotland; ed Prince of Wales Sch, Nairobi; George Watson's Coll, Edinburgh; Edinburgh Univ. Vice-pres, Liberal International. Mbr, British Cl of Churches, 1971-75. Rector, Univ of Edinburgh, 1982-85.
Mrs **Shirley Finlay-Maxwell** was a senior executive with a textile finishing company. Mbr, Kirklees MDC, 1978-82 and 1983-86. B Feb 27 1935; ed Galashiels Acad; St Leonard's Sch, St Andrews.
Mr **Neil Glen**, building society business development officer. B Jun 5 1950; ed Macalpine Primary Sch and Kirkton HS, Dundee. Chmn, Cunninghame North CLP; Ayrshire Fabian Soc; Dalby branch LP. ASTMS; nat exec mbr, Halifax Building Soc Staff Assocn.
Mr David Steel
Mr **Andrew Lumsden** runs his own knitwear business. SNP's first regional cllr in the Borders. B 1959; ed Herriot-Watt Univ.

TWICKENHAM — No change

Electorate %Turnout	64,661	81.5%	**1987**	64,116	77.8%	**1983**
*Jessel, T.F.H. (C)	27,331	51.9%	+1.5%	25,110	50.4%	(C)
Waller, J. (L/All)	20,204	38.3%	-2.4%	20,318	40.8%	(L/All)
Vaz, Ms V.C.M. (Lab)	4,415	8.4%	+0.9%	3,732	7.5%	(Lab)
Batchelor, D.S. (Grn)	746	1.4%	+0.5%	424	0.9%	(Eco)
				274	0.5%	(Other)
L/All to C swing 2.0%	52,696	C maj 7,127 13.5%		49,858	C maj 4,792 9.6%	

Mr Toby Jessel was elected in 1970; contested Hull North, at by-election and general election, 1966, and Peckham, 1964. Mbr, Cl of Europe and WEU, since 1976; exec and organizing cmtes, European Music Year, 1985; Liveryman, Worshipful Company of Musicians. B Jul 11 1934; ed RNC Dartmouth; Balliol Coll, Oxford. Mbr, GLC, for Richmond upon Thames, 1967-73; Southwark BC, 1964-66; Metropolitan Water Boards, 1967-70; London Airport Consultative Cmte, 1967-70. Jt vice-chmn, Cons back-bench arts and heritage cmte, 1979-82, chmn, 1983- ; chmn, Anglo-Belian parly gp; sec, Indo-British gp.

Mr John Waller, computer systems engineer and company chairman, contested this seat in 1983 and 1979. Mbr, London Borough of Richmond uopon Thames Cl, since 1973. B Apr 14 1940; ed Sir Roger Manwood's Sch, Sandwich; Caius Coll, Cambridge.

Ms Valerie Vaz, lawyer. B Dec 7 1954; ed Twickenham CS; Bedford Coll, London.

Mr David Batchelor, economist. B Mar 8 1963; ed Hampton GS; St John's Coll, Oxford. Cl election agent, 1986.

Mr Toby Jessel

TYNE BRIDGE — No change

Electorate %Turnout	58,152	63.1%	**1987**	60,808	61.5%	**1983**
*Clelland, D.G. (Lab)	23,131	63.0%	+6.6%	21,127	56.5%	(Lab)
Bates, M.W. (C)	7,558	20.6%	-4.6%	9,434	25.2%	(C)
Mansfield, J.C. (SDP/All)	6,005	16.4%	-1.9%	6,852	18.3%	(L/All)
C to Lab swing 5.6%	36,694	Lab maj 15,573 42.4%		37,413	Lab maj 11,693 31.3%	

Mr David Clelland was elected at the 1985 by-election. Mbr, Select Cmte on Home Affairs, 1985-87; Select Cmte on Parliamentary Commissioner for Administration, 1985-87. B Jun 27 1943; ed Kelvin Grove Boys' Sch, Gateshead; Gateshead and Hebburn Tech Colls. Electrical tester, 1964-81. Mbr, Gateshead BC, 1972-86 (leader, 1984-85). Nat sec, Assocn of Councillors, 1981-85. Sponsored by AEU.

Mr Michael Bates, investment adviser. Chmn, Northern Area YCs, 1985- ; mbr, nat YCs advisory cmte; nat union exec cmte. Vice-pres, Gateshead YCs; vice-chmn, Northern Area Cons Central Cl. B May 26 1961; ed Heathfield Senior HS, Gateshead; Gateshead Tech Coll. Mbr, Tyne and Wear Community Relations Cl; chmn, Gateshead Inter-Church youth cmte.

Dr John Mansfield, house officer. Has served on Newcastle and Gateshead SDP area pty cmtes. B Oct 14 1961; ed Merchant Taylors', Northwood; St John's Coll, Oxford; Newcastle Medical Sch. BMA.

Details of 1985 by-election on Page 285

Mr David Clelland

TYNEMOUTH — No change

Electorate %Turnout	74,407	78.1%	**1987**	74,549	74.6%	**1983**
*Trotter, N.G. (C)	25,113	43.2%	-5.4%	27,029	48.6%	(C)
Cosgrove, P. (Lab)	22,530	38.8%	+7.5%	17,420	31.3%	(Lab)
Mayhew, D.F. (L/All)	10,446	18.0%	-2.1%	11,153	20.1%	(L/All)
C to Lab swing 6.4%	58,089	C maj 2,583 4.4%		55,602	C maj 9,609 17.3%	

Mr Neville Trotter, chartered accountant, has been on the Select Cmte on Transport, since 1983. A director of William Bairds plc; consultant with Grant Thornton, formerly Thornton Baker (former partner), parly adviser to British Marine Equipment Cl. Chmn, ABTA parly cmte; sec, Cons back-bench industry cmte, 1979-83; ex-chmn, shipping and shipbuilding cmte; jt sec, aviation cmte. Elected in Feb 1974; contested Consett, 1970. B Jan 27 1932; ed Shrewsbury Sch; King's Coll, Durham. Mbr, Newcastle City Cl, 1963-74; Tyne and Wear MBC, 1973-74; vice-chmn, Northumberland Police Authority, 1970-74. Mbr, Public Expenditure Cmte and its trade and industry sub-cmte, 1974-79; Northern Economic Planning Cl, 1969-74. Sponsored private Bills on consumer safety, licensing amendment, and intoxicating substances supply.

Mr Patrick Cosgrove, barrister and former teacher in Newcastle comprehensive schools, contested the seat 1983 and 1979. Cllr, Whitley Bay, then mbr, North Tyneside Cl, 1970- . B Apr 29 1947; ed St Cuthbert's GS, Newcastle; Leeds Univ. TGWU.

Mr David Mayhew, development officer for Toc H, contested this seat 1983. B Jul 31 1951; ed St Paul's Sch, London; Christ Church, Oxford; Wycliffe Hall, Oxford; Newcastle Poly.

Mr Neville Trotter

ULSTER MID — No change

Electorate %Turnout	67,256	77.4%	**1987**	63,899	84.3%	**1983**
*McCrea, Rev R.T.W. (DUP)	23,004	44.2%	+14.2%	16,174	30.0%	(DUP)
Haughey, P.D. (SDLP)	13,644	26.2%	+3.8%	16,096	29.9%	(PSF)
Begley, S. (PSF)	12,449	23.9%	-6.0%	12,044	22.4%	(SDLP)
Bogan, P. (All)	1,846	3.5%	+0.3%	7,066	13.1%	(OUP)
McClean, P.J. (WP)	1,133	2.2%	+0.8%	1,735	3.2%	(All)
				766	1.4%	(Other)
SDLP to DUP swing 5.2%	52,076	DUP maj 9,360 18.0%		53,881	DUP maj 78 0.1%	

The Rev William McCrea, a minister of the Free Presbyterian Church of Ulster since 1967, was elected in 1983; resigned seat in 1985 in protest at Anglo-Irish Agreement and retained it at 1986 by-election. Member for Mid Ulster, N Ireland Assembly, 1982-86. Gospel recording artist; director, Daybreak Recording Co. B Aug 6 1948; ed Cookstown GS; Theological Coll, Free Presbyterian Church of Ulster. Member, Magherafelt DC, since 1973 (chmn, 1977-81); vice-pres, Assocn of NI Local Authorities, 1980-81.
Mr Denis Haughey, former teacher now full-time agent for pty ldr, Mr John Hume. B Oct 3 1944. Chmn, SDLP, 1973-78. SDLP Assembly mbr, Mid Ulster, 1982-86. Fought Fermanagh and South Tyrone, 1974, and Mid Ulster, 1983. ,
Mr Sean Begley, chmn, Mid-Ulster PSF exec. Aged 34. Engineer.
Mr Patrick Bogan, teacher, is president, Alliance Pty. B Mar 27 1941; ed Christian Brothers GS, Omagh; St Joseph's Coll of Ed.
Details of 1986 by-election on Page 285

The Rev William McCrea

UPMINSTER — No change

Electorate %Turnout	66,613	75.2%	**1987**	66,445	72.1%	**1983**
*Bonsor, Sir Nicholas (C)	27,946	55.8%	+3.3%	25,153	52.5%	(C)
Martin, J. (SDP/All)	11,089	22.1%	-3.6%	12,339	25.8%	(SDP/All)
O'Flynn, D.R. (Lab)	11,069	22.1%	+1.6%	9,829	20.5%	(Lab)
				566	1.2%	(Other)
SDP/All to C swing 3.4%	50,104	C maj 16,857 33.6%		47,887	C maj 12,814 26.8%	

Sir Nicholas Bonsor, barrister, farmer and underwriting member of Lloyd's, won this seat in 1983; MP for Nantwich, 1979-83; fought Newcastle under Lyme, Feb and Oct 1974. Vice-chmn, Standing Cl of the Baronetage, 1987- . Chmn, Food Hygiene Bureau Ltd. B Dec 9 1942; ed Eton; Keble Coll, Oxford. Mbr, CLA Legal and Parly sub-cmte, since 1978. Fellow, Royal Soc of Arts. Chmn, Cyclotron Trust for Cancer Treatment, 1984- ; vice-chmn, Cons backbench foreign and Commonwealth affairs cmte, 1981-83; trustee, Baronets' Trust, 1986- ; Verdin Trust for Mentally Handicapped, 1983- . Mbr, Royal Yacht Squadron.
Mr John Martin, chmn and managing director of Planning Research and Systems, supplier of automative market and product information, contested Hornchurch 1983, and Worcester 1964 for Lab. Mbr, Haringey BC, 1964-68; Hornsey BC, 1962-64. B Apr 6 1936; ed GS and LSE. Former sec, Consumer Cl.
Mr Denis O'Flynn, trade union organiser. Contested Havering, Romford Feb and Oct 1974 and Hitchen 1979. Mbr, Havering Borough Council, 1971- . B Jan 21 1933; ed St Patrick's Sch, Cork. AUEW.

Sir Nicholas Bonsor

UPPER BANN — No change

Electorate %Turnout	64,540	65.6%	**1987**	60,795	72.0%	**1983**
*McCusker, J.H. (OUP)	26,037	61.5%	+4.6%	24,888	56.9%	(OUP)
Rodgers, Mrs B. (SDLP)	8,676	20.5%	+2.6%	7,807	17.8%	(SDLP)
Curran, B.P. (PSF)	3,126	7.4%	-2.0%	4,547	10.4%	(DUP)
Cook, Mrs M.F.A. (All)	2,487	5.9%		4,110	9.4%	(PSF)
French, T. (WP)	2,004	4.7%	-0.7%	2,392	5.5%	(WP)
SDLP to OUP swing 1.0%	42,330	OUP maj 17,361 41.0%		43,744	OUP maj 17,081 39.0%	

Mr Harold McCusker won the seat in 1983; resigned it in 1985 in protest at Anglo-Irish Agreement and retained it at 1986 by-election; MP for Armagh, Feb 1974-83. Teacher, 1961-68; personal officer-production manager, 1968-74. B Feb 7 1940; ed Lurgan Coll; Stranmillis Coll, Belfast. Chief whip, UU Pty, Westminster, 1975-76. Chmn, Northern Ireland Gas Employers' Board, 1977-81. Member, NI Assembly, 1982-86. Fellow, Industry and Parliament Trust.
Mr Brid Rodgers, chaired the SDLP in 1978; pty gen Sec, 1981-1983. Mbr, Irish Republic Senate, 1983-86; Craigavon BC, 1985- .
Mr Brendan Curran, unemployed electrician. Aged 37. PSF member, Craigavon BC, 1985- . Spent 7<OS> years as prisoner in the Maze.
Ms Fionnuala Cook, teacher, is Alliance spokeswoman on women's rights. B May 3 1946; ed Convent of Mercy Primary Sch, Lurgan; Univ Coll, Dublin. Vice-chmn (1979), N Ireland cmte, International Yr of the Child. Chmn, Banbridge Alliance Assocn.
Details of 1986 by-election on Page 285.

Mr Harold McCusker

UXBRIDGE — No change

Electorate %Turnout	63,157	76.5%	1987	61,615	72.3%	1983
*Shersby, J.M. (C)	27,292	56.5%	+2.9%	23,875	53.6%	(C)
Keys, D. (Lab)	11,322	23.4%	+1.8%	11,038	24.8%	(SDP/All)
Goodman, A. (SDP/All)	9,164	19.0%	-5.8%	9,611	21.6%	(Lab)
Flindall, I. (Grn)	549	1.1%				
Lab to C swing 0.5%	48,327	C maj 15,970 33.0%		44,524	C maj 12,837 28.8%	

Mr **Michael Shersby,** member of the Public Accounts Cmte and the Chairmen's Panel, since 1983. Elected as MP for Hillingdon, Uxbridge, in 1972 by-election. Director General, British Sugar Bureau, since 1977 (director, 1966-77); sec, UK Sugar Industry Assocn, since 1978. B Feb 17 1933; ed John Lyon Sch, Harrow-on-the-Hill. Chmn, Cons back-bench trade cmte, 1974-76; food and drink sub-cmte, 1979- . Jt sec, 1977-80, and vice-pres, 1980-83, parly and scientific cmte. Vice-chmn, Cons environment cmte, 1979-1983; Cons smaller businesses cmte, 1979-80 and 1983. Mbr, cl, Food and Drink Fed; treas, World Sugar Research Organization. Mbr, Court, Brunel Univ, 1975- ; Paddington BC, 1959-64; Westminster City Cl, 1964-71; Dep Lord Mayor, 1967-68.
Mr **David Keys,** journalist. B Apr 4 1950. Mbr, Hillingdon CND.
Mr **Anthony Goodman,** marketing and research executive, new projects, with financial services company. B Jul 30 1963; ed state schools and New Coll, Oxford. Founder, Nat Young Social Democrats; member CSD; SDP nat cmte's youth working gp; Tawney Soc nat cmte; David Owen advisory research group. ASTMS.

Mr Michael Shersby

VALE OF GLAMORGAN — No change

Electorate %Turnout	65,310	79.3%	1987	62,885	74.2%	1983
*Gower, Sir Raymond (C)	24,229	46.8%	-1.3%	22,421	48.0%	(C)
Smith, J.W.P. (Lab)	17,978	34.7%	+8.9%	12,028	25.8%	(Lab)
Davies, D.K. (SDP/All)	8,633	16.7%	-7.2%	11,154	23.9%	(SDP/All)
Williams, P.G. (Pl C)	946	1.8%	-0.5%	1,068	2.3%	(Pl C)
C to Lab swing 5.1%	51,786	C maj 6,251 12.1%		46,671	C maj 10,393 22.3%	

Sir Raymond Gower has been a Vice-President of the National Chamber of Trade since 1956. Solicitor; director of Airport Hotels Ltd, British Soil Ltd and Broughton and Co (Bristol) Ltd. Elected for this seat 1983; MP for Barry, 1951-83; contested Ogmore, 1950. B Aug 15 1916; ed Neath GS; Cardiff HS; Univ Coll, Cardiff; Cardiff Sch of Law. PPS to ministers, 1951-60. Chmn, Welsh Cons MPs, 1970-97 and since 1979; vice-chmn, 1974-79. Treas, Welsh parly pty (all-pty), 1966- . Mbr, Speaker's conference on electoral reform, 1967-69 and 1971-74; Select Cmte on Welsh Affairs, 1979-83. Governor, Univ Coll, Cardiff, since 1954; mbr, Court of Governors, Nat Museum of Wales, since 1952; Nat Library of Wales, since 1951, and Univ Coll, Aberystwyth, since 1955.
Mr **John Smith,** tutor for the TUC. Mbr, Barry DC (Ldr, Lab gp). B Mar 17 1951. Mbr, WEA, Anti-Apartheid, AUT.
Mr **Keith Davies,** fitter and turner in petro-chemical industry, contested Neath 1983. B Jul 24 1946. Former trade union convenor and shop steward.
Mr **Penri Williams,** electrical engineer at Aberthaw Power Station. Mbr, Mid Glamorgan CC. Aged 36; ed Cowbridge GS; Poly of Wales, Pontypridd.

Sir Raymond Gower

VAUXHALL — No change

Electorate %Turnout	66,538	64.0%	1987	64,867	60.5%	1983
*Holland, S.K. (Lab)	21,364	50.2%	+3.7%	18,234	46.5%	(Lab)
Lidington, D.R. (C)	12,345	29.0%	+2.3%	10,454	26.7%	(C)
Acland, S.H.V. (SDP/All)	7,764	18.2%	-6.0%	9,515	24.3%	(SDP/All)
Owens, Ms J. (Grn)	770	1.8%		508	1.3%	(NF)
Cook, D.J.S. (Comm)	223	0.5%		266	0.7%	(Loony Soc)
Oluremi, K. (RF)	117	0.3%		199	0.5%	(Com)
				38	0.1%	(Other)
C to Lab swing 0.7%	42,583	Lab maj 9,019 21.2%		39,214	Lab maj 7,780 19.8%	

Mr **Stuart Holland** became Opposition spokesman on overseas development and co-operation in 1983. Political economist and supervisor of doctoral theses at Sussex Univ; Visiting Fellow, Sussex European Research Centre, since 1979; associate, Inst of Development Studies, 1974- . Mbr, economic cmte, Socialist International, 1984- . Chmn, Public Enterprise Group, 1973-75; asst economic, Cabinet Office, 1966-67, and personal asst to Prime Minister, 1967-68. Elected in 1979. B Mar 25 1940; ed Christ's Hospital, Univ of Missouri, Balliol Coll and St Antony's Colls, Oxford. Exec mbr, Labour Coordinating Cmte, 1978-81; European Nuclear Disarmament Campaign, 1980-83. Special adviser, Commons Expenditure Cmte, 1971-72; consultant, economic and social affairs cmte, Cl of Europe, 1973; and to Ministry of Overseas Development, 1974-75; OECD, 1977; UN University, 1977-82.
Mr **David Lidington,** press officer. B Jun 30 1956; ed Haberdashers' Aske's Sch; Sidney Sussex Coll, Cambridge
Mr **Simon Acland,** venture capital executive with United Bank of Kuwait. Mbr, Lambeth BC 1982- (ldr, Alliance gp, 1986-). B Mar 27 1958; ed Eton; Lincoln Coll, Oxford.
Mr **Dave Cook,** Comm Pty official. Nat sec, Campaign against Racist Laws. Aged 45.

Mr Stuart Holland

WAKEFIELD — No change

Electorate %Turnout	69,580	75.6%	1987	68,416	69.3%	1983
Hinchliffe, D.M. (Lab)	24,509	46.6%	+6.2%	19,166	40.4%	(Lab)
Hazell, N.J. (C)	21,720	41.3%	+1.7%	18,806	39.6%	(C)
Kamal, Dr L. (SDP/All)	6,350	12.1%	-7.2%	9,166	19.3%	(SDP/All)
				295	0.6%	(Other)
C to Lab swing 2.3%	52,579	Lab maj 2,789 5.3%		47,433	Lab maj 360 0.8%	

Mr David Hinchcliffe, social work tutor with Kirklees MBC. Member, Wakefield Met DC, 1979- (chmn, employment and economic development cmtes); Wakefield health authority; former mbr, Wakefield City Cl; former chmn, Wakefield Trades Cl. B Oct 14 1948; ed Wakefield Tech Coll; Leeds Poly; Bradford Univ. NUPE.
Mr Norman Hazell, draughtsman, contested the seat in 1983. Mbr, Wakefield MDC, 1982- ; chmn, Wakefield East Con Assocn, 1974- . B Apr 17 1932; ed Thornes House GS and Wakefield Tech Coll. Partner, Titan Flooring Ltd, Wakefield.
Dr Lufte Kamal, medical practitioner. Mbr, SDP nat cmte, 1983-86; SDP finance cmte, 1983-86; working pty on health, local govt and aid to the third world. Chmn, Hemsworth TC, 1981-82; mbr, Wakefield City Cl, 1978-86 (ldr, SDP gp, 1982-86). B Dec 31 1939; ed Univ of Dacca, Bangladesh. Chmn, Wakefield Division BMA, 1983-85, previously vice-chmn and sec.

Mr David Hinchcliffe

WALLASEY — No change

Electorate %Turnout	67,216	79.8%	1987	68,462	72.6%	1983
*Chalker, Mrs L. (C)	22,791	42.5%	-3.5%	22,854	46.0%	(C)
Duffy, L. (Lab)	22,512	41.9%	+9.5%	16,146	32.5%	(Lab)
Richardson, J.K. (SDP/All)	8,363	15.6%	-6.0%	10,717	21.6%	(SDP/All)
C to Lab swing 6.5%	53,666	C maj 279 0.5%		49,717	C maj 6,708 13.5%	

Mrs Lynda Chalker was appointed Minister of State for Foreign and Commonwealth Affairs in 1986; Minister of State for Transport, 1983-86; Under Secretary of State for Transport, 1982-83; Under Secretary of State for Health and Social Security, 1979-82; an Opposition spokesman on social services, 1976-79. Elected in Feb 1974. B Apr 29 1942; ed Roedean; Heidelberg Univ; Westfield Coll, London Univ; Central London Poly. Statistician; chief exec, international division, Louis Harris International Ltd, 1972-74; dep market research manager, Shell Mex and BD Ltd, 1969-72; Research Bureau Ltd (Unilever), 1963-69. Mbr, General Advisory Cl of BBC, 1975-79. Ex-parly adviser, Market Research Soc. Nat vice-chmn, YCs, 1970-71. Has served on Cons Nat Union Exec Cmte; CPC Nat Advisory Cmte; Select Cmte on Race Relations and Immigration.
Mr Lawrence Duffy, welfare rights resource officer and former steelworker. B Apr 19 1955. Was sec, occupation strike cmte to save Cammell Lairds shipyard, Birkenhead. Chmn, Merseyside Campaign Against Security Cuts. TGWU.
Mr Jonathan Richardson, teacher, contested the seat 1983. First chmn, Wallasey SDP; mbr, CSD, 1982-84. B Feb 18 1951; ed Lancaster and Liverpool Univs; St John's Coll of Ed, York. NUT.

Mrs Lynda Chalker

WALLSEND — No change

Electorate %Turnout	76,688	75.0%	1987	76,268	71.1%	1983
*Garrett, W.E. (Lab)	32,709	56.8%	+7.8%	26,615	49.1%	(Lab)
Milburn, D. (C)	13,325	23.2%	-2.8%	14,101	26.0%	(C)
Phylactou, Mrs J. (SDP/All)	11,508	20.0%	-4.9%	13,522	24.9%	(SDP/All)
C to Lab swing 5.3%	57,542	Lab maj 19,384 33.7%		54,238	Lab maj 12,514 23.1%	

Mr Edward Garrett, an engineer, was elected in 1964; contested Hexham, 1955; Doncaster, 1959. Chmn (and former sec), all-party group for chemical industry. Employed by and union organiser at ICI, 1946-64. B Mar 21 1920; ed Prudhoe elementary sch; LSE. Delegate to Cl of Europe and WEU, 1979- . Parliamentary adviser to Machine Tools Trades Assocn and to BAT Industries. Chmn, British-Czech parly gp. Mbr, exec cmte, UK branch CPA, 1986-87; Public Expenditure Cmte, 1971-79; Select Cmte on Agriculture, 1966-69; Prudhoe UDC, 1946-64; Northumberland CC, 1955-64. Sponsored by AUEW.
Mr David Milburn, technical sales agent and engineer. B 1940; ed Clegwell Modern Sch; Hebburn Tech Coll. Former constituency pty chmn; mbr, Northern CPC cmte.
Mrs Joan Phylactou, senior lecturer in industrial psychology at Newcastle Poly. Contested the seat, 1983. Dep ldr, Alliance gp, North Tyneside MBC; mbr, CSD; SDP national cmte. B 1947; ed Univ Coll and Birkbeck Coll, London.

Mr Edward Garrett

WALSALL NORTH — No change

Electorate %Turnout	68,331	73.8%	1987	68,868	71.0%	1983
*Winnick, D.J. (Lab)	21,458	42.6%	+0.1%	20,782	42.5%	(Lab)
Hertz, Mrs L. (C)	19,668	39.0%	+2.3%	17,958	36.7%	(C)
Shires, I. (L/All)	9,285	18.4%	-2.3%	10,141	20.7%	(L/All)
Lab to C swing 1.1%	50,411	Lab maj 1,790 3.6%		48,881	Lab maj 2,824 5.8%	

Mr **David Winnick** has been on the Select Cmte on Home Affairs since 1983; on Select Cmte on Environment, 1980-83. Jt vice-chmn, PLP foreign affairs cmte, 1985- ; vice-chmn, West Midlands Group of Lab MPs, 1985- . Regained seat for Labour in 1979; MP for Croydon South, 1966-70; contested Harwich 1964; Croydon Central, Oct 1974, and Walsall, Nov 1976. B Jun 26 1933; ed secondary schools and LSE. Chmn, Tribune Group, 1984-85; chmn (unpaid), UK Immigrants Advisory Service, 1984- . Mbr, Select Cmte on Race Relations and Immigration, 1969-70; Willesden Cl, 1959-64; Brent Cl, 1964-66. Vice-pres, APEX, since 1983; sponsored by APEX.

Dr Leah Hertz, entrepreneur and academic; chmn, Crochetata gp of companies; senior visiting fellow, City Univ business sch. Mbr, Barnet BC. B Sep 27 1937; ed Hebrew Univ of Jerusalem; City of London Univ; Darwin Coll, Cambridge. Holds karata black belt (1st Dan).

Mr Ian Shires, production supervisor, has been on Walsall MBC since 1979; leader, Lib gp. B Sep 1 1944; ed Pelsall Sec Mod Sch; Walsall Tech Coll; Wednesbury Commercial Coll. MATSA.

Mr David Winnick

WALSALL SOUTH — No change

Electorate %Turnout	66,746	75.5%	1987	67,257	74.3%	1983
*George, B.T. (Lab)	22,629	44.9%	+1.4%	21,735	43.5%	(Lab)
Postles, G.E. (C)	21,513	42.7%	+0.6%	21,033	42.1%	(C)
King, L.A. (L/All)	6,241	12.4%	-0.8%	6,586	13.2%	(SDP/All)
				632	1.3%	(Other)
C to Lab swing 0.4%	50,383	Lab maj 1,116 2.2%		49,986	Lab maj 702 1.4%	

Mr Bruce George, a mbr of the Select Committee on Defence since 1979, was elected in Feb 1974; contested Southport, 1970. Author and lecturer on defence and foreign policy subjects. B Jun 1 1942; ed Mountain Ash GS;, Univ Coll of Wales, Swansea; Warwick Univ. Visiting lecturer, Essex Univ, 1985-86; senior lecturer in politics, Birmingham Poly, 1970-74. Chmn, political cmte, N Atlantic Assembly, 1976- . Served on former Select Cmte on Violence in the Family; former sec, all-pty parly gp on widows and one-parent families; patron, Nat Assocn of Widows; vice-pres, Psoriasis Assocn; hon consultant, Confed of Long Distance Pigeon Racing Assocns; co-founder, sec and captain, House of Commons Football Club; pres, Walsall and District Gilbert and Sullivan Soc. Apex and NATFHE.

Mr Graham Postles, marketing and development manager for an insurance broking group. B Aug 21 1957; ed Aldridge GS; Selby GS; City of Birmingham Poly.

Mr Lionel King, senior lecturer TV production, Sandwell Coll of Further and Higher Ed, W Midlands, fought Kidderminster 1964, Sutton Coldfield 1970. Chmn, W Midlands Regional Lib Pty, 1962-63; mbr, pty nat exec, 1963-64. B Jul 7 1936; ed Leyton County HS; Birmingham Univ. NAS/UWT 1961-85; NATFHE since 1985.

Mr Bruce George

WALTHAMSTOW — C gain

Electorate %Turnout	48,691	72.4%	1987	48,324	68.8%	1983
Summerson, H.H.F. (C)	13,748	39.0%	+3.1%	13,241	39.8%	(Lab)
*Deakins, E.P. (Lab)	12,236	34.7%	-5.1%	11,936	35.9%	(C)
Leighton, P.L. (SDP/All)	8,852	25.1%	+3.5%	7,192	21.6%	(SDP/All)
Malik, Dr Z.I. (DC)	396	1.1%		444	1.3%	(NF)
				424	1.3%	(Other)
Lab to C swing 4.1%	35,232	C maj 1,512 4.3%		33,237	Lab maj 1,305 3.9%	

Mr Hugo Summerson, chartered surveyor, contested Barking 1983. B Jul 21 1950; ed Harrow; Royal Agricultural Coll.

Mr Eric Deakins was a mbr of the Public Accounts Committee, 1983-87, and jt hon sec, all-pty gp on overseas development; hon sec, British-American parly gp. Author. MP for this seat, Feb 1974-87; for Walthamstow West, 1970-74; contested Finchley, 1959; Chigwell, 1966 and Walthamstow West, 1967. Former Opposition spokesman on agriculture and food. Mbr, Select Cmte on Foreign Affairs and Overseas Development sub-cmte, 1979-82. Under Secretary of State, DHSS, 1976-79; Under Secretary of State for Trade, 1974-76. B Oct 7 1932; ed Tottenham GS and LSE. With FMC (Meat) Ltd, 1956-71, being general manager, Pigs Division, from 1969. Mbr, Tottenham BC, 1958-61, 1962-63. TGWU.

Mr Peter Leighton, barrister, a founder-mbr of SDP. Contested the seat 1983. B Oct 16 1943; ed Leyton Cty HS; Univ Coll, London. Labour mbr, Waltham Forest BC, 1970-78; chmn, educ cmte, 1972-78; represented cl on AMA and London Boroughs Assocn educ cmtes. Chmn, Waltham Forest SDP, 1981- . School, coll and poly governor.

Mr Hugo Summerson

WANSBECK — No change

Electorate %Turnout	62,639	78.0%	**1987**	63,398	72.9%	**1983**
*Thompson, J. (Lab)	28,080	57.5%	+10.4%	21,732	47.0%	(Lab)
Mitchell, Mrs S. (L/All)	11,291	23.1%	-7.0%	13,901	30.1%	(L/All)
Walton, D. (C)	9,490	19.4%	-3.4%	10,563	22.9%	(C)
L/All to Lab swing 8.7%	48,861	Lab maj 16,789 34.4%		46,196	Lab maj 7,831 17.0%	

Mr John Thompson, a mbr of the Select Committee on Education, Science and Arts since 1985; vice-chmn, PLP education, science and arts cmte, 1985-86; sec, Northern group of Lab MPs. Elected in 1983. Former electrical engineer at Ellington Colliery. B Aug 27 1928; ed Bothal Sch and Ashington Mining Coll. Mbr, board, Northumberland Water Authority, 1981-83; Northumberland CC, 1974-83 (Leader of opposition, 1978-81, vice-chmn and leader of cl, 1981-83); Wansbeck DC, 1974-79; Newbiggin by the Seas UDC, 1970-74. Sponsored by NUM.

Mrs Sarah Mitchell, consultant social worker and social work tutor. Mbr, Alnwick DC; Northumberland Family Practitioner Cmte. B 1951; ed Kesteven and Sleaford HS; Ipswich Civil Coll.

Mr David Walton, investment adviser with firm of stockbrokers. B Aug 11 1959; ed Bedlington County HS, Northumberland. EETPU.

Mr John Thompson

WANSDYKE — No change

Electorate %Turnout	75,239	81.3%	**1987**	71,094	79.0%	**1983**
*Aspinwall, J.H. (C)	31,537	51.6%	+1.0%	28,434	50.6%	(C)
Blackmore, R.B. (L/All)	15,393	25.2%	-2.2%	15,368	27.4%	(L/All)
White, I. (Lab)	14,231	23.3%	+1.6%	12,168	21.7%	(Lab)
				213	0.4%	(Other)
L/All to C swing 1.6%	61,161	C maj 16,144 26.4%		56,183	C maj 13,066 23.3%	

Mr Jack Aspinwall, a mbr of the Select Cmte on Parliamentary Commissioner for Administration since 1983; jt sec, Cons back-bench aviation cmte, 1985- . Director of an investment company and consultant; director of family business of retail shops, 1956-66. Won this seat 1983; MP for Kingswood, 1979-83; contested it Feb and Oct 1974 as a Liberal. B Feb 1933; ed Prescott GS, Bootle; Marconi Coll, Chelmsford. Mbr, Avon CC and Kingswood DC.

Mr Roger Blackmore, college lecturer, contested Devon North 1983, Gainsborough 1979, twice in 1974, 1970. B Dec 30 1941; ed Abingdon Sch; Shebbear Coll, N Devon; Leicester Univ.

Mr Ian White, solicitor. B Apr 8 1945. Ed Merrywood GS, Bristol.

Mr Jack Aspinwall

WANSTEAD AND WOODFORD — No change

Electorate %Turnout	57,921	72.4%	**1987**	57,705	68.4%	**1983**
Arbuthnot, J.N. (C)	25,701	61.3%	+1.0%	23,765	60.3%	(C)
Bastick, J.R. (L/All)	9,289	22.1%	-1.7%	9,411	23.9%	(L/All)
Hilton, Mrs L. (Lab)	6,958	16.6%	+3.1%	5,334	13.5%	(Lab)
				932	2.4%	(Other)
L/All to C swing 1.4%	41,948	C maj 16,412 39.1%		39,442	C maj 14,354 36.4%	

Mr James Arbuthnot, a Chancery barrister, contested Cynon Valley in 1983 and 1984 by-election. Mbr, Royal Borough of Kensington and Chelsea Council, since 1978, being chmn of works cmte, Deputy Mayor, vice-chmn of housing, and chief whip. Specialises in tax, company law, landlord and tenant law, probate and trust law. B Aug 4 1952; ed Eton; Trinity Coll, Cambridge.

Mr John Bastick, managing director of advertising and marketing company, contested Harlow 1983. Press officer, Brentwood Lib Assocn; chmn of branch organisations, Brentwood. B Apr 12 1942; ed Malmesbury GS; Regent St Poly.

Mrs Lesley Hilton contested Wanstead and Woodford 1983. B Jul 30 1949; ed Maidstone GS. Mbr, Nat Union of Students.

Mr James Arbuthnot

WANTAGE — No change

Electorate %Turnout	66,499	77.9%	**1987**	63,950	76.9%	**1983**
*Jackson, R.V. (C)	27,951	54.0%	+1.1%	25,992	52.9%	(C)
Tumin, Mrs W. (SDP/All)	15,795	30.5%	-1.8%	15,867	32.3%	(SDP/All)
Ladyman, S. (Lab)	8,055	15.5%	+1.1%	7,115	14.5%	(Lab)
				183	0.4%	(Other)
SDP/All to C swing 1.4%	51,801	C maj 12,156 23.5%		49,157	C maj 10,125 20.6%	

Mr Robert Jackson

Mr Robert Jackson was appointed an Under Secretary of State for Education and Science in Jun 1987. Mbr, Select Cmte on Energy, 1987. Jt sec, Cons back-bench agriculture, fisheries and food cmte, 1985-87; and to foreign affairs cmte, 1985-87. Political adviser to Lord Soames when Governor of Rhodesia in 1980. Elected in 1983; contested Manchester Central, Oct 1974. Mbr, European Parliament, for Upper Thames, 1979-84, being rapporteur for the EP on the 1983 EEC budget. B Sep 24 1946; ed Falcon Coll, near Bulawayo, and St Edmund Hall and All Souls, Oxford (Pres of Union, 1967; Fellow, 1968-86). Mbr, Oxford City Cl, 1969-71. Served in private office of the then Sir Christopher Soames, Vice-President of EEC Commission, 1974-76; Chef de Cabinet to chmn of EEC's Economic and Social Cmte, then Mr Basil de Ferranti, 1976-78.
Mrs Winifred Tumin, freelance lecturer and writer on deafness and disability; chmn, Royal Nat Inst for the Deaf. Mbr, Warnock Cmte on special education. Contested the seat in 1983. Member, CSD, 1982-86; chmn, working pty on disabled. B Jun 3 1936; ed North Fordland Lodge Sch; Lady Margaret Hall, Oxford.
Dr Stephen Ladyman, computer scientist. B Nov 6 1952; ed Liverpool Poly; Strathclyde Univ. ASTMS.

WARLEY EAST — No change

Electorate %Turnout	55,706	69.4%	**1987**	57,439	68.9%	**1983**
*Faulds, A.M.W. (Lab)	19,428	50.2%	+4.7%	18,036	45.6%	(Lab)
Antoniou, A. (C)	13,843	35.8%	-1.2%	14,645	37.0%	(C)
Jordan, J.J. (SDP/All)	5,396	14.0%	-3.0%	6,697	16.9%	(SDP/All)
				217	0.5%	(Other)
C to Lab swing 2.9%	38,667	Lab maj 5,585 14.4%		39,595	Lab maj 3,391 8.6%	

Mr Andrew Faulds

Mr Andrew Faulds, actor who, in the Register of MPs' Interests, says he has a "valuable voice", was Opposition spokesman on the arts, 1970-73, and 1979-82. Elected for this seat, Feb 1974; MP for Smethwick, 1966-74; contested Stratford upon Avon, 1963 and 1964. B Mar 1 1923; ed George Watson's, Louth GS, Daniel Stewart's, Edinburgh, Stirling HS and Glasgow Univ. Mbr, Commons Services Cmte, since 1983. Delegate to Cl of Europe and WEU, 1975-80. Mbr, Equity (cl member, 1966-69). Jt chmn, all-pty heritage group. Chmn, British branch, Parly Assocn for Euro-Arab Cooperation, 1974- . Exec cmte mbr, GB-China Centre, 1976- ; Franco-British Cl, 1978- ; IPU, British section, 1983- .
Mr Anthony Antoniou, banker with Coutts & Co since 1977; active in running family business. Mbr, London Borough of Barnet Cl, 1986- . B Apr 26 1953; ed Friern Barnet GS for Boys; Boreham Wood CFE; Middlesex Poly. Member, NWSA, clearing bank union; branch rep, 1984-86.
Mr Jonathan Jordan, teacher. Founder mbr of SDP. Gen sec, Sandwell area pty, 1982-86; policy officer, W Midlands reg cl, 1986- . B May 28 1951; ed Wallingford GS, Oxford; City of Birmingham Coll of Ed; Birmingham Poly; Warwick Univ. Member, Bournville Hockey Club. NAS.

WARLEY WEST — No change

Electorate %Turnout	57,526	70.0%	**1987**	57,165	67.8%	**1983**
*Archer, P.K. (Lab)	19,825	49.2%	+2.1%	18,272	47.1%	(Lab)
Williams, W. (C)	14,432	35.8%	+2.3%	13,004	33.5%	(C)
Todd, Miss E. (L/All)	6,027	15.0%	-4.3%	7,485	19.3%	(L/All)
Lab to C swing 0.1%	40,284	Lab maj 5,393 13.4%		38,761	Lab maj 5,268 13.6%	

Mr Peter Archer

Mr Peter Archer, QC, has been chief Opposition spokesman on Northern Ireland since 1983. Elected to Shadow Cabinet in 1981; chief Opposition spokesman on legal affairs, 1981-82, and on trade, 1982-83. Solicitor General, 1974-79; PPS to Attorney General, 1967-70. Elected in Feb 1974; MP for Rowley Regis and Tipton, 1966-74; contested Brierley Hill, 1964, and Hendon South, 1959. Recorder. B Nov 20 1926; ed Wednesbury HS, LSE and Univ Coll, London. Chmn, Soc of Labour Lawyers, 1970-74, and 1979- ; exec cmte, Fabian Soc, 1980- ; Amnesty (British section), 1971-74. Jt vice-chmn, all-pty parly war crimes gp. Sponsored by APEX.
Mr Wallace Williams, manufacturer's agent and sales consultant, contested Stoke-on-Trent Central 1979 and 1974, and Stafford and Stone, 1970, when Liberal. Mbr, Leek RDC, 1971-73; Staffordshire Moorlands DC, 1974- (chmn, 1977). Chmn, W Midlands Provincial Cl, 1975-85. B Mar 17 1930; ed King Edward VI GS, Stafford. Mbr, exec cmte, Nat Housing and Town Planning Cl.
Miss Elaine Todd, advisory teacher responsible for liaison between education and industry in Dudley; chairs Birmingham Northfield Lib Pty. B Aug 9 1950; ed Bolling GS, Bradford; N Counties Coll of Ed, Newcastle; Keele Univ.

WARRINGTON NORTH · No change

Electorate %Turnout	75,627	75.2%	**1987**	69,850	72.6%	**1983**
*Hoyle, E.D.H. (Lab)	27,422	48.2%	+7.0%	20,873	41.2%	(Lab)
Jones, L. (C)	19,409	34.1%	+3.4%	15,596	30.8%	(C)
Bithel, C. (SDP/All)	10,046	17.7%	-9.9%	13,951	27.5%	(SDP/All)
				267	0.5%	(Other)
C to Lab swing 1.8%	56,877	Lab maj 8,013 14.1%		50,687	Lab maj 5,277 10.4%	

Mr Douglas Hoyle, member of Select Cmte on Trade and Industry since 1984. Elected for this seat 1983; MP for Warrington, 1981-83; and for for Nelson and Colne, Oct 1974 to 1979; contested it in Feb 1974, and 1970; Clitheroe, 1964. Member, Lab Party NEC, 1978-82 and 1983-85. B Feb 17 1930; ed Adlington Sch, Horwich Tech Coll and Bolton Tech Coll. Sales engineer, Charles Weston Ltd, Salford, 1953-75. Member, Cl of "Get Britain Out" (of EEC) Campaign; Manchester Reg Hosp Board, 1968-74; NW RHA, 1974-75. Pres of ASTMS, 1977-81 and since 1985; vice-pres, 1981-85; mbr, nat exec, since 1968, and of union since 1958. Sponsored by the union.
Mr Laurence Jones, undertaker. B 1948; ed Wirral GS; Liverpool Poly.
Mr Colin Bithel, senior production controller with Vauxhall Motors, Cheshire. Contested Crewe 1979 as Liberal candidate. Pres, local SDP branch. Mbr, Flintshire Cl, 1970-74; Alyn and Deeside DC, 1974- . B Apr 28 1935; ed Deeside Comprehensive Sch.

Mr Douglas Hoyle

WARRINGTON SOUTH · No change

Electorate %Turnout	76,219	77.6%	**1987**	72,803	74.5%	**1983**
Butler, C.J. (C)	24,809	42.0%	+0.0%	22,740	41.9%	(C)
Booth, A. (Lab)	21,200	35.9%	+5.9%	16,275	30.0%	(Lab)
Marks, I. (L/All)	13,112	22.2%	-5.2%	14,827	27.3%	(L/All)
				403	0.7%	(Other)
C to Lab swing 2.9%	59,121	C maj 3,609 6.1%		54,245	C maj 6,465 11.9%	

Mr Christopher Butler, political adviser, market researcher and freelance journalist, contested Brecon and Radnor in the 1985 by-election. Served in Cons Research Dept, 1977-80; political office, 10 Downing Street, 1980-83; special adviser, Secretary of State for Wales, 1983-85; and to Minister for the Arts, 1986-87. B Aug 12 1950; ed Cardiff HS for Boys; Emmanuel Coll, Cambridge.
Mr Albert Booth, Secretary of State for Employment, 1976-79, and chief Opposition spokesman on transport, 1979-83, was MP for Barrow-in-Furness, 1966-83, when he unsuccessfully contested Barrow and Furness; contested Tynemouth 1964. Technical director; qualified draughtsman. Former Lab Pty treas. Minister of State for Employment, 1974-76; chmn, Select Cmte on Statutory Instruments, 1970-74; an Opposition spokesman on trade and industry, 1973-74. B May 28 1928; ed St Thomas's, Winchester; South Shields Marine Sch; Rutherford Coll of Tech. Mbr, Tynemouth BC, 1962-65. Was an AUEW(Tass) sponsored MP.
Mr Ian Marks, marketing manager, fought this seat 1983. Mbr, Warrington BC, 1983- ; Lymm PC. B Apr 12 1948; ed Bedford Sch; Churchill Coll, Cambridge; Liverpool Univ.

Mr Christopher Butler

WARWICK AND LEAMINGTON · No change

Electorate %Turnout	72,763	76.0%	**1987**	70,858	73.6%	**1983**
*Smith, Sir Dudley (C)	27,530	49.8%	-1.1%	26,512	50.8%	(C)
O'Sullivan, K.P. (SDP/All)	13,548	24.5%	-1.4%	13,480	25.9%	(SDP/All)
Christina, Ms A. (Lab)	13,019	23.5%	+1.6%	11,463	22.0%	(Lab)
Alty, Ms J.A. (Grn)	1,214	2.2%	+0.9%	685	1.3%	(Eco)
SDP/All to C swing 0.1%	55,311	C maj 13,982 25.3%		52,140	C maj 13,032 25.0%	

Sir Dudley Smith was Under Secretary of Defence for the Army, 1974; Under Secretary of State for Employment, 1970-74; an Opposition spokesman on employment and productivity, 1969-70; an Opposition whip, 1964-66. Elected at 1968 by-election; MP for Brentford and Chiswick, 1959-66; contested Peckham, 1955. Vice-chmn, Select Cmte on Race Relations and Immigration, 1974-79. B Nov 14, 1926; ed Chichester HS. Management consultant with clients who include American Express, the Smith Kling Beckman Corporation and Bass plc. Journalist and senior exec with nat and provincial newspapers, 1943-66. Divisional director, Beecham Group, 1966-70. Mbr, Cl of Europe and WEU, 1979- (Sec-General of European Democratic Gp, 1983- ; chmn, WEU budget cmte, 1984-87); Middlesex CC, 1958-63. Chmn, Wilderness Foundation (UK), 1981- ; United and Cecil Club, 1975-80. Governor, Mill Hill Sch.
Mr Kevin O'Sullivan, consulting engineer, contested East Berkshire 1983. Chmn, SDP third world and development gp. B Apr 28 1938; ed Cambridge and Yale Univs. Partner, T.P. O'Sullivan and Partners; mbr of Lloyds.
Ms Ann Christina, social worker. Aged 37. Nalgo.
Ms Janet Alty, lecturer. B Feb 20 1937; ed Manchester HS for Girls; Bryn Mawr Coll, Penn, US; Geneva and Vienna Univs.

Sir Dudley Smith

WARWICKSHIRE NORTH — No change

Electorate %Turnout	70,687	79.9%	**1987**	68,625	78.0%	**1983**
*Maude, F.A.A. (C)	25,453	45.1%	+3.1%	22,452	41.9%	(C)
O'Brien, M. (Lab)	22,624	40.1%	+3.0%	19,867	37.1%	(Lab)
Neale, Mrs S.J. (SDP/All)	8,382	14.8%	-6.1%	11,207	20.9%	(SDP/All)
Lab to C swing 0.1%	56,459	C maj 2,829 5.0%		53,526	C maj 2,585 4.8%	

Mr Francis Maude

Mr Francis Maude was appointed Under Secretary of State for Trade and Industry in Jun 1987; an assistant Government whip, 1985-87. Elected for this seat 1983. Barrister. B Jul 4 1953; ed Abingdon Sch; Corpus Christi Coll, Cambridge. mer, Westminster City Cl, 1978-84. PPS to Mr Peter Morrison, Minister of State for Employment, 1984-85. Mbr of chambers of Sir Michael Havers QC, from 1978. Son of Lord Maude of Stratford-upon-Avon.
Mr Michael O'Brien, lecturer in law at coll of further ed, contested Ruislip Northwood 1983. B Jun 19 1954; ed Worcester Tech Coll; North Staffs Poly. NATFHE.
Mrs Suzan Neale, Birmingham City Cl's welfare officer for the disabled; home help organiser with cl, 1979-82. Founder mbr, SDP; vice-chmn, Warwickshire SDP. Mbr, N Warwickshire DC and Warwickshire CC. B Jul 25 1933; ed Bailey Sec Sch, Fleetwood; Blackpool and Bristol tech colls.

WATFORD — No change

Electorate %Turnout	73,540	77.9%	**1987**	71,992	76.1%	**1983**
*Garel-Jones, W.A.T.T. (C)	27,912	48.7%	+0.8%	26,273	48.0%	(C)
Jackson, M.J. (Lab)	16,176	28.2%	+2.2%	14,267	26.0%	(SDP/All)
Beckett, Mrs F.M. (SDP/All)	13,202	23.0%	-3.0%	14,247	26.0%	(Lab)
C to Lab swing 0.7%	57,290	C maj 11,736 20.5%		54,787	C maj 12,006 21.9%	

Mr Tristan Garel-Jones

Mr Tristan Garel-Jones became Vice-Chamberlain of the Royal Household in 1986; a Lord Commissioner of the Treasury (Government whip), 1983-86; an asst Govt whip, 1982-83. Mbr of Lloyd's. Principal of language sch in Madrid, Spain, 1960-70; now owns sch; merchant banker, 1970-74; at Cons Central Office from 1974, being personal asst to party chmn, 1978-79. Gained seat for Cons in 1979; contested Caernarvon, Feb 1974, and Watford, Oct 1974. Former exec mbr, Hemel Hempstead Cons Assocn. B Feb 28 1941; ed Llangennech Primary Sch and King's Sch, Canterbury. Sec, Cons back-bench constitutional cmte, until 1982. ASTMS.
Mr Michael Jackson, area officer, Nupe. Mbr, Watford Cl, 1980- (chmn, housing cmte). B May 6 1948; ed Verulam Sch, St Albans; Warwick Univ; Garnet Coll. Mbr, Lab Pty local govt advisory cmte.
Mrs Fiona Beckett, school governor; bd mbr, Watford YMCA; mbr, CPRE. Contested Hertfordshire in 1984 Euro election. Mbr, CSD; SDP nat cmte; SDP finance and communications cmtes; SDP health policy gp; chair, community care working pty. B Aug 22 1948; ed Exeter Univ.

WAVENEY — No change

Electorate %Turnout	81,889	78.4%	**1987**	77,960	75.3%	**1983**
Porter, D. (C)	31,067	48.4%	-3.4%	30,371	51.8%	(C)
Lark, J.A. (Lab)	19,284	30.0%	+2.6%	16,073	27.4%	(Lab)
Beaven, D. (SDP/All)	13,845	21.6%	+0.7%	12,234	20.8%	(SDP/All)
C to Lab swing 3.0%	64,196	C maj 11,783 18.4%		58,678	C maj 14,298 24.4%	

Mr David Porter

Mr David Porter, former teacher; Conservative Party agent. Mbr, Waveney DC, 1974-84 and 1985-87. B Apr 16 1948; ed Lowestoft GS; New College of Speech and Drama, London. Taught in East End of London, New Barnet and Lowestoft where he was Head of Drama at the Benjamin Britten HS, 1978-81. Became pty agent 1982 holding posts in Eltham, Norwich North and became agent and sec to Waveney Cons Assocn in Jan 1985.
Mr Alan Lark, safety manager with Leyland Trucks, contested Waveney 1983 and Lowestoft 1979. Ldr, Lab gp, Waveney DC; dep ldr and education spokesman, Suffolk CC. Vice-chmn, CLP. B Oct 18 1936; ed Roman Hill Sch; Lowestoft CFE. Governor, Lowestoft and Gt Yarmouth CFEs.
Mr David Beavan, farmer and former journalist. Contested Hitchin, Feb 1974. Former mbr, CSD. B Aug 24 1951; ed Stowe Sch; Essex Univ.

WEALDEN | | | | | | No change

Electorate %Turnout	73,057	75.0%	**1987**	69,244	71.8%	**1983**
*Johnson Smith, Sir Geoffrey (C)	35,154	64.2%	0.0%	31,926	64.2%	(C)
Sinclair, D. (SDP/All)	15,044	27.5%	-2.2%	14,741	29.6%	(SDP/All)
Ward, C. (Lab)	4,563	8.3%	+2.2%	3,060	6.2%	(Lab)
SDP/All to C swing 1.1%	54,761	C maj 20,110 36.7%		49,727	C maj 17,185 34.6%	

Sir Geoffrey Johnson Smith, company director and consultant, won this seat 1983; MP for East Grinstead, 1965-83, and for Holborn and St Pancras South, 1959-64. Non-exec director, London Weekend Television (Holdings) Ltd; Brands Hatch Leisure plc; Taylor Alden Ltd (industrial public relations and marketing); Glengate Holdings Ltd (commercial and industrial property); and MDA (Benelux) SA (construction consultants and quantity surveyors). Consultant to Eagle Star Gp, and to Philips Business Systems Ltd, Colchester. Former BBC TV broadcaster, reporter and interviewer, 1953-59. Parly Sec, Civil Service Dept, 1972-74; Under Sec of State for Defence for the Army, 1971-71; Opposition whip, 1965-66; a PPS, 1960-63. Chmn, Select Cmte on Members' Interests, 1980- ; mbr, exec, 1922 Cmte, 1979- ; vice-chmn, Cons back-bench defence cmte, 1980- . B Apr 16 1924; ed Charterhouse; Lincoln Coll, Oxford. Mbr, N Atlantic Assembly, 1980- , being chmn of Military Cmte since 1985.
Mr David Sinclair, self-employed consultant, was constituency agent/organiser 1983. Mbr, Tunbridge Wells BC, 1983-87; Kent CC, 1985- .
Mr Charles Ward, teacher. Sec, Wealden CLP, 1983-84; delegate from E Sussex Lab Pty to East Sussex CC Lab gp, 1984-87. B Dec 5 1949; ed Wisbech GS; Northumberland Coll of Ed; Newcastle Poly. NAS/UWT: vice-pres, E Sussex Fed.

Sir Geoffrey Johnson
Smith

WELLINGBOROUGH | | | | | | No change

Electorate %Turnout	70,450	78.1%	**1987**	67,598	77.8%	**1983**
*Fry, P.D. (C)	29,038	52.7%	+3.9%	25,715	48.9%	(C)
Currie, J. (Lab)	14,968	27.2%	+1.2%	13,659	26.0%	(Lab)
Stringer, L.E. (L/All)	11,047	20.1%	-4.6%	12,994	24.7%	(L/All)
				228	0.4%	(Other)
Lab to C swing 1.3%	55,053	C maj 14,070 25.6%		52,596	C maj 12,056 22.9%	

Mr Peter Fry, a former Conservative spokesman on transport, has been on the Select Cmte on Transport since 1979. Won the seat at 1969 by-election; fought Nottingham North, 1964; Willesden East, 1966. Insurance broker. B May 26 1931; ed Royal GS, High Wycombe; Worcester Coll, Oxford. Chmn, all-pty footwear and leather industries group; jt chmn, all-pty roads study group; sec, parly Road Passenger Transport gp. Chmn, British-Bahamian and British-Yugoslav parly gps. Mbr, Bucks CC, 1961-67. Director, Political Research and Communications International Ltd, public affairs consultants, and two other companies.
Mr Jim Currie, local govt officer. B Jan 2 1958; ed St Alban's HS.
Mr Leslie Stringer, operations, administration and industrial relations manager, contested this seat 1983 and 1979. Mbr, Wellingborough BC, 1976- . B Nov 28 1927; ed Woolwich Poly.

Mr Peter Fry

WELLS | | | | | | No change

Electorate %Turnout	67,195	79.6%	**1987**	62,159	77.6%	**1983**
*Heathcoat-Amory, D.P. (C)	28,624	53.5%	+0.9%	25,385	52.6%	(C)
Butt Philip, A.A.S. (L/All)	20,083	37.6%	-1.5%	18,810	39.0%	(L/All)
James, P. (Lab)	4,637	8.7%	+0.9%	3,747	7.8%	(Lab)
Fish, J.S. (Falkland)	134	0.3%		273	0.6%	(Ind)
L/All to C swing 1.2%	53,478	C maj 8,541 16.0%		48,215	C maj 6,575 13.6%	

Mr David Heathcoat-Amory, chartered accountant, company director and underwriting member of Lloyd's, was elected in 1983; contested Brent South, 1979. PPS to Financial Secretary to the Treasury, 1985- . B Mar 21, 1949; ed Eton and Oxford Univ. Asst finance director, British Technology Group, 1980-83. Director, Lowman Manufacturing Co Ltd, since 1979, and London and Devonshire Trust Ltd.
Dr Alan Butt Philip, university lecturer, fought this seat 1983, 1979, twice in 1974; also contested Somerset in 1979 Euro election. B Aug 15 1945; ed Eton; St John's Coll and Nuffield Coll, Oxford. AUT.
Mr Peter James, an operating dept assistant, NHS, contested Devon North 1983. B Sep 9 1953; ed West Bridgeford GS. Sch governor.

Mr David
Heathcoat-Amory

WELWYN HATFIELD — No change

Electorate %Turnout	73,607	80.9%	**1987**	72,644	79.4%	**1983**
Evans, D.J. (C)	27,164	45.6%	-2.1%	27,498	47.7%	(C)
Granshaw, Miss L.P. (SDP/All)	16,261	27.3%	+0.9%	15,252	26.5%	(SDP/All)
Pond, C.R. (Lab)	15,699	26.4%	+0.5%	14,898	25.8%	(Lab)
Dyson, B.I. (Ind C)	401	0.7%				
C to SDP/All swing 1.5%	59,525	C maj 10,903 18.3%		57,648	C maj 12,246 21.2%	

Mr David Evans

Mr David Evans, chmn, Luton Town Football Club, since 1984, a director since 1976. Was professional footballer with Aston Villa; professional cricketer with Gloucestershire, Warwickshire and Hertfordshire. Mbr, MCC; Middlesex CCC general and finance cmtes. Captained Club Cricket Conference, 1968-74, and tour to Australia, 1971; manager of 1975 tour. Founder, chmn and managing director, Brengreen (Holdings) plc, mainly operating in contract cleaning with local authority contracts for refuse collection and street cleaning. Master, Guild of Master Cleaners, 1981-82; Dep Master, 1982-83. Freeman, City of London; mbr, Worshipful Company of Horners. B Apr 23 1935; ed Raglan Road Sch; Tottenham Tech Coll. Mbr, St Albans City Cl, 1980-84; Wheathampstead PC, since 1979; exec cl, St Albans Cons Assocn, 1979-84. Chmn, Lord's Taverners, 1982-84; chaired sponsorship cmte, 1981-82, cricket cmte, 1978-81, and covenant cmte, 1982-85; cl mbr, 1978- ; mbr of foundation cmte. Chmn, Hundred Guinea Club, which raises money for children's charities.
Dr Lindsay Granshaw, univ lecturer, contested the seat 1983. Member, SDP health and social services and pharmaceutical industry policy gps. B Aug 21 1954; ed Brighton and Hove HS; St Anne's Coll, Oxford; Bryn Mawr Coll; Pennsylvania Univ.
Mr Chris Pond, director of Low Pay Unit; hon Visiting Professor, Surrey Univ. B Sept 25 1952; ed Michenden Sch, Southgate; Sussex Univ. Long distance runner. TGWU.

WENTWORTH — No change

Electorate %Turnout	63,886	72.5%	**1987**	62,057	69.7%	**1983**
*Hardy, P. (Lab)	30,205	65.2%	+6.1%	25,538	59.1%	(Lab)
Hague, W.J. (C)	10,113	21.8%	-0.4%	9,603	22.2%	(C)
Eglin, D.M. (SDP/All)	6,031	13.0%	-5.7%	8,082	18.7%	(SDP/All)
C to Lab swing 3.2%	46,349	Lab maj 20,092 43.3%		43,223	Lab maj 15,935 36.9%	

Mr Peter Hardy

Mr Peter Hardy was elected for this seat in 1983; MP for Rother Valley, 1970-83; contested Scarborough and Whitby, 1964; Sheffield, Hallam, 1966. Teacher, 1953-70. Chmn, PLP energy cmte, 1974- . Energy consultant to Nalgo. Delegate to Cl of Europe and WEU, 1976- ; leader, Lab delegation, 1983- ; chmn, cmte on environment, Cl of Europe. B Jul 17 1931; ed Wath upon Dearne GS; Westminster Coll, London; Sheffield Univ. Mbr, cl, Royal Soc for Protection of Birds; exec cmte, NSPCC. PPS to Secretary of State for Environment, 1974-76, and to Foreign Sec, 1976-79. Sponsored Badgers Act 1973, the Conservation of Wild Creatures and Wild Plants Act 1975, the Protection of Birds (Amendment) Act 1976 and the Education (Northern Ireland) Act 1978. Patron, Yorkshire Wildlife Trust. Mbr, Wath upon Dearne UDC, 1960-70 (chmn, 1968-69). Sponsored by Nacods.
Mr William Hague, management consultant. B Mar 26 1961; ed Wath-on-Dearne Comprehensive Sch; Magdalen Coll, Oxford (Pres of Union, 1981; pres, Univ Cons Assocn, 1981).
Mr David Eglin runs a small family farm near Coventry. Mbr, SDP working pty on agriculture. Cmte mbr, then chmn, Nuneaton SDP. B May 5 1941; ed De Aston GS, Market Raisen; West of Scotland Agric Coll.

WEST BROMWICH EAST — No change

Electorate %Turnout	58,239	73.2%	**1987**	59,391	70.2%	**1983**
*Snape, P.C. (Lab)	18,162	42.6%	+4.5%	15,894	38.1%	(Lab)
Woodhouse, R.F. (C)	17,179	40.3%	+2.9%	15,596	37.4%	(C)
Smith, M.G. (L/All)	7,268	17.1%	-7.4%	10,200	24.5%	(L/All)
C to Lab swing 0.8%	42,609	Lab maj 983 2.3%		41,690	Lab maj 298 0.7%	

Mr Peter Snape

Mr Peter Snape became an Opposition spokesman on transport in 1983; a spokesman on home affairs, 1982-83; and on defence and disarmament, 1979-82. Lord Commissioner of the Treasury (Govt whip), 1977-79; asst Govt whip, 1975-77. Elected in Feb 1974. Clerical officer, British Rail, 1970-74; goods guard, 1967-70; regular soldier, 1961-67; railway signalman, 1957-61. Served on Select Cmte on Channel Tunnel Bill, 1986-87. B Feb 12 1942; ed St Joseph's Sch, Stockport. Mbr, Bredbury and Romily UDC, 1971-74 (chmn, finance cmte, ldr of Lab gp). Delegate, Cl of Europe and WEU, 1975; N Atlantic Assembly, 1979-80. Sponsored by NUR. Hon parly adviser to Musicians' Union. Chmn, West Midlands Lab MPs, 1985- . Fellow, Industry and Parliament Trust.
Mr Roger Woodhouse, employed in an accountancy firm. Mbr, Sandwell MBC 1976-79; 1980- . B 1942; ed West Bromwich GS. Treas, West Bromwich East Con Assocn; sec Wednesbury Con and Unionist Club.
Mr Martyn Smith, sec, West Birmingham CHC, contested this seat 1983 and 1979; Stoke-on-Trent North Oct 1974, Stoke-on-Trent South Feb 1974. B Feb 16 1946; ed Wyggeston Boys' Sch, Leicester; Jesus Coll, Cambridge. Mbr, Sandwell MBC, 1980- (Gp ldr); Newcastle-under-Lyme BC, 1972-74.

237

WEST BROMWICH WEST — No change

Electorate %Turnout	58,944	67.0%	**1987**	58,341	63.8%	**1983**
*Boothroyd, Miss B. (Lab)	19,925	50.5%	-0.3%	18,896	50.7%	(Lab)
Betteridge, F.A. (C)	14,672	37.2%	+4.3%	12,257	32.9%	(C)
Collingbourne, A. (SDP/All)	4,877	12.4%	-4.0%	6,094	16.4%	(SDP/All)
Lab to C swing 2.3%	39,474	Lab maj 5,253 13.3%		37,247	Lab maj 6,639 17.8%	

Miss Betty Boothroyd

Miss Betty Boothroyd, member of Commons Chairmen's Panel since 1979 and House of Commons Commission since 1983, was elected to the Labour Party NEC in 1981. Asst Govt whip, 1974-76. Elected for this seat, Feb 1974; MP for West Bromwich, May 1973 to Feb 1974; contested Rossendale, 1970; Nelson and Colne by-election, 1968; Peterborough, 1959; Leicester SE by-election, 1957. Mbr, BBC Gen Advisory Cl, 1987- ; European Parliament, 1975-77; delegate to N Atlantic Assembly, 1974. B Oct 8 1929; ed Dewsbury Coll of Commerce and Art. Mbr, exec cmte, UK branch, CPA, 1986- ; court, Birmingham Univ, 1982- . Select Cmte on Foreign Affairs, 1979-81; Hammersmith BC, 1965-68. Sponsored by GMB.
Mr Frank Betteridge, director of his own company. Mbr, Sandwell MBC; former mbr, West Midlands CC; mbr, West Midlands RHA, 1980- . B 1932; ed Blue Coat Sec Mod Sch; Walsall Tech Coll. Sec, West Bromwich West Con Assocn.
Mr Anthony Collingbourne, microbiologist and brewer, contested the seat 1983. Founder mbr, SDP; chmn, area SDP. B Nov 12 1947; ed Northwood Sec Mod; Huntingdon GS; Ferndale GS; Llandaff Coll of Tech.

WESTBURY — No change

Electorate %Turnout	84,860	78.2%	**1987**	80,244	75.5%	**1983**
*Walters, D.M. (C)	34,256	51.6%	+0.2%	31,133	51.4%	(C)
Hughes, D.J. (L/All)	24,159	36.4%	-1.0%	22,627	37.4%	(L/All)
Thomas, H.W. (Lab)	7,982	12.0%	+2.0%	6,058	10.0%	(Lab)
				740	1.2%	(Other)
L/All to C swing 0.6%	66,397	C maj 10,097 15.2%		60,558	C maj 8,506 14.0%	

Mr Dennis Walters

Mr Dennis Walters, chairman of the Conservative Middle East Cl since 1980. Director, Cluff Oil Inc, and Gulf Development Co; mbr, Kuwait Investment Advisory Cmte; adviser to Canadian investment and finance company; trustee, ANAF Foundation; consultant to Balfour Beatty Construction Ltd and to Robert Fraser and Partners Ltd (investment and finance). Elected in 1964; contested Blyth, 1959 and 1960 by-election. B Nov 1928; ed Downside; St Catharine's Coll, Cambridge. Governor, British Inst of Florence, 1965- . Jt sec, 1965-71, and jt vice-chmn, 1974-79, Cons back-bench foreign affairs cmte. Chmn, Asthma Research Cl, since 1969; jt chmn, Euro-Arab Parly Assocn, 1978-81; Cl for Advancement of Arab-British Understanding, 1970-82.
Mr David Hughes is head of the Cl for Environmental Conservation. Fought this seat 1983; Southampton Test, 1979. Vice-chmn, Lib Pty, 1987- ; chmn, Lib party candidates' assocn, 1984- ; former chmn, ULS. B Apr 10 1956; ed St Paul's Sch; Southampton Univ.
Mr Haydn Thomas, teacher in further education, contested this seat 1983. CLP sec; mbr, South West Lab Pty reg exec. B Feb 3 1951; ed North London Poly; London Univ. Mbr, Westbury TC. Nupe; TUC delegate, West Wilts.

WESTERN ISLES — Lab gain

Electorate %Turnout	23,507	70.2%	**1987**	22,822	66.5%	**1983**
Macdonald, C.A. (Lab)	7,041	42.7%	+12.6%	8,272	54.5%	(SNP)
Smith, I. (SNP)	4,701	28.5%	-26.0%	4,560	30.1%	(Lab)
MacIver, K. (SDP/All)	3,419	20.7%	+14.9%	1,460	9.6%	(C)
Morrison, M. (C)	1,336	8.1%	-1.5%	876	5.8%	(L/All)
SNP to Lab swing 19.3%	16,497	Lab maj 2,340 14.2%		15,168	SNP maj 3,712 24.5%	

Mr Calum Macdonald

Mr Calum Macdonald, crofter on Isle of Lewis; former teaching fellow in political philosophy, Univ of California. B May 7 1956. TGWU.
Mr Ian Smith manages his own family import/export business. Contested Argyll and Bute 1983, Kinross and West Perthshire 1979. SNP spokesman on transport; former mbr, SNP nat exec; has served on various SNP cmtes. B Jan 1937; ed Nicholson Inst, Stornaway.
Mr Kenneth MacIver, broadcaster. Mbr, Western Isles Cl, 1979-83. B Oct 2 1950; ed Nicolson Inst, Stornoway; Aberdeen Univ. NUJ.
Mr Murdo Morrison, public relations manager for an oil company, contested the seat 1983 and 1979. B Jun 13 1938; ed Nicolson Inst, Stornoway. Mbr, Motherwell DC, 1974-84 (Cons gp ldr). Life mbr, Gaelic League of Scotland.

WESTMINSTER NORTH | No change

Electorate %Turnout	59,263	71.1%	**1987**	68,988	64.2%	**1983**
*Wheeler, J.D. (C)	19,941	47.3%	+4.1%	19,134	43.2%	(C)
Edwards, Ms J.F. (Lab)	16,631	39.5%	+0.1%	17,424	39.4%	(Lab)
De Ste Croix, R.J. (SDP/All)	5,116	12.1%	-3.6%	6,956	15.7%	(SDP/All)
Stutchfield, D. (Grn)	450	1.1%		527	1.2%	(Eco)
				221	0.5%	(Other)
Lab to C swing 2.0%	42,138	C maj 3,310 7.9%		44,262	C maj 1,710 3.9%	

Mr John Wheeler

Mr John Wheeler, director-general, British Security Industry Assocn, since 1976 and trustee of its benevolent fund, was elected for this seat 1983; MP for City of Westminster, Paddington, 1979-83. Asst governor, Wandsworth Prison, 1968-72, and Brixton, 1972-73. Director, International Fire Security and Safety Exhibitions and Conferences Ltd, Major Exhibitions and Conferences Ltd, and other companies. Mbr of Lloyd's. B May 1 1940; ed Bury St Edmunds Cty Sch; Prison Services Staff Coll. Director, Nat Supervisory Cl for Intruder Alarms, 1977- . Chmn, Nat Inspectorate of Security Guard Patrol and Transport Services, 1982- . Mbr, Home Office standing cmte on crime prevention, 1976- ; Home Affairs Select Cmte, 1979- , being chmn of its sub-cmte on race relations and immigration, 1980- . Chmn (1986-) and vice-chmn (1979-86), all-pty penal affairs gp. Jt sec, Cons back-bench home affairs cmte, 1980- ; chmn, Cons Greater London MPs' cmte, 1983- ; jt treas, all-pty parly war crimes gp.
Ms Jennifer Edwards, local govt officer in Camden. B Dec 26 1954; ed Brighton and Torquay Girls' GSs; Cambridge Univ. Nalgo.
Mr Richard de Ste Croix, solictor, contested Chertsey and Walton 1983. Member, wider share ownership policy gp. B Jul 15 1947; ed Victoria Coll, Jersey; Pembroke Coll, Oxford.
Mr David Stutchfield, mechanical engineer. Mbr, Central London energy management gp. B Jul 1958; ed Ashville Coll, Harrogate; Imperial Coll, London Univ; Hatfield Poly.

WESTMORLAND AND LONSDALE | No change

Electorate %Turnout	70,237	74.8%	**1987**	67,161	72.3%	**1983**
*Jopling, T.M. (C)	30,259	57.6%	-3.7%	29,775	61.3%	(C)
Collins, S. (L/All)	15,339	29.2%	+2.0%	13,188	27.2%	(L/All)
Halfpenny, S. (Lab)	6,968	13.3%	+3.4%	4,798	9.9%	(Lab)
				805	1.7%	(Other)
C to L/All swing 2.9%	52,566	C maj 14,920 28.4%		48,566	C maj 16,587 34.2%	

Mr Michael Jopling

Mr Michael Jopling was Minister of Agriculture, Fisheries and Food, 1983-87; Parliamentary Secretary to the Treasury and Government Chief Whip, 1979-83. An Opposition spokesman on agriculture, 1974-79. Lord Commissioner of the Treasury (Govt whip), 1973-74; asst Govt whip, 1971-73. Won this seat in 1983; MP for Westmorland, 1964-83; contested Wakefield, 1959. Farmer and mbr of Lloyd's. B Dec 10 1930; ed Cheltenham Coll and King's Coll, Durham Univ. Former mbr, select cmtes on science and technology and on agriculture. Mbr, NFU nat cl, 1962-64; Thirsk RDC, 1958-64. Jt sec, Cons back-bench agriculture cmte, 1966-70. PPS, Minister of Agriculture, 1970-71.
Mr Stanley Collins, business systems analyst. Mbr, South Lakeland DC, 1979- . B Aug 10 1948; ed Roundhay Sch, Leeds; UMIST. Former mbr, Lib nat exec, pty cl; past constituency chmn. ASTMS since 1971.
Mr Shaun Halfpenny, teacher. Mbr, Cumbria CC (vice-chmn, ed cmte; chmn, public protection). B May 9 1950; ed Ulverston GS; Ulverston Comprehensive; De La Salle Coll, Manchester. Nupe.

WESTON-SUPER-MARE | No change

Electorate %Turnout	76,341	75.6%	**1987**	71,439	73.0%	**1983**
*Wiggin, A.W. (C)	28,547	49.4%	-4.1%	27,948	53.6%	(C)
Crockford-Hawley, J.R. (SDP/All)	20,549	35.6%	+0.2%	18,457	35.4%	(SDP/All)
Loach, P.J. (Lab)	6,584	11.4%	+0.3%	5,781	11.1%	(Lab)
Lawson, Dr R.H. (Grn)	2,067	3.6%				
C to SDP/All swing 2.2%	57,747	C maj 7,998 13.9%		52,186	C maj 9,491 18.2%	

Mr Jerry Wiggin was Under Secretary of State for the Armed Forces, 1981-83; Parliamentary Secretary, Ministry of Agriculture, Fisheries and Food, 1979-81. Returned at 1969 by-election; contested Montgomeryshire, 1964 and 1966. B Feb 24 1937; ed Eton and Trinity Coll, Cambridge. Company director, consultant and mbr of Lloyd's; former tenant farmer. PPS to Lord Balniel, Minister of State for Defence, 1970-74, and to Sir Ian Gilmour, Minister of State for Defence Procurement, 1971-73. Jt sec, Cons defence cmte, 1974-75; vice-chmn, Cons agriculture cmte, 1975-79; chmn, Cons West Country MPs, 1978-79. General rapporteur, economic cmte, N Atlantic Assembly, 1976-79. Director, SH Services Ltd and Copyright Services Ltd; consultant to British Sugar plc.
Mr John Crockford-Hawley, teacher; head of geography dept, Wyvern Sch, Weston-super-Mare. Chmn, constituency Alliance co-ordinating cmte. Mbr, Weston-super-Mare DC, 1976-86 (Cons 1976-85 when he joined SDP). Mayor of Weston-super-Mare, 1984-85. B Nov 8 1946; ed Bishop Otter Coll, Chichester. FRGS.
Mr Paul Loach, economist. Chmn, finance cmte, Haringey Cl.
Dr Richard Lawson, medical practitioner. Mbr, Woodspring DC 1986- . B Jul 20 1946; ed Churchers Coll, Petersfield; King's Coll, London; Westminster Hospital.

Mr Jerry Wiggin

239

WIGAN · No change

Electorate %Turnout	72,064	76.6%	**1987**	72,390	75.6%	**1983**
*Stott, R. (Lab)	33,955	61.5%	+7.0%	29,859	54.6%	(Lab)
Wade, K.R. (C)	13,493	24.5%	+1.9%	12,554	22.9%	(L/All)
White, K.J. (L/All)	7,732	14.0%	-8.9%	12,320	22.5%	(C)
C to Lab swing 2.5%	55,180	Lab maj 20,462 37.1%		54,733	Lab maj 17,305 31.6%	

Mr Roger Stott, an Opposition spokesman on transport, 1980-83, and since 1985; a spokesman on trade and industry with responsibilities for information technology, 1983-85. Elected for this seat 1983; MP for Westhoughton, 1973-83; contested Cheadle, 1970. PPS to Secretary of State for Industry, 1975-76; to the Prime Minister, 1976-79; Leader of the Opposition, 1979-80. Telephone engineer, 1964-73; hon adviser, Nat Fed of Post Office and British Telecom Pensioners. B Aug 7 1943; ed Rochdale Tech Coll; Ruskin Coll. Mbr, Select Cmte on Agriculture, 1979-81; Rochdale Cl, 1970-74. Pres, Bass Wingates Band, since 1980. Vice-chmn and treas, North-West Lab MPs. Sponsored by NCU, engineering section.
Mr Kenneth Wade, company director. B 1940; ed Queen Elizabeth's GS, Blackburn; Imperial Coll of Science and Technology; Hatfield Coll of Advanced Technology. Mbr, North West RHA.
Mr Kevin White, accountant. Election agent at Windsor and Maidenhead, 1979. Mbr, Royal Borough of Windsor and Maidenhead Cl, 1979-87. B Mar 11 1952; ed sec mod sch.

Mr Roger Stott

WILTSHIRE NORTH · No change

Electorate %Turnout	80,712	79.3%	**1987**	76,150	76.6%	**1983**
*Needham, R.F. (C)	35,309	55.2%	+2.1%	30,924	53.0%	(C)
Graham, C.S.M. (L/All)	24,370	38.1%	-2.6%	23,692	40.6%	(L/All)
Reid, Mrs C. (Lab)	4,343	6.8%	+1.8%	2,888	5.0%	(Lab)
				791	1.4%	(Other)
L/All to C swing 2.3%	64,022	C maj 10,939 17.1%		58,295	C maj 7,232 12.4%	

Mr Richard Needham was appointed an Under Secretary of State for Northern Ireland in 1985. Elected for this seat 1983; MP for Chippenham, 1979-83; contested Pontefract and Castleford, Feb 1974; Gravesend, Oct 1974. Former chmn, RGM Print Holdings Ltd; former director, Radio Somerset Ltd; mbr of Lloyd's. Personal and political asst to Mr James Prior, 1974-79; then PPS to Mr Prior as Secretary of State for Northern Ireland, 1983-84; PPS to Secretary of State for the Environment, 1984-85. Mbr, PAC, 1982-83; jt vice-chmn, Cons backbench employent cmte, 1981-83; chmn, all-pty productivity cmte. B Jan 29 1942; ed Eton. Founder mbr, Anglo-Japanese 2000 Gp. Mbr, Somerset CC, 1967-74. Former mbr, Tobacco Workers' Union and Slade.
Mr Christopher Graham, BBC TV producer of current affairs programmes, contested this seat 1983. Mbr, Lib Pty policy cmte; Treasury affairs panel; Lib Commission on Future of Work. B Sep 21 1950; ed St Edward's Sch, Oxford; Liverpool Univ. Mbr, Liverpool City Cl, 1971-74. ACCT and NUJ.
Mrs Christine Reid, part-time teacher. B Aug 2 1943; ed Nottingham Univ.

Mr Richard Needham

WIMBLEDON · No change

Electorate %Turnout	63,353	76.1%	**1987**	64,132	72.4%	**1983**
Goodson-Wickes, Dr C. (C)	24,538	50.9%	-1.2%	24,169	52.1%	(C)
Slade, A.C. (L/All)	13,237	27.5%	+0.3%	12,623	27.2%	(L/All)
Bickerstaff, Mrs C.M. (Lab)	10,428	21.6%	+2.7%	8,806	19.0%	(Lab)
				831	1.8%	(Other)
C to L/All swing 0.7%	48,203	C maj 11,301 23.4%		46,429	C maj 11,546 24.9%	

Dr Charles Goodson-Wickes, occupational physician and barrister, contested Islington Central 1979. Medical adviser to Barclays Bank, RTZ, McKinsey, the Royal Society, Meat and Livestock Commission. Mbr, medical advisory cmte, Industrial Soc; fitness advisory panel, Inst of Directors. Surgeon Captain, Life Guards, 1973-77; now Capt, Regular Army reserve of officers. Chmn, appeal bd, asbestos licensing regulations. B Nov 7 1945; ed Charterhouse; St Bartholomew's Hosp; Inner Temple. Author, *The New Corruption* which instigated setting up of Widdicombe cmte inquiry into conduct of local govt. Mbr, public affairs cmte, British Field Sports Soc; Medico-Legal Soc; International Associa of Physicians for Overseas Service; Soc of Occupational Medicine; BMA.
Mr Adrian Slade is President-elect (for 1987-88) of the Liberal Party; chmn, London Lib Pty. Contested Putney 1966 and twice in 1974. Managing director and principal shareholder of advertising agency. GLC mbr for Richmond and leader of Alliance gp, 1981-86. B May 25 1936; ed Eton; Trinity Coll, Cambridge.
Mrs Christine Bickerstaffe, acoustics engineer/physicist, British Aerospace. B Jan 30 1946. AUEW/TASS.

Dr Charles Goodson-Wickes

WINCHESTER — No change

Electorate %Turnout	76,507	80.4%	**1987**	72,792	76.2%	**1983**
*Browne, J.E.D. (C)	32,195	52.3%	-5.2%	31,908	57.6%	(C)
MacDonald, J.L. (SDP/All)	24,716	40.2%	+6.2%	18,861	34.0%	(SDP/All)
Inglis, F.C. (Lab)	4,028	6.5%	-1.6%	4,512	8.1%	(Lab)
Walker, Ms J.P. (Grn)	565	0.9%		155	0.3%	(W Reg)
C to SDP/All swing 5.7%	61,504	C maj 7,479 12.2%		55,436	C maj 13,047 23.5%	

Mr John Browne has served on the Select Cmte on the Treasury and Civil Service since 1982. Managing director, Falcon Finance Management Ltd, since 1978; director, Churchill Private Clinic, 1980- and of two other companies; adviser to Barclays Bank, 1978-84. Elected in 1979. Mbr, Westminster City Cl, 1974-78. Jt sec, Cons back-bench finance cmte, 1982-84; sec, Cons back-bench defence cmte, 1982-83, and to Cons Middle East Cl, 1980-82. Chmn, Cons back-bench smaller businesses cmte, 1984- ; vice-chmn, 1983-84. B Oct 1938; ed Malvern Coll, RMA Sandhurst, Cranfield Inst of Technology, Harvard Business Sch. Served in Grenadier Guards; retired as captain, 1967; TA since 1981. Liveryman, Goldsmiths' Company, 1982- ; Freeman, City of London. Mbr, Court of Southampton Univ, 1979- ; Royal Utd Services Inst for Defence Studies; NFU. Governor, Malvern Coll, 1981- .
Mr John MacDonald, sixth form master at Winchester Coll, joining staff in 1965. Contested this seat 1983. Chmn, Winchester SDP, 1983-84. Mbr, Winchester City Cl, 1982- (ldr, Alliance gp). B Dec 8 1938; ed Glenalmond Coll; Oriel Coll, Oxford.
Dr Frederick Inglis, reader in education, Bristol Univ, contested W Derbyshire 1970, Feb 1974; Cheltenham Oct 1974. B May 17 1937; ed Oundle; Cambridge Univ. NUT/AUT.

Mr John Browne

WINDSOR AND MAIDENHEAD — No change

Electorate %Turnout	79,319	75.4%	**1987**	78,619	70.3%	**1983**
*Glyn, Dr A. (C)	33,980	56.8%	-1.4%	32,191	58.2%	(C)
Jackson, S.J. (L/All)	16,144	27.0%	+1.7%	13,988	25.3%	(L/All)
De Lyon, Ms H.B. (Lab)	6,678	11.2%	-0.4%	6,383	11.5%	(Lab)
Board, W.O. (Ind C)	1,938	3.2%	-0.1%	1,842	3.3%	(Ind C)
Gordon, P. (Grn)	711	1.2%		511	0.9%	(NF)
Stephenson, Ms P.H. (BT)	328	0.5%		300	0.5%	(Ind)
				68	0.1%	(Other)
C to L/All swing 1.5%	59,779	C maj 17,836 29.8%		55,283	C maj 18,203 32.9%	

Dr Alan Glyn was elected in Feb 1974; MP for Windsor, 1970-74, and for Clapham, 1959-64. Barrister and medical practitioner. B Sep 29 1918; ed Westminster Sch; Caius Coll, Cambridge; St Bartholomew's Hosp and St George's Hosp. Former chmn, Cons foreign affairs Far East sub-cmte; chmn, Danish, Swedish, Mongolian and Indonesian parly groups of IPU. Mbr, bd of governors, national heart and chest hospitals, 1982- ; Kensington, Chelsea and Westminster Local Medical Cmte, 1974- ; Chelsea BC, 1959-62; governing body, British Postgraduate Medical Fed, 1967-82; Greater London Central Valuation Panel, 1967- . Freeman, Worshipful Society of the Art and Mystery of Apothecaries of the City of London, 1961.
Mr Stanley Jackson, company director, pensions consultant and author. Director, Target Financial Consultants; managing partner, TFC Partnership.B Apr 8 1945; ed Glyn GS, Epsom.
Ms Hilary de Lyon, education officer. B Apr 8 1956; ed Roseberry GS, Epsom; Liverpool Univ.

Dr Alan Glyn

WIRRAL SOUTH — No change

Electorate %Turnout	62,251	79.4%	**1987**	60,864	75.8%	**1983**
*Porter, G.B. (C)	24,821	50.2%	-3.5%	24,766	53.7%	(C)
Swarbrooke, J.S. (Lab)	13,858	28.0%	+5.4%	10,928	23.7%	(SDP/All)
Gilchrist, P.N. (L/All)	10,779	21.8%	-1.9%	10,411	22.6%	(Lab)
C to Lab swing 4.5%	49,458	C maj 10,963 22.2%		46,105	C maj 13,838 30.0%	

Mr Barry Porter has served on the Select Cmte on Trade and Industry since 1985; former mbr, Select Cmte on Transport. Elected in 1983; MP for Bebington and Ellesmere Port, 1978-83; contested Chorley, Oct 1974; Newton, Feb 1974; Liverpool, Scotland Exchange, Apr 1971. Solicitor; director, Leisure Investments plc. Sec, all-pty solicitors gp. B Jun 11 1939; ed Birkenhead Sch and Univ Coll, Oxford. Parly adviser to Hearing Aid Assocn. Mbr, Birkenhead CBC, 1967-74; Wirral BC, 1975-79. Served as officer, back-bench leisure industries cmte and all-pty tourism cmte.
Mr John Swarbrooke, marketing officer. B Apr 25 1956; ed Birmingham and Liverpool Univs. Mbr, Maidstone BC, 1982-84. ASTMS.
Mr Phillip Gilchrist, education liaison officer, contested Bebington and Ellesmere Port 1979 anbd Liverpool, West Derby Feb 1974. Mbr, Wirral MBC, 1977- ; Merseyside CC, 1977-86. B Nov 21 1951; ed King's Sch, Chester; York Univ; Edge Hill Teacher Training Coll.

Mr Barry Porter

WIRRAL WEST — No change

Electorate %Turnout	63,597	77.9%	**1987**	61,646	73.4%	**1983**
*Hunt, D.J.F. (C)	25,736	51.9%	-3.9%	25,276	55.9%	(C)
Dunn, A.H. (Lab)	13,013	26.3%	+4.5%	10,125	22.4%	(L/All)
Brame, A.J. (L/All)	10,015	20.2%	-2.2%	9,855	21.8%	(Lab)
Burton, D. (Grn)	806	1.6%				
C to Lab swing 4.2%	49,570	C maj 12,723 25.7%		45,256	C maj 15,151 33.5%	

Mr David Hunt was appointed Treasurer of HM Household and Government Deputy Chief Whip in Commons in Jun 1987; Under Secretary of State for Energy, 1984-87; Lord Commissioner of the Treasury (Govt whip), 1983-84; asst Govt whip, 1981-83. Vice-chmn, Conservative Pty, 1983-85. Solicitor. Elected for this seat 1983; MP for Wirral, 1976-83; contested Bristol South 1970, and Kingswood 1974. B May 21 1942; ed Liverpool Coll; Montpellier and Bristol Univs; Guildford Coll of Law. Mbr of Lloyd's. Pres, British Youth Cl, 1978-80, its chmn, 1971-74; nat YC chmn, 1972-73, vice-pres, 1986- . Vice-pres, Cons Group for Europe, 1984- (chmn, 1981-82; vice-chmn, 1978-81); vice-chmn, all-pty parly youth lobby, 1978-79. PPS to Secretary of State for Trade, 1979-81; and to Secretary of State for Defence, 1981. Vice-pres, Nat Playbus Assocn, 1981- .
Mr Alexander Dunn, teacher; head of dept at catholic sch in Liverpool. Aged 27; ed Edinburgh Univ. Dep ldr, Lab gp, Wirral BC.
Mr Allan Brame, teacher. Mbr, Merseyside CC, 1981-86. B Jan 20 1952; ed Birkenhead Sch; Selwyn Coll, Cambridge; Goldsmiths Coll, London.
Mr David Burton, commercial manager of waste paper processors. B Oct 16 1950; ed Oldershaw GS, Wallasey.

Mr David Hunt

WITNEY — No change

Electorate %Turnout	75,284	77.3%	**1987**	69,362	74.7%	**1983**
*Hurd, D.R. (C)	33,458	57.5%	+2.1%	28,695	55.4%	(C)
Burton, Mrs M.E. (L/All)	14,994	25.8%	-5.1%	15,983	30.8%	(L/All)
Collette, Ms C. (Lab)	9,733	16.7%	+2.9%	7,145	13.8%	(Lab)
L/All to C swing 3.6%	58,185	C maj 18,464 31.7%		51,823	C maj 12,712 24.5%	

Mr Douglas Hurd was appointed Home Secretary in 1985; Secretary of State for N Ireland, 1984-85; Minister of State, Home Office, 1983-84; Minister of State for Foreign and Commonwealth Affairs, 1979-83; Opposition spokesman on Europe, 1976-79; head of Mr Edward Heath's political office, 1968-74; Cons Research Dept, 1966-68. Elected for this seat 1983; MP for Mid-Oxon, Feb 1974-83. B Mar 8 1930; ed Eton and Trinity Coll, Cambridge (Pres of Union, 1952). In Foreign Service, 1952-66, in China, the United States and Europe, becoming a chief secretary. Visiting Fellow, Nuffield Coll, Oxford, 1978. Author of political thrillers.
Dr Muriel Burton, adult education organiser, contested Mid-Oxon in 1979 and Oct 1974, Oldham East in 1964; also Cotswolds in 1984 and 1979 Euro elections. Mbr, Lib Pty Cl and Lib Euro panel. B Jun 17 1934; ed Counthill GS, Oldham; Manchester, Oxford and Reading Univs. Former mbr, Oldham BC and S Oxon DC. ASTMS.
Mrs Christine Collette is researching modern history. B Jun 4 1947; ed Oxford Univ. Full-time Nalgo official, 1976C80. Sch governor. Founder mbr, Labour Heritage.

Mr Douglas Hurd

WOKING — No change

Electorate %Turnout	82,476	75.1%	**1987**	78,327	71.7%	**1983**
*Onslow, C.G.D. (C)	35,990	58.1%	-0.2%	32,748	58.3%	(C)
Goldenberg, P. (L/All)	19,446	31.4%	+2.0%	16,511	29.4%	(L/All)
Pollack, Ms A.J. (Lab)	6,537	10.5%	-1.1%	6,566	11.7%	(Lab)
				368	0.7%	(Other)
C to L/All swing 1.1%	61,973	C maj 16,544 26.7%		56,193	C maj 16,237 28.9%	

Mr Cranley Onslow, elected chairman of 1922 Committee of all Conservative backbenchers in 1984; mbr, its exec, 1968-72, 1981-82 and 1983-84. Minister of State for Foreign and Commonwealth Affairs, 1982-83; Under Secretary of State for Trade and Industry (Aerospace and Shipping), 1972-74; Opposition spokesman on health and social security, 1974-75; and on defence, 1975-76. Chmn, Select Cmte on Defence, 1981-1982, and a member, 1980-82; chmn, Cons back-bench aviation cmte, 1970-72, 1979-82. Elected in 1964. Director, Argyll Group plc,1983- ; Rediffusion plc, 1985- , and Rediffusion Radio Systems; consultant to Bristow Helicopters; associate, Management consultants. Chmn, Nautical Museums Trust, 1983- . B Jun 8 1926; ed Harrow; Oriel Coll, Oxford; Geneva Univ. Mbr, UK delegation, Cl of Europe, 1972-83; Dartford RDC, 1960-62; Kent CC, 1961-64; British Field Sports Soc; Anglers' Coop Assocn, Salmon and Trout Assocn, and Nat Rifle Assocn.
Mr Philip Goldenberg, solicitor. Mbr, Woking BC, 1984- ; Lib Pty Cl, 1975- ; nat exec, 1984-85 (co-opted) and since 1986. Contested this seat 1983; Eton and Slough, 1979 and twice in 1974. B Apr 26 1946; ed St Paul's Sch, London; Pembroke Coll, Oxford.
Ms Anita Pollack, political researcher, contested London South West in 1984 Euro election. Exec mbr, Greater London Lab Pty; vice-chair, Newham NE CLP; nat exec mbr, London Coordinating Cmte. B Jun 3 1946; ed City of London Poly; Birkbeck Coll, London Univ.

Mr Cranley Onslow

WOKINGHAM — No change

Electorate %Turnout	85,474	75.9%	**1987**	71,725	76.0%	**1983**
Redwood, J.A. (C)	39,808	61.4%	+1.0%	32,925	60.4%	(C)
Leston, J.C. (L/All)	19,421	29.9%	-1.7%	17,227	31.6%	(L/All)
Morgan, P.J. (Lab)	5,622	8.7%	+0.7%	4,362	8.0%	(Lab)
L/All to C swing 1.3%	64,851	C maj 20,387 31.4%		54,514	C maj 15,698 28.8%	

Mr John Redwood, industrialist and banker, was, from 1984, head of the Prime Minister's policy unit; adviser on nationalized industries to Treasury and Civil Service Select Cmte, 1981. Contested Southwark, Peckham, 1982 by-election. Deputy chmn, Norcros plc; investment manager and director, N M Rothschild and Sons, 1977- ; investment adviser, Robert Fleming and Co, 1973-77. B Jun 15 1951; ed Kent Coll, Canterbury; Magdalen and St Antony's Colls, Oxford. Fellow, All Souls, 1972. Mb, Oxfordshire CC, 1973-77.
Mr John Leston, company director, leads Alliance gp on Berkshire CC, to which he was elected in 1981. Contested this seat 1983. B Nov 26 1953; ed Chesterfield Sch; City Sch, Lincoln; Queen Elizabeth's GS, Blackburn; Magdalen and Nuffield Colls, Oxford. Director, business consultancy - Research Solutions Ltd.
Mr Peter Morgan, finance officer, Medical Research Cl. Vice-chair, Wantage CLP and Wiltshire Euro constituency; Wantage branch sec. Mbr, Wantage TC, 1983-87. B Jun 24 1955; ed Upper Sch, Banbury. Soc of Civil and Public Servants.

Mr John Redwood

WOLVERHAMPTON NORTH EAST — C gain

Electorate %Turnout	63,464	74.3%	**1987**	63,716	70.3%	**1983**
Hicks, Mrs M. (C)	19,857	42.1%	+2.5%	17,941	40.1%	(Lab)
Purchase, K. (Lab)	19,653	41.7%	+1.6%	17,727	39.6%	(C)
Pearson, M. (L/All)	7,623	16.2%	-2.9%	8,524	19.0%	(L/All)
				585	1.3%	(Other)
Lab to C swing 0.5%	47,133	C maj 204 0.4%		44,777	Lab maj 214 0.5%	

Mrs Maureen Hicks, lecturer, tourism consultant and director, Stratford-upon-Avon Motor Museum. Mbr, Stratford on Avon DC, 1979-84 (chmn, tourism cmte; vice-chmn, Stratford tourism markcting gp; vice-chmn, ammenities cmte); former mbr, Heart of England Tourist Bd executive; former sch governor; chmn, Stratford Junior Business and Professional Women's Club, 1985-86; former mbr, management team, CAB and Bishopton Community Assocn. Former asst staff manager, Marks and Spencer; ex-teacher. B Feb 23 1948; ed Ashley Sec Sch; Brockenhurst GS; Furzedown Coll of Ed.
Mr Kenneth Purchase, adviser to worker-controlled co-operatives who has worked for Aerospace, British Leyland and as a housing manager. Mbr, Wolverhampton Cl, 1970- ; Wolverhampton DHA; Wolverhampton and Dist Manpower Bd; DHSS Benefits Tribunal. Ed Wolverhampton Poly. TGWU.
Mr Malcolm Pearson, engineer in Wolverhampton factory. Mbr, Wolverhampton BC, 1987- . Chmn, Wolverhampton NE Lib Assocn, 1984-86. B Apr 21 1931; ed primary sch; St Mary's Sec Mod Sch, Willenhall.

Mrs Maureen Hicks

WOLVERHAMPTON SOUTH EAST — No change

Electorate %Turnout	55,710	72.5%	**1987**	56,428	69.1%	**1983**
Turner, D. (Lab)	19,760	48.9%	+4.2%	17,440	44.7%	(Lab)
Mellor, J.P. (C)	13,362	33.1%	+1.2%	12,428	31.9%	(C)
Whitehouse, R.F. (L/All)	7,258	18.0%	-5.4%	9,112	23.4%	(L/All)
C to Lab swing 1.5%	40,380	Lab maj 6,398 15.8%		38,980	Lab maj 5,012 12.9%	

Mr Dennis Turner, partner and director of Springvale sports, social and leisure cooperative, contested Halesowen and Stourbridge, Feb and Oct 1974. Mbr, West Midlands CC, 1974-86; Wolverhampton BC, 1966- (currently deputy leader; former chmn, education, housing, social services). Director, Springvale Training Centre; West Midlands Enterprise Board; Black Country Cooperative Development Agency; Wolverhampton Enterprise Ltd. B Aug 26 1942; ed Stonehead Sec Mod Sch; Bilston CFE. ISTC.
Mr John Mellor, retired police superintendent; in police force 1949-84. Mbr (for Graiseley ward), Wolverhampton Cl, 1987- ; vice-chmn constituency Cons assocn. B Nov 29 1928; ed Uttoxeter; Burton Tech Coll.
Mr Richard Whitehouse, school master, contested Derby North 1979. Chmn, Hull ULS 1971-73; chmn, Hull Central, 1973; mbr, exec, Wolverhampton SE Libs, 1974- ; exec, NLYL, 1972-74. Mbr, Wolverhampton MBC, 1984- . B Nov 27 1951; ed Hull Univ. NUT.

Mr Dennis Turner

WOL

WOLVERHAMPTON SOUTH WEST — No change

Electorate %Turnout	68,586	75.5%	**1987**	68,847	72.4%	**1983**
*Budgen, N.W. (C)	26,235	50.7%	+0.1%	25,214	50.6%	(C)
Lawrence, R. (Lab)	15,917	30.7%	+3.3%	13,694	27.5%	(Lab)
Lamb, B. (SDP/All)	9,616	18.6%	-2.9%	10,724	21.5%	(SDP/All)
				201	0.4%	(Other)
C to Lab swing 1.6%	51,768	C maj 10,318 19.9%		49,833	C maj 11,520 23.1%	

Mr Nicholas Budgen, barrister, has been a mbr of the Select Cmte on Treasury and Civil Service, since 1983; Public Accounts Cmte, 1980-81. Elected in Feb 1974; contested Birmingham, Small Heath, 1970. Asst Govt whip, 1981-82. Sec, Cons backbench finance cmte, 1979. B Nov 3 1937; ed St Edward's Sch, Oxford; Corpus Christi Coll, Cambridge. Chmn, Birmingham Bow Group, 1967-68.
Mr Roger Lawrence, local govt officer and former lecturer and researcher. B Nov 9 1951. Mbr, Wolverhampton BC, 1983- . Nalgo.
Mr Beris Lamb, building contractor. B Mar 14 1942; ed sec sch; Wolverhampton Coll; Bilston Coll. Vice-chmn and former chmn, SDP area pty. Mbr, ISTC until redundancy; was chmn, management branch, Bilston Steelworks.

Mr Nicholas Budgen

WOODSPRING — No change

Electorate %Turnout	76,289	79.1%	**1987**	71,280	77.8%	**1983**
*Dean, Sir Paul (C)	34,134	56.6%	-1.0%	31,932	57.6%	(C)
Coleman, Mrs C.R. (L/All)	16,282	27.0%	-3.3%	16,800	30.3%	(L/All)
Chapple, D.L.T. (Lab)	8,717	14.4%	+2.7%	6,536	11.8%	(Lab)
Keeble, Dr B.R. (Grn)	1,208	2.0%		177	0.3%	(W Reg)
L/All to C swing 1.1%	60,341	C maj 17,852 29.6%		55,445	C maj 15,132 27.3%	

Sir Paul Dean was appointed First Deputy Chairman of Ways and Means and Deputy Speaker in Jun 1987; Second Dep Chmn and Dep Spkr, 1982-87. Mbr, Chairmen's Panel, 1979-82; Select Cmte on Members' Salaries, 1981-82; Select Cmte on Commons Services, 1979-82; Select Cmte on Overseas Development, 1978-79. Consultant to Grand Metropolitan Brewing, Foods, Leisure and Retailing plc; consultant on pension schemes; former director, Watney Mann and Truman Holdings Ltd. Chmn, Cons back-bench health and social services cmte, 1979-82. Under Secretary of State for Health and Social Security, 1970-74. Elected for this seat 1983; MP for North Somerset, 1964-83; contested Pontefract by-election, 1962. B Sep 14 1924; ed Ellesmere Coll, Shropshire; Exeter Coll, Oxford. Resident tutor, Swinton Coll, 1956-57; joined Cons research dept, 1958; asst director, 1962-64. Chmn, Watchdog gp for self-employed, 1975-79.
Mrs Ruth Coleman, mathematics teacher, contested Macclesfield 1983 and Liverpool, Toxteth 1979. B Jan 21 1947; ed Manchester HS for Girls; York and Manchester Univs.
Mr David Chapple, postman. Chmn, Woodspring CLP; previously TU liaison officer for CLP; former sec, Clevedon branch. B Dec 7 1951; ed Nailsea Comprehensive Sch. Nupe shop steward; UCW.

Sir Paul Dean

WOOLWICH — No change

Electorate %Turnout	58,071	70.7%	**1987**	56,297	68.0%	**1983**
*Cartwright, J.C. (SDP/All)	17,137	41.7%	+1.2%	15,492	40.5%	(SDP/All)
Austin Walker, J. (Lab)	15,200	37.0%	+3.6%	12,767	33.4%	(Lab)
Salter, A. (C)	8,723	21.2%	-3.9%	9,616	25.1%	(C)
				384	1.0%	(Other)
SDP/All to Lab swing 1.2%	41,060 SDP/All maj 1,937 4.7%			38,259 SDP/All maj 2,725 7.1%		

Mr John Cartwright, Vice-President of the SDP, was Alliance spokesman on defence in its election team; SDP spokesman on defence and foreign affairs since 1983, and environment, 1981-83. Mbr, Select Cmte on Defence, 1979-82 and since 1986. SDP whip, 1983- . Director, Royal Arsenal Co-operative Society, 1972-74, being its political sec, 1967-72. Elected as Labour MP for Woolwich East in Oct 1974; resigned party and joined SDP, 1981. Won this seat 1983; contested Bexleyheath, Feb 1974, and Bexley, 1970. Parly adviser to Professional Assoc of Teachers. B Nov 29 1933; ed Woking CGS. Jt chmn, Cl for Advancement of Arab/British Understanding, 1983- vice-chmn, GB-USSR Assocn, 1983- ; vice-pres, AMA, 1974- . Exec civil servant, 1952-55; Lab Pty organizer, 1955-67; chmn, Nat Union of Lab Organizers, 1969-70. Ldr of Greenwich BC, 1971-74 and chief whip, London Boroughs Assocn, 1971-75. Mbr, Lab Pty NEC, 1971-75 and 1976-78. Trustee, Nat Maritime Museum, 1976-83.
Mr John Austin-Walker, popularly known as "Jaws", is a community relations officer in Bexley; former sec/agent, Greenwich Lab Pty. Member, Greenwich BC, 1980- (ldr of cl, 1982-87). Vice-chmn, ALA. B Aug 21 1944; ed Glyn GS, Epsom; Goldsmiths Coll, New Cross. Governor, Greenwich Theatre. ASTMS.
Mr Anthony Salter, publisher, former journalist. Mb, Lewisham BC, 1982- . B 1949; ed Gravesend GS; Lancaster Univ.

Mr John Cartwright

244

WORCESTER — No change

Electorate %Turnout	68,980	76.7%	**1987**	66,531	74.1%	**1983**
*Walker, P.E. (C)	25,504	48.2%	-1.3%	24,381	49.4%	(C)
Webb, M.J. (Lab)	15,051	28.4%	+5.7%	13,510	27.4%	(SDP/All)
Caiger, J.J. (SDP/All)	12,386	23.4%	-4.0%	11,208	22.7%	(Lab)
				208	0.4%	(Other)
C to Lab swing 3.5%	52,941	C maj 10,453 19.7%		49,307	C maj 10,871 22.0%	

Mr **Peter Walker** was appointed Secretary of State for Wales in Jun 1987; Secretary of State for Energy, 1983-867; Minister of Agriculture, Fisheries and Food, 1979-83. Chief Opposition spokesman on defence, 1974-1975, and on trade and industry, 1974. Secretary of State for Trade and Industry, 1972-74; Secretary of State for Environment, 1970-72; Minister of Housing and Local Government, Jun-Oct 1970. Opposition spokesman on Treasury and economic affairs, 1964-66, on transport, 1966-68, on local govt, housing and land, 1968-70. Elected at 1961 by-election. B Mar 25 1932; ed Latymer Upper Sch, Hammersmith. Former chmn, Lloyd's insurance brokers and former director of other companies.
Mr **Mike Webb**, senior lecturer in economics at Worcester Coll of HE. B Mar 13 1952; ed St Joseph's Coll and Trinity Coll, Oxford. Trained as teacher in Coventry. Former researcher for BR. Set up Worcestershire's Education and Industry Centre, 1981.
Mr **John Caiger**, merchant banker. B Jul 11 1936; ed Dover Coll; RMA Sandhurst.

Mr Peter Walker

WORCESTERSHIRE MID — No change

Electorate %Turnout	80,591	76.6%	**1987**	74,254	74.6%	**1983**
*Forth, M.E. (C)	31,854	51.6%	+0.7%	28,159	50.9%	(C)
Pinfield, P. (Lab)	16,943	27.4%	+2.2%	13,954	25.2%	(Lab)
Harwood, E. (SDP/All)	12,954	21.0%	-2.3%	12,866	23.2%	(SDP/All)
				386	0.7%	(Other)
C to Lab swing 0.8%	61,751	C maj 14,911 24.1%		55,365	C maj 14,205 25.7%	

Mr **Eric Forth** was elected in 1983; contested Barking, Feb and Oct 1974. Mbr, European Parliament, for North Birmingham, 1979-84; chmn, back-bench cmte, European Democratic Group. PPS, Minister of State for Education and Science, 1986- . Vice-chmn, Cons back-bench European Affairs cmte, 1983-86; mbr, Select Cmte on Employment, 1983-87; sec, Cons back-bench sports cmte, 1985-86. B Sep 9 1944; ed Jordanhill Coll Sch, Glasgow; Glasgow Univ. Mbr, Brentwood UDC, 1968-72. Non-exec company director, Business Link (Europe) Ltd.
Mr **Peter Pinfield**, social worker. B Jan 27 1948; ed Exeter and Open Univs. Former personnel and training manager and sch governor.
Mr **Edgar Harwood**, regional director in steel stockholding, contested Wolverhampton South West in 1983. B Sep 4 1939; ed Aston Univ. Runner-up, Town Crier World Championship, 1986.

Mr Eric Forth

WORCESTERSHIRE SOUTH — No change

Electorate %Turnout	77,237	75.6%	**1987**	73,278	73.6%	**1983**
*Spicer, W.M.H. (C)	32,277	55.3%	-0.5%	30,095	55.8%	(C)
Chandler, P.J. (L/All)	18,632	31.9%	-2.7%	18,706	34.7%	(L/All)
Garnett, R.J. (Lab)	6,374	10.9%	+3.2%	4,183	7.8%	(Lab)
Woodford, G.M.H. (Grn)	1,089	1.9%	+0.3%	866	1.6%	(Eco)
				113	0.2%	(Other)
L/All to C swing 1.1%	58,372	C maj 13,645 23.4%		53,963	C maj 11,389 21.1%	

Mr **Michael Spicer** was appointed Under Secretary of State for Energy in Jun 1987; Under Secretary of State for Transport, 1984-87, being Minister for Aviation, 1985-87. Elected, Feb 1974; contested Easington, 1966 and 1970. Vice-chmn, Cons Party, 1981-83; dep chmn, 1983-85. Former economic consultant. PPS to Ministers of State for Trade, 1979-81. Mbr, Cons Research Dept, 1966-68; director, Cons Systems Research Centre, 1968-70. B Jan 22 1943; ed Wellington Coll and Emmanuel Coll, Cambridge. Managing director, Economic Models Ltd, 1970-80; former director, Argus Press Group.
Mr **Paul Chandler**, computer programmer, is a director of Computer Department Ltd, Malvern, and of the Travel Club, Upminster. Mbr, Malvern Hill DC, 1982- ; Hereford and Worcester CC, 1985- . B Nov 9 1949; ed Felsted Sch, Essex; Essex Univ.
Mr **Robert Garnett**, teacher. Has served on management and exec cmtes, Halesowen and Stourbridge CLP. B Jun 27 1948; ed Stoneham Boys' Sch, Reading; Berkshire Coll of Ed; Reading and Surrey Univs. Mbr, Reading BC, 1973-79 (Lab gp ldr, 1976-78). Vice-pres and former pres, Dudley NUT.

Mr Michael Spicer

245

WORKINGTON — No change

Electorate %Turnout	56,911	80.6%	**1987**	56,119	79.6%	**1983**
*Campbell-Savours, D.N. (Lab)	24,019	52.4%	+0.3%	23,239	52.0%	(Lab)
McIntosh, Miss A.C.B. (C)	17,000	37.1%	+1.0%	16,111	36.1%	(C)
Badger, G.W. (L/All)	4,853	10.6%	-1.3%	5,311	11.9%	(L/All)
Lab to C swing 0.3%	45,872	Lab maj 7,019 15.3%		44,661	Lab maj 7,128 16.0%	

Mr Dale Campbell-
Savours

Mr Dale Campbell-Savours has served on the Public Accounts Commmittee, the Select Committee on MPs Interests and the Select Committee on Procedure since 1983. Regained Workington for Labour in 1979; contested Darwen, Feb and Oct, 1974. Director, clock manufacturing company, 1971-76. B Aug 23 1943; ed Keswick Sch and Sorbonne. Mbr, Ramsbottom UDC, 1972-74. TGWU. Sponsored by Cohse.
Miss Anne McIntosh, political adviser. B Sep 20 1954; ed Harrogate Coll; Edinburgh Univ; Aarhus Univ, Denmark.
Mr William Badger, official of an education authority. B 1944; ed Warwick Sch; Exeter, Birmingham and Lancaster Univs.

WORSLEY — No change

Electorate %Turnout	73,208	77.2%	**1987**	71,987	74.7%	**1983**
*Lewis, T. (Lab)	27,157	48.1%	+7.8%	21,675	40.3%	(Lab)
Horman, Mrs V. (C)	19,820	35.1%	+2.5%	17,536	32.6%	(C)
Cowpe, D. (L/All)	9,507	16.8%	-10.2%	14,545	27.1%	(SDP/All)
C to Lab swing 2.6%	56,484	Lab maj 7,337 13.0%		53,756	Lab maj 4,139 7.7%	

Mr Terence Lewis

Mr Terence Lewis, a personnel officer, was elected in 1983. Jt vice-chmn, PLP health and social security cmte, 1985- . B Dec 29 1935; ed Mount Carmel Sch, Salford. Member, Bolton BC, 1975- ; education cmte chmn, 1982-83; member, Kearsley UDC, 1971-74. Sponsored by TGWU.
Mrs Veronica Horman, mathematics teacher. Mbr, Mid-Sussex DC, 1981-87; Reading BC, 1973-79. Mayor of East Grinstead, 1985-86. Mbr, South East Area Advisory Cmte on Education. B Mar 15 1949; ed St Joseph's Convent, Reading; St Mary's Coll, Twickenham.
Mr David Cowpe, journalist, has served on Salford City Cl. B Jan 14 1942; ed Chetham's Hospital Sch, Manchester. NUJ.

WORTHING — No change

Electorate %Turnout	77,000	72.8%	**1987**	75,772	71.2%	**1983**
*Higgins, T.L. (C)	34,573	61.7%	+0.9%	32,807	60.9%	(C)
Clare, B.A. (L/All)	16,072	28.7%	-3.9%	17,554	32.6%	(L/All)
Deen, J. (Lab)	5,387	9.6%	+3.8%	3,158	5.9%	(Lab)
				395	0.7%	(Other)
L/All to C swing 2.4%	56,032	C maj 18,501 33.0%		53,914	C maj 15,253 28.3%	

Mr Terence Higgins

Mr Terence Higgins, an economist, became chairman of the Select Cmte on Treasury and Civil Service in 1983; mbr since 1980. Chmn, Select Cmte on Procedure (Finance), 1981-82; House of Commons Liaison Cmte, 1984- . Special Fellow, Policy Studies Inst, 1986-87. Mbr, Public Accounts Commission, 1984- . Chmn, Cons back-bench transport cmte, 1979-82, and since 1985. Opposition spokesman on trade, 1974-76; a spokesman on Treasury and economic affairs, 1974. Financial Secretary to the Treasury, 1972-74; Minister of State, Treasury, 1970-72. Elected 1964. B Jan 18 1928; ed Alleyn's Sch, Dulwich; Gonville and Caius Coll, Cambridge, and Yale. Opposition spokesman on Treasury and economic affairs, 1966-70. Economist with Unilever, 1959-64; director, Lex Service Group, 1980- . Former Olympic and Commonwealth Games athlete. Chmn, Cons back-bench sports and recreation cmte, 1979-82; mbr, exec, 1922 Cmte, 1980- . Cl mbr, Royal Inst of International Affairs, 1980-86; Inst of Advanced Motorists, 1980- . Governor, Dulwich Coll, 1980- . Trustee, Industry and Parliament Trust.
Mr Robert Clare, biologist, has been a mbr of Worthing BC since 1975. B Feb 13 1941; ed St John's Sch, Leatherhead; Brunel Univ.
Mr James Deen, journalist, chairs Worthing CLP. B Mar 6 1946; ed Queen Elizabeth GS, Wakefield; Manchester Univ. NUJ.

WREKIN, THE — Lab gain

Electorate %Turnout	82,520	78.3%	**1987**	77,226	75.5%	**1983**
Grocott, B. (Lab)	27,681	42.8%	+6.1%	22,710	39.0%	(C)
*Hawksley, P.W. (C)	26,225	40.6%	+1.6%	21,379	36.7%	(Lab)
Cook, G. (SDP/All)	10,737	16.6%	-7.8%	14,208	24.4%	(SDP/All)
C to Lab swing 2.3%	64,643	Lab maj 1,456 2.3%		58,297	C maj 1,331 2.3%	

Mr **Bruce Grocott**, television producer, was MP for Lichfield and Tamworth, Oct 1974-1979; contested this seat 1983; SW Hertfordshire 1970. PPS to Mr John Silkin, 1975-78 (Minister for Local Government and Planning then Minister of Agriculture, Fisheries and Food). Chmn, all-party penal reform gp, 1976-79. Mbr, Select Cmte on Overseas Development, 1978-79; Bromsgrove DC, 1971-74 (chmn, finance cmte). B Nov 1 1940; ed Hemel Hempstead GS; Leicester and Manchester Univs. NUJ; ASTMS.

Mr **Warren Hawksley** served on the Select Cmte on Employment in 1987; jt sec, Cons backbench urban and new towns cmte, 1985-87. Worked for Lloyds Bank, 1960-79. MP for this seat, 1979-87; contested Wolverhampton North-East, Feb and Oct 1974. B Mar 10 1943; ed Mill Mead, Shrewsbury; Denstone Coll, Uttoxeter. Mbr, Shropshire CC, 1970-81; West Mercia Police Authority, 1977-81. Governor, Wolverhampton Poly, 1973-77. Dep chmn, Oswestry Cons, 1975-77.

Mr **George Cook**, teacher. Sec, S Staffs area SDP; Labour mbr, Walsall BC, 1970-73. B Feb 2 1937; ed County GS, Hyde; Chester Diocesan Training Coll. NAS/UWT.

Mr Bruce Grocott

WREXHAM — No change

Electorate %Turnout	62,401	80.9%	**1987**	60,707	77.5%	**1983**
*Marek, J. (Lab)	22,144	43.9%	+9.6%	16,120	34.3%	(Lab)
Graham-Palmer, R.H.W. (C)	17,992	35.6%	+2.3%	15,696	33.4%	(C)
Thomas, M. (L/All)	9,808	19.4%	-10.3%	13,974	29.7%	(L/All)
Watkins, D. (Pl C)	539	1.1%	-1.6%	1,239	2.6%	(Pl C)
C to Lab swing 3.7%	50,483	Lab maj 4,152 8.2%		47,029	Lab maj 424 0.9%	

Dr **John Marek** joined the Opposition's DHSS front bench team in 1985 as a spokesman on health. Mbr, Select Cmte on Welsh Affairs, 1983-86; PAC, 1985; all-pty road study gp. Lecturer in applied maths, Univ Coll of Wales, Aberystwyth, 1966-83. Elected in 1983; contested Ludlow, Oct 1974. B Dec 24 1940; ed London Univ. Sec, Aberystwyth Lab Party, 1971-79; chmn, Dyfed County Lab Pty, 1978-80. Mbr, Ceredigion DC, 1979-83; International Astronomical Union. Fellow, Industry and Parliament Trust. Sponsored by NUR.

Mr **Roger Graham-Palmer**, farmer, hotel owner and company director, contested the seat 1979. Mbr, Wrexham Maelor BC, 1973-83. B Feb 15 1941; ed Radley Coll, Abingdon; Emmanuel Coll, Cambridge. Director, Wrexham and East Denbyshire Water Co; chmn, Wrexham Training Ltd.

Mr **Martin Thomas, QC**, Recorder of Crown Court, contested this seat 1983, 1979 and twice in 1974; West Flint 1970, 1966 and 1964. Vice-chmn, Marcher Sound, independent local radio for Wrexham and Chester. Mbr, Criminal Injuries Compensation Bd. Welsh rugby coach and referee. B Mar 13 1937; ed Grove Park GS, Wrexham; Peterhouse, Cambridge.

Mr **Dennis Watkins**, optician, contested Newport West 1983. Pl Cymru's treas. Mbr, Taff Ely BC, 1987- .

Dr John Marek

WYCOMBE — No change

Electorate %Turnout	71,918	72.8%	**1987**	70,065	71.7%	**1983**
*Whitney, R.W. (C)	28,209	53.9%	-0.4%	27,221	54.2%	(C)
Hayhoe, T.E.G. (SDP/All)	14,390	27.5%	-0.5%	14,024	27.9%	(SDP/All)
Huddart, J.R.W. (Lab)	9,773	18.7%	+1.5%	8,636	17.2%	(Lab)
				327	0.7%	(Other)
SDP/All to C swing 0.1%	52,372	C maj 13,819 26.4%		50,208	C maj 13,197 26.3%	

Mr **Raymond Whitney** was Under Secretary of State for Health and Social Security, 1984-86; Under Secretary of State for Foreign and Commonwealth Affairs, 1983-84. Former company chmn and export consultant. Elected at by-election in 1978. Mbr, PAC, 1981-83. Jt vice-chmn, Cons back-bench employment cmte, 1980-83; chmn, Cons back-bench foreign and Commonwealth affairs cmte, 1981-83. B Nov 28 1930; ed Wellingborough Sch; Sandhurst; London Univ. In diplomatic service: First Sec, Peking, 1966-68; Head of Chancery, British Embassy, Buenos Aires, 1969-72; Asst Head, East African Dept, Foreign and Commonwealth Office, 1972-73; Dep High Commissioner and Economic Counsellor, Dacca, 1973-76; Head of Information Research Dept and Overseas Information Dept, FCO, 1976-78. PPS to Treasury ministers, 1979-80.

Mr **Thomas Hayhoe**, corporate planning manager with W.H. Smith. Research asst and speechwriter for Mr Peter Walker, 1978-81. Member, SDP health and social services policy gp, 1982- . B Mar 3 1956; ed Woodruffe Comp Sch, Lyne Regis; St Paul's Sch, London; Corpus Christi Coll, Cambridge (Pres of Union, 1977-78); Stanford Univ.

Mr **John Hoddart**, chmn and director, subsidiary companies, Booker plc. Former cllr and Lab chief whip, Newcastle City Cl. B May 25 1926; ed lea schs; Durham Univ; LSE.

Mr Raymond Whitney

WYRE — No change

Electorate %Turnout	67,066	75.4%	**1987**	65,934	71.4%	**1983**
Mans, K.D.R. (C)	26,800	53.0%	-3.4%	26,559	56.4%	(C)
Murdoch, I.C. (SDP/All)	12,139	24.0%	-0.9%	11,748	25.0%	(SDP/All)
Ainscough, P. (Lab)	10,725	21.2%	+2.6%	8,743	18.6%	(Lab)
Brown, R. (Grn)	874	1.7%				
C to SDP/All swing 1.2%	50,538	C maj 14,661 29.0%		47,050	C maj 14,811 31.5%	

Mr **Keith Mans**, manager with John Lewis Partnership. Former RAF pilot and now pilot in RAF Reserve. Contested Stoke-on-Trent Central, 1983. B Feb 10 1946; ed Berkhamsted Sch; RAF Coll, Cranwell; Open Univ. Leader, New Forest DC; chmn, New Forest Conservatives; mbr, New Forest local government liaison gp. Mbr, Bow Gp; Con Gp for Europe. Past winner of the Wessex area speaking competition.
Mr **Iain Murdoch**, teacher; head of general studies. Treas, NW Reg Cl, SDP; chmn, Lancaster and Wyre area pty, 1982-83; mbr, SDP fishing policy cmte. B Oct 16 1950; ed Oxford and Edinburgh Univs.
Mr **Paul Ainscough**, works for a pharmaceutical company. B Feb 12 1961. Former sec, Socialist Students' Assoc, Preston Poly.

Mr Keith Mans

WYRE FOREST — No change

Electorate %Turnout	70,784	77.6%	**1987**	68,298	75.1%	**1983**
Coombs, A.M.V. (C)	25,877	47.1%	-1.2%	24,809	48.4%	(C)
Batchelor, A.J. (L/All)	18,653	34.0%	+1.6%	16,632	32.4%	(L/All)
Knowles, N. (Lab)	10,365	18.9%	-0.3%	9,850	19.2%	(Lab)
C to L/All swing 1.4%	54,895	C maj 7,224 13.2%		51,291	C maj 8,177 15.9%	

Mr **Anthony Coombs** is a director of several Midlands based companies; interests in finance and building development. Contested Coventry North West in 1983. Mbr, Birmingham City Cl, since 1978. B Nov 18 1952; ed Charterhouse Sch, Surrey; Worcester Coll, Oxford.
Mr **Anthony Batchelor** is head of business and social studies, Kidderminster Coll, and an Open Univ tutor. Contested this seat 1983, Kidderminster twice in 1974, Worcestershire South 1964, and Birmingham South in 1979 Euro election. Mbr, Wyre Forest DC, 1973-87 (chmn, 1986-87; ldr, 1979-83 and 1984-86). B Apr 6 1941; ed King Charles I Sch, Kidderminster; Univ Coll, London; Birmingham Poly; Keele Univ. NATFHE.
Mr **Nigel Knowles**, trade union educ officer, contested Hastings and Rye 1983 and Bodmin 1979. B Dec 5 1946; ed Birmingham Poly; Essex Univ; Worcester Coll of HE. Served on Haringey Cl.

Mr Anthony Coombs

YEOVIL — No change

Electorate %Turnout	70,390	79.7%	**1987**	66,102	79.8%	**1983**
*Ashdown, J.J.D. (L/All)	28,841	51.4%	+1.0%	26,608	50.5%	(L/All)
Sandeman, G.D.S. (C)	23,141	41.3%	-2.7%	23,202	44.0%	(C)
Fitzmaurice, J. (Lab)	4,099	7.3%	+1.8%	2,928	5.6%	(Lab)
C to L/All swing 1.9%	56,081	L/All maj 5,700 10.2%		52,738	L/All maj 3,406 6.5%	

Mr **Paddy Ashdown** was Alliance spokesman on education in its election team. Liberal spokesman on trade and industry since 1983. Director (unpaid), Election Technology Ltd. Won this seat in 1983; contested it, 1979. B Feb 24 1941; ed Bedford Sch; Hongkong University. Qualified Chinese interpreter. Capt in Royal Marines, 1959-71, in Commando units and Special Boat Service in Far East. First Secretary to UK mission to UN in Geneva, 1971-76; in commercial manager's dept, Westland Helicopters, Yeovil, 1976-78; senior manager, Morlands, Yeovil, 1978-81; local govt officer, Dorset CC, 1981-83.
Mr **Dugald Sandeman**, farmer. Mbr, Somerset CC, 1979-85 (chmn, ed cmte, 1983-85). B Sep 9 1949; ed Sherborne Sch; Magdalene Coll, Cambridge. NFU.
Mr **John Fitzmaurice**, international civil servant; administrator in general secretariat, EEC Commission, Brussels. B Nov 18 1947; ed Shaftesbury GS; Bristol Univ. Mbr, European Civil Service Union.

Mr Paddy Ashdown

YNYS MON					PI C gain
Electorate %Turnout	52,633	81.7%	**1987**	50,359	79.6%	**1983**
Jones, I.W. (Pl C)	18,580	43.2%	+10.0%	15,017	37.5%	(C)
Evans, R. (C)	14,282	33.2%	-4.2%	13,333	33.3%	(Pl C)
Parry, C. (Lab)	7,252	16.9%	-0.1%	6,791	16.9%	(Lab)
Evans, I.L. (SDP/All)	2,863	6.7%	-5.7%	4,947	12.3%	(SDP/All)
C to Pl C swing 7.1%	42,977	Pl C maj 4,298 10.0%		40,088	C maj 1,684 4.2%	

Mr **Ieuan Wyn Jones**, a solicitor, contested this seat 1983; West Denbigh in 1979 and Oct 1974, and North Wales in Euro elections, 1979. Nat Pl Cymru chairman, 1978-82; dep treas of party. B May 22 1949; ed Ysgol-y-Bermyn, Y Bala, Gwynedd; Liverpool Poly.
Mr **Roger Evans**, barrister, contested Warley West 1979 and Oct 1974. B Mar 1947; ed City of Norwich Sch; Bristol GS; Trinity Hall, Cambridge (Pres of Union, 1970). Chmn, Cambridge Univ Cons Assocn, 1969.
Mr **Colin Parry**, former research chemist and production controller in the metal industry, now runs a village supermarket near Holyhead, with his wife. B Oct 3 1939; ed Holyhead Comprehensive Sch; Cardiff Univ. Brother-in-law of Mr Neil Kinnock. ASTMS.
Mr **Ieuan Evans**, local govt officer with Gwynedd CC, became vice-chmn of the SDP Cl for Wales in 1987; mbr, CSD; SDP policy cmte for Wales; policy coordinator for Alliance in Wales. Mbr, Arfon BC, 1985-87. B Jul 11 1956; ed Ysgol Glan Clwyd, St Asaph; Univ Coll of N Wales, Bangor.

Mr Ieuan Wyn Jones

YORK					No change
Electorate %Turnout	79,297	78.4%	**1987**	78,311	75.1%	**1983**
*Gregory, C.R. (C)	25,880	41.6%	+0.3%	24,309	41.3%	(C)
Bayley, H. (Lab)	25,733	41.4%	+6.3%	20,662	35.1%	(Lab)
Cable, J.V. (SDP/All)	9,898	15.9%	-7.1%	13,523	23.0%	(SDP/All)
Dunnett, A.D. (Grn)	637	1.0%		204	0.3%	(Ind)
				148	0.3%	(Other)
C to Lab swing 3.0%	62,148	C maj 147 0.2%		58,846	C maj 3,647 6.2%	

Mr **Conal Gregory**, an international wine consultant (being a Master of Wine) and lecturer, since 1977, won the seat from Labour in 1983. B Mar 11 1947; ed King's Coll, Wimbledon, Univ of Sheffield and Worshipful Company of Vintners. Editor, International Wine & Food Society's Journal, 1980-83. Nat vice-chmn, Bow Group, 1976-77; mbr, nat advisory cmte, CPC, 1984- . Mbr, CPA; IPU; all-pty disablement gp; all-pty arts and heritage gp. Jt sec, Cons back-bench transport cmte, 1983- . Vice-chmn, Cons food and drinks sub-cmte, 1985- ; jt vice-chmn, Cons tourism cmte, 1985- ; sec, all-pty tourism cmte, 1983- . Mbr, Norfolk CC, 1977-81; E Anglia Tourist Bd, 1979-81. Non-exec director, Westwick Vintners Ltd; parly consultant to Consort Hotels Ltd, the Market Research Soc and Jan Morris and Associates Ltd; and consultant to International Exhibitions Ltd. Mbr, court of governors, Sheffield, York and Hull Univs. Fellow, Industry and Parliament Trust.
Mr **Hugh Bayley**, univ lecturer and freelance television producer; former nat officer, Nalgo. Chaired St Pancras North CLP, 1982; sec, London Lab co-ordinating cmte, 1982-85; mbr, Lab housing gp and Lab aid and development cmte. Mbr, Camden Cl, 1980-86 (chaired employment cmte, 1981-82, and Lab gp, 1982-85) B Jan 9 1952; ed Haileybury Sch; Bristol and York Univs. Mbr, nat cmte, Anti-Apartheid Movement; nat cl, International Yr of Shelter for the Homeless. ACTT and AUT.
Mr **Vincent Cable**, an economist and adviser to the Commonwealth Sec-General; previously dep director, Overseas Development Inst and special adviser to Mr John Smith, when Secretary of State for Trade. Contested this seat for SDP 1983 and Glasgow, Hillhead for Labour 1970. Mbr, SDP policy cmte on development. B May 9 1943; ed Nunthorpe GS, York; Cambridge and Glasgow Univs. Mbr, Glasgow City Cl, 1971-74. ASTMS.
Mr **Alan Dunnett**, coll lecturer. Founder mbr, York Grn Pty. B May 27 1946; ed Gonville and Caius Coll, Cambridge. NATFHE.

Mr Conal Gregory

Rise and fall of the parties 1945-87

The following table gives the parties after each election from 1945 to 1987

	1945	1950	1951	1955	1959	1964	1966	1970	Feb 1974	Oct 1974	1979	1983	1987
Consevative	213	298	321	345	365	303	253	330	296	276	339	397	375
Labour	393	315	295	277	258	317	363	287	301	319	268	209	229
Lib/SDP/All	12	9	6	6	6	9	12	6	14	13	11	23	22
Others	22	3	3	2	-	2*	2*	7*	24*	27*	17*	21	24
(*includes the Speaker)													
Total	640	625	625	630	630	630	630	630	635	635	635	650	650

Abbreviations

The following abbreviations have been used in the biographies of MPs:

ABA	Amateur Boxing Association
Acad	Academy
ACC	Association of County Councils
ACTT	Association of Cinematograph, Television and Allied Technicians
AHA	Area Health Authority
AMA	Association of Metropolitan Authorities
Apex	Association of Professional Executive clerical and Computer Staff
APT	Association of Polytechnic Teachers
Aslef	Associated Society of Locomotive Engineers and Firemen
Assocn	Association
ASTMS	Association of Scientific, Technical and Managerial Staffs
Asst	Assistant
AUEW/TASS	Amalgamated Union of Engineering Workers (Technical Administrative and Supervisory Section)
AUT	Association of University Teachers
B	Born
BC	Borough Council
Bd	Board
BEC	Building Employers' Confederation
BIFU	Banking Insurance and Finance Union
BMA	British Medical Association
CBC	County Borough Council
CBI	Confederation of British Industries
CC	County Council
CFE	College of Further Education
CHC	Community Health Council
Chmn	Chairman
Cl	Council
CLA	Country Landowners' Association
Cllr	Councillor
CLP	Constituency Labour Party
Cmte	Committee
CND	Campaign for Nuclear Disarmament
Cohse	Confederation of Health Service Employees
Coll	College
Confed	Confederation
Cons	Conservative
Co-op	Co-operative Party
Corpn	Corporation
Cosla	Convention of Scottish Local Authorities
CPA	Commonwealth Parliamentary Association
CPC	Conservative Political Centre
CSD	Council for Social Democracy
DC	District Council
Dept	Department
DHA	District health authority
DHSS	Department of Health and Social Security
Dist	District
Div	Division
DTI	Department of Trade and Industry
E	East
Ed	Education
EEC	European Economic Community
EETPU	Electrical, Electronic, Telecommunications, and Plumbing Union
EIS	Educational Institute of Scotland
EPEA	Electrical Power Engineers Association
Exec	Executive
FCO	Foreign and Commonwealth Office
Fed	Federation
FIMechE	Fellow, Institute of Mechanical Engineers
FOC	Father (chairman) of Chapel (branch), NUJ
FRS	Fellow of Royal Society
GLC	Greater London Council
GMB or GMBATU	General, Municipal, Boilermakers and Allied Trades Union
GMC	General management committee
Govt	Government
Gp	Group
GS	Grammar School
Hosp	Hospital
HS	High School
ICE	Institution of Civil Engineers
ILEA	Inner London Education Authority
Inst	Institute
IOJ	Institute of Journalists
IPCS	Institution of Professional Civil Servants
IPU	Interparliamentary Union
ISTC	Iron and Steel Trades Confederation

Jt	Joint
Lab	Labour
Lancs	Lancashire
Ldr	Leader
Lib	Liberal
LP	Liberal Party
LSE	London School of Economics
Mass	Massachusetts
MATSA	Managerial Administrative Tech Staff Assoc
MBC	Metropolitan Borough Council
Mbr	Member
MDC	Metropolitan District Council
MEP	Member of European Parliament
N	North
Nacods	National Association of Collierymen etc
NAHT	National Association of Head Teachers
Nalgo	National Association of Local Government Officers
NAS	National Association of Schoolmasters
Nat	National
NATFHE	National Association of Teachers in Further and Higher Education
NCB	National Coal Board
NCER	National Council for Electoral Reform
NCU	National Communications Union
NE	North East
NEC	National executive committee
NFBTE	National Federation of Building Trades Employers
NFU	National Farmers' Union
NGA	National Graphical Association
NI	Northern Ireland
NLVA	National Licensed Victuallers' Association
NLYL	National League of Young Liberals
Notts	Nottinghamshire
NUJ	National Union of Journalists
NUM	National Union of Mineworkers
NUPE	National Union of Public Employees
NUR	National Union of Railwaymen
NUS	National Union of Seamen
NUS	National Union of Students
NW	North West
PAC	Public Accounts Committee
Parly	Parliamentary
PAT	Professional Association of Teachers
PC	Parish Council
PLP	Parliamentary Labour Party
Poly	Polytechnic
PPS	Parliamentary Private Secretary
Pres	President
Pty	Party
RCVS	Royal College of Veterinary Surgeons
RDC	Rural District Council
Reg	Regional
Rep	Representative
RHA	Regional Health Authority
RMA	Royal Military Academy
RNC	Royal Naval College
S	South
Sch	School
SDP	Social Democratic Party
SE	South East
Sec	Secretary
Sec Mod Sch	Secondary Modern School
SFHEA	Scottish Further and Higher Education Assocn
SLP	Scottish Liberal Party
Soc	Society
Sogat '82	Society of Graphical and Allied Trades '82
SSTA	Scottish Secondary Teachers Association
SW	South West
TC	Town Council
Tech	Technical or Technology
TGWU	Transport and General Workers' Union
Treas	Treasurer
TSSA	Transport Salaried Staffs Association
TV	Television
Ucatt	Union of Construction, Allied Trades and Technicians
UCW	University College of Wales
UDC	Urban District Council
ULS	Union of Liberal Students
UMIST	Univ of Manchester Inst of Science and Tech
UNA	United Nations Association
Univ	University
USDAW	Union of Shop, Distributive and Allied Workers
W	West
WEA	Workers Educational Association
WEU	Western European Union
YHA	Youth Hostels Association
YCs	Young Conservatives
YLs	Young Liberals
Yorks	Yorkshire

250

How the Nation Voted - June 1987

	C	Lab	All	SNP/Pl C	Others	Total
England						
Electorate						35,988,364
Votes	12,521,946	8,005,826	6,466,974	-	137,706	27,132,452
% of vote/turnout	46.2	29.5	23.8	-	0.5	75.4
MPs	357	155	10	-	1*	523
Candidates	522	523	523	-	214	1782
						Swing -1.2%
Scotland						
Electorate						3,952,465
Votes	713,499	1,258,177	570,043	416,873	10,069	2,968,661
% of vote/turnout	24.0	42.4	19.2	14.0	0.3	75.1
MPs	10	50	9	3	0	72
Candidates	72	72	72	71	21	308
						Swing -5.8%
Wales						
Electorate						2,151,332
Votes	501,302	765,267	304,258	123,589	3,742	1,698,158
% of vote/turnout	29.5	45.1	17.9	7.3	0.2	78.9
MPs	8	24	3	3	0	38
Candidates	38	38	38	38	6	158
						Swing -4.5%
N. Ireland						
Electorate						1,089,160
Votes	-	-	-	-	730,152†	730,152
% of vote/turnout	-	-	-	-	100	67.0
MPs	-	-	-	-	17	17
Candidates	-	-	-	-	77	77
United Kingdom						
Electorate						43,181,321
Votes	13,736,747	10,029,270	7,341,275	540,462	881,669	32,529,423
% of vote/turnout	42.2	30.8	22.6	1.7	2.7	75.3
MPs	375	229	22	6	18*	650
Candidates	632	633	633	109	318	2325
						Swing -1.7%

* Including the Speaker

Swings from Lab to C

How the Nation Voted - June 1983

	C	Lab	All	SNP/Pl C	Others	Total
England						
Electorate						35,142,369
Votes	11,711,970	6,862,616	6,714,910	-	183,416	25,472,912
% of vote/turnout	46.0	26.9	26.4	-	0.7	72.5
MPs	362	148	13	-	0	523
Candidates	523	523	523	-	431	2,000
						Swing +4.3%
Scotland						
Electorate						3,886,899
Votes	801,312	990,644	692,367	331,975	7,820	2,824,118
% of vote/turnout	28.4	35.1	24.5	11.8	0.3	72.7
MPs	21	41	8	2	0	72
Candidates	72	72	72	72	26	314
						Swing +1.7%
Wales						
Electorate						2,113,854
Votes	499,310	603,858	373,312	125,309	7,151	1,608,940
% of vote/turnout	31.0	37.5	23.2	7.8	0.4	76.1
MPs	14	20	2	2	0	38
Candidates	38	38	38	38	17	169
						Swing +4.2%
N. Ireland						
Electorate						1,050,222
Votes	-	-	-	-	764,925†	764,925
% of vote/turnout	-	-	-	-	100	72.8
MPs	-	-	-	-	17	17
Candidates	-	-	-	-	95	95
United Kingdom						
Electorate						42,193,344
Votes	13,012,592	8,457,118	7,780,589	457,284	963,312	30,670,895
% of vote/turnout	42.4	27.6	25.4	1.5	3.1	72.7
MPs	397	209	23	4	17	650
Candidates	633	633	633	110	569	2,578
						Swing +3.9%

† Separate table on page 282

Swings from Lab to C

Ministers in House of Lords

Lord Havers

Viscount Whitelaw

Lord Young of Graffham

Lord Cameron of Lochbroom

Lord Havers, appointed Lord Chancellor 1987. Called to the Bar, Inner Temple, 1948. MP for Wimbledon, 1970-87; Attorney General, 1979-87; Solicitor General 1972-74; Opposition spokesman on law, 1974-79. Former chmn, Conservative Legal Cmte. Mbr, Cmte of Privileges, 1976-87; Select Cmte on MPs' Interests, 1974-79. B Mar 10 1923; ed Westminster Sch; Corpus Christi Coll, Cambridge. Recorder of Dover, 1962-68; Recorder of Norwich, 1968-71; Master of the Bench, 1971; Chancellor of Dioceses of St Edmundsbury and Ipswich, 1965-73; Ely 1969-73.

Viscount Whitelaw, Lord President of the Council, Leader of the House of Lords and Mrs Thatcher's deputy in the Cabinet from 1983. Home Secretary 1979-83; Deputy Leader of the Opposition, 1975-79. Chief Opposition spokesman on devolution, 1974-76; home affairs and broadcasting, 1976-79. Chairman of the Conservative Party, 1974-75; Secretary of State for Employment, 1973-74; Secretary of State for Northern Ireland, 1972-73; Lord President of the Council and Leader of the Commons, 1970-72. President, National Union of Conservative and Unionist Assoc 1971. Opposition chief whip, 1964-70; Parliamentary Secretary, Ministry of Labour, 1962-64. MP for Penrith and the Border, 1955-83; contested East Dunbartonshire 1950 and 1951. B Jun 28 1918; ed Winchester; Trinity Coll, Cambridge. Farmer and landowner. Former captain, Royal and Ancient Golf Club.

Lord Young of Graffham, Secretary of State for Trade and Industry, 1987- ; Secretary of State for Employment, 1985-87; Minister without Portfolio, 1984-85. Mbr, Nat Economic Development Cl, 1982- ; English Industrial Estates Corporation, 1980-82. Chmn, Manpower Services Commission, 1982-84; industrial adviser, 1979-80, and special adviser, 1980-82, Dept of Ind; director, Centre for Policy Studies, 1979-82 (mbr, management bd, 1979). B Feb 27 1932; ed Christ's Coll, Finchley; Univ Coll, London. Solicitor. Exec, Great Universal Stores Ltd, 1956-61; chmn, Eldonwall Ltd, 1961-75; Hanover Property Services Ltd, 1974-84; director, Town and Country Properties Ltd, 1972-75; chmn, British ORT, 1975-80, pres, 1980-82; administrative cmte,

World ORT Union, 1980-84. Chmn, International Cl of Jewish Social and Welfare Services, 1981- .

Lord Cameron of Lochbroom, appointed Lord Advocate 1984. President, Pensions Appeal Tribunal for Scotlandn 1975-84; chmn, cmte of investigations under 1958 Agricultural Marketing Act, 1980-84; Advocate Depute, 1981; Home Advocate Depute, 1982. B Jun 11 1931; ed Edinburgh Acad; Oxford and Edinburgh Univs. Admitted to Faculty of Advocates 1958; QC in 1972. Chmn, industrial tribunals in Scotland, 1966-81; mbr, Legal Aid Central Cmte 1974-81.

Lord Belstead, appointed Minister of State for the Environment 1987; Minister of State, Agriculture, Fisheries and Food, 1983-87; Minister of State, Foreign and Commonwealth Office, 1982-83; Under Secretary of State, Home Office, 1979-82; Under Secretary for Education and Science, 1970-73; Under Secretary, Northern Ireland Office 1973-74. B Sep 1932; ed Eton; Christ Church, Oxford. Deputy Leader of House of Lords, 1983- .

Lord Glenarthur, appointed Minister of State, Foreign and Commonwealth Office, 1987; Minister of State, Scottish Office, 1986-87; Under Secretary of State, Home Office, 1985-86; Under Secretary of State for Health and Social Security, 1983-85; Lord-in-Waiting (Government Whip), 1982-83. Commissioned 10th Royal Hussars (PWO) 1963; ADC to High Commissioner, Aden, 1964-65; captain 1970; Major 1973; retired 1975. B Oct 7 1944; ed Eton.

Lord Trefgarne, Minister of State for Defence Procurement since 1986; Under Secretary of State for the Armed Forces, 1983-86; Under Secretary of State for Health and Social Security, 1982-83; Under Secretary of State for Foreign and Commonwealth Affairs, 1981-82; Under Secretary, Department of Transport, 1981; Lord-in-Waiting (Government Whip), 1979-81; Opposition Whip in Lords, 1977-79. B Mar 31 1941; ed Haileybury; Princeton Univ, US.

The Earl of Caithness, Minister of State, Home Office, since 1986; Under Secretary of State for Transport, 1985-86; a Lord-in-Waiting (Government Whip), 1984-85. B Nov 3 1948; ed Marlborough; Royal Ag Coll, Cirencester.

Lord Denham

Lord Belstead

Lord Trefgarne

Lord Sanderson
of Bowden

Lord Skelmersdale, appointed Under Secretary of State for Health and Social Security 1987; Under Secretary of State for the Environment, 1983-87; a Lord-in-Waiting (Government Whip), 1981-86. B Apr 2 1945; ed Eton; Lord Wandsworth Coll, Basingstoke; Somerset Farm Inst; Hadlow Coll.

Lord Sanderson of Bowden, appointed Minister of State at the Scottish Office, 1987. Partner, Charles P Sanderson, wool and yarn merchants, Melrose, since 1958. Chmn, Edinburgh Financial Trust, since 1983; Shires Investment Trust, since 1984. B April 30 1933; ed St Mary's Sch, Melrose; Trinity Coll, Glenalmond; Scottish Coll of Textiles, Galashiels; Bradford Coll.

Lord Denham, Government Chief Whip and Captain, Gentlemen at Arms, since 1979; Opposition Chief Whip, 1978-79; Opposition Deputy Chief Whip, 1974-78; Captain, Yeoman of the Guard (Government Deputy Chief Whip), 1971-74. B Oct 3 1927; ed Eton; King's Coll, Cambridge.

Viscount Davidson, Captain, Yeomen of the Guard (Government Deputy Chief Whip) 1986- .; a Lord-in-Waiting (Government Whip), 1985-86. B Dec 22 1928; ed Westminster Sch; Pembroke Coll, Cambridge.

Lord Brabazon of Tara, Under Secretary of State for Transport since 1986; a Lord-in-Waiting (Government Whip), 1984-86. B Dec 20 1946; ed Harrow. Mbr, Stock Exchange, 1972-84.

Lord Lyell, Under Secretary of State for Northern Ireland since 1984; a Lord-in-Waiting (Government Whip), 1979-84; an Opposition Whip, 1974-79. B Mar 27 1939; ed Eton; Christ Church, Oxford. Chartered accountant. Mbr, Queen's Bodyguard for Scotland (Royal Company of Archers).

Lady Trumpington, Parliamentary Secretary, Agriculture, Fisheries and Food, was made a life peer in 1980. Appointed a Government whip, 1983. Spokesman for the Home Office and on health and social security, 1983-85; Under Secretary of State, Health and Social Security, 1985-87. Cambridge city councillor, 1963-73; Mayor of Cambridge, 1971-72. Cambridgeshire county councillor, 1973-75. Born, October 1922. Educated privately in England and France.

Lady Hooper was appointed Under Secretary of State of State for Education and Science, 1987; Baroness-in-Waiting (Government Whip), 1985-87. B May 25 1939; ed Univ of Southampton; Universidad Central, Quito, Ecuador. MEP, Liverpool, 1979-84. Vice-chmn, Environment and Consumer Affairs Cmtes, European Parlt, 1979-84; EDG Whip, European Parlt, 1982-84. Contested Merseyside West, European Parly elections 1984. Partner, Taylor Garrett, 1974-84. Fellow, Industry and Parly Trust, 1983.

Viscount Long, a Lord-in-Waiting (Government Whip), 1979- ; Opposition Whip, 1974-79. B Jan 30 1929; ed Harrow.

Lord Hesketh, a Lord-in-Waiting (Government Whip) 1986- . B Oct 28 1950; ed Ampleforth.

Lord Beaverbrook, a Lord-in-Waiting (Government Whip) 1986- . B Dec 29 1951; ed Charterhouse; Pembroke Coll, Cambridge. Chmn, Beaverbrook Foundation since 1985.

Earl of Dundee, a Lord-in-Waiting (Government Whip) 1986- . B June 5 1949; ed Eton; St Andrews Univ. Contested Hamilton by-election May 1978.

The Earl of Arran, a Lord-in-Waiting (Government whip) 1987- . Co-founder, Gore Publishing Ltd, 1980; co-chmn, Children's Country Holidays Fund. B Jul 14 1938; ed Eton; Balliol Coll, Oxford.

Election of haves and have-nots

By David Butler, Fellow of Nuffield College, Oxford and Robert Waller, Harris Research Centre

The 1987 General Election returned the same Prime Minister to office for the third time in succession – an event without precedent since the coming of mass democracy in 1932. The Conservatives did win in 1951, in 1955, and again in 1959, but that was under different leaders. Coincidentally their third victory then was, like Margaret Thatcher's third triumph, by a margin of 101 seats over all other parties.

A 1.7 per cent swing from Conservative to Labour left the governing party 11.4 per cent ahead: a lead 4.4 per cent greater than in any postwar contest except 1983 when the Conservatives enjoyed a gap of 14.9 per cent over Labour.

Compared with 1983, the Conservatives suffered a net loss of 21 seats and Labour a net gain of 20. But in fact 47 seats ended in different hands. More seats moved against the predominant Labour tide than in any election since the 1920s. The Conservatives gained five seats from Labour (Battersea, Walthamstow, Thurrock, Wolverhampton NE and Ipswich) and regained Fulham, which Labour had captured in a by-election in 1986. The Scottish Nationalists lost both their existing seats but gained three others in NE Scotland. The Alliance parties suffered eight losses but picked up three constituencies in compensation: Southport, NE Fife and Argyll and Bute, all previously held by the Conservatives.

The Conservatives were victorious with only 43.2 per cent of the UK vote, and only 42.2 per cent of the GB vote – less than their share in any election won by them, save 1922. They did so because the opposition was, once again, divided. Fifty-seven per cent of the electorate in Great Britain supported non-Conservative candidates, though it might also be pointed out that 68 per cent voted non-Labour and 77 per cent non-Alliance.

Under the majoritarian ('first past the post') electoral system, 43 per cent of the United Kingdom Vote sufficed to secure 57 per cent of the seats. Labour with 31.5 per cent of the vote won 34 per cent of the seats. The Alliance's 23 per cent won only 3½ per cent of the seats. If there had been a pure system of proportional representation, the Conservatives would have got 279 instead of 375 seats, Labour 202 instead of 229, and the Alliance 149 instead of 22.

The Conservatives distributed their vote in the most efficient way of the three main party groupings. Labour piled up majorities in the rock-solid areas of Scotland and Wales, and also improved their vote in some constituencies, including those in the South where they came a poor third in 1983 and had no chance of winning in 1987. The 28 safest seats in Britain (majorities from 46.8 per cent up to 64.4 per cent) are now all Labour. Twenty-two Labour seats have majorities of over 50 per cent, compared with three in 1983; no Conservative seat exceeds Chelsea's 46.6 per cent majority. In other words, even more than before Labour wastes votes in superfluously large margins of victory.

At the other - marginal end - of the constituency scale, Labour will be left with a difficult task in 1991 and 1992, when it will need 51 gains to deny the Conservatives a clear majority. In 1987 it needed to win 72 of the Conservatives' 1983 seats, with majorities ranging up to 12 per cent. Now the 51 targets have majorities up to 8.3 per cent. A swing of about 4 per cent will be required to prevent the Tories from winning a fourth term of power, while for Labour on its own to reach the critical 326 it must gain 97 seats, and that will need a swing of over 8 per cent, as against 10.5 per cent needed after the 1983 election.

All this ignores the Alliance. They made less impact on the 1987 contest than expected. Yet they still won 23 per cent of the vote, only 3 per cent less than in 1983. They still remained in second place in 228 of the 375 Conservative seats, fully 63 per cent of them. Only in 37 instances did Labour overtake the Alliance to become the principal challengers to the Conservatives. Yet apart from their 22 victories, the Alliance found themselves within 10 per cent of winning in only 27 seats; in 17 cases a Liberal candidate was second and in 10 cases an SDP candidate was runner-up. In 20 of the 27 the Conservatives now hold the seat; in seven Labour do so.

The turnout was 75.5, 2.8 per cent more than in 1983. It rose in almost every part of the country except in Northern Ireland, where stricter rules against personation (and perhaps a lack of enthusiasm for the current political scene) reduced it from 72.8 per cent to 67.0 per cent. The highest turnout was in Brecon and Radnor (84.4 per cent), which incidentally also produced the closest three-party result (5.6 per cent covering the Liberal, Conservative and Labour candidates). The lowest turnout, 55.4 per cent in Hackney South and Shoreditch, was 3.6 per cent higher than the 1983 minimum, recorded by the City of London and Westminster South.

It was widely said that the register was even more inaccurate than in 1983, when at least 7 per cent of eligible voters were omitted and an equal number of duplicate or 'dead' names was included. The postal vote, now permitted for holidaymakers, was up, probably by a third, and there was also an increase in proxy voting. But only 12,000 British citizens domiciled abroad took advantage of their new opportunities to vote provided by the Representation of the People Act of 1985.

   That Act also reduced the level for lost deposits from 12.5 per cent to 5 per cent (to compensate for an increase in the sum of the deposit from £150 to £500) and only one major party candidate in Britain failed to reach 5 per cent, (Margot Von Romberg, the Liberal fighting Dundee East). However, apart from the Nationalists, only one minor party candidate or independent saved his deposit, the Orkney and Shetland Movement's representative who secured 14.5 per cent of the vote. The higher deposit was used by the National Front as an excuse for fielding no candidates for the first time since their formation in 1968. It did not deter the Greens from putting up 113, but their highest vote was 3.6 per cent, obtained by local councillor Richard Lawson at Weston-Super-Mare, and their average was 1.3 per cent. The Green vote exceeded the Conservative majority over Labour in two seats, York and Dulwich.

   The Scottish and Welsh nationalists each made one net gain. Plaid Cymru held their two existing seats in NW Wales and added a third, Ynys Mon (Anglesey), where the Conservatives had been disrupted by the resignation of the sitting MP Keith Best just before the election. The SNP had a very mixed election, losing the idiosyncratic Western Isles on the retirement of their former leader Donald Stewart, and losing their present leader Gordon Wilson to Labour at Dundee East, but picking up Moray, Angus East and Banff and Buchan in compensation, all from the Tories. The Mrs Ewing elected at Moray was not the former member for the seat, Winnie Ewing, but her daughter-in-law Margaret, who had held East Dunbartonshire for the SNP, as Mrs Bain, from 1974-79.

   Northern Ireland had its own special pattern, as ever; no mainland parties stood (apart from a single Green). The rival unionist parties formed an electoral pact and won safely in all their 1983 seats except Newry and Armagh (lost even more heavily to the SDLP than in the 1986 by-election) and South Down where Enoch Powell's 37 year parliamentary career was finally ended. Note may be taken of Robert McCartney's performance in cutting James Kilfedder's majority in North Down to under 4,000 on a 'Real Unionist' anti-abstentionist ticket. The SDLP, with three seats instead of the one gained in 1983, were nevertheless disappointed that Gerry Adams of Sinn Fein again inflicted a clear defeat on their candidate in the ever more Catholic West Belfast, while Mid Ulster and Fermanagh and South Tyrone were once again denied to Catholic candidates as Sinn Fein and the SDLP split the republican vote almost equally.

   Some expected variations in the vote in Britain did not materialise. As in 1983 the ethnic origin of candidates had little effect. Four black MPs were elected with swings comparable to those in neighbouring seats: Keith Vaz did particularly well to oust Peter Bruinvels the active Conservative MP in Leicester East. Diane Abbott (Hackney North) was the first ever black woman MP to be elected. The highest ever number of women were elected as MPs: 41 in all, compared with 23 in 1983. Twenty-one of these were Labour, equalling their all-time record (1945); 18 were Conservative, breaking their record of 16 in 1970; the first ever SDP woman MP to be returned in a General Election was Rosie Barnes who held on to the Greenwich seat she gained from Labour in the by-election earlier in 1987; and Ray Michie was the first woman to win in a General Election as a Liberal since Lady Megan Lloyd George held Anglesey in 1950.

   Conspicuous association with the far left had little adverse effect on Labour candidates' chances; the existing two Militant supporters Terry Fields (Liverpool Broadgreen) and Dave Nellist (Coventry SE) were returned with increased majorities, and were joined by Pat Wall, who gained Bradford North, and Ronnie Campbell, who just held Blyth Valley. All of the five Labour MPs defeated in the election could be classed as being on the moderate wing of the party.

   There were exceptional results in individual constituencies. The young SDP MP Charles Kennedy increased his majority from 4.9 per cent to 29.7 per cent in Ross, Cromarty and Skye. Norman Godman increased the Labour majority over the Alliance in Greenock and Port Glasgow from 10.5 per cent to 46.0 per cent. Philip Oppenheim increased the Conservative vote in Amber Valley by 10.7 per cent. The SNP vote in Western Isles dropped by 26.0 per cent as Labour's Calum Macdonald took the seat after an SNP interregnum of 17 years.

   Some seats showed notable switch backs from by-election figures. In Penrith and the Border the Conservatives turned a 552 majority into 17,366, and in Ryedale a loss by 4,940 into a win by 9,740. They also won back Fulham and Portsmouth South, but just failed in Brecon and Radnor, their other by-election loss.

   In general there was little evidence of fresh tactical voting over and above that which took place in 1983. The Labour vote grew in many seats where in 1983 they had been squeezed into a humiliating third place, for example doubling at the Isle of Wight and Cornwall North, and exceeding the Alliance deficit to the Conservatives at places such as Richmond and Barnes, Bath, Hereford and Hazel Grove. Alliance efforts to get Labour support to switch where only they could defeat the Conservatives met with little reward: only in Southport did the Labour vote slip when the Alliance made a gain. Where the Alliance vote fell sharply, it seems to have gone if anything to the Conservatives rather than to Labour. One place where a species of tactical voting does seem to take place is Scotland, where SNP support seems to have shifted to the Alliance to oust the Tories in Argyll and nearly do so in Kincardine and Deeside, while the Alliance performed poorly as the SNP vanquished the Tories at Moray, Banff and Angus East.

   The new father of the House of Commons will be Sir Bernard Braine, the member for Castle Point, who was first returned for an Essex constituency in 1950 and has an unbroken record of service since then. Also elected in 1950 was the former Prime Minister, Edward Heath, but Sir Bernard took his oath of allegiance a few minutes before him. Denis Healey is the Labour member with the longest continuous service, having been in Parliament since 1952. Michael Foot is now the sole survivor of the 1945 intake, but he spent five years out of the House between 1955 and 1960. He is also the only MP to have contested a seat before the war, Monmouth in 1935. Mr Foot is the oldest MP, having been re-elected at the age of 73 years and 11 months. Sir Bernard is the oldest Conservative, turning 73 a fortnight after the 1987 election. Only five MPs in all were septuagenarians at the time of their election, compared with nine in 1983. The youngest MP to be returned was Matthew Taylor, the Liberal by-election victor at Truro earlier in the year, who was still only 24 years of age. The largest majority was gained by Allan Rogers, the Labour member for Rhondda (30,754); the largest Conservative margin was that of John Major at Huntingdon (27,044). The narrowest majorities were 56 for the Liberal Richard Livsey at Brecon and Radnor, and 56 for Labour's Alan Meale at Mansfield. The closest Conservative win was by 147 votes (Conal Gregory at York).

The biggest variations from the standard national pattern were regional. Labour fared very well in the metropolitan areas of the North of England especially Merseyside, in Wales and in Scotland, which was clearly a disaster area for the Conservatives as they lost over half of their 21 seats. The Conservatives resisted the movement to Labour in the Midlands and the South and actually made three net gains in London, where they now have 58 of the 84 seats. This table tells a clear story:

	C% ±	Lab% ±	All% ±
London and rest of South	+1.2	+1.1	-2.0
Midlands	+0.9	+2.1	-2.7
North	-1.8	+5.4	-3.5
Wales	-1.5	+7.5	-5.3
Scotland	-4.4	+7.3	-5.3
Great Britain	-0.1	+3.0	-3.0

But these figures should not be taken as simple evidence of a North-South divide. The Conservatives held on notably in some northern areas such as Bury, Bolton and most strikingly Batley and Hyndburn, while their vote went down west of Bristol, and Labour made gains in some areas in the South and Midlands, such as Oxford East, Norwich South, Leicester South and Leicester East. Even in London, Labour secured positive swings in some boroughs, such as Lambeth, Camden, and Islington. One explanation may lie in the pattern of housing tenure.

A Harris/ITN exit poll on election day suggested that the Tories led Labour by two to one among owner occupiers, while Labour led among council tenants by over two to one. This may help to account for the Conservatives' very strong performance in the heavily owner occupied Pennines marginals such as Hyndburn (77 per cent home owning back in 1981 according to the most recent census) and the two Bury seats. Another explanation may lie in the pattern of unemployment: Labour led by over two to one among the jobless, who are particularly numerous in Merseyside, in Tyne and Wear, and in Scotland, but less so in London and the Midlands. The two sides of the mining dispute of 1984-5 were clearly reflected in the significant move to Labour in the Yorkshire coalfield, and to the Conservatives in the Nottinghamshire coalfield. All evidence still points to a massive vote for Labour among non-whites, especially Afro-Caribbeans.

All in all, it has to be concluded that this was the election of the Two Nations, not North and South so much as the haves and have-nots, the rich and poor. It was an election of social and political bifurcation, and the most polarized election within living memory. There were swings of approximately 10 per cent to both Labour and Conservative. Large parts of the country strongly rejected Mrs Thatcher's government; there are now no Tory MPs in the cities of Glasgow, Liverpool, Manchester, Newcastle upon Tyne, Bradford, Stoke on Trent, Hull or Leicester. On the other hand, other areas endorsed the third Conservative term with even greater enthusiasm than before. Problems of legitimacy and consensus must arise in a nation which has once again returned a large and potentially invulnerable Conservative majority when of the 72 MPs in Scotland only 10 are Tories, of the 38 in Wales only 8 are, and of the 17 in Northern Ireland none at all. Mrs Thatcher quickly announced as an early priority for her new government an increase in the attention shown to the inner cities. The 1987 election results bear out the fact that she has not as yet won undivided or even consistent support amongst the citizens of the United Kingdom, even in the hour of her unprecedented triumph.

Regional, metropolitan, city and county voting patterns

The Times has calculated the following analyses of voting in the General Election on June 11 1987 in which the same 650 constituencies were contested as in 1983, enabling comparisons to be made between the two elections. There are 523 parliamentary seats in England, 72 in Scotland, 38 in Wales and 17 in Northern Ireland. The separate analysis of voting in Ulster is on Page 282.

The election statistics for England have been divided into the official standard nine regions of the country: South-East (108 seats); South-West (48 seats); Greater London (84 seats); East Anglia (20 seats); East Midlands (42 seats); West Midlands (58 seats); Yorks and Humberside (54 seats); North-West (73 seats) and Northern (36 seats).

Statistics are also set out for the metropolitan areas; counties and cities and boroughs with more than two seats. Scotland has been analysed on a regional basis and Wales by county.

SOUTH-EAST			C	Lab	All	Other	Total
1987 Electorate	7,988,668	Votes	3,382,849	1,023,521	1,653,544	27,603	6,087,517
Turnout %	76.2	Votes %	55.6	16.8	27.2	0.5	100.0
Swing %	0.0	Seats	107	1	0	0	108
Lab to C		Candidates	108	108	108	44	368
1983 Electorate	7,658,245	Votes	3,076,607	893,325	1,636,717	36,597	5,643,246
Turnout %	73.7	Votes %	54.5	15.8	29.0	0.6	100.0
		Seats	106	1	1	0	108
		Candidates	108	108	108	81	405
		Change 83-87	1.1	1.0	-1.8	-0.2	

SOUTH-WEST			C	Lab	All	Other	Total
1987 Electorate	3,506,075	Votes	1,386,857	436,358	906,288	13,048	2,742,551
Turnout %	78.2	Votes %	50.6	15.9	33.0	0.5	100.0
Swing %	-1.0	Seats	44	1	3	0	48
C to Lab		Candidates	48	48	48	22	166
1983 Electorate	3,342,700	Votes	1,295,737	370,544	836,547	19,099	2,521,927
Turnout %	75.4	Votes %	51.4	14.7	33.2	0.8	100.0
		Seats	44	1	3	0	48
		Candidates	48	48	48	50	194
		Change 83-87	-0.8	1.2	-0.1	-0.3	

GREATER LONDON			C	Lab	All	Other	Total
1987 Electorate	5,111,379	Votes	1,655,905	1,136,892	770,109	50,867	3,613,773
Turnout %	70.7	Votes %	45.8	31.5	21.3	1.4	100.0
Swing %	0.2	Seats	57	23	3	1	84
Lab to C		Candidates	83	84	84	63	314
1983 Electorate	5,093,471	Votes	1,517,154	1,031,435	853,332	55,874	3,457,795
Turnout %	67.9	Votes %	43.9	29.8	24.7	1.6	100.0
		Seats	56	26	2	0	84
		Candidates	84	84	84	151	403
		Change 83-87	1.9	1.6	-3.4	-0.2	

EAST ANGLIA			C	Lab	All	Other	Total
1987 Electorate	1,495,371	Votes	601,421	249,894	297,041	5,217	1,153,573
Turnout %	77.1	Votes %	52.1	21.7	25.7	0.5	100.0
Swing %	0.0	Seats	19	1	0	0	20
C to Lab		Candidates	20	20	20	7	67
1983 Electorate	1,413,994	Votes	539,418	216,902	298,624	2,934	1,057,878
Turnout %	74.8	Votes %	51.0	20.5	28.2	0.3	100.0
		Seats	18	1	1	0	20
		Candidates	20	20	20	10	70
		Change 83-87	1.1	1.2	-2.5	0.2	

257

EAST MIDLANDS

		C	Lab	All	Other	Total
1987 Electorate	2,992,872	Votes	1,127,237	696,780	486,768	9,128	2,319,913
Turnout %	77.5	Votes %	48.6	30.0	21.0	0.4	100.0
Swing %	-0.3	Seats	31	11	0	0	42
C to Lab		Candidates	42	42	42	17	143
1983 Electorate	2,891,369	Votes	1,013,406	600,624	517,098	17,266	2,148,394
Turnout %	74.3	Votes %	47.2	28.0	24.1	0.8	100.0
		Seats	34	8	0	0	42
		Candidates	42	42	42	26	152
		Change 83-87	1.4	2.1	-3.1	-0.4	

WEST MIDLANDS

		C	Lab	All	Other	Total
1987 Electorate	3,943,327	Votes	1,346,505	984,023	615,699	10,401	2,956,628
Turnout %	75.0	Votes %	45.5	33.3	20.8	0.4	100.0
Swing %	-0.8	Seats	36	22	0	0	58
C to Lab		Candidates	58	58	58	17	191
1983 Electorate	3,863,281	Votes	1,261,738	874,172	655,982	12,444	2,804,336
Turnout %	72.6	Votes %	45.0	31.2	23.4	0.4	100.0
		Seats	36	22	0	0	58
		Candidates	58	58	58	32	206
		Change 83-87	0.5	2.1	-2.6	-0.1	

YORKS & HUMBERSIDE

		C	Lab	All	Other	Total
1987 Electorate	3,729,620	Votes	1,040,749	1,128,875	602,709	7,811	2,780,144
Turnout %	74.5	Votes %	37.4	40.6	21.7	0.3	100.0
Swing %	-3.3	Seats	21	33	0	0	54
C to Lab		Candidates	54	54	54	16	178
1983 Electorate	3,690,001	Votes	1,013,315	925,483	669,377	13,516	2,621,691
Turnout %	71.0	Votes %	38.7	35.3	25.5	0.5	100.0
		Seats	24	28	2	0	54
		Candidates	54	54	54	30	192
		Change 83-87	-1.2	5.3	-3.9	-0.2	

NORTH-WEST

		C	Lab	All	Other	Total
1987 Electorate	4,842,068	Votes	1,401,453	1,518,698	758,141	8,996	3,687,288
Turnout %	76.2	Votes %	38.0	41.2	20.6	0.2	100.0
Swing %	-3.6	Seats	34	36	3	0	73
C to Lab		Candidates	73	73	73	19	238
1983 Electorate	4,820,148	Votes	1,405,468	1,266,111	822,241	23,179	3,516,999
Turnout %	73.0	Votes %	40.0	36.0	23.4	0.7	100.0
		Seats	36	35	2	0	73
		Candidates	73	73	73	44	263
		Change 83-87	-2.0	5.2	-2.8	-0.4	

NORTHERN

		C	Lab	All	Other	Total
1987 Electorate	2,378,984	Votes	578,970	830,785	376,675	4,635	1,791,065
Turnout %	75.3	Votes %	32.3	46.4	21.0	0.3	100.0
Swing %	-4.2	Seats	8	27	1	0	36
C to Lab		Candidates	36	36	36	9	117
1983 Electorate	2,369,160	Votes	589,127	684,020	424,992	2,507	1,700,646
Turnout %	71.8	Votes %	34.6	40.2	25.0	0.1	100.0
		Seats	8	26	2	0	36
		Candidates	36	36	36	7	115
		Change 83-87	-2.3	6.2	-4.0	0.1	

ENGLISH REGIONS: TOTALS

		C	Lab	All	Other	Total
1987 Electorate	35,988,364	Votes	12,521,946	8,005,826	6,466,974	137,706	27,132,452
Turnout %	75.4	Votes %	46.2	29.5	23.8	0.5	100.0
Swing %	-1.2	Seats	357	155	10	1	523
C to Lab		Candidates	522	523	523	214	1782
1983 Electorate	35,142,369	Votes	11,711,970	6,862,616	6,714,910	183,416	25,472,912
Turnout %	72.5	Votes %	46.0	26.9	26.4	0.7	100.0
		Seats	362	148	13	0	523
		Candidates	523	523	523	431	2000
		Change 83-87	0.2	2.6	-2.5	-0.2	

Metropolitan analysis

Athough the Greater London Council and the six Metropolitan County Councils have been abolished by the Conservative Government, the Metropolitan county boundaries are still in place and thus these areas still provide a basis for comparison of voting between 1983 and 1987 in the areas of heaviest population in England.

The Metropolis has been divided into two areas – Outer London and Inner London. Outside London there are 36 Metropolitan district authorities in the six metropolitan areas. None of the parliamentary constituencies crosses a metropolitan county boundary.

Seats making up Metropolitan counties and the voting in them was as follows:

OUTER LONDON			C	Lab	All	Other	Total
1987 Electorate	3,394,270	Votes	1,231,367	666,192	528,693	38,276	2,464,528
Turnout %	72.6	Votes %	50.0	27.0	21.5	1.6	100.0
Swing %	0.5	Seats	44	10	0	1	55
Lab to C		Candidates	54	55	55	26	190
1983 Electorate	3,350,019	Votes	1,120,377	604,258	601,815	25,618	2,352,068
Turnout %	70.2	Votes %	47.6	25.7	25.6	1.1	100.0
		Seats	44	11	0	0	55
		Candidates	55	55	55	67	232
		Change 83-87	2.3	1.3	-4.1	0.5	

Barking, Beckenham, Bexleyheath, Brent East, Brent North, Brent South, Brentford and Isleworth, Carshalton and Wallington, Chingford, Chipping Barnet, Croydon Central, Croydon North East, Croydon North West, Croydon South, Dagenham, Ealing Acton, Ealing North, Ealing Southall, Edmonton, Enfield North, Enfield, Southgate, Erith and Crayford, Feltham and Heston, Finchley, Harrow East, Harrow West, Hayes and Harlington, Hendon North, Hendon South, Hornchurch, Hornsey and Wood Green, Ilford North, Ilford South, Kingston upon Thames, Leyton, Mitcham and Morden, Newham North East, Newham North West, Newham South, Old Bexley and Sidcup, Orpington, Ravensbourne, Richmond and Barnes, Romford, Ruislip, Northwood, Surbiton, Sutton and Cheam, Tottenham, Twickenham, Upminster, Uxbridge, Walthamstow, Wanstead and Woodford, Wimbledon.

INNER LONDON			C	Lab	All	Other	Total
1987 Electorate	1,717,109	Votes	424,538	470,700	241,416	12,591	1,149,245
Turnout %	66.9	Votes %	36.9	41.0	21.0	1.1	100.0
Swing %	-0.6	Seats	13	13	3	0	29
C to Lab		Candidates	29	29	29	37	124
1983 Electorate	1,743,452	Votes	396,777	427,177	251,517	30,256	1,105,727
Turnout %	63.4	Votes %	35.9	38.6	22.7	2.7	100.0
		Seats	12	15	2	0	29
		Candidates	29	29	29	84	171
		Change 83-87	1.1	2.3	-1.7	-1.6	

Battersea, Bethnal Green and Stepney, Bow and Poplar, Chelsea, City Of London and Westminster South, Dulwich, Eltham, Fulham, Greenwich, Hackney North and Stoke Newington, Hackney South and Shoreditch, Hammersmith, Hampstead and Highgate, Holborn and St Pancras, Islington North, Islington South and Finsbury, Kensington, Lewisham Deptford, Lewisham East, Lewisham West, Norwood, Peckham, Putney, Southwark and Bermondsey, Streatham, Tooting, Vauxhall, Westminster North, Woolwich.

WEST MIDLANDS			C	Lab	All	Other	Total
1987 Electorate	1,991,176	Votes	616,375	575,279	249,433	4,384	1,445,471
Turnout %	72.6	Votes %	42.6	39.8	17.3	0.3	100.0
Swing %	-0.8	Seats	14	17	0	0	31
C to Lab		Candidates	31	31	31	10	103
1983 Electorate	1,984,318	Votes	583,127	521,819	285,092	6,984	1,397,022
Turnout %	70.4	Votes %	41.7	37.4	20.4	0.5	100.0
		Seats	13	18	0	0	31
		Candidates	31	31	31	20	113
		Change 83-87	0.9	2.4	-3.2	-0.2	

Aldridge-Brownhills, Birmingham Edgbaston, Birmingham Erdington, Birmingham Hall Green, Birmingham Hodge Hill, Birmingham Ladywood, Birmingham Northfield, Birmingham Perry Barr, Birmingham Selly Oak, Birmingham Small Heath, Birmingham Sparkbrook, Birmingham Yardley, Bromsgrove, Burton, Cannock and Burntwood, Coventry North East, Coventry North West, Coventry South East, Coventry South West, Dudley East, Dudley West, Halesowen and Stourbridge, Hereford, Leominster, Ludlow, Meriden, Newcastle-under-Lyme, Nuneaton, Rugby and Kenilworth, Shrewsbury and Atcham, Shropshire North, Solihull, Stafford, Staffordshire Mid, Staffordshire Moorlands, Staffordshire South, Staffordshire South East, Stoke-on-Trent Central, Stoke-on-Trent North, Stoke-on-Trent South, Stratford-on-Avon, Sutton Coldfield, Walsall North, Walsall South, Warley East, Warley West, Warwick and Leamington, Warwickshire North, West Bromwich East, West Bromwich West, Wolverhampton North East, Wolverhampton South East, Wolverhampton South West, Worcester, Worcestershire Mid, Worcestershire South, The Wrekin, Wyre Forest.

METROPOLITAN ANALYSIS

GREATER MANCHESTER

GREATER MANCHESTER			C	Lab	All	Other	Total
1987 Electorate	1,945,586	Votes	526,361	644,966	290,881	2,113	1,464,321
Turnout %	75.3	Votes %	35.9	44.0	19.9	0.1	100.0
Swing %	-2.3	Seats	10	19	1	0	30
C to Lab		Candidates	30	30	30	6	96
1983 Electorate	1,944,856	Votes	508,273	557,571	332,005	6,907	1,404,756
Turnout %	72.2	Votes %	36.2	39.7	23.6	0.5	100.0
		Seats	11	18	1	0	30
		Candidates	30	30	30	21	111
		Change 83-87	-0.2	4.4	-3.8	-0.3	

Altrincham and Sale, Ashton- under-Lyne, Bolton North East, Bolton South East, Bolton West, Bury North, Bury South, Cheadle, Davyhulme, Denton and Reddish, Eccles, Hazel Grove, Heywood and Middleton, Leigh, Littleborough and Saddleworth, Makerfield, Manchester Blackley, Manchester Central, Manchester Gorton, Manchester Withington, Manchester Wythenshawe, Oldham Central and Royton, Oldham West, Rochdale, Salford East, Stalybridge and Hyde, Stockport, Stretford, Wigan, Worsley.

MERSEYSIDE

MERSEYSIDE			C	Lab	All	Other	Total
1987 Electorate	1,117,029	Votes	242,431	397,647	195,653	2,696	838,427
Turnout %	75.1	Votes %	28.9	47.4	23.3	0.3	100.0
Swing %	-6.8	Seats	4	11	2	0	17
C to Lab		Candidates	17	17	17	5	56
1983 Electorate	1,140,132	Votes	285,452	325,170	193,137	11,223	814,982
Turnout %	71.5	Votes %	35.0	39.9	23.7	1.4	100.0
		Seats	5	11	1	0	17
		Candidates	17	17	17	10	61
		Change 83-87	-6.1	7.5	-0.4	-1.1	

Birkenhead, Bootle, Crosby, Knowsley North, Knowsley South, Liverpool Broadgreen, Liverpool Garston, Liverpool Mossley Hill, Liverpool Riverside, Liverpool Walton, Liverpool West Derby, St Helens North, St Helens South, Southport, Wallasey, Wirral South, Wirral West.

SOUTH YORKSHIRE

SOUTH YORKSHIRE			C	Lab	All	Other	Total
1987 Electorate	997,096	Votes	180,327	405,189	136,323	1,085	722,924
Turnout %	72.5	Votes %	24.9	56.0	18.9	0.2	100.0
Swing %	-5.2	Seats	1	14	0	0	15
C to Lab		Candidates	15	15	15	4	49
1983 Electorate	994,249	Votes	193,784	337,515	158,924	1,464	691,687
Turnout %	69.6	Votes %	28.0	48.8	23.0	0.2	100.0
		Seats	1	14	0	0	15
		Candidates	15	15	15	4	49
		Change 83-87	-3.1	7.3	-4.1	-0.1	

Barnsley Central, Barnsley East, Barnsley West and Penistone, Doncaster Central, Doncaster North, Don Valley, Rotherham, Rother Valley, Sheffield Attercliffe, Sheffield Brightside, Sheffield Central, Sheffield Hallam, Sheffield Heeley, Sheffield Hillsborough, Wentworth.

WEST YORKSHIRE

WEST YORKSHIRE			C	Lab	All	Other	Total
1987 Electorate	1,543,576	Votes	441,722	478,135	242,848	4,177	1,166,882
Turnout %	75.6	Votes %	37.9	41.0	20.8	0.4	100.0
Swing %	-2.4	Seats	9	14	0	0	23
C to Lab		Candidates	23	23	23	8	77
1983 Electorate	1,538,890	Votes	412,584	394,733	287,454	10,196	1,104,967
Turnout %	71.8	Votes %	37.3	35.7	26.0	0.9	100.0
		Seats	11	10	2	0	23
		Candidates	23	23	23	20	89
		Change 83-87	0.5	5.3	-5.2	-0.6	

Batley and Spen, Bradford North, Bradford South, Bradford West, Calder Valley, Colne Valley, Dewsbury, Elmet, Halifax, Hemsworth, Huddersfield, Keighley, Leeds Central, Leeds East, Leeds North East, Leeds North West, Leeds South and Morley, Leeds West, Normanton, Pontefract and Castleford, Pudsey, Shipley, Wakefield.

TYNE & WEAR

TYNE & WEAR			C	Lab	All	Other	Total
1987 Electorate	887,856	Votes	177,639	344,987	119.452	1,815	643,893
Turnout %	72.5	Votes %	27.6	53.6	18.6	0.3	100.0
Swing %	-6.0	Seats	1	12	0	0	13
C to Lab		Candidates	13	13	13	5	44
1983 Electorate	892,200	Votes	193,966	281,015	144,090	478	619,549
Turnout %	69.4	Votes %	31.3	45.4	23.3	0.1	100.0
		Seats	2	11	0	0	13
		Candidates	13	13	13	1	40
		Change 83-87	-3.7	8.2	-4.7	0.2	

Blaydon, Gateshead East, Houghton and Washington, Jarrow, Newcastle Upon Tyne Central, Newcastle Upon Tyne East, Newcastle Upon Tyne North, South Shields, Sunderland North, Sunderland South, Tyne Bridge, Tynemouth, Wallsend.

ENGLISH METROPOLITAN COUNTIES TOTALS			C	Lab	All	Other	Total
1987							
Electorate	13,593,698	Votes	3,840,760	3,983,095	2,004,699	67,137	9,895,691
Turnout %	72.8	Votes %	38.8	40.3	20.3	0.7	100.0
Swing %	-2.0	Seats	96	110	6	1	213
C to Lab		Candidates	212	213	213	101	739
1983							
Electorate	13,588,116	Votes	3,694,340	3,449,258	2,254,034	93,126	9,490,758
Turnout %	69.8	Votes %	38.9	36.3	23.7	1.0	100.0
		Seats	99	108	6	0	213
		Candidates	213	213	213	227	866
		Change 83-87	-0.1	3.9	-3.5	-0.3	

Non-Metropolitan Counties

There are 39 non-Metropolitan counties containing 310 parliamentary constituencies, none of which cross county boundaries. The Isle of Wight has just one seat (its detailed analysis is in the election results). The analysis in these counties plus comparisions with 1983 is as follows:

AVON			C	Lab	All	Other	Total
1987 Electorate	722,493	Votes	271,205	135,627	152,739	6,227	565,798
Turnout %	78.3	Votes %	47.9	24.0	27.0	1.1	100.0
Swing %	0.5	Seats	9	1	0	0	10
Lab to C		Candidates	10	10	10	8	38
1983 Electorate	708,399	Votes	251,487	129,026	146,791	4,073	531,377
Turnout %	75.0	Votes %	47.3	24.3	27.6	0.8	100.0
		Seats	9	1	0	0	10
		Candidates	10	10	10	13	43
		Change 83-87	0.6	-0.3	-0.6	0.3	

Bath, Bristol East, Bristol North West, Bristol South, Bristol West, Kingswood, Northavon, Wansdyke, Weston-super-Mare, Woodspring.

BEDFORDSHIRE			C	Lab	All	Other	Total
1987 Electorate	378,631	Votes	159,155	71,026	62,047	1,257	293,485
Turnout %	77.5	Votes %	54.2	24.2	21.1	0.4	100.0
Swing %	0.8	Seats	5	0	0	0	5
Lab to C		Candidates	5	5	5	2	17
1983 Electorate	364,167	Votes	141,424	62,686	72,981	344	277,435
Turnout %	76.2	Votes %	51.0	22.6	26.3	0.1	100.0
		Seats	5	0	0	0	5
		Candidates	5	5	5	1	16
		Change 83-87	3.3	1.6	-5.2	0.3	

Bedfordshire Mid, Bedfordshire North, Bedfordshire South West, Luton North, Luton South.

BERKSHIRE			C	Lab	All	Other	Total
1987 Electorate	543,926	Votes	230,951	70,618	101,798	4,311	407,678
Turnout %	75.0	Votes %	56.7	17.3	25.0	1.1	100.0
Swing %	0.3	Seats	7	0	0	0	7
Lab to C		Candidates	7	7	7	6	27
1983 Electorate	508,697	Votes	202,447	59,121	103,957	4,514	370,039
Turnout %	72.7	Votes %	54.7	16.0	28.1	1.2	100.0
		Seats	7	0	0	0	7
		Candidates	7	7	7	10	31
		Change 83-87	1.9	1.3	-3.1	-0.2	

Berkshire East, Newbury, Reading East, Reading West, Slough, Windsor and Maidenhead, Wokingham.

COUNTY ANALYSIS

BUCKINGHAMSHIRE			C	Lab	All	Other	Total
1987 Electorate	455,378	Votes	196,565	53,246	93,182	1,570	344,563
Turnout %	75.7	Votes %	57.0	15.5	27.0	0.5	100.0
Swing %	-0.4	Seats	6	0	0	0	6
C to Lab		Candidates	6	6	6	2	20
1983 Electorate	421,010	Votes	176,161	44,574	88,385	1,277	310,397
Turnout %	73.7	Votes %	56.8	14.4	28.5	0.4	100.0
		Seats	6	0	0	0	6
		Candidates	6	6	6	4	22
		Change 83-87	0.3	1.1	-1.4	0.0	

Aylesbury, Beaconsfield, Buckingham, Chesham and Amersham, Milton Keynes, Wycombe.

CAMBRIDGESHIRE			C	Lab	All	Other	Total
1987 Electorate	468,911	Votes	189,284	66,061	99,359	1,977	356,681
Turnout %	76.1	Votes %	53.1	18.5	27.9	0.6	100.0
Swing %	0.3	Seats	6	0	0	0	6
Lab to C		Candidates	6	6	6	3	21
1983 Electorate	435,650	Votes	165,272	54,977	102,392	1,396	324,037
Turnout %	74.4	Votes %	51.0	17.0	31.6	0.4	100.0
		Seats	5	0	1	0	6
		Candidates	6	6	6	4	22
		Change 83-87	2.1	1.6	-3.7	0.1	

Cambridge, Cambridgeshire North East, Cambridgeshire South East, Cambridgeshire South West, Huntingdon, Peterborough.

CHESHIRE			C	Lab	All	Other	Total
1987 Electorate	725,907	Votes	254,639	195,389	117,190	1,424	568,642
Turnout %	78.3	Votes %	44.8	34.4	20.6	0.3	100.0
Swing %	-2.7	Seats	7	3	0	0	10
C to Lab		Candidates	10	10	10	3	33
1983 Electorate	698,915	Votes	237,733	154,931	127,307	1,158	521,129
Turnout %	74.6	Votes %	45.6	29.7	24.4	0.2	100.0
		Seats	7	3	0	0	10
		Candidates	10	10	10	3	33
		Change 83-87	-0.8	4.6	-3.8	0.0	

City Of Chester, Congleton, Crewe and Nantwich, Eddisbury, Ellesmere Port and Neston, Halton, Macclesfield, Tatton, Warrington North, Warrington South.

CLEVELAND			C	Lab	All	Other	Total
1987 Electorate	417,669	Votes	107,007	141,469	66,115	1,786	316,377
Turnout %	75.7	Votes %	33.8	44.7	20.9	0.6	100.0
Swing %	-4.4	Seats	2	4	0	0	6
C to Lab		Candidates	6	6	6	1	19
1983 Electorate	417,197	Votes	105,909	112,168	77,708	412	296,197
Turnout %	71.0	Votes %	35.8	37.9	26.2	0.1	100.0
		Seats	1	4	1	0	6
		Candidates	6	6	6	2	20
		Change 83-87	-1.9	6.8	-5.3	0.4	

Hartlepool, Langbaurgh, Middlesbrough, Redcar, Stockton North, Stockton South.

CORNWALL			C	Lab	All	Other	Total
1987 Electorate	351,115	Votes	131,194	34,994	111,064	373	277,625
Turnout %	79.1	Votes %	47.3	12.6	40.0	0.1	100.0
Swing %	-2.9	Seats	4	0	1	0	5
C to Lab		Candidates	5	5	5	1	16
1983 Electorate	330,129	Votes	126,182	22,838	104,365	2,604	255,989
Turnout %	77.5	Votes %	49.3	8.9	40.8	1.0	100.0
		Seats	4	0	1	0	5
		Candidates	5	5	5	7	22
		Change 83-87	-2.0	3.7	-0.8	-0.9	

Cornwall North, Cornwall South East, Falmouth and Camborne, St Ives, Truro.

CUMBRIA

			C	Lab	All	Other	Total
1987 Electorate	377,178	Votes	142,338	97,876	55,480	319	296,013
Turnout %	78.5	Votes %	48.1	33.1	18.7	0.1	100.0
Swing %	-0.3	Seats	3	3	0	0	6
C to Lab		Candidates	6	6	6	1	19
1983 Electorate	368,063	Votes	129,940	86,730	60,654	805	278,129
Turnout %	75.6	Votes %	46.7	31.2	21.8	0.3	100.0
		Seats	3	3	0	0	6
		Candidates	6	6	6	1	19
		Change 83-87	1.4	1.9	-3.1	-0.2	

Barrow and Furness, Carlisle, Copeland, Penrith and The Border, Westmorland and Lonsdale, Workington.

DERBYSHIRE

			C	Lab	All	Other	Total
1987 Electorate	712,462	Votes	241,124	201,785	114,593	291	557,793
Turnout %	78.3	Votes %	43.2	36.2	20.5	0.1	100.0
Swing %	0.2	Seats	6	4	0	0	10
Lab to C		Candidates	10	10	10	1	31
1983 Electorate	691,972	Votes	214,730	180,598	117,228	5,311	517,867
Turnout %	74.8	Votes %	41.5	34.9	22.6	1.0	100.0
		Seats	6	4	0	0	10
		Candidates	10	10	10	3	33
		Change 83-87	1.8	1.3	-2.1	-1.0	

Amber Valley, Bolsover, Chesterfield, Derby North, Derby South, Derbyshire North East, Derbyshire South, Derbyshire West, Erewash, High Peak.

DEVON

			C	Lab	All	Other	Total
1987 Electorate	763,638	Votes	297,174	78,426	219,748	5,415	600,763
Turnout %	78.7	Votes %	49.5	13.1	36.6	0.9	100.0
Swing %	-2.6	Seats	10	0	1	0	11
C to Lab		Candidates	11	11	11	9	42
1983 Electorate	727,001	Votes	292,254	61,441	196,131	3,954	553,780
Turnout %	76.2	Votes %	52.8	11.1	35.4	0.7	100.0
		Seats	10	0	1	0	11
		Candidates	11	11	11	12	45
		Change 83-87	-3.3	2.0	1.2	0.2	

Devon North, Devon West and Torridge, Exeter, Honiton, Plymouth, Devonport, Plymouth, Drake, Plymouth, Sutton, South Hams, Teignbridge, Tiverton, Torbay.

DORSET

			C	Lab	All	Other	Total
1987 Electorate	507,372	Votes	222,200	43,414	118,346	244	384,204
Turnout %	75.7	Votes %	57.8	11.3	30.8	0.1	100.0
Swing %	-0.9	Seats	7	0	0	0	7
C to Lab		Candidates	7	7	7	1	22
1983 Electorate	476,807	Votes	201,441	35,163	102,097	4,944	343,645
Turnout %	72.1	Votes %	58.6	10.2	29.7	1.4	100.0
		Seats	7	0	0	0	7
		Candidates	7	7	7	7	28
		Change 83-87	-0.8	1.1	1.1	-1.4	

Bournemouth East, Bournemouth West, Christchurch, Dorset North, Dorset South, Dorset West, Poole.

DURHAM

			C	Lab	All	Other	Total
1987 Electorate	463,800	Votes	99,903	183,306	69,379	0	352,588
Turnout %	76.0	Votes %	28.3	52.0	19.7	0.0	100.0
Swing %	-4.3	Seats	1	6	0	0	7
C to Lab		Candidates	7	7	7	0	21
1983 Electorate	462,737	Votes	101,975	152,761	80,275	406	335,417
Turnout %	72.5	Votes %	30.4	45.5	23.9	0.1	100.0
		Seats	1	6	0	0	7
		Candidates	7	7	7	2	23
		Change 83-87	-2.1	6.4	-4.3	-0.1	

Bishop Auckland, Darlington, City Of Durham, Durham North, Durham North West, Easington, Sedgefield.

ESSEX

		C	Lab	All	Other	Total
1987 Electorate	1,167,472	Votes	481,794	168,591	237,399	3,061	890,845
Turnout %	76.3	Votes %	54.1	18.9	26.6	0.3	100.0
Swing %	0.5	Seats	16	0	0	0	16
Lab to C		Candidates	16	16	16	6	54
1983 Electorate	1,118,378	Votes	424,932	145,600	243,679	4,927	819,138
Turnout %	73.2	Votes %	51.9	17.8	29.7	0.6	100.0
		Seats	15	1	0	0	16
		Candidates	16	16	16	10	58
		Change 83-87	2.2	1.2	-3.1	-0.3	

Basildon, Billericay, Braintree, Brentwood and Ongar, Castle Point, Chelmsford, Colchester North, Colchester South and Maldon, Epping Forest, Harlow, Harwich, Rochford, Saffron Walden, Southend East, Southend West, Thurrock.

GLOUCESTERSHIRE

		C	Lab	All	Other	Total
1987 Electorate	399,484	Votes	159,609	57,557	99,450	283	316,899
Turnout %	79.3	Votes %	50.4	18.2	31.4	0.1	100.0
Swing %	-0.9	Seats	5	0	0	0	5
C to Lab		Candidates	5	5	5	1	16
1983 Electorate	382,197	Votes	148,692	49,044	94,245	1,218	293,199
Turnout %	76.7	Votes %	50.7	16.7	32.1	0.4	100.0
		Seats	5	0	0	0	5
		Candidates	5	5	5	3	18
		Change 83-87	-0.3	1.4	-0.8	-0.3	

Cheltenham, Cirencester and Tewkesbury, Gloucester, Gloucestershire West, Stroud.

HAMPSHIRE

		C	Lab	All	Other	Total
1987 Electorate	1,158,235	Votes	489,846	128,880	266,289	1,393	886,408
Turnout %	76.5	Votes %	55.3	14.5	30.0	0.2	100.0
Swing %	0.2	Seats	15	0	0	0	15
Lab to C		Candidates	15	15	15	3	48
1983 Electorate	1,099,940	Votes	446,697	119,281	242,498	1,745	810,221
Turnout %	73.7	Votes %	55.1	14.7	29.9	0.2	100.0
		Seats	15	0	0	0	15
		Candidates	15	15	15	6	51
		Change 83-87	0.1	-0.2	0.1	-0.1	

Aldershot, Basingstoke, Eastleigh, Fareham, Gosport, Hampshire East, Hampshire North West, Havant, New Forest, Portsmouth North, Portsmouth South, Romsey and Waterside, Southampton Itchen, Southampton Test, Winchester.

HEREFORD & WORCESTER

		C	Lab	All	Other	Total
1987 Electorate	504,138	Votes	200,824	69,574	115,061	2,191	387,650
Turnout %	76.9	Votes %	51.8	17.9	29.7	0.6	100.0
Swing %	-1.6	Seats	7	0	0	0	7
C to Lab		Candidates	7	7	7	2	23
1983 Electorate	478,844	Votes	187,965	55,097	112,997	3,420	359,479
Turnout %	75.1	Votes %	52.3	15.3	31.4	1.0	100.0
		Seats	7	0	0	0	7
		Candidates	7	7	7	7	28
		Change 83-87	-0.5	2.6	-1.8	-0.4	

Bromsgrove, Hereford, Leominster, Worcester, Worcestershire Mid, Worcestershire South, Wyre Forest.

HERTFORDSHIRE

		C	Lab	All	Other	Total
1987 Electorate	744,762	Votes	305,252	116,404	163,027	2,113	586,796
Turnout %	78.8	Votes %	52.0	19.8	27.8	0.4	100.0
Swing %	0.4	Seats	10	0	0	0	10
Lab to C		Candidates	10	10	10	4	34
1983 Electorate	720,597	Votes	279,184	105,213	167,638	2,696	554,731
Turnout %	77.0	Votes %	50.3	19.0	30.2	0.5	100.0
		Seats	10	0	0	0	10
		Candidates	10	10	10	6	36
		Change 83-87	1.7	0.9	-2.4	-0.1	

Broxbourne, Hertford and Stortford, Hertfordshire North, Hertfordshire South West, Hertfordshire West, Hertsmere, St Albans, Stevenage, Watford, Welwyn Hatfield.

HUMBERSIDE			C	Lab	All	Other	Total
1987 Electorate	653,219	Votes	202,098	168,061	111,537	1,087	482,783
Turnout %	73.9	Votes %	41.9	34.8	23.1	0.2	100.0
Swing %	-3.8	Seats	4	5	0	0	9
C to Lab		Candidates	9	9	9	2	29
1983 Electorate	645,004	Votes	200,486	133,356	122,360	1,025	457,227
Turnout %	70.9	Votes %	43.8	29.2	26.8	0.2	100.0
		Seats	5	4	0	0	9
		Candidates	9	9	9	2	29
		Change 83-87	-2.0	5.6	-3.7	0.0	

Barnsley Central, Barnsley East, Barnsley West and Penistone, Batley and Spen, Beverley, Boothferry, Bradford North, Bradford South, Bradford West, Bridlington, Brigg and Cleethorpes, Calder Valley, Colne Valley, Dewsbury, Doncaster Central, Doncaster North, Don Valley, Elmet, Glanford and Scunthorpe, Great Grimsby, Halifax, Harrogate, Hemsworth, Huddersfield, Hull East, Hull North, Hull West, Keighley, Leeds Central, Leeds East, Leeds North East, Leeds North West, Leeds South and Morley, Leeds West, Normanton, Pontefract and Castleford, Pudsey, Richmond (Yorks), Rotherham, Rother Valley, Ryedale, Scarborough, Selby, Sheffield Attercliffe, Sheffield Brightside, Sheffield Central, Sheffield Hallam, Sheffield Heeley, Sheffield Hillsborough, Shipley, Skipton and Ripon, Wakefield, Wentworth, York.

KENT			C	Lab	All	Other	Total
1987 Electorate	1,144,091	Votes	468,984	167,612	226,508	4,959	868,063
Turnout %	75.9	Votes %	54.0	19.3	26.1	0.6	100.0
Swing %	-0.3	Seats	16	0	0	0	16
C to Lab		Candidates	16	16	16	8	56
1983 Electorate	1,109,631	Votes	437,349	150,703	218,030	5,609	811,691
Turnout %	73.1	Votes %	53.9	18.6	26.9	0.7	100.0
		Seats	16	0	0	0	16
		Candidates	16	16	16	15	63
		Change 83-87	0.1	0.7	-0.8	-0.1	

Ashford, Canterbury, Dartford, Dover, Faversham, Folkestone and Hythe, Gillingham, Gravesham, Kent Mid, Maidstone, Medway, Sevenoaks, Thanet North, Thanet South, Tonbridge and Malling, Tunbridge Wells.

LANCASHIRE			C	Lab	All	Other	Total
1987 Electorate	1,053,546	Votes	378,022	280,696	154,417	2,763	815,898
Turnout %	77.4	Votes %	46.3	34.4	18.9	0.3	100.0
Swing %	-3.4	Seats	13	3	0	0	16
C to Lab		Candidates	16	16	16	5	53
1983 Electorate	1,036,245	Votes	374,010	228,439	169,792	3,891	776,132
Turnout %	74.9	Votes %	48.2	29.4	21.9	0.5	100.0
		Seats	13	3	0	0	16
		Candidates	16	16	16	10	58
		Change 83-87	-1.9	5.0	-3.0	-0.2	

Blackburn, Blackpool North, Blackpool South, Burnley, Chorley, Fylde, Hyndburn, Lancashire West, Lancaster, Morecambe and Lunesdale, Pendle, Ribble Valley, Preston, South Ribble, Rossendale and Darwen, Wyre.

LEICESTERSHIRE			C	Lab	All	Other	Total
1987 Electorate	658,556	Votes	270,098	141,617	105,091	2,564	519,370
Turnout %	78.9	Votes %	52.0	27.3	20.2	0.5	100.0
Swing %	-0.3	Seats	6	3	0	0	9
C to Lab		Candidates	9	9	9	6	33
1983 Electorate	639,897	Votes	244,053	122,069	109,262	6,648	482,032
Turnout %	75.3	Votes %	50.6	25.3	22.7	1.4	100.0
		Seats	8	1	0	0	9
		Candidates	9	9	9	14	41
		Change 83-87	1.4	1.9	-2.4	-0.9	

Blaby, Bosworth, Harborough, Leicester East, Leicester South, Leicester West, Leicestershire North West, Loughborough, Rutland and Melton.

LINCOLNSHIRE			C	Lab	All	Other	Total
1987 Electorate	436,369	Votes	177,166	60,789	90,160	1,337	329,452
Turnout %	75.5	Votes %	53.8	18.5	27.4	0.4	100.0
Swing %	-1.4	Seats	6	0	0	0	6
C to Lab		Candidates	6	6	6	3	21
1983 Electorate	414,281	Votes	162,402	46,074	95,802	802	305,080
Turnout %	73.6	Votes %	53.2	15.1	31.4	0.3	100.0
		Seats	6	0	0	0	6
		Candidates	6	6	6	2	20
		Change 83-87	0.5	3.3	-4.0	0.1	

Gainsborough and Horncastle, Grantham, Holland With Boston, Lincoln, Lindsey East, Stamford and Spalding.

COUNTY ANALYSIS

NORFOLK			C	Lab	All	Other	Total
1987 Electorate	562,950	Votes	224,842	101,027	113,612	960	440,441
Turnout %	78.2	Votes %	51.0	22.9	25.8	0.2	100.0
Swing %	0.2	Seats	7	1	0	0	8
Lab to C		Candidates	8	8	8	1	25
1983 Electorate	536,846	Votes	200,775	88,871	112,636	1,303	403,585
Turnout %	75.2	Votes %	49.7	22.0	27.9	0.3	100.0
		Seats	8	0	0	0	8
		Candidates	8	8	8	5	29
		Change 83-87	1.3	0.9	-2.1	-0.1	

Great Yarmouth, Norfolk Mid, Norfolk North, Norfolk North West, Norfolk South, Norfolk South West, Norwich North, Norwich South.

NORTHAMPTONSHIRE			C	Lab	All	Other	Total
1987 Electorate	417,140	Votes	166,926	87,433	67,049	1,274	322,682
Turnout %	77.4	Votes %	51.7	27.1	20.8	0.4	100.0
Swing %	0.6	Seats	6	0	0	0	6
Lab to C		Candidates	6	6	6	3	21
1983 Electorate	395,078	Votes	146,075	76,079	75,284	733	298,171
Turnout %	75.5	Votes %	49.0	25.5	25.2	0.2	100.0
		Seats	6	0	0	0	6
		Candidates	6	6	6	2	20
		Change 83-87	2.7	1.6	-4.5	0.1	

Corby, Daventry, Kettering, Northampton North, Northampton South, Wellingborough.

NORTHUMBERLAND			C	Lab	All	Other	Total
1987 Electorate	232,481	Votes	52,083	63,147	66,249	715	182,194
Turnout %	78.4	Votes %	28.6	34.7	36.4	0.4	100.0
Swing %	-4.8	Seats	1	2	1	0	4
C to Lab		Candidates	4	4	4	2	14
1983 Electorate	228,963	Votes	57,337	51,346	62,265	406	171,354
Turnout %	74.8	Votes %	33.5	30.0	36.3	0.2	100.0
		Seats	1	2	1	0	4
		Candidates	4	4	4	1	13
		Change 83-87	-4.9	4.7	0.0	0.2	

Berwick- upon-Tweed, Blyth Valley, Hexham, Wansbeck.

NOTTINGHAMSHIRE			C	Lab	All	Other	Total
1987 Electorate	768,345	Votes	271,923	205,156	109,875	3,662	590,616
Turnout %	76.9	Votes %	46.0	34.7	18.6	0.6	100.0
Swing %	-0.8	Seats	7	4	0	0	11
C to Lab		Candidates	11	11	11	4	37
1983 Electorate	750,141	Votes	246,146	175,804	119,522	3,772	545,244
Turnout %	72.7	Votes %	45.1	32.2	21.9	0.7	100.0
		Seats	8	3	0	0	11
		Candidates	11	11	11	5	38
		Change 83-87	0.9	2.5	-3.3	-0.1	

Ashfield, Bassetlaw, Broxtowe, Gedling, Mansfield, Newark, Nottingham East, Nottingham North, Nottingham South, Rushcliffe, Sherwood.

OXFORDSHIRE			C	Lab	All	Other	Total
1987 Electorate	408,019	Votes	166,089	63,961	84,012	1,196	315,258
Turnout %	77.3	Votes %	52.7	20.3	26.6	0.4	100.0
Swing %	-0.3	Seats	5	1	0	0	6
C to Lab		Candidates	6	6	6	3	21
1983 Electorate	391,782	Votes	150,537	53,866	85,625	2,314	292,342
Turnout %	74.6	Votes %	51.5	18.4	29.3	0.8	100.0
		Seats	6	0	0	0	6
		Candidates	6	6	6	9	27
		Change 83-87	1.2	1.9	-2.6	-0.4	

Banbury, Henley, Oxford East, Oxford West and Abingdon, Wantage, Witney.

SHROPSHIRE			C	Lab	All	Other	Total
1987 Electorate	296,518	Votes	110,136	58,068	59,470	660	228,334
Turnout %	77.0	Votes %	48.2	25.4	26.0	0.3	100.0
Swing %	-2.4	Seats	3	1	0	0	4
C to Lab		Candidates	4	4	4	1	13
1983 Electorate	280,369	Votes	101,881	44,268	61,785	135	208,069
Turnout %	74.2	Votes %	49.0	21.3	29.7	0.1	100.0
		Seats	4	0	0	0	4
		Candidates	4	4	4	1	13
		Change 83-87	-0.7	4.2	-3.6	0.2	

Ludlow, Shrewsbury and Atcham, Shropshire North, The Wrekin.

SOMERSET			C	Lab	All	Other	Total
1987 Electorate	347,983	Votes	138,541	32,545	104,587	134	275,807
Turnout %	79.3	Votes %	50.2	11.8	37.9	0.0	100.0
Swing %	-0.5	Seats	4	0	1	0	5
C to Lab		Candidates	5	5	5	1	16
1983 Electorate	327,540	Votes	128,794	29,564	93,134	273	251,765
Turnout %	76.9	Votes %	51.2	11.7	37.0	0.1	100.0
		Seats	4	0	1	0	5
		Candidates	5	5	5	1	16
		Change 83-87	-0.9	0.1	0.9	-0.1	

Bridgwater, Somerton and Frome, Taunton, Wells, Yeovil.

STAFFORDSHIRE			C	Lab	All	Other	Total
1987 Electorate	781,841	Votes	271,589	204,928	127,594	1,233	605,344
Turnout %	77.4	Votes %	44.9	33.9	21.1	0.2	100.0
Swing %	-0.5	Seats	7	4	0	0	11
C to Lab		Candidates	11	11	11	2	35
1983 Electorate	763,045	Votes	255,472	187,142	125,652	716	568,982
Turnout %	74.6	Votes %	44.9	32.9	22.1	0.1	100.0
		Seats	7	4	0	0	11
		Candidates	11	11	11	2	35
		Change 83-87	0.0	1.0	-1.0	0.1	

Burton, Cannock and Burntwood, Newcastle- under-Lyme, Stafford, Staffordshire Mid, Staffordshire Moorlands, Staffordshire South, Staffordshire South East, Stoke-On-Trent Central, Stoke-On-Trent North, Stoke-On-Trent South.

SUFFOLK			C	Lab	All	Other	Total
1987 Electorate	463,510	Votes	187,295	82,806	84,070	2,280	356,451
Turnout %	76.9	Votes %	52.5	23.2	23.6	0.6	100.0
Swing %	-0.5	Seats	6	0	0	0	6
C to Lab		Candidates	6	6	6	3	21
1983 Electorate	441,498	Votes	173,371	73,054	83,596	235	330,256
Turnout %	74.8	Votes %	52.5	22.1	25.3	0.1	100.0
		Seats	5	1	0	0	6
		Candidates	6	6	6	1	19
		Change 83-87	0.0	1.1	-1.7	0.6	

Bury St Edmunds, Ipswich, Suffolk Central, Suffolk Coastal, Suffolk South, Waveney.

SURREY			C	Lab	All	Other	Total
1987 Electorate	792,847	Votes	361,831	68,173	165,039	2,369	597,412
Turnout %	75.4	Votes %	60.6	11.4	27.6	0.4	100.0
Swing %	0.4	Seats	11	0	0	0	11
Lab to C		Candidates	11	11	11	3	36
1983 Electorate	770,406	Votes	331,879	61,285	159,676	5,945	558,785
Turnout %	72.5	Votes %	59.4	11.0	28.6	1.1	100.0
		Seats	11	0	0	0	11
		Candidates	11	11	11	7	40
		Change 83-87	1.2	0.4	-0.9	-0.7	

Chertsey and Walton, Epsom and Ewell, Esher, Guildford, Mole Valley, Reigate, Spelthorne, Surrey East, Surrey North West, Surrey South West, Woking.

267

COUNTY ANALYSIS

SUSSEX EAST

SUSSEX EAST			C	Lab	All	Other	Total
1987 Electorate	550,235	Votes	235,529	61,887	107,244	2,795	407,455
Turnout %	74.1	Votes %	57.8	15.2	26.3	0.7	100.0
Swing %	-1.1	Seats	8	0	0	0	8
C to Lab		Candidates	8	8	8	5	29
1983 Electorate	533,686	Votes	220,859	51,301	103,040	3,265	378,465
Turnout %	70.9	Votes %	58.4	13.6	27.2	0.9	100.0
		Seats	8	0	0	0	8
		Candidates	8	8	8	6	30
		Change 83-87	-0.6	1.6	-0.9	-0.2	

Bexhill and Battle, Brighton, Kemptown, Brighton, Pavilion, Eastbourne, Hastings and Rye, Hove, Lewes, Wealden.

SUSSEX WEST

SUSSEX WEST			C	Lab	All	Other	Total
1987 Electorate	546,378	Votes	246,678	48,497	113,266	2,579	411,020
Turnout %	75.2	Votes %	60.0	11.8	27.6	0.6	100.0
Swing %	-0.9	Seats	7	0	0	0	7
C to Lab		Candidates	7	7	7	2	23
1983 Electorate	525,725	Votes	230,234	37,867	112,801	3,753	384,655
Turnout %	73.2	Votes %	59.9	9.8	29.3	1.0	100.0
		Seats	7	0	0	0	7
		Candidates	7	7	7	6	27
		Change 83-87	0.2	2.0	-1.8	-0.3	

Arundel, Chichester, Crawley, Horsham, Shoreham, Sussex Mid, Worthing.

WARWICKSHIRE

WARWICKSHIRE			C	Lab	All	Other	Total
1987 Electorate	369,654	Votes	147,581	76,174	64,141	1,933	289,829
Turnout %	78.4	Votes %	50.9	26.3	22.1	0.7	100.0
Swing %	-0.1	Seats	5	0	0	0	5
C to Lab		Candidates	5	5	5	2	17
1983 Electorate	356,705	Votes	133,293	65,846	70,456	1,189	270,784
Turnout %	75.9	Votes %	49.2	24.3	26.0	0.4	100.0
		Seats	5	0	0	0	5
		Candidates	5	5	5	2	17
		Change 83-87	1.7	2.0	-3.9	0.2	

Nuneaton, Rugby and Kenilworth, Stratford-On-Avon, Warwick and Leamington, Warwickshire North.

WILTSHIRE

WILTSHIRE			C	Lab	All	Other	Total
1987 Electorate	413,990	Votes	166,934	53,795	100,354	372	321,455
Turnout %	77.6	Votes %	51.9	16.7	31.2	0.1	100.0
Swing %	-0.1	Seats	5	0	0	0	5
C to Lab		Candidates	5	5	5	1	16
1983 Electorate	390,627	Votes	146,887	43,468	99,784	2,033	292,172
Turnout %	74.8	Votes %	50.3	14.9	34.2	0.7	100.0
		Seats	5	0	0	0	5
		Candidates	5	5	5	7	22
		Change 83-87	1.7	1.9	-2.9	-0.6	

Devizes, Salisbury, Swindon, Westbury, Wiltshire North.

YORKSHIRE NORTH

YORKSHIRE NORTH			C	Lab	All	Other	Total
1987 Electorate	535,729	Votes	216,602	77,490	112,001	1,462	407,555
Turnout %	76.1	Votes %	53.1	19.0	27.5	0.4	100.0
Swing %	-2.9	Seats	7	0	0	0	7
C to Lab		Candidates	7	7	7	2	23
1983 Electorate	511,858	Votes	206,461	59,879	100,639	831	367,810
Turnout %	71.9	Votes %	56.1	16.3	27.4	0.2	100.0
		Seats	7	0	0	0	7
		Candidates	7	7	7	4	25
		Change 83-87	-3.0	2.7	0.1	0.1	

Harrogate, Richmond (Yorks), Ryedale, Scarborough, Selby, Skipton and Ripon, York.

NON-METROPOLITAN COUNTIES: TOTALS			C	Lab	All	Other	Total
1987 Electorate	22,523,256	Votes	8,641,011	4,018,105	4,428,542	213,968	17,301,626
Turnout %	76.8	Votes %	49.9	23.2	25.6	1.2	100.0
Swing %	-0.9	Seats	260	45	4	4	313
C to Lab		Candidates	309	309	309	132	1059
1983 Electorate	21,690,180	Votes	7,982,726	3,411,530	4,422,469	253,136	16,069,861
Turnout %	74.1	Votes %	49.7	21.2	27.5	1.6	100.0
		Seats	263	40	6	4	313
		Candidates	309	309	309	230	1157
		Change 83-87	0.3	2.0	-1.9	-0.3	

United Kingdom Cities and Boroughs

Voting in principal cities and boroughs in England, Scotland, Wales and Northern Ireland, together with comparison with the results in 1983, was as follows:

BELFAST			OUP	DUP	All	PSF	SDLP	Other	Total
1987 Electorate	227,284	Votes	40,918	20,372	20,408	23,603	24,704	13,394	143,399
Turnout %	63.1	Votes %	28.5	14.2	14.2	16.5	17.2	9.3	100.0
		Seats	2	1	0	1	0	0	4
		Candidates	3	1	3	4	3	5	19
1983 Electorate	230,153	Votes	46,085	32,855	22,197	23,619	20,613	17,685	163,054
Turnout %	70.8	Votes %	28.3	20.1	13.6	14.5	12.6	10.8	100.0
		Seats	2	1	0	1	0	0	4
		Candidates	4	4	3	4	4	8	27
		Change 83-87	0.3	-5.9	0.6	2.0	4.6	-1.5	

Belfast East, Belfast North, Belfast South, Belfast West.

BOLTON			C	Lab	All	Other	Total
1987 Electorate	195,157	Votes	60,931	66,906	24,157	0	151,994
Turnout %	77.9	Votes %	40.1	44.0	15.9	0.0	100.0
Swing %	-2.3	Seats	2	1	0	0	3
C to Lab		Candidates	3	3	3	0	9
1983 Electorate	193,799	Votes	58,594	57,752	30,789	586	147,721
Turnout %	76.2	Votes %	39.7	39.1	20.8	0.4	100.0
		Seats	2	1	0	0	3
		Candidates	3	3	3	3	12
		Change 83-87	0.4	4.9	-4.9	-0.4	

Bolton North East, Bolton South East, Bolton West.

BIRMINGHAM			C	Lab	All	Other	Total
1987 Electorate	673,871	Votes	180,810	207,964	74,194	3,595	466,563
Turnout %	69.2	Votes %	38.8	44.6	15.9	0.8	100.0
Swing %	-1.3	Seats	5	6	0	0	11
C to Lab		Candidates	11	11	11	8	41
1983 Electorate	684,843	Votes	180,354	195,577	83,250	3,558	462,739
Turnout %	67.6	Votes %	39.0	42.3	18.0	0.8	100.0
		Seats	5	6	0	0	11
		Candidates	11	11	11	11	44
		Change 83-87	-0.2	2.3	-2.1	0.0	

Edgbaston, Erdington, Hall Green, Hodge Hill, Ladywood, Northfield, Perry Barr, Selly Oak, Small Heath, Sparkbrook, Yardley.

269

CITY ANALYSIS

BRADFORD

			C	Lab	All	Other	Total
1987 Electorate	207,781	Votes	58,521	68,014	23,422	0	149,957
Turnout %	72.2	Votes %	39.0	45.4	15.6	0.0	100.0
Swing %	-2.5	Seats	0	3	0	0	3
C to Lab		Candidates	3	3	3	0	9
1983 Electorate	207,233	Votes	50,688	52,533	37,406	4,852	145,479
Turnout %	70.2	Votes %	34.8	36.1	25.7	3.3	100.0
		Seats	1	2	0	0	3
		Candidates	3	3	3	5	14
		Change 83-87	4.2	9.2	-10.1	-3.3	

Bradford North, Bradford South, Bradford West.

BRISTOL

			C	Lab	All	Other	Total
1987 Electorate	277,806	Votes	92,948	69,919	48,076	2,265	213,208
Turnout %	76.7	Votes %	43.6	32.8	22.5	1.1	100.0
Swing %	0.8	Seats	3	1	0	0	4
Lab to C		Candidates	4	4	4	5	17
1983 Electorate	284,549	Votes	87,266	68,263	48,528	2,357	206,414
Turnout %	72.5	Votes %	42.3	33.1	23.5	1.1	100.0
		Seats	3	1	0	0	4
		Candidates	4	4	4	7	19
		Change 83-87	1.3	-0.3	-1.0	-0.1	

Bristol East, Bristol North West, Bristol South, Bristol West.

CARDIFF

			C	Lab	All	Nat	Other	Total
1987 Electorate	223,761	Votes	67,968	66,367	37,987	2,562	0	174,884
Turnout %	78.2	Votes %	38.9	37.9	21.7	1.5	0.0	100.0
Swing %	-4.9	Seats	2	2	0	0	0	4
C to Lab		Candidates	4	4	4	4	0	16
1983 Electorate	225,250	Votes	66,167	48,789	44,427	3,199	517	163,099
Turnout %	72.4	Votes %	40.6	29.9	27.2	2.0	0.3	100.0
		Seats	3	1	0	0	0	4
		Candidates	4	4	4	4	2	18
		Change 83-87	-1.7	8.0	-5.5	-0.5	-0.3	

Cardiff Central, Cardiff North, Cardiff South and Penarth, Cardiff West.

COVENTRY

			C	Lab	All	Other	Total
1987 Electorate	238,016	Votes	61,386	82,359	32,218	789	176,752
Turnout %	74.3	Votes %	34.7	46.6	18.2	0.4	100.0
Swing %	-3.6	Seats	1	3	0	0	4
C to Lab		Candidates	4	4	4	2	14
1983 Electorate	236,724	Votes	62,464	70,512	38,227	749	171,952
Turnout %	72.6	Votes %	36.3	41.0	22.2	0.4	100.0
		Seats	1	3	0	0	4
		Candidates	4	4	4	3	15
		Change 83-87	-1.6	5.6	-4.0	0.0	

Coventry North East, Coventry North West, Coventry South East, Coventry South West.

EDINBURGH

			C	Lab	All	Nat	Other	Total
1987 Electorate	352,964	Votes	85,059	98,564	59,956	18,531	878	262,988
Turnout %	74.5	Votes %	32.3	37.5	22.8	7.0	0.3	100.0
Swing %	-4.6	Seats	2	4	0	0	0	6
C to Lab		Candidates	6	6	6	6	2	26
1983 Electorate	351,644	Votes	86,286	76,402	70,992	13,456	1,256	248,392
Turnout %	70.6	Votes %	34.7	30.8	28.6	5.4	0.5	100.0
		Seats	4	2	0	0	0	6
		Candidates	6	6	6	6	3	27
		Change 83-87	-2.4	6.7	-5.8	1.6	-0.2	

Central, East, Leith, Pentlands, South, West.

270

GLASGOW

			C	Lab	All	Nat	Other	Total
1987 Electorate	566,845	Votes	50,772	249,600	59,965	41,015	2,262	403,614
Turnout %	71.2	Votes %	12.6	61.8	14.9	10.2	0.6	100.0
Swing %	-8.1	Seats	0	11	0	0	0	11
C to Lab		Candidates	11	11	11	11	7	51
1983 Electorate	578,938	Votes	75,295	207,731	84,724	30,200	2,011	399,961
Turnout %	69.1	Votes %	18.8	51.9	21.2	7.6	0.5	100.0
		Seats	0	10	1	0	0	11
		Candidates	11	11	11	11	9	53
		Change 83-87	-6.2	9.9	-6.3	2.6	0.1	

Cathcart, Central, Garscadden, Govan, Hillhead, Maryhill, Pollok, Provan, Rutherglen, Shettleston, Springburn.

HULL

			C	Lab	All	Other	Total
1987 Electorate	197,581	Votes	37,949	72,937	26,203	0	137,089
Turnout %	69.4	Votes %	27.7	53.2	19.1	0.0	100.0
Swing %	-5.4	Seats	0	3	0	0	3
C to Lab		Candidates	3	3	3	0	9
1983 Electorate	202,282	Votes	40,585	60,341	33,128	222	134,276
Turnout %	66.4	Votes %	30.2	44.9	24.7	0.2	100.0
		Seats	0	3	0	0	3
		Candidates	3	3	3	1	10
		Change 83-87	-2.5	8.3	-5.6	-0.2	

Hull East, Hull North, Hull West.

LEEDS

			C	Lab	All	Other	Total
1987 Electorate	380,125	Votes	91,963	108,287	71,978	1,434	273,662
Turnout %	72.0	Votes %	33.6	39.6	26.3	0.5	100.0
Swing %	-2.6	Seats	2	4	0	0	6
C to Lab		Candidates	6	6	6	3	21
1983 Electorate	388,542	Votes	91,722	93,719	75,479	2,815	263,735
Turnout %	67.9	Votes %	34.8	35.5	28.6	1.1	100.0
		Seats	2	3	1	0	6
		Candidates	6	6	6	8	26
		Change 83-87	-1.2	4.0	-2.3	-0.5	

Leeds Central, Leeds East, Leeds North East, Leeds North West, Leeds South and Morley, Leeds West.

LEICESTER

			C	Lab	All	Other	Total
1987 Electorate	207,437	Votes	66,129	71,131	20,416	678	158,354
Turnout %	76.3	Votes %	41.8	44.9	12.9	0.4	100.0
Swing %	-1.3	Seats	0	3	0	0	3
C to Lab		Candidates	3	3	3	3	12
1983 Electorate	208,335	Votes	59,666	60,438	25,707	3,010	148,821
Turnout %	71.4	Votes %	40.1	40.6	17.3	2.0	100.0
		Seats	2	1	0	0	3
		Candidates	3	3	3	7	16
		Change 83-87	1.7	4.3	-4.4	-1.6	

Leicester East, Leicester South, Leicester West.

LIVERPOOL

			C	Lab	All	Other	Total
1987 Electorate	372,293	Votes	47,568	155,083	69,814	699	273,164
Turnout %	73.4	Votes %	17.4	56.8	25.6	0.3	100.0
Swing %	-10.7	Seats	0	5	1	0	6
C to Lab		Candidates	6	6	6	2	20
1983 Electorate	389,199	Votes	79,627	128,467	55,389	8,071	271,554
Turnout %	69.8	Votes %	29.3	47.3	20.4	3.0	100.0
		Seats	0	5	1	0	6
		Candidates	6	6	6	5	23
		Change 83-87	-11.9	9.5	5.2	-2.7	

Liverpool Broadgreen, Liverpool Garston, Liverpool Mossley Hill, Liverpool Riverside, Liverpool Walton, Liverpool West Derby.

271

CITY ANALYSIS

MANCHESTER

		C	Lab	All	Other	Total
1987 Electorate	309,615	Votes	60,750	120,050	39,020	993	220,813
Turnout %	71.3	Votes %	27.5	54.4	17.7	0.4	100.0
Swing %	-3.5	Seats	0	5	0	0	5
C to Lab		Candidates	5	5	5	3	18
1983 Electorate	319,540	Votes	65,856	109,073	40,382	1,477	216,788
Turnout %	67.8	Votes %	30.4	50.3	18.6	0.7	100.0
		Seats	1	4	0	0	5
		Candidates	5	5	5	4	19
		Change 83-87	-2.9	4.1	-1.0	-0.2	

Manchester Blackley, Manchester Central, Manchester Gorton, Manchester Withington, Manchester Wythenshawe.

NEWCASTLE-UPON-TYNE

		C	Lab	All	Other	Total
1987 Electorate	192,229	Votes	42,025	66,517	31,213	891	140,646
Turnout %	73.2	Votes %	29.9	47.3	22.2	0.6	100.0
Swing %	-5.9	Seats	0	3	0	0	3
C to Lab		Candidates	3	3	3	3	12
1983 Electorate	191,706	Votes	46,345	54,165	36,352	478	137,340
Turnout %	71.6	Votes %	33.7	39.4	26.5	0.3	100.0
		Seats	1	2	0	0	3
		Candidates	3	3	3	1	10
		Change 83-87	-3.9	7.9	-4.3	0.3	

Newcastle Upon Tyne Central, Newcastle Upon Tyne East, Newcastle Upon Tyne North.

NOTTINGHAM

		C	Lab	All	Other	Total
1987 Electorate	210,693	Votes	65,131	64,106	20,316	1,091	150,644
Turnout %	71.5	Votes %	43.2	42.6	13.5	0.7	100.0
Swing %	-2.4	Seats	2	1	0	0	3
C to Lab		Candidates	3	3	3	2	11
1983 Electorate	209,504	Votes	58,609	51,068	27,282	2,605	139,564
Turnout %	66.6	Votes %	42.0	36.6	19.5	1.9	100.0
		Seats	3	0	0	0	3
		Candidates	3	3	3	2	11
		Change 83-87	1.2	6.0	-6.1	-1.1	

Nottingham East, Nottingham North, Nottingham South.

PLYMOUTH

		C	Lab	All	Other	Total
1987 Electorate	180,047	Votes	53,951	31,927	53,283	493	139,654
Turnout %	77.6	Votes %	38.6	22.9	38.2	0.4	100.0
Swing %	-6.0	Seats	2	0	1	0	3
C to Lab		Candidates	3	3	3	1	10
1983 Electorate	174,086	Votes	60,828	24,304	45,492	1,018	131,642
Turnout %	75.6	Votes %	46.2	18.5	34.6	0.8	100.0
		Seats	2	0	1	0	3
		Candidates	3	3	3	5	14
		Change 83-87	-7.6	4.4	3.6	-0.4	

Plymouth, Devonport, Plymouth, Drake, Plymouth, Sutton.

SHEFFIELD

		C	Lab	All	Other	Total
1987 Electorate	417,590	Votes	74,652	151,269	73,042	940	299,903
Turnout %	71.8	Votes %	24.9	50.4	24.4	0.3	100.0
Swing %	-5.4	Seats	1	5	0	0	6
C to Lab		Candidates	6	6	6	3	21
1983 Electorate	420,191	Votes	85,726	128,832	75,777	1,464	291,799
Turnout %	69.4	Votes %	29.4	44.2	26.0	0.5	100.0
		Seats	1	5	0	0	6
		Candidates	6	6	6	4	22
		Change 83-87	-4.5	6.3	-1.6	-0.2	

Sheffield Attercliffe, Sheffield Brightside, Sheffield Central, Sheffield Hallam, Sheffield Heeley, Sheffield Hillsborough.

STOKE-ON-TRENT

STOKE-ON-TRENT		C	Lab	All	Other	Total
1987 Electorate	210,977	Votes	50,759	74,095	26,796	0	151,650
Turnout %	71.9	Votes %	33.5	48.9	17.7	0.0	100.0
Swing %	0.3	Seats	0	3	0	0	3
Lab to C		Candidates	3	3	3	0	9
1983 Electorate	212,785	Votes	45,968	69,526	30,694	504	146,692
Turnout %	68.9	Votes %	31.3	47.4	20.9	0.3	100.0
		Seats	0	3	0	0	3
		Candidates	3	3	3	1	10
		Change 83-87	2.1	1.5	-3.3	-0.3	

TEESSIDE

TEESSIDE		C	Lab	All	Other	Total
1987 Electorate	269,790	Votes	63,953	93,214	46,663	0	203,830
Turnout %	75.6	Votes %	31.4	45.7	22.9	0.0	100.0
Swing %	-4.8	Seats	1	3	0	0	4
C to Lab		Candidates	4	4	4	0	12
1983 Electorate	270,464	Votes	62,712	71,905	54,665	412	189,694
Turnout %	70.1	Votes %	33.1	37.9	28.8	0.2	100.0
		Seats	0	3	1	0	4
		Candidates	4	4	4	2	14
		Change 83-87	-1.7	7.8	-5.9	-0.2	

WOLVERHAMPTON

WOLVERHAMPTON		C	Lab	All	Other	Total
1987 Electorate	187,760	Votes	59,454	55,330	24,497	0	139,281
Turnout %	74.2	Votes %	42.7	39.7	17.6	0.0	100.0
Swing %	-0.9	Seats	2	1	0	0	3
C to Lab		Candidates	3	3	3	0	9
1983 Electorate	188,991	Votes	55,369	49,075	28,360	786	133,590
Turnout %	70.7	Votes %	41.4	36.7	21.2	0.6	100.0
		Seats	1	2	0	0	3
		Candidates	3	3	3	2	11
		Change 83-87	1.2	3.0	-3.6	-0.6	

UK NON-METROPOLITAN CITIES & BOROUGHS: TOTALS

UK NON-METROPOLITAN CITIES & BOROUGHS: TOTALS		C	Lab	All	Nat	Other	Total
1987 Electorate	5,872,338	Votes	1,372,679	1,973,639	863,216	62,108	17,008	4,288,650
Turnout %	73.0	Votes %	32.0	46.0	20.1	1.4	0.4	100.0
Swing %	-3.9	Seats	25	67	2	0	0	94
C to Lab		Candidates	94	94	94	21	44	347
1983 Electorate	5,938,605	Votes	1,420,127	1,678,472	967,050	46,855	38,748	4,151,252
Turnout %	69.9	Votes %	34.2	40.4	23.3	1.1	0.9	100.0
		Seats	32	57	5	0	0	94
		Candidates	94	94	94	21	85	388
		Change 83-87	-2.2	5.6	-3.2	0.3	-0.5	

Scotland

There are 72 parliamentary constituencies in Scotland. The analysis of the voting in the nine regions of Scotland is as follows (the voting in the island areas of Orkney and Shetland and Western Isles is in the constituency details elsewhere):

BORDERS

			C	Lab	All	Nat	Other	Total
1987 Electorate	81,015	Votes	21,037	6,264	30,987	4,246	0	62,534
Turnout %	77.2	Votes %	33.6	10.0	49.6	6.8	0.0	100.0
Swing %	-1.7	Seats	0	0	2	0	0	2
C to Lab		Candidates	2	2	2	2	0	8
1983 Electorate	78,777	Votes	20,853	4,526	32,788	2,307	0	60,474
Turnout %	76.8	Votes %	34.5	7.5	54.2	3.8	0.0	100.0
		Seats	0	0	2	0	0	2
		Candidates	2	2	2	2	0	8
		Change 83-87	-0.8	2.5	-4.7	3.0	0.0	

Roxburgh and Berwickshire, Tweeddale, Ettrick and Lauderdale.

CENTRAL

			C	Lab	All	Nat	Other	Total
1987 Electorate	209,705	Votes	37,271	78,595	20,230	25,565	0	161,661
Turnout %	77.1	Votes %	23.1	48.6	12.5	15.8	0.0	100.0
Swing %	-5.0	Seats	1	3	0	0	0	4
C to Lab		Candidates	4	4	4	4	0	16
1983 Electorate	205,391	Votes	39,114	63,008	30,823	19,556	334	152,835
Turnout %	74.4	Votes %	25.6	41.2	20.2	12.8	0.2	100.0
		Seats	1	3	0	0	0	4
		Candidates	4	4	4	4	1	17
		Change 83-87	-2.5	7.4	-7.7	3.0	-0.2	

Clackmannan, Falkirk East, Falkirk West, Stirling.

DUMFRIES & GALLOWAY

			C	Lab	All	Nat	Other	Total
1987 Electorate	112,776	Votes	35,377	16,590	14,065	19,310	579	85,921
Turnout %	76.2	Votes %	41.2	19.3	16.4	22.5	0.7	100.0
Swing %	-3.3	Seats	2	0	0	0	0	2
C to Lab		Candidates	2	2	2	2	2	10
1983 Electorate	109,425	Votes	36,309	13,228	15,165	16,645	0	81,347
Turnout %	74.3	Votes %	44.6	16.3	18.6	20.5	0.0	100.0
		Seats	2	0	0	0	0	2
		Candidates	2	2	2	2	0	8
		Change 83-87	-3.5	3.0	-2.3	2.0	0.7	

Dumfries, Galloway and Upper Nithsdale.

FIFE

			C	Lab	All	Nat	Other	Total
1987 Electorate	264,033	Votes	47,133	89,929	43,883	21,042	0	201,987
Turnout %	76.5	Votes %	23.3	44.5	21.7	10.4	0.0	100.0
Swing %	-7.1	Seats	0	4	1	0	0	5
C to Lab		Candidates	5	5	5	5	0	20
1983 Electorate	256,899	Votes	53,329	66,330	50,080	15,304	1,724	186,767
Turnout %	72.7	Votes %	28.6	35.5	26.8	8.2	0.9	100.0
		Seats	1	4	0	0	0	5
		Candidates	5	5	5	5	4	24
		Change 83-87	-5.2	9.0	-5.1	2.2	-0.9	

Dunfermline East, Dunfermline West, Fife Central, Fife North East, Kirkcaldy.

GRAMPIAN

			C	Lab	All	Nat	Other	Total
1987 Electorate	387,573	Votes	90,584	62,313	69,791	54,533	299	277,520
Turnout %	71.6	Votes %	32.6	22.5	25.1	19.7	0.1	100.0
Swing %	-4.3	Seats	1	2	1	2	0	6
C to Lab		Candidates	6	6	6	6	1	25
1983 Electorate	366,885	Votes	95,412	47,734	67,106	42,063	367	252,682
Turnout %	68.9	Votes %	37.8	18.9	26.6	16.6	0.1	100.0
		Seats	4	1	1	0	0	6
		Candidates	6	6	6	6	1	25
		Change 83-87	-5.1	3.6	-1.4	3.0	0.0	

Aberdeen North, Aberdeen South, Banff and Buchan, Gordon, Kincardine and Deeside, Moray.

HIGHLAND

			C	Lab	All	Nat	Other	Total
1987 Electorate	150,391	Votes	22,235	22,715	48,569	13,864	1,019	108,402
Turnout %	72.1	Votes %	20.5	21.0	44.8	12.8	0.9	100.0
Swing %	-7.9	Seats	0	0	3	0	0	3
C to Lab		Candidates	3	3	3	3	2	14
1983 Electorate	142,917	Votes	30,473	14,674	46,318	11,826	0	103,291
Turnout %	72.3	Votes %	29.5	14.2	44.8	11.4	0.0	100.0
		Seats	0	0	3	0	0	3
		Candidates	3	3	3	3	0	12
		Change 83-87	-9.0	6.7	0.0	1.3	0.9	

Caithness and Sutherland, Inverness, Nairn and Lochaber, Ross, Cromarty and Skye.

LOTHIAN

			C	Lab	All	Nat	Other	Total
1987 Electorate	594,684	Votes	122,752	186,679	92,030	45,670	1,895	449,026
Turnout %	75.5	Votes %	27.3	41.6	20.5	10.2	0.4	100.0
Swing %	-4.5	Seats	2	8	0	0	0	10
C to Lab		Candidates	10	10	10	10	5	45
1983 Electorate	586,116	Votes	128,363	150,686	110,923	31,481	1,455	422,908
Turnout %	72.2	Votes %	30.4	35.6	26.2	7.4	0.3	100.0
		Seats	4	6	0	0	0	10
		Candidates	10	10	10	10	4	44
		Change 83-87	-3.0	5.9	-5.7	2.7	0.1	

East Lothian, Central, East, Leith, Pentlands, South, West, Linlithgow, Livingston, Midlothian.

STRATHCLYDE

			C	Lab	All	Nat	Other	Total
1987 Electorate	1,796,515	Votes	261,472	723,590	213,361	156,387	2,485	1,357,295
Turnout %	75.6	Votes %	19.3	53.3	15.7	11.5	0.2	100.0
Swing %	-7.1	Seats	2	30	1	0	0	33
C to Lab		Candidates	33	33	33	33	8	140
1983 Electorate	1,789,316	Votes	317,090	577,717	294,162	117,109	3,399	1,309,477
Turnout %	73.2	Votes %	24.2	44.1	22.5	8.9	0.3	100.0
		Seats	6	26	1	0	0	33
		Candidates	33	33	33	33	14	146
		Change 83-87	-5.0	9.2	-6.7	2.6	-0.1	

Argyll and Bute, Ayr, Carrick, Cumnock and Doon Valley, Clydebank and Milngavie, Clydesdale, Cumbernauld and Kilsyth, Cunninghame North, Cunninghame South, Dumbarton, Eastwood, East Kilbride, Glasgow Cathcart, Glasgow Central, Glasgow Garscadden, Glasgow Govan, Glasgow Hillhead, Glasgow Maryhill, Glasgow Pollok, Glasgow Provan, Glasgow Rutherglen, Glasgow Shettleston, Glasgow Springburn, Greenock and Port Glasgow, Hamilton, Kilmarnock and Loudoun, Monklands East, Monklands West, Motherwell North, Motherwell South, Paisley North, Paisley South, Renfrew West and Inverclyde, Strathkelvin and Bearsden.

TAYSIDE

			C	Lab	All	Nat	Other	Total
1987 Electorate	301,219	Votes	69,343	60,466	24,827	71,555	308	226,499
Turnout %	75.2	Votes %	30.6	26.7	11.0	31.6	0.1	100.0
Swing %	-4.5	Seats	2	2	0	1	0	5
C to Lab		Candidates	5	5	5	5	1	21
1983 Electorate	298,264	Votes	73,685	45,516	34,752	64,265	541	218,759
Turnout %	73.3	Votes %	33.7	20.8	15.9	29.4	0.2	100.0
		Seats	3	1	0	1	0	5
		Candidates	5	5	5	5	2	22
		Change 83-87	-3.1	5.9	-4.9	2.2	-0.1	

Angus East, Dundee East, Dundee West, Perth and Kinross, Tayside North.

Wales

Wales has 38 parliamentary seats in its eight counties and the analysis of the voting in the Principality is as follows:

CLWYD

			C	Lab	All	Nat	Other	Total
1987 Electorate	308,892	Votes	96,009	94,600	48,051	8,299	0	246,959
Turnout %	79.9	Votes %	38.9	38.3	19.5	3.4	0.0	100.0
Swing %	-4.7	Seats	2	3	0	0	0	5
C to Lab		Candidates	5	5	5	5	0	20
1983 Electorate	298,103	Votes	90,234	67,486	62,372	8,563	0	228,655
Turnout %	76.7	Votes %	39.5	29.5	27.3	3.7	0.0	100.0
		Seats	3	2	0	0	0	5
		Candidates	5	5	5	5	0	20
		Change 83-87	-0.6	8.8	-7.8	-0.4	0.0	

Alyn and Deeside, Clwyd North West, Clwyd South West, Delyn, Wrexham.

DYFED

			C	Lab	All	Nat	Other	Total
1987 Electorate	262,598	Votes	59,679	75,213	46,432	26,512	1,302	209,138
Turnout %	79.6	Votes %	28.5	36.0	22.2	12.7	0.6	100.0
Swing %	-4.2	Seats	1	2	1	0	0	4
C to Lab		Candidates	4	4	4	4	2	18
1983 Electorate	255,702	Votes	63,804	62,010	45,473	27,124	1,944	200,355
Turnout %	78.4	Votes %	31.8	31.0	22.7	13.5	1.0	100.0
		Seats	1	2	1	0	0	4
		Candidates	4	4	4	4	6	22
		Change 83-87	-3.3	5.0	-0.5	-0.9	-0.3	

Carmarthen, Ceredigion and Pembroke North, Llanelli, Pembroke.

GLAMORGAN MID

			C	Lab	All	Nat	Other	Total
1987 Electorate	402,890	Votes	55,878	200,112	37,486	18,204	1,521	313,201
Turnout %	77.7	Votes %	17.8	63.9	12.0	5.8	0.5	100.0
Swing %	-5.9	Seats	0	7	0	0	0	7
C to Lab		Candidates	7	7	7	7	2	30
1983 Electorate	402,015	Votes	55,852	158,940	59,112	23,239	3,216	300,359
Turnout %	74.7	Votes %	18.6	52.9	19.7	7.7	1.1	100.0
		Seats	1	6	0	0	0	7
		Candidates	7	7	7	7	4	32
		Change 83-87	-0.8	11.0	-7.7	-1.9	-0.6	

Bridgend, Caerphilly, Cynon Valley, Merthyr Tydfil and Rhymney, Ogmore, Pontypridd, Rhondda.

GLAMORGAN SOUTH

			C	Lab	All	Nat	Other	Total
1987 Electorate	289,071	Votes	92,197	84,345	46,620	3,508	0	226,670
Turnout %	78.4	Votes %	40.7	37.2	20.6	1.5	0.0	100.0
Swing %	-4.9	Seats	3	2	0	0	0	5
C to Lab		Candidates	5	5	5	5	0	20
1983 Electorate	288,135	Votes	88,588	60,817	55,581	4,267	517	209,770
Turnout %	72.8	Votes %	42.2	29.0	26.5	2.0	0.2	100.0
		Seats	4	1	0	0	0	5
		Candidates	5	5	5	5	2	22
		Change 83-87	-1.6	8.2	-5.9	-0.5	-0.2	

Cardiff Central, Cardiff North, Cardiff South and Penarth, Cardiff West, Vale Of Glamorgan.

GLAMORGAN WEST

			C	Lab	All	Nat	Other	Total
1987 Electorate	283,448	Votes	52,436	126,443	33,693	7,304	469	220,345
Turnout %	77.7	Votes %	23.8	57.4	15.3	3.3	0.2	100.0
Swing %	-4.9	Seats	0	5	0	0	0	5
C to Lab		Candidates	5	5	5	5	1	21
1983 Electorate	280,930	Votes	53,494	103,726	44,520	8,675	709	211,124
Turnout %	75.2	Votes %	25.3	49.1	21.1	4.1	0.3	100.0
		Seats	0	5	0	0	0	5
		Candidates	5	5	5	5	3	23
		Change 83-87	-1.5	8.3	-5.8	-0.8	-0.1	

Aberavon, Gower, Neath, Swansea East, Swansea West.

GWENT

			C	Lab	All	Nat	Other	Total
1987 Electorate	332,443	Votes	73,565	142,740	41,219	5,328	450	263,302
Turnout %	79.2	Votes %	27.9	54.2	15.7	2.0	0.2	100.0
Swing %	-4.5	Seats	1	5	0	0	0	6
C to Lab		Candidates	6	6	6	6	1	25
1983 Electorate	327,686	Votes	71,073	114,865	60,463	5,761	0	252,162
Turnout %	77.0	Votes %	28.2	45.6	24.0	2.3	0.0	100.0
		Seats	2	4	0	0	0	6
		Candidates	6	6	6	6	0	24
		Change 83-87	-0.2	8.7	-8.3	-0.3	0.2	

Blaenau Gwent, Islwyn, Monmouth, Newport East, Newport West, Torfaen.

GWYNEDD

			C	Lab	All	Nat	Other	Total
1987 Electorate	182,788	Votes	44,914	26,330	21,519	52,487	0	145,250
Turnout %	79.5	Votes %	30.9	18.1	14.8	36.1	0.0	100.0
Swing %	-1.5	Seats	1	0	0	3	0	4
C to Lab		Candidates	4	4	4	4	0	16
1983 Electorate	176,532	Votes	45,815	23,993	23,702	45,455	0	138,965
Turnout %	78.7	Votes %	33.0	17.3	17.1	32.7	0.0	100.0
		Seats	2	0	0	2	0	4
		Candidates	4	4	4	4	0	16
		Change 83-87	-2.0	0.9	-2.2	3.4	0.0	

Caernarfon, Conwy, Meirionnydd Nant Conwy, Ynys Mon.

POWYS

			C	Lab	All	Nat	Other	Total
1987 Electorate	89,202	Votes	26,624	15,484	29,238	1,947	0	73,293
Turnout %	82.2	Votes %	36.3	21.1	39.9	2.7	0.0	100.0
Swing %	-6.0	Seats	0	0	2	0	0	2
C to Lab		Candidates	2	2	2	2	0	8
1983 Electorate	84,751	Votes	30,450	12,021	22,089	2,225	765	67,550
Turnout %	79.7	Votes %	45.1	17.8	32.7	3.3	1.1	100.0
		Seats	1	0	1	0	0	2
		Candidates	2	2	2	2	2	10
		Change 83-87	-8.8	3.3	7.2	-0.6	-1.1	

Brecon and Radnor, Montgomery.

What did the polls portend?

By Robert M. Worcester, MORI

The Tories under Mrs Thatcher began their campaign late. The 1979 General Election campaign was announced on 29th March for 3rd May with the Easter Holiday bisecting the campaign period. In that first spring election, the Conservative Party did not officially launch its campaign until half way (18 days) into the 35 day campaign. In 1983, the Tories began on the ninth day of the month long election period and this time held their fire until day eight of this election's 31 day election period.

There was a narrowing of the Tory lead over Labour in the last week of the 1979 campaign, a 12 point Tory lead midway in the campaign being squeezed to just three a week before polling day, finally widening to seven. In 1983, an entirely different pattern occurred, with the hapless Labour Party campaign nine points behind when the Tories launched their effort, widening to 22 before narrowing to 10, and finally ending on 16.

There was a more stable pattern this time with the Conservative Party never in any serious danger. While the Alliance enjoyed a rise in three of the last four elections, only the October 1974 election the exception, in 1987 they slid from around 25 per cent at the outset to the low 20's and finished on 22 per cent.

During the 1987 campaign, there were some 54 national, nationwide, marginal and national panel surveys plus an estimated 60 regional and individual constituency polls published and an estimated 70-80 private surveys carried out for the political parties. There were six 'predictive' pools giving their best guess as to the outcome of the election plus two polling day/exit polls from which the television programmes projected seat estimates. In 1979, and again in 1983, and yet again in 1987, all final polls were within the pollsters' margin of error of plus or minus 3 per cent on the share of each Party. The record of the polls going back to their first effort, in a British general election in 1945, shows that, on average, the error per Party up to now has been plus or minus 1.5 per cent.

The issues of unemployment and jobs were seen from the outset of the campaign for most people to be among the two or three most important issues they would take into account when deciding which Party to vote for in the general election. At the outset of the campaign, the National Health Service /health related issues were in second place with one third of electors saying that this issue would be among the most important for them. This rose to over 40 per cent during the campaign but was overtaken in the third week of the campaign by education and schools, which had begun by being selected by around 26 per cent but by election week had risen to 43 per cent. The other issue of importance was defence which rose sharply following the two Kinnock interviews on the subject but fell off in importance in the final week. Other issues which were expected to play an important role, such as nuclear power, financial scandals in the City, and the environment, really never took off. Labour's strengths were seen in jobs, education and health care, while the Tories captured a greater share of confidence on defence and law and order.

From the outset, the Conservatives were thought to have the best leaders, the best policies and the best image, but the Labour Party and their leader Neil Kinnock, caught up somewhat on Mrs Thatcher during the campaign. At the beginning of the campaign, 46 per cent felt Mrs Thatcher would make the most capable Prime Minister, more than double the 21 per cent who felt Mr Kinnock would. Mrs Thatcher's rating held constant through the campaign, dropping but one point at the end to 45 per cent, while Mr Kinnock's capability rating rose steadily starting at 21 per cent then going to 24 per cent in week two, and 26 per cent in week three, and finally 27 per cent in the last week.

The MORI poll conducted for *The Sunday Times* before the campaign began found that while in 1979 52 per cent of the public lived in owner/occupier houses, in 1987 66 per cent do. In 1979, 30 per cent of the electorate were members of trade unions, now 22 per cent are. When Mrs Thatcher took office, seven per cent of the electorate owned shares of a British company, now 19 per cent do, and in 1979 a third of the electorate (33 per cent) were identified as middle class, now four electors in 10 are designated middle class.

The campaign began with the Conservatives at 43 per cent, Labour at 32 per cent and the Alliance at 23 per cent, in the poll carried out by MORI for *The Times* with the fieldwork conducted the evening Mrs Thatcher called the election and finishing two days later. MORI's final poll, published in *The Times* on election day, was Conservatives 44 per cent, Labour 32 per cent and the Alliance 22 per cent, and predicted on a uniform swing a result of 'just over a 100 seat majority'. The result of the vote on election day was Conservatives 43 per cent, Labour 32 per cent, the Alliance 23 per cent, and a majority of 101 seats for Mrs Thatcher's Government.

The Poll of Polls

JUNE 1987 GENERAL ELECTION CAMPAIGN VOTING TRENDS

Dates	Fieldwork Sampling	Company (Publication)	C %	Lab %	Aln %	Other %	Total %	C-L %	C/Lab swing %
6-11.5	1,735(180)	NOP (Standard)	46	28	25	1	100	+18	-1
7.11.5	1,085(110)	GALLUP (Telegraph)	39	28	30	3	100	+11	+2.5
8-12.5	1,445(103)	MARPLAN (Guardian)	43	29	25	3	100	+14	+1
8-12.5	1,934(178)	MORI (Sunday Times)	44	31	23	2	100	+13	+1.5
11-13.5	1,424(73)	MORI (Times) (Adj)	43	32	23	2	100	+11	+2.5
11-14.5	1,521(65)	MORI (S/T) (Pnl)	44	30	25	1	100	+14	+1
13.5	1,020(50)	MARPLAN (D.Express)	41	30	26	3	100	+11	+2.5
13-15.5	1,040(97)	HARRIS (Observer)	42	33	23	2	100	+9	+3.5
13-15.5	3,164(100)	HARRIS (W/W) (Adj)	40	34	25	1	100	+6	+5
14-17.5	2,410(60)	NEWSNIGHT (Adj)	40	34	24	2	100	+6	+5
16-17.5	1,058(97)	HARRIS (TV-AM)	42	32	24	2	100	+10	+3
18.5	1,072(54)	MARPLAN (Today)	41	33	24	2	100	+8	+4
19.5	1,976(52)	NOP (I'dent) (Adj)	42	34	23	1	100	+8	+4
19-20.5	2,640(197)	GALLUP (Telegraph)	42	33	23	2	100	+9	+3.5
18-21.5	1,079(98)	HARRIS (TV-AM)	43	36	20	1	100	+7	+4.5
20-21.5	1,328(65)	MORI (S/T) (Pnl)	44	31	24	1	100	+13	+1.5
20-21.5	1,066(97)	HARRIS (Observer)	41	34	22	3	100	+7	+4.5
21.5	1,517(103)	MARPLAN (Guardian)	41	33	21	5	100	+8	+4
20-22.5	1,432(140)	GALLUP (S'graph) (Pnl)	42	33	23	2	100	+9	+3.5
20-22.5	1,386(66)	HARRIS (WW) (Adj)	42	35	22	1	100	+7	+4.5
22-25.5	1,075(98)	HARRIS (TV-AM)	42	37	21	0	100	+5	+5.5
26.5	1,035(69)	MARPLAN (Today)	42	35	20	3	100	+7	+4.5
26.5	1,978(52)	NOP (I'dent) (Adj)	42	35	21	2	100	+7	+4.5
26-27.5	2,506(194)	GALLUP (Telegraph)	44.5	36	18	1.5	100	+8.5	+3.8
27-28.5	1,188(65)	MORI (S/T) (Pnl)	44	32	23	1	100	+12	+2
27-28.5	1,072(98)	HARRIS (Observer)	41	37	21	1	100	+4	+6
27-28.5	1,296(66)	HARRIS (W/W) (Adj)	41	37	21	1	100	+4	+6
26-29.5	1,067(97)	HARRIS (TV-AM)	45	32	22	1	100	+13	+1.5
28.5	1,553(103)	MARPLAN (G'dian)	44	32	21	3	100	+12	+2
27-29.5	1,271(140)	GALLUP (S'graph) (Adj)	41.5	34	22.5	2	100	+7.5	+4.3
29.5	1,302(50)	MARPLAN (S.E'ss) (Adj)	45	31	23	1	100	+14	+1
29-30.5	1,420(73)	MORI (Times) (Adj)	44	32	22	2	100	+12	+2
30.5-1.6	2,116(60)	NEWSNIGHT (Adj)	40	36	22	2	100	+4	+6
30.5-2.6	1,573(100)	HARRIS (TV-AM)	42	36	20	2	100	+6	+5
1.6	1,063(69)	MARPLAN (Today)	44	33	21	2	100	+11	+2.5
2.6	1,989(52)	NOP (I'dent) (Adj)	43	34	20	3	100	+9	+3.5
2-3.6	2,553(200)	GALLUP (Telegraph)	40.5	36.5	21.5	1.5	100	+4	+6
3-4.6	1,305(65)	MORI (S/T) (Adj)	43	32	24	1	100	+11	+2.5
3-4.6	1,087(98)	HARRIS (Observer)	44	33	21	2	100	+11	+2.5
4.6	1,576(103)	MARPLAN (Guardian)	44	34	20	2	100	+10	+3
3-5.6	1,100(60)	HARRIS (W/W) (Adj)	40	35	24	1	100	+5	+5.5
3-5.6	1,275(145)	GALLUP (S'graph) (Pnl)	41.5	34.5	22.5	1.5	100	+7	+4.5
3-6.6	2,102(98)	HARRIS (TV-AM)	43	33	22	2	100	+10	+3
5.6	1,300(23)	MARPLAN (S.E'ss) (Adj)	47	30	21	2	100	+17	-0.5
5.6	1,065(69)	MARPLAN (Today)	43	35	21	1	100	+8	+4
5-6.6	1,443(73)	MORI (Times) (Adj)	43	34	21	2	100	+9	+3.5
8.6	1,575(103)	MARPLAN (Guardian)	45	32	21	2	100	+13	+1.5
8-9.6	2,122(99)	HARRIS (TV/AM)	42	35	21	2	100	+7	+4.5
8-9.6	2,005(195)	GALLUP (Telegraph)	41	34	23.5	1.5	100	+7	+4.5
9.6	1,086(69)	MARPLAN (Today)	43	35	21	1	100	+8	+4
9.6	1,702 *	ASL (The Sun)	43	34	21	2	100	+9	+3.5
9-10.6	1,668(165)	MORI (Times)	44	32	22	2	100	+12	+2
10.6	1,633(103)	MARPLAN (Guardian)	42	35	21	2	100	+7	+4.5
10.6	1,668(52)	NOP (I'dent) (Adj)	42	35	21	2	100	+7	+4.5
June 11		**Final Result**	**43**	**32**	**23**	**2**	**100**	**+11**	**+2.5**

Abbreviations: 'Adj' indicates a marginals poll adjusted to reflect the whole country; 'Pnl' indicates a panel survey; W/W – Weekend World; I'dent – The Independent; S/T – Sunday Times; S'graph – Sunday Telegraph; S.Ex'ss – Sunday Express; ASL – Audience Selection Ltd. * – Telephone poll. 11.5 Thatcher announces election date

Marginal seats

Labour's Mansfield and Liberal/Alliance Brecon and Radnor share the somewhat dubious privilege of heading the 1987 list of marginal constituencies, both being won by 56 votes (0.1%) majority. They are followed by Conservative held York where Mr Conal Gregory retained the seat by 147 votes (0.2%). The second most marginal Tory seat is that just held by Mr George Younger, Secretary of State for Defence. At Ayr, his majority over Labour was 182 votes (0.3%).

After the June 1987 election, there are 151 MPs representing constituencies which they won by majorities of 10.0% or less; in 1983 the comparable number was 155. The 151 comprises 76 Conservatives, 56 Labour, 10 Liberal/Alliance, two SDP/Alliance, three Scottish National Party, one Plaid Cymru and three in Northern Ireland.

The following table is in percentage majority order showing that figure and the voting majority. The third column identifies the party who were runners-up and the last two columns shows the number of votes and the identity of the party in third place.

Conservative marginals

York	0.2%	147 Lab	9,898 SDP/All
Ayr	0.3%	182 Lab	7,859 L/All
Portsmouth South	0.4%	205 SDP/All	7,047 Lab
Wolverhampton N E	0.4%	204 Lab	7,623 L/All
Dulwich	0.5%	180 Lab	5,664 SDP/All
Wallasey	0.5%	279 Lab	8,363 SDP/All
Nottingham East	1.0%	456 Lab	6,887 L/All
Stockton South	1.3%	774 SDP/All	18,600 Lab
Thurrock	1.4%	690 Lab	7,970 SDP/All
Bolton North East	1.7%	813 Lab	6,060 SDP/All
Ipswich	1.7%	874 Lab	6,596 SDP/All
Battersea	1.8%	857 Lab	5,634 SDP/All
Stirling	2.1%	948 Lab	6,804 L/All
Lancashire West	2.2%	1,353 Lab	8,972 SDP/All
Batley & Spen	2.3%	1,362 Lab	8,372 SDP/All
Delyn	2.3%	1,224 Lab	8,913 L/All
Cambridgeshire N E	2.5%	1,428 L/All	4,891 Lab
Edinburgh West	2.5%	1,234 L/All	10,957 Lab
Bath	2.7%	1,412 SDP/All	5,507 Lab
Hereford	2.7%	1,413 L/All	4,031 Lab
Colne Valley	3.0%	1,677 L/All	16,353 Lab
Hornsey & Wood Green	3.0%	1,779 Lab	8,928 SDP/All
Ellesmere Port & Neston	3.2%	1,853 Lab	8,143 SDP/All
Langbaurgh	3.3%	2,088 Lab	12,405 L/All
Corby	3.4%	1,805 Lab	7,805 L/All
Hazel Grove	3.4%	1,840 L/All	6,354 Lab
Richmond & Barnes	3.9%	1,766 L/All	3,227 Lab
Nottingham South	4.2%	2,234 Lab	7,517 SDP/All
Kincardine & Deeside	4.3%	2,063 L/All	7,624 Lab
Walthamstow	4.3%	1,512 Lab	8,852 SDP/All
Tynemouth	4.4%	2,583 Lab	10,446 L/All
Hyndburn	4.6%	2,220 Lab	7,423 SDP/All
Cardiff Central	4.8%	1,986 Lab	12,062 L/All
Birmingham, Selly Oak	4.9%	2,584 Lab	8,128 L/All
Cannock & Burntwood	4.9%	2,689 Lab	8,698 L/All
Hampstead & Highgate	4.9%	2,221 Lab	8,744 SDP/All
Darlington	5.0%	2,661 Lab	6,289 L/All
Warwickshire North	5.0%	2,829 Lab	8,382 SDP/All
Pendle	5.1%	2,639 Lab	12,662 L/All
Bury South	5.2%	2,679 Lab	6,772 SDP/All
Basildon	5.3%	2,649 Lab	9,139 L/All
Streatham	5.7%	2,407 Lab	6,663 L/All
Birmingham, Northfield	5.9%	3,135 Lab	8,319 SDP/All
Birmingham, Yardley	6.0%	2,522 Lab	8,734 L/All
Stockport	6.1%	2,853 Lab	10,365 L/All
Warrington South	6.1%	3,609 Lab	13,112 L/All
Coventry South West	6.2%	3,210 Lab	10,166 L/All
Barrow & Furness	7.2%	3,927 Lab	7,799 SDP/All
Swindon	7.2%	4,857 Lab	13,114 SDP/All
Slough	7.3%	4,090 Lab	7,490 SDP/All
Conwy	7.4%	3,024 L/All	9,049 Lab
Kingswood	7.5%	4,393 Lab	10,382 SDP/All
Sherwood	7.7%	4,495 Lab	9,343 SDP/All
Cheltenham	7.8%	4,896 L/All	4,701 Lab
Plymouth, Sutton	7.9%	4,013 L/All	8,310 Lab
Westminster North	7.9%	3,310 Lab	5,116 SDP/All
Plymouth, Drake	8.0%	3,125 SDP/All	9,451 Lab
Devon North	8.1%	4,469 L/All	3,467 Lab
Bolton West	8.2%	4,593 Lab	10,936 SDP/All
Bristol East	8.2%	4,123 Lab	10,247 L/All
Isle of Wight	8.2%	6,442 L/All	4,626 Lab
Edinburgh, Pentlands	8.3%	3,745 Lab	11,072 SDP/All
Lewisham West	8.3%	3,772 Lab	7,247 L/All
Rossendale & Darwen	8.3%	4,982 Lab	9,097 L/All
Galloway & U Nithsdale	8.9%	3,673 SNP	6,001 L/All
Oxford W & Abingdon	9.0%	4,878 SDP/All	8,108 Lab
Feltham & Heston	9.1%	5,430 Lab	9,623 SDP/All
Chester, City of	9.2%	4,855 Lab	10,262 L/All
Falmouth & Camborne	9.3%	5,039 SDP/All	11,271 Lab
Cambridge	9.4%	5,060 SDP/All	15,319 Lab
Stevenage	9.5%	5,340 SDP/All	14,229 Lab
Luton South	9.6%	5,115 Lab	9,146 L/All
Cornwall North	9.8%	5,682 L/All	3,719 Lab
Elmet	9.8%	5,356 Lab	8,755 SDP/All
Croydon North West	10.0%	3,988 Lab	6,363 L/All
Pembroke	10.0%	5,700 Lab	14,832 L/All

Labour marginals

Mansfield	0.1%	56 C	11,604 SDP/All
Bradford South	0.6%	309 C	9,109 SDP/All
Norwich South	0.6%	336 C	12,896 SDP/All
Dewsbury	0.8%	445 C	8,907 SDP/All
Glanford & Scunthorpe	0.9%	512 C	7,762 SDP/All
Blyth Valley	1.8%	853 SDP/All	7,823 C
Crewe & Nantwich	1.9%	1,092 C	8,022 SDP/All
Islington S & Finsbury	2.0%	805 SDP/All	8,482 C
Carlisle	2.1%	916 C	7,655 SDP/All
Halifax	2.1%	1,212 C	8,758 SDP/All
Clwyd South West	2.2%	1,028 C	10,778 SDP/All
Dundee East	2.2%	1,015 SNP	5,938 C
Walsall South	2.2%	1,116 C	6,241 L/All
West Bromwich East	2.3%	983 C	7,268 L/All
Wrekin, The	2.3%	1,456 C	10,737 SDP/All
Leicester West	2.4%	1,201 C	6,708 SDP/All
Oxford East	2.6%	1,288 C	7,648 L/All
Aberdeen South	2.8%	1,198 C	8,844 SDP/All
Bristol South	2.8%	1,404 C	9,952 SDP/All
Tooting	3.0%	1,441 C	6,423 SDP/All
Derby South	3.2%	1,516 C	7,608 SDP/All
Bradford North	3.3%	1,633 C	8,656 SDP/All
Leicester South	3.3%	1,877 C	7,773 L/All
Nottingham North	3.3%	1,665 C	5,912 SDP/All
Walsall North	3.6%	1,790 C	9,285 L/All
Leicester East	3.7%	1,924 C	5,935 SDP/All
Edinburgh South	3.8%	1,859 C	10,900 SDP/All
Brent East	4.2%	1,653 C	5,710 SDP/All
Copeland	4.3%	1,894 C	4,052 SDP/All
Strathkelvin & Bearsden	4.8%	2,452 C	11,034 L/All
Wakefield	5.3%	2,789 C	6,350 SDP/All
Newcastle Central	5.4%	2,483 C	7,304 SDP/All
Edinburgh Central	5.5%	2,262 C	7,333 L/All
Sheffield, Hillsborough	5.5%	3,286 L/All	10,396 C
Dagenham	5.9%	2,469 C	7,088 SDP/All
Newport West	6.0%	2,708 C	5,903 L/All
Dudley East	6.4%	3,473 C	7,965 SDP/All
Birmingham, Erdington	6.6%	2,467 C	5,530 SDP/All
Derbyshire North East	6.7%	3,720 C	9,985 SDP/All
Manchester, Withington	6.7%	3,391 C	9,978 L/All
Hammersmith	6.9%	2,415 C	5,241 L/All
Glasgow, Hillhead	7.8%	3,251 SDP/All	6,048 C
Ashfield	8.0%	4,400 C	13,542 L/All
Carmarthen	8.0%	4,317 C	12,457 Pl C
Tottenham	8.2%	4,141 C	8,983 L/All
Wrexham	8.2%	4,152 C	9,808 L/All
Renfrew W & Inverclyde	9.0%	4,053 C	9,669 SDP/All
Cardiff West	9.1%	4,045 C	7,300 SDP/All
Newham South	9.3%	2,766 C	6,607 SDP/All
Bridgend	9.5%	4,380 C	5,590 SDP/All
Leeds West	9.6%	4,692 L/All	11,276 C
Newcastle-under-Lyme	9.6%	5,132 L/All	14,863 C
Stoke-on-Trent South	9.7%	5,053 C	7,669 L/All
Blackburn	9.8%	5,497 C	5,602 SDP/All
Barking	9.9%	3,409 C	7,336 L/All
Newcastle North	10.0%	5,243 L/All	12,915 C

Liberal/Alliance marginals

Brecon & Radnor	0.1%	56 C	12,180 Lab
Southport	3.4%	1,849 C	3,483 Lab
Fife North East	3.6%	1,447 C	2,947 Lab
Argyll & Bute	3.8%	1,394 C	6,297 SNP
Liverpool, Mossley Hill	4.9%	2,226 Lab	8,005 C
Rochdale	5.4%	2,779 Lab	9,561 C
Southwark & Bermondsey	7.7%	2,779 Lab	4,522 C
Montgomery	8.1%	2,558 C	3,304 Lab
Truro	8.2%	4,753 C	5,882 Lab
Ceredigion & Pembroke N	9.7%	4,700 C	8,965 Lab

SDP/Alliance marginal

Woolwich	4.7%	1,937 Lab	8,723 C
Greenwich	5.7%	2,141 Lab	8,695 C

SNP marginals

Angus East	3.3%	1,544 C	4,971 Lab
Banff & Buchan	5.6%	2,441 C	4,211 SDP/All
Moray	8.2%	3,685 C	5,118 Lab

Plaid Cymru marginal

Ynys Mon	10.0%	4,298 C	7,252 Lab

SDLP marginal

Down South	1.3%	731 OUP	2,363 PSF

Sinn Fein marginal

Belfast West	5.4%	2,221 SDLP	7,646 OUP

UPUP marginal

Down North	9.7%	3,953 Real U	7,932 All

Women MPs

It was a record-breaking election for women. The largest number of women candidates produced the largest number of women MPs; the first black woman MP was elected; and Mrs Margaret Thatcher, the first woman to lead a British political party and the first woman Prime Minister, became the first Prime Minister this century to win three consecutive general election victories.

The major parties fielded a total of 243 women candidates (Labour: 92; SDP: 60; Conservative: 46; and Liberal: 45) and the minor parties had another 84 women candidates, making a grand total of 327.

At the 1983 general election, 23 women had been elected to Parliament and a further five women won seats in by-elections, making a total of 28 women MPs before the dissolution.

Four retired — Mrs Sally Oppenheim (Gloucester, C); Mrs Renèe Short (Wolverhampton North East, Lab); Dame Judith Hart (Clydesdale, Lab); and Miss Joan Maynard (Sheffield, Brightside, Lab). And three were defeated — Mrs Anna McCurley (Renfrew West and Inverclyde, C); Dr Oonagh McDonald (Thurrock, Lab) who was an Opposition spokesman on Treasury and economic affairs; and Mrs Elizabeth Shields (Ryedale, Lib/All).

The remaining 21 were re-elected and were joined by another 16 women taking their seats for the first time and four returning to Parliament after absences.

The total of 41 was a record and comprised 21 Labour; 17 Conservative; two Liberal/SDP Alliance; and one Scottish National Party.

The by-election victors were: Mrs Virginia Bottomley, who held Surrey South West for the Conservatives in May 1984 and joined her husband Peter, MP for Eltham and later a junior minister; Mrs Ann Clwyd, who on the same day held Cynon Valley for Labour; Mrs Elizabeth Shields, who won Ryedale for the Liberal/SDP Alliance in May 1986, overturning a Conservative majority of more than 16,000; Mrs Llin Golding, who held Newcastle-under-Lyme for Labour in July 1986, replacing her husband John who resigned the seat shortly after his election as general secretary of the National Communications Union; and Mrs Rosie Barnes, who won Greenwich for the SDP/Liberal Alliance in February 1987, the first time the SDP had captured a Labour-held seat.

Four of the five held their seats at the general election, but Mrs Shields, who became the first Liberal woman MP since Lady Megan Lloyd George 35 years earlier, lost Ryedale back to the Conservatives after just 13 months in Parliament.

Among the 16 newcomers to the Commons were Ms Diane Abbott who won Hackney North and Stoke Newington for Labour and so became the first black woman MP; Ms Hilary Armstrong who won Durham North West, succeeding her father Ernest, the Deputy Speaker and former junior minister and whip, who represented the seat for 23 years; Miss Emma Nicholson, a vice-chairman of the Conservative Party with special responsibility for women, who won Devon West and Torridge; and Mrs Joan Ruddock, former chairman of the Campaign for Nuclear Disarmament, who won Lewisham Deptford.

The others making their parliamentary debut were, for Labour: Mrs Maria Fyfe who won at Glasgow, Maryhill; Mrs Mildred Gordon at Bow and Poplar; Ms Alice Mahon at Halifax; Dr Marjorie Mowlam at Redcar; Ms Dawn Primarolo at Bristol South; Ms Joyce Quin at Gateshead East; and Ms Joan Walley at Stoke-on-Trent North. For the Conservatives: Mrs Teresa Gorman who won at Billericay; Mrs Maureen Hicks at Wolverhampton North East; Mrs Gillian Shephard at Norfolk South West; and Miss Ann Widdecombe at Maidstone. And for the Liberal/SDP Alliance: Mrs Ray Michie at Argyll and Bute.

The most experienced of the women MPs returned to the Commons after an absence was Miss Joan Lestor who won Eccles for Labour, having been defeated in Slough at the 1983 election. She represented that seat for 17 years, during which time she held junior ministerial posts in the Education department and the Foreign Office.

The others making a come-back were: Mrs Ann Taylor, who won Dewsbury for Labour, having represented Bolton West from October 1974 until 1983, and was a former assistant Government whip and later an Opposition spokesman on education and then housing; Mrs Audrey Wise, who won Preston for Labour, having represented Coventry South West from February 1974 until 1979; and Mrs Margaret Ewing, who won Moray for the SNP, having represented Dunbartonshire East from October 1974 to 1979 as Mrs Margaret Bain.

The women MPs in this Parliament are:

Conservative
Mrs Virginia Bottomley (*Surrey South West*); Mrs Lynda Chalker (*Wallasey*); Mrs Edwina Currie (*Derbyshire South*); Dame Peggy Fenner (*Medway*); Miss Janet Fookes (*Plymouth, Drake*); Mrs Teresa Gorman (*Billericay*); Mrs Maureen Hicks (*Wolverhampton North East*); Mrs Elaine Kellett-Bowman (*Lancaster*); Dame Jill Knight (*Birmingham, Edgbaston*); Miss Emma Nicholson (*Devon West and Torridge*); Mrs Elizabeth Peacock (*Batley and Spen*); Mrs Marion Roe (*Broxbourne*); Mrs Angela Rumbold (*Mitcham and Morden*); Mrs Gillian Shephard (*Norfolk South West*); Mrs Margaret Thatcher (*Finchley*); Miss Ann Widdecombe (*Maidstone*); and Mrs Ann Winterton (*Congleton*).

Labour
Ms Diane Abbott (*Hackney North and Stoke Newington*); Ms Hilary Armstrong (*Durham North West*); Mrs Margaret Beckett (*Derby South*); Miss Betty Boothroyd (*West Bromwich West*); Mrs Ann Clwyd (*Cynon Valley*); Mrs Gwyneth Dunwoody (*Crewe and Nantwich*); Mrs Maria Fyfe (*Glasgow, Maryhill*); Mrs Llin Golding (*Newcastle-under-Lyme*); Mrs Mildred Gordon (*Bow and Poplar*); Ms Harriet Harman (*Peckham*); Miss Joan Lestor (*Eccles*); Ms Alice Mahon (*Halifax*); Dr Marjorie Mowlam (*Redcar*); Ms Dawn Primarolo (*Bristol South*); Ms Joyce Quin (*Gateshead East*); Ms Jo Richardson (*Barking*); Mrs Joan Ruddock (*Lewisham Deptford*); Ms Clare Short (*Birmingham, Ladywood*); Mrs Ann Taylor (*Dewsbury*); Ms Joan Walley (*Stoke-on-Trent North*); and Mrs Audrey Wise (*Preston*).

SDP/Alliance
Mrs Rosie Barnes (*Greenwich*).

Liberal/Alliance
Mrs Ray Michie (*Argyll and Bute*).

Scottish National Party
Mrs Margaret Ewing (*Moray*).

Only one argument

By Richard Ford, The Times correspondent in Belfast

The political landscape is rarely fundamentaly altered by elections in Northern Ireland but 1987 will be remembered throughout the United Kingdom for the end of Enoch Powell's 37 year long House of Commons career.

His defeat by the Social Democratic and Labour Party in South Down was the only change in representation in any of the North's 17 constituencies. Elections come and elections go but the longest running sore in British politics goes on. The Prime Minister was surrounded by unprecedented security to guard her from possible attack by the Provisional IRA and the Secretary of State for Northern Ireland was forced to make a speech from a place in his constituency named "somewhere" yet the reason for this security was hardly mentioned during the campaign.

The election in the Province was entirely separate with different parties, candidates and above all only one argument. The constitutional issue has dominated Northern elections since the foundation of the State and in 1987 it was there in the form of the Anglo Irish Agreement, signed in 1985 and giving the Irish Republic a consultative role in the affairs of the Province.

Loyalist politics had until the Agreement been dominated by the Rev Ian Paisley's attempt to make his Democratic Unionist Party supplant the Official Unionists led by Mr James Molyneaux as the leading voice of the majority community. But the pan-Unionist front forged to fight the accord resulted in a truce in which neither party opposed each other's sitting MPs. It was bitterly resented by young ambitious members of the DUP but was enforced by threats of expulsion, the actual expulsion of an official Unionist Party member and appeals for Unionist Unity.Undoubtedly the Loyalist community wanted Unionist Unity but this did not prevent them greeting their candidates with strong criticism of the tactics used to oppose the Agreement.

In North Down voters were given the chance to pass judgment on the tactics, strategy and future options for Unionism when an official Unionist Constituency Association defied the leadership and chose a candidate who headed the campaign for integration as opposed to devolution. The sitting MP retained the seat with a reduced majority but only after a campaign in which many of the Unionist leadership were drafted into the constituency to prevent an electoral upset.

When the votes were counted the disolusion within the Loyalist community was shown by a drop in the total Unionist vote compared with both the 1983 general election and the bye elections held in 1986 to test opposition to the deal. The largest drop was in votes for the three DUP MPs indicating that many official Unionists were not prepared to support Mr Paisley's brasher brand of loyalism. Similarly DUP voters did not flock to OUP candidates they suspected of being less than whole hearted in their opposition to the Agreement.

The polls of 1986 and 1987 have seen Unionists lose seats in Newry and Armagh and South Down to the Social Democratic and Labour Party. With three MPs at Westminster the party of constitutional nationalism received a major boost in defeating Mr Powell and tightened its grip on Newry and Armagh. In private Unionists say that both seats have been lost to them forever. Despite these successes the SDLP failed to capture West Belfast where the Provisional Sein Fein president Mr Gerry Adams held his seat on a reduced majority but having increased his vote by 483.

It was an election of paradoxies with the Unionists, one time allies of the Conservative Party, hoping for a Tory defeat or a hung Parliament in which they would be able to exert maximum pressure and the SDLP privately wanting a victory by Mrs Thatcher to ensure strong support for the deal. The unhappy faces among unionists and the increasing calls for dialogue in the days following the results reflected the problems facing the Unionist leadership entering a new Parliament.

	June 1983				June 1987			
	total votes	% total votes	MPs	candi- dates	total votes	% total votes	MPs	candi- dates
OUP	259,952	34.0	11	16	276,230	37.8	9	12
DUP	152,749	20.0	3	14	85,642	11.7	3	4
All NI	61,275	8.0	0	12	72,671	10.0	0	16
PSF	102,701	13.4	1	14	83,389	11.4	1	14
SDLP	137,012	17.9	1	17	154,087	21.1	3	13
Others	51,236	6.7	1	22	58,133	8.0	1	18
Totals	764,925	100	17	95	730,152	100	17	77
Electorate	1,050,222		(turnout 72.8%)		1,089,160		(turnout 67.0%)	

282

Defeated members

The election produced only 41 casualties among sitting MPs, compared with 63 in 1983 – when many MPs who had switched to the SDP swelled the ranks of the defeated.

Most notable among defeated MPs at the 1987 election were Mr Enoch Powell, rejected by the electorate for the first time in his parliamentary career, and Mr Roy Jenkins, one of the founders of the Social Democratic Party. Four members of the Government lost their seats in Wales and Scotland where the Government suffered several reverses.

Mr Powell entered Parliament when he won Wolverhampton South West for the Conservatives in 1950 with a majority of 691, a margin which he had turned into a safe 14,467 when he last fought the seat in 1970. Four years later he decided not to stand again for the Conservative Party, but was out of Parliament for only a few months. In the second election of 1974, he was chosen as the United Ulster Unionist candidate for South Down.

He began his ministerial career in junior office at the old Ministry of Housing and Local Government, and then became Financial Secretary to the Treasury, a post from which he resigned in protest at Government spending policies, but he returned to office as Minister of Health from 1960 to 1963. His attempt to gain leadership of the Conservative Party in 1965 was unsuccessful and three years later, Mr Edward Heath dismissed him from the shadow cabinet after a controversial speech about immigration.

Mr Jenkins also had a parliamentary career split clearly into two chapters. In the first he held high office in the Labour Governments under Mr Harold Wilson, and became Deputy Leader of the Labour Party, a post from which he resigned over the issue of Britain's Common Market membership. Mr Jenkins then had a four-year spell as President of the EEC Commission, from which he returned to become a leading figure in establishing the SDP, and then the Alliance. He first failed to win Warrington in a by-election, but then took Glasgow, Hillhead, for the SDP. He resigned as leader of the new party immediately after the 1983 election, but took a leading part in the Alliance's parliamentary work as Treasury spokesman.

The Conservative Party's heaviest losses were in Scotland, Wales and the North of England. Defeated ministers were Mr Michael Ancram and Mr John Mackay, who had been Under Secretaries of State at the Scottish Office, Mr Mark Robinson, Under Secretary of State, Welsh Office, and Mr Gerry Malone, a Government whip.

The Labour Party had only six MPs defeated but they included Dr Oonagh McDonald, a valued member of the front bench team, who had been a Treasury and economic affairs spokesman for most of the 1983-87 Parliament.

Mr Kenneth Weetch had held the marginal seat of Ipswich since October 1974, a lonely outpost for Labour in the last Parliament. In London, Mr Alfred Dubs, Mr Eric Deakins and Mr Nick Raynsford, who had won a by-election, succumbed to a swing against the party which did not conform to the national trend.

Mr Clement Freud, who first entered Parliament at a by-election in 1973, lost Cambridgeshire North East to a swing against the Alliance of more than 6 per cent.

The Scottish Nationalist Party suffered the bitter blow of losing their chairman, Mr Gordon Wilson, Dundee East, at a time when they gained three seats elsewhere in Scotland, although they also lost the seat of the retiring leader of the party, Mr Donald Stewart, the Western Isles, regained by Labour after a gap of many years.

Defeated MPs were:

Conservative
Ancram, M.A., *Edinburgh South;*
Bruinvels, P.N.E., *Leicester East;*
Corrie, J.A., *Cunninghame North;*
Fletcher, Sir A., *Edinburgh Central;*
Fraser, P.L., *Angus East;*
Galley, R., *Halifax;*
Harvey, R.L., *Clwyd South West;*
Hawksley P., *The Wrekin;*
Henderson, J.F.B., *Fife North East;*
Hickmet, R.S., *Glanford and Scunthorpe;*
Hirst, M., *Strathkelvin and Bearsden;*
Hubbard-Miles, P.C., *Bridgend;*
Lawler, G.J., *Bradford North;*
McCurley, Mrs A.A., *Renfrew West and Inverclyde;*
MacKay, J.J., *Argyll and Bute;*
McQuarrie, A, *Banff and Buchan;*
Malone, G. P., *Aberdeen South;*
Merchant, P.R.G., *Newcastle upon Tyne Central;*
Norris, S.J., *Oxford East;*
Ottaway, R.G.J., *Nottingham North;*
Pollock, A., *Moray;*
Powley, J.A., *Norwich South;*
Robinson, M.N.F., *Newport West;*
Silvester, F.J., *Manchester, Withington;*
Spencer, D.H., *Leicester South;*
Terlezki, S., *Cardiff West;*
Whitfield, J, *Dewsbury;*

Labour
Deakins, E.P., *Walthamstow;*
Dubs, A., *Battersea;*
Hamilton, W.W., MP for *Fife Central,* defeated in *South Hams;*
McDonald, Miss O.A., *Thurrock;*
Raynsford, W.R.N., *Fulham;*
Weetch, K.T., *Ipswich;*

Alliance:
Freud, C.R., *Cambridgeshire, North East;*
Hancock, M.T., *Portsmouth South;*
Jenkins, R.H., *Glasgow, Hillhead;*
Meadowcroft, M.J., *Leeds West;*
Shields, Mrs E.L., *Ryedale;*
Wrigglesworth, I.W., *Stockton South;*

Scottish National Party
Wilson, R.G., *Dundee East*

Official Unionist Party
Powell, J.E., *Down South*

By-Elections

The 31 by-elections since June 1983 included 15 in Northern Ireland, after the mass resignation of all the Unionist MPs in protest at the Anglo-Irish Agreement, leading to a mini general election in Ulster in January 1986.

All but one successfully retained their seats, amassing votes for their "Ulster Says No" campaign which they had portrayed as a referendum on the Agreement, and then operated a partial boycott of Westminster. Mr James Nicholson of the OUP lost Newry and Armagh to Mr Seamus Mallon of the SDLP.

In several seats where no other candidate was standing against the Unionists, a dummy candidate was put up, in order to force a vote, with the name of Mr Peter Barry, the foreign minister of the Irish Republic.

The motion allowing for the 15 by-election writs to be issued was moved by Sir Peter Emery, Conservative MP for Honiton and chairman of the all-party Select Committee on Procedure, in the absence of any Unionist MPs. It was an unprecedented parliamentary event and the motion, which could have led to 15 individual debates in the event of any objections, was passed unchallenged.

The record for the highest number of candidates ever to stand in a single constituency was broken by one when 17 people contested Chesterfield in March 1984 and Mr Tony Benn won the seat. The new record is unlikely to be beaten because in October 1985 the Representation of the People Act came into effect, raising the deposit from £150 to £500 in a move designed to discourage the proliferation of fringe candidates.

When Mr Matthew Taylor retained Truro for the Liberals in March 1987, he became the youngest MP in the Commons at 24, taking over the title from his Alliance colleague, Mr Charles Kennedy of the SDP, then aged 27.

Of the 16 by-elections held in Great Britain, the Conservatives held five seats and lost two to the Liberals (one of which they regained at the 1987 general election), and one each to Labour and the SDP (both of which they also regained in 1987); Labour held five and lost one to the SDP; and the Liberals held one.

The three by-election victors in Great Britain who had each overturned large Conservative majorities but then failed to retain their seats at the 1987 general election when they were regained by the Tories were: Mr Michael Hancock, who won Portsmouth South for the SDP in June 1984; Nr Nick Raynsford, who won Fulham for Labour in April 1986; and Mrs Elizabeth Shields, who won Ryedale for the Liberals in May 1986.

In Northern Ireland, 14 of the 15 by-election victors retained their seats at the general election but Mr Enoch Powell, a Conservative MP for 24 years and a Unionist MP for 13 years, lost South Down to the SDLP.

When the election was announced by-elections were pending in two seats — Kirkcaldy (Labour) following the death of Mr Harry Gourlay and Lewisham, Deptford (Labour) following the death of Mr John Silkin.

1983

July 28: **Penrith and the Border** (caused by the elevation to the peerage of Mr William Whitelaw): D. Maclean (C) 17,530 (46%); M. Young (L/All) 16,978 (44.6%); L. Williams (Lab) 2,834 (7.4%); D. Sutch (Loony) 412 (1.1%); E. Morgan (Rtd Naval Off) 150 (0.4%); H. Anscomb (Death Off Rds) 72 (0.2%); J. Connell (Peace) 69 (0.2%); P. Smith (New Nat) 35 (0.1%). C maj: 552. No change.

1984

March 1: **Chesterfield** (caused by the resignation of Mr Eric Varley who took a job in industry): T. Benn (Lab) 24,633 (46.5%); M. Payne (L/All) 18,369 (34.7%); N. Bourne (C) 8,028 (15.1%); B Maynard (Ind) 1,355 (2.6%); D. Sutch (Loony) 178; D. Bentley (Four Wheel Drive) 116; J. Davey (No Dental Increases) 83; T. Layton (Spare The Earth) 46; H. Anscomb (Death Off Rds) 34; J. Bardwaj (Yoga) 33; D. Butler (Chesterfields in Thame) 24; P. Nicholls-Jones (Welshman) 22; S. Shaw (Elvis Presley) 20; C. Hill (Prisoner) 17; G. Piccaro (Acne) 15; D. Cahill (Reclassify Sun As Comic) 12; J. Connell (Peace) 7. Lab maj: 6,264. No change.

May 3: **Cynon Valley** (caused by the death of Mr Ioan Evans): Mrs A. Clwyd (Lab) 19,389 (58.8%); F. Aubel (SDP/All) 6,554 (19.9%); C. Jones (Pl C) 3,619 (10.9%); J. Arbuthnot (C) 2,441 (7.4%); Mrs M. Winter (Comm) 642 (1.9%); N. Recontre (Womble) 215 (0.7%); P. Nicholls-Jones (Ind) 122 (0.4%). Lab maj: 12,835. No change.

May 3: **Stafford** (caused by the death of Sir Hugh Fraser): W.Cash (C) 18,713 (40.4%); D. Dunn (SDP/All) 14,733 (31.8%); M. Poulter (Lab) 12,677 (27.4%); C. Teasdale (Soon To Be Unemployed) 210 (0.4%). C maj: 3,980. No change.

May 3: **Surrey South West** (caused by the death of Viscount Maurice Macmillan): Mrs V. Bottomley (C) 21,545 (49.3%); G. Scott (L/All) 18,946 (43.4%); Mrs B. Roche (Lab) 2,949 (6.7%); V. Litvin (Pro Nuclear Holocaust) 117 (0.3%); Miss H. Anscomb (Freight Off Rds) 82 (0.2%); P. Smith (Full Hearing) 29 (0.1%). C maj: 2,599. No change.

June 14: **Portsmouth South** (caused by the death of Mr Bonner Pink): M. Hancock (SDP/All) 15,358 (37.6%); P. Rock (C) 14,017 (34.3%); Mrs S. Thomas (Lab) 10,846 (26.5%); G. Knight (NF) 226 (0.5%); T. Mitchell (Eco) 190 (0.5%); A. Evens (Ind

Lib) 113 (0.3%); T. Layton (Spare The Earth) 50 (0.1%); A. Andrews (Vote Educ) 42 (0.1%); P. Smith (New Nat) 41 (0.1%). SDP/All maj: 1,341. SDP gain from C.

December 13 : **Enfield, Southgate** (caused by the murder of Sir Anthony Berry in the IRA Brighton bomb outrage): M. Portillo (C) 16,684 (49.6%); T. Slack (L/All) 11,973 (35.6%); W. Hamid (Lab) 4,000 (11.9%); A. Polydorou (Turkish Troops Out Of Cyprus) 687; J. Kershaw (Nat) 80; R. Shenton (English Nat) 78; I. Burgess (Restore Middlesexshire) 50; G. Weiss (Cpt Rainbow Universal) 48; H. Anscomb (Death Off Rds) 45. C maj: 4,711. No change.

1985

July 4: **Brecon and Radnor** (caused by the death of Mr Tom Hooson): R. Livsey (L/All) 13,753 (36%); R. Willey (Lab) 13,194 (34%); C. Butler (C) 10,631 (28%); Mrs J. Davies (Pl C) 435; D. Sutch (Loony) 202; R. Everest (One Nation C) 154; A. Genillard (Cure MS) 43. L/All maj: 559. L/All gain from C.

December 6: **Tyne Bridge** (caused by the death of Mr Harry Cowans): D. Clelland (Lab) 13,517 (57.8%); R. Kenyon (SDP/All) 6,942 (29.7%); Mrs J. Lait (C) 2,588 (11%); J. Connell (Peace) 250; G. Weiss (Cpt Rainbow Universal) 38; P. Smith (New Nat) 32. Lab maj: 6,575. No change.

1986

January 23: 15 seats in Northern Ireland (caused by the mass resignation of the Unionist MPs in protest at the Anglo-Irish Agreement):

Antrim East: R. Beggs (OUP) 30,386 (84.9%); S. Neeson (All) 5,405 (15.1%). OUP maj: 24,981. No change.

Antrim North: Rev I. Paisley (DUP) 33,937 (97.4%); P. Barry (AIA) 913 (2.6%). DUP maj: 33,024. No change.

Antrim South: C. Forsythe (OUP) 30,087 (94.1%); P. Barry (AIA) 1,870 (5.9%). OUP maj: 28,217. No change.

Belfast East: P. Robinson (DUP) 27,607 (81.0%); D. Napier (All) 5,917 (17.4%); F. Cullen (WP) 578 (1.7%). DUP maj: 21,690. No change.

Belfast North: C. Walker (OUP) 21,649 (71.5%); P. Maguire (All) 5,072 (16.7%); S. Lynch (WP) 3,563 (11.8%). OUP maj: 16,577. No change.

Belfast South: Rev M. Smyth (OUP) 21,771 (71.3%); D. Cook (All) 7,635 (25.0%); G. Carr (WP) 1,109 (3.6%). OUP maj: 14,136. No change.

Down North: J. Kilfedder (UPUP) 30,793 (79.2%); J. Cushnahan (All) 8,066 (20.8%). UPUP maj: 22,727. No change.

Down South: E. Powell (OUP) 24,963 (48.4%); E. McGrady (SDLP) 23,121 (44.9%); H. McDowell (PSF) 2,936 (5.7%); S. Magee (WP) 522 (1.0%). OUP maj: 1,842. No change.

Fermanagh and South Tyrone: K. Maginnis (OUP) 27,857 (49.7%); O. Carron (PSF) 15,278 (27.2%); J. Currie (SDLP) 12,081 (21.5%); D. Kettyles (WP) 864 (1.5%). OUP maj: 12,579. No change.

Lagan Valley: J. Molyneaux (OUP) 32,514 (90.7%); T. Lowry (WP) 3,328 (9.3%). OUP maj: 29,186. No change.

Londonderry East: W. Ross (OUP) 30,922 (93.9%); P. Barry (AIA) 2,001 (6.1%). OUP maj: 28,921. No change.

Newry and Armagh: S. Mallon (SDLP) 22,694 (45.5%); J. Nicholson (OUP) 20,111 (40.3%); J. McAllister (PSF) 6,609 (13.2%); P. McCusker (WP) 515 (1.0%). SDLP maj: 2,583. SDLP gain from OUP.

Strangford: J. Taylor (OUP) 32,627 (94.2%); P. Barry (AIA) 1,993 (5.8%). OUP maj: 30,634. No change.

Ulster Mid: Rev W. McCrea (DUP) 23,695 (46.1%); D. Morrison (PSF) 13,998 (27.2%); A. Colton (SDLP) 13,021 (25.3%); T. Owens (WP) 691 (1.3%). DUP maj: 9,697. No change.

Upper Bann: H. McCusker (OUP) 29,311 (80.8%); T. French (WP) 6,978 (19.2%). OUP maj: 22,333. No change.

April 10: **Fulham** (caused by the death of Mr Martin Stevens): N. Raynsford (Lab) 16,451 (44.4%); M. Carrington (C) 12,948 (34.9%); R. Liddle (SDP/All) 6,953 (18.7%); J. Birdwood (Repatriation) 226; D. Sutch (Loony) 134; J. Creighton (Wine Connoisseurs) 127; J. Black (Dem Rights For NI) 98; G. Rolph (Fellowship) 39; J. Swinden (Humanist) 38; L. Duke (Cpt Rainbow Universal) 37; R. Simmerson (Anti-EEC) 33. Lab maj: 3,503. Lab gain from C.

May 8: **Derbyshire West** (caused by the resignation of Mr Matthew Parris who took a job in television): P. McLoughlin (C) 19,896 (39.6%); C. Walmsley (L/All) 19,796 (39.4%); W. Moore (Lab) 9,952 (19.8%); C. Sidwell (Crocodile Tears) 348; R. Goodall (Ind) 289. C maj: 100. No change.

May 8: **Ryedale** (caused by the death of Mr John Spence): Mrs E. Shields (L/All) 27,612 (50.3%); N. Balfour (C) 22,672 (41.3%); S. Haines (Lab) 4,633 (8.4%). L/All maj: 4,940. L/All gain from C.

July 17: **Newcastle-under-Lyme** (caused by the resignation of Mr John Golding after his election as general secretary of the National Communications Union): Mrs L. Golding (Lab) 16,819 (40.8%); A. Thomas (L/All) 16,020 (38.8%); J. Nock (C) 7,863 (19.1%); D. Sutch (Loony) 277; J. Gaskell (Rainbow All Prince Charles) 115; J. Parker (Referendum On Nuclear Energy) 83; D. Brewster (Rainbow All Bob Geldof) 70. Lab maj: 799. No change.

November 13: **Knowsley North** (caused by the resignation of Mr Robert Kilroy-Silk who, after a prolonged battle with Militant supporters in his local party, left to take a job in television): G. Howarth (Lab) 17,403 (56.3%); Miss R. Cooper (L/All) 10,679 (34.6%); R. Brown (C) 1,960 (6.3%); D. Hallsworth (RCP) 664; R. Weiss (Rainbow All) 111; D. Cory (Ind) 88. Lab maj: 6,724. No change.

1987

February 26: **Greenwich** (caused by the death of Mr Guy Barnett): Mrs R. Barnes (SDP/All) 18,287 (53.0%); Mrs D. Wood (Lab) 11,676 (33.8%); J. Antcliffe (C) 3,852 (11.2%); G. Bell (Grn) 264; M. Hardee (Rainbow) 124; I. Bell (Brit Nat) 116; J. Pearce (NF) 103; K. Marshall (Rev Comm) 91. SDP/All maj: 6,611. SDP/All gain from Lab.

March 12: **Truro** (caused by the death in a road accident of Mr David Penhaligon): M. Taylor (L/All) 30,599 (60.4%); N. St Aubyn (C) 15,982 (31.5%); J. King (Lab) 3,603 (7.1%); J. Hoptrough (Grn) 403; H. Anscomb (Death Off Rds) 75. L/All maj: 14,617. No change.

Farewell to Knights of the Shires

Eight former members and one current member of Mrs Thatcher's cabinets since she came to office in 1979 along with Sir James Callaghan, the former Labour Prime Minister, and one of his cabinet ministers, were among the 87 MPs who did not stand at the general election. Two others who served in the cabinets of Mr Edward Heath also called it a day.

These 87 departures represented the largest exodus of MPs at any general election since the war and even in 1935. However, among them were seven whose farewell to the Commons was somewhat involuntary because their constituency Labour parties de-selected them.

From the Tory backbenches there was a veritable exit of knights of the shires, 18 in all, plus two ex-cabinet ministers also knights. On both sides of the House, a number of former junior ministers did not seek re-election. Among the Labour departees were Mr Jack Dormand, chairman of the Parliamentary Labour Party since 1981, and Mr Ernest Armstrong, the Deputy Speaker, whose daughter Hilary won his seat of Durham North West.

Some 43 Conservative MPs, 41 Labour, two Liberals and the well-liked leader of the Scottish National Party, Mr Donald Stewart, made up the 87 not seeking re-election to Westminster. The nearest comparable number of departures was in 1970 when 79 MPs - 50 Labour, 27 Tory and two Liberal - did not seek re-election. In 1983 it was 77 made up of 38 Labour, 34 Tory and five others including the then Mr George Thomas, Speaker. In February 1974, some 70 MPs left and in 1945 there were 68.

The eight ex-Thatcher cabinet ministers and the one current cabinet office holder who retired were: **Sir Humphrey Atkins** (Spelthorne) - Lord Privy Seal and chief Government spokesman in the Commons on foreign and Commonwealth affairs, 1981-82 when he resigned following the Argentinian invasion of the Falklands. Until January 1987, he was chairman of the Select Committee on Defence.

Mr Mark Carlisle (Warrington South) - Secretary of State for Education and Science, 1979-81, and a Home Office minister, 1970-74.

Mr Nicholas Edwards (Pembroke) - Secretary of State for Wales, 1979-87.

Mr Patrick Jenkin (Wanstead and Woodford) - From 1979 he served as Secretary of State for Social Services, then Industry and finally Environment.

Sir Keith Joseph (Leeds North East) - Secretary of State for Education and Science, 1981-86; Secretary of State for Industry, 1979-81, and in the

Heath administration he spent four years as Secretary of State for Social Services.

Mr James Prior (Waveney) - chairman of GEC since leaving Mrs Thatcher's cabinet in which he was first Secretary of State for Employment and then Secretary of State for Northern Ireland.

Mr Francis Pym (Cambridgeshire South East) - was asked to resign as Secretary of State for Foreign and Commonwealth Affairs within 48 hours of the 1983 election result. He became Foreign Secretary in 1982, previously being Leader of the Commons, 1981-82, and Secretary of State for Defence, 1979-81. Under Mr Heath, he was Government Chief Whip.

Mr Peter Rees (Dover) - in the Cabinet as Chief Secretary to the Treasury, 1983-86.

Mr Norman St John-Stevas (Chelmsford) - Chancellor of the Duchy of Lancaster, Leader of the Commons and Minister for the Arts, 1979-81.

Also retiring were **Sir Michael Havers** (Wimbledon), Attorney General from 1979, and **Sir Ian Percival** (Southport), Solicitor-General, 1979-83. After the election, Sir Michael became the new Lord Chancellor upon the retirement of Lord Hailsham of St Marylebone.

The two other members of the Heath administration who left the Commons were **Mr Geoffrey Rippon** (Hexham) - Chancellor of the Duchy of Lancaster, 1970-72, and then Secretary of State for Environment, and the former Secretary of State for Wales (1970-74), **Mr Peter Thomas** (Hendon South).

The other Conservative MPs not standing were: Sir Frederic Bennett (Torbay); Mr Keith Best (Ynys Mon); Mr Timothy Brinton (Gravesham); Sir Paul Bryan (Boothferry); Mr Esmond Bulmer (Wyre Forest); Sir Adam Butler (Bosworth); Sir Walter Clegg (Wyre); Mr Eric Cockeram (Ludlow); Viscount Cranborne (Dorset South); Mr David Crouch (Canterbury); Sir Edward du Cann (Taunton); Sir Reginald Eyre (Birmingham, Hall Green); Sir Edward Gardner (Fylde); Sir Paul Hawkins (Norfolk South West); Sir Philip Holland (Gedling); Sir Anthony Kershaw (Stroud); Sir Kenneth Lewis (Stamford and Spalding); Sir Carol Mather (Esher); Sir Peter Mills (Devon West and Torridge); Mr Christopher Murphy (Welwyn Hatfield); Mr Tom Normanton (Cheadle); Mrs Sally Oppenheim (Gloucester); Sir John Osborne (Sheffield Hallam); Sir John Page (Harrow West); Sir Reginald Prentice (Daventry); Mr Harvey Proctor (Billericay); Sir William van Straubenzee (Wokingham); Sir Patrick Wall (Beverley); Mr John Watson (Skipton and Ripon); Sir John Wells (Maidstone).

Among these are ex-Ministers of State like Sir Adam Butler and Sir William van Straubenzee who both served at the Northern Ireland Office. Sir Edward du Cann is an ex-junior Treasury minister who was chairman of the 1922 Committee from 1972 to 1984 and of the Select Committee on the Treasury and Civil Service from 1979-83. Other personalities include Sir Reginald Prentice, the ex-Labour Secretary of State for Education who on crossing the floor to join the Conservative Party subsequently became Minister of State for Social Security. Mr Tom Normanton had the distinction of being the last Tory in the Commons to have the dual mandate of MP and MEP.

Sir James Callaghan, made a Knight of the Garter by the Queen in April, became Prime Minister in April 1976 following his election as Labour leader in succession to the then Sir Harold Wilson. Following Labour's defeat in 1979, Sir James, MP for Cardiff South and Penarth, led the party until his resignation in 1980.

The one retiring MP who served under Mr Callaghan in the cabinet is **Mr Roy Mason**, Secretary of State for Northern Ireland from 1976-79 and Secretary of State for Defence, 1974-76.

Among other Labour ex-ministers leaving was **Dame Judith Hart** who had a brief spell from 1967-68 in the then Cabinet as Paymaster General. She served twice outside the Cabinet as Minister for Overseas Development and is an ex-chairman of the Labour Party. **Mr Don Concannon** served as Minister of State for Northern Ireland and **Mr Reginald Freeson**, de-selected at Brent East, is a former Minister for Housing and Construction. **Mr Walter Harrison** put in continuous service as a whip in Government or Opposition from 1966 to 1983 being deputy chief Labour whip from 1970.

Labour also lost the long serving **Mr Ian Mikardo** (Bow and Popular) who was first elected to Westminster for Reading in 1945 and apart from 1959 to 1964 was there ever since, in recent years being openly, honourably and humourously acknowledged as the Commons bookie!

Those leaving the Commons from the Labour benches were:

Mr Leo Abse (Torfaen); Mr Ernest Armstrong (Durham North West); Mr Norman Atkinson* (Tottenham); Mr Gordon Bagier (Sunderland South); Mr Hugh Brown (Glasgow Provan); Mr Robert Brown (Newcastle North); Sir James Callaghan (Cardiff South and Penarth); Mr Ian Campbell (Dumbarton); Mr Lewis Carter-Jones (Eccles); Mr Michael Cocks* (Bristol South); Mr Don Concannon (Mansfield); Mr Bernard Conlan (Gateshead East); Mr James Craigen (Glasgow, Maryhill); Mr Jack Dormand (Easington); Mr Robert Edwards (Wolverhampton South East); Mr Raymond Ellis (Derbyshire North East); Mr John Forrester* (Stoke-on-Trent North); Mr Reginald Freeson* (Brent East); Mr James Hamilton (Motherwell North); Mr Walter Harrison (Wakefield); Dame Judith Hart (Clydesdale); Dr Mark Hughes (Durham, City of); Mr Ronald Lewis (Carlisle); Mr Gregor Mackenzie (Glasgow, Rutherglen); Mr Roy Mason (Barnsley Central); Miss Joan Maynard (Sheffield, Brightside); Mr Hugh McCartney (Clydebank & Milngavie); Mr Michael McGuire* (Makerfield); Mr Ian Mikardo (Bow and Poplar); Dr Maurice Miller (East Kilbride); Mr George Park (Coventry North East); Mr Laurie Pavitt (Brent South); Mr Ernest Roberts* (Hackney North and Stoke Newington); Mr John Ryman (Blyth Valley); Mrs Renee Short (Wolverhampton North East); Dr Roger Thomas (Carmarthen); Mr Stanley Thorne (Preston): Mr Thomas Torney (Bradford South); Mr James Tinn (Redcar); Mr James White (Glasgow, Pollok); Mr Alec Woodall* (Hemsworth).

* denotes de-selected by constituency Labour Party.

The Alliance bade farewell to two of its MPs, both Liberals - Mr Stephen Ross (Isle of Wight) and Mr Richard Wainwright (Colne Valley) who for some years had been the Liberal spokesman on Treasury and economic affairs. Finally, Mr Donald Stewart, SNP leader since 1974, stood down at Western Isles which he first won in 1970.

'The Next Moves Forward'

FOREWORD by The Rt. Hon. Margaret Thatcher

In the last eight years our country has changed — changed for the better.

We have discovered a new strength and a new pride. We have fostered a new spirit of enterprise. We have risen to fresh challenges at home and abroad. Once again, our economy is strong. Our industries are flourishing. Unemployment is falling.

Founded on this new prosperity, we are building a better Health Service and providing more care for those in need. Living standards are higher than ever before. Our people have the protection of a stronger defence and more police.

Britain has come right by her own efforts. We trusted in the character and talents of our people. The British instinct is for choice and independence. Given the opportunities provided by Conservative policies, many more families now enjoy the pride of ownership — of homes, of shares and of pensions.

Together we are building One Nation of free, prosperous and responsible families and people. A Conservative dream is at last becoming a reality.

This Manifesto points the way forward.

THE BRITISH REVIVAL

This manifesto sets out our vision for the Britain of the 1990s and beyond, a future based on the aspirations of millions of individuals and their families — their hopes, their needs, their security. For the first time in a generation this country looks forward to an era of real prosperity and fulfilment.

A vast change separates the Britain of today from the Britain of the late 1970s. Is it really only such a short time ago that inflation rose to an annual rate of 27 per cent? That the leader of the Transport and General Workers' Union was widely seen as the most powerful man in the land? That a minority Labour Government, staggering from crisis to crisis on borrowed money, was nonetheless maintained in power by the Liberal Party in return for the paper concession of a Lib-Lab pact? And that Labour's much-vaunted pay pact with the unions collapsed in the industrial anarchy of the "winter of discontent", in which the dead went unburied, rubbish piled up in the streets, and the country was gripped by a creeping paralysis which Labour was powerless to cure?

It seems in retrospect to be the history of another country. Yet these things happened and people had to accept them as an unavoidable part of everyday life.

REVERSING THE DECLINE

Remember the conventional wisdom of the day. The British people were "ungovernable". We were in the grip of an incurable "British disease". Britain was heading for "irreversible decline".

Well, the people were *not* ungovernable, the disease was *not* incurable, and the decline *has* been reversed.

Britain today is in the seventh successive year of steady economic growth. We have moved from the bottom to the top of the growth league of major European countries.

In Britain today, inflation has reached its lowest levels for almost twenty years.

In Britain today, the number of strikes has dropped to the lowest levels for 50 years.

In Britain today, far from being in debt to the IMF, we have built up our net overseas assets to their highest level since the Second World War — higher than France, Germany and the United States, second only to Japan.

In Britain today, living standards are higher than ever before in our history.

But these are bald statistics. What matters is the feel of the country — the new enthusiasm for enterprise, the new spirit that Britain can make it, that we can prosper with the best. Investment in British industry is rising strongly. Our services sector, employing almost two-thirds of our workforce, generates a vast surplus of foreign earnings. And our manufacturers are travelling the globe with a new confidence born of the knowledge that Britain is internationally competitive again.

THE WORLD STAGE

This national revival is not confined to increased economic strength. Britain is also playing a major part on the international stage. From the White House through Europe to the Kremlin, our voice is heard on arms control, on East-West issues, on human rights, on the Middle East and on African affairs.

With the Conservative Government, Britain has played a strong and responsible role internationally. We have defended civilised values by fighting terrorism relentlessly. We have secured our national interests, as when we liberated the Falklands. We have been ready to settle long-standing issues like Hong Kong where we reached an agreement to safeguard the way of life of the people.

Time and again we have shown that we possess the essential requirements of successful diplomacy:

we stand firm on principles yet are ready to negotiate and prepared to take decisive action.

FOUNDED IN STRENGTH

The ability to act internationally does not come without effort. It must be founded on a strong economy and a robust defence. This Government took the necessary steps to build up both. Success has followed.

Prudent financial policies have made Britain one of the world's largest creditors. Today we are able to shape world efforts to sustain trade and promote international monetary co-operation.

We gave a lead in Nato and installed Cruise missiles. Today, as a result, the Soviet Union is at last prepared to negotiate to remove its own missiles targeted against us.

This Government is modernising our own independent deterrent. Today Britain retains an independent influence in arms control negotiations between the superpowers.

By such steadfastness, we have not only rebuilt our economy and re-established our world reputation; we have also regained our national self-respect. But restoring a country's greatness is not easy. The new Conservative policies met bitter resistance every step of the way.

REMEMBER ....

The year-long coal strike, with its violence and intimidation on a massive scale. It failed and mining productivity has since soared.

The battle we have had to fight to ensure that Britain paid no more than its fair share of the European Community Budget. We now get automatic rebates – this year, over £1.3 billion.

The doubling of the oil price which confronted the new Government with a world-wide recession – and, more recently, an equally dramatic fall in the oil price which halved government oil revenues and in earlier times would have threatened a collapse of confidence in the pound. Both these oil "shocks" were sucessfully withstood by prudent policies which have produced a sustained growth of prosperity.

And let us not forget the challenge of the Falklands War.

How many of the alternative governments on offer would have stood firm, overcome, or even survived such difficulties? Does anyone suppose that the Labour Party would have resisted, let alone defeated, the violence and intimidation in the coal strike? Or that the Liberals or the Social Democrats would have fought so hard for our rebate from the European Community? Or that *any* of the Opposition parties would have persevered through all these difficulties to break the back of inflation and restore honest money?

A STRONG AND STABLE GOVERNMENT

How has it been done? All these improvements in the wealth and standing of our country have only been possible because we have had a strong government with sound policies and a decisive majority in Parliament. A weak government with uncertain policies would not have known how to withstand the pressures upon it; a government without a good overall majority in Parliament would not have been allowed to do so; and a strong government with unsound policies would have been a positive force for disaster.

In this election, only the Conservative Party is offering strong, decisive and united government.

THE NEXT MOVES FORWARD

The next Conservative Government will build on the achievements of the past eight years with a full programme of positive reform. We will continue:

● to pursue policies of sound financial management, the conquest of inflation, the promotion of enterprise and the growth of employment;

● to spread the ownership of homes, shares, pensions and savings ever more widely to give families greater financial independence;

● to give people greater choice and responsibility over their own lives in important areas such as housing and education;

● to improve the well-being of the people through better health care, and to safeguard the living standards of those who have to depend on the community;

● to improve the quality of life by conserving the best of our heritage and our countryside, and by fostering provision for the arts and sport;

● to exercise strong leadership where government needs to be strong – in protecting the nation against potential aggression and the citizen against lawlessness.

We intended to press on with the radical Conservative reform which we embarked upon in 1979, and which has already revived the spirit of our people and restored the reputation of our country.

WIDER OWNERSHIP AND GREATER OPPORTUNITY

Conservatives aim to extend as widely as possible the opportunity to own property and build up capital, to exercise real choice in education, and to develop economic independence and security.

Our goal is a capital-owning democracy of people and families who exercise power over their own lives in the most direct way. *They* would take the important decisions – as tenants, home-owners, parents, employees, and trade unionists – rather than having them taken for them.

Of course, it is not possible to *give* people independence. That is something we must all achieve by

by our own efforts. But what this Conservative Government *has* done is to make it easier for people to acquire independence for themselves:
● by introducing the right to buy council houses;
● by returning nationalised industries to the people in ways that encourage the widest possible spread of ownership;
● by making it easier to buy shares in British industry through employee share schemes and Personal Equity Plans.

These opportunities − all too often introduced in the teeth of fierce resistance from the Opposition parties − have achieved spectacular results. There has been a surge of home-ownership, share-owner-ship, and self reliance.

And because these first-time shareholders and home-owners *are* more independent, they develop a more independent outlook. They are no longer content that some of the most important decision in their lives − what school their children attend, for example, or whether or not to go on strike − should be taken by officialdom or trade union bosses. People want to decide such things for themselves.

In this way the scope of individual responsibility is widened, the family is strengthened, and volun-tary bodies flourish. State power is checked and opportunities are spread throughout society. Ownership and independence cease to be the privileges of a few and become the birthright of all.

In this way One Nation is finally reached − not by a single people being conscripted into an organised socialist programme but by millions of people building their own lives in their own way.

BETTER HOUSING FOR ALL
Home Ownership
Nowhere has the spread of ownership been more significant than in housing. Buying their own home is the first step most people take towards building up capital to hand down to their children and grandchil-dren. It gives people a stake in society − something to conserve. It is the foundation stone of a capital-owning democracy.

A home should be a source of pride and independence to the family living in it, regardless of whether it is owned or rented. We will ensure that every family in the land has an opportunity to make it so.

Home-ownership has been the great success story of housing policy in the last eight years. One million council tenants have become home-owners and another one and a half million more families have become home-owners for the first time.

Two out of every three homes are now owned by the people who live in them. This is a very high proportion, one of the largest in the world. We are determined to make it larger still.

Some people are still deterred by the costs and complications of house purchase. That is why we must look for new ways to make house-buying simpler and easier. Our abolition of the conveyancing monopo-ly has already made it cheaper.

We will keep the present system of mortgage tax relief.

We will target improvement grants to where they are most needed − the least well-off. To meet the special needs of old people, we will ensure that all local authorities have powers to give improvement grants, where necessary, for properties where elderly people move in with relatives. We will extend the 30 per cent housing association grant to help schemes for old people.

A right to rent
Most problems in housing now arise in the rented sector. Controls, although well-meant, have dramati-cally reduced the private rented accommodation to a mere 8 per cent of the housing market.

This restricts housing choice and hinders the economy. People looking for work cannot easily move to a different area to do so. Those who find work may not be able to find rented accommodation nearby. Those who would prefer to rent rather than buy are forced to become reluctant owner-occupiers or to swell the queue for council houses. Some may even become temporarily homeless.

And it is not only these people and their families who suffer from the shortages of homes for rent. The economy as a whole is damaged when workers cannot move to fill jobs because there are no homes to rent in the neighbourhood.

This must be remedied. We have already taken some modest steps in this direction by making it easier to part-own or part-rent homes through shared ownership; by bringing in and widening the scheme for assured tenancies; by our system of shortholds; and by providing a new 30 per cent housing association grant to build hostels for young workers. We have also directly tackled the problem of homelessness through new grants to housing associations and other measures.

More must now be done. The next Conservative Government, having already implemented the right to buy, will increase practical opportunities to rent.

We must attract new private investment into rented housing − both from large institutions such as building societies and housing associations as well as from small private landlords. To do this we intend, in particular, to build on two initiatives we have already taken.

First, to encourage more investment by institutions, we will extend the system of *assured tenancies.* This will permit new lettings in which rents and the period of lease will be freely agreed between tenants and landlords. The tenant will have security of tenure and will renegotiate the rent at the end of the lease, with provision for arbitration if necessary.

Second, to encourage new lettings by smaller landlords, we will develop the system of *shorthold.* The rents of landlords will be limited to a reasonable rate of return, and the tenant's security of tenure will be limited to the term of the lease, which would not be less than six months. This will bring back into use many of the 550,000 private dwellings which now stand empty because of controls, as well as making the provision of new rented housing a more attractive investment.

And we will revise the *housing benefit* system to ensure that it prevents landlords from increasing rents to unreasonable levels at the taxpayer's expense.

All existing private and housing association tenants will continue to have their present protection in respect of rents and security of tenure.

We will strengthen the law against harassment and unlawful eviction.

Rights for Council Tenants

Many council estates built in the Sixties and Seventies are badly designed, vulnerable to crime and vandalism, and in bad repair. In many areas, rent arrears are high. In all, over 110,000 council dwellings stand empty. Yet it is often difficult for tenants to move. If they are ever to enjoy the prospect of independence, municipal monopoly must be replaced by choice in renting.

We will give groups of tenants the right to form tenant co-operatives, owning and running their management and budget for themselves. They will also have the right to ask other institutions to take over their housing. Tenants who wish to remain with the local authority will be able to do so.

We will give each council house tenant individually the right to transfer the ownership of his or her house to a housing association or other independent, approved landlord.

In some areas more may be necessary. The success of Estate Action and Housing Action Areas shows how a carefully targeted approach can transform the area of poor housing and give people there new hope. Our Urban Development Corporations have been successful in restoring derelict industrial areas. We believe that a similar approach could be adopted for housing in some places. We will take powers to create Housing Action Trusts – initially as a pilot scheme – to take over such housing, renovate it, and pass it on to different tenures and ownerships, including housing associations, tenant co-operatives, owner-occupiers or approved private landlords.

We will reform the structure of local authority housing accounts so that public funds are directed at the problems of repair and renovation; maintenance and management are improved; resources are directed to the areas where the problems are greatest; rent arrears are reduced; and fewer houses are left empty.

Housing is the biggest single investment that most people make – whether in money or in time, skill and effort. In the last eight years, as a result of our policies, we have seen a dramatic increase in home-ownership. In the next five years, we will complement that with policies designed to improve the supply and condition of the rented housing stock.

A CAPITAL-OWNING DEMOCRACY
Share ownership

Home-ownership leads naturally to other forms of financial provision for the future – notably to pensions and share-ownership. Half of the working population are in occupational pension schemes, but in 1979 only seven per cent of the population held shares.

People were deterred by the sheer unfamiliarity of owning shares. Young people were reluctant to save for a retirement which seemed far away. And most tax incentives encouraged saving through institutions rather than directly.

With a Conservative Government, all that has been changing. We were determined to make share-ownership available to the whole nation. *Just as with cars, television sets, washing machines and foreign holidays, it would no longer be a privilege for the few; it would become the expectation of the many.* We achieved this historic transformation in three ways:

First, we introduced major tax incentives for employee share-ownership. Seven out of the last eight budgets have included measures to encourage people to purchase shares in the company in which they work.

Second, starting this year, we brought in Personal Equity Plans, which enable people to invest in British industry entirely free of tax.

Third, we embarked on a major programme of privatisation, insisting that small investors and employees of the privatised companies should have a fair chance to join in the buying.

The results have been dramatic, and the direct consequence of government policy. Share ownership has trebled. Almost one in five of the adult population now owns shares directly. And the figure will continue to rise. Of this total, the majority are first-time shareholders and most of them own shares in either privatised companies or the TSB group. One-and-a-half million people hold shares in the companies where they work.

After eight years of Conservative Government, Britain is now in the forefront of a world-wide revolution in extending ownership. One in every five British adults now owns shares compared to one in ten Frenchmen, and one in twenty Japanese. Only the Americans, where a quarter of the people are shareholders, remains ahead – and the gap is narrowing.

This is the first stage of a profound and progressive social transformation – popular capitalism. Owning a direct stake in industry not only enhances personal independence; it also gives a heightened sense of involvement and pride in British business. More realistic attitudes to profit and investment take root. And the foundations of British economic achievement are further strengthened.

We will press on with the encouragement of popular capitalism.In the next Parliament:

We will continue to extend share-ownership as we have done with home-ownership.

We will re-introduce our proposed tax incentives for profit-related pay.

We will privatise more state industries in ways that increase share-ownership, both for the employees and for the public at large.

RAISING STANDARDS IN EDUCATION

Parents want schools to provide their children with the knowledge, training and character that will fit them for today's world. They want them to be taught basic educational skills. They want schools that will encourage moral values: honesty, hard work and responsibility. And they should have the right to chose those schools which do these things for their children.

Raising Standards in our Schools

How can all this best be done? Resources obviously matter. This Government has provided more resources for pupils than ever before.With the Conservatives:

● Spending per primary school pupil has risen by 17 per cent after allowing for inflation and per secondary pupil by 20 per cent under our Government.

● There are more teachers in proportion to pupils than ever before.

● British schools are world leaders in the use of computers in the classroom.

But money alone is not enough. Increased resources have not produced uniformly higher standards. Parents and employers are rightly concerned that not enough children master the basic skills, that some of what is taught seems irrelevant to a good education, and that standards of personal discipline and aspirations are too low. In certain cases education is used for political indoctrination and sexual propaganda. The time has now come for school reform.

Four Major Reforms

First, we will establish a National Core Curriculum.

It is vital to ensure that all pupils between the ages of 5 to 16 study a basic range of subjects – including maths, English, and science. In each of these basic subjects syllabuses will be published and attainment levels set so that the progress of pupils can be assessed at around ages 7, 11 and 14, and in preparation for the GCSE at 16. Parents, teachers and pupils will then know how well each child is doing. We will consult widely among those concerned in establishing the curriculum.

Second, within five years governing bodies and head teachers of all secondary schools and many primary schools will be given control of their own budgets.

They know best the needs of their schools. With this independence, they will manage their resources and decide their priorities, covering the cost of books, equipment, maintenance and staff. Several pilot schemes for financial devolution to schools have already proved their worth, such as those in Cambridgeshire and Solihull.

Third, we will increase parental choice.

The most consistent pressure for high standards of schools comes from parents. They have a powerful incentive to ensure that their children receive a good education. We have already done much through the 1980 and 1986 Education Acts so that parents can make their voice heard. But parents still need better opportunities to send their children to the school of their choice. That would be the best guarantee of higher standards. To achieve this:

We will ensure that Local Education Authorities (LEAs) set school budgets in line with the number of pupils who will be attending each school.

Schools will be required to enrol children up to the school's agreed physical capacity instead of artificially restricting pupil numbers, as can happen today. Popular schools, which have earned parent support by offering good education, will then be able to expand beyond present pupil numbers.

These steps will compel schools to respond to the views of parents. But there must also be variety of educational provision so that parents can better compare one school with another.

We will therefore support the co-existence of a variety of schools – comprehensive, grammar, secondary modern, voluntary controlled and aided, independent, sixth form and tertiary colleges – as well as the reasonable rights of schools to retain their sixth forms, all of which will give parents greater choice and lead to higher standards.

We will establish a pilot network of City Technology Colleges. Already two have been announced and support for more has been pledged by industrial sponsors.

We will expand the Assisted Places Scheme to 35,000. This highly successful scheme has enabled 25,000 talented children from less-well-off backgrounds to gain places at the 230 independent schools currently in the scheme.

We will continue to defend the right to independent education as part of a free society. It is under threat from all the other parties.

Fourth, we will allow state schools to opt out of LEA control.

If, in a particular school, parents and governing bodies wish to become independent of the LEA, they will be given the choice to do so. Those schools which opt out of LEA control will receive a full grant direct from the Department of Education and Science. They would become independent charitable trusts.

In the area covered by the Inner London Education Authority, where entire borough councils wish to become independent of the LEA, they will be able to submit proposals to the Secretary of State requesting permission to take over the provision of education within their boundaries.

Village Schools
We recognise the important contribution made by small rural primary schools to education and to the community life of our villages.

We will ensure, therefore, that the future of these schools is judged by wider factors than merely the number of pupils attending them.

Pre-School Education
Eighty per cent of all three- and four-year-olds in this country attend nursery classes, reception classes or playgroups. Formal nursery education is not necessarily the most appropriate experience for children. Diversity of provision is desirable. LEAs should look to support the voluntary sector alongside their own provision.

A Better Career for Teachers
We recognise the importance of teachers and wish to enhance their professional status. The Government has provided a record amount of money to increase their pay by an average 16.4 per cent this year — 25 per cent over 18 months. Our new pay award will encourage able young people to enter the career of teaching and reward the many good teachers already in the profession.

The Burnham negotiating machinery finally broke down and has been temporarily replaced by an Interim Advisory Committee. The Government wants an effective and permanent machinery for settling teachers' pay, in which the interests of all parties will be recognised.

The Government will produce a Green Paper setting out the various alternatives and will enter into wide consultations with a view to establishing a new and effective machinery.

HIGHER AND FURTHER EDUCATION
The British system of higher education is among the best in the world. It ranges from universities to further education colleges providing skills and qualifications. We recognise the value of research and scholarship for their own sake. At the same time, we must meet the nation's demand for highly qualified manpower to compete in international markets.

Building on our achievements since 1979 — 157,000 more full-time and part-time students — we want to expand higher education opportunities still further. By 1990, we plan to increase student numbers by a further 50,000 and to raise the proportion of 18-year-olds in higher education.

We will replace the University Grants Committee with an independent statutory body on the lines recommended by the Croham Committee. The new body will be called the Universities Funding Council (UFC) and will have broadly equal numbers of academic and non-academic members with a chairman who has substantial experience outside the academic world. The primary responsibility of the UFC will be the allocation of funds to individual universities under new contractual agreements.

Polytechnics are today strong, successful and mature institutions. They are complementary to the universities. Their present structure, under local authorities, is inappropriate for an expanding national role.

As part of our policy to delegate power and responsibility, we will legislate to convert the polytechnics and other mainly higher education colleges in England to free-standing corporate bodies under boards of governors.

We will set up a new Polytechnics and Colleges Funding Council independent of central Government, in place of local authority control.

As part of our aim to widen access to higher education we have begun a review of student support which is the most generous in the western world. We need to modernise this system which has not changed for 25 years. The purpose of the review is to improve the overall prospects of students so that more are encouraged to enter higher education. No final conclusions have been reached, but we believe that top-up loans to supplement grants are one way, among others, of bringing in new finance to help students and relieve pressure on their parents.

We will take care to ensure that the best aspects of the present system are retained in any new proposals which we bring forward.

TRADE UNIONS
It is not only in relation to government, however, that people's right to choice and independence must be safeguarded and extended. Great social institutions can sometimes become too powerful and cease to represent their members, denying them any control over the decisions taken in their name and even forcing them to act against their own interests. That was the case with trade unions before 1979.

Since then, Conservative reforms have redressed the balance between the individual and his union, preventing coercion of the majority by activists and militants. These highly successful and popular measures have encouraged democracy within the unions, restrained the abuses of secondary action and picketing, reversed the growth of closed shops, restored the rights of redress against unions acting unlawfully, and removed the immunity of unions that call a strike without a fair ballot.

The result has been a transformation of shop-floor relations, allowing management and workforce to co-operate to improve working practices and introduce new technology to mutual gain. In the next Parliament we will protect the rights of individual trade union members.

We will introduce legislation to:

● empower individual members to stop their unions calling them out on strike without first holding a secret ballot of members;

● protect individual members from disciplinary action if they refuse to join a strike they disagree with;

● ensure that all members of trade union governing bodies are elected by secret ballot at least once every five years;

● make independently supervised postal ballots compulsory for such elections;

● limit further abuse of the closed shop by providing protection against unfair dismissal for all non-union employees, and removing any legal immunity from industrial action to establish or enforce a closed shop;

● provide new safeguards on the use of union funds;

● establish a new trade union commissioner with the power to help individual trade unionists to enforce their fundamental rights.

BUILDING PROSPERITY AND EMPLOYMENT

Since this Government took office in 1979, we have restored honest money and established a stable economic framework in which business can flourish. We have been careful not to spend money before we earned it. We have brought the nation back to living within its means. We have massively rebuilt our international assets. We have refused to be drawn into an auction of pledges for higher spending that the country simply could not afford. We have balanced the books. We have paid our way.

The results of been dramatic:

● Despite the coal strike and the collapse of the oil price, Britain has moved from being bottom to the top of the growth league of major European countries.

● Inflation has reached its lowest levels for almost 20 years.

● The basic rate of income tax has been cut from 33 pence to 27 pence, four taxes have been abolished, and almost a million and a half people have been taken out of the income tax altogether.

● Over a million extra jobs have been created since 1983 — more than in the rest of the European Community put together.

● Unemployment, a problem throughout Europe, is now firmly on a downward trend — with youth unemployment in this country below the European average.

● We have rebuilt our net overseas assets to some £110 billion from a mere £12 billion when we first took office. This will provide substantial foreign earnings in the years ahead and a cushion, should oil revenues fall.

While the Opposition parties cling to the failed policies of the past, our strategy has become widely accepted abroad. Socialist Spain as well as Christian Democratic Germany, Social Democratic Sweden as well as France, Labour New Zeealand and Conservative Canada, all accept that governments must reduce their borrowing, curb state spending, reduce taxation, privatise state firms and do away with unnecessary controls. What we began in 1979 is today common international practice.

STABLE PRICES

Our greatest economic challenge on entering office was to defeat inflation. Rampant inflation under the Labour Government, when money lost a quarter of its value in a single year, had reduced our economy to "the sick man of Europe".

Nothing erodes a country's competitive edge faster than inflation. Nothing so undermines personal thrift and independence as to see the value of a lifetime's savings eaten away in retirement through spiralling prices. And nothing threatens the social fabric of a nation more than the conflicts and divisiveness which inflation creates.

Our success in the battle against inflation has been the key to Britain's economic revival. It required firm control of public expenditure, a substantial reduction in government borrowing, curbing the growth of money in circulation, maintaining financial discipline, stimulating competition and moderating trade union power.

The Opposition parties opposed nearly every aspect of this strategy. If even some of their policies were implemented today, higher borrowing and higher spending would once again unleash inflation.

There is no better yardstick of a party's fitness to govern than its attitude to inflation. Nothing is so politically immoral as a party that ignores that yardstick.

The Conservative Government will continue to put the conquest of inflation as our first objective. We will not be content until we have stable prices, with inflation eradicated altogether.

LOWER TAXES

We are the only Party that believes in lower taxation.

As the Party determined to achieve growing prosperity we recognise that it is people who create wealth, not governments. Lower taxation, coupled with lower inflation, makes everyone better off. It encourages people to work harder, to be inventive and to take risks. It promotes a climate of enterprise and initiative.

Lower tax on earnings enables people to build up savings to give them financial security in later life.

Lower taxation, by increasing take-home pay without adding to industry's costs, improves competitiveness and helps with jobs. And tax relief for charitable donations encourages more people to give — and to give more generously.

There is a strong moral case for reducing taxation. High taxes deprive people of their independence and make their choices for them. The desire to do better for one's family is one of the strongest motives in human nature. As a party committed to the family and opposed to the over-powerful State, we want people to keep more of what they earn, and to have more freedom of choice about what they do for themselves, their families and for others less fortunate.

Governments should trust people to spend their own money sensibly and decently; high taxation prevents them doing so.

That is why we have:

● cut the basic rate from 33 pence to 27 pence in the £, and increased the personal allowances (the starting point for paying tax) by 2 per cent more than inflation.

If Labour's tax regime were still in force, the family man on average earnings would today be paying more than £500 per year in extra income tax: a headmaster married to a nurse would be paying more than £1,300 extra;

● reduced sharply the absurd top rates of tax inherited from Labour which were causing so many of our most talented people to work abroad;

● increased greatly the tax relief for charitable donations. Giving to charities has doubled since we first took office;

● abolished four taxes completely: the national insurance surcharge — the tax which Labour put on jobs — the investment income surcharge, the development land tax and the lifetime gifts tax;

● reformed and simplified corporation tax, and cut its rate to the lowest of any major industrial country;

● cut the small business corporation tax rate by more than a third, and extended it to many more small businesses;

● reformed and reduced capital taxes as well as slashing stamp duty.

In every case where taxes have been reformed and reduced there has been an increase in the amount of tax collected.

Labour totally fail to understand the benefits this brings to everyone. Today they openly threaten to raise taxation. To fulfil their plans, they would have to raise taxes substantially. Indeed, all the Opposition parties — Labour, Liberals and SDP — would raise taxation. We believe that it is precisely the wrong thing to do.

It will be our aim to do the opposite.

In the next Parliament:

We aim to reduce the burden of taxation.

In particular, we will cut income tax still further and reduce the basic rate to 25 pence in the £ as soon as we prudently can.

We will continue the process of tax reform.

SPENDING WE CAN AFFORD

Over the past eight years we have managed the nation's finances with care. Even allowing for inflation, this has enabled us to spend substantially more on the Health Service (up by 31 per cent), defence (up by 23 per cent), roads (up by 17 per cent), education per pupil (up by 18 per cent), the police and the battle against crime (up by 47 per cent), the disabled and long-term sick (up by 72 per cent), and government training schemes (up by 120 per cent).

How have we been able to do this without running into the financial crises which Labour's spending policies invariably set off?

First, we have been prudent with the nation's money. We have slashed public borrowing and sought savings in government expenditure wherever they could sensibly be found.

Second, we are engaged in steadily reducing the share of the nation's income taken by the State. This means that more will be left for families and for business to invest — the only safe route to higher growth in the economy.

Third, we have constantly improved the efficiency of the public services, ensuring that we get more value for every pound spent.

For the next Parliament:

Our aim is the ensure that public expenditure takes a steadily smaller share of our national income.

Within that objective, we will continue to spend more on our priorities. We have set out our plans for further increased spending in these areas over the next three years.

CREATING NEW JOBS

High unemployment is one of the most intractable problems facing all Western industrial countries.

We understand the anxiety and stress which unemployment can cause. For almost a year unemployment in the United Kingdom has fallen faster than among any of our major competitors in Europe, and faster than at any time since 1973. It is falling because of the growth and enterprise we have achieved, assisted by the unemployment and training programmes we have developed.

Since we were last re-elected in 1983, the number of jobs has risen by over 1 million – more than in the rest of the European Community put together. This Government has established the conditions in which business can prosper and create new jobs. This has not just been achieved through the revitalisation of traditional industries. We have encouraged growth in those crucial areas of new enterprise which provide the foundation for the jobs of the future – self-employment, small firms, the creation of new enterprise, the expanding service sector – particularly tourism and leisure – and new technology.

Self-employment is the seedcorn of the new enterprises of tomorrow. Without sufficient people to start new businesses, the future of our whole economy is in jeopardy. Today we have the highest number of self-employed for over 60 years. One worker in ten is now his own boss – or her own boss, since a quarter of the self-employed are women. Indeed, the eighties have seen almost three-quarters of a million people become self-employed. More and more of our young people today seek self-employment as a worthwhile career. It is particularly encouraging that almost half of the growth in self-employment since 1983 has been in the Northern part of our country.

Small firms, along with all businesses, have benefitted from our management of the economy. Since this Government took office, the number of registered businesses has shown a net increase of more than 500 a week – and the number has increased in every region of the country.

HELPING UNEMPLOYED PEOPLE INTO JOBS

As well as creating a climate in which business could employ more people, we have developed programmes to help those out of work.

The *Youth Training Scheme (YTS)* caters for school-leavers aged 16 and 17 who wish to participate in training and work experience. Every trainee is given the opportunity of working towards a recognised qualification.

The new *Job Training Scheme (JTS)*, which started in April this year, will offer a chance to any person over 18 who has been unemployed for six months or more, who wants to work and train with an employer for a recognised qualification. This year it will help nearly a quarter of a million people.

Under our *Community Programme*, each year over 300,000 people who have been out of work for some time gain valuable experience working on community projects. They have a reference to show potential employers.

We will improve the Community Programme to make it full-time and better able to help those with families. We shall pay those working on the programme an allowance giving a premium over and above their social security payments.

Under the *Enterprise Allowance Scheme*, 230,000 unemployed people have started to work for themselves. Many of them have now become employers themselves.

JobClubs were first opened in 1985 to help the unemployed help themselves back into jobs. Over 1,000 have been established. At present two-thirds of those leaving JobClubs go into employment.

The JobClubs programme has been a great success. We aim to expand it.

Our economic success means that we can now do more to help those out of work.

Although youth unemployment has declined in the last year, it still remains a problem. Far too many of our youngsters leave school with an education that has failed to prepare them for the world of work. At the same time, by maintaining high starting wages comparable to those of fully trained craftsmen, trade unions have kept many of them out of work.

In 1983 we introduced the first Youth Training Scheme. It is now a national two-year programme aimed at giving young people qualifications for work.

The First Guarantee

We will now guarantee a place on the Youth Training Scheme to every school-leaver under 18 who is not going directly into a job.

As a result, none of these school-leavers need be unemployed. They can remain at school, move to college, get a job, or receive a guaranteed training. YTS will serve as a bridge between school and work.

We will take steps to ensure that those under 18 who deliberately choose to remain unemployed are not eligible for benefit. We will, of course, continue to protect other young people, such as those who suffer from disabilities.

The Second Guarantee

There are still too many young people without the right qualifications for employment in today's world.

Within a year we aim to guarantee a place, either on the Job Training Scheme or on the Enterprise Allowance Scheme or in a JobClub, for everyone aged between 18 and 25 years who has been unemployed for between six and twelve months.

The Third Guarantee

In addition to these major programmes we have taken one further important step.

Restart is a programme we have set up for interviewing and counselling the long-term unemployed to help them into a job or training. Everyone who has been unemployed for more than one year has already given an interview.

We will guarantee to provide the Restart service in the future at six-monthly intervals, to all those who have been unemployed for more than six months.

Over the next five years we will aim, through the Restart interviews, to offer everyone who is under 50, and who has been unemployed for more than two years, a place in the Job Training Scheme or in the new Community Programme, in a JobClub or in the Enterprise Allowance Scheme.

Regional Assistance

Money spent on earlier programmes attracting firms to regions has sometimes created very few jobs. Our new system of regional assistance, introduced in 1984, ensures that aid is directly targeted towards the creation of new jobs. New activities in the service sector from which so many of the jobs comes have also been made eligible for assistance. Under the new policy, offers of assistance have already been made which should secure almost 300,000 jobs. We will continue to ensure that assistance is directed where it is most needed.

THE EMPLOYMENT AND TRAINING SERVICE

We will take further steps to provide a comprehensive service to the unemployment. We will consult the Manpower Services Commission about transferring JobCentres to the Department of Employment so that they can work more closely with Unemployment Benefit Offices.

The Manpower Services Commission would then become primarily a training agency. It is employers who are best equipped to assess their training needs.

We will increase employer representation on the Commission and its advisory bodies.

More jobs are being created by business and industry. Nothing would destroy whole industries more effectively than a return to the overmanning and restrictive practices of the 1970s. Our policies form a practical and realistic approach to help people back into work. We will build on prosperity to create more employment.

A FRAMEWORK FOR BUSINESS AND INDUSTRY

British business is in a healthier state than it has been for a generation. Output has been rising steadily for six years. Productivity has increased at a rate second only to Japan. Company profitability is at its highest for over twenty years. Industry has a confidence in the future that would have been unthinkable seven years ago.

Moreover, setting new records has not been confined to the private sector. Since 1983 productivity in the coal industry has risen by over 50 per cent. British Steel has more than doubled its productivity since 1979 and made a profit last year for the first time in over ten years. British Rail will cost the taxpayer 25 per cent less in subsidy this year than in 1983 and without any major route closures.

The Conservative Government has created a framework in which once again enterprise can flourish — by cutting red tape, by denationalising state-owned companies, by removing unnecessary restrictions, by abolishing exchange control, by enabling the City of London to become the foremost financial centre in the world, by keeping down prices through extending competition, and by ensuring access to open trade so that British exporters and consumers can both benefit.

PRIVATISATION

Over a third of the companies and industries which used to be owned by the State have been returned to free enterprise. Productivity and profitability have soared in the newly privatised companies.

● In 1980 Jaguar made 14,000 cars a year, losing well over £3,000 on each car sold. Now the company is hard put to keep up with overseas demand and last year sold over 40,000 cars, making a pre-tax profit of over £120 million.

● Since the National Freight Consortium was sold to management and staff in 1982, pre-tax profits have increased sevenfold.

● British Aerospace, Cable & Wireless, Amersham International and Associated British Ports have all strikingly increased their profits.

It is no mystery why privatisation has succeeded. The overwhelming majority of employees have become shareholders in the newly privatised companies. They want their companies to succeed. Their companies have been released from the detailed controls of Whitehall, and given more freedom to manage their own affairs. And they have been exposed to the full commercial disciplines of the customer. Even former monopolies now face increased competition.

We will continue the successful programme of privatisation.

In particular, after the privatisation of the British Airports Authority, we will return to the public the Water Authorities, leaving certain functions to a new National Rivers Authority.

Following the success of gas privatisation, with the benefits it brought to employees and millions of consumers, we will bring forward proposals for privatising the electricity industry subject to proper regulation.

COMPETITION

Competition forces the economy to respond to the needs of the consumer. It promotes efficiency, holds down costs, drives companies to innovate and ensures that customers get the best possible value for money. Accordingly, this Government has:

● deregulated long-distance coach services – creating over 700 new services with improved quality and lower fares;

● removed the monopoly on conveyancing of houses in England and Wales;

● removed the opticians' monopoly, making it easier and cheaper to buy spectacles;

● relaxed advertising controls on accountants, solicitors, stockbrokers and vets, and permitted greater fee competition for architects and surveyors;

● increased competition on air routes within the UK and between certain European countries, which has resulted in cheaper fares, a more responsive service and greater choice of carriers for the passenger;

● deregulated telecommunications, so that customers can now choose between suppliers when buying telephones and private exchanges, and business can choose between two alternative telecommunications networks;

● suspended the Post Office monopoly of time-sensitive and valuable mail, stimulating a dramatic increase in the number of private courier companies.

We will continue this approach.

But competition must be supplemented by legal protection for consumers. Those who make their living from their ideas and creations also require protection against theft.

We will introduce further measures to impose tighter controls on pyramid selling.

We will introduce measures to reform the law on copyright, design and performance protection.

THE CITY

The City of London is the world's leading market place in foreign exchange, international bank lending and international insurance. It is a major source of funds for British companies. The financial services sector as a whole accounts for nearly 6 per cent of our national income, generates a net £7 billion per year to our balance of payments, and employs over one million people.

Like other sections of British industry, however, the City was held back by restrictive practices until they were swept away in last year's "big bang". This has brought nearer the day when shares can be bought and sold over the counter in every high street. We have also given building societies greater freedom to make a wider range of services available to the average family.

At the same time, the Conservative Government has introduced a legal framework to protect investors and consumers:

● The Companies Acts of 1980 and 1981 strengthened the powers of investigators and increased the courts' power to disqualify directors for misconduct in the City as elsewhere.

● The Insolvency Act of 1985 made it easier to disqualify directors who had been guilty of unlawful trading.

● And now the Financial Services Act of 1986 provides the first comprehensive system of investor protection we have had in this country. It also contains stringent new powers to investigate insider dealing which was first made a criminal offence by the Conservative Government in 1980.

The Conservative Party is the party of law and order. That applies just as much to City fraud as to street crime.

Parliament has just approved our proposals for establishing a Serious Fraud Office to improve the work of investigating and prosecuting the worst cases of fraud and for streamlining court procedure. After the election, we will reintroduce our proposals to reform the outdated rules on evidence, as recommended by the Roskill Committee.

TRADE

Britain exports 30 per cent of all that it produces. If this country is to remain a key trading nation, industry must remain competitive. That is one reason why the Conservative Government attaches great value to maintaining an open multinational trading system. Another is that increased trade is a major way of encouraging growth and prosperity in the Third World. There is little point in demanding more aid for these countries and then refusing them the opportunity to trade.

We will continue to fight for free and fair trade in international negotiations and resist the growth of protectionism.

We will press for international rules of fair trading to be extended to international investment, trade in services and the protection of intellectual property such as patents, trade-marks and copyright.

We will continue to exert pressure on countries such as Japan to open up their markets and provide the same freedom to trade for our exporters as they expect us to provide for theirs.

As well as creating the commercial and legal framework in which industry can flourish, the Government must also ensure that the practical services on which industry and the citizen rely – transport, energy, research and development, and an efficient civil service – are provided to a high standard.

EFFICIENT TRANSPORT

The Conservative Government is proud of a record that has:

- modernised the transport system by investing over £10 billion in the nation's motorways, roads, airports, seaports and railways;
- since 1979 completed over 680 miles of motorway and trunk roads, and 67 by-passes;
- secured greater efficiency by privatising British Airways, the National Freight Corporation, Sealink and Associated British Ports;
- increased competition by deregulating long-distance coach services and abolishing local bus licensing.

These measures have laid the foundations of an efficient and more flexible transport system. We will develop it further along these lines. We are now returning the nationalised bus companies to the private sector — in many cases to management buy-outs. We are also privatising the former British Airports Authority — the world's leading international airports group.

We are committed to a major capital investment programme through:

new investment to build an extra 450 miles of motorway and trunk roads to 1989/90;

British Rail's plans to invest £500 million a year over the next three years;

private sector financing, construction and operation of the Dartford Bridge and the Channel Tunnel.

ENERGY

Britain is the only major Western industrial country that is a net exporter of energy. This owes much to North Sea oil so successfully developed by free enterprise. But it is an advantage that will not last indefinitely.

Coal will continue to meet much of the steadily rising demand for electricity. Renewable sources of energy can make some contribution to the nation's energy needs, which is why government-sponsored research has been increased. Nevertheless, to reject, as our opponents do, the contribution of nuclear energy to supplying reliable, low-cost electricity, and to depend on coal alone, would be short-sighted and irresponsible.

The world's resources of fossil fuels will come under increasing strain during the 21st century; so may the global environment if the build-up of carbon dioxide — the so-called "greenhouse effect" — significantly raises temperatures and changes climates.

After the most careful and painstaking independent assessment of the safety case for a new pressurised water reactor at Sizewell, therefore, the Government has decided to proceed with the next phase of our nuclear programme. It is vital that we continue to give the highest priority to safety. Our nuclear industry has a record of safety and technical excellence second to none.

We intend to go on playing a leading role in the task of developing abundant, low-cost supplies of nuclear electricity, and managing the associated waste products.

SCIENCE AND R & D

Government support for research and development amounts to more than £4½ billion per year. It is larger as a share of our national income than that of the United States, Japan or Germany. A country of our size cannot afford to do everything. These resources need to be better targeted. The task of government is to support basic research and to contribute where business cannot realistically be expected to carry all the risks.

We will ensure that government spending is firmly directed towards areas of high national priority, by extending the role of the Advisory Council on Applied Research and Development, drawing on the full range of advice from the academic community and from business.

THE CIVIL SERVICE

We have long had in this country a professional and dedicated public service which is the envy of the world. We are now building on those traditional qualities which can too easily be taken for granted — with new strengths and skills: a greater readiness to adapt efficiently to change, including technological change, to manage the public service more effectively, and to see that the taxpayer gets value for money. The size of the Civil Service at under 600,000 people today is the smallest since the war. This is already saving the taxpayer £1 billion a year.

We will press on with long-term management reforms in order to improve public services and reduce their cost.

AGRICULTURE AND THE RURAL ECONOMY
Farming

Britain's farmers serve the nation well. They produce 80 per cent of the food we grow compared with 60 per cent only 10 years ago. They have made us into the world's sixth largest exporter of cereals when we had been a net importer for decades before. They look after 80 per cent of the British countryside. And consumer food prices have risen less than the cost of living, unlike the Labour years.

But farmers world-wide are under pressure because of rising surpluses and the huge costs of disposing of them. It is just as much in the farmers' interest as in the consumers' and taxpayers' that this over-production be stopped and a radical overhaul of the Common Agricultural Policy achieved. Farmers need a more sustained environment in which to plan ahead.

We will continue:

to play a leading part in European Community negotiations to reform the CAP;

to strive for even-handed and fair treatment between Member States and between the different regions of the UK;

to work for an early devaluation of the Green Pound, especially in relation to beef;

to uphold the interests of the efficient family farm;

to reduce costs and tackle surpluses, by bringing supply and demand in the Community into better balance by a combination of measures including price restraint;

to reduce the role for intervention.

At home we will continue:

to promote competitiveness and innovation in British farming and horticulture;

to give particular assistance to farmers in the Less Favoured Areas, recently extended, where farming is difficult;

to encourage better marketing of agricultural and horticultural products and to ensure that the consumer has as much information about the contents of food as is necessary to make sensible choices.

We will not introduce rating on agricultural land and will oppose two-tier pricing in the CAP, which would greatly disadvantage our farmers and benefit their competitors.

The rural economy

Farming is, and will remain, the major industry in the countryside, and food production will continue to be the farmer's basic purpose. The higher production resulting from greater efficiency and modern techniques initially means more land coming out of agriculture. A new balance of policies has to be struck, with *less* support for expanding production of commodities already in over-supply, and *more* support for diversifying into other activities.

We have recognised the new needs of the countryside and rural economies in two ways. First, we now place more emphasis on support for the environment and the beauty of the countryside; we now give grants to plant hedgerows, not dig them up. Second, we encourage alternative uses of land and more diverse job opportunities to maintain thriving communities in the rural economy.

We will, therefore:

emphasise environmental protection and promotion of non-farming rural businesses in the planning system;

continue to support the Development Commission in developing rural enterprises;

extend the Environmentally Sensitive Areas scheme which makes conservation a more integral part of farming;

introduce new schemes to assist diversification of new enterprises on farms;

introduce a new Farm Woodland Scheme to assist alternative land use.

The UK fishing industry

Our fishing industry supplies two-thirds of the fish we eat. It is an important source of jobs and income in many areas.

The Government's success in further improving the Common Fisheries Policy has meant that international policies has been made more effective; and increasingly stringent conservation measures have secured the future for our fleets.

We will introduce legislation to ensure that UK quotas are reserved for UK fishermen. We are pledged to measures to enable our fishermen to take full advantage of all their opportunities and to improve and modernise their boats.

Animal welfare

The Conservatives have a proud record over the years of promoting animal welfare. Most of the legislation was either initiated by Conservative governments or introduced as Private Members' measures by Conservative MPs when the Conservatives were in office.

Since 1979 we have:

● set up the Farm Animal Welfare Council which advises the Government on the welfare of farm animals. We will continue to care for them with the advice and guidance of the Farm Animal Welfare Council.

● honoured our commitment to replace the 1876 legislation with the Animals (Scientific Procedures) Act 1986 – the most effective in Europe. It imposes tight new controls on the use of animals for experiments. The number of experiments has declined in each of the last nine years, and we expect that decline to continue.

BETTER HEALTH, BETTER CARE
Achievements in Health

The health of the British people is steadily improving. Quite simply, we live longer. Life expectancy has increased and infant mortality has declined.

Over the last eight years the Government has spent more on the Health Service than any previous government, Labour or Conservative. In 1979, the outgoing Labour Government planned to spend less than £8 billion on the nation's health. This year, the Conservative government will spend nearly £21 billion. After allowing for inflation, that is an increase of almost a third. This extra money has been spent wisely and well. The Health Service today is treating more patients than ever before in its history.

Money is important, but the success of the NHS depends still more on the dedication of the people working in it. There are over 75,000 more doctors, dentists and nurses than in 1978. These extra staff hve enabled the NHS to treat 6 million *more* patient cases – in-patients, day cases, out-patients – than when we took office. Sometimes they work in very difficult conditions. That is why the Government has reduced nurses' basic hours from 40 to 37½ hours per week and increased their pay by 30 per cent after allowing for inflation. We will continue to improve the Health Service.

Future tasks for the health service

Our policies rest on six principles:

First, we will give greater emphasis to the prevention of avoidable illness and the promotion of good health – to make the NHS more truly a health service and not merely a sickness service.

Much progress has been made in the past eight years.

● The improvement of the maternity services has helped to reduce by a third the death rate among babies in the weeks around birth.

● The expansion of vaccination and immunisation has prevented illness and death among children.

● Screening for cervical cancer has been improved and death rates from the disease have fallen by almost ten per cent in the past decade.

● We have already embarked on a major campaign to tackle the problem of coronary heart disease.

● To fight AIDS, the Government has undertaken the biggest health education campaign ever seen in this country – one much admired abroad – and is fully supporting the Medical Research Council in a special programme of research towards treatments and vaccines.

These are welcome advances.

In the next Parliament, we will build on this work by:

completing the network of computerised 'call and recall' systems for cervical cancer screening and extending them to younger women;

developing a national programme for breast cancer screening;

backing the newly established and powerful Health Education Authority.

Second, we will continue to show our support for the million people working in the NHS, of whom half are nurses.

Nurses wanted the assurance that, without recourse to strike action, they would receive fair treatment over pay. That is why we set up the independent Nurses' Pay Review Body. After the latest award, we will have *increased* nurses' pay by 30 per cent since 1979, after allowing for inflation. That compares to the severe *reduction* of more than 20 per cent, which they suffered under the last Labour Government.

Nurses also want a training and career structure which reinforces their professionalism, rewards experience, and offers opportunities for managerial responsibility without being removed to a distant desk. We share those views, and will seek to further them. We are particularly keen to attract experienced nurses back into the profession, and to encourage others to take up nursing as a new career.

Hospital doctors and consultants, too, are a vital part of the Health Service. We have already increased the number of consultant posts and we will continue to work for improvements in the medical career structure.

The NHS could not function without ancillary services. Some of these – cleaning, catering, and laundry – have been put out to competitive tender to enable health authorities to select the best and most effective way of providing these services. Savings are now approaching £100 million a year and they have gone directly and immediately into better patient care.

We have undertaken consultation on the improvement of primary care. Our aim is to develop the strength and flexibility of the services provided by GPs, dentists, pharmacists, opticians and nurses who work in the community.

There are particular problems affecting health care in inner cities. Doctors and nurses there take on a particularly tough and difficult job. We shall continue to look for new ways of helping them and improving health care, especially primary care in the inner cities.

Our third principle is to modernise the whole framework of the health service – its hospitals, its clinics, its equipment.

In the face of economic collapse, the last Labour Government cut the hospital building programme by a third. This Government has embarked on the biggest building programme ever. It will cost £3 billion. In seven years we have already carried through over 200 major building projects from start to finish.

We will complete some 125 further major new building schemes in the next three years, and get many more under way.

New hospitals, too, are being built in areas lacking the provision they need. Old and inefficient Victorian building are being replaced with purpose-built modern hospitals. Much modern medicine and surgery is better carried out in the new larger hospitals, equipped with new medical technology. Wherever possible, however, small old hospitals have found a new role as community hospitals staffed by local GPs.

Fourth, elderly, disabled, mentally ill and mentally handicapped people should be cared for within the community whenever this is right for them.

In the past some people who should have been cared for in other ways have remained in hospitals, sometimes for years. That is changing. The number of children in long-stay hospitals for the mentally handicapped has fallen by almost three-quarters. The number of adults in long-stay mental handicap and mental illness hospitals has fallen by around 11,000.

This changing pattern has already brought a better life to many thousands of people. It has the potential to do so for many thousands more. But we need to examine carefully various alternatives to discover what is now best for patients. We have set in hand the first ever full scale review of community care.

We will develop our policies in the light of its findings.

Our fifth principle is to strengthen management.

The NHS is a large and complex organisation. It needs good management. It is not a business, but it must be run in a business-like way.

The reduction of waste and inefficiency has released hundreds of millions of pounds for better patient care. The sale of property which the NHS no longer needs — for example, because of new hospital developments — is currently raising £200 million a year for better health care.

We will continue to ensure that the Health Service is as efficient as possible.

But good management is not just a matter of efficiency. We value enterprise in the public service just as much as in the private sector. We will continue to encourage district and regional managers to devise new ways of providing better patient care.

Finally, the ultimate purpose of the Health Service is to serve the patient: that principle is the heart of the Government's policy.

The time some patients have to wait for treatment is the most widespread concern in the NHS. The Government has given priority to reducing waiting lists and times. We have set up a special £50 million two-year programme. This year it will give treatment to over 100,000 people who are waiting for operations. We have set targets for more hip operations for old peole, and more bone marrow transplants for children.

Putting patients first was the theme of our consultative document on primary care. We want the patient to have more information about services available from family doctors so that they can make a more informed choice.

SOCIAL SECURITY — A FAIR DEAL FOR THOSE IN NEED

We are spending about £46 billion this year on social security benefits — over £800 a year for every man, woman and child in the country. Expenditure on pensions and other benefits has risen by £13 billion on top of inflation, since we came into office. Most of this, an extra £9 billion, has gone to provide better standards of help and support to more elderly people, families with children, disabled people and those suffering long-term illness. The other £4 billion has gone to help the unemployed. But we have done more than provide extra resources — massive as the increase has been.

For the first time for 40 years the Government has undertaken an overall review of the social security system. The review showed a social security system which was too complex and which too often did not provide help for those most in need. The 1986 Social Security Act tackled these problems and reformed the position so that the system is simpler to understand and to run. It will be fairer in the way it directs help to those who need it most. And it will be a system in which people can look forward to independence and security in retirement.

Our policies for social security have four main aims.

First, to ensure that those in retirement have a secure standard of living through state provision and their own pensions and savings.

This Government has honoured its pledge to the pensioner and more than maintained the buying power of the state pension. Total spending on state pensions and benefits for elderly people has risen by 29 per cent after allowing for inflation.

We will continue to maintain the value of the state retirement pension.

But retired people value their independence. They do not want to rely on the State alone for their income nor, increasingly, are they doing so. We share Beveridge's original goal of a good basic pension from the State, together with a second income from occupational and personal pensions and savings.

Pensioners have benefitted from our success against inflation. Almost three-quarters of all pensioners have savings. Their income from these has grown by over seven per cent on average every year since 1979. Income from savings fell by 3½ per cent every year under the last Labour Government, eaten away by inflation.

Occupational pensions, pensioners' savings, social security benefits and the state retirement pension have all increased. The total increase in income for the average pensioner is more than double that achieved during the last Labour Government.

We are now offering new opportunities for people to obtain additional pensions from their jobs or their own savings. We have already improved the treatment of those now retiring early and of the pension rights of people changing jobs.

We wish to encourage the ten million employees who do not yet have their own occupational pension scheme to have a pension of their own. Every employee should have the right to take out a personal pension, fully portable from job to job. That is why we are extending favourable tax treatment from employers' schemes to personal pensions.

As a result of these reforms, millions more people will have the opportunity to take out additional pensions of their own.In the next Parliament:

We will reintroduce measures to give substantial tax incentives to personal pensions, and to enable members of occupational schemes to make additional voluntary contributions to a pension plan that is completely separate from their employers' schemes. These measures will further increase choice for millions of employees.

Second, to bring more help to low income families.

Child benefit will continue to be paid as now, and direct to the mother. Families on income support – which replaces supplementary benefit – will benefit from the new family premium. In addition, we will introduce the new family credit which will benefit twice as many low income families in work as family income supplement. The new system will also help tackle both the unemployment and poverty traps.

Third, to improve the framework of benefits for disabled people.

Spending on benefits for disabled people and those suffering long-term sickness has been increased by 72 per cent after inflation to £6 billion. The amount spent on mobility allowances has been doubled, invalid care allowance extended, the new severe disablement allowance introduced and the invalidity trap abolished. The introduction of the new disablement premiums will bring an extra £50 million per year to disabled people.

We are carrying out a major new survey of the needs of disabled people. This will be completed next year.

Fourth, to reform the tangled web of income-related benefits which has grown up piecemeal over forty years.

For the first time all the income-related benefits will be calculated in the same way. Where people are working, the amount of benefit they get will depend on their pay *after* tax and national insurance contributions. Thus people will not be made worse off by taking a job and will not lose money when their gross pay rises.

The new rules, which come into effect in April next year, will be easier for claimants to understand and staff to run. In addition, our programme of computerisation – the biggest programme ever in this country – will help staff to deliver benefits to all who are entitled to them quickly, accurately and courteously.

Success in social policy depends on growth in national prosperity. Labour's economic failure led to damaging cuts in health care and benefits. Our increasing economic strength means that resources for care have grown and are growing – with programmes better managed, better adapted to changing demands, and better directed to those most in need.

FREEDOM, LAW AND RESPONSIBILITY

Conservatives have always believed that a fundamental purpose of government is to protect the security of the citizen under the rule of law. There can be no half-heartedness, no opting out, in the fight against crime and violence: all of us, not just the Government or the police, share a responsibility to make safer our streets and homes.

The fight against crime

We do not underrate the challenge. Crime has been rising steadily over the years; not just in Britain, but in most other countries, too. The origins of crime lie deep in society: in families where parents do not support or control their children; in schools where discipline is poor; and in the wider world where violence is glamourised and traditional values are under attack.

Government *alone* cannot tackle such deep-rooted problems easily or quickly. But Government must give a lead: by backing, not attacking the police; by providing a tough legal framework for sentencing; by building the prisons in which to take those who pose a threat to society – and by keeping out of prison those who do not; and by encouraging local communities to prevent crime and to help the police detect it. All this we have done; and we will intensify these efforts.

● The manpower available to the police has been increased by 16,500 since 1979.

● We have given the police more powers to avert public disorder.

● We have encouraged tougher sentences for violent criminals. The maximum penalties for trafficking in hard drugs and for attempted rape have been raised to life imprisonment. The courts have been empowered to strip drug traffickers of their profits.

● We have brought forward a number of reforms to help tackle child abuse and make it more likely that offenders will be successfully prosecuted.

● We have embarked on the biggest prison building and modernisation programme this century, and increased staff numbers by almost a fifth.

Care for the innocent

At the same time we have extended protection for innocent people and for the victims of crime.

● We have strengthened the safeguards against any abuse of police power by setting up an independent Police Complaints Authority, providing for the tape-recording of police interviews and setting down clear rules on the proper treatment of the individual citizen.

● We have given special priority to helping the victims of crime. Police treatment of rape victims has been made more sensitive. More criminals now pay compensation to their victims. We are providing more money to help local Victim Support Schemes.

● We have launched a determined drive to improve the administration of justice by providing for time limits by which the cases of those held in custody must be heard. 58 more Circuit Judges have been appointed, and 43 court building projects have been completed.

Better justice

The challenge before us remains great; but much has been done. The great majority of those who commit serious crimes of violence are brought to book. There are more police, better equipped to fight crime. Those who commit serious crimes can now expect much tougher punishment.

Early in the new Parliament the Criminal Justice Bill will have to be reintroduced. It will:

enable child victims of physical and sexual abuse to give evidence by a live video link in order to reduce the anguish which they would otherwise face;

raise to life imprisonment the penalty for carrying firearms while committing a crime;

tackle, by providing for reference to the Court of Appeal, the problem of lenient sentences which undermine public confidence in the criminal justice system;

give victims of crime a statutory right to compensation under the Criminal Injuries Compensation Scheme;

build on our previous measures stripping drug traffickers of the proceeds of their crimes and extend the same approach to other serious crimes.

We have already signed an extradition treaty with the United States which will make it more difficult for terrorists to escape British justice: now we will reform our own law on extradition so as to make still more effective the international war against crime.

Building on strength

We will continue to put a high priority on the fight against crime, so that the citizen can feel safe on the street or in his home. We will:

increase the number of police further to ensure a stronger police presence on our streets, to combat crime and to protect the public;

strengthen the law dealing with the sale and possession of offensive weapons;

maintain the operational independence of the police and resist pressure from the Opposition parties to politicise the police by letting local authorities decide policing priorities;

continue our present prison building programme and achieve more professional and efficient working practices in the prison service;

institute a thorough review of the workings of the parole system.

Our approach in all these cases is strongly supported by the general public. We will go further in drawing on that support by promoting crime prevention. Already more than 29,000 Neighbourhood Watch Schemes have sprung up since the last Election. We are committed to the success of this popular anti-crime movement.

We will build on the support of the public by establishing a national organisation to promote the best practices in local crime prevention initiatives.

We will seek ways to strengthen the special constabulary.

Tackling drug abuse

We have taken the battle against drugs into every corner of the globe where production or trafficking flourishes. We have more than doubled the number of customs specialist drugs investigators. We have strengthened the effectiveness of the police in the fight against drug abuse. Traffickers can now be sentenced to life imprisonment. They also stand to lose all the wealth generated by their evil trade under the most far-reaching asset seizure provisions anywhere in the world.

We have funded about 200 new drug treatment facilities. Our prevention campaign, targetted on youngsters at risk, is encouraging a strong resistance to hard drugs amongst teenagers.

The battle against drugs can and must be won. Already there are some signs that the heroin problem may have passed its peak. The cocaine explosion has never happened. It need never happen.

We will continue to make the defeat of the drug trade a key priority.

Immigration and race relations

Immigration for settlement is now at its lowest level since control of Commonwealth immigration first began in 1962. Firm but fair immigration controls are essential for harmonious and improving community relations.

We will tighten the existing law to ensure that control over settlement becomes even more effective.

We now require visas for visitors from the Indian sub-continent, Nigeria and Ghana, but to protect genuine travellers and to guard against bogus visitors seeking to settle here illegally. We are tackling the problem of those who fraudulently pose as refugees and who seek to exploit Britain's long tradition of giving refuge to the victims of persecution.

We want to see members of the ethnic minorities assuming positions of leadership alongside their fellow citizens and accepting their full share of responsibility. Racial discrimination is an injustice and can have no place in a tolerant and civilised society. We are particularly concerned about racial attacks. They require effective and sympathetic attention from the police, and we have ensured that increasingly they receive it.

Progress towards better community relations must be on a basis of equality. Reverse discrimination is itself an injustice and if it were to be introduced, it would undermine the achievement and example of those who had risen on their merits.

Immigrant communities have already shown that it is possible to play an active and influential role in the mainstream of British life without losing one's distinctive cultural traditions. We also want to see all ethnic minorities participating fully in British culture. They will suffer permanent disadvantage if they remain in linguistic and cultural ghettos.

Reforming the law

Since the last election the Government has made a number of important reforms of family law. These cover the law of maintenance and distribution of property following divorce, measures to prevent the abduction of children and the law of illegitimacy.

Particular laws which are not enforced or which are full of obvious anomalies risk bringing the law itself into disrepute. Changing tastes also require the reform of out-dated laws which govern personal habits and behaviour: such reform should, where possible, be on the basis of a wide consensus.

The present laws on Sunday trading and licensing contain innumerable anomalies. They are frequently flouted.

We will, therefore, look for an acceptable way forward to bring sense and consistency to the law on Sunday trading.

And we will liberalise the laws on liquor licensing hours so as to increase consumer choice, but we will also keep a sensible limit on late-night opening.

We have already extended absent voting rights to new categories of electors. In particular, we have enfranchised British citizens who have lived abroad for less than 5 years.

We propose to extend this eligibility.

Northern Ireland

The British people have shown their commitment to the people of Northern Ireland in the common fight against terrorism, and in helping improve the economic and social situation in the Province. We resolutely support the security forces in their outstanding service to the whole community.

We were determined that terrorism will not succeed; that the vital principles of democracy will be upheld; and that the people of Northern Ireland themselves should determine their constitutional position.

We will maintain, against Socialist opposition, for as long as necessary the special powers which the police need throughout the UK to prevent terrorism and bring terrorists to justice.

There will be no change in the present status of Northern Ireland as part of the United Kingdom unless the people of Northern Ireland so wish it.

That is at the heart of the Anglo-Irish Agreement, which was signed with the Republic of Ireland in 1985. The Agreement offers reassurance to both sides of the community that their identities and interests will be respected, and that any change in the status of Northern Ireland would only come about with the consent of a majority of the people of the Province. It commits both governments to work together in the fight against terrorism.

We will continue to work within the Province for a developed government in which both communities can have confidence and will feel able to participate.

LOCAL GOVERNMENT AND INNER CITIES

The Conservative view of local government is that local people should look after the interests of the local community which they were elected to serve, maintaining and improving essential services at a price people can afford. That is an honourable tradition of public service, still upheld by councillors in most local authorities.

But the abuses of left-wing Labour councils have shocked the nation. The Labour Party leadership pretends that this is a problem in only a few London boroughs. The truth is that the far Left control town halls in many of our cities.

The extremists have gained power in these areas partly because too few ratepayers have an interest in voting for responsible councillors pursuing sensible policies. Many people benefit from local services yet make little or no contribution towards them: this throws too heavy a burden on too few shoulders.

There is much else wrong with the present system of domestic rates. They seem unfair and arbitrary. And companies are left with little protection against huge rate rises levied by councils controlled by Labour, Liberals and Social Democrats, which drive them out of business and destroy jobs.

We have acted to protect ratepayers' interests in a number of ways. The wasteful and unnecessary tier of the GLC and metropolitan counties has been eliminated – to the substantial benefit of rate-payers. Our rate-capping legislation – so bitterly opposed by the Labour, SDP and Liberal parties in Parliament – has protected ratepayers from huge rate increases. This year alone, twenty councils will be rate-capped – nineteen of them Labour and one controlled by the Liberals and the SDP – saving rate-payers several hundred million pounds.

We will now tackle the roots of the problem. We will reform local government finance to strengthen local democracy and accountability.

Local electors must be able to decide the level of service they want and how much they are prepared to pay for it.

We will legislate in the first Session of the new Parliament to abolish the unfair domestic rating system and replace rates with a fairer Community Charge.

This will be a fixed rate charge for local services paid by those over the age of 18, except the mentally ill and elderly people living in homes and hospitals. The less-well-off and students will not have to pay the full charge – but everyone will be aware of the costs as well as the benefits of the local services. This should encourage people to take a greater interest in the policies of their local council and getting value for money. Business rate-payers will pay a Unified Business Rate at a standard rate pegged to inflation.

We will require local authorities to put out to tender a range of services, including refuse collection, the cleaning of streets and buildings, vehicle maintenance, catering and ground maintenance.

Ratepayers expect councils to provide their services as efficiently as possible. Yet some local authorities steadfastly oppose private sector companies tendering for services even though they could provide them more cheaply and more effectively. The independent Audit Commission has estimated that some £500 million a year could be saved if all councils followed the practices of the best – sums which could be used to lower rates or improve services.

The Widdicombe Report into the conduct of local authority business painted a disturbing picture of the breakdown of democratic processes in a number of councils. We will take action to strengthen democratic processes in local authorities.

Inner cities

The regeneration of the inner cities must be tackled. The growth in our national prosperity in recent years has been founded on a rebirth of enterprise. But in many of our inner cities the conditions for enterprise and pride of ownership have been systematically extinguished by Socialist councils. For the sake of those living in our inner cities we must remove the barriers against private investment, jobs and prosperity which such councils have erected.

We are setting up five new Urban Development Corporations which will have the powers, resources, and management structure to reclaim and redevelop great tracts of derelict land: these new Corporations will follow the model successfully applied in London Docklands and on Merseyside.

Our Unified Business Rate will ensure that companies and jobs are are not driven out of inner city areas by the high rates of profligate councils.

We have roughly doubled the resources to reclaim derelict land. We will improve procedures to accelerate the process of bringing vacant and under-used public sector land back into productive use.

We will build on the experience of Urban Development Corporations by creating new mini-UDCs. These will operate on a smaller scale in areas where there is clear economic potential, but where the local authorities are failing to tackle the problem.

Our Urban Programme provides a range of grants to help industry and local councils undertake projects that will improve the environment and encourage new investment.

We are helping to lead local action through our five City Action Teams, sixteen Inner City Task Forces and the Inner City Partnerships. All of them draw on government assistance and work with local business and local people to promote enterprise, employment and training.

Great cities are built on the enterprise and vitality of the individuals who live there. Our aim is to create a climate which encourage and harnesses that energy in the interest of all.

A BETTER SOCIETY
Planning and the environment

Conservatives are by instinct conservationists – committed to preseve all that is best of our country's past. We are determined to maintain our national heritage of countryside and architecture. Since taking office we have:

● more than doubled the area of specially protected Green Belt: we will continue to defend it against unsuitable development;

● established new arrangements, backed with public funds, to make farming more sensitive to wildlife and to conservation;

● completed the work of listing pre-war buildings which receive legal protection and extended such protection to the best post-war buildings;

● established a new, powerful Pollution Inspectorate;

● passed new laws on the control of pesticides and implemented new controls on the pollution of water;

● put in hand plans for cleaning up Britain's beaches, costing over £300 million over the next four years;

● more than doubled spending after allowing for inflation on countryside and nature conservation since 1979;

● set in hand the establishment of the new Norfolk Broads Authority – a major environmental initiative;

● established a huge programme, costing over £4,000 million, to clean up the environment of the Mersey Basin by the early years of the next century.

We are determined to maintain the Green Belt. We will protect the countryside for its own sake and conserve its wildlife, while allowing for those small scale and well planned developments which are needed to provide jobs and keep country areas thriving.

Wherever possible we want to encourage large-scale developments to take place on unused and neglected land in our towns and cities rather than in the countryside. We want to improve on our performance in 1986 when nearly half of all new development took place on reused land.

A practical agenda

Only the Conservatives have a serious costed agenda for further environmental action for another five years of Government. We will:

continue our £600 million programme of modifying power stations, to combat acid rain;

adopt improved standards, in concert with Europe, for reducing pollution from cars. We have already reduced tax on lead-free petrol and will encourage its wider use;

introduce new laws on air pollution and dangerous wastes;

double the funding for Environmentally Sensitive Areas;

introduce new laws giving extra protection to the landscape of our National Parks;

encourage more small woodlands in lowland areas through new grants;

legislate to safeguard common land on the basis of the Common Land Forum, and continue to protect public access to the countryside through footpaths;

support scientifically justified, international action to protct the atmosphere and the sea from damage from pollutants;

establish a National Rivers Authority to take over responsibilities for ensuring strict safeguards against the pollution of rivers and water courses and to pursue sound conservation policies. The water supply and sewage functions of the water authorities will be transferred to the private sector;

set up safe facilities for disposing of radioactive waste from power stations, hospitals and other sources: we have aksd UK NIREX to come forward with proposals for deep disposal.

The arts

Our international reputation in the arts has never been higher. Tourists flock to this country to enjoy the highest standard of theatre, music, artistic excellence and our museums. Art centres have nearly doubled in number since 1979. Attendances at theatres, concerts, cinemas and historic houses have all risen significantly.

Under the Conservatives, spending on the arts has risen by 15 per cent since 1979 after allowing for inflation. Over the same period, the Arts Council grant has risen from £61 million to nearly £139 million. And schemes like the Business Sponsorship Incentive Scheme have pushed the value of such sponsorship from £½ million to £25 million over the last decade.

In future years:

We will maintain government support for the arts and continue to encourage private support.

We will make it a major objective to ensure that excellence in the arts is available in all parts of the country.

We will continue to safeguard our heritage, particularly through the National Heritage Memorial Fund, created by this Government in 1980 to assist the preservation, maintenance and acquisition of items of outstanding merit which might otherwise be lost to the nation.

We will encourage our great national museums and galleries to make the national treasures which they house more widely accessible.

Sport

We have increased funding for the Sports Council from £15 million in 1978/79 to £37 million in 1987/88.

We will continue to work with the Council and through our funding of the Sports Council National Centres, we will encourage the pursuit of excellence in our sports.

We want to encourage competitive sports through schools and clubs and we strongly oppose any attempts to ban competitive sports in schools.

We will continue to encourage schools and colleges to open their facilities for community use wherever possible to co-operate with other owners to achieve public access to sport premises.

Football hooliganism has tarnished the good name of British sportsmanship. We have acted to control the sale of alcohol at sports grounds. We have enhanced police powers to stop and search at football grounds and we have encouraged tougher sentencing of hooligans.

Broadcasting

Our objectives for broadcasting are to provide consumers with a wider range of programmes, to encourage independent producers, and to preserve the high standards which we have traditionally enjoyed in British broadcasting.

Vital decisions will need to be made in the next Parliament. We have already published proposals for a less regulated and more diverse radio system. We shall follow a policy of more competition, variety and innovation in our domestic networks and encourage the export of British programmes to international audiences and markets. The development of the broadcasting industry will be allowed to occur, wherever possible, commercially.

We will therefore introduce a major new Broadcasting Bill in the new Parliament. It will enable the broadcasters to take full advantage of the opportunities presented by technological advances and to broaden the choice of viewing and listening.

The broadcasters owe it to the lively talent in the independent sector to take more programmes from them.

We will ensure that at least 25 per cent of programmes broadcast on both ITV and BBC will be supplied by independent producers as soon as possible.

The responsibility for enforcing broadcasting standards must rest with the broadcasting authorities. The present Broadcasting Complaints Commission has a relatively narrow remit. But there is deep public concern over the display of sex and violence on television. We will therefore bring forward proposals for stronger and more effective arrangements to reflect that concern.

We will remove the current exemption enjoyed by broadcasters under the Obscene Publications Act 1959.

BRITAIN AND THE WORLD
Britain is once again giving a lead in world affairs. We are forthright in support of freedom and justice. We stand up vigorously for Britain's interests abroad. Our voice is heard with respect on the crucial issues of war and peace, of finance and trade.

Defending the nation
The first duty of government is the defence of the realm and the preservation of peace. Nuclear weapons are vital to that task. In the 40 years since 1945, more than 10 million people have died in wars around the globe. But there has been peace in Europe.

Conventional weapons did not succeed in deterring war. But nuclear weapons have prevented, not only nuclear war, but conventional war in Europe as well. A strong defence policy has proved to be the most effective peace policy.

Labour's policy is to give up Britain's independent nuclear deterrent without asking anything in return. The Labour Party would require the United States to withdraw its nuclear weapons from our soil and to close down Nato nuclear bases in Britain. It would remove Britain altogether from the protection of the United States' nuclear umbrella.

That policy would abandon the defence policy followed by every British government, Labour or Conservative since the Second World War. It would expose us to nuclear blackmail from the vast Soviet armoury, to which we would have no reply. It would inflict damage, perhaps fatal damage, on the Atlantic Alliance on which we and Western Europe depend for our security. It would strike at our relations with our most important ally, weakening the American commitment to Europe's defences. It would, in short, be the biggest victory for the Soviet Union in 40 years.

The defence policy of the Liberals and Social Democrats is muddled and confused. They would cancel Trident and they have no clear idea of what to put in its place. Their suggested replacements are much more expensive than Trident, which costs only 3p in every £ of defence spending. None would be available in time. None would provide equal security.

The Liberal and SDP defence policy would be one-sided disarmament by default or inadvertence. The only difference between it and Labour policy is a matter of timing. Labour would scrap Britain's deterrent immediately upon entering office. The Liberals and Social Democrats would allow it to wither on the vine.

Only the Conservative Party stands by the defence policy which every post-war government has seen to be necessary and which has kept the peace of Europe for more than a generation. We are not prepared to take risks with Britain's security.

We will stand fully by our obligations to our European and American allies in Nato.

We will retain our independent nuclear deterrent and modernise it with Trident. Because of improvements in Soviet defences we need a greater capability of Trident to retain the necessary deterrence which Polaris gives. No amount of money spent on conventional defence would ever buy us the same degree of deterrence.

We will continue to increase the effectiveness of our conventional forces, to provide them with the most modern equipment and to obtain better value for money from the defence budget. We have already increased defence spending by more than 20 per cent in real terms since 1979 and restored the pay and conditions of our servicemen.

But we also want to see a world in which there are fewer nuclear weapons. That is why Britain is at the forefront of arms control negotiations.

We will strive with our allies to achieve balanced and verifiable agreements for:
the elimination of medium-range nuclear missiles in Europe and preferably world-wide;
agreed constraints on shorter-range missiles;
a 50 per cent cut in strategic nuclear missiles;
and a world-wide ban on chemical weapons.

Western strength and resolution are essential to achieve these aims. That is why the Conservative Government deployed Cruise missiles. All the Opposition parties – Labour, Liberals and SDP – voted against deployment in the House of Commons. Yet it was the deployment of Cruise and Pershing missiles which brought the Soviet Union back to the negotiating table. We can look forward to an agreement this year which will, for the first time, reduce the numbers of nuclear weapons.

With the Conservatives Britain is also taking the lead in working towards greater trust and confidence between East and West, and to encourage changes in the East, where disillusion with totalitarian Socialism grows inexorably. The Prime Minister's historic visit to Moscow was a major contribution to this. We shall welcome any move by the Soviet Union towards respect for basic human rights. But we must not lower our guard. Strong defence is still the surest foundation for building peace.

Europe grows in strength

This Government has taken Britain from the sidelines into the mainstream of Europe. But being good Europeans does not prevent us from standing up for British interests. The agreement we negotiated on the Community Budget has saved Britain £4,500 million since 1984.

We will continue to work for strict controls on the Community Budget.

Britain has led the way in establishing a genuine common market, with more trade and services moving freely across national boundaries.

We will campaign for the opening of the market in financial and other services and the extension of cheaper air fares in Europe.

We will also continue to work with our European partners to defend our own trading interests and press for freer trade among all nations.

All of this will help safeguard existing jobs and create new ones.

We will continue to play a responsible leading role in the development of the Community, while safeguarding our essential national interests.

Firm against terrorism and aggression

Britain has stood at the forefront in the fight against international terrorism. No democracy has a better record than Britain in standing up to the terrorists, who threaten the most basic values of civilised life.

We will seek the support of other democratic nations for the provisions of the European Convention on the Suppression of Terrorism.

We stood up to aggression in the Falklands and would do so again, if necessary. We want normal relations with Argentina. We have made numerous proposals to that end. But we stand by our pledges to the Islanders. We will not negotiate on the sovereignty of the Falklands.

The wider world

When other countries are prepared to act in good faith, the Conservative Government has shown the will and the diplomatic skill to find solutions to age-old conflicts and misunderstandings. Our record of tackling longstanding problems in Hong Kong, Zimbabwe, and Gibraltar demonstrates our determination to seek peaceful and imaginative settlements of difficult international disputes. We have played a prominent part in bringing Israel and the moderate Arab states closer to peace negotiations in the framework of an international conference.

We believe that the issues of Southern Africa, too, will be tackled best by dialogue, not violence. We want to see an end to apartheid in South Africa. But trade and economic sanctions would only serve to entrench apartheid, increase the risk of bloodshed, and inflict severe hardship on black South Africans without bringing a settlement any nearer. Negotiations between the leaders of the South African people are the best way to resolve the problems of that unhappy country.

Overseas aid

We have the sixth largest aid programme in the western world, and the third largest in Europe, spending about £1,300 million each year. Britain pioneered the reform of Europe's food aid policy, to make it more rapid and effective. We have substantially increased our support for the disaster, famine and refugee relief activities of voluntary agencies, as well as for their long-term development work. We have led the way in giving help to the people of Ethiopia, ravaged by famine. Our "Aid and Trade Provision" funds have helped win good development contracts for British firms worth over £2 billion since 1979.

We will maintain our substantial aid programme and direct it ever more effectively.

We will bring more young people from Commonwealth and other countries to train and study in Britain.

We ourselves have made positive and practical proposals for international action to help some of the poorest and most indebted countries of sub-Saharan Africa.

Labour's proposal of selective import controls would damage developing countries, open the door to protectionism, and harm those poorest countries which most need our help. It would also be bad for Britain. The best contribution Britain can make to developing countries is to champion open trade and free enterprise abroad and to practise them at home.

A fateful choice

For decades there was basic agreement between political parties on defence and foreign policy. That agreement was firmly in the national interest. It has been torn up by our opponents.

Labour's policy would mean not a secure Britain, but a neutralist Britain. And eventually – for there can be no trifling with Soviet power – a frightened and fellow-travelling Britain. The Liberals and Social Democrats would take us more slowly down that same disastrous road.

This election matters more for our safety and freedom than any election since the Second World War.

CONCLUSION: THE WAY FORWARD

The proposals outlined in this manifesto are the extension of policies which have already proved outstandingly successful.

Today Britain is a stable and well-governed country which exercises great influence in the world.

We seek the support of the British people to make the achievement truly secure, to build upon it and to extend its benefits to all.

No previous government with eight years of office to its credit has ever presented the electorate with such a full programme of radical reform.

No other party, presenting its manifesto proposals to the nation, has been able to support them with such a solid record of achievement.

We commend them with confidence to the British people.

'Britain Will Win'

INTRODUCTION by Mr Neil Kinnock, leader of the Labour Party

Every election is a time of decision. But this General Election on June 11 faces the British people with choices more sharp than at any time in the past fifty years.

The choices are between Labour's programme of work for people and Tory policies of waste of people: between investment in industrial strength, and acceptance of industrial decline; between a Britain with competitive, modern industries, and a Britain with a low tech, low paid, low security economy increasingly dependent upon imports.

The election will decide whether we and our children are to live in a country that builds high standards of care for all who need treatment for illness, pensions in retirement, good grounding in education, fair chances to get on; or in a country where the Conservatives go on running down the vital health, education and social services of every community, imposing higher charges and lower standards.

This election will decide whether our country is to be a United Kingdom or a divided kingdom; one that is brought together by proper provision, prudent investment and concern for the interests of the whole nation, or one that is pulled apart by poverty, cuts, increased privilege for the richest and neglect for the rest.

This election will decide whether we put our resources into the real defence provided by a modern, well-equipped army, navy and airforce safeguarding our country and supporting Nato; or spend those sums on maintaining an ageing system of nuclear weapons, while buying a new generation of missiles which cannot give our country effective defence. It will decide whether Britain is part of the international process of nuclear build-down or ruled by a government uniquely intent upon nuclear build-up.

We already know what a third term for Mrs Thatcher would mean for the people of Britain.

Under the Tories there have been:

● Eight years of record unemployment, relentless industrial closures and redundancies, of flooding imports and shrunken investment.

● Eight years of the highest ever tax burden on the family and the nation as VAT, National Insurance, rates and fees have all been put up in a shift to taxes on spending and employment.

● Eight years of cuts and closures and charges, of intensified means tests and reduced services.

● Eight years of increased state control, of centralising government, of abolition of rights of representation and negotiation.

● Eight years of rising crime, of greater insecurity on the streets and housing estates and in the home.

● Eight years of meanness towards the needy in our country and towards the wretched of the world.

● Eight years of growing division — in health, in opportunity, in housing conditions, in work and in income — between regions, communities, classes, families, white and black, rich and poor.

The Tories say they are "proud of their record". So proud indeed that they would want to do more of the same if they were re-elected.

Their plans for a poll tax would penalise millions of families, pensioners and young people. Their refusal to provide the resources needed for the Health Service and their plans for imposing further payment and privatisation will hit everyone in the service and everyone needing to use it.

They would, if they won power again, privatise water, electricity, steel and other services, and industries built up by public investment over past years. They want to impose penal increases in rents for private and public tenants. They are committed to introducing compulsory labour for young unemployed people.

All this and worse would come with a third term of Tory government. Britain cannot afford more of that run-down, sell-off and split-up, nor all the costs and waste that they bring. Britain does not have to. Britain can stop the rot — but only by voting Labour. There is no other way to prevent thirteen years of Thatcherism.

No party other than Labour can possibly win enough seats to form a government. The Liberals and SDP know that. Their hope is to profit from confusion. To divide the non-Conservative vote in such a way as to make them the "hook" in a "hung" Parliament and have power far beyond their responsibility. And, while one of their leaders clearly favours an arrangement to sustain a Conservative government, the other hasn't the strength to stop him. That offers no way ahead for a nation that needs to get on with investing for change, for quality, for confidence in the future.

Proper support for education, strengthened research and development and long-term, low interest finance for industrial growth are all essential if Britain is to gain the vitality necessary to outpace competitors who have been building these assets for years.

They are essential, too, if we are to generate the wealth needed for the security, care and opportunity fundamental to the individual freedom of women and men of all ages and origins. When our country faces the common pressures on the environment, the common dangers of crime, the common costs of unemployment, under-investment and under-performance together, our country has every common sense reason to meet those challenges together.

That is democratic socialism in action. And just as a family uses its combined spirit and resources to overcome crisis, so Britain can once again make common cause to achieve common good.

Only a Labour government can give that lead. Only we are committed to such concerted action. Only we believe that the whole nation should win and can win.

That is why Britain will win, with Labour.

BRITAIN WILL WIN

Britain is crying out for change. Only a Labour government can bring it about. Mending divisions, building new strengths will need determination and realistic priorities. Commonsense and the common interest require that the Tory philosophy of selfishness and short-term gain is replaced by the democratic socialist philosophy of community and caring, of investment in people and in production.

We must as a priority tackle the immediate tragedy and waste of unemployment. We must commit resources to modernising and strengthening the industries and services that earn Britain a living. We must ensure the continuity of expansion that is necessary for a lasting economic recovery. That is our strategy.

It begins from the understanding that people are Britain's most precious resource. It is rooted and in the confidence that, with the right skills, the right equipment and the backing of a government that is committed to encouraging enterprise and innovation, Britain's people can make our country more efficient, more competitive and more socially just. It is a message of hope and confidence – the alternative to the divisive and dictatorial approach of the Conservatives.

We do not believe that everything could or should be done by government. But we know, from our own history and from the example set by our competitors, that national economic success cannot be achieved without government.

Britain will win with a Labour government that invests to enable people to use their abilities and to stimulate modern training, research, development, production and marketing. These are the ingredients of economic vitality, and the foundations of fairness.

THE PRIORITY PROGRAMME

For our first two years in government we will concentrate resources on the essential tasks of combating unemployment and poverty. In the course of that action, we will strengthen the health, housing, education, social services and crime-fighting services that are vital to social and economic well-being, and begin to rebuild our manufacturing industry.

Clearly, all other programmes that require substantial public finance must take lower priority in terms of timescale and public resources.

THE JOBS PROGRAMME

Immediately after the election the Labour Government will call together a National Economic Summit to assess fully the condition of the economy and set the recovery programme in motion – producing the jobs that need to be done by people who need to do them in a country that wants them done.

The Summit will establish the first stage of the National Economic Assessment. This will identify the concerted action that will need to be taken by government, employers in the private and public sectors and trade unions to increase investment, contain inflation and achieve sustained recovery.

We will reduce unemployment by one million in two years as the first instalment in beating mass unemployment.

Half a million jobs will be generated in private industry and in the public sector by the repairing and building of the houses, the hospitals and schools, the transport improvements and sewers that the nation needs. This will be achieved by public investment and by reducing employers' National Insurance contribution in targeted areas.

Another 360,000 new jobs and training places will be created. These will provide new skills for young people and adults – with proper opportunities for women.

A further 300,000 new jobs will improve the health and education services and the neglected community and caring services. The depleted customs services will be strengthened in the fight against drugs. The revenue and benefit departments will be staffed to increase efficiency.

We will extend the voluntary Job Release Scheme to men over 60 so that those who want to retire early vacate jobs for those who are currently unemployed. This could take as many as 160,000 people out of unemployment and into work.

THE ANTI-POVERTY PROGRAMME

The spread of poverty in the past eight years has stained the whole nation, and widened misery and disadvantage amongst old and young. Much of it is the result of deliberate government policies. Millions of poor people endure it in despair. Millions who are not poor regard it as a disgrace. The Labour government will combat poverty directly.

We will immediately increase the single pension by £5 a week and the pension for a married couple by £8, as the first step in re-establishing a link between pensions and average earnings or living costs, whichever is the most favourable to pensioners. We will begin the abolition of the TV licence fee for pensioners.

We will provide pensioners on supplementary benefit and others on low incomes with a £5 winter premium to help with fuel bills. We will begin discussions with the fuel industries with a view to phasing out standing charges.

We will fully restore the State Earnings Related Pension Scheme as part of the process of achieving our objective of a pensions level of one-third average earnings for single people and half average earnings for married couples.

We will restore and increase the death grant.

We will increase child benefit by £3 a week for all children, raise the allowance to the first by £7.36 and increase one-parent family benefit by £2.20.

We will restore and increase the maternity grant.

We will start to phase in a new disability income scheme and provide resources to give special support to young people with disabilities. Our special Minister for the Disabled will be put in charge of our programme for the disabled.

We will extend the long-term supplementary benefit rate to the long-term unemployed.

We will implement a comprehensive strategy for ending low pay, notably by the introduction of a statutory national minimum wage. This will be of particular benefit to women workers, and will help lift families out of poverty.

THE ANTI-CRIME PROGRAMME
We will introduce crime prevention for home-owners and tenants.

We will work with the police to get more police on the beat. Uniformed police officers will be relieved of non-law-and-order tasks which take them away from crime prevention, pursuit and detection.

We will reverse the Tory cuts in the number of those who can claim criminal injuries compensation. We will give the Criminal Injuries Compensation Board more staff to cut the all-time record 64,000 queue awaiting compensation.

PAYING FOR THE RECOVERY PROGRAMME
These immediate programmes will cost £6 billion a year net for the first two years.

We will pay for them by:

● Putting directly into generating 300,000 jobs the money that would be used up by the Thatcher government on its 2p income tax bribe.

● Adopting the same practice as most successful industrial countries and companies, by prudently borrowing £3 billion for useful wealth generating national investment.

We will reverse the extra tax cuts which the richest 5 per cent have received from the Tory government and allocate that money instead to the most needy. We will also bring forward other reforms to capital taxation – including the introduction of a wealth tax, which, whilst applying to only the wealthiest one per cent of the population, will, over the years, bring a significant contribution from those in our society best able to pay.

CHANGES WITHOUT CHARGES
Apart from legislating where necessary for the Recovery Programme, the new Parliament will swiftly enact many other worthwhile measures. These will cost little to implement but produce significant improvement in the quality of administration, provision and response to the needs of ordinary citizens.

They will include:

● A Minister for Women, with a place in the Cabinet.

● A Freedom of Information Act, to be accompanied by the repeal of Section Two of the Official Secrets Act.

● Parliamentary scrutiny of the Security Services.

● Appointment of an Education Ombudsman

● Appointment of an Ombudsman for Police Complaints.

● An Energy Efficiency Agency to co-ordinate conservation programmes for domestic and industrial energy users.

● A new Ministry of Environmental Protection.

PROGRAMME FOR A FIVE-YEAR PARLIAMENT
Labour's Programme for Recovery will be the start of a strategy for a full Parliament. We have to halt the decline in manufacturing industry, not only to generate jobs and increase our world trade share but to create the wealth to finance the rescue and expansion of education, health, housing and the social services.

NEW STRENGTH FOR INDUSTRY
For eight years British industry has been left to drift and decline. Our oil revenues have been wasted and the City has concentrated upon short-term movements of capital at the expense of British manufacturing industry. The huge capital outflow of £110 billion since 1979 is ruinous evidence of the Tories' lack of

concern for the strength of the British economy.

Labour is committed to rebuilding our industrial base. Our country must make the best use of computers and information technology to develop the modern means of making a living as the oil runs down and the pressures of technical change and international competition intensify.

We will:

● Establish a capital repatriation scheme using the tax system to attract and retain British savings and investment in Britain.

● Set up the British Industrial Investment Bank, with strong bases in Scotland, Wales and English regions, to ensure finance for industry where it is needed, when it is needed and on terms which encourage long term development.

● Implement a dynamic and properly funded regional policy. This will include the establishment of Regional Development Agencies (starting with the North, North-West, Yorkshire and Humberside); the promotion of local and regional enterprise boards; greater scope for local authorities to participate constructively in economic development; and creating high technology innovation centres throughout Britain.

● Create a new Ministry of Science and Technology to promote a major increase in research and development.It will co-ordinate the activities and budgets of government departments involved in these areas and will encourage, in conjunction with industry and the scientific community, the full application of science to industrial processes and products.

● We shall extend social ownership by a variety of means, as set out in Labour's detailed proposals. In particular, we will set up British Enterprise, to take a socially owned stake in high-tech industries and other concerns where public funds are used to strengthen investment.

Social ownership of basic utilities like gas and water is vital to ensure that every individual has access to their use and that the companies contribute to Britain's industrial recovery, for instance, by buying British. We shall start by using the existing 49 per cent holding in British Telecom to ensure proper influence in their decisions. Private shares in BT and British Gas will be converted into special new securities. These will be bought and sold in the market in the usual way and will carry either a guaranteed return, or dividends linked to the company's growth.

● Encourage the establishment and success of co-operatives of all forms.

● Strengthen the Department of Trade and Industry as the spearhead of this new national industrial strategy.

● Bring in a stronger regulatory framework to ensure honest practice in the City of London and introduce new safeguards on mergers, takeovers and monopolies to protect our national industrial, technological and research and development interests.

PLAN FOR TRAINING

For modern, wealth-creating industry we need a well-trained workforce. British industry now carries out less than half of the training of our main competitors. Labour will therefore establish a national training programme to bring about a major advance in the spread and standard of skills.

For young people we will establish an integrated, high quality Foundation Programme that will guarantee for all 16 year olds at least two years of education, training and work experience according to their needs.

The Adult Skillplan will develop lifelong training and education for everyone needing to supplement and update skills in work, with particular emphasis given to training for women.

The Jobs, Enterprise and Training Programme will expand existing programmes for unemployed people with a guarantee of a job or new skill for the long-term unemployed.

A SENSIBLE ENERGY POLICY

Efficiency in industry and security in the community both depend on reliable and safe supplies of energy available at acceptable cost. Britain's oil reserves have a limited life. We have huge reserves of coal which will last for centuries. Labour's co-ordinated energy programme will ensure the most sensible use of our reserves while protecting our environment and stimulating employment.

Labour will initiate a major energy conservation programme and ensure that Britain develops the full potential of its coal, oil and gas resources, whilst gradually diminishing Britain's dependence upon nuclear energy.

We will invest substantially in research into, and development of, the renewable energy resources as part of the alternative means of power.

We will not proceed with the building of the proposed Pressurised Water Reactor at Sizewell.

We share national concern about the problem of nuclear waste. We will ensure a safe future for Sellafield and develop a new strategy for the monitoring, storage and disposal of nuclear waste.

Labour will take effective steps to improve the service provided by the energy industry to energy consumers. These will cover quality of supply, frequency of metering, general service arrangements and proper provision for the disabled, those in poverty and others with special needs.

A PROSPEROUS AGRICULTURE

A more efficient agricultural industry can clearly make a valuable contribution to Britain's recovery. We will support good environmental practices in agriculture.

To give Britain's producers the backing they need, the burden of agricultural support must be shifted from consumers. The direction of support must be shifted away from blanket support for commodities, towards helping the farmers who need it most, such as those who work in the hills or on marginal land. To help bring this about we will introduce new, long-term programmes for agriculture.

We will also help new farmers and young farmers by offering farms to rent. And we will reverse the cuts in the Agricultural Development and Advisory Service and research.

FREEDOM AND FAIRNESS FOR ALL BRITAIN'S PEOPLE

We are determined to make Britain a fairer and freer society.

To us and to the majority of the British people a civilised community is one in which citizens band together to provide, out of community resources to which all contribute, essential services like health, education and pensions that the great majority of people can not afford to provide for themselves at time of need.

When the Tories talk of freedom, they mean freedom for the few, for those who can afford to buy privilege. What they mean, as their record so plainly shows, is more tax cuts for the rich and less help for the poor and for the great majority who are neither rich nor poor.

Labour's objective is to broaden and deepen the liberty of all individuals in our community; to free people from poverty, exploitation and fear; to free them to realise their full potential; to see that everyone has the liberty to enjoy real chances, to make real choices.

It means collective provision for private use. The British people know that this is the most effective way for them to secure their freedom as individuals whilst meeting the moral obligations which they feel towards others and seeing that fairness is a way of national life, not just a fine word.

These values are the essence of our democratic socialism.

INVESTING IN HEALTH

Labour's proudest achievement is the creation of the National Health Service. The Conservatives voted against it then. All who use and value the service know only too well how it has been neglected and downgraded by today's Tories.

Labour will establish the NHS in its rightful place as a high quality service for the prevention and treatment of illness, free at the time of use to all who need attention, equipped to meet the changing pressures of need as they relate, for instance, to an ageing population and the requirements of proper provision for people suffering from mental illness.

The biggest single deficiency in the NHS today is the excessively high hospital waiting lists which, under the Tories, are increasing year by year. We shall speedily reduce them by computerising bed allocation, encouraging more consultants to work full-time for the NHS and targeting increased resources where waiting lists remain excessive.

The basis of the NHS is the Family Doctor Service. We shall act to improve it, with shorter GP patient lists, more convenient surgery hours, more choice and information for patients. We will develop local family health care teams and more local health centres.

Women's health care has been seriously neglected. Our Charter for Womens' Health will include a network of Well-Women Clinics, and a computerised call and recall screening system as a universal service for all women at risk of cervical and breast cancer. We shall see that all women have the chance to see a woman doctor if they choose.

We will step up the fight against AIDS by increasing research resources to find a vaccine or cure and also ensure adequate resources for the supply of drugs capable of arresting the affliction.

We will improve outpatient and emergency facilities and ambulance services and repair and build hospitals. We intend to improve both the quantity and quality of services for the National Health. The Tories have increased prescription charges twelve fold. We will begin to reduce them with the purpose of securing their eventual abolition.

Labour will ensure that nurses get proper and justified pay increases by right and regularly, not exceptionally as pre-election sweeteners. Other hospital staff, on whom the effective running of the service depends, must also be fairly rewarded as part of the effective health team.

Privatisation means a Health Service run for profit rather than in the patients' interests. Labour will end privatisation in the NHS, relieve the pressure on NHS facilities by beginning to phase out pay beds and remove public subsidies to private health.

A CARING COMMUNITY

The quality of life of the elderly and of disabled people can and must be improved by community services. We believe that retirement should be comfortable and interesting – a time of freedom and choice, not anxiety and loneliness. We believe that disability should not be a disqualification from good standards of living and liberty.

Apart from our commitment to higher pensions and the beginning of a new disablement allowance, Labour will support the National Health Service and local government in providing more meals on wheels, home helps, chiropody services and health visitors.

We also recognise the immense contribution of the three million people – mostly women – who care for their elderly, infirm and disabled relatives at home. They save the community huge sums of money, often at considerable sacrifice to themselves. The Labour government will consequently provide a carer's allowance to give extra help to those who serve their loved ones and our society so well.

We appreciate and will support voluntary efforts that supplement services which are essential to the community. We share the view of many who are engaged in such efforts that they achieve best results working in the context of high quality public provision.

EDUCATION FOR BRITAIN'S FUTURE

Our children are our future. We have a moral and material duty to see that children and young people are fully equipped to deal with the complexities and challenges which face them now and which they will meet as citizens; parents and workers in the future.

They must be provided with a system of education that enables them to control that future. We must see that it is democratic and just, that it is creative and compassionate, and that it is one in which they can fully exploit the advantages of science and technology with confidence and in safety.

In pursuit of those objectives, Labour will invest in education so that the abilities of all children and adults from all home backgrounds and in every part of our country are discovered and nourished.

We will make nursery education available for all three-and four-year-olds whose parents want this opportunity. We will make provision for smaller classes and ensure that children have up-to-date books, equipment and buildings without having to depend on fund-raising for those essentials.

The entitlement to free school meals and the restoration of nutritional standards are, like the strengthening of the school health service, commitments which are necessary to safeguard the physical and social wellbeing of growing children.

We will see that teachers are recognised properly as well qualified professionals, in their systems of rewards, in the procedures for negotiation of their employment conditions and in participation in the development of education.

In addition we shall work with local education authorities to secure a flexible but clear core curriculum agreed at national level, a School Standards Council, and a new profile of achievement recording individual progress through school for all pupils. We will improve links between schools and home so that parents and teachers act in partnership to foster the best interests of children.

We shall foster achievement with other policies such as providing proper funding for the GCSE curriculum and examination, for improved supply of teachers and equipment for science subjects so that girls as well as boys increase science learning. There will be maintenance allowances for 16 to 18-year-olds whose family circumstances would otherwise impede their further education.

We will spread the provision of a comprehensive tertiary system of post-school education.

These policies will all contribute to raising standards of performance in schools. At the same time as we improve the quality of publicly provided education, we shall end the 11 plus everywhere and stop the diverting of precious resources that occurs through the Assisted Places Scheme and the public subsidies to private schools.

Labour values the research and teaching contribution made by Britain's higher education system. We will ensure that our universities and polytechnics get the resources they need to restore and expand the opportunity for all qualified young people seeking higher education to secure places. We will ensure that more adults have access to higher education to give them the "second chance" of personal development.

We will also invest in research in higher education, in order to provide the facilities and opportunities necessary to sustain standards of excellence, to retain and attract the highest talents and to encourage the industrial and commercial application of research output.

Education for life through a well-funded adult education services will help to provide the means by which rapid economic and social change can be embraced.

REAL CHOICE IN HOUSING

Public funding for housing has fallen by 60 per cent during Mrs Thatcher's eight years in office. Far fewer homes are being built. Millions of dwellings are in serious disrepair. Yet there is record unemployment among building workers. This policy is immoral and grossly inefficient. Labour will reverse it. We will also improve the quality of housing workmanship and establish a new system of registration in the construction industry.

We will launch a major housebuilding and public and private sector housing renovation drive as part of our jobs programme and to combat the problems of bad housing, overcrowding and homelessness. Owner-occupiers will benefit from increased availability of improvement grants.

We will maintain mortgage tax relief, at the standard rate of income tax. To assist house-purchasers we will introduce a housing "log book", giving each dwelling's history, condition and construction so that purchasers will know exactly what they are buying. This will be transferred with the sale.

For council tenants, we will maintain the right to buy. Local authorities, at present limited by the Tories in using the receipts from council house sales, will be required to use these proceeds to invest in new housing. For the millions who choose to remain council tenants, we will give a legal right to be consulted about rents, charges, repair and improvement programmes. Tenants' associations will be given representation in the decision-making structure and a say in spending budgets on their estates.

Groups of tenants who want to take over the running of their homes will have the right to set up management co-operatives.

Leaseholders who own their homes will be given the legal right to acquire their freeholds at fair prices and without the costly current impediments to that right. Leaseholders in flats will get the legal right to hire and fire the managing agents in block of flats. They will be empowered to have the freeholder's accounts examined by an auditor of their choice and be given the legal right to extend their lease.

Security of tenure will be protected for private tenants. These tenants will be given a legal right to get repairs done.

PROTECTING OUR PEOPLE

The Thatcher government has broken its promises on law and order. Last year 4,311,000 crimes were committed in Britain. The clear-up rate fell to 32 per cent. Millions of women are scared to go out at night. Many old people lock themselves into their homes. Drug trafficking is increasing.

Labour will take urgent action to make people safer. Our crime prevention programme will:

● Help local councils to implement a Safer Streets policy, with more street-lighting, more caretakers, park-keepers and other public employees whose presence deters crime.

● Bring in a Safe Estates Policy, assisting councils to provide stronger locks, stouter doors and vandal-proof windows for tenants and home-owners — especially older citizens — who have difficulty in meeting the costs of such security improvements.

● Introduce a Safer Transport policy, to protect passengers and crews, including better services, especially at night, adequate staffing, better sited bus stops and well-lit stations with alarm buttons.

● Lay down crime prevention standards for buildings, open spaces and vehicles to combat vandalism and to deter criminals.

● Combat violence against women — specially domestic violence — by seeing that the laws that already exist against beating and abuse are vigorously enforced.

Our victim support programme will fund a national network of victim support schemes, providing practical help to victims of all crime, ranging from victims of rape and child abuse to mugging and burglary victims.

We shall assist family and support groups in their efforts to work with professionals in the health, education and other services and within the community to deal with the great and growing problem of drug abuse.

Locally elected police authorities will be given clear statutory responsibility with the police to enforce the law and uphold the Queen's peace. The police themselves will remain responsible for all operational matters.

Fraud in the City of London is a serious crime. Too many get away with it. Labour will bring in effective regulation by establishing an independent statutory commission.

MAKING TRAVEL EASIER

Efficient, inexpensive public transport is essential in any society. Tory policies have made travel more difficult by cutting services and pushing up fares. Deregulation of buses has brought chaos to many parts of the country both in towns and cities and in the rural areas where efficient and cheap public transport is so important.

Labour will invest to co-ordinate and improve bus and rail services, which will improve travel and reduce congestion. There will be Local Transport Plans for every area.

Action will be taken to keep fares down. There will be good concessionary fare schemes for local travel for pensioners and people with disabilities.

We shall promote services for those with special needs, such as dial-a-ride and taxicard schemes offering cheap travel for the disabled.

We shall invest to ensure a continuing future for British Rail Engineering as high quality supplier both for British Rail and to world markets.

A SAFER ENVIRONMENT

The countryside and the urban areas all suffer from pollution and the misuse of the environment. Labour will establish a Ministry of Environmental Protection to take positive action to safeguard the quality and safety of life. We will:

● Set up an Environmental Protection Service and a Wildlife and Countryside Service.

● Extend the planning system to cover agricultural forestry and water developments requiring them, and industry, to take account of environmental considerations.

● Invest more in land reclamation and cleaning up, in recycling and conservation, in development of new products, processes and pollution control equipment. This will not only make the country cleaner but will create jobs as well.

● Take action to deal with acid rain.

● Stop radio-active discharges into our seas and oppose the dumping of nuclear waste at sea.

● Provide for better monitoring, inspection and enforcement of pollution control, to cover areas ranging from air pollution to beaches, from hazardous chemicals to food additives, and from water quality to vehicle emissions.

● Protect green belts and other specially designated areas.

● Bring in a new Wildlife and Countryside Act and provide for public access to all common land, mountain, moor and heath.

● End all forms of organised hunting with hounds. Special account will be taken of the conditions applying in National Parks. These changes will not affect shooting and fishing.

● Update animal protection legislation − for example, to eliminate unnecessary experimenting on live animals.

STRENGTHENING DEMOCRACY

We will seek to strengthen parliamentary democracy and introduce state aid for political parties, along the lines of the Houghton Report.

We shall establish a new democractically elected strategic authority for London and consult widely about the most effective regional structure of government and administration in England and Wales.

SCOTLAND

We shall legislate in the first Parliamentary session to establish a democratically-elected Scottish Assembly in Edinburgh. This will have a wide range of powers over health, education and housing and over significant aspects of industrial and economic policy. It will take responsibility for changes in the structure of Scottish local government.

WALES

Wales and the Welsh economy will clearly benefit from Labour's programme for investment in jobs and vital services. In addition, the Welsh Development Agency will be given greater powers and funds − and there will be a new Wales Economic Planning Council. Welsh agriculture will benefit from our measures to help the livestock farmers − especially the marginal and hill farmers.

A separate Arts Council for Wales will be established and the development of the use and choice of the Welsh language will be encouraged.

NORTHERN IRELAND

Labour's policies for economic renewal are essential to combat the record unemployment and social deprivation in Northern Ireland and to encourage the economic security which is fundamental to the development of harmony and trust in the community.

We believe in a united Ireland: to be achieved peacefully, democratically, and by consent. We consequently support the Anglo-Irish Agreement and its commitment that there should be no change in the constitutional position of Northern Ireland without the consent of the majority of the people who live there. No group or party will be allowed to exercise a veto on political development, or on policies designed to win consent.

We will combat para-military violence from wherever it comes. We will promote discussions aimed at encouraging mutual confidence and eliminating conflict whilst ensuring that the respective identities and basic rights of both communities will be protected. We will replace present strip-searching practice with more effective and acceptable security measures.

LOCAL DEMOCRACY

The Tory government has undermined local democracy and plans to continue to diminish the importance of votes in local elections.

It has made huge cuts in rate support grant and imposed financial penalties to prevent councils maintaining and improving the quality of essential local services. Employment, and sensible and sensitive investment in local communities and their services, have been damaged.

Labour will restore the right of councils to decide their own policies and plans, which will be subject to the decisions of local people at annual local elections.

We will halt the cuts in rate support grant and end financial penalties. We will make the legal liabilities of councillors similar to those of Ministers and Company Directors by ending surcharge and disqualification except for criminal offences.

We will abolish the Rates Act and repeal the legislation which established the poll tax in Scotland.

We will give local authorities the necessary powers to enable them to build on existing successful initiatives for enterprise and employment, to develop new technologies and to train young people.

Labour will examine the structure of local government to ensure that it is democratic and effective. We will establish a new Quality Commission to ensure the spread of "best practice", efficiency and high standards of local authority provision and response to the public.

NEW LIFE FOR INNER CITIES

Except where it has turned areas over to speculators so that they can create luxury accommodation at astronomical prices, this government has left inner-city areas to rot.

Experience has shown that the Conservatives' City Action Teams have never had the means or the purpose of making any real impact on inner city problems.

Tory cuts in funding and in housing, together with mass unemployment, have turned too many of our urban areas into dingy, hopeless places.

Yet the people who live there, given the chance, have the zest and initiative to make these areas thrive socially and economically.

Labour will launch a drive against inner-city deprivation both as a way of generating employment and as a means of making such areas safer and better places to live.

Labour's approach will be to develop the partnership between central and local government, with the direct participation of the voluntary and private sectors.We will:

● Give local authorities in key areas the power to declare Public Action Zones. In these areas, local councils will have additional resources and powers to undertake programmes of investment. Land will be identified for housing, jobs and amenities and extra government resources allocated to help with comprehensive regeneration. Local people will be fully consulted about their needs and ideas.
● Strengthen the Urban Programme and Partnership Schemes.
● Make Urban Development Grants available for local needs.
● Increase resources for reclaiming derelict land.

RURAL AREAS

Under the Tories, the problems of the rural areas have become steadily more serious – the lack of jobs, the poor housing, and the loss of buses, post offices, shops and schools.

Labour will give our rural communities the chance to thrive again. Our policies include better public transport, new mobile facilities for health care and social services – and extra help to keep open local schools and post offices.

ENHANCING RIGHTS, INCREASING FREEDOM

Under the Conservatives, Britain has become a harsher place. Freedoms built up over generations have been weakened or removed. Labour will restore and enhance those freedoms in a Britain where life can be more pleasant and fulfilling.

We believe that positive steps are needed to help women and ethnic minorities get a fair deal, and to attain more democracy in the workplace. In addition, we will take steps to ensure that homosexuals are not discriminated against.

WOMEN'S RIGHTS

More than half of Britain's people – the women of our country – are still denied many essential rights. Labour's Ministry for Women will make sure that, in framing their policies, all government departments listen and respond to women's needs and concerns.

In particular, women must have the right to work and equal rights at work. In addition to our new provision for training opportunities and protection against discrimination, Labour will help the large number of women who are part-time workers. We will legislate for them to have the same hourly rates, rights to sick pay, paid holidays and job security as full-time workers.

We will give homeworkers the status and rights of employees; introduce effective laws for equal pay for work of equal value; provide better-paid leave for parents when their child is born; and encourage a shorter, more flexible working week.

DEMOCRACY IN THE WORKPLACE

Workers' rights have been eroded, or in some cases removed entirely, during the Thatcher years. Labour's policy for new rights and responsibilities means legislation to foster good industrial relations and democratic participation in industry and trade unions. We believe that the law should be used to enlarge, not diminish, the freedom of workers to control their environment. We will:

● Replace Tory legislation that gives employers and non-unionists the means to frustrate legitimate trade union activity. New laws will strengthen the legal right rights of representation, bargaining and trade unionism that are essential in a modern democracy.
● Improve the protection available against unfair dismissal. We shall make the legislation apply from the time of employment. Reinstatement will be the normal outcome of a successful finding of unfair treatment. We will ensure that justice is done in cases where miners have been unfairly dismissed.
● Extend employment protection to all workers, including part-timers.
● Improve statutory protection in respect of health and safety at work.
● Restore provision for fair pay, such as the Fair Wages Resolution, Schedule 11 of the 1975 Employment Protection Act and the powers of the Wages Council.
● Strengthen ACAS to put more emphasis on conciliation and arbitration.
● Take steps to develop stable and effective negotiating machinery, promote trade union membership and organisation, and encourage union recognition by employers.
● Restore the right to belong to a trade union to every employee – including those at GCHQ.
● Ensure that the law guarantees the essential legal freedom of workers and their unions to organise effective industrial action.
● Provide a statutory framework of measures to underpin the participative rights of union members, for example by laying down general principles for inclusion in union rule books. These will be based on a right for union members to have a secret ballot on decisions relating to strikes, and for the method of election of union executives to be based on a system of secret ballots.
● In consultation with the TUC, we will establish new independent tribunal, presided over by a legally-qualified person. This will have the duty of acting on complaints by union members if they consider that these statutory principles have been breached.

319

EQUALITY FOR ETHNIC MINORITIES

All the people of this country — whatever their race, colour or religion — must enjoy the full rights of citizenship.

Our policies for employment, education, housing, health care, local government and much else will clearly be of benefit to people of the ethnic minorities as they will be to the whole community.

In addition, Labour will take firm action to promote racial equality, to attack racial discrimination and to encourage contract compliance and other positive means of ensuring equity for all citizens. We will strengthen the law on public order to combat racial hatred and take firm action against the growing menace of racial attacks. We will make prosecution easier in order to encourage the reporting of offences.

Labour's policy of firm and fair immigration control will ensure that the law does not discriminate on the basis of race, colour or sex.

A BETTER DEAL FOR CONSUMERS

When people make a purchase, they often feel they are treated unfairly, or even cheated. Labour's Charter for Consumers will provide proper safeguards suited to modern conditions.

There will be firmer protection against unsafe goods. We will make producers strictly liable for defective products.

We will provide easier means of redress for purchasers and stiffer penalties to deter illegal practices.

We will take action to make sure that public bodies respond better to the needs and complaints of people who use their services.

We will bring in a statutory code of advertising practice. There will be powers to order the correction of misleading advertisements.

We will improve access to legal services where necessary.

There will be more safeguards for customers when companies go bankrupt.

TOWARDS A FULLER LIFE

Life is not only work. Labour will make provision for the co-ordination and development of leisure amenities and the leisure and cultural industries.

Our Support Sport programme will provide more resources for physical education and training through more playing fields and facilities, better equipment and well-trained teachers and instructors. We will nourish special talents and encourage wider participation in sport.

We will encourage schools to open up their recreational facilities to the whole community and prevent the selling off of school and other sports grounds.

We will set up a Sports Trust to channel resources into the development of community sporting facilities and the attraction of major international sporting events to Britain.

We will establish a Ministry for the Arts and Media with responsibility for the arts, crafts, public libraries, museums, film, publishing, the press, the record industry, the development of broadcasting and access to it, fashion, design, architecture and the heritage. The Home Office will remain responsible for regulatory and statutory powers in relation to broadcasting.

The development of central and local government support for the arts, culture and entertainment is essential to the extension of choice, access and participation, and to the development of the related industries.

We will protect the independence of the BBC and the independent broadcasting organisations. We reject subscription TV for the BBC and the auctioning of ITV franchises.

We will legislate to ensure that ownership and control of the press and broadcasting media are retained by citizens of Britain and to place limits on the concentration of ownership. We will strengthen the Press Council and set up a launch fund to assist new publications in order to encourage the diversity necessary in a healthy democracy.

MODERN BRITAIN IN A MODERN WORLD

The globe is torn by strife and oppression. A Labour Britain must play its part in promoting freedom and reducing conflict.

Labour will play a full part in the United Nations Organisation and the Commonwealth.

Under the Conservatives, Britain picks and chooses which authoritarian countries to condemn and which to befriend. Labour will stand up for freedom wherever it is oppressed — whether in Eastern Europe, Latin America, Asia or Africa.

The Thatcher government has made no real effort to foster freedom in South Africa and Namibia. Labour will make the arms embargo complete, halt investment and commercial loans and ensure that British measures against apartheid embrace those already adopted by the US Congress, the Commonwealth and the EEC. We will support the imposition by the UN Security Council of comprehensive mandatory economic sanctions and provide help to the Front Line States who bear the brunt of South African military and economic attack.

We uphold the principle that it is wrong for one country to dominate or threaten another. We oppose the Soviet presence in Afghanistan. We oppose United States intervention in Nicaragua and the financing and arming of the Contra terrorists.

Labour will actively seek a stable peace in the Middle East which protects the security of Israel and recognises the right of Palestinians to self-determination.

Labour supports genuine guarantees for the independence, sovereignty and territorial integrity of Cyprus and supports the efforts of the United Nations to achieve them.

We support the human rights movement throughout the world. We champion the demand for free trade unions in Poland. We will press the Russians to honour their obligations under international human rights agreements.

International terrorism is a growing menace to liberty and security. Labour is firmly committed to strengthening national provision and international co-operation in combating and defeating it.

Labour's aim is to work constructively with our EEC partners to promote economic expansion and combat unemployment. However, we will stand up for British interests within the European Community and will seek to put an end to the abuses and scandals of the Common Agricultural Policy. We shall, like other member countries, reject EEC interference with our policy for national recovery and renewal.

DEFENDING OUR COUNTRY

Labour has a proud record of acting in defence of Britain. It was a Labour government which helped to establish the North Atlantic Alliance. It was a Labour government which in the 1970s put resources into rebuilding the Royal Navy and equipping the Royal Air Force with the most up-to-date aircraft.

At the same time, Labour has always linked necessary defence with the need to reduce hostility between East and West. We must be alert in protecting our country and equally alert in helping to keep away the scourge of war and nuclear destruction.

The incoming Labour government will maintain that record of effective defence whilst working to lower international tension, fear and distrust.

Labour's defence policy is based squarely and firmly on Britain's membership of Nato. We are determined to make the most useful possible contribution to the alliance. We can best do that by concentrating our resources on the non-nuclear needs of our army, navy and air force.

The Polaris system of nuclear delivery is ageing and will soon be obsolete. The Tories are buying the expensive American Trident system — a policy which increases nuclear armament without increasing security and, at the same time, diminishes our effective defences. Trident's cost of up to £10 billion will take up so much of our defence budget as to deny modern and necessary equipment to our front line forces. Indeed, this process is already happening.

Labour rejects this dishonest and expensive policy. We say that it is time to end the nuclear pretence and to ensure a rational conventional defence policy for Britain.

So Labour will decommission the obsolescent Polaris system. We will cancel Trident and use the money saved to pay for those improvements for our army, navy and air force which are vital for the defence of our country and to fulfil our role in Nato. We will maintain a 50-frigate and destroyer navy. We will play a full part in the development of the European Fighter Aircraft. We will invest in the best up-to-date equipment for the British Army of the Rhine.

That commitment to conventional defence will be based wherever possible on buying British-made rather than foreign equipment. This policy will provide greater security for workers in our vital industries like aerospace, shipbuilding and engineering where jobs are in danger from the reductions which the Tories are making in conventional defence.

We have always recognised that a properly negotiated and monitored international agreement to remove nuclear weapons from European soil would provide the most effective guarantee against the horrors of nuclear war. It would be the most significant step towards an eventual worldwide renunciation of, and ban upon, nuclear weapons. That is why we were the first to propose to the superpowers the zero option in respect of intermediate nuclear weapons.

Labour therefore strongly supports the talks between the United States and Soviet governments aimed at reducing nuclear armaments. Success in these efforts to negotiate the removal of all intermediate nuclear missiles in Europe would be warmly welcomed. It would mean the removal of America's Cruise missiles here in Britain and in the rest of Europe, as well as Pershing IIs in Germany and the Soviet SS20s and other short-range missiles.

We naturally, therefore, want to assist that process in every way possible. If, however, it should fail we shall, after consultation, inform the Americans that we wish them to remove their cruise missiles and other nuclear weapons from Britain. We would then become the ninth — of the sixteen Nato members — which do not have US nuclear weapons on their territory. This change would, of course, not affect the other US, British and joint defence and early warning systems in the United Kingdom.

We will oppose the extension of the arms race into outer space and will seek an international agreement to abolish chemical weapons.

THE WAR WE MUST FIGHT

The world is aware, as never before, of the horrors of famine and poverty in many countries. A Labour Britain will play its full part in defeating these scourges.

We will set up a Department of Overseas Development and Co-operation, headed by a Cabinet Minister. We will double Britain's aid budget in order to achieve the United Nations' target of 0.7 per cent of national income within five years. We will restore funding for development education. We will give greater support to voluntary agencies. We will promote international action to lift the burden of third world debt and improve the trading conditions of the developing countries.

In all of our policies for making our aid commitment more effective we shall consult the agencies and the men and women of the communities that use the aid to help to win their freedom from want and poverty.

BRITAIN WILL WIN WITH LABOUR

On June 11, the people of Britain have the opportunity to put behind them the bleak years of Thatcherism and to give our country a fresh start. Labour's plans, carefully costed, prudently programmed, can provide that start.

To go on under Toryism is to accept lower expectations and narrower horizons: it is to surrender to national decline and national division.

We must not shackle ourselves or burden our children with that future of failure. Together, we can be successful not just in material and economic terms, though these are vitally important, but also in terms of our sense of purpose, our freedom, independence and confidence.

That success can come only when the nation is restored to strength and unity in their fullest sense.

Labour has the policies to generate efficient production and secure high standards of justice. Labour has the vision and commitment to stimulate the energies, the skills and the will to succeed of the British people.

In our precious democratic tradition, a general election passes power back from Parliament to the people. We urge the people to use their power in their own interests, their families' interests, their country's interests.

Britain will win with Labour.

Britain United
'The Time Has Come'

FOREWORD by Mr David Steele, leader of the Liberal Party and Dr David Owen, leader of the Social Democratic Party

The Alliance's vision is of a Britain united, a Britain confident, compassionate and competitive. We know that it is possible to unite our country. We know the British people want greater unity. But we also know the task of drawing Britain together again can only be achieved through political, economic and social reform on a scale not contemplated in our country for over forty years.

At the last election, about a third of the nation's voters didn't even both to turn out.

It's hard to think of a more damning condemnation of politics in this country.

But it is not hard to understand why so many people feel cynical and uninterested.

Since the last war the Tories and Labour have each had six turns at Government.

Many honourable men and women on both sides have worked hard for the nation but the system has defeated all but a few.

Rigid dogmas, the overriding need for party unity, and indiscriminate three-line whips have all helped to create a climate of conflict and rancour.

Listen to Parliamentary question time and count how many times the Speaker has to call for order. We've had forty years of yah-boo politics and where has it got us?

We live in a country that is patently unfair to many of its citizens. While politicians brandish statistics at each other on TV chat shows, we can all see with our own eyes what is happening to our schools, hospitals and inner cities.

We know there is more crime because our own homes have been broken into, our own neighbours have been mugged, our own children have been offered drugs.

We know that unemployment remains a huge problem because few families haven't been touched by its shadow.

For many, the situation seems hopeless. Unable to contemplate five more years of uncaring government under Mrs Thatcher, they still do not trust the Labour Party.

Mr Kinnock tries hard but for how long can he keep the lid on the extremists of the Left?

They already dominate some of the Town Halls. When the election is over, will they emerge again to claim the rewards of their silence?

Many of these people feel that the Alliance is the answer — but they ask what chance does it have of changing things? The answer is — every chance.

At the last election, the Alliance won nearly 8 million votes, little less than the Labour Party.

If just 12 more people in every 100 vote for the Alliance this time, we will be the single largest party in Parliament. If just 5 more people in every 100 support us, we would have over 70 seats and almost certainly hold the balance of power.

Think of it. Issues would be judged on their merits. We would curb the Tories' divisive policies and stop the destructive antics of the Labour Left.

Politicians would be forced to listen to each other and work together. The two-party, two class pantomime would finally be over.

It's not an impossible dream. It's closer now than at any time in our history.

All you have to do to make it happen is vote Alliance on June 11th.

INTRODUCTION

There has never been an election like this in modern times. All the evidence and all the commentators confirm that it is a three-way contest which the Alliance enters from a position of unprecedented strength and promise. The Official Opposition is falling apart and is now quite unable to present itself as a realistic alternative to a Government which presides over the worst unemployment ever known in the lifetime of those who are of working age. The two-party system has broken down because it is rooted in outdated battles of class and ideology, and provides no outlet for the vast numbers of people who want individual freedom to go hand-in-hand with social justice, who want the state to back industry without trying to take it over, who want power to be given back to communities instead of concentrated in Whitehall and who want a nation which is soundly defended but takes the lead in the quest for negotiated disarmament and a fairer world.

In any Government the policies which have been set out in the election programme can only tell part of the story of how they will behave in office. It is at least as important to know and trust the values and principles for which they stand, and which will guide their response to the new events and new problems with which governments have to deal. These values, we believe, are embodied in this Joint Programme. They are our guide-book for government.

● Governments are there to protect and preserve the freedom of citizens, to whom they should be accountable and open;

● Freedom must extend to all the people, and Governments must therefore widen the opportunities of those whose liberty is limited by lack of employment, education, health care, housing or help in dealing with disability;

● Governments should not try to do what can be better done by individuals, by communities, by voluntary organisations or by private enterprise, but should set about enabling people to help themselves; however governments should be ready to enter into partnership with these organisations to tackle the problems that neither it nor they can solve alone;

● Decisions of Government should be taken democratically at the most local level compatible with effective action;

● Governments should learn to listen to the people to whom they are accountable;

● Governments should exercise the creative leadership to enable society as a whole to match its needs and resources with the work to be done – of which there is an abundance in Britain today;

● Government must challenge and curb all those who threaten individual freedom by the abuse of monopoly power, by the denial of rights or by crime and violence;

● It is the business of Government to act fairly in the pursuit of a united society, not to identify itself solely with any one section of society or region of the country;

● Government should take positive steps to ensure equal opportunities for women –who make up 52% of the population – and for minority groups such as the ethnic communities.

● Government must enable society to take the longer view, setting the right balance between present consumption and future investment and ensuring that economic development is sustainable and environmentally responsible.

● These values must also guide foreign policy, where the defence of the nation goes hand-in-hand with the promotion of peace and fairness in a world marked by severe inequality and injustice.

We believe that Government at all levels can be more open, more accountable, more fair and more in tune with the wishes of the people of this country if it is allowed to break free of the two-party system and the old class conflict which that system feeds. Our country and its people deserve better, and here is how we believe it can be done.

THE GREAT REFORM CHARTER

Democracy in Britain did not just happen. It was the product of reform – reform against vested interests of both left and right. In 1832 Britain took the first step with the Great Reform Act. Further instalments of reform followed in 1867, 1884, 1918 and 1928 before all men and women had gained the vote. Yet, since then, our democracy has stood still despite the tremendous changes in the economy and society. The Alliance believes that it is time for a new era of reform. For, without getting the structure of our democracy right, we will get nothing right.

The Alliance, if empowered by the British people, will:

● Replace the undemocratic "first past the post" electoral system with proportional representation based on a single transferable vote for all Westminster and local authority elections;

● Introduce PR for elections to the European Parliament. We support a common system for all member states;

● Repeal the Official Secrets Act and replace it with Freedom of Information legislation providing for a public right of access to all official information, subject to limited and specific exemptions to protect national security and proper law enforcement and privacy;

● Reform the law of confidentiality to ensure that freedom of expression on matters of public interest is not unnecessarily restricted;

● Incorporate the European Convention on Human Rights and its protocols into British law in a Bill of Rights;

● Remove the right of the Prime Minister to determine the date of general elections and replace it with fixed-term parliaments;

● Devolve power to a legislative Scottish Assembly, establish a Welsh Senedd and decentralise decision-making to the English regions in accordance with the wishes of their electors;

● Extensively reform Whitehall procedures in order to make the governmental system more responsive to the wishes and needs of the people;

● Reform the House of Commons procedures;

● Reform the House of Lords.

BETTER GOVERNMENT

Most of the problems facing our country cannot be solved unless we get better government. That means government which can carry the people with it in its major policies, and it means government which the citizens can call to account. Our system is currently failing in both respects, and it is getting worse. Under our proposals no government will be able to ride roughshod over the rights of its citizens.

● *First, we insist that the voting system should be reformed* so that no minority – which is what Mrs

Thatcher's Party was at the last election — is given an inflated Parliamentary majority. Fewer people voted Conservative at the last election than the one before, yet the system gave the absolute power of a massively increased majority to Mrs Thatcher, and ensured that the House of Commons could be little more than a talking shop. No wonder Labour leaders join with the present Conservative leadership in wanting to keep the old system — they can see that it offers the only hope of inflicting on the nation policies which the majority of the people reject. The Alliance will introduce community proportional representation, using the well-tried single-transferable vote system with constituencies based on local communities. This system also gives the voters the chance to show which candidates they prefer and would increase the opportunities for women to be elected to Parliament, and make the election of representatives of ethnic minorities more likely. We will reform the voting system for local government on a similar basis, which is the real answer to the abuse of power by the Town Hall extremists. Fairly elected local councils can and should be entrusted with important responsibilities because they are not run as one party states. We will end the scandal whereby England, Scotland and Wales are denied fair representation in the European Parliament; we will introduce a new Great Reform Charter covering a range of specific legislation, all aimed at strengthening our democracy both locally and nationally.

● *We will open the doors of government* so that incompetence and deceit cannot be hidden behind them. We will repeal Section Two of the Official Secrets Act and introduce a Freedom of Information Act so that the public have access to government information to give people access to their personal files, including medical files, held about them by public bodies and to build on the foundation laid by the Access to Personal Files Act, which was introduced as a private members bill by a Liberal MP. We hope to strengthen data protection laws. In areas of government where secrecy is needed, we will introduce new safeguards including a committee of Privy Counsellors to oversee the security services;

● *We do not believe that Whitehall knows best.* British government has never been more centralised than it has become under Mrs Thatcher. In education, health and every aspect of local government, power has been taken over by Ministers. As a result of what the Conservatives have done, an extremist government would have far more opportunities than ever before to control people's lives. This centralisation is inefficient as well as dangerous. How on earth can the man or woman in Whitehall know the needs, the problems and the potential of every community from Shetland to the Scillies? The Alliance will reverse this trend.

● *We will introduce a code for the public service* and reassert the safeguards of ministerial responsibility and civil service impartiality which have been severely eroded under Mrs Thatcher's Government as the handling of the Westland affair showed.

● *We will devolve power to the nations and regions of Britain.* We aim to establish an elected Scottish Parliament, Welsh Senedd and elected regional assemblies throughout England. Public support is essential for progress to be made within the framework of an initial Devolution Act. The devolved structure will require a step-by-step process starting with establishing a Scottish Legislative Assembly with wide powers and self-government in her domestic affairs. This would be created within an overall framework in a devolution bill which sets out the objectives and principles for devolution of powers within the UK. Wales already has a well established, but unaccountable, layer of devolved administration; we therefore aim to create a Welsh Senedd and would publish an early Green Paper on its powers and responsibilites. The abolition of the Greater London Council and the six metropolitan county councils has created a vacuum. London is now the only major capital city in the democratic world without a democratically elected local authority. Greater London is of sufficient size and importance to be a region in itself and there is already widespread support for such a regional assembly, which should be established as soon as possible. We shall publish an early Green Paper with proposals for an elected Greater London regional assembly and setting out the proposal, as the need and demand is established, for the creation of democratically elected regional governments in England.

● *Local government needs a fair system of local finance* which the rates no longer provide. The Government's alternative of a poll tax is unacceptable because it is grossly unfair: it does not relate taxation to the ability to pay. We are committed to the planned introduction of a local income tax as the main source of local government revenue in place of domestic rates. We believe that business rates should be related to ability to pay and we will consult with industry and commerce as to how this can be achieved.

● *Parliament itself needs a shake-up.* A fair electoral system will have that effect but even under the present system many existing Parliamentary practices will not survive for long after this election, because three major political forces will be strongly represented. It will no longer be possible for two political parties to run the House of Commons to suit their own convenience. We intend to put the control of parliamentary business and parliamentary time in the hands of an All-Party Business Committee and to make much more use of select committees: we want widely-supported private members bills to have sufficient time to be debated and decided upon. In recent years the House of Lords has proved the value of a second chamber by its careful scrutiny of bills which got little attention in the Commons and by its willingness to defeat the government on issues of national concern. But there can be no justification for basing the membership of the second chamber so largely on heredity and on the whim of Prime Ministers. The Alliance will work towards a reform of the second chamber linked with our devolution proposals so that it will include members elected from the regions and nations of Britain and will phase out the rights of hereditary peers to vote in the Lords;

● *We will greatly strengthen the rights of the individual.* British Governments have sought to lull citizens into a false sense of security by claiming that our rights are protected by an unwritten constitution. Hundreds of British people find out every year that these protections are inadequate and they have to go to Strasbourg to seek protection from the European Convention on Human Rights. We will enact the European Convention into British law, so that the citizen can secure redress in the British courts.

● *We will establish a Human Rights Commission,* which will take over the work of the Equal Opportunities and Racial Equality Commissions, and counter all discrimination on grounds of race, sex, creed, class, disability or sexual orientation. The Commission would be able to initiate action in the courts;

● *We will open up opportunities for women at work and in public life.* Today, fewer than one in five of Government appointees on public bodies are women. We will secure equal representation of women on all appointed public bodies within a decade; our social and tax policies aim to give women equal rights and freedom to choose their way of life;

● *The Alliance accepts the need for immigration controls* and for clear legal definition of British nationality, but also accepts that the law in this area is fundamental to individual rights and should be fair to everyone regardless of race and regardless of whether they are men or women. There should be effective rights of appeal against refusal of citizenship and referral to an independent body in cases of deportation, and immigration procedures should be revised so as to promote family unity without significantly affecting immigration totals, which remain lower than rates of emigration from Britain.

● *We will combat discrimination against black people in housing and employment* and take positive steps through such measures as contract compliance to secure equal opportunities for racial minorities, and we will devote more police resources to dealing with racial harassment;

● *We will combat prejudice against and misunderstanding of people with disabilities,* to improve their quality of life, and to extend educational opportunities for disabled young people.

● *We will restore the principle that anyone born in Britain is entitled to British citizenship.* We are adamantly opposed to discrimination and we will repeal the sexist and racist aspects of the British Nationality Act 1981.

Opportunities for women

The Alliance is committed to the principle that women should have equal opportunities and in government we will take positive steps to ensure this ideal becomes a reality.

● We will open up opportunities for women in public life by securing equal representation of women on all appointed bodies within a decade.

● We will strengthen the rights of women at work through equal pay for work of equal value, equal treatment, ensuring that all public authorities and private contractors are equal opportunity employers. We will restore the maternity grant and improve benefits for families.

● We will offer a tax allowance to help with the costs of childcare and remove the tax on the use of workplace nurseries.

● We will ensure that girls and women have equal opportunities in education and training.

● We will promote measures that give employees with family responsibilities rights to parental and family leave.

● The Alliance wants to see more women in Westminster. Changing the electoral system to a form of proportional representation will increase the opportunities for women to be elected to Parliament.

Northern Ireland

We intend to secure progress towards a peaceful and secure life for the people of Northern Ireland. That depends on the acceptance of three fundamental principles;

● Rejection of violence;

● Recognition that both Unionist and Nationalist traditions have their legitimate place;

● Acceptance that Northern Ireland should not cease to be a part of the UK unless a majority of the people of Northern Ireland so wish.

The government of Northern Ireland must be based on a partnership between the two traditions. The Alliance welcomes the Anglo-Irish agreement as a genuine attempt to achieve the objectives we set out. We wish to see a UK/Irish Parliamentary Council, and a devolved assembly where responsibilities and power will be shared. We would improve arrangements for considering Northern Ireland legislation at Westminster.

Our commitment to incorporate the European Convention on Human Rights into UK law will strengthen individual rights in Northern Ireland and we would reform the Diplock courts so that three judges preside over non-jury trials; in this and other respects we believe that the passing of identical anti-terrorist measures in Northern Ireland and the Republic can increase the authority those measures carry in a divided community. We also support the establishment of a joint security commission.

We would encourage the participation of people from the minority tradition in the RUC and believe that a totally independent police complaints procedure should be established. We would introduce the 110-day limit on the time in which a prisoner may be held in custody before appearing in court, as we propose for England and Wales.

We would encourage those who are working for reconciliation in Northern Ireland and who are seeking to eliminate sectarianism and discrimination in religious life, education, housing and politics.

We believe that the membership of the EEC offers not only practical help to Northern Ireland, but also prospects for the long-term development of a confederal relationship between UK and the Republic of Ireland which could offer a solution to a problem which has claimed over 2,500 lives in the last 18 years.

FIGHTING CRIME

Crime rates have soared in this Government's last eight years. Overall, crime is up by over 60%, burglaries have almost doubled, while robberies have increased two and a half times over. People, particularly elderly people, live in fear in their homes and in the streets and women feel increasingly unable to go out at night.

Detection rates have dropped from over two-fifths in 1979 to under a third in 1986. Increases in police numbers have been largely offset by special duties like policing strikes and demonstrations, and by a drop in the working week. There are few extra bobbies on the beat.

The Alliance would tackle both crime and the causes of crime. Some Labour-controlled boroughs refuse to co-operate with the police in combatting crime. The Conservative Government refuses to recognise that homelessness, unemployment and aimless bed-and-breakfast regimes are breeding-grounds of delinquency. Both are wrong.

The Police

The Alliance firmly supports the police in the battle against crime; that fight can only be effective if the police get the support of the whole community, through community policing and policemen on the beat. Many police forces are still under strength: yet more officers are needed to provide the kind of local policing which we believe is essential. An Alliance Government will finance a further 4,000 police officers over and above the present Government plans and 1,000 more civilians, so releasing police officers for patrol duties.

Proportional representation for local government would stop unrepresentative extremists from controlling police authorities. It would mean more sensible police authorities and make possible a democratically accountable police authority for London. We oppose the police monitoring units by which some Labour councils attempt to undermine the police. The Alliance fully accepts the need for chief officers to have full operational control of their force. The Alliance supports a fully independent system for investigating complaints against the police. We reject moves towards a national police force. We would appoint a Royal Commission to review the question of police accountability.

Lifeline

Too many elderly people suffer from isolation, fear and cold.
● We intend to give them the safety, security and warmth they deserve. Britain has 6 million people aged 70 or over. For them our "Lifeline" programme will:
● include free installation of a telephone;
● protect them against the criminal by free installation of secure locks;
● cut their heating bills by free home insulation;
● abolish standing charges on electricity, gas and telephones.

These 6 million people live in 4.5 million households and this will cost £180million. "Lifeline" will build on present schemes and will also be a part of our long-term job guarantee.

Crime crisis areas

An Alliance Government will target "Crime Crisis Areas", those with the highest rates of crime, for special anti-crime measures. Chief Constables, in consultation with Community/Police Liaison Committee and police authorities, would define these areas. They will have:
● More police on the streets;
● Local police stations re-opened. Police Posts should be established where no station is close by;
● Security grants to pay for entry phones and security locks;
● Projects to make crime danger spots safe and to provide effective street lighting and more caretakers on estates;
● New housing estates designed to minimise opportunities for crime and hazardous public areas will be redesigned;
● A legal obligation imposed on British Telecom to keep all public telephones in constant repair. In London up to half our public telephones are broken at any one time — many of them the only lifeline in high crime areas.

Upholding the law

● *We will create a new Ministry of Justice.* Its responsibilities will include the strengthening of the rights of the citizen to legal aid and advice and improving court and tribunal procedures. We will establish a family court system and set up a new legal services council.

Sentencing Policy. Sentencing is often seen as arbitrary, with the same crime attracting widely divergent punishments. For the criminals, sentences become more of a lottery than a deterring force. We will strengthen the role of the Judicial Studies Board in setting guidelines for sentencing. This will mean that any judge stepping ouside the Board's recommendations would be asked to explain the reason and any special circumstances. This would maintain a judge's flexibility, while keeping sentencing broadly consistent. It would also limit the ever-increasing upward trend in sentencing.

A Royal Commission on the Presentation of Violence in the Media. We will establish a Royal Commission to report within a year on the public presentation of violence on TV and the reporting of crime in newspapers, to make recommendations on the possible link between these and violent crime on the streets.

Crime Prevention Units. There would be a duty on all local authorities to establish Crime Prevention Units, and to work closely with the police to help in setting up Neighbourhood Watch schemes. They would advise on security in all new planning and building.

Insuring Against Crime. We aim to make insurance available to all council tenants, who are twice as likely to be burgled as home owners and far less likely to be insured.

Curbing the Sale of Offence Weapons. We will curb the sale of knuckle dusters, battle knives, spiked shoe straps, cross-bows and catapults.

DEALING WITH OFFENDERS

The prison scandal
The prisons are bursting at the seams, yet Home Office projections show numbers increasing until the end of the decade 1985-1995. Of the 13,000 increase, 5,000 people will be untried and unsentenced.

The Alliance believes drastic action is needed to reduce the prison population, while ensuring that those responsible for violent and serious crime are kept out of society for as long as the Courts think necessary. Imprisonment rarely rehabilitates the prisoner. Three-fifths of all men who receive a prison sentence re-offend within two years of being released.

● The minimum standards for prisons proposed by NACRO, and accepted in principle by the then Home Secretary as long ago as 1981, should be adopted as a target to be achieved within two years.

● A limit of 110 days should be laid down as soon as possible for remand prisoners. If not prosecuted within that period, they would be released. This systems operates successfully in Scotland.

● Probation authorities should be required to provide bail hostels adequate to accommodate their own needs. The Home Office should make a special 100% grant for the purpose.

● The "short, sharp, shock" has failed. As the Magistrate's Association has recommended there should be a single youth custody sentence. Detention centres, already under-used by the Courts, should be abolished, and the accommodation released to be used for remand centres.

Alternatives to prison
● Every effort should be made to ensure that fine defaulters, elderly shoplifters and drunks are not sent to prison.

● Police cautions and intermediate treatment should be more widely used. Where punishment is appropriate, it should normally be community service rather than prison; but many of these offenders are more appropriately dealt with by rehabilitation or medical treatment.

● The probation service must be expanded to enable bail and non custodial sentences to be supervised where necessary under appropriate supervision.

● The Home Office should consider extending the period of automatic remission for less serious offences.

● We strongly support victim support schemes.

● Offenders should recompense their victims, either directly or indirectly. Community service orders oblige offenders to undertake work for the community. They should be more widely used.

These changes should ease the frustration that threatens to erupt in the prisons, and enable prison officers to do the professional job they want to do. We welcome "Fresh Start", which proposes shorter hours and less reliance on overtime, but recognise that unless overcrowding is tackles, this reform may not work.

BUILDING THE FUTURE
A generation ago, Britain was among Europe's richest countries. Today Britain is falling down the league of industrialised nations. Real income per head is well below that of Sweden, Germany or France. Our manufacturing trade has gone into the red. In every year since 1983 we have imported more goods than we exported, the first time that has happened since the Industrial Revolution.

Worst of all is unemployment. Many more than the three million people registered as unemployed have no jobs. The Government has juggled the figures and brought in cosmetic devices to hide the truth. But the facts won't go away. The dole queue is three times what it was in 1979. Unemployment has been a low priority for this Government, used to keep down inflation. Tax cuts have had a higher priority than job creation. The cost in human misery and hardship, loss of confidence and self-respect, not least among young people, has been incalculable.

Britain, like other industrial countries, has to cross the gulf between the first industrial revolution, based on steel, engineering and railways, and the second, based on the sunrise technologies of micro-electronics, biotechnology and new materials. To cross that gulf demands investment in new buildings, plant and machinery, and above all in the research and development on which new products and new processes are based. Yet under Mrs Thatcher's Government, investment in manufacturing industry and in R & D has fallen substantially. We must give a much higher priority to training and education. There has been a huge decline in apprenticeships and skill training in Britain in the last eight years, although the new technologies demand much higher qualifications and regular updating of knowledge.

The Government has failed to use the once-in-a-lifetime opportunity North Sea oil gave us to invest in our industry and in our people. High interest rates have crippled businesses of all sizes; sudden ups and downs in the sterling exchange rate have handicapped exports. Even the proceeds from selling-off state assets — *our* assets — have gone into cutting taxes to buy votes.

These are our objectives:

● *to reduce unemployment*, first amongst those unemployed for a year or more, and amongst young people; in three years we will reduce unemployment by one million;

● *to bridge the gap between the older industrial areas and the areas of prosperity.* The older industrial areas have lost a million jobs. We would encourage regional development agencies and local employment initiatives to harness the energy and enthusiasm of the local people in these hard-hit areas. The South-East would benefit too, for house prices are now soaring far beyond the ability of most families to pay, and attractive countryside is besieged by developers.

● *to build a new partnership between business and government*, to re-equip our factories, tackle the blight of our inner cities, and draw up a strategy for a competitive and successful industry;

● *to abolish class division in the workplace* by encouraging a single status for white collar and blue collar workers, and creating opportunities for all employees to share in the profits, decisions and ownership of firms;

● *to strengthen the rights of women at work* including equal pay for work of equal value and equal treatment. We will ensure that all public authorites and private contractors are equal opportunity employers and we will promote changes to enable those with domestic responsibilities to secure access to employment. We would restore maternity grants and give a tax allowance to help with child-care costs. We would remove the tax on the use of workplace nurseries and encourage wider provision of child-care facilities.

Unemployment

Unemployment at present levels is not the inevitable result of new technology or world recession — Japan has only 2.5% unemployment and US unemployment has fallen by two million since 1983. It can be reduced in Britain. The key is to ensure that in creating new jobs the nation does not embark on another round of severe inflation which will damage competitiveness and cost us jobs in the long run. Labour ignores this danger and the Conservatives use it as an excuse for allowing unemployment to remain high. The Alliance is prepared to take the difficult steps necessary to create jobs *and* control inflation at the same time.

● *Therefore we will expand the economy by targeting resources to increase output and exports rather than consumption and imports.* New capital investment building up to £1.5 billion per annum will support the framework of services on which industry and society depend, like transport, homes, schools, hospitals and drainage. We will give more spending power to the poorest people in our society, which will itself generate more economic activity with much less impact on imports than general cuts in income tax;

● *We will control inflation by winning the support of the British people for our incomes strategy;* as a back-up we will legislate for reserve powers for a counter-inflation tax on companies — under which inflationary increases would be unattractive because they would go in extra tax: profit-sharing would be exempted. We would introduce fairer arrangements for public sector pay, with an independent pay and information board whose findings would inform and assist negotiations, arbitration procedures and incentives to negotiate no-strike agreements in essential services;

● *We will join the exchange rate mechanism of the European Monetary System*, enabling us to make our currency more stable and to reduce current interest rates by as much as 2%. We would also seek to develop the role of the EMS within the world economy.

For the long-term unemployed we will provide a guarantee of a job through:

a) a building and investment programme aimed at providing 200,000 jobs in such essential areas as transport, housing, insulation, urban renewal and new technologies;

b) a new recruitment incentive to encourage companies to take on over 270,000 jobless people;

c) a crash programme of education and training, offering new skills to the unskilled unemployed, with 200,000 places;

d) 60,000 extra jobs in the health and social services to improve care in the community and more jobs in nursery education;

e) an expanded job release scheme, opening up 30,000 jobs by allowing men to benefit from the scheme at 62 years of age.

Backing Small Business

● We will build a partnership between government, entrepreneurs and investors to encourage new businesses and create new jobs. We will especially encourage small businesses, which will be a major motor of growth and employment in the 1990's.

● We will reduce the tax and administrative burdens on small businesses.

329

● We will promote the establishment of Small Firms Investment Companies to provide equity and loan finance.
● We will introduce a Bill to enable business to charge interest on overdue payment of bills, if they so wish.
● We will ensure that there are business start-up schemes and expansion schemes specifically geared to encouraging enterprise by women.
● We will ensure small businesses get their fair share of public contracts from both central and local government.
● We will encourage local public/private initiatives, such as Enterprise Agencies, which we identified in our Worksearch Campaign.

Industrial Investment Bonds

● We will introduce Industrial Investment Bonds to liberate many new and small businesses from the high cost of borrowing start-up capital.

These bonds will help bridge the gap between the new businessman who needs access to low-cost funds and the investor, including individuals, who would like to back him or her provided the balance between risk and reward is reasonable. We will accordingly allow new and growing companies to raise funds through the issue of Industrial Investment Bonds which will pay interest free of tax to investors.

A similar scheme is already providing a valuable kick-start for many new companies in the United States. Together with the Business Expansion Scheme, our Industrial Investment Bonds will give the next generation of businesses the most favourable climate ever to build up employment for the community and profits for themselves and their investors.

Rebuilding British Industry

Manufacturing and services go hand in hand, but only a quarter of services are tradeable and two thirds of our exports depend on manufacturing. Britain cannot survive on a basis of low tech service jobs. Nor can business flourish without a thriving industry to buy their products. Manufacturing industry is the driving force at the core of our economy. Its decline must be reversed. Therefore:

● *We will introduce Industrial Investment Bonds* to attract investors into industry, a new industrial credit scheme to provide medium-term finance for manufacturing companies and a tax allowance for investment in new technologies;

● *We will work in partnership with industry* and put industry first. There will be a new Cabinet Industrial Policy Committee responsible for overseeing the development and implementation, in co-operation with industry, of a broad industrial strategy with long-term priorities;

● *We will encourage employers to take on more staff by a 25% cut in their National Insurance Contribution payments* targeted on assisted areas and areas of high unemployment;

● *We will introduce a training incentive with rebates for companies who spend more money on training* and contributions from those who do not provide it themselves; our new Department of Education and Training will monitor standards and turn youth training into a fully comprehensive, high quality vocational and educational programme for 16-19 years old;

● *We will increase the lamentable low funding of civil research and development,* placing emphasis both on commercial exploitation of new technology using the British Technology Group, and on boosting basic scientific research; we would give greater support to European Community joint research programmes;

● *We will give more backing to exports* using the Export Credit Guarantee Department and the Aid and Trade Provision (funded from the DTI) more effectively than the present Government has done in recent years because of its ambivalent attitude towards public sector support. We will press the European Community to take stern action against dumping. We will launch a more determined attack on unfair restrictions on our trade, including those imposed by Japan on a wide range of products and services and by the US on our high-technology exports;

● *We will insist on a strong competition policy to promote efficiency and give consumers a fair deal*: the Office of Fair Trading will be strengthened and will take on the responsibilities of the Monopolies and Mergers Commission and companies seeking mergers will have to justify them; individuals and institutions will have power to seek redress in court against anti-competitive practices;

● *We will continue to judge whether industries should be in the public or private sector on objective criteria related to competition and efficiency.* We opposed the privatisation of British Gas and British Telecom – although we would not reverse it but instead concentrate on improving consumer choice and protection. We supported the privatisation of Rolls Royce. We would not privatise water authorities and the Central Electricity Generating Board on ground of public policy relating to safety standards and care for the environment. We welcome the fact that British Steel is now operating profitably. We believe it should be retained as a single entity to withstand international competition and should be considered for privatisation providing its success can be maintained;

● *We will work with the people of the hard-hit regions to stimulate new economic activity* and new prospects for jobs through regional development agencies. We will encourage the setting up of a local venture capital funds to finance new enterprise. We do not believe that government always knows best, so we will support local initiatives through appropriate fiscal and financial means.

We will promote partnership

For too long the industrial sector has been a battleground between opposing forces of capital and labour, instead of a mutually beneficial and equal partnership.

● *We will legislate for employee participation* but believe that flexibility must be allowed in working out the detail for employee councils at the place of work. These councils should have the information and the rights to enable them to contribute to strategic decisions; opportunity must be provided for participation at top level — for example by employee directors or a representative or supervisory council, or by directors elected by shareholders and employees jointly;

● *We will encourage other forms of industrial participation,* including co-operatives in which it is workers who hire capital and management skill; we will establish an Industrial Partnership Agency incorporating the Co-operative Development Agency to take a lead in this field.

● *We will strengthen the law in relation to Directors' statutory obligation* to have regard to the interests of their employees as well as their shareholders; this should include a requirement to consult employees before making a recommendation in response to any take-over bids;

● *We will extend incentives* to employees' share-ownership and profit-sharing which were introduced at Liberal insistence in 1987;

● *We will encourage wider share ownership* by a scheme which gives more people a direct tax incentive to become small investors;

● *We have long been committed to trade union reform* aimed at giving unions back to their members and we have taken the lead in promoting the extension of postal ballots and internal elections and have vigorously opposed pre-entry closed shops. Trades unions are an essential element in the protection of the employees' interests, which is why we would return union recognition to GCHQ members. Our central aim is to make unions democratic and accountable and therefore entitled to positive rights including the right to recognition and the right to strike balanced by the acceptance of their responsibilities to their members, their industries and to the wider community.

● *To reduce industrial conflict we support a system of referring disputes to independent arbitration* prior to any industrial action. We will also encourage the establishment of freely negotiated strike-free agreements especially in the provision of essential public services.

● *We will take action through equal opportunity* and contract compliance policies to eliminate discrimination against ethnic minorites and women;

● *We will actively promote* measures that give employees with family responsibilities *minimum rights* to parental and family leave.

Agriculture

The Alliance will promote a healthy farming industry. We must arrest the precipitous decline in farm incomes of recent years. Our policies for aligning supply and demand of agricultural produce are designed to secure fair returns for farmers' efforts. Adequate price and income support is required to enable necessary farming adjustments to be made.

● *We will join the exchange rate mechanism of the European Monetary System* to lower interest rates, promote financial stability and prevent unfair discrimination against British farmers through over-valuation of the green pound.

● *The Alliance will work to reform the CAP*: the policy has achieved secure food supplies but has gone on unchecked to produce wasteful and hugely expensive surpluses. Many farmers who borrowed heavily on inflated land prices to meet production demands are now threatened with bankruptcy. The Alliance will secure the income of British family farms by negotiating adequate guaranteed prices for determined quantities of production, with additional quantities disposed at much lower floor intervention prices: a two-tier pricing system. An eligible tonnage for each member-state will be agreed to take into account the differing farm structures in the Community.

● *We will seek a fairer share of milk quota* for British producers and the retention of the right to quota transfer and leasing. Transfer of quotas through an agency would create a pool of quota to be administered by the Milk Marketing Board and would help small family farms.

● *We are committed to supporting the less favoured areas,* and ensuring that the upland beef and sheep industries are safeguarded through differential premia and retention of the sheepmeat regime.

● *We shall increase Government support for effective marketing* schemes for farm produce at home and abroad. Farm-based processing and marketing co-operatives will be assisted to retain more of the selling price of foodstuffs in rural communities.

● *We will encourage conservation,* the reduced use of chemical inputs, organic farming and less intensive methods of livestock production. The Government's cuts in agricultural research, education and advice will be reversed. Special efforts will be devoted to lowering input costs. The Alliance will sponsor partnership between Government and industry to promote both research into new uses for farm produce which will help to sustain incomes and into the improvement of animal welfare.

● *We will encourage farmers to diversify* taking account of the needs of tenant farmers and other small family farms. We will make annual payments for the upkeep of important amenities such as walls, hedges, footpaths and meadows. We will provide further support for the custodianship of areas of environmental importance, and the encouragement of mixed forestry on the farm with establishment grants and annual payments for growers. We will propose clear guidelines for land use to assist diversification and to protect the countryside.

● *The Alliance rejects proposals to rate farm land or buildings.* We also reject the Government's proposals for a poll tax which will apply to farmers and farm workers and, unlike Alliance proposals for local government income tax, is not based on the ability to pay;

● *The Alliance wishes to support new entrants* to the farming industry, and therefore proposes the retention of County Council smallholdings and the promotion of tax incentives to encourage landlords to let more land.

● *We would promote local rural employment,* including farm-based tourism, through properly funded rural development agencies and by means of a credit scheme which would provide working capital at low rates of interest to agricultural and rural industries.

● *We will also encourage* the establishment of a Credit Union (or Farm Bank) designed to help farmers secure finance at fair and reasonable rates.

Fishing

The Alliance in government will act to strengthen the contribution the fishing industry can make to the livlihood of rural communities.

After many years of turmoil from the loss of traditional distant water fishing grounds and the protracted negations for a fair Common Fishing Policy, what British fisherman now need above all is stability to plan and invest for the future. We will:

● *Improve the conservation of fish stocks* by the use of licensing and technical means that will safeguard stocks and decentralise the administration of quantitative controls so as to give fishermen greater responsibility for the management of necessary conservation measures with the flexibility to recognise regional differences..

● *Strengthen the European Community Inspectorate* so as to achieve fair enforcement by all member-states.

● *We will support better vocational training,* fish processing and marketing and export promotion under the co-ordination of the Seafish Industry Authority.

● *We would not impose light dues on fishing vessels.*

The Alliance believes that these policies will help to secure jobs, greater prosperity, greater fairness, and a sense of pride in the industries upon which our future depends.

HEALTH AND COMMUNITY CARE

The National Health Service is in a state of fundamental crisis and malaise. It is suffering shortages and declining standards. Our people are seeing their services cut, their waiting lists lengthened, and more and more needs going unmet. Unless a Government is elected again which is committed to the ideas and ideals of a National Health Service, one of the great achievements of 20th century civilised society could be in irreversible decline.

● *We will back the National Health Service by increasing its budget* so that by year five it will be £1 billion per annum higher than that planned by the Conservatives. Our Health Service was once the envy of the world: now the strains under which it is working are well known, and we are losing some of the best health professionals who can no longer do the job they were trained to do because of inadequate resources. We aim to restore a sense of pride in the Health Service and to give it a new sense of direction. Our priorities for change are:

● *To provide prompt medical treatment for those who need it,* regardless of who they are or where they live. There are huge inequalities between and within regions of the country in availability of hospital treatment and family doctor services. We would set aside special funds — building on the recently introduced funds to cut waiting lists — to back good practice. The Conservative Government has increased *prescription charges* by 240% over the last eight years which is much higher than inflation. We will not increase prescription charges beyond the inflation rate.

● *To promote good health, not merely to treat illness.* This means targeting resources in health education, promoting healthy eating, tightening up food labelling and facing up to the problems presented by smoking and alcohol abuse. We will ban advertising of tobacco products. Our policies to deal with unemployment, poverty and poor housing are crucial in reducing ill-health. The primary health care team working with family doctors must be built up and their preventive work expanded. There should be more screening, including well-women clinics, with efficient follow-up for known risk groups.

● *To create a new innovation fund,* to tackle inequalities in health care, improve the "cinderella services", and to fund new developments and new priorities in health care; this will have an initial life of five years, with a budget which will total £250 million in the first three years. This will be in addition to money spent on creating new jobs caring in the community.

● *To make "care in the community" a reality.* We are not prepared to see patients turned out of the old institutional hospitals without adequate facilities to care for them in the community. We want to support "carers" who look after elderly and handicapped people in their own families and their own homes. We intend to introduce a carers' benefit, and we want carers to have more opportunities for a break from their responsibilities.

However, we recognise that for some people good institutional care remains the best solution.

● *To strengthen patients' rights,* through statutory access for the individual to his or her own medical files, through more opportunities for patients to participate in decisions and through stronger community health councils.

● *To give real independence to the Health Education Authority.*
● *To restructure the nursing profession* along the lines proposed in Project 2000.

In the longer term we want to see health authorities brought under democratic control through regional assemblies and, for the districts, democratic control at local level, but the NHS has suffered so many bouts of reorganisation under successive governments that for the moment the priority must be to let those running the service get on with the job.

● *We would remove the centralising pressure to make all authorities do things in the same way,* and we would leave authorities with more freedom to decide, for example, whether privatisation of services was likely to improve patient care or not; we would give these authorities more direct control over their budgets.

● *We uphold the right of individuals to use their own resources to obtain private medical care,* but we will not allow private medicine to exploit the NHS by using facilities at subsided cost and we will work to end the delays which give rise to "queue-jumping" through private medicine.

Right to treatment
No client of the NHS should have to wait longer than six months for hospital treatment. No-one should be kept waiting for years in pain, with unnecessary crippling disabilities for lack of a hospital bed. Patients should have the right to treatment in other authorities where there is spare capacity.

The Alliance will work to ensure that every patient receives hospital treatment for routine operations within six months of referral by a GP. The backlog of people waiting is now of crisis proportions. We estimate it will take two years to reduce the maximum waiting time to one year. We aim to reduce this to within six months during our first term of office.

To end long waiting lists District Health Authorities and Health Boards will be empowered to:
● Buy and sell hospital treatment from each other to obtain the best and quickest service;
● Buy services from other Districts with surpluses. Selling services between DHAs would be a new incentive for good management practice rather than penalize success;
● Pay travelling costs for patients who cannot afford transport out of their districts.
● Appoint more hospital doctors and negotiate with consultants so that they give priority to their NHS waiting lists rather than on private practice.
● Ensure an increased number of places in local hospitals for convalescence and community care to release beds for acute treatment.

GPs will need to have full computerised information on waiting lists when they make their first referrals. They are already substantial funds within the NHS for computerisation and the Alliance will ensure all GPs can be linked to hospitals nationwide.

In consultation with the medical profession, we will draw up and regularly review a list of routine operations such as hip replacement for which all patients should expect treatment within our six month target.

In consultation with District Health Authorities, we will agree allocations of extra resources, taking into account the numbers of patients from outside their area that Districts are already treating.

The vital role of the voluntary sector
In health and in many other fields of service the work of volunteers and voluntary organisations is vital: the Alliance sees no benefit in state monopoly, and welcomes the dedication, innovation and diversity which the voluntary sector can bring. We want a more stable framework for the voluntary organisations making them less dependent on short-term funding which can be misused by local councils and govern-ment departments as a means of exerting political control in the voluntary sector. We will:
● Expand opportunities for individual voluntary effort, giving young people, for example, the chance to volunteer full-time for a year without losing their social security entitlements and by linking existing voluntary groups with new initiatives;
● Ensure that experience gained by volunteers is given proper accreditation to enable those without traditional qualifications to gain access to further and higher education;
● Ensure adequate public core funding to enable voluntary organisations to take full advantage of tax concessions on payroll giving and individual donors;
● Support services which advise voluntary organisations on how to develop their management skills and structures to ensure staff development and better service delivery;
● Support and help to widen the network of Citizens Advice Bureaux, Law Centres and other legal advice services.

ENDING POVERTY
We can and will relieve many thousands of people from the burden of poverty.
Poverty in Britain is getting worse. The Conservatives' taxation and benefit policies have redistributed income from the poor to the rich, from people with dependent children to single people and childless couples, and from one group of the poor to another group of the poor. This is unjust and unacceptable. The Alliance will tackle poverty by targetting much higher benefits to those with the lowest incomes in relation to their needs. We will help families with children. We will improve benefits for the disabled and those caring for elderly and disabled relatives at home.

Our proposals fall into two parts:

First, we will, over the first two years, improve the incomes of pensioners, families with children, the unemployed, disabled and carers. These improvements will be paid for in part by increasing public expenditure by a net £1.75 billion by the second year. The remainder will be paid for from increased tax revenues and from changes which will make the tax system fairer.

The second phase of our proposals will be a restructuring of the tax and benefits systems to create one integrated system which will be simpler and fairer.

THE IMMEDIATE PACKAGE
Pensioners
● *We intend to concentrate the bulk of extra spending on helping poorer pensioners* with incomes on and just above the state retirement pension. We will increase the basic state retirement pension by £2.30 a week for a single person and £3.65 for a married couple. This will include the forecast update of the pension in 1988. For poorer pensioners we will introduce an additional benefit of £3.70 a week for single people and £5.75 for couples. This will increase the incomes of poorer pensioners in total by £6 per week (single person) and £9.40 per week (couple).

● *We will introduce a Death Grant of £400*, recoverable from the estate of the deceased, specifically designed to help pensioners with a small amount of savings feel confident that most of their, or their spouses, funeral costs will be covered by the Grant;

● *We will require standing charges for gas, electricity and telephones to be abolished for everyone.*

Double pension at Christmas
The £10 Christmas bonus has become hopelessly inadequate to meet the extra spending pensioners and widows face at Christmas.

We will increase the bonus by paying a double pension in the first week of December. A single person will receive £39.50 and a married couple £63.25. The net cost will be £268 million.

Child Benefit
● *We will increase child benefit by £1 per child a week* in the first year and by a further £1 per child a week in the second year.

Maternity Grant
● *We will introduce a maternity grant of £150* for the first child born in every family and of £75 for the births of each subsequent child.

Families in Work
● *We will add £5 per week to the family credit* due to be introduced in April 1988 as a replacement to family income supplement. These families will also gain from the extra child benefit. Unlike the Conservatives we will retain at this stage free school meals and milk for family credit recipients regardless of whether the families are in work or not; this will ensure equal treatment with families dependent on benefits.

Families out of Work
● *We will increase the family premium* under the income support scheme by £5 per week and, in this first phase, we will increase the net amount per child received by income support families by £2 per child per week.

Single Parents
● *We will increase the single parent premium* for income support recipients by £1.10 a week, single parents will also benefit from the increased child benefit and, if their earnings are low, from the extra £5 on family credit. If they are not in paid employment they will benefit from higher family premium and the child additions.

Young People
● The Conservatives' benefit changes include setting a new low personal allowance for unemployed 18-24 year olds with a higher Personal Allowance for single people 25 and over. We do not support this discrimination based on age and *we will abolish the 18-24 income support rate* to ensure that all single people receive the same amount of benefit.

Long-term Unemployed
● *We will establish a new premium* under the income support scheme for the long-term unemployed without dependent children of £3.50 a week for a single person and £5 for a couple.

Social Fund
● *We will not place cash limits on the Social Fund* and we will replace loans with grants. We will establish clear criteria of eligibility for special payments and a right of independent appeal and will ensure that the very poor receive extra money to cover heating costs.

Housing Benefit

● *We will not impose a 20% rates charge* on those with very low incomes as the Conservatives plan to do from April 1988. We will not implement the Conservatives' proposed cuts in the funding of Housing Benefit.

The total gross cost of this immediate package over two years is £3.6 billion and the net cost is £1.75 billion, which will be met from our planned expansion of the economy. Part of the cost of the package will be met by changes to the tax system, and by starting to phase in independent taxation for married women.

We will change the current personal tax allowances into a standard allowance worth the same value for all taxpayers and will not uprate the Married Man's Tax Allowance. Pensioners', Single Person's and Wife's Earned Income Allowances will continue to be uprated with inflation. We will confine Mortgage Tax Relief to the basic rate of tax, so that all taxpayers benefit equally from it at the same rate.

PEOPLE WITH DISABILITIES
Charter for Independence

The biggest handicap faced by people with disabilities is the barriers put up by the rest of us to their participation in society. The Alliance therefore supports measures which reduce the physical and attitudinal obstacles faced by those with disabilities and which enable all to enjoy as many as possible of the opportunities which are often taken for granted by the able-bodied.

We believe that the majority of people with disabilities wish to live an independent life in the community and in their own home. In support of this we will:

● Speed up the full implementation of the Disabled Persons Act 1986;

● Increase the income of people with disabilities who are dependent on benefits by £3.50 per week and provide additional financial support through our tax and benefit proposals.

● ensure that "care in the community" policies are properly co-ordinated and funded, unlike the current situation which has been described by the Audits Commission as resulting in "poor value for money and unnecessary suffering".

● Tackle discrimination against disabled people through our proposed new Bill of Rights and the Human Rights Commission.

● Support the voluntary organisations of and for disabled people and ensure that they are properly consulted on matters which affect them.

● Ensure that the needs of disabled people are taken into account in housing, public buildings and by public transport operators. We would expand support for the specialised transport which can often be the key to independent living for people with limited mobility.

● Improve the provision of education for those with special needs, in colleges as well as in schools, backed by a National Advisory Committee.

People Caring for Dependent Relatives

● We will legislate through the Carers' Charter for carers needs. We will replace Invalid Care Allowance by a more generous Carers' Benefit.

● We will seek to improve the position of people with disabilities in our society.

THE SECOND STAGE

The next stage will be to implement our structural changes to the tax and benefit systems. We will replace income support and family credit by a new basic benefit, for those in or out of work. Basic benefit entitlement will be gradually reduced as income rises. Child benefit will be payable to all alike, whether they are in or out of work.

We will introduce legislation to merge the tax and benefits systems, and employees' NICs with income tax at a high threshold. These structural changes will not come into effect until the second Parliament.

In the meantime we will continue to freeze the Married Man's Tax Allowance, and this extra revenue will enable us further to improve benefits for families with children, people with disabilities and carers.

OUR LONGER-TERM OBJECTIVES

● We will reform capital taxation to encourage wider distribution of gifts and legacies;

● Wider tax relief for savings, including savings directly invested in small businesses, ending the artificial distinction between income from earning and income from investment.

● We would move towards an equal and flexible retirement age for men and women giving everyone the right to retire at any age from 60 to 70, with a reduced pension for those retiring below 65 but protection for women currently approaching 60;

● We will aim to restore the link between pensions and average earnings, broken by the present Government, which will become more feasible if our plans to achieve growth while restraining inflation are given the chance to succeed.

EDUCATION: THE ESSENTIAL INVESTMENT

We will increase investment in education and training by an additional £2 billion per annum beyond that planned by the Conservatives by the fifth year.

Britain lags far behind our main industrial competitors in the proportion of our people who receive higher education, further education and skill training. Basic research is seriously underfunded. As a result, industry lacks the qualified and skilled people it needs, and individuals are not given the chance to develop their potential.

We aim:
- To *widen access* to education;
- To *raise standards* in schools;
- To *increase research*;
- To provide more effective *training and skills.*

Our schools are in turmoil. The decision of the two largest teachers unions to conduct a series of strikes in protest at the removal of their bargaining rights by the Teachers Pay and Conditions Act, means another term of disrupted education for the children of England and Wales, with especially serious consequences for those taking public examinations this summer. Many of these pupils have suffered repeated disruption of their schooling over the past three years; they are innocent victims of other people's actions.

To continue with the current Government's present policy, which would deny to the teachers negotiating rights for the next three eyars, cannot create the mutual trust between the teachers, the local education authorities and the Secretary of State that is essential to improve morale in the profession. Without an improvement in morale, pledges of higher standards in the schools can only be achieved by a committed, self-respecting teaching profession.

The teachers unions have been divided among themselves on pay and conditions. That is why the Alliance urged earlier this year in the House of Lords that an independent review body should put forward recommendations as a basis for negotiation. That was done by the Main Committee in Scotland; after an agreed settlement disruption ceased in Scottish schools.

The Alliance believes that the Government should make it clear that teachers pay and conditions would be imposed for the current settlement only; and that an independent review body would be established to make proposals on teacher's pay and conditions as a basis of negotiation. We understand and sympathise with the teachers anger at the removal of their negotiating rights. We would restore them. But the action by the teacher's unions should cease. It does nothing to achieve their aims. It is damaging pupils' education, is alienating public opinion and undermining the standing of teachers in the community. It is in no-one's interest that it continues.

The Alliance plans:

- *To create a united Department of Education, Training and Science,* and put local education authorities in charge of much of the local training work of the MSC;
- *To restore negotiating rights to teachers* and to create a General Teaching Council to enhance professional standards, which will also be supported by more in-service training and appraisal to ensure that good teachers do not have to leave the classroom to become administrators in order to achieve adequate rewards and status;
- *To raise standards in schools* through increased resources for books and materials, doubling teacher training in shortage subjects such as maths, science and computing, through special funds for innovation, through a stronger Inspectorate and through a broad and balanced curriculum established by consensus providing for a core range of subjects to be studied by all pupils but allowing for local needs to be reflected and innovation to be tried.
- *To make available one year's pre-school educational experience for all children.*
- *To develop the potential of each young person* by the wider use of profiles and records of achievement, by discouraging early specialisation by reforming A-level examination so that it covers a wide range of subjects over the arts-science divide, by positive action to encourage girls to take up subjects previously dominated by boys, and by seeking to build on achievements rather than merely penalising failure.
- *To enable schools to have full charge of their own budgets,* as the Alliance has done in Cambridgeshire, ensuring that a fully representative governing body is accountable for making the most effective use of the available money.
- *To get rid of artificial divisions at 16* by taking steps towards a single system of education and training allowances, replacing the present arrangements which make YTS schemes more financially attractive than further study.
- *To develop tertiary colleges* where local conditions are appropriate.
- *A crash programme to overcome skills shortages,* with an expansion of training and re-training facilities under the guidance of local education authorities, giving representation to trainees in the management of schemes.
- *A training incentive scheme* to encourage employers to increase their commitment to training; companies spending above a certain quota on training would receive a rebate.
- *To enable the long term unemployed to take up vacant places in further and higher education courses* without losing benefit, with the student able to leave the course immediately a job becomes available.
- *To widen access to further and higher education* by an immediate restoration of benefits taken away by the Tories, plus a 15% phased real improvement in student support.
- *To recognise that education is a life-long process,* and that more people need to return to it at different stages of life either to learn new skills or to acquire basic skills; we will seek to make access to higher and

further education for mature students easier and to strengthen those institutions which are specially geared to their needs; the European Social Fund should be widened to help in this area.

● *To guarantee a period of free further education* based on Open University levels of funding for everyone over 18 to be taken at a time of their choice.

● *To restore confidence in our Universities, Polytechnics and Colleges* by according proper recognition to their value and increasing so far as possible the resources available to them, by expanding scientific research, which has been severely cut, and widening access. We will increase the number of students by 20% over five years as a step towards our goal of doubling the proportion of our young people going into higher education by the year 2000. The higher education sector would have a major part to play in our crash programme to overcome skill shortages; we intend to create a Higher Education Council to co-ordinate the planning of both sectors of higher education; we support corporate status for Polytechnics but oppose the Government's plans to bring them under national control

● *Improved education provision for those with special needs,* in colleges as well as in schools, backed by a National Advisory Committee.

We recognise and would uphold the rights of those who wish to pay for independent education in the private sector. We would phase out the Assisted Places scheme without affecting pupils already in the scheme, so that money which has been diverted from the state system can once again be used to raise the standards in state schools. We believe that charitable tax reliefs in private education should only go to genuinely philanthropic activities, and would review the workings of charity law with that object in view. We will encourage greater co-operation between state and independent schools.

INVESTING IN QUALITY

A national programme for raising educational standards – The Alliance TEN POINT PLAN.

Encouraging progress

We will require all schools, both maintained and independent, to publish indicators showing progress in academic results related to intake and social factors such as community involvement, truancy, and delinquency.

Setting goals

We will ask each school to set targets for improvement – in the case of maintained schools, in consultation with their local education authority.

Assisting improvement

We will institute "special inspections" of all schools which regularly fall below a certain level in terms of progress achieved.

Reward excellence

We will institute an annual "Queen's Award" for schools, to be judged by an independent panel of experts, for outstanding progress, teaching progress, teaching and curriculm innovation and success.

Promoting professionalism

We will establish "teacher fellowships" as one year awards to outstanding teachers.

Spreading technology

We will develop Information Technology Centres as resources of technological expertise in collaboration with local colleges, polytechnics and universities and computing.

Enriching experience

We will initiate a pilot project of summer schools, targeted on inner city children, to enhance performance across the curriculum; we will approach independent schools to participate and make their facilities available for these summer schools.

Boosting numeracy

We will inaugurate a national numeracy campaign, backed by advertising and television.

Involving parents

We will launch pilot projects for parental involvement in schools.

Empowering parents

We will establish a "code of good practice" for local education authorities including:
Parents having a voice on education committees;
LEAs publishing their policies on home/school links;
LEAs appointing an advisory officer with special responsibility for developing a closer partnership with parents;
The training of parent governors.

AN ALLIANCE FOR YOUNG PEOPLE

The Alliance seeks to give young people the opportunity to shape their own lives and play a full part in their community. Our policies are designed to provide a platform for young people to speak out and to increase their financial independence.

● We will build on the YTS to turn youth training into a fully comprehensive, high quality vocational and educational programme for 16-19 year old.

● We will offer a job guarantee for our young people who have been unemployed for over a year.

● Our "Rent-a-Room" scheme will help to satisfy the need, particularly, for rented accommodation and will make it easier for them to travel to seek work.

● We will abolish the 18-24 income support rate so that all single people will receive the same rate of personal allowance.

● We will review the duties of local authorities to house the homeless and in the first instance will aim to give 16-18 year olds leaving local authority care, a statutory right to be housed.

● We will get rid of artificial divisions at 16 by taking steps towards a single system of education and training allowances, replacing the present arrangements which discourage young people from continuing in full time education.

● We will restore student benefit entitlements, make a 15% phased real improvement in student support, increase the number of full time equivalent students by 140,000 (20%) in five years and double the number by the end of the century.

● We will reduce the age of candidature to eighteen to enable young people to take a full part in local and central government.

GREEN GROWTH

There cannot be a healthy economy without a healthy environment.
We will take proper care of our environment.

Under an Alliance government every aspect of policy would be examined for its effect on our environment, which we hold in trust for future generations.

● *We will ensure Britain takes the lead in promoting sustainable economic growth* and investment in new technologies designed to remove pollution and thereby create new job opportunities.

● *The Alliance will set up a new Department of Environmental Protection* headed by a Cabinet Minister who will be responsible for environmental management, planning, conscrvation and pollution control, and promoting environmental policies throughout government. Among the priorities of this department will be:

● *Powerful disincentives to polluters* based on tougher penalties and implementation of a "polluter pays" principle for cleaning up the damage backed by support for good practice;

● *The safest possible containment and disposal for industrial waste,* with recycling wherever feasible;

● *Clean Air legislation* setting new standards, with tough measures to deal with acid rain and an acceleration of the phasing out of lead in petrol;

● *Introducing a statutory duty for both private and public sector companies* to publish annual statements on the impact of their activities on the environment and of the measures they have taken to prevent, to reduce and eliminate their impact.

● *Protection of the green belt* round our cities.

The Alliance is opposed to privatisation of the water authorities, which would hand over vital environmental responsibilities affecting rivers, sewerage, water quality, pollution control and fisheries to private hands. These functions should be restored to democratic control.

Energy and the environment

We will institute an energy policy which meets the needs of industry and the domestic consumer and has full regard to the environment. Britain is in a better position than many other countries to do this because of the natural assets we have. Alliance energy policy avoids dependence on any single source of supply and is based on:

● *More prudent use of our oil and gas resources* so that they are not depleted too quickly.

● *Continued modernisation and development of the coal industry,* including new coal-fired power stations with measures to prevent acid rain and more help to areas affected by pit closures; the power to license coal mines would be transferred from British Coal to the Department of Energy to prevent abuse of monopoly;

● *Much more research and development work on renewable energy sources;* including wind, solar, wave and geothermal energy; we will vigorously pursue proposals for tidal barrages such as those suggested for the Severn and the Mersey; subject to taking the environmental impact into account;

● *Far more effort into energy efficiency and conservation,* including higher standards of insulation in homes and encouragement of Combined Heat and Power schemes; nevertheless there will need to be a programme of replacement and decommissioning for power stations which are reaching or have reached the end of their design lives.

● Existing capacity and planned coal-fired power stations are enough to meet our needs for some time to come and *we see no case for proceeding with a PWR at Sizewell or other nuclear power stations at the present time.* Safety must come first and after Chernobyl there is clearly a need for a wider investigation into the safety of nuclear power, and there is also a need for a thorough and independent review of the economics of nuclear power generation.

We will continue research into nuclear fission power including research into the fast breeder reactor which may be needed if renewable resources prove to be less viable than we believe. We remain committed to the Joint European Torus (Jet) nuclear fission project.

There is a serious problem concerning the disposal of nuclear waste, and further studies will be commissioned to solve the problem as satisfactorily as possible. We do not believe that this critical matter should be rushed and therefore advocate on-site storage until suitable methods which have proved to be safe are available.

● *We would abide by the international convention (the London convention) which prohibits marine dumping of nuclear waste.*

The environment is under particular stress in two areas; the cities and the countryside. The Alliance is determined to protect and improve the quality of life in both.

Improving the quality of life in the inner cities

Our cities are in danger of changing from having been centres of initiative and activity in the past into industrial deserts, pessimistic about their future. The division and bitterness in Britain that Conservative neglect in central government and Labour control in local government have brought about are seen at their worst in our major cities.

Urban neighbourhoods need be no less distinct and individual than rural communities but the Labour and Conservative attitude has been to regard the city – and particularly the inner city – as one huge problem area and as a battleground for the class struggle. Those who live there know better and are appalled at the damage inflicted on the close, caring communities of the past.

The Alliance believes that the strong city cannot survive without strong neighbourhoods. We have confidence in the ability of those who live in the inner city to renew their own communities, but they must be given the political and economic tools to do the job. Too many of the people who serve the inner cities in professional jobs live in suburbs remote from local problems.

● Through a partnership of the public and private sectors we would invest in housing, schools and the infrastructure to encourage those who work in the inner cities to live there.

● *We will make attractive residential accommodation available* and close to the city centre to end the twilight ghettos that assist the mugger and the burglar.

● *We will support opportunities* for local people to work in their own community, to establish new businesses through local enterprise agencies and to train for needed skills.

● *The Alliance will use the Urban Programme* to establish community centres, enhance voluntary groups and assist tenants to manage their own estates.

● *We will promote the establishment* of elected Neighbourhood Councils with statutory parish status, where there is clear demand.

Genuine law and order depends on communities supporting the police in preventing crime and being confident enough to end the anonymity on which criminal activity thrives. Renewing our cities and enabling urban communities to develop a real sense of stability and security is the only sound way of preventing and detecting crime.

Protecting and enhancing our countryside

The Alliance seeks to provide better opportunities for those who live and work in the countryside, to check decline and depopulation, (especially of young people), to support small businesses and to encourage self-help solutions to rural problems.

● Our agricultural policies are designed to allow farmland to remain in use rather than being set aside. However, our planning strategy will allow for alternative land use which is in keeping with, and makes a sensitive contribution to the local rural economy.

● *We will give strong support to the Development Commission* and COSIRA, in their efforts to promote local enterprise and re-use existing buildings for these purposes. In regions where Development Agencies are set up they will promote a co-ordinated approach to the rural economy. Rural areas with severe economic problems should be designated to receive aid from the European Community regional fund;

● *We will encourage imaginative schemes* to maintain essential facilities in the countryside such as rural transport, village schools, call boxes and sub-post offices, all of which have been threatened under the Conservatives; nationalised industries and privatised monopolies such as British Telecom should be placed under stronger obligations to recognise rural needs;

● *We will conserve our heritage* of buildings.

● National Parks, areas of outstanding natural beauty and green belts should be fully protected, with those who live and work in these areas having a full, democratic voice in planning policies and recognition given of the added problems they face;

● Forestry policy should place more emphasis on broad-leaved species, and larger scale afforestation should be subject to a special system of planning controls.

● *We oppose the privatisation of the Forestry Commission.*

Home start

A new deal for first-time buyers.

Owning a home of one's own is most people's dream but not everyone can afford the high cost of taking the first step. We will open the door to home-ownership for thousands more — the young and the not-so-young — to enable them to cope with the initial problem, buying a home, when their resources are most stretched.

We will build on and considerably improve the existing Capital Home Loan Scheme with a tax credit of up to £1,000 for every new buyer. This will give first time buyers the benefit of lower monthly repayments at the start of their mortgages.

All those eligible will have average incomes for the two previous years not exceeding £20,000 (joint) or £10,000 (single). A ceiling will be worked out, region by region, on the price of the home purchased, so as to exclude people rich enough to buy very expensive homes. We estimate this will cost around £50 million per annum once the scheme is fully underway.

Stamp Duty. We will abolish Stamp Duty on house purchases for every one participating in "Home Start". Stamp Duty now stands at 1% on purchases priced at above £30,000. Abolition would be worth at least £300 and could in the south-east be worth £600 to a first-time buyer.

Better housing
We will take action to deal with homelessness and bad housing. Housing is a vivid example of the Conservatives' cynicism. The Government decided the narrow rules restricting local housing powers, cut back the capital sums available and is now blaming the local housing authorities for the housing crisis such national decisions cause. In particular the restriction of spending on housing to only 20% of the money coming to local authorities from capital sales make no financial or social sense. We will remove the restriction.

● *We will tackle the problem of homeslessness;*
● *We will give tenants more control* over their environment and more choice.
● *We will provide more choices* for private tenants;
● *We will give the elderly and disabled* more opportunities to move to more suitable housing or to adapt their present homes;
● *We will stop housing problems* from restricting economic opportunities — it is no use getting "on your bike" to find work if the only available jobs are in places where there is no affordable housing accommodation;
● *We will require each housing authority* to draw up a housing strategy to determine what are the areas of need and how they can best be met working with voluntary organisation, housing associations, building societies and the private sector, as Alliance groups on local councils are already doing;
● *We will open up a new "partnership" sector of rented housing* funded by building societies and institutions with a central government contribution to keep rents at reasonable levels; these schemes would be run by their tenants as co-operatives with the support of local councils and Housing Associations. In the long run we want public support for housing costs to be even-handed between those who rent and those who buy;
● We will target our housing assistance on those who most need it. We will promote mortgage schemes which can open up home ownership to a wider variety of people, such as index-linked mortgages and shared ownership; we will improve the availability of home improvement grants to home owners to maintain the fabric of their properties for the benefit of the whole community;
● We will retain the right to buy. We also wish to give local authorities enough discretion to deal with local housing shortages. Parliament must ensure that limits are set on such discretion to ensure that it is not used to deny the right to buy to tenants in general, and that anyone who is precluded from buying his or her present home is given the opportunity to buy another property on comparable terms through portable discounts.
● We would restore to councils the right to spend the proceeds of council house sales on replacing and repairing housing stock;
● We will insist on higher design standards in public housing, more and greater recognition of the contribution that good community architecture can make to the quality of life and we want investment directed at improving exisiting properties wherever justified rather than demolition.
● We will incorporate rights for council tenants to control and improve their houses in a statutory tenants' charter.
● We will set up a national mobility scheme covering all sectors of housing;
● Once more homes are available because of the Alliance's housing strategy, we will extend the statutory duty of local authorities to provide for the homeless, phasing in extensions to the 1977 Act beginning with single people over 40 and young aged 16-18 leaving care or who are otherwise homeless.

Rent a room
There is a desperate need for rented accommodation, particularly for single people and couples. There are millions of owner-occupied houses and council houses in Britain with spare rooms.

Many are deterred from renting by the present rentals red tape. Another crucial factor is to make it easier for people to travel to seek work. We will act to enable owner-occupiers and council tenants wishing to let a room in their own home to do so more easily, and to their financial advantage.
● Rental income up to £60 per week will not be subject to income tax or capital gains tax.

● We will legislate to invalidate clauses in mortgage contracts or local authority letting contracts that prohibit such lettings.

● Re-possession of such rooms will be made easier.

The "Rent-a-Room" scheme will be restricted to owner-occupier, council tenants, or tenants of housing associations, letting a maximum of two rooms in their home.

The rent will be determined by the market, but only rental income up to a total of £60 per week will be disregarded by the Inland Revenue.

We will legislate to impose a duty on local authorities to issue and regularly review licences to approved agencies, such as housing associations, housing aid centres, or commercial agencies, in their area to operate the scheme. Such agencies will enter into contracts with both landlord and tenant, and will be responsible to the landlord for ending any tenancy arrangement within a fortnight. Court· procedures will be speeded up to ensure that possession in all genuine cases is obtainable in that time.

The "Rent-a-Room" scheme will benefit many people.

First, it will help single people and couples, particularly the young, and those moving in order to get work to find suitable accommodation where at the moment it is bot scarce and expensive.

Second, it will help owner-occupiers, including elderly people, to increase their income, to assist with mortgage repayments or with the maintenance for their homes; it should help some young families to be able to afford to become home owners for the first time.

Home income plan

For many elderly people their only capital is their home and they do not have a regular income. Elderly home owners on low incomes, in fact, are becoming one of the most deprived sections of the community. The proportion in low standard homes is double that of the population as a whole and many others in good homes are short of spending money.

To enable Britain's elderly home owners to live more comfortable, independent and happier lives we will introduce a tax-assisted Home Income Plan. It will significantly increase their income or provide money for essential house expenses and repairs.

The Home Income Plan wil enable them, if they choose, to unlock the capital value of their homes to meet their need for more income now.

They will be able to take out a mortgage on part of the value of the house and use it to buy an annuity providing regular income. The interest on the loan will be added to the capital sum so that neither interest nor capital need be repaid during the borrower's lifetime.

Although several leading building societies and life assurance companies offer home income plans at present, they are of limited value because the interest has to be paid gross after the death of the borrower. Yet tax relief is allowed if the borrowers reduce their income by repaying the interest during their lifetime. Neither method gives really fair value and so only 25,000 home income plans have been taken out.

We will make Home Income Plans a really worthwhile benefit for older people by allowing them to postpone the interest repayments and qualify for tax relief when the interest is finally repaid. This could, on life assurance industry calculations give an 80% boost to the income of a woman in her 70s.

Tax relief for pensioners aged 70 or over who take out Home Income Plans would cost less than £40 million, assuming a 70% take-up. The cost would take time to build up and would not be incurred all at once.

TRANSPORT

We will maintain public transport.

Wider car ownership has improved the quality of life and enhanced the freedom of millions of people, which we welcome; at the same time, transport policy has to deal with the problems of congestion and road safety, which arise from busier roads, and has to ensure adequate public transport for those who do not have access to a car, including many women, young people and the elderly. While so many people have greater freedom of travel than ever before, significant minorities now have significantly less opportunity to travel than previously, especially in rural areas and some outlying housing estates.

The Alliance believes that:

● Deregulation of bus services under the Conservatives was botched. Bus services could only survive if they paid for themselves, leaving many elderly people and single-parent families isolated in their own homes. The Alliance supports comprehensive competitive tendering for a network of necessary bus services, with local councils involved in planning and financing them. This combines greater enterprise and new ideas with more care for deprived groups and areas. Local councils and transport authoritiesa should use their subsidy powers to ensure that essential services are maintained and that public transport in cities is attractive enough to reduce congestion resulting from commuting by car;

● *We will undertake a major renewal of road, rail and port infrastructure* as part of our programme of measures to tackle unemployment; we will build more by-passes and a designated national heavy lorry network to get more of the vehicles out of the towns, villages and residential areas;

● *We will support investment in our rail network* both to encourage the transfer of freight from road to rail and to ensure that the nations and regions of Britain all share in the economic advantages of the Channel fixed link.

● The Conservative Government has presided over a decline in our merchant fleet which threatens our national economic and security interest. We would entrust the lead role in co-ordinating maritime policy to a senior member of the Cabinet; and we would seek to help the industry through the present crisis by positive financial support and a determination to ensure fair play in world shipping markets.

ARTS, BROADCASTING AND RECREATION

We will ensure that people have the opportunity to enjoy the arts and physical recreation and to develop their own potential through these activities. To help achieve this aim we will double arts funding within the lifetime of one Parliament.
- *The Alliance will set up a unified Ministry,* headed by a Cabinet Minister, to have responsibility for the arts, broadcasting, films, publishing, leisure and recreation — these activities are at present scattered amongst Ministries within which they are of a minor significance and are subject to control rather than enhancement.
- *We will further decentralise funding for the arts,* channelling it through enhanced regional arts associations and the Scottish and Welsh Arts Councils.
- *Wherever possible we will replace grants* with endowment trusts providing greater stability and independence for the arts with a mix of public and private funding.
- *We will co-operate with artists to achieve better deals* through stronger copyright and public lending right laws;
- *We regard the BBC World Service, the British Council and the provision of educational facilities for overseas students* as very effective cultural ambassadors and we will ensure that increased funds are available to carry out that task;
- *We will secure the maximum access to sport facilities* for the whole community.

ANIMALS

- *We will strengthen the protection of animals.*
A civilised society treats animals with care and compassion. An Alliance Government will therefore set up an Animal Protection Commission which will considerably improve control over the welfare of animals in laboratories, farms, zoos, slaughter houses and circuses, as well as domestic and wild animals, and at a reduced cost, by unifying all existing Government responsibilities in this field. The Commission will be given extensive powers to advise, inspect and enforce legislation, and to review the effectiveness of existing legislation to deal with cruelty, in particular police entry powers and the power of the courts. The Commission will include fair representation from animal welfare organisations as well as users.

BRITAIN, EUROPE AND THE WORLD

The Alliance will ensure that Britain's foreign and defence policies help to bring a fairer and safer world. The things we want to achieve in our own country will not be possible unless we co-operate with other countries to achieve a fairer and safer world. Our concern that people should have basic human rights and a decent life cannot stop at the Channel. The huge public support for famine relief, the vigorous public debates on peace and defence and the public compassion for those suffering from oppression in many parts of the world refute the narrow-minded view that world affairs are not an election issue in Britain.

Our Aims

The Alliance is firmly internationalist. Opportunities for international co-operation have been thrown away by the Governments of the post-war years, when Britain needed to develop a new role and new relationships in a changed world.

We see the future of the United Kingdom as being bound up with the future of the European Community. As an enthusiastic and committed member of that Community Britain can significantly influence political and economic decisions.

Britain is also a member of the Commonwealth and should be using that position to develop concerted policies on eradicating hunger and on issues such as South Africa and Namibia, yet Mrs Thatcher has made such agreement impossible and treats respected Commonwealth leaders with disdain.

Britain should take the lead in seeking international agreement on selective, targeted sanctions, backed by help for the Front Line States, as a means of increasing the pressure for an end to apartheid in South Africa.

Britain should have a sufficiently mature relationship with the United States for the British Prime Minister to make clear where British foreign policy departs from that of the President of the day. The British Prime Minister should disavow such ventures as the bombing of Libya and support for the Contras, as so many Americans do, rather than allying with the most conservative forces in the White House.

On defence and disarmament, Britain should be firmly committed to the achievement of multilateral disarmament and firm in our acceptance of our responsibility towards collective security through Nato: the Alliance rejects the one-sided approach which characterises both the escalation of our present nuclear capacity through Trident and Labour's decision to remove all nuclear weapons from British soil without securing the removal of those weapons which could threaten us.

The Alliance believes that Britain should take a lead in seeking international efforts to tackle the basic problems of the poorest countries of the world, particularly the burden of debt which is crippling their efforts to feed their own people and the need to get a fairer system of international trade which is not biased against the poorer countries.

EUROPE

The European Community must be the basis of a united Europe which has common policies on trade, technology and social policy, and encourages Europe's scientific and industrial development. We believe Labour's negative attitude to the European Community, and the obstructiveness of Mrs Thatcher's Government, not least in vetoing the proposed European Community programme for co-ordinated research and development, is short-sighted and unconstructive. In a world of super powers, Europe has to speak with a united voice.

The Alliance would:
● Ensure fair elections to the European Parliament by proportional representation to give proper rights to the people of this country;
● Seek reform of the Community's political institutions so that the bureaucracy is properly accountable to the European Parliament, and that the Council of Ministers shares power effectively with the Parliament;
● Work for reform of the Common Agricultural Policy so that it no longer dominates the Community budget, and to develop Community policies on regional development, social and employment issues;
● Support European initiatives to put effort and resources into developing advanced technology; we would accept the negotiated European Community co-ordinated research and development programme;
● Make it easier for companies to sell throughout Europe;
● Extend the common rights of citizenship in Europe.

GLOBAL CO-OPERATION

An Alliance Government will:
● Increase British support for the United Nations, develop its capacity for peacekeeping, restore Britain's membership of UNESCO and increase British backing for the UN agencies such as the High Commission for Refugees.
● Develop Commonwealth and European co-operation on a wide range of issues, including sanctions against South Africa designed to increase pressure for an end to apartheid and peaceful change before war become inevitable; we are also determined to end South Africa's illegal occupation of Namibia.
● Increase efforts through international co-operation to deal with the threat of terrorism.

Peace and Security

We will promote disarmament while maintaining sound defence.
Everything we prize most highly could be threatened by the destruction of our freedom through armed intervention or threat, or by the destruction of a world which now contains a massive arsenal of nuclear weapons. But at long last there is now an opportunity to halt the arms race. The Alliance is determined to combine sound defence against any possible threat with determined efforts to reduce and even remove the massive nuclear stockpile, which causes increasing anxiety to the peoples of the world. New opportunities for arms agreements are being opened up by the changed priorities of a new Soviet leadership; we cannot afford to assume that this new and welcome trend in Moscow will continue unchecked, but at this delicate and hopeful stage it is vital that we have a British Government determined to seize the opportunity to drive sensible bargains on arms control which are secure because they are seen on each side as being realistic. Britain cannot defend itself or the values of western democracy alone, just as it cannot achieve international disarmament solely by its own actions; both the other Parties have chosen in different ways to ignore the reality that our defence and disarmament efforts are interdependent with those of other countries.
● *The Alliance is committed to Nato,* and we accept the obligations of Nato, including the presence of Allied bases and nuclear weapons on British soil on the basis of clear arrangements for a British veto over their operations including where appropriate, dual-key systems; we believe it is essential to strengthen the European contribution to Nato;
● *The Alliance welcomed the outline agreement discussed at Reykjavik* to remove all intermediate nuclear weapons from Europe, and Mr Gorbachov's later acceptance that such a deal should not be linked to the future of the US Strategic Defence Initiative; the Alliance believes that this must be only the first, vital step in a continuing process which will include both shorter-range nuclear weapons and conventional forces.
● *The Alliance would withdraw UK support for President Reagan's Strategic Defense Initiative,* which clearly involves breaching the ABM Treaty, is destabilising and is likely to lead to further escalation.
● *We will seek to revive negotiations on a Comprehensive Test Ban.* In the meantime Britain should itself ban nuclear weapons testing and should encourage the US to do likewise.
● *We would seek a battlefield-nuclear-weapon-free-zone in Central Europe* extending 150km in each direction from the East-West divide.
● *We believe that Nato relies too heavily on nuclear weapons at all levels for deterrence.* A strengthened European pillar, involving effective defence co-operation and improved conventional strength would

better enable Western Europe to move towards the elimination of dependence on first use of nuclear weapons. Nato should adopt strategies and weapons which are more self-evidently defensive in intent and which are concerned with minimum deterrence;

● *We want to see a new initiative achieve Mutual and Balanced Force Reductions* and we would be prepared to include Britain's nuclear weapons in disarmament negotiations.

● *We would continue Britain's efforts to achieve a multilateral treaty prohibiting the manufacture, development and possession of chemical weapons.* In the meantime, we would oppose any manufacture of fresh stocks of chemical or biological weapons.

● *In the government we would maintain with whatever necessary modernisation our minimum nuclear deterrent until it can be negotiated away, as part of a global arms negotiation process, in return for worthwhile concessions by the USSR which would enhance British and European security. In any such modernisation we would maintain our capability in the sense of freezing our capacity at a level no greater than that of the Polaris system.* We would cancel Trident because of its excessive number of warheads and megatonnage, high cost and continued dependence on US technology. We would assign our minimum deterrent to Nato and seek every opportunity to improve European co-operation on procurement and strategic questions.

● *We would seek to reduce the flow of arms to areas of conflict and to ensure that arms fromBritain are not supplied to repressive regimes,* particularly for their internal security operations.

Shared Earth

The Alliance will:

● Increase the share of Britain's GNP which goes in development aid, which has gone down from 0.52% to 0.33% under the Conservatives, so that we reach the UN target of 0.7% by the end of a five-year Parliament;

● Concentrate aid on raising the living standards of the poorest through more rural development, environmentally sustainable resource use, promotion of self-sufficiency, recognition of the role of women, appropriate technology, training and education, making full use of experience and expert voluntary agencies;

● Seek to increase awareness of development issues through more resources being devoted to development education;

● Change the situation in which many poor countries pay more in debt repayments to rich countries than they receive in aid by seeking international agreement on debt rescheduling and cancellation;

● Combine the Aid-Trade Provision and the Overseas Development Administration's "soft-loan" facility with the Overseas Projects division of the Department of Trade and Industry and the Export Credit Guarantee Department into one division of the DTI – help to British industry will no longer be taken from the aid budget.

CONCLUSION

The Alliance came into being to achieve these things. From three sources came the political ideas and momentum which are now carrying the Alliance forward. One was Liberalism, a long and honoured political tradition from which we draw not only the philosophy of individual freedom but also a record of achievement in the establishment of the modern welfare state and the championing of local communities. The SDP combines a commitment to social justice and ending poverty with a dynamic approach to wealth creation and its leaders have extensive experience of government. A third element, which has ensured that the strength of the Alliance is infinitely greater than the sum of its parts, is the support of those who have never before been members of a political party, because no party seemed to offer them the chance to realise their aims. Their numbers continue to grow.

The Alliance is therefore different. It involves two political parties working together, and taking along with them the great mass of people who are dissatisfied with the politics which is so dismally displayed in the shouting match of the House of Commons at Prime Minister's Question Time. All political parties involve compromises between different views and different strands of opinion – the Labour and Conservative parties each embrace an enormously wide range of opinion. But for them the spirit of compromise, if it operates at all, has to be concealed, kept within the party and denied in public. We make no secret of the fact that our programme draws on the ideas of our two parties and that we are keen to work together to achieve shared goals. Like the others we seek to put our entire programme forward for endorsement and to form a majority Alliance Government, but unlike the others the whole approach of the Alliance underlines our belief that if we are in a balanced Parliament we must heed the message of the voters and work with the other parties to seek an agreed programme which commands the widest possible support.

The Alliance is different also because it is not the voice of any one section of interest. It is not paid for and controlled by the trade union movement, as is the Labour party, and it does not have the massive dependence which the Conservatives have on the City and big business. These links makes each of the other parties powerless to reform their own institutional backers and incapable of understanding or winning the confidence of their institutional opponents. The Alliance has a capacity to be fair which is based on its independence and on the breadth of its support, typified by the fact that we have been able to win by-elections in the heart of the countryside in a former Conservative stronghold in Ryedale and in a former Labour stronghold in Greenwich, both seats now held by Liberal and SDP women MPs.

The Alliance is different in another respect. It is not merely seeking to become the elected government of the country, but to overhaul the system of government so that all future governments, of whatever party, are based on real public consent and full participation in an open society. Our intention is not simply to get into the driving seat but to re-design the vehicle. Once the Alliance has reformed the voting system, no future government will be awarded the power of a majority without the support of a majority of the people, and no kind of extremism, whether of the left or of the right, will be able to get in through the back door. Not only that – if we find ourselves exercising power in a Parliament with no overall majority, we guarantee that we will use that power to block extremism and to fight for the kind of reforms which make sure that governments cannot push people around and individuals have the opportunity and the means to achieve their full potential.

The Alliance is different, too, in its belief about the nature of society. Our aim is a civilised society in which individual freedom goes hand-in-hand with care for others. Individual freedom is central to our beliefs, but if it is not accompanied by social responsibility it becomes freedom only for those who can afford it, or the survival of the fittest. But when society as a whole tries to meet human needs it must respect individual choice and be aware of the dangers and limitations of state provision, otherwise there will be no freedom, and public services will be both inhuman and inefficient. Declining public services and the inhuman scale of organisations like the DHSS and the big council housing departments have contributed to a widespread feeling of apathy and despair, and many young people in particular feel that this society has no place for them and does not want to listen to them. Government must work in partnership with people, enabling them to use their own organisations, their own local communities and their own skills, and giving them effective democratic control over those services which can only be provided by the community as a whole. Our society is one that recognises that the arts are not an optional extra, to be grudgingly afforded when the economy is booming, but play an essential part in meeting the wider needs of individuals and in broadening the vision of communities. Our aim is a society in which values other than the purely economic are recognised and valued. Our society is one that recognises the importance of the environment in which we live – even those who are successful do not want to live in a shoddy society whose values are dominated by greed and selfishness. We recognise the crucial need to live in harmony with our environment and we will support those developments in our industrial and social activities which are environmentally enhancing and benign. We aim to join the nations which lead the field in environmental protection instead of trailing amongst the last.

The Alliance is also different in being concerned about both unemployment *and* inflation. The Conservative Party concentrate all its attention on inflation and ignores unemployment and its consequences. The Labour Party concentrates all its attention on unemployment and ignores the fact that increased inflation undermines expansion and inevitably puts brakes on efforts to get people back to work. We must have sustainable growth. That is why our proposals for expanding the economy are accompanied by plans for an incomes strategy and for a firm monetary and exchange rate discipline through entry to the exchange rate mechanism of the European Monetary System. But in the long term we will only succeed if we give the top priority to industry. The service and manufacturing sectors of industry are mutually dependent, but manufacturing industry has been devastated in recent years. We believe it is the engine of growth and our competitors in Japan, in Germany and in the US demonstrate that only too well.

Much of what the Alliance wants to do to ensure basic standards in the public services and to encourage people to find new ways of caring for one another depend on achieving success through our economic and industrial policies, which are designed to enable us to achieve greater prosperity. Some of what we want to do will have to wait until we have earned the resources with which to do it. We are not prepared to enter an electoral auction seeing who can make the largest bids to spend money which is not there and will not be there unless taxes and borrowing are increased to unreasonable and imprudent levels. Investment in industry and particularly in new and high technology industry is the key to creating the wealth we all want. We deplore the way in which windfall benefits such as oil revenues and the proceeds from privatisation have been frittered away instead of being used to enhance the basic fabric of our society.

The other parties know that the Alliance is different, and they fear it, even to the extent of burying their own fundamental disagreements with each other so as to co-operate against us. In the House of Commons they have voted together against electoral reform, and against some of the measures designed to put trades unions fully under the control of their members. They work with each other in an attempt to preserve the appearance of a two-party system long after it is dead: Conservatives carefully protect Labour's privileges in the House of Commons to ensure that latterly only Labour and Conservative working peers have been appointed to the Lords, in the vain hope of silencing the Alliance voice. We do not rule out the possibility that after the next election there could be an informal "Lab-Con pact" to keep the Alliance out, as there has been on several local councils: it would be the old parties way of attempting to stagger on as if nothing had happened after the two-party system had suffered a shattering defeat. Indeed we believe that Labour and Conservative supporters should now be asking their candidates "In a balanced Parliament will you work with the Alliance or with our traditional opponents?"

That is why our prime aim is an Alliance majority government, an aim that can certainly be realised at this election. Indeed, such are the absurdities of the voting system that quite small increases in Alliance support can make the difference between fifty Alliance seats and three hundred. If we get that majority we will at once set out to reform the system under which we gained it. But we will also be able to get on with the job of bringing down unemployment while managing the economy on a sound basis so as to prevent inflation from increasing dramatically again. We will be able to embark on immediate improvements in basic services like education and health, while we open the way to the longer-term proposals in these and other fields which will give people more chance to realise their full potential and build a caring community. We will be able through our tax and benefit proposals to improve the lot of those who now find themselves on or near the poverty line. We will be able to make the conservation of the environment a priority of government, and pay special attention to the needs of cities and country-side. We will be able to house many of the homeless through more imaginative housing policies involving partnership between public and private housing. We will pursue policies on defence and foreign affairs which will make Britain a force for good in the world, recognising our interdependence with other nations.

All this is possible, and our Joint Programme sets out the main steps we will take. These aims and values are also a clear guide to the way we would use the power we had if no party had an overall majority. We would insist that the views of the substantial section of the electorate who had voted for us went into the process by which the programme of a new government was decided. If other parties seek to cheat the electorate of that right, we shall seek to bring the matter back before the voters as soon as possible. We are not prepared to see the views of so many voters ignored any longer.

An election of opportunity
We believe that our priorities are right, that our proposals are practical and that our values are those which are most urgently needed in the government of this country. We make no claim to have a monopoly on good ideas. We seek from the voters the chance to give back to them the power and the opportunities which are rightly theirs. Their times has come.

Alongside this Programme for Government the Alliance is publishing manifestos for Scotland and Wales, setting out our policies on those issues which we believe should be dealt with by devolved power.

National Freedom with a Scottish Parliament

Play the Scottish Card

The Scottish National Party manifesto *Play the Scottish Card* said:

The principal aim of the Scottish National Party is to win support for the establishment of an independent Scottish Parliament. This Parliament would allow the Scottish people to win their national freedom and provide the power to change our country for the better.

At this election, Scotland will reach a crossroads in her political future. The North/South divide and the prediction of the Registrar General for Scotland that, alone among the Western democracies, Scotland will experience a loss of ten per cent of our population over the next 50 years, spells out a stark warning of the dangers our country faces without independence.

An independent Scotland will be governed by a democratic parliament, elected on proportional representation by the Scottish people. This parliament will decide on all matters relating to the government of Scotland within recognised boundaries of Scotland and will negotiate international treaties on behalf of Scotland.

In arguing for Scottish independence, the SNP has maintained that the Scottish people must be allowed to decide their own constitutional future. Decisions taken in London will be designed to divert Scotland's energies away from gaining real political power. This was the case in the 1974-79 period, when only toy-town assemblies with no useful power, were on offer.

One of the interim demands of the SNP is the establishment of a Scottish Constitutional Convention through which representatives elected by Scots by proportional representation can decide on the most acceptable framework for self-government. The Convention would sit for only a short period in time and would draw together proposals to change the Constitution in Scotland.

One of the greatest advantages of winning independence will be that Scotland can take part in the affairs of the world and make a positive contribution to peace and security. The aims of Scottish international policy will be to establish cooperation and friendliness between countries in the preservation of peace and the protection of our people and territory.

The condition of any country can be measured by the strength of its economy and its industrial base. If such a measurement was made of Scotland today the conclusion would without doubt show Scotland to be weak.

Only self-government, and the return of real power to Scotland, will allow us the opportunity to rebuild the economic and industrial fabric of our nation.

Scotland has suffered a heavy economic and industrial price during the years of the Thatcher Government. The dramatic rise in unemployment and the consequent decline in Scotland's economic and industrial base have had a devestating effect on the ability of the country to compete in an international context.

Scotland desperately needs a serious injection of capital to boost its infrastructure, create the capacity to expand, and encourage new initiatives in research and development.

The SNP rejects the principle that unemployment is inevitable, and would approach employment in the same way as do many small European countries who have minimal levels of unemployment.

Much more is needed, however, to provide long-term stability for the Scottish economic and industrial sectors. An independent Scotland must decide its priorities for economic development and establish the conditions and institutions that will create such an environment.

The need for Scottish self-government is just one example of the failure and injustice of the British system. An independent Scotland must learn from this failure and take firm decisions to create a new and open society.

A new Scotland will carry out the provisions of a written constitution and will guarantee rights and opportunities afforded to each citizen. Our society will be driven by a desire to create openness and promote justice and freedom for the individual.

Winning for Wales: Senate needed

In its manifesto *Winning for Wales*, Plaid Cymru said:

Satisfying employment for the whole population is the key to the regeneration of the Welsh economy, just as it is the key to the high standard of living enjoyed by the small Scandinavian countries. The policies of this manifesto have been designed to achieve the basic aim of full employment, with a minimum wage, good working conditions and genuine equality for men and women.

A single body — Action Wales — will be established under the direction of a Welsh Senate and work closely with a more independent Wales TUC to create work and improve living standards. Action Wales will combine the roles of all the public agencies responsible for economic development, thus avoiding the duplication that is a feature of Wales today.

The growth of strategic industries will be initiated by a flexible range of financial incentives to attract capital and skills into the Welsh economy and by direct investment.

The decline in the coal industry must now be reversed; the sinking of a new Margam mine must be followed by more investment in deep mines and more research into the potential of our coalfield.

Wave and wind generation of electricity are becoming competitive in price. Wales must take advantage of a long, exposed coastline and an under-employed engineering industry to develop the renewable and non-polluting sources to meet our own energy needs and as a major export industry.

Plaid Cymru, the Party of Wales, will oppose any further nuclear power stations and demand regular safety inspections of the existing stations.

Wales must be directly represented in Brussels and recognised as a separate region within the Common Agricultural Policy. A Minister for Welsh Agriculture should be appointed immediately to the Welsh Office, pending the establishment of a Welsh Senate.

Plaid Cymru is totally opposed to the storing of nuclear waste on site or the discharge of nuclear waste into the Irish Sea and will resolutely oppose any plan to dispose of nuclear waste in any part of Wales.

Plaid Cymru propose a Welsh Transport Authority under the direction of a Welsh Senate to co-ordinate all forms of transport and communication and to pay special attention to the transport needs of rural Wales.

Plaid Cyrmru will press the Government to pass a new Welsh language act to ensure the same status and the same opportunities for the Welsh and English languages in all aspects of the national life of Wales in accordance with the recommendations of the Arfe report as adopted by the European Parliament.

We oppose any reduction in income tax which will enable the rich to get richer and afford more luxuries while the problems of unemployment, education cuts, poor housing and ill-health get worse and worse.

If necessary, we will support an increase in income tax provided it is accompanied by a raising of the tax threshold to take low income out of taxation altogether and provided that there is a cut in military expenditure.

We demand immediate unilateral nulcear disarmament by Britain and the removal from Wales of all American military installations. An independent Wales would withdraw from Nato.

We are campaigning for a Senate to assume all the powers of the Secretary of State within the Welsh Office. It will consist of 100 members elected for a fixed term of four years.

The Senate will have the power to initiate legislation to be presented to the Westminster Parliament and the power to scrutinise all Westminster and European legislation.

Its most important task will be the regeneration of the Welsh economy, acting through a single authority, developing Wales.

Greenprint for an age of understanding

The belief that planning to secure the welfare of the earth automatically secures the welfare of the people was emphasized in The Green Party election manifesto. It stated:

Green politics provides each of us with the challenge to reject the path of false technology and to recapture not some 'romantic golden age' but a truly satisfying and sustainable future for both ourselves and our earth. It is a greenprint for an age of understanding. We need to stop building on the quicksand of materialism, patriarchy, competition and aggression. We are sinking faster than most people think.

Growth takes power out of the hands of local communities and gives it to multinational corporations which have no connection with the places where people live and work. Competition sets communities and nations against each other, and progress often leads us down untested and unsafe technological paths.

A Green economy would reduce waste and pollution to a minimum; support socially useful products and services, not just commercially viable ones; secure greater democratic control over economic decision-making, questioning and challenging the power of capital.

The manifesto stresses that, contrary to popular mythology, the Green Party is not anti-technology and that it favours technology which is "good and satisfying to work with, produces useful end results and is kind to the environment." It would set up independent technological boards to assess technologies. There would be health and safety checks, too.

On unemployment, the manifesto calls for a fresh approach to the organization of work and says the first step is to bring together the people and the work that needs to be done. A basic income scheme would remove the 'tax on jobs' and introduce an array of flexible alternatives such as job sharing, more part time arrangements, and time off for study, caring for small children or dependent relatives, "or just digging the garden."

Self employment would become easier as a basic income scheme would provide for bad patches. The scheme would guarantee economic security to all as a right. The scheme would be financed, among other ways, by pollution charges, a reduction of income tax personal allowances and a higher company tax on large firms.

Among taxation proposals is one for an automatic, tax-free weekly payment for everyone.

Conservation taxes would discourage waste of valuable resources and there would be consumption taxes on goods and services. Pollution charges would ensure that the polluter "pays the full cost of pollution, whether intentional or accidental" and these would be set at levels to ensure that they could never constitute a 'licence to pollute.'

Relief for the Third World's burdens would include agreements being sought with those countries wanting to restructure their economies on sustainable lines, and creative ways of working together would be explored. "For example, debts owed to UK-based banks could be bought at a discount and then cancelled, meaning a loss to the bank. Or a proportion of the debt could be paid in local currency into a development fund for local sustainable projects."

On defence and disarmament, "The Green Party would pursue immediate and unconditional British nuclear disarmament." It would renounce deployment and use of nuclear weapons by British forces and ban deployment of these weapons by any foreign country in Britain.

Other manifesto proposals:

● Energy: A move from dependence on finite fossil fuels and phase out nuclear power while developing conservation and introducing renewable energy supplies;

● Health: Emphasis on prevention of disease and health promotion.

● Transport: Reduce travel needs, especially journeys to work, by encouraging more integrated communities. Reduce reliance on cars.

The manifesto concluded: The Green Party stands for a new kind of politics. We must take control of our own lives and learn to work together for a better future. We cannot allow ourselves to be ruled by remote control government, the power of big business and the media, and the lottery of market forces. We must begin by taking personal responsibility for the state of the planet and for the job of changing it. We can only do it by choosing what we know is right. We can begin by voting Green, but that is only the beginning.

'Make Britain a Power for Peace'

The Communist Party manifesto calls for a public ownership programme to help tackle unemployment, for greater rights for the trade unions and for a non-nuclear Britain.

The manifesto says that big, privately-owned business puts more and more of its money overseas to get even bigger profits rather than investing in industry and jobs in Britain.

To deal effectively with the disastrous state of the economy there must be government power to plan investment, to control the export of capital needed for investment, the document says. "It means, too, a public ownership programme with genuine democratic control." All this meant opposing the restraints and policies of the EEC. And a large scale public works programme should be started to help the jobless.

The manifesto also wants an immediate cut in working hours as a first step to a 35 hour week. It says money for investment and expanded social services would come from cutting military spending. Increased employment would save on benefits and generate revenue.

The manifesto condemns the attacks it says have been made by "the Tories and big employers" on trade union rights. It continues: "Communists call for the repeal of all anti trade union legislation and its replacement by an Act giving positive rights, including the right to strike. Trade unions — the main defence of people at work — need full rights to organise and negotiate."

There should be more effective safety regulations, too. Unions and employees should have the right to information and consultation on investment plans. "Legislation for equal pay for work of equal value is essential in order to end the undervaluing of women's skills."

The Thatcher government is accused of weakening local democracy, and the Communists believe councils should have more rights and that the GLC and Metropolitan County Councils should be restored. The "unjust" rates system would be ended and replaced by a local income tax.

Both black and white have a shared interest in opposing racism which has been made worse by Tory policy, says the document. "The racist immigration and nationality laws must go. Family reunion is a basic human right. We need citizens' laws and entry procedures which do not discriminate on grounds of sex and colour. The Race Relations Act must be given real teeth."

Under the heading "Make Britain a Power for Peace" the manifesto declares that the Tory government is holding up agreement on removing nuclear weapons from Europe, which is now possible. "Pressure from the peace movement and from public opinion, and the proposals from the Soviet Union, have created an opening for change. But the Tory government stands in the way."

"Communists campaign for unilateral nuclear disarmament by Britain, removal of cruise, the scrapping of Trident, closure of all US nuclear bases in Britain and a substantial cut in arms spending.

"We work for closer cooperation between the British and Soviet people. Britain should support proposals for nuclear free zones in Europe, the Pacific and elsewhere, and work for a total test ban."

Civil nuclear power must go, too; it is dangerous and no cheaper than other energy sources, the document asserts.

The manifesto also calls for:
- More money for health care and an end to inequality in the health service;
- Proportional representation with a single transferable vote for the electoral system;
- Scottish and Welsh assemblies;
- Building of more homes, mostly for renting, and reduced council rents;
- A Freedom of Information Act to protect the people's right to know;
- A police service answerable to society;
- British withdrawal from Ireland, creating conditions for a united and independent Ireland;
- A good education and equality of opportunity for all children, rich and poor.

Index to Candidates

Those elected are named in bold type.

D

I

J

L

K

INDEX TO CANDIDATES

M

360

INDEX TO CANDIDATES

Q

R

S

T

INDEX TO CANDIDATES

Y

Z